THE COUNT—DUKE OF
OLIVARES

1. Diego de Velázquez, *Count-Duke of Olivares on Horseback.*

THE COUNT—DUKE OF
OLIVARES

The Statesman in an Age of Decline

J. H. ELLIOTT

YALE UNIVERSITY PRESS
NEW HAVEN AND LONDON · 1986

Designed by Gillian Malpass

Set in Linotron Bembo and printed in Great Britain by The Bath Press, Avon

Library of Congress Cataloging-in-Publication Data

Elliott, John Huxtable.
  The Count-Duke of Olivares
  Bibliography: p.
  Includes index.
  1. Olivares, Gaspar de Guzmán, conde-duque de,
1587–1645.   2. Statesmen—Spain—Biography.   3. Spain—
Politics and government—1621–1665.   I. Title.
DP185.9.06E45   1986   946'.05'0924 [b]   85-26450
ISBN 0-300-03390-7

CONTENTS

PART IV   THE LOSS OF REPUTATION (1635–1645)

PREFACE

I first became aware of the Count-Duke of Olivares when, as a Cambridge undergraduate on my first visit to Spain, I came face to face with the great equestrian portrait by Velázquez in the Prado Museum. That imperious figure with his commanding manner, his swirling mustachios, his wary eyes, is not easy to ignore. Yet when I later came to consult the standard historical literature on seventeenth-century Europe, it seemed that I was wrong. References tended to be cursory and unilluminating, and he was given little more than a walk-on part in studies of the Thirty Years' War. For a man in command of the destinies of Spain and its empire in the 1620's and 1630's, during its last two decades as the dominant world-power, this looked a rather ungenerous treatment, even allowing for the fact that his career ended in failure and defeat.

Subsequent inspection of works written by Spanish historians suggested that he had fared little better at the hands of his compatriots. The seventeenth century, as the Golden Age of Spanish literature and art, has always attracted the attention of scholars, and has inspired work of high quality. But Spain's other seventeenth century—the century of military defeat, political disaster and economic decline—has received on the whole a meagre treatment by the standards of the best European historical scholarship, and remains to this day relatively unknown. Olivares, although Spain's outstanding statesman of the century, shared this neglect. In the later nineteenth century Antonio Cánovas del Castillo, the great statesman of Restoration Spain, discussed his career with intelligence and mounting sympathy in three works on Spain under the House of Austria,[1] but was unable to do much more than suggest that his ideas and actions had all too often been misunderstood, and deserved more serious attention than they had yet been given.

It took some fifty years for Cánovas' call to be heeded. In 1936 the Count-Duke received his first and only biography to date. This

---

[1] *Historia de la decadencia española* (Madrid, 1854), *Bosquejo histórico de la Casa de Austria* (Madrid, 1869), and *Estudios del reinado de Felipe IV*, 2 vols. (Madrid, 1888).

was the work, not of a trained historian, but of a brilliant physician and man of letters, Gregorio Marañón. His book, *El Conde-Duque de Olivares*, was essentially concerned with Olivares the man, and treated only summarily his ministerial policies and career. These were depicted as reflections of a personality whose dominant characteristic was *la pasión de mandar*—the passion to command—and in turn the personality was seen as the prisoner of a biological organism which Dr. Marañón dissected with professional skill. It is doubtful whether the particular psychoanalytical approach adopted by Marañón would now command very wide support, but his book remains a fascinating and often suggestive examination of a complex character, based on a range of archival and printed sources which place all future historians of the period in the author's debt.

Dr. Marañón's *Olivares*, however, is primarily a psychoanalytical case-history that happens to have a seventeenth-century background, and it displays little awareness of the political and social realities of the age. It therefore seemed to me that there was room for a closer scrutiny of Olivares in his role as a Spanish and European statesman, and as the principal minister for twenty-two years of Philip IV of Spain. At the time when I first began historical research, I planned to devote myself to his reform programme of the 1620's and his confrontation with what has come to be known in European historiography as the 'decline of Spain'. This original plan was frustrated by the belated discovery that the Olivares archive had been destroyed by fire in the eighteenth century, and that the surviving documentation appeared inadequate to undertake the kind of study I had in mind. I therefore turned instead to one of the most significant domestic events during his tenure of power, the revolution of Catalonia in 1640 against his government, hoping in this way to illuminate at least one aspect of his political programme and the reactions that it provoked.

In the resulting book, *The Revolt of the Catalans*, I suggested that the destruction or disappearance of the bulk of Olivares' personal papers made it unlikely that he could ever be given the kind of detailed study that had been accorded his great, and ultimately successful, rival, Cardinal Richelieu. While engaged on other things, however, I continued to keep my eyes open for documentation on the Count-Duke and his period in office, in the feeling that he was a sufficiently important figure in the history of Spain and of Europe to deserve more comprehensive study. Spain's great national archive at Simancas in fact contains a vast amount of documentation on Spanish foreign policy during the Olivares years, including many policy discussions by the Count-Duke himself. Since a substantial part of his time was occupied by foreign affairs, it seemed to me that this documentation

could form the basis of a more extensive treatment, especially if supplemented by papers from other public and private archives, both
inside and outside Spain.

The pursuit of these papers extended over a number of countries
and a number of years. I should not, however, have been able to
continue it, or settle down to write up the results, without the opportunities for research and writing provided by my appointment to
the Institute for Advanced Study in 1973. At this point, the full-scale
political biography of the Count-Duke which until then had been
no more than a gleam in the eye became for the first time a practical
possibility. But other complementary or related projects had first
priority. It seemed to me that the first need was to collect, collate
and establish the texts of the Count-Duke's principal surviving
papers, at least in the field of domestic policy, and edit them with
a series of introductory essays designed to set them into context.
The resulting two volumes, written in collaboration with José F.
de la Peña, were published in 1978–80 under the title of *Memoriales
y Cartas del Conde Duque de Olivares*. The documents in those volumes,
and the essays that accompany them, constitute the bed-rock of the
present book.

During the same period I became increasingly interested in the
cultural history of the reign of Philip IV, and collaborated with Professor Jonathan Brown of the Institute of Fine Arts in New York
on a study of the principal building project of the Olivares years,
the palace of the Buen Retiro in Madrid. In our book, *A Palace
for a King* (1980), we sought to give a 'total' history of the building
and furnishing of Philip IV's new pleasure palace, combining political
and social history with the history of art. This book should be seen
as complementing the present political biography of the Count-Duke,
where his cultural policies are given less attention than they would
otherwise have demanded.

In spite of a relatively summary treatment of the cultural history
of the period, and also of the origins of the Catalan revolution of
1640—both of them extensively treated in these earlier publications—
the present work remains, as I am acutely aware, very long. I have
discussed the Count-Duke in shorter compass, and attempted to compare his statesmanship with that of his French counterpart, in my
Richelieu and Olivares (1984). I felt, however, that at this stage in
the development of Spanish and European historiography, a case
existed for attempting as full a study as the surviving documentation
and the present state of the bibliography allow. When I first began
exploring the reign of Philip IV, the Spain of this period was almost
deserted territory, apart from the remarkable pioneering work of
Don Antonio Domínguez Ortiz on Spanish society and on crown

finances in the seventeenth century, and of Don José Antonio Maravall on the political culture of the age. But in the last few years
a new wave of pioneers, Spanish and non-Spanish, has been coloniz-
ing previously neglected areas and greatly extending our knowledge
of the terrain. The work published by José Alcalá-Zamora and
Jonathan Israel on Spain and the Netherlands, by Eberhard Straub
on the Count-Duke's foreign policy, by James Casey on seventeenth-
century Valencia, and by Jean Vilar on the movement for reform
in Castile, has raised the history of seventeenth-century Spain to new
levels of scholarship, while other historians, and particularly a
younger generation of Spanish historians, are now undertaking
important and much-needed work on Castilian demographic and
local history. All these studies, together with the important work
of Don Felipe Ruiz Martín on finance and the economy during the
'century of the Genoese', have brought us significantly closer to the
day when we can begin to rethink the old problem of 'the decline
of Spain', not simply as a problem in economic history, but as one
in which domestic and international politics, the state of the economy
and the crown's finances, cultural attitudes and the structure of society
are all closely interwoven.

Political biography is not at present very fashionable among historians of Early Modern Europe. While it is not an economical way
of examining some of the questions at present in the forefront of
historical debate, it does, however, have certain advantages. The role
of decision-making, the politics of power, and the conduct of foreign
policy have tended to be relegated to the sidelines in much of the
most innovative historical work produced during the last two or
three decades, but there is a growing appreciation of the price that
has been paid for their neglect. If we are to achieve a genuinely
'total' history, they will sooner or later have to be reintegrated. A
biography of a prominent statesman who touches national life at
a whole variety of points can contribute to this reintegration by providing a focus that brings into perspective different aspects of his
times all too easily left in isolation. Unless artificially compartmenta-
lized into segments bearing such wan headings as 'domestic policy',
and 'foreign policy', it also demands a chronological narrative that
seeks to combine as far as possible domestic and international developments into a single frame of reference. This is what I have attempted
here.

No one is more conscious than I of the extent to which I have
fallen short of what I hoped to do. Ideally, more space should be
devoted in a political biography of the Count-Duke to questions
of domestic politics and government. But in many years of searching
I have not come across sufficient documentation of the kind required.

For the time being, at least, the inner workings of the Olivares administration preserve their mysteries. The heavy emphasis on foreign policy, however, is not purely an accident deriving from the bias of the documentation. With Olivares, as with Richelieu, foreign policy came to dominate everything else, and the careers of both men are likely to be distorted if this cardinal fact is ignored. I have done my best not to lose myself and the reader in the complexities of diplomatic detail when describing a policy which swept over the broad expanses of Europe during two full decades. My guiding principle, here and elsewhere, has been to discover wherever possible Olivares' *intentions*, in the belief that this would yield useful insights into attitudes of mind and problems of power and policy in seventeenth-century Europe. The exact reasons why those intentions were all too often not realized in practice will for a long time continue to elude us.

While the figure of Olivares himself will, I hope, emerge as a creature of flesh and blood, the same cannot be said of many of the lesser characters in the cast. When I began work, many of them were not even names, and their lives and careers had to be reconstructed from sketchy and inadequate sources. Nor, in most instances, do we have the kind of contemporary reportage which enables the historian to turn them with a few strokes of the pen into living and breathing personalities. Perhaps, as more information appears, others will be more successful than I. But it is not entirely inappropriate that they should be overshadowed here, as they were overshadowed in the court of Philip IV, by the towering figure of the king's principal minister. I cannot claim, after many years of acquaintance, to understand this complicated and often exasperating personality, although I have at least come to recognize (and occasionally sympathize with) some of his moods. He was, as Fernand Braudel once described him, not so much a single personality as a 'cortège of personalities, and he requires a cortège of explanations.' 'I must confess', continues Braudel, 'that if I had the desire to study the Count-Duke of Olivares, I should recoil before the immensity of the task.'[2] As one who has undertaken the task, I can only hope that the reader does not similarly recoil before the immensity of the resulting book.

I have acquired numerous debts of gratitude in the preparation of this book. My first thanks go to the directors and staff of the many archives in which I have worked for their unfailing help and courtesy.

[2] Fernand Braudel, 'En Espagne au temps de Richelieu et d'Olivarès', *Annales*, 2 (1947), pp. 354–58.

While it would be invidious to name some and not others, the days and weeks spent in Spain's great archive of Simancas linger in the memory as especially enjoyable, because the archivists of that unique castle-archive have succeeded over the generations in creating and maintaining ideal working conditions for the obsessive reader of other people's papers. I am deeply indebted, too, to the many owners of Spanish private archives, who have generously allowed me access and left me free to explore their contents. No one knows the full extent of the treasures that still lie in these archives, but the soundings that I have taken suggest the wealth of the riches still to be uncovered by historians of Early Modern Spain.

Many historians in Spain have given me not only help and encouragement, but also the privilege of their friendship. In particular, I owe more than I can ever repay to Antonio Domínguez Ortiz, José Antonio Maravall, and Felipe Ruiz Martín, who have generously exchanged with me over many years the ideas and information they have accumulated in the course of their own researches into the history of Habsburg Spain. José F. de la Peña, of the University of Alcalá de Henares, worked side by side with me in Princeton on the Count-Duke's papers, and together we have experienced the excitements and frustrations of the chase.

I owe a deep debt of gratitude also to Jonathan Brown, of the Institute of Fine Arts at New York University, as a companion and collaborator who for many years has lived with me mentally in the court of Philip IV. Over the years I have tried out my ideas on Orest Ranum and Richard Kagan, of the Johns Hopkins University, both of whom have responded generously to my requests for help, and have not hesitated to tell me when they felt I was going wrong. Professor Helmut Koenigsberger of King's College, University of London, has read much of the text of the book, and has, as always, been an acute and sympathetic critic. The Institute for Advanced Study has provided me during the past twelve years with unparalleled opportunities for the exchange of ideas with scholars working in my own and other fields, and, even if they are unaware of it, traces of their influences are to be found on numerous pages of this book. The Institute has also allowed me to appoint a succession of research assistants, and my gratitude goes out especially to David Lagomarsino, James Amelang, and Xavier Gil Pujol, whose thoughtful assistance and solicitude did much to lighten my task.

Richard Ollard, whose generous enthusiasm is accompanied by a close attention to detail, read the text in typescript and made many helpful observations. At the Yale University Press, John Nicoll, apparently undaunted by the scale of the enterprise, managed it with the competence and shrewdness which those fortunate enough to work with him have come to expect. I am deeply indebted both to him and to Gillian Malpass for the skill, discernment and care with which they have transformed the typescript into such a handsome volume.

My secretary, Peggy Van Sant, has assisted at every stage of the book since its inception, has spent long hours on the various drafts, and has cheerfully found a solution to every problem that presented itself along the way. Peter Bakewell, of the University of New Mexico, generously agreed to read the proofs, and detected, with his skilled editorial eye, many errors which had escaped me. Above all, my thanks go to my wife, who has provided constant support and encouragement, laboured heroically on the index, and has uncomplainingly lived in the Count-Duke's company for more years than I care to think.

Finally, I am grateful to the Institute for Advanced Study and its Director, Dr. Harry Woolf, for generous help from the publications fund towards the costs of printing.

Princeton, 24 February 1986

LIST OF ILLUSTRATIONS, TABLES AND MAPS

TABLES

MAPS

The maps were drawn by Elizabeth Dawlings and were based on the following:

Map 1 on the map of Spain in John Lynch, *Spain under the Habsburgs* (Basil Blackwell: Oxford, 1981).

Maps 2 and 3 on the maps of Europe during the Thirty Years' War in Geoffrey Parker, *The Thirty Years' War* (Routledge and Kegan Paul: London, 1984).

Map 4 on the map of the Low Countries in Jonathan I. Israel, *The Dutch Republic and the Hispanic World, 1606–1661* (Clarendon Press: Oxford, 1982).

PHOTOGRAPHIC SOURCES

Photographs have been supplied by owners, with the exception of the following:

Achenbach Foundation for Graphic Arts, California Palace of the Legion of Honor, 14.

British Library, 7.

The Hispanic Society of America, 18.

Mas, 10, 12, 24.

1. The Spain of Olivares

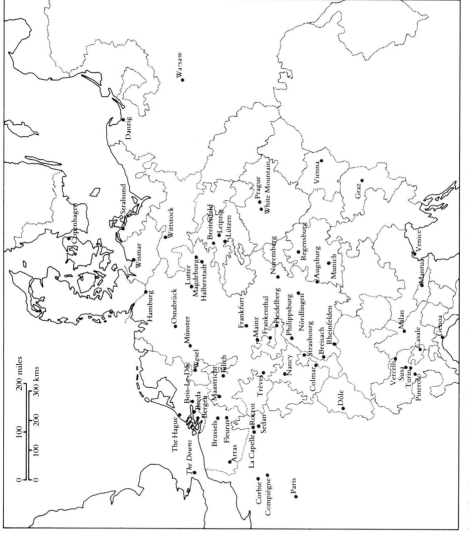

2. The Europe of the Thirty Years' War: towns and state boundaries

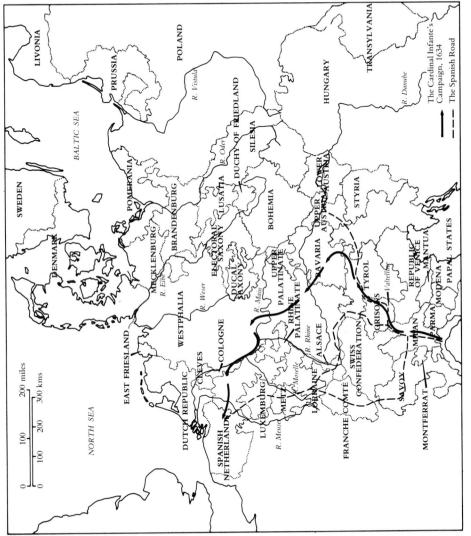

3. The Europe of the Thirty Years' War: military and political

Spanish Netherlands

Independent Bishopric of Liège

Territories conquered or reconquered
by the Dutch 1626–1648

EAST
FRIESLAND

Emden

GRONINGEN

FRIESLAND

R. Ems

TERRITORY
OF DRENTE

Hoorn   Enkhuizen

HOLLAND   OVERIJSSEL   Lingen

Haarlem   Amsterdam   R. Ijssel

Deventer   Oldenzaal

Leiden   Utrecht   GELDERLAND

The Hague   Arnhem   Grol

Delft

Rotterdam   R. Waal   Schenkenschans

Dordrecht   Nijmegen   Cleves

R. Maas   Gennep   Rees

Bois-Le-Duc   Wesel

ZEELAND   MEIERIJ

Middelburg   Breda   Rheinberg

Flushing   Bergen-op-Zoom   Geldern   Orsoy

Zandvliet   Eindhoven   Venlo

Ostend   Brugge   Hulst   Antwerp   Roermond

Dunkirk   Sas van Gent   Düsseldorf

Ghent   Maastricht   R. Rhine

FLANDERS   R. Lys   Jülich

St Omer   Leuven

Hesdin   Brussels

Lille   BRABANT   Liège

ARTOIS   R. Scheldt

HAINAULT

R. Sambre

LUXEMBURG

R. Meuse

0   50   100 kms

0   50 miles

4. The Netherlands, 1621–1648

LIST OF ABBREVIATIONS

1. Archives and Libraries

AAE	Archives du Ministère des Affaires Étrangères, Paris
ADI	Archivo del Duque del Infantado, Madrid
ADM	Archivo del Duque de Medinaceli, Seville
AGI	Archivo General de Indias, Seville
AGI Indif.	Indiferente General
AGR	Archives Générales du Royaume, Brussels
AGR CPE	Conseil Privé Espagnol
AGR SEG	Secrétairerie d'État et de Guerre
AGS	Archivo General de Simancas
AGS CJH	Consejos y Juntas de Hacienda
AGS Est.	Estado
AGS GA	Guerra antigua
AHN	Archivo Histórico Nacional, Madrid
AHN Est.	Estado
AHP	Archivo Histórico de Protocolos, Madrid
AMT	Archivo Municipal de Toledo
AS	Archivio di Stato
ASF	Archivio di Stato, Florence
ASG	Archivio di Stato, Genoa
ASL	Archivio di Stato, Lucca
ASM	Archivio di Stato, Mantua
ASV	Archivio Segreto Vaticano, Rome
ASVen	Archivio di Stato, Venice
BAV	Biblioteca Apostolica Vaticana, Rome
BL	British Library, London
BL Add.	Additional Mss.
BL Eg.	Egerton Mss.
BNM	Biblioteca Nacional, Madrid
BNP	Bibliothèque Nationale, Paris
BPM	Biblioteca del Palacio, Madrid
MSB	Bayerische Staatsbibliothek, Munich

PRO   Public Record Office, London
PRO SP   State Papers, Spain
RAH   Real Academia de la Historia, Madrid

2. *Other abbreviations*

Actas   Las actas de las Cortes de Castilla, 60 vols. (Madrid,
           1877–1974)
BAE   Biblioteca de Autores Españoles
BRAH   Boletín de la Real Academia de la Historia
Codoin   Colección de documentos inéditos para la historia de España
Hoz   Pedro de la Hoz, *Relación diaria desde 31 de marzo de 1621
           a 14 de agosto de 1640* (Ms. in author's possession. See
           p. 45n. 139)
leg.   legajo
lib.   libro
MC   J. H. Elliott and J. F. de la Peña, *Memoriales y cartas
           del Conde Duque de Olivares* (see Bibliography)
MHE   Memorial Histórico Español (13–19, *Cartas de algunos PP.
           de la Compañía de Jesús*)
Novoa   Matías de Novoa, *Historia de Felipe III, rey de España;
           Historia de Felipe IV, rey de España* (see Bibliography)

PART I

THE INHERITANCE
(1587–1622)

PROLOGUE

'On 31 March of this year 1621, at nine in the morning, His Majesty the King, Don Felipe III, passed to a better life.'[1] So began the *Grand Annals of Fifteen Days*, a brilliant piece of absentee reporting by that luminary of Spanish letters, Don Francisco de Quevedo, at this moment suffering the temporary inconvenience of banishment to his estate of La Torre de Juan Abad. Quevedo's *Annals* enjoyed an immediate success. They were passed from hand to hand, copied and recopied (for their author was unwilling to run the risk of publication) and attained enormous popularity with a public more than usually eager to hear the latest news from court.

Quevedo's absence from the scene of these great events did not prevent him from conveying the mood of hope and apprehensive excitement that swept Madrid during those first weeks of the reign of the sixteen-year old Philip IV—conveying it, indeed, almost too successfully, for he would later have cause to regret some of his more fulsome passages on the men of the new regime. The mood was captured, too, in the more ephemeral productions of the moment—in the satirical verses that made the rounds of the capital, in the newsletters from court correspondents to their provincial readers, and in the despatches of foreign envoys assiduously relating the latest scraps of gossip. The new king, according to a letter written from Madrid at the end of May, had 'in a few short days filled the world with hope.'[2] The accuracy of the comment was not substantially reduced by the suspect nature of its source; for it came from a man with a larger stake than most in the success of the new regime—Don Gaspar de Guzmán, Count of Olivares, now generally acknowledged as the new king's favourite.

Hope was a commodity that had been in short supply, and if it now made an exaggerated reappearance, this may in part be attributed to the suddenness of the change. In retrospect, however, the death

[1] Francisco de Quevedo, 'Grandes anales de quince días', in *Obras completas*, ed. Felicidad Buendía (6th ed., Madrid, 1966), 1, p. 731.
[2] BNM Ms. 7377, fo. 325, Olivares to Count of Guimerá, 29 May 1621.

2. The Alcázar of Madrid as it appeared after the modernization of the main facade by the court architect Juan Gómez de Mora in the reign of Philip III. The principal apartments were located on the third story, and the king's study, overlooking the river Manzanares, was in the left of the two towers, on the south-west corner.

of Philip III at the age of only forty-two should have come as no surprise. As Quevedo observed, the king's health had been uncertain and his colour suspicious since he fell ill on his return in 1619 from a state visit to Lisbon, where his son, Prince Philip, had received the oath of allegiance as heir to the Portuguese Crown. But there was no undue alarm when he came down with a fever on 1 March 1621, just as he was leaving his rooms in the palace for a visit to the convent of the Incarnation. The ministrations of his physicians, however, brought no improvement. The king was afflicted by a deep melancholy; and his confessor, Fray Luis de Aliaga, whose preoccupation with the affairs of this world was at least as great as his preoccupation with those of the next, failed to shake his conviction that his had been a life ill-spent. It had in fact been unusually blameless, as the lives of ordinary men go; and Philip III was the most ordinary of men. But he also happened to be the ruler of the most powerful state in Christendom, and as his otherwise insignificant life ebbed away, he could not banish his remorse for his failings as a king. The self-condemnation of Philip III on his death-bed made a profound impression on all those who saw him, and the memory of it would return to haunt his son.[3]

[3] For contemporary references to the state of mind of Philip III on his deathbed, see Ruth Lee Kennedy, '"El condenado por desconfiado"; its ambient and date of composition', *Homenaje a Guillermo Gustavino* (Madrid, 1974), pp. 27–33. The king's last days are described by Matías de Novoa, 'Historia de Felipe III, rey de España', *Codoin* 61, pp. 329–43.

As it became clear that the king's life was indeed drawing to an end, the gloomy royal palace of the Alcázar became the centre of intensive political manoeuvering (Pl. 2). Its physical layout made it a good setting for gossip and intrigue. Perched above the river Manzanares on the western side of Madrid, it was built around two large courtyards, where shopkeepers transacted their business, news-mongers came to hear and retail the latest 'novelties' (*novedades*)—a highly suspect word in a society which regarded any form of *novedad* as, by definition, dangerous[4]—and where courtiers, suitors and sup-plicants passed endless days of waiting. For the Alcázar, while it was a royal residence, was also the seat of government. Around the queen's courtyard, to the right of the principal entrance, were the council-chambers of the tribunals that governed the Spanish Monarchy—most notably the Councils of Castile, Aragon, Portugal and the Indies, and the first among them all, the Council of State.

On the upper floor were to be found the royal apartments—the queen's on the east side, the king's on the west. Since the death of Margaret of Austria in 1611 the queen's apartments had lacked an occupant. On the other hand the palace—most unusually for the Spanish Habsburgs—contained several royal offspring. Anne, the eldest of Philip and Margaret's children, had left home in 1615 on her marriage to Louis XIII, King of France. But the king had exchanged his daughter for a daughter-in-law by simultaneously marrying his ten-year old son Philip, Prince of Asturias, to the King of France's sister, Elizabeth of Bourbon. The prince and princess occupied a suite of rooms running northwards towards the river—a suite that Philip, as king, would later hand over to his first minister, the Count of Olivares.[5] The remaining royal children had their own apartments, but not their own households: the Infante Don Carlos, a shy retarded youth; his vivacious brother, the Cardinal-Infante Don Fernando, inappropriately destined for an ecclesiastical career as Cardinal-Archbishop of Toledo; and the Infanta María, no less inappropriately destined, at least by James I of England, to become Princess of Wales.

The king's quarters, on the western side, were approached through a series of galleries and antechambers, darkly furnished and hung with tapestries or paintings from the splendid royal collection. Here the king lived behind a barricade of protocol, eating solitary meals in his private dining chamber, and working, when the spirit moved

<hr>

[4] For *novedades* see especially José Antonio Maravall, *La cultura del barroco* (2nd. ed., Madrid, 1980), pp. 455–6.

[5] Ernst Werner, 'Caída del Conde-Duque de Olivares', *Revue Hispanique*, 71 (1927), p. 127. The plan of this floor of the Alcázar is reproduced in Jonathan Brown and J. H. Elliott, *A Palace for a King* (New Haven and London, 1980), p. 35.

him, in a study overlooking one of the palace gardens, known from
its Roman statuary as the Garden of the Emperors. Always he was
surrounded by the same few faces, those of the select group of nobles
and gentlemen who occupied the various ceremonial offices around
his royal person, and screened him from contact with the outside
world. Now, in March 1621, he lay dying in his bed-chamber, the
central figure, as always, in that elaborate court ritual which enve-
loped the lives of the Spanish Habsburgs from the cradle to the grave.

This was the moment for which many had been waiting with varying degrees of hope and fear: the Duke of Lerma, the fallen favourite
of Philip III, still dreaming of a return to power; the Duke of Uceda,
Lerma's son and his uneasy successor in the management of government business; Fray Luis de Aliaga, the ambitious royal confessor;
Prince Philibert of Savoy, whose response to the news of the king's
illness was to leave his naval command in the Mediterranean and
hurry to the court;[6] and Don Fernando de Borja, who had been elevated out of harm's way to the viceroyalty of Aragon, but was still
thought to retain the affections of the prince. But, as the bells of
the Madrid churches tolled out their message on the morning of
31 March, two men had a clearer idea than most of what the future
held in store. One was the Duke of Lerma's former henchman, Don
Rodrigo Calderón, who heard the tolling of the bells from his prison
cell and prophetically exclaimed: 'The King is dead, and I am dead!'[7]
The other was Don Gaspar de Guzmán, the Count of Olivares.

[6] Franz Christoph Khevenhüller, *Annales Ferdinandei*, 1 (Leipzig, 1724), pp. 1270–1.
[7] Novoa, *Codoin* 61, p. 373.

I

THE GUZMÁN INHERITANCE

The House of Guzmán

The enemies of Don Gaspar de Guzmán liked to say that he was born in Nero's palace in Rome. He was in fact born, on 6 January 1587, in the Spanish Embassy. Since 1582 his father, Don Enrique de Guzmán, had been Spain's ambassador to the pope—a mission which he accomplished with an arrogance and irascibility that made him a suitable match for that tempestuous pontiff Sixtus V.

As a third son of a junior branch of the great Andalusian house of Guzmán, Don Gaspar could not ordinarily have looked forward to great fame or great fortune. But the fact that he had been born in Rome as the son of the Spanish ambassador did give him certain initial advantages. Cardinal Aldobrandini, the future Pope Clement VIII, officiated at his baptism, and later conferred on him a canonry in Seville cathedral, together with a number of benefices intended to pave the way for a successful ecclesiastical career. If everything went according to plan he might one day rise to eminence as Cardinal Guzmán. This at least was the hope of his father, who arranged a rigorous tutoring for his son.[1] Many years later, when Don Gaspar himself was discussing the upbringing of a bastard son of Philip IV, he laid down the essentials for a good education, which was very probably patterned on his own. The child, he wrote, must be thoroughly grounded in the rudiments of piety; be given a good reading knowledge of Latin, French and Italian; and attain proficiency in fencing, dancing and horsemanship. 'Above all', concluded Don Gaspar, 'beat him and train him well.'[2]

Even the plans of so meticulous a planner as the second Count of Olivares were not exempt, however, from the vagaries of chance. The eldest of his three sons died as a result of a fall from a balcony in Salamanca in 1587, the year of Don Gaspar's birth. The second,

---

[1] There is very little information on Olivares' early years. Most of what we have comes from the manuscript *Epítome de las Historias de la Gran Casa de Guzmán*, completed in 1638 by Juan Alonso Martínez Sánchez Calderón, BNM Ms. 2258 (Libro XVIII). See also Gregorio Marañón, *El Conde-Duque de Olivares* (3rd. ed., Madrid, 1952), ch. 2.

[2] BL Eg. Ms. 347, fos. 79–80v. *Instrucción* of Olivares for Don Juan de Isassi, 1 June 1630. The child in question was Francisco Fernando, who died in 1634 at the age of nine.

Don Jerónimo, fell ill and died in 1604, at the age of twenty-one. There remained Don Gaspar and his three sisters, Francisca, Inés and Leonor. (See family tree, between pp. 22 and 23). Don Gaspar, as a result of these family misfortunes, now found himself heir at the age of seventeen to the title and estate, along with all that complementary baggage which any noble family in Early Modern Europe accumulated over the course of the centuries—hopes, aspirations, grievances, lawsuits and debts. The house of Guzmán, as one of the greatest and most prolific houses in Spain, was furnished with all of these.

The titular head of the family in the opinion of most people was that great Andalusian magnate, the Duke of Medina Sidonia. In 1600 the seventh duke, who had led the Invincible Armada to defeat, was the lord of some 90,000 vassals and enjoyed, at least nominally, an annual income of 170,000 ducats.[3] The centre of his domains was Seville's port of Sanlúcar de Barrameda, where his hereditary control of the customs dues yielded him rich benefits, some of them more licit than others. Even if his estates, like those of his fellow magnates, were encumbered with debts, his resources were so vast as to make him unsinkable. His position as captain-general of the Andalusian coast reinforced the impressive local influence which he derived from his wealth and his splendid lineage. The Spanish Crown, for all its success in creating an elaborate bureaucracy, still looked to the magnates for assistance in their local spheres of influence, and a Duke of Medina Sidonia was bound to be a major political figure, even if, like the seventh duke, he shunned the politics of the court. One man who had no illusions on this score was the Duke of Lerma, Philip III's favourite and principal minister. He married his daughter to the Count of Niebla, the duke's son and heir, who became eighth Duke of Medina Sidonia in 1615.

In a lengthy memorandum on the Guzmáns and their ancestry which Don Gaspar inflicted on the king in 1625, he began the family history with Ruy Pérez de Guzmán in 1015.[4] Over the centuries the Guzmán family tree had put forth many branches, and it was from one of the most recent of these that the Counts of Olivares sprang. Pedro de Guzmán, who was created first Count of Olivares by the Emperor Charles V in 1535,[5] was the son of the third Duke of Medina Sidonia by Leonor de Zúñiga, his second wife. As a younger son, Pedro de Guzmán saw his two elder brothers succeed in turn to

---

[3] Pedro Núñez de Salcedo, 'Relación de los títulos que hay en España . . .', BRAH, 73 (1918), pp. 468–92, gives late sixteenth-century estimates for the income of Medina Sidonia and his fellow aristocrats.

[4] MC, 1, Doc. VII.

[5] Sánchez Calderón, Epítome, fo. 566, for this and other details of his career.

the ducal title; but he contested their succession in the courts, alleging matrimonial irregularities which left him as the eldest legitimate son. The failure of his claim left him with a sense of burning injustice, which he transmitted to his descendants along with his title.

The unsatisfied aspiration after the Medina Sidonia title and fortune was one of the driving elements in the career not only of Don Pedro himself, but also of his son and grandson, the second and third Counts of Olivares. Their constant harping on the importance of their services to the crown and on the inadequacy of their rewards suggests a dogged determination to compensate for their failure to secure recognition of the family primacy which they considered theirs of right. 'It is only right', reads a petition of Don Pedro to Philip II, 'that everyone should recognize the high esteem in which my services are held ... and that I should retire to my *patria* with the honour that befits so ancient a servant of Your Majesty and Your Majesty's father.'[6]

Traditionally it was through service to the crown, coupled wherever possible with a profitable marriage, that younger sons sought to build their own family fortunes. In spite of his expressions of dissatisfaction, Don Pedro managed reasonably well on both counts. He won the favour of Charles V by helping to crush the Comunero uprisings in Seville and Toledo in 1521, and accompanied the Emperor on his travels in Germany, Italy and Flanders. He was majordomo to both Charles V and Philip II, and was rewarded, in addition to the title of Count of Olivares, with the governorship of the royal palace (Alcázar) and dockyards in Seville, and with a knighthood in the military order of Calatrava. He died in 1569, having established in the name of his eldest son a *mayorazgo*—an entailed estate—with its principal seat in the small town of Olivares near Seville.

Don Pedro de Guzmán's career, which firmly established him and his family among the titled nobility of Castile, was an obvious success story except in his own terms, which required nothing less than accession to the dukedom of Medina Sidonia. Indeed it stands as a perfect illustration of the kind of opportunities available in early sixteenth-century Spain to the untitled sons of the upper nobility and to members of the *hidalgo* or gentry class. The growing military and administrative needs of the crown in an age of warfare and territorial expansion created numerous possibilities for service and reward. Government service could lead to dramatic social advancement, as the career of Charles V's secretary, Francisco de Los Cobos, spectacularly demonstrated.[7]

If not everyone who entered government service did as well as Los Cobos, the little group of secretaries and officials recruited by

[6] AGS Expedientes de Hacienda leg. 973. Undated petition of the first Count of Olivares.
[7] See Hayward Keniston, *Francisco de los Cobos* (Pittsburgh, 1960).

Ferdinand the Catholic still managed to obtain rich pickings. The best known among them was Los Cobos' first patron, the Aragonese Lope Conchillos, who married María Niño de Ribera, a cousin of the Duke of Infantado.[8] It was their daughter, Francisca de Ribera Niño, who became the wife of Pedro de Guzmán in 1539; and the bond between new wealth and old lineage was drawn still closer when in due course one of the daughters of this marriage, Doña Ana Félix de Guzmán, married Los Cobos' grandson. A jocular wedding guest arrived for the ceremony with his hat stuck full of pens—an allusion to the origins of both families' fortunes that may not have struck either the Count of Olivares or the Marquis of Camarasa, the bridegroom's father, as being in the best of taste.[9]

Considerable wealth and a family bureaucratic tradition were not all that Francisca de Ribera Niño brought to her marriage to the first Count of Olivares. Her father, Lope Conchillos, was not only an Aragonese, but also, like so many of the officials in Ferdinand's secretariat, an Aragonese of Jewish ancestry.[10] Lope Conchillos himself moved easily in the *converso*—the Christianized Jewish—circles of early sixteenth-century Toledo, and his wife's family was apparently related by marriage to another *converso*, Juan Sánchez de Toledo, the grandfather of St. Teresa of Avila.[11] These relationships, which were reasonably acceptable at the time but which grew more and more socially embarrassing as Castilian society became obsessed by the issue of purity of blood (*limpieza de sangre*) were concealed by later generations as best they could. The seventeenth-century historian of the house of Guzmán blandly remarks that 'the ancient family of the Conchillos was and is one of the most esteemed and highly regarded in the kingdom of Aragon';[12] but everybody knew that the grandmother of Don Gaspar de Guzmán, third Count of Olivares, was the daughter of a *converso* family, and when Quevedo came to describe the imaginary isle of the Monopantos with its dissembling Jewish inhabitants, he called its prince *Pragas Chincollos*[13]—an anagram of Gaspar Conchillos, clearly recognizable as the Count of Olivares himself.

As is only to be expected, the descendants of converted Jews in sixteenth- and seventeenth-century Spain reacted in different ways to the knowledge that 'tainted' blood ran in their veins, and it is impossible to determine the extent to which this awareness of an

[8] *Ibid.*, p. 48.

[9] *Ibid.*, p. 331.

[10] Julio Caro Baroja, *Los judíos en la España moderna y contemporánea* (Madrid, 1962), 2, p. 16.

[11] José Carlos Menor Fuentes, *El linaje toledano de Santa Teresa de Jesús y de San Juan de la Cruz* (Toledo, 1970). I owe this reference to the kindness of Dr. José Francisco de la Peña.

[12] Sánchez Calderón, *Epítome*, fo. 583.

[13] 'La fortuna con seso y la hora de todos', *Obras completas*, 1, p. 266.

inherited social stigma—itself not unusual among the Castilian nobility—played any part in the psychological make-up of the second and third Counts of Olivares. Their eagerness to secure entry into the exclusive circle of the grandees is explicable without reference to a *converso* ancestry; and an alleged predilection for the company of Jews, of which Don Gaspar's enemies accused him, may have been no more than a reflection of the crown's financial necessities. Yet in a discussion in the Council of State in 1625 on the *limpieza* laws, which excluded so many qualified men from office and honour on the grounds of dubious ancestry, he spoke with unusual feeling: 'The law prohibiting honours is unjust and impious, against divine law, natural law, and the law of nations . . . . . Without crime, without sin or offence against God, they find themselves—even when they excel all others in virtue, sanctity and scholarship—condemned not only without being heard, but without even the possibility of being heard . . . . . In no other government or state in the world do such laws exist . . . . .'[14] The words, perhaps, of a man who knew something of the suffering and indignities experienced by those of 'tainted' blood; but against them must be set a clause in his will—or was it no more than a conventional formula?—which stipulated that no one of tainted ancestry should succeed to his inheritance.[15]

The first Count of Olivares' marriage to the daughter of Lope Conchillos brought him three sons and two daughters who survived into adult life. Besides Ana Félix, who married the Marquis of Camarasa, there was Leonor, who married into the family of Mexía, and whose descendants bore the title of Marquis of Loriana.[16] The third son, Don Pedro de Guzmán, was a gentleman of the chamber to Philip II and Philip III; the second, Don Félix, died on military service in Flanders. The eldest, Don Enrique, who was born in 1540, succeeded his father as second Count of Olivares in 1569. Able, ambitious, and as meticulous in his attention to detail as his master Philip II, he spent his long and distinguished career in the service of the crown. He accompanied Philip to England at the time of his marriage to Mary Tudor; was wounded in the leg at the battle of St. Quentin; and proceeded to hold a succession of important posts outside Spain— the embassy at Rome from 1582 to 1591, the viceroyalty of Sicily

---

[14] *MC*, 1, p. 73 n. 42.

[15] RAH Salazar, M-189, *Testamento*, 16 May 1642, p. 30. The will (but not the list of individual bequests) is published in *Testamentos de 43 personas del Madrid de los Austrias*, ed. Antonio Matilla Tascón (Madrid, 1983), pp. 171–94. See p. 190 for this clause, which seems to go beyond the merely formulaic in its insistence that the Council of Castile, by secret individual votes, should decide whether the claimant to the title was indeed of blood 'clean of all bad race, and of all infection and taint.' How this is to be squared with Olivares' comments of 1625 on the *limpieza* laws remains a mystery.

[16] Sánchez Calderón, *Epítome*, fo. 579v.

from 1591 to 1595, and that of Naples from 1595 to 1599. His viceregal career was characterized by an unusual attention to good financial management, which did not, however, preclude attention to his own financial well-being.[17]

In 1579 Don Enrique married Doña María Pimentel de Fonseca, the daughter of the fourth Count of Monterrey. The marriage brought him a dowry of 60,000 ducats, and a connection with some of the most distinguished houses of Castile, notably those of Monterrey, Fuentes and Frías (the Constables of Castile). It was while she was lying ill as a child in the Monterrey palace in Salamanca, that Doña María was visited by St. Teresa, and made an apparently miraculous recovery.[18] Not surprisingly, she revered the memory of St. Teresa; and her son, Don Gaspar, who inherited this devotion, was the proud possessor of the saint's heart set with diamonds, which he would bequeath to the queen.[19] During her husband's terms of office in Rome and Palermo the countess, as practical in her piety as St. Teresa herself, became known for her charitable works among the poor and her efforts to reform and rescue prostitutes. She seems to have had a good head for business, and was left by her husband to manage both the household and the household accounts. But it was her devoutness that most impressed her contemporaries. She and her husband amassed an enormous collection of relics, some of them still dustily preserved in the collegiate church of Olivares; and whatever Sixtus V may have thought of the count, he had nothing but admiration for the 'holy countess.' She died in childbed in 1594 at the age of forty-four, when her third son, Don Gaspar, was seven.[20]

Don Enrique had made his career in the service of Philip II, and like many another loyal servant of the old king, he never quite adjusted to the very different regime which came with the accession of Philip III in 1598. The frivolity and self-indulgence of the government exercised by the Duke of Lerma on behalf of Philip III must have been deeply distressing to a man accustomed to the austere morality of the Prudent King. While Lerma could hardly ignore the impressive record of service of the Count of Olivares, he was in no great hurry to add this potentially awkward colleague to his team. The count returned to Spain from Naples in 1600, and it was only

---

[17] Don Enrique's career is summarized in Sánchez Calderón's *Epítome*, lib. XVII, and Marañón, *Olivares*, pp. 12–19. See also H. G. Koenigsberger, *The Government of Sicily under Philip II of Spain* (London, 1951), pp. 193–4. [Emended version, *The Practice of Empire* (Ithaca, 1969)].

[18] Efrén de la Madre de Dios and O. Steggink, *Tiempo y vida de Santa Teresa* (Madrid, 1968), p. 434.

[19] *Testamento*, 29v.

[20] Sánchez Calderón, *Epítome*, fos, 607–607v.; Marañón, *Olivares*, p. 20; Juana Gil-Bermejo, 'Olivares y su colegial', *El Correo de Andalucía*, 29 December 1971, for the collegiate church of Olivares and its relics.

in November 1601 that he obtained the expected reward for his labours—a seat on the Council of State.[21] He was also appointed principal financial minister of the crown, an occupation which can only have been a source of despair to so fastidious a public servant in the prevailing climate of royal liberality. But his real mortification came from the king's refusal to give him the reward which he most coveted, a grandeeship for himself and his house. There was, he was told, no hope.[22] Like his father before him, he felt bitterly the lack of recognition, and made no attempt to hide his resentment. Matías de Novoa, a court official who found an outlet for his frustrations in a verbose and spiteful chronicle of the history of his times, tartly observed that to be a grandson of the Duke of Medina Sidonia is an insufficient qualification for grandeeship, and that the supreme privilege of the grandee—the right to be covered in the presence of the king—was properly reserved for 'great men, great deeds, great victories and great enterprises.'[23] The theory was admirable, but under the Duke of Lerma its application left much to be desired.

A grandeeship would have given the junior branch of the house of Guzmán that unassailable position among the great houses of Castile which the first Count of Olivares had resolved to secure for his family when the dukedom of Medina Sidonia eluded his grasp. As it was, the second count could do no more than transmit the family ambition to the next generation, in the hope that one of his sons would succeed where he and his father had failed. But before his death on 26 March 1607 at the age of sixty-seven, he took whatever steps were needed to ensure that his son and heir Don Gaspar should be well placed to fight for that supreme prize which had so persistently been denied him by the enemies of his house. Always the prudent manager, he made the most careful arrangements for the disposal of his estate, without, however, neglecting the salvation of his soul.

The entail established by the first count in 1563 and inherited by Don Gaspar is described by him as being worth 60,000 ducats a year.[24] While this did not begin to compete with the annual incomes— at least on paper—of the great families of Castile, like the Dukes of Alba, Infantado, Medina Sidonia and Medina de Ríoseco, it placed the Counts of Olivares high in the middle ranks of the titled nobility. In a 1592 listing of Castile's fifty-two titled families, ten were stated to have an annual income of over 100,000 ducats, and another four

[21] P. L. Williams, 'The Court and Councils of Philip III of Spain' (University of London, doctoral dissertation, 1973), p. 30; Luis Cabrera de Córdoba, *Relaciones de las cosas sucedidas en la corte de España desde 1599 hasta 1614* (Madrid, 1857), p. 156, says that he took the oath as councillor on 24 September 1602.

[22] Cabrera de Córdoba, p. 191.

[23] *Codoin* 61, p. 86.

[24] 'El Nicandro', *MC*, 2, p. 263.

of between 60,000 and 100,000. There followed a further group of ten in the 40,000 to 60,000 range, including the Counts of Olivares. Below them were another ten in the 20,000 to 40,000 range, and eighteen with under 20,000 a year.[25]

The entailed portion of the Olivares estate consisted almost entirely of landed property in the region of Seville: the town of Olivares, with its seigneurial dues and rents, and the produce of its olive groves, vineyards and cornfields; similar dues and rents from the little towns of Castilleja de la Cuesta, Castilleja de Guzmán and Heliche, and from an estate at Miraflores on the outskirts of Seville; and some houses in Seville itself, along with their gardens outside the city boundaries. Investments in municipal taxes and customs dues on the Indies trade yielded a further 4,000 ducats a year.[26]

As was common with entailed estates, however, the real as distinct from the nominal annual income of the Olivares entail seems to have been substantially less than this figure of 60,000 ducats. Although entails were technically inbarrable, the Castilian nobility had found a means of circumventing the intentions of their ancestors by petitioning the crown for special dispensations from the clause of their entails prohibiting the right to mortgage.[27] Profiting from this device, Don Enrique had raised loans on his entail, on which he paid 20,370 ducats a year in interest. The estate also had to bear the salaries of stewards and other officials, and was inevitably subject to fluctuations in the yield of rents and dues. In the early 1620's the average annual income from the entail was assessed at 40,500 ducats,[28] which suggests either a sharp fall in its value since the time of Don Gaspar's succession, or else that the figure of 60,000 was only nominal.

But Don Enrique's legacy was not confined to an entailed estate carrying a burden of debt. He also left substantial reserves of wealth outside the entail, including a charitable foundation, the *monte de Olivares*, whose annual income of 14,000 ducats was initially to be used for the endowment of the church at Olivares, and later for the foundation of a convent of twelve nuns and the provision of financial assistance to members of the family. Inventories drawn up at the time of his death show that he possessed considerable wealth, too, in the form of urban properties, and household effects like tapestries, carpets and silverware. He owned cattle and sheep—a flock

---

[25] Núñez de Salcedo, 'Relación de los títulos . . .'; Charles Jago, 'The influence of debt on the relations between crown and aristocracy in seventeenth-century Castile', *Economic History Review*, 26 (1973), p. 221 n. 1. The accuracy of contemporary estimates of aristocratic income is of course highly suspect.

[26] AHP leg. 1824, fos. 798 ff., 'El Conde de Olivares Don Enrique. Inventario de sus bienes'; Sánchez Calderón, *Epítome*, fos. 612v.–615.

[27] Jago, 'Influence of debt', p. 222.

[28] BL Add. Ms. 34,447, fo. 229, statement on income and properties of the Count of Olivares.

of over a thousand—and his estates produced wine which was exported to the Indies.[29] As a former Italian viceroy—always one of the more lucrative assignments for the Spanish nobility—and as a landowner in an Andalusia which still displayed unmistakeable signs of prosperity, Don Enrique had clearly added substantially to the wealth of his line, and had laid firm foundations for his son's career.

The early years

Don Gaspar succeeded to his father's title, as third Count of Olivares, at the age of twenty. He was unusual among the titled nobility of Spain in having spent the first years of his life outside the peninsula. It was not until he was thirteen, when he returned in 1600 with his father from Naples, that he first saw the land of his ancestors. Although he was never again to leave the Iberian peninsula, those childhood years in Italy and Sicily at least gave him an awareness of a world beyond Spain, together with a knowledge of Italian and an acquaintance with Italian literature. He studied Dante and Bembo with his tutor, and in later life his personal library contained a large section devoted to 'Tuscan' books. Like other Spanish nobles of the sixteenth and early seventeenth centuries he admired Italian culture; and although he can hardly have had any clear recollection of the 'buildings and gardens of Rome', about which he sustained an animated monologue with the Modenese ambassador many years later,[30] it is clear that the Italian experience of those early years had made its mark upon him.

Don Gaspar was also unusual among titled Spanish nobles in receiving a university education. Although a few titled families traditionally sent their sons to the university, the majority were educated at home.[31] As a younger son, destined for the church, there was a good case for sending Don Gaspar to study canon law at Salamanca, where the Counts of Monterrey, his relatives on his mother's side, had their family palace. In 1601, at the age of fourteen, he was sent off from Seville to Salamanca accompanied by nineteen servants, including eight pages and four footmen, and by a tutor—a relative, Dr. Laureano de Guzmán—who was armed with a sheaf of minutely detailed instructions drafted by an anxious father.[32]

Above all, Don Enrique insisted, his son was to be a good Christian, taking communion on all the major feast days, and attending mass

[29] AHP leg. 1824, fos. 798 ff.
[30] Brown and Elliott, *A Palace*, p. 89.
[31] Richard L. Kagan, *Students and Society in Early Modern Spain* (Baltimore, 1974), pp. 183–4.
[32] BNM Ms. 10,846, fos. 1–23, 'Instrucción que Don Enrique de Guzmán ... dió a Don Laureano de Guzmán ...', 7 January 1601.

'infallibly' every day. He was to examine his conscience carefully each night before retiring to bed, and one tenth of his monthly expenditure was to be devoted to alms-giving—a standard practice in the Count of Olivares' household.[33] He was to attend the courses needed for graduation in canon and civil law, but during his first year he was also to spend time at home improving his Latin, 'because every one insists on the importance of this.' On his way to lectures he must avoid being sidetracked into conversation with bad students, and in the lecture hall he was always to sit at the same bench, accompanied by a page and other members of his household. On returning home (at ten on summer mornings and at eleven in winter) he could indulge in a little croquet or ninepins before his midday meal. He would be read to after lunch (on no account would card games be allowed). In the afternoon there were more lectures to attend. When they were finished he might engage his lecturers in a little conversation in the cloisters, as long as he listened more than he talked—a habit which Don Gaspar never seems to have acquired. He would then return home and take some light refreshment. The evening hours from six to nine were to be devoted to the study of lecture notes. Each day six new precepts and their glosses were to be memorized, for it was essential to confide to memory all the rules of canon and civil law. After supper there would be a general discussion of the day's classes before the household retired for the night.

There is some conflict of opinion as to how far the fourteen-year old Don Gaspar actually followed this rigorous regimen and did any work.[34] If, as seems probable, he read extensively at some stage of his life, this may have been after his university days were over. But the years at Salamanca do seem to have given him an abiding love of books and learning. 'From the school of Salamanca', one of his eulogists would write, 'he retained a determination never to leave learning bereft of a patron, wherever it was to be found.'[35] At Salamanca, too, he made the acquaintance of promising scholars of his own generation, like Don Juan de Isassi,[36] whom he would later recommend for appointment as tutor to Philip IV's young son. As far as his own studies were concerned, even a superficial introduction to the rudiments of canon and civil law would have given him

[33] Sánchez Calderón, *Epítome*, fo. 615.

[34] Sánchez Calderón, fo. 672v. says that Don Gaspar 'se graduó en los sagrados canones con particular ingenio y aplicación', while the Conde de la Roca, *Fragmentos históricos de la vida de D. Gaspar de Guzmán*, in Valladares, *Semanario Erudito*, 2, p. 150, says that he 'cursó en la facultad del derecho con más ingenio que aplicación.' Sánchez Calderón, who tends to follow Roca closely, may here have decided to improve upon him.

[35] BNM Ms. 2237, fo. 132. Joseph Pellicer de Tovar, *Templo de la fama, alcázar de la fortuna levantado a las acciones de Don Gaspar de Guzmán, Conde Duque de Olivares*.

[36] BL Eg. Ms. 347, fo. 76. Olivares to king, Good Friday, 1630.

some training in the arts of casuistry which he was to display in his political career. Was it in his university years that he developed a tendency to produce his epithets in groups of three—'it is a common, agreed, and special belief . . .'; '. . . with great application, care and skill . . .'?[37] He also learnt how to speak in public and engage in debate—his father's instructions included arrangements for fort-nightly debates between himself and his servants—and in later years he was famed for what his admirers described as eloquence and his enemies loquacity.

In the speeches with which Don Gaspar would one day harangue the Council of State there was always liable to be an element of rhetorical overkill, combined with a degree of circumlocution which must have tried the patience of his hearers. The contrast between his rhetorical style and that of a statesman of the older generation, like the Count of Gondomar, is as sharp as the contrast in architectural style between the convolutions of Sevillian Baroque and the classical sobriety of the Escorial. Complexity and artifice were to be at a premium among Spaniards of Don Gaspar's generation, who revelled in the flights of Jesuit oratory. The contrived obscurities of the Flemish scholar Justus Lipsius—that oracle of their age—held a greater attrac-tion for them than his Tacitean brevity.[38] It was characteristic of Don Gaspar's taste that he should have felt an instinctive affinity for the writings of his famous Bolognese contemporary, Virgilio Malvezzi, whom he would summon to Madrid in 1636 to chronicle the triumphs of his regime.[39] Malvezzi, who—like Lipsius—drew his inspiration from Tacitus and Seneca, sought by means of startling paradoxes, and of sudden discontinuities and digressions, to convey to his readers an impression of oracular inspiration. It was somewhat the same with Don Gaspar's speeches and state papers. Their argu-ments were forcefully marshalled, their phraseology occasionally enlivened by some surprising colloquialism or popular proverb, but they also convey an impression of prolixity and diffuseness with their frequent digressions from the main line of argument. It remains unclear to what extent the overblown sentences and the tendency to digress reflect the influence of contemporary models, and how far they simply derive from a lack of mental discipline.

Don Gaspar's greatest distinction in his university career was to be elected rector in November 1603 by his fellow students—a post

---

[37] *MC*, 1, p. 220.
[38] For the Lipsian rhetorical tradition, and its Italian interpreter, Malvezzi, see Marc Fumaroli, *L'âge de l'éloquence* (Geneva, 1980), pp. 216–19. I am indebted to Dr. Fumaroli for his advice and guidance on the various rhetorical traditions in seventeenth-century Europe. The Spanish rhetorical tradition in this period needs more systematic study.
[39] For Malvezzi, in addition to Fumaroli, see especially D. L. Shaw's introduction to his edition of Malvezzi's *Historia de los primeros años del reinado de Felipe IV* (London, 1968).

which was traditionally filled by a student of noble birth. Presumably it was while he was fulfilling his duties as university rector that an incident occurred which he would recall with pride in 1637 during the insurrection in the Portuguese town of Evora. One night he and three or four servants found themselves confronted by a mob of a thousand or more students armed with stones, 'and students being what they are, I stopped them single-handed . . . and not one of them dared pass.'[40] As a reward for his services as rector, Philip III appointed him to the commandery of Vívoras in the Military Order of Calatrava;[41] and on his death-bed his last recorded words were: 'When I was rector, when I was rector!'[42]

It was just after the conclusion of his year as rector that the sudden death of his elder brother, Don Jerónimo, changed the course of his life. The ecclesiastical career was hastily abandoned, and his father summoned him to Valladolid, to which the court had recently moved.[43] The university education was to be exchanged for an education in the ways of the court, in which Don Gaspar, under his father's tutelage, would prove an adept pupil. As heir to his father's frustrated ambitions, it would be for him to secure the outward recognition of royal approval which would vindicate the honour of the family. This was to be one of the abiding themes of his life; and near the end of it, defeated and disgraced, he would write of his 'reputation and honour, which is all I have wished to preserve even to the grave, so as not to appear the unworthy son of such great parents as God was pleased to bestow on me.'[44]

As soon as he inherited his father's title in 1607, the new count started spending, and spending with abandon. Mobilizing all the resources he could muster, he embarked on an extravagant courtship of his cousin, Doña Inés de Zúñiga y Velasco, one of the queen's ladies-in-waiting. In the process, he is said to have spent the enormous sum of 300,000 ducats,[45] presumably on the assumption that money was the only language that the court of Philip III could understand. Lavish spending would strengthen his claims to a grandeeship, especially if Doña Inés' own claims on the royal bounty were taken into account. She was the daughter of Don Gaspar de Zúñiga y Acevedo, the fifth Count of Monterrey, who had died in Lima the preceding year leaving enormous debts[46]—such an

[40] BL Add. Ms. 28,429, fos. 58–58v., Olivares to Conde de Basto, 16 November 1637.
[41] Pellicer, *Templo de la fama*, fo. 122v.–123.
[42] Marañón, *Olivares*, p. 27. See also Urbano González de la Calle, *Relaciones del Conde Duque de Olivares con la Universidad de Salamanca* (Madrid, 1931).
[43] Marañón, *Olivares*, p. 29.
[44] AHN Est. lib. 869, fo. 249v., Olivares to Antonio Carnero, 22 December 1643.
[45] Pellicer, *Templo de la fama*, fo. 132; Roca, *Fragmentos*, p. 151.
[46] AGI Indif. leg. 754, copy of royal cédula of 11 May 1608; ADI Montesclaros Mss., lib. 31, Olivares to Montesclaros, 24 August 1626.

for grand theatrical gestures, like the building of the largest and most pompous of all the monumental catafalques erected to commemorate the triumphs and virtues of the late Philip II.[56]

In moving back to Seville, where he had inherited his father's honorific post as governor of the Alcázar—the old royal palace of the Moorish kings—the Count of Olivares took his place among the small group of titled nobles whose presence added lustre to the city's life. Renaissance and post-Renaissance Seville prided itself on its dedication to letters and the arts. The city's leading families, who dominated both the city council and the cathedral chapter, vied with each other as patrons, and graced with their presence the literary salons which were a feature of Sevillian life. The first Count of Olivares, Don Gaspar's grandfather, used to gather the city's poets together for sessions in the rooms of the Alcázar.[57] Another meeting-place was the Casa de Pilatos, the splendid Renaissance palace of the Dukes of Alcalá, where the third duke, Don Fernando Afán de Ribera, boasted one of the best private libraries in Spain, and a fine collection of pictures, sculptures and Roman antiquities.[58]

Olivares, four years the junior of Alcalá, was not the kind of man to let himself be outdone in friendly rivalry. If Alcalá was a great book-collector, he would be a greater; if Alcalá was a brilliant patron, he would none the less outshine him. On returning to Seville in 1607 he began to patronize poets and artists with a lavishness which earned him the sobriquet of Manlio, after the munificent Roman patron, M. Manlius Capitolinus.[59] Some of the most distinguished figures in the city's cultural life were to be found in his company, like Seville's leading artist, Francisco Pacheco, who painted a portrait of Olivares which has unfortunately not survived.[60] Pacheco's house was the meeting-place for one of Seville's private academies, which in its time had been attended by Cervantes and Lope de Vega. Through the Pacheco circle Olivares made new friendships and strengthened old ones. One of his most intimate friends was a younger brother of the Marquis of Orellana, a relative on his mother's side—Don

[56] For the splendours of Renaissance Seville, see Vicente Lleó Cañal, *Nueva Roma: mitología y humanismo en el renacimiento sevillano* (Seville, 1979). The *túmulo* of Philip II is described and discussed in pp. 138–49.

[57] Lleó Cañal, p. 86.

[58] For the Seville academies, see Jonathan Brown, *Images and Ideas in Seventeenth-Century Spanish Painting* (Princeton, 1978), ch. 1, and the references there given. For the Duke of Alcalá, see Joaquín González Moreno, *Don Fernando Enríquez de Ribera, tercer duque de Alcalá de los Gazules, 1583–1637* (Seville, 1969).

[59] Cayetano Alberto de la Barrera y Leirado, *Poesías de Don Francisco de Rioja* (Madrid, 1867), pp. 13–14.

[60] Berwick y Alba, Duque de, *Discursos leídos ante la Real Academia de Bellas Artes de San Fernando en la recepción pública del Excmo. Sr. Duque de Berwick y de Alba* (Madrid, 1924), pp. 23–4.

Juan de Fonseca y Figueroa, a canon of the cathedral, and a historian and amateur painter, of whom he later wrote: 'we were close friends from early youth, the foundations of our friendship being ties of kinship and his great natural talents . . .'.[61] Another was Francisco de Rioja, a member of Pacheco's academy—'a person of singular letters, deeply read in Greek and Latin authors', in Olivares' words.[62] Rioja celebrated Don Gaspar and his love affairs in his poetry—an art at which Don Gaspar himself also tried his hand, writing verses both in Latin and Spanish which he later burnt.[63] During these years an enduring friendship was forged between the two men. Rioja was to become Olivares' private librarian, and perhaps his closest confidant, remaining with him to the end.

There was much that was trivial and pedantic in the cultural life of early seventeenth-century Seville, but the city enjoyed the supreme advantage of easy access to the outside world, and its ties with Italy and Flanders were close. The young Diego de Velázquez, serving his apprenticeship in the studio of his future father-in-law, Francisco Pacheco, had the opportunity to study Italian paintings and Flemish engravings, while books from the Spanish Netherlands figured regularly in the return cargoes of the ships that had carried Spanish wine, wool and oil to the north. Among the most popular of these books with the local intelligentsia were the works of Justus Lipsius, humanist, neo-Stoic and editor of Tacitus. His *De Constantia* of 1584 had earned him a circle of Spanish admirers, one of them being Olivares' uncle, Don Baltasar de Zúñiga, who came to know Lipsius in person while on diplomatic service in Brussels.[64] But it was in Seville, as the distinguished biblical scholar Benito Arias Montano wrote to assure Lipsius in 1593, that many of his most devoted followers were to be found.[65] It was in Seville, too, that the Spanish translation of *De Constantia* was published in 1616. This book profoundly influenced both the form and the content of *The Ambassador*, a vademecum for diplomats, published in Seville in 1620 by another of Olivares' close friends, Juan de Vera y Figueroa, Count of La Roca.[66]

---

[61] BAV Barb. Lat. Ms. 8599, fo. 2, Olivares to Cardinal Ludovisi, 12 July 1622.

[62] BAV Barb. Lat. Ms. 8599, fo. 20, Olivares to Cardinal Barberini, 18 December 1623.

[63] Marañón, *Olivares*, p. 31.

[64] Four letters from Lipsius to Zúñiga are included in Alejandro Ramírez, *Epistolario de Justo Lipsio y los Españoles, 1577–1606* (Madrid, 1966).

[65] *Ibid.*, letter 11. Unfortunately, Gerhard Oestreich, *Neostoicism and the Early Modern State* (Cambridge, 1982), has little to say about the influence of Lipsius in Spain, which is the subject of a doctoral thesis by Jean Gottigny, 'Juste-Lipse et l'Espagne' (Louvain, 1968).

[66] G. A. Davies, 'The influence of Justus Lipsius on Juan de Vera y Figueroa's *Embaxador* (1620)', *Bulletin of Hispanic Studies*, 42 (1965), pp. 160–73. For the international fame of Vera's *Ambassador* see Garrett Mattingly, *Renaissance Diplomacy* (London, 1955), ch. 22. A facsimile of the 1620 edition, *El Embaxador*, with the author's name appearing as Don Juan Antonio de Vera y Zúñiga, was published in Madrid in 1947.

In the dialogues of *The Ambassador*, it is not difficult to catch echoes of the debates to which Olivares would have been exposed in sessions with his literary friends in Seville—debates possibly continued in the gardens of the Alcázar or in those of the Olivares·estate at Mira-flores. Vera's dialogues are pervaded by the influence of two men—Tacitus and Justus Lipsius—and it is to these twin luminaries that the participants turn for guidance as they wrestle with the problem of how to conduct their public and private lives. Should a man prefer the pleasures of country life to the perils of the court? In what circum-stances was the resort to deceit legitimate? The great merit of Tacitus in the eyes of an anti-Machiavellian generation which could not dis-pense with Machiavellian methods, was to offer historical lessons in statecraft which were as relevant to its own times as to those of ancient Rome. 'Men may change, but their ways remain the same', wrote Vera y Figueroa, quoting Tacitus.[67] The same quotation appeared on the dedicatory page of the *Spanish Tacitus*, a translation, accompanied by aphorisms, published in 1614 by Baltasar Alamos de Barrientos, the friend and disciple of Philip II's renegade secretary, Antonio Pérez.[68] In the storehouse of historical experience provided by Tacitus, the seventeenth-century statesman—a Machiavellian in spite of himself—could find the wisdom to equip him for his voyage through perilous and uncharted seas.

For the young Olivares, contemplating a career at court, the attrac-tions of Tacitus were great. Here were a set of general rules, of incal-culable value to the fledgeling statesman. But at the same time, they were not so universal in their application as to foreclose the area properly left to the exercise of free will. 'Universal rules are insufficient to govern individual affairs', remarks one of Vera's characters.[69] 'The first rule of all', Olivares was later to observe, 'is to be for ever on the lookout for the unforeseen and accidental.'[70] There always came a moment when no rule or maxim could help, and when the statesman was forced back on personal instinct and experience. And what if he should fail? From the works of Justus Lipsius, which were well represented in Olivares' library, he could derive the austere comforts of a neo-Stoic philosophy which counselled personal fortitude and Christian resignation in the face of disaster.

The actual extent of Olivares' reading during those eight years

---

[67] *El Embaxador*, fo. 100v.
[68] *Tácito Español* (Madrid, 1614). Spanish Tacitism has not been adequately studied, but see Francisco Sanmartí Boncompte, *Tácito en España* (Barcelona, 1951), and the brief but perceptive survey, 'La corriente doctrinal del tacitismo político en España', in José Antonio Maravall, *Estudios de historia del pensamiento español*, 3 vols (Madrid, 1983–4), 3, pp. 73–98.
[69] *El Embaxador*, fo. 11v.
[70] AGS Est., leg. 2054, *El Conde Duque sobre el reparo de las cosas de Alemania*, 23 October 1639.

in Seville is impossible to determine, not least because it was one
of his maxims that 'great men never cite authors, only reason.'[71]
He clearly enjoyed the company of learned men, and apparently took
pleasure in hearing them discuss even the more abstruse points of
Latin philology.[72] In 1641, towards the end of his political career,
when his world was collapsing around him, he was described as
spending long periods every day closeted with Rioja, and with his
companion of student days, Juan de Isassi, reputedly the most learned
man in Spain.[73] For a man with the intellectual curiosity of Olivares
and his overwhelming passion for detail there was solace to be found
in the company of scholars, and perhaps also refreshment and
renewal.

There was solace to be found, too, in the company of books. It
was presumably during the Seville years that Don Gaspar began to
build up what was to become one of the greatest private libraries
in seventeenth-century Europe. Although he patronized artists, there
is no indication that he ever became a picture collector; but as a
collector of books he was insatiable. According to the Flemish Jesuit,
Claude Clément, who visited it around 1635, 'the library of Don
Gaspar de Guzmán, Count of Olivares and Duke of San Lúcar, is
one of the most excellent, both for its size and for the selection of
the best books of every kind. Its fame is universal and it very much
deserves a visit. The count has an uncontrollable urge to go on adding
to it every day, on account of his singular love of letters.'[74]

When catalogued in the mid-1620's, the Olivares library contained
some 2,700 printed books and 1,400 manuscripts.[75] Some of his books
were probably inherited: the numerous Americana, for instance,
which included a manuscript of Bernal Díaz's history of the conquest
of Mexico, could well have been acquired by his father-in-law, the
Count of Monterrey, when he was viceroy of Mexico and Peru.

---

[71] AGS Est., leg. 2050, *El Conde Duque sobre los últimos despachos . . .*, 7 December 1635.
[72] Printed memorandum *Al Excelentísimo Señor Conde Duque de San Lúcar la Mayor . . .el Dr.
Francisco de Figueroa, médico del Santo Oficio de Sevilla* (Seville, 30 August 1633), in BL 593.h.17
(122). The word under debate was *acia*, as used by Cornelius Celsus.
[73] Letter from the *licenciado* Hurtado de la Puente, 8 October 1641, cited by Barrera, *Poesías
de Rioja*, p. 98
[74] Quoted by Gregorio de Andrés, 'Historia de la biblioteca del Conde-Duque de Olivares
y descripción de sus códices', *Cuadernos Bibliográficos* 28 (1972), p. 12 n. 33.
[75] A catalogue of the Olivares library was prepared between 1625 and 1627 by Padre Lucas
de Alaejos, who was Olivares' librarian until his appointment as prior of the Escorial in 1627.
Three copies survive, one in RAH Ms. D.119, one in the Biblioteca del Palacio Real, and
a third, which is the one I have used, in BAV Barb. Lat. Ms. 3098 (*Bibliotheca Selecta Comitis
Ducis de San Lucar*). This Vatican copy is not identical with the copy in the Real Academia
de la Historia, and includes a section of 'prohibited books' which does not appear in the
RAH version. The contents and history of the library are briefly discussed by Gregorio Marañón,
Olivares, pp. 160–6, and 'La biblioteca del Conde-Duque de Olivares', *BRAH* 107 (1935),
pp. 677–92, and more fully by Gregorio Andrés in the article cited above, but the catalogue
still awaits a systematic analysis.

Once he had become a great public figure, and his mania for book-collecting common knowledge, it was natural, too, that he should have received numerous gifts, like the group of manuscripts which the canons of Saint Bavon in Ghent despatched to him from their cathedral library in 1627. Some of these gifts were more voluntary than others. His visit with the king to Aragon and Catalonia in 1626 yielded him a rich harvest of precious codices plucked from the hands of reluctant monks. The inmates of the Charterhouse of Aula-Dei in Zaragoza found themselves parted from their fabulous collection of Greek, Latin and Arab codices which had once belonged to the Aragonese historian Zurita; and more codices came from the monasteries of Poblet, Montserrat and San Juan de la Peña. Everywhere he travelled, Olivares would leave in his wake a trail of plundered monasteries, which Juan de Fonseca and Francisco de Rioja, his advisers on such matters, had systematically stripped of their most precious bibliographical treasures.[76]

Ancient codices, both classical and biblical, obviously held an irresistible attraction for Olivares; and once acquired they were bound in handsome bindings stamped with the Guzmán family arms.[77] But these codices, although bibliographically the jewels of the Olivares library, constituted only a small part of it. The collection was divided into printed books and manuscripts, with sub-divisions for works in Latin (including Greek and Hebrew), Spanish (Catalan, Portuguese and Valencian, as well as Castilian), French (including German and Flemish), and 'Tuscan'. There was also a substantial section of 'prohibited' works on the official Index of forbidden and expurgated books, which he was allowed to possess by virtue of special dispensations from the Inquisitor General, the papal nuncio, and the papal legate who visited Madrid in 1626, Cardinal Barberini.

A large private library of a seventeenth-century noble is, at best, an ambiguous index of its owner's literary tastes, and all the more

---

[76] Andrés, pp. 5–6.

[77] The arms (see Pl. 14) are divided in the form of a saltire cross into four quarters: the first and fourth on a blue ground have a chequered cauldron in red and gold, the handle terminating each end in seven green serpents' heads; the second and third quarters in ermine. All within a border composed of fourteen alternating compartments containing the lion and castle of León and Castile (silver and red, lion; red and gold, castle). I am grateful to Mr. Donald Davis for his help with this description. According to a commemorative sermon preached in 1624 for the late Count of Olivares and his ancestors, the lions and castles, symbolizing vigilance and fortitude, came to the family through the marriage into it of the Infanta Doña Beatriz, daughter of Henry II of Castile; the ermine as a symbol of loyalty and purity was inherited from the Dukes of Brittany and Count Ramiro de León; and the two cauldrons were originally the insignia of the *ricos hombres* of Castile, in commemoration of the hospitality they provided at their tables for noble warriors. The serpents on the handles were symbols of prudence. (*Sermones funebres predicados dominica infra octava de todos santos de 1624 años en la provincia del andalucia del orden de la Santísima Trinidad de Redemptores ... recopilados por el muy reverendo maestro fray Luis de Cordova Ronquillo*, pp. 33–6).

so when, as with Olivares, it drew heavily upon voluntary or involuntary gifts. Imaginative literature is conspicuous by its absence—there
is not even a copy of *Don Quijote* to hint at the brilliant literary
achievements of the Golden Age of Spain. Yet his own youthful
efforts at writing poetry, and his enthusiastic patronage of poets and
playwrights both in Seville and during his ministerial career, suggest
a lively interest in the writings of his Spanish contemporaries, many
of whom dedicated their books to him. On the other hand, the library,
as might have been expected, was notably strong in works of history
and in political treatises. It contained an impressive array of the chronicles of Castile; and Diego Hurtado de Mendoza's *War of Granada*,
from which he would quote in his Great Memorial for the king in
1624,[78] is represented several times over. The great Roman historians
were there, too, with the 1611 Herrera translation of the Annals
of Tacitus among them. Bodin, Guicciardini and Machiavelli (*The
Prince, The Discourses* and *The Art of War*) had a place—all three among
the authors on the Index. There was an extensive collection of medical
treatises, and religion was also well represented, as befitted the library
of a man originally intended for an ecclesiastical career. The theology
was unorthodox as well as orthodox. The section devoted to prohibited books contained Melanchthon and Calvin (but not Luther),
along with no less than thirteen of Erasmus' works that had found
their way onto the Index, together with a number of other Erasmian
or heterodox writings—not least Bartolomé Carranza's notorious
Catechism. This section also included the Koran and numerous Hebrew
works. The fact that Olivares was granted a special licence by the
Inquisitor General in 1624 to 'have and read any books by rabbis
who may have translated, paraphrased or commented in the Spanish
language on the Old Testament or any part of it,'[79] suggest that his
interest in these works of theology went further than the beauty
of their bindings.

The cast of Olivares' mind as it was revealed over the course of
the years was that of a man whose thought-processes tend more
to vigour than coherence. In his letters and state papers his ideas
tended to run away with themselves, and symmetry and proportion
were sacrificed to repetitious detail. The sources of his ideas are difficult to trace, but it would be very much in keeping with his personality if he became a voracious, if undisciplined, reader during those
days in Seville, soaking up ideas and information which he would
later unleash on a captive audience. When he took the Modenese

[78] *MC*, 1, p. 75.

[79] AHN Inquis., lib. 592, fo. 404, licence dated 19 January 1624. I am indebted to Professor
Antonio Domínguez Ortiz for bringing this document to my attention and providing me
with a transcript of it.

poet Fulvio Testi to see a play in the palace of the Buen Retiro in 1635, he talked without stopping throughout the entire performance, expatiating on the wonders of the palace, and then moving on to the beauties of Rome, and from there to 'perspectives and painting, theatres, fiestas and tournaments, and finally poetry.'[80]

A restless, ambitious, hyper-active man, who wanted to be every-thing, know everything, do everything—this was the Olivares who at last, in 1615, at the age of twenty-eight, achieved his ambition of a court appointment. The heir to the throne was to be given a household of his own on his marriage to Elizabeth of Bourbon; and the Duke of Lerma—perhaps to fend off the importunities of this tiresome young member of the house of Guzmán—consented to his selection as one of the gentlemen of the prince's chamber. It was a move he would later have cause to regret, but it is probable that he had not yet taken the measure of Don Gaspar, who at this stage of his life is likely to have conveyed an impression of being all sound and fury. The sheer guile and craftiness of the man were kept well out of sight.

Although there might have been some reason to fear the influence of so domineering a figure on the youthful heir to the throne, Philip III still seemed to have a long reign ahead of him, and in any event Don Gaspar was not a very seductive personality. Heavy and squat, with a bulbous nose, black moustachios and a splayed black beard, his appearance was far from prepossessing (Pl. 3). Indeed, the exag-gerated torso and shoulders gave him a hunch-backed look; and he may already have been making those sudden involuntary movements of head, hands and legs on which later observers remarked, and which perhaps betrayed an epileptic inheritance.[81] Although he was a first-class horseman, his physical health was never good—like so many members of the Spanish nobility he is likely to have suffered from syphilis[82]—and there must be some question also about the state of his mental health. In the later 1630's it was alleged that, as a boy, he suffered from periods of mental disorder,[83] but it is difficult to know whether this was anything more than the malicious gossip of his enemies. Contemporaries, however, were struck by the sudden changes of mood, the alternation of an almost excessive gentleness with violent outbursts of temper.[84] Periods of euphoria, too, would

---

[80] Brown and Elliott, *A Palace*, p. 89.
[81] ASF Mediceo, filza 4963, coded enclosure in letter of 14 November 1637 from Bernardo Monanni to Grand Duke of Tuscany. Marañón, *Olivares*, pp. 122–4, for possible epileptic inheritance.
[82] Marañón, p. 21.
[83] Monanni despatch of 14 November 1637.
[84] Marañón, p. 123.

alternate with bouts of deep depression, when he asked only to be allowed to bury himself in some remote corner and be forgotten by the world. But these may be no more than the reactions of a statesman under strain; and if, as contemporaries seemed to feel, there was something extravagant about Olivares' personality, he apparently succeeded in developing an inner discipline which helped to keep his emotions under tight control.

The move to court in 1615 marked the formal end of those Seville years during which Don Gaspar learnt to develop and display talents that would later be put to use on a larger stage. Although in future he would rarely see or be seen in his native Andalusia, he always thought of himself as a 'son of Seville'.[85] Even when settled in Madrid, he continued to take seriously his duties as governor of Seville's Alcázar, where he arranged for the construction in 1626 of a splendid public theatre, known as the Montería, to the benefit of both civic culture and the royal revenues.[86] He also took an interest in Seville university, of which he was named 'protector' in 1623, and it was through him that the university was raised to the status of a *colegio mayor*. This allowed its graduates to compete on an equal footing with those of the *colegios mayores* of Salamanca, Alcalá de Henares and Valladolid, which traditionally monopolized the senior administrative and judicial posts in the gift of the crown.[87]

Olivares' continuing interest in Seville derived at least in part from its political and commercial importance. It was, as he himself said, 'the principal city of these realms',[88] and no ruler of Spain could afford to neglect it. He would like to have seen it better governed, but he never managed to wrest control of the city council from the hands of a faction led by the Ortiz de Melgarejo family.[89] The most he could do was to see that the crown's principal representative in Seville, known as the *asistente*, was a figure in whom he had complete personal confidence, like Don Fernando Ramírez Fariñas, appointed *asistente* at the end of 1622.[90]

Yet over and above a natural preoccupation with the well-being of a city whose fortunes were critical to the survival of the Monarchy,

[85] AHN Est., leg. 727, Olivares to Comendador Mayor de León, 14 February 1626, commenting on the recent flooding in the city.
[86] Víctor Pérez Escolano, *Juan de Oviedo y de la Bandera* (Seville, 1977), p. 48; AGS Casas y Sitios Reales, leg. 308, fo. 262, consulta of Junta de Obras y Bosques, 18 March 1631.
[87] AHP 1718, fos. 21–27v., *Patronazgo del Colegio Mayor de Sevilla al señor Conde de Olivares*, 19 November 1623; Domínguez Ortiz, *Historia de Sevilla*, pp. 116–7; Kagan, *Students and Society*, p. 98.
[88] *MC*, 1, p. 66 (*Gran Memorial*).
[89] Domínguez Ortiz, *Historia de Sevilla*, p. 92; José Velázquez y Sánchez, *Estudios Históricos* (Seville, 1864) for Don Diego Ortiz Melgarejo.
[90] For Ramírez Fariñas, see *MC*, 1, p. 66 n. 39.

3. A massive impression of personal power is conveyed by Velázquez's first portrait of Olivares (1624), which shows him with the
attributes of his two household offices, the golden key of the *sumiller
de corps* and the golden spurs of the master of the horse.

Olivares had a deep affection for it, and took immense pride in showing off its splendours to the king during an eleven-day royal visit in March 1624.[91] He was, after all, a native of Andalusia; it was here that his family had their estates; and he shared many of the characteristics of the Andalusians—their sense of the theatrical, their love of pageantry and display, their lavish generosity, and (not least) their loquacity.[92] But from 1615 Madrid, not Seville, was to be the centre of his life, and it was here, if at all, that his fortunes would be made. In November of this year a letter from Quevedo to his patron, the Duke of Osuna, gives us a fleeting glimpse of Don Gaspar during the ceremonial return of the court to Madrid after the royal marriage celebrations on the Franco-Spanish frontier. The Duke of Sessa, surrounded by a splendid entourage, had the great Lope de Vega at his side; but Olivares, not to be outdone, was accompanied not by one but by *two* poets.[93] The men in power might refuse him his grandeeship, but none the less he would out-grandee them all.

'Now everything is mine'

Once established in the household of the heir to the throne, Olivares found himself subjected to a series of humiliations and snubs. The prince was a petulant and spoilt youth, surrounded by courtiers competing for his favour, and he does not seem to have found Don Gaspar much to his liking (Pl. 4). The snubs culminated one day in a disdainful remark by the prince that he was tired of the count's presence. Olivares, who happened at this moment to be carrying the prince's chamber-pot, reverently kissed it before withdrawing in silence from the room. But his request to leave the prince's service and retire to Seville was not granted. Gradually, the fawning and the self-abasement yielded results. By playing in particular on Philip's passion for riding and his taste for the theatre, Olivares began to win for himself a commanding position in his entourage.[94]

Simultaneously, Don Gaspar was deftly taking advantage of the cracks and fissures now beginning to open up in the elaborate edifice of power and patronage so skilfully constructed by the Duke of

[91] Domínguez Ortiz, *Historia de Sevilla*, p. 68; Jacinto de Herrera y Sotomayor, *Jornada que Su Magestad hizo a la Andaluzia* (Madrid, 1624).

[92] For contemporary images of the Andalusian, see Miguel Herrero García, *Ideas de los Españoles del siglo XVII* (2nd. ed., Madrid, 1966), ch. 5.

[93] Luis Astrana Marín, *Epistolario completo de Don Francisco de Quevedo Villegas* (Madrid, 1946), letter 10, 21 November 1615.

[94] Roca, *Fragmentos*, p. 156; Raffaele Ciasca, *Istruzioni e Relazioni degli Ambasciatori Genovesi*, 2 (*Spagna*) (Rome, 1955), p. 72.

4. Prince Philip, here portrayed by Rodrigo de Villandrando with his dwarf Soplillo, not long before his accession to the throne at the age of sixteen in 1621.

Lerma.[95] Since 1598 Don Francisco Gómez de Sandoval y Rojas, first Duke of Lerma, had been master of the king and his government—a position formally legitimized by a royal decree of 1612 to the effect that orders issued by the duke carried as much authority as if they had been personally issued by the king himself.[96] The first minister of the crown in practice, even if not in name, Lerma owed his power to his position as the *privado* or *valido*—the royal favourite. Although he was a member of the Council of State, he rarely attended its meetings, preferring to exercise his power from behind the scenes. This power derived exclusively from his personal ascendancy over Philip III—an ascendancy fostered by assiduous attendance on the king, to whom he enjoyed free access by virtue of his occupancy of the three principal palace offices of groom of the stole (*sumiller de corps*), master of the horse, and chief majordomo (Pl. 5).

The pattern of the Lerma administration, which tends too easily to be viewed through the distorting lens subsequently applied to it by the Olivares faction, was shaped by the temperamental characteristics of king and favourite.[97] Philip III had none of his father's addiction to the business of government, and spent as much time as he could away from the seat of his administration, in one or other of his country residences. As a result, the court and the administration were for much of the time physically divorced. Lerma, for his part, derived immense satisfaction from the pleasure and pomp of power, but had no taste for the hard work that normally accompanies it, and made use of a pronounced tendency to melancholy to avoid unwelcome business. Vain, devious, facile and astute, he was deft at the exercise of patronage, bored by the routine of administration, and, wherever possible, tended to take the easy way out, rather than wrestle with hard problems and risk unpleasant confrontations. As a result, much of the business of government during the Lerma years devolved upon others, even while Lerma reserved for himself as many as possible of the major decisions that determined royal policy.

The effect of this devolution was simultaneously to bureaucratize

---

[95] There is no serious study of the Duke of Lerma, but C. Pérez Bustamante, *Felipe III. Semblanza de un monarca y perfiles de una privanza* (Madrid, 1950), provides a general introduction to the period, with pp. 58–62 devoted to Lerma and his character. The same author's posthumously published volume on 'La España de Felipe III', Ramón Menéndez Pidal, *Historia de España*, 24 (Madrid, 1979), adds nothing substantially new to the received picture.

[96] See Francisco Tomás Valiente, *Los validos en la monarquía española* (Madrid, 1963), pp. 71–2, and Appendix I.

[97] Lerma's preference for governing through the spoken rather than the written word makes his administration particularly difficult to study. Some initial steps towards a reassessment have been taken by P. L. Williams in his dissertation on 'The Court and Councils of Philip III of Spain', cited above and his article on 'Philip III and the restoration of Spanish Government, 1598–1603', *The English Historical Review*, 88 (1973), pp. 751–69, which I have used for the brief sketch that follows.

5. Pedro Antonio Vidal, *Duke of Lerma*.

and to personalize the workings of government. The various councils seized the opportunity to formalize their routines and consolidate their areas of special jurisdiction; and, as their business grew, their secretariats expanded. In 1598 they employed twenty-two secretaries; the number had more than doubled by the 1620's.[98] This tentative assertion of independence by the bureaucratic organs of the government posed a potential threat to Lerma, which he attempted to counter by developing an extensive clientage system embracing court and government alike. Here he was in his element, dispensing royal patronage on a massive scale to relatives, friends and dependents, and creating in the process a powerful Sandoval faction, which justifiably regarded the duke as the founder of its fortunes. For a decade or more this Sandoval faction helped to keep the system dependent on the favourite. But in order to lubricate the machinery and ensure the continuing contentment of his growing army of clients, he was constantly having to devolve more responsibility on subordinates—selected secretaries or outsiders who for one reason or another had caught his fancy. As a result, the royal favourite himself became the tool of favourites, on whom he placed an excessive reliance in his anxiety to spare himself the trials and torments generally considered part and parcel of the exercise of power. The effect of this was on the one hand to deflect criticism from his own person onto his henchmen and minions, but on the other to leave him increasingly isolated as hostility mounted towards a government which gave every appearance of drifting rudderless in a Sargasso Sea of corruption.

Olivares had originally sought to curry favour with Lerma's chief favourite, Don Rodrigo Calderón; but by the time of Don Gaspar's appointment to the prince's chamber in 1615, Calderón's influence was on the wane. His own venal practices and the unremitting hostility of the royal confessor, Fray Luis de Aliaga, had combined to undermine him, and only Lerma's protection still saved him from disgrace. But the longer Lerma stood by Calderón, the more he risked jeopardizing his own pre-eminence. At this point Lerma's own son, the Duke of Uceda, whose very mediocre talents included an instinct for the preservation of his family even at the expense of sacrificing his father, made common cause with Aliaga against Calderón. Lerma responded to this filial revolt by turning for support to his nephew and son-in-law, the Count of Lemos, who arrived back at court in 1616 with a high reputation for his political and administrative skills after completing six successful years of service as viceroy of Naples.

This manoeuvre was not a success. Aliaga exploited his hold over

---

[98] Williams, 'Philip III and the restoration', p. 769.

the king's conscience to thwart Lerma's efforts to have his son-in-law appointed to the Council of State. Olivares, as he sniffed the political winds, rightly calculated that the Count of Lemos and an ageing Lerma were likely to be out-matched by the Uceda-Aliaga alliance, and with some justification he saw Lemos as potentially a more formidable long-term rival than Uceda for supreme power at court. He had already shifted his allegiance from Calderón to Uceda, using Uceda's secretary, Juan de Salazar, as a go-between.[99] He now set out to fan the rivalry between Uceda and Lemos.

Failing to win the favour of Philip III, Lemos, who had his own political ambitions, fastened his hopes on the heir to the throne. The power struggle that now developed in the prince's household was at this stage less a struggle between competing families than a struggle between competing factions in a single family—that of the Duke of Lerma, which had dominated the court and Spanish political life for the best part of twenty years, but had now fallen out over the duke's political inheritance. On one side was the Duke of Lerma himself, supported by his son-in-law, the Count of Lemos and his cousin, Don Fernando de Borja, a gentleman in Prince Philip's chamber. On the other were ranged his two sons, the Duke of Uceda and the Count of Saldaña, the prince's master of the horse. Olivares, for so long an isolated figure in the household, had become a close ally of the sons against Lemos and their father.

If the future lay with the prince and with those who could gain his confidence, the present still rested in the feeble hands of Philip III. The king was now paying less attention to the admonitions of the Duke of Lerma than to those of his confessor, Aliaga, who was in the position—always advantageous where Philip III was concerned—of having the deity on his side. In 1617, in a bid to restore his slipping fortunes, the favourite invited the king and his family to the splendid palace he had built for himself in the ducal town of Lerma, where he entertained them with the largesse and pomp that he so loved to parade. But by now his game was as good as lost. Aliaga succeeded in convincing the king that the Count of Lemos was acquiring a dangerous influence over his son, and when the court returned to Madrid Lemos was forbidden access to the prince's chambers on all but official occasions.[100] Lerma, Calderón and Lemos were now fighting for their political lives. With characteristic foresight where his own interests were concerned, Lerma had already taken out an insurance policy with Rome. A widower, although with

[99] Novoa, *Codoin* 61, p. 127; Pérez Bustamante, *Felipe III*, pp. 100–1 for the various court manoeuvres. There is a biography of Lemos by Alfonso Pardo Manuel de Villena, Marqués de Rafal, *Un mecenas español del siglo XVII. El conde de Lemos* (Madrid, 1911).
[100] Novoa, *Codoin* 61, pp. 142–3.

children and grandchildren, he aspired to become a prince of the church. In March 1618 Pope Paul V reluctantly yielded to the pressure from Madrid and raised him to the purple.

The Cardinal-Duke, as he now became, was not yet resigned to the loss of power. All through the first half of 1618 the struggle continued, with Calderón, the most vulnerable member of the trio, as the prime target of the enemy attack. Although the battle was being fought within the ruling family, Olivares, the outsider, was quietly making his dispositions. He had found an ally in the prince's household in the Marquis of Castel Rodrigo, the son of Philip II's Portuguese minister and favourite, Don Cristóbal de Moura. Castel Rodrigo, disappointed at Lerma's refusal to transform the personal grandeeship bestowed on his father into a hereditary grandeeship for his house, had decided to throw in his lot with Olivares. 'Now for the battle', said Calderón one day, finding himself in the company of Olivares and Castel Rodrigo, and of two of Lemos' allies in the prince's household, Don Diego de Aragón and Don Fernando de Borja. 'If the duke [of Lerma], my master, wins, it is all up with you [Olivares and Castel Rodrigo]; and if the Duke of Uceda wins, with you'—turning to Aragón and Borja.[101]

But the two sides were unevenly matched, and Uceda and Aliaga had primed the king on what needed to be done. Uceda, on the king's orders, summoned Don Fernando de Borja into his presence and commanded him to hand over the keys to the prince's chamber. Shortly afterwards he was despatched to Zaragoza as viceroy of Aragon. A number of lesser household officers were then made to follow suit. Although Lerma himself still clung to power, this 'revolution of the keys'[102] of 1618 was a shattering defeat both for him and his party. The Count of Lemos, a patrician to his fingertips, read the omens correctly, and retired to his Galician estates.

Lerma was shrewd enough to realize that the long-term beneficiary of this family feuding could well be the Count of Olivares, and he made one last attempt to remove him from the prince's household. Using as his intermediary the Marquis of San Germán, a relative of Olivares, he offered him a place in the king's household instead of that of the prince. But Olivares refused the bait, to the exasperation of Lerma, who told him that he was too wilful to be tamed.[103] In any event, it was late to engage in this kind of manoeuvre, for Lerma's political life could be counted in days. On 4 October 1618 the unfortu-

---

[101] *Ibid.*, p. 148.

[102] 'La revolución, y mudanza de llaves', Roca, *Fragmentos*, p. 156.

[103] 'En V. S., señor Conde, no es domesticable la dureza', Roca, *Fragmentos*, p. 158. The Marquis of San Germán later became Marquis of La Hinojosa, and appears under this title in Roca's narrative.

nate prior of the Escorial, Fray Juan de Peralta, found himself entrusted by the king with the delicate mission of informing the Cardinal-Duke that His Majesty, who would never forget his great services, had graciously given him leave to enjoy the peace and quiet which he had so richly earned.[104] The fallen favourite, who was not unprepared for the blow, left for his ducal palace at Lerma, and Don Rodrigo Calderón withdrew to his house in Valladolid, where he was to be arrested on 20 February 1619.

The fall of Lerma marked the end of an age, but not, at least in the short run, the end of a dynasty. His place in the king's favour, and to some extent also in the government of Spain, was taken by Uceda. But Uceda's power never equalled that of his father in the days of his greatness. Some time later he was described as 'occupying the first place' in the king's favour, and as the 'prime minister' (primer ministro).[105] But only a month after he succeeded his father, the king rescinded his 1612 decree and declared that orders and appointments would carry authority only if signed by the royal hand.[106] In reality the royal favour after 1618 was shared between Uceda and Aliaga, who seems to have intervened extensively in government business.[107] But since Uceda was a less skilful politician than his father and apparently had little grasp of the problems of government, power flowed back to the councils, and in particular to the Council of State, of which Uceda himself was not a member until the last days of the reign. Spain was never more truly a conciliar monarchy than in the last three years of the reign of Philip III.[108]

The change of favourites did not immediately affect Don Gaspar's personal position. As Uceda's ally in the power struggle he naturally gained some ground with Lerma's fall; but there were many other aspirants for place and favour, and Lerma's empire was still firmly in the hands of the Sandoval connection. To break the hold of the Sandovals it was essential to build up an alternative power base at the very centre of the court. One possible ally was the president of the Council of Castile, Don Fernando de Acevedo, Archbishop of Burgos. Acevedo, a relative, claims in his memoirs to have given Olivares valuable advice at a critical moment in his palace career.[109]

---

[104] Novoa, Codoin 61, pp. 154–5.
[105] Tomás Valiente, Los validos, Appendix III (Accusation against Uceda by Don Juan de Chumacero de Sotomayor).
[106] Ibid., Appendix II.
[107] Novoa, Codoin 61, p. 159.
[108] This point is made by the Genoese ambassador Saluzzo in his relation of 1622 (Ciasca, Istruzioni, 2, pp. 161–2).
[109] Mateo Escagedo Salmón, 'Los Acebedos', Boletín de la Biblioteca Menéndez y Pelayo, 8 (1926), p. 243. Acevedo also reports a growing intimacy between Olivares and Fray Juan de Peralta, the prior of the Escorial.

While this may well be true, Acevedo was too much a creature of the Sandovals to be a dependable ally. But Olivares had another and much closer relative who was rapidly gaining in authority and influence at court. This was his uncle, Don Baltasar de Zúñiga.

It was Olivares himself who seems to have engineered Zúñiga's summons to court in June 1617. Born in Salamanca around 1561, Don Baltasar was the son of the fourth Count of Monterrey. After attending Salamanca University he became a soldier, and sailed with the Armada against England in 1588. This experience may have persuaded him that his vocation lay elsewhere, and he joined his brother-in-law, the Count of Olivares, in the embassy in Rome, to acquire an apprenticeship in the art of diplomacy. He then went to court, where he was one of the gentlemen at the king's table, but was disappointed in his hope of a post in the household of the prince.[110] Although Philip II let it be known that he had singled him out for great things, it was only at the beginning of the reign of Philip III that he was given a major appointment. For four years, from 1599 to 1603, he was Spanish ambassador to the court of the Archdukes Albert and Isabella in Brussels, where he married a Flemish wife. From 1603 to 1606 he was ambassador in Paris, and then, between 1608 and 1617, to the Imperial Court in Prague. From Prague he was destined for the embassy in Rome, but Olivares apparently urged Uceda to secure his recall to Madrid, on the grounds that his intimate knowledge of the Empire and its problems made his presence in the Council of State indispensable at a time when uncertainty over Bohemia and the Imperial succession threatened to throw Central Europe into turmoil.[111] On 1 July 1617 he duly took his seat in the Council.[112] As Olivares had anticipated, his long diplomatic experience, combined with his intellectual ability and a certain austerity of manner soon made him the dominant voice in the Council's increasingly worried discussions of foreign policy, and enabled him to rise rapidly in the estimation of the king. A grateful monarch created him Comendador Mayor of León in the Order of Santiago, and appointed him tutor to the heir to the throne (Pl. 6).

Zúñiga was made tutor to the prince on 22 April 1619, the day

---

[110] Zúñiga is a figure of the first rank who has been absurdly neglected by historians, although he makes an occasional appearance in accounts of early seventeenth-century international relations, notably in Bohdan Chudoba, *Spain and the Empire, 1519–1643* (Chicago, 1952), esp. pp. 194–8. Details of his biography can be gleaned from the one-page printed eulogy written on his death in October 1622 by the royal chronicler Antonio de Herrera, *Elogio a Don Baltasar de Zúñiga*, of which there is a copy in AGS Est., leg. 7038, lib. 3081, and also from Malvezzi, *Historia de los primeros años del reinado de Felipe IV*, ed. Shaw, pp. 86–7.

[111] Novoa, *Codoin* 61, p. 159.

[112] Peter Brightwell, 'The Spanish Origins of the Thirty Years' War', *European Studies Review*, 9 (1979), p. 411.

6. Anonymous seventeenth-century artist, *Don Baltasar de Zúñiga*.

on which king and prince set out from Madrid on their state visit to Portugal. The Count of Olivares was also of the party, but while the court was still in Lisbon he suddenly decided to return home to Seville. The Count of La Roca offers a number of explanations for this unexpected decision, including Olivares' financial troubles, which were no doubt acute.[113] But the general tenor of Roca's words suggests a sudden personal crisis, almost as if the strain of the struggle to establish himself at court had brought him to breaking-point. The opening dialogue in Roca's *The Ambassador* might almost have been a dialogue between Roca and Olivares himself at this very moment, as the two participants, Julio and Ludovico, talked of the squalid traffic of courts, the penalties of place-hunting, and the tranquillity of Julio's garden, 'never to be sufficiently praised.'[114]

But the tranquillity, if such it was, proved of short duration. The king's sudden illness in October, on the way back from Portugal, threw the court into turmoil. Zúñiga sent a hasty message to his nephew to come at once to Casarrubios, where the court had come to its unexpected halt, but Don Gaspar appears to have replied that he would only come if the prince would assure him in advance of high office in the event of his father's death.[115] If, as Matías de Novoa alleges, no one at this time was talking about either Olivares or Zúñiga as possible successors to Uceda,[116] the response was shrewd.

Olivares duly returned to the court in his own good time. Here he reestablished himself in the favour of the prince, with the assistance of an attendant in his chamber, Antonio de Losa.[117] The fact that in March 1620 he bought a house in Madrid for 9,000 ducats—a house conveniently close to the Alcázar in the quarter of San Juan[118]—suggests that he had put the temptation of his Seville garden firmly behind him. But the hazards of court life were forcefully brought home to him in the following month, when an attempt was made on his life as he went by coach after dark.[119] A subsequent inquiry revealed only that the attempt was made on the orders of persons unknown.

In the poisoned atmosphere of court feuds and vendettas, nothing was predictable, but Olivares and Zúñiga quietly made their disposi-

---

[113] Roca, *Fragmentos*, p. 159.

[114] *El Embaxador*, fos. 5–5v.

[115] Sánchez Calderón, *Epítome*, fo. 673.

[116] Novoa, *Codoin* 61, p. 247.

[117] Ciasca, *Istruzioni*, 2, p. 72; Escagedo Salmón, 'Los Acebedos', 8, p. 338.

[118] Marañón, *Olivares*, p. 425.

[119] Miguel Muñoz de San Pedro, 'Un extremeño en la corte de los Austrias', *Revista de Estudios Extremeños*, 2 (1946), pp. 390–3.

tions, and the king's new illness in March 1621 found them well prepared. As soon as its gravity became clear a family council of war was held in Olivares' house. Don Gaspar's elder sister, Doña Francisca de Guzmán and her husband, the Marquis of Carpio, of the Haro family, were away on their Córdoban estates at the time, but his other two sisters and their husbands were there: Doña Inés, married to the inconsequential Marquis of Alcañices, and Doña Leonor and her husband, the Count of Monterrey.[120] The Guzmán-Zúñiga-Haro family connection, excluded from the inner circle of power during the long years of Sandoval dominance, stood poised in March 1621 for the moment of decision.

The family council could reckon on the near certainty that Uceda would soon be out of power if the king should die. But would the prince really put Olivares in his place? Don Gaspar appeared to have ingratiated himself successfully with the heir to the throne, but prominent men like Prince Philibert of Savoy were waiting in the wings, and the heir to the throne gave every indication of being as pliable a figure as his father. The real danger came not from Uceda, but from that wily fox, Lerma, who had still not reconciled himself to his fall from grace. When the Cardinal-Duke learnt from an understandably agitated Duke of Uceda that the king was dying, he decided to stake everything on a dramatic return to Madrid, in the hope that a last-minute intervention might save the fortunes of his house.

Zúñiga and Olivares knew their Cardinal-Duke, just as they also knew their king. Lerma must at all costs be stopped. But how was this to be managed? They now had important allies in the king's bed-chamber, including the Marquis of Malpica and the Duke of Infantado.[121] As councillors of state, Infantado and Don Baltasar de Zúñiga might perhaps succeed in persuading their fellow-councillors to advise the king to refuse Lerma permission to enter the court, on the grounds that criminal prosecutions were pending against some of his former associates, and notably Don Rodrigo Calderón.[122] A riskier, but possibly more effective device, would be to forbid Lerma entry on the authority of the prince acting in his father's stead. Antonio de Losa, the prince's confidant, is alleged to have advised him that he must choose between Lerma and Olivares, and that Lerma's age made the choice of Olivares inevitable.[123] One way or another, the prince was persuaded of what needed to be done, and signed

[120] Novoa, *Codoin* 61, pp. 335–6.
[121] *Ibid.*, p. 337.
[122] *Ibid.*, p. 339.
[123] This story is reported in a despatch of 22 September 1625 by the papal nuncio, the Bishop of Gravina (ASV, Spagna, 65, fo. 334).

an order to the effect that Lerma was not to enter Madrid. It is not clear whether the document bore his signature as prince or as king, but whatever its validity, it had the desired effect. The Cardinal-Duke, on receiving it from the hands of a royal official, Don Alonso de Cabrera, halted his journey in Villacastín; and later, as the news of Philip III's death reached him, he disconsolately took the road back to Valladolid.[124]

The gamble of Zúñiga and Olivares had worked. Even before knowing the final outcome, Olivares was so confident that when Uceda accosted him to say that everything was ready for the prince's accession, he was able to remark: 'Now everything is mine.' 'Everything?' asked Uceda. 'Yes, without exception.'[125] Shortly afterwards, on 31 March 1621, the king died, aged only forty-two.

The prince, now Philip IV, was still in bed when Fray Antonio de Sotomayor, his Dominican confessor, entered the bed-chamber to tell him that his father was dead. The bed curtains were drawn again as Sotomayor withdrew, but the new king was not allowed much time for solitary meditation. The late king's servants, having kissed the hands of their dead master, were now on their way to his successor's quarters to perform a similar, if less macabre, ritual. Entering the bed-chamber, Olivares told his master that this was no time to be in bed. Philip, giving his first orders as king, commanded that the curtain be drawn, and asked for his shirt. It was at this moment that Uceda arrived at the door, accompanied by his right-hand man, the royal secretary, Juan de Ciriza. The duty of Uceda, as the prince's groom of the stole, was to attend upon him when he dressed or undressed; but on this occasion Philip rose from his bed with unwonted alacrity and ordered that only a gentleman and an attendant should enter his room while he was dressing. The symbolic gesture told its own story.[126]

When Uceda eventually obtained entry it was only to be ordered to leave the state papers and his keys of office on the table, and withdraw. Philip's brothers, the Infantes Don Carlos and Don Fernando, then came to kiss hands, followed by the grandees, the titled nobility, the bishops, the councillors, and the foreign envoys. When the ceremony was over, the king summoned Don Baltasar de Zúñiga, and formally entrusted him with the state papers. The secretarial duties performed by Juan de Ciriza were transferred to the secretary for

---

[124] There are various accounts of the discomfiture of Lerma, notably Novoa, *Codoin* 61, pp. 340–1 and 345; Acevedo's memoirs (Escagedo Salmón, 'Los Acebedos', 8, pp. 257–9); Quevedo, 'Grandes Anales', *Obras*, 1, p. 733; Roca, *Fragmentos*, pp. 162–3.

[125] Roca, *Fragmentos*, p. 162.

[126] This episode is recounted in Novoa, *Codoin* 61, p. 344.

Italian business, Antonio de Aróztegui, whose appointment seems to have been formalized under a new title, that of *secretario del despacho*, or personal secretary to the king.[127]

Zúñiga and Olivares had clearly worked out the division of duties between themselves well in advance. The age difference of the two men was itself sufficient to explain their decision. Zúñiga, described by Quevedo as 'a man for all seasons and for his own business',[128] was now in his sixtieth year, and had spent his life in public service, while his nephew was only thirty-four, and had no political or administrative experience at home or abroad. Court rumour had it that the new king had wanted to entrust the state papers to Olivares rather than Zúñiga, whom he seems to have found a forbiddingly austere tutor,[129] but that Olivares declined, on the pretext that he had neither the health nor the capacity to handle matters of state.[130] The plea of poor health was genuine—at one moment during these days Don Gaspar was having to be carried around in a chair.[131] But the plea, if genuine, was hardly adequate, and Olivares had obviously calculated that he stood more to gain at this stage by 'modesty'[132] than by pushing himself forward.

In any event it was highly desirable to present as sharp a contrast as possible with the regime of the Duke of Lerma, as a man of manifest incompetence for conducting the government. Zúñiga, with his gravity and experience, presented exactly the right image at a moment when, in the words of the Mantuan ambassador, 'the true support of this monarchy, which is little less than collapsing, lies in maintaining reputation.'[133] The new king's choice of Zúñiga as his principal minister was therefore received with 'universal applause',[134] but no one had any doubt that the man with the real influence behind the scenes was the Count of Olivares.

From the very first day of the new reign, it was clear that Zúñiga and Olivares meant business. There were immediate changes both in the administration and in the palace. Two members of the Council of Castile, Drs. Tapia and Bonal, were forcibly retired, perhaps more

---

[127] *Cartas de Andrés de Almansa y Mendoza* (Madrid, 1886), p. 11. For the *secretario del despacho*, see José Antonio Escudero, *Los secretarios de estado y del despacho*, 1 (Madrid, 1969), pp. 253–5.

[128] Quevedo, *Obras*, 1, p. 735.

[129] Ciasca, *Istruzioni*, 2, p. 72.

[130] ASM, Archivio Gonzaga, Serie E.XIV.3, busta 615, Celliero Bonatti to Duke of Mantua, 11 April 1621.

[131] BNM Ms. 7377, fo. 298v. (*Relación de la enfermedad de S.M.*).

[132] Quevedo, *Obras*, 1, p. 735.

[133] ASM, Archivio Gonzaga, Serie E.XIV.3, busta 615, Celliero Bonatti to Duke of Mantua, 31 March 1621.

[134] Archivo del Duque de Frías, sección Fuensalida (cat. III, no. 1597), Juan de Eraso to ?, 4 April 1621.

as an earnest of the new king's intentions than because of any unique degree of venality in their ministerial careers.[135] Prominent nobles banished from court under the old regime were allowed to return. Among them was that dazzling courtier, and poet, the Count of Villamediana, whose friends feared—and with good reason—that he would prove incapable of holding his malicious tongue for long.[136] But, for the moment at least, he was busily singing the praises of the new regime, revelling in the downfall of Uceda and Aliaga, and saluting the young Philip IV as the 'restorer of Spain'. The 'great goodness' of Philip III had destroyed his realm, but his son, for all his tender years, would set things right again.[137] As an indication of his intentions, the new king, who was passing the official period of mourning at the convent of San Jerónimo on the eastern outskirts of Madrid, summoned into his presence on 3 April the judges in the case of Don Rodrigo Calderón, whose case had been languishing. Four days later, the great Duke of Osuna, whose high-handed actions as viceroy of Naples had made him many enemies, was taken into custody after delivering himself of some intemperate and insulting remarks about the gratitude of kings.

In the palace, too, changes began almost at once. The Duchess of Gandía, who belonged to the influential house of Borja, was given back her post as mistress of the queen's household, while members of the king's household too closely identified with Uceda were suspended from the exercise of their office. In a society in which an office was regarded as a piece of private property, it was not easy to dismiss people from their posts. But it was decided that in future no one was to hold more than one household office. Uceda himself held two—those of lord high steward (*mayordomo mayor*) and groom of the stole (*sumiller de corps*). Under the new dispensation he was now compelled to renounce the second of these posts, which went to Olivares;[138] and on 23 April he was banished from court, and then placed under arrest. A pretext was also found for depriving Uceda's brother, the Count of Saldaña, of his post as master of the horse, and transferring it to his father-in-law, the Duke of Infantado, who held the office until December 1622, when it was given to

---

[135] Quevedo, *Obras*, 1, pp. 735–7.

[136] ASM, Archivio Gonzaga, Serie E.XIV.3, busta 615, Celliero Bonatti to Duke of Mantua, 11 April 1621.

[137] Teófanes Egido, *Sátiras políticas de la España moderna* (Madrid, 1973), nos. 15–20 ('Ciclo de Villamediana'), esp. pp. 87–8.

[138] Novoa, *Codoin* 61, pp. 355–6.

Olivares.[139] The rule about duplication of household offices clearly applied more to some than others.

Everything that happened in those first hectic days of the reign of Philip IV indicated a determination on the part of the sixteen-year old king and his advisers to wipe the slate clean. But one event above all made it clear that the age of the Duke of Lerma was over, and that a bright new star had risen in the skies. On 10 April the Jesuit court preacher, Father Jerónimo de Florencia, preached a sermon before the king in which he praised the despatch with which business was now being conducted. After hearing the sermon, the king took lunch in a large room in the convent of San Jerónimo. The room was already thronged with nobles when Olivares entered and modestly went over to one side. When the table had been cleared, the king suddenly said: 'Count of Olivares, be covered'—the formal words with which a grandeeship was traditionally bestowed. Don Gaspar, coming forward, threw himself at the king's feet and kissed his hand. One after another his relations followed suit, and Don Baltasar's normally grave features could not conceal their joy.[140] For the king's action marked something more than the personal triumph of Olivares. It also marked the triumph of a clan, and a cause.

---

[139] Angel González Palencia, *Noticias de Madrid, 1621–1627* (Madrid, 1942), p. 43, which gives the date of the appointment as 20 December 1622. These *Noticias* were transcribed by González Palencia from a manuscript in the Biblioteca Nacional of Madrid. I have in my possession another version of this manuscript which continues to 1640, although from mid-1637 the number of monthly entries declines sharply. This version, transcribed in 1703 by Fray Pedro de La Hoz under the title of *Madrid. Relación diaria*, contains variations from the manuscript used by González Palencia, and gives the date of Olivares' appointment to the mastership of the horse as 22 December (p. 47). Unless there are significant variations I cite, for convenience, from the version published by González Palencia. Entries taken from Pedro de La Hoz's manuscript will appear simply as Hoz, with the page number and date.
[140] Novoa, *Codoin* 61, p. 355; Hoz, p. 4.

EL FER·NANDO
O
SEVILLA RESTAVRADA
POEMA HEROICO
ESCRITO CON LOS VERSOS DE LA GERVSALEMME
LIBERATA DEL INSIGNE
TORQVATO TASSO
OFRECIDO
ALLA MAGESTAD DE
FILIPPO IV. EL GRANDE
MONARCA DE ESPAÑA,
EMPERADOR DE LAS INDIAS,
POR D. IVAN ANTONIO DE VERA,
Y FIGVEROA, CONDE DELA ROCA, COMENDA-
DOR DELA BARRA, GENTILHOMBRE DE LA
BOCA DE SV CONSEIO, Y CONTADVRIA
MAIOR DE HACIENDA, EMBAXADOR
ESTRAORDINARIO EN SAVOIA, Y
ORDINARIO EN VENECIA.

DE INTERES.   DE VALOR.

PARA SVSTENTAR MEIOR, EL GRAVE PESO QVE VES, LA LEALTAD YACE OCVLTO
DESNVDA AQVI DE INTERES, VESTIDA ALLI DE VALOR.

ANNO   EN MILAN   1632

Con Privilegio   POR HENRICO ESTEFANO.   Y Licencia.

7. The title page of the Count of La Roca's *El Fernando* (1632), depicting Olivares as Atlas holding the globe aloft. On the left he appears naked of interest, and on the right clothed with valour.

II

THE ZÚÑIGA INHERITANCE

The burden of Atlas

One evening around 1630 two friends, a priest and a *caballero*, were enjoying the shade of the trees and the murmuring of the fountains in the gardens of the old Moorish Alcázar palace in Seville, of which the Count of Olivares was governor. In their imaginary conversation—the invention of a Sevillian parish priest with literary pretensions, Juan de Robles—the *caballero* asked his friend a leading question that was often asked by seventeenth-century Spaniards, but could in some circumstances be dangerous: should the king have a favourite? Momentarily taken aback, the priest then proceeded to marshal a series of arguments justifying the existence of the *privado*. He could hardly have done otherwise, since Robles' book was dedicated to Olivares. Kings, the priest remarked, were the most heavily burdened of men, and he reminded the *caballero* of the fable of Atlas, who asked his friend Hercules for a moment's help while he shifted from one shoulder to the other the burden of the globe that he was condemned for ever to hold aloft.[1]

This burden was Spain's global Monarchy, the *monarquía española*, the title by which the world-wide dominions owing allegiance to the King of Spain were collectively known. Within two years of Philip IV's accession the full weight of it was to be placed on the massive shoulders of Olivares, who himself would be saluted by contemporaries as 'a new Atlas',[2] and even depicted as such in the Count of La Roca's long epic poem, *El Fernando*, where his burden appears improbably light (Pl. 7).[3] The global image was entirely appropriate. Spanning the world, from Italy to the Philippines, and from Portugal to Ceylon, the Monarchy of the King of Spain—an

---

[1] Juan de Robles, *Tardes del Alcázar, doctrina para el perfecto vasallo*, ed. Miguel Romero Martínez (Seville, 1948), p. 96. The work, which is undated, is thought to have been written around 1631.

[2] Córdoba Ronquillo, *Sermones fúnebres*, pp. 31–2.

[3] Juan Antonio de Vera y Figueroa, Count of La Roca, *El Fernando, o Sevilla restaurada* (Milan, 1632). E. Zudaire, 'Ideario político de D. Gaspar de Guzmán, privado de Felipe IV', *Hispania*, 25 (1965), pp. 413–25, notes other and later references to the Atlas image as applied to Olivares (p. 414).

empire in all but name—was one on which, like the Roman empire, the sun never set.[4]

To sustain it, however, was every year becoming a harder task. Triumphalists, like the Benedictine Fray Juan de Salazar, might proclaim that 'the Spanish Monarchy will last for many centuries and be the final one',[5] but not everyone was so confident. The Romans, too, had had their empire, and before them the Assyrians, the Medes, the Persians and the Greeks; and one after another they had vanished. Could Spain alone hope to escape that cyclical process of rise and decline to which, if history was any guide, all empires were inexorably subject? Sixteenth-century Spaniards liked to see themselves as the Romans of their century, but they could hardly avoid facing the implications of the analogy, and many of them would find themselves in agreement with Giovanni Botero, who, after asking in his *The Reason of State* (1589) 'Whether it is a greater task to extend or preserve a state?', answered his own question as follows: 'Clearly it is a greater task to preserve a state, because human affairs wax and wane as if by a law of nature, like the moon to which they are subject. Thus to keep them stable when they have become great and to maintain them so that they do not decline and fall is an almost superhuman undertaking.'[6]

Philip II, in the last years of his reign, had visibly been faltering in the 'superhuman undertaking' of conserving his world-wide Monarchy. The revolt of the Netherlands, the war with England, the intervention in the civil wars in France, had all taken a heavy toll of the Monarchy's resources, and imposed enormous strains on Castile. In 1598, the last year of his life, the old king had sought to reduce the crown's commitments and smooth the path for his son by negotiating a treaty of peace with France, and arranging for his daughter, the Infanta Isabella (Isabel Clara Eugenia) and her future husband, the Archduke Albert, to become 'sovereign princes' of the provinces of the southern Netherlands that had remained loyal to Spain. The extent to which this arrangement was intended to represent a real transfer of sovereignty from Madrid to Brussels remains unclear,[7] but it offered his successor some additional room for

[4] Pedro Fernández Navarrete, *Conservación de Monarquías* (Madrid, 1626), fo. 33 (Discurso II), quoting Claudian. Ariosto's *Orlando Furioso*, echoing Virgil, helped give the image its sixteenth-century currency. See Marcel Bataillon, *Etudes sur Bartolomé de las Casas* (Paris, 1965), p. 113.

[5] Juan de Salazar, *Política española* (1619; ed. Miguel Herrero García, Madrid, 1945), p. 199.

[6] Book I, 5. Trans. P. J. and D. P. Waley (London, 1956), pp. 5–6.

[7] For the practical limitations on the Archdukes' independence of action during the reign of Philip III, see Geoffrey Parker, *Spain and the Netherlands, 1559–1659* (London, 1979), ch. 9 ('The Decision-making Process in the Government of the Catholic Netherlands under "the Archdukes", 1596–1621').

manoeuvre in his dealings with the seven rebellious United Provinces of the northern Netherlands, now well on their way to emerging as an independent Dutch Republic with its own distinctive identity.

The rulers of Early Modern Europe tended to devise their foreign policies with little or no thought for the budgetary resources that would be needed to sustain them. This was especially true for the Spanish Monarchy, which carried with it such an accumulated weight of commitments and concerns, and possessed—at least in theory— such vast reserves, that financial realities ranked relatively low in the scale of priorities when set against the protection of dynastic or strategic interests, and considerations of prestige. Yet from time to time there would come a moment of reckoning, as in 1596, when the crown's debts became so massive and its bankers so reluctant to make further loans that some reassessment of policy became inescapable. But Philip II's desire to reduce the Monarchy's over-extended commitments with an eye to the succession of his young and untried son seems to have evoked little enthusiasm in Madrid once the new reign had begun. Philip III came to the throne with every intention of proving himself a great warrior and crusading king.[8] In spite of his precarious financial inheritance, and serious economic dislocation in Castile following the ravages of famine and plague in 1599–1600, the new king and his advisers launched out on major new military enterprises, despatching expeditionary forces to Algiers and Ireland in 1601, and making a fresh bid to bring the Dutch rebels to heel.

The Irish and North African expeditions, however, were expensive failures, and in 1604 a peace treaty was signed with England. This enabled Spain to bring the weight of its resources to bear on the war in the Netherlands, where a seemingly hopeless situation looked like being salvaged by a promising new commander. Ambrogio Spinola, a member of the great Genoese banking family and a wealthy man in his own right, had arrived in the Netherlands from Italy in 1602 at the head of an expeditionary force of 9,000 men.[9] In 1604 he achieved a major success for the Archdukes Albert and Isabella by recapturing Ostend. As a reward, Madrid appointed him commander of the Spanish army of Flanders, a post that he would occupy for more than two decades, and from which he wielded enormous influence over the policies of the archducal court in Brussels. Madrid

[8] See Williams, 'Philip III and the restoration of Spanish Government', p. 756.
[9] See Geoffrey Parker, *The Dutch Revolt* (Ithaca, 1977), p. 236. The Spinolas became intermarried with the Spanish nobility, and for reasons of consistency Ambrogio Spinola will appear under the hispanicized form of his name, Ambrosio Spínola, in this book. The most comprehensive account of his career remains that of Antonio Rodríguez Villa, *Ambrosio Spínola, primer marqués de los Balbases* (Madrid, 1904).

would soon learn to grow wary of him, as an excessively persuasive advocate with the Archdukes of policies which it suspected of being framed with too much of an eye to his own personal and financial interests; but in its first flush of enthusiasm it was willing to give him massive support for a new round of operations against the rebellious Dutch.

The need to crush, or at least contain, the Dutch before it was too late had been forcefully brought home to Madrid by their recent successes in the Far East, West Africa and the Caribbean.[10] Their increasingly confident incursions into overseas regions held or claimed by the Spanish and Portuguese crowns had added a new, global, dimension to their initial revolt, and opened up vast areas of vulnerability for a Monarchy whose possessions were too geographically widespread for the effective military protection of all of them. From the standpoint of Madrid it therefore made sense to strike hard at the Dutch in their homeland, on the assumption that this would tie down their forces and reduce their appetite for dangerous overseas ventures. If this assumption was not quite as well founded as Madrid believed, Spínola's new offensive at least worried the Dutch sufficiently to induce them to contemplate the possibility of some sort of negotiated settlement. But it also had less advantageous consequences for Spain, adding to the growing war-weariness of the loyal provinces of the southern Netherlands—'Flanders', as they were known to the Spaniards—and imposing new strains on Spain's already overstretched finances. The Spanish crown had to produce around three million ducats a year to support the operations of an army of Flanders of around 70,000 men, and a long history of mutinies showed what could be expected if the men did not receive their pay on time.[11] In the winter of 1606 a new mutiny broke out in the ranks; an eight months' ceasefire was agreed in the spring of 1607; and in November of the same year the crown, unable to service its debts or to extract further loans from the bankers, followed the precedents set by Philip II and declared a new 'bankruptcy', suspending its payments to them.

In Madrid the financial emergency of 1607 created a climate in which for the first time the possibility either of a peace settlement or of a long-term truce with the Dutch rebels could be seriously considered. Spínola himself, lacking the resources to sustain his offen-

---

[10] See Jonathan Israel, *The Dutch Republic and the Hispanic World, 1606–1661* (Oxford, 1982), p. 2.

[11] Geoffrey Parker, *Spain and the Netherlands*, ch. 5 ('Mutiny and Discontent in the Spanish Army of Flanders, 1572–1607'), and, for a detailed study of the Spanish army in the Netherlands and its problems, see the same author's *The Army of Flanders and the Spanish Road, 1567–1659* (Cambridge, 1972).

sive, favoured a settlement, although his advocacy was hardly a recommendation to his enemies on the Council of State, who began to constitute an anti-peace party.[12] Behind the scenes the Duke of Lerma manoeuvred adroitly to win support for an end to the war in the Netherlands. His motives were probably mixed. The belligerency of the first years of the reign had not brought the expected results; it was hard to see how additional funds could be found for the war without resorting to unpleasant and unpopular measures; and the endless conflict in the Netherlands was consuming an excessive proportion of Spain's money and energies at a time when other dangers were threatening. In particular, he is likely to have been disturbed by the revival of French power under Henry IV after the long quiescence imposed on France by the civil wars of the later sixteenth century. The French occupation of Savoy in 1600, and the subsequent Franco-Savoyard peace treaty of Lyon of 1601 which brought French territory to within a stone's throw of one section of the vital military road along which Spanish soldiers had to travel in their journey from Milan to Flanders,[13] made it necessary to reassess Madrid's priorities. So, too, did the growing dangers posed by the pirate state of Algiers to Spain's maritime links with Italy, which may have suggested the desirability of some shift of forces from the northern to the Mediterranean theatre.[14] The sheer number and range of the Monarchy's commitments made it difficult for its rulers to concentrate exclusively for any length of time on any one problem, and there was always some new crisis to grip the attention and compel them to realign the pieces on the board.

Peace came between Spain and the United Provinces in 1609, but it came almost by default, and not in the form of a definitive peace, but of a truce which the two parties agreed to observe for twelve years. The decisive step had already been taken in the ceasefire of 1607, when, to the surprise and indignation of the Council of State, the Archduke Albert effectively conceded the existence of the United Provinces as an independent state, while failing to secure in return any written promise from the Dutch that they would evacuate the East Indies.[15] For all its indignation, however, the Council of State proved impotent in face of the realities of the situation, and the Twelve Years' Truce of 1609 was approved as a virtual *fait accompli* on the basis of the concessions that had already been made. In the first

[12] Julián María Rubio, *Los ideales hispanos en la tregua de 1609 y en el momento actual* (Valladolid, 1937), p. 49.

[13] Parker, *The Army of Flanders*, pp. 68–9; Rudolf Bolzern, *Spanien, Mailand und die katholische Eidgenossenschaft* (Luzern/Stuttgart, 1982), p. 78.

[14] R. A. Stradling, *Europe and the Decline of Spain* (London, 1981), p. 42.

[15] Israel, *The Dutch Republic*, p. 5.

of its thirty-eight articles, the Archdukes and the Spanish crown agreed to treat the seven provinces as 'free provinces and states', and the fourth article about overseas trade was so ambiguously phrased as in effect to leave the Dutch free to continue their activities in the East and West Indies.[16]

The truce of 1609 meant the winding up, at least for a season, of the last of the great wars on which Spain had embarked in the reign of Philip II. To the other states of Europe, these wars were a standing testimony to Spain's thirst for universal monarchy. To the Spanish crown they were wars fought on behalf of the faith and in defence of its own legitimate interests. Now that they were over, other ways had to be found to protect those interests effectively. For the moment, the soldiers yielded precedence to the diplomats, and the years immediately preceding 1618 were to be the culminating years of the *pax hispanica*, in which the Spain of Philip III took advantage of the skills of its agents and ambassadors to maintain its influence in Europe during a time of precarious peace.[17]

The *pax hispanica* had always been something of a sleight of hand. In particular it depended on the passivity of France, or at least on its complicity in preserving the European peace—a complicity that could not be taken for granted as long as Henry IV was on the throne. For contemporaries the mutual hostility of the French and Spanish crowns was regarded as a constant of international life; and it was reinforced by an assumed 'natural' antipathy between Spaniards and Frenchmen, which—as described in 1617 by a Spaniard resident in France—was reflected even in their contrasting gastronomic and sartorial tastes.[18] There were a number of actual or potential points of friction in Franco-Spanish relations, any one of which might provoke a direct confrontation between the two crowns if the will to compromise was lacking.[19] While France was afraid of the massive reassertion of Spanish power in northern Europe that would inevitably follow from a victory over the Dutch, Spain worried about open or covert French help to the United Provinces, and about the possibilities of sudden French action designed to block the military corridor running from Milan to Brussels. This lifeline of the Spanish Monarchy

[16] Israel, pp. 11–12. The text of the truce is to be found in *Prontuario de los tratados de paz*, 4 vols. (Madrid, 1749–52), 1, pp. 100–129, with an explanatory secret agreement relating to article 4 on trade, pp. 130–32.
[17] For the *pax hispanica* see in particular H. R. Trevor-Roper, 'Spain and Europe 1598–1621', *The New Cambridge Modern History*, 4 (Cambridge, 1970), ch. 9.
[18] Carlos García, *La oposición y conjunción de los dos grandes luminares de la tierra, o la antipatía de franceses y españoles*, ed. Michel Bareau (Edmonton, 1979).
[19] For a good analysis of Franco-Spanish relations in the reign of Henry IV, based on Spanish documentation, see Antonio Eiras Roel, 'Política francesa de Felipe III: las tensiones con Enrique IV', *Hispania*, 31 (1971), pp. 245–336.

in Europe looked like a noose to the French. But, as Spaniards and French were well aware, it was a lifeline or noose that might be cut with reasonable ease at a number of critical points—the French border with Savoy, the Swiss valley of the Valtelline, or along the northern reaches of the Rhine, especially if, as the Spaniards feared, France succeeded in annexing or bringing under its own control the independent duchy of Lorraine.

Italy was also a potential theatre of conflict between France and Spain in the early seventeenth century, although it remained secondary to the Netherlands. Since the victories of Charles V, the Italian peninsula had lived in the shadow of Spanish power, which was massively reinforced by Spain's possession of Naples, Sicily, and the duchy of Milan—that parade-ground of Spanish arms from which it dominated northern Italy. Among the leading princes and states of Italy, the popes were invariably subject to heavy pressure from Madrid, exercised through the Spanish ambassador in Rome; Venice was surrounded by Habsburg territory; the Grand Dukes of Tuscany were too weak to represent a challenge; and Charles Emmanuel, Duke of Savoy, had been brought into the Spanish system through his marriage to the younger daughter of Philip II. All of them, however, cast wistful glances towards Paris as a potential counterforce to Madrid, and Henry IV did what he could to encourage their aspirations, without, however, committing himself to a confrontation with Spain in a region where he could hardly avoid being worsted.

In Italy and northern Europe alike, Henry IV's policies seem to have been designed to extract the maximum advantages for France without precipitating war with Spain, although there were obvious risks involved in the plans he was making for military intervention in the conflict over the succession to the German duchies of Cleves-Jülich at the time of his assassination in 1610. The following years of regency government in France during the minority of Louis XIII not only reinforced the tacit complicity between Paris and Madrid to avoid pushing their differences to extremes, but saw the culmination of Lerma's patient diplomatic efforts to incorporate France into the Spanish system by means of a dynastic alliance. The Franco-Spanish royal marriages of 1615 were, at first sight, a triumph for the moderate and pacific policies with which the Duke of Lerma had come to be identified, and which he believed could maintain Spain's predominant position in Europe without loss to its reputation.[20] But in practice the new friendship between the crowns proved short-lived. They fell out again in 1616 in the aftermath of

[20] See Antonio Eiras Roel, 'Desvío y "mudanza" de Francia en 1616', *Hispania*, 25 (1965), pp. 521–60 for the changes in the Franco–Spanish relationship in 1615–16.

an armed conflict between Spain and Savoy that arose out of Duke Charles Emmanuel's seizure of the strategic north Italian marquisate of Montferrat from its rightful holder, the Duke of Mantua.[21] Thereafter, Franco-Spanish relations returned to their usual state of suspicion and hostility, although the domestic preoccupations of the royal government in France would for several more years limit its diplomatic effectiveness and prevent it from pursuing coherent anti-Spanish policies. It was only in 1624, with the advent to power of Cardinal Richelieu, that the coherence would begin to return.

The continuing inability of the French to set their own house in order during the opening years of the reign of Louis XIII was a stroke of fortune for the Duke of Lerma, as Olivares came to appreciate in the 1620's and 1630's when he found himself faced by the formidable political skills of Richelieu. But every adjustment of position made by Lerma in his efforts to avoid major military confrontations increased the risks of his stumbling. In particular, the tilt to France represented by the marriage alliance of 1615 introduced new strains into his relationship with the court of the Emperor in Vienna, which had long suspected him of being insufficiently concerned with maintaining the ties between the Spanish Habsburgs and their Austrian cousins.[22]

The preservation of a close relationship between Vienna and Madrid had been the traditional cornerstone of Spain's international policies, cemented into place by generations of dynastic intermarriage and by a broad similarity of political and religious objectives. The King of Spain and the Holy Roman Emperor each had need of the other.[23] Although the Austrian branch of the family was the junior branch, its possession of the Imperial title conferred upon it a unique authority. At the same time, Philip II and his successors took their effective superiority to the Emperor for granted, based as it was on far more extensive territorial possessions and infinitely greater resources. This very superiority placed them, at least in their own eyes, in an almost tutelary relationship to their Austrian cousins, who, they believed, were likely to come to grief in a hostile world unless they turned constantly to Madrid for support and guidance. Generations of Spanish ambassadors at the Emperor's court had therefore assiduously promoted the close and continuing union of the two branches of

---

[21] See Antonio Bombín Pérez, *La cuestión de Monferrato, 1613–1618* (Vitoria, 1975).

[22] Edouard Rott, 'Philippe III et le Duc de Lerme', *Revue d'Histoire Diplomatique*, 1 (1887), pp. 201–16, and 363–84. For Lerma's tense relationship in the earlier years of the reign with the Dowager Empress María and Philip III's queen, Margaret of Austria, see María Jesús Pérez Martín, *Margarita de Austria, Reina de España* (Madrid, 1961). Margaret's death in 1611 removed an important obstacle to the Duke's plans for a marriage alliance with France.

[23] For the Imperial-Spanish relationship in this period, see especially Chudoba, *Spain and the Empire*, and Eberhard Straub, *Pax et Imperium* (Paderborn, 1980), ch. 3.

the family, which was seen as the only secure guarantee for the retention of the Imperial title in the Habsburg family, and the furtherance of those ideals to which the House of Austria was devoted—the defence of the church and the maintenance of the faith. It was also fundamental to the conservation of Spain's own territorial interests in both southern and northern Europe. The King of Spain, in his capacity as Duke of Milan and Duke of Burgundy, was a vassal of the Emperor twice over, and any upheaval in the Empire could have serious consequences for Spain's position in Italy and the Netherlands. Yet upheaval in the Empire seemed very close when Don Baltasar de Zúñiga, Spain's ambassador to the Imperial Court, returned to Madrid in the summer of 1617 to take up his seat in the Council of State; and nothing in the Duke of Lerma's record suggested that he would respond to the impending crisis with resolution or energy.

The end of the pax hispanica

From the early years of the reign of Philip III there had been divisions in the Council of State between the hardliners—many of them representatives of the older generation who had worked in close association with Philip II—and those who preferred Lerma's more moderate and conciliatory approach to international politics.[24] Lerma's opponents believed that his unwillingness to deploy the full panoply of Spanish power at moments of international tension was creating a fatal impression of weakness and little by little was destroying the credibility of the Spanish crown—its 'reputation' in seventeenth-century parlance. They saw the Twelve Years' Truce with the Dutch as a profound humiliation, and they were equally scandalized by the terms of the Peace of Asti of 1615 which ended the war between Spain and Savoy over Charles Emmanuel's occupation of Montferrat. Although the marquisate was returned to the Dukes of Mantua, the terms of the peace, negotiated under French auspices and accepted by Lerma's cousin, the Marquis of La Hinojosa, in his capacity as governor of Milan, were generally thought to be discreditable to Spain, and were a cause of rejoicing to Venice and other Italian states which wanted to see the end of Spain's predominance in Italy.[25]

Among those who felt these humiliations most deeply were its representatives in foreign parts—ambassadors and viceroys who were concerned to uphold the reputation of their royal master, and who

[24] Eiras Roel, 'Política francesa', p. 305.
[25] Bombín, *La cuestión de Monferrato*, ch. 3.

felt that Madrid was doing little or nothing to give them the support they deserved. They were profoundly disturbed by what they saw as the deterioration of the Habsburg and Catholic position in Europe, and were bitter at the failure of the ministers in Madrid to stand fast when the vital interests of the Monarchy were at stake. For a man like Don Pedro de Toledo, Marquis of Villafranca, who restored the prestige of Spanish arms in northern Italy after the recall of Hinojosa in disgrace from his government of Milan, the temptation to take the law into his own hands, acting first and explaining afterwards, was difficult to resist. But the effect of such independent behaviour was to erode still further the dwindling authority of the Lerma regime.

While Madrid's proconsuls—the Duke of Osuna in Naples, the Marquis of Villafranca in Milan—and its ambassador to Venice, the Marquis of Bedmar, were sending home urgent warnings about Venetian and Savoyard threats to Spain's position in Italy, equally shrill warnings were coming from the court of the Emperor. Here, the Count of Oñate, Zúñiga's successor as Spanish ambassador, fretted over the prospects for the Habsburg succession in the Empire and became increasingly anxious for the future of the Catholic cause throughout central Europe. The strength of Protestant and anti-Habsburg forces in Bohemia raised the alarming possibility that it would not cast its electoral vote for the devoutly Catholic Archduke Ferdinand of Styria as successor to the Emperor Matthias; and if the Empire were lost to the Habsburgs, the last dikes against a Protestant inundation of central Europe would be breached beyond repair.[26]

As Spain's envoys surveyed the darkening scene from their different vantage-points, they were persuaded that the enemies of the House of Austria—the forces of international Calvinism, the Venetians and the Dutch—were engaged in a vast conspiracy to secure its overthrow.[27] The Bohemian rebellion of 1618 helped to confirm the correctness of their verdict, and one after another they seem to have come to the same conclusion: that in this gathering international crisis, attack represented the best form of defence. Military intervention—to save Bohemia for Ferdinand, and to guarantee the corridors and lifelines linking Spain's military base in Milan to Vienna and Brussels—

[26] For Oñate and his reactions, see Chudoba, *Spain and the Empire*, pp. 210–28; and, for Madrid's reactions to the rebellion of Bohemia, Straub, *Pax et Imperium*, ch. 4, and Peter Brightwell, 'The Spanish Origins of the Thirty Years' War', which draws on his unpublished doctoral dissertation, 'Spain and the Origins of the Thirty Years' War' (Cambridge University, 1967). Other parts of this dissertation have appeared in article form under the titles of 'Spain and Bohemia: the decision to intervene', *European Studies Review*, 12 (1982), pp. 117–141, and 'Spain, Bohemia and Europe, 1619–1621', *European Studies Review*, 12 (1982), pp. 371–99.
[27] For the connection made by the Marquis of Villafranca between the Bohemian rebellion and Venetian intrigue, see Bombín, *La cuestión de Monferrato*, p. 266 n. 5.

was indispensable if the great Hispanic system established by Philip II were not to be destroyed beyond repair. For these men looked back with a growing nostalgia to the reign of the Prudent King, who had not been afraid to discharge the responsibilities of world-wide power.

But could Philip III be induced to act as his father would have done? So long as he was dominated by the Duke of Lerma, it seemed clear that he could not. But Zúñiga's influence at court was growing as Lerma's declined, and Zúñiga, with his intimate knowledge of European and Imperial affairs, was a persuasive supporter of Oñate's interventionist proposals when they came before the Council of State.

In the event, Lerma lacked the authority to withstand pressure from the powerful combination of Oñate, Zúñiga and the Imperial ambassador in Madrid, Franz Christoph Khevenhüller, for financial and military assistance to the Austrian Habsburgs. During the summer of 1618 Madrid was sucked by almost imperceptible stages into the central European quagmire. A Spanish foot regiment and five hundred cavalrymen had been stationed in Friuli to help enforce the peace settlement of 1617 between the Archduke Ferdinand of Styria and the Venetians, and had then been lent to Ferdinand until 1 June 1618 to overawe a session of the Hungarian Diet. Instead of licensing these troops on the agreed date, Oñate offered on his own initiative to place them under Imperial command. He then urged Madrid to send money for their upkeep, because of the unrest in Bohemia. Lerma was anxious to disavow the ambassador's commitment, but Zúñiga argued that the Emperor could not be abandoned, 'for such a withdrawal of Your Majesty's protection would deprive him of all his reputation.'[28] The words were characteristic of Zúñiga, always acutely sensitive to the importance of 'reputation'—of prestige and face-saving—as an essential component of power.

By mid-July, Philip III had been persuaded that it was his duty to help his Austrian cousins, and overruled protests from the harassed President of the Council of Finance, the Count of Salazar, that the treasury could not afford 200,000 ducats for Oñate. Lerma informed Salazar that Philip insisted on prompt help for Ferdinand, 'since if the Empire should be lost to the House of Austria through the lack of it, nothing in Italy will be safe . . .'[29] The domino theory had established itself during the reign of Philip II as a standard argument in favour of military action to preserve Spain's far-flung interests,[30]

[28] Quoted Brightwell, 'Spanish Origins', p. 422, which I have followed for this summary account of the stages of Spanish intervention.
[29] AGS CJH, leg. 555, no. 212, consulta, 26 August 1618, and note from Lerma to Salazar, 8 September 1618.
[30] See H. G. Koenigsberger, 'The Statecraft of Philip II', *European Studies Review*, 1 (1971), p. 20.

and in this instance the status of the Duchy of Milan as an Imperial fief gave the theory an additional force.

A few weeks after reluctantly acceding to a measure of support for the Austrian Habsburgs, the Duke of Lerma fell from power. Even if the principal cause of his fall was discontent at his mismanagement of domestic affairs, his handling of foreign policy also played its part. The activists, both inside and outside Spain, resented the sight of the Monarchy subjected to one humiliation after another by the inertia and indecisiveness of Madrid. They knew that, where foreign policy was concerned, Lerma was at his most vulnerable in his dealings with the Empire, simply because the close relations between the Spanish and Viennese branches of the House of Austria had created a powerful Imperial lobby in Madrid, with easy access to the king. By playing on Philip's sense of family loyalty this lobby was well placed to bring home to him the inadequacies of his favourite.

Lerma's fall left Zúñiga the dominant figure in the field of foreign policy. Like so many Spaniards who remembered the days of Philip II, Zúñiga was deeply worried by the decline of the Monarchy's reputation. Later, when discussing the termination of the truce with the Dutch, he is alleged to have said: 'In my view, a monarchy that has lost its *reputación*, even if it has lost no territory, is a sky without light, a sun without rays, a body without a soul.'[31] The words were no doubt embellished for the record, but the sentiments were authentic. The preoccupation with reputation came naturally to men educated in the aristocratic tradition of Early Modern Europe, but Zúñiga regarded reputation both as an end in itself and as an instrument for the conduct of foreign policy. Appearance could, in certain circumstances, be as effective as the reality of power: and when real power was diminishing—as many of Zúñiga's generation believed it to be—then the maintenance of appearances became all the more important.

But Zúñiga, although sympathizing with the impatience of his colleagues serving abroad, was equally determined to avoid precipitate action. A man with few illusions, he had reached the conclusion that an early commitment of men and money to Archduke Ferdinand was the least of the various evils which faced Spain in 1618, and might save it much larger disbursements in the years to come. But the Bohemian crisis had to be set into the context of a wider, European, strategy. He had no wish to precipitate a general European conflict, and regarded Spain's support for Ferdinand as essentially preventive. It was also a cardinal element in his policy that England

[31] Speech as given by Juan Yáñez, *Memorias para la historia de don Felipe III* (Madrid, 1723), p. 117.

should be neutralized. This would isolate the Dutch, and would introduce a moderating element in Germany, where James I of England could be expected to exercise a restraining influence over the Protestant princes, and in particular over his son-in-law, Frederick V, the Elector Palatine. Spain's ambassador in London, the Count of Gondomar, had left England for Spain in July 1618; but Madrid was sufficiently confident of James' reaction to request his mediation, and he responded at the end of September by letting it be known that English help would not be forthcoming for the Bohemian rebels.[32] Throughout the German troubles of the next few years, Madrid worked to retain the benevolent neutrality of England, reviving the old idea of a marriage between the Prince of Wales and the Infanta María, the younger daughter of Philip III.

As long as the Emperor Matthias lived, there was a lingering possibility of compromise between the crown and the dissidents in Bohemia. But the death of Matthias on 20 March 1619 removed this possibility, to the relief of Oñate and Zúñiga, who feared that any further concessions to rebels and heretics would destroy the authority of the Austrian Habsburgs beyond repair. In the following months, while Philip III was making his state visit to Portugal, the battle-lines were drawn in Bohemia and Germany. At Oñate's request, six thousand men from the army of Flanders left the Netherlands for Bohemia in April, and in June the Council of State approved the despatch to Germany of an equal number of men from Spanish Italy.[33]

On 28 August 1619, Zúñiga and Oñate achieved their first objective when the Imperial electors, meeting in Frankfurt, elected the Archduke Ferdinand Emperor, unaware that the Bohemians had just offered their own crown to Frederick, the Elector Palatine. On 28 September, disregarding the agitated warnings of James I, Frederick accepted the offer. The new Emperor, Ferdinand II, who was facing revolt in Hungary as well as Bohemia, was desperately in need of help, and early in October, at Oñate's instigation, he made a verbal agreement with Duke Maximilian of Bavaria. In return for Bavarian military assistance, Maximilian would be made an Imperial elector, and would be allowed to retain (although under exactly what conditions remained unclear) any of the Elector Palatine's territories that his forces managed to occupy.[34]

The deteriorating position of the Habsburgs in central Europe could not be treated in isolation from Spain's problem in the Netherlands. In Brussels, the Archduke Albert, as brother to the late Emperor, was deeply committed to the family cause, and urged on Philip III

[32] Chudoba, *Spain and the Empire*, p. 222.
[33] Chudoba, p. 223; Brightwell, 'Spain and Bohemia', p. 125.
[34] Straub, *Pax et Imperium*, p. 151.

the necessity for large-scale Spanish intervention against the Protestant rebels in the Habsburg lands.[35] The Bohemian rebels for their part were attempting to enlist Dutch support,[36] and the United Provinces were likely to play a decisive role in any anti-Habsburg coalition. A rebel victory in Bohemia would have profound consequences for Spain's position in the Netherlands, where the Twelve Years' Truce between Madrid and the Dutch had only some eighteen months to run.

During the last two years of the reign of Philip III, therefore, the hour-glass was running low. Could the problems of the Empire be settled before the truce expired? Could, or should, the truce be prolonged? During 1619 this was the subject of much debate both inside and outside the Council of State.[37] Quite apart from the humiliation represented by the effective concession of sovereignty to the United Provinces in article I of the truce, it could be argued that other articles had also proved highly prejudicial both to Spain and to the loyalist provinces of the southern Netherlands. The Spanish negotiators had failed to obtain toleration for Dutch Catholics, and they had failed to lift the blockade of Antwerp by securing the re-opening of the river Scheldt to trade. In addition, the calculated ambiguities of clause IV on the participation of the Dutch in European and overseas trade had gravely damaged the economic interests both of Spain and Portugal, as Philip III was certainly reminded on his visit of 1619 to Lisbon.

Zúñiga approached the question of the expiry of the truce with a hard-bitten realism, well aware that the days were long since passed for the military suppression of the revolt of the Netherlands.

> We cannot by force of arms [he told the secretary, Juan de Ciriza, in April 1619] reduce those provinces to their former obedience. Whoever looks at the matter carefully and without passion, must be impressed by the great armed strength of those provinces both by land and by sea, their strong geographical position ringed by the sea and by great rivers, lying close to France, England and Germany. Furthermore, that state is at the very height of its greatness, while ours is in disarray.

In his eyes, peace or war with the Dutch constituted a choice of evils, and one that must be made on the basis of careful calculations.[38]

---

[35] Albert to Philip III, in H. Lonchay and J. Cuvelier, *Correspondance de la cour d'Espagne sur les affaires des Pays-Bas au XVIIᵉ siècle*, 1 (Brussels, 1923), Doc. 1432.

[36] J. V. Polisensky, *The Thirty Years War* (London, 1971), p. 110.

[37] For the debate on the truce, see especially Peter Brightwell, 'The Spanish System and the Twelve Years Truce', *English Historical Review*, 89 (1974), pp. 270–92, and Jonathan Israel, *The Dutch Republic*, ch. 2.

[38] Quoted Brightwell, 'Spanish System', p. 289.

During the second half of 1619, the Council of State began assembling opinions and recommendations on the truce, and in particular sought the views of the Councils of Portugal and the Indies, whose areas of jurisdiction were those most directly affected by Dutch naval and commercial activity. The massive Dutch incursion into the Pacific and Indian oceans during the years of truce was inevitably a source of profound concern to the government in Madrid, not only because of the loss of trade and wealth to the Portuguese crown and Portuguese merchants, but also because of the consequences of that loss for the delicate relationship between Portugal and Castile. For all the splendours of Philip III's reception in Lisbon in the spring of 1619, the Portuguese remained far from reconciled to the union of the Crowns of Castile and Portugal in 1580, and the inability of the Spanish crown to protect their overseas possessions could only deepen their disillusionment. It is therefore not surprising that the strongest pressures for the resumption of the war came from the Councils of Portugal and the Indies, which believed that the Dutch would only relax their effort overseas when they were faced with the need to defend themselves at home.[39]

The Council of State met on 25 December 1619 to consider the replies of the two councils to the king's request for their views on the desirability of prolonging the truce.[40] The councillors agreed that they should be forwarded to the Archduke Albert for his comments, and insisted on the importance of pressing ahead with a previously agreed decision to build up a fleet in northern waters. Zúñiga again reiterated his pessimistic assessment of the general situation, which was more serious than the gravest emergencies faced by Charles V and Philip II. Confronted by the combined forces of Germany, Holland, England and Venice, acting in collusion with the Turk, he believed that the Monarchy as a whole, 'and even these kingdoms', were as good as lost. The treasury was empty, the nobility indebted, the peasantry poverty-stricken. Only the church remained, and it would be better to take the wealth of the church than to hear the doctrines of Luther and the Koran being preached from the pulpits of Madrid.

The council responded by suggesting a reduction to 5% or 4% of the interest on some or all government bonds (*juros*), and a prohibi-

---

[39] In a meeting of the Council of State on 22 October 1625 Fray Iñigo de Brizuela observed that 'the principal reason given in the consultas of 1619 and 1621 for not continuing the truce was that, while it was in force, the Dutch had entered the Indies.' (AHN Est. lib. 738, fo. 316.) The Council of Portugal had already given its views in May 1618 in response to an earlier royal request for information. In its consulta it dwelt on the disastrous consequences of the truce for the Portuguese East, with the English following in the footsteps of the Dutch (AGS Est., leg. 634, no. 344).

[40] Archivo de los Condes de Oñate, leg. 104, consulta of Council of State.

tion on the export of unminted silver by the crown's bankers. It also agreed with Zúñiga on the need to capitalize on Spain's ecclesiastical wealth, even to melting down the communion cups if this should be necessary (a proposal to which the Inquisitor General Aliaga appended a formal objection).

This discussion took place in an atmosphere of growing pessimism about the course of events in central Europe. Two days earlier a despatch had arrived from Oñate reporting that Vienna was threatened by the Hungarian rebel forces of Bethlen Gabor. On 28 December the council met again, this time to discuss whether the Archduke Albert should send an army into the Palatinate. The advocates of military intervention in Germany from the Netherlands argued that it would reduce the pressure on the Emperor, prevent the Protestant forces from occupying Alsace, induce Maximilian of Bavaria to come to Ferdinand's aid in Bohemia, and frighten the Dutch into agreeing to the continuation of the truce on more favourable terms. Oñate, Zúñiga and the Archduke Albert all favoured intervention, and their arguments carried the day.[41] But it was not until 9 May 1620 that Philip III formally wrote to Albert to say that he approved an invasion of the Palatinate.[42]

By this time, events in central Europe were already turning to the advantage of the Habsburgs. Imperial and Spanish diplomacy worked effectively during the first six months of 1620 to isolate the Bohemian rebels and their new king, the Elector Palatine. Bethlen Gabor failed in his offensive against Vienna and signed a truce with Ferdinand in February. Then in March the Elector of Saxony was successfully detached from the Bohemian cause, and by the summer it was clear that Frederick was out on his own, and that he could expect effective help neither from inside nor outside Germany.[43] The Emperor was receiving subsidies from Spain and the papacy; he had secured the promise of military assistance from Maximilian of Bavaria and the German Catholic League; and Spínola was preparing to invade the Palatinate with an army of 25,000 men.

In July 1620 the Habsburg cause scored a new and unexpected success when the Catholic inhabitants of the Valtelline turned on their Protestant overlords of the Grisons and appealed for Spanish help. The Duke of Feria, who in 1618 had succeeded Villafranca in the governorship of Milan, sent his troops into the valley, and established a chain of Spanish strong-points. Neither France nor Venice was in a position to send effective help to the Grisons; and although

[41] Brightwell, 'Spain and the Origins', p. 308.
[42] Lonchay and Cuvelier, *Correspondance*, 1, Doc. 1477; Anna Egler, *Die Spanier in der Linksrheinischen Pfalz, 1620–1632* (Mainz, 1971), p. 31.
[43] Polisensky, *Thirty Years War*, p. 110.

there followed a period of complicated diplomatic manoeuvring, the peace settlement eventually signed in September 1622 confirmed for a while the striking success of the Spaniards. They were now the masters of the Alpine passes, and the safety of the military corridor leading from Italy to the Tyrol and northwards to Flanders was assured.[44]

In September Spínola launched his invasion of the Rhine Palatinate, and in a triumphant campaign secured the second of Spain's great strategic objectives—the control of the Rhine valley, and with it another vital link in the chain of communications between Italy and Flanders.[45] Simultaneously the combined forces of the Emperor and the Catholic League were on the move against the Bohemians, and on 8 November, at the battle of the White Mountain, the Bohemian cause was annihilated and the Elector Palatine fled for his life. It was a dramatic reversal of fortune. At the end of 1619 Zúñiga was foreseeing the end of the Spanish Monarchy. Now, a year later, the Habsburg and Catholic cause was triumphant in central Europe; the activists were vindicated, and the effective deployment of military power had secured unrestricted passage along the 'Spanish road' from Milan to Brussels.

The achievement of victory in Germany before the expiration-date for the Twelve Years' Truce gave Zúñiga and his colleagues some leeway before reaching a final decision on the problem of the Netherlands. The Archduke Albert, anxious to save the loyal provinces of the south from another round of warfare, urged on Madrid at least a short renewal of the truce.[46] But while Zúñiga was not eager for a resumption of the conflict, the very successes of Habsburg arms in Germany made it all the harder to accept the perpetuation of a temporary settlement which was perceived as being so prejudicial to Spain. Zúñiga and his fellow-members of the Council of State were not the men to be swept off their feet by the providentialist rhetoric of a work like Fray Juan de Salazar's *Política Española*, which, although published in 1619, was something of a throwback to a more self-confident age. But, like Salazar, they did see the Spanish Monarchy as standing for certain fundamental principles—not, like some states, for the 'rules of the impious Machiavelli, called by the atheists "Reason of State"'; nor for lust of conquest or the 'ambition to acquire new vassals without just title'; but rather for 'religion'

---

[44] Polisensky, p. 160; Antonio Bombín Pérez, *Los caminos del imperio español* (inaugural lecture, Vitoria, 1974); Pedro Marrades, *El camino del imperio* (Madrid, 1943), ch. 7; Bolzern, *Spanien, Mailand*, pp. 329–36.

[45] Jürgen Kessel, *Spanien und die Geistlichen Kurstaaten am Rhein während der Regierungszeit der Infantin Isabella, 1621–1633* (Frankfort, 1979), pp. 42–4, and see Geoffrey Parker, *The Army of Flanders*, pp. 54–5 and 253 for the Palatinate and its place in the Spanish strategic network.

[46] Lonchay and Cuvelier, *Correspondance*, 1, Doc. 1519, Albert to king, 28 December 1620.

and for the 'zeal and honour of serving God.'[47] These attitudes and aspirations were instinctive to them, and if they reached their day-to-day decisions on the basis of more mundane calculations, they had as their point of reference a view of the world in which the King of Spain had certain rights and responsibilities, the first of which he could not forfeit nor the second evade without grave offence to God and betrayal of His cause.

Given the demonstrable harm done to Spanish interests by the truce of 1609—the damage to Spanish and Portuguese overseas commerce, the covert assistance given by the Dutch to the enemies of the Habsburgs—could the king honorably agree to its prolongation? The Archduke Albert's request for even a short renewal seems to have been discussed at a meeting of the Council of State on 21 January 1621, two months before the death of Philip III.[48] Don Carlos Coloma, governor of Cambrai and a veteran of the wars of Philip II, had argued in a memorandum of June 1620 that the only way out of the impasse in the Netherlands was a good peace, or a good war.[49] A 'good peace' he defined as a peace treaty or a long truce in which the Dutch renounced their 'ill-founded liberty', withdrew from the Indies trade, and opened the Scheldt to shipping. A 'good war' was one in which four years' resources were concentrated into two, and three armies were sent on campaign with orders to devote themselves exclusively to an invasion of Holland. The Council of State's decision pointed inexorably towards a 'good war'. The archduke was informed that even a short-term prolongation of the truce would only be acceptable if the Dutch were to allow freedom of worship to their Catholics, renounce their trade with the Indies, and re-open the Scheldt.[50]

But Zúñiga was not yet quite prepared to face the consequences of this decision. Albert was simultaneously authorized to treat with the Stadholder Maurice of Nassau in the hope of making a private deal;[51] and indeed during the winter months of 1620 Mme. T'Serclaes, a Dutch Catholic, had been crossing and recrossing the border between the United Provinces and the Spanish Netherlands on a secret mission designed to win Maurice's support for a prolongation of the truce on better terms.[52] The covert negotiations with Maurice—

[47] Salazar, pp. 53–4 (proposición tercera).

[48] I have not come across this consulta, but its existence is established by a reference to it in the consulta of the Council of State of 17 July 1621, in the Archivo de los Condes de Oñate, leg. 104.

[49] Printed in Rodríguez Villa, Ambrosio Spínola, pp. 342–8.

[50] Lonchay and Cuvelier, Correspondance, 1, Doc. 1527, king to Albert, 4 February 1621.

[51] Ibid., Doc. 1530, Powers given to Archduke Albert, 4 February 1621.

[52] Charles Howard Carter, The Secret Diplomacy of the Habsburgs, 1598–1625 (New York and London, 1964), p. 258, and see also J. J. Poelhekke, 't Uytgaen van den Treves. Spanje en de Nederlanden in 1621 (Groningen, 1960), for the last months before the expiry of the truce.

which the internal feuds in the United Provinces made appear more promising at the time than they look in retrospect—were followed by a final attempt to salvage the truce, in the form of a mission led by the chancellor of Brabant, Pierre Pecquius, to the States General of the United Provinces towards the end of March. But neither Maurice nor the States General seemed prepared to countenance a continuation of the truce on terms more favourable to Spain; and on 31 March 1621, the day of Philip III's death, the archduke wrote to Madrid to report the failure of the mission.[53] He pointed out that, by the time his letter reached Madrid, the truce would already have expired. He had therefore asked Spínola to negotiate a suspension of arms in the Palatinate, and hurry home with his army to Flanders. On 22 April the new king, Philip IV, approved this decision.[54] Spain was back at war.

Spain at war

The Twelve Years' Truce expired formally on the tenth day of the new reign. The effect of Madrid's decision to let it lapse was to condemn Spain to another twenty-seven years of warfare with the Dutch, in the continuing quest for a solution to the problem of the Netherlands which had eluded the Spanish Crown ever since the outbreak of revolt in 1566. No event did more to shape the history of the Olivares years than the resumption of the war in the Netherlands, although it passed unmentioned by the court gazetteers, preoccupied by the comings and goings of the great during those first hectic days of the reign of Philip IV.

Of what use were the Netherlands to Spain? *'Flandes, quid nobis prodest?'*, asked Pedro López de Reino, an official of the Council of Indies, in 1624. 'If they refuse to abandon their obstinacy, why should we pursue a ruinous war that has gone on for sixty-six years, and is leading us to destruction—a war fought in provinces which are by nature unyielding, from which we extract nothing of benefit, and which supply us with nothing that we need?'[55] At the time when López de Reino asked his awkward question, it is unlikely that anyone in government circles in Madrid envisaged that the decisions of 1621 would lead to a further quarter century of war. Disillusionment spread only by degrees, until eventually the resumption of the war in the Netherlands became one of the principal charges of accusation against Olivares.[56] But all the crucial decisions, including the final decision

[53] Lonchay and Cuvelier, *Correspondance*, 1, Doc. 1557, Albert to king, 31 March 1621.
[54] *Ibid.*, 2, Doc. 10, Philip IV to Albert, 22 April 1621.
[55] José Larraz López, *La época del mercantilismo en Castilla, 1500–1700* (Madrid, 1943), p. 96.
[56] 'Cargos contra el Conde Duque', *MC*, 2, p. 235.

not to renew the truce in its 1609 form, had in fact been taken before Olivares possessed any voice in the government of Spain.

His subsequent behaviour, however, suggests that Olivares fully accepted the arguments for resuming the war with the Dutch. He was always scathing in his indictments of the 1609 Truce,[57] and he clearly shared his uncle's view that the terms on which it had been negotiated, and the uses to which it had been put by the Dutch, had been an unmitigated disaster for Spain. Total victory over the Dutch might be out of the question, but only war, it seemed, could halt the Dutch in their tracks, and bring about a settlement that was neither dishonourable to Spain nor harmful to its interests.

The exact nature of those interests, however, was not easily defined. The commitment to defend the loyal provinces of the southern Netherlands had become over the years an article of faith, questioned by some, like Pedro López de Reino, but apparently never seriously examined at the highest levels of government. Although Flanders represented a terrible drain on Castile's resources, it was seen, together with that other relic of the old Burgundian inheritance, the Franche-Comté, as an integral part of that structure of Hispanic power which held the French in check and gave the King of Spain his European hegemony. It was also argued that Spain, by fighting the enemy in those distant northern lands, was preserving the Iberian peninsula itself from the miseries of war, although the exact mechanism by which this process operated was never spelt out in detail.[58]

Beyond this, there was a complex of ties—made up of religion, loyalty, sentiment and interest—which bound Flanders to Spain, perhaps too closely for the good of either party. Zúñiga himself, through his Flemish wife, was a living embodiment of that Spanish-Flemish connection which could never be left out of account when the affairs of the Netherlands were discussed in Madrid. Flanders had become a training-ground not only for Spanish soldiers, but also for ministers and officials, who might well move on to posts in the upper echelons of the government in Madrid—men like Don Agustín Mexía, once a *maestre de campo* in the army of Flanders, and now a Councillor of State; or Don Fernando Carrillo, President of the Council of the Indies from 1617. These were men whom Zúñiga had come to know during his years in Brussels, as indeed he also knew all the leading figures at the court of the Archdukes Albert and Isabella.[59]

---

[57] 'La tregua que tanto he abominado...', Olivares to Marquis of Los Balbases (Ambrosio Spínola), draft letter of 29 August 1629 (AGS Est. leg. 2713).

[58] For a classic statement of this standard argument, see the king's speech to the Castilian Cortes of 1621, *Actas*, 36, p. 18.

[59] BL Eg. Ms. 2079, fos. 236–46v., 'Relación de las cosas de Flandes y de las personas de importancia que sirven a SM, escrita por Don Baltasar de Zúñiga.'

There were personal links of shared experience among the Spaniards who had braved those cold northern winters, just as there were links between Spaniards and Flemings who had worked side by side in the service of the crown. Zúñiga's personal staff included his Flemish secretary, Jacques Bruneau, who in due course joined the distinguished group of Flemish diplomats in the royal service,[60] and Antonio Carnero, whose family history epitomizes the interplay of Spain and Flanders over the course of three generations. The first Carnero to serve in the Netherlands was Alonso, accountant to the army of Flanders from 1584–7 and again from 1589–95.[61] While serving in the Netherlands he married a Flemish wife, Anne Trogner. Alonso's nephew, the first Antonio Carnero, was a financial official in the household of Don Enrique de Guzmán, Count of Olivares, leaving it in 1584 to assist his uncle in Brussels, where he in turn served as accountant of the army from 1587–9. Many years later, after service in Spain and Milan, he returned to Brussels, where he published in 1625 a *History of the Wars in the Low Countries*.[62] Alonso's son, the second Antonio, was born in Brussels around 1586, grew up speaking perfect French,[63] and spent the early years of his secretarial career in the Netherlands before being called to Madrid in 1621 to assist Zúñiga with his papers. On Zúñiga's death in the following year, he entered the service of Olivares (whose father his own father had served), becoming his private secretary and his right-hand man.[64]

The men who constituted the powerful Spanish-Flemish lobby in Madrid were unlikely to feel any sympathy for those who dared to ask: *'Flandes, quid nobis prodest?'* Ties of loyalty and sentiment were always liable to get in the way of any attempt to calculate the value of the Netherlands connection purely in terms of interest. But, by the same token, the lobby was unlikely to press for war to the death with the Dutch. These men had seen, and no doubt personally benefited from, the precarious revival of prosperity in the southern provinces of the Netherlands during the years of truce. While they might

---

[60] Other members of this group were the Baron d'Auchy, and Gabriel de Roy (Roye). See José Alcalá-Zamora y Queipo de Llano, *España, Flandes y el mar del norte, 1618–1639* (Barcelona, 1975), p. 38.

[61] Parker, *Army of Flanders*, p. 284.

[62] *Historia de las guerras civiles que ha avido en los Estados de Flandes* (Brussels, 1625). Information on the family's history in AHN Ordenes Militares (Santiago), Expte. 1572.

[63] Almost the only Spaniard in Madrid capable of doing so, according to the Council of State in 1639, when looking for a special emissary to send to Paris (AGS Est. K. 1419, consulta, 22 August 1639).

[64] AHN Est., lib. 259, fos. 183v.–184, royal cédula of 18 September 1622 on Antonio Carnero's career and services. The complications of the Carnero family are further compounded by the fact that Antonio Carnero, Olivares' secretary, had a brother, also called Antonio Carnero, who served the crown in various capacities in Italy and in due course became secretary of the Council of Italy and *ayuda de cámara* to the king.

not share the passionate desire for peace of the Archdukes and Ambrosio Spínola, whose relationship to the family banking house had always made his motivations suspect,[65] they would have liked, if they could, to have spared Flanders the devastations of war. At best they were reluctant warriors, and Zúñiga himself, who was a friend of Spínola,[66] would willingly have staved off the conflict if there had been any way of obtaining an honourable peace.

But in the spring of 1621 there was no hope of this. Although Prince Maurice himself may have had his hesitation about the resumption of hostilities, the triumph of his Orangist party in the United Provinces in 1618 had led to at least a temporary eclipse of the party favouring peace, and had created a climate in which there was no possibility of renegotiating the truce of 1609 in such a way as to take account of Spanish susceptibilities.[67] The militancy of the Dutch in 1621 therefore made the agonized debate in Madrid about terms and conditions almost wholly irrelevant. Neither side had any overwhelming urge to prevent the resumption of the war, and the only hope remaining to Archduke Albert and his circle was that Spain would simply not have the resources to send the army on campaign. On 24 June Albert wrote to inform Madrid that it would be necessary to increase the allocation of the army of Flanders to 300,000 ducats a month if it was expected to take the offensive. Failing this the only option was to renew the truce on the best terms available.[68] This was to be his last despairing attempt to shield from war the provinces which he and the Archduchess Isabel Clara Eugenia had cherished with a parental solicitude for twenty-three years. He died on 13 July; and although the government was formally entrusted to his widow, the southern Netherlands now lost their nominal independence and reverted to direct dependence on the Spanish Crown.[69]

The archduke was fully aware that his insistence on a substantial increase in the budgetary allocation for Flanders would embarrass Madrid. Already the king had convoked the first meeting of the Cortes of Castle to be held in his reign, in order to levy new taxes for his wars. The royal speech, read to the thirty-six assembled depu-

[65] Juan Roco de Campofrío, 'Relación de la jornada que su alteza el Archiduque Alberto... hizo a Flandes en el año de 1595', published under the title of *España en Flandes* (Madrid, 1973), pp. 291–2. A secret report in 1616 by the inspector-general of the army of Flanders, Don Francisco de Andía y Irarrazábal (the future Marquis of Valparaíso), concluded that Spínola disposed of the army's funds as he wished; but Spínola, an energetic and skilful lobbyist, managed to retain the royal confidence. See Miguel Angel Echevarría Bacigalupe, *La diplomacia secreta en Flandes, 1598–1643* (Bilbao, 1984), pp. 79–80.

[66] ASM, Gonzaga, E.XIV.3, busta 615, Bonatti to Duke of Mantua, 2 August 1621.

[67] See Israel, *The Dutch Republic*, pp. 63–4, 80–1, for the attitudes of the Dutch and of Maurice.

[68] Lonchay and Cuvelier, *Correspondance*, 2, Doc. 49.

[69] *Ibid.*, Doc. 68, Bedmar to king, 26 July 1621.

ties on 22 June, dwelt on the heavy military expenses that had been incurred since the convocation of the last Cortes of Philip III in 1617. Four million ducats had been needed for Flanders and Germany, to save the Emperor. In addition, the expiration of the truce in the Netherlands had made it necessary to increase the ordinary annual assignations of $1\frac{1}{2}$ million ducats for Flanders by a further 120,000 ducats a month, 100,000 of which were needed to reinforce the army, and the remaining 20,000 to fit out a Dunkirk squadron of twenty ships.[70]

The crown insisted that this increased expenditure was unavoidable, and asked the Cortes for a prompt vote on the traditional subsidies, known as the ordinary and extraordinary *servicios*. These would supplement the *millones* of two million ducats a year over a nine-year period, conceded by the last Cortes of the reign of Philip III. It duly obtained its vote, although not without a certain friction which augured badly for the future relations of the Cortes and the new regime. But one or two subsidies conceded by the Cortes of Castile would not go very far towards alleviating the pressing problems of the royal *hacienda*, as contemporaries called the king's patrimonial income and the other revenues that accrued to him primarily in his capacity as King of Castile and the Indies.[71]

At the start of the new reign the royal *hacienda* was in a deplorable state, and the prognostications of the *Consejo de Hacienda*—the Council of Finance—were, with good reason, uniformly bleak. It reported again in July 1621, as it had consistently reported in the later years of Philip III,[72] that the treasury was so depleted that there was simply no way to meet the crown's outstanding obligations to its bankers for the current year, and still less to arrange the *asientos*, or contracts, with the bankers for the years ahead.[73] To meet the current year's expenses it had already been forced to draw on anticipated revenues

[70] *Actas*, vol. 36, pp. 23–9. The facts and figures for the royal speech were prepared by Juan de Ciriza in response to a request from the royal secretary, Pedro de Contreras, who read the speech to the Cortes (AGS Est., leg. 2710, letter from Contreras to Ciriza, 15 May 1621, and Ciriza's reply, 18 May).

[71] Since the taxes granted by the Cortes of the Crown of Aragon also figured in the estimates of the Consejo de Hacienda if the money was remitted to Madrid, the *hacienda* cannot properly be described as being limited to Castile and the Indies. But since tax revenues from the Crown of Aragon constituted only a small fraction of the king's income for general uses, and the tax revenues from Italy were consumed locally, the royal *hacienda* was overwhelmingly concerned with Castilian and Indies revenues. For a detailed description of the royal *hacienda* in the later sixteenth century, see Modesto Ulloa, *La hacienda real de Castilla en el reinado de Felipe II* (Madrid, 1977). The most comprehensive account to date of royal finances in the reign of Philip IV is Antonio Domínguez Ortiz, *Política y hacienda de Felipe IV* (Madrid, 1960).

[72] See J. H. Elliott, *The Revolt of the Catalans* (Cambridge, 1963), pp. 187–90.

[73] AGS CJH, leg. 573, consulta, 17 July 1621; and see Domínguez Ortiz, *Política y hacienda*, pp. 12–13.

up to 1625, and this in turn presupposed higher rates of interest for the bankers. The *alcabala* or sales tax and the king's ordinary revenues were burdened with interest payments that exceeded their annual yield; the *servicios* voted by the Cortes were mortgaged to the bankers until 1625, as were the clerical subsidies of the *cruzada* and the *excusado*; and the other major source of crown revenue in Castile, the *millones* levied on the basic commodities of wine, olive-oil, vinegar and meat, were so inefficiently administered by the commission of the Cortes established for this purpose, that the actual return bore little relation to their nominal worth.

During the final years of the reign of Philip III the crown's annual expenditure had been of the order of nine million ducats, of which court expenses and the payment of ambassadors accounted for about one million ducats, while military and naval expenses, together with the servicing of debts, were responsible for most of the rest.[74] A realistic increase in military and naval expenditure to take account of the resumption of hostilities with the Dutch would mean an additional two million ducats a year for the army of Flanders, over and above the 1½ million normally assigned to it, and a doubling of the assignment for the Atlantic fleet, which stood at half a million ducats at the end of the reign of Philip III.[75]

The problem of finding the money to meet this increased expenditure was compounded by the recent spectacular fall in the value of silver remittances from the Indies. In the opening years of the reign of Philip III the crown could count on receiving some two million ducats of American silver a year. In 1615 and 1616 this dropped to one million ducats, and the figure for 1620 was only 845,000.[76] Important long-term changes were under way in the economic relationship between Spain and the American viceroyalties of Mexico and Peru as these approached self-sufficiency in foodstuffs and other commodities traditionally provided by Spain, and became increasingly reliant on north European manufactures shipped to the Indies by way of Seville.[77] Costs of silver production, too, were rising in the New World, as the easier veins were exhausted, and shortages developed in the supply of mercury needed for the refining process. Officials of the Council of Finance explained in 1613 that every thousand *quintales* of mercury which failed to reach the mines involved a loss to the king of 200,000 ducats worth of silver in Peru, and

[74] Elliott, *Catalans*, p. 188.
[75] AGS CJH, leg. 573, fo. 11, statement of provisions agreed with bankers for 1621, dated 28 January 1621; AGS CJH, leg. 578, fo. 303, consulta, 10 December 1621.
[76] Elliott, *Catalans*, p. 189.
[77] The problems of Seville's Atlantic trade in the early seventeenth century are exhaustively examined in vol. 8, 2 (2) of Pierre Chaunu, *Séville et l'Atlantique, 1504–1650* (Paris, 1959).

100,000 in Mexico.[78] But it is doubtful whether the problem of the mercury supply had yet become critical, and the shortfall in silver remittances in the last years of Philip III is more easily explained by the decision of the American viceroys to hold back silver for local needs, of which the most pressing was the strengthening of the coastal defences against Dutch attack.[79]

Traditionally American silver constituted somewhere between a quarter and a fifth of the crown's annual income, so that even a temporary decline in remittances was of serious concern. It was all the more serious because it was silver that the crown's Genoese bankers wanted, and not the copper coinage known as *vellón*. Much of the Castilian tax yield was paid into the treasury in *vellón*, and while this could be used domestically to meet the crown's expenses, it was of no value (beyond its copper content) outside Castile. It was bullion that was needed for payments to the army of Flanders or for subsidies to the Emperor, just as it was bullion that the European banking and commercial community needed for its international transactions. To offset the disadvantages arising from receipt of payments in *vellón*, the crown's bankers insisted on receiving, over and above the normal interest payments, a premium designed to cover the discrepancy between current silver and *vellón* rates. The premium varied from place to place and year to year, but in 1620 it stood at around 5%.[80] The need to pay the premium inevitably pushed up the price to the crown of every *asiento* or contract negotiated between the Council of Finance and the royal bankers, and added to the great and growing burden of crown indebtedness.

The Council of Finance issued repeated warnings about the gravity of the financial situation, but these warnings had no marked impact on the foreign policy decisions taken by the Council of State between 1618 and 1621. It is, after all, in the nature of financial advisers to warn that further expenditure will infallibly bring disaster, just as it is in the nature of politicians to reply that there are certain things more important than money. In any event, the Spanish Council of State was not, by character or composition, a body unduly sensitive to the problems of financial management. Most of its members, drawn as they were from the high nobility, were accustomed to living well beyond their means. Personal experience had led them

[78] AGS CJH, leg. 520, nos. 12 and 39, Junta de Hacienda, 17 April and 23 November 1613; and see P. J. Bakewell, *Silver Mining and Society in Colonial Mexico* (Cambridge, 1971), ch. 7, for the problem of the mercury supply for the American mines.

[79] AGS CJH, leg. 555, no. 212, consulta, 26 August 1618, which anticipates a poor year for silver remittances because of heavy local expenditure by the viceroys.

[80] Earl J. Hamilton, *American Treasure and the Price Revolution in Spain, 1501–1650* (Cambridge, Mass., 1934), Table 7 (premiums on silver in terms of *vellón*).

to assume that promises, coupled with the occasional judicious down-payment, could indefinitely postpone the threatened catastrophe. In this they were largely right.

The Council of State which approved Spain's military intervention in Germany and led Spain back into war with the Dutch had about eight active members.[81] Although the accession of Philip IV brought some changes in the council's composition, it involved no break in the continuity of its policies because Zúñiga and his friends had in practice been in control of foreign policy-making since the summer of 1617. There had, however, always been cross-currents in the council which prevented Zúñiga from automatically getting his way. On the Valtelline, for example, the Duke of Feria, as Governor of Milan, had been pressing for an uncompromising stand by Spain, even at the expense of alienating France. In this he enjoyed the support at the council table of the Count of Benavente, President of the Council of Italy, and of the Duke of Infantado, who was related to Feria by marriage. Zúñiga, on the other hand, was anxious to avoid new wars at a time when Spanish arms were heavily committed in Germany and the Dutch truce was nearing its end, and therefore seems to have preferred to reach a negotiated settlement with the French on the status of the valley, even if this involved Spain's abandonment of its Valtelline forts.[82] On this occasion the council was divided enough for Philip III to call it into his presence. His decision apparently went in favour of a negotiated settlement. Marshal Bassom-pierre, whose mission to Madrid as extraordinary ambassador for France coincided with Philip III's illness and death, was able to negotiate a treaty by which the Valtelline would be restored to the Grisons. This Treaty of Madrid, signed on 25 April 1621, remained a dead letter, however, because the cantons refused to ratify it—an outcome highly satisfactory to Feria and his friends.[83]

The accession of Philip IV allowed Zúñiga to place his own stamp more firmly on the council. Two of its members most closely asso-ciated with the Lerma regime—the Inquisitor General Aliaga and the Marquis of La Laguna—were excluded from its sessions, the first permanently and the second temporarily, at the beginning of the

---

[81] No fully reliable list of councillors of state is yet available. Luis de Salazar y Castro, *Advertencias históricas* (Madrid, 1688) lists appointments to the council under Philip III (pp. 223–7) and Philip IV (pp. 227–37), but the lists contain inaccuracies. The following councillors attended the session of 25 December 1619 which debated the Truce with the United Provinces (Archivo de los Condes de Oñate, leg. 104): Duke of Infantado, Marquis of Villafranca, Don Agustín Mexía, Marquis of La Laguna, Count of Benavente, Inquisitor General (Fray Luis de Aliaga), Don Baltasar de Zúñiga, Cardinal Zapata.

[82] ASF Mediceo, filza 4949, fos. 746–8, ambassadorial despatch, 30 January 1621.

[83] Marrades, *Camino del imperio*, pp. 59–60; and see also for the Valtelline, Rémy Pithon, 'Les débuts difficiles du ministère de Richelieu et la crise de Valteline, 1621–1627', *Revue d'Histoire Diplomatique*, 74 (1960), pp. 289–322.

new reign.[84] A third, the Duke of Uceda, who had only been appointed to the council in the last days of Philip III, was also forbidden to attend. In turn, the Marquis of Villafranca, bellicose by temperament but erratic in his judgments, resumed the seat which he had temporarily forfeited when the Duke of Uceda had exiled him from the court.[85]

Four new councillors were appointed in April—the Duke of Monteleón, the Marquis of Aytona, Don Diego de Ibarra, and the Marquis of Montesclaros. The first two of these were appointed, in part at least, as a gesture to the Aragonese and the Catalans. Don Diego de Ibarra, an old soldier and a member of the Council of War, was a close friend of Zúñiga. Don Juan Manuel de Mendoza, third Marquis of Montesclaros, may partly have owned his appointment to his membership of the Mendoza family. The Mendozas were already represented on the council by the head of the family, the Duke of Infantado, but it was important that they should be wooed away from the Sandovals and brought into the Zúñiga-Guzmán camp. Montesclaros, however, had impressive personal credentials. He had served as viceroy of both Mexico and Peru, and was the first former viceroy in the Indies ever to reach the Council of State. His comparative youth—he was only fifty-one—his experience of government overseas, and his obvious talents augured a long and influential ministerial career, but it was cut short by his sudden death in 1628.[86]

On 17 July this renovated Council of State, still unaware of the Archduke Albert's death, met to discuss his final plea that Madrid should either increase the allocation for the army of Flanders, or else agree to a further truce on the best terms available.[87] The Duke of Infantado, speaking first, set the tone for the meeting when he argued that finding an extra 300,000 ducats a month was not as bad as perpetuating a truce which had cost Spain its reputation. The Marquis of Villafranca, militant as always, denounced the Twelve Years' Truce as the work of two men, the Archduke Albert, a pacifist by temperament, and Spínola, who had taken advantage of it to recover his debts. The king, he argued, was strong on land and the Dutch on the sea; and it was because the army of Flanders had left them unmolested for the past twelve years that they had been able to make themselves masters of the East Indies, and would soon be masters of the West Indies, too. There is no indication that Villafranca and

[84] ASF Mediceo, filza 4949, fo. 852, ambassadorial despatch, 29 April 1621.
[85] ASG, Lettere Ministri, Spagna, 2429, ambassadorial despatch, 17 April 1621.
[86] Ibid., 30 April 1621. For the Marquis of Montesclaros, see Francisco Layna Serrano, Historia de Guadalajara y sus Mendozas en los siglos XV y XVI, 3 (Madrid, 1942), pp. 236–8, and Nicolás Cabrillana, 'Un noble de la decadencia: el virrey marqués de Montesclaros, 1571–1628', Revista de Indias, 29 (1969), pp. 107–50.
[87] Archivo de los Condes de Oñate, leg. 104, consulta, 17 July 1621.

his colleagues had ever given any serious thought to the archduke's earlier attempts to expose the fallacy of this argument about the relationship of peace on land with war at sea. He had made efforts to explain to Madrid that Dutch overseas enterprise was privately financed and would not automatically cease with renewal of the war, but clearly to no avail.[88]

The French, according to Villafranca, could also be expected to think again once the army of Flanders moved against the Dutch. With war so close to their own frontiers, they would show less enthusiasm for interfering in Italy, as they had during the truce. 'We can hope, therefore, that there will be peace everywhere else if there is a good war in Flanders.' Apart from its diversionary benefits, the resumption of war in the Netherlands would also, as Don Agustín Mexía emphasized, have the advantage of giving the army of Flanders something to do. No one knew better than a Flanders veteran the dangers of having an idle and underpaid army on one's hands. The Count of Benavente, who followed Mexía, spoke even more forcefully in favour of sending the army of Flanders on campaign. In a Monarchy as large as that of Spain, he argued, there would always be a war somewhere, and it was best that it should be in Flanders, where the wars had served as a school of arms for Spaniards. War would force Spaniards to take up their arms again, and would prevent a martial people from growing effeminate. He had always understood that there were four prerequisites for the conservation of the Monarchy: good financial management; well-run armies and fleets; peace in Italy; war in Flanders. 'Either we have a good war, or we lose everything.'

Not all the members of the Council of State were quite as uncomplicated in their attitudes to war and peace as Villafranca and Benavente. Montesclaros, who stated that the 'principal object of war must be peace', at least paid some attention to the internal situation in the United Provinces—their reported shortage of money and credit, and the feuds between Arminians and Gomarists—in order to justify his conviction that the time had come for all-out war. Ibarra, the professional soldier, also believed that at this moment the army of Flanders was likely to hold the advantage, although he was concerned about the readiness of the fleet. In general the councillors, including Zúñiga, Aytona and Monteleón, give the impression of having reached the conclusion that anything would be preferable to the continuation of an unsatisfactory truce, and that somehow, and somewhere, the money for campaigning must be found.

Unanimously, then, although with varying degrees of enthusiasm,

---

[88] Lonchay and Cuvelier, *Correspondance*, 2, Doc. 26, Albert to Philip IV, 30 April 1621.

the Council of State committed Spain to the renewal of full-scale war against the United Provinces. The king, in reply to the *consulta* which embodied its recommendations, decreed that from the beginning of August the army of Flanders should receive its 300,000 ducats a month, and that the campaign was to start forthwith. All that was now needed was the money to pay for the war.

The methods of war finance adopted during those opening months of the reign were to cast a long shadow over the years to come. Even where they had been recommended or approved in the reign of Philip III, the fact that they were implemented by the men of the new regime—men who were proclaiming the need to break with the immediate past—inevitably associated them in the public mind with the incoming administration rather than with the old. They were not calculated to inspire confidence either in the integrity of the crown or in the king's choice of ministers, and helped to sour opinion which had welcomed with enthusiasm the change of regime.

The first measure, and one for which Olivares would later have to pay a heavy penalty, was the large-scale minting of *vellón* coins of pure copper. Under Philip III the Cortes of Castile had made the cessation of *vellón* minting for a period of twenty years one of the conditions for the voting of the *millones*. This condition was accepted by the king in June 1618,[89] but in the last weeks of his reign a majority of the eighteen cities represented in the Cortes agreed under pressure to the minting of a further 800,000 ducats to help the king pay his bankers. It soon became clear that 800,000 ducats were nothing like enough, and in May 1621, within a week or two of the beginning of his reign, Philip IV ordered the Council of Finance to resume minting. When the council hesitated, it received a sharp royal reminder that the king's principal obligation was to defend his realm against his enemies. Any further delay in minting was therefore inexcusable.[90] In July the crown made an attempt to preserve appearances by securing an authorization from the Cortes to mint a further 600,000 ducats;[91] but in reality shortage of copper proved the only restraint on the output of the mints over the next five years, and the objections of the Cortes were simply overruled. When minting was at last suspended on 8 May 1626, nearly twenty million ducats had been manufactured over a five-year period, with an effective yield to the treasury of thirteen million after the deduction of expenses.[92] By this time the damage had been done. The bad money drove out the good—*vellón* became the chief circulating medium

[89] Hamilton, *American Treasure*, p. 78.
[90] AGS CJH, leg. 581, no. 1, consulta, 16 February 1622, outlining sequence of events.
[91] Domínguez Ortiz, *Política y hacienda*, p. 254.
[92] *Ibid.*, p. 256.

in Castile around 1622–3[93]—and the premium on silver in terms of *vellón* rose to 18% or 20% in Madrid by 1622 and to over 50% by 1626.[94]

The easiest way to raise money for internal uses was no doubt to manufacture it, but the crown still needed silver for its foreign transactions. Following a decision taken in principle in the reign of Philip III, the government sequestered 800,000 ducats in silver (one eighth of the total) consigned in the 1620 Indies fleet to the account of private individuals, and compensated the unfortunate owners in *vellón*.[95] There were precedents from earlier reigns for impounding silver from the treasure fleets, but the immediate benefit to the royal treasury was far outweighed by the long-term damage to the delicate mechanism of the Indies trade.

Having shaken the confidence of mercantile and financial circles in Seville and Madrid, Zúñiga's government then proceeded to reduce interest rates on *juros* and *censos*. Seventeenth-century Castile was a *rentier* society, with people at many social levels drawing a substantial portion of their annual income from *rentas*, in the form of annuities on state bonds (*juros*) and individual or corporate bonds (*censos*). Rates of return varied. A 'pragmatic', or royal decree, of 1608 reduced interest rates on all future *juros* and *censos*, but not on existing ones, so that the yield on future *juros perpetuos* would be 5% instead of 7.1%, while single life annuities (*juros de por vida*) came down to 10%.[96] This brought some limited relief to the royal treasury, which at that time was having to devote half its annual income to interest payments on *juros*. But the underlying problems remained. The crown had a staggering burden of indebtedness; and, in the opinion of the Council of Finance, one of the major reasons for the decline of industry and agriculture in Castile was the availability of *juros* and *censos* 'at such advantageous rates that their yield is considered to be higher than the profits to be made in trade, agriculture and stock-raising'. The result was that people tried to live on annuities, instead of using their capital for more productive forms of investment.[97]

This was not a new argument. That acute observer of the contemporary Castilian scene, Martín González de Cellorigo, had inveighed

[93] Hamilton, *American Treasure*, p. 212.

[94] Hamilton's table of premiums on silver in terms of *vellón* (*American Treasure*, p. 96) shows a premium of only 6% in 1622, but in March 1622 the king expressed his concern to the President of the Council of Castile about the excessive premiums, and subsequent documentation indicates that the prevailing rate at court was at that time 18% or 20% (BL 1322.1.12, *Papeles varios*, ms. 3).

[95] AGS CJH, leg. 573, no. 104, consulta, 30 May 1621; no. 194, consulta, 8 August 1621; Antonio Domínguez Ortiz, 'Los caudales de Indias y la política exterior de Felipe IV', *Anuario de Estudios Americanos*, 13 (1957), pp. 336–7.

[96] Domínguez Ortiz, *Política y hacienda*, p. 318.

[97] AGS CJH, leg. 547, no. 58, consulta, 3 September 1617.

in 1600 against the way in which wealth in Castile disappeared into 'thin air, into papers, contracts, *censos*, letters of exchange, into coins and silver and gold', instead of into investment which increased the national income.[98] A reduction in the prevailing rates of interest might divert wealth into more productive channels, and would certainly reduce the pressure on the royal treasury; but against this it could be argued that for the crown to tamper with interest rates was to default on its moral obligations.[99] Don Fernando de Acevedo, the President of the Council of Castile, set his face against any such tampering, and resisted all attempts by Baltasar de Zúñiga to make him put his signature to a new pragmatic.[100] This was no doubt an additional reason for getting rid of a minister who anyhow was too closely associated with the Lerma and Uceda regimes for the comfort of Zúñiga and Olivares; and the first law signed by his successor, Don Francisco de Contreras, was a pragmatic dated 7 October 1621 which reduced interest rates on all *juros* and *censos* to 5%.[101] Like the pragmatic of 1608 this new measure brought at least temporary relief to the treasury, but at the expense of many small investors and corporate institutions which had been getting a return of some 7.5% on their *censos*.[102] It is not clear that it had any beneficial effects on the Castilian economy, but it certainly eroded public confidence in the word of the king. This in turn was not likely to help the regime when it embarked on its efforts to win support for its plans for economic and fiscal reform.

These early measures of the new regime made it possible for the army of Flanders to go out, rather belatedly, on campaign. Traditionally, campaigning in the Netherlands consisted largely of long and expensive siege warfare, designed to pick off one by one the strongly fortified cities of the United Provinces. Spínola opened the war in traditional style, first laying siege to the Dutch-occupied town of Jülich, which capitulated in February 1622 (Pl. 8), and then moving on to besiege Bergen-op-Zoom.

The long and ultimately abortive siege of Bergen helped to confirm what many had long suspected—that a war of protracted sieges was not only intolerably expensive, but also was unlikely to bring the

---

[98] Martín González de Cellorigo, *Memorial de la política necessaria y útil restauración a la república de España* (Valladolid, 1600), fo. 29.
[99] See the arguments of Ldo. Juan de Samaniego, 2 August 1621, in Angel González Palencia, *La Junta de Reformación* (Valladolid, 1932), Doc. XXIV.
[100] Escagedo Salmón, 'Los Acebedos', *Boletín de la Biblioteca Menéndez y Pelayo*, 9 (1927), pp. 76–8.
[101] Faustino Gil Ayuso, *Noticia bibliográfica de textos y disposiciones legales de los reinos de Castilla impresos en los siglos XVI y XVII* (Madrid, 1935), no. 784.
[102] ASG, Lettere Ministri, Spagna, 2429, despatch, 18 October 1621.

Dutch to heel.[103] In 1619 the Count of Gondomar, drawing on his first-hand experience of life in northern Europe, commented in the course of a letter to the king that 'warfare today is not a question of brute strength, as if men were bulls, nor even a question of battles, but rather of winning or losing friends and trade, and this is the question to which all good governments should address themselves.'[104]

How then should war against the Dutch be waged? One method, already chosen by Madrid at the end of Philip III's reign, was to create a special Flanders squadron, in order to carry the war more effectively onto the sea.[105] Another was to use the weapons of economic warfare. There was a growing appreciation in Madrid of the sources of Dutch prosperity, and of the way in which that prosperity was founded on the impoverishment of Spain. As long as the Dutch dominated the north-south carrying trade, on which Spain was dependent both for imports and exports, there was bound to be a heavily adverse balance of trade with northern Europe. This in turn meant an outflow of Spanish bullion, which was then used by the Dutch to build up their own military and commercial strength and to subsidize Spain's enemies. To add insult to injury the Dutch were also suspected of smuggling large quantities of counterfeit copper coinage into the peninsula, and carrying off silver in return.[106]

As soon as hostilities were resumed in 1621, the crown ordered the expulsion of Dutch ships from all ports in the king's dominions, and placed an embargo on Dutch goods and assets.[107] But while an embargo had an obvious appeal to protectionist circles in cities of the interior, like Toledo, anxious to save local industries from being overwhelmed by foreign competition, it was less welcome to the mercantile communities of port cities like Seville, which were likely to suffer from any impediments to trade.[108]

In any event, an embargo was at best a crude weapon, which would not in itself go far towards wresting economic hegemony from the Dutch. This was particularly appreciated by those who had

[103] See pp. 42–3 of Jonathan Israel, 'A Conflict of Empires: Spain and the Netherlands, 1618–1648', *Past and Present*, 76 (1977), pp. 34–74, for the disillusionment created by Spínola's failure to take Bergen-op-Zoom.

[104] *Correspondencia Oficial de don Diego Sarmiento de Acuña, Conde de Gondomar* in *Documentos inéditos para la historia de España*, 2 (Madrid, 1943), p. 140 (Gondomar to Philip III, 28 March 1619).

[105] Alcalá-Zamora, *España, Flandes*, pp. 156–8.

[106] Jonathan Israel, 'Spain and the Dutch Sephardim, 1609–1660', *Studia Rosenthaliana*, 12 (1978), p. 3.

[107] Israel, *The Dutch Republic*, pp. 93–4.

[108] For protectionist tendencies in Toledo, see Jean Vilar, 'Docteurs et marchands: l'"école" de Tolède', communication to Fifth International Congress of Economic History (Moscow, 1970), and his introduction to Sancho de Moncada, *Restauración política de España* (Madrid, 1974).

8. In this representation of the surrender of Jülich (1622), painted by Jusepe Leonardo for the Hall of Realms of the palace of the Buen Retiro in 1634, Ambrosio Spínola is offered the keys of the city. On horseback beside him is Olivares' cousin, Don Diego Mexía, the future Marquis of Leganés.

first-hand experience of the Dutch and their methods, like Manuel López Pereira, who had moved with his family to Seville, after long years of residence in Holland. López Pereira was a member of that group of Portuguese merchants, many of them *conversos* or New Christians of Jewish origin, who had steadily expanded their role in the commercial and financial life of Castile since the Union of the Crowns of Castile and Portugal in 1580.[109] In a memorandum

[109] There is a large, and growing, literature on the Portuguese New Christians. See particularly vol. 2 of Caro Baroja, *Los judíos*, and 'La sociedad criptojudía en la corte de Felipe IV', in his *Inquisición, brujería y criptojudaismo* (2nd. ed., Barcelona, 1972). Also Antonio Domínguez Ortiz, *Los judeoconversos en España y América* (Madrid, 1971). The figure of Manuel López Pereira has so far not received the attention it deserves. The detail about his years of residence in Holland comes from an undated consulta of a junta presided over by the Marquis of Montesclaros to examine a number of papers he had submitted to the government (ADI Montesclaros Mss., volume entitled *Flandes y Alemania*, fo. 37).

which he submitted for ministerial consideration at the start of the reign he explained that the prosperity of the Dutch sprang from their trading ventures and from the reserves of Spanish silver which they had succeeded in accumulating.[110] As one possible answer he proposed—like a fellow-Sevillian, Tomás de Cardona[111]—an increase in the currency value of Indies silver, on the grounds that it was currently undervalued and therefore impossible to retain in the peninsula. He also wanted the government to get to grips with the problem of the debased *vellón* coinage, either by reducing it to the intrinsic worth of its copper content, or by issuing better quality coins. He opposed the embargo on Dutch goods, since he believed that this merely encouraged the Dutch to develop alternative trading outlets with even more damaging consequences to Spain; and he wanted Spain to concentrate all its efforts on challenging the Dutch on sea, and not on land.

López Pereira's memorandum, which is of special interest because its author would later become one of Olivares' financial advisers, takes its place as one among many in a wide-ranging debate in the Castile of the early 1620's—a debate sharpened by the advent to power of a new regime and by the simultaneous resumption of the war with the Dutch, with all the economic and financial problems that this involved. It was a debate which touched on fundamental issues of policy—currency reform, protectionism versus free trade, and the most effective methods for waging economic warfare and promoting economic growth. However simplistic the pronouncements of some of their more bellicose colleagues in the Council of State, Zúñiga and Olivares were alive to these wider issues, and well aware that the future of the Monarchy depended on the skill and determination with which they were confronted.

The legacy of Zúñiga

In the memorable words of the Count of La Roca, Don Baltasar de Zúñiga was a man who 'although he seemed to be asleep, was not asleep within.'[112] It was he who, between 1617 and 1621, steered Spain back into war—war first in Germany, and then in the Nether-

---

[110] AHN Consejos, lib. 1428, fos. 263–70. The assessment of his memorandum by Juan de Hoces is printed in González Palencia, *La Junta de Reformación*, Doc. XXX.
[111] For Tomás de Cardona, see Jean Vilar, 'Una pauta del pensamiento monetarista castellano: la "proposición" Cardona, 1618–1628', reprinted from *Dinero y crédito (siglos XVI al XIX)*, ed. Alfonso de Otazu (Madrid, 1978), pp. 449–57. Hoces, in his assessment, considers López Pereira's proposal inferior to Cardona's.
[112] Roca, *Fragmentos históricos*, p. 162.

lands. Of the man himself we know all too little. Prudent, phlegmatic, rather too fond of women—these are the images conjured up by contemporaries.[113] It is perhaps more revealing of the cast of his temperament that he was an admirer of Justus Lipsius and a translator of Montaigne, although his translations (criticized for their inaccuracy) have not survived.[114] He was a man who looked out warily on the world around him; not a man for heroic gestures, but one who preferred to calculate the risks, and then to steer the ship as best he could, fully aware that any sudden squall might cause it to capsize.

When Zúñiga was entrusted by the king with the government of the Monarchy in April 1621, he had only another eighteen months to live. Although death came suddenly to him in October 1622, he was sixty when he became the king's principal minister, and it is likely that he saw himself as essentially a caretaker and custodian, although one upon whom the highest responsibilities had devolved. He was, first of all, the custodian of his house and family—of the Guzmán-Zúñiga connection—which over the generations had served the crown with such distinction. He had learnt his first lessons in statecraft in the Spanish embassy in Rome from his brother-in-law, the second Count of Olivares, and now he was grooming his nephew, the third count, in the same tradition.

Contemporaries were naturally on the lookout for any signs of discord between uncle and nephew, and the relationship does indeed seem to have deteriorated in the last months of Don Baltasar's life, in part at least because of a dispute between their wives.[115] But each was well aware that he needed the other. Don Baltasar had the experience of the world that Olivares lacked; but Olivares for his part had the favour of the king. It was natural, therefore, that they should devise a partnership in which Zúñiga managed affairs of state, and gradually inducted his nephew into the art of government business, while Olivares consolidated his position in the palace.

At the start of the reign, when Olivares was loudly disclaiming any desire to meddle in affairs of state, Zúñiga was reported to be running the government with the assistance of the king's secretary Antonio de Aróztegui. The other prominent figure in the regime was the Count of Benavente, of the house of Pimentel, a close relative of Zúñiga, who called him in for frequent consultation.[116] Benavente, however, died in November, and Zúñiga added to his other duties that of the presidency of the Council of Italy, vacated by Benavente's

[113] Roca, *ibid*; Malvezzi, *Reinado de Felipe IV*, pp. 85–7.
[114] Juan Marichal, 'Montaigne en España', *La voluntad del estilo* (Madrid, 1971), p. 102.
[115] Malvezzi, *Historia*, p. 86.
[116] ASF Mediceo, filza 4949, fo. 844, despatch, 17 April 1621.

death.[117] There were those who believed that, from the very beginning, Zúñiga danced to Olivares' tune.[118] No doubt he and his nephew spent long hours together devising policy and discussing government business, in which Olivares, for all his disclaimers, became heavily involved before the end of the year.[119] But there is no reason to believe that the two men were not at one in their principal objective, even if at times they disagreed on how best to carry out their policies.

Zúñiga outlined this objective in an interview with the Genoese ambassador in April 1621.[120] The aim of the new administration, he said, was to 'restore everything to the state it was in during the reign of Philip II and to abolish the large number of abuses introduced under the recent government.' To return to the age of Philip II—an age in which (at least in retrospect) the very name of the King of Spain commanded instant respect both at home and abroad: there could be no higher ideal for the survivors of a generation which had known and served the Prudent King, and which had watched with dismay the erosion of the Monarchy's greatness during the reign of his successor. Zúñiga saw himself as the custodian of the great traditions of the Monarchy. It was his task to restore it, as far as possible, to its former grandeur, and to pass on the precious trust to the next generation, in the person of his nephew.

The insistence on 'reputation' that ran through his policy was an integral part of this determination to conserve and restore. Reputation meant asserting the rights and interests of the King of Spain, by war if necessary, so that he should occupy the position in the world to which he was entitled. Olivares, who in this respect proved an apt pupil of his uncle, later expressed the concept in the following words: 'I have always been deeply anxious to see Your Majesty enjoying throughout the world *opinión* and *reputación* equal to your greatness and parts.'[121]

During the five years in which he directed Spanish foreign policy Zúñiga went far towards restoring Spain's 'reputation in the world'. The Austrian Habsburgs saved; Frederick an unhappy exile in The Hague, his temporary kingdom of Bohemia lost to him, and his lands in the Palatinate occupied; the humiliation of the 1609 truce with the Dutch effaced by the resumption of hostilities, with every hope that a more effective style of warfare would bring the United Provinces to their senses: all these were achievements on which he

---

[117] BL microfilm M854, Gondomar papers (1621), Zúñiga to Gondomar, 15 November 1621: 'murió el buen Conde de Benavente, que ha hecho gran soledad en esta corte.'
[118] ASM, Gonzaga, E.XIV.3, busta 615, despatch, 8 June 1621.
[119] ASM, Gonzaga, E.XIV.3, busta 615, Celliero Bonatti to Giovanni Magno, December 1621.
[120] ASG, Lettere Ministri, Spagna, 2429, despatch, 6 April 1621.
[121] AGS Est. leg. 2039, consulta, 29 June 1625.

could look back with pride. But at the same time Zúñiga knew enough of the ways of God and the world to appreciate that each success carried within itself the seeds of possible future defeat; that no victory was permanent, no achievement definitive, in a world that was eternally subject to change. Already, in the final months of his life, the problems were crowding in on him. The very extent of the Habsburg triumph had alerted Spain's traditional enemies to the new dangers, their fears fed and their suspicions confirmed by the interception and publication in the spring of 1622 of secret correspondence which showed a clear design to recatholicize the Empire and transfer the Elector Palatine's title to Maximilian of Bavaria.[122]

Zúñiga himself was fully alive to the possibility that any rash move could extend the war in Germany into a European conflict. In the Valtelline he advocated compromise through papal mediation, and reached an agreement with the French under the Treaty of Aranjuez of May 1622 for the Spanish fortresses to be temporarily entrusted to the papacy until a definitive settlement was produced.[123] Where the Rhenish Palatinate was concerned, he favoured an eventual restitution to a duly penitent Frederick, in the belief that this was essential in order to retain the goodwill of England.[124] As for Frederick's electoral dignity, he and his colleagues were strongly opposed to any unilateral move by the Emperor to transfer it to Maximilian of Bavaria. This would not only compromise Spain's relations with England, but would threaten an indefinite extension of the war in Germany, jeopardizing Spain's prospects in its war with the Dutch. 'If the transfer is effected', said the Marquis of Aytona in the Council of State, 'there cannot be peace.'[125] This is what Zúñiga had always feared, and what he worked to prevent; but events were slipping out of Madrid's control, and in February 1623, three months after Zúñiga's death, the Emperor's formal conferment of the electoral title on Maximilian made the continuation and extension of the German conflict a foregone conclusion.

Perhaps Zúñiga was fortunate in the timing of his death. In 1622 it was easy to count the successes which his policies had achieved, but less easy to detect their long-term implications. A document would later circulate in Madrid, purporting to contain Don Baltasar's last instructions to his nephew. The document—which looks like a fabrication by the partisans of the fallen Duke of Lerma—expressed the fear that Olivares' arts and talents would diminish rather than

---

[122] See Dieter Albrecht, *Die auswärtige Politik Maximilians von Bayern, 1618–1635* (Göttingen, 1962), p. 71.
[123] Marrades, *Camino del imperio*, p. 100.
[124] Straub, *Pax et Imperium*, p. 176.
[125] AHN Est., lib. 739, fo. 162, consulta, 28 September 1622.

increase the greatness of the Monarchy; and it advised him to follow the maxims by which Lerma had maintained peace for so long.[126] But the attempt by the friends of Lerma to appropriate Zúñiga posthumously for themselves looks strangely unconvincing. Zúñiga, in so far as he was a man of peace, was always a man of peace with reputation, and his nephew in turn would adopt the same posture. The willingness to resort to war where this appeared necessary was an essential part of a policy which aimed, in the broadest sense, to renew and regenerate the Spanish Monarchy. It was to that task, both at home and abroad, that Zúñiga and Olivares were totally committed.

[126] For one of many copies in circulation, BAV Lat. Ms. 10,445, fos. 91–96v.

III

THE REFORMIST INHERITANCE

The ills of Castile

The regeneration of the Spanish Monarchy could only be brought about by the regeneration of Castile. On this, everyone was agreed. Castile was the head and the heart of the Monarchy—its exact position in the organism was variously located—and if Castile was sick, then the whole body suffered. This medical analogy was a commonplace of the times. 'I imagine Spain like a human body', runs a characteristic commentary. 'Although at present so debilitated and weak as to appear on the point of death, it ought to be strong and robust.'[1] If the analogy held, then the conclusion was obvious. 'Your Majesty is the doctor of this republic.'[2] It was for the king to effect the cure.

Modern diagnoses have concentrated primarily on the economic ailments of Spain and Castile under the later Habsburgs.[3] These, while numerous, were by no means uniquely Spanish; but by the end of the sixteenth century their number and gravity were beginning to have a cumulative effective, with one acting and reacting upon

[1] Pedro Hurtado de Alcocer (1621) in Angel González Palencia, *La Junta de Reformación*, p. 169. For other examples of the medical analogy, see p. 49 of J. H. Elliott, 'Self-perception and Decline in Seventeenth-century Spain', *Past and Present*, 74 (1977), pp. 41–61.

[2] Jerónimo de Ceballos, *Arte real para el buen gobierno de los reyes y príncipes, y de sus vassallos* (Toledo, 1623), fo. 30.

[3] The starting-point for modern discussion is the article by Earl J. Hamilton, 'The Decline of Spain', *Economic History Review*, 8 (1938), pp. 168–79. For a reexamination of the question in the light of work done in the twenty years following the publication of Hamilton's article, see J. H. Elliott, 'The Decline of Spain', *Past and Present*, 20 (1961), pp. 52–75. Since the 1960's a large, and growing, body of writing has been produced on different aspects of the historical problem conventionally and conveniently labelled 'the decline of Spain'. Some of the most important of this work relates to the crown finances, but in recent years there has been a surge of interest in the demographic history of Spain and in its rural and urban history. This welcome development has led to some excellent local and regional studies, which have still to be integrated into a satisfactory analysis of the problem of 'decline'. Reflections of this work, and bibliographical references to it, may be found in recent general histories of Habsburg Spain, notably John Lynch, *Spain under the Habsburgs*, 2 vols., (2nd. ed., Oxford, 1981); Henry Kamen, *Spain, 1469–1714. A Society of Conflict* (London, 1983); Bartolomé Bennassar, *La España del siglo de oro* (Barcelona, 1983; Spanish trans. of *Un siècle d'or espagnol*, Paris, 1982). For a recent economic survey of the sixteenth and seventeenth centuries see vol. 3 (*Los siglos XVI y XVII*) by V. Vázquez de Prada, of the *Historia económica y social de España*, ed. V. Vázquez de Prada (Madrid, 1978).

another in such a way as to make Spain's general condition proportionately more severe than that of its enemies and competitors.[4]

Like other parts of Europe, sixteenth-century Spain had seen a significant increase in population—perhaps from $7\frac{1}{2}$ to $8\frac{1}{2}$ million for the peninsula, excluding Portugal (whose population numbered rather over a million) between 1541 and 1591.[5] Of this total population, almost $1\frac{1}{2}$ million were inhabitants of the Crown of Aragon; 350,000 of Navarre and the Basque provinces; and some 6,600,000 of the lands of the Crown of Castile.[6] While population increased throughout the peninsula, rates of growth were uneven, but by the 1570's and 1580's the growth was faltering through much of Castile, where it had been intense in the earlier decades of the century, and many communities were entering a new phase of demographic stagnation. In its early stages the increase in demand created by the expansion of Castile's population had served as a stimulus to economic growth, and had led to an impressive extension of land under cultivation. But much of this land was poor and arid, and by the 1570's there were growing signs that the expansion had reached its limits. Demand for food was outstripping supply; commodity prices, forced up by unsatisfied demand, and sustained at a high level by annual injections of American silver into the Castilian economy, ran ahead of those of Spain's competitors; and Castile was transformed into an importing society, dependent on the Mediterranean and Baltic lands for additional stocks of grain, and on Italy and northern Europe for an increasing range of manufactured goods to meet both its own needs and those of the growing American market.

If the secular expansion of the Castilian economy came to an end around 1580, some of the cities of Castile and Andalusia, sustained by the flow of Indies silver and by their *rentier* and commercial wealth, maintained their prosperity to 1600 and beyond; and one of them, Madrid, selected by Philip II in 1561 as the capital of his world-wide Monarchy, was still only on the verge of its dazzling career of urban growth and conspicuous consumption, battening like a gaudy parasite on the wealth of the empire and of its own hinterland of central Castile.[7] It was in the countryside rather than the cities that the first signs of strain appeared. Traditionally there had been a somewhat precarious balance in Castile between arable and pasture, between

---

[4] For a useful brief account of the condition of Spain at the end of the sixteenth century see James Casey, 'Spain: a Failed Transition', in *The European Crisis of the 1590s*, ed. Peter Clark (London, 1985), pp. 209–28.

[5] See Jordi Nadal, *La población española. Siglos XVI a XX* (2nd. ed., Barcelona, 1984), p. 17.

[6] Antonio Domínguez Ortiz, *The Golden Age of Spain, 1516–1659* (London, 1971), p. 175.

[7] See David R. Ringrose, *Madrid and the Spanish Economy, 1560–1850* (Berkeley and Los Angeles, 1983).

cereal production for home consumption and sheep-farming, which was the basis not only of Castilian textile production but also of a major export trade in wool. The pressure to bring more land under cultivation to feed an expanding population disturbed this balance in the later sixteenth century, by stimulating a massive encroachment on good pasture-land, and a consequent fall in the numbers both of non-migratory flocks and of the transhumant flocks belonging to owners banded together in the great association known as the *Mesta*.[8]

While sheep-farming was running into trouble, the same was also true of arable farming. Peasant farmers had taken out loans in order to finance their cultivation of new land; and, as land became more marginal, profits—initially so tempting—began to decline, and growing numbers of peasants had difficulty in meeting their interest payments. Their difficulties were aggravated by the heavy burden of seigneurial, ecclesiastical and royal dues, which together took from them more than 50% of the value of their harvest.[9] As their debts mounted, many of them chose the simplest way out, leaving their villages for the greater security of an anonymous life in the cities. The indebtedness of rural Castile had therefore created a highly vulnerable society, and one that was ill-equipped to respond to the challenge of a succession of disastrously wet summers in the 1590's.[10] A run of bad harvests produced famine conditions, and famine was followed by plague. The great plague epidemic of 1596–1602, which struck Castile with particular savagery, carried off 600,000 inhabitants, or 10% of the population. Recovery would be slow and uncertain. Castile was now deep into a long phase of demographic stagnation and recession that would continue until the later years of the seventeenth century—a phase characterized by sporadic periods of high mortality provoked by subsistence crises.[11]

The crown's growing financial difficulties in the reign of Philip II did much to aggravate the dislocation of life in the Castilian countryside during the last years of the sixteenth century. Taxes in Castile, having tripled in the 1560's and 1570's, were barely able to keep

[8] Felipe Ruiz Martín, 'Pastos y ganaderos en Castilla; La Mesta, 1450–1600', in M. Spallanzini (ed.), *La lana come materia prima* (Florence, 1974), pp. 271–85; Miguel Caxa de Leruela, *Restauración de la abundancia de España* (1631), ed. Jean Paul Le Flem (Madrid, 1975), introduction, pp. xviii–xix, and xxiii. Julius Klein, *The Mesta. A Study in Spanish Economic History, 1273–1836* (Cambridge, Mass., 1920) remains the standard institutional history.

[9] Noël Salomon, *La campagne de Nouvelle Castille à la fin du seizième siècle d'après les 'Relaciones topográficas'* (Paris, 1964), p. 250.

[10] Casey, 'Spain: a failed transition', p. 214.

[11] Nadal, *La población española*, p. 37; Bartolomé Bennassar, *Recherches sur les grandes epidémies dans le nord de l'Espagne à la fin du XVIe siècle* (Paris, 1969), p. 11; Vicente Pérez Moreda, *Las crisis de mortalidad en la España interior, siglos XVI–XIX* (Madrid, 1980), chs. 12 and 13.

pace with inflation in the 1580's and 1590's.[12] In its increasingly desperate attempts to narrow the gap between income and expenditure, the crown sold off to private purchasers lands and villages that were under royal jurisdiction, and in particular gave permission for sales of large tracts of *tierras baldías*, crown lands with free-use privileges and traditionally in the public domain, which played an important part in the economic life both of townsmen and peasants.[13] These sales, which reached their peak in the 1580's,[14] had a profound impact on the distribution of wealth and property in Castile, creating new possibilities for the privileged and the tax-exempt to reinforce their position at the expense of the rural and urban masses.

The late sixteenth century therefore saw the acceleration of a process that was to cast a long shadow over the future history of Castile—the consolidation of a *rentier* oligarchy of *poderosos* (powerful ones), who took advantage of the needs of the crown and the distress of the peasantry to concentrate land, jurisdiction and revenues overwhelmingly into their own hands. This oligarchy was drawn from the ranks of the nobility and the urban patriciates, of the upper echelons of the bureaucracy, and of the wealthy peasant proprietors who had known how to play the market.[15] Benefiting from their tax-exempt status and their monopoly of local and urban power, members of the city councils of Castile would buy up the lands of indebted peasants and take into private possession large strips of the *tierras baldías*. Similarly, nobles with easy access to the crown would make the most of their opportunities, like Olivares' Haro relatives, whose marquisate of El Carpio, near Córdoba, would be vastly extended over the course of the seventeenth century.[16]

This oligarchy, which was so busily establishing itself in the later sixteenth century, showed every sign of being more interested in the passive enjoyment of its income than the active management of its wealth. The aristocratic ethos inherent in Castilian society, as in all European societies of the period, was massively reinforced by the fiscal policies of the state, which penalized the productive and discouraged the entrepreneur. Not only fiscal and economic policies but also mental attitudes had therefore to be changed if new sources

---

[12] I.A.A. Thompson, 'The impact of war', in Clark, *The European Crisis of the 1590's*, p. 267.

[13] For the *tierras baldías* see the important study by David E. Vassberg, *Land and Society in Golden Age Castile* (Cambridge, 1984).

[14] *Ibid.*, p. 174.

[15] See Jaume Torras i Elías, 'L'economia castellana el segle XVI', *Recerques*, 16 (1984), pp. 159–69 for a succinct analysis of the background to this development.

[16] José Ignacio Fortea Pérez, *Córdoba en el siglo XVI. Las bases demográficas y económicas de una expansión urbana* (Córdoba, 1981), p. 102 n. 66. For other examples, in the Segovia region, see Angel García Sanz, *Desarrollo y crisis del antiguo régimen en Castilla la Vieja. Economía y sociedad en tierras de Segovia, 1500–1814* (Madrid, 1977), part 2.

of wealth were to be generated; and by the early seventeenth century there was a small but increasingly vociferous group of people in Castilian society who had become aware of this, and were worried enough by what was happening to bombard the crown with proposals, and publish their concerns to the world. These people were collectively, and pejoratively, known as *arbitristas*, because they recommended *arbitrios* or expedients to the king, some of them so wild or obsessive as to give them all a bad name.[17] Reacting somewhat defensively to this contemptuous dismissal of the breed, Juan de Robles' fictional priest conversing in the gardens of the Alcázar of Seville argued that 'the *arbitrio* is not only not intrinsically bad, but is one of the most useful of things for the service of kings and the welfare of kingdoms; for it is nothing else than a project to carry out with the minimum of discomfort what is necessary and proper.'[18]

These *arbitristas*—clerics, lawyers, merchants, royal officials, or plain adventurers—saw themselves as men with a special responsibility. They were the look-out men on the *atalayas*—those stone watchtowers along the coast from which observers kept constant watch for Turkish and Moorish sails; men who saw farther than their fellows and were therefore able to advise them how to avoid the perils that lay ahead.[19] Alternatively, they were physicians who had successfully diagnosed the ailments of the body politic, and who could supply appropriate (and indeed infallible) remedies. Some of them, inevitably, were charlatans; but others, like González de Cellorigo in his great *Memorial for the Restoration of the Republic* (1600), displayed a remarkable diagnostic acumen, and had wise counsel to offer. And all of them, in spite of the gravity of their diagnoses, were imbued with the belief that something must, and could, be done.

This optimism seems at first sight hardly compatible with the fatalism inherent in the concept of decline, which González de Cellorigo discussed in the first section of his book, entitled: 'how our Spain, for all its fertility and abundance, is subject to the decline (*declinación*) to which all republics are prone.' There were, he pointed out, various opinions as to why states declined. Some attributed decline to the movements of the planets, some to the natural instability of all things human, and others to the processes of nature itself, which made every organism subject to birth, maturity and decay. But no Christian could accept a natural or astrological determinism that constricted the free

---

[17] For the *arbitristas* and their image, see Jean Vilar, *Literatura y economía* (Madrid, 1973); also J. H. Elliott, 'Self-perception and decline', pp. 41–61. The nearest seventeenth-century English equivalent to *arbitrista* is 'projector'.
[18] Robles, *Tardes del Alcázar*, pp. 38–9.
[19] Michel Cavillac, *Gueux et marchands dans le 'Guzmán de Alfarache', 1599–1604* (Bordeaux, 1983), pp. 296–307.

movement of God's will.[20] Even in the darkest of times, then, a glimmer of hope remained. God's judgments were inscrutable, His ways unknown to man; and a Christian resignation in the face of God's will did not preclude vigorous efforts by men to help themselves. For example, the doctor must always do the best by his patient. If, as Cellorigo argued, wise doctors had found ways of checking the fever 'against its natural course', the same should be possible for those entrusted with the care of the body politic. Cellorigo's own prognosis for Spain at the start of the new century was that 'the illness of our republic is not so malign as to remove all hope of a remedy, if it is properly applied.'[21]

What, then, was the illness from which Castile was suffering—an illness which all considered grave, but which none wished to regard as incurable? Although there were as many diagnoses as doctors, there was a certain convergence on what were perceived to be the most serious symptoms. Although it is their *economic* diagnoses and remedies which have most attracted the attention of later generations, many of the would-be reformers in the Castile of Philip III in fact saw the problems of their native land as preeminently problems of manners and morals.[22] Living, like the majority of their European contemporaries, in a world where the ordering of events reflected a special relationship between the purposes of God and the conduct of men, seventeenth-century Castilians saw a natural equation between morality and national well-being. There would be no more victories, the historian, moralist and reformer Fray Juan de Mariana warned his readers, until morals were reformed.[23] This equation between morality and success, immorality and failure, was reinforced by the ever-present lesson of Rome. For those who had read their Sallust and their Seneca—that most Spanish of Romans—the parallels between their own situation and that of Imperial Rome were uncomfortably close. Idleness; hypocrisy concealed beneath a veneer of religious observance; sexual promiscuity; an excessive indulgence in food, drink and ostentatious apparel—these were the external signs of an inner decay. The Franciscan Fray Juan de Santamaría, one of Philip III's chaplains and author of the enormously influential *República y policía cristiana* (1615), quoted Sallust to the effect that 'when a kingdom reaches such a point of moral corruption that men dress like women, . . . that the most exquisite delicacies are imported for

[20] *Memorial*, fos. 1–4.

[21] *Ibid.*, fo. 55v.

[22] Michael D. Gordon rightly emphasizes this point in his 'Morality, reform and the empire in seventeenth-century Spain', *Il Pensiero Politico*, 11 (1978), pp. 3–19.

[23] Juan de Mariana, *De spectaculis*, in his *Obras* (*BAE*, 31, Madrid, 1854), p. 460.

its tables, and men go to sleep before they are tired, . . . then it can be regarded as lost, and its empire at an end.'[24]

The careless ostentation of court life under Philip III, so shocking to contemporary moralists, only served to underline the loss of ancient virtue. It was clear that Castilians were no longer what they formerly had been. 'If we turn our gaze', wrote Quevedo in his *España Defendida* (1609), 'towards those good men of Castile of some fourteen or fifteen hundred years ago, what sanctity, what virtue, and what trustworthiness we see! None of these do we imitate or bequeath to our heirs . . . . When we were poor, we conquered foreign riches. Now that we are rich, our very riches conquer us.'[25] Quevedo's Castile—a land of valiant men and virtuous women living a life of heroic austerity—was located in the mists of antiquity, although it had remained true enough to itself into the relatively recent past to produce a Hernán Cortés and a Ximénez de Cisneros. There was indeed no clear consensus as to when the decline had begun, although the peak of achievement tended to be located some hundred years earlier in an (idealized) reign of Ferdinand and Isabella. 'Our Spain', wrote Cellorigo, 'in all things reached its highest degree of perfection . . . in those times', and then a decline set in, 'to which no certain beginning can be given.'[26]

For those who were writing at the beginning of the reign of Philip III, in the aftermath of the disasters of the late sixteenth century, it was natural to think of the reign of Ferdinand and Isabella as the true golden age of Castile. By the end of Philip III's reign, as that of Philip II slowly receded into history, this in turn began to appear an age of epic achievements, in comparison with what followed. Zúñiga and Olivares could therefore proclaim their intention of restoring things to the state they had been in during the reign of Philip II,[27] which itself was already beginning to acquire some of the tints of a golden age, while the men they displaced—like Don Fernando de Acevedo, the President of the Council of Castile—criticized them for attempting to 'discredit everything past, for badly understood reasons of state.'[28] When he spoke of 'everything past', Acevedo was referring to the immediate past, the years 1598 to 1621, the reign of Philip III.

But why should the reign of Philip III—a period of relative international peace and of a high degree of internal stability—have provoked such intense soul-searching in Castile, and in the end, such

[24] Juan de Santa María, *República y policía christiana*, (ed. Lisbon, 1621), p. 200.
[25] *Obras*, 1, pp. 523–4 (Cap. 5).
[26] *Memorial*, fo. 31.
[27] Above, p. 82.
[28] Escagedo Salmón, 'Los Acebedos', *Boletín de la Biblioteca Menéndez y Pelayo*, 8, p. 339.

a massive repudiation? The moralists' denunciations of contemporary behaviour themselves point to an underlying malaise—to the need to find an explanation for something which seemed to have gone badly wrong, as if the collective expectations of Castile had somehow been defrauded. Here the fact of defeat in war, or at least of the failure to score a clear-cut victory, was of great psychological importance. For a society which had been taught to think of itself as a warrior nation, as a chosen people holding the standards of God aloft amidst the smoke of battle, military failure was not just unpalatable. It was also inexplicable. Under the promptings both of Christian doctrine and Roman example, the agonizing attempt to explain was therefore likely to turn towards an assumed loss of ancient virtue.

The death in 1598 of the old king, Philip II, further contributed to the dissolution of old certainties. Philip, for all his defects, had impressed upon the Castilian consciousness a particular image of kingship—just, firm, authoritative, and intensely personal. His son had abandoned the duties of government to favourites, to the discomfiture of a society which expected its kings to be kings. The elaborate administrative machinery which had been developed during the sixteenth century in fact continued to work with considerable smoothness and efficiency during the reign of Philip III, maintained as it was by the highly professional caste of officials with a legal training—the *letrados*—produced by Castile's universities.[29] No doubt it was corrupt, but this was nothing new. Yet somehow the corruption, which may indeed have grown worse (although this hardly lends itself to proof) seemed symptomatic of a fundamental failure of kingship. In place of the aura of integrity and austerity that surrounded the late king, people saw only the self-serving behaviour of the new king's ministers, who had visibly prospered on the perquisites of office. All the inadequacies of government therefore led to a great and growing demand for more effective kingship, as if an ineffectual Philip III could still be transformed by exhortation and persuasion into another Philip II.

Just as the Castile of Philip III fell short when measured against the ideal of a martial society built on heroic virtues, so too, then, it fell short when measured against the ideal of a just society, ruled by a Prudent King. In both instances there seemed to be a falling away; and for those who looked around them, there was no shortage of evidence. The corruption of ministers; the indebtedness of a crown which still lavishly bestowed *mercedes*, or grants and favours, from an empty royal treasury; and the breakdown of so-called 'distributive

---

[29] For the *letrados*, see Kagan, *Students and Society*, and Jean-Marc Pelorson, *Les Letrados, juristes castillans sous Philippe III* (Le Puy-en-Velay, 1980).

justice',[30] by which relative proportion was maintained between the various parts of Castilian society—all this seemed clear evidence of an accelerating process of decline, and of the urgent need to halt it by reform and exhortation.

But alongside, and often interwoven with, the moralizing preoccupations and the ethical remedies, there was also a more strictly secularist train of thought, which looked to the world of politics and economics for solutions to political and economic problems. 'Matters of state, justice, government . . .', wrote Santamaría, 'are a science' deserving of care and study.[31] 'In reality', argued Sancho de Moncada in his *Political Restoration of Spain* (1621), 'there is a science of government', even though some might argue to the contrary.[32]

In arguing for the existence of a 'science of government', Moncada and other Spaniards of his generation were affirming their belief that its practitioners could identify the ailments of a sick society, with as much precision as a skilled doctor could identify the ailments of a sick patient, and then set about curing them in the same way—by the systematic application of rules and principles derived from a corpus of knowledge and experience. This belief, which lay at the heart of European 'mercantilist' doctrines of the early seventeenth century, had been fostered by men like Giovanni Botero, whose *Reason of State* and *Relazioni*, disseminated in particular by the Jesuits, were widely read and discussed in Spain.[33] Botero provided a set of criteria for measuring and assessing the power of states, such as the revenues of the prince, the prosperity of agriculture and industry, and, most of all, the size of population. Spaniards of the reign of Philip III, who took these as the indicators of national wealth and power, could not fail to be deeply perturbed by the fact that in Castile they pointed sharply downwards. While Botero's own observations about Spain were neither original nor profound, his criteria answered to the needs of seventeenth-century Castilians by setting their problems simultaneously into a temporal and a spatial context. From a temporal perspective, Castile had suffered a diminution and decline in population and resources. From a spatial perspective it was failing to compete effectively with other European states. These twin themes of decline

[30] Santa María, *República*, fo. 103.

[31] *Ibid.*, dedication.

[32] Moncada, *Restauración*, p. 229, and introduction by Vilar, pp. 63–4. Similarly he would later claim that a treatise he had written on the value of silver was designed to reduce the question of currency to a demonstrable science (*ciencia demonstrativa*), guided by 'universal scientific principles'. (AGS Gracia y Justicia, leg. 889, undated *memorial* of Sancho de Moncada, with royal *decreto* of 5 February 1622.)

[33] 'The book (i.e. *Reason of State*) is common', Angel Manrique, *Socorro del clero al estado* (Salamanca, 1624; repr. Madrid, 1814), p. 55. The influence of Botero in Spain deserves attention. See Pelorson, *Les Letrados*, pp. 350, 356 n. 54, and pp. 431–6, and Cavillac, *Gueux et marchands*, p. 292.

and backwardness were to provide the material for Spain's great seventeenth-century debate.

Although Sancho de Moncada made use of parish registers to document the decline in marriage rates in his native Toledo,[34] accurate statistics were inevitably in short supply, and much of the evidence used in the debate tended to be impressionistic. Yet there was a profound seriousness about many of the contributions, which began with a flurry of treatises in 1598–1605, the opening years of the reign of Philip III, and then resumed with a new intensity around 1614, building up to a climax between 1617 and 1620.[35] Major problems of the Castilian economy were correctly identified—the *rentier* mentality, the neglect of the mechanical arts, the lack of productive investment, the weakness of the agricultural sector, the export of raw materials and the consequent decay of native Castilian industries. Along with the diagnoses went the remedies, and any government capable of picking its way amidst the welter of conflicting advice would have found to hand a number of highly intelligent proposals for remedial action. But the party of reform had good reason to wonder whether anyone in high places was willing to hear what it had to say.

The pressure for reform

It was one of the traditions of Spanish kingship that every vassal had the right to a hearing from his prince, who in turn had a duty to seek the best counsel he could find. Petitions, memoranda (*memoriales*) and *arbitrios* therefore flowed in to Madrid from hopeful subjects in every corner of Castile and the Monarchy, piling up on the tables of the secretaries, cluttering the archives of the councils, and sometimes, when the writer was fortunate or had the advantage of well-placed friends, receiving careful conciliar scrutiny, and even arriving, at least in digested form, on the royal desk. There were occasions when the process was accelerated by the direct intervention of the royal favourite or some other powerful minister, and some or all of the intervening stages might be omitted, but in general it was to the relevant council that proposals for reforms or improvements were directed—fiscal proposals, for instance, to the Council of Finance, and more general recommendations on a wide range of subjects to the Council of Castile.

The Council of Castile, or Royal Council (*Consejo Real*), was Castile's supreme governing body, and its president was regarded as

---

[34] *Restauración*, ed. Vilar, p. 137.
[35] Vilar, *Literatura y economía*, p. 189.

the second person in the realm after the king.[36] In the reign of Philip III it consisted, according to the ordinances, of a president, sixteen councillors, and two general procurators (*fiscales*), but the actual size of the council was rather larger because of the presence of a number of supernumary councillors. It met every day in plenary session, except Sundays and holidays,[37] but was also divided into chambers or committees for specific areas of competence and jurisdiction, including most notably the *cámara de Castilla*, which controlled patronage and appointments. Every Friday, by tradition, there was held the famous *consulta de viernes*, when the entire council, with much ceremonial, reported to the king, with the president remaining behind after the session for a secret audience.[38]

On assuming his new duties as president of the Council of Castile in 1616, Don Fernando de Acevedo claims to have moved the king deeply with his description of the miserable state of his realm.[39] But his council had so far proved itself singularly ineffective in promoting the reforms that were now being widely demanded, and it would probably remain so as long as the Duke of Lerma held power. To enlightened opinion in the cities and at court, the duke stood as a prime obstacle to thorough-going reform both by virtue of his personality and of the position that he held. When Fray Juan de Santamaría, the spokesman of the increasingly powerful anti-Lerma faction at the court of Philip III, wrote that 'kings have a duty in conscience to attend in person to serious matters of state', and to follow the advice of good councillors and 'working ministers' like those whom Philip II had employed, he was in reality calling for the end not only of the Lerma regime but of the whole system of government by a single, all-powerful favourite.[40] True kingship should be consultative, and, by implication, Castile found itself in its present sorry state because the king did not know what was happening in his own realms, and entrusted their care to a man who put his own interests above those of the commonwealth. A more open and conciliar form of government, in which the freely tendered advice of concerned subjects received proper ministerial attention, was the only means of bringing about the restoration of Castile.

[36] There is no institutional history of the Council of Castile, and the inadequacies of the documentation would make it difficult to write. A brief account of the competence and operations of the council is to be found in the introduction to Janine Fayard, *Les membres du Conseil de Castille à l'époque moderne, (1621–1746),* (Geneva, 1979), a valuable prosopographical study of the councillors.

[37] Fayard, p. 111.

[38] Fayard, pp. 122 and 147.

[39] Escagedo Salmón, 'Los Acebedos', *Boletín de la Biblioteca Menéndez y Pelayo,* 6, p. 239.

[40] Santa María, *República,* fos. 217 and 37–8v. See also for Santamaría and the opposition to Lerma, Jean Vilar's introduction to Sancho de Moncada's *Restauración,* pp. 17–18, and Pérez Martín, *Margarita de Austria,* pp. 178–9.

Unable, or unwilling, to take the initiative, the Council of Castile—
the proper body for advising the king on the needs of his kingdom—
found itself increasingly buffeted by the reformist winds. By the
later years of Philip III these were blowing with particular strength
from an unexpected quarter, the Cortes of Castile. Although the
Cortes were the parliament of Castile, they were not, except in the
most restrictive sense, a truly representative body. They spoke for
the towns—the eighteen towns or cities of Castile allowed to send
representatives to the sessions—and within the towns, they spoke
largely for the town councils, each of which chose two *procuradores*,
or deputies. In his *De Rege* of 1599, Juan de Mariana was scathing
about a parliamentary body from which nobles and clergy were
excluded. 'Do not the people complain at every turn of the corruption,
by means of gifts and promises, of the *procuradores* of the cities—the
sole survivors of the shipwreck—and especially since they have ceased
to be elected and have come to be chosen by the random drawing
of lots?'[41] Yet, for all the defects of their composition and the corruption of their members, the Castilian Cortes in the reign of Philip
III were showing unmistakeable signs of a new vitality, which gradually impelled them to the forefront of the movement for reform.[42]

Already in the second half of the reign of Philip II the Cortes
were speaking out with a new-found confidence. The crown's growing financial needs had led to more frequent, and longer, sessions,[43]
and there were lively debates on the condition of Castilian agriculture
and the crown's requests for more taxes. One of the weaknesses
of the Cortes of Castile had been their inability to establish the principle that redress of grievances should precede supply, but the introduction in 1590 of a new tax—the *millones*—gave the *procuradores* a fiscal
weapon of considerable potential. Under agreements patiently
worked out between king and Cortes at the beginning of the reign
of Philip III, the *millones* were to be granted to the crown by the
cities of Castile, operating through the Cortes, on the basis of a mutual
contract that was to be periodically renewed. Under the terms of
this contract, the revenues collected by the cities in the form of *sisas*,
or excise dues, were to be controlled, not by the Council of Finance,

---

[41] Juan de Mariana, *Del rey y de la institución real,* in *Obras, BAE,* 31, p. 487.

[42] The Cortes of Castile are at present the subject of historical reassessment. See in particular
Charles Jago, 'Habsburg Abolutism and the Cortes of Castile', *The American Historical Review,*
86 (1981), pp. 307–26; I.A.A. Thompson, 'Crown and Cortes in Castile, 1590–1665', *Parlia-
ments, Estates and Representation,* 2 (1982), pp. 29–45; Pablo Fernández Albadalejo, 'Monarquía,
Cortes y "cuestión constitucional" en Castilla durante la edad moderna', *Revista de las Cortes
Generales,* 1 (1984), pp. 11–34.

[43] Thompson, 'Crown and Cortes', p. 31, which contrasts the period 1539–1572, with the
Cortes in session for two months a year on average, with the period 1573–1665, when it
was in session for an average of nearly eight months a year.

but by a special commission of the Cortes, the Junta de Millones, and were to be dispensed only for purposes determined by the Cortes, and under the conditions that the Cortes imposed.[44]

These agreements gave a new lease of life to Castilian constitutionalism. By 1621 the *millones* accounted on average for 30% of the revenue available to the crown each year to finance its current expenditures.[45] The narrow representative basis of the Cortes and the lack of integrity of individual *procuradores* remained a continuing weakness, but at least they now had a formidable bargaining counter in their hands if they knew how to use it. During the reign of Philip III there is evidence that the Cortes were moving with some success to establish themselves as a genuine consultative partner in the government of Castile. The cities were deeply concerned by the decay of industry and agriculture that they saw all around them. Toledo, for instance, was experiencing a sharp decline of population, especially after 1610, a drastic diminution of its textile production, and a dwindling of its position as an urban trade centre as the rapid growth of Madrid reduced it to second-class provincial status.[46] The contrast between its former greatness and its current miseries helped to make it one of the principal centres of reformist thought and writing;[47] and in the Cortes it would find a natural forum for the expression of its concerns, and for the advocacy of the protectionist measures which it saw as a solution to its own problems, and, by extension, to those of Castile as a whole.

The progressive crumbling of the Lerma regime left a vacuum at the centre of political life which the new Cortes that met in 1617 were therefore not unprepared to fill. They were, indeed, positively invited to do so, when Acevedo, as President of the Council of Castile, confessed to them 'behind closed doors' the 'general weakness in this body of the kingdom', and appealed to the *procuradores* to come forward with remedies.[48] They responded by requesting a written account of the state of the crown's finances, which only served to confirm the need for root and branch reform. A special junta—the *junta de desempeño*—had been set up in 1602 for the amortization (*desempeño*) of the royal debts.[49] But its affairs had been grossly mismanaged, and the crown had been compelled to resort in 1607 to a suspension of payments to its bankers, barely a decade after the

[44] Jago, 'Habsburg Absolutism', pp. 311–16 for this contract and its implications.
[45] Jago, *ibid.*, p. 317.
[46] Michael Weisser, 'The Decline of Castile Revisited: the Case of Toledo', *The Journal of European Economic History*, 2 (1973), pp. 614–40.
[47] See Jean Vilar, 'Docteurs et marchands'.
[48] *Actas*, 29, pp. 423–7 (29 May 1617).
[49] AGS CJH, leg. 542, Don Fernando Carrillo to king, 4 August 1616, for a summary history of this junta.

last 'bankruptcy' of Philip II. Although the immediate crisis was
averted by a well-tried formula of compromise, the *medio general*,
whereby short-term debts were converted into long-term debts, the
underlying problems of an over-committed and debt-ridden treasury
remained unresolved. When the Cortes requested information in 1617
about the progress of the amortization scheme, the only possible
answer was that no progress had in fact been made.[50]

The Cortes of 1617 therefore added their voice to the general cry
for reform. The *procurador* for Córdoba, for instance, Don Baltasar
de Góngora, presented a list of evils from which Castile was suffering—the doubling of the staff of the royal households since the death
of Philip II; the large disbursements from the treasury on grants
and *mercedes*; the *asientos* with foreign bankers at exorbitant rates of
interest; the import of foreign textiles which were killing the Castilian cloth industry.[51] On 6 June 1618 the Duke of Lerma, struggling
for survival, sent a note to Acevedo in which the king asked the
Council of Castile to provide a 'remedy' that would save Castile
from collapse. On 1 February 1619, after Lerma himself had fallen,
the council responded by producing its famous reform *consulta*,
drafted by one of its members, Don Diego de Corral y Arellano
(Pl. 9).[52]

The *consulta*, suitably decked out with reverential rhetoric, was
not an intellectually distinguished document. In comparison with
the best treatises of the time, and notably those of González de Cellorigo and Sancho de Moncada, it fell short both as an analysis of Castile's
problems and as a recipe for their cure. But it has historical importance
as an official recognition by the highest tribunal in Castile of the
gravity of Castile's problems—'the illness', as it observed, 'is very
grave, and incurable with ordinary remedies'[53]— and as an agenda
for action. This agenda in turn was fed into the contemporary debate
as a result of the extended gloss on the *consulta*, written by Pedro
Fernández Navarrete, and officially published in 1626 under the title
of *Conservación de Monarquías*.[54]

The *consulta* followed the contemporary wisdom in representing
a large population as the key to greatness and wealth. Castile, it
argued, was suffering from a loss of population unprecedented in

[50] AGS CJH, leg. 547, no. 58, consulta, 3 September 1617.

[51] *Actas*, 30, pp. 453–65 (14 October 1617).

[52] The reference to Lerma's *billete* of 6 June 1618 comes in the opening paragraph of the
reform consulta (Doc. IV of González Palencia, *Junta de Reformación*). Corral's authorship
is affirmed by Fernández Navarrete, *Conservación de monarquías*, p. 21. See also León Corral
y Maestro, *Don Diego de Corral y Arellano, y los Corrales de Valladolid* (Valladolid, 1905), p. 40.

[53] González Palencia, *Junta de Reformación*, p. 29.

[54] An early edition was published in Barcelona in 1621 under the title of *Discursos políticos*
(Gordon, 'Morality, reform', p. 5 n. 11).

9. Don Diego de Corral, the author of the Council of Castile's famous
consulta of 1619 putting forward a programme of reform. Velázquez painted
this portrait close to the time of Corral's death in 1632.

its history, and it attributed this to the excessive burden of taxation, especially on agricultural labourers, 'who are rapidly disappearing.' It proposed a number of legal changes to improve their situation, and made several wide-ranging suggestions for reform—none of them novel—which would help alleviate the tax burden and restore prosperity to the countryside. The king should cut down on his liberal distribution of *mercedes*—the pensions, offices and honours which imposed such a heavy strain on the resources of the treasury. People of quality at court should be ordered to return to their native towns and estates, in order to clear the court of its hordes of parasites. New sumptuary legislation was essential for the reform of manners and morals, and would reduce Castile's dependence on foreign imports. The Council of Castile also wanted to restrict the number of new religious foundations, and curb the entry into convents and monasteries of those who lacked a true religious vocation.

During the regime of the Duke of Uceda little was done to give effect to these reforms. Shortly before his death, Philip III informed the council that he saw no signs of progress in halting the depopulation of Castile. The council replied that it had put into effect such measures as lay within its powers.[55] It had issued a pragmatic, for example, on 18 May 1619 designed to improve the situation of farmers and labourers by removing the *tasa del trigo*, the price ceiling on the sale of their grain. In theory, this would encourage cultivation, but in practice this does not seem to have happened, and the new freedom in the grain market lasted only nine years before the council, frightened by rising prices, reimposed the regulations in September 1628.[56] Similarly, applications to set up new religious foundations were being carefully scrutinized. But on some of the questions of greatest moment, like the introduction of new sumptuary laws and the revocation of *mercedes*, the king himself had intervened to prevent immediate action.

The council was, of course, correct. In their fear of offending vested interests, Uceda and his colleagues were dragging their feet. The ritual obeisance of ministers to the idea of reform meant little when it was set against their lavish bestowal of patronage on a scale that showed no sign of diminution. Between 1 January 1619 and 1 December 1620 the crown made grants to the value of nearly 400,000 ducats on the recommendation of two councils alone, those of War and State.[57] The Cortes, in exasperation, responded by incorporating important reform proposals into their conditions for the granting

---

[55] González Palencia, *Junta de Reformación*, Doc. XII (4 March 1621).
[56] AHN Consejos, leg. 51,438, no. 3, consulta, 23 August 1628. For the *tasa del trigo* see Hamilton, *American Treasure*, pp. 255–6.
[57] AGS CJH, leg. 573, *Relación de las mercedes y ayudas de costa . . .*

of the *millones*, and stipulating the exact purposes for which the funds would be released.[58] The ministers in turn resorted to their usual practice of attempting to manipulate the city councils. For example, they approached the poet Góngora, now a court chaplain, to influence the votes of two of his relatives on the municipal council of Córdoba.[59] But, at a time when the reform movement was floundering for lack of firm direction from the government, the Cortes, although subjected to pressure, were beginning to make the running. The advent of a new king and a new regime in 1621, promised real reform at last. But the change also carried with it the potential for constitutional conflict, as the Cortes and the city councils awoke to their new-found strength.

The new golden age?

Philip IV was receiving advice, both solicited and unsolicited, from the moment of his accession, but he is likely to have paid particular attention to the views of Fray Juan de Santamaría. A leading advocate of reform, the Franciscan seems to have had close links with Philip III's nephew, Prince Philibert, the son of Charles Emmanuel of Savoy, and Grand Prior of the Order of St. John. The memoirs of Don Fernando de Acevedo represent Santamaría as the moving spirit in a conspiracy in 1620 to overthrow the Duke of Uceda and Fray Luis de Aliaga.[60] Had the plot succeeded, Prince Philibert would presumably have stepped into Uceda's shoes. But nothing came of it; Philibert went back to his post as commander of the Mediterranean fleet; and although he returned post haste to Spain on the news of Philip III's death, he was forbidden entry to the court and had to stop at Barajas. When he finally managed to kiss the new king's hand at Aranjuez in late May, Olivares, who knew a potential rival when he saw one, did not let him out of his sight.[61] In the end he had to be content with the viceroyalty of Sicily.[62]

---

[58] Jago, 'Habsburg Absolutism', p. 316, and *Actas*, 34, for the conditions of the *millones* (1619).

[59] The two relatives concerned were Don Alonso de Guzmán and Don Francisco de Góngora y Argote. 'Con estos dos caballeros es muy poderoso Don Luys de Góngora, capellán de SM, que asiste en esta corte; es tío del uno y cuñado del otro, y le tienen respeto.' From a printed letter of 10 January 1619 from Don Jerónimo Zapata Ossorio, corregidor de Córdoba, to the President of the Council of Castile, in BL Add. Ms. 9,936, fos. 255–268v. For Góngora's Córdoban background and relatives, see Robert Jammes, *Études sur l'oeuvre poétique de Don Luis de Góngora y Argote* (Bordeaux, 1967), introduction.

[60] Escagedo Salmón, 'Los Acebedos', *Boletín de la Biblioteca Menéndez y Pelayo*, 8, pp. 23–9, 156–62.

[61] ASM, Gonzaga, E.XIV.3, busta 615, despatch, 15 May 1621; Khevenhüller, *Annales Ferdinandei*, 1, pp. 1270–1.

[62] González Palencia, *Noticias de Madrid*, p. 14 (2 November 1621), recording the appointment. He died of the plague on 3 August 1624.

No doubt sensing that, with his candidate out of the country, the battle was already lost, Santamaría threw in his lot with the new favourites. On 6 April, a week after the accession, he presented a paper entitled: 'What His Majesty should do with all speed, and the principal causes of the destruction of this Monarchy.'[63] The corruption from which the Monarchy was at present suffering, he wrote, was a result of the 'wickedness and inadequacy of those who have governed it.' Unless the king took immediate action, the same thing would happen to him as happened to his father, who on his deathbed lamented over and over again how he had been deceived throughout his life. Philip must act at once to 'clean out the entire fishpond'. He must get rid of the men who had deceived his father and had packed the palace with their creatures and confidants—all of them men who were 'unworthy and ridiculous, in Spain and outside it.' His four candidates for immediate removal were the Inquisitor General, Aliaga, who—as Philip III realized too late—had deceived him in everything; the Patriarch of the Indies, Don Diego de Guzmán; the President of the Council of Castile, Acevedo, who had perverted justice in pursuit of his own interests; and the royal secretary Juan de Ciriza, 'the source of all the contagion.' It was this gang of four, acting in complicity with Uceda, whose 'oppression and tyranny had prevented the king from recovering his power after he had thrown out the Duke of Lerma.'

Santamaría recommended that—however zealous and prudent Don Baltasar de Zúñiga might be—the king should leave people in no doubt that the decision to remove these men was his own. This advice no doubt struck a responsive chord. While Philip was still a prince, Olivares lectured him on the responsibility of kings to govern personally,[64] and may even have placed a copy of Santamaría's book in his hands. The very first day of his reign, according to a newsletter, 'the new king said he had read in a book by a good author that kings should not have favourites, but good councillors. They say this is the book by Fray Juan de Santamaría.'[65]

The sixteen-year old king certainly started his reign with the best of intentions, and set out to provide an example of kingship very different from that of his father. The Imperial ambassador, Khevenhüller, reported at the end of May that he was despatching business promptly, and that his ministers, following his lead, were up by five in the morning, and in bed by ten at night, 'something very

[63] AHN Est., lib. 832, *Lo que SM debe executar con toda brevedad* ... Another copy in BL Add. Ms. 10,236, fos. 323–8. The first of these says that he presented it to the king on 6 April, and the second that he gave it to Olivares for communication to the king.
[64] Novoa, *Codoin* 61, p. 319.
[65] BNM Ms. 7,377, fo. 294v., *Principios e ingreso del reinado de Felipe III de Aragón* ... Cited also in Tomás Valiente, *Los validos*, p. 14.

different from the time of Philip III.' The new regime, indeed, could hardly have begun better. The king wanted to 'conform his government to that of his grandfather Philip II'. He had stripped ministers of their perquisites, and, where possible, was appointing to office men who had served in his grandfather's reign. If things continued in this way, Philip IV would be one of the greatest kings the House of Austria had ever produced, and the Spanish Monarchy would be restored to its former grandeur.[66]

Things, unfortunately, did not continue in this way. Philip soon tired of the novelty of kingship, and abandoned the study for the hunting-field.[67] But for the first weeks and months of the reign the new spirit of purposeful activity emanating from the court was symbolized by the young king himself. At the end of August Andrés de Almansa y Mendoza, a professional writer of newsletters from court, was sufficiently uplifted to write: 'the reign of the king our lord, Philip IV, is a golden age (siglo de oro) for Spain, and such happy beginnings promise a prosperous end.'[68]

No doubt these were the effusions of a professional court panegyrist, but Zúñiga and Olivares did succeed at the beginning of the reign in catching the mood of the moment. The population of Madrid—a town that was little more than a vast appendage to the court—was normally regarded as fickle and volatile. But the rejection of the age of Philip III went beyond mere volatility. The late king's ministers had made themselves deeply unpopular, and a regime which moved against these bloodsuckers of the commonwealth was automatically assured a warm welcome.

The initial measures of the new administration were well calculated to create an impression of purification and renewal, although Santamaría's guilty men escaped more lightly than he would have wished. It was not easy to remove office-holders without good legal cause. The Patriarch of the Indies, Don Diego de Guzmán, was left untouched; Ciriza, although he lost his influence, still managed to retain a foothold in the secretariat; the regime was still worrying in August about what to do with Aliaga, after 'gentle measures' to ease him out of his post as Inquisitor General had failed, but it eventually managed to force his resignation;[69] and Don Fernando de Acevedo, to some extent shielded by his relationship with Zúñiga and Olivares, clung to the presidency of the Council of Castile until September, when he was retired with reasonable dignity to his Arch-

---

[66] State Archive, Litoměřice-Žitenice (Czechoslovakia), B. 228, Khevenhüller to Lobkowicz, 2 May 1621.
[67] Ciasca, Istruzioni, 2, p. 72 (Relazione di Giulio della Torre, 1622).
[68] Cartas, p. 53.
[69] AGS Gracia y Justicia, leg. 266, king to Francisco de Contreras, 8 August 1621; and see Henry Charles Lea, A History of the Inquisition of Spain, 1 (New York, 1906), pp. 307–8.

bishopric of Burgos, on the pretext that, because of his past association with them, he could not properly be involved in the criminal
investigations of Lerma and Uceda.[70]

But if the purge was initially somewhat muted, the symbols of
change were from the beginning very much in evidence. Zúñiga
and Olivares set a startling example of personal rectitude by refusing
to receive presents, and amazed the world by ending Lerma's and
Uceda's practice of accepting a gift of 100,000 *escudos* from the king
every time they reported the safe arrival of the treasure fleet.[71] Fray
Juan de Santamaría had defined a 'gift' as something given out of
'pure love', without any form of 'obligation, interest, or necessity'.
Any other form of giving was nothing but bribery.[72] This rigorous
definition of a gift, if consistently implemented, would have brought
confusion to a society where the fabric of social relations was held
together by gift-giving. Fortunately the new practice did not prove
contagious.

Clean hands—*limpieza de manos*—would always remain an ideal
of the Olivares administration, although one honoured more in the
breach than in the observance. Olivares himself would accumulate
honours, offices and grants over the years, and some of his relatives,
especially his brother-in-law, Monterrey, would become by-words
for self-enrichment through high office. But, by contemporary standards, Olivares' own hands were clean, and when enemies pointed
to the numerous royal favours he had received, he could argue, with
some justification, that the service of the crown had involved him
in heavy personal expenditure and left him without the time to attend
to his estates.[73]

Almost the first act of the new administration was to set up a
special body, the Junta de Reformación, to raise the standard of public
morality. The creation of committees or juntas of ministers for special
purposes had become a common practice under Philip III, and Uceda
seems to have attempted to set up some kind of reform junta under
the presidency of Acevedo in the preceding year.[74] The preamble

---

[70] Roca, *Fragmentos*, p. 170.

[71] Amadeo Pellegrini, *Relazioni inedite di Ambasciatori Lucchesi alla corte di Madrid* (Lucca, 1903),
Appendix VIII, p. 59 (relation of Cesare Burlamacchi, 20 July 1622). The *escudo*, a gold
coin whose value was fixed at 440 *maravedís* in 1609, was worth somewhat more than the
ducat, a unit of account valued at 375 *maravedís*.

[72] Santa María, *República*, fo. 52v.

[73] AHN Consejos, leg. 7,126, royal cédula of 22 December 1625, cited in *MC*, 1, pp. 140–1;
and cf. the *Nicandro* (*MC*, 2, pp. 261–5).

[74] Cf. Vilar's introduction to Moncada, *Restauración*, p. 28, citing Manuel Colmeiro, *Historia
de la economía política en España*, ed. Gonzalo Anes Alvarez (Madrid, 1965), p. 787, where
no reference is given. The history of the various *juntas de reformación* still needs elucidation.
For an incomplete listing of juntas, see Cristóbal Espejo, 'Enumeración y atribuciones de
algunas juntas de la administración española desde el siglo XVI hasta el año 1800', *Revista
de la Biblioteca, Archivo y Museo*, año VIII, 32 (1931), pp. 325–62.

to the royal decree of 8 April ordering the creation of this new junta[75] made the obligatory reference to the 'Christian piety' of Philip III, but also spoke of Philip II, with his 'attention to government and severe discipline'—that Roman and military ideal which Justus Lipsius had sought to carry over into the world of the state and social relations.[76] The king declared his intention of establishing a 'kind of censorship (*censura*) to uproot vices and abuses and bribery'. Once again, Santamaría's book was an apparent source of inspiration. 'The Romans', he wrote, 'had another council, which was called the council of the *censura*, or customs, to prevent public delinquents from disturbing the commonwealth and to ensure that they did not go unpunished'.[77]

The ten-man junta was supposed to meet every Sunday in the lodgings of Acevedo, who did not take it seriously and soon ceased to attend.[78] Among those entrusted with the onerous task of restoring morality to Castile were Fray Antonio de Sotomayor, the royal confessor, Jerónimo de Florencia, the Jesuit preacher and confessor to the king's brothers, Don Diego de Corral, the author of the 1619 *consulta* on reform, and Dr. Alvaro de Villegas, administrator of the archbishopric of Toledo. A moving spirit on the junta was that relic of the age of Philip II, the seventy-seven year old Don Francisco de Contreras, who had come out of his retirement to serve as one of the judges of Don Rodrigo Calderón. In 1611, while serving on the Council of Castile, he had drafted a set of sumptuary laws 'so obscure, petty and cruel', according to Acevedo, that they had to be abandoned. Now he had a second chance to secure their enforcement. The confidant of Zúñiga, and a suitably austere symbol of the dawning puritanical era, he was appointed to succeed Acevedo as President of the Council of Castile on 10 September.[79]

This first attempt at setting up a body of censors of Castilian manners and morals was not, as Acevedo indicated, a glowing success. The junta produced one or two *consultas*—on moderation of dress, and the expulsion of vagrants from court[80]—and then seems to have

[75] Gonzalo Céspedes y Meneses, *Historia de Don Felipe IV, Rey de las Españas* (Barcelona, 1634), fo. 35; BNM Ms. 18,670, cédula real.
[76] See Oestreich, *Neostoicism*, ch. 15.
[77] *República*, fos. 71–71v.
[78] Escagedo Salmón, 'Los Acebedos', *Boletín de la Biblioteca Menéndez y Pelayo*, 8, pp. 340–1. For this junta and its successors (which are again not satisfactorily differentiated) see Angel González Palencia, 'Quevedo, Tirso y las comedias ante la Junta de Reformación', *Boletín de la Real Academia Española*, 25 (1946), pp. 43–84. This article contains some useful biographical information on members of the reforming juntas.
[79] For Contreras' career see *MC*, 1, p. 79 n. 43 and the references there given. His own complacent account of his life is printed in Diego de Colmenares, *Historia de la insigne ciudad de Segovia* (ed. Segovia, 1975), 3, pp. 161–77.
[80] González Palencia, *Junta de Reformación*, Docs. XIX and XX.

petered out. But it struck momentary terror into the hearts of ministers and officials by ordering all ministers who had held office since
1603 to produce registers of their property—following, it was said,
the example of the Emperor Galba, described by Tacitus as having
restored the treasury in the wake of Nero by forcing the recipients
of his bounty to disgorge their spoils.[81]

This order may be regarded as the precursor of a more systematic
attempt at the beginning of 1622 to investigate the sources of ministerial wealth. On 14 January a decree was issued to the effect that all
office-holders in the Monarchy appointed since 1592 should present
to the justices sworn inventories of their properties and possessions
within ten days. Future office-holders were to be subjected to the
same procedure.[82] The idea of demanding inventories from office-
holders had been under discussion for many years. Juan Márquez,
the author of a treatise on the Christian Governor (1612), had rejected
it as likely to achieve very little.[83] But Juan de Santamaría had
endorsed the idea with enthusiasm. Because corruption was growing
worse every day, he wrote, a law should be introduced ordering
all those appointed to office to present an inventory of their possessions, so that the treasury could at any moment establish whether
they were lining their own coffers. The Emperor Antoninus Pius
had made just such a law.[84]

Orders to this effect were duly sent out to local officials in January,[85]
and a special junta for inventories was set up. But the results were
disappointing. Some inventories were undoubtedly compiled in
Spain, although little trace of them has remained.[86] Only in Mexico,
which in 1621 acquired a zealously reforming viceroy in the person
of the Marquis of Gelves, does the order appear to have been systematically put into effect, but these Mexican inventories, which in due
course were shipped back to Spain, were never opened, and kept
their seals intact.[87] By the time of their arrival, the attempt to keep

[81] Roca, *Fragmentos*, p. 166. Quevedo, *El Chitón de las Tarabillas* (*Obras*, 1, p. 813) also cites
the Galba precedent, for which see Tacitus' *Histories*, Book 1, ch. 20.
[82] Gil Ayuso, *Noticia bibliográfica*, nos. 787 and 789 (decrees of 14 January and 1 February
1622).
[83] Juan Márquez, *El governador christiano* (Salamanca, 1612), fo. 177.
[84] *República*, fo.51.
[85] AGS Gracia y Justicia, leg. 889, *copia de las cartas que se escriben sobre el cumplimiento del
decreto,* and *recibo de los pliegos* . . .
[86] Among the papers of the Marquis of Caracena in the Archivo del Duque de Frías at Montemayor is a folder of drafts marked *Traslado de los inventarios que hizo el Marqués de Caracena* . . .
de todos sus bienes en virtud del real decreto de SM. So far this is the only Spanish inventory
drawn up in response to the decree to have come to light. On 9 November 1623 the royal
secretary Bartolomé de Anaya wrote to the king about a complaint he had lodged over the
way in which he was being treated by the Junta de Inventarios (AGS Gracia y Justicia, leg. 889).
[87] For the Mexican inventories, see José F. de la Peña, *Oligarquía y propiedad en Nueva España,*
(*1550–1624*) (Mexico City, 1983), ch. 1.

a check on ministerial fortunes seems to have been abandoned, for reasons which Francisco de Contreras was unwilling to commit to paper.[88] It is probable that office-holders consistently dragged their feet, with the encouragement of a central administration whose members were no more anxious than the rest to see their fortunes exposed to public scrutiny. Juan Pablo Mártir Rizo, in a life of Maecenas which he dedicated to Olivares, wrote with approval of Maecenas' order for a registration of personal property, but alluded to the arguments of opponents that it was 'inhuman' to let the poverty of some be exposed to public ridicule, and the wealth of others provoke public envy.[89] In seventeenth-century Castile, where appearance counted for so much, any attempt to assess wealth realistically was bound to flout so many established conventions as to threaten the very ordering of society.

There was, however, less scruple about recovering the ill-gotten gains of the fallen favourites of Philip III. Following the arrest of the Duke of Uceda, and the placing of a sequestration order on the Duke of Lerma's estate, a special judicial tribunal was appointed to investigate their affairs. Whether the fallen ministers would get a fair hearing was open to doubt. Although some of their judges were indebted to them for past favours, they had their own careers to consider.[90] But in the trial of Don Rodrigo Calderón on a variety of charges ranging from murder to peculation, one judge—Don Diego de Corral—was brave enough to resist the intense pressures brought to bear upon him. Of the three judges, Don Francisco de Contreras voted for the death sentence, and Don Luis de Salcedo declined to vote before hearing Corral's decision. Corral argued that Calderón had already suffered sufficiently in his person, estate and honour, and refused to vote with Contreras. Finally Salcedo succumbed to ministerial pressure, but Calderón appealed, and additional judges were appointed. These confirmed the death sentence, with Corral holding out to the end.[91]

---

[88] BL Eg. Ms. 347, fo. 112, Contreras to Olivares, 14 October 1627. In the viceroyalty of Naples, on the other hand, the Duke of Alba issued an order in 1627 that no minster appointed to the *regia cámara* should take possession of his office without having first produced a sworn inventory of his possessions, which suggests that here at least a further effort was being made to enforce the 1622 decree. Whether such inventories were in fact compiled in Naples is not clear. See Giovanni Muto, *Le finanze pubbliche napoletane tra riforme e restaurazione, 1520–1634* (Naples, 1980), p. 114.

[89] Juan Pablo Martyr Rizo, *Historia de la vida de Mecenas* (Madrid, 1626), fos. 91v.–92v.

[90] For Acevedo's condemnation of the behaviour of Garcí Pérez de Araciel, a leading member of the tribunal, see Escagedo Salmón, 'Los Acebedos', *Boletín de la Biblioteca Menéndez y Pelayo,* 9, p. 73.

[91] The story of the trial and death of Calderón is narrated at length by Novoa, *Codoin* 61, pp. 369–91. See also Angel Ossorio, *Los hombres de toga en el proceso de D. Rodrigo Calderón* (Madrid, 1918).

Zúñiga and Olivares had clearly decided that they needed an exemplary victim, but they miscalculated badly. The news was brought to Calderón in his cell on 14 July and he devoted his final weeks to preparing for death. Stripped of his titles, offices and possessions he was brought to the Plaza Mayor on 21 October, and executed before an enormous crowd. By his proud bearing on the scaffold he redeemed in a few moments the reputation of a lifetime. Instead of the approval it had so confidently expected, the ritual murder planned by the new regime to serve as a symbol of cleansing and regeneration brought only a massive condemnation. The Duke of Alba wrote to Olivares that he had watched the death not simply of a Roman, but of a Roman and an apostle.[92]

To the enemies of the new administration it was appropriate that Fray Juan de Santamaría, that inveterate persecutor of the ministers of Philip III, should not long have survived Calderón.[93] But well before Santamaría was found dead in the cell of his convent, it had become clear that the programme of national restoration, which he had done so much to promote, was running into trouble. Much of the goodwill surrounding the advent of the new regime was dissipated during the course of its first summer, and more was lost in the reaction to the martyr's death of Don Rodrigo. The new golden age was looking tarnished even before it had fully dawned.

Much of the antagonism to the new ministers was only to be expected. The campaign against the Lerma-Uceda faction stirred up a host of enemies, who buzzed like hornets as they found themselves dislodged from the nooks and crannies of the palace. The favours lavished by the king on members of the Guzmán-Haro-Zúñiga connection—the grandeeship in July for Monterrey, the appointment of the Marquis of Carpio, another of Olivares' brothers-in-law, to a post in the king's chamber[94]—added insult to injury. A rival group of families was replacing the Sandovals at the centre of power, and this process in turn created new centres of intrigue and opposition.

The price of reform, in any event, is bound to be enmity. Too many interests are threatened, too many influential people likely to be disturbed. The real question was whether Zúñiga and Olivares could carry with them the body of opinion favourable to reform in principle, even when baulking at the details. If they were to have any hope of success they had to retain, or build up, support in the court itself, in the ranks of the administration, and in the urban patriciates of Castile. With the latter they failed almost before they had begun.

[92] Novoa, *Codoin* 61, p. 390.
[93] *Ibid.*, p. 103.
[94] González Palencia, *Noticias de Madrid*, p. 5 (15 July 1621).

Their initial test came with the first Cortes of the new reign in June 1621. The crown's prime motive in summoning the Cortes was to secure new taxes, but a number of deputies had ideas of their own about the session. The ordinary *servicio* was voted on 19 July. The voting of the extraordinary *servicio* was to be accompanied by the voting of a special tax, the *chapín de la reina*, traditionally granted on the occasion of royal marriages, which the deputies were not empowered to vote without referring back to their cities.[95] On 24 July, while the deputies were waiting for their additional powers, the *procurador* for Murcia, Don Juan de Belástegui, proposed a joint commission of ministers and deputies to examine possible remedies for the ills of the realm.[96] This unusual proposal for joint action by king and people was followed four days later by the presentation of a reform programme by the *procurador* for Granada, Don Mateo de Lisón y Biedma.[97] Insisting on the indissoluble unity of king and kingdom and their common interest in survival, Lisón listed the areas in which action should be taken: depopulation and abuses in tax collection; the over-production of *vellón* coinage; the need for sumptuary laws; the excessive number of new religious foundations and the dangers of mortmain; and the urgent need for judicial and administrative reform, and a reduction in the number of office-holders. Again, as with Belástegui, it was joint action that Lisón demanded.

The Cortes responded by appointing a six-man committee to prepare a memorandum for the king and to represent the realm in discussions with the ministers. In addition to the initiators of the movement in the Cortes—Belástegui and Lisón—the committee included one of the *procuradores* for Seville, Juan de Vargas, and the Count of Chinchón, who held a post in the royal administration as Treasurer-General in the Council of Aragon, and sat in the Cortes as *procurador* for Segovia.

Lisón and his friends were making a bid to start the new reign in a new way, appealing directly to the king to take personal charge of a great reform programme which would harmonize the interests of the ruler and the ruled. It was a bold step, following logically on the expressions of concern voiced in the last Cortes of the reign of Philip III, but potentially extending the activities of the Cortes into areas where it was not expected to trespass. Not surprisingly, the appeal elicited no response from the court. The ministers were

---

[95] AMT Cartas y Varios (1621), Don Isidro del Cerro and Don Jerónimo de Figueroa to city of Toledo, 4 August 1621.
[96] *Actas*, 36, p. 164.
[97] *Ibid.*, pp. 179–83. For Lisón's relations with the regime, see the important article by Jean Vilar, 'Formes et tendances de l'opposition sous Olivares: Lisón y Viedma, *Defensor de la Patria', Mélanges de la Casa de Velázquez*, 7 (1971), pp. 263–94.

not about to enter into partnership with a body which they despised as being unrepresentative of opinion in the cities and a byword for corruption. Lisón then sought to make the granting of the *servicio* conditional on the creation of his joint commission,[98] and Vargas and Chinchón supported him in the attempt. But, as was usual in the Cortes of Castile, blandishments and blackmail made it almost impossible for the deputies to maintain a common front for any length of time. Lisón failed in his bid to tie the subsidy to the redress of grievances, and his subsequent campaign to reduce the financial dependence of his fellow-deputies on the crown only succeeded in earning for him the odium of his colleagues and repudiation by the municipal council of his native city of Granada.[99] Many of the deputies shared Lisón's concern for reform, but personal ambitions were always liable to take precedence over collective ideals. Lisón was left to wage his patriotic campaign single-handed, turning to the printing-press to make his ideas better known and understood, and exasperating the ministers with his vigilant concern for Castilian liberties.[100]

When the session was concluded on 19 November, probably none too soon for the court, Olivares and Zúñiga are likely to have been left with a mixture of irritation and contempt—irritation with Lisón and his friends for interfering in matters of high policy, and contempt for the self-seeking behaviour of the majority of the *procuradores*. But it may have been unwise to dismiss in so high-handed a fashion the overtures of the reformist group in Philip IV's first Cortes. To carry through a broad-based programme of reform, they needed at least the goodwill of that class of municipal notables from which the *procuradores* were drawn. Madrid might choose instead the path of confrontation, but if so it would have to find enough ministers and officials who identified themselves more closely with the crown than with the provincial elites to which many of them were bound by the ties of family.

If Zúñiga and Olivares failed to capitalize at a critical psychological moment on the impulse to reform this may partly have been because of their other pressing preoccupations. Zúñiga was heavily involved in foreign affairs, and Olivares, although increasingly absorbed by the crown's financial problems, was still consolidating his position at court. Both men presumably had their contacts with reformist groups, but neither had yet had time to sort through the many reform

---

[98] *Actas*, 37, pp. 11–12.
[99] Vilar, 'Formes et tendances', p. 272.
[100] See Vilar's 'Formes et tendances' for the printing of Lisón's papers, which were collected and clandestinely published under the title of *Discursos y apuntamientos* (BL 5384.aaa.47 for a rare surviving copy).

proposals. The sudden intervention of the Cortes in matters of high policy at this early stage of the reign naturally came as an unwelcome distraction. The Cortes of Castile might have their uses as an instrument for mobilizing public opinion in support of royal initiatives, but they were not expected, at least in Olivares' vision of the world, to take initiatives on their own.

In that vision of the world, Olivares himself held the centre of the stage—a fact which he was unable to conceal for very long. By the end of the first three months of the reign, his behaviour was drawing adverse comment. The Genoese ambassador reported early in July that he was *odiatissimo*, and ascribed this partly to envy, but also to Olivares' own temperament, 'little inclined to give pleasure in his personal relations.'[101] The Mantuan ambassador, a month later, was more explicit. He expected a change of government, and especially the removal of Olivares, who had shown himself to be 'odious, and ill-bred.'[102]

Foreign ambassadors naturally picked up their gossip from disaffected courtiers, who were riled by Don Gaspar's abrasive treatment of them. Yet this alleged abrasiveness contrasts oddly with a comment of Acevedo: 'His Excellency was laughing, as was his habit, because he was suave by nature.'[103] Was this, then, a selective abrasiveness, reserved for those whom Olivares deliberately wished to cross and humiliate? He appears to have singled out for harsh treatment the court nobility and grandees, whom he took to addressing as *Vuestra Señoría*, in place of the more hyperbolic forms of address that had come into vogue. Not unnaturally they found this cadet member of the house of Guzmán arrogant and offensive, and began to look back with a growing nostalgia to the courteous days of Lerma.[104]

Olivares himself once confided to Gondomar that he was not 'rigorous by temperament', but only when it was incumbent upon him to be so;[105] and his arrogant demeanour towards his fellow-nobles was at least in part deliberate policy. He believed that the grandees had acquired excessive influence and were pressing too close upon the throne. The inflation of courtesy titles was symptomatic of an underlying social disorder which the 1611 sumptuary legislation had attempted to correct by restricting the form of address in almost all the upper levels of the social hierarchy to *Vuestra Señoría*. Olivares was clearly determined to show that this legislation should not, after all, be regarded as a dead letter, and it would in fact be repeated

---

[101] ASG, Lettere Ministri, Spagna, 2429, despatches of 25 June and 7 July 1621.
[102] ASM, Gonzaga, E.XIV.3, busta 615, despatch, 2 August 1621.
[103] Escagedo Salmón, 'Los Acebedos', *Boletín de la Biblioteca Menéndez y Pelayo*, 9, p. 166.
[104] ASM, Gonzaga, E.XIV.3, 615, despatch, 10 August 1621.
[105] BPM Ms. 11,817, Olivares to Gondomar, 17 January 1625.

word for word in the articles of reformation published in February 1623.[106] But while there was a policy behind his behaviour to his fellow-grandees, it was a policy which he seems to have pursued with a certain relish. His own family resentments against the great houses of Castile, and perhaps even the resentments of a younger son, may at some level of his personality have inspired a wish to take revenge.

Most of all, however, the grandees were enraged by the dominance which Don Gaspar had acquired over the young king, and for a moment in the summer of 1621 it seemed that a scandal had made him suddenly vulnerable. Olivares was reported to be accompanying the king on nocturnal expeditions round the streets of Madrid, and since Philip was widely believed to have lost interest in the charms of the queen,[107] the natural conclusions were drawn. Galcerán Albanell, formerly Philip's tutor and now Archbishop of Granada, rebuked the count for encouraging the king in 'illicit affairs'. Olivares replied tartly that, while he did indeed accompany the king on his sorties from the palace, nothing improper occurred. Indeed, it was only right that the king should see with his own eyes what his excessively sheltered father had only heard about from others.[108] The exchange of letters soon became public property, and Olivares' explanation failed to convince. The Marquis of Mirabel, who read the exchange in Paris where he was serving as ambassador, wrote sardonically to Gondomar that he now realized 'there was nothing in this life for which men could not find some excuse.'[109]

A puritanical reformer who leads his monarch astray is an easy target for his critics. There was an ostentatious rallying to the queen, who was said to be deeply offended with her husband's favourite,[110] and much talk that autumn about his being on the brink of disgrace. In September and October he was indisposed—afflicted, it was said, with a deep melancholy, as if already foreseeing his downfall.[111] More prosaically, he seems to have been suffering from sciatica.[112] The king's response to his favourite's illness was to put off his trip to his country-seat of Valsaín, and to pay him repeated visits.[113] This hardly indicated a loss of favour, and the rumours died down; but they were always liable to flare up again at the least hint of royal disapproval, as in May 1622 when Philip, annoyed by Olivares' ab-

---

[106] González Palencia, *Junta de Reformación*, Doc. LXVI, article 15, p. 434.

[107] Ciasca, *Istruzioni*, 2, p. 72.

[108] For this episode, and references to the correspondence, see Marañón, *Olivares*, pp. 38–9.

[109] BNM Ms. 18,428, fo. 30, Mirabel to Gondomar, 10 March 1622.

[110] ASF, Mediceo, filza 4949, fo. 911, despatch, 20 July 1621.

[111] ASM, Gonzaga, E.XIV.3, busta 615, despatch, 28 September 1621.

[112] ASF, Mediceo, filza 4949, fo. 1024, despatch, 20 October 1621.

[113] ASM, Gonzaga, E.XIV.3, busta 615, despatches of 20 October and 11 November 1621.

sence from the bedchamber when he should have been handing him his shirt, disconcerted him by saying that if his health prevented him from carrying out his duties he should ask permission to retire.[114]

For all his ill health—and how much of it was the result of nervous tension?—Don Gaspar was firmly establishing himself as the king's indispensable guide and counsellor in the ways of the world and the palace. The first known state paper from his hands, dated 28 November 1621, took the form of a little lecture to Philip on the dangers of excessive liberality in kings (as exemplified by his late father), followed by a proposal that no more *mercedes* and favours should be granted at the expense of the royal treasury.[115] This advice reflected his growing awareness of the crown's financial problems. He was said to be devoting much of his time to financial business, hoping to make economies wherever he could, starting with the royal household.[116]

Coming on the heels of the highly unpopular order requiring personal inventories from all royal officials, any attempt to check the flow of *mercedes* was bound to run into trouble. 'Reward and punishment' were, as the Marquis of Villafranca observed, 'the two poles of monarchy', and he and a number of other ministers were inexorably opposed to the introduction of any general law by which the king placed limitations on his own powers of patronage. The need for economy, which was generally recognized, ran directly counter to the traditional conception that liberality was an integral part of kingship. How could government be carried on, if the king were unable to reward the deserving? Don Francisco de Contreras expressed the dilemma neatly, when he described the attempt to restrict *mercedes* as 'absolutely essential', but continued: 'Everyone serving Your Majesty in peace or war aspires to *mercedes* and rewards . . .; and if they were to learn that Your Majesty actually prevents himself by law from giving such rewards, they would either cease to serve, or else would serve half-heartedly.'[117] Could economy and austerity be made compatible with majesty? It was a dilemma that Olivares would never succeed in resolving.

In the spring of 1622 an anonymous well-wisher offered some private advice to Olivares about reactions to the new regime.[118] His enemies were many and influential, for the fallen ministers were not only part of a vast family network, but also had a large following

---

[114] ASM, Gonzaga, E.XIV.3, busta 615, despatch of 22 May 1622.

[115] *MC*, 1, Doc. I. Also in Roca, *Fragmentos*, pp. 175–81.

[116] Ciasca, *Istruzioni*, 2, pp. 73–4.

[117] AHN Est., lib. 738, fos. 236 and 227v., replies of Villafranca and Contreras to royal request for advice on anonymous proposals for reform (March and April 1622).

[118] AHN Consejos, lib. 1431, fos. 202–205v., anonymous paper for Olivares, 19 May 1622.

of friends and clients, who were to be found whenever conversation turned to the actions of the government. Critics noted the disparity between the regime's words and its achievements—all the talk of introducing a holy commonwealth, while wicked ministers still went unpunished; the failure to do anything about increasing the royal revenues, apart from reducing interest rates on *juros*, for which there could be no theological sanction. The inventories of private property had merely brought ministers into disrepute and forfeited their good-will. Where people had expected to see the *vellón* currency reformed, it was simply driving out good silver; and where they expected to see morals reformed, vice flourished as never before.

It did indeed seem as if there was all too little to show at the end of the first year of an administration which had first been greeted with high—excessively high—hopes. One year later it was still floundering in a morass of conflicting advice. Cogent arguments were adduced against every new proposal. A law restricting *mercedes* would discourage the deserving. Increased taxation to reduce the burden of royal debt would destroy what little prosperity remained.[119] The Mantuan ambassador in Madrid, in a despatch of June 1622, drew up an overwhelmingly negative balance-sheet on the regime. The new ministers, he wrote, had indulged in excessive condemnation of the Lerma regime, but time had shown how different were words from actions.[120]

Olivares and Zúñiga were well aware that their plans for the regeneration of the Monarchy were faltering, and that action must be taken. The financial situation alone was enough to cause them deep concern. The crown's bankers were refusing to negotiate new *asientos*,[121] and early in July the Council of Finance protested when the king asked for an additional 300,000 ducats to be sent to Milan. It still had to find four million ducats for the current year's expenditure, and it had already mortgaged future tax revenues until the end of 1626. 'The population and substance of these kingdoms of Castile have been destroyed, and they are incapable of supporting the burdens imposed upon them.' The king must reduce costs, avoid granting *mercedes*, and secure help from the other kingdoms of the Monarchy, since Castile no longer had sufficient resources for its own preservation.[122]

The royal response, as usual, was that the new expenditure could not be avoided. But it was obvious that the whole weight of the regime must be placed behind a concerted programme of reform.

---

[119] Don Diego de Corral to king, 17 May 1622, cited in Corral, *Don Diego de Corral*, pp. 43–4.
[120] ASM, Gonzaga, E.XIV.3, busta 615, despatch of 25 June 1622.
[121] ASM, Gonzaga, E.XIV.3, busta 615, despatch of 8 June 1622.
[122] AGS CJH, leg. 581, fo. 68, consulta, 13 July 1622.

The Junta de Reformación had proved a failure. A new and more impressive body was needed, which would fully reflect the commitment of the king and his principal ministers to the cause of reform. This body, the Junta Grande de Reformación, came into existence in August 1622, and held its first meeting in the palace in the presence of the king on 11 August. Its membership was suitably impressive: Olivares himself, the presidents of all the councils, the new Inquisitor General (Andrés Pacheco), the king's confessor (Fray Antonio de Sotomayor), and Olivares' confessor, the Jesuit Hernando de Salazar, whose influence in policy discussions was beginning to attract attention.[123] A further six members were drawn from the Councils of Castile, Indies and Finance, while the *corregidor* of Madrid, Don Juan de Castro y Castilla, and his fellow-*procurador* for Madrid in the Cortes represented the realm. The secretary of the junta was Pedro de Contreras, who had served as secretary to its predecessor. The administration clearly meant business, for even Sundays and holidays were to be used for meetings.[124]

The Junta Grande

The news of the existence of this august body was officially communicated in a royal letter of 3 September 1622 to the eighteen cities represented in the Cortes of Castile.[125] After the difficulties experienced with Lisón and his fellow-dissidents in the Cortes of 1621, Zúñiga and Olivares had obviously decided this time to prepare the ground for reform by appealing directly to the municipalities for 'remedies' for the ills of Castile, which would be placed before the junta. Unfortunately the junta's working papers have not survived, and it is not possible to determine the relative parts played by Olivares and the other members of the junta in its deliberations, or the specific origins of the proposals that were placed before it. It presumably had at its disposal the papers of the Junta de Reformación set up at the beginning of the reign, and at least a sample of the vast mass of documentation generated inside and outside the administration in the attempt to bring about the restoration of Castile.

The junta worked fast, and at Valsaín on 20 October, two weeks after the death of Don Baltasar de Zúñiga, the king put his signature

---

[123] ASM, Gonzaga, E.XIV.3, busta 615, despatch of 30 August 1622.

[124] González Palencia, *Noticias de Madrid*, p. 32.

[125] González Palencia, *Junta de Reformación*, p. 379 for a reference to this letter, at the start of king's letter to the cities of October 1622 (Doc. LXII).

to a long letter listing its recommendations.[126] This letter was sent out in the course of the next few days to the principal cities of Castile, and a version of it to leading members of the nobility. While the letter to the cities expressed confidence that with God's help the affairs of the realm would be restored to a prosperous state, the letter received by one noble, the Count of Montalbán, expressed confidence that He would 'not allow this realm to come to an end in my time',[127] thus conjuring up an alarmist vision which was apparently only to be shared with those of high birth. The letter asked for suggestions as to how the proposed reforms might be improved, but its tone and contents made it clear that the proposals were to be promulgated substantially as they stood. It was not, as the newsletter writer Almansa y Mendoza hastened to assure his readers, that the king lacked the power to publish the proposals in the form of a pragmatic, but simply that he wanted the junta's decisions to be considered by men of authority, intelligence and learning so that the final resolution should be a mature one, and could be observed as an inviolable law.[128]

The reforms outlined in the king's letter were in general a medley of those which had been propounded and discussed in court and country ever since the idea of a general reformation of Castile had been in the air. One group of reforms was concerned with justice and administration, and included a proposal for a two-thirds reduction in the number of scribes, tax-receivers and *alguaciles* (the principal police officials in the towns). Another group attempted to tackle the problem of superfluous and unnecessary expenditure which had been such a consistent preoccupation of the reform movement. Dowries, now so large as to be a deterrent to marriage, were not to rise above the level permitted by law; and the sumptuary proposals which were so dear to the heart of Don Francisco de Contreras were once again taken down from the shelf and given a dusting. Far too much money, according to the junta, was spent on household servants, and the king, to set an example, had decided to cut back the size of his household to what it had been under Philip II.

The junta also paid much attention to what it considered the greatest danger threatening the Monarchy—the decline of population, and the loss of inhabitants in so many towns and villages. To reverse this process of decline, it produced a mixed bag of recommendations

---

[126] *Junta de Reformación*, Doc. LXII, where the letter is dated 28 instead of 20 October. For a valuable discussion of this letter and the responses to it, see Felipe Ruiz Martín, 'La banca en España hasta 1782', in F. Ruiz Martín *et al.*, *El banco de España: una historia económica* (Madrid, 1970), pp. 74–96.

[127] Archivo del Duque de Frías, C 21/20 (Montalbán), king to Montalbán, 30 November 1622 (compare the wording in *Junta de Reformación*, p. 408).

[128] *Cartas*, p. 147.

of the kind which Botero had suggested in his *Reason of State*:[129] an order (yet again) that the nobility should leave the court for their estates; a prohibition on emigration, including emigration to the Indies; a ban on the movement of families to the overpopulated cities of Madrid, Granada and Seville. Foreign workers, so long as they were Catholics, would be encouraged to settle in Spain. Special exemptions and privileges were to be given to the newly married and to anyone with six male children or more, while, conversely, anyone still unmarried at the age of twenty-five was to be penalized. Charitable foundations were to be induced to provide financial assistance towards dowries for orphans and the poor. Brothels, those 'houses of abomination', would no longer be tolerated.

Two other themes, which had also been discussed in the Cortes, received the junta's attention. It favoured protectionist measures to save Castilian industry, but did not go into details. But it approached at greater length, although rather gingerly, another burning issue of the day, *limpieza de sangre*. The exclusion from a large number of public offices of those with 'tainted' Jewish blood was a source of great personal distress and of deep divisions in Castilian society. In the Cortes of 1618 the deputy for Avila, Don Gabriel Cimbrón, asserted that many people wanted to see changes in the present system, including Inquisitors General, but that 'as this is such a dangerous, and even odious, subject, there are few who dare to broach it.' The operation of the laws, he said, encouraged perjury, bribery, and slander for motives of personal revenge. He managed to persuade the Cortes, although with several opposing votes, to make as one of its conditions for the voting of the *millones* the creation of a special junta to look into the question, but the crown rejected this condition.[130]

The members of the city councils, many of them of suspect ancestry, were bound to live with a deep sense of insecurity under the existing *limpieza* laws. The influx of Portuguese of Jewish ancestry—the so-called *marranos* or 'New Christians'—into Castile following the annexation of Portugal in 1580 had added to this insecurity by bringing the question of Jewish blood to the forefront again.[131] But the presence of these marranos, who began to infiltrate the Seville trade and the administration of royal rents and taxes, also raised larger questions of public policy which, for all the resistance of Uceda and Aliaga, could not be indefinitely ignored. Might not the New Christians, including those who had fled the Iberian peninsula, be capable of rendering some service to the crown? This was

[129] *Reason of State*, pp. 153–6.
[130] *Actas*, 31, pp. 342–6, and 32, p. 540.
[131] Domínguez Ortiz, *Los judeoconversos*, p. 65.

argued by González de Cellorigo, who, as a professional advocate
of prisoners of the Inquisition, produced in 1619 a long printed statement in their defence.[132] 'In all Portugal', he wrote, with a little
exaggeration, 'there is not a business-man who does not belong to
this nation.'[133] If, instead of being harassed, they were guaranteed
security, many who had left the peninsula would return, including
those who had taken up residence in the rebellious northern provinces
of the Netherlands, where they had done so much to strengthen
the economic power of the Dutch. Bringing with them their entrepreneurial skills and their capital, they would be able, as loyal vassals
of the crown, to undertake the *asientos* and other financial operations
which at present were monopolized by rapacious foreigners.

The New Christians themselves, who were active lobbyists in their
own cause, petitioned the new administration of Philip IV to pardon
the prisoners of the Inquisition, and suspend the *autos de fe*.[134] A
three-man junta, including the royal confessor, Sotomayor, was set
up to examine their plea, and reported in a *consulta* of 11 July 1621
on the advantages which the crown could hope to obtain from the
New Christians in its present financial extremity. They would certainly provide a substantial down-payment in cash for any concessions, and could be expected to offer their services as royal bankers
and revitalize the fairs of Medina del Campo and Burgos. But nothing
came immediately of this sympathetic consideration of the New
Christians' case. The king himself, in a characteristic manifestation
of hereditary piety, seems to have been reluctant to allow any change.
In 1623 Olivares referred to two occasions of great financial necessity
when His Majesty had refused to accede to their petitions and 'make
it easier for them to sin.'[135] But there would be ways of circumventing
the royal obstinacy when the time was ripe.

The royal letter of 1622 itself marked a step forward from the
response of Philip III to the request of the Cortes. The proposed
changes in the operation of the *limpieza* statutes were modest,
although they went some way towards clipping the wings of those

---

[132] 'Alegación', ed. I. S. Révah, 'Le plaidoyer en faveur des *Nouveaux Chrétiens* portugais
du licencié Martín González de Cellorigo', *Revue des Études Juives*, 4ᵉ série, 2(1963), pp. 279–398.
[133] *Ibid.*, p. 390.
[134] Petitions and consultas in AGS Est., leg. 2645. I am indebted to Dr. José F. de la Peña
for drawing my attention to these documents. *Autos de fe* ('acts of faith') were the public
or private ceremonies at which 'penitent' heretics were 'reconciled' to the church. The principal
features of the public *autos* were the procession, the mass, the sermon and the reconciliation,
in which the sinners abjured their errors and swore to avoid their sin in the future. Some,
but not all, *autos* were accompanied by the burning at the stake of condemned heretics (or
their effigies), who had been 'relaxed' or handed over to the secular authorities to carry out
the sentence of death decreed by the Inquisition. See Henry Kamen, *Inquisition and Society
in Spain in the sixteenth and seventeenth centuries* (London, 1985), pp. 189–97.
[135] AHN Est., lib. 742, fo. 232, consulta, 20 January 1623.

unscrupulous people who produced anonymous denunciations or sought for malicious purposes to reopen cases that were theoretically closed. At least those who were rightly or wrongly classified as Old Christians would be able to sleep a little more easily at night. But the underlying problem—discrimination in appointment to secular and ecclesiastical office on the grounds of ancestry—was left untouched, as the city council of Valladolid made clear in its reply to the king's letter. It wanted the crown to go further, and ensure that genealogical investigations did not extend beyond a person's grandparents, unless absolute evidence of Judaism could be produced, 'because it is impossible to establish anything for certain by mere allegation and hearsay, and Your Majesty is losing the potential services of great subjects.'[136] This was an argument that Olivares would make his own.[137]

Even if he already appreciated the practical advantages that would come from making Castile a more open society—and they were certainly borne in upon him as he got to grips with the intractable problems of economic revival and administrative reform—Olivares was well aware of the need to tread with the delicacy of an Agag where questions of *limpieza* were concerned. It was easier, and politically safer, to begin with what he hoped would be less controversial reforms. Everyone was agreed on the need to restore trade and industry—'the sole basis for the conservation and increase of monarchies', in the words of the royal letter.[138] Yet so far, in spite of all the pious expressions of hope, nothing of substance had been achieved. One of the difficulties was that there had been no ordering of priorities, no real attempt to select one or two of the innumerable 'remedies' that had been suggested, and make them then the central features of the programme for reform. It was exactly this that the final section of the king's letter attempted to do.

Explaining that the principal reason for the 'decline' of the kingdom was the failure to replenish its expended capital, the letter stated that the junta, after carefully considering how other republics maintained themselves, had concluded—in language borrowed straight from the *arbitristas*—that the very salvation of the Monarchy lay in the foundation of deposit savings banks (*erarios*) and *montes de piedad* (state-owned pawnshops).

There was nothing new about this idea. *Monti di pietà* were well established in Italy by the sixteenth century, and were designed to provide credit for ordinary people at non-usurious rates of interest.

[136] AGS Patronato Real, leg. 91, fo. 120, Procurador General of Valladolid to king, October 1622.
[137] See *MC*, 1, p. 73 n. 42.
[138] González Palencia, *Junta de Reformación*, p. 397.

A number of sixteenth-century Spaniards were attracted by them, and they found a fervent advocate at the end of the century in the Franciscan Fray Francisco Ortiz Lucio.[139] The idea of a national banking system for Spain also had its origins in the sixteenth century.[140] It originated in the 1570's in a proposal presented to Philip II by a Fleming, Peter van Oudegherste, and subsequently taken over by two Spaniards serving in the Netherlands, Luis Valle de la Cerda and Juan López de Ugarte. The scheme failed to find favour with Philip, but Valle de la Cerda managed to attract the interest of members of the urban patriciate, and his book was published in 1600 at the expense of the Cortes of Castile. This work offered proposals for liquidating the debts of the crown through the creation of a savings bank in every Castilian city, and the same building was also to house a *monte de piedad*, in which those in need of money could obtain loans at lower rates of interest than in Italy, in exchange for pledges.[141] After Valle de la Cerda's death in 1607 the Cortes frequently returned with interest to the proposal, and the book was reissued in 1618. In July 1621 Juan López de Ugarte, the last survivor of the original begetters of the scheme, seized the opportunity afforded by the coming of a new regime to present a memorial recommending the adoption of Valle de la Cerda's proposals.[142]

There was, then, a vigorous lobby, both inside and outside the Cortes, for the establishment of a network of deposit banks. The junta, for its part, picked up the idea with enthusiasm, and gave such a glowing account of the advantages to be expected of the scheme as to suggest that it would bring about the millennium. The banks, in the form proposed by the junta, would sell redeemable annuities at 5% and would lend at 7% to all who needed capital. Their presence would guarantee that financial resources would be readily available for agricultural and industrial enterprise: farmers and stockowners, for instance, would be able to borrow to increase output, and would be protected from ruin when times were bad. Taxes would be more punctually paid, bankruptcies reduced, and usury checked. The drain of gold and silver out of the peninsula would be stemmed, and *asientos* with foreign bankers would no longer be needed, since the crown would draw on the banks for its expenditures in Flanders or Italy without resorting to middle-men. The banks could be used, too,

[139] Brian Pullan, *Rich and Poor in Renaissance Venice* (Oxford, 1971), p. 466; Cavillac, *Gueux et marchands*, pp. 202–3.
[140] For antecedents of the scheme, see especially Ruiz Martín, 'La banca', pp. 64–73, and Earl J. Hamilton, 'Spanish Banking Schemes before 1700', *The Journal of Political Economy*, 57 (1949), pp. 134–56.
[141] Luis Valle de la Cerda, *Desempeño del patrimonio de su magestad* (Madrid, 1600), ch. 2.
[142] González Palencia, *Junta de Reformación*, Doc. XXII.

to 'consume' the *vellón* currency, which had brought ruin to crown and vassals alike.

Valle de la Cerda, comparing the miserable state of his native town of Cuenca with the prosperity of Genoa blessed by its deposit banks, had made similarly enthusiastic claims.[143] But if, as seems likely, the members of the junta had read their Valle de la Cerda, some of them had apparently also been reading the draft treatise of another and more recent advocate of the banks, Jerónimo de Ceballos, a lawyer and town-councillor of that most reform-minded of Castilian cities, Toledo.

The extent of Olivares' own reading in the works of the *arbitristas* is unclear. Only three of them appear in his library catalogue—which may, or may not, be a complete record of his holdings—but they form a lively trio. One was Martín González de Cellorigo, whose *Memorial* listed in the catalogue was presumably his great *Memorial* on the restoration of Spain; the second was Damián de Olivares, the Toledo merchant, represented by his *Memorial* of 17 July 1620, an aggressively mercantilist treatise on wool and silk manufacture; the third was Jerónimo de Ceballos, whose *Arte regia y política para el gobierno de los reinos* appears in the manuscript section of the catalogue.

Ceballos, whose treatise received in 1621 the warm approbation of the Council of Castile's censor for political works,[144] was a tireless advocate of his native Toledo at the Spanish court, where Olivares would have got to know him well. He probably encouraged Ceballos to publish his manuscript, for he received both the dedication and a printed copy when it came out at Toledo in 1623 under the title of *Arte real para el buen gobierno de los reyes y príncipes*.[145] This work reads at many points like a blueprint for the reform programme adopted by Olivares, and the parallels with the king's letter of October 1622 are unmistakeable.

Ceballos puts the case for the foundation of *erarios* in the third discourse of his treatise. The advantages of a national banking system were undeniable, but, as Ceballos appreciated, the critical problem was how to finance it. The system must be instituted, he argued, with the maximum gentleness (*suavidad*). The registration of wealth as a basis for compulsory contributions would cause people to lose their credit and reputation if the extent of their wealth became public knowledge, and it was discovered—as it was bound to be—that they were worth less than they said.[146] For its part the junta promised,

[143] *Desempeño*, fos. 64 ff.
[144] Vilar, introduction to Moncada, *Restauración*, p. 31 n. 55.
[145] Escorial Ms. K.1.17, *Fragmento del catálogo del Conde Duque*, fo. 162, records the gift from Ceballos under the heading *Libros*.
[146] *Arte real*, fos. 30–30v.

although without revealing details, that a gentle (*suave*) and easy way had been devised for securing valuations, without expense or vexation to property-owners.[147] *Suavidad* was also claimed for the system by which the banks were to be financed.[148] All vassals of the crown, clerical and lay, would have to invest a twentieth of their estates in the purchase from the banks of permanent annuities yielding 3%.

This funding from private resources was necessary because the banks would not be viable if they were financed only from the royal revenues. These revenues were automatically to be channelled into the banks—a system which in itself would reduce the costs of tax-collection, since there would be a bank in each administrative area. The funds would then be available for royal expenditure on such necessary items as the maintenance of the fleet.

The scheme was ingenious—indeed far too ingenious—and depended, as the subsequent course of events made clear, on a degree of public confidence in the word of the king that simply did not exist in seventeenth-century Castile. But the reforming zeal of the junta did not end with its enthusiastic endorsement of the banking project. The other major proposal in the king's letter was for a radical tax reform. In this, too, it kept company with Ceballos, who inveighed against the social injustice of the existing tax system, and especially of the *millones*. These, as taxes on the basic domestic commodities of wine, oil, vinegar and meat, inevitably bore hardest on the poor.[149] In order to do away with this iniquitous fiscal system and with the horde of tax-collectors who were destroying Castile, he proposed that from 1625 the *millones, alcabalas* and royal monopolies should be abolished, and replaced by a single consolidated tax on flour, the proceeds of which were to be deposited in the *erario* of each locality.[150]

The Junta Grande similarly recommended the abolition of the *millones*, as from 1624, but it ingeniously tied this proposal to a new plan for the financing of national defence. The junta proposed that, in place of the *millones*, which traditionally were used for the upkeep of the frontier fortresses and the high seas fleet, the towns and villages of Castile should take it upon themselves to maintain the 30,000 soldiers needed for the country's defence. On the calculation that there were some 15,000 of them—a figure which also appears in the treatise of Ceballos[151]—this would come to two soldiers (at a monthly rate

[147] González Palencia, *Junta de Reformación*, p. 403.
[148] *Ibid.*, p. 402.
[149] *Arte real*, fos. 106v.
[150] *Ibid.*, fos. 114–116v.
[151] *Ibid.*, fo. 115. A similar estimate is given by the *procurador* for Salamanca in the Cortes of 1617 (*Actas*, 31, p. 142).

of pay of six ducats each) for every centre of population, although adjustments would be made in accordance with wealth. Castile, therefore, would be providing a grand total of two million ducats a year for its own defence. This was the current nominal yield of the *millones*, but under the new system there would be far fewer overheads, and consequently far less opportunity for waste and peculation, because each locality would be responsible for raising its dues in its own way and depositing them in the nearest local bank. The scheme, then, had the double advantage of drastically simplifying the present wasteful system of tax-collection, and of ensuring that the garrisons would be regularly paid.

Madrid had long been groping, without much success, for a better system of organizing Spain's land and sea defences. By the end of Lerma's tenure of power both the fleet and the frontier garrisons were badly run down, but after 1617, under pressure from the Council of War, the crown belatedly embarked on a new naval construction programme.[152] At the suggestion of Prince Philibert of Savoy, appropriations were set aside for the construction of a special squadron for the Straits of Gibraltar. By the summer of 1622 this squadron had eighteen ships, and the high seas fleet—the *Armada del Mar Océano*—twenty-three, with the promise of more to come. For all the success of this programme, which had largely been achieved under contract arrangements, it was still necessary to maintain a high level of regular financial appropriations for the upkeep of the strengthened fleet, and it was hoped that the new banking system would make this possible.[153]

The problem of land defence had proved particularly intractable. Neither Philip II nor Philip III had succeeded in establishing a satisfactory national militia, and the militia—such as it was—was disbanded at the request of the Cortes in 1619.[154] As long as the pay was hopelessly in arrears, there was no enthusiasm for military service at home, and the frontier fortresses were badly undermanned. The junta clearly hoped that its proposed system of budgetary allocations for the *presidios*—the frontier garrisons—would provide that guarantee of regular and punctual pay which would attract volunteers to the colours.

But the system had another and important advantage. Ministers, Cortes and *arbitristas* had been demanding with increased stridency

[152] AGS CJH, leg. 554, paper by Martín de Aróztegui, secretary of Council of War, 15 August 1617; and see I.A.A. Thompson, *War and Government in Habsburg Spain, 1560–1620* (London, 1976), pp. 198–200.

[153] González Palencia, *Junta de Reformación*, p. 416 (introduction to the *capítulos de reformación* of 10 February 1623).

[154] See *MC*, 2, introduction to Doc. XII for the question of defence, and the sources there cited.

that the other kingdoms and provinces of the Iberian peninsula, and of the Monarchy as a whole, should give Castile greater financial support in bearing the intolerable burdens of empire.[155] As seen from Castile, these provinces were under-taxed, but their various laws and privileges made it almost impossible to raise the level of taxation without risking serious constitutional conflict. The Lerma regime, for instance, had attempted to introduce the *millones* into Vizcaya, but had been forced to make a humiliating retreat.[156] But it might be possible to circumvent the resistance to new taxes by insisting, instead, that each kingdom and province should bear the costs of its own defence. The Council of Finance made a plea to this effect in a *consulta* of 10 April 1622,[157] and the Junta Grande took up the theme. The king's letter explained that, under the new system by which Castile was to pay for its own defence, the other provinces— 'Aragon, Portugal, Navarre, Vizcaya and Guipúzoca'—would be expected to do the same. This was only equitable; and in any event no laws and liberties could justify fiscal exemption where the defence and conservation of the Monarchy was at stake.[158] In this brief paragraph of the royal letter was to be found in embryo Olivares' great project for a Union of Arms, and with it half the history of his regime.

The Junta Grande's proposals, as embodied in the letter of October 1622, constituted a major programme for reform. They were certainly the clearest expression to date of the hopes and intentions of the new regime; and the two central proposals in the programme—the national banking project and the replacement of the *millones* by a new fiscal system tied to the needs of national defence—promised, if carried into effect, a new and more rational organization of resources, designed to pave the way for the regeneration of Castile.

But what were the chances that they would, indeed, be put into effect? The letter was persuasively argued, and it put the case for reforms most of which had already been widely canvassed over the past twenty years. There was a general recognition that Castile was suffering from a variety of ills, and a hope, if not a firm expectation, that a new king, with new ministers, would apply the remedies that would restore the patient to health. At the same time, many of the remedies themselves were open to one kind of objection or another,

[155] See *MC*, 1, pp. 174–5 and Elliott, *Catalans*, pp. 190–2.
[156] C. Weiss, *España desde el reinado de Felipe II* (Madrid, 1846), p. 461.
[157] Elliott, *Catalans*, p. 192.
[158] González Palencia, *Junta de Reformación*, p. 406.

and there was a deep-seated sense of unease about the ways in which they were to be introduced.

The campaign to persuade the city councils of the virtues of the junta's proposals was carefully orchestrated.[159] The *corregidores*, who were carefully briefed, called an extraordinary meeting of their respective councils to discuss the contents of the king's letter. Their task, as they can hardly have failed to be aware, was a delicate one. As nominees of the crown they were working in an environment naturally suspicious of any intervention from Madrid. They were anxious to curry favour with the court, on which they depended for reappointment or promotion when their three years in office came to an end, but anxious also not to make life too difficult for themselves in their local communities; and somehow they had to sell to the city councillors—the *regidores*—of cities with a vote in the Cortes, a programme of reforms which the Cortes had not discussed. The programme itself was bound to arouse opposition, and it could easily be predicted that this would be concentrated on the two proposals by which the crown set most store—the banking project and the tax reform.

The fragmentary register of Olivares' correspondence shows that he followed closely the reaction of the towns. Under the heading of *Erarios* the register records correspondence on: ' . . . what happened in the town council of Madrid on 31 October 1622 about the response to His Majesty's letter on the *erarios* . . . . Opinion of the university of Alcalá . . . . Letter of the *corregidor* of Toledo on the *erarios* . . . . What happened in Seville with the Count of La Fuente, the *asistente*, in the matter of *erarios*, with sworn testimony . . . .'[160] In some cities, where the *corregidor* was unusually persuasive and the opposition disorganized, it was possible to report success—in Soria, Guadalajara, Madrid, Toledo and Cuenca.[161] But elsewhere the results were not encouraging. Some of the junta's recommendations were well received, but on the fiscal proposals the majority of the towns were adamant, and insisted that the Cortes were the proper forum for such matters.[162]

The members of the city councils were the spokesmen of a Castilian urban patriciate which—however much it approved reform in principle—did not want it for itself. This patriciate, combining somewhat uneasily old *hidalgo* families with 'new' families which had made their money in stock-raising, or land, or government service—or, in a town like Segovia, in manufactures—was an overwhelmingly

---

[159] For this campaign and the cities' responses, as recorded in the correspondence preserved in AGS Patronato Real, leg. 91, see Ruiz Martín, 'La banca', pp. 74–96.
[160] Escorial Ms. K.1.17, *Fragmento del catálogo del Conde Duque*, fo. 146v.
[161] Ruiz Martín, 'La banca', pp. 80–1.
[162] *Ibid.*, pp. 92–3.

rentier class. It lived on *juros* and *censos*, on which it had already seen its interest rates fall as a result of the decree of October 1621.[163] Since many of its *juros* were guaranteed by the *millones*, the suppression of the *millones* could have adverse effects on its income. Nor did the patriciate take kindly to the idea of a compulsory contribution of 5% of its wealth to get the new banks started. It had its money locked up, not only in paper credit, but in land, houses, furnishings and worked and unworked silver. Three years later, Manuel López Pereira estimated that twelve to fifteen million ducats of silver in coins and bars were being hoarded in Castile.[164] One of the objects of founding the banks was to get this silver into circulation and use it for productive investment; but the patriciate, understandably sceptical about the government's intentions and fearful of losing its assets, was not disposed to cooperate.

In the city of Granada, which roundly rejected the junta's proposals,[165] that doughty opposition figure, Lisón y Biedma, devoted the second of his *Discursos* to them.[166] Two million ducats a year for the upkeep of soldiers; a 5% compulsory contribution to the *erarios*; and the heavy expense of buying out superfluous office-holders—all this was too much for the long-suffering vassals of the crown. 'These kingdoms of Castile' deserved to be relieved of their burdens, and not subjected to 'taxes upon taxes and scourges upon scourges.' Lisón also had his doubts about the practicability of the proposed schemes. He did not believe that the towns and villages had the resources to raise two million ducats a year, especially as by no means all of them had municipal lands and other assets which they could dispose of on profitable terms. He thought, too, that the registration of property for the compulsory contribution to the banks would lead to enormous abuses, and he doubted whether the banks would achieve their aims. In principle, the idea was a good one, but everything depended on the way it was carried out; and on his reckoning the 119 proposed banks would absorb fourteen of the twenty million ducats in circulation in Castile, leaving only six for ordinary business transactions and for essential expenses.

The scepticism felt by Lisón was also to be found at the highest level of the administration. That wily politician, the Marquis of Montesclaros, who had rapidly become one of the principal ministers of the crown, replied to the king's letter with a letter of his own in which the diplomatic turns of phrase did not conceal the depth

[163] Above, p. 77.
[164] AHN Consejos, leg. 51,359, exp. 4, paper of López Pereira for Olivares, 10 March 1625.
[165] Vilar, 'Formes et tendances', p. 274.
[166] Lisón y Biedma, *Discursos y apuntamientos*, fos. 15–22v., *segunda parte*, dated 21 November 1622.

and extent of his doubts.[167] However desirable the ends, great circumspection and skill would be needed, and a close attention to timing. It was best to introduce reforms little by little, so that opposition to one did not prevent acceptance of another. Montesclaros then proceeded to cast doubts on the wisdom of the sumptuary proposals, on the grounds that this was not the time to put people out of work, as was bound to happen if austerity of dress became the order of the day. As for the banking project, it was true that such schemes existed in other countries, and could yield similar benefits in Castile. But the system by which the banks were to be financed needed a little 'sweetening'. It was hard to see how they could be adequately funded without taking too much money out of circulation; and if it came to coercion, nobles and ecclesiastics could find themselves in a state of serious financial embarrassment. It would be wiser, then, to scale down the size of the operation in its initial stages, reduce the level of contributions, and, above all, be patient.

But patience was not easy when so much needed to be done. Olivares, who was increasingly shouldering the burden of government since the death of Zúñiga, was desperate for results. The king's finances were in a terrible state; war and defence were consuming enormous sums; and Castile was simply not generating the kind of wealth that was needed to cover these expenses. Faced with the opposition of the towns to proposals which he believed to be essential to the Monarchy's salvation, Olivares might be forced to change his tactics. But the foundations of his programme were now in place; and if the country would not cooperate in the way he would have wished, then he would push through the programme with all the resources at his disposal, and save Castile in spite of itself.

[167] Escorial Ms. 1.III.31, fos. 70–72v., *carta del Marqués de Montesclaros en respuesta de la de SM*, 7 November 1622 (also to be found in ADI Montesclaros Mss., lib. 130, no. 27).

PART II

REFORM AND REPUTATION
(1622–1627)

IV

POWER AND RESISTANCE

The making of the Olivares regime

When Don Baltasar de Zúñiga died in his rooms in the palace on 7 October 1622 Olivares was away at the Escorial with the king, who had gone there for the hunting season. His uncle's death came as a shock. Who, he wrote to Francisco de Contreras, could possibly take his place? He himself would like nothing better than to retire to some quiet corner if the choice were left to him ... Contreras asked in reply whether Olivares had one or several ministers in mind for discharging Don Baltasar's duties.[1] His question reflected the speculation at court, where it was thought—and hoped—that the count's palace duties and the uncertain state of his health might prevent him from stepping into Don Baltasar's shoes.[2]

Olivares surprised those who expected him to grasp for power by taking the hint in Contreras' letter. His brother-in-law, Monterrey, was given Zúñiga's post as President of the Council of Italy, and he himself now belatedly accepted a seat on the Council of State.[3] But he declined to assume responsibility for the management of government business. Perhaps on the model of the famous Junta de Noche in the last years of Philip II, a triumvirate of three ministers was appointed—the Marquis of Montesclaros, Don Agustín Mexía, and Don Fernando Girón, a veteran of the wars in the Netherlands, who was now promoted from the Council of War to that of State. For three years this triumvirate carried out on a collective basis the duties discharged by Zúñiga; and although it sometimes met by royal order

---

[1] AGS Gracia y Justicia, leg. 889, Olivares to Contreras, 8 October 1622, and Contreras' draft reply, 9 October.

[2] ASM, Gonzaga, E.XIV.3, busta 615, despatch, 18 October 1622.

[3] In a letter of 18 October 1622 to Dudley Carleton, Walter Aston reports that Olivares 'is lately sworne' of the Council of State (PRO SP.95, pt. 2, fo. 239v), and Almansa y Mendoza, *Cartas*, p. 147, reports similarly in his letter of 16 November 1622. While it has not been possible to establish the exact date of the appointment, October 1622 looks the most likely month. It seems impossible to accept as early a date as January, as given in Straub, *Pax et Imperium*, p. 165, on the strength of *avisos* from Madrid. I am grateful to Dr. Patrick Williams for the Aston reference and for his advice.

in Olivares' rooms to discuss special business, he himself ostentatiously refrained from taking part in its ordinary deliberations.[4]

The forms, then, were carefully observed. The Council of State remained the forum for the discussion of all major policy questions, although there now existed an inner council of three ministers to pass judgment on the numerous *consultas* which were sent up for decision by the king. Nobody, however, had any doubt as to where the real power lay. 'Olivares', wrote the British ambassador, Sir Walter Aston, in December, 'is as absolute with this king as the Duke of Lerma was with his father.'[5]

In deciding to take refuge behind a triumvirate of more experienced ministers, Olivares certainly hoped to disarm criticism of his allegedly inordinate lust for power. He also seems to have had a genuine dislike of some of the functions normally associated with a favourite and principal minister, especially the handling of requests for jobs and favours. These were dealt with by the triumvirate, and the count's defenders claimed that only once, in the minor matter of a single appointment, did the king ever depart from its recommendations.[6] But, for all his desire to avoid some of the duties which had given earlier favourites a bad name, he could not really hope to escape for long either the appearance, or the responsibilities, of power. Circumstance, the structure of government and his own personality were all pushing him from October 1622 towards the centre of the stage.

The process was accelerated by the startling arrival in March 1623 of the Prince of Wales and the Duke of Buckingham. The presence in Madrid of the first minister of the King of England naturally made it desirable that he should have a Spanish counterpart, and Olivares inevitably became the principal spokesman for the Spanish side in the negotiations over the Infanta's marriage. In any event the conduct of foreign relations—the audiences with ambassadors and papal nuncios, the communication with the ministers of other princes—called for a minister who was known to have the ear of the king. In November 1622 Olivares was already deeply engaged in discussions with the papal nuncio on the Valtelline question,[7] and his personal involvement in such negotiations automatically added to his influence in the Council of State.

Yet initially there was bound to be some ambiguity in Don Gaspar's relationship with a council in which seniority traditionally counted for so much. In the other councils the junior councillors spoke first,

---

[4] For the triumvirate, see Roca, *Fragmentos*, pp. 183–4. On 8 February 1623 a meeting of the triumvirate was held in Olivares' rooms, on the orders of the king, to discuss the Valtelline question (AHN Est., lib. 738, fos. 64–66v.).
[5] BL Add. Ms. 36,449, fo. 34, Aston to Calvert, 19/29 December 1622.
[6] Roca, *Fragmentos*, p. 184.
[7] AHN Est., lib. 739, fo. 172, draft consulta of Council of State, 24 November 1622.

but in the Council of State the gravity of the issues under discussion was thought to require the wisdom of age and experience, and the order of speaking was by seniority of appointment.[8] During his first year or more as a councillor, therefore, he was among the last to speak.[9] Where Don Baltasar de Zúñiga, in spite of joining the Council of State relatively late in his career, had dominated it from the first by the sheer weight of his expertise, his nephew had no administrative experience and no real knowledge of the world outside Spain, except for childhood memories. This was a deficiency that it was too late to remedy for himself, although his later insistence on the importance of foreign travel for nobles and ministers shows that he was anxious to prevent it arising in others.[10] He was hampered, too, by his youth. Aged only thirty-five, he was surrounded by men considerably older than himself, some of them—like Don Pedro de Toledo, Marquis of Villafranca, who was thirty years his senior—men of great experience and extremely strong opinions. It is not surprising, then, that during the first years of his ministry his attendance at council meetings tended to be sporadic, and that he preferred whenever possible to operate from behind the scenes.

If at the beginning there was some excuse for uncertainty, he never quite seems to have made up his mind what he wanted of the Council of State. Early in 1622 he had had little windows cut into the walls of the council chambers, so that the king could follow the discussions from behind a screen without being visible.[11] This would give Philip an insight into the workings of government, and encourage the councillors to watch their words. Occasionally, when matters of great moment were discussed, the king by tradition would attend in person, sitting at a small table with a handbell on it, while the councillors were seated on bare benches at a discreet distance, and the secretaries stood in attendance.[12] But the king's presence, open or concealed, seems to have made little difference. Speeches continued to be long on rhetoric, and the preliminary sifting of business by the triumvirate apparently failed to expedite its despatch.

Much clearly depended on the calibre of individual councillors.

[8] Francisco Bermúdez de Pedraza, *El secretario del rey* (Madrid, 1620; repr. Madrid, 1973), fos. 73v.–74.

[9] See, for example, the discussion of 23 November 1623 on the Valtelline, where he was preceded by the Duke of Infantado, the Marquis of Villafranca, Don Agustín Mexía, the Marquis of La Laguna, and the Marquis of Aytona, and followed by Don Fernando Girón and the Count of Gondomar. (AHN Est. lib. 739, fos. 357–8v.).

[10] *MC*, 2, p. 88 ('between the ages of eighteen or twenty, and thirty, they should see the world, or Europe, or at least all Spain'), and p. 96 ('Italy and France'). *Memorial sobre la crianza*, 1632 and 1635.

[11] Brown and Elliott, *A Palace*, p. 41. González Palencia, *Noticias de Madrid*, p. 21, dates this to 15 March 1622. See also Céspedes y Meneses, *Reinado de Felipe IV*, fo. 79v.

[12] Bermúdez de Pedraza, *El secretario*, fos. 72v.–73.

When Olivares joined the Council of State in October 1622 it seems to have had ten or twelve active members. On 18 April 1624 a further thirteen were added.[13] Some of the new members, like the Duke of Medina Sidonia, were absentee, and their appointment was largely honorific. The nomination of others, like Monterrey and the royal confessor, Sotomayor, could be expected to strengthen Olivares' position at the council table. One of the Venetian ambassadors would later assert that councillors who had never been outside Spain had an exaggerated notion of Spanish power, and were consequently more inclined to war than peace.[14] Although it is true that Flanders veterans tended to be pessimistic about Spain's prospects in the Netherlands wars, it is doubtful whether a voting analysis of seventeenth-century councillors of state would sustain this interesting proposition. A good deal of foreign experience, however, was represented on the Council of State in the early 1620's, and more would be added with the new appointments of 1624—notably Fray Iñigo de Brizuela, who had been the confessor of Archduke Albert in Brussels, Don Luis de Velasco, a former general of the cavalry in Flanders, and the Marquis of Gelves, a veteran soldier and diplomat, whose tumultuous three years as a reforming viceroy in Mexico were at this moment drawing to an ignominious close.[15]

The larger the council, however, the more cumbersome its proceedings, and Olivares floated a number of ideas for its reform.[16] Was it really necessary, for instance, to subject the king to fifty-five page *consultas* when he could listen to the discussion from his little window? Could the length of speeches perhaps be reduced by ordering councillors not to justify their arguments? Coming from Olivares, who soon proved to be the most long-winded of them all, there is a certain hollowness about this call for reformation.

Throughout his career Olivares stoutly upheld the standard Castilian ideal of government by counsel—'with all the considerations, *pro* and *con*, duly laid before the prince so that he can choose the policy he considers most appropriate'[17]—but he was quite determined that the chosen policy should be his own. To ensure this happy outcome, he had to make certain that his views were well supported, and for this he needed friends and adherents well distributed through

[13] González Palencia, *Noticias de Madrid*, pp. 93–4.

[14] Francesco Corner (ambassador to Madrid 1631–4) in N. Barozzi and G. Berchet, *Relazioni degli stati europei. Serie I, Spagna*, 2 (Venice, 1860), p. 35.

[15] For a brief account of the Gelves viceroyalty and the 'tumult' of January 1624 in Mexico City, see J. I. Israel, *Race, Class and Politics in Colonial Mexico, 1610–1670* (Oxford, 1975, ch. 5).

[16] BL Add. Ms. 25,452, fos. 3–7, *Unos puntos que hizo el marqués de Montesclaros y la respuesta a la margen del conde de Olivares*, 9 May 1624

[17] 'Instrucción al marqués de Leganés', *MC*, 2, p. 57.

the court and the government. This was not necessarily easy to achieve in an administrative system where men could not be deprived of office without judicial process, and where there was a standard pattern of appointments and promotions which it was difficult to breach. Little by little he did begin to create a genuine 'Olivares regime', but it took time and patience, and he had to begin by gathering around him a team of supporters and dependents whom he could place in strategic positions as the opportunity arose.

The creation of a durable regime depended on a judicious use of patronage—an exercise in which the Duke of Lerma had excelled. However loudly Olivares might proclaim his determination to break with the evils of the Lerma administration, he had no choice but to imitate Lerma's methods when it came to building up an administration of his own. But in some respects his task was harder than Lerma's, since Lerma had not come to power loaded with the heavy ideological baggage of puritanical reform. Don Gaspar's own pronouncements, indeed, had helped to box him in. It was impossible to win supporters without the promise of *mercedes*, but he was committed to steering clear of any patronage system which involved Lerma's practice of raiding the treasury. Equally, it was impossible to consolidate his position in the palace without placing his adherents in major court offices, but he was no less committed to reforms in the royal households and reductions of their staff. Add to this the tenacity of dynastic and proprietary attitudes to office in society at large, and the chances of any quick transformation of court and administration were severely limited.

These problems, some institutionalized and some of Olivares' own making, were partially offset by the formidable powers naturally accruing to anyone who was seen to enjoy the favour of the king. While some of Lerma's most committed supporters were bound to skulk in their chambers and wait for better days, many members of the court and the administration would automatically turn towards the rising star. But expectations had to be satisfied if allegiances were not to shift again, and this remained a cause for constant concern. There were few among the grandee houses of Castile who could resist the offer of a lucrative viceroyalty or a major court post, and by dangling high offices and honours before them Olivares could hope to secure supporters in strategic positions, and neutralize his enemies. A prize capture was the Duke of Infantado, the head of the Mendoza clan and a leading figure in the Sandoval connection. 'This old man', wrote Novoa bitterly as he recorded his betrayal, 'was extremely vain, and more Mendoza than others.' Playing on this vanity, Olivares lured him away from the Sandoval camp at the start of the reign with the offer of the mastership of the horse.[18] The size and importance of the Mendoza clientage system made this a major defection; and it is significant that a year later, in 1622, Olivares felt confident enough of his man to have him appointed to the lord high stewardship—the post of *mayordomo mayor*, vacated as a result of the judicial sentence passed on its nominal holder, the Duke of Uceda.[19]

The *mayordomo mayor* was a dominant figure in the labyrinthine world of the Spanish court, as the man responsible for the palace arrangements and control of the palace staff.[20] In 1623 the total number of household officials and service staff on the court books was around 1,700.[21] Any royal favourite with his wits about him would take care to keep a close eye on this horde of functionaries and servants, and Olivares, by virtue of his unique right to living quarters in the palace in his capacity as *sumiller de corps*, was ideally placed to keep a supervisory watch—an occupation that sat well with his busy and suspicious temperament. The most sensitive posts, and at the same time the most coveted, were those giving direct access to the royal chamber and the royal person; twelve majordomos, nine grooms, forty-three gentlemen of the chamber, nine valets (*ayudas de cámara*) and forty-seven gentlemen-in-waiting, according to a list drawn up in 1623.[22] If Olivares could not remove, he could at least appoint, and the faces of more and more of his own relatives and dependents were to be seen in the ranks of those who clustered round the king.

There was an obvious incompatibility between the new supernumerary appointments and the regime's proclaimed intention to reduce the size and cost of the household administration, but this could be at least partially mitigated by making as many court posts as possible purely honorific. A similar policy dictated the granting of *mercedes*. If pensions from the treasury were no longer to be allowed, alternative sources of patronage became all the more important. The Olivares administration, following in the steps of its predecessor, had no compunction in charging against the revenues of

---

[18] Above, p. 44.

[19] See Novoa, *Codoin* 61, pp. 358 and 394–5 for these appointments.

[20] For a brief survey of the court, see J. H. Elliott, 'Philip IV of Spain. Prisoner of ceremony', in *The Courts of Europe*, ed. A. G. Dickens (London, 1977), ch. 8. Detailed information on palace functions and offices is to be found in Antonio Rodríguez Villa, *Etiquetas de la casa de Austria* (Madrid, 1913) and Dalmiro de la Valgoma y Díaz-Varela, *Norma y ceremonia de las reinas de la casa de Austria* (Madrid, 1958).

[21] Gil González Dávila, *Teatro de las grandezas de la villa de Madrid* (Madrid, 1623), p. 333.

[22] BL Add. Ms. 36,446, fos. 247–59v., *Relación de todos los criados que ay en la casa real de España este año de 1623 años*.

Spanish bishoprics pensions to nobles, ministers and anyone else it wished to reward. In this way vast sums were transferred from church to state.[23] The other major traditional source of patronage enjoyed by the Spanish crown derived from the king's mastership of the military orders of Calatrava, Santiago and Alcántara. Between them, these had 183 revenue-producing *encomiendas* or commanderies, but prior commitments and family interests severely restricted their free disposal by the crown. On the other hand, there were no restraints on the creation and bestowal of knighthoods (*hábitos*) in the Orders. While these yielded no income, their conferment after due investigation of ancestry served as a guarantee of the holder's purity of blood, and this made them highly coveted, especially among those over whose ancestry there hovered a shadow of suspicion. The Olivares administration capitalized heavily on this deep-rooted social anxiety, and its bestowal of *hábitos*—so cheap to itself, so precious to the recipients—showed an immediate and spectacular increase on the number of those bestowed by its predecessor: 515 in the Order of Santiago alone between 1621 and 1625, as against 168 between 1616 and 1620.[24]

While Olivares, always anxious to see that soldiers got their due reward, made sure that some of these *hábitos* went to military men—thirty, for instance, to soldiers of the army of Flanders in 1621[25]—he also distributed them generously as a means of winning adherents and rewarding supporters. 'From his tightness in the granting of *mercedes* from the royal treasury', wrote the Count of La Roca, 'was born the superfluity of honours.'[26] How successful he would be with a patronage policy based so heavily on honours rather than emoluments remained to be seen: there was a hungry multitude both inside and outside the palace waiting to be fed. Initially, however, his careful disposal of the patronage resources of the crown created a climate of expectation in which he could set about the major enterprise of fashioning an administration that would reflect his hopes and desires.

The men to whom he was turning during these first years of the reign were some of them his 'natural adherents', in the sense of being bound to him by ties of kinship, friendship, dependence and regional affiliation. Others were men from inside the administration itself, who for one reason or another attracted his attention and became, in the language of the period, his *hechuras*—his 'creatures'. Still others were outsiders with some special expertise.

[23] See Antonio Domínguez Ortiz, *La sociedad española en el siglo XVII*, 2 vols. (Madrid, 1963–70), 2, pp. 160–7.

[24] Figures as given in L. P. Wright, 'The Military Orders in Sixteenth and Seventeenth Century Spanish Society', *Past and Present*, 43 (1969), pp. 34–70.

[25] *Ibid.*, p. 54.

[26] *Fragmentos*, p. 181.

It was inevitable that his family should play a critical part in buttressing and maintaining his power. Lerma had packed the court with his relatives, and it was only by countering with the appointment of their own kinsmen that Zúñiga and Olivares could guard against a palace *coup*. Not surprisingly, then, the dominant theme of the first years of the reign as depicted in Matías de Novoa's secret history is the rise of what he calls the *parentela*—the clan.[27] Acidly he depicts the rising fortunes of the houses of Zúñiga, Guzmán and Haro, as their members were appointed to court posts which—as he saw it—belonged of right to the vast family network of the Sandovals. The most ambitious, and the most dangerous, of Don Gaspar's relatives was his brother-in-law, the Count of Monterrey, a man of diminutive stature but high ambition (Pl. 10).[28] Raised to the grandeeship in July 1621, President of the Council of Italy in 1622, councillor of state in 1624, he was rapidly launched on a lucrative career which took him to Italy in 1628 as ambassador to the Holy See. He served as viceroy of Naples from 1631 to 1636 and then—a richer as well as a more cynical man—returned to his seat on the Council of State to give Olivares the dubious benefit of his advice during his final years of power.

Don Gaspar's other brothers-in-law were made of less promising material, but he made of them what he could. For the Marquis of Alcañices, a man devoid of political or administrative talents, a place was found in January 1622 as principal huntsman (*montero mayor*) to the king.[29] The third brother-in-law, and the only one to have children, was Don Diego López de Haro, Marquis of Carpio. He was named a gentleman of the king's chamber in July 1621, and his elder son, Don Luis Méndez de Haro, who was one day to succeed his uncle as the king's principal minister, was given a court appointment in October 1622 as gentleman-in-waiting to the royal table (*gentilhombre de la boca*).[30] Carpio's younger son, Don Enrique de Guzmán, whom the Count and Countess of Olivares treated more as a son than a nephew,[31] was given a vacant deanery in Seville in 1624 as a result of their personal intercession with the Pope, and was raised to the purple two years later. But his premature death within a few months of his elevation dashed the high hopes that

[27] Novoa, *Codoin* 61, p. 352.

[28] For contemporary descriptions of Monterrey's appearance and personality, see Angela Madruga Real, *Arquitectura barroca salamantina. Las Agustinas de Monterrey* (Salamanca, 1983), p. 33.

[29] González Palencia, *Noticias de Madrid*, p. 18. Alcañices was raised to a grandeeship in January 1640.

[30] *Ibid.*, pp. 5 and 39.

[31] BAV, Barb. Lat. Ms. 8599, fo. 26, Countess of Olivares to Cardinal Barberini, 28 March 1624.

10. The funerary monument which the Count of Monterrey, Olivares' brother-in-law, commissioned from Giuliano Finelli in the 1630's while he was viceroy of Naples. It was destined for the church of an Augustinian convent that he was founding in Salamanca.

Don Gaspar had placed in the family's new cardinal. Carpio's younger brother, Don García de Haro, was more fortunate. 'He had been bred up', wrote the Earl of Clarendon, 'in the study of law in Salamanca, where he had been eminent; and upon his stock in that knowledge came early into the court . . .'[32] The combination of ties of kinship with the favourite and the right professional qualifications was irresistible. Appointed to the Council of Castile in 1624, Don García soon worked his way into the inner circle of Olivares' advisers. Under the name of the Count of Castrillo—a title inherited through his wife at the end of 1629—he became a councillor of state and one of the most important figures of the Olivares regime.

Other relatives also shared in the family's change of fortune. A cousin, the Marquis of Camarasa, became groom of the stole to the Cardinal Infante.[33] Another cousin, Don Diego Mexía, hurried back to Madrid from active service in Flanders,[34] and laid the foundations of a career which—under the title of the Marquis of Leganés—would in effect make him the favourite's favourite. Two more distant relatives, Don Jaime Manuel de Cárdenas and Don Manrique de Silva, were summoned to court from Oran and Portugal respectively, and given posts as gentlemen of the chamber.[35]

The effect of these various court appointments was to give Don Gaspar a power-base at the point where power was won or lost—in the palace itself. The appointments also placed under obligation a group of relatives whom he could use for various kinds of government business, including political and diplomatic missions. Novoa's remarks make it clear that the rise of the *parentela* was deeply resented; but the Duke of Lerma had fortified his own position in just the same way twenty years before. One group of families was simply displacing another. But the exact implications of that displacement for the balance of political and social power in seventeenth-century Spain continue to escape us. The Venetian ambassador observed that 'the count is not related to the principal houses of the court, as was the Duke of Lerma';[36] but the families of Guzmán, Haro, Zúñiga, Fonseca and Pimentel, with all of which Olivares was connected, represented neither new blood nor new wealth. Nor did they constitute a solid territorial or regional bloc. The Zúñigas, who had Galician estates, lived in Salamanca; the Haros, although originally coming from Vizcaya, had their family seat in Córdoba. The Andalusian affi-

---

[32] Clarendon, Edward, Earl of, *The History of the Rebellion and Civil Wars in England*, ed. W. D. Macray, 5 (Oxford, 1888), p. 95.

[33] González Palencia, *Noticias de Madrid*, p. 27 (12 June 1622).

[34] Novoa, *Codoin* 61, p. 352; ASG, Lettere Ministri, Spagna, 2429, despatch, 12 August 1621.

[35] BAV, Vat. Lat. Ms. 10,422 *Relazione della corte di Spagna*, fo. 37.

[36] Barozzi and Berchet, *Relazioni*, 2 (Venice, 1860), p. 14.

liations of the Haros and the Guzmáns may suggest a tilt towards the aristocracy of the south, but it would be hard to maintain that the establishment of the Olivares regime represented the capture of Madrid by the great southern landowners.

There was a more distinctly Andalusian flavour to his inner circle of friends and confidants, like his librarian Francisco de Rioja, and Juan de Fonseca y Figueroa, who was appointed in 1622 to the post of *sumiller de cortina* in the royal chapel.[37] As a 'son of Seville', Don Gaspar naturally offered a helping hand to fellow-Sevillians. Juan de Jáuregui, who dedicated his *Orfeo* to Olivares in 1624, became a groom to the queen in 1626,[38] and an appointment in the royal secretariat went to another Sevillian poet, Francisco de Calatayud, who would also serve as secretary to at least two of the special juntas—for population and education—to which Olivares increasingly resorted for his programme of reform.[39] But of all the Sevillians on whom he bestowed his patronage, it was Diego de Velázquez who, more than any other, would reciprocate in full measure. Summoned to court by Fonseca in 1623 at Olivares' bidding,[40] he would create those haunting images of king and favourite which would ensure their immortality.

To the friends and dependents of his Sevillian years, Don Gaspar added men who had been in the service of Don Baltasar de Zúñiga, like his secretaries, Francisco de Alviz[41] and Antonio Carnero. For advice on public and private affairs he turned to his Jesuit confessor, Fray Hernando de Salazar, 'the cleric in Spain to whom I owe most and whom I love most, and a man who, in my fallible judgment, is a person of rare and superior parts both in virtue and letters.'[42] Ten years older than Olivares, and a native of Cuenca, Salazar had been a professor of theology in Murcia and Alcalá before moving to the Colegio Imperial of the Jesuits in Madrid.[43] He was soon serving on a variety of juntas, especially those concerned with fiscal questions, and acquired notoriety as Olivares' *éminence grise*, although—unlike his French counterpart, Father Joseph—he seems to have confined his interests exclusively to domestic affairs.

During the next few years others would be added to this circle of friends and confidants—the *licenciado* José González, an advocate

[37] Hoz, pp. 5–6, 23 April 1621; Carl Justi, *Diego Velázquez and his Times* (London, 1889), p. 86.

[38] For Jáuregui's career, see José Jordán de Urriés y Azara, *Biografía y estudio crítico de Jáuregui* (Madrid, 1899).

[39] Barrera, *Poesías de Rioja*, p. 288; *MC*, 1, p. 99 n. 54; *MC*, 2, p. 67.

[40] Julián Gállego, *Velázquez en Sevilla* (Seville, 1974), pp. 108–9.

[41] Almansa y Mendoza, *Cartas*, p. 18; *MC*, 1, pp. 27–8.

[42] BAV, Barb. Lat. Ms. 8599, fo. 81, Olivares to Cardinal Barberini, 18 December 1623.

[43] José Simón-Díaz, *Historia del Colegio Imperial de Madrid*, 1 (Madrid, 1952), p. 549, for a brief biography.

in the chancellery of Valladolid,[44] and Jerónimo de Villanueva, the Protonotario of the Crown of Aragon.[45] Olivares wanted around him men in whom he could place absolute trust, and who shared his own views about the need for reform. But at the same time he needed expert advice, especially where economic and financial questions were concerned.

The proposals for economic reform that were flowing in from all sides in the early 1620's obviously required careful scrutiny. What, for instance, was the regime to make of the numerous memoranda with which it was bombarded by the English adventurer, Sir Anthony Sherley, who had finally come to rest in Granada? His brain teeming with projects, Sherley turned hopefully to Olivares as 'the sole minister of the king and kingdom', and 'the *maestro* who moves all the wheels of that great clock', and dedicated to him his *Peso político de todo el mundo*, a survey of the world from China to Peru.[46] Don Gaspar reciprocated in kind—Sherley, he said, was 'a man of great experience, who has seen much', and he reminded the sceptics that, however wild some of Sherley's projects might appear, similar criticisms had been made of Christopher Columbus and his schemes, 'and think of the benefits which they brought to this Monarchy!'[47] But not every would-be reformer was a new Columbus, and hardheaded advisers were needed to pronounce on new projects and to order priorities.

Under the impetus of the renewal of the war with the Dutch, one of the first areas in which Olivares moved to take action was that of naval policy. Traditionally he has been accused of neglecting the sea, with fatal consequences for Spain, but the record of his years in office belies the accusation.[48] The naval reconstruction programme, already under way before the accession of Philip IV,[49] was vindicated in the opening months of the reign when Don Fadrique de Toledo won a victory in the Straits of Gibraltar in August 1621 against a superior Dutch fleet.[50] The *Junta de Armadas*—a special committee

[44] Janine Fayard, 'José González (1583?–1668) "créature" du comte-duc d'Olivares et conseiller de Philippe IV', in *Hommage à Roland Mousnier*, ed. Yves Durand (Paris, 1981), pp. 351–68.

[45] For biographical details and references, see *MC*, 1, p. 80 n. 44. See also below, p. 260.

[46] See Xavier-A. Flores' edition, *Le "Peso político de todo el mundo" d'Anthony Sherley* (Paris, 1963). Olivares as the *maestro*, p. 145. The listings of Spanish manuscripts in the catalogue of Olivares' library include the following entry: 'Conde Escherley un libro de razón de estado y gobierno al Conde Duque de S. Lucar en que da relación de las cosas antiguas de las provincias y potentados del mundo y el remedio del reino y monarquía de España.'

[47] AGS Est. leg. 2645, no. 23, consulta of junta held in Olivares' rooms, 8 September 1626. I am grateful to Dr. Conrad Kent for bringing this consulta to my notice.

[48] See C. Fernández Duro, *Armada española*, 4 (Madrid, 1898), p. 7, for a vindication of Olivares' naval record. José Alcalá-Zamora's *España, Flandes y el Mar del Norte* provides much material for a reassessment.

[49] Above, p. 123.

[50] Almansa y Mendoza, *Cartas*, pp. 66–8; Israel, *The Dutch Republic*, p. 112.

for naval affairs—was revived under Olivares' presidency in January 1622,[51] and during his early years in office he prepared a memorandum on the fleet which appears to have been lost.[52] While Don Gaspar's interest in naval matters extended to ship design,[53] the creation of a special junta gave him access to the advice of experts like Juan de Pedroso of the Council of Finance, a man with long experience of fitting out fleets.

Among the many figures who advocated concentration on the fleet was a remarkable survivor from the age of Philip II, Baltasar Alamos de Barrientos. A friend and disciple of the notorious Antonio Pérez, Alamos paid for his loyalty with long years in prison. The translator of Tacitus and the author of an important treatise for Philip III on the government of the Spanish Monarchy, he also wrote, either for Lerma or Olivares, a long memorandum on questions of policy and government which included a section on the need to make the King of Spain the master of the seas.[54] He proposed the issuing of licences for privateering—a policy which the government adopted in December 1621[55]—and the construction of two fleets, one for northern waters, and the other to guard the Straits. His was just the kind of mind—informed, wide-ranging, curious—that Olivares appreciated, and it seems probable that the reform programme owed much to his thinking. He was appointed to the Council of Finance in 1626 and served on a number of juntas until his death in 1634 at the age of eighty-four.[56]

Plans for the revival of Spanish naval power went hand in hand with schemes for encouraging trade, like those put forward by a Portuguese merchant, Duarte Gómez Solís, whose book on the East and West Indies trade, published in Madrid in 1622, was in effect

---

[51] Fernández Duro, *Armada*, 4, p. 10. The members were: Don Diego Brochero, Don Fernando Girón, Don Juan de Pedroso, and Miguel de Ipeñarrieta, with Martín de Aróztegui serving as secretary.

[52] It is recorded as being in vol. 3 of the Colección Vega, which is not among those that are now held by the AHN.

[53] In 1635 he outlined his requirements for an armed troop transport ship capable of approaching close to shore (AGS Est. leg. 2655, *proposición del Sr. Conde Duque*, 17 February 1635).

[54] Hispanic Society of America, New York, Ms. HC 380/80, *Advertencias políticas sobre lo particular y público de esta monarchía*, fos. 97–100v. The dedication of this copy is to Olivares, but the dating of Alamos' treatises is difficult, and he may originally have written it to curry favour with Lerma in a bid to restore his fortunes during or after his imprisonment.

[55] See MC, 2, p. 143 n. 48.

[56] ASF, Mediceo, filza 4960, despatch by Monanni, 14 February 1634, reports his death and gives a brief account of his career, which includes the remark that Olivares had him released from prison. On fo. 2 of the *Advertencias* he acknowledges his indebtedness to Olivares for 'el bien de mi libertad', but it is generally said to have been Lerma who released him. Cf. the introduction to his *L'art de gouverner*, ed. J. M. Guardia (Paris, 1867), 24, p. xxiv. There are many unresolved mysteries about the life of this interesting figure, whose ideas on statecraft are examined by J. A. Fernández-Santamaría, *Reason of State and Statecraft in Spanish Political Thought, 1595–1640* (Lanham, 1983), pp. 194–208.

a compendium of mercantilist proposals for the salvation of Spain. Trade, Gómez argued, makes princes more powerful than war. He wanted merchants to be given more weight in Spanish government and society, and special attention to be paid to the fleet, and to the founding of trading companies 'like those of Holland'.[57] Partly as a result of pressure from Portuguese merchants like Gómez Solís, the mercantilist tide was running strongly in the Madrid of the early 1620's, and there were high hopes that the new regime would come to the help of the merchant community. Once again it was the renewal of the war with the United Provinces that provided the stimulus to action. On 1 December 1622 the king appointed the Marquis of Montesclaros president of a special committee to deal with the problem of the illicit entry of goods originating in the rebellious provinces of the Netherlands.[58]

This committee, which became known as the *Junta de Comercio*, was soon being asked to consider schemes for the encouragement of trade submitted to the government by projectors like Anthony Sherley and merchants like Manuel López Pereira. Its members included the Count of Gondomar, whose long period of service in England had made him a keen analyst of the reasons for the prosperity of the trading nations of the north, and Mendo da Mota, once a professor of law at the University of Coimbra, and now a member of the Council of Portugal. One of the earliest and most important documents to be considered by the junta was a memorandum prepared by Mota himself on the need to promote Spanish trade by encouraging merchants and founding trading companies.[59] Spain, in his opinion, was suffering from two principal weaknesses, lack of people and of money—both of them accidental rather than natural weaknesses. He denied that either was the result of a sin 'peculiar to Spaniards, because we know that until they became distracted by their conquests in the Indies, they applied themselves to trade with the nations of Europe, and there were numerous wealthy merchants in Spain.' Unfortunately these merchants had failed to grasp that the way to conserve the wealth of the Indies was to continue their domestic and international trade. This would have prevented

[57] *Discursos sobre los comercios de las dos Indias* (Madrid, 1622; facsimile reprint, ed. Moses Bensabat Amzalak, Lisbon, 1943), especially fos. 38, 85v., 209v.

[58] AGS Est. leg. 2847, royal order to Marquis of Montesclaros, 1 December 1621. The founding members of the junta were Don Diego de Ibarra, Don Juan de Villela, the Count of Gondomar, and Mendo da Mota, of the Council of Portugal. Several of its papers are to be found in this *legajo*. An account of some of the junta's activities is to be found in Israel, *The Dutch Republic*, pp. 138–42.

[59] AGS Est. leg. 2847, memorial of Mendo da Mota, 5 March 1623, and royal order to Montesclaros, 8 March.

the exploitation of Spain by foreign merchants, who drained the country of its American silver.

Mota's 'unique and exclusive remedy' was that Spaniards should rededicate themselves to trade, instead of simply living off their annuities. But how was this to be achieved? While he approved the project for the establishment of banks, he did not think this was the entire solution. Banks could provide the means, but they could not provide the incentive, and for this he advocated the founding of '*consulados* or juntas of native Spaniards, whose purpose would be none other than to search out all possible ways and means ... of making Spaniards devote themselves to commerce.' This was an idea which would have a strong appeal for Olivares. He was to devote much time and thought both to devising institutional forms for the promotion of commercial enterprise, and to finding ways of removing the social stigma connected with trade.

It seems likely that the *Junta de Comercio* was a disappointment to him. It led a rather chequered career because of the heavy involvement of its members in their other duties, and in 1624 it had to be ordered back to work after many months of inactivity.[60] But by now Olivares had his own close advisers in matters of trade and finance—an indispensable prerequisite for a man who considered one of his most important ministerial duties to be a personal engagement in the annual negotiations with the crown's Genoese bankers for the next year's *asientos*. In theory this was the task of the Council of Finance, but although this was overhauled in November 1621, Olivares remained profoundly dissatisfied with its low level of performance. The Marquis of Montesclaros was made its President in July 1623, but even the appointment of so capable a figure seems to have brought no lasting improvement. Instead, Olivares turned increasingly to individual experts—to the Portuguese New Christian, Manuel López Pereira; to Alamos de Barrientos; and to a distinguished minister of the previous regime, the *licenciado* Gilimón de la Mota, whose close association with the Duke of Lerma did not prevent him from rapidly gaining the confidence of his successor. In the summer of 1625 Olivares proposed a drastic reform of the Council of Finance, and when this was put into effect in January 1626, Montesclaros was replaced by Gilimón as the presiding figure in the Council.[61]

Inevitably it was a slow business to build up a reliable team of advisers and officials. Over the years, new ones would be added, while others would fail to stay the course. Don Gaspar proved to

---

[60] AGS Est. leg. 2847, royal order of 23 August 1624.
[61] For Olivares' reform of the Council of Finance, see *MC*, 1, Doc. VI. For Gilimón's earlier career, Pelorson, *Les Letrados*, pp. 263–4.

be a hard taskmaster; but if he asked much of others, he did not spare himself. Since the death of his uncle in the autumn of 1622 he had been systematically concentrating authority in his own hands, even if he attempted to hide that movement behind the all too transparent screen of the triumvirate. As the king's minister—and increasingly as his principal minister—he had no doubt that it was his duty to deploy royal power to the full in order to save Castile, and the Monarchy, from ruin. His was to be an active, interventionist government, its philosophy inspired by that common assumption in the Europe of the 1620's and 1630's that the state had a central role to play in the management of human and economic resources. Such a government required a strong principal minister, with access to the best minds in the country, whether inside or outside the bureaucracy. War and economic recession were both working to this end. It may therefore have been something more than accident that led to the almost simultaneous emergence in the Spain of Philip IV and the France of Louis XIII of two ministers—Olivares and Richelieu—whose methods of government were startlingly similar and whose policies seemed to have been cast in the same mould.

The resistance of the cities

Authoritarian by instinct, mercantilist by conviction, the Olivares regime revealed its true colours with the publication of its famous Articles of Reformation on 10 February 1623.[62] By now it was clear that the urban oligarchies of Castile were not prepared to accept the king's proposal for the establishment of a national banking system, unless some alternative and less painful means of financing it could be found. It was also apparent that the cities were unlikely to cooperate with Madrid in any general reform programme that had not won the assent of the Cortes of Castile. Olivares responded by adopting what was to prove one of his favourite political devices, a 'middle way'. On the one hand, he sought to uphold the authority of the crown by issuing a list of twenty-three Articles of Reformation, which were 'to have the force of law and pragmatic sanction (as if made and promulgated in the Cortes)'.[63] On the other, he followed this up three days later with a gesture to the cities, in the form of a royal letter convoking the Cortes.

The preamble to the Articles reiterated the king's intention to found the deposit banks and commission new squadrons for the fleet. The

[62] González Palencia, *Junta de Reformación*, doc. LXVI; English translation, *A Proclamation for Reformation . . .* (London, 1623).
[63] González Palencia, p. 417.

Articles themselves, which immediately assumed the force of law, were essentially a recapitulation of the measures outlined in the king's letter of October 1622, with the addition of one or two measures from earlier reform programmes, like Article XXII, which harked back to the great reforming *consulta* of 1619[64] and restricted the number of grammar schools in Castile in the belief that uneducated agricultural labourers were of more value to the community than half-educated students. Sumptuary legislation figured heavily in the Articles; so, too, did measures designed to encourage marriage and population growth, including tax relief for foreign immigrants. In a valiant attempt to prune the bureaucracy, the king ordered a two-thirds reduction of local and municipal offices. Article XX, relating to the requirements of purity of blood for offices and honours, showed that the crown had not responded to the requests of some of the cities for a greater degree of liberalization, and preferred to confine itself to forbidding anonymous denunciations and making a modest attempt to prevent unnecessary harassment. In matters of trade, Article XIII made it clear that it was the protectionist forces, representing the industrial cities of central Castile, that had triumphed, at least for the moment. From the day of promulgation, the import of a wide range of foreign manufactures (with the exception of Flemish tapestries) was forbidden.

In his brilliant 'Satirical epistle against the present customs of the Castilians', Quevedo celebrated in verse the new programme of austerity and reform promulgated by Olivares, whom he hailed as Spain's restorer.[65] But the austerity so admired by Quevedo proved an early casualty. When the Prince of Wales suddenly materialized in Madrid on the night of 17 March, all thoughts of austerity were put to flight, and four days later a royal decree suspended the sumptuary articles for the duration of the prince's visit, with the exception of the prohibition on the starched ruff.[66] The impetus now lost was never regained, and the king's adoption of the stiff cardboard *golilla* in place of the ruff turned out to be the only lasting bequest of the 1623 laws to Spanish sartorial fashion.

The suspension of the new sumptuary laws coincided with a new convocation of the Cortes, which would not be dissolved until 1629. The government seems to have prepared for this Cortes with more than normal care. Nobles and ministers were unusually thick on the ground, and Olivares himself secured a seat by arranging to be

---

[64] *Ibid.*, p. 28; and see above, p. 98.

[65] Francisco de Quevedo, *Obra poética*, ed. José Manuel Blecua, 1 (Madrid, 1969), no. 146.

[66] AHN Consejos, leg. 7126, cédula of 21 March 1623, suspending pragmatics. For the *golilla*, see Ruth Matilda Anderson, *The Golilla: a Spanish Collar of the Seventeenth Century* (Hispanic Society of America, New York, n.d. Reprinted from *Waffen-und Kostümkunde*, 11 [1969]).

selected as one of Madrid's two deputies.[67] The king's speech, read on 6 April, contained the customary brief survey of international events, and a reference to the lamentable state of the treasury. It declared the Monarchy to be suffering from a 'complication of evils', but asserted that a comprehensive remedy had been found for the process of decline in the proposed establishment of the deposit banks and the creation of a standing force of 30,000 men and a number of naval squadrons to be maintained by the various provinces.[68]

The first and most important subject for the consideration of the Cortes was the banking scheme. In vain the deputies protested that the king had exceeded his authority in founding them by decree in his Articles of Reformation. The President of the Council of Castile rebuked them on 31 May for their presumption in questioning the king's authority, and informed them that their duty was simply to consider the funding of the banks by means of the 5% compulsory contribution.[69]

There were the makings here of a major constitutional conflict similar to the one that was developing in England between crown and parliament. Several of the cities, anticipating strong pressure by the crown, had withheld full powers from their deputies, and had allowed them only a consultative, as distinct from a decisive, vote. This meant that any money grants would have to be referred back to the cities for ratification, which—in the present circumstances— was bound to be more than usually conditional.[70] The court also found that the deputies were unhealthily inquisitive about the crown's finances. Contreras reported to Olivares on 20 June that two deputies had been to ask him for detailed information on the state of the treasury and on the progress that was being made in amortizing the royal debt.[71] Anxious to preserve the goodwill of the Cortes, the court responded on 6 July with a breakdown of expenditures which revealed a horrifying debt of nearly 116 million ducats.[72]

It soon became apparent that opposition in the Cortes to the banking system was as strong as the opposition in the cities when the project was first mooted. The 5% compulsory contribution was an impossible stumbling block; and although by the autumn nine cities had been talked or browbeaten into some sort of assent,[73] it was obvious that there was an insufficient degree of trust in the crown to make the scheme viable. Olivares' hopes for a new and rationalized

[67] Vilar, 'Formes et tendances de l'opposition', p. 275.
[68] Actas, 38, pp. 23–38.
[69] Hamilton, 'Spanish banking schemes', pp. 145–6.
[70] Lynch, Spain under the Habsburgs, 2, p. 98.
[71] RAH Salazar K.8, fo. 76, Don Francisco de Contreras to Olivares, 20 June 1623.
[72] Actas, 39, pp. 15–22.
[73] MC, 1, p. 19.

tax system were similarly being thwarted. Although the *millones* were generally agreed to be an inefficient, costly and iniquitous tax, there was no agreement on a possible alternative. In the summer of 1623 the Cortes toyed with the idea of a flour tax, but found insuperable objections.

The reluctance of the Cortes to approve the abolition of the *millones* is partly to be explained by the vested interest of the urban patriciates in the administration of the tax and in the security which it afforded for their holding of *juros*. But the events of the last two decades had also made it clear that the periodical voting of the *millones* with a long list of attached conditions was one of the few bargaining counters at the Cortes' disposal. The cities and the deputies were genuinely afraid that the disappearance of the *millones* might also entail the disappearance of the Cortes. These fears were not entirely groundless. In chapter XX of his *Arte real*, published in this same year 1623, Jerónimo de Ceballos asked whether kings had a right to demand taxes for public needs even if the Cortes objected. His answer was unhesitating. Necessity, he claimed, overrode all other considerations 'because the salvation of the people is the supreme law'. This convenient doctrine of 'necessity', to which the Olivares regime would resort with growing frequency in the difficult years ahead, had important implications for the relationship of king and Cortes. In cases of necessity, Ceballos argued, concessions and donations were no longer a matter of grace, but simply the obligatory payment of a debt owed by vassals to their king. Where necessity prevailed, the power of the monarch was superior both to the laws and the Cortes, and he therefore had every right to impose new taxes on his subjects. 'And since it is not the *procuradores* of the Cortes but the cities who concede the service of *millones*, and they cannot refuse a just contribution, these meetings of the Cortes could be avoided, along with the resulting expenses, to the benefit of the poor.'[74]

There was a close similarity between Ceballos' reform proposals and those being put forward by the government.[75] Why should there not also be an identity of views on the future of the Cortes? Olivares alluded to the existence of fears about his constitutional intentions in a speech that he delivered in the Cortes on 16 September.[76] There would always, he said, be occasions when the Cortes would have to be summoned, and with so much important work to be done, this was no time to harbour such suspicions.

The speech itself was a stirring call to the deputies to approve the

[74] Ceballos, fo. 114.
[75] Above, p. 121.
[76] *Actas*, 39, pp. 353–9, reprinted in *MC*, 1, Doc. II.

funding of the banks and a new form of taxation for paying 30,000 men. The time had come to relieve the king of his burden of debt and place the crown finances on firm foundations. Within the week His Majesty would embark on the reform of his household. The time had come, too, to lift the burden of the *millones* from the backs of 'the poor, miserable labourers'; to save the Monarchy from 'final ruin' and restore it to 'supreme felicity', and to put an end to the 'miserable slavery' to which it had been subjected by those 'infamous rebels', the Dutch. 'Each of us should be able to stand comparison with the greatest of the Romans and the Greeks, who in war and peace restored and redeemed their monarchies and republics.'

The count's eloquent appeal for support of his reforms failed to sway the Cortes. When the financial vote was taken on 4 October 1623, the deputies were already falling back on the traditional sources of revenue—the *millones*, and a variety of fiscal expedients to be selected at the Cortes' discretion.[77] Yet the amount of money voted was unprecedented: sixty million ducats payable over twelve years, together with the twelve million still outstanding from the previous grant.[78] This was more than double the existing *millones*, and while it would not do much to reduce the crown's debts, it might at least make possible the achievement of a reasonable balance between income and expenditure. To ensure strict control of disbursements, specific allocations were made: 1,200,000 ducats for frontier garrisons and fortresses, and 1,300,000 for the fleets; 300,000 for ministerial salaries, and 610,000 for the royal households.[79] The regime responded with an announcement made by Olivares in the Cortes on 8 February that 67,000 ducats a year would be saved on the king's household expenses, and over 80,000 a year on those of the queen by reducing staff and limiting the number of courses served to ladies-in-waiting (in future, a maximum of six for lunch, and four for dinner).[80] These heroic gestures would no doubt make sacrifice more palatable to the cities of Castile.

For ultimately the fate of the reform programme and of the enormous tax grant would turn on the reaction of the cities, and on both fronts there were signs of serious trouble. The unpopularity of the regime's banking project was reflected in the decision of the Cortes on 2 February 1624 to make it a condition of the new tax grant that the king should fund the banks and the *montes de piedad* from his own resources, and abandon the proposed monopoly rights of

[77] *Actas*, 39, pp. 450–6.
[78] BL Add. Ms. 36,449, fo. 85, Aston to Conway, 6/16 March 1624.
[79] Domínguez Ortiz, *Política y hacienda*, pp. 24–5.
[80] *Actas*, 40, pp. 424–9; and see 'Los gastos de corte en la España del siglo XVII', in Antonio Domínguez Ortiz, *Crisis y decadencia de la España de los Austrias* (Madrid, 1969), pp. 73–96.

the banks in making mortgage loans. Two weeks later, the crown rejected this condition; but without the concurrence of the Cortes and the cooperation of the cities the banking scheme was doomed.

There were difficulties, too, over another of the government's reform proposals—the plan for a two-thirds reduction in the number of municipal offices in Castile.[81] In February 1623 the enforcement of this programme of municipal reform was entrusted to the *licenciado* Baltasar Gilimón de la Mota, whom Olivares would later describe as 'the most learned, discreet, informed and prudent minister I have known in my life.'[82] His commission stipulated that all the offices of town councillors, *alguaciles*, scribes, *procuradores* and lesser municipal officials, whether or not they were held on a hereditary basis, should be treated as disposable. One-third were to be competed for by lot, and the remaining two-thirds abolished. Those who succeeded in the lottery would compensate the dispossessed either by purchasing their offices from them, or paying them regular dues. The process was to be accompanied by a royal promise that neither Philip, nor his successors in perpetuity, would create new offices.[83]

This ambitious scheme ran into immediate trouble. On 9 June 1623 the Cortes protested against a 'novelty' which would transfer the government of the cities from the hands of the tried and the true to those of the new and inexperienced. In other words, the proposed reform was perceived as a grave threat to the power of the urban oligarchies. The Cortes wanted the whole business taken out of Gilimón's hands and entrusted to the cities themselves. They also insisted that, before any offices were abolished, compensation to the full value of the office should be given to those threatened with dispossession.[84] In October the Cortes asked Olivares to intercede with the king to terminate Gilimón's commission, and warned that this would be one of the conditions for the granting of the *millones*.[85] Next month the crown, worried about its tax prospects, made its first retreat. It accepted the principle of compensation before dispossession, the compensation to come from a fifth of the proceeds of the sale of the last five offices in each category.[86]

Gilimón made some progress in abolishing offices as he moved from town to town, but, as observed in a letter intended for the eyes of Olivares, 'the towns and cities have no voice—it is the town councillors who speak for them. And in practice they speak only

[81] Above, p. 116.
[82] *MC*, 1, p. 87.
[83] AHN Consejos, lib. 1428, fos. 76–78v., printed paper: *El licenciado Baltasar Gilimón de la Mota . . .*, 11 February 1623.
[84] *Actas*, 38, pp. 412–14.
[85] *Actas*, 39, p. 496.
[86] *Actas*, 40, pp. 84–6.

for themselves, and against any reduction in the number of offices, because half of them will lose their jobs.'[87] Outside the ranks of the municipal oligarchies the reform, not surprisingly, was welcomed; but town councils, especially those in Andalusia, put up a stiff resistance, using the Cortes as a line of defence.[88]

The turmoil in the city councils over Gilimón's commission came at a bad moment for the government, which was dependent on those same councils for the ratification of the Cortes' vote on the *millones*. Even without this further complication, ratification was far from being a foregone conclusion. The sheer size of the subsidy provoked reactions of outrage. Moreover it was the members of the urban patriciates who stood to lose most from the measures proposed in the Cortes for raising the additional tax revenue, since these involved levies on office-holders, bond-holders and the propertied classes.[89] Objections were particularly loud in the cities of Andalusia—not least in Olivares' native Seville—and on 8 February 1624, with very little warning, the king left Madrid for a tour of southern Spain.

Philip's sixty-nine day royal progress of 1624 represents the only occasion in the seventeenth century when a King of Spain visited the cities of the south.[90] In taking his royal master to his own native kingdom, Olivares was motivated in part by the pride of an Andalusian patriot. But he was also well aware that there was now more wealth to be found on the periphery of the peninsula—in the eastern kingdoms, in Andalusia and in Portugal—than in the exhausted heartland of Castile. This wealth had somehow to be tapped for the crown. A royal visit could play an important part in this process, and the British ambassador was probably right in suspecting that the prime reason for the journey was to bring pressure to bear on the recalcitrant cities of Andalusia to ratify the tax grant provisionally voted by the Cortes.[91]

The royal party, which included the Infante Don Carlos and three councillors of state in addition to Olivares, reached Córdoba on 22 February, after being entertained on his estates by Olivares' brother-in-law, the Marquis of Carpio. The obvious misery of Córdoba—a city of 'noble inhabitants, but poor and depopulated'[92]—graphically

[87] AHN Consejos, lib. 1428, fos. 118–19, Gilimón to ?, 13 February 1624.
[88] AHN Consejos, lib. 1428, fo. 113, 'Lo que se advierte acerca de la reducción de los oficios'. Complaints were said to be coming from Granada, Málaga, Antequera, Écija, Alcalá la Real and Loja.
[89] Charles Jago, 'Habsburg absolutism and the Cortes of Castile', p. 320.
[90] Domínguez Ortiz and Aguilar Piñal, *Historia de Sevilla*, 4, p. 68.
[91] BL Add. Ms. 36,449, fo. 85, Aston to Conway, 6/16 March 1624. For a contemporary account of the king's journey, see Herrera y Sotomayor, *Jornada que Su Magestad hizo a la Andaluzia*.
[92] Herrera y Sotomayor, fo. 2.

illustrated the reasons for its objections to the recent vote in the Cortes. Failing, after four days in the city, to break its resistance, the king and his entourage moved on to Ecija and to further lavish entertainments, provided this time by the Duke of Arcos, who was sworn in as a member of the Council of State. On 1 March the party entered Seville, and the king moved into the Alcázar for a stay of eleven days. The firework displays and *fiestas* organized by the city in a splendid manifestation of loyalty to the new monarch did not conceal the underlying tension. The attitudes and convictions of the city councillors of early seventeenth-century Seville are elo-quently expressed in a remarkable play, *La estrella de Sevilla*, which may conceivably have been written around this time with an eye to the royal visit.[93] In this play the king, Don Sancho, is received with every honour by Seville, but in the course of his stay is firmly lectured on the character, and the limitations, of royal authority. As against the royal favourite, Don Arias, who maintains that his master can do as he likes, civic dignitaries insist on the existence of a higher law which even kings must recognize.

Led by Don Fernando Melgarejo, the civic dignitaries of 1624 con-fronted Don Gaspar as their forefathers had confronted Don Arias. As governor of the Alcázar, Olivares, together with his deputy, had a seat on the city council. He rallied the loyalists with the help of the king's representative, the *asistente* Don Fernando Ramírez Fariñas; and a council meeting which he chaired on 13 March approved the vote in the Cortes, although on stringent terms, and added as a sweet-ener a special gift of 30,000 ducats.[94] Olivares wrote to Gondomar the next day expressing his gratification that his native city should have responded so loyally.[95] But sentiment in the city was running high, and, according to the British ambassador, 'in most of the ser-mons the friars animated those that it concerned, not to consent upon any respect to such a destruction of their country as would follow if they should proceed unto the levying of these millions.'[96] A few weeks later, after the royal party had left, fresh trouble broke out when Ramírez Fariñas summoned another meeting to put the finish-ing touches to the vote, 'and the people having gotten notice, upon

[93] For this play, see Ruth L. Kennedy, '"La Estrella de Sevilla", reinterpreted', *Revista de Archivos, Bibliotecas y Museos*, 78 (1975), pp. 385–408. Both date and authorship remain a mystery.

[94] Velázquez y Sánchez, *Estudios históricos*, p. 90; Domínguez Ortiz, *Política y hacienda*, p. 26; Joaquín Guichot, *Historia del excelentísimo ayuntamiento de Sevilla*, 1 (Seville, 1896), p. 187. Charles Jago, 'Habsburg absolutism', p. 320, points out that Olivares' speech to the city council of Seville was identical to that delivered by the *corregidor* in Valladolid—an indication of the planning behind the campaign to win ratification of the *millones* vote by the cities.

[95] AGS Est. leg. 7003, Olivares to Gondomar, 14 March 1624.

[96] BL Add. Ms. 36,449, fo. 90, Aston to Conway, 29 March/8 April 1624.

the breaking up of the meeting, of what had been there propounded, in a tumultuous manner ran after the Asistente', who barely escaped with his life.[97]

The browbeating of the city councils into acceptance of the new grant of *millones* was not the only purpose of the king's visit to Andalusia. The presence of the king and his favourite in the great port cities of Seville and Cadiz would emphasize in suitably dramatic form the crown's commitment to the commercial and naval revival of Spain, and would enable them to hear at first hand the complaints and suggestions of merchants engaged in the overseas trade. These were likely to be numerous. The embargo on trade with the Dutch following the resumption of hostilities in 1621, and then the new legislation in the Articles of Reformation of 1623 forbidding the import of foreign manufactures, had launched Spain into a new protectionist era which might—if all went well—promote an industrial revival, but would certainly have a far-reaching and potentially damaging impact on established patterns of trade. Toledo's triumph, in other words, was Seville's loss. It was to prevent just such a triumph that Captain Tomás de Cardona, as a self-appointed champion of the free trade interest, had lobbied for a 25% debasement of gold and silver, as a better means than protectionism for preventing the outflow of precious metals from Spain.[98] His efforts had so far been unsuccessful, and his solution had many opponents, even in his native Seville; but the trading interest that he represented was a powerful one, and Seville's merchant community, which included many foreigners, could be expected to make the most of the royal visit to press its case on the king and his minister.

It was important that the foreign merchants in Seville, and especially the Flemish merchants, should not be antagonized. They had been badly hit by the trade embargo and they were subject to endless harassment and vexation. Just before the king's visit to Andalusia the Council of State had been discussing the possibility of appointing a 'protector of the foreign nations' to defend their interests. Such a post already existed, but only on a localized basis. Its current holder was Juan Gallardo de Céspedes, who was deputy governor of the Seville Alcázar for Olivares and an influential figure in city politics, but the Council of State felt that a post of such delicacy and importance required a figure of the highest authority.[99] The Council's discussions

---

[97] BL Add. Ms. 30,449, fo. 117, Aston to Conway, 6/16 June 1624. The *asistente* of Seville was the equivalent of the *corregidor* in other cities, a royal nominee executing royal policy.

[98] Above, p. 80; Vilar, 'Un pauto del pensamiento monetarista castellano'; Hamilton, *American Treasure*, pp. 66–7; Jaime Carrera Pujal, *Historia de la economía española*, I (Barcelona, 1943), pp. 570–2.

[99] AGS Est. leg. 2645, consulta of Council of State, 8 January 1624. I am grateful to Dr. Enriqueta Vila Vilar for information about Gallardo.

pointed inexorably to Olivares himself,[100] but although the king approved the idea, the count declined the appointment, perhaps as the result of a private letter from the Count of Gondomar, who warned him that he would earn nothing but unpopularity from a formal association with foreign merchants accused by 'manufacturers' of destroying Spain with their imported goods.[101]

Even if he did not formally become their protector, Olivares was anxious to keep the foreign merchant community contented. As Gondomar had argued in the Council of State on 8 January, it would be ideal if all trade were in Spanish hands, but since in Spain's present state there were not enough native ships or merchants, 'it would be better to have some trade than none', and this meant courting foreign merchants. A deputation of the Flemish merchants in Seville was in fact received in audience by Olivares on 9 March, and presumably at this meeting there was an exchange of ideas about possible ways of restoring Spanish trade with the north.[102] At almost the same moment the Junta de Comercio in Madrid was discussing memoranda by Manuel López Pereira and Francisco de Retama, a merchant from Jerez de la Frontera and—like López Pereira—a recent arrival from Holland,[103] proposing the foundation of Spanish trading companies on the Dutch model. The Junta advised the king that 'it would be a good thing to resort to imitation, in so far as this is compatible with our temperament and disposition', and advocated a study of the charters of the English and Dutch East India Companies, with a view to founding 'trading companies in Spain for different parts of Europe, and in Portugal for the Indies.'[104]

Domestic necessity and foreign example were therefore both working to persuade the regime of the virtue of the schemes already proposed by Mendo da Mota, Duarte Gómez Solís and Sir Anthony Sherley for a collaborative endeavour by crown and merchants to revive Spanish trade through the organization of monopoly companies. It is likely that when Olivares received the Flemish merchants in audience he floated the idea of a North European trading company with them. It is equally likely that they used the occasion to request that the loyal provinces of the southern Netherlands should be given the privilege of direct participation in the Iberian overseas trades, as Retama and López Pereira proposed. But this was to ask too much.

[100] AGS Est. leg. 2645, consulta of 29 January 1624.
[101] AHN Est. lib. 869, fo. 34, Gondomar to Olivares, ? January 1624. Olivares' refusal of the appointment is reported in a consulta of the Council of State of 8 February 1624 (AGS Est. leg. 4126).
[102] Antonio Domínguez Ortiz, 'El almirantazgo de los países septentrionales y la política económica de Felipe IV', *Hispania* 7 (1947), pp. 272–90.
[103] AGS Est. leg. 2847, petition from Retama, 11 May 1624.
[104] AGS Est. leg. 2847, fo. 50, consultas of 13 and 16 March 1624.

The Junta de Comercio suspected that Flemish participation in trade with the East or West Indies would open the door to covert Dutch participation, and it rejected the idea out of hand.[105]

While Olivares made use of his visit to Seville to sound out the possibilities for some new form of commercial organization to wrest from the Dutch their monopoly of Europe's north-south trade, he is also likely to have used the occasion to inquire into the state of Seville's trade with the Indies. This fell within his area of responsibility as Grand Chancellor of the Indies. The office was one which had lapsed in 1575 on the death of the Marquis of Camarasa, and in acknowledgment of Don Gaspar's own services, and those of father and grandfather, the king revived it in his person in July 1623, and attached it to his family in perpetuity.[106] Although the Grand Chancellorship carried with it a seat in the Council of the Indies, he does not seem to have attended its sessions, and there is no sign in his surviving papers of personal intervention in the government of the American viceroyalties. On the other hand, he had a deep and continuing preoccupation with the fortunes of Spain's American trade, which he rightly regarded as critical for the crown's finances.

The fall in silver remittances from the Indies and the general decline of Spain's American trade had given rise in recent years to much discussion, and had provoked a flurry of memoranda and suggestions. Apart from major changes of demand in the American market, which, as López Pereira argued in one of his papers, was overstocked,[107] it was well known that the trade was subjected to fraud on a massive scale. This occurred both in the outward shipment of goods to the Indies, which were grossly underregistered in an attempt to avoid the payment of dues, and also in the handling of bullion and other merchandise on the return journey to Seville. According to a confidential report submitted to the Council of State in 1617, when the returning fleets arrived at Sanlúcar large quantities of unregistered silver would be extracted from the galleons by night, and secretly placed on board ships from northern Europe that were hovering around the port, together with more silver brought from Seville to Sanlúcar, allegedly to pay for the imported merchandise.[108] The organization of the Indies trade was in the hands of a monopoly

[105] Consulta of 13 March 1624.

[106] Conferment of title 27 July 1623, printed as Appendix IV of Tomás Valiente, Los validos, and as Appendix VIII of Antonio León Pinelo, El Gran Canciller de Indias, ed. Guillermo Lohmann Villena (Seville, 1953). For the history of the Grand Chancellorship, see the introduction to this edition, and Ernesto Schäfer, El consejo real y supremo de las Indias, 1 (Seville, 1935), pp. 217–27.

[107] AGS Est. leg. 2847, undated memorandum accompanying consulta of Junta de Comercio of 16 March 1624; and see above, p. 70.

[108] ADI Montesclaros Mss. lib. 130, no. 22, Proposiciones que hizo a SM en su consejo de estado Liven Wanequer en 13 de abril 1617.

association of merchants, the Consulado of Seville, and the Casa de la Contratación (the House of Trade that supervised the American trade for the crown) accused the Consulado of being deeply implicated in the frauds. But in reality there was fraud and corruption at every level, from the generals of the fleets to the merchants of the Consulado, and from the the officials of the Casa de la Contratación to the Council of the Indies itself.[109]

It was easy enough to allege fraud, but not so easy to know how to stop it. In order to compensate for the losses, the crown had made a practice of raising the dues on goods, but every time the dues increased, so too did the contraband. Olivares no doubt took a close look at the Consulado during his visit, but he was as well aware as anyone of what was happening, and he had his own private agents in Seville, like Sebastián de Casaus, to keep him informed.[110] His problem was that, while the merchants of the Consulado might be frightened of the prospect of judicial inquiry and the imposition of penalties, their fears could all too easily be translated into a panic which would have a disastrous impact on Seville's trade with the Indies. Confidence had already been shaken by confiscation of silver from the 1620 treasure fleet,[111] and nothing would be better calculated to undermine it further than an attempt at radical reform. Subsequent events suggest that Olivares finally came to the conclusion that the price was too high to pay. In the very month of his visit, the 1624 fleet left Seville for Portobelo in Panama. Two years later a royal accountant, Cristóbal de Balbas, who seems to have been in Olivares' confidence, produced evidence that more than 85% of the merchandise carried in this fleet was in fact contraband. The documentation was unprecedented in its precision, and the evidence of fraud overwhelming. But the crown needed the Consulado of Seville at least as much as the Consulado needed the crown. As a result, a deal was struck, and the threatened inquiry was dropped in return for the payment by the Consulado of a fine of 206,000 ducats.[112]

The Indies trade, then, was one area which the reform programme was unlikely to reach. For all his zeal for reformation, Olivares dared not kill the goose that laid the silver eggs. The only alternative was a complicity in corruption between crown and Consulado to keep the supply running, and it was on this tacit basis that Olivares reached his *modus vivendi* with the Seville merchant community, putting such pressure as he could on the Consulado, but trying—within the limits

[109] Enriqueta Vila Vilar, 'Las ferias de Portobelo: apariencia y realidad del comercio con Indias', *Anuario de Estudios Americanos*, 39 (1982), pp. 275–340.

[110] Escorial Ms. K.1.17, *Fragmento del catálogo del Conde Duque*, fo. 180v. ('D. Sebastián de Casaos, grande amigo del Asistente Fariña y confidente del conde').

[111] Above, p. 76.

[112] See Vila Vilar, 'Las ferias de Portobelo', for this important case-history of the 1624 fleet.

imposed by the increasingly tight financial constraints on the crown—
to avoid driving it to despair.

The king and the count extended their education into the affairs
of the Indies trade by paying a visit to Seville's port of Sanlúcar
de Barrameda, where the Duke of Medina Sidonia rose from his
sickbed to greet them. From here they embarked for Puerto Santa
María and Cadiz, where the king spent five days. The visit provided
Olivares with a splendid opportunity to demonstrate publicly the
concern of his administration for the restoration of Spanish naval
power. The king, dressed as a soldier, inspected the coastal defences,
which might soon be needed against an English attack. He conferred
honours and awards on soldiers and sailors, reviewed the ships of
the Atlantic and Mediterranean fleets, and was entertained with a
mock naval battle.[113] From Cadiz the royal party travelled to Gibraltar, where, to Don Gaspar's fury, the gate of entry was too narrow
for the royal coach, and the king had to enter on foot. But in the
governor of Gibraltar Olivares met his match. 'The gate', he
explained, 'was not constructed to let carriages in, but to keep the
enemy out.'[114] After Gibraltar came Málaga and Granada, where the
king spent six days, and was voted a subsidy of 20,000 ducats. From
Granada he travelled north at speed by the way of Jaén and was
back in Madrid on 18 April.

As a sight-seeing tour of Andalusia the journey had no doubt been
a valuable educational experience for the king, but the political dividends were disappointing. With the exception of Seville, the Andalusian cities had obstinately refused to ratify the vote of their deputies
in the Cortes, and even Seville had second thoughts.[115] The opposition
in the cities to the new round of taxes was so fierce that the papal
nuncio, writing in early August, prophesied revolt.[116]

Faced by the resistance of the Andalusian cities to a ratification
of the Cortes vote, the crown convened a special Junta Grande, apparently composed of the councillors of State and Castile, some time
in August 1624.[117] According to the British ambassador, Sir Walter

[113] Herrera y Sotomayor, fos. 3v.–6; Fernández Duro, *Armada española*, 4, p. 26.
[114] Quoted by Carrera Pujal, *Historia de la economía española*, 1, p. 490.
[115] Novoa, *Codoin* 61, p. 450.
[116] ASV, Spagna, 65, nuncio, 9 August 1624.
[117] The convocation of this junta has apparently passed unnoticed, and no documents relating
to its activities have so far come to light. The information about its purpose and activities
comes from the court letter-writer Almansa y Mendoza, *Cartas*, pp. 295–6, and from Sir
Walter Aston, the British ambassador, in letters of 8/18 August and 2/12 September 1624
(BL Add. Ms. 36,449, fos. 135–6 and 148). There is also a reference to the discussion as
to whether the king can levy taxes outside the Cortes in Khevenhüller's *Annales Ferdinandei*,
2, pp. 636–7. Among the ambassadors in Madrid, Aston, perhaps equating the Castilian Cortes
with the House of Commons, is the only one to pay regular attention to the Cortes and
to problems of parliamentary taxation.

Aston, it was summoned to advise the king 'whether he may not give order for the levying the said millions granted unto him in parliament, notwithstanding the opposition since made by the cities.' The junta's reaction showed what strength the Castilian constitutionalist tradition still possessed in spite of the weakness of institutional barriers against the exercise of the royal prerogative. The Marquis of Montesclaros, in particular, spoke out against the proposal in terms which scandalized Cardinal Zapata, who sat at the king's right hand. According to Aston the junta, while not denying the reserve powers of the king, felt that 'such unlimited authority is only to be put in execution in time of extreme necessities, of which they say there is at present no appearance, and do therefore rather wish that His Majesty would here proceed in a calmer manner, and represent his occasions to the cities, and leave it to them to resolve upon such a concession.' The junta was dissolved in late August or early September, after deciding that it was not convenient for the king 'to take that course, neither can His Majesty put it in execution without injustice and tyranny.'

The negative verdict of the Junta Grande and the resistance of the cities forced Olivares to turn again to the Cortes, in the hope that they could come up with a set of fiscal proposals more acceptable to the towns. The deputy for Toledo warned his city that time was running out—'if a decision is not taken promptly, His Majesty will take it, because the financial situation is acute.'[118] On 19 October 1624 the Cortes agreed to a service of twelve million ducats payable in six years, regretting that this was the best that could be managed.[119] The service was voted, as Sir Walter Aston pointed out in a letter to Buckingham, 'instead of their great concession of 70 millions, which the Conde of Olivares did much to boast of to His Highness and Your Grace at your being here.'[120]

The great retreat, therefore, was beginning. Olivares' grand scheme for a rational attempt to match income and expenditure by guaranteeing a large and fixed tax yield over a long period, was rapidly coming unravelled; and although in December the crown launched an appeal for a *donativo*—voluntary contributions throughout the country for the reduction of its debts—the relative success of this appeal under the impact of the outbreak of hostilities with England was no compensation for the failure to establish the crown's finances on a sounder basis.[121] Even the more modest proposition approved by the Cortes

---

[118] AMT Cartas (1624), Angel Sánchez to city of Toledo, 23 September 1624.
[119] *Actas*, 41, pp. 519–21.
[120] BL Add. Ms. 36,449, fo. 175, 24 December/3 January 1624/5.
[121] For the first and most successful of the *donativos* of this period, see Domínguez Ortiz, *Política y hacienda*, p. 299.

in October soon ran into trouble. There was endless discussion about ways of raising the money, and a decision taken by the Cortes in November to levy a 1% sales tax[122] proved to be highly controversial. But gradually the cities fell into line: by 30 June 1625 twelve of the eighteen cities in the Cortes had approved the vote,[123] although Toledo still held out. According to the *corregidor*, who was too frightened to write personally to Olivares about the behaviour of a city to which he had close ties, the *regidores* of Toledo were holding back, partly out of fear of each other, and partly out of fear of popular reactions.[124]

But already by this time it was clear that Olivares would have to abandon much more than his proposals for fiscal reform. His urgent need of money for day-to-day expenses left him hopelessly vulnerable to pressure from the cities exerted through the Cortes. After the loss of the seventy-two million tax vote, it was the turn of the plan for reducing the number of municipal offices. In January 1625 the Cortes made it a condition for the granting of the *millones* that Gilimón's commission should be revoked, and offices restored to all those who had been deprived of them without being compensated in ready cash. The crown accepted this condition in November.[125] Last of all, the scheme for the deposit banks was decently interred. As another condition for the *millones*, the Cortes continued to insist that the banks should be funded out of the crown's financial resources (which were known to be non-existent) and conduct their business under tight constraints. On 7 February 1626 this condition, too, was accepted by the king.[126]

'The towns and cities have no voice', Gilimón had written; 'it is the town councillors who speak for them.' It was inevitable that Olivares should come up against the solid resistance of these urban patriciates as soon as he threatened their interests. One of his difficulties was the lack of alternative power groupings in Castilian society. His high-handed methods and his relative success in stemming the bounteous flow of royal patronage had alienated the nobility; the administration was, by nature, conservative and sluggish; the people, whose burdens he genuinely wished to alleviate, carried no political weight. Certain aspects of his programme no doubt possessed a considerable sectional appeal: those of *converso* ancestry were likely to welcome his cautious steps towards a more liberal approach to the question of 'tainted' blood; the cities of the interior were natural

---

[122] *Actas*, 42, pp. 39–40.

[123] AMT Cartas y varios (1625), Francisco de Contreras to city of Toledo, 30 June 1625.

[124] AGS Patronato Real, leg. 91, fo. 227, corregidor of Toledo to Pedro de Contreras, 8 July 1625.

[125] *Actas*, 43, p. 242.

[126] See Hamilton, 'Spanish banking schemes'.

supporters of his protectionist policies. But there was little scope for building up a broad-based alliance which would favour a general reform programme, and different groups withdrew support as soon as they saw their own interests in jeopardy.

The reform programme was bedevilled, too, by a fundamental lack of trust between the crown and those it most wished to encourage—the more enlightened and entrepreneurial sections of Castilian urban society. The resistance of the cities to Olivares' fiscal reforms was motivated, at least in part, by the arbitrary and high-handed manner in which they were put forward. Could a crown so cavalier in its approach to what the urban patriciates regarded as their constitutional rights be trusted to keep its word about the uses to which the funds in the deposit banks would be put? What was to prevent it from raiding the banks when a financial emergency arose? Similar doubts attended the administration's proposals for the restoration of trade that followed in the wake of the royal visit to Andalusia. Could trading companies on the model of those of England and the Dutch Republic be satisfactorily transplanted to the soil of Spain, where there was no substantial check on the exercise of the prerogative power? To judge from the reactions, there were many who suspected that they could not.

On 4 October 1624 a royal decree announced the creation of the *Almirantazgo de los Países Septentrionales*, a company of Flemish merchants with its headquarters in Seville, and trading with northern Europe. Other projects were to follow—a Levant Company in Barcelona, an India Company in Lisbon—but the example of the Almirantazgo was not encouraging. The convoy system envisaged for the company proved unsuitable for northern trade; the plans raised questions about the extent of royal participation and intervention which were never satisfactorily resolved; and the merchants resented the tight procedures and the high rates to which the fledgling organization was subjected.[127] Once again it was a question of trust, and it was characteristic of the political and intellectual climate in which it was introduced that the one reasonably effective feature of the new Almirantazgo proved to be its activity as a regulating agency. As a trading company it never worked, but it rapidly spawned an impressive bureaucracy designed to check and regulate the trade between Spain and northern Europe. An army of officials established itself in the ports of the peninsula, with powers to board ships, inspect certificates, check warehouses and confiscate contraband. Since the officials were remunerated from the confiscations they effected, they performed their duties with zeal, and the Almirantazgo can be credited with

[127] See Domínguez Ortiz, 'El almirantazgo'; Carrera Pujal, *Historia de la economía española*, 1, pp. 526–8; Israel, *The Dutch Republic*, p. 205.

some success in stemming the flood of Dutch imports into Spain.[128] But it wielded at best a blunt weapon, and its activities are more likely to have been effective in arbitrarily driving up prices than in creating a climate in which native Castilian industries could embark on a sustained recovery. At bottom, it had been asked to do the impossible—to stimulate Spanish trade with northern Europe, while curbing the flow of northern goods into Spain—and this flaw in its conception dogged it from the start.

Olivares, however, was both resourceful and determined. His whole political career can be read as a gloss on the words of one of the many Tacitean writers of the age, Alvia de Castro, who observed in his *True Reason of State* that the good statesman 'must always make for one goal—to achieve what he sets out to do.'[129] To do this, Olivares would tack and turn, but there remained throughout the whole of his twenty-two years of power a formidable consistency about his long-term aims. In his struggle with the Cortes and the cities, he might have lost a battle, but he had not yet lost the war. In his struggle to revive commerce and industry he would come back again and again to his original objectives, brushing up his plans, and adding new refinements to make them more acceptable. There would be moments of depression and despair; but as long as the king continued to require his services, he would not give up the fight.

The Count-Duke

For all the criticisms which his policies were arousing, the king gave every sign of absolute confidence in his minister. Philip's interests in these early years of the reign were directed more towards the theatre and the hunt than towards the ceaseless flow of *consultas* and despatches on which he was expected to reach a decision. To some extent the triumvirate served as a filter, but it still remained for the king to take the final decision and give the necessary orders. Here, the presence of Olivares at his side was immensely reassuring. Young, inexperienced, unsure of himself and not yet very interested in affairs of state and government, Philip needed someone to guide and instruct him. Don Gaspar, with an apparently infinite capacity for work, and an obsequious deference towards the young man who was at once his master and his pupil, filled the part to perfection. Philip in turn expressed his gratitude by showering his favourite with honours.

[128] See Israel, pp. 206–9.
[129] Quoted by Maravall in 'La corriente doctrinal del tacitismo político en España', p. 101.

As groom of the stole and, from December 1622, as master of the horse, Olivares had access to the king at all times, both inside and outside the palace. His appointment as a councillor of state in October 1622 gave him for the first time ministerial status. As Grand Chancellor of the Indies from 1623 he acquired a high-sounding title and broad jurisdiction. The salary attached to the Grand Chancellorship was small—a mere 2,000 ducats a year—but it carried with it valuable perquisites, like the right of appointment in perpetuity to the offices of chancellor and registrar in each of the eleven chancelleries and *audiencias* of the Indies, although by no stretch of the imagination could the emoluments have been worth almost 25,000 ducats a year, as Novoa alleged.[130] Indeed it was partly because the revenues seem to have been less than expected that the king also granted his Grand Chancellor the right to send a 200-ton ship each year from Acapulco to the Philippines, but he apparently decided not to take advantage of this lucrative concession.[131] The principal attraction of the office is likely to have been the title, which conferred status and prestige at a time when Don Gaspar was trying to establish himself in the ranks of the high aristocracy. The Duke of Alba, after all, was Grand Chancellor of Navarre. By 1626, when he devolved the office and its accompanying privileges on his son-in-law, he would have less need of such trappings.

'Amidst his public cares', wrote the Count of La Roca delicately, 'the count did not neglect the private concerns of his house. He wished to enhance its greatness, but not at the expense of the royal patrimony or the treasury.'[132] The most inexpensive way for the crown to reward him was out of the income of the commanderies (*encomiendas*) of the military orders. From his early years he had held the commandery of Vívoras in the Order of Calatrava. In 1624, having duly but inaccurately been found free of any taint of the blood of 'Jew, Moor, converted Jew, heretic or villein',[133] he was admitted to the Order of Alcántara, of which he became *Comendador Mayor*, and in which he was also given, by special papal dispensation, the revenues of the commandery of La Garza, held by his daughter María. From these commanderies he derived an annual income of some 17,500 ducats.[134]

---

[130] Novoa, *Codoin* 61, p. 401. Cf. Schäfer, 1, pp. 224–5. A list of Olivares' revenues, dating from c. 1624, estimates his emoluments as Grand Chancellor as worth rather more than 4,000 ducats a year, excluding the fees and dues accruing to him from appointments to the offices of *registradores* and *cancilleres* in the eleven *audiencias* of the Indies (BL Add. Ms. 34,447, fos. 229–230v.).

[131] Roca, *Fragmentos*, p. 230.

[132] *Ibid.*, p. 231.

[133] AHN Ordenes militares (Alcántara), Expte. 697, Informaciones.

[134] BL Add. Ms. 34,447, fo. 230v., statement on the income and properties of the Count of Olivares.

With these revenues and the income from his court appointments, he embarked on the two not entirely compatible tasks of paying off his debts and establishing his house as one of the greatest in Spain. His family had long been fighting a legal suit with the Dukes of Medina Sidonia over a debt settlement arising from the collapse of the Espinosa bank in 1576. In January 1624 the case was won by Olivares on appeal in the Chancellery of Valladolid, possibly with the assistance of that skilful advocate José González. The case was said to be worth at least 300,000 ducats to him: he would not, after all, as he feared, have to watch his children die of hunger.[135] But his finances remained in a precarious state, and at the end of 1625 a grateful king was forced to come to his rescue. A letter patent of 22 December explained how Don Gaspar, following in the tradition of his father and grandfather, had incurred heavy debts in the service of his king, and had been too busy with the duties of government to attend to his estates. Gilimón de la Mota had therefore been designated to assume responsibility for the administration of his estates and the redemption of his debts.[136] There was a certain irony, which no doubt passed unnoticed, that the crown should be attempting to redeem the debts of Olivares at the same time as Olivares was attempting to do the same for those of the crown. In neither instance was the operation a success. Four years after the arrangement of 1625 he was complaining that he found himself without silver, without jewels, without even fifty *reales* to pay for his own funeral expenses, and with debts of 800,000 ducats.[137]

The complaint has to be taken with a grain of salt, and against the debts one has to set the assets, starting with the handsome gifts that anyone in his position was bound to receive, despite all his attempts to decline them: a set of tapestries depicting the acts of the apostles, presented by the king and valued at 10,000 ducats; a gold and diamond ring worth 7,000 ducats from the Infante Don Carlos; and a jewel set with diamonds, valued at 25,000 ducats, the gift of the Prince of Wales during his visit to Madrid.[138] A few trifling

---

[135] AGS Gracia y Justicia, leg. 889, Olivares to Francisco de Contreras, 30 November 1623. Reports of the case in González Palencia, *Noticias de Madrid*, pp. 89 and 121, and Almansa y Mendoza, *Cartas*, p. 265. The 1624(?) list of revenues (fo. 230v.), cited in the preceding note, gives the figure of 300,000 ducats as being recoverable from Alonso de Espinosa and the Duke of Medina Sidonia as the result of steps already taken, with a further 125,000 outstanding.

[136] AHN Consejos, leg. 7126, cédula, 22 December 1625. The procedure was one followed in other cases of crippling aristocratic indebtedness. See Ignacio Atienza Hernández, 'La "quiebra" de la nobleza castellana en el siglo XVII. Autoridad real y poder señorial; el secuestro de los bienes de la casa de Osuna', *Hispania*, 44 (1984), pp. 49–81.

[137] *MC*, 2, p. 48, Olivares to Count of Castro, 13 August 1629.

[138] 1624(?) statement on income, BL Add. Ms. 34,447, fo. 230.

presents such as these might be regarded as some compensation for the financial sacrifices of office.

But the heaviest expenditure came not from the obligations of office, but from the purchase of the most permanent of all assets, land. He was now in a position to realize the dream of his father and grandfather, and establish the allegedly junior branch of the house of Guzmán as at least the equal of the ducal branch of Medina Sidonia. His estates and jurisdictions clustering around the town of Olivares formed a promising nucleus, but these Andalusian properties needed to be consolidated and rounded out. Unfortunately this could only be achieved at the expense of the city of Seville, to which they were inconveniently close; for Seville, too, had its eyes on the pockets of royal demesne located in its hinterland.

Although the principal object of the king's visit to Andalusia in 1624 was to introduce him to his vassals in southern Spain and to overawe the recalcitrant Andalusian cities with the majesty of his presence, the visit fitted admirably into the context of Don Gaspar's personal and family strategy, which indeed some contemporaries saw as the real motive behind it. His family, they said, had always been 'much inferior' to the ducal families of Alcalá and Medina Sidonia, and he now wanted an opportunity to display himself in his new-found glory to his fellow-Andalusians. He also wanted to 'enlarge more easily his estate and its confines, especially by arranging to purchase the castle of San Lúcar la Mayor . . . a pleasant and noble town only two leagues from Seville.' So far, this prize had eluded him, but once secured he would persuade the king to make it the seat of a dukedom.[139]

The prediction proved accurate. Don Gaspar's grandfather had made strenuous efforts to purchase from the crown its rights of juris-diction over San Lúcar la Mayor, but in the end the lordship had been acquired by the city of Seville, with a prohibition on its aliena-tion. In December 1623, presumably under pressure from the court, the city council of Seville was induced to sell San Lúcar to Don Gaspar. The crown duly authorized Seville to alienate the lordship, and—in recognition of the great financial services of a city which claimed to generate a third of all the king's Castilian revenues—to pocket the proceeds.[140] The purchase of San Lúcar, with its eight hundred vassals, seems to have cost Don Gaspar just under 100,000 ducats.[141] A similarly complicated transaction also enabled him to

[139] AAE Corresp. Espagne, no. 13, fos. 230–1, copy of letter from Cadiz, 26 March 1624.
[140] AHN Est. lib. 1826, fos. 337–9v., *consulta de la cámara*, 17 December 1623; Antonio Herrera García, *El Aljarafe sevillano durante el antiguo régimen. Un estudio de su evolución socioeconómica en los siglos XVI, XVII y XVIII* (Seville, 1980), pp. 66–7.
[141] BL Add. Ms. 34,447, fo. 229v.

buy additional rights of jurisdiction that would give him full possession of another town close to Seville, Castilleja de la Cuesta.[142] This
was followed by further local purchases in the immediately succeeding years, and then a new round of acquisitions at the very end of
his political career, in 1641, including the town of Mairena. On his
death he still owed the royal treasury some 85,000 ducats for the
various purchases.[143]

Once Don Gaspar was in full possession of these additional lord-
ships, the next step followed logically. The new acquisitions were
incorporated into the Olivares entail, drawn up by the notary on
10 October 1624;[144] and on 5 January 1625 the king created him Duke
of San Lúcar la Mayor, the title to pass with the entail in perpetuity.[145]
His official style was now Count of Olivares, Duke of San Lúcar
la Mayor. He began to sign his letters *El Conde Duque de San Lúcar*,
and it was as the Conde Duque, the Count-Duke, that he would
henceforth be known to the world.[146]

The Counts of Olivares were dukes at last, and there only remained
the question of the succession. Don Gaspar still continued to hope
for a son, but no child had been born to Doña Inés for many years,
and it looked increasingly as though it would fall to their daughter
María to perpetuate the line. Olivares had already made the necessary
dispositions with this prospect in mind. From the time of his rise
to power there had been intense speculation at court about his choice
of a husband for his daughter. One possibility was that he might
select the Count of Niebla, son and heir of the Duke of Medina
Sidonia, and so unite the two rival branches of the house of Guzmán.[147]
But Olivares was never a man to do the obvious. Living in genteel
poverty in León was a remote and obscure relative, Ramiro Pérez
de Guzmán, Marquis of Toral, still only a child, who was summoned
to court along with his mother and sister. The Marquises of Toral

---

[142] Domínguez Ortiz and Aguilar Piñal, *Historia de Sevilla*, p. 90; Herrera García, *El Aljarafe*,
pp. 68–9; Olivares' letter of thanks, Archivo Muncipal de Sevilla, papeles importantes, 2,
20 January 1625.
[143] Herrera García, *El Aljarafe*, pp. 71–6, including a map of the family properties.
[144] AHP 1718, *aumento de mayorazgo*.
[145] Text in Roca, *Fragmentos*, pp. 233–5.
[146] It has been argued that 'Conde Duque de Olivares' has no warrant as a title in contemporary
usage, and that Don Gaspar was known in his own times either as the 'Conde de Olivares',
or simply as the 'Conde-Duque'. (See E. Zudaire, 'Un error de inercia: el supuesto Conde-
Duque de Olivares', *Hidalguía*, 11 (1963), pp. 599–610.) But Malvezzi speaks of him as 'el
Conde-Duque de Olivares' in his *Historia . . . del reinado de Felipe IV* (p. 87), and he is named
in a royal decree of 1627 as 'Don Gaspar de Guzmán, Conde Duque de Olivares, Duque
de Sanlúcar la Mayor' (*Defensas legales por la Señora D. Inés de Zúñiga y Velasco . . . contra
el Señor Don Luis Méndez de Haro, Conde Duque de Olivares*, Madrid, 1646, discurso jurídico,
fo. 2v.). It is not therefore wrong that he should have passed into history as 'the Count-Duke
of Olivares'.
[147] Roca, *Fragmentos*, pp. 236–7, for the possible bridegrooms.

claimed the titular headship of the ancient house of Guzmán,[148] and it gradually became apparent that Olivares was planning to steal a march on the Dukes of Medina Sidonia by marrying his daughter to the nominal head of the family.

In September 1624 Toral's sister was married to the Constable of Castile[149]—an alliance that brought the family into the inner circle of Spanish magnates. This marriage was followed on 10 October by the signing in the palace of a marriage contract between Ramiro Pérez de Guzmán, Marquis of Toral, aged twelve, and Doña María de Guzmán, Marchioness of Heliche, aged fourteen.[150] The marriage was to be celebrated at a time decided by the bride's father, and the married couple were to live in his household for as long as he wanted. Toral would take the title of Marquis of Heliche on marriage, and the descendants of the union were to bear the name of Pérez de Guzmán, and sport the arms of the house of Olivares.

The engagement was not well received in the Olivares family circle, particularly by Olivares' nephew, Don Luis de Haro, who had himself been mentioned as a potential husband for María, and who saw his hopes of eventual succession to the Olivares entail rapidly receding.[151] It also led to a sharp exchange between Olivares and his brother-in-law Monterrey, who had taken a dislike to Toral, and did not relish the prospect of his succeeding to the Monterrey estates in lieu of any children of his own. Olivares tartly replied that he and Doña Inés still hoped for male heirs who would succeed to both their houses.[152]

Didactic as always, Olivares wrote a set of instructions for his future son-in-law the day before the signing of the marriage contract.[153] These were generally of a rather bland character, with their insistence on the need for piety and a modest comportment at court, but they contained one or two characteristic touches. In particular, the future Marquis of Heliche was to patronize learning and letters, which, to the detriment of the Spanish Monarchy, had for too long been neglected. He was also advised to make his own way in the world, without banking on his father-in-law's remaining in a post so subject to sudden change: 'and I promise you, my son, that I never applied for or sought the position that I hold, and since I have been in it I have not been so foolish as to let a day pass without

[148] Novoa, *Codoin* 61, p. 452. The family is celebrated in Lope de Vega's play, written in the early years of the century, *Los Guzmanes de Toral.*
[149] González Palencia, *Noticias de Madrid*, p. 104.
[150] AHP 1718, *capitulaciones*, 10 October 1624.
[151] Novoa, *Codoin* 61, p. 452.
[152] ASV, Spagna, 65, fo. 40, nuncio, 17 July 1624.
[153] Berkeley, Bancroft Mss. MM. 1755, no. 15, *Instrucción del Conde Duque para su yerno,* 9 October 1624.

expecting that I would be out of it by the next. This is the truth, and anything said to the contrary is without foundation.'

Olivares' instructions made it clear that he looked forward to his future son-in-law assisting him with his duties in the palace. Toral was still very young, but he proved a model courtier and rapidly endeared himself to the king. His later career suggests what his father-in-law may have been the first to perceive—that there was more to him than met the eye. As Duke of Medina de Las Torres he was to show in the later years of Olivares' government that he had a mind of his own; and in the post-Olivares period he emerged as an intelligent realist with an acute perception of Spain's international situation, although his easy-going ways and natural laziness deprived him of the decisive political influence that he might otherwise have enjoyed.[154]

The marriage was celebrated on 9 January 1625, four days after Olivares' elevation to his dukedom. Looking back over the events of the preceding four years, the new duke could hardly fail to consider his record with pride. To all intents and purposes he was the king's principal minister and had realized beyond all expectations the ambitions of his father and grandfather. He had upheld the honour of his house, and had avenged the wrongs done it by the Dukes of Medina Sidonia. The olive tree, the emblem of the Counts of Olivares, was now securely rooted, and would soon, with the help of God and the king, be raising its branches to the skies.

---

[154] For his later career, see R. A. Stradling, 'A Spanish Statesman of Appeasement: Medina de las Torres and Spanish Policy, 1639–1670', *Historical Journal*, 19 (1976), pp. 1–31.

V

A PROGRAMME FOR RENEWAL

The rise of the 'planet king'

By conferring a dukedom on Don Gaspar in January 1625, Philip once again affirmed his confidence in the man who was both his favourite and his minister. Olivares' enemies, who were numerous, found this confidence incomprehensible, and—following an old tradition about the power of favourites—attributed it to the exercise of a malign influence over the king by the use of magic arts. In 1622 stories were circulating at court about a woman called Leonor and magic potions which Olivares gave the king to retain his favour.[1] Some months later, a member of the royal Guard of Archers, Don Antonio de Beaufort, was accused of conspiring to kill Olivares, 'either by witchcraft, poison or some other means', in order to restore the Duke of Lerma to power.[2] Magic was clearly the antidote to magic.

The *valido* or *privado* was a man who had succeeded in capturing the favour of the king, usually—it was assumed—by sinister means. In the popular imagination Don Alvaro de Luna, the fifteenth-century favourite of John II of Castile, was the very image of the *privado*, and the spectacular downfall and execution of Don Alvaro in 1453 was seen as a salutary warning to those who rose above their stations and usurped the royal authority. The Duke of Lerma was regarded by his enemies as having done exactly this, and Olivares therefore had every inducement to disclaim for himself the title of favourite, with its pejorative connotations. Instead, he liked to call himself a 'minister'—the king's 'faithful minister'[3]—emphasizing the official, and not the personal, character of the high position in which he found himself.

But from very early in the reign contemporaries regarded him

---

[1] 'Informe que hizo don Miguel de Cárdenas... sobre los hechizos que se decía daba el conde Olivares al rey don Felipe IV', printed as *libro séptimo* of Adolfo de Castro, *El Conde-Duque de Olivares y el Rey Felipe IV* (Cadiz, 1846). See also Marañón, *Olivares*, pp. 195–8.

[2] BL Add. Ms. 36,449, fo. 54, Aston to Calvert, 28 July/7 August 1623; also AHN Inquis. leg. 3683, caja 4, for documentation on Beaufort, which Don José Martínez Barra plans to publish.

[3] Tomás Valiente, *Los validos*, p. 95.

not just as a minister but as the principal or first minister. He himself wrote as early as February 1623 that evil-intentioned people were clamouring against him as *'primer ministro'* of the king; and although he eschewed the title of 'first' or 'prime' minister, others had no such compunctions.[4] Yet at the same time they persisted in seeing him as a *privado*, and he himself seems to have harboured the suspicion that there was some justice in their view.

At least in theory, a working king required no favourite, but only ministers. The perfect example was Philip II; and Olivares, who was committed from the beginning to Fray Juan de Santamaría's insistence on the need for a return to personal kingship,[5] naturally set before the young Philip IV the awesome example of his grandfather. In 1626, when he felt compelled to rebuke the king for his persistent idleness, he explained that if only Philip were willing to change his ways, 'the very reason for the name of *privado* would disappear'.[6] Yet, a year later, he was saying that, while it would be fine to have no *privado*, there had been nobody since the time of Jesus Christ who did not turn to someone for support—'slave or confidant, call him what you will.'[7]

The ambiguity of Olivares' words reflected the ambiguity of his relationship to the king. It was by capturing Philip's favour while he was still a prince that he had attained his present eminent position, and once he lost that favour he would fall from power. In this respect he remained the true *privado*. His *privanza* depended, as he knew, on a personal relationship, and this could never be taken for granted, but changed and developed over the years, as Philip reached maturity.

Even at the beginning, before long years in each other's company added new layers of complexity, the exact psychological components of that relationship are inevitably blurred. The sheer masterfulness of Olivares obviously exercised a powerful attraction over an adolescent who was conscious of the heavy inheritance to which God had called him, and yet at the same time profoundly uncertain of his own abilities. He needed both reassurance and flattery, and these are exactly what Olivares, with his extraordinary combination of self-confidence and self-abasement, was able to supply. Olivares' enemies saw him as cynically manipulating the king for his own nefarious designs, but he had as much need of Philip as Philip of him. The king, half his age, was the son he never had. He was also the man chosen by God to govern the greatest Monarchy on earth, and Oli-

---

[4] See *MC*, 1, pp. 203–4.

[5] See above, p. 102.

[6] *MC*, 1, p. 207 (*Reflexiones políticas y cristianas*, 4 September 1626).

[7] *Ibid.*, p. 217 (*Papel del Conde Duque . . . sobre los naturales de los señores infantes*, 10 October 1627).

vares' reverence for the mystery of Spanish kingship was almost over-whelming. If his expressions of loyalty and gratitude come close at times to idolatry, this was because he saw Philip as the embodiment of a more than earthly majesty. By some mysterious providence this greatest of all kings had plucked him from among his fellows to help him bear his burdens; and he in turn must be worthy of the confidence that his monarch had reposed in him.

It was precisely because such a precious trust had been committed to his charge that he conceived it as the most important of all his duties to train his royal master in the art of kingship. He had observed in him a quick wit and a natural intelligence. Philip had also proved to be a good athlete and horseman, and his bearing and manner were potentially those of a king. But both mentally and emotionally he lacked discipline, and his education had in many respects been hope-lessly inadequate. A few days from his sixteenth birthday at the time of his accession, he was, however, still young enough to be trained and moulded to conform to the ideal image of a King of Spain. This image, as envisaged by Don Gaspar, was a composite one. Philip must become as politically astute as Ferdinand the Catholic, the greatest of all the kings of Spain in Olivares' eyes.[8] He must be as glorious and triumphant as the Emperor Charles V. From his grand-father Philip II, 'the first of kings in prudence',[9] he must learn impas-sivity, sobriety, and the art of government, with all the relentless dedication to paper-work which this entailed. From his father he could learn, if nothing else, a notable lesson in piety.

By persuading Philip that kingship was an art that had to be learned, and by offering to guide his first hesitant steps, Olivares helped to counter his deep sense of inadequacy, while at the same time enhanc-ing his own indispensability during the formative years. The first task was to complete his education and transform him into the para-gon of the cultivated prince (Pl. 11). The arrival in Madrid in 1623 of Charles, Prince of Wales, came as a welcome stimulus. Charles' fastidiousness and refinement, and his discerning eye for the arts, could not fail to suggest to Philip how much he still had to learn. Already he had embarked on a programme of reading, which Olivares probably helped him to devise.[10] According to his own account, he had read by 1622–3 some at least of the books on his impressive reading list—a list that included Roman histories, Castilian chronicles, histories of France, England and Germany, books on geography, and foreign works either in the original or in translation. This reading programme continued throughout the 1620's, and by the early 1630's,

[8] *MC*, 2, p. 75, Olivares to Cardinal Infante, 27 September 1632.
[9] *Ibid.*, p. 214, Olivares to Don Juan Chumacero, 22 October 1641.
[10] See Brown and Elliott, *A Palace*, pp. 40–42.

when he set himself to translate into Castilian Books VIII and IX
of Guicciardini's *History of Italy*, he had become a highly cultivated
man, capable—as Olivares had planned—of setting a splendid example to the Spanish nobility:

> In all Spain there is not a single private person who can ride in
> both styles of saddle like our master the king, while performing
> all the equestrian exercises I have described with almost equal skill.
> And although they did not teach him much Latin, he has some;
> and his knowledge of geography is outstanding. He understands
> and speaks French, he understands Italian and Portuguese as well
> as he understands Castilian; and although he cannot travel to foreign
> parts as he would if he were a private person, he has been round
> all the provinces of Spain observing them with particular care.[11]

The metamorphosis of Philip from a gauche and ignorant prince
into a royal aesthete and a model of gentility constituted an important
element in Olivares' programme for the renewal of Spanish greatness.
The King of Spain, as the first of monarchs, could and should set
an example, not only to his own nobility but also to the other kings
of Europe. It followed that his court must be the most brilliant in
the world. Arms and letters, as Philip himself would observe, were
'the two poles which govern the movement of monarchies, and are
the foundations on which they rest, because together they form a
perfect harmony, each supporting the other.'[12] This was a piece of
conventional wisdom, but—as Olivares saw it—one that in recent
years had been forgotten. Just as the profession of arms in Spain
had fallen on bad times, so too had the pursuit of letters. In the
letter of instruction that he wrote to his future son-in-law in October
1624, his exhortation to hold men at arms in high esteem was immediately followed by an exhortation to 'respect and favour' letters,
and 'encourage men of talent' (*grandes ingenios*).[13]

Presumably he missed no opportunity to give similar advice to
his royal pupil, whose own inclinations anyhow led him in the same
direction. Surrounded by great works of art from the splendid royal
collection, Philip—who himself had taken drawing lessons from an
excellent artist, the Dominican friar Juan Bautista Maino[14]—soon
showed that he had a discriminating eye for a painting. An increasingly close relationship with his new court artist, Velázquez, and
the opportunity for conversations with the great Peter Paul Rubens

---

[11] *MC*, 2, Doc. XIIa, Olivares to Archbishop of Granada, 18 September 1632.
[12] 'Autosemblanza de Felipe IV', printed as appendix II of Carlos Seco Serrano, ed., *Cartas de Sor María de Ágreda y de Felipe IV* (*BAE*, 109, Madrid, 1958), p. 236.
[13] Berkeley, Bancroft Mss. MM. 1755, no. 15, fos. 184–5.
[14] Brown and Elliott, *A Palace*, p. 44.

11. Possibly Velázquez's first portrait of Philip IV, executed on his arrival at court in August 1623. The collar worn by Philip is the *golilla*, in conformity with the new austerity measures introduced by the Articles of Reformation earlier in the year.

during his nine months' visit to Madrid on a diplomatic mission in 1628–9, helped to complete his artistic education, and make him a great patron and collector.[15] From his early years Philip also delighted in music and the theatre. On occasion he would visit one or other of the two public theatres in Madrid, the Corral de la Cruz and the Corral del Príncipe,[16] and the *salón de comedias* in the palace of the Alcázar provided the setting for an increasingly important court theatre, which helped to stimulate the new vogue for elaborate 'machine plays' with spectacular scenic effects.[17]

Olivares did everything he could to encourage these tastes, partly to give pleasure to Philip, and partly because they so perfectly suited his plans to endow Spain with a brilliant cultural life revolving round the court. He himself was cast in the great tradition of aristocratic patronage, and when the artists in Madrid attempted in 1624 to set up an Academy he was happy to accept the role of patron and protector. Like so many other projects of the Olivares era, the plans for an Academy came to nothing, probably because of internal disputes among the community of painters.[18] But Olivares himself took naturally to the part of a new Maecenas as described by his admirer Juan Pablo Mártir Rizo—'father of good letters, protector of the muses, defender of philosophy, for which his name will be immortalized in times to come.' He would become the minister, as Mártir Rizo expressed it, 'if not of the Emperor Augustus, of a more august emperor, to whom peace owes greater successes, and war more glorious triumphs.'[19] The reign of Philip IV, then, was to be a new Augustan age, and, between them, king and minister were equipped to make it so. The times, too, were propitious, thanks to the galaxy of literary and artistic talent in Castile and Andalusia. Here at least there was no sign of the creeping decay that appeared to be affecting the other parts of the body politic and social—a fact duly celebrated by the royal chronicler Tomás Tamayo de Vargas, when he explained in 1629 that although Spain, 'as if prevented by the exercise of arms', had come late to letters, 'it has made such progress in them in so

---

[15] For Philip as patron and collector see especially Jonathan Brown, *Velázquez, Painter and Courtier* (New Haven and London, 1986).

[16] For the latter, see John J. Allen, *The Reconstruction of a Spanish Golden Age Playhouse. El Corral del Príncipe, 1583–1744* (Gainesville, 1983).

[17] For court theatre under Philip IV, see especially chs. 10 and 11 of N. D. Shergold, *A History of the Spanish Stage from Medieval Times until the end of the seventeenth century* (Oxford, 1967).

[18] *Actas*, 41, pp. 124–5 for the Cortes' discussion of the artists' petition. For other texts relating to the proposed academy, see Francisco Calvo Serraller, *Teoría de la pintura del siglo de oro* (Madrid, 1981), pp. 157–77. I am grateful to Professor Jonathan Brown for bringing these passages to my notice.

[19] *Historia de la vida de Mecenas*, fo. 80 and dedication.

little time that they may even be thought to have taken the lead; and it is now inferior to no nation in one or the other.'[20]

Since most contemporary poets, playwrights and men of letters lived precariously on the borderline between survival and starvation, there was no lack of candidates for court patronage. Góngora, Lope de Vega, Quevedo, and a host of lesser talents, hurried to pay obeisance to the new king and his minister. Some, indeed, sensing the way the winds were blowing at court in the final years of Philip III, may already have made the necessary adjustments before the change of regime. The poet and playwright Antonio Hurtado de Mendoza, a protégé of Lerma's son, the Count of Saldaña, seems to have eased himself into Don Gaspar's graces in time to share in the glories of 1621. Within two months of the new king's accession he was given his first court post, as an official of the wardrobe. In August 1621 he was promoted to the coveted position of *ayuda de cámara* to the king—an office which allowed him to act as Olivares' eyes and ears in the royal chamber—and was appointed a royal secretary in 1624. Mendoza was to be seen at every court function in the Olivares years. The combination of literary facility and personal subservience made him indispensable to a minister who appreciated both characteristics and knew exactly how to put them to use.[21]

Don Gaspar, making the most of his new eminence, dispensed and withheld his patronage as the fancy took him. He no doubt derived a special satisfaction from righting the injustices inflicted by the Lerma regime. In particular he took steps to rehabilitate Spain's greatest historian, the octogenarian Juan de Mariana, who had suffered persecution at the hands of Lerma's ministers for his outspoken views on a number of sensitive subjects, including the consequences of flooding Castile with *vellón*.[22] In August 1622 it was agreed to award him a thousand ducats to print a new edition of his *History of Spain*, and Philip invited him to continue the work down to his own reign in the post of royal chronicler.[23] Mariana's rehabilitation reflected Olivares' conviction of the importance of history and his reverence for the past—a reverence which would later make him take in hand the preservation of Charles V's crumbling palace at Yuste, as a fitting memento to a glorious monarch.[24] It may also have reflected some personal indebtedness to Mariana's writings. It was natural that a man concerned with the political education of

[20] *Actas*, 48, p. 223.
[21] See Gareth A. Davies, *A Poet at Court: Antonio Hurtado de Mendoza, 1586–1644* (Oxford, 1971).
[22] Georges Cirot, *Mariana, historien* (Paris, 1905), pp. 96–101.
[23] AHN Consejos leg. 4422, no. 184, consulta de cámara, 29 August 1622; Cirot, pp. 121–2.
[24] AGS Cámara de Castilla, leg. 1247, petition of 5 July 1638.

his king should turn for advice to that great manual for the instruction of princes, Mariana's *De Rege*, and the similarity between some of Olivares' reform projects and those discussed by Mariana suggests some direct influence of the historian on the statesman.[25]

As writers fell over themselves to pen suitably fulsome epistles of dedication to the new favourite, they must have wondered how to hit the right note in addressing themselves to a man of such capricious tastes. He seems, for instance, to have appreciated the stylistic conceits of Góngora, a fellow-Andalusian, although the great poet appears to have felt in the end that he did not get his deserts.[26] While Lope de Vega remained a favourite court playwright, his assiduous dedication of his works to the Count and Countess of Olivares apparently failed to win their personal patronage.[27] Tirso de Molina quickly fell foul of the new regime, in part perhaps because of bitter disputes within the Mercedarian Order which pitted him against a relative of Olivares, Fray Pedro de Guzmán.[28] On the other hand, offices, honours and commissions were showered on Luis Vélez de Guevara, the Andalusian playwright, famed for his 'machine plays'.[29] It clearly paid to be an Andalusian, and in transferring to Madrid the taste for spectacle of Sevillian theatre, Vélez had hit on the perfect formula for an exacting patron.

For all the private disappointments of individual writers, the Olivares regime enjoyed wide support among Spain's men of letters, at least in its early years. Disillusionment came later.[30] They naturally welcomed the flattering attention paid to them by the men of the new regime, and were happy to sing the praises of king and minister. Olivares in turn welcomed the outpouring of plays, poems and treatises that greeted the dawn of a new age. The very concentration of *ingenios* at the court shed lustre on the king, and would ensure his lasting glory. He was well aware, too, of the more immediate benefits which their presence would bring. While he would continue to lament the weakness of history-writing in Spain, as 'one of the many subjects of neglect among us',[31] he was quick to realize that the talented authors, playwrights and artists who clustered around the fringes of the court could do much to present the world with a favourable image of the king and vindicate the record of his minis-

[25] See especially *MC*, 2, pp. 145–6.

[26] Marañón, *Olivares*, pp. 152–3; Jammes, *Don Luis de Góngora*, p. 337.

[27] Hugo Albert Rennert, *The Life of Lope de Vega, 1562–1635* (Glasgow, 1904), pp. 314–15.

[28] Fr. Gabriel Téllez, *Historia General de la Orden de Nuestra Señora de las Mercedes*, ed. Fray Manuel Penedo Rey, 2 vols. (Madrid, 1973–4), 1, pp. lxxvii and cxxviii–cxlv.

[29] See Ruth Lee Kennedy, *Studies in Tirso, 1: The Dramatist and his Competitors, 1620–26* (Chapel Hill, 1974), pp. 222–3.

[30] Charles Vincent Aubrun, *La Comédie Espagnole, 1600–1680* (Paris, 1966), p. 48.

[31] AGS Est. leg. 2335, consulta of Council of State, 27 October 1634.

ters. Living in hope and expectation of reward, they were all too ready to oblige.

Although undercurrents of dissent ran through many of the works published in Spain's Golden Age, the general tenor of court poetry and court theatre was well calculated to reinforce the exalted image of kingship that Olivares was so anxious to purvey.[32] Time and again the king was presented on the stage as a God on earth whose very presence was sufficient to restore light and harmony to a world of darkness and confusion. It is hardly surprising that the young Philip, after being nurtured on this theatrical fare, had one day to be rebuked by the President of the Council of Castile, Don Fernando de Acevedo, when he attempted to dispose arbitrarily of a court post. 'No, sire,' Acevedo reports himself as saying, 'Your Majesty is not able to do absolutely everything you want in your kingdom. You would do well to remember that you can alienate nothing in it—not even this post, however insignificant, because it has been agreed by compact with the realm.' The king responded with a blush to this unwelcome lesson in constitutionalism.[33]

Such frankness, inevitably, was the exception, although Olivares' rebuke to the king for his idleness in 1626 shows that he, too, was capable of it when the occasion required. But extravagant flattery was the order of the day, as paeans of praise were showered on king and minister. In time its effect would be to isolate the court by encouraging its natural tendency to confuse rhetoric with reality. But in the early years of the reign it served its purpose well. Stage presentations conveyed a suitably confident impression of Spanish power, as in Lope de Vega's play of 1622, *La nueva victoria de Don Gonzalo de Córdoba*, written to celebrate the somewhat ambiguous victory over Mansfeld's Protestant forces at Fleurus; and in turn the victories of Spanish arms were used to enhance the glory of the king. 'Felipe', wrote Lope in *La nueva victoria*, 'is coming out like the sun, chasing these dark clouds away.'[34] This image of Philip as the sun was quickly taken up by the court poets and playwrights, and was to provide a central theme for the reign. The sun as the fourth planet seemed a particularly appropriate emblem for the fourth King Philip, and the conceit of the *rey planeta*—the planet king—may already have been hit upon by 1623.[35] It was as the Planet King that Philip was

---

[32] See José Antonio Maravall, *Teatro y literatura en la sociedad barroca* (Madrid, 1972), ch. 11, and José María Díez Borque, *Sociología de la comedia española del siglo XVII* (Madrid, 1976), part 2, ch. 1.

[33] Escagedo Salmón, 'Los Acebedos', *Boletín de la Biblioteca Menéndez y Pelayo*, 9, p. 150.

[34] *Obras de Lope de Vega (BAE*, 233), p. 337.

[35] 'El planeta real' appears in Tirso de Molina's *Tanto es lo de más como lo de menos*, but there is some disagreement about the dating of this play. See J. C. J. Metford, 'Tirso de Molina and the Conde-Duque de Olivares', *Bulletin of Hispanic Studies*, 36 (1959), pp. 15–27.

to appear before the world and before posterity—the central figure in a dazzling court, dispensing light and favour. *Illuminat et fovet*—'he shines and warms'—Philip's motto ran.[36] Olivares in turn chose as his own device the sunflower, inclining towards the sun.[37]

Like a skilled stage manager, Don Gaspar orchestrated to brilliant effect the court of the Planet King. Pageants, plays and literary disputations, tournaments and equestrian sports, all helped to create the sense of a revitalized monarchy. Philip himself, warming to his part, held the stage with ease. But if the world of the theatre and the theatre of the world were always liable to change places in seventeenth-century Europe, Olivares had something more in mind than a simple stage performance for an actor-king. There were other and less congenial duties that could not be escaped, and the young monarch still had to complete his education in the art of government.

Instruction in government

Philip himself describes how, 'in order to learn my office of king', he began by listening to the deliberations of the councils through the little windows that had been cut in the walls, and then graduated to appearing, and speaking, at council meetings. He also tried his hand at writing state papers 'on matters of importance', and finally, six years after his accession, took to reading by himself, and without a secretary, all *consultas* that came to him on matters of government and appointment to offices.[38] This was rather a bland retrospective description of what in fact had proved a difficult and painful process. As Olivares' rebuke to the king in 1626 made clear, there were times when he despaired of ever getting Philip to settle down systematically to his papers, and a year later he was still complaining that 'the king is young and little inclined to paper-work.'[39] But a serious illness during the autumn of 1627 helped to shake Philip out of his lethargy, and he began to put in long hours at his desk.

It might be thought that, in attempting to transform Philip IV into a new Philip II, Olivares was working himself out of a job. There were times, as the cares of office closed in upon him, when he could have wished for nothing better. Expressions of his profound wish to retire, and actual requests for leave to do so, punctuated Olivares' political career.[40] While these are not necessarily to be taken

---

[36] Juan de Caramuel y Lobkowitz, *Declaración mystica de las armas de España invictamente belicosas* (Brussels, 1636), p. 58.

[37] Brown and Elliott, *A Palace*, p. 200.

[38] 'Autosemblanza de Felipe IV', *BAE*, 109, p. 233.

[39] BL Add. Ms. 14,006, fo. 40, Olivares to Infanta Isabel, 12 October 1627.

[40] Eg. *MC*, 1, pp. 156–7.(*Memorial genealógico*, 26 July 1625); and see Marañón, *Olivares*, p. 75.

at face value—they were, after all, a useful device for eliciting from the king a statement of continuing confidence in his favourite—there was something perversely satisfying about being able to say, as he said in 1629, that he no longer seemed to be needed, because the king had taken such effective control of business.[41] Retirement now would set the seal on his labours, for it would mean that he had succeeded in realizing his aim of creating a king who could govern by himself. At the same time, he knew Philip well enough to appreciate that this was never likely to happen. The king's persistent doubts about his own abilities, his need for someone to whom he could turn for advice and reassurance, and the sheer quantity of paper-work involved in the government of the Spanish Monarchy, made it improbable that he could dispense with the services of an intimate counsellor. As the king learnt how to govern, the most that could be hoped was that the intimate counsellor should lose the characteristics of a favourite, thus relieving Olivares of a cause for continuing embarrassment, and be seen as exercising no more than the proper duties of a principal minister.

In order to prepare Philip for that happy day when he would be ready to exercise the full duties of kingship, it was necessary to provide him with some essential information about his realms, and offer him a programme for the reign. The realms themselves were numerous. Among his titles, Philip was King of Castile, León, Aragon, the 'two Sicilies', Portugal, Navarre, Granada, Valencia, Majorca, Sardinia, the Canary Islands, 'the East and West Indies and Tierra Firme of the Ocean Sea'; Duke of Brabant and Milan; Count of Flanders and Barcelona; and *señor* of Vizcaya. These various kingdoms and territories had their own traditions, their own individual institutions, and their own unique problems. Any general set of instructions governing the Monarchy as a whole was therefore almost impossible to produce. But Olivares seems to have decided that the king should be given guidance on at least some of the major realms, beginning with those of the Iberian peninsula. It was with this object in mind that he drafted the most celebrated of all his state papers, the secret instruction, or Great Memorial, dated 25 December 1634.[42] There are some indications that this was to have been followed by a separate document on the Indies, but either this has disappeared or it was never written.[43]

The Great Memorial is, first and foremost, a document designed

[41] AGS Est. leg. 2713, Olivares to Monterrey, 17 August 1629.

[42] *MC*, 1, Doc. IV. See the editors' introduction to this document, which we have entitled the *Gran Memorial*, for variations in the text, and for general considerations on authorship and contents.

[43] *Ibid.*, p. 100.

for the education of the king. It was intended for his eyes alone, and large parts of it were purely descriptive and informative. These parts could easily have been prepared by a secretary, or perhaps by Francisco de Rioja, working to Olivares' orders. But other parts are didactic, or put forward plans for action. These sections bear more directly the stamp of Olivares' inspiration, and offer the best surviving clue to his ideas and intentions in the first years of his ministry.

For all the diversity of its contents, the Great Memorial reflects a consistent underlying philosophy. The starting-point of Olivares' analysis was that 'the present state of these kingdoms is, for our sins, quite possibly the worst that has ever been known.'[44] Considering his awareness of the anarchy and disorders of the fifteenth century—an awareness that lies behind much of his discussion of the dangers represented by the high nobility—it is hard to know how seriously he takes his own diagnosis. The vision of Castilian history which appears in Lope de Vega's plays, and was no doubt shared by Lope's contemporaries, was of three distinctive epochs—a heroic early medieval period, when Castile brought to the summit of perfection the austere military virtues that made the country what it was; a period of disorder in the fourteenth and fifteenth centuries, when a turbulent nobility reduced the state to anarchy by challenging the power of the crown; and the period distinguished by the recovery of royal power and the restoration of good government, begun by the Catholic Kings and culminating in the reign of Philip II.[45] Olivares, inspired by this same view of Castile's past, conveys the impression that under Philip III the gains of the preceding century of strong government had been thrown away, and that the Castile inherited by Philip IV was in process of reversion to the unbalanced, disordered and fundamentally unjust society of the years immediately preceding the advent of Ferdinand and Isabella.

The need of the moment was to 'resuscitate Your Majesty's Monarchy',[46] at a time when it was being subverted by its own inner weaknesses and threatened by the military and economic power of its enemies. This process of resuscitation demanded, as he saw it, a combination of political management with administrative, constitutional and economic reform. At least part of the economic reform programme was under way by the end of 1624: as he pointed out in the document, trading companies were being planned, and legislative measures had been taken to deal with the problem of depopulation. Other projects still remained to be discussed or implemented,

---

[44] *Ibid.*, p. 52.
[45] For Lope's sense of the past, see Renato I. Rosaldo Jr., 'Lope as a poet of history: history and ritual in *El testimonio vengado*', *Estudios de Hispanófila* (1978), pp. 9–32.
[46] *MC*, 1, p. 98.

like the settlement in Castile of colonies of foreign immigrants, but he could reasonably claim that his government had given momentum to the economic policies which it considered necessary for the salvation of Castile.[47]

Much of the document, however, was occupied with problems of government, justice and administration, for it was on better government that everything turned. Better government meant, for Olivares, stronger kingship, and the true key to the salvation of Spain was to be found in the restoration and assertion of royal power. Once this restoration had been achieved, the Spanish Monarchy could realize the high aims for which it existed—the 'spread of the Catholic religion' and the devotion of its energies to the 'extirpation of the Church's enemies.'[48]

Reforming statesmen of the early seventeenth century had a natural tendency to see in the exaltation of kingship the best solution to the problems of their times. Only firm royal government could provide 'justice', 'discipline', and 'economy'—those watchwords of a generation profoundly impressed with the example of Imperial Rome through its reading of Tacitus and Justus Lipsius[49]—which seemed to offer the best, and indeed the only, hope of maintaining some degree of control over men who suffered from the defect of original sin, and over a world in a state of constant flux. The corollary to a pessimistic vision of the world and of man was therefore an authoritarian conception of the state. The iron fist—cloaked whenever expedient in the velvet glove—was the proper response to the forces of disorder. Yet at the same time there existed among these seventeenth-century statesmen a confidence in the advantages to be derived from the expansion and deployment of state power, which belied the pessimism of their vision. The contradiction between their dark assessment of the problems they faced and their luminous belief in the capacity of the state to master them by a supreme assertion of authority, was to set up profound, if creative, tensions in the Europe of the 1620's and the 1630's.

The word 'state' figured less prominently in the vocabulary of Olivares than in that of Cardinal Richelieu, whom Louis XIII recalled to his government in this same year, 1624. Although Don Gaspar spoke of 'reason of state' or 'matters of state', he does not seem to have thought in terms of 'the state' as an abstract entity. Instead, he saw the king as the embodiment of public power, and would

---

[47] *Ibid.*, p. 60.
[48] *Ibid.*, p. 99.
[49] Cf. Pierre Roose writing to Olivares on 15 December 1632 about the importance of restoring in Flanders 'la justicia distributiva', which 'gave the Romans discipline and economy, and through them universal empire.' (AGR CPE, Reg. 1502. fo. 9).

use some such phrase as 'the royal authority' where Richelieu spoke of the 'state'.[50] This may in part have reflected the traditionalism of Castilian political thinking, at a time when the idea of the sovereign state as a form of public power distinct from both the ruler and the ruled was gaining ground in Europe.[51] Although Bodin had been translated into Spanish in 1590,[52] the organic conception of the relationship of king and kingdom continued to dominate the Castilian political mentality, as testified by Olivares' speech to the Cortes in 1623, in which he observed that 'there is no kingdom without a king, nor king without a kingdom'.[53] But it may not only have been traditionalism that militated against the adoption by Olivares of the concept of the state. The word itself seemed peculiarly inapplicable to the Spanish Monarchy, composed as it was of such a multitude of territories. Where and what was the 'state' in this curious medley of kingdoms, each with its own institutions and laws?

Precisely because the king constituted the only unifying element in this worldwide Monarchy, apart from its common faith, it was natural that Olivares should constantly revert to his majesty and power. His examination of the ordering of Castilian society in the first part of the Great Memorial was written with an eye to what he called 'the conservation of the dignity and authority of Your Majesty,'[54] which he saw as essential to the general health of the body politic. His ideal, like that of Ferdinand and Isabella more than a hundred years before him, was one of a society in which the crown preserved a harmonious balance between the different social orders. Unfortunately, recent and not so recent developments had profoundly disturbed the equilibrium; and it was entirely in keeping with contemporary preconceptions that Olivares should see its restoration as a question of political management rather than social engineering.

The church, with its five archbishoprics and thirty dioceses,[55] was the first of the three orders of Castilian society, and the one which, in Olivares' opinion, had most overstepped the bounds. 'I am afraid that it is today the most powerful in wealth, revenues and possessions', and well on the way to becoming 'master of everything.'[56] Olivares' concern at the accumulation of land and riches in ecclesiasti-

[50] J. H. Elliott, *Richelieu and Olivares* (Cambridge, 1984), pp. 44–5.

[51] Cf. Quentin Skinner, *The Foundations of Modern Political Thought* (Cambridge, 1978), 2, p. 353 and William F. Church, *Richelieu and Reason of State* (Princeton, 1972), p. 350.

[52] By Gaspar de Anastro. See José Antonio Maravall, *La Philosophie Politique Espagnole au XVIIe siècle* (Paris, 1955), p. 157.

[53] *MC*, 1, p. 19.

[54] *Ibid.*, p. 53.

[55] Domínguez Ortiz, *La sociedad española*, 2, p. 17.

[56] *MC*, 1, pp. 50 and 51.

cal hands was shared by several of his contemporaries, both lay and clerical. Jerónimo de Ceballos in his *Arte Real*, which coincided on so many issues with the diagnoses and remedies put forward by Olivares, believed that the church in Castile, through its accumulation of lands in mortmain, had now become richer than the laity.[57] At almost the same moment as the drafting of the Great Memorial, the Cistercian Fray Angel Manrique, a professor of moral philosophy at Salamanca, produced a powerful treatise urging the Castilian clergy to come to the help of king and kingdom. At this time of critical shortage both of men and money, he advocated a reduction in the numbers of the clergy, and the release from mortmain of part of the church's property.[58]

Olivares made only a passing mention of the excessive number of ecclesiastics,[59] which so troubled Manrique and other contemporary critics of the church, but he gave his views on the matter in a *consulta* written thirteen years later. If those going into the church had a genuine vocation, there could never be too many of them; but if they were motivated simply by the desire to obtain privileges and tax-exemption, then indeed the number was excessive.[60] The proportion of religious and secular clergy relative to the lay population was certainly increasing during this period, although contemporaries had no exact figures to confirm their impression. But if the trend seemed to them disturbing, the proportion was probably still considerably smaller than they imagined it to be. In 1591, the nearest date for which reasonable statistics are available, it is estimated that Castile—with a population of some 6,500,000—had 33,087 secular clergy, 20,697 regular clergy, and 20,369 nuns, a grand total of 74,000 or 1.1%.[61] This seems to have been much the same proportion as in seventeenth-century France.[62]

What was to be done about the numbers and riches of the clergy? Olivares' response was notably cautious, and reflected his awareness of the complexity of a problem which had to be set into the wider

[57] Ceballos, Doc. XXIII. Annual ecclesiastical revenues in the seventeenth century have been estimated at around a sixth or a seventh of total national income. See Domínguez Ortiz, *La sociedad española*, 2, p. 131, who, however, admits the impossibility of making any precise estimate.

[58] *Socorro del clero al estado*. For Manrique and his discussion of the Spanish church see Quintín Aldea Vaquero, 'Iglesia y estado en la época barroca', *Historia de España Ramón Menéndez Pidal*, 25 (Madrid, 1982), ch. 4, pp. 561–9.

[59] *MC*, 1, p. 99.

[60] *MC*, 2, Doc. XIV, p. 157. Consulta of 1637.

[61] Felipe Ruiz Martín, 'Demografía eclesiástica de España', in Quintín Aldea, ed., *Diccionario de historia eclesiástica de España*, 1 (Madrid, 1972), p. 683. For all Spain, excluding Portugal, the figures are: secular clergy, 40,599; regular clergy, 25,445; nuns, 25,051. Total—91,085 (*ibid.*, p. 685).

[62] Roland Mousnier, *Les Institutions de la France sous la Monarchie Absolue*, 1 (Paris, 1974), p. 252.

context of Spain's relations with the papacy. The prickly character of Spain's dealings with Rome during Olivares' two decades of power is evidence that he saw himself as standing in the severe regalist tradition of Philip II, firmly rejecting any attempt at papal intervention in Spain's domestic affairs, while claiming privileged treatment for Spaniards as the 'firstborn' of the Church.[63] At the same time, he had to move with care, in the awareness that any conflict with the papacy would have grave international, as well as domestic, consequences for Spain. The whole question of clerical wealth and taxation, therefore, was one for complex negotiation with the papacy, through the papal nuncio in Madrid and the Spanish ambassador in Rome.

While determined to prevent the church from trespassing beyond the boundaries of its own domain, Olivares had no compunction about using clerics where they could serve the purposes of the crown. Their independence made them useful as *visitadores* for conducting judicial inquiries, and they had proved their value as presidents of the chancelleries and of some of the councils, especially the Council of Castile. Although Olivares did not think that ecclesiastics should necessarily preside over the Council of Castile,[64] all the presidents appointed during his ministry after the retirement of Contreras in 1627 were in fact bishops.[65] He was looking, he said, for men of 'virtue, integrity and independence', although his difficult relations with Cardinal Trejo, President of the Council from 1627 to 1629, suggest that his enthusiasm for the last of these qualifications was at best qualified.

The counterpart of Olivares' willingness to appoint ecclesiastics to high secular positions was his determination to exclude the upper nobility. His treatment of the magnates in the Great Memorial shows him once again, as in his treatment of the church, to be firmly and consciously following the tradition of the Catholic Kings and Philip II. At the time he was writing, there were around 160 titled nobles in Castile—an increase of about forty since 1600. A list drawn up for the Council of Finance in 1627 broke down this titled nobility into twenty-five dukes (all of them grandees), seventy marquises (nine grandees) and seventy-three counts (seven grandees)—a grand total of 168, of whom a quarter (forty-one) were grandees.[66] The number of grandees in particular is impressive—twice what it had

---

[63] Olivares to papal nuncio, 8 December 1623, cited in Pedro de Leturia S. J., *Relaciones entre la Santa Sede e Hispanoamérica*, 1 (Analecta Gregoriana 101, Rome, 1959), p. 378.

[64] *MC*, 1, p. 51.

[65] See the list in *MC*, 2, p. 260 n. 34, where the date of the death of Miguel Santos de San Pedro appears by a misprint as 1638 instead of 1633.

[66] AGS CJH, leg. 632, Junta del donativo, 9 August 1627. For other contemporary listings see *MC*, 1, p. 56 n. 32.

been in the early sixteenth century—and indicates something of the problem that confronted Olivares as he contemplated the distribution of privilege and power in Castile.

'The nobility', according to Olivares, 'consists of the Infantes, grandees, *señores, caballeros* and *hidalgos.*'[67] One of the most striking features of this classification is the inclusion among the nobles of the Infantes Don Carlos and Don Fernando. In devoting a section to them under the general heading of the nobility, Olivares was conscious that he was dealing with a special problem. His preoccupation with the Infantes, which seems at moments during the next few years to border on obsession, is only comprehensible in the wider context of Castilian history. Philip IV still had no heir; and for the first time in the history of the Spanish Habsburgs there were young adult Infantes in Castile.[68]

The medieval examples of the part played by the Infantes in the political life of Castile, especially in times of uncertainty over the succession, were disturbing enough to suggest the need for special precautions. An opposition group of grandees clustering round an Infante who was heir presumptive to the throne, represented a threat, not only to the power of the favourite, but also to the stability of the throne itself. Only a few weeks before Olivares presented his Great Memorial, the papal nuncio reported that the Infantes were the first to resent his dominance over the king;[69] and Olivares, who had no doubt studied the character of the Infante Don Carlos as closely as he had studied that of his elder brother, had every reason to believe that the resentment of this docile prince was incited by men who were plotting his own downfall. His best hope was to win the confidence of the Infantes as he had succeeded in winning that of the king, and about this time he wrote a private memorandum for the tongue-tied Don Carlos, with encouraging advice on how to conduct himself in public audiences.[70]

But even if he did succeed in winning their confidence—and the spirited temperament of the Cardinal-Infante Don Fernando suggested that, with him at least, this might not be easy—he was determined not to run any risks with the Infantes. He advised the king to take the greatest care in selecting their servants, and to make sure that they were shut off from 'all communication with grandees and

[67] *MC*, 1, p. 52. For this classification, see Domínguez Ortiz, *La sociedad española*, 1, pp. 190–1.

[68] The one partial exception to this is Ferdinand, the younger brother of Charles V, who was hurried out of the country within a few months of Charles' arrival in 1517. 'Infante' was used only of the younger brothers or younger sons of a monarch. The eldest son and heir to the throne was styled the Prince of Asturias.

[69] ASV, Spagna 65, fo. 74, nuncio's despatch, 30 October 1624.

[70] Marañón, *Olivares*, Appendix XXI.

important ministers, other than those who have Your Majesty's confidence and favour.' When the time came, they should be settled through marriage in some kingdom or province outside the Spanish Monarchy; and in the meantime Philip should welcome them with open arms, but with bridle in hand.[71]

Within a few months of writing these words, Olivares rather incongruously incorporated a paragraph into a memorandum on reform of the Council of Finance which addressed itself to what he called 'the great and arduous business of what is to be done with the Infantes Don Carlos and Don Fernando.' They should not, he wrote, be maintained in such subjection that the maliciously inclined could assert that they were being kept in 'a kind of prison' (which is what the maliciously inclined were indeed asserting).[72] In October 1625, when Don Carlos was eighteen and the Cardinal-Infante sixteen, he followed up this warning with a paper listing possible brides for Don Carlos, and suggesting more or less implausible destinations and occupations for the two young men. Don Carlos, for instance, might be appointed to the viceroyalty of Sicily, or lead a campaign against the Turks, while the Cardinal-Infante could be sent to Oran.[73] A year later a special junta of senior ministers, including Olivares, was still brooding on the question, and, after much cogitation, came up with tentative solutions which would be formally adopted some years later—Portugal for Don Carlos, and Flanders for his younger brother.[74] But by then fate, too, was ready to take a hand.

The troubles of Louis XIII with his younger brother, Gaston d'Orléans, suggest that Olivares' anxieties over the careers of the Infantes were not entirely wide of the mark. But Charles V and Philip II had tamed their aristocracies much more effectively than the sixteenth-century Valois; and—at least in retrospect—the House of Austria had less to fear from its high nobility. The danger in Spain, as Olivares seems instinctively to have realized, was less of aristocratic uprising than of oligarchical control; and he saw himself as the staunch upholder of royal authority against the encroaching power of the magnates, who had profited from the complicity and weakness of the Duke of Lerma to press too close around the throne. Here again he placed himself in the tradition of Ferdinand the Catholic and Philip II, who kept the grandees out of major judicial, financial and court offices, while simultaneously favouring and 'keeping them under' by sending them on expensive missions abroad.[75] With the utmost

---

[71] MC, 1, p. 53.
[72] Ibid., p. 130 (4 June 1625).
[73] Ibid., Doc. VIII (Papel del Conde Duque . . . sobre el estado de los señores infantes).
[74] Ibid., p. 163.
[75] Ibid., p. 55.

secrecy Philip should make sure that the grandees were never allowed to become too rich.

The techniques recommended by Don Gaspar for controlling the aristocracy were modelled on the sixteenth-century Habsburg practice of dividing in order to rule. 'Emulation' should be encouraged between the nobility and the other social orders in Castile, and also between the different ranks of the nobility—for example, between the grandees and the titled nobility, whose collective power was greater than that of the grandees, although individually they counted for less. This was the class on which Philip II had drawn for his household and conciliar appointments, as being less dangerous than the grandees. By the same token, the king should give special encouragement to the lowest ranks of the nobility, the *caballeros* and *hidalgos*, and tempt them, with the prospect of rewards and promotion, into military and naval service, as the 'sole means of restoring the reputation of Spanish arms on sea and land.'[76]

Implicit in all these comments on the higher and lower nobility is Olivares' belief—developed with increasing urgency as the years went by—in the need to create a genuine service nobility in Spain. He was persuaded that the nobles and *hidalgos* of Castile had lost their sense of vocation, and become idle and effete. How was this sense of vocation to be restored? Even if he did not approach the question directly in the Great Memorial, he was already devoting attention to the manners, morals and education of the young. In January 1624 the Junta de Reformación was revived,[77] and, after studying the documents produced for it in the first months of the reign, decided to make sexual immorality its first priority. It also devoted its attention to the theatre, and on 6 March 1625, after consultation with Olivares, proposed a ban on the printing of 'plays, novels and other works of this kind, because of their unfortunate effect on the manners of the young.' The first and most spectacular casualty of this new wave of puritanism was Tirso de Molina, who was banished from Madrid to one of the distant houses of his Order for his 'profane comedies' which set such 'bad examples.'[78] For the next ten years—until 1635—the Council of Castile refused to grant licenses for the publication of such corrupting works, and if they appeared at all,

---

[76] *Ibid.*, p. 59.

[77] González Palencia, 'Quevedo, Tirso y las comedias', p. 44.

[78] *Ibid.*, p. 83; Téllez, *Historia General*, introduction, pp. cxlii–cxlv; Kennedy, *Studies in Tirso*, pp. 351–5. It remains unclear whether Tirso's exemplary punishment is to be explained in terms of personal vendettas, literary vendettas, or the hostility of Olivares, on the grounds of subversive criticism in Tirso's recent plays. Tirso's many enemies obviously saw in the Junta de Reformación a useful agency for silencing him and getting him away from the court.

it was under a clandestine imprint, or else in the Crown of Aragon, which fell outside the council's jurisdiction.[79]

The sons of the Spanish nobility, however, were not only to be shielded from the bad; they were also to be encouraged to pursue the good. In December 1623 the king and Olivares wrote to the General of the Jesuits in Rome announcing their intention to establish *Estudios Reales*—a royal college—at court, using for this purpose the Jesuit foundation of the Colegio Imperial of Madrid. The statutes for this new foundation were drawn up in January 1625, with a pre-amble in which the king observed that the felicity of a commonwealth depended largely on the way in which its young—and especially its noble young—were educated. There were to be twenty-three chairs, and the subjects for study in the upper college were to include the classical languages, history, natural philosophy, mathematics, the military arts, 'politics and economics, including those of Aristotle, adjusting reason of state to conscience, religion and the Catholic faith.'[80] Don Juan de Villela, President of the Council of the Indies, was to superintend the founding of the college, which was to remain, like its predecessor, under Jesuit direction.

The plans for the Estudios Reales of the Colegio Imperial came under immediate attack from the universities, which feared for their educational monopoly, and also from the various religious orders, which resented the growth of Jesuit influence at court. Olivares himself was awkwardly caught between his circle of Jesuit friends on one side—Hernando de Salazar, Juan Bautista Poza, and the court preacher Jerónimo de Florencia—and on the other the Dominican Order which claimed his first loyalty, because, as he once explained, the blood of its founder ran in his veins.[81] On this occasion, however, he stood firmly with the Jesuits, and, in spite of the carefully orches-trated assault, the Estudios Reales were formally opened with much pomp in February 1629. But they proved a sad disappointment. In 1634 the upper college had only sixty pupils, none of them of high social standing, and the Cámara de Castilla described the enterprise as a failure.[82] The universities and the aristocracy between them had contrived to sabotage the Colegio Imperial.

After examining the church and nobility, Olivares turned briefly to the people. They must be fed, and humoured, and kept firmly in their place; but at the same time 'it is always necessary to pay

---

[79] *Ibid.*, and Jaime Moll, 'Diez años sin licencias para imprimir comedias y novelas en los reinos de Castilla: 1625–1634', *Boletín de la Real Academia Española*, 54 (1974), pp. 97–103.

[80] Cited by José Simón-Díaz, *Historia del Colegio Imperial*, 1, p. 68, which is the standard history of the college.

[81] AGS Est. leg. 2332, consulta of Council of State, 25 September 1631.

[82] Domínguez Ortiz, *La sociedad española*, 2, Appendix XXVIII.

attention to the voice of the people.'[83] The principal danger was that members of the nobility might place themselves at the head of a popular cause. Olivares made an oblique reference, too, to his difficulties with the cities, where members of the patriciate had been claiming to speak for the people when they opposed the taxes voted by the Cortes. Riots and tumults should be harshly repressed, but if this failed, there was nothing for it but to 'lengthen the reins' in the knowledge that the general confusion and lack of leadership would sooner or later make exemplary punishment possible.

Jerónimo de Ceballos, in his *Arte Real*, had compared government to the mastering of an unbroken horse, which 'unless controlled with prudence and art' would throw anyone who attempted to mount it.[84] Olivares, the skilled rider, resorted instinctively to this same image. The government of Castile, like good horsemanship, was a matter of skill, cunning and control. Imbued with a deeply pessimistic sense of human nature—'our inclinations are evil and always lead us to choose the worst'[85]—he was not the man to spare either bridle or bit. Yet at the same time he was intensely proud of that very spirit which made Castile so hard to govern. Was not the '*brío* and the freedom of the most wretched peasant in Castile' without parallel in the other kingdoms of the Monarchy, and the reason for the superiority of Castilian infantry on the battlefield?[86]

But the people had to be properly governed, and, as he turned to administration and justice, Olivares lamented the prevailing abuses, especially in the government of the towns, where the city councillors 'do what they want, seizing the property of the poor, trampling on them and harassing them', while the *corregidores* stood by, unwilling or unable to act.[87] When had a municipal official, an *alcalde* or a *corregidor* last been executed for his crimes? Olivares was to be perennially concerned, although to no very visible effect, with the lack of qualified office-holders. He was always keeping an eye open for talent, and he regarded the office of *corregidor* as the 'first school of government' in Castile. But Castile's sixty-nine *corregimientos*[88] had lost their former prestige, and everyone now aspired to more important posts.[89]

---

[83] *MC*, 1, p. 62.
[84] Ceballos, fo. 96.
[85] *MC*, 1, p. 65.
[86] *Ibid.*, p. 91.
[87] *Ibid.*, p. 65.
[88] The figure tentatively given in Pelorson, *Les Letrados*, pp. 122–33 for the reign of Philip III. The immediate auxiliaries of the *corregidores* numbered some two hundred (p. 111). For a map of the *corregimientos* at the end of the sixteenth century, see Bennassar, *La España del siglo de oro*, p. 62.
[89] *MC*, 1, p. 64.

Between them, the royal councils and the high legal tribunals in the Crown of Castile had around 150 seats to be kept filled,[90] and Olivares was much exercised by the shortage of suitable candidates for the major judicial tribunals—the *audiencias* of Seville and Galicia, and the chancelleries of Valladolid and Granada. A prime reason for this shortage was the narrowness of the criteria for selection. The six Colegios Mayores in the major universities exercised a stranglehold over administrative and judicial appointments, and he wanted to see graduates of other colleges and universities considered for important posts, since 'these kingdoms have suffered seriously from the failure to make use of such people.'[91] There was also another and still more pernicious form of discrimination, and he expressed his horror at a system which excluded those of Jewish ancestry as far back as the fourth, fifth or even seventh generation.[92]

From the chancelleries, he turned to the councils, each of which he described, although omitting the Councils of State and War. Apparently he also drafted a separate accompanying document, unfortunately lost, giving his personal opinion of each of the fifty or more councillors.[93] Most of the councils had weaknesses, and especially the Council of Aragon, 'which is the one that most needs men of stature, and the one that today has fewest of them.'[94] At this point he was already touching on the question which was to occupy the last part of the Great Memorial—the government of the kingdoms and provinces of the Iberian peninsula other than Castile. Unlike the other councils, that of Aragon was presided over by a vice-chancellor, and Olivares doubted whether a native vice-chancellor was really equipped to tackle the problems of nepotism, corruption and partiality which made the Council of Aragon's jurisdiction notorious. To the indignation of the provinces concerned, he had in fact already made an attempt to appoint a Castilian vice-chancellor, although his candidates—first his cousin Pedro de Guzmán, and then Dr. Garci Pérez de Araziel of the Council of Castile—died before they could effectively take up their duties. Eventually, in 1628, he got his way by allowing the office of vice-chancellor to lapse, and creating a new office of president, which Castilians could occupy.[95]

He was equally prepared, or so he suggested in the Great Memorial, to have a native of the Crown of Aragon appointed to the presidency

---

[90] Kagan, *Students and Society*, p. 83. With the inclusion of the *audiencias* of the Indies, the number rises to around 225.
[91] *MC*, 1, p. 72.
[92] *Ibid.*, p. 73.
[93] *Ibid.*, p. 80.
[94] *Ibid.*, p. 81.
[95] See Elliott, *Catalans*, pp. 254–6. The first holder of the post was the Marquis of Montesclaros.

of the Council of Castile.[96] For him, the most satisfactory of the councils was the Council of Italy because it combined Italians and Spaniards; and it was this kind of combination which—by counteracting local and national influences—seemed to him to offer the best hope for the future of the Monarchy.

A programme for unity

The government of the non-Castilian kingdoms of Spain, and the relationship of those kingdoms to Castile, was for Olivares the most difficult and the most important of all the problems confronting Philip IV. In Castile, the authority of the crown might have diminished in recent years, but with wise policies it could be revived. But elsewhere in the peninsula—in the Crown of Aragon, Portugal and Vizcaya—its very foundations were weak. The laws, the privileges, the immunities, the parliamentary institutions all hampered the exercise of effective kingship, and this at a time when the Monarchy had never been more endangered by domestic weaknesses and foreign enmity.

For a statesman surveying the world from Madrid, diversity was bound to seem a profound source of weakness in an age which looked to a greater concentration of power as the most effective answer to economic depression and military attack. Olivares was highly critical of those who had preceded him in the government of Spain. They had, he said, turned a monarchy into an 'aristocracy', and—where the need was for unity—their methods of government had reduced everything to division.[97] By this he meant that Madrid's traditional distrust of the king's non-Castilian vassals, and its tendency to treat them as foreigners by excluding them from offices and honours, had deprived the crown of much of its potential authority. Nothing was more symptomatic of this divisive approach than the survival of customs barriers between the different kingdoms of the peninsula after their nominal union under the rule of a single king.[98] This was a point to which he returned more forcefully in his reform memorandum of 1637: 'only neglect of the rules of government could have maintained these customs posts, to the prejudice and total ruin of Spain'.[99] The *Nicandro*, the apologia for his career written after his fall in 1643, placed the blame for the Portuguese Revolution of 1640 squarely on the shoulders of Philip II, who had

[96] *MC*, 1, p. 81.
[97] *Ibid.*, p. 94.
[98] *Ibid.*, p. 96.
[99] *MC*, 2, p. 160.

failed to appoint Portuguese to Castilian offices and Castilians to Portuguese, and who could well have abolished the customs barriers between Portugal and Castile, for 'the preservation of this Monarchy was worth more than 200,000 ducats.'[100]

Division and separation must therefore be replaced by unity. This was to be an abiding theme of Olivares' political career, extending also to his foreign policy, where he was persistently striving to establish leagues of union. It was as if he could never get out of his mind the discussion in Botero's *Reason of State* on 'whether compact or dispersed states are more lasting.'[101] 'Now we should say that without doubt', wrote Botero,

> a great empire is more safe from enemy attacks and invasions because it is powerful and united, and unity confers strength and firmness; yet on the other hand it is more vulnerable to the internal causes of ruin, for greatness leads to self-confidence, confidence to negligence and negligence to contempt and loss of prestige and authority.

What, then, of the scattered empire? Botero considered this

> weaker than a compact one because the distance between the parts is always a source of weakness and if the different parts are so weak that none of them is able to stand alone against the attacks of a neighbouring power, or if they are so placed that one cannot come to the aid of another, then the empire will not last long. But if they are able to help each other and if each is large and vigorous so that it need not fear invasion, the empire may be accounted as strong as a compact one . . .,

and potentially even stronger.

Ironically, Botero turned for proof of the durability of the scattered empire to the Spanish Monarchy—that same Monarchy which Olivares saw as disunited, defenceless and close to ruin. But thirty-five years had elapsed between Botero's *Reason of State* and Olivares' Great Memorial, and the ties between the different parts of the Monarchy, which had seemed strong and resilient in 1589, looked to Olivares dangerously fragile. Was it the Monarchy that had changed in the intervening period, or the outside world, or both? There is no doubt that the weakness of the Castilian economy, the drain on Castilian manpower, and the decline of Castilian self-confidence had begun to produce important changes in the internal balance of the Monarchy. Castile still dominated the Monarchy, but where once it had dominated it from a position of strength, it was now beginning to do

[100] *Ibid.*, p. 252.
[101] Botero, Book 1, section 7 (trans. Waley, pp. 9–12).

so from one of weakness. Nor were the revenues from the Indies what they had been in the great silver age of Philip II, while the strain of raising additional sources of income had taken its toll both of Castile and of other parts of the Monarchy, especially the Italian viceroyalties. At the same time, the world too had changed. The rebellious provinces of the Netherlands had won effectual independence and had become an aggressive mercantile power that was draining Spain of its life-blood. France, if still suffering from religious disunity, was no longer being torn to pieces by civil war, and had shown extraordinary powers of recuperation. Peace, whether in the Netherlands or Germany, remained elusive, and the consequent commitment of Castile's already over-extended resources to massive military and naval expenditure suggested that there were only two means of ensuring survival in such troubled times—the promotion of economic growth, and the rationalization of the Monarchy's resources.

But how could the crown organize more effectively the resources of the Monarchy for the benefit of all, when there was no mutual confidence between its various parts? Its many kingdoms and provinces clung to their own laws and forms of government, resentful—and understandably so, in the opinion of Olivares—at their lack of access to a king who, as far as they were concerned, was a more or less permanent absentee. Why should natives of Portugal or Aragon not have the same chance of office and honour in the Monarchy as those born in Castile and Andalusia?[102] Why should they not see their monarch more frequently? Could he not, for instance, spend some time with his Portuguese subjects?[103] And how could they be expected to respond with loyalty and enthusiasm as long as confidence was withheld from them? The Portuguese, the Aragonese, the Catalans were not foreigners—they were hereditary vassals of the king, and deserved to be treated as such. As long as mistrust prevailed, it was impossible to comply with one of the essential rules of good government, that superior ministers should not be natives of the provinces which they administered. 'And when Your Majesty can place in these kingdoms [of Castile] ministers who are natives of those others, then you will certainly be able to introduce Spanish governors and ministers into foreign provinces. And then it will be possible to call this Monarchy fortunate, and Your Majesty a true monarch, because you will have the greatest united empire that has ever been seen.'[104]

The Monarchy, then, was to be welded into a whole, starting with the Iberian peninsula itself. Behind this vision of a united Spain lurked

[102] *MC*, 1, p. 93.
[103] *Ibid.*, p. 90.
[104] *Ibid.*, p. 95.

the shadowy image of *Hispania*—the Hispania of Rome and the Visi-goths. The jurist and councillor of Castile, Dr. Gregorio López Madera, who republished in 1625 his *Excelencias de la Monarquía de España* (1597), sought to show that as a consequence of the succession of the Kings of Castile and León to the Hispania of the Visigoths 'the kingdom of Spain is truly one, although because of the victories of its kings it is divided into many titles.'[105] He wrote in the tradition of the fifteenth-century humanists who had promoted the idea of a united peninsula and looked back to Hispania for their inspiration. But the dynastic union which had joined together the crowns of Castile and Aragon under Ferdinand and Isabella, and then, in 1580, the crowns of Castile and Portugal, had come to appear an inadequate and incomplete form of union to members of the Castilian ruling class. Ever since the union of the crowns there had been those who advocated the destruction of Aragonese laws and liberties and the reduction of the states of the Crown of Aragon to conformity with Castilian laws. Their voices were joined in the reign of Philip III by the voices of a growing chorus of Castilians who felt that the laws and liberties of the non-Castilian kingdoms of the peninsula stood in the way of an equitable sharing of the fiscal and military burden which now threatened to crush Castile beneath its intolerable weight.

The point was eloquently made in the great reform *consulta* of the Council of Castile in 1619, which insisted that it was not only Castile that found itself 'obligated and interested' in helping the king meet his costs, but also 'the other kingdoms and provinces of this Crown and Monarchy. It is only right that these, being less burdened and more populous, should offer themselves, and should even be asked to help, so that the whole weight and burden should not fall' on an enfeebled Castile.[106] As he studied the financial problems of the crown, Olivares could not fail to appreciate the urgency of this demand that he now heard rising all around him. Were not all the kingdoms of the Monarchy equally interested in the war in Flanders, asked the *procurador* for Valladolid in the Cortes of 1623? Should they not all share in the expenses of the war, and should not the Crown of Aragon pay for the defence of its own frontiers, instead of leaving the responsibility to Castile?[107]

[105] *Excelencias* (Madrid, 1625), fo. 86. See Straub, *Pax et Imperium*, pp. 96–7, for the suggestion that Olivares was attempting to renew the Visigothic monarchy of *Hispania*, following the old humanist ideal. Given his strong sense of history there may indeed be a gothicizing element in his schemes, but there is no evidence for this in his surviving papers, and the theme of *Hispania* does not seem to have been developed in the political imagery of the Olivares years.

[106] González Palencia, *Junta de Reformación*, p. 16.

[107] *Actas*, 39, pp. 389–92; and see Elliott, *Catalans*, pp. 189–92, for similar contemporary demands.

Financial pressures, then, and the problems of defence were pushing Madrid towards a reconsideration of the relationship between the constituent parts of the Monarchy even before Olivares settled down to write for the king, in the greatest secrecy, his ideas for the unification of Spain. If these ideas all have a recognizable ancestry, the way in which they were formulated and synthesized was very much his own, and reflected the time and thought he had given to a question which he had come to see as critical for the survival of the Spanish Monarchy. His approach to this delicate question in the Great Memorial suggests that he was attempting to weld together into a coherent political programme a set of differing and sometimes contradictory assumptions about the nature of Spain and the Monarchy.

The theory behind the Monarchy inherited and transmitted by Philip II was clear, and indeed found its expression in the conciliar system, as described by Olivares himself in the Great Memorial: 'Because in Your Majesty's person, although it is singular, there are diverse representations of royalty, thanks to the incorporation into this crown of different kingdoms retaining their individual and separate status, it is necessary to have in this court a council for each of them; and in this way Your Majesty is considered to be in each of his kingdoms.'[108] But the theory of the autonomy and parity of the different provinces and kingdoms had given way in practice to a system in which, if all were equal, Castile was considerably more equal than the others. This practical hegemony had not been reflected in any institutional changes, and the disparity between theory and practice proved a continuous cause of friction. The non-Castilian kingdoms of the peninsula and Monarchy resented Castilian predominance, and a treatment that relegated them to second-class status. Castile, for its part, was embittered by the sacrifices it was called upon to make, and resentful that the other kingdoms of the peninsula took shelter behind their laws and liberties whenever the king approached them for men and money for his wars.

Castile, then, demanded parity of sacrifice, while the non-Castilian kingdoms demanded parity of benefits. Olivares realized that a way must be found to strike a balance between these two demands; and to find it he may have turned back to sixteenth-century policy proposals that had never received the imprimatur of royal approval. Cardinal Granvelle, for one, seems to have conceived of the Spanish Monarchy as a genuinely international community, in which the natives of one kingdom would be appointed to high office in another. But while Philip II was prepared to accept, within limits, the conventional maxim of sixteenth-century statecraft that men served better

[108] *MC*, 1, p. 74.

outside their native provinces, he was never willing to elevate this to a theory of empire.[109] His viceroy of Sicily, Marc Antonio Colonna, also adopted an internationalist approach, and urged the sharing of resources between the different kingdoms, but again Philip was unwilling to raise the idea to the level of a general principle. 'Except in the most urgent cases', he wrote, 'it is not the custom to transfer the burdens of one kingdom to another.'[110]

Suggestions for a reorganization of the Monarchy on the basis of genuine reciprocity between the various kingdoms were thwarted under Philip II by the king's innate conservatism and his devotion to the principle that the dynasty had a duty to maintain each of its possessions as a distinctive entity governed in accordance with the laws and constitutions in force at the time of its acquisition. But there were also enormous practical difficulties in the way of any such reorganization. A general redistribution of burdens and benefits within the Monarchy would encounter on the one hand the intransigence of Castilians unwilling to abandon their primacy in appointments to office and their exclusive rights in the Indies, and on the other the intransigence of non-Castilians, determined not to surrender their treasured laws and liberties. Philip II was always too cautious a ruler to run the risk of stirring up passions without good cause.

For Olivares, however, disunity elevated to a principle was a luxury that the Monarchy could no longer afford. The different kingdoms and provinces could no longer be permitted to remain strangers to each other. Instead, they must be brought together in a genuine partnership. But how was he to achieve this integration of the different parts of the Monarchy, beginning with the Iberian peninsula itself? He knew that any attempt to introduce change would provoke resistance, for 'the strength of custom is so great in matters of government that it often impedes and wrecks the most sensible designs.' It was therefore necessary to proceed step by step, gradually 'breaking the ice, and letting it be known that it is Your Majesty's opinion that foreigners should be admitted into the honours, offices and dignities' of Castile. Then, by degrees, and after testing the reactions, it would also be possible to start introducing Castilians into posts in the other kingdoms.[111]

After this general explanation of his grand design, Olivares proceeded in the final section of the Great Memorial to recapitulate and elaborate upon it in a way that was to earn him much posthumous notoriety. 'The most important piece of business in your Monarchy', he wrote in a famous passage,

---

[109] Koenigsberger, 'The Statecraft of Philip II', pp. 7–8.
[110] Koenigsberger, *Government of Sicily*, pp. 56–7.
[111] *MC*, 1, p. 95.

is for Your Majesty to make yourself King of Spain. By this I mean, Sir, that Your Majesty should not be content with being King of Portugal, Aragon, and Valencia, and Count of Barcelona, but should work and secretly scheme to reduce these kingdoms of which Spain is composed to the style and laws of Castile, with no differentiation in the form of frontiers, customs posts, the power to convoke the Cortes of Castile, Aragon and Portugal wherever it seems desirable, and the unrestricted appointment of ministers of different nations both here and there.... And if Your Majesty achieves this, you will be the most powerful prince in the world.[112]

The most shocking part of this proposal to nineteenth and twentieth-century historians who did not belong to the Castilian centralist tradition was the scheme to reduce the non-Castilian regions of the peninsula to the 'style and laws of Castile'.[113] To them, this was the point in the Great Memorial at which Olivares finally revealed himself in the colours of a true Castilian. The imposition of Castile's legal and political system on the Crown of Aragon and Portugal was seen as the culmination of a long-standing plan by Castile's ruling class to make Spain and Castile synonymous.

This conspiratorial interpretation smacks more of nineteenth-century phobias than of seventeenth-century realities. For a seventeenth-century statesman the most powerful argument in favour of using Castile as the model for the rest of Spain was that the king's authority in Castile was infinitely greater than in the other kingdoms of the Iberian peninsula. Uniformity of law throughout the peninsula—a law which was that of Castile—would therefore guarantee an impressive extension of the power and authority of the crown. When Olivares went around repeating the aphorism 'Multa regna, sed una lex',[114] there is good reason to believe that this Andalusian was talking, not as a Castilian bent on 'Castilianizing' the peninsula, but as a minister who was determined to raise his king to new pinnacles of preeminence.

The greater the degree of homogeneity the less that preeminence would be frustrated by the anomaly of customary rights and constitutions inhibiting the effective workings of royal power. It was for this reason that Olivares preferred the first of the three possible methods that he advanced for securing a closer union of the kingdoms of the peninsula:

The first, Sir, and the most difficult to achieve, but the best, if it can be achieved, would be for Your Majesty to favour natives

[112] *Ibid.*, p. 96.
[113] See Elliott, *Catalans*, p. 200.
[114] Cited Elliott, *Catalans*, p. 199, from Vittorio Siri's *Mercurio* (2nd. ed., Casale, 1648), 2, p. 43.

of those kingdoms by introducing them into Castile, arranging marriages between them and Castilians, and so smoothing their way with favours that—with their admission into the offices and dignities of Castile—they forget their privileges in their enjoyment of those of Castile. In this way it would be possible to negotiate this most advantageous and necessary union.[115]

It was presumably in pursuance of this policy of intermarriage among the distinctive peninsular aristocracies that the Duke of Medina Sidonia's daughter was married to Portugal's leading magnate, the Duke of Braganza, in 1633.

The other two possible methods were more direct, and more brutal. One was for the king, with an army behind him, to negotiate a satisfactory settlement from a position of strength. The other, 'not so justified, but the most effective', would be for the king to visit a kingdom or province in person, and seize the pretext of some prearranged popular uprising to call on his army and 'settle and dispose the laws in conformity with those of Castile' under the guise of restoring order.

These coldly calculating proposals, intended solely for the eyes of the king, were hardly of a kind to endear the image of Olivares to the liberal conscience of later generations. His first method, which represented a gradualist approach, was in fact very close to the one advocated by Alamos de Barrientos in a treatise of 1598 for Philip III. Alamos, the heir to the tradition of the Prince of Eboli and Antonio Pérez, had made similar proposals for securing a gradual unification of the peninsula—intermarriage between the Castilian and non-Castilian aristocracies, the appointment of members of the non-Castilian nobility to posts outside their native territories, and royal visits to the various kingdoms. In this way, 'Castile would easily remain Castile, and Aragon and Portugal would become Castile.' And the ultimate objective was that 'all should be one, with one king of all and everything.'[116]

This objective was also Olivares' objective, and one which he now saw as so urgent that nothing could be allowed to stand in its way. The Hispania which he envisaged would no doubt have a strongly Castilian complexion. Convenience alone was enough to dictate this; and the preeminence of Castile within the peninsula was a matter of historical fact. Eleven years later he would write, in a moment of great pressure, of Castile becoming 'head of the world, as it is already head of Your Majesty's Monarchy',[117] and there were Casti-

---

[115] *MC*, 1, p. 97.

[116] Alamos de Barrientos, *L'Art de Gouverner*, ed. J. M. Guardia (Paris, 1867), p. 267.

[117] In his paper of 14 June 1635 on the war with France, cited Elliott, *Catalans*, p. 310.

lian jurists, like López Madera, who claimed that this headship enjoyed legal sanction, and that in the time of Alfonso VI the other realms of the peninsula had recognized the 'superiority' of the kings of Castile and León.[118] But if Olivares took this superiority for granted, he was not, as he later insisted, *nacional*.[119] His loyalties were not to a particular nation, but to the king, and for him the salvation of the Monarchy lay in rising above regional ties and affiliations, and putting the needs of the whole before those of any of its parts.

At the beginning of the century that strange Italian Dominican, Thomas Campanella, had written a treatise on the Spanish Monarchy, which contained some proposals strikingly similar to those of Olivares. It first appeared in print in a German translation in 1620, but there is no evidence that Olivares had any knowledge of the book. For Campanella, too, it was an 'undoubted truth, that every great empire, if it be united within itself, is so much the safer from the enemies' incursions, because it is not only great but universal also; whence chiefly is derived all its strength and power.' Considering the 'several sorts of people in Spain', Campanella urged its king to

labour especially that there may be all fair correspondence and friendship betwixt the Castilians, Arragonians and the Portuguese and let him confer equal office upon them in court, and let him bestow preferments upon the Portuguese in the Kingdom of Castile; and upon the Castilians in the Kingdom of Portugal; and let him, as it were, tie them one to the other by the common bond of marriages betwixt each other, and by the community of navigation... and let all these be brought to a familiarity one with another, notwithstanding they are so far distant in place from one another... And by little and little their old customs are also to be abolished; but not upon a sudden...[120]

Was the Spanish statesman as utopian a visionary as the Italian political theorist? The very failure of his plans for union would seem at first sight to suggest that they lay outside the realm of political possibility. Olivares' own reference to the 'strength of custom' shows that he was not unaware of the difficulties; but he seems to have persuaded himself that the prize justified the risks. What he had in mind was a supra-national Monarchy, its focal point of loyalty a

[118] *Excelencias*, fo. 85.
[119] BNM Ms. 1630, fo. 186v., Olivares to Marquis of Torrecuso, 4 January 1640. See below, p. 564.
[120] *A Discourse Touching the Spanish Monarchy* (Eng. trans., London, 1654), pp. 125–6; and see Elliott, *Catalans*, p. 198 n. 2. The German translation was followed in 1640 by editions in Latin, which gave the book its European fame. It did not appear in Spanish until 1982, under the title of *La Monarquía Hispánica*, trans. Primitivo Mariño (Madrid, 1982).

king who commanded the obedience of a cosmopolitan service nobility, and who governed a complex of kingdoms which recognized
their obligations to each other, and shared a common set of laws
and institutions. It was by any measure an ambitious ideal; and in
the conditions of the early seventeenth century its creation would
test the powers of adjustment of state and society to their very limits,
and quite possibly beyond.

Yet it was not necessarily an impossible way forward for the
Spanish Monarchy. As long as the nineteenth-century nation-state
appeared to be the logical culmination of centuries of European political development, all attempts to create supra-national political organizations were liable to be consigned by historians to the rubbish-heap
of the past. But a new age brings new perspectives; and a century
that has seen the leviathan of the nineteenth-century nation-state
weakened from within by local and regional loyalties and from without by the rise of international organizations, may well judge more
sympathetically than its nineteenth-century predecessor the attempts
of earlier generations to establish supra-national political structures.

In the wake of the suppression of the Bohemian rebellion, the
Austrian Habsburgs did indeed move to organize their own territories
in the way that Olivares had signalled for Spain, and gradually succeeded in creating an international service aristocracy with the court
in Vienna as the supreme focus of loyalty.[121] It was in good measure
the prestige gained from victory in their wars which enabled them
to reconstruct their Monarchy. The military defeats of Spain—
Olivares' inability to secure the clinching victory—deprived the
crown of that extra element of power and prestige which might have
made all the difference between success and failure in its attempts
to establish its system of government on new and firmer foundations.
As a result, it would be left to the new and victorious dynasty of
the Bourbons to take up the task again two generations later, and
to resume under more favourable conditions his projects for the unification of Spain.

At the time when Olivares drafted his Great Memorial, however,
the possibilities still seemed open, and there appeared—for all the
difficulties—to be some room left for manoeuvre. The Great Memorial was conceived as a new programme for a new reign, as a programme for restoration and revival. Towards the end of it, Olivares
himself recapitulated the major themes of this programme, and then,
some time between 1624 and 1629, produced an additional resumé
which at some stage became incorporated into the text of the original
Memorial.[122] Between them, these two summaries indicate, if in a

[121] See R. J. W. Evans, *The Making of the Habsburg Monarchy, 1550–1700* (Oxford, 1979).
[122] *MC.*, 1, p. 86–9.

rather disorganized manner, his own sense of priorities. The most important part of the entire programme was, as he made clear,[123] his plan for union. 'The remaining business in these kingdoms comes down to concern for justice and its good administration, preserving equity among Your Majesty's subjects, and keeping them dependent on you.' Then there was the question of ensuring regular assignations for the frontier garrisons and the fleets. As far as commercial revival was concerned he pithily summarized his scheme as one for 'controlling Spain's trade by means of companies and consulates, bending all our efforts to turning Spaniards into merchants.' Then, almost as an afterthought, he remembered the depopulation of Castile, and hastily recapitulated some of the standard remedies—the establishment in the peninsula of colonies of foreign workers, Italians, Flemings, or German Catholics; privileges for the married; a limitation (in so far as conscience would allow) on religious foundations and on the number of those entering the church.[124]

In his later recapitulation, he mentioned some of the same points, but added others to the list, addressing himself particularly to fiscal questions that had been ignored in the original Memorial. Once again, as at the very beginning of the reign, he insisted on the need to avoid the granting of *mercedes* from the patrimonial revenues, and on the importance of freeing those revenues from their burden of debt. He wanted to see order restored to the currency, with the *vellón* coinage reduced to its proper value. He also put forward in summary form his programme for taxation: the avoidance, wherever possible, of new taxes, the abolition of old ones, and—if abolition proved impossible—their replacement by a single tax, in order to remove the obstacles to trade.[125]

Like his plans for the reorganization of the Monarchy, these were ambitious proposals, which were bound to unsettle established interests and stir lively opposition. Already the failure to abolish the *millones* had shown how hard it was to introduce change from above in the Spain of the seventeenth century. Olivares was asking for radical changes, including the most difficult of all, a change of attitude. To turn 'Spaniards into merchants' was to challenge a prevailing set of values which not only had deep roots in the past, but had been reinforced by more recent developments like the gradual squeezing of the *conversos* to the margins of society, and the encouragement of a *rentier* mentality through ill-conceived fiscal policies. Moreover, Olivares was hoping to bring about these changes at a time when the Monarchy was deeply engaged in war, and when the most

---

[123] *Ibid.*, p. 98.
[124] *Ibid.*, p. 99.
[125] *Ibid.*, p. 88.

pressing of all ministerial preoccupations was to find new sources of income. Yet if war was an obstacle, it also constituted the principal impetus to reform. Unless resources were rationalized and Spain united there seemed little chance of defending the Monarchy successfully against its many enemies.

VI

'PHILIP THE GREAT'

The English dilemma

When Olivares appealed to his fellow-deputies in his stirring speech to the Cortes of Castile in September 1623 to emulate the Greeks and Romans by rallying to the salvation of the republic, he tried to persuade them that a vote to set the king's armies and fleets on firm financial foundations would bring both 'the glory of peace, and glory in war.'[1] Glory, in peace and war alike, was his ambition for his king. Philip was to be the greatest of all the kings of Spain—triumphant in war, magnanimous in victory, glorious in the peace and prosperity which he would bring to his peoples.

There were moments in the first years of his ministry when this high ambition looked to be almost within Olivares' grasp. Don Baltasar de Zúñiga had laid down the guidelines, and as a mere apprentice in the field of foreign policy he set himself to follow them as best he could. Under Zúñiga's skilled direction, the Council of State had committed itself to a policy which took as its first priority the recourse to war (if possible more on sea than on land) in order to induce the Dutch to agree to a peace that would be honourable to Spain. Once the Austrian Habsburgs had defeated their Bohemian rebels the other major priority was the restoration of a settled order in the Empire, and a solution to the problem of the Valtelline which would safeguard Spain's strategic interests without provoking a conflict with France.

None of these problems could be treated in isolation. A lasting settlement in Germany—one which recognized the rights both of the Emperor and the princes, including their religious rights—was the only solid guarantee for the long-term security of Flanders and Milan.[2] Similarly, the diplomatic isolation of the United Provinces was an important precondition for the success of Spanish arms, and as long as there was friction with France over the Valtelline, and with the Protestant princes in Germany, the Dutch would not be without friends in the world. Among these friends must be counted

[1] *MC*, 1, p. 22; and see above, p. 150.
[2] See Straub, *Pax et Imperium*, p. 178.

the English, if only because of common religious sympathies, and Madrid therefore placed a high value on the achievement of a close understanding between the Crowns of Spain and England. A special junta which had been set up to advise on the advantages and disadvantages of a marriage between Philip's sister, the Infanta María, and Charles, Prince of Wales, reported in December 1621 that an Anglo-Spanish alliance could indeed bring great temporal advantages to Spain 'because of this crown's need of the King of England; and with such an alliance a settlement would be reached in Germany, the Dutch and the French would be held in check, the safety of Flanders and the Indies would be assured, and with their fleet (the largest in Europe) acting in unison with ours we could clear the seas of corsairs.'[3]

The Count of Gondomar, Spain's ambassador in London since 1613, had worked hard and with considerable success to woo James I away from the Dutch-Palatine connection and draw him closer to the Habsburg camp.[4] In spite of the differences of religion, the prospect of an Anglo-Spanish marriage treaty had begun to be taken seriously in the last years of Philip III, although more seriously by James than by Philip, since it was assumed in Madrid that the pope would never grant a dispensation for the marriage on terms likely to prove acceptable to the English crown. Yet with each new round of negotiations the commitment of all three parties—Rome, Madrid and London—increased, and with it the dangers that would follow a breakdown.[5]

Inevitably, the expulsion of James' son-in-law Frederick from his Palatine territories added new complications to the inevitably tortuous negotiations between London and Madrid. As the result of Spínola's invasion of the Rhenish Palatinate in September 1620 the strategic Rhine valley had fallen under Spanish control; and in September 1622, Tilly, acting as general for Maximilian of Bavaria and the forces of the Catholic League, completed the conquest of Frederick's territories by occupying his capital of Heidelberg. There

[3] AHN Est. lib. 738, fo. 168v., consulta of 3 December 1621.

[4] For the shift in James I's foreign policy in these years, see pp. 88–9 of Simon Adams, 'Spain or the Netherlands? The Dilemmas of Early Stuart Foreign Policy', in *Before the English Civil War*, ed. Howard Tomlinson (New York, 1984), ch. 4.

[5] The most comprehensive treatment of the negotiations remains S. R. Gardiner, *Prince Charles and the Spanish Marriage*, 2 vols. (London, 1869), subsequently incorporated into his *History of England from the Accession of James I to the Outbreak of the Civil War, 1603–1642* (repr. New York, 1965). Gardiner also edited for the Camden Society (vol. 101, 1869), a contemporary account by Fray Francisco de Jesús, *Narrative of the Spanish Marriage Treaty*, which includes important documentary material. The Marqués de Alcedo, *Olivares et l'Alliance Anglaise* (Bayonne, 1905) adds little to Gardiner. See also D. H. Willson, *King James VI and I* (London, 1956), and Roger Lockyer, *Buckingham. The Life and Political Career of George Villiers, First Duke of Buckingham, 1592–1628* (London, 1981), which contains (ch. 5) an excellent account of the Prince of Wales' visit to Madrid in 1623 and its antecedents.

remained only the stronghold of Frankenthal, held by an English garrison. Frederick's position was hopeless, and in April 1623 the English troops marched out of Frankenthal after the signing of an agreement by which the town was placed in the hands of the Infanta Isabella for eighteen months, on the understanding that the English would be readmitted if Frederick and the Emperor had not by then been reconciled.[6] The agreement was a farce, and Madrid had no difficulty in finding pretexts for retaining Frankenthal once the eighteen months had elapsed.

Spain had an obvious strategic interest in the Rhenish Palatinate, since its possession would allow its soldiers to use the Rhineland corridor on their journey from Italy to Flanders. But an alternative route existed, whereby troops coming from the Tyrol could avoid the Rhine Palatinate and, crossing the Rhine at Breisach, could reach Spanish Luxemburg by way of the friendly duchy of Lorraine.[7] The existence of this alternative route made it possible for Madrid at least to contemplate the eventual restitution of his lands to a chastened Frederick if generally acceptable terms could be found. The price was well worth paying if it brought Spain the friendship of England, but a further and potentially fatal complication was introduced by the ambitions of Maximilian of Bavaria. Maximilian's demand that the Emperor should invest him with Frederick's electoral dignity and the Upper Palatinate not only threatened to keep the Empire in a state of continuing unrest, but also placed Madrid in an impossible position as it sought on the one hand to win the active friendship of James I, and on the other to avoid alienating Maximilian, whose long-term ambitions it profoundly mistrusted.[8] But already before the formal transfer of the Upper Palatinate and the electoral title to Maximilian in February 1623, it was obvious that the Emperor would succumb to Bavarian pressure, in spite of all Madrid's attempts to stiffen his resolution and prevent him from taking the fatal step.

If Olivares looked—and looked in vain—to the Emperor to leave him some room for manoeuvre in his negotiations with James I, James for his part looked to Spain as the best and only hope for the restoration of his wayward son-in-law. Although his ambassador in Madrid, the Earl of Bristol, was conducting continuous negotiations on the marriage alliance and on the Palatinate, there was a discrepancy between the optimism of his despatches and the seemingly endless delays in concluding an agreement. James therefore decided to send a special envoy to Madrid to assess the intentions

---

[6] Gardiner, *History of England*, 5, p. 74; Alcalá-Zamora, *España, Flandes*, p. 220; Egler, *Die Spanier*, pp. 66–9.

[7] See Parker, *Army of Flanders*, pp. 54–5.

[8] See Straub, *Pax et Imperium*, p. 179; Albrecht, *Die auswärtige Politik*, p. 93.

of the Spanish ministers.[9] He chose for this mission a man who had close connections not only with Spain but with Olivares himself, Endymion Porter, or Don Antonio Porter, as he was known to his Spanish friends. Porter was the grandson of Giles Porter, who had married Doña Juana de Figueroa y Montsalve while serving in the embassy in Madrid in the 1560's. The family kept up its Spanish connection, and in 1605 Endymion took service in the household of the Count of Olivares, whose son, Don Gaspar, was the same age as himself. There is no indication that he and the future Count-Duke ever became intimate friends, but Olivares, who later described Porter as 'a very good man, and one with a particularly strong sense of obligation', clearly valued him as a trustworthy contact at the British court.[10]

This was the man whom James sent to Madrid in November 1622. Porter also carried a secret order from the Prince of Wales and the Marquis of Buckingham to find out from Gondomar, now back in Madrid, what kind of reaction could be expected if the prince should come to Spain in person.[11] From the beginning the mission went badly. The Earl of Bristol resented Porter's interference, and he secured an interview with Olivares on his own initiative. This interview, which began warmly enough, turned sour when Porter asked Olivares to confirm an assurance which Bristol claimed to have received from Philip himself that Spanish troops would be used to restore the Elector Palatine. Olivares replied in high indignation at the outrageous suggestion that Spain would ever use its forces against those of the Emperor, and allegedly ended the interview with the words: 'As for the marriage, I know not what it means.'[12]

It was hardly surprising if Olivares lost his temper, for he found himself in an awkward position. While anxious to avoid provoking the English, he was equally anxious to do nothing which would weaken the Imperial and Catholic cause in Germany. Porter's blunt question about the Palatinate therefore touched him on an especially raw nerve, and all the more so since the king may have given Bristol some verbal commitment, although the ambassador subsequently failed to get it in the same form on paper.[13] Moreover the Infanta, who was not without spirit, had apparently told her brother that

[9] Lockyer, *Buckingham*, p. 129.

[10] AGS Est. leg. 2056, *consulta* of Council of State, 31 May 1641. Malvezzi, in his *Reinado de Felipe IV*, p. 93, describes Porter as 'an Englishman, a presumed Catholic, who had been a servant of the Conde-Duque'. Fray Francisco de Jesús in his *Narrative*, p. 44, says that 'he had served a few years previously in the chamber of the Conde de Olivares, in whose grace he was as advanced as he was in his zeal for the Catholic religion.' See also Gervas Huxley, *Endymion Porter* (London, 1959).

[11] Gardiner, *History*, 4, p. 370; Huxley, *Endymion Porter*, p. 66.

[12] Gardiner, 4, pp. 383–4.

[13] Lockyer, *Buckingham*, p. 131.

she had no intention of marrying a heretic. Consequently, Olivares was under heavy pressure to give nothing away, and was promptly instructed by the king to find some way of escape from the marriage.[14] His problem was to achieve this without driving England to war, and in this he was eventually to fail. His enemies would accuse him of disastrously mishandling the affair,[15] but it is not easy to see how—given the temperament of Buckingham and the intensity of anti-Spanish sentiment in England—he could have extricated himself with elegance. Several of his ministerial colleagues favoured continuing the negotiations, either because they were afraid of the consequences of breaking them off, or because they were counting on a marriage to bring major advantages to Spain. Some years later, Olivares claimed in a private letter that he alone, working single-handed, had undone the English match.[16] This may well be true; and if his colleagues did indeed drive him further in the direction of a marriage than he personally would have wished, they only succeeded in adding to his difficulties.

He first attempted to find a way out of the dilemma by proposing to the Council of State in early December that the Prince of Wales should marry not the Infanta but the eldest daughter of the Emperor, while the Elector Palatine's son should be given a Catholic education at the Imperial court.[17] This ingenious solution failed to find favour with the Council of State, which feared that it might lead to war with England. The charade therefore went on, until it turned into melodrama when the Prince of Wales and Buckingham arrived in Madrid on 17 March 1623, travelling under the improbable names of Tom and John Smith.

Gondomar, who learnt the news from the Earl of Bristol, hurried late at night to Olivares' apartments in the palace, and arrived looking so full of himself that Olivares, who enjoyed teasing him about his anglophilia, asked whether he had the King of England in Madrid. 'If not the king', Gondomar replied, 'at least I have the prince.' Olivares in turn hastened to the king's apartments and was up for much of the night making suitable arrangements for a hospitable reception (Pl. 12).[18]

The king and Olivares can be forgiven for assuming that the Prince of Wales would never have undertaken the hazardous journey to Spain unless he was seriously thinking of conversion to Catholicism. The Earl of Bristol himself was under the same impression.[19] It was,

[14] Gardiner, 4, pp. 387–91.
[15] Novoa, *Codoin* 61, p. 427.
[16] BL Add. Ms. 24,909, fo. 154, Olivares to Padre Diego de Quiroga, 30 January 1630.
[17] Gardiner, 4, p. 393; Francisco de Jesús, *Narrative*, pp. 48–50; Roca, *Fragmentos*, pp. 193–6.
[18] Roca, *Fragmentos*, pp. 197–8.
[19] Lockyer, *Buckingham*, p. 143.

after all, not usual for the heir to a European throne to risk life and reputation by travelling in disguise across the continent in the off-chance of picking up a wife. His intentions must surely be serious; and since differences in religion constituted the principal stumbling-block to the conclusion of the marriage, it was natural to assume that the prince had suddenly seen the light. The Spanish court was no doubt encouraged in this belief by the tenor of the despatches that Gondomar had sent from London over the course of the years. Although he had frankly, and correctly, reported that, if Madrid insisted on full freedom of worship for English Catholics, there was no chance of concluding the match, he had also reported that James I would do everything in his power to ease their situation, and con-veyed a general impression that the conversion of Charles was by no means impossible.[20]

If Charles did not after all intend to change his faith—and it soon became apparent that he did not—his presence only added to the embarrassments of an already embarrassing situation. The arrival of despatches from the Count of Oñate in Vienna reporting the formal transfer of the Palatine electorate to Maximilian of Bavaria com-pounded still further the difficulties of the Council of State, which foresaw with alarm the outbreak of a new and greater war in Ger-many, with England intervening against the House of Austria. Now that Maximilian had been formally vested with his new title, there was no possibility of full restitution for the Elector Palatine, and Olivares was afraid that any hint of Spanish disapproval would only drive Bavaria into the arms of the French.[21]

There remained one last hope—that the pope would continue to withhold the dispensation for the marriage. But early in April, to Madrid's acute embarrassment, it became clear that the cardinals, impressed by the Prince of Wales' extraordinary gesture in travelling to Spain, had decided that the dispensation could no longer be with-held. Dated 12 April 1623, it reached Innocenzo De Massimi, the papal nuncio in Madrid, on 4 May. The papal terms were stiff, demanding as they did additional religious guarantees for the Infanta, her servants and her future offspring, and requiring the prior agree-ment of the Privy Council and Parliament.[22]

Bitter at Rome's inclusion of additional clauses, Buckingham had a stormy meeting with Olivares.[23] The two favourites had conceived an intense dislike for each other, and Olivares' register of correspon-dence contains the following laconic entries under Buckingham's

[20] *Correspondencia oficial de don Diego Sarmiento*, 2, pp. 293–9 (letter of 2 April 1620).
[21] AHN Est. lib. 739, fos. 228–30, draft consulta of Council of State, 8 April 1623.
[22] Gardiner, 5, pp. 31–3 and 37–8.
[23] Gardiner, 5, p. 38.

12. The great Plaza Mayor of Madrid, built by Juan Gómez de Mora in the last years of Philip III, was the setting for tournaments and equestrian games in honour of the Prince of Wales' visit in 1623, as depicted here by Juan de la Corte.

name: 'opposed to the marriage .... tries to disturb the peace ... the evil intentions with which he left Spain ... Buckingham and the devil have their seat in England.'[24] The prince, on the other hand, still fancied himself in love with the Infanta, at whom he would gaze longingly for half an hour on end at court festivities, 'as a cat does a mouse', in Olivares' graphic words.[25]

Olivares did not believe that James I or the Prince of Wales would or could perform any promises they might make about suspending the penal laws against the English Catholics, and he was therefore insistent that the Infanta should not be allowed to leave Spain until they had taken effect. This was the line he took at a meeting of the Council of State on 17 May, where he described the possibility of a marriage alliance between the Crowns of England and Spain as the 'greatest matter ever to present itself to this Monarchy.'[26] 'Lawful marriages', he continued, 'are a means of securing friendship between princes, but they are not sufficient of themselves if there are other

[24] Escorial, Ms. K.1.17, fo. 133.

[25] James Howell, *Epistolae Ho-Elianae* (11th ed., London, 1754), p. 135 (10 July 1623).

[26] Draft consulta in AHN Est. lib. 739, fos. 247–9. Olivares' speech is printed in Francisco de Jesús, *Narrative*, pp. 67–71 and Roca, *Fragmentos*, pp. 204–12. The draft appears to be the speech as taken down by a secretary while it was being delivered. Francisco de Jesús has a more polished and rounded version.

interests involved.' An English match, as he pointed out, raised two major questions. Was it lawful, and was it necessary? Whether it was licit for the Infanta to marry a heretical prince was a matter for the theologians—he disclaimed any professional competence in this area. As for necessity, he reverted to his theme of interests of state. He argued, with a certain remoteness from historical reality, that there had 'always been goodwill between Spain and England' and that this had been sustained without family alliances. The best foundation for friendship between two monarchies was 'common interests of state, such as have existed and do exist between these two crowns; from which it follows that this marriage, even if licit, is not necessary.' The principal benefits to be derived from a marriage would therefore be religious rather than secular, but there was no guarantee that the King of England and his son would be able to keep their word as far as religious concessions were concerned, and he did not see how pressure on them to do so would serve to keep their friendship. Only actual conversion, or an act of toleration approved by Privy Council and Parliament, would make him change his mind; and even then he would delay the Infanta's departure for England until the conditions were met.

This was a harder line than that taken by some of his colleagues on the Council of State, who seemed to think that a little more pressure would bring the English to heel. But it was the line later to be adopted by a junta of theologians who were asked to give their opinions on the match.[27] It also revealed a shrewder appreciation of British realities than that of Gondomar, whom Olivares believed to have been excessively anglicized by his many years in London. Two years later, when the marriage negotiations had ignominiously foundered and Spain was threatened by an English invasion, Olivares wrote disparagingly to Gondomar of the '*sancta sanctorum* of your Great Britain', and while conceding that it possessed great power at sea, doubted whether this power was substantial enough to allow the British to make any real conquests.[28] He was also sceptical, and justifiably so, of James' ability to induce Parliament to repeal the penal laws. But beyond this he had grasped that the Crowns of Spain and England had certain common needs and interests which could make their courses converge even without the formalized bonds of a royal marriage.

England needed Spain if it were to have any hope of securing the restoration of the Elector Palatine. Spain, for its part, needed English friendship for the development of its northern strategy for the isolation and defeat of the Dutch. A few weeks before the arrival

[27] Francisco de Jesús, *Narrative*, p. 67.
[28] *MC*, 1, Doc. V, Olivares to Gondomar, 2 June 1625.

of the Prince of Wales, the Junta de Comercio reported favourably on a proposal originally presented to Gondomar in London for the transfer of the cloth mart from the United Provinces to Antwerp; and it used the occasion to point out that Spain, for its own preservation and that of the Indies, needed a close alliance with England more than with any other nation.[29] A benevolently neutral England would provide a safe protective flank for Spanish shipping on its way to the Flemish ports. It would provide, too, some of those ships and naval stores so badly needed by the Spanish fleet. Beyond this there lay the possibility of a revitalized economic relationship linking the British Isles, the Iberian peninsula and the loyal provinces of the Southern Netherlands in a powerful trading community which would get the better of the upstart Dutch.

This vision, which looked back to the old Anglo-Burgundian relationship, had obvious merits in the circumstances of the 1620's. The growing friction between English and Dutch economic interests created opportunities for Spain and Flanders which skilful Spanish diplomacy might hope to exploit. The markets of Spain and the silver of the Indies presented an attractive bait for an English merchant community in the grips of an economic recession. Olivares also knew that James was dependent on his help for the recovery of the Palatinate. All this suggested that, in the long run at least, Madrid might be able to win the tacit cooperation of England without having to make any substantial sacrifice. This is in effect what happened in the 1630's. The sharp deterioration of Anglo-Spanish relations following the collapse of the marriage plans proved to be no more than a spectacular interlude, a temporary disturbance of an official relationship based on a somewhat grudging recognition that common needs created a common concern.[30]

The long view, however, was clouded by the great storm that was brewing over the Prince of Wales' marriage—a storm that threatened to wreck all possibility of that Anglo-Spanish understanding which was essential to Madrid's northern policy. The storm, as might have been expected, blew up fast. Buckingham wanted to cut his losses and get the prince out of Spain as quickly as possible; and on 22 May Olivares told his colleagues that the critical moment had arrived, with either an agreement or a total rupture of negotiations imminent. There were obvious drawbacks in acceding to the prince's request to return immediately to England, and it would be best to hold him in Madrid a little longer, and induce him to send home Sir Francis Cottington to report to James and return with further

---

[29] AGS Est. leg. 2516, consulta, 13 February 1623.
[30] This point emerges clearly from Part IV, ch. 2 of Alcalá-Zamora, *España, Flandes*.

instructions.[31] Charles allowed himself to be persuaded without excessive difficulty to remain in Madrid until the junta of theologians produced its report.

This august body of forty divines met on 26 May, and was asked to pronounce on whether the proposed marriage would further the cause of the Catholic religion. It was also asked what security would be necessary to allow Philip to swear to the pope that he was morally certain of the conditions being fulfilled. The junta reported on 2 June that the marriage would indeed be beneficial if the King of England fulfilled the conditions stipulated by Rome, but that, although a marriage might now be formally agreed, the Infanta's departure should be deferred for at least a year to ensure that the promises of toleration for English Catholics were kept.[32]

At ten o'clock that same night Olivares went to the prince's rooms in the palace to report the junta's decision. Again Buckingham lost his temper; again the prince threatened to leave; and again Olivares persuaded him to change his mind. Cottington left for England, and so too did Olivares' confidant, the Marquis of La Hinojosa, appointed ambassador extraordinary to the Court of St. James's. The two men reached London within a few days of each other, and it is not clear which made the stronger impression—Cottington with his gloomy tidings, or the syphilitic Hinojosa with his face so deformed that he needed 'corke and like instruments to help his speech'.[33] James I wept at the terrible predicament in which his son and his favourite found themselves, but despairingly decided to comply with Spain's conditions.

In Madrid Charles still hoped that these might be modified, and Olivares played along with him. In the process he sacrificed the president of the Council of Finance, Juan Roco de Campofrío, an outspoken opponent of the marriage in the junta of theologians. Roco was nominated to a bishopric, and the presidency given on 19 July to the Marquis of Montesclaros.[34] 'The divines have not yet recalled their sentence', Charles wrote to his father on 6 July, 'but the Conde tells us he has converted very many of them, yet keeps his old form in giving us no hope of anything till the business speaks it itself.'[35] Still swept up in romantic notions of marriage, he startled Olivares

[31] National Maritime Museum, Greenwich, Ms. PHB/1a, fos. 302–16, consulta of Council of State, 22 May 1623.

[32] Francisco de Jesús, *Narrative*, pp. 75–6.

[33] *The Diary of Sir Simonds D'Ewes, 1622–1624*, ed. Elisabeth Bourcier (Paris, 1974), p. 141.

[34] Roco de Campofrío, *España en Flandes*, introduction, xiv. The circumstances of Roco's disgrace are not clear, and his opposition to the match may have been no more than a useful pretext for removing him. Olivares' register of correspondence (Escorial Ms. K.1.17) contains the following entry (fo. 178): 'Roco de Campofrío does not approve of the English marriage and refuses to sign, and how he left the presidency, and the causes of it.'

[35] Quoted in Martin Hume, *The Court of Philip IV* (2nd. ed., London, 1928), p. 112.

and the Spanish court by accepting the conditions on 17 July. The news was celebrated in Madrid with fireworks and bonfires, and the prince and his bride were permitted to be seen together in public.[36] On 7 September Charles took a solemn oath to observe the articles of the marriage, duly approved by his father and the Privy Council, which Cottington had brought back from England. Philip in turn promised that the marriage should take place on the arrival of the pope's consent, with the possibility that the Infanta, now known as the Princess of England, would leave for her new homeland in the spring.

The oath-taking was in reality a face-saving ceremony, opening the way to retreat from a marriage that would never take place. The long delay, the constant prevarications of Olivares, the angry altercations over matters of religion between the Spaniards and the members of his suite, had begun to disillusion even the Prince of Wales. Buckingham, who took no trouble to conceal his antipathy to Olivares, wanted no more of the marriage, and was now only anxious to get himself and the prince out of Spain. In London it was becoming increasingly clear that the only justification for a highly unpopular marriage would be effective Spanish help in the recovery of the Palatinate. Olivares showed no sign of being willing or able to promise this; and the public sale in London in August of booty from the Portuguese Asian outpost of Hormuz, captured by a joint force of English and Persians in February of the preceding year,[37] was hardly calculated to strengthen his confidence in English protestations of amity.

But Olivares' problem remained, as always, how to break free of the English commitment without involving Spain in another northern war. On the surface, all was cordiality as the Prince of Wales took his leave of the Spanish royal family. Charles' departure from Madrid on 9 September was preceded by a lavish exchange of gifts, in the course of which Olivares was presented with a jewel of eight diamonds, valued at 25,000 ducats. He later explained that he would never have accepted it if the king had not commanded him to do so.[38] But the courtesies meant little, and even they were disregarded by Buckingham, who insulted Olivares again just before leaving.[39] Charles was now persuaded that the Spaniards meant to trick him, and that—as Olivares had suggested in one of his papers—

---

[36] González Palencia, *Noticias de Madrid*, p. 68; Lockyer, *Buckingham*, p. 158.

[37] Malvezzi, *Reinado de Felipe IV*, introduction, xliii. For Hormuz and the significance of its capture, see Niels Steensgaard, *The Asian Trade Revolution of the Seventeenth Century* (Chicago, 1974).

[38] BL Add. Ms. 24,909, fo. 134, Olivares to Padre Diego de Quiroga, 30 December 1629; and see above, p.164.

[39] Gardiner, 5, p. 116.

the Infanta might retreat to a nunnery in order to avoid going through with the marriage. To forestall the humiliation of rejection, he wrote from Segovia one letter to Philip reaffirming his desire to marry the Infanta, and another simultaneously to the Earl of Bristol revoking the ambassador's powers to conclude the betrothal on the arrival of the pope's consent. The opening duplicity of one party was thus matched by the closing duplicity of the other in a negotiation in which the dishonours were ultimately even.

The collapse of the English marriage negotiations led, as the Council of State had feared, to a rapid deterioration in relations between the English and Spanish crowns. During 1624 Olivares played for time by attempting to refloat his project of a Palatine-Imperial marriage,[40] but it remained obstinately grounded. He still banked on James I's hatred of war, but James was growing old and feeble, Buckingham was determined on revenge for his treatment in Madrid, and Parliament was gripped by an anti-Spanish fever. The Spanish ambassadors, Hinojosa and Don Carlos Coloma, did their best to rally the 'Spanish' party of Buckingham's enemies, but their efforts were hampered by the inability of Madrid to offer James the concessions on the Palatinate that would have enabled him to stand against the tide of popular and parliamentary opinion. 'War with Spain is England's best prosperity', declared Sir Edward Coke, and by the early summer of 1624 James found himself irrevocably committed to a war he did not want.[41]

Alliance-building (1624–5)

The gradual movement in 1624 towards Anglo-Spanish hostilities placed in jeopardy the northern strategy which had been evolving in Madrid since 1619. This strategy had been formulated on the assumption that the grain and naval supplies of northern Europe and the Baltic were essential to Spain; that the naval, commercial and financial power of the Dutch endangered the very foundations of the Spanish Monarchy; and that the retention of Flanders was indispensable to Spain, not only for reasons of religion and honour, but also because of its practical value as a base for the protection of Spain's maritime supply-lines, and as a source of military supplies and technical expertise.[42] In order to defend what it conceived to be its vital

[40] Alcalá-Zamora, España, Flandes, p. 220
[41] Robert E. Ruigh, The Parliament of 1624 (Cambridge, Mass., 1971), pp. 205, 300.
[42] The assumptions behind Spain's northern policy are admirably discussed in Alcalá-Zamora, España, Flandes, although, in a deliberate attempt to redress the balance of traditional historiography, the author is largely concerned with the economic and strategic importance of Flanders to Spain, and says little about cultural, religious and emotional ties.

interests in the north, Madrid had spent the last few years painfully re-evaluating and reformulating its aims and methods, until by 1624 it had achieved something approaching a coherent plan of campaign.

In this, as in so much else, Olivares was the inheritor of ideas and policies enunciated before he came to power, but he injected a new energy and urgency into their realization. The first plank in Madrid's revised anti-Dutch policy was to be a major strengthening of Spain's naval power in northern and Atlantic waters. For over twenty years the Dunkirk squadron, formed in 1621–2, ravaged Dutch shipping and preyed with sometimes devastating effect on the fishing fleets which the Spaniards had rightly come to see as major contributors to the prosperity of the United Provinces.[43] But the creation of the Dunkirk squadron was only one element in Olivares' general programme for Spain's naval revival. A few weeks after the king's return from his symbolic visit to the Andalusian ports, the British ambassador reported that 'the Conde of Olivares (who hath taken upon himself the care of the sea business here) intends to put to sea this summer 70 sail of men of war to be divided into seven squadrons . . .'[44]

The events of that spring of 1624 underlined the importance of his decision to give high priority to the fleet. In May a Dutch expeditionary force sailed into the Bay of All Saints in Brazil, and seized the city of Bahía, which was evacuated by its panic-stricken Portuguese inhabitants.[45] The news reached Lisbon in July, and preparations were hastily begun for the fitting out of a combined Spanish-Portuguese expedition under the command of Don Fadrique de Toledo. With 12,000 men and fifty-two ships it left the Cape Verde islands for Brazil in February 1625.[46]

The creation of the Dunkirk squadron and the despatch of Don Fadrique's armada for the recovery of Pernambuco in Brazil were the first visible manifestations of the enormous effort that was to be made by the Spain of Olivares to defeat the Dutch in their own element, on water. Spain's shortage of timber and naval supplies put it at a serious disadvantage in the international maritime contest, but the 1620's and 1630's were to be a period of intensive activity in the dockyards of the Iberian peninsula, which are said to have turned out some fifty galleons a year.[47] Olivares took a characteristically personal interest in questions of design: in 1635 he is to be

---

[43] See R. A. Stradling, 'The Spanish Dunkirkers, 1621–1648: a record of plunder and destruction', *Tijdschrift voor Geschiedenis*, 93 (1980), pp. 541–58.

[44] BL Add. Ms. 36,449, fo. 45, Aston to ?, 18/28 April 1624.

[45] C. R. Boxer, *Salvador de Sá and the Struggle for Brazil and Angola, 1602–1686* (London, 1952), pp. 48–50. For '8 May 1625' on p. 48, read '1624'.

[46] Boxer, p. 60.

[47] Alcalá-Zamora, *España, Flandes*, p. 92, citing Fernández Duro.

found outlining the need for a blunt-ended craft with a shallow draught, capable of carrying twelve pieces of artillery and 150 musketeers.[48]

As he pored over the maps in his map room—and he amazed Flanders veterans with his intimate knowledge of every port, reef and estuary[49]—he was deeply concerned about the need to secure harbours and bases in northern waters. From 1622 onwards he was involved in a number of complex diplomatic manoeuvres designed to obtain for Spanish use a chain of naval bases stretching from the Channel to the Baltic.[50] This was to be a major element in his global strategy: he would bring the Dutch to their knees by crippling their trade. But this trade was not confined to the oceans—it followed, too, the waterways that flowed into the North Sea. Any attempt to cut the lifelines of the United Provinces therefore had to include the blockade of their river-routes; and it was decided in January 1624, after consultation with Brussels, to close to Dutch shipping the Scheldt, the Meuse, the Rhine and the Lippe. The Duke of Neuburg, who was given a magnificent reception when he arrived in Madrid on a state visit in October,[51] was to be asked for his assistance in closing the Weser, while it was hoped that Tilly would use his army to block shipping on the Elbe.

If Olivares' plans were properly executed, the combination of a series of river blockades with a naval blockade of the Netherlands coastline by the Dunkirk squadron could be expected to place heavy strains on the Dutch economy. But Dutch merchants were resourceful, and the international ramifications of their trading network were so complex that contraband and collusion could only be held in check by a massive campaign of regulation and control, organized by Madrid on an equally international basis. In this campaign, the new system of the Almirantazgo, which officially came into being in October 1624 with the formation of the Flanders trading company in Seville,[52] had a central part to play. Combining as it did regulatory and trading functions, it faithfully reflected its mixed paternity, derived partly from the protectionist preoccupations of the Iberian peninsula, and partly from the commercial preoccupations of the Flanders-Seville merchant community. The crown had been bombarded with petitions and proposals by members of this community, anxious for Spain to move onto the offensive commercially, and wrest control of the

---

[48] AGS Est. leg. 2655, *proposición del Sr. Conde Duque*, 17 February 1635.
[49] Roca, *Fragmentos*, pp. 266–7. He called this map room the '*cuadra del obrador*' or '*oficio*' and retired to it to think and plan, according to Roca.
[50] Alcalá-Zamora, *España, Flandes*, pp. 98–9.
[51] Almansa y Mendoza, *Cartas*, p. 305.
[52] Above, p. 161.

north-south trade from the hands of the Dutch. One such proposal came from Manuel Sueyro, a member of a Portuguese Jewish merchant family settled in Antwerp from the mid-sixteenth century. Like his father, Diego López Sueyro, Manuel served as a secret agent for Madrid in Flanders, while pursuing his own mercantile and financial interests.[53] A similar proposal, which received careful and sympathetic consideration from the Council of State, came in 1623 from a German long resident in Spain, Agustín Bredimus, a strong advocate of a Spanish-Flemish trading company, who, like Sueyro, had ambitious plans for cutting the Dutch and the Hanse out of the north-south trade.[54] But the most influential and flamboyant of these northern advocates of a Spanish-Flemish commercial drive into northern waters was Gabriel de Roy, a native of Artois who had built up contacts over the years with officials in Madrid, and who inhabited—like Sueyro—the shadowy in-between world of trade and espionage.[55]

Olivares seems to have had a penchant for figures like Manuel Sueyro and Gabriel de Roy—men of somewhat unorthodox background and wide international contacts, who could supply him with private information behind the backs of government officials, and be sent on confidential missions from which Madrid could easily disassociate itself if they turned out unsuccessfully. In Gabriel de Roy he detected the kind of talents needed for the advancement of his northern commercial strategy. In 1624 de Roy was made a member of the junta that recommended the establishment of the Almirantazgo.[56] He was then sent to Brussels to recruit merchants for the new company and to establish Flemish inspectorates of ships and their cargoes to complement the work of those being set up in Iberian ports as dependencies of a central board in Madrid, the Junta del Almirantazgo.[57] From Brussels he would be despatched on important missions designed to broaden the scope of the northern strategy.

There was no doubt in Olivares' mind that the participation of the Emperor and the Empire was critical to the success of this northern

---

[53] Echevarría Bacigalupe, *La diplomacia secreta*, p. 174. Manuel was also a man of broad cultural interests, and published Castilian translations of Tacitus and Sallust. See chs. 4 and 5 of *La diplomacia secreta* for the careers of father and son.

[54] Alcalá-Zamora, *España, Flandes*, p. 180; M. E. H. N. Mout, '"Holendische Propositiones". Een Habsburgs plan tot vernietiging van handel, visserij en scheepvaart der Republiek (ca. 1625)', *Tijdschrift voor Geschiedenis*, 95 (1982), pp. 345–62.

[55] Alcalá-Zamora, *España, Flandes*, p. 142. I am grateful to Jonathan Israel for letting me see in typescript the text of a forthcoming article on de Roy, 'The Politics of International Trade Rivalry during the Thirty Years' War: Gabriel de Roy and Olivares' Mercantilist Projects (1623–45),' to be published in *The International History Review*.

[56] Israel, *The Dutch Republic*, pp. 204–5; Eddy Stols, *De Spaanske Brabanders of de Handelsbetrekkingen der Zuidelijke Nederlanden met de Iberische Wereld, 1598–1648* (2 vols., Brussels, 1971), 1, pp. 18–19.

[57] Mout, '"Holendische Propositiones"', p. 353.

strategy. By early 1624 the triumph of the Habsburg and Catholic cause in Germany appeared complete. The Emperor Ferdinand II owed at least part of this success to the military and financial support of Spain, which claimed to have remitted to its ambassador to the Imperial court, the Count of Oñate, a total of 4,747,018 florins (some three million ducats) for military and embassy expenses between April 1617 and April 1622.[58] In return for this assistance, Olivares felt that he could reasonably look to the Emperor for cooperation in Spain's struggle against the Dutch, especially now that Ferdinand's own rebels in Bohemia had been subdued. The collapse of the English marriage negotiations had further improved prospects for closer collaboration between the two branches of the House of Austria, and in the autumn of 1624 the Emperor took soundings through Franz Christoph Khevenhüller, his ambassador in Madrid, as to whether the Spanish court now considered the way open for a formal proposal of marriage between the Infanta María and his son.[59]

In November 1624, as part of that continuing process by which the two branches of the family kept in personal touch, Ferdinand's brother, the Archduke Charles, arrived in Spain for a visit which was also to be used for discussion of the Infanta's marriage plans. The visit came to an abrupt end with the archduke's death of a fever contracted shortly after his arrival,[60] but a member of his entourage, the Count of Schwarzenberg, stayed on in Madrid. Here he had extensive conversations with Olivares about the possibilities for a new dynastic alliance, and also about his Almirantazgo project.[61] Schwarzenberg returned to Vienna in the spring of 1625 an enthusiastic supporter of the plans for a joint Spanish-Imperial trade war against the United Provinces. As part of these plans, which involved detaching the towns of the Hanseatic League from the Dutch, the Emperor was to seek means of gaining control of two ports in the nominally independent but Dutch-occupied county of East Friesland.[62] It was also hoped to set up a chain of Almirantazgo agencies along the North German coastline, and to bring the Hanse towns into a great new

[58] AGS Est. leg. 2327, fo. 311, *Relación del dinero que se ha remitido* . . ., 25 April 1623.

[59] State Archives, Prague. Mnichovo Hradiště, Autografy 1623–30/288/49, no. 141, Olivares to Khevenhüller, 27 September 1624.

[60] Céspedes y Meneses, *Historia de Don Felipe IV*, fo. 214v. The Emperor, his brother, suspected that the illness was brought on by a drinking spree in Barcelona, according to a letter to the Count-Duke from the Count of Osona, Spain's ambassador in Vienna. Letter 5 (10 February 1625) in Jesús Gutiérrez, 'Don Francisco de Moncada. El hombre y el embajador. Selección de textos inéditos', *Boletín de la Biblioteca de Menéndez Pelayo*, 56 (1980), pp. 3–72.

[61] Mout, '"Holendische Propositiones"', pp. 351–6; and see the first part of the two-part article by F. Mareš, 'Die maritime Politik der Habsburger in den Jahren 1625–1628', *Mitteilungen des Instituts für Oesterreichische Geschichtsforschung*, 1 (1880), pp. 541–78, and 2 (1881), pp. 49–82.

[62] Rafael Ródenas Vilar, *La política europea de España durante la guerra de los treinta años* (Madrid, 1967), p. 74.

Habsburg trading network designed to extend all the way from the Baltic to the Iberian peninsula.

Some fifty years earlier, when rather similar plans were discussed between Philip II and the Emperor Maximilian II, they came to nothing, but if the Imperial court felt some scepticism, the proposal nevertheless secured Ferdinand's approval. International complications, however, delayed action for some months, and further time was lost as Brussels, Vienna and Madrid sought to orchestrate the diplomatic manoeuvres that would be needed to bring the Baltic states and the cities of the Hanseatic League into line—a process in which the indispensable Gabriel de Roy would have a leading part to play. It was not, therefore, until early in 1626 that the first of the various envoys would be despatched on his mission, but already it was becoming clear that any attempt to involve the Empire in Dutch affairs was likely to be strenuously resisted, especially by Bavaria.[63] There was a profound suspicion of Spanish intentions throughout the German lands, and Munich in particular could be counted upon to raise objections whenever Madrid seemed to be exercising excessive influence over Imperial policy.

The plans anyhow demanded a degree of coordination and control that were beyond the powers of temporary diplomatic agents, and perhaps indeed of seventeenth-century diplomacy itself. Even the more localized but still ambitious plans for a river blockade of the United Provinces ran rapidly into trouble, and for similar reasons. They involved the cooperation of the Rhineland states, all of them dependent on river traffic for their economic survival. As small states that found themselves reluctantly caught up in great-power conflicts, the ecclesiastical electorates of Mainz, Trèves and Cologne had other reasons, too, for unhappiness.[64] They had welcomed the Spanish occupation of the Rhine Palatinate as rescuing them from the danger of being submerged by the forces of Protestantism; but, once rescued, they came to resent the continuing and burdensome presence of Spanish troops, and began to fear—like the other German states and principalities—that an excessive deployment of Spanish power would lead to the loss of German liberties. They were distressed, too, by Spain's unwillingness to restore to the Catholics the ecclesiastical properties that had been alienated from them in the Palatinate—an unwillingness brought about by Olivares' anxiety not to offend English susceptibilities at the time of the marriage negotiations.[65] Now they were being called upon by Madrid to make further sacrifices in

[63] Albrecht, *Die auswärtige Politik*, p. 159.
[64] See Kessel, *Spanien und die geistlichen Kurstaaten* for their dilemmas, and their attempts to escape from them.
[65] Kessel, pp. 156–8.

a cause which had failed to bring them the expected benefits. Yet they could not protest too long or too loud. As long as France was unable or unwilling to intervene effectively on their behalf, they had nowhere else to turn for help but to Madrid in the event of a new attempt by the Protestant states to restore the Elector Palatine.

The Elector of Cologne, whose bishoprics of Münster, Osnabrück, Paderborn and Minden would be ruined if his electorate became embroiled in hostilities with the Dutch, did everything possible to preserve his neutrality. It was primarily as a result of pressure from Cologne that the Catholic League refused to countenance the incursion of Imperial forces into East Friesland.[66] Behind the scenes, too, the Elector and his colleagues manoeuvred to thwart the economic blockade of the United Provinces. The Dutch for their part adopted a retaliatory policy of counter-blockade. This brought severe privations to the Spanish army of Flanders, and reduced by about 300,000 ducats (the same amount of money as was needed to maintain the Dunkirk squadron) the revenues of the Brussels treasury, which derived part of its income from the dues paid by Dutch shipping for use of the rivers.[67]

In these circumstances it is not surprising that Madrid's policy for the economic strangulation of the United Provinces was never fully effective, and that the river blockade had eventually to be called off at the request of Brussels in 1629.[68] But, however imperfect, the Spanish blockade had a damaging impact on the life and economy of the United Provinces, interrupting the flow of Dutch exports to neighbouring territories and precipitating a slump in shipping and trade.[69] As Olivares saw the situation in 1624, it certainly represented a potentially more promising approach to the intractable problem of the Netherlands than the old and increasingly discredited policy of siege warfare favoured by Spínola, who was inclined to be sceptical about projects for developing Spanish naval power. Spínola had pinned his hopes on an Anglo-Spanish alliance as a means of forcing the Dutch to agree to a reasonable settlement with Spain. When the negotiations between London and Madrid collapsed he had no choice but to take to the field again, and in July 1624 he made his first cautious moves towards laying siege to Breda, an allegedly impregnable garrison town guarding the entrance to Holland.[70]

[66] Kessel, pp. 136–8.
[67] Alcalá-Zamora, *España, Flandes*, pp. 184–6; also Jonathan Israel, 'The States General and the Strategic Regulation of the Dutch River Trade, 1621–1636', *Bijdragen en Mededelingen Betreffende de Geschiedenis der Nederlanden*, 95 (1980), pp. 461–91.
[68] Israel, 'The States General', p. 483.
[69] Israel, *The Dutch Republic*, pp. 149–53.
[70] For Spínola's views, see Straub, *Pax et Imperium*, pp. 169–70.

The prospect of a long, expensive and possibly unsuccessful siege left the Council of State divided.[71] Only Don Pedro de Toledo and Don Diego de Ibarra spoke out strongly in favour of a continued, and largely open-ended, Spanish commitment in Flanders. On the assumption, traditional in Spanish ruling circles, that war was unavoidable for a great power like Spain, since the multiplicity of its interests and the jealousy of its enemies were bound to involve it in conflicts in one part of the world or another, they argued that it was preferable that it should fight its wars in Flanders rather than in the Indies or Italy, or the Iberian peninsula itself. But Don Fernando Girón, whose years of service in Flanders had made him deeply pessimistic about the chances of victory, urged the king to think hard about ways of extricating the Monarchy from that interminable war; and Cardinal Zapata, speaking for many of the councillors, argued that while Spain was being lost, Flanders was not being won. Olivares himself was not present at this meeting, but the subsequent royal order that the army of Flanders should receive its full allocation of money suggests that he was prepared to gamble on Spínola achieving a spectacular success.

It was obvious that hostilities with England would make it more difficult to send provisions by sea to Spínola's army of Flanders, and enhanced the need for armed convoys as envisaged in the plans for the Almirantazgo. The impending war also raised the alarming prospect of a Protestant maritime coalition against the Spanish Monarchy, and the restoration of the Anglo-Dutch collaboration that had been the undoing of Philip II. In spite of Louis XIII's preoccupation with the Huguenot question it seemed by no means impossible that France might seek to associate itself with such a coalition and turn Spain's difficulties to its own advantage.

The chances of this were greatly increased by the governmental changes in Paris during the course of 1624. The administration of La Vieuville had not distinguished itself in the field of foreign affairs, and on 29 April Cardinal Richelieu was admitted to the royal council on the insistence of the Queen Mother, Marie de Médicis. Between May and August La Vieuville negotiated for a marriage between the Prince of Wales and Louis' sister, Henrietta Maria; and simultaneous discussions with the Dutch culminated in June in the treaty of Compiègne, by which France committed itself to annual loans to the United Provinces for the the next three years if they continued their war with Spain.[72]

When La Vieuville was dismissed from office in August, French

---

[71] AGS Est. leg. 2038, consulta, 14 September 1624.
[72] Richard Bonney, *The King's Debts. Finance and Politics in France, 1589–1661* (Oxford, 1981), p. 122.

foreign policy was already showing signs of a firmer sense of direction, although Richelieu was still far from being the Olivares of Louis XIII.[73] Much would depend on how skilfully he handled the two great foreign policy questions facing France in the autumn of 1624—the marriage alliance with England, and the undecided fate of the Valtelline. The key to both these questions lay with Rome, where the death of Gregory XV in July 1623 and his replacement by Maffeo Barberini as Pope Urban VIII marked the beginnings of a shift in papal policy to a less pro-Spanish stance. The French had actively supported Barberini's candidacy, and the policies he would pursue during his long pontificate would convince Madrid—and not without justification—that the head of the church was the enemy of Spain.[74]

Although Olivares received the congratulations of Urban VIII and his apostolic benediction for the devotion to the Faith that he had displayed in his handling of the English marriage negotiations,[75] Richelieu was the one to carry off the prize. The Cardinal succeeded in persuading the papacy that an English marriage would redound to the benefit of the English Catholics and of the church as a whole. Urban gave his consent, and in May 1625, a few weeks after his accession to the English throne, Charles was married by proxy to Henrietta Maria.[76] The conclusion of the Anglo-French marriage was perhaps the first clear indication to Olivares that a formidable opponent now faced him in France.

On the Valtelline, too, Richelieu turned to Urban for help, but with less success. As agreed between France and Spain in 1622, the papacy was holding the Valtelline forts in trust. It showed no eagerness to comply with Richelieu's wishes and abandon or demolish these forts without first receiving financial compensation. In November 1624, following an agreement between France, Savoy and Venice, a Franco-Swiss army of 9,000 men under the command of the Marquis of Coeuvres marched into the Grisons with the object of restoring the Valtelline to the Protestants. By the end of the year the papal garrisons had been expelled, and the only fortress still to hold out was Riva, where the Duke of Feria had hastily installed a Spanish garrison in response to a belated appeal by the pope.[77]

[73] For the changes in French government and foreign policy in 1624, see especially A. D. Lublinskaya, *French Absolutism: the Crucial Phase, 1620–1629* (Cambridge, 1968), pp. 262–71, and Rémy Pithon, 'Les débuts difficiles . . . de Richelieu'.

[74] A. Leman, *Urbain VIII et la rivalité de la France et de la Maison d'Autriche de 1631 à 1635* (Lille, 1920) tries laboriously but not entirely convincingly to absolve Urban VIII of partiality to France. Various aspects of papal diplomacy in the 1620's are examined by Georg Lutz, *Kardinal Giovanni Francesco Guidi di Bagno* (Tübingen, 1971).

[75] Papal brief of 27 April 1624 in Roca, *Fragmentos*, pp. 216–17.

[76] Lutz, *Kardinal Bagno*, p. 148.

[77] Pithon, 'Les débuts dificiles', p. 15; Marrades, *El camino del Imperio*, pp. 126–7.

The new vigour injected by Richelieu into French foreign policy was deeply disturbing to Madrid. French diplomacy was everywhere active—in London, the Hague, and in Germany, where it was working to detach Bavaria and the Catholic League from the Emperor, and to promote an alliance of England, Denmark, Sweden and the United Provinces for the restoration of the Elector Palatine.[78] Over the winter months of 1624–5 it looked as though a great European coalition against the House of Austria was in the making, with Richelieu pulling the strings from Paris. By early 1625 Christian IV of Denmark—determined to steal a march on his rival, Gustavus Adolphus of Sweden—was planning to march his troops across the Elbe in defence of German Protestantism without even waiting for the conclusion of a formal agreement with the other Protestant powers.[79] In England, the Duke of Buckingham, bent on getting his revenge, was fitting out a great fleet, which was presumably intended for use against Spain.[80] In northern Italy Charles Emmanuel of Savoy married his younger son, Prince Thomas, to a French wife, Marie de Bourbon, in January 1625; and, acting in collusion with the French, was engaged in assembling an army for an attack on Spain's ally, the republic of Genoa.[81]

It is likely that Olivares on the one side, like the Duke of Buckingham on the other,[82] failed to take into account the obstacles in the way of France entering an anti-Habsburg coalition in support of the Protestant cause. Richelieu had entered the government as the candidate of the *dévot* party, which was committed to a Catholic foreign policy, and it was difficult at this stage of his political career for him to move too far in the direction of a rapprochement with the Protestant states of Europe. His problems were compounded in January 1625 when he was caught off balance by the revolt of the Huguenot Seigneur de Soubise—a revolt joined a few weeks later by his brother, the Duke of Rohan.[83] A Huguenot rebellion ruled out any possibility of effective French participation in a predominantly Protestant anti-Habsburg coalition. It was only in northern Italy that the Cardinal could safely take overt anti-Spanish action without being accused by his enemies of playing into the hands of

---

[78] Rafael Ródenas Vilar, *La política europea* pp. 23–5; Straub, *Pax et Imperium*, pp. 207–10.

[79] For Christian IV and the Danish intervention, see Geoffrey Parker, *The Thirty Years' War* (London, 1984), pp. 71–81.

[80] Lockyer, *Buckingham*, pp. 249–50.

[81] Romolo Quazza, *Storia Politica d'Italia. Preponderanza Spagnuola, 1559–1700* (2nd. ed., Milan, 1950), p. 445. Prince Thomas was given the title of Prince of Carignano on his marriage. For his later military career with Spain, see Romolo Quazza, *Tomaso di Savoia-Carignano nelle campagne di Fiandra e di Francia, 1635–1638* (Turin, 1941). The activities and intrigues of the Princess of Carignano were to become a source of constant anxiety to Olivares.

[82] Adams, 'Spain or the Netherlands?', p. 98.

[83] Bonney, *The King's Debts*, p. 123.

international Protestantism, and even in Italy his policies were running into trouble. The Venetians were unwilling to join in an attack on Genoa, and the papacy had been antagonized by French assistance to the Protestant Grisons and the occupation of the Valtelline.

In spite of all the difficulties encountered by the anti-Habsburg forces in constructing a European-wide coalition, Madrid was deeply preoccupied by the threat from its enemies. In October 1624 the Infanta Isabella was instructed to explore the possibility of a settlement with the Dutch,[84] in order to free Spain's hands for dealing with the French. At the end of December the papal nuncio reported that Olivares and the councillors of state were resolved to go to war over the Valtelline rather than accept any modification of the Treaty of Aranjuez.[85]

The overwhelming need, as Olivares saw it, was to build up an effective alliance of the Habsburgs and their friends as a counterforce to the coalition that Richelieu was constructing. At least since 1618 there had been sporadic discussion in the Catholic courts of the desirability of a close union between Spain, the Emperor, the Catholic League and the Italian princes against a combination of the Protestant powers.[86] The events of 1624 gave a fresh impetus to the idea. At the same time as Olivares began seeking the economic co-operation of the Empire against the United Provinces, he also began to explore the possibilities for military co-operation against the Protestant powers, including the Dutch. His first proposals for a league, or formal alliance, between Spain, the Emperor and the princes of the Empire seem to have been drawn up in October 1624. Since he was well aware of the suspicions with which any actions taken by Spain were greeted in Germany, he took care to arrange, by way of the Imperial ambassador Khevenhüller, that the initiative should appear to come from the Emperor.[87]

At a time when Denmark was preparing to challenge Habsburg and Catholic supremacy in Germany, the Emperor welcomed a project which seemed to guarantee further assistance from Spain, and instructed Khevenhüller to press ahead with the plans in Madrid. But the construction of an alliance of the Habsburgs and their friends was to prove as difficult and frustrating as the construction of an anti-Habsburg alliance. Everyone in principle was in favour of a close understanding between the leading Catholic powers, but in practice each interpreted the plans for collaboration in the light of his own particular interests. Maximilian of Bavaria, while paying lip service

---

[84] Lonchay, *Correspondance*, 2, Doc. 583, Philip IV to Infanta, 11 October 1624.
[85] ASV, Spagna, 65, fo. 110, nuncio, 20 December 1624.
[86] Straub, *Pax et Imperium*, p. 219.
[87] Heinrich Günter, *Die Habsburger-Liga, 1625–1635* (Berlin, 1908), pp. 5–6.

to Catholic unity, was quick to reject proposals which seemed likely to involve the Empire in Spain's war with the Dutch.[88] The Emperor, too, had his own priorities, and Denmark at this moment ranked higher than the Netherlands among them. Spain, for its part, was preoccupied with the Flanders war, and had no wish to become engaged in yet another conflict by committing itself to a war against the Danes.[89]

Olivares' proposal for a League of Alliance was therefore to turn into a long and exhausting quest for an elusive prize—a quest that would provoke misunderstandings and recriminations between Madrid and Vienna for almost the whole length of his political career. So eager was he to create his alliance, that at times he gives the appearance of seeing the alliance as an end in itself, rather than as simply a means to an end. As it formed itself alluringly in his mind, the alliance would bring the Dutch war to an end. It would save Spain from battling single-handed against the forces of Protestantism. And it would relieve Castile of its crushing burden by distributing the costs of warfare more equitably among the participants in the Habsburg and Catholic cause.

Any relief of this kind would come none too soon. His difficulties with the cities of Castile in 1624 had frustrated Olivares' plans for a reorganization of the tax system which would establish the crown's finances on more solid foundations. Six months of negotiations were needed with the Genoese bankers to arrange for the 1625 *asiento*, which was finally concluded in December 1624.[90] The *asiento*, which was for 3,250,000 ducats, but would cost the crown 4,180,000 ducats by the time gratifications for the bankers and foreign exchange rates had been taken into account, was described by the Council of Finance as being one of the most unfavourable in years. Interest rates were intolerable, and it was in the hope of bringing them down by reducing its arrears of debt that the crown launched its appeal for voluntary contributions—the *donativo*—at the end of the year. By February 1625, however, the Council of Finance was urging that the income from the *donativo* should be used to meet current expenses rather than pay off old debts—a proposal rejected by the crown, which suggested as an alternative the sale of vassals and jurisdictions from the royal patrimony.[91] This was exactly the kind of resort to easy expedients that Olivares' frustrated plans for fiscal and budgetary

---

[88] Albrecht, *Die auswärtige Politik*, pp. 161–2.
[89] Ródenas Vilar, *La política europea*, pp. 54–5.
[90] AGS CJH, leg. 602, fo. 285, consulta, 10 December 1624; also Domínguez Ortiz, *Política y hacienda*, p. 29.
[91] AHN Consejos, lib. 1427, fos. 408–9 and 412–13, consultas of Consejo de Hacienda, 8 and 20 February 1625.

reform had sought to avoid, but in 1625 all other considerations paled before those of national defence.

The annus mirabilis (1625)

In spite of the setback to his fiscal plans, Olivares looked to be well in command in those opening weeks of 1625. His elevation to the dukedom of San Lúcar la Mayor confirmed his high standing with a grateful king, who must have glimpsed in that secret document, the Great Memorial, something of the glorious future to which his minister was calling him. The new Count-Duke dominated, although not yet with absolute security, both the court and the Council of State. He conducted all major negotiations with foreign ambassadors. He was the principal architect of the policies that were being designed to restore the fortunes of Castile and the Monarchy. And with his restless energy and his consuming concern with the minutiae of business as well as with the broader issues of policy, he was beginning to reveal himself as Sir Anthony Sherley had described him—'the *maestro* who moves all the wheels of that great clock.'

Many wheels had to be laboriously moved in the early spring of 1625 in order to make Spain ready for war. The Count-Duke's scheme for the raising and maintenance in Castile of a permanent force of 30,000 men had at least temporarily foundered, together with his project for the abolition of the *millones*. But, as his Great Memorial made clear, he was still determined to bring some order and system into the country's defences by earmarking, 'if possible', annual budgetary allocations for the upkeep of fortresses, frontier garrisons and the fleet.[92] The expectation of an English attack on the coast some time during the course of the year might help to bring opponents of his schemes to their senses. The initial response to the appeal for a *donativo* suggested that the danger had touched a patriotic chord. By 17 January 1½ million ducats had already been contributed, and a combination of pressure and propaganda would swell the figure in the coming months.[93] A few days later the Cortes requested that the militia system, at present confined to the coasts, should be extended to cover the whole of Castile; and in the Council of State the veteran Don Fernando Girón begged the king for leave of absence to organize the defence of Cadiz.[94]

While Spain was preparing its defences against a possible attack, Olivares and the Council of State were engaged in continuous discus-

[92] *MC*, 1, p. 98.
[93] *Actas* 42, p. 154; Domínguez Ortiz, *Política y hacienda*, p. 299.
[94] *Actas* 42, pp. 281–2; AGS Est. leg. 7034, consulta, 8 February 1625.

sion about how best to handle the international crisis and break up the potential coalition of Spain's enemies. The Count-Duke's awareness of the crown's financial problems helped incline him to caution, although he was being pressed to respond aggressively to the challenge from France. The Duke of Feria, as governor of Milan, and Spain's ambassador in Paris, the Marquis of Mirabel, were both urging a massive display of military strength as a response to the revival of French interest in the affairs of northern Italy. They had their supporters in the Council of State, particularly the Marquis of Montesclaros and Don Pedro de Toledo. But the Count-Duke's instinct was to resolve the Valtelline question without recourse to war, and he astutely handled it as a question to be settled between France and the papacy.[95] Anything that would embroil the French with Urban VIII was to the obvious advantage of Madrid, and Olivares welcomed Urban's decision to send his nephew, Cardinal Francesco Barberini, as a legate to Paris with what looked like the unrewarding task of trying to negotiate a settlement.[96]

Olivares' preference, whenever possible, was to play for time, and he was encouraged in this by Mirabel's report in January of fresh trouble in France with the revolt of Soubise. A general Huguenot uprising was likely to frustrate Franco-Savoyard plans for a joint campaign against Genoa and avert the expected confrontation with France. But would Madrid be justified in giving active support to French heretics and in encouraging rebellion in the Huguenot city of La Rochelle? The issue was brought before the Council of State at the beginning of February. In the same month, the Duke of Rohan rebelled in Languedoc and appealed to Mirabel for Spanish help. Secret negotiations began; a junta of theologians, customarily assembled to pronounce where questions of conscience impinged on matters of state, gave its blessing; and although Olivares swore to the papal nuncio in July that Madrid had never given the Huguenots a subsidy,[97] all the indications would seem to point the other way.[98]

The Huguenot uprising, in any event, failed to prevent the attack on Genoa. The armies of France and Savoy, led by Lesdiguières and by Charles Emmanuel, joined forces at Asti on 4 March, and marched across the neutral territory of Montferrat to invade the Genoese Republic. Their campaign was designed to cut communications between Genoa and Milan, interrupting the movement of Spain's

[95] Ródenas Vilar, *La política europea*, pp. 29–32; Straub, *Pax et Imperium*, p. 211.

[96] ASV, Spagna, 65, fo. 202, nuncio, 20 March 1625.

[97] ASV, Spagna, 65, fo. 285, nuncio, 30 July 1625.

[98] For the discussions about aid for the Huguenots, see Ródenas Vilar, *La política europea*, pp. 32–7, and the modifications to his account in Straub, *Pax et Imperium*, p. 212 n. 11, which includes a reference to the theologians' verdict.

troops to the Valtelline, and thence into central and northern Europe.[99] By the middle of April only the demoralized city of Genoa stood between the invading armies and victory, although Spanish land and sea forces were being hastily assembled to come to the city's rescue.

The French campaign in Italy increased the uneasiness and impatience of those councillors who felt that the crown's foreign policy was being too hesitant and too cautious, and that great opportunities were being missed. Highly critical voices were raised at a meeting of the Council of State on 30 April, which Olivares did not attend. The council was supposed to be discussing the situation created by the death of James I the previous month, and deciding whether the Count of Gondomar, who was thought to be unacceptable to the new King Charles I, should still undertake a conciliatory mission to London for which he had been selected earlier in the year.[100] Instead, it embarked on a discussion that was as much concerned with France as with England.

Don Pedro de Toledo, whose militant views were so influential that Olivares apparently resorted to holding extraordinary meetings at which he would not be present,[101] wanted Gondomar to go ahead with his mission but to travel by way of Germany. Here he could use his remarkable diplomatic skills to promote Madrid's plans for a League of Alliance, and persuade the Emperor to assist the Spanish cause in northern Italy by undertaking a diversion against the Venetians in Friuli.

The Marquis of Montesclaros showed himself on this occasion even more of a hawk than Don Pedro de Toledo. As President of the Council of Finance he was as well informed as Olivares about the state of the treasury, but unlike Olivares he argued for attack instead of defence. Behind every clash of arms since the start of the reign were to be found the intrigues and machinations of the King of France. But Spain now had the largest army it had ever had in Flanders, and another large army in Italy. While the wretched condition of the crown's finances made it hard enough to keep these armies in existence, if they were once disbanded it would be even more difficult to assemble them again. Bearing this in mind, what today passed as 'prudence' might look to future generations like supine behaviour in the face of provocation. The king should not curb his military ardour at the cost of his future reputation. Instead, he should send an ambassador to Louis XIII to announce that France would be

[99] Lublinskaya, *French Absolutism*, p. 277.

[100] AGS Est. leg. 2516, consulta, 30 April 1625. Gondomar had already left Madrid on 16 April.

[101] ASV, Spagna, 65, fo. 214, nuncio, 8 April 1625.

invaded unless he withdrew his troops from Italy. Part of the army
of Flanders would enter France by way of Picardy; the galleys of
the Marquis of Santa Cruz would attack the coast of Provence; and
His Majesty should place himself at the head of his troops and invade
from Catalonia. God and time, concluded Montesclaros, had offered
the king evenly balanced scales—on one side perpetual unrest in all
his dominions if he failed to act, and on the other absolute and honourable security if he resorted to war in defence of his kingdoms and
his allies.

The 'prudence' attacked by Montesclaros was clearly that of Olivares; and he appealed directly over the head of the favourite to the
king himself. Two other councillors normally associated with Olivares' policies followed Montesclaros' lead. Peace, for the Marquis
of La Hinojosa, was 'not achieved simply by running away from
war, but rather by deciding to have recourse to it when this becomes
necessary.' Olivares' brother-in-law, Monterrey, joined forces with
Montesclaros and Hinojosa, arguing that it would be better to raise
the siege of Breda and use Spínola's army for an invasion of France,
since the capture of one more stronghold would not bring the Flanders
war to an end. Nor would a continuation of the siege of Breda get
the French out of Italy. He, too, wanted the king to lead an invading
force from Catalonia, drawing on the resources of the Crown of
Aragon as the region of Spain least burdened by taxes.

During the next few weeks the tide was beginning to turn in Italy,
as the Duke of Feria came to Genoa's relief by land, and the Marquis
of Santa Cruz by sea. But in Madrid the partisans of open war with
France continued to make the running. On 15 May Don Pedro de
Toledo again put the case for a simultaneous invasion of France from
Flanders, Navarre and Catalonia.[102] The atmosphere in Madrid was
conducive to this kind of talk. The French and Spanish crowns were
engaged in a campaign of mutual reprisals against the property of
citizens resident in each other's countries,[103] and war fever was rising.
It was about this time that Philip IV had himself portrayed in armour
on horseback—'like a Caesar', reported Sacchetti, the papal nuncio.[104]
The nuncio alleged that Olivares did nothing to discourage these bellicose gestures, partly because he suspected that there was no real
danger of the king actually going to war, and partly to avoid the
impression of any lack of enthusiasm. But in his heart the Count-
Duke did not want war, which would undermine his own position
and ruin the exchequer.

[102] Ródenas Vilar, *La política europea*, p. 46.
[103] Albert Girard, 'La saisie des biens français en Espagne en 1625', *Revue d'Histoire Économique et Sociale*, 19 (1931), pp. 297–315.
[104] ASV, Spagna, 65, fo. 245, nuncio, 10 June 1625.

Something of Olivares' state of mind at this moment is revealed by a remarkable letter that he wrote to Gondomar on 2 June 1625.[105] Gondomar, now aged and infirm, was reluctantly making his way northwards to Brussels, in order to keep a close eye on English affairs. From Irún he wrote what seems to have been a long and highly critical letter to Olivares about his handling of recent questions of foreign policy, and the general state of Spain. He apparently wanted Madrid to be more conciliatory towards the papacy over the Valtelline, and more conciliatory towards England over the restitution of the Palatinate—partly out of an exaggerated notion of English power, in Olivares' opinion.[106] On the other hand, like Montesclaros and Don Pedro de Toledo, he wanted Spain to break with France as soon as Breda fell.

Through Olivares' reply there ran a refrain—the extreme difficulty of making the right decision. Men could only do their best, and the disposal of events was in God's hand. The disagreements in the Council of State were not over the ends, but over the ways of getting there. Such disagreements were, after all, legitimate. Over the question of war with France he largely agreed with Gondomar; but making war was not quite the same as the creation of the world when 'God said let there be light and there was light.' From the four armies which the king had in the field, how exactly was he to produce another two or three for the invasion of France?

Olivares struck back when he turned to Gondomar's comments on the condition of Spain, which had clearly touched him on the raw. According to Gondomar, the ship of state was sinking—se va todo a fondo.[107] This was something, he riposted, that the old and the discontented had been saying since the beginning of the world, and yet their countries had not only survived but flourished for centuries to come. By this he did not mean to imply that these were happy times, as none knew better than the king himself. And yet, think what had happened in the four years since his accession in 1621! At that time government and the administration of justice were notoriously bad, the treasury was exhausted and revenues mortgaged up to the end of the current year, 1625. 'I do not infer or presume to claim that our present state is any better, or that things have improved in any way. But thanks to the care, the resolution and the vigilance of the king', Spain had got through the past four years without rebellions at home or mutinies in its armies. Ministers were no longer robbing the treasury, and the king was handling by himself

---

[105] MC, 1, Doc. V.
[106] Ibid., p. 114.
[107] Ibid., p. 110.

more business than Philip III or Philip II—this last an extremely improbable claim. As for the defence of the king's dominions, everything humanly possible had been done. The army of Flanders was guaranteed its pay for the whole of 1625, and a million ducats were already assured it for 1626. A million had also been provided for the army of Italy, and another million would be forthcoming within the week. The state of the Monarchy, then, was not unlike that of Gondomar himself—infirm and mortally ill, but all the same capable of sitting for six hours at a council meeting, and of crossing the Pyrenees in a litter.

I conclude, *señor conde*, by saying that I do not consider it useful to indulge in a constant despairing recital of the state of affairs, because the intelligent are already aware of it, and to make them despair of a remedy can only weaken their resolution, while it can do positive harm to the rest by undermining their confidence . . . But there is no risk in your writing all this to me, for I know it and lament it, without letting it weaken my determination or diminish my concern; for the extent of my obligation is such as to make me resolve to die clinging to my oar till not a splinter is left.

Was Olivares, then, as pessimistic as Gondomar about the future of Spain? Or was the image of the oarsman a nice piece of baroque rhetoric which would look well for the record? The defeatism of Gondomar was perhaps permissible in an old man of fifty-eight with only one more year to live, but it would hardly have come well from the man twenty years his junior who found himself entrusted with the government of the Monarchy. A resolute realism was therefore the obvious response to a letter of this sort, although the reference to Gondomar's age and infirmities was gratuitously (and characteristically) offensive. Things were bad, but they might have been worse; and for this the regime could no doubt claim some credit.

A similar realism distinguishes the Count-Duke's assessment of the European scene at this moment. He was obviously anxious not to push the enemies of the House of Austria to extremes, and so provoke a general European conflagration which Spain might be unable either to control or survive. This unwillingness was reflected in his refusal to be stampeded into war with France. It was also reflected in his response to the interest shown by the Emperor that spring in the plans for a League of Alliance. A special junta of the Council of State was set up at the beginning of May to consider the papers submitted by Khevenhüller on the Emperor's behalf. At the beginning of June it reported back to the king with a generally favourable verdict on Vienna's proposals.[108] It saw great advantages in the project to each of the principal participants, the Emperor, Bavaria and Spain itself, especially if (as it hoped) the king could take advantage of his status as a prince of the Empire to secure its involvement in the war with the Dutch. But, to embrace the maximum number of states, this must be a non-confessional alliance, created for the 'defence, peace and tranquillity of the Empire, and the provinces of Germany and Italy, against all those who attempt to disturb them.' This would allow the inclusion of Lutheran Saxony along with the pope (in his role as a temporal prince) and the King of Poland.

The Count-Duke, in a separate paper,[109] warmly endorsed the Junta's report, insisting that Saxony's inclusion was critical to the success of the League. It was very important not to drive the German Lutheran princes to despair; and the pope—who himself was at this very moment courting 'the most perfidious of all heretics condemned by the church, namely the Jews'—should feel no scruple about entering an alliance that included Lutheran princes, since this was the way to disunite the forces of Protestantism, setting Lutheran against Calvinist. In effect, the Count-Duke, like Richelieu on the other side, was acutely aware that a militantly confessional policy, of the kind advocated by the Emperor's Jesuit confessor Lamormaini[110] and by the *dévots* in France, simply did not respond to the complexities of seventeenth-century European life. At present, in the Count-Duke's words, the king was 'exhausting himself by taking on single-handed all the power of Europe.' This could not continue. Spain needed allies, and it needed stability in Germany; and this stability could never come if militantly Catholic policies drove the Lutherans into the arms of the Calvinists.

One of the inducements to realism in Olivares' assessment of Spains' situation and possibilities in the early summer of 1625 was his acute awareness of the financial constraints under which he was operating, although those same constraints could be turned to advantage when he found himself having to resist expensive policies of which he did not approve. Only two days after replying to Gondomar he drafted a confidential paper about the Council of Finance, in which he referred to his difficulties in organizing the defence of the Monarchy because of the total exhaustion of the treasury and the royal patrimony. He had, he said, spent a lot of time and thought on possible

---

[108] AGS Est. leg. 2327, fos. 370 and 371, consulta of Junta, 6 June 1625, enclosing *Parecer de la Junta* of 2 June.

[109] AGS Est. leg. 2327, fo. 372, *Parecer del Señor Conde Duque.*

[110] See Robert Bireley, *Religion and Politics in the Age of the Counterreformation. Emperor Ferdinand II, William Lamormaini, S. J., and the Formation of Imperial Policy* (Chapel Hill, 1981).

remedies, and had made himself innumerable enemies by closing the door on *mercedes* drawn from the king's exhausted reserves. He now proposed an end to the present system of direct administration of royal revenues by the Council of Finance and its officials—a system which had led to endless corruption and abuses—and a return to the farming of revenues and taxes. He also wanted sweeping changes in the composition of the council, which should be reconstituted with a president, two councillors and a secretary, all to hold office for only two years.[111]

A secret committee, convened to consider the Count-Duke's proposals, held several meetings during June, and reported favourably. But it would be a long time before any reforms in the machinery of financial administration would begin to show positive results in the form of increased revenues. In the meantime the enormous cost of paying for the campaigns of Spínola's army in Flanders and Feria's in Milan was straining the crown's credit to its limits. The armies, it was true, were poised for victory, but it soon became apparent that victory had its problems, no less than defeat.

On 5 June the defeated Dutch garrison under Justin of Nassau marched out of Breda with full battle honours.[112] The news reached Madrid on the 15th and was greeted with great rejoicings, Olivares rewarding the messenger with five hundred doubloons.[113] On the same day, at a meeting of the Council of State to discuss the latest information about the intentions of the British fleet, he again seized the opportunity to talk about the desperate financial straits to which Spain's enemies had reduced her.[114] With Spínola's triumph in Flanders, the pressure on him for a pre-emptive strike against France was bound to increase.

When the Council of State came to discuss the surrender of Breda and its implications, two of the activists—Hinojosa and Don Pedro de Toledo—were absent on duty, the first in Lisbon and the second in Galicia.[115] This was probably deliberate. In March the nuncio had reported that the two men were being sent to supervise the preparation of the fleet in order to thwart their ambitions and to keep them away from the Council of State, where they were opposing a negotiated settlement on the Valtelline.[116] Their absence did not,

[111] *MC*, 1, Doc. VI.
[112] Rodríguez Villa, *Ambrosio Spínola*, p. 431; and, for reactions to the event, Brown and Elliott, *A Palace*, pp. 178–84, and Simon A. Vosters, *La rendición de Bredá en la literatura y el arte de España* (London, 1973).
[113] González Palencia, *Noticias de Madrid*, p. 120.
[114] AGS Est. leg. 2645, consulta, 15 June 1625.
[115] AGS Est. leg. 2039, consulta, 29 June 1625 (draft version in AHN Est., lib. 740, fos. 342–5v.).
[116] ASV, Spagna, 65, fo. 199, 13 March 1625.

however, silence the demands for a massive strike against France. Again it was Montesclaros, supported by Monterrey, who wanted immediate action. Had he not represented to the king on numerous occasions how important it was not to be pushed around by those who wished the Monarchy no good? The crown had now assembled an enormous and highly expensive military machine which would be impossible to reconstitute if it were once disbanded. Everything, therefore, suggested that the time had come to declare war on the French and their allies and to invade France simultaneously from Piedmont and Flanders.

Olivares was prepared to recognize that the behaviour of the French amply justified a declaration of war. Their military activities in the Valtelline and the republic of Genoa, and the help they were giving the Dutch, left no doubt that they were aiming to destroy the Monarchy. And yet . . . Louis XIII was, after all, the king's brother-in-law. Nor were the fortunes of war predictable. Then came a disquisition on the problem of being a great power in a hostile world. The King of Spain needed no new conquests to maintain his reputation, for he was already, by a long way, the greatest king on earth. If he acquired still more territory he would only alarm all his rivals. In any event, it was good government, not new conquests, which made princes truly famous. Admitting his perplexity, Olivares advised the king to avoid arousing the fears of his fellow-princes. This meant that he should never be the first to declare war. The best approach to France was to induce Louis' ministers to negotiate by stirring up internal dissensions and by massing troops on its frontier.

Towards the end of the meeting it was clear that he had failed to carry his colleagues, and he spoke up again, this time ready with hard facts and figures to buttress his argument. On the day that the king declared war on France, the English and French crowns would consolidate their alliance, the Huguenots would lay down their arms, and the German Protestant princes would join a grand anti-Spanish coalition consisting of France and the Protestant powers of the north. And how would Spain pay for such a war, bearing in mind that war with France was not quite the same thing as war with Venice or Savoy? Then, for the benefit of innumerate colleagues, he totted up the costs of such a war for a single year. Allocations of fourteen to sixteen million ducats would be needed for 1626— figures that were simply out of the question at present. The breakdown of these figures gives some idea of the scale of costs with which Olivares found himself confronted, at a time when the crown's tax revenues were already mortgaged before collection, and when receipts of two million ducats a year in American silver were regarded as something of a windfall by treasury officials:

Army of Flanders	3,600,000	ducats (to be doubled if a second army was needed for the invasion of France)
Army of Milan	3,000,000	
Spanish fleet (60–70 ships)	1,500,000	
Flanders fleet (at its present strength)	250,000	
Frontier defences and royal households	2,500,000	
Interest payments, and exchange and conversion rates	3,500,000	
	14,350,000	

Olivares' figures, which are in line with costs and estimates given in the budget statements drawn up by the Council of Finance, tell their own story. In particular, they show that at this moment a quarter of the crown's expenditure was going on interest payments to the bankers and on the premium required for the conversion into silver of payments in *vellón*. It was not his wish, Olivares concluded, to be the odd man out, or to persist obstinately in his opinion, but it was his obligation to represent all this to His Majesty, 'so that in all times and circumstances he can refer to the counsel he has given.'

He did not, however, quite leave it to the king to make up his mind without benefit of further advice. The documents accompanying the *consulta* in its draft form show that on 1 July the king ordered Don Agustín Mexía, who had not attended the council meeting, to read the *consulta* alone and give his opinion. Everyone, Mexía reported diplomatically, had argued cogently; but in his opinion it would be wrong to declare war on France, for the reasons put forward by the Count-Duke.[117] In the light of this response the king ordered that copies of the opposing arguments should be forwarded to the Infanta Isabella in Brussels for her consideration. It was a well-tried method of playing for time.

Olivares' problem was to strike the right balance between the high expectations created by Spínola's victory at Breda, and the harsh financial realities implicit in the fact that when the besieged marched out of the surrendered fortress they were in considerably better shape than the besiegers.[118] The wretched state of Spínola's victorious but

[117] AHN Est. lib. 740, fos. 346–8, consulta of Mexía, 1 July 1625.
[118] Alcalá-Zamora, *España, Flandes*, p. 209.

underpaid army drove home the real lesson of Breda—that the traditional style of siege warfare practised in Flanders was impossibly expensive, and that the future pattern of war against the Dutch must be defence on the land and offence at sea. On 13 July instructions to this effect would be sent to Spínola, whose reward for Breda was appointment to the prestigious *encomienda mayor* of Castile (its revenues unfortunately mortgaged for the next twelve years).[119]

It was all the more difficult to strike the balance when victories were taken as visible manifestations of divine favour—as they were, not least by Olivares himself. On 6 July news of another great victory reached Madrid: the Dutch garrison at Bahía in Brazil had surrendered to Don Fadrique de Toledo on 1 May.[120] 'These are events', wrote Olivares of Breda and Brazil, 'which show that God aids His cause'; 'God is Spanish and favours our nation these days. Let us not waste them.'[121] But he also wrote to Don Carlos Coloma that they demanded a careful response if they were not to irritate the enemy rather than deter him.[122]

The caution was more than justified, in view of a report from the Council of Finance on 6 July that the bankers would stop all further payments, including the monthly payments to the royal households, until they were issued with drafts on the *millones* for 1626 and 1627.[123] It was not surprising, therefore, that Olivares should choose this moment to make another bid for that elusive prize, peace with the Dutch. On 11 July the Infanta was ordered to make discreet moves towards opening a new round of negotiations.[124] Once again, however, they would come to nothing. In the wake of the victories of that autumn, Olivares, perhaps deliberately, set his demands too high. However dispiriting for the Dutch the loss both of Breda and Brazil, Madrid's insistence that they should accept some form of Spanish sovereignty and give toleration to their Catholics was quite unacceptable.[125]

For all the Count-Duke's insistence on the need for caution, the papal nuncio, as he observed him, felt that he was in danger of being swept along by the rising tide of anti-French hysteria. He denounced Richelieu to the nuncio as the friend of heretics, and urged that the pope should declare him to have forfeited his cardinal's hat and even, perhaps, his life.[126] The expectation of an English invasion and of

---

[119] *Ibid.*, p. 210; Rodríguez Villa, *Ambrosio Spínola*, pp. 440–1.
[120] González Palencia, *Noticias de Madrid*, p. 122.
[121] BPM Ms. 1817, Olivares to Gondomar, 8 July and 3 July 1625.
[122] Rodríguez Villa, *Ambrosio Spínola*, p. 434.
[123] AGS CJH, leg. 602, consulta, 6 July 1625.
[124] Lonchay, *Correspondance*, 2, Doc. 718.
[125] Ródenas Vilar, *La política europea*, pp. 59–61; Israel, *The Dutch Republic*, pp. 223–4.
[126] ASV, Spagna, 65, fo. 284v., nuncio, 30 July 1625.

war with France had created a highly charged atmosphere at court. On 25 July the standards of the militia were raised[127] and Castile braced itself for the coming battle.

At this, of all moments, Olivares tendered his resignation to the king. He did so in a long and extraordinary document, dated 26 July.[128] With its long relation of family and personal services to the crown it read less like a letter of resignation than a standard petition for some favour from the king—except that the favour requested was leave to retire. Being drafted, too, by Olivares, it constantly broke away from the standard format to dwell on personal and family details which would normally have seemed superfluous and irrelevant. But this was more than a petition; it was a vindication—the vindication of a house and a man whose legitimate grievances had been more than cancelled by the overwhelming generosity of the greatest of kings.

Olivares began his story (how often he must have heard it in his childhood!) with Ruy Pérez de Guzmán fighting the Moors in 1015. Name by name the long line of descent was carefully chronicled. So, too, was the process by which the Counts of Olivares were deprived of the succession to the dukedom of Medina Sidonia. His father, his grandfather, each of his ancestors—they had all loyally served their kings; and his father in particular, how little rewarded! Then came the story of Olivares' own struggles to serve Philip honourably while he was still a prince—services which again went unacknowledged and unrewarded until suddenly, on his accession, Philip had been pleased to raise him to his present undeserved eminence. Thanks to His Majesty's favour and munificence 'this house and this slave' had been 'born again'.

After this long personal introduction, full of the self-demeaning rhetoric in which Olivares was always liable to indulge, he abruptly switched to the theme which he had broached eight weeks earlier in his reply to Gondomar—a comparison between the condition of Spain at the moment of Philip's accession and its present condition in 1625. Not only the theme but some of the turns of phrase were lifted from the letter to Gondomar; but this time the sketch was filled out with detail, and the dark and the light were placed in sharp relief. 1621 was a time of almost total darkness: a ruined treasury, corrupt ministers, neglected and demoralized armies and fleets. And today? As a result of the recent subsidy voted by the Cortes, His Majesty had three million more ducats in revenues than on his accession. He had also been given a *donativo*, which had already reached

---

[127] Alcalá-Zamora, *España, Flandes*, p. 114.
[128] *MC*, 1, Doc. VII.

four millions, for redeeming his debts. For his part, Philip had reduced his household expenses and closed the door on *mercedes* in cash. The administration of justice, if not yet perfect, was 'on the road to perfection', and ministers no longer accepted bribes. At the age of twenty, Philip was personally handling forty-four out of every fifty *consultas*, and making his own decisions on a vast range of appointments and *mercedes*. Ecclesiastical appointments he handled with his confessor, without the papers being seen by Olivares. Juntas and tribunals were now sitting on every issue of substance that had come up in the last three hundred years—trade and shipping, internal navigation and repopulation schemes, the exploitation of Spain's disused mines, the manufacture of armaments, and the reform of government and the royal finances.

No less impressive was the military record at a time when France, England, Denmark, Sweden, Venice, Savoy, the Palatinate, the German Protestant princes and the Dutch had all lined up against His Majesty—when in 'Asia, Africa and Europe' he had been taken on single-handed by all the rest of the world. The defence preparations told their own story: 140,000 men under arms in the Iberian peninsula; 70,000 paid men in Flanders, 70,000 in Lombardy, 12,000 in Genoa; North Africa, Naples and Sicily all well defended; 70 galleys (compared with 5 or 6 in 1621), 20 galleons in Flanders, 56 in Brazil, 52 in Lisbon, 8 in Genoa, not counting those in the treasure fleets. Breda had been captured, Brazil recovered, and the latest news from Genoa was that the enemy had been put to ignominious flight.

As Olivares stepped back and surveyed the scene, he found it inconceivable that so much could have been achieved by unaided human efforts. It was the work of God—and of the king. As for himself, he was no more than the weary servant of His Majesty, who had felt it wrong to leave his place at the oar so long as the skies were overcast. But now that God had placed the king on the road to felicity and had exalted his greatness and his power, he humbly asked leave to retire to his corner, more than satisfied with the honours lavished upon him by munificent royal hands.

What are we to make of this extraordinary outpouring, this strange amalgam of cringing self-abasement and complacency? And how, too, explain its peculiar timing, the day after the raising of the colours for the country's defence, and when Spain was 'awaiting hourly' the appearance of an English invading fleet of '130 ships'?[129] The sombre tones of the letter to Gondomar had given way to the roseate hues of a victorious Spain. Thanks to Breda, Genoa and Brazil, it is to be assumed that the skies were no longer 'overcast'. Nor was

---

[129] *Ibid.*, p. 152.

it any longer a question of clutching the last splinter of the oar, but of voluntarily exchanging the rowing bench for a quiet retreat. There is no reason to doubt Olivares' word when he speaks of his exhaustion—it had, after all, required a heroic effort to get the fleets fitted out and the armies paid. Even if some of his statistics are over-enthusiastic, it is hard to imagine any other contemporary European state being capable of building up so massive a war-machine in such a short space of time. The mighty administrative structure of ministers and officials, provisioners and supervisors may have creaked and groaned, but when it was driven hard it could still mount a major operation, like the organization and despatch of Don Fadrique de Toledo's Brazilian armada of 56 vessels in a mere six months. Could the England of Charles I compare with that?

There was, then, good reason to be proud of the record of achievement, which it was politic to ascribe to Philip's leadership. But this great vindication of four years of government would hardly seem necessary if the record had not been under attack. Gondomar's sense that the ship was sinking was no doubt widely shared, at least among the older generation in the ruling group. No doubt, too, efforts had been made to communicate the feeling of alarm to the king. There had also been the sharp divisions over whether or not to go to war with France, and again Olivares' leadership had been called into question. In the circumstances it may well have seemed a good moment for the Count-Duke to strike back. Breda and Brazil told their own story. These were glorious victories which had raised the King of Spain's prestige to unprecedented heights. What better moment—with an English invasion hourly expected—to ask for leave to retire? How could the king, in the moment of victory and with new dangers threatening, conceivably agree to such a request?

The pilot, then,—or, rather, the oarsman—would not be dropped. Instead, he reinforced his position by having his offer turned down, and skilfully emphasized his own indispensability. Only the Count-Duke, with his determination and his unflagging energy, could ensure that the national defences were adequate to withstand the impending English attack. Throughout the autumn he laboured tirelessly. Never since entering the royal service had he been so overwhelmed with great affairs of state, he wrote to Gondomar in September. The activities of the English, the French and the Danes, all coming together at one and the same time, had put him under intolerable strain.[130]

The final dispositions were taken in October, as the English fleet under the command of Sir Edward Cecil struggled to put out to sea. Olivares himself was named general of the Spanish cavalry; Don

---

[130] BPM, Ms. 1817, Olivares to Gondomar, 14 September 1625.

Augustín Mexía, general of the Castilian Armada; Don Pedro de Toledo, general in Aragon, Catalonia, Valencia and Navarre; and Olivares' cousin, Don Diego Mexía, *maestre de campo general* of the army of Castile.[131] But the intentions of the English were still unknown, and the appearance of an Anglo-Dutch fleet of ninety ships in the Bay of Cadiz on 1 November came as a surprise.

The news reached Madrid on the 5th,[132] and the next day Olivares commented in a letter to the Spanish ambassador at Vienna on the extraordinary secrecy with which the English had managed to carry out their enterprise.[133] But his letter exuded confidence. Don Fernando Girón had everything prepared in Cadiz, where fourteen galleons of Don Fadrique de Toledo's fleet, now safely returned from Brazil, were among the ships that faced the enemy.[134] Moreover, the nobles and gentry were flocking to Andalusia in such large numbers that some of them had to be held back to prevent confusion. Olivares himself, as the newly appointed general of the Spanish cavalry, donned his armour and went riding in the riding-school behind the Alcázar. His intentions, as usual, were regarded as suspect. 'Under this pretext of governing and of raising men', reported the papal nuncio, the Count-Duke was thought to have succeeded in clearing Madrid of real or potential enemies, although he was so consumed by suspicion that he distrusted even his own nephew, Don Luis de Haro—always a favourite of the king—and derived no pleasure from his great position.[135]

Even if he had some fears for the safety of the treasure fleet on its homeward journey, Olivares was confident enough of Spain's newly achieved naval strength to believe that the English would meet a satisfactorily hostile reception. His confidence was fully justified. Sir Edward Cecil's expedition was a fiasco. Soon after being put ashore, the English landing-force, hot and exhausted, came across great vats of wine in deserted farmhouses on the road to Cadiz, and quickly degenerated into a drunken rabble. An assault on Cadiz itself was now out of the question, and on 6 November Cecil ordered the re-embarkation of his hungry and demoralized men. Still hoping to catch the treasure ships, the English fleet then stationed itself off the southern coast of Portugal until 26 November, when its increasingly unseaworthy condition compelled Cecil to order it to sail for home.[136] Three days later the galleons of Tierra Firme and the *flota*

[131] Khevenhüller, *Annales Ferdinandei*, 2, p. 1033.
[132] González Palencia, *Noticias de Madrid*, p. 126.
[133] ADM, leg. 79, Olivares to Count of Osona, 6 November 1625.
[134] Chaunu, *Séville et l'Atlantique*, 5, p. 105.
[135] ASV, Spagna, 65, fo. 371, nuncio, 12 November 1625.
[136] Gardiner, *History of England*, 6, pp. 20–21; Lockyer, *Buckingham*, pp. 281–4.

of New Spain put safely into Cadiz.[137] In gratitude for their safe arrival, the king gave orders that the sacrament should be celebrated in the churches of Spain in perpetuity every 29 November.[138]

The defeat of the English at Cadiz was a triumph for the Conde-Duque, and one that must have given him particular personal satisfaction. For if, as he claimed, it was he who had prevented the conclusion of the English marriage in 1623, then this was his war, and was widely regarded as such. Gondomar and his other critics had warned him of the overwhelming power of England, and the events of Cadiz had proved him, and not them, to be right. This 'horrible power' of England[139] had been revealed as a sham.

This vindication of Olivares' policies set the seal on a year of great victories for Spain, which were promptly commemorated by reenactments on the stage.[140] Brazil, Breda, Genoa, Cadiz—together with the repulse of a Dutch attack on Puerto Rico in September,[141] the news of which had yet to reach Madrid—would show the world that Spanish power was not in decline. The Count-Duke looked to be well on the way to achieving his ambition of overawing the world with his master's fame. It seems to have been now, in this year of victory, 1625, that Philip first came to be officially styled *Felipe el Grande*, a king great in the arts of war and peace.[142] In 1634 and 1635, when pictures were being commissioned for the new palace of the Buen Retiro, five of the twelve battle paintings in the great series for the Hall of Realms were devoted to the victories of 1625: Cadiz, Breda, Genoa, Bahía, and San Juan de Puerto Rico. If Velázquez's *Surrender of Breda* has acquired the greatest fame, the most revealing picture in the series is Juan Bautista Maino's depiction of the recovery of Brazil. Within the painting is another painting to which Don Fadrique de Toledo points. It depicts Philip the Great in armour being crowned with laurels by Minerva and the Count-Duke of Olivares. The Count-Duke stands back from his royal

---

[137] Chaunu, *Séville et l'Atlantique*, 5, p. 113.

[138] Céspedes y Meneses, *Historia de Felipe IV*, fo. 255v.

[139] *MC*, 1, p. 115.

[140] Calderón's *El sitio de Bredá*, and Lope de Vega's *El Brasil restituido*. For the first of these see Shirley B. Whitaker, 'The First Performance of Calderón's *El sitio de Bredá*', *Renaissance Quarterly*, 31 (1978), pp. 515–31.

[141] Enriqueta Vila Vilar, *Historia de Puerto Rico, 1600–1650* (Seville, 1974), pp. 137–50.

[142] Martin Hume (*The Court of Philip IV*, p. 155) says that Olivares, following these victories, 'caused the title to be officially accorded to his young master', but I have found no indication of any official declaration to this effect. Nor does Juan de Tapia's panegyric of Philip's greatness, *Ilustración del renombre de grande* (Madrid, 1638) mention any formal proclamation or indicate when the title first began to be used. In 1625 Velázquez painted the king in armour on horseback, and, according to Palomino, inscribed the painting: PHILIPPUS MAGN. HVIVS NOM. IV. POTENTISSIMUS HISPANIARUM REX., INDIAR. MAXIM. IMP. ANNO CHRISTI. XXV, SAECULI XVII. ETA. XX. A. (Elías Tormo y Monzó, *Pintura, escultura y arquitectura en España* [Madrid, 1949], p. 169).

13. This detail from Juan Bautista Maino's *Recapture of Bahía*, painted in 1635 for the Hall of Realms, shows Don Fadrique de Toledo, the commander of the Brazil expeditionary force, before a painting of Philip IV being crowned with laurels by Minerva and the Count-Duke, while Heresy, Discord and Treachery lie under foot.

master, but he stands back rather in the manner of the marionette-player who pulls the strings (P1. 13).[143]

Felipe el Grande was the Count-Duke's creation. He was the figure envisaged in the Great Memorial of 1624, the king who ruled with justice at home, while laying down the law to his enemies abroad. The Monarchy was at last on the road to revival; and Olivares took this as clear evidence that God had chosen to look on his royal master with special favour. But if '*el Grande*' was a recognition of achievement, it was also in part a statement of intent. Much still remained to be done, and there was no better time than the present. Philip, King of Portugal, Aragon and Valencia, and Count of Barcelona, was not yet King of Spain. With the country mobilized for war and still under threat, this was the moment to embark on the great task of uniting the arms of his various peoples as a necessary prelude to the still greater task of uniting their hearts.

[143] For the battle paintings, see Brown and Elliott, *A Palace*, pp. 161–90.

VII

THE UNION OF ARMS

The project unveiled

In a surprisingly expansive letter written in December 1625 to his old rival Don Fernando de Borja, now languishing in Zaragoza as viceroy of Aragon, the Count-Duke explained that, ever since entering the king's service, he had been trying to find some way by which the various kingdoms could be made to act 'each for all, and all for each.'[1] Since the Monarchy contained so many realms, all so diverse in their 'humours', there would no doubt be some difficulty in persuading them to accept the scheme he had in mind—a common programme for defence, a 'union of arms'—even though this would entail no alteration in their laws and institutions. For this reason, he had been waiting for the moment when events themselves would predispose people in its favour. This moment had now come. Spain's enemies could do her a good turn if their enmity were to bring about a 'firm and perpetual union of kingdom to kingdom.'

The Count-Duke had in fact already prepared on 15 October a document putting the case for a programme for mutual defence that would bring to an end the 'separation of hearts' between the various kingdoms of the Monarchy.[2] The news of the English invasion provided just the scenario he needed for unveiling his scheme to his colleagues on the Council of State. The day chosen was 13 November 1625; the occasion, an order from the king on the 11th for the council to consider the general situation resulting from the shortage of men and money at a time when all Spain's enemies were up in arms against her.

If, as seems possible, this was the meeting of the Council of State ironically described by Matías de Novoa,[3] then it was carefully stage-

---

[1] Bodleian Library, Oxford. Arch. Seld. A. Subt. 22, Olivares to Borja, 2 December 1625.

[2] See *MC*, 1, Doc. IX, for the (slightly revised) version of this document, as prepared for publication and distribution. The draft of 15 October, entitled *Papel que escribió el Conde Duque deseando entablar la unión de los reinos de esta Monarquía* is in BL Eg. Ms. 347, fos. 119–26.

[3] Novoa, *Codoin* 69, pp. 11–13. There is a brief summary of Olivares' speech in AHN Est., lib. 738, fos. 39–40. The whole consulta is in the Archivo de los Condes de Oñate, leg. 104, expte. 1638. I am much indebted to the Marqueses de Torre Blanca for allowing me to see it.

managed, with Philip and his brothers listening to the proceedings behind the grilled window that served as a peep-hole into the council chamber. The first three councillors to speak—Don Agustín Mexía, Cardinal Zapata and the Marquis of Aytona—all argued for a truce with the United Provinces because of the crippling shortage of money. Only three weeks before, on 1 November, the king had in fact decided to appropriate two-fifths of the silver due to arrive on private account in the eagerly awaited treasure fleet, compensating the unfortunate owners in the much-debased *vellón* coinage—a proceeding which in practice meant the loss of one-fifth of their capital.[4] The Marquis of Montesclaros, although nominally in charge of the crown's finances, brushed these difficulties aside. The king should trust in God and his vassals, instead of attempting to balance his commitments against his resources. The time to press for peace was later, after more victories had been won. Don Diego de Ibarra, who followed Montesclaros, favoured a truce with the Dutch if it could be obtained on better terms than those of 1609, and thought that the best hope of peace lay in Germany.

It was now the turn of Olivares. Rising to his feet and—according to Novoa—inserting the tip of his cane between his hair-piece and his bald patch, he paused a shade too long in order to create the maximum effect, and then embarked on a two-hour speech. The king, he began, was fighting on God's side, in the Valtelline and in Genoa, and against the English and the Dutch. He agreed with Montesclaros that this was not the moment to initiate negotiations for peace. The area of first priority was Italy; and here it was necessary to await the arrival of Cardinal Barberini, still on his mission to Paris, to see if the pope could be induced to join a grand alliance against the northern heretics, offering him in return a general Italian settlement. The next priority was to press hard for the proposed League of Alliance with the Emperor and friendly German princes, and at the same time send his old Sevillian friend Juan de Vera y Figueroa to Warsaw to see if Sigismund III of Poland, too, could be persuaded to participate. Spanish troops, in the meantime, should be massed along the frontier with France.

Never, he continued, had the Monarchy found itself so beleaguered, and at this point, 'although with some trepidation', he broached his grand design. Although the king had more territory, power and resources than all his enemies, he could not but view with concern the unsatisfactory relationship between Castile and the

---

[4] For this sequestration, see Domínguez Ortiz, *Política y hacienda*, p. 287. The Council of the Indies, discussing the terms of the compensation in a consulta of 10 November 1625 (AGI Indif. leg. 755) estimated that, at the current official conversion rate of silver to *vellón*, they would get the equivalent of no more than eighty ducats on every hundred of silver.

other kingdoms of the Monarchy, which were separated from it and
were looked upon with mistrust. The Count-Duke therefore recommended that the king should 'form a league' with his kingdoms to
make the Monarchy entirely secure. Each of them should be asked
to send two plenipotentiaries to Madrid. After discussing matters
of mutual concern with the king, they would all be assembled, along
with two deputies from Castile and two from León, to hear him
speak about the state of his Monarchy, the dangers that faced it,
and his intention that all his kingdoms should be treated on an equal
footing. Following the king's speech they would be instructed to
arrange among themselves the quota of paid men to be levied by
each kingdom as a contribution to an army that could be used to
repel an invasion of any part of the Monarchy, or to take the offensive
when needed. As a tailpiece to this proposal, which Olivares seemed
to think would win general acceptance on its merits, he recommended
that the fortresses of Castile should be garrisoned by non-Castilians,
and those of the other kingdoms by men from Castile and elsewhere.

It is clear that the Count-Duke envisaged his plan for the Union
of Arms both as a desirable end in itself, and as a means of working
towards that integration of the peoples and kingdoms of the
Monarchy which he had proposed to Philip as the principal objective
of his reign. What better method than to begin with the most 'natural'
of instincts, self-preservation?[5] This itself persuaded him that the
Union of Arms would secure the approval of those whom it was
intended to help. Who could fail to see its advantages when the enemy
was battering at the gates? But, unfortunately for the Count-Duke,
there was rather less battering at some gates than at others. Would
Aragon really be interested in coming to the help of Flanders? Or
was Valencia really preoccupied with the threat from the French?
Yet his scheme was worked out on the basis of assumed mutual
interests deriving from a common danger which was presumed to
threaten all to an equal degree.

It is improbable that the Union of Arms sprang fully formed from
the Count-Duke's fertile brain, and in his speech he himself referred
to the circles (*Kreise*) of the Holy Roman Empire as a working model
of the system he had in mind. Its general character was implicit
in Botero's comments about the weaknesses of 'dispersed states',[6]
but it is likely that more specific proposals were also in circulation,
and that the Count-Duke drew on these for the formulation of his
scheme. One such proposal is outlined in the *Politico-Christianus*, a
book published in Antwerp in 1624 by a Flemish Jesuit, Carolus

[5] 'El fin de la propria conservación es natural'—Olivares in his letter of 2 December 1625
to Don Fernando de Borja.
[6] Above, p. 192.

Scribani, who sent complimentary copies to the king and the Count-Duke with fulsome letters of dedication.[7] In his book, Scribani refers to a project devised in 1615 by a 'great man' who was an expert in Spanish affairs, although apparently not himself a Spaniard. This 'great man'—in all probability Spínola—suggested that the burdens of the war in the Netherlands could be more easily borne if they were shared out on the basis of a quota system among the kingdoms and provinces of the Iberian peninsula. Between them these would be responsible for providing a reserve force of 221,000 paid infantry and 89,900 cavalry, a quarter of which would be called on to serve at any one time. The combined quota for Aragon and Catalonia would be 36,000 infantry and 14,000 cavalry; the Portuguese quota, 20,000 infantry and 10,000 cavalry; Valencia and Murcia together would be responsible for 16,000 infantry and 8,000 cavalry; the rest would be provided by the Crown of Castile, and by Vizcaya and Navarre, with the military orders and the titled nobility producing their own quotas according to rank. While the author of the scheme admitted that the Crown of Aragon and Portugal might raise objections, he thought that a royal visit would succeed in dispelling them.[8]

Although this 1615 proposal envisaged a much larger reserve of paid men than the one that the Count-Duke now planned to establish, it could well have been a source of inspiration for the Union of Arms, which in other respects resembled it closely. Once it became clear, as it quickly did, that the Count-Duke's idea for an assembly of plenipotentiaries of the various kingdoms was unlikely to work, he prepared a document justifying the scheme and expounding its method of operation in detail.[9] As in the scheme described by Scribani, a quota system would be established. Under this system the different parts of the Monarchy would commit themselves to providing and maintaining a fixed number of paid men, who would constitute a common military reserve for the Monarchy as a whole. These quotas, which were presumably determined on the basis of population estimates of varying degrees of unreliability, were assigned as follows:

Catalonia	16,000
Aragon	10,000
Valencia	6,000
Castile and the Indies	44,000

[7] L. Brouwers, *Brieven van Carolus Scribani (1561–1629)* (Antwerp, 1972), letters 15 and 16. I am grateful to Professor Robert Bireley for first bringing Scribani to my notice, and to my colleague Professor Glen Bowersock for his help with Scribani's text.

[8] Carolus Scribani, *Politico-Christianus* (Antwerp, 1624), pp. 596–609. L. Brouwers, *Carolus Scribani SJ., 1561–1629* (Antwerp, 1961), p. 459 n. 117, takes the identification of the 'great man' with Spínola for granted.

[9] *MC*, 1, Doc. IX.

Portugal	16,000
Naples	16,000
Sicily	6,000
Milan	8,000
Flanders	12,000
Mediterranean and Atlantic islands	6,000

These 140,000 men would not be permanently under arms, but would be trained on holidays, like the militia, and would be available in case of emergency. If any part of the Monarchy were attacked, one seventh of this reserve force—20,000 infantrymen together with 4,000 cavalry—would be assigned to its defence, with each province providing one seventh of its quota. Similarly, if there were three wars simultaneously, three sevenths of the total reserve would be called to arms.

Olivares was prepared to promise that the levying and payment of these troops should be handled entirely by local officials, and that if it proved impossible for any one kingdom to fulfil its quota, the shortfall would be made good from another. But it was open to question whether a scheme which looked eminently just and sensible when studied in Madrid, would commend itself to kingdoms congenitally suspicious of Castile's intentions. Even the way in which the Union should be presented to those kingdoms raised delicate questions, as the Marquis of Caracena pointed out in the meeting of the Council of State on 13 November at which Olivares outlined his plan. Taking into account the proximity of Aragon and Catalonia to France (always a source of anxiety to Madrid), he thought it advisable that such a project should be formally presented to the Cortes of the various kingdoms, with His Majesty present.

The Count-Duke seems to have accepted that, at least in the Crown of Aragon, it would be necessary to hold meetings of the Cortes to obtain approval for the Union of Arms. But his need for money and men was pressing, and he worked out a timetable which revealed little awareness of the likely reactions to his project. Four regents of the Council of Aragon were issued on 15 November with letters to be delivered in person to the local elected authorities—the Deputies or Estates—of Catalonia, Aragon, Valencia, and the Balearic Islands; and each was instructed to outline the Union of Arms to them in his respective kingdom or province, and to expound its merits.[10]

If the regents reported back to Madrid that a royal visit to the Crown of Aragon seemed likely to win acceptance for the Union, orders should be sent to the Duke of Alba in Naples and the Marquis of Tavara in Sicily to press ahead with it in their respective viceroyal-

---

[10] RAH G.43. D. J. Dormer, *Anales de la Corona de Aragón en el reinado de Felipe IV el Grande*, lib. 2, ch. 1. The instructions themselves have not come to light.

ties. As for Milan, where the Count-Duke understood the royal government to be as 'absolute as it is in the Indies', it should be possible to settle the matter in the Council of Italy. He thought that the loyal provinces of the Southern Netherlands would willingly participate in a project designed for their own defence, and the Infanta Isabella would be asked to proceed with the necessary arrangements.[11] Simultaneously the three Cortes of Aragon, Valencia and Catalonia should be summoned to meet in mid-December, all in the same town. The king, travelling as lightly as if he were going to his Pardo palace just outside Madrid, would take the oath there to guarantee their constitutional rights and would seek to persuade the three Cortes to accept the Union. It was to be hoped that everything could be concluded by the end of January, but it might be necessary to offer a return visit for an entire year at a later date.[12]

The Count-Duke's projected timetable, however, did not end with January, for the Union was seen as part of a wider offensive and defensive movement against Spain's enemies. At the Council of State's meeting on 20 November it was agreed that the only proper response to the English attack on Cadiz was an invasion of Ireland. This would be launched from the Iberian peninsula with a hundred ships and some twenty thousand men. The invasion force would be supported by another fleet from Flanders which would ravage the English coast, or even attempt to establish a base on English soil. Meanwhile, as previously agreed, peace negotiations should be pursued with the Dutch on the basis of a recognition of the rights of Dutch Roman Catholics and of some sort of Spanish sovereignty; and troops should be massed along the frontiers of France, which would be kept quiet over the winter by being given (in the Count-Duke's words) a 'bone to gnaw' in the form of possible concessions on the Valtelline.

The timetable therefore demanded that, as soon as the Union of Arms was approved by the Cortes of Aragon, Catalonia and Valencia, troops should be moved up to the French frontier at both ends of the Pyrenees, in Catalonia and Guipúzcoa. The king himself would then travel to Llerena in south-west Spain, where Don Agustín Mexía would be assembling the paid infantrymen who were to embark at Cadiz. By the beginning of March preparations would be sufficiently advanced for His Majesty to take up residence in Lisbon, where he would remain until the invasion armada would be ready to sail to Ireland.

[11] AHN Est. lib. 738, fos. 41–2v. and 43–4v., undated summaries in Carnero's hand, headed *Sobre la unión en Flandes* and *Sobre unión en Italia*, following the summary (fos. 39–40) of Olivares' *voto* in the Council of State of 13 November 1625.

[12] AGS Est. leg. 2041, consulta, 20 November 1625.

This vastly complex operation would not, Olivares admitted, be easy to mount, and time was of the essence. Indeed, if he had not 'seen God work miracles' on behalf of His Majesty, he would regard it as an impossibility. This sense of the identification of God's cause and that of Spain, triumphantly reinforced by the chain of victories from Breda to Cadiz, had undoubtedly created a new psychological climate at court. Winter was always the season for dreams, but the grand designs were all too soon dispelled as a new year imposed its own realities. Those last weeks of 1625, made glorious by the rout of the English at Cadiz, were more than usually conducive to dreams. But how far was the Count-Duke really swayed by his own rhetoric? He had, it seemed, thrown his caution of June and July to the winds, and all the talk was now of massing armies and fitting out armadas. But the papal nuncio believed that it was all for the sake of appearances; that 'he always wants to demonstrate that he does not want what he really wants'; and that the best minds in the Council of State were agreed that the shortage of men and money made peace necessary, but that this peace would be more secure if the king appeared formidably armed.[13]

The Count-Duke's tightly drawn timetable for mobilizing the Monarchy could be thrown into disarray, as he was well aware, by local resistance, by a shortage of money, or by both. A succession of letters to Madrid from the viceroys in Aragon, Catalonia and Valencia had emphasized the resentment aroused in the Crown of Aragon by the failure of the new king to pay a state visit and take the oath to observe their laws and liberties.[14] Where kingship was looked upon, as it was by the Crown of Aragon, as a contractual agreement, this failure was easily interpreted as representing a deliberate intent to subvert cherished laws and institutions. The Aragonese and Catalans had long felt themselves neglected and slighted by Madrid, and there existed a whole backlog of grievances which could only be remedied in the correct constitutional manner—by the holding of Cortes presided over, as their constitutions required, by the royal person. Even Olivares, unattuned as he was to these provincial sensibilities, had some doubts about a rapid royal visit which would allow time only for the king's swearing-in and for the formal adoption by the Cortes of the Union of Arms. Yet he wanted to prevent a situation in which the king was endlessly delayed in the Crown of Aragon by the determination of the Cortes to attend to other matters; and he left it to Don Fernando de Borja, with his greater knowledge of the local scene, to advise whether a possible alternative

[13] ASV, Spagna 65, fo. 388v., nuncio, 6 December 1625.
[14] See Elliott, *Catalans*, ch. 6.

14. Olivares wrote to Rubens in August 1626 thanking him for this allegorical portrait as engraved by Pontius. He appears in it wearing the sash of captain-general of the cavalry, the appointment given him at the time of the English attack on Cadiz in 1625. The emblems of Minerva and Hercules, on the left and right, symbolize his combination of wisdom and valour, while the globe, baton and rudder above his head allude to his skilful and prudent policy. In the poem, by Gaspar Gevaerts, the triumphant olive spreads its peace-bringing leaves across the world.

in Aragon might not be a short royal visit followed by a continuation of the Cortes under the presidency of some suitably qualified figure.[15]

It very soon became apparent that these doubts were well-founded. The Regent Castelví 'surpassed Demosthenes' in the eloquence with which he expounded the Union of Arms to the Noble Estate of Valencia;[16] and the Regent Fontanet, with his own ambitions for higher office, spared no efforts with the Catalans.[17] But the replies sent back to Madrid were uniformly discouraging. Where information was scarce, rumours abounded; and the arrival of these emissaries of the court had aroused the darkest suspicions in Barcelona, Zaragoza and Valencia. What did they really want? A request for troops was perhaps no more than a cover, and there was talk of Olivares planning to introduce 'one crown, one law, one coinage'.[18]

The Great Memorial of 1624 presumably remained a secret between the Count-Duke and the king, although it is hard to believe that the playwright Mira de Amescua was drawing a bow entirely at a venture when he had the clown Pablillos in the *Próspera fortuna de Don Alvaro de Luna* produce a project with an uncanny resemblance to the centrepiece of the Great Memorial: '*arbitrio* to make the King of Castile, King of Granada, Aragon, Navarre, Portugal, the Antipodes and the New Worlds.'[19] But if Olivares was indeed in the habit of going around murmuring *multa regna, sed una lex*,[20] it is not difficult to understand the rumours about 'one crown, one law.' 'One coinage' remains more problematical, but in a discussion in the Council of State on 1 November about the *vellón* inflation in Castile, which was now reaching crisis proportions, the Count-Duke had mentioned the possibility of introducing a new silver coinage with an admixture of copper which would be interchangeable with similar coins in the other realms of the peninsula, and even in Italy and Flanders.[21] Montesclaros, in some draft notes, went even further, and suggested that efforts should be made to get Castilian *vellón*

[15] Olivares to Borja, 2 December 1625.

[16] The text of Castelví's speech, delivered on 20 December 1625, is printed in Dámaso de Lario Ramírez, *Cortes del reinado de Felipe IV. 1. Cortes Valencianas de 1626* (Valencia, 1973), xx–xxiii. I owe to Dr. J. G. Casey the analogy to Demosthenes, which is taken from Mossèn Porcar's *Coses evengudes en la ciutat y regne de València*, ed. V. Castañeda Alcover (Madrid, 1934).

[17] Luca Assarino, *Le rivolutioni di Catalogna* (Bologna, 1648), p. 22.

[18] Elliott, *Catalans*, citing the diary of Dr. Pujades, now published as *Dietari de Jeroni Pujades*, ed. Josep Maria Casas Homs (4 vols., Barcelona, 1975–6), 3, p. 236.

[19] Mira de Amescua, *Comedia famosa de Ruy López de Avalos (Primera parte de don Alvaro de Luna)*, ed. Nellie E. Sánchez-Arce (México, 1965), p. 53 (jornada primera). The allusion appears to have escaped notice, but it would reinforce the editor's tentative dating of the play to 1623–4 (p. 15). Mira de Amescua's authorship of this play and its companion-piece, *Adversa fortuna de don Alvaro de Luna*, seems probable, but has not been definitively established.

[20] Above, p. 197.

[21] AHN Est. lib. 741, fo. 118, consulta, 1 November 1625.

to circulate throughout the peninsula, 'since it is not unreasonable that this infirmity should be spread through all the members of the body.'[22] In effect he was advocating that Castile should export its inflation; and this is exactly what the urban oligarchies of the Crown of Aragon feared.

It was the fears of the provincial ruling class in Aragon, Catalonia and Valencia about the intentions that lurked behind Madrid's new-fangled proposals, which wrecked the Count-Duke's timetable from the beginning, and almost immediately brought into question the prospects for the long-term success of his plans. Peoples who had not seen their monarch for twenty years or more—the last royal visit was that of Philip III to Valencia in 1604—were unlikely to respond with much enthusiasm to the idea of a brief, token visit, even if it were accompanied by a promise to return at a later date and spend a whole year in the Crown of Aragon. Too many grievances cried out for royal attention; too many provincial nobles were eager for *mercedes*.

Royal progresses were expensive, which is one reason why, four years after his accession, Philip IV had still not been to visit his subjects in the Crown of Aragon. But it was clear that the Union of Arms had no chance of acceptance without approval by the Cortes; and constitutionally the Cortes could only be held if the king were present. On 21 December 1625, therefore, after the viceroys and the emissaries from the Council of Aragon had sent back their reports to Madrid, the Council of State recommended a royal visit; and the king, in replying, fixed it for 7 January.[23] The Aragonese Cortes were summoned to meet at Barbastro on 15 January, the Valencian Cortes at Monzón, and the Catalan Cortes at Lérida—a location which aroused such indignation that Olivares found it expedient to have them transferred to Barcelona even before the king set foot in the Principality.[24]

Before the king could leave Madrid, extensive preparations had first to be made. The most pressing problem was the provision of money for 1626. The Genoese bankers, their own credit increasingly battered,[25] were described by their ambassador as very reluctant to undertake assignations; and on the eve of the king's departure the *asientos* had still not been agreed.[26] But at the last moment, after the Count-Duke had spent an entire night haggling with the

---

[22] ADI Montesclaros Mss. lib. 130, no. 29, *borrador*.

[23] Elliott, *Catalans*, p. 214.

[24] *Ibid.*, p. 216.

[25] Ruiz Martín, 'La banca en España', pp. 97–8.

[26] ASG, Lettere ministri, Spagna, 2432, despatch of G. B. Serra, 7 January 1626.

bankers,[27] agreement was reached for the provision of three million ducats in Flanders and another three million in Spain.

There were, too, some administrative changes to be made. The time had come to carry out the clean sweep of the Council of Finance which Olivares had advocated six months earlier.[28] One of the problems was to ease Montesclaros out of the presidency without damaging his reputation; and for this the king's visit to Aragon provided a convenient opportunity. On the pretext that he was needed to accompany the king and undertake special duties in the Crown of Aragon he could be honourably replaced. On 7 January 1626 he was succeeded by Gilimón de la Mota, although with the title of Contador Mayor de Cuentas, instead of President.[29] Gilimón's closeness to Olivares made him an attractive replacement at a moment when the Count-Duke was attempting to obtain a tighter control over the receipt and disbursement of the royal revenues. Montesclaros had proved an awkward colleague, always liable to take an independent line both on foreign and domestic issues, and recently he had been at odds with Olivares over ways of curbing inflation in Castile.[30] Olivares may also have had another consideration in mind. The fact that Montesclaros' departure was much regretted by the Genoese bankers[31] suggests that a mutually beneficial relationship may have grown up between them, and the Count-Duke was already laying plans for breaking their stranglehold over the crown's finances.

Gilimón's appointment was followed on 24 January by the reconstitution of the Council of Finance with a new membership, including the septuagenarian Alamos de Barrientos and the Count-Duke's cousin, Don Francisco Dávila, Marquis of La Puebla.[32] One further administrative change coincided with the king's departure from Madrid, this time in the royal secretariat. Since 1567 there had been two secretaries of state, one for Northern Europe (*Norte*) and one for Italy.[33] The death on 8 December 1625 of Andrés de Losada y Prada, secretary for northern affairs, and the infirmities of the head of the Italian secretariat, Juan de Ciriza, made a change necessary. Olivares decided to place the two secretariats in the hands of one man, whose status would be higher than that normally accorded to the secretaries. His choice for the post was Don Juan de Villela, who held it until his death in 1630.

---

[27] AGS CJH, leg. 621, fo. 7, consulta, 1 February 1626.

[28] Above, p. 233, and *MC*, 1, Doc. VI.

[29] González Palencia, *Noticias de Madrid*, p. 128.

[30] See below, pp. 267–8.

[31] ASG, Lettere ministri, Spagna, 2432, despatch of G. B. Serra, 7 January 1626.

[32] *MC*, 1, pp. 123–4.

[33] See José Antonio Escudero, *Los secretarios de estado y del despacho*, especially 1, pp. 222–58, for developments under Philip III and Philip IV.

With thirty years of ministerial service in Peru, Mexico, Spain and Flanders, Villela's credentials were impeccable. President of the Council of the Indies since 1623, he had just been made a member of the Council of State.[34] To the papal nuncio he was a paragon—a man of great goodness, outstanding letters, unusual experience of the world, personal sanctity, and a total lack of ambition.[35] He was, however, sufficiently upset at losing the presidency of the Council of the Indies (now entrusted on an interim basis to Olivares' relative, Don García de Haro) to take to his bed with a fever.[36] Ciriza, therefore, instead of going into immediate retirement, had to accompany the king to Aragon, and it was only in March that Villela was well enough to travel to Monzón and assume his duties.

The Crown of Aragon

It was on 7 January 1626—a cold Madrid morning—that the king set out for Zaragoza, together with his brother, the Infante Don Carlos.[37] He was supposed to be travelling light, and, apart from the Count-Duke himself, was accompanied by only three councillors of state—Montesclaros, Monterrey, and the Marquis of Aytona, whose Catalan origins would have made him a useful intermediary in the Cortes at Barcelona, had he not died in Barbastro on 24 January.[38] The king was to be away from Madrid for just over four months, not returning to his capital until 14 May. This was a much longer absence than Olivares had planned, and added greatly to the complications of government. Inevitably, foreign ambassadors chose to join the king and Olivares when they saw that the royal visit to Aragon was likely to be prolonged; and by mid-March the concourse of foreign envoys in Monzón, and their unhealthy curiosity about the relations between the king and his vassals in the Crown of Aragon, was causing considerable embarrassment.[39] The previous summer a decision had been taken to imitate the French example and create a new office, that of *conductor de los embajadores*, who would

[34] On 30 December 1625 (González Palencia, *Noticias de Madrid*, p. 127). For his career and services see González Dávila, *Teatro de las grandezas*, p. 484, and AGS Est. leg. 634, Villela to king, 30 June 1622.
[35] ASV, Spagna, 66, fo. 28, nuncio, 29 January 1626.
[36] ASG, Lettere ministri, Spagna, 2432, despatch of G. B. Serra, 7 January 1626.
[37] González Palencia, *Noticias de Madrid*, p. 128.
[38] Dormer, *Anales*, lib. 2, ch. 7. He was succeeded in the title by his son, Don Francisco de Moncada (1586–1635), who, under the title of Count of Osona, was at this moment serving as Spain's ambassador to the Imperial court in Vienna.
[39] Manuel Danvila y Collado, *El poder civil en España*, 6 vols. (Madrid, 1885–6), 6, Doc. 948, consulta of Council of State, 15 March 1626.

be responsible for looking after ambassadors and arranging audiences for them. Perhaps to bring order to the chaos of Monzón, the post was now set up, and harassed envoys welcomed the appointment of its first holder, Don Francisco Zapata.[40]

Even if the councils remained in Madrid, the major decisions were being taken where the king was to be found—first in Barbastro and Monzón, and then in Barcelona. This was especially true of foreign policy decisions, where there were obvious advantages to Olivares in working with a mere rump of the Council of State—Montesclaros, Monterrey, Don Juan de Villela and the royal confessor. The papal nuncio suspected from the first that this would make it easier for him to secure a settlement of the Valtelline question,[41] and he was not disappointed. By the early spring of 1626 Richelieu was as anxious as Olivares for peace in Italy. During the winter he had found himself faced simultaneously with a Huguenot revolt and with the possibility of war with Spain. Since Louis XIII's finances were as precarious as those of Philip IV, this was not the moment to take unnecessary risks. Moreover, the party of the *dévots* at the French court were strongly critical of Richelieu's Valtelline policy as being offensive to the papacy, and were starting to denounce him as a friend to heretics.[42] He therefore began to withdraw from his excessively exposed position, negotiating a peace with the Huguenots which was duly ratified on 5 February, and instructing Du Fargis, the French ambassador in Spain, to attempt to secure a Valtelline settlement.

Olivares and Du Fargis reached agreement at Monzón on 5 March. From the standpoint of both parties it was an ambiguous settlement, carefully avoiding a definitive decision on the fate of the Alpine passes. Spain made an apparent concession in agreeing to the sovereignty of the Protestant Grisons over the Roman Catholic inhabitants of the Valtelline; but this was so hedged about with guarantees of autonomy and the free exercise of their religion, that the sovereignty was no more than nominal. In return for this, Spain obtained the withdrawal of French troops from the valleys. Madrid also secured important psychological advantages. France had once again left its allies— Venice, Savoy and the Dutch—in the lurch in pursuit of a unilateral settlement with the King of Spain. It is not therefore surprising that Richelieu, faced with a great outburst of indignation both at home

[40] ASG, Lettere ministri, Spagna, 2432, despatch of G. B. Serra, 4 May 1626; and see Albert J. Loomie, 'The *Conducteur des Ambassadeurs* of Seventeenth Century France and Spain', *Revue belge de philologie et d'histoire*, 53 (1975), pp. 333–56, for the history of the post.
[41] ASV, Spagna, 66, fo. 16, nuncio, 10 January 1626.
[42] For Richelieu's policy at this time, see Pithon, 'Les débuts dificiles'; Lublinskaya, *French Absolutism*, pp. 277–81; Luis Suárez Fernández, *Notas a la política anti-española del Cardenal Richelieu* (Valladolid, 1950), pp. 14–19.

and abroad, should have found it expedient to disown Du Fargis for making an unauthorized agreement. But it is also not surprising that he should have found it expedient to ratify the treaty after the uproar had begun to die down. It inaugurated an official era of good relations with Spain which would allow him to attend to his first priority, the preparation of a war against La Rochelle intended to extinguish the Huguenot 'state within the state'. In the short term, the success belonged to Olivares; but in the longer term Richelieu's very setback contained within itself the potentialities for a major reversal of fortunes.[43]

While he was engaged in his negotiations with Du Fargis, Olivares was also heavily involved in the process of attempting to steer the Cortes of Aragon and Valencia towards acceptance of the Union of Arms. By holding the Aragonese Cortes in the king's presence at Barbastro, while summoning those of Valencia to Monzón, only a few days journey away, he hoped to despatch two provincial assemblies before moving on to Catalonia. He had calculated, quite correctly, that the indignation provoked among the Valencians by the convocation of their Cortes for an Aragonese rather than a Valencian city would not lead to much beyond formal protests. In dealing with Valencia he was dealing with a society which had still to recover from the loss of a third of its population through the expulsion of its Morisco inhabitants between 1609 and 1612. Traditionally it was regarded as more politically docile than its sister states, Aragon and Catalonia, largely because its standing committee of the Estates, the *Diputació*, had never evolved beyond a revenue-collecting body into an institution actively engaged in the defence of the contractual constitution. If, on top of this, Valencia was now demographically and economically weakened, it was unlikely to put up a very effective resistance to Madrid's demands.[44]

Yet at this moment the weakness proved in some respects to be a source of strength. The plan for the Union of Arms, in requiring the Valencians to provide 6,000 paid men, would in effect mobilize one in eleven adult males.[45] It is not clear what statistics, if any, were available to Olivares when he devised his scheme—the figure of 16,000 required of Catalonia seems to have been based on an estimated population of one million, when the actual population was

---

[43] This interpretation of the Treaty of Monzón is based on Lublinskaya, *French Absolutism*, pp. 279–81.

[44] For the condition of Valencian society in the decades after the expulsion of the Moriscos, see the admirable study by James Casey, *The Kingdom of Valencia in the Seventeenth Century* (Cambridge, 1979). Table 1 (p. 5) gives an estimate of 31,715 Moorish and 65,016 Old Christian households in the kingdom of Valencia on the eve of the expulsion in 1609.

[45] Casey, p. 252.

probably of the order of 360,000,[46] and Madrid normally assumed a working ratio for Catalonia, Aragon and Valencia of 3:2:1. The sheer impossibility of meeting a manpower demand of this order, especially on any continuing basis, was probably the strongest weapon in the hands of the Valencian Cortes.

On 5 March, the day he agreed to the treaty of Monzón with the French ambassador, the Count-Duke wrote to Don Francisco de Contreras, the President of the Council of Castile, reporting on current progress and future prospects.[47] The king had already put the plan for the Union of Arms to the Cortes of Aragon and Valencia. In the first, the Count-Duke thought the day had been won; in the second, matters were in hand; and when the king went to Catalonia agreement should be easier 'because inevitably they will understand the advantages better.' He admitted that his policy had run into so many difficulties that 'if they had not been foreseen they would have discouraged those of us most committed to the service of the king.' But he claimed that each new difficulty had enhanced his enthusiasm for the fray. He was busy talking, writing, arguing, and distributing printed papers which would open the eyes of the blind and the sceptics—and all without yielding ground, although at a terrible cost in sweat and toil.

All this activity was, no doubt, beginning to yield results, although there was still a long way to go, and the price already threatened to be a good deal more than wear and tear on the ministers. The attempt to introduce change had aroused deep suspicions in societies which thought instinctively in terms of the sanctity of an immemorial and allegedly unchanging contractual relationship between the king and his subjects. The government's printed manifesto attempting to explain and justify the Union of Arms was soon answered by counter-manifestoes pointing out its defects. A true union, it was argued, would not be a mere military union, but one in which offices were fairly distributed, honours given without parsimony, and economic policies coordinated to prevent the export of raw materials from Spain.[48]

Behind these arguments there lurked a deep suspicion of Castile's intentions, which was heightened by the growing awareness of the Castilians' inability to put their own house in order. But the opposition was not confined to natives of the Crown of Aragon. A Catalan diarist reports the arrest of a Castilian, Don Andrés de Mendoza,

---

[46] See Elliott, *Catalans*, p. 238.

[47] *MC*, 1, Doc. X.

[48] BL Add. Ms. 13,997, fos. 17–19v., *Discurso de quan poco útil sea en la forma que se pretende la unión de las Coronas de Castilla y Aragón.*

for writing answers to the government's manifestoes.[49] Montesclaros might sycophantically write of the Union of Arms as a divinely inspired idea that had come to the Count-Duke for giving the king a 'monarchy of monarchies',[50] but some of Olivares' opponents at court would shed no tears if his policies were shipwrecked in the Crown of Aragon.

Some of the greatest magnates in Spain, like the Dukes of Infantado, Lerma, and Sessa, had large properties in the Crown of Aragon, and retained their provincial connections and influence, although spending most of their time in Madrid. Consequently they were liable to be sensitive to any challenge to provincial liberties. Beyond this, too, there lurked a feeling that what Olivares did today in Aragon, he might well do tomorrow in Castile. In the journal of that disgruntled courtier Matías de Novoa, who accompanied the king on his visit to Aragon, there was a strong undercurrent of sympathy for the Aragonese, Catalans and Valencians, combined with indignation at the way in which Olivares chose to handle them.[51] For a significant section of opinion in Castile, as well as in the Crown of Aragon, the Count-Duke had already come to symbolize a tyrannical determination to ride roughshod over rights and privileges.

Olivares' methods were, as might have been expected, those of a man in a hurry, exasperated by the resistance, the petty impediments and the delays inherent in the whole creaking machinery of traditional parliamentary institutions. In some respects, however, the character of these institutions worked to his advantage, since the Estates in the Cortes of Aragon, Valencia and the principality of Catalonia, deliberated separately, and differed so sharply in their interests that it was not hard to play off one against another.[52] The clerical Estate, dominated by bishops dependent on the crown for further promotion, was always the most pliable, while the third Estate had no wish

---

[49] Pujades, Dietari, 4, p. 43. The identity of this Andrés de Mendoza is not certain, but there are grounds for thinking that he may well have been the Andrés de Almansa y Mendoza who wrote such glowing newsletters from Madrid in the opening years of the reign. If so, he must have had a change of heart and joined the ranks of Olivares' enemies. For a discussion of this question, see the second edition of Maravall, La cultura del barroco, p. 160 n. 70.

[50] ADI Montesclaros Mss., lib. 130, no. 30, undated draft on monetary problems.

[51] Eg. Novoa, Codoin 69, p. 16. As tension mounted in the later years of the ministry he became increasingly outspoken (cf. Codoin 77, p. 331, and Codoin 80, p. 225).

[52] The best contemporary account, although stronger for Aragon and Valencia than for Catalonia, is provided by Dormer in his Anales. There is no modern account of the Aragonese Cortes of 1626, but these are now being studied by Xavier Gil Pujol of the University of Barcelona. For those of Valencia, see Casey, The Kingdom of Valencia, and Dámaso de Lario's introduction to his edition of the Cortes del reinado de Felipe IV, together with his articles on 'Cortes valencianas de 1626: problemas en torno al pago del servicio ofrecido', Estudis, 4 (1975), pp. 115–27, and 'Un conato de revuelta social en Valencia bajo el reinado de Felipe IV', in Homenaje al Dr. Juan Reglà Campistol (Valencia, 1975), 1, pp. 571–81. For the Catalan Cortes, see Elliott, Catalans, ch. 8.

to alienate a king to whom it looked for the confirmation of municipal privileges and exemptions. It was the noble Estates in all three provinces—packed with penurious, fractious and discontented gentry—which gave the ministers most difficulty and proved most resistant to being dragooned into anything approaching a unanimous vote for the men and the money needed for the Union of Arms.

While Olivares employed all his own formidable powers of bullying, cajolery and blandishment to bring recalcitrant Aragonese and Valencian gentlemen to heel, he also worked through a small group of ministers and officials, together with natives of the Crown of Aragon who could exert their influence on behalf of the court, like the Duke of Gandía, who was used to solicit support among the Valencian nobility.[53] Certain ministers, known as *tratadores*, served as intermediaries between the Cortes and the king, and those chosen for this delicate duty were either relatives of the Count-Duke, or his dependents. It was in the Valencian Cortes that his nephew, Don Luis de Haro, gained his first practice in the art of discreet political management which would later stand him in such good stead. Haro's fellow *tratadores* were the Marquis of Valdonquillo, and a Portuguese, the Count of Castro, who had won the Count-Duke's favour.[54] His son-in-law, the Marquis of Heliche, and his cousin, Don Diego de Mexía, were appointed *tratadores* in the Aragonese Cortes; and when the king decided on 20 March to move on to Barcelona, leaving the Cortes still in session, they reluctantly had to accept Monterrey as their president.[55]

One other minister—this one not a member of the Olivares clan—also made his name and his fortune in the course of these 1626 Cortes. This was the protonotary (*protonotario*) of the Crown of Aragon, Don Jerónimo de Villanueva, 'whose intelligence was from then on recognized as fitting him for greater employments.'[56] A member of an Aragonese family of royal officials—probably of Jewish origin[57]—he had been appointed to his father's old post of protonotary in 1620 at the age of twenty-six. The Villanuevas seem to have been closely associated with the Duke of Lerma, and with his son Uceda, so that the change of régime in 1621 represented a moment of grave danger

[53] Casey, *The Kingdom of Valencia*, pp. 239–40.

[54] Novoa, *Codoin* 69, pp. 229.

[55] *Ibid.*, p. 20; Dormer, *Anales*, lib. 2, ch. 13.

[56] Novoa, *Codoin* 69, p. 18.

[57] There seems no good reason to doubt the allegation, which was made with substantial supporting evidence by the *fiscal* of the Inquisition, Don Pascual de Aragón, in a statement dated 23 February 1652 during Villanueva's trial (AHN Inquis., leg. 3687²). For further biographical information on Villanueva, see *MC*, 1, p. 80 n. 44, and Mercedes Agulló y Cobo, 'El monasterio de San Plácido y su fundador, el madrileño Jerónimo de Villanueva, protonotario de Aragón', *Villa de Madrid*, 13 (1975), pp. 59–68. Also Elliott, *Catalans*, pp. 256–9.

for the family fortunes. By this time Don Jerónimo was already known for his unhealthy interest in astrology, which would one day be a contributory cause of his undoing.[58] But, perhaps guided by the stars, he survived this particular crisis, and bided his time. Hitherto he had been quietly buried in his office in Madrid, but his performance of official duties connected with the Cortes brought him to Olivares' attention. He showed all the proper zeal of a loyal official, and narrowly avoided creating an incident when he was heard muttering at the door of the aristocratic chamber in the Valencian Estates that a particularly recalcitrant noble deserved to be garrotted.[59] He was rewarded in July for his services with the offer of membership in the Order of Calatrava—an offer which he may have had some trepidation in accepting, since it would require a careful investigation of his dubious ancestry.[60] But by one means or another he safely established his credentials, and embarked on what was to prove a spectacular ministerial career as one of Olivares' most trusted confidants.

Villanueva and his colleagues worked hard under the watchful eyes of the Count-Duke to secure acceptance by the Cortes of the Union of Arms in its original form. The Valencians, as anticipated, were the first to crack under the pressure, but the crown was also forced to make a significant retreat. During the first week of March there was rising tension at Monzón as the crown pressed the nobility for their vote, which had to be *nemine discrepante*. On 7 March Don Luis de Haro entered to announce that the king intended to abolish the *nemine discrepante* requirement;[61] and although the threat was not carried out,[62] resistance began to crumble. But the court had now seen the need for concessions, and on the same day Haro reported to the third Estate that 1,666 paid men, instead of the original 6,000, would be acceptable to the king. The first and third Estates now signified their compliance, and so, up to a point, did the nobility. But, worried by the continuing manpower shortage, it baulked at voting for paid men, and was only willing to offer cash for the payment of Valencian or non-Valencian volunteers. This itself ran counter to the whole spirit of the Union of Arms, but Olivares was in a hurry to move on to Barcelona, and was disinclined to haggle further. On 21 March, therefore, the king accepted the offer of a subsidy

[58] AHN Consejos, lib. 1431, fos. 214–7, anonymous attack on Fray Luis de Aliaga.
[59] Dormer, *Anales*, lib. 2, ch. 10.
[60] AHN Inquis., leg. 3688¹, fo. 263, royal order of 12 December 1626, and the comments of Don Pascual de Aragón, who says that he asked for a delay during which he took the opportunity to consult the devil.
[61] Dormer, *Anales*, lib. 2, ch. 14.
[62] Casey, *The Kingdom of Valencia*, pp. 227–8, 241.

of 1,080,000 *lliures* (regarded as sufficient to maintain 1,000 men for
a period of fifteen years[63]), and set off for Barcelona.

The king and the Count-Duke left behind them a sullen, angry
people. On the day after the Cortes voted the subsidy, a poster was
stuck up on a wall in the city of Valencia. At the top left sat the
king on his throne. At the top right were the Valencian coat of arms,
and representatives of the three Estates, with the words '*Fear. Ambition*' beside them. Below was the Count-Duke, surrounded by flames,
and dragging down the king and the Estates with ropes. 'Where
are you taking these people, count?' asks the king. 'When they feel
the heat they will know', the Count-Duke replies.[64]

The hostility felt by the Valencians towards the Count-Duke, and
their sense of the betrayal of the fatherland by its nominal defenders,
proved to be a common reaction throughout the Crown of Aragon.
In communities that were traditionally hostile to Castile and fearful
of Madrid's intentions there was a growing sense of the *patria* in
danger. The kingdom of Valencia itself lacked the cohesion, the
strength and the confidence to mount a strong resistance to policies
which it profoundly distrusted; but as the king and the Count-Duke
crossed the frontier from Aragon into Catalonia they came face to
face with a society more tenacious of its privileges, and hitherto less
exposed to the corroding process of Castilian linguistic and cultural
penetration, than the one they left behind them.

The royal party entered Barcelona on 26 March—the king, incredi-
bly blond to Catalan eyes,[65] mounted on horseback and dressed in
rose, with a plumed hat adorned with diamonds. Along, too, 'came
a fine coach and inside it there was only one person, a very fat man
with a thick beard.'[66] It was Barcelona's first sight of Olivares, 'duke,
or devil, of San Lúcar'.[67]

On the following day the king took his long-deferred oath to
observe the Principality's privileges and constitutions, and the Cortes
opened in the monastery of Saint Francis on the 28th with a speech
from the throne which emphasized the crown's need of help, but
tactfully made no specific requests of the Catalans. Just as Olivares
had used the leading magnate of Valencia, the Duke of Gandía, to
create the nucleus of a royal party in the Valencian Cortes, so he
attempted to use the Duke of Cardona for similar purposes in the
Cortes of Catalonia. Although Cardona, like the other great nobles
of the Crown of Aragon, belonged to the court nobility, his posses-

---

[63] *Ibid.*, p. 252.
[64] See Dámaso de Lario, 'Un conato de revuelta'.
[65] Pujades, *Dietari*, 4, p. 45.
[66] Elliott, *Catalans*, p. 218, from the diary of Miguel Parets.
[67] Pujades, *Dietari*, 4, p. 60.

sion of large estates in the Principality and the Catalan origins of his family gave him substantial local influence. This made him useful to the king, but it also had its dangers, since it was liable to embroil the crown in local vendettas, with Cardona's enemies casting themselves in the role of patriots defending the fatherland from tyrannical ministers. The destructive possibilities of the situation were obvious from the opening day of the Cortes, when only the intervention of Olivares prevented Cardona and the Count of Santa Coloma from drawing swords on each other.[68]

The decision to give special tokens of favour to Cardona also had its repercussions in the jealous circle of aristocrats who clustered round the king. In this little world, proximity to the monarch was all-important, and was carefully regulated by rank and office. On the journey from Madrid, Olivares, as favourite, groom of the stole and master of the horse, sat immediately on the right of the king and Don Carlos. The carriage was also shared by the Duke of Medina de Ríoseco, Admiral of Castile, 'the first man in Spain', and by Olivares' son-in-law, Heliche, and his brother-in-law, the Marquis of Carpio, acting as first groom.[69] At Valdoncellas, on the last lap of the journey to Barcelona, the king, just as he was stepping into his coach, called for Cardona. The Admiral was already on the point of taking his seat, and Philip turned to him to say that there was no room for him in the coach today, and that he should go to the coach reserved for his entourage. The Admiral, who was not accustomed to this kind of treatment, went white, and replied: 'I never thought in Spain to find myself without a seat in this coach.' Unfortunately Cardona could not be found, and the Admiral was called back to take his accustomed place; at which moment Cardona turned up, and the Admiral smartly sat down. The cortège, with Cardona now excluded from the royal coach, made its way to his palace, where the royal party was to lodge—the king furious, the Count-Duke embarrassed, and the Admiral no doubt preening himself on his revenge.[70]

It was at this moment, according to Matías de Novoa, whose horizons did not extend beyond the bickering world of the court, that the royal cause was lost. The Catalans sided with the Admiral, a descendant of the Catalan family of Cabrera; and the incident did Cardona, and the king himself, no good. But it was only the beginning of a major breach between Olivares and the first grandee in

[68] *Ibid.*, 4, p. 47.
[69] Novoa, *Codoin* 69, p. 28.
[70] Novoa, *ibid.*, tells the story, and there is also an account in BL Eg. Ms. 347, fos. 126–8, *Relación de lo que pasó al Almirante de Castilla*. For Olivares' subsequent relations with the Admiral, see D. L. Shaw, 'Olivares y el Almirante de Castilla (1638)', *Hispania* 27 (1967), pp. 342–53.

Castile. Two weeks later, on Maundy Thursday, 9 April, when the king was performing his usual Easter ritual of washing the feet of the poor, he turned to the Marquis of Heliche for the towel. It was the task of the groom of the stole to hand the king the towel, but Olivares was absent; and to ask Heliche for the towel was tantamount to recognizing him as his father-in-law's deputy. The Admiral immediately objected and withdrew. That evening—prompted, as Olivares later discovered through his spies, by the Marquis of Castel Rodrigo[71]—the Admiral entered the king's chamber to protest. When the king replied that 'the person to whom I gave the office of *sumiller* is as good as you', the Admiral took from his neck the chain from which hung the golden key that gave access to the royal chamber, kissed it, handed it back to the king, and requested leave to retire to his estates.[72] After an abortive intervention by Montesclaros, whose frustrations and ambitions were moving him into Olivares' camp,[73] the king put his signature that same night to a document for the consideration of the Council of State, in which the Admiral was witheringly described as 'this poor, badly-brought up *caballero*.'[74] The council seems to have been in some uncertainty as to what was expected of it, but the Admiral was placed under house arrest, and then banished to his estates.

This absurd episode, the cause of intense excitement both in Barcelona and Madrid, where the entire nobility went to call on the Admiral's mother, who in turn called on the queen,[75] suggests something of the passions which were never far below the surface in the rigidly formalized court of Philip IV. As the house of Guzmán consolidated its hold on power, so the bitterness increased among the dispossessed Lerma kinship, to which the Admiral belonged. With the king still lacking a male heir—although a daughter, who was soon to die, had been born to him in November—this faction placed its hopes in the silent and enigmatic figure of the Infante Don Carlos, whose relations with the Admiral were close.[76] In the person of the Admiral the faction now had its not very heroic martyr. Family loyalties, reinforcing the disillusionments of the disappointed and the dispossessed, were in the process of creating an embryonic opposition.

As long as the king survived, and his confidence in the Count-Duke remained undiminished, this opposition could not hope to achieve much beyond intrigue. But in the delicate political situation in Catalonia

[71] Novoa, *Codoin* 69, p. 42.
[72] *Ibid.*, p. 41; Pujades, *Dietari*, 4, p. 51.
[73] Novoa, *Codoin* 69, pp. 46–7.
[74] Instituto de Valencia de Don Juan, Madrid, envío 109 (91). Novoa, p. 48, ascribes this document to Olivares.
[75] Pujades, *Dietari*, 4, pp. 59–60.
[76] Novoa, *Codoin* 69, p. 56.

in the spring of 1626, intrigue could itself be dangerous. In these same weeks the Duke of Cardona was formally linked to the new ruling houses when his daughter married Don Luis de Haro, the Count-Duke's nephew.[77] Haro's friendship with the king, and his recent success with the Valencian Cortes, had already begun to make the Count-Duke uneasy;[78] but the Guzmán-Haro nexus looked formidably strong to those outside the magic circle, and it was beginning to seem as if only the failure of the Count-Duke's policies could bring about its downfall. In the circumstances it would not be surprising if opposition to the crown in the Catalan Cortes, where Cardona acted as one of the *tratadores*, was discreetly abetted by the Count-Duke's enemies in the royal entourage.

Olivares hoped by initial gestures of conciliation to get the Cortes into the right frame of mind to respond favourably to his scheme for the Union of Arms. The crown agreed that the Cortes should first consider their own business before turning to that of the king. In addition, the Count-Duke, still full of his plans for commercial revival, sent his confessor Hernando de Salazar to discuss with the city authorities of Barcelona a project for a trading company which would once again make it a great centre of Mediterranean and Levantine trade.[79]

These inducements did not work. The proposals for a trading company provoked no great enthusiasm in Barcelona's mercantile community; and after twenty-seven years without a Cortes there was too much to discuss, and too many interests at stake, for the Estates to be willing to curtail their business. Olivares was anxious to get the king away from Barcelona as quickly as possible, not least because of fears for his health. The cardinal legate, Barberini, had recently arrived in Barcelona after his abortive mission to France, and had promptly fallen ill, along with several of his entourage.[80] With sickness making the rounds, and the summer heat not far away, the Count-Duke's growing concern to despatch the Cortes with speed was understandable.[81] He himself was confined to his lodgings with stomach trouble, which prevented him from receiving visitors.[82]

On 16 April the Protonotario horrified the Cortes by informing them that all private business must be concluded within two days; and two days later he read on behalf of the king an eloquent plea

[77] *Ibid.*, p. 49.
[78] *Ibid.*, p. 27. Already on 12 November 1625 the papal nuncio was referring to Olivares' distrust of his nephew (ASV, Spagna 66, fo. 371v.).
[79] Elliott, *Catalans*, p. 226.
[80] Pujades, *Dietari*, 4, p. 50.
[81] RAH 11-13-3, Olivares to Duke of Alcalá, 14 April 1626.
[82] BAV Barb. Lat. Ms. 8599, fo. 69, Olivares to Barberini, 12 April 1626.

for Catalan help.[83] But the eloquence counted for nothing beside the revelation that the crown was asking for 16,000 paid men. From this point the Cortes degenerated into a series of angry altercations, as Cardona and the court faction struggled to secure discussion and acceptance of the royal proposal, while the king issued threats of imminent departure. In a last bid to obtain agreement, Olivares followed the Valencian precedent and asked for money rather than soldiers; but he was thinking in terms of a subsidy of four million *lliures* spread over fifteen years, while the Catalans had in mind a figure in the region of one million.[84] Finally, in exasperation, the Count-Duke attempted to force a vote on 3 May. Only the bishops proved amenable. In the other two Estates there was uproar, and the representatives of the towns and all but a rump of the nobility marched out of the session in disgust.

At dawn the next morning the king and the Count-Duke slipped out of Barcelona and away. As much as sheer exasperation this may have been a calculated move to bring the Cortes to their senses, but, if so, it was unsuccessful. Numerous votes were now cast in the Cortes for subsidies of varying sizes, but there was no unanimity and the king ignored pleas to return. He was alleged to have said on leaving that he had arrived in Barcelona without knowing what to expect, but that next time he would come prepared.[85] As he took the road to Zaragoza was Olivares turning over in his mind the possibility that one day Philip would come back at the head of his army?

The king's return to Madrid was precipitate. After a brief stop in Zaragoza to attend mass at the Pilar, he was back in his capital on 14 May. The Count-Duke was so exhausted by his wrangling with the Cortes and the fatigues of the journey that he was forced to take to his bed for several days. He seems to have been suffering from gastric trouble, and during the first week of June Cardinal Barberini reported that his indisposition, which his doctors were treating with constant purging, still kept him in seclusion, and had brought all business to a standstill.[86]

The extension of the Union

The delays and difficulties encountered on the king's visit to the Crown of Aragon played havoc with Olivares' timetable for the spring and summer of 1626. There was no longer any question of

---

[83] Elliott, *Catalans*, pp. 230–1. A *lliura* was worth slightly less than a Castilian ducat.
[84] *Ibid.*, pp. 237–8.
[85] Pujades, *Dietari*, 4, p. 58.
[86] BAV Barb. Lat. Ms. 8321, fo. 178, Cardinal Barberini to secretariat, 6 June 1626.

Philip moving on to Llerena and Lisbon, and the plan for the invasion of Ireland was shelved. The papal nuncio thought that the fleet was simply not strong enough at present to attack the British Isles.[87] The enormous effort of the siege of Breda and the other great military and naval enterprises of 1625 had produced clear signs of exhaustion. In May, the Emperor, hard pressed by Christian IV of Denmark's invasion of northern Germany, appealed to Madrid for financial help. After a difficult discussion on 10 June the Council of State finally acceded to the request, but the treasury had such trouble laying hands on the money that the Emperor did not receive his 200,000 ducats until September 1627.[88]

There were other indications, too, of a growing financial emergency. The source of the crown's troubles was a continuous shortfall of silver to meet its vast foreign commitments, coupled with an internal monetary situation that was slipping out of control. The continuous striking of *vellón* coins of pure copper in order to meet each new budgetary deficit was having consequences both intended and unintended. It furthered Olivares' policy of bringing hoarded silver out into the open, as its fortunate owners sought to take advantage of the rising value of silver in relation to *vellón* to make new purchases or settle old debts. Once released into circulation, this silver played its part in helping the crown to meet the enormous military expenses of the opening years of the reign. The price was paid by the mass of Castile's population, which saw the purchasing power of its coins rapidly eroding as *vellón* lost its value, and its living standards fall as commodity prices began to climb.[89] But the crown also stood to lose as a result of having to pay higher and higher premiums to its foreign bankers for the conversion into silver of tax revenues collected overwhelmingly in *vellón*. An attempt made in March 1625 to fix the premium on silver in terms of *vellón* at an artificial 10%[90] was, predictably, a total failure. By the end of October it stood at around 20% in Seville and 46% in Madrid.[91] Throughout 1625 this rising silver premium was the subject of agitated ministerial debate.

Inevitably opinions were sharply divided both as to the cause of the trouble and its cure. The Marquis of Montesclaros, while still President of the Council of Finance, produced some interesting calculations about the chronic shortage of silver, which for him was at the root of the problem.[92] On the assumption that most of the world's

---

[87] ASV, Spagna 66, fo. 52v., nuncio's despatch, 17 June 1626.
[88] Ródenas Vilar, *La política europea*, p. 137, n. 356.
[89] Bennassar, *La España del siglo de oro*, p. 111.
[90] Gil Ayuso, *Noticia bibliográfica*, Doc. 858.
[91] AGI Indif., leg. 755, consulta, 10 November 1625.
[92] ADI Montesclaros Mss., lib. 130, no. 29, undated *borrador*.

silver reserves were in Spanish hands, he argued that the correct
policy was to stem the outflow of silver, and he examined the various
routes by which it left Castile. By his reckoning, five million ducats
in silver went abroad each year as a consequence of the crown's *asientos*
with the bankers: 3,800,000 ducats to Flanders, 600,000 for the purchase of foreign naval stores, and 300,000 for the maintenance of
Spain's armies in Italy. A further four million were spent on importing foreign manufactures, together with corn for Portugal (and sometimes Andalusia), and on freighting the Indies fleets. There was also
a continuous drain of Spanish silver to Rome, and a further drain
through the illegal export of silver without a licence. Foreigners
smuggled into the country large quantities of counterfeit *vellón* coins
which they then exchanged for silver, and the counterfeit coins helped
to depreciate still further a coinage already depreciated by over-
production.

If Montesclaros was right, there were two questions to which
the crown had to address itself. One was the over-production of
vellón, which was at least partly responsible for the present high prices
in Castile, although there were other causes too, including the prohibition on imports imposed by the Articles of Reformation of 1623.
The other major problem was the licensed or unlicensed export of
silver from Spain, with much of the licensed export being used for
the crown's military commitments abroad.

During 1625 majority opinion among ministers, both in the Council of Castile and the Council of State, favoured what seemed a relatively painless solution to these problems. The Council of Castile
urged the immediate cessation of the minting of *vellón*; and the Council of State, which in some bemusement examined the whole question
in November 1625,[93] supported the Council of Castile's plea for an
end to *vellón* manufacture, while at the same time advocating an
attempt to prevent the illegal entry of *vellón* and the exit of silver
by employing officials of the Inquisition as inspectors of goods at
ports and frontier posts. It also recognized that the king himself
was the principal silver-exporter, and that it lay in his power to reduce
this export by choosing which wars to fight and which to avoid.

The Count-Duke and his closest financial advisers—Manuel López
Pereira, Alamos de Barrientos and Father Hernando de Salazar—were
clearly not persuaded that these measures would be adequate. The
desirability of stopping the minting of *vellón* coins was obvious,
although it was doubtful whether the crown could afford to do this
in its present predicament. But Olivares was coming to the conclusion
that, with so much *vellón* already in circulation, the only effective

[93] AHN Est. lib. 741, fos. 114–115v., and 117–119v., draft consultas, 1 November 1625.

cure—even if minting were to cease—would be a massive dose of deflation. Deflation, however, could have serious political consequences, as the Council of State hastened to point out in its *consulta* of 1 November, following almost word for word a draft prepared by Montesclaros.[94] Between 1621 and 1625, said the Council, the crown had indeed greatly enhanced its reputation, but it had also adopted a number of measures which had not been universally well received—the decree ordering ministers to produce inventories of their possessions, the reduction of interest rates on *juros*, which had hit 'everybody', and the 1623 pragmatics on the reformation of manners. Since then there had been the voluntary *donativo* and the vast tax grants of the Cortes. Was this really the right moment, then, to indulge in a massive deflation, and cut private wealth by half? Might not deflation, coming on top of all the earlier grievances, lead to some considerable *inconveniente*—a euphemism implying anything from a local riot to a Comunero revolt?

The Council of State's resolute refusal to contemplate an immediate and drastic deflation meant that the problem of *vellón* was left in suspense while further expert opinions were solicited. But Olivares kept a close watch on the situation while away in Aragon, and wrote from Barcelona at the beginning of April 1626 to warn the President of the Council of Castile of the serious consequences of any further delay in reaching a decision.[95] In addressing itself once again to this vexing question, the Council of Castile had before it papers prepared by two of the Genoese bankers, Carlos Strata and Bartolomé Espínola, and a third drafted jointly by Hernando de Salazar and Alamos de Barrientos. They all agreed that a 75% reduction in the nominal value of *vellón* coins was essential, although they differed as to the best way of achieving it. They recognized that, if the estimated 28 million ducats in circulation were reduced in value overnight to seven million, those who suffered most would be the poor, since most of the *vellón* coins were in their hands. Should they be compensated, and, if so, how? Carlos Strata advocated the establishment of a chain of banks across Castile to 'consume' the *vellón* and to operate an annual levy on the wealthy, whose estates would be subject to a yearly valuation. The others, too, wanted some form of levy, although Espínola preferred to leave its actual operation to the good faith of the individual citizen.[96]

The Council of Castile drew back at the prospect of such drastic measures. One of its members, Pedro de Marmolejo, thought that

---

[94] ADI Montesclaros Mss., lib. 130, no. 36, undated *borrador*.
[95] BL 1322.1.12 (*Papeles varios*), Ms. 15, President of Council of Castile to Dr. Don Pedro Marmolejo, 8 April 1626.
[96] These three printed papers are to be found in BL 1322.1.12, nos. 56–8.

a 75% deflation, coming on top of the reduction in the interest rate on *juros* and the concession by the Cortes of an additional two million ducats a year, would ruin trade and lead to a spate of bankruptcies. In his view, no instant cure existed. The Cortes and the cities, he thought, should be asked to advise on possible means of providing compensation, and the king in the meantime should bring all *vellón* production to a halt.[97]

It was this last recommendation that was most easily accomplished, and it was one on which the Cortes were insisting as a condition for the *millones*.[98] But its consequences for the royal revenues were bound to be drastic, since the crown received so much of its income in *vellón*. Yet with the conversion rate of *vellón* to silver now 70%,[99] the easy answer of continuous minting of more *vellón* coins was every day becoming less palatable. On 8 May 1626, a week before the king's return from the Crown of Aragon, the government at last grasped the nettle and suspended *vellón* production.[100] Five years, and twenty million ducats, had slipped by. The days when the crown had financed its foreign policy by striking large quantities of low-grade coins were over—but for how long?

The consequences of that profligate minting were all too soon apparent, and it was with these that the government now found itself having to grapple. Once again the Council of Castile drew back as it contemplated the likely social effects of *vellón* deflation, and instead attempted to fix prices by decree at their 1624 level.[101] The cure was worse than the disease. As royal officials attempted to enforce the price-fixing decree, traders concealed their goods, shops emptied mysteriously, imports abruptly ceased, and prices rose still higher under the impact of artificially induced shortage.[102] The fall in imports—itself something that the government's economic policies had sought to achieve—led to a fall in customs receipts, and a consequent further loss to the treasury at a time when it had deprived itself of a major source of income through the cessation of *vellón* minting and was struggling to persuade the bankers to advance more credit. 'The crown's resources are not infinite', complained the Council of Finance, 'and every year expenditure exceeds revenue.'[103]

It was in order to make those resources a little less finite that Olivares had embarked on his great plan for the Union of Arms. The king's journey to the Crown of Aragon had not worked out

[97] BL 1322.1.12, Ms. 16, paper by Marmolejo, 20 April 1626.
[98] Almansa y Mendoza, *Cartas*, p. 336.
[99] AGS CJH, leg. 621, *Relación de lo que S.M. ha menester en cada un año . . .* (1626).
[100] Domínguez Ortiz, *Política y hacienda*, p. 256.
[101] Gil Ayuso, *Noticia bibliográfica*, Doc. 891.
[102] AGS CJH, leg. 621, no. 71, consulta, 12 July 1626.
[103] AHN Est. lib. 739, fos. 429–30v., draft consulta of Council of Finance, 9 August 1626.

quite as anticipated, but it had not been a total failure. The Catalans, admittedly, had agreed to nothing. The Valencians had offered money, but not men. The Aragonese Cortes, continuing in session under the presidency of Monterrey, eventually came up with an offer of 2,000 paid men for fifteen years, or the monetary equivalent.[104] It was only a fifth of the number which Olivares originally had in mind for Aragon, but at least it was a beginning to a real Union of Arms. It was enough, in any event, for him to feel justified in moving towards the second, and more grandiose, stage of the project.

On 25 July the king officially decreed the inauguration of the Union of Arms,[105] and three days later the President of the Council of Castile read the decree to the assembled Cortes.[106] In view of the many services already rendered by Castile, and also of the present monetary disorders, the king undertook to pay from his own revenues the 24,000 infantrymen allocated to Castile under the terms of the Union. The pay of one third of these men was to come from revenues specifically set aside for the purpose. It is not clear whether the Cortes felt any great surge of gratitude for this grand but empty gesture.

With Castile officially participating in the Union, it was now the turn of Flanders, the burden of whose defence had fallen so heavily, and for so long, on the Castilian tax-payer. The Breda campaign had left Brussels penniless and the army in poor shape.[107] Here, if anywhere, major reforms were necessary if the defence and financing of the Monarchy were to be more soundly established. A royal order on 5 August to Don Juan de Villela explained what was intended.[108] Of all the king's dominions only the loyal provinces of the Netherlands were now under attack; and by the terms of the Union, if they agreed to participate, they would receive the help of an army of twenty thousand men from other parts of the Monarchy. Since the war in the Netherlands was now being shifted from land to sea, Olivares hoped that a force of 20,000 infantry and 4,000 cavalry provided by the Monarchy as a whole would be sufficient, if complemented by an additional 20,000 infantrymen raised by the Southern Netherlands themselves for manning their fortresses.[109]

If this plan were realized, it would represent a massive scaling-down of the military establishment in the Netherlands. At this time the army of Flanders was almost 70,000 men strong, and of these

[104] Dormer, *Anales*, lib. 2, ch. 20.
[105] Elliott, *The Revolt*, p. 246.
[106] *Actas*, 45, pp. 250–1.
[107] Alcalá-Zamora, *España, Flandes*, p. 212.
[108] AGS Est. leg. 2040, *El Rey Nuestro Señor, a 5 de agosto de 1626* . . .
[109] AGS Est. leg. 2040, *El Señor Conde-Duque sobre la forma en que se podría encaminar en Flandes lo de la unión.*

30,000 were tied down in garrison duty.[110] Could it possibly make do with less? The Infanta, who was told of the king's plans with the greatest secrecy in a letter of 9 August,[111] was clearly sceptical about the whole idea. She read the letter, with her usual shrewdness, as an attempt to induce the Netherlands to shoulder a greater share of the war effort, and declared that this was frankly impossible.[112] Olivares, on the other hand, obviously believed that he could drastically cut the scale and cost of the war in the Netherlands if his great northern strategy for crippling Dutch trade could be brought to fruition. In January 1626 a Flemish noble, Jean de Croy, the Count of Solre, a founder member of the recently constituted *Junta de Población* in Madrid, had been sent to Warsaw to negotiate for the acquisition of ships for a Spanish Baltic squadron. It soon became clear that Sigismund III was interested in something more ambitious— Spanish military help against the Swedes, and the transfer of the Dunkirk squadron to the Baltic, where it would make use of Polish ports while Imperial forces occupied the north German coast.[113]

On 27 August 1626 the Danes under Christian IV were routed at Lutter, and Denmark lay open to attack by the new Imperial army which Albrecht von Wallenstein had contracted to raise for the Emperor in 1625. Olivares' Baltic dreams now began to acquire some semblance of contact with reality. At the end of September a victorious Ferdinand II intimated to the Marquis of Aytona, the Spanish ambassador, that he would be willing to assist Spain in its attempt to secure a Baltic port.[114] Some form of cooperation between Spain, Poland and the Empire for the control of the Baltic trade therefore began to look feasible just when the groundwork for the Union of Arms was being laid in Madrid. In union lay salvation—a Union of Arms between the kingdoms of the Monarchy, and a League of Alliance between Vienna and Madrid. The Count-Duke seems to have coupled them in his mind as the answer to Spain's troubles,[115] and by the autumn of 1626 it was beginning to seem as if both of them might soon be achieved.

At a meeting on 6 October[116] the Council of State had before it a paper by Olivares on the extension of the Union of Arms to

---

[110] Parker, *Army of Flanders*, pp. 272 and 11.

[111] Lonchay, *Correspondance*, 2, Doc. 885.

[112] *Ibid.*, Doc. 891, Infanta to Philip IV, 27 August 1626.

[113] Alcalá-Zamora, *España, Flandes*, pp. 236–9; Ródenas Vilar, *La política europea*, pp. 83ff.

[114] Ródenas Vilar, pp. 83–4.

[115] It is significant that Khevenhüller, in his *Annales Ferdinandei*, moves immediately from a discussion of Olivares' proposals for the Union of Arms to a discussion of his proposals for the League of Alliance. As a man with inside knowledge of the Count-Duke's plans, he clearly saw the relationship between the two projects. (*Annales Ferdinandei*, 2, pp. 1037–42.)

[116] AGS Est. leg. 2040, consulta, 6 October 1626.

Flanders, and a statement outlining the possible objections of Flanders to new forms of taxation. But the difficulties in Aragon and Valencia, Olivares asserted, had finally been overcome; Sardinia and Majorca had voluntarily joined, and it was believed that other kingdoms, including Portugal, would accept the scheme. Catalonia was notably absent from this optimistic assessment.

One or two of the more independently minded councillors showed a less than whole-hearted enthusiasm for the Union, although they were careful to season their speeches with the obligatory words of praise. Don Pedro de Toledo, in particular, while describing it as 'the only cure for the Monarchy', warned against the danger that the search for an advantageous union might lead to irremediable disunion. Rumblings of discontent were to be heard in Naples, and he feared the same for Flanders. Don Fernando Girón, too, believed it would be wise to suspend the introduction of the Union into Flanders until the rest of the Monarchy had joined. But the other councillors showed themselves fervent partisans of the scheme, and not least among them the Marquis of Montesclaros, over whom a mysterious change seems to have come since his removal from the presidency of the Council of Finance earlier in the year. The expense of accompanying the king to the Crown of Aragon had forced him to pawn his wife's jewels and most of his silverware,[117] and it is possible that financial embarrassments were taking their toll. In mid-August he had a two-hour conversation with the Count-Duke in the north gallery of the palace, and he followed this with a letter in which he was unable to conceal his frustration at being passed over for offices and honours.[118] The Count-Duke remarked in reply that Montesclaros had always seemed to him to possess ambition, 'a vice common to almost everyone'.[119] Later he forwarded to him an anonymous paper that had fallen into his hands, which referred to Montesclaros' straitened circumstances and his hopes of appointment to the post of treasurer-general of the Crown of Aragon, now being vacated by the nomination of the Count of Chinchón to the viceroyalty of Peru.[120] The device, while hardly subtle, proved effective. On 10 January 1627 Montesclaros was appointed to replace Chinchón.[121] So it was that men of spirit lost their independence.

In response to the Council of State's *consulta* the king gave orders that all the relevant papers should be forwarded to the Infanta. Olivares was clearly determined to press ahead with the Union, a 'most

[117] ADI Montesclaros Mss., lib. 125, undated draft letter from Montesclaros to Olivares.
[118] ADI Montesclaros Mss., lib. 31, no. 52, Montesclaros to Olivares, 15 August 1626.
[119] ADI Montesclaros Mss., lib. 31, no. 52, Olivares to Montesclaros, 24 August 1626.
[120] ADI Montesclaros Mss., lib. 31, no. 55, Olivares to Montesclaros, 17 November 1626 and enclosure.
[121] González Palencia, *Noticias de Madrid*, p. 153.

justified measure' as long as the original conditions were scrupulously observed.[122] The Council of the Indies, asked to advise on the possibilities of extending it to America, replied that there could be no question of raising troops. Instead it suggested that the two viceroyalties of New Spain and Peru might be persuaded to provide between them 600,000 ducats a year over the next fifteen years, to be used to establish and maintain a squadron of twelve galleons and three smaller vessels. Four of these galleons would help protect the silver fleets, and the remaining eight would be added to the Atlantic fleet to guard the shipping lanes between Gibraltar and the English Channel. Orders to this effect were sent to the viceroys in April 1627.[123]

As for the Union in Flanders, the Infanta continued to prevaricate, and the Count-Duke felt that she had not fully grasped its advantages. The proposed new system would relieve the loyal provinces of having to billet some 30,000 underpaid soldiers, most of them undisciplined Germans.[124] In order to push through the scheme in face of the Infanta's scepticism, Olivares decided to send a personal emissary. His choice fell on his cousin, Don Diego Mexía, whose star was rising fast. A younger son of the Marquis of Loriana and of Olivares' aunt, Doña Leonor de Guzmán, Mexía knew the Netherlands well. He had fought with the army of Flanders as long ago as 1600, and had also served in the household of the Archduke Albert. Olivares must have decided at an early stage to promote this relative of his, who combined an amiable character and some administrative and military ability with a discerning eye for the arts—he would in due course become one of the great picture collectors of the age.[125] Although some ten years older than the Count-Duke, his lack of money as a cadet member of his family made him totally dependent on the favour of his cousin, who knew how to turn the financial necessities of his relatives to his own advantage, but who also came to look upon him as a son. He helped organize the defence preparations in Castile when the English attack on Cadiz was expected, and accompanied the king and Olivares on their journey to the Crown of Aragon. His services were rewarded in July 1626 by his appointment to the Council of State. On 10 April 1627 he was created Marquis of

[122] AHN Est. lib. 870, *Copia de una representación del Conde Duque con motivo del buen estado en que camina el negocio de la unión*, 3 February 1627. See Roca, *Fragmentos*, pp. 262–6.

[123] See Fred Bronner, 'La Unión de las Armas en el Perú. Aspectos político-legales', *Anuario de Estudios Americanos*, 24 (1967), pp. 1133–71. For New Spain, J. I. Israel, *Race, Class and Politics in Colonial Mexico*, pp. 178–80.

[124] AGS Est., Reg. 2041, paper by Olivares, 28 January 1627.

[125] Cf. Mary C. Volk, 'New light on a seventeenth-century collector: the Marquis of Leganés', *Art Bulletin*, 52 (1980), pp. 256–68, and Brown and Elliott, *A Palace*, pp. 115–6. For his career, a petition from him which was discussed in the Council of State on 19 November 1641 is especially useful (AHN Consejos, lib. 7157), and the Tuscan ambassador in Madrid writes about him at some length on 29 September 1635 (ASF Mediceo, filza 4961).

Leganés,[126] and that June he was betrothed to a lady-in-waiting to the queen, Doña Polixena Spínola, daughter of the great Ambrosio Spínola, who brought with her an enormous dowry of 200,000 ducats (Pl. 15).[127]

Around the time of his engagement Leganés was selected for the mission to Flanders, where it was no doubt hoped that the family ties now linking him to Spínola would help smoothe the way for the Union of Arms. He arrived in Brussels on 9 September and spent the next few weeks negotiating with the Estates of the different provinces of the Spanish Netherlands. By the end of the year it was agreed that they should join the Union, offering as their contribution 12,000 paid infantry.[128] The success of Leganés' mission came as a welcome relief to the Count-Duke. He felt that his own reputation and that of Leganés himself were deeply committed,[129] and in this he was right. The Union of Arms was his own brainchild, and in 1625–6 he invested a great deal of time and effort in preparing for its entry into the world. The birth had not been easy, but future prospects looked reasonably promising, and the rest of the world watched with interest, and even, it seems, with some thought of emulation. 'Our union at home is that which most importeth us', wrote Secretary Coke for the benefit of Charles I, 'and therefore His Majesty may be pleased to consider whether it be not necessary upon the same grounds of State as the Spaniards have built to unite his three kingdoms in a strict union and obligation each to other for their mutual defence when any of them shall be assailed, every one with such a proportion of horse, foot or shipping as may be rateably thought fit.'[130] The way to strength lay through unity.

Leganés' success also meant much to Olivares on purely personal grounds. For 1626, the year of the Union of Arms, had been a year of terrible personal tragedy. On 21 June his twenty-two-years-old nephew, Enrique de Guzmán, a young man in whom he had placed the highest hopes, died within two months of being made a cardinal.[131] A few weeks later he was struck by a still more devastating blow. In July his daughter María gave premature birth to her first child, a stillborn daughter. A new-born infant was hastily found and

[126] González Palencia, *Noticias de Madrid*, pp. 144 and 158.
[127] *Ibid.*, p. 161.
[128] Echevarría Bacigalupe, *La diplomacia secreta*, pp. 121–2; AGS Est. leg. 2042, acceptance of union by the Infanta in the name of Philip IV, 23 December 1627 (also in Lonchay, *Correspondance*, 2, Doc. 1146).
[129] BL Add. Ms. 14,006, fo. 37v., Olivares to Leganés, 12 October 1627.
[130] *Calendar of State Papers. Domestic. Addenda 1625–1649*, 77, pp. 241–2. I owe this citation to the kindness of Professor Conrad Russell, who refers to it in his 'Monarchies, Wars and Estates in England, France, and Spain, c.1580–c.1640', *Legislative Studies Quarterly*, 7 (1982), pp. 205–20.
[131] González Palencia, *Noticias de Madrid*, p. 143.

15. Peter Paul Rubens, *Marquis of Leganés.*

presented to the mother as if it were her own.[132] The deception worked, but María was very weak, and on 28 July her father wrote sadly to the Marquis of Aytona that there was little hope of saving her life.[133] She died two days later, and with her died Olivares' prospects for the founding of a great new Guzmán dynasty.

Over the next few months Don Diego Mexía moved in to fill the gaping void, so far as it could ever be filled. When he was created Marquis of Leganés in April 1627 he changed his name to Don Diego Felípez de Guzmán, following the style recently adopted by Olivares himself, who had added Felípez to the family names in honour of the king.[134] Although Olivares still cherished hopes of having more children of his own, it looked as though it would fall to Don Diego to perpetuate the line. At the same time he needed an intimate within the family circle. In establishing the Union of Arms in Flanders Leganés was able to show that he was not unworthy of the confidence placed in him by the patron who had become to him a father. Many years later he would claim to have followed consistently 'the directions of the Count-Duke', to have been 'entirely his creature', and to have done his best to imitate the Count-Duke's 'zeal and love' for the king.[135] But where 'zeal and love' for the king were concerned, the Count-Duke was inimitable.

---

[132] The story is told by Cassiano dal Pozzo, who accompanied Cardinal Barberini on his visit to Spain. Extracts from his diary, including this one of 19 July, are printed with a commentary in José Simón Díaz, 'Dos privados frente a frente: el Cardenal F. Barberini y el Conde-Duque de Olivares (Madrid, 1626)', *Revista de la Biblioteca, Archivo y Museo*, 7–8 (1980), pp. 7–53.

[133] ADM leg. 79, Olivares to Aytona, 28 July 1626.

[134] ASG, Lettere ministri, Spagna, 2434, despatch, 19 June 1627.

[135] AHN Consejos, lib. 7157, petition of Leganés (1641).

VIII

THE FIRST MINISTER

The new Spanish Seneca

His daughter's death in July 1626 left the Count-Duke numbed. There was now nothing to hope for, and nothing to fear, as far as the things of this world were concerned.[1] In October when he had to leave his wife alone for the first time since the loss of María in order to accompany the king to the Escorial, he wrote to Fray Tomás de la Virgen, a Trinitarian friar, of his terrible sadness at leaving Doña Inés 'without her companion of eighteen years' standing, without a granddaughter, without the other son and daughter we had, who died; in fact, she has nobody, and her heart, like mine, is broken . . .'[2]

After his wife, his first thought was for his bereaved son-in-law, 'reduced to a state which could never have been imagined, and with his fortunes so low that only the most signal demonstrations of favour could hope to restore them.'[3] These demonstrations took the form of treating him as if his wife and child had survived. On 16 August, still only thirteen years old, he was created Duke of Medina de las Torres and given a grandeeship. To maintain the new duke in proper style Olivares conferred upon him extensive revenues, made him heir to his entail unless he himself should produce a male heir ('which today is very possible'[4]), and transferred to him his own palace office of groom of the stole. 'With all this', it was unkindly observed, 'they wiped away his tears on the death of his wife.'[5]

It was to be a long time before Olivares abandoned all hope that Doña Inés would bear him the son for which he yearned, and there would be dark murmurings at court about potions and sorcery and sacrilegious couplings in an oratory chapel of the Madrid convent

---

[1] ADM leg. 79, Olivares to Aytona, 8 August 1626.

[2] José María Martínez Val and Margarita Peñalosa E.-Infantes, *Un epistolario inédito del reinado de Felipe IV* (Ciudad Real, 1961), letter 57 (17 October 1626). The two children he mentions died in infancy.

[3] BAV Barb. Lat. Ms. 8600, fos. 3-5v., Olivares to Cardinal Barberini, 22 August 1626. A copy of this letter, undated and without the name of the recipient, survives in the Archive of the Duke of Alba, and was partially published in Marañón, *Olivares*, pp. 282-3.

[4] *Ibid.*

[5] González Palencia, *Noticias de Madrid*, p. 147.

of San Plácido, of which the Protonotario Jerónimo de Villanueva was founder and patron.[6] Olivares' career had been planned on the assumption that with God's favour and that of the king he would found a great house which would bring fresh lustre to the name of Guzmán. Until July 1626 everything had been going according to plan; and now, without warning, the plan had collapsed. Not unnaturally, it proved agonizingly difficult to adjust to the new situation, and in the process the Count-Duke became a more sombre, and superficially a harder, man, although perhaps one with a deeper and more instinctive reaction to the sorrows of the afflicted.[7]

If he had been no more than conventionally religious in his early years, the effect of his daughter's death was to leave him profoundly disenchanted with the world and its works. In the midst of his tragedy he found some consolation in the writings of the sixteenth-century Flemish mystic, Abbot Blosius;[8] and observers noted how from now on he became almost fanatically punctilious in the observance of his religious exercises, confessing and taking communion every day.[9] The Venetian ambassador's report that he had a coffin set up in his room, and would lie in it while the *De profundis* was recited over him,[10] may well be one of those macabre stories so appealing to seventeenth-century tastes; but the consciousness of the nearness of death and an overwhelming sense of his own sinfulness were his ever-present companions. As someone who had achieved more than he ever dreamt possible, and then 'lost it all in a single hour' with his daughter's death, he was convinced that this was an act of God's mercy designed to force upon him the realization that 'salvation is all that counts', and that everything else was but 'vanity and madness.'[11]

The religious melancholy into which he settled was accompanied by a new austerity in his personal life. He abandoned the pleasures of the table, ordinarily drinking water, and turning to wine only for medicinal purposes.[12] The sexual promiscuity of his early years

---

[6] 'Vida licenciosa y hechos escandalosos y sacrilegos de Don Gaspar de Guzmán', BNM K.141, published in Basilio Sebastián Castellanos, *El Bibliotecario* (Madrid, 1841), pp. 71–2. See also Marañón, *Olivares*, pp. 285–6.

[7] Cf. his letter of condolence to Rubens on the death of Isabella Brant, Max Rooses, *Correspondance de Rubens*, 3 (Antwerp, 1900), letter ccccvii (8 August 1626). In this same letter he thanks Rubens for his engraved portrait (Pl. 14) which he sees as a testimonial of Rubens' love for him, and expatiates on the power of love.

[8] Martínez Val, *Un epistolario inédito*, letter 50 (Olivares to Fray Tomás de la Virgen, n.d.). Blosius was also among the favourite devotional writers of Philip II (see Baltasar Porreño, *Dichos y hechos del rey D. Felipe II* (Madrid, 1942), p. 67).

[9] Sánchez Calderón, *Epítome*, fo. 690v.

[10] Barozzi and Berchet, *Relazioni. Spagna*, 2, p. 16.

[11] BL Eg. Ms. 2053, fo. 34, Olivares to Duke of Carpiñano, 20 October 1628.

[12] BAV Vat. Lat. Ms. 10,422, *Relazione della corte di Spagna*, fo. 32v.

was now a thing of the past. Although he would make the occasional jocular remark about women in response to the Cardinal-Infante's letters from Flanders in the 1630's recounting his troubles with some new mistress,[13] his own life became a model of marital fidelity.[14] He and Doña Inés were brought closer to each other by their shared loss, and this austere and pious woman imposed herself in their marriage as the calm and stable support of a husband who was subject to periodic bouts of deep mental depression.

These bouts of depression have been diagnosed as those of a cyclothymic personality, sharply oscillating between melancholy and euphoria.[15] But the alternating phases of exaltation and depression gave way to a more deep-settled depression in the years after 1626, even though—by what must often have been a tremendous effort of the will—the Count-Duke would emerge from some fresh set-back with new hopes, new plans, and a display of resilience and stamina which deeply impressed those who were privy to the mental anguish that he suffered. This was particularly true of the last, terrible years of power, when disaster followed disaster in quick succession. A few days before his fall in 1643 his secretary Carnero wrote to a friend: 'My master is utterly worn out and broken, but even with the water over his head, he keeps swimming.'[16] This refusal to give up was characteristic of the Count-Duke, and it was only at the end of his life, when there was nothing left to live for, that something finally snapped and he crossed the farther boundary of the no-man's land between abnormality and madness.

It would be natural to assume that Olivares' political judgment was liable to be clouded by his temperamental instability; but this is perhaps to reckon without his iron determination to counteract the tendencies to which his 'melancholic' temperament made him prone. It was as a true neo-Stoic, combining classical fortitude with Christian resignation in the tradition of Justus Lipsius, that he chose to face the world. This was nowhere more apparent than in his reaction to the loss of his daughter. His immediate instinct was to think of retiring from the king's service, 'disillusioned with the brevity of all things, and mindful of my salvation.'[17] But personal inclination took second place to duty. With icy self-control he held his usual audiences on the day of María's death—an act of stoicism that earned

[13] MSB Cod. Hisp. 22, Olivares to Cardinal Infante, 18 September 1636.

[14] See Marañón, *Olivares*, pp. 174–5.

[15] Marañón, ch. 6, discusses these mood swings and the nature of the cyclothymic personality, which he relates to Olivares' physique, following the German psychologist, Ernst Kretschner. See Elliott, *Richelieu and Olivares*, pp. 13–16.

[16] AGR CPE Reg. 1504, fo. 238v., Carnero to Pierre Roose, 16 January 1643.

[17] Letter to Cardinal Barberini, 22 August 1626.

him the grudging admiration even of his enemies, and was to be celebrated by Quevedo in his play of 1629, *Cómo ha de ser el privado*, where the Marquis of Valisero (a transparent anagram of Olivares) refuses to cancel his audiences on being informed of the death of his son and heir.[18]

In the play, which was based on the biographical sketch of Olivares written by his Sevillian companion the Count of La Roca,[19] Valisero loses all his personal ambitions on the extinction of his line, and—turning away from all thoughts of further aggrandisement of himself and his house—dedicates himself exclusively to the royal service. 'I have no children; I am heir to myself,'[20] he says, and the only favour he accepts of the king is a grant of twelve thousand ducats for the construction of his tomb. This was the image that Olivares liked to project of himself in the years after 1626—the image of a man for whom nothing existed beyond the service of his king and the salvation of his soul. 'I have neither father, child nor friend other than he who serves the king well, who risks his life and honour and will sacrifice everything for the royal service, leaving the rest to our Lord who alone disposes events . . .'[21]

The image never conformed exactly to the reality, and the urge to found a dynasty returned with a new insistence during Olivares' last years in power, at a moment when he could no longer conceal the extent of his political failure even from himself.[22] But 1626 did mark a great change both in the man and in his attitude to the world. In comparison with Lerma he had always shown a degree of restraint in taking advantage of the enormous opportunities available to a royal favourite. But until now his profound sense of loyalty to his monarch had been accompanied by a fierce determination—spurred on by his contempt for many of the heads of the grandee houses of Castile—to establish the superiority of his own house beyond dispute. With this ambition irretrievably shattered by María's death, he found compensation in an almost defiant identification of himself with the service of his royal master. The personal austerity, the total absorption in the business of government, which were such striking features of his life in the years after 1626, were a means of justifying to others, and perhaps also to himself, that tenacious dedication to the exercise of power which was all that remained to him after the extinction of his hopes of succession.

[18] Quevedo, *Obras completas*, 2, p. 609.
[19] *Fragmentos históricos*. In one of the ms. copies of the *Fragmentos* in the Royal Library at Copenhagen (Gl. kgl. saml. 590,2°) the dedication to the king carries the date 19 July 1628.
[20] *Obras completas*, 2, p. 628.
[21] ADM leg. 79, Olivares to Aytona, 30 December 1633.
[22] See below, p. 619, for the recognition of his bastard son.

Olivares' secretary, Antonio Carnero, once described him as 'indefatigable'.[23] Hard work and a regular routine provided the sheet-
anchor for this driven spirit. Much of the routine was provided by
the requirements of the court. At the beginning of the reign Don
Gaspar had moved into the royal palace of the Alcázar, together
with his wife and daughter; and although he retained and improved
his Madrid town house in the Calle de Santiago, close to the Alcázar,[24]
he remained in residence in the palace throughout his years of power.
A plan of the Alcázar drawn in 1626 by the court architect, Juan
Gómez de Mora,[25] shows the Countess of Olivares occupying rooms
on the second story, while the Count-Duke's, like those of the king
and the queen, were located on the third. His suite, which ran out
into a projecting extension at the rear of the palace, included four
unspecified apartments, together with a private oratory and an
audience-chamber, a gallery and a large study, lined with books,
where Cardinal Barberini found him despatching business with Carnero when he came to present his condolences on the death of María.[26]
One of the rooms, which he called his 'work-room or office', was
devoted to his extensive collection of maps and charts.[27] In December
1627, when a joint Franco-Spanish invasion of the British Isles was
being contemplated, he took the Genoese ambassador to this room
and showed him 'six very clear and distinct maps' of England and
Ireland, from which he was able to explain to the ambassador just
how easily the invasion could be accomplished.[28]

From Olivares' apartments a passage led through the north gallery
to the king's quarters; and if the normal procedure was for the Count-
Duke to visit the king, it was not unknown in the early years of
the reign for the traffic to be in the other direction, as on one famous
occasion when the king entered Olivares' study and found him working with a towel wrapped round his head.[29] Contemporaries found
this highly improper, and Olivares felt it advisable to ask his royal
master to desist from making these personal visits.

---

[23] AGR CPE Reg. 1504, fo. 115v., Carnero to Roose, 20 September 1636.
[24] He had purchased this house, in a ruined condition, in 1620 for 9,000 ducats (see Marañón,
Olivares, Appendix 6). In his newsletter of 15 August 1623 Almansa y Mendoza mentions
the fact that the count's house in the Calle de Santiago was under construction (Cartas, p.
198). It was in effect being rebuilt. He seems to have housed some of his personal staff there,
and also to have used it himself as a quiet place for meeting friends away from the court.
[25] BAV Barb. Lat. Ms. 4372, Relación de las casas que tiene el Rey en España . . . . See Brown
and Elliott, A Palace, plate 14, for a reproduction of the plan of the main floor, where the
Count-Duke's rooms are numbered 75 to 84.
[26] Simón Díaz, 'Dos privados', pp. 36–7.
[27] Roca, Fragmentos, pp. 266–7 (quadra del obrador, u oficio).
[28] ASG, Lettere ministri, Spagna, 2434, despatch, 18 December 1627.
[29] See 'Cargos contra el Conde Duque' (1643) in MC, 2, Doc. XX[a], p. 242.

Residence in the palace was incumbent on the Count-Duke as long as he held the office of groom of the stole (*sumiller de corps*), or the post (especially revived for him in 1636[30]) of grand chamberlain (*camarero mayor*). The duties of groom of the stole involved, at least nominally, not only dressing and undressing the king, but also sleeping in the royal bedroom.[31] By transferring these duties to Medina de las Torres in 1626 he reduced the amount of obligatory time spent each day in ceremonial attendance on the king, although as master of the horse he still had to accompany Philip on his hunting trips and on any excursion beyond the palace confines.

Since Philip was a passionate huntsman who spent long hours in the saddle, the post of master of the horse was an onerous one. The king's principal huntsman, Juan Mateos, published in 1634 a treatise on *The Origins and Dignity of the Hunt,* which was dedicated to Olivares as master of the horse, and contained an engraving of him in the hunting-field.[32] But already by this time the Count-Duke had lost much of his enthusiasm for the chase. 'Tomorrow', he wrote in February 1631, 'His Majesty goes to Guisando, where he will spend some days hunting. It is not a resort that is very good for my infirmities and all my endless troubles, but I will bear with pleasure anything that gives pleasure to His Majesty.'[33] But in earlier years the various duties that devolved on him as master of the horse, which included booting and spurring the king, supervising the running of the stables, and riding with the king not only when he was out hunting but also in jousts and tourneys,[34] appealed to a man who had always been proud of his horsemanship. No doubt it offered, too, a pleasant relaxation from interminable paper-work.

For it was among papers that the Count-Duke spent the greater part of his life, and at least in the imagination of his contemporaries he was never separated from them. He was said to resemble a scarecrow as he went around the palace with documents stuck in his hatband and dangling from his belt.[35] When he took an outing in his coach, he carried stacks of state papers with him, and dictated to his secretaries as he went. His working day—apart from his ceremonial attendance on the king, who rose at eight, lunched at midday,

---

[30] Hoz, p. 245 (8 April 1636).
[31] González Dávila, *Teatro de las grandezas*, p. 314. According to the *Etiquetas* of 1636 relating to the royal chamber (Royal Library, Copenhagen, Ny.kgl.S., no. 190) a portable bed would be set up for him in the bed-chamber; but the king could dispense him from the obligation to spend the night there, so long as he was in the palace. There is no indication as to whether Olivares normally received such a dispensation.
[32] *Origen y dignidad de la caza* (Madrid, 1634; new ed., Madrid, 1928).
[33] BL Add. Ms. 24,909, fo. 189, Olivares to Padre Diego de Quiroga, 5 February 1631.
[34] González Dávila, *Teatro*, pp. 314–5.
[35] BAV Vat. Lat. Ms. 10,422, *Relazione della corte di Spagna*, fos. 76–76v.

and dined at eight[36]—was that of a hard-pressed bureaucrat.[37] His first waking hours, until seven, were set aside for religious exercises. Then he would draw the curtains of the king's bed and brief Philip on the day's business; and the rest of the morning would be spent with secretaries going through the *consultas* to be placed before the king, although he also had to make time to interview petitioners.

He regarded the granting of audiences as one of the less congenial duties of his office. How, he asked Don Francisco Lanario de Aragón, Duke of Carpiñano, could he deal with prolix petitioners and not send them away discontented? 'My difficulty is that I have numerous occupations, and am more anxious to do the right thing in audiences than anything else, even though I do not consider them the most substantial part of my work. But I can only spare two or three hours for them.' What did Carpiñano recommend? Little more, it transpired, than a great deal of patience—not one of the qualities for which Don Gaspar was renowned.[38] One way to limit the amount of time spent on audiences was to leave as far as possible to the king the business of appointments, along with the distributions of *mercedes* or favours. In September 1626 Olivares told Philip that if only he would handle by himself 'the current business of private persons' it would free his ministers from those innumerable preoccupations which prevented them from devoting their full time to his service.[39]

Such a rigid division of functions, however, was neither practical nor, from Olivares' point of view, entirely desirable, whatever he might say to the contrary. The dispensing of patronage was in reality such an integral part of the exercise of power that no principal minister of the King of Spain could have survived if he once allowed it to slip from his hands. Olivares' concern that the king should occupy himself with petitions and *mercedes* cannot, therefore, be taken entirely at face value; and, where appointments were concerned, Philip inevitably turned to him for advice, as when the post of Inquisitor General fell vacant in 1626, and the Count-Duke, at the king's request, produced a list of candidates, the most prominent of whom was in due course appointed.[40] But it was true that a vast amount of paper-work was generated by requests for pensions, places and favours, if only

[36] Barozzi and Berchet, *Relazioni. Spagna*, 2, p. 10.
[37] Sánchez Calderón, *Epítome*, fos. 690v.–91 for Olivares' working day, following Roca, *Fragmentos*, pp. 245–6.
[38] BL Eg. Ms. 2053, fos. 26–32v., *Preguntas del Conde Duque sobre las audiencias*; and see Enrique Tierno-Galván, 'Acerca de dos cartas muy poco conocidas del Conde Duque de Olivares', *Anales de la Universidad de Murcia* (1951–2), pp. 71–6.
[39] *MC*, 1, Doc. XI (*Reflexiones políticas y cristianas*), p. 207.
[40] AGS Gracia y Justicia leg. 621, Olivares to king, 26 August 1626. Olivares listed five names, but refused to rank them, on grounds both of conscience and lack of knowledge. But he noted that many were of the opinion that the post should go to a jurist rather than a theologian, and the senior jurist on his list was Cardinal Zapata, who received the appointment.

because the organization of patronage, like everything else in the Spanish Monarchy, had become highly bureaucratized. There were endless routine decisions to be taken about pensions for the widows of Flanders veterans, or requests for arrears of wages, or petitions from petty officials to be allowed to transfer their office to a son or nephew. All these petitions were channelled through the councils, but it was for the king, with or without the guidance of his favourite, to take the final decision, even if it only meant endorsing a *consulta* with the words 'yes'—*Así*— or 'no'—*No ha lugar.*

The Count-Duke would break his morning at twelve for a light lunch. By three he would be back at work, 'receiving and despatching letters, giving more audiences, holding meetings ... and then despatching documents with his secretaries until eleven o'clock at night.' Much of his most important business, however, was conducted in privacy, away from the palace. His meetings with Barberini during the legate's visit to Madrid in 1626 were held almost invariably out of doors, in the gardens of the Casa del Campo, or walking along the banks of the Manzanares, or—most of all—in his well-appointed coach with its embossed leather hangings, drawn by six fine mules. His coach, indeed, became his second office, where he could transact business and discuss high matters of state with a single travelling companion in conditions of absolute secrecy.[41] So it was that 'from his bedroom to his study, in his coach, in corners, and pausing on the staircase, he heard and despatched the business of an infinite number of people.'[42]

With this routine, it is not surprising that he overworked his secretaries, just as he overworked himself. In the early 1620's he was building up a secretarial team which would serve him with devotion over the years. Francisco de Elosu y Alviz, whom he inherited from Baltasar de Zúñiga, died in October 1624. Elosu's death, which Olivares felt keenly,[43] led to a reorganization of his secretariat.[44] Andrés de Rozas, formerly secretary to Archbishop Acevedo, President of the Council of Castile,[45] was given responsibility for foreign despatches and for the papers of the Councils of State, Italy and Flanders, 'and anything else that I order.' Francisco Gómez de Lasprilla took over the papers of the remaining councils, and the correspondence with the ministers at court. Antonio Carnero was to handle Spanish correspondence and the business of the Council of War, and to deal with everything relating to the Count-Duke's palace posts. All three

[41] Simón Díaz, 'Dos privados', pp. 47–8; Marañón, *Olivares*, pp. 108–9.
[42] Sánchez Calderón, *Epítome*, fo. 691.
[43] AGS Est. leg. 7033, Olivares to Gondomar, 25 October 1624.
[44] *MC*, 1, Doc. III (*Copia del orden del Conde Duque*, October 1624).
[45] *Actas*, 36, p. 211.

men were to regard themselves as subordinate to the secretary Antonio de Contreras, who belonged to one of the best-entrenched families in the Spanish bureaucracy.

Of these various secretaries, Antonio Carnero became the one closest to Olivares. In December 1626 the nuncio reported that he had been made *ayuda de cámara* to the king, with access at any hour to the royal apartments, and that he was advancing steadily in the Count-Duke's favour.[46] 'A very honest man and a very good friend (though he stole my dog)', remarked the English ambassador, Sir Arthur Hopton.[47] Although one or two other secretaries entered his personal service over the course of the years—notably, in the 1630's, Jerónimo de Lezama, whose father had been employed in naval administration in Vizcaya[48]—Olivares seems to have used Carnero for his most important letters and memoranda. Carnero, more than anyone, knew the Count-Duke's secrets, and his bold, clear hand—obviously sometimes working at speed to his master's dictation—appears at every turn in a documentation that extends over twenty years. Like Olivares' other secretaries, he was also appointed secretary to the king, so that the close personal relationship between king and minister was maintained at a lower level in their respective secretariats. The Count-Duke saw to it that a series of appointments and perquisites came his way—all the more necessary as he eventually had eleven children to support.[49] Carnero in turn gave unstinting loyalty to his patron in the years of his disgrace as much as in the years of high fortune.

The perquisites given to Carnero and his colleagues over and above their salaries were well deserved because, as Olivares warned them on appointment, he drove his secretaries hard. 'My disposition', he explained, 'is not a very good one', partly because as a man in authority he had to act with rectitude in the service of the king, and partly because of his 'almost habitual' poor health.[50]

Ill-health was a recurring theme throughout his correspondence. 'I have read your long letter, as full of hypochondria as if it were my own', he wrote to his brother-in-law, Monterrey, in 1629.[51] In 1626 he was complaining of severe headaches, made 'gigantic' by his melancholy temperament,[52] and he suffered increasingly from

[46] ASV, Spagna 66, fo. 92v., 12 December 1626
[47] BL Eg. Ms. 1820, fo. 22, Hopton to Cottington, 14 April 1631.
[48] AHN Est. leg. 727, La Junta de Reformación de Presidios, 9 October 1633, on a petition from Jerónimo de Lezama.
[49] AHN Est. lib. 869, fo. 104, Olivares to Carnero, 28 December 1644. He married in 1631 Doña Ana María de Zárate, the daughter of his predecessor in the secretariat of Italy.
[50] MC, 1, Doc. III, p. 33.
[51] AGS Est. leg. 2713, Olivares to Monterrey, 30 October 1629.
[52] BAV Barb. Lat. Ms. 8599, fo. 74, Olivares to Cardinal Barberini, 10 May 1626.

insomnia. Gout, too, was a recurrent problem, and he was constantly being bled and purged. Although a fine horseman, his official duties left him less and less time for exercise; and a sedentary existence helped to undermine his constitution still further. By the early 1630's his gout and his growing corpulence made his life one of almost continuous suffering. 'I am so racked by my illnesses', he wrote to the Marquis of Aytona in 1633, 'that when I tried to mount a horse the other day I couldn't manage it. This is the worst thing that could happen to me, because I always used to recover my spirits and vitality once I was on horseback.'[53]

His physical infirmities were no doubt partly responsible for the asperity and the sudden outbursts of temper which frightened or antagonized so many of those who did business with him. But, as he indicated in his instructions to his secretaries, his asperity was also a direct consequence of his conception of his official duties. As the new 'Spanish Seneca',[54] austere and beyond reproach, he could not afford to give an impression of weakening when personal inclination pointed in one direction and the king's interests in another. At heart he seems to have been a generous man, capable of inspiring deep devotion, and genuinely solicitous for the well-being of servants and ministers who cringed before the lash of his tongue.[55] Indeed, something of this quality is captured in an unusually informal portrait drawing, possibly by Velázquez, which makes him look mild and even benign (Pl. 16).[56] But, like other public figures of his age, he was deeply conscious of playing a part in the 'theatre of the world';[57] and it is thus that he appears in the official image created by Velázquez—stern and imperious, whether (as in the portrait of c. 1625) holding his riding whip as master of the horse (Pl. 17), or as the supreme commander and grand strategist in the great equestrian portrait of the later 1630's (Pl. 1). This is the Olivares intended for the eyes of posterity, a man impressively in control both of himself and of events. But there is one late portrait where the reality breaks through, and the caved-in mouth and sunken eyes (although they have lost nothing of their astuteness) show how the years and the cares of office have taken their toll (Pl. 28).

[53] ADM leg. 79, Olivares to Aytona, 21 January 1633.
[54] Quevedo, 'Cómo ha de ser el privado', Obras completas, 2, p. 625.
[55] Cf. his personal note of 22 October 1625 to Andrés de Prada, one of the king's secretaries, expressing solicitude for his health and advising him on the importance of a suitable regime for convalescence, especially during the autumn months (AGS Est. leg. 2847).
[56] Published and discussed by Jonathan Brown, 'A Portrait Drawing by Velázquez', Master Drawings, 14 (1976), pp. 46–51.
[57] In Quevedo's Cómo ha de ser el privado, the Marquis of Valisero complains that Fortune has left him exposed in the theatre of the world as the target for envy and complaint (Obras completas, 2, p. 596).

16. This drawing, showing Olivares as captain-general of the cavalry, has been attributed to Velázquez. It may have provided a model for the allegorical Rubens portrait engraved by Pontius (Pl. 14).

17. In this portrait of *c.* 1625 Velázquez shows Olivares wearing the green cross of the order of Alcántara, of which he became a member in 1624.

c/ Conde Duque

It is not surprising if this complex figure, for whom joyless hard work became a way of life, was misunderstood by his contemporaries. 'His name is known to all Europe, but his person to very few, and they all have different impressions', wrote the French poet, Vincent Voiture, who visited Madrid in 1632 on behalf of Gaston d'Orléans, and commented admiringly on the Count-Duke's constancy in the face of adversity and on his success in preventing a total Spanish collapse.[58]

Foreign ambassadors tended to speak of Olivares with dislike in their despatches from Madrid, partly because they were the natural recipients of malicious gossip in a court rife with malice, and partly because they so often found themselves at the receiving end of the Count-Duke's verbal barrages. When he turned on the Genoese ambassador in an angry interview, banging his fist against the window-frame in his fury,[59] it is not surprising that the ambassador's despatches related his activities with something less than enthusiasm. The papal nuncios, who found him a determined supporter of the crown's prerogatives where church-state relations were concerned, were almost uniformly unfavourable, although at least one of them, Giulio Sacchetti, gradually came round to a grudging recognition of his qualities. 'The Count of Olivares', he wrote in 1625, 'although jealous of his office and violent in his conduct, acts with upright intentions, and is endowed with a mind superior to what might be expected of his age and experience.'[60] But occasionally a foreign envoy showed a sympathetic insight into the enormous difficulties that faced him, and Sir Arthur Hopton, the English envoy in Madrid for most of the 1630's, was a constant if somewhat naif admirer: 'I for my part am of those that think that having (as he hath in all his actions) virtue for his guide, he cannot fail for fortune for his companion.'[61] The correlation, unfortunately, proved less close than Hopton imagined.

Although the asperity which Olivares displayed in his personal relations may sometimes have been the result of deliberate intent, the comments of observers on the damaging consequences of his behaviour for his own best interests suggest that asperity was an integral part of a personality which they described as naturally choleric. There is indeed something deeply distasteful about the hectoring, bullying tone which he adopted in some of his reported interviews, even after allowance is made for the bias of the reporting. When that persistent critic of the crown's fiscal policies, Lisón y Biedma,

---

[58] Vincent Voiture, *Les Oeuvres de M. de Voiture* (Paris, 1691), 2, pp. 249–54.
[59] ASG, Lettere Ministri, Spagna, 2434, despatch, 20 December 1628.
[60] ASV, Spagna 65, fo. 216v., letter of 8 April 1625.
[61] BL Eg. Ms. 1820, fo. 173, Hopton to Cottington, 11 May 1632.

protested in the course of a stormy interview in June 1627 that it was hardly necessary to go to so much trouble to crush a mere 'ant' like himself, he was curtly told by Olivares that he was not even an ant, or as much as half an ant, and that he would be given the kind of punishment that would serve as an example to the rest.[62]

The impression created by such accounts is of a man who found it difficult to curb his outbursts of exasperation when, as so often happened, men and events failed to conform to his designs. Temperamentally, he wanted to organize everything. He was a man with the '*ambizione di dominare*', in the words of one of the Venetian ambassadors.[63] It is a plausible hypothesis that the various facets of his temperament were in fact all of a piece—that the harshness and irritability were the reverse side of a basic generosity of character, and that, in a man of Olivares' character and constitution, these traits are frequently accompanied by the will to dominate.[64]

That the Count-Duke was domineering, impulsive and strident was generally agreed. Contemporary observers spoke, too, of a certain extravagance in his deportment,[65] of a tendency to seek the unexpected solution and to do things in the unexpected way, as if he were inspired by a wilful capriciousness; and they dwelt on his apparently excessive ingenuity, and his constant contriving of novel and grandiose designs which bore little relation to practical possibilities. One of the Genoese ambassadors described him as 'by nature very inclined to novelties, without taking account of where they may lead him.'[66] Another reported that 'his character is dangerous because of his sudden outbursts of anger, his love of novelties and of dangerous counsels.'[67]

These characteristics may point to a certain kind of personality, but they also very much belonged to the age in which Olivares lived. The theatrical gestures, the rhetoric, the grand design, were the stock in trade of the great public personalities of his generation. If Olivares loved complicated machinations, so did Richelieu. If he pursued grandiose and chimerical schemes that seemed far removed from reality, so too did Wallenstein—and Olivares, unlike Wallenstein, had no use for astrology.[68] An apparent predilection for vast and complicated schemes was, in any event, accompanied by an astute perception

[62] Lisón's record of the interview has been published by Jean Vilar in his 'Formes et tendances de l'opposition'.

[63] Barozzi and Berchet, *Relazioni. Spagna*, 2, p. 15.

[64] Marañón, *Olivares*, p. 121.

[65] *Ibid.*, p. 106.

[66] ASG, Lettere Ministri, Spagna, 2435, despatch, 20 January 1629.

[67] Ciasca, *Istruzioni,* 2, p. 264 (Luca Pallavicino, 18 October 1628).

[68] In 1633 he described the situation in Germany as being 'all in the air and governed by astrology, which is the worst thing of all, the greatest *liviandad*' (AGS Est. leg. 2334, consulta, 24 May 1633).

of the strong and weak points of the men who would be involved in them, and by an extreme capacity for attending to the minutest details of organization.

Nor should the Count-Duke's pronouncements be necessarily taken at face value. Contemporaries were well aware of his guile, and his capacity for deceit was a byword. In particular, he had a reputation for taking the opposite line in important council meetings to the one which he really favoured. 'It is usually his manner of proceeding', wrote Hopton, 'to deliver his opinion in public contrary to what he thinks and means shall take effect, because on either side he finds his justification, in the good success of the action by the success itself, in the bad by his voice ...'[69] The Count-Duke's tendency to put up a smokescreen in order to cover his trail was not simply a device, as Hopton assumed, to make sure that he emerged with credit, however events turned out. It certainly served this purpose, but it could also be used to conceal a cautious policy behind a display of bravado. Behind all the loud talk and the apparent impulsiveness, there was a caution that at times bordered on timidity—and, indeed, a lack of that ultimate ruthlessness which characterized his great rival, Richelieu.

Rhetoric, therefore, featured strongly in Olivares' style of government, and the Count-Duke was never at a loss for words. It is true that he told the Infante Don Carlos in 1624 that he was still overcome with confusion at the thought of having to speak at a council meeting in the presence of the king, and would bring his speech ready written to prevent him from tying himself in knots.[70] But in fact words cascaded from him in a powerful, if turbulent, stream which overwhelmed his hearers. He cajoled, he dazzled, he infuriated. Novoa, after summarizing his presentation to the Council of State of his plan for the Union of Arms, remarks: 'that was the substance of it; but the powder which he expended unnecessarily was excessive, embarking as he did on a two-hour prologue where an expression of opinion was more than sufficient. But he was always a great embellisher.'[71]

His rhetoric spilled over into his memoranda and correspondence, most of which appears to have been dictated—usually to the faithful Carnero—although he would often scrawl a few lines of his own as a personal postscript. His letters are punctuated with vivid collo-

---

[69] BL Eg. Ms. 1820, fo. 266, Hopton to Lord Treasurer, 9 May 1632. For a similar comment in relation to his vote on the Mantuan War, see Barozzi and Berchet, *Relazioni. Spagna*, 1, p. 651.
[70] 'Advertimientos del Conde-Duque al Señor Infante Don Carlos', Marañón, *Olivares*, Appendix 21, p. 452.
[71] Novoa, *Codoin* 69, p. 13.

quialisms and popular refrains which obviously emerged sponta-
neously in the course of dictation. He had the natural letter-writer's
gift, too, of conforming the letter to the character of the recipient.
There was a sharp edge to his correspondence with the Count of
Gondomar, along with a rather forced conviviality which occasionally led him into pieces of doggerel verse—almost the only verse
that survives from his pen after he burnt his youthful poems.[72] It
was as if two rivals, each with a healthy respect for the other, had
chosen for their test of strength the device of a weekly literary competition.

The letters and state papers reinforce the image conveyed by contemporaries of an extravagant, out-size personality with a gift for
endless self-dramatization. His inflated and tortuous prose wanders
down interminable labyrinths. He digresses, he repeats himself, he
consumes an enormous quantity of words to make a relatively simple
point. He blames himself, he blames the world, he clothes himself
in sackcloth and ashes, he prostrates himself before God and the
king, and in general seems to use the device of a state paper as a
mixture of advocate's brief and confessional. Through it all comes
an impression of energy, of a barely controlled elemental force, which
sweeps the reader along, half-admiring, half-bemused. There is an
undigested quality about the state papers—of which only a small
portion survives out of the vast quantity he must have produced
during twenty-two years of power—as if his ideas and arguments
came to him with such irresistible urgency that there was no time
to sift and classify. It was characteristic of the Count-Duke that
one state paper after another would refer to the latest event or problem
as 'without exception the most important thing that has happened
in Your Majesty's Monarchy.'[73] From here he would launch into
a vehement disquisition in which every contingency, probable and
improbable, would be considered, every aspect of the problem
attacked, but whose conclusions were all too frequently muddied,
as if the waters had not been given time to settle.

Yet the attitudes and reactions are those of a man who had worked
hard to master the rules of statecraft and steeped himself in its theory—
too much so, if some of his enemies are to be believed. The Portuguese
noble and man of letters, Francisco Manuel de Melo, who saw him
at work in the 1630's, wrote of him:

The political and historical books which he read had left him with
a number of maxims which were unsuited to the humour of our

---

[72] Cf. his letters of 27 March and 11 April 1625 in the Gondomar correspondence (BPM
Ms. 1817). A youthful effusion is reproduced in Marañón, Appendix 16.
[73] Eg. the marriage alliance with England (AHN Est. lib. 739, draft consulta, 17 May 1623).

times. From this sprang a number of harsh actions, whose only object was to imitate the ancients; as if Tacitus, Seneca, Paterculus, Pliny, Livy, Polybius and Procopius, of whom he took counsel, would not have altered their views if they had been alive now, considering the differences which every age introduces into the customs and interests of men.[74]

But was this criticism just?

The Count-Duke had clearly fashioned for himself a stock of general maxims, the first of which was the necessity to be on one's guard against unexpected accidents. This sense of the contingent, against which no maxim was infallible, constantly recurred. 'I have always understood', he wrote in a note to Juan de Villela, 'that one should never be discouraged if a desirable outcome is delayed, or things seem to go awry, because it always depends on different accidents, and these change daily and hourly.'[75] Very often the maxims he liked to enunciate ran directly counter to the kind of political behaviour which contemporaries tended to associate with him. They accused him of wanting to introduce novelties, but, as he himself insisted on one occasion, 'although many things would be better if they were other than they are, to change them would be worse.'[76] They accused him, somewhat inconsistently, of being both Machiavellian and chimerical; but, as Diego de Corral reminded him on one occasion, 'I have heard Your Excellency say very wisely that the art of government does not consist in being acute, but in being moral and practical, pursuing policies that can easily be put into practice—ones that are so massive and dense that they can be cut with a knife—and avoiding metaphysical and plausible-sounding propositions.'[77]

An extravagant, disordered personality whose constant demand was for the neo-Stoic virtues of order, discipline, economy; a Machiavellian statesman with impossibly chimerical schemes; a practitioner of a statecraft derived from maxims who harboured a profound scepticism about the validity of general rules—the contradictions abound. Yet beneath all the enigmas of this complex character, there remain certain constant traits. The Count-Duke as a statesman was almost agonizingly aware of the scale and complexity of the problems which, as the first minister of the King of Spain, he was called upon to face. He knew that they demanded of him infinite resourcefulness and tireless energy. Hoping for the best, yet fearing the worst, he was acutely conscious of charting a course through turbulent seas

---

[74] *Epanáforas* (ed. E. Prestage, Coimbra, 1931), p. 93.
[75] AGS Est. leg. 2329, 20 March 1629.
[76] AGS Est. leg. 2042, Olivares in Junta del aposento del Conde Duque, 27 June 1628. For the occasion, see below, p. 353.
[77] BL Eg. Ms. 340, fo. 254v., Corral to Olivares, 6 December 1626.

with very inadequate navigational aids. If anyone was capable of doing this, he believed it to be himself; but he could never forget that the ultimate disposition of events did not lie in the hands of men. All he could do was to live up to the highest responsibilities of his post, working, planning, ordering, supervising with unremitting vigilance, in the belief that God would ultimately favour His own, and that the king must be well served.

The struggle with the system

The Count-Duke's relationship with the king was the foundation of his power. This relationship was both personal and ministerial. At the personal level, Philip was still in 1626 the uneasy and often aberrant pupil of an overbearing master, grateful for the care and attention that Olivares lavished upon him, but at the same time chafing at the discipline. At the ministerial level, Olivares was determined to draw the king into a working partnership, since he knew that his plans for national revival stood no chance of success unless the king personally identified himself with the programme of his minister, and was seen to take an active part in promoting Olivares' policies. This helps explain the anguished tones of the personal letter which he wrote to the king on 4 September 1626, at a time when he was still reeling from the blow of his daughter's death. Unless Philip were prepared to devote time and attention to government business, his own position would become untenable. Even then, he could not assure the king of success, for Spain's ills were deeply rooted, its financial reserves exhausted, its ministers lax, disobedient and corrupt. But, if any remedy was to be found, it lay in the king's willingness to get down to work. It is to Philip's credit that he accepted the rebuke, and promised to keep a copy in his archives so that later generations could see how a minister should talk to his king.[78]

When Olivares wrote of the laxity and self-interest of ministers, he was still smarting from recent setbacks in his dealings with the Council of Castile. It had been clear from the beginning that, as a reforming minister, he would sooner or later come into conflict with the council, even though its president, Don Francisco de Contreras, had been hand-picked by Zúñiga and himself.

Part of the trouble rose from those conflicts of jurisdiction which were endemic in the Spanish administrative system, and were a constant source of despair to Olivares. He found it exasperating that 'with the kingdom in such a state as to leave scarcely a moment to look for remedies', so much time and energy should be spent

---

[78] MC, 1, Doc. XI; and see above, p. 170.

resolving disputes over demarcation lines.[79] But his own methods
of government made the problem worse. In order to by-pass the
cumbersome bureaucratic procedures and speed up the process of
reform, he increasingly resorted to the appointment of *ad hoc* committees, or juntas, to take responsibility for particular areas of administration which had previously been under conciliar control. By 1626
these juntas were beginning to proliferate. There were the two juntas
created in 1622 for the fleet (*Armadas*) and for trade (*Comercio*);[80] there
was the *Junta de Reformación*, itself reformed in 1624 to watch more
effectively over manners and morals,[81] and the *Junta del Almirantazgo*,
with Antonio Carnero as its secretary, for the governance of the
new trading companies and control of contraband.[82] Then in 1625
came a *Junta de Minas* for the exploitation of Spain's mines,[83] and
the very important *Junta de Población y Comercio*. This latter, consisting
of six members under the presidency of Olivares, was set up to devise
schemes for increasing the population of Castile (for example by
establishing settlements of foreign artisans), and for making rivers
navigable, and promoting manufactures.[84] These juntas were only
the beginning. By the time of Olivares' fall in 1643 there were more
than thirty of them in existence, and yet another junta had to be
created to discuss their abolition.[85]

The recourse to juntas was nothing new in the history of Spanish
administration, but Olivares carried it to unprecedented lengths. By
creating juntas he was in effect setting up an alternative administration
alongside the councils. From his point of view this had obvious advantages. The average junta had six to eight members, while the Council
of Castile, which would have handled at least some of the business
now transferred to juntas, had twenty members by 1627, excluding
the president.[86] The smaller numbers meant greater secrecy and speed;
and juntas were able to concentrate their attention on a particular
problem without the time-consuming distractions of routine busi-

[79] AGS Gracia y Justicia, leg. 621, Olivares to President of Council of Castile, 2 February
1625.
[80] Above, pp. 142–3 and 144.
[81] González Palencia, 'Quevedo, Tirso y las comedias', p. 44.
[82] AGS Est. leg. 2847, royal order to Andrés de Prada, 10 February 1625.
[83] AHN Consejos, leg. 7145, President of Council of Castile, 6 October 1626.
[84] Khevenhüller, *Annales Ferdinandei*, 2, pp. 1056–7; Carrera Pujal, *Economía española*, 1, pp.
522–4; Eugenio Larruga, *Memorias políticas y económicas*, 11 (Madrid, 1791), pp. 266–75. The
Junta's papers have not so far come to light. Apart from Olivares, its membership, according
to Khevenhüller, consisted of the Marquis of La Hinojosa; Gilimón de la Mota; the Count
of Solre; Don García de Haro; Jerónimo Caimo, of the Council of Italy; and Mendo da Mota,
of the Council of Portugal. The secretary was the Sevillian poet and man of letters, Francisco
de Calatayud.
[85] AHN Consejos, leg. 12,432, consulta de la junta particular, 8 March 1643.
[86] Biblioteca de la Universidad de Salamanca, Ms. 2064 no. 15, consulta of Cardinal Trejo,
31 December 1627.

ness. Above all, the members of a junta could be hand-picked by Olivares himself, whereas the councils, with their long-established appointment procedures, were much less amenable to his personal control. This, indeed, was the principal reason for the unpopularity of the juntas, and the Count-Duke's recourse to them was one of the major charges levelled against him after his fall from power. 'In the juntas which he created, he pursued his own interests, and if any minister opposed him, he would be excluded from it, and replaced by one of his own men.'[87]

Members of the councils who found themselves excluded from the juntas naturally resented the proliferation of these upstart bodies which arrogated to themselves traditional conciliar business. They resented, too, the rise to power of figures who had not followed their own laborious climb up the ladder of promotion by well-established stages. In practice, most of these men shared their own background, moving from the universities to lesser judicial and administrative posts, and then into the councils where they were lucky enough to attract Olivares' attention, and found themselves summoned to serve on juntas. These ministers—such men as Antonio de Contreras, Francisco Antonio de Alarcón, Luis Gudiel y Peralta, Francisco de Tejada—were in fact of impeccable *letrado* origins, no different from their fellow-councillors except in their ability to win Olivares' confidence.[88] Indeed, as far as is known, the only rank outsider to break into the highest reaches of the administration was Olivares' special protégé, José González, who, as his advocate in the chancellery of Valladolid, had helped him to acquire his ducal estate of San Lúcar la Mayor. In December 1624 González was appointed *fiscal* (prosecuting attorney) of the Valladolid chancery, the first stepping-stone on the path to high office. Already by this time he described himself as a rich man,[89] although, as the son of a lawyer in the province of Logroño, his origins seem to have been relatively modest.[90] In 1626 he was summoned to Madrid to serve as *fiscal* of the *sala de alcaldes de Casa y Corte*, and thereafter his ascent was rapid. In January 1628 he entered the Council of Castile as its *fiscal*, and—by the unusual device of a royal decree instead of the customary process of selection by the Cámara de Castilla—he was made a councillor of Castile in October 1629.

The Council of Castile was naturally jealous of its role as the tribunal responsible for justice, order and good government in the realms

---

[87] *MC*, 2, p. 242 ('Cargos contra el Conde Duque').
[88] For the background and careers of these ministers, see Fayard, *Les membres du Conseil de Castille* and Pelorson, *Les Letrados*.
[89] AHN Consejos, leg. 4422 no. 34, consulta of Consejo de Cámara, 12 February 1622.
[90] For Gonzalez's spectacular career, see Fayard, 'José González'.

of the Crown of Castile. Its members, having reached their high
office by laborious stages, tended to be elderly; and age reinforced
the natural conservatism that was inculcated by their legalistic training. They disliked 'novelties'; they were fearful of any measure which
might provoke public disorder; and they were bound by close ties
of friendship, kinship and common interest to the members of Castile's urban patriciate.

Not surprisingly, the reaction of these venerable figures to the
Count-Duke's initiatives tended to range from scepticism to hostility
and downright obstructionism. In 1625, for instance, Olivares proposed the conferment of special honours on men who served the
king in his armies and his fleets, or devoted their lives to trade.[91]
His proposals included the revival of a medieval military order of
knighthood, the Order of the Banda, founded by Alfonso XI, and
also some modification to the statutes relating to purity to blood,
so that a distinguished record of military or mercantile service might
remove the taint of impurity and qualify the deserving for titles of
nobility. These proposals were approved by various juntas of ministers, and even by the Council of State; but before putting them into
effect the king wanted them to be seen by the Council of Castile
and its select committee, the Cámara de Castilla. Here they ran into
fierce opposition. The proposal for the revival of the order of the
Banda threatened the privileged status of the three military orders
of Santiago, Alcántara and Calatrava; while any suggestion for
improving the lot of the *conversos* aroused strong emotions among
those who had successfully established their own purity of blood
and were determined to exclude the rest. Inevitably the Cámara de
Castilla became the last redoubt of all the opponents of the proposed
reforms. Contreras, as President of the Council, warned the king
in the most solemn terms of the serious consequences of attempting
to confer nobility and purity of blood on those who did not naturally
possess them. So intense was the opposition that during the summer
of 1626 the plan for the introduction of a new system of honours
was quietly interred.

From Olivares' standpoint the Council of Castile's obstructionism
was still more serious in the vexed matter of the Castilian currency.
The Council's policy of attempting to check inflation by recourse
to price-fixing was manifestly failing, but it remained adamantly
opposed to deflation by decree. In spite of this, rumours abounded
during the autumn of 1626 that the nominal value of the *vellón* coinage
would be called down as soon as the treasure fleet arrived, and people
with large holdings of *vellón* hastened to unload them on others before

---

[91] For these proposals, see *MC*, 2, pp. 145–8.

the day of reckoning.[92] When the galleons returned to Sanlúcar at the end of November, they brought a rich haul, partly because they were also carrying merchandise that should have arrived in 1625 but had been held up by fears of English and Dutch attacks.[93] Olivares understood that there were more than twenty millions in silver on board,[94] and orders were given that none of it should be released to its owners until the arrival of instructions from Madrid.[95]

Although it seemed certain that something was being prepared, the days passed without publication of the expected deflationary decree. In reality the councils were so fiercely opposed to deflation that Olivares, even if privately convinced that a 75% reduction in the nominal value of *vellón* was now the only solution,[96] found it impossible to get his way. The Council of Castile was still busily casting around for that elusive elixir, a painless cure for inflation. There was certainly no shortage of private nostrums. In particular, a Milanese businessman, Gerardo Basso, was touting a scheme for 'consuming' the *vellón* currency by setting up a network of *diputaciones*, or banking consortia, in the major towns of Castile. He coupled this with a plan for ending the system of annual contracts (*asientos*) between the crown and its Genoese bankers, and for retaining the bullion of the Indies in Spain.[97] The credentials of Basso, who had originally made his name by importing copper into Castile and was now solemnly proposing to remove it again, certainly raised questions about the soundness of his scheme; and Diego de Corral warned Olivares not to be taken in by such a speculative project.[98] The Count-Duke may well have shared Corral's suspicions, but something had to be done, and if the Council of State was persuaded by Basso, then he would be willing to go along with it. In the present conjuncture any action was beginning to seem preferable to none.[99]

By the end of 1626 it was clear that a major financial crisis was looming, and it was significant that the contracts with the bankers for 1627 had still to be agreed.[100] Ever since the 1550's a handful

[92] AHN Osuna, leg. 240, expte. 414, Don Pedro de Nava Valdivia to Duke of Béjar, 21 October and 3 December 1626.

[93] Chaunu, *Séville et l'Atlantique*, 8, 2 (2), p. 1616.

[94] ADM leg. 79, Olivares to Aytona, 21 November 1626.

[95] AGS CJH, leg. 621, no. 19, consulta of Consejo de Hacienda, 10 December 1626.

[96] Roca, *Fragmentos*, p. 279.

[97] BNM Ms. 14,997 (14), *Arbitrio* . . . (see Carrera Pujal, *Economía española*, 1, p. 567). There is a résumé of his proposal, in the hand of Antonio Carnero, in BL Eg. Ms. 340, fos. 255–6v.

[98] BL Eg. Ms. 340, fos. 254–5v., Diego de Corral to Olivares, 6 December 1626.

[99] Olivares' lack of enthusiasm for Basso's scheme can be deduced from the disparaging reference to it in the king's paper for the Council of Castile of late September 1627 (*MC*, 2, Doc. XIII, p. 247). Such evidence as survives tends to bear out the contention that Olivares, in the name of the king, had been pressing for deflation since 1624.

[100] AGS CJH, leg. 632, fo. 16, paper by the Contador Mayor (Gilimón de la Mota), 24 January 1627.

of Genoese bankers—the Espínolas, the Centurions, and the Imbreas prominent among them—had dominated the Spanish crown finances, providing payments abroad in anticipation of the arrival of treasure fleets and the collection of tax revenues, under the terms worked out with the crown's financial ministers in agreed *asientos* or contracts. They had made enormous profits out of this relationship with the crown, which granted them licences for the export of silver, and effectively gave them control of the market in *juros*, or government bonds.[101] But persistent overspending and defaulting by the crown had progressively increased the strain on their resources, and weakened their international credit standing. From the beginning of the new reign, doubts had been growing about their capacity to sustain for much longer their leading role as the purveyors of cash and credit to the King of Spain.[102] The crown had failed to provide them with sufficient silver to keep their balances healthy, and instead they found themselves palmed off with *juros* and *vellón*, both of which were rightly coming to be seen as doubtful assets. With their position weakening in the international money markets, they no longer enjoyed quite the impregnability they had displayed in the financial crisis of 1575–7, when Philip II had tried and failed to dispense with their services.[103]

The growing weakness of the Genoese coincided with the advent, in the person of Olivares, of a minister who shared the desire, so often expressed by Cortes and *arbitristas*, to see the crown's finances handled by vassals of the king. But it was one thing to criticize the Genoese for exploiting the crown's financial needs, and another to find an adequate replacement for their professional services. Among Philip IV's own subjects, only one group possessed the skills, the contacts and the resources to aspire to a place in the international financial league. This was the mercantile community of Portuguese Jews, or crypto-Jews, popularly known as marranos. Although earlier attempts to secure a more sympathetic hearing for the marranos had foundered on the rock of Philip's obstinacy, the times were changing, and Olivares knew his mind. In 1623 Jacob Cansino, a Jew from Oran who came from a family of Arabic interpreters, received permission to come to Madrid to divulge some secret information to the king.[104] This—the first of a number of visits—marked the beginning of a friendship with Olivares, to whom Cansino later dedicated his translation of a sixteenth-century work on the greatness of Constanti-

---

[101] For the rise of the Genoese, and their method of operation, see F. Ruiz Martín, *Lettres marchandes échangées entre Florence et Medina del Campo* (Paris, 1965), introduction.
[102] See Ruiz Martín, 'La banca en España', p. 97.
[103] *Ibid.*, p. 99.
[104] AHN Est. lib. 741, fo. 244, consulta of Consejo de Estado, 6 December 1623.

nople, embellished with a striking engraving which showed the Count-Duke, sword in hand, slaying a dragon (Pl. 18).[105]

Through Cansino and through his financial adviser, Manuel López Pereira, Olivares was able to obtain first-hand information on the workings of the international marrano community, and was persuaded that it possessed the expertise and the resources to be able to render important services to the Spanish Crown. If he played his hand skilfully, he could use the Portuguese to break the stranglehold of the Genoese financial system, but he had to move with care. Apart from the opposition of Church and Inquisition to concessions to the Portuguese New Christians, he could not afford to ignore the likely reactions of the Seville merchant community, already worried by the extent of Portuguese penetration into the American trade.[106]

The Portuguese themselves, well aware of the enormous profits to be gained from handling the Spanish royal finances, and anxious to reduce the harassment by the Inquisition of the marrano community, were eager to proffer their services; and in August 1626 a trial run was undertaken. A consortium of Portuguese business-men— Manuel Rodríguez de Elvas, Nuño Díaz, Duarte Fernández, Manuel de Paz, Simón Suárez and Juan Núñez Saravia—offered to arrange an *asiento* of 400,000 *escudos* for the crown in Flanders. While the Council of Finance was unhappy about the proposed conditions, it approved the idea in principle, as a means of giving the Genoese some healthy competition.[107] By November 1626 the papal nuncio was sufficiently alarmed by rumours of a forthcoming pardon for the Portuguese Jews to request an audience of Olivares, who assured him that the rumours were unfounded, and that the theologians had approved the *asiento* solely on account of the emergency in Flanders.[108] But the nuncio remained unconvinced. During the winter months soundings continued, and proved sufficiently encouraging to persuade Olivares that the time was ripe for his long premeditated *coup*.

On 31 January 1627 the crown suspended its payments to the bankers.[109] The first royal 'bankruptcy' of the reign of Philip IV bore obvious similarities to the 'bankruptcies' which had punctuated

---

[105] *Extremos y grandezas de Constantinopla* (Madrid, 1638). The dedication lists some of his own services and those of his family. For this obscure figure, see Yosef Hayim Yerushalmi, *From Spanish Court to Italian Ghetto* (New York, 1971), pp. 167–8.
[106] James C. Boyajian, *Portuguese Bankers at the Madrid Court, 1626–1650* (New Brunswick, 1982), p. 20.
[107] AGS CJH, leg. 621, fol 92, consulta of Consejo de Hacienda, 17 August 1626. See also Domínguez Ortiz, *Política y hacienda*, p. 130; Caro Baroja, 'La sociedad criptojudía', *Inquisición*, ch. 5; and Boyajian, *Portuguese Bankers*, ch. 2, for negotiations with the Portuguese.
[108] ASV, Spagna 66, fo. 77, despatch, 16 November 1626.
[109] Domínguez Ortiz, *Política y hacienda*, p. 31; Ruiz Martín, 'La banca', pp. 101–3.

18. An engraving of Olivares slaying the dragon from a book published in 1638 by Jacob Cansino, a Jewish interpreter from Oran, who enjoyed the Count-Duke's favour and protection.

the reigns of Philip II and Philip III. A ritual had been established, by which the crown defaulted on its payments, the bankers protested, negotiations were opened, and a settlement was eventually reached by which short-term were converted into long-term debts. But this time there were differences. For one thing, the decree of suspension was directed specifically against the Genoese, and excluded the now relatively insignificant Fuggers. While Olivares had no chance of dispensing entirely with Genoese services, he had a trump card to play in the willingness of the Portuguese consortium to lend money to the crown. On this occasion, therefore, the negotiations with the Genoese did not proceed quite so smoothly as their previous experiences of suspension of royal payments had led them to expect. The Genoese ambassador was still complaining in March that everything would have been settled but for the 'caprice' of the Count-Duke, who was determined to bring the Portuguese into play, even though they lacked the resources and expertise to arrange payments outside Spain.[110]

The ambassador had no real reason for surprise. The Count-Duke had more than once made it clear that he was not going to stand for a situation in which three or four Genoese bankers acting in collusion could hold the king to ransom. With the decree of 31 January 1627 he at last broke free from the intolerable dependence which had so limited his scope for financial manoeuvre. For the remainder of his years in office, he used the Portuguese to hold in check the demand of the Genoese for higher rates of interest. To the original group of *asentistas* new names would be added—Duarte Brandón Suárez, Simón and Lorenzo Pereira, and the wealthiest and most notorious of them all, Manuel Cortizos.[111] These men, of uncertain ancestry and no less uncertain orthodoxy, congregated in Madrid with their families and friends, allured by the attractions of lucrative financial dealings with the crown, and at least partly reassured by the willingness of the most powerful man in Spain to place them under his protection. This time, evading the need for recourse to a papal pardon, Olivares managed to arrange for them a temporary edict of grace from the Inquisition. This edict, issued on 26 June 1627, was followed in November 1629 by the concession of complete freedom of movement, in return for a benevolence.[112] Life was still precarious, as Núñez Saravia would discover when he found himself in the cells of the Inquisition in 1631.[113] The Portuguese community

[110] ASG, Lettere Ministri, Spagna, 2432, despatch, 19 March 1626.
[111] Domínguez Ortiz, *Política y hacienda*, pp. 130–1. For Cortizos, see Caro Baroja, *Los judíos*, 2, pp. 103ff.
[112] Domínguez Ortiz, p. 130.
[113] Caro Baroja, *Inquisición*, p. 58.

in Madrid was highly visible and highly unpopular; but the dangers of high visibility were recompensed by the glittering rewards.

If the Count-Duke had won himself a little more latitude, he was well aware that his freedom of movement was still very cramped. He had brought an alternative group of financiers into play, and later in the year he attempted to improve the financial system by creating a new post, that of *factor general*, which was given to Barto-lomé Espínola, a member of the distinguished Hispano-Genoese banking family.[114] The *factor general*, who was given a seat on the Council of Finance, seems to have acted as the crown's broker, but one who drew on his own very substantial fortune, and that of his family, to provide security for advances to the king. Espínola held the post until his death in 1644, but it is not clear that this attempt to give a veneer of royal respectability to what had previously been private banking transactions made any appreciable difference to the workings of the *asiento* system. No cosmetic changes could long conceal the unpalatable truth that the Spanish Crown was still living far beyond its means.

Having taken on the Genoese bankers with some success, the Count-Duke turned again to the currency crisis, which would jeopardize all his financial arrangements if it were not soon brought under control. On 2 February 1627 jurisdiction in the trials of counterfeit *vellón* smugglers was transferred to the Inquisition in an attempt to tighten control over contraband activities by northern ships putting in at Spanish ports. This implicit equation between heresy and economic subversion was made explicit in an extraordinary piece of allegorical theatre, *El Monte de la Piedad*, written around this time by Mira de Amescua, which made the case for a sound currency alongside the case for a sound faith.[115]

It was not enough, however, to prevent the entry of counterfeit coins. It was also essential to 'consume' the excessive quantity of *vellón* coins, legal and illegal, now circulating through Castile. Unable to get his way on revaluation, Olivares fell in with the Council of Castile's recommendations, based on Gerardo Basso's scheme, for a supposedly painless liquidation of the surplus currency. One reason for his willingness to comply with this scheme seems to have been the possibility of turning to the crown's advantage the discomfiture of the Genoese, who were anxious to save what they could from the wreckage created by the recent suspension of payments. Their

---

[114] AGS CJH, leg. 632, no. 137, consulta, 21 September 1627. See also Domínguez Ortiz, *Política y hacienda*, pp. 101–2 and 110–11, and Boyajian, *Portuguese Bankers*, p. 39.

[115] See James C. Maloney, *A Critical Edition of Mira de Amescua's 'La Fe de Hungría' and 'El Monte de la Piedad'* (Tulane Studies in Romance Languages and Literature, no. 7, 1975). For the transfer of jurisdiction to the Inquisition, see lines 849–61 of the *Monte de la Piedad*.

expertise made them the obvious people to run the machinery required for the 'consumption' of *vellón*. On 27 March the crown decreed the establishment of '*diputaciones* for the consumption of *vellón*'—initially a network of banks in ten cities of Castile, to be managed by a *diputación general* of the leading Genoese financiers subject to the ultimate control of a special ministerial junta.[116] These *diputaciones*, funded with the income from the recent *donativo*, or voluntary benevolence, and with 100,000 ducats from the *millones* approved by the 1626 Cortes, were to accept deposits in *vellón* currency at 5%, and return 80% of the principal four years later in the form of silver. They were also given a monopoly of mortgage loans, fixed at 7%, and were permitted to buy and sell *juros*, deal in foreign and domestic exchange, and organize a lottery. Their operations would be financed by the sale of lottery tickets, and by the allocation of various royal dues, including a 2% levy on income and capital.

The Cortes of Castile were officially informed of the royal pragmatic establishing the *diputaciones* in a message from the new President of the Council of Castile, Cardinal Trejo.[117] He had been chosen on 23 March, four days before the publication of the pragmatic, to replace the aged Don Francisco de Contreras, whose initial enthusiasm for the reform programme had long since cooled. Trejo's selection for this sensitive post came as a surprise. Born in 1562, and one-time professor of canon and civil law at Salamanca, he had been raised to the purple in 1615, and had commonly been regarded as the creature of Don Rodrigo Calderón.[118] Why Olivares should have agreed to the appointment of a man so closely identified with the discredited Lerma regime is not clear; but in principle he favoured a churchman for the presidency, and Trejo's name was first among the ecclesiastics in a list of possible lay and clerical nominees submitted a few months earlier to the king by the court preacher, Fray Hortensio Palavicino—a list that also included the names of the Marquis of Montesclaros, Don Juan de Chaves and Don Diego de Corral.[119]

Trejo's satisfaction at his unexpected elevation is likely to have proved short-lived, and he would soon have cause to remember a sentence he once penned when Campanella sought his protection: 'The kingdom is a kind of beautiful prison, and the administration of the republic is a gilded cage.'[120] Hardly had the Cortes

---

[116] Pragmatic of 27 March 1627 (copy in BL 593.h.17 [80]). For the working of the system, see Ruiz Martín, 'La banca', pp. 104–5; Vilar, 'Formes et tendances', pp. 280–1; Domínguez Ortiz, *Política y hacienda*, pp. 256–7; and Hamilton, 'Spanish Banking Schemes', pp. 147–8.

[117] *Actas*, 44, pp. 31–2.

[118] For Trejo's career, see José López de Toro, 'Respuesta del cardenal Trejo a una carta de Tomás Campanella', *Revista de Estudios Políticos* 122 (1962), pp. 161–78.

[119] New York Public Library Mss., Spanish Miscellany 1626–1755, *copia de proposición que hizo de doce sujetos para presidente de Castilla el Maestro Hortensio* . . .

[120] For the text of this letter, see López de Toro, 'Respuesta'.

congratulated him on his appointment when the bars of the cage closed around him.

There was extreme agitation in the city councils of Castile when they learnt of the pragmatic. They were indignant at the creation of a monopoly banking system by royal *fiat* so soon after their defeat of Olivares' plans for the foundation of the *erarios*, for this looked suspiciously like the 1622 scheme decked out in a new garb. They were also indignant that its operation should be placed in the hands of the Genoese, whose predominance in Castile's financial life, at the local and the national level, they had long resented.[121] The city of Granada, where Lisón y Biedma kept alive the opposition to the Olivares regime, addressed a letter of protest to the Cortes complaining that the pragmatic contravened the conditions under which the *millones* had been voted, and entailed the imposition of new levies for which parliamentary consent had not been obtained.[122] Other cities—Burgos, Seville, Salamanca, Murcia—ranged themselves alongside Granada, and a junta was appointed by the Cortes to discuss the pragmatic. This brought down upon the Cortes a vigorous reprimand from Cardinal Trejo for interfering with a law that had already been published. The reprimand was accompanied by a threat to revalue the currency forthwith if they did not desist.[123]

Once again it was Lisón y Biedma who spoke up most forcefully for the opposition. In a memorial for the king he insisted yet again on the crown's contractual obligations, and warned that the failure to abide by them would absolve the population of its obligation to pay taxes.[124] Lisón was allowed to present his memorial in person on 31 May, but Olivares was not the man to let a deputy of the Cortes get away with this kind of threat. In a stormy interview on 1 June the Count-Duke subjected him to a furious tirade, and shortly afterwards had him banished to his estates in Algarinejo, effectively ending his political career.[125] Thereafter he was a marked man. In 1629 a royal commissioner inquiring into the fate of crown lands in the kingdom of Granada reported rumours that some six thousand acres of sugar-growing land in the region of Almuñecar and Motril had been appropriated by Don Mateo Lisón, *regidor* of Granada, 'who brags of being a patriot' (*repúblico*). It would not be difficult, the commissioner added, to investigate the allegation if His Majesty so ordered.[126]

[121] Ruiz Martín, 'La banca', p. 106.
[122] *Actas*, 45, pp. 447.
[123] AHN Consejos, leg. 50,036, fo. 125, Cardinal Trejo to Rafael Cornejo, 29 April 1627.
[124] Lisón y Biedma, *Discursos y apuntamientos*, fos. 79–85v.
[125] Vilar, 'Formes et tendances', pp. 283–4.
[126] AGS Dirección general del tesoro. Inventario 24. Leg. 582, Juan Moreno to king, 23 November 1629.

The banishment of Lisón was not the Count-Duke's only attempt to silence criticism. Stringent censorship laws already existed, but the system by which authors had to submit their manuscripts to the Council of Castile did not prevent the open or clandestine publication of a great deal of material that was obnoxious to the authorities on moral or political grounds. On 13 June 1627, therefore, as the agitation over rising prices became daily more pronounced, a new censorship law was published in an attempt to close the loopholes in the existing regulations.[127] The printing of 'letters and relations, apologies and panegyrics, gazettes and newsheets, sermons, discourses and papers on affairs of state and government, . . . *arbitrios*, verses, dialogues or anything else, even if short and of very few lines', was rigorously forbidden unless official approval had first been obtained. Coming twelve days after the interview with Lisón, who none the less succeeded in printing (without date or place of publication) a collection of his discourses, *arbitrios* and dialogues, the new law was clearly designed to address an abuse which the government now regarded as flagrant.

The regime's nervousness was understandable. As a result of the depreciation in the value of *vellón*, real wages in Castile had fallen by more than 20% since 1622.[128] During 1626 the average price indices rose 13.68 points,[129] and the upward movement continued into 1627. The month of May was exceptionally cold, and the crops could not withstand the unseasonable weather.[130] With grain and livestock prices soaring, and uncertainty over the fate of the currency becoming acute, there were fears for public order. The crown was faced, too, with an intransigent Cortes and the bitter resistance of the urban patriciate to its banking scheme. Although the *diputaciones* were able to begin their operations, the unwillingness of the public to entrust them with their money ruined their prospects from the outset.[131] The patriciate's hatred of the Genoese and its natural distrust of any banking system under state control meant that the *diputaciones* were unable to accumulate the funds required for the effective working of the scheme.

While Olivares inveighed against the blindness of the commonwealth,[132] an intense debate was raging, both inside and outside the Cortes, over the coinage, the *diputaciones*, and the causes of inflation.

[127] *Novísima recopilación de las leyes de España* (3 vols., Madrid, 1805), lib. 8, tit. 16, ley 9.

[128] Hamilton, *American Treasure*, p. 281.

[129] *Ibid.*, p. 218.

[130] González Palencia, *Noticias de Madrid*, p. 159; and see Fernando Urgorri Casado, 'Ideas sobre el gobierno económico de España en el siglo XVII', *Revista de la Biblioteca, Archivo y Museo* (Ayuntamiento de Madrid), 19 (1950), pp. 123–230, esp. p. 189.

[131] Urgorri Casado, p. 172.

[132] AHN Consejos, leg. 51,359, expte. 6, Olivares to Trejo, 30 July 1627.

In particular there was sharp disagreement as to how far high prices were to be attributed to an excess of low-grade coinage in circulation.[133] Members of the *diputación general* were inclined to blame not only the surfeit of *vellón* in Castile, but also the increase in taxes and the 1623 prohibition on the import of foreign goods. They therefore proposed a return to free trade, and the annual fixing of prices.[134] The unhappy Cardinal Trejo believed that the root cause of the trouble was the continuing belief that the *vellón* coinage was about to lose half its nominal value by governmental decree. While he himself favoured a currency reform along these lines—and it may have been this that won him the approval of Olivares—the Council of Castile was convinced that the country could not stand the shock. The cardinal for his part thought that the Council's fears were not entirely groundless—the people was a many-headed beast, and there was real danger, 'if not of sedition, at least of the most scandalous talk.'[135]

Philip's reply to this *cri du coeur* of 22 August was sharp and unsympathetic. The Council of Castile, he said, had tied his hands by rejecting revaluation of the coinage and by approving the *diputaciones.* It was therefore up to the Council, having brought Castile to the brink of disaster, to find the way of escape. The king's exasperation at the supine response of the Council to the economic crisis—'do something, even if you do it badly, in this business of prices'—bears the Count-Duke's impress. The document carried a somewhat shaky signature, but this may well have been the full extent of royal intervention, for on the day after Trejo produced his memorandum, the king became seriously ill.

The king's illness

Philip had been unwell for several weeks, but on 23 August 1627 he suffered a relapse.[136] For a short time there were fears for his life, and during those agonizing days the sea and sky changed places, in Olivares' graphic words.[137] As far as the Count-Duke's own fortunes were concerned, the king's illness could hardly have come at

---

[133] The debate remains unsettled. Where Hamilton, ('Spanish Banking Schemes') advances a monetarist explanation of the 1627 crisis, Urgorri Casado, in the most extensive treatment of the subject to date ('Ideas sobre el gobierno'), lays special emphasis on other possible causes of the high prices, notably bad weather and poor harvests.

[134] AHN Consejos, leg. 51,359, expte. 6, paper by *diputados*, 2 August 1627; and see González Palencia, *Junta de Reformación*, Doc. LXXVI (consulta of the Junta de Diputación, 7 August 1627).

[135] AHN Consejos, leg. 51,359, expte. 6, Cardinal Trejo to king, 22 August 1627.

[136] González Palencia, *Noticias de Madrid*, p. 164.

[137] ADM leg. 79, Olivares to Aytona, 6 September 1627 ('acá hemos visto estos días la mar por el cielo').

a worse moment. He himself had fallen ill in mid-August while tend-ing the king,[138] and rose with difficulty from his sick-bed to come to that of his master.[139] He now had to face all the uncertainties of a royal illness at a time when the Castilian ruling class was begin-ning to turn solidly against his government, and rising food prices threatened a general insurrection. What if, at this of all moments, Philip IV should die?

Uncertainty over the succession made the danger all the worse. Philip's only surviving child, the Infanta María Eugenia, had died in July,[140] and although the queen was again pregnant, she had a record of miscarriages. If she did carry the child to term, the country would be subjected to the incalculable hazards of a regency. If she miscarried, or the child died in infancy, the succession would devolve on Philip's brother, the Infante Don Carlos. Throughout Philip's illness Don Carlos displayed the extreme discretion, bordering on total self-effacement, which was to characterize all his brief and inef-fectual life (Pl. 19). But close behind him stood his younger brother, the Cardinal-Infante Don Fernando, who already showed signs of a very different spirit—'acute and incomparably more active' in the Count-Duke's words.[141] And behind both the Infantes stood the dis-sident nobles, whose potentiality for mischief had so exercised the Count-Duke when he first discussed the problem of the Infantes in his Great Memorial of 1624.[142]

Through his spies—like his relative, the Marquis of Camarasa, the Cardinal-Infante's groom of the stole—the Count-Duke had kept a close watch on the doings of the royal princes. He was no doubt well aware that Don Carlos kept up a secret correspondence with the Admiral of Castile, still living in banishment on his estates follow-ing his discourtesy to the king on the royal visit to Barcelona in 1626.[143] He had been sufficiently alarmed, too, by the growing influence over the Cardinal-Infante of Lerma's nephew, Don Melchor de Moscoso, to engineer his exit from court by securing his elevation to the bishopric of Segovia.[144] But to avoid antagonizing Don Fer-nando, he replaced Don Melchor by his brother, Don Antonio Mos-coso, on whom he thought he could rely. It was an over-subtle move that he would later have cause to regret.

Palace intrigues are by their nature obscure, but there was much

[138] Roca, *Fragmentos*, p. 253.
[139] González Palencia, *Noticias de Madrid*, p. 164.
[140] *Ibid.*, p. 163.
[141] 'Papel del Conde-Duque de Olivares ... sobre la educación de los Señores Infantes', Valla-dares, *Semanario erudito*, 29, p. 253.
[142] Above, p. 185.
[143] Novoa, *Codoin* 69, p. 56.
[144] *Ibid.*

19. Diego de Velázquez, *Infante Don Carlos*.

coming and going of disgruntled aristocrats in the apartments of the Infantes during the king's illness. The composition, and even the intentions, of this dissident group remain mysterious, for the grandees were still hesitant about signalling too openly their opposition to a minister who enjoyed the favour of the king. The old Duke of Lerma had died in 1625, outliving by a few months his son, the Duke of Uceda; but in spite of the loss of their leaders, the members, friends and dependents of the Sandoval family, like Lerma's brother-in-law, the exiled Admiral of Castile, still constituted a powerful court faction. Family divisions, however, were not clear-cut, since the grandee families were so extensively intermarried. Although Olivares' mother was a Pimentel, the Pimentel family, which had enjoyed great power and influence in the reign of Philip III, seems to have moved into opposition early in the reign, and entertained itself with private performances of plays by Tirso de Molina satirizing the Count-Duke and his policies.[145]

During Cardinal Barberini's stay in Madrid in the summer of 1626, seven nobles are recorded as refusing to pay him a courtesy call: the Dukes of Lerma, Híjar, Maqueda, Feria and Alcalá, the Marquis of Castel Rodrigo, and Don Pedro de Toledo. It is probable that these seven were either in the camp opposed to Olivares, or at least temporarily out of sympathy with him.[146] The presence among them of Don Manuel de Moura, Marquis of Castel Rodrigo, suggests a recent rift between him and Olivares, since they had been allies in the palace intrigues that led to Lerma's fall.[147] Although Castel Rodrigo was rewarded with a grandeeship at the beginning of the new reign, this apparently failed to satisfy his ambitions, for there are indications that he was the moving spirit in the plotting that went on during those late August days when it seemed that the king might die.[148]

There is no evidence that the dissidents had any political programme beyond the replacement of Olivares. Everything else was subordinate to this, and Olivares for one had no illusions on this score. But the degree of hostility towards himself and his government revealed during those terrible weeks must have shaken him badly. Even worse, it extended to the king, whose illness was ascribed in pasquinades and palace gossip either to a venereal infection, or to a sword-thrust

[145] See Ruth Lee Kennedy, *Studies in Tirso*, pp. 211–14.
[146] The names are recorded in the journal of the visit kept by Cassiano dal Pozzo. See José Simón Díaz, 'El arte en las mansiones nobiliarias madrileñas de 1626', *Goya* 154 (1980), pp. 200–5. For Barberini's visit, see also, by the same author, in addition to 'Dos privados', 'La estancia del Cardenal Legado Francesco Barberini en Madrid el año 1626', *Anales del Instituto de Estudios Madrileños*, 17 (1980), pp. 159–213.
[147] Above, p. 36.
[148] Novoa, *Codoin* 69, pp. 69–72.

received during one of his amorous assignations. 'Most amazing of all', reported the nuncio, 'is the people's lack of love for their king, because of their dissatisfaction with his government.'[149] The churches were almost empty when public prayers were offered for Philip's recovery.[150] Novoa, usually so prone to exaggeration, was probably not far off the mark when he noted in his journal that many people hoped the king would die, in the belief that this would liberate them from the Count-Duke's tyrannical government.[151] Ironically, the French had displayed similar reactions a month or two earlier in the illness of Louis XIII, which offered some hope of release from the tyranny of Richelieu.[152] In France as in Spain the fates of king and favourite were inexorably intertwined.

Lucca's ambassador, hesitant to put pen to paper for fear of his despatch being opened *en route*, attributed the universal desire for a change of regime to heavy taxation, high prices, and the 'rigorous character' of the Count-Duke, who took everything upon himself, excluded all but a handful of dependents from the business of state, and was parsimonious with his patronage. In spite of his gesture in appointing Trejo to the presidency of the Council, he had deeply offended the Lerma connection, which included the best families in Spain. But the ambassador also believed that Olivares was paying the price for circumstances beyond his control: Spain's weakness after the years of Lerma's government; the high costs of war; and the effects of a debased *vellón* currency.[153]

The Count-Duke's behaviour during the king's illness did nothing to endear him to his enemies. To the fury of the grandees he took the unprecedented step of refusing them access to the royal bedroom. The Duke of Feria, not a man to be easily silenced, was loud in his complaints. But the Count-Duke was undeterred. He and the king exchanged continuous messages from their respective sick-beds through Olivares' confidant, Dr. Alvaro de Villegas, administrator of the archdiocese of Toledo, who moved to and fro between their apartments.[154] In the meantime, those two ambitious marquises, Hinojosa and Montesclaros, served as Olivares' eyes and ears, reporting everything said and done in the Infantes' entourage.

The gravity of the king's illness made it essential that a last will and testament should be available in the event of his death. This

[149] ASV, Spagna 66, fo. 196v., 28 August 1627.
[150] ASL, Anziani al tempo dalla libertà, 647 (Lettere di Spagna), no. 37, Iacopo Arnolfini, 25 September 1627.
[151] Novoa, *Codoin* 69, p. 62.
[152] Lutz, *Kardinal Bagno*, pp. 79–80; Elliott, *Richelieu and Olivares*, pp. 90–3.
[153] Letter of Iacopo Arnolfini, 25 September 1627.
[154] ASV, Spagna 66, fo. 209, nuncio, 4 September 1627; Novoa, *Codoin* 69, p. 59.

was drawn up by Villegas and the Protonotario, Jerónimo de Villa-nueva, apparently on the the basis of some notes drafted by Montes-claros, who also prepared (possibly for his own benefit) a judicious paper on the proper behaviour of a councillor of state in the event of the illness and death of a king. The essence of his advice was at all costs to avoid committing oneself.[155] As for the king's testament, this was a strange document. The queen was to act as regent for the as yet unborn child; and if this should be a girl, she was in due course to be married to her uncle, the Infante Don Carlos—a device for keeping him 'grateful and respectful'. The two Infantes would advise the queen mother, and the Count-Duke would continue to conduct government business, 'because of His Majesty's satisfaction at the way he has served him', and to provide essential continuity. In matters of state the three royal votes should always be accompanied by the vote of a councillor of state or the president of the relevant council, and also of the Count-Duke, who was made responsible for the education of the still unborn monarch.[156]

These arrangements do not bear out the Count of La Roca's contention that Olivares planned to retire permanently to his estates in the event of his master's demise.[157] Fully aware that, in Roca's words, he would be 'the target of the world's hostility' if Philip should die,[158] he was clearly using the king's last wishes to guarantee his position against attack. But how successful would he have been? Everything turned on his relationship with the king's younger brothers, and he hastened to rebuild his fences after an unpleasant brush with the Cardinal-Infante when the king's illness was at its height.[159] But even if he succeeded in winning over the Infantes, he would find it difficult to maintain his position in the face of strong aristocratic and popular unrest.

None of Olivares' contingency plans, however, was put to the test. Amidst all the turmoil, the event anticipated with varying degrees of fear and hope failed to occur. On 4 September Philip's health took a turn for the better,[160] and by the 10th he was well enough to get out of bed.[161] Was it mere coincidence that the Count-Duke himself recovered on exactly the same day?[162]

Physically and psychologically those weeks of strain left their mark. Olivares wrote to the Marquis of Aytona on 19 September that he

[155] ADI Montesclaros Mss., lib. 130, no. 2.
[156] ADI Montesclaros Mss., lib. 130, no. 1. Notes in Montesclaros' hand.
[157] Roca, *Fragmentos*, p. 257.
[158] *Ibid.*, p. 256.
[159] Novoa, *Codoin* 69, pp. 63–4.
[160] ADM, leg. 79, Olivares to Aytona, 6 September 1627.
[161] González Palencia, *Noticias de Madrid*, p. 165.
[162] Olivares to Aytona, 6 September 1627.

was back again at work, but still very weak; and he found himself without the assistance of two valuable royal secretaries, Pedro de Contreras and Juan de Insausti, both of whom had died in the past month. 'It is all toil and care. God give me strength.'[163] Three weeks later he told Leganés that he still felt painfully weak, and would like nothing better than to retire. But he had no intention of fleeing from office. The king's illness had opened his eyes: he was living in hell; and instead of lightening his burden, Philip simply thrust more work upon him. To crown it all, the death of the Duchess of Gandía on 19 September left vacant the post of *camarera mayor* to the queen, and the king had chosen the Countess of Olivares to fill the post and become nurse to the still unborn baby. Neither he nor his wife had wanted this honour—or so at least Olivares protested to Leganés—and he only allowed Doña Inés to accept the appointment because it would give her less time to brood on her daughter's death (Pl. 20).[164]

The king's illness brought home to Olivares, as nothing else could have done, the terrible unpopularity of his government, and his own vulnerability. Public opinion appeared uniformly hostile; the faction round the Infantes was plotting his overthrow; and at every turn his policies were blocked by a tacit alliance of the urban patriciate and highly-placed ministers, especially those of the Council of Castile. As long as supplies remained scarce and prices high, there was danger of revolt. The king's urgent appeal to the Council of Castile to 'do something, even if you do it badly' had failed to break the Council's resistance to currency reform. It preferred instead to issue a pragmatic on 13 September which again fixed prices (somewhat above the 1624 level) and lifted the 1623 ban on the import of foreign goods.[165]

The pragmatic was vigorously enforced, and its immediate results were spectacular. Prices tumbled, shops were stripped bare,[166] and for a few weeks Cardinal Trejo basked in a sudden popularity.[167] But this consumer's paradise was unlikely to last for long. There was an instant outcry from merchants and shopkeepers, who chose to risk stringent penalties and conceal their wares rather than sell them at artificially low prices.[168] The Genoese ambassador, while conceding the necessity for the pragmatic, thought it could only be effec-

[163] ADM, leg. 79, Olivares to Aytona, 19 September 1627.

[164] BL Add. Ms. 14,006, fo. 34, Olivares to Leganés, 12 October 1627.

[165] For the pragmatic and the tariff of prices, see Carmelo Viñas Mey, 'Cuadro económico-social de la España de 1627–8', *Anuario de historia económica y social*, 1 (1968), pp. 720–5. See also Urgorri Casado, 'Ideas sobre el gobierno', pp. 193–5.

[166] ASG, Lettere Ministri, Spagna, 2434, despatch, 2 October 1627.

[167] ASV, Spagna 66, fo. 247, nuncio, 31 October 1627.

[168] González Palencia, *Noticias de Madrid*, pp. 165–6; Domínguez Ortiz, 'El Almirantazgo', pp. 14–15.

20. The king and the Count-Duke, the queen and the Countess of Olivares. Details from an engraving by Francisco Herrera the elder, commissioned in 1627 by Andalusian members of the Trinitarian order as a gift for Olivares. The engraving depicts the adoration of the Trinity.

tive if the *vellón* coinage were reformed.[169] This remained Olivares' view, and, as opposition to the pragmatic gathered strength, he seized the opportunity to vindicate his record and recover the initiative.

His first action, taken while the king was still convalescing, was to send an order to each of the councils demanding specific reform proposals.[170] Then, in late September or early October, he wrote on the king's behalf a long state paper, directed initially at the Council of Castile, but designed for publication and distribution.[171] The paper purported to be by the king: 'I have wanted to write this paper, so that you should know how I have personally put my shoulder to the wheel. I have corrected a large number of evils from which my kingdoms were suffering at the start of my reign, and have set to work on the others.' The victories of the opening years of the reign were proudly listed, the reforms no less proudly described.

[169] ASG, Lettere Ministri, Spagna, 2434, 18 September 1627.
[170] Roca, *Fragmentos*, p. 259.
[171] *MC*, 1, Doc. XIII. For the evidence of Olivares' authorship of this paper, see the introductory study to this document.

But the glowing record of achievement was punctuated by sharp sallies against the Council of Castile for its refusal to grapple effectively with the currency question. 'I cannot forebear to tell you that, in refusing to adopt my decisions, you hold a heavy share of the blame for the public unrest . . .'

The king's shafts were not, however, confined exclusively to the Council of Castile. He also referred mysteriously to the malice of unnamed enemies who were spreading poisonous allegations and fomenting popular unrest. This may have been a reference to pasquinades and placards which were discovered in various parts of the palace on the morning of Sunday 5 October. Cardinal Trejo, who was embarrassed to find his own praises sung in these pasquinades, attempted to placate Olivares by quoting from a scurrilous sonnet, clandestinely printed in Salamanca, on his own sexual proclivities, although he omitted to quote the opening lines about 'a king who is a count, and a count a king', and the concluding words: 'no silver, no bread, no justice.'[172] But Olivares was in no mood to follow Trejo's advice and laugh off the attacks. If the authors went unpunished, 'sedition would break out, just as we had reason to fear over these past days.'[173]

It is hard to know whether the Count-Duke in his present state of agitation was genuinely fearful of some uprising in Madrid, or whether he was simply preparing the way for a move against his enemies. It was not easy for a seventeenth-century minister to assess the scope and character of the dangers to his government. There was no police service to keep a systematic watch, although the reign of Philip III saw the appointment of an official who came to be known as the principal spy, the *espía mayor*.[174] This post was held in the early years of Philip IV by the Marquis of Charela, and then by Don Gaspar de Bonifaz, well known in the court as an excellent bull-fighter, a skilled horseman and an indifferent poet.[175] But in addition to making use of the services of the *espía mayor* and his subordinates, the Count-Duke appears to have built up his own espionage network. Novoa makes frequent references to the spies he planted in different parts of the palace, including the royal chamber,[176] and three months after Philip's illness, Olivares' right-hand man,

---

[172] A copy of this sonnet, with additional verses, found its way into the hands of the Catalan diarist Jeroni Pujades, and is printed in his *Dietari*, 4, p. 111. It is also printed in mutilated form from a ms. in the Biblioteca Nacional, in Danvila, *El poder civil*, 3, p. 68.

[173] BL Eg. Ms. 347, fos. 109–110v., undated letter of Trejo to Olivares, and the latter's marginal reply of 6 October 1627.

[174] Miguel Gómez del Campillo, 'El espía mayor y el conductor de embajadores', *Boletín de la Real Academia de la Historia*, 119 (1946), pp. 317–39.

[175] *Epistolario de Quevedo*, ed. Astrana Marín, p. 115, n. 2. Bonifaz died in 1639.

[176] See Marañón, *Olivares*, pp. 109–10.

the Protonotario Villanueva, was put in charge of the king's secret expense account.[177] This was used for a variety of confidential purposes on the king's behalf, and would have provided the Count-Duke with funds for the payment of spies and agents. But such agents had their disadvantages, and not the least of them was the need to provide information which would justify their existence. For a royal favourite who depended on the eyes and ears of these men, every considerable figure at court was inclined to be a potential enemy, and every whisper in the street a potential call to rebellion.

By dwelling on the failings of the Council of Castile and on the sinister activities of unnamed fomenters of sedition, the Count-Duke hoped to clear his own record in the eyes of the world, while simultaneously absolving himself of any responsibility for the current troubles in the eyes of his king. But the world at least never seems to have received the message, since the Council of Castile apparently succeeded in hushing it up.[178] In spite of this, the Count-Duke had no intention of letting matters rest. He needed the king's help to rid himself of his enemies, and he concentrated his attack at the point of greatest potential danger—the position of the Infantes.

On 10 October 1627 he wrote a characteristically devious memorandum for the king.[179] After the events of the last few days, which had confirmed his sense of the vanity of life and the inconstancy of men's behaviour, all he wanted was a little peace, so that he could contemplate the problem of his own salvation. His debts were large, his estates neglected, and he begged for permission to retire from office.

He then launched into a disquisition of extreme obscurity. It had come to his notice, he wrote, that during His Majesty's illness people had been talking in the streets, in the confessional, and in the corners of the palace with an unprecedented lack of restraint about the king himself, while praising his brothers to the skies. This was bad enough, but there had also been dangerous talk within the palace itself. The Count-Duke had grounds for believing that M—here he had recourse to a private cypher shared between himself and the king—had sought to bring about an inseparable union of the two Infantes, making use of A and abetted by S. Between them, the three conspirators had managed to win over Don Carlos, just as the Council of Castile had feared would happen when it recommended that M should be discreetly removed from the Infantes' presence.

If the king acceded to his request to retire, all the troubles provoked

---

[177] BNM, Ms. 7797, volume of *gastos secretos*.
[178] Roca, *Fragmentos*, p. 259.
[179] Printed in part in Antonio Valladares de Sotomayor, *Semanario erudito*, (34 vols., Madrid, 1787–91), 29, pp. 255–65. There is a longer version in BL Eg. Ms. 2081, fos. 248–260v.

by hatred of his ministers would be at an end. But if not, then His Majesty must look hard to his own interests and those of the queen, for the danger was all the greater now that the conspirators knew that they had been unmasked. The first priority was to reach a decision on the future of the Infante Don Carlos, but if the king took action, it must be seen to be his own, and taken without reference to the Count-Duke. The only alternative was to cast Jonah into the sea ... But would even this satisfy men whose one desire was high office?

Once again, therefore, Olivares placed his resignation in the hands of the king. Confident that he was the target of so much hatred only because of his unswerving loyalty to his royal master, he again sought to reinforce his position by securing endorsement from the king. But he needed this endorsement also for his own reassurance. The extent of his depression at this time is apparent from his correspondence with Leganés and from a remarkable letter he wrote on 12 October to the Infanta in Brussels. The contrast in tone between this letter and the confident manifesto produced a few days earlier for the benefit of the Council of Castile is very striking. The royal service was being neglected, complained Olivares, 'because nobody obeys.' The ambition of the king's ministers was incredible, and 'the king, God preserve him, is a boy, and has little taste for paper work. They all know this, and they laugh at me.' They were all against him, while he was working himself to death and achieving nothing.[180]

But relief was on its way. As he lay on his sick-bed, Philip no doubt recalled the death agonies of his father reproaching himself to the end for his failure to govern. In any event, the illness changed him. In November the Genoese ambassador reported that since his recovery the king had been attending closely to business, despatching documents without even a minister or secretary in attendance. The ambassador had actually seen several long documents written entirely in the king's hand, in which he reached decisions that were contrary to the recommendations of his ministers but were 'based on good and sound reasoning.'[181] Philip himself, in the autobiographical introduction which he wrote in the early 1630's to his translation of Guicciardini, states that 'after six years of my reign'—that is, in 1627—'I decided, in order to achieve what I had set out to do, to despatch personally (without even the assistance of a secretary to read them to me) all the *consultas* relating to government and appointments.'[182] The traits of his grandfather, Philip II, were beginning to assert themselves just at the moment when Olivares despaired of turning him into a royal bureaucrat.

[180] BL Add. Ms. 14,006, fos. 40–43, Olivares to Infanta, 12 October 1627.
[181] ASG, Lettere Ministri, Spagna, 2434, 27 November 1627.
[182] *BAE*, 109 (Seco Serrano, *Cartas de Sor María*), p. 233.

A working monarch might well choose to dispense with the services of a favourite, and this was clearly the hope of Olivares' enemies. Their best means of obtaining access to the king was through his court chaplains and preachers, who knew how to play on his fears and superstitions. Olivares was well aware of this. In the aftermath of the royal illness his relations were noticeably cool with the most eloquent of the court preachers, the Jesuit Father Jerónimo de Florencia, who was too closely associated for comfort with the Cardinal-Infante and his friends; and even his own confessor, Hernando de Salazar, seems temporarily to have fallen from favour.[183] The Count-Duke's suspicions of the backstairs activities of these bustling clerics were not ill-founded. When the queen gave birth prematurely on 30 October to an Infanta who survived for only twenty-four hours[184]—the child for whom a regency government was being so anxiously planned only a few weeks before—the king's domestic chaplain, Father Cogolludo, was there to point the moral. Had he not warned Philip when the last baby Infanta died that His Majesty would have no happiness, and the queen no living progeny, until the Count-Duke was dismissed?[185]

If these warnings moved Philip, he kept his own counsel, and gave his favourite his full support. The Infante Don Carlos continued to live in the palace, perhaps because of the difficulty of finding a reliable minister to accompany him to Portugal, but elaborate measures were taken to seal him off from undesirable influences. After various plans had been unsuccessfully mooted, the Marquis of Castel Rodrigo (perhaps the mysterious 'M' in Olivares' document) was despatched to Lisbon to supervise the fitting out of the India fleet. But in an apparent bid to reconcile some of the opposition, the Admiral of Castile was recalled to court. The most surprising and baffling event, however, was the appointment of the Count-Duke's brother-in-law, Monterrey, as ambassador extraordinary in Rome, with the promise of future succession to the viceroyalty of Naples. Naples was an attractive prospect for a man of Monterrey's avaricious disposition, but it is hard to avoid the suspicion that this ambitious grandee had not displayed quite the loyalty expected of him in the gravest court crisis of Olivares' career.[186]

The Count-Duke, however, had emerged from this crisis with his authority strengthened. The opposition had been nipped in the bud, and his enemies exposed. The king had once again expressed his confidence in his minister, and for the first time since the opening months

---

[183] ASV, Spagna 66, fo. 247v., nuncio, 31 October 1627.
[184] González Palencia, *Noticias de Madrid*, p. 167.
[185] ASV, Spagna 66, fo. 264, nuncio, 27 November 1627.
[186] Novoa, *Codoin* 69, pp. 69–72.

of the reign showed signs of taking seriously the business of government. At last there was a prospect of establishing that genuine working partnership which Olivares had always aimed to create. Then
the word 'favourite' would disappear from the political lexicon (or
so he fondly believed), and king and minister would labour side
by side to restore Spain's battered fortunes.

PART III

THE FAILURE OF REFORM
(1627–1635)

IX

THE OPTIONS OPEN

Grand designs

The court feuds of 1627, bitter as they were, proved puny in comparison with the feuds engendered by the contemporaneous battle of the saints. The tutelary saint of Castile had for centuries been St. James the Greater, whose body had been miraculously transported by boat from Palestine to Galicia, performing the voyage, in the words of the incomparable Richard Ford, 'in seven days, which proves the miracle, since the modern Alexandria Steam Company can do nothing like it.'[1] St. James, however, now had to submit to the challenge of a new saint, Teresa of Avila, canonized as recently as 1622. Her adherents were determined to crown their success by securing her nomination as the patron saint of Spain. The Count-Duke, whose family associations with the newly canonized saint were strong, warmly endorsed the move, congratulating the Cortes of Castile in May 1626 on their decision in her favour, and sending Cardinal Barberini a copy of her *Life*, with a plea for Urban VIII's support.[2] In July 1627 a papal brief duly proclaimed her patron saint of Spain, although with no diminution of the honours due to St. James. But the devotees of Santiago were not to be assuaged.[3] Among them were the members of the Council of Castile, who in October refused to take part as a corporate body in a procession being organized in her honour. The king, already at odds with his council over its attitude to currency reform and the reform programme in general, insisted on compliance.[4]

For the next two years the rival partisans of St. James and St. Teresa battled for supremacy. Quevedo, who had spared no effort to enter into the good graces of Olivares, undid all the hard work by penning an indignant manifesto in defence of St. James, and found

[1] Richard Ford, *A Handbook for Travellers in Spain* (London, 1845), 2, p. 662.
[2] *Actas*, 45, p. 52; BAV, Barb. Lat. Ms. 8599, fo. 80, Olivares to Barberini, 27 May 1626.
[3] For the co-patronage controversy, see Américo Castro, *La realidad histórica de España* (3rd ed., Mexico, 1966), pp. 391–9, and T. D. Kendrick, *Saint James in Spain* (London, 1960), ch. 4.
[4] AHN Consejos, leg. 7145, expte. 34, consulta, 9 October 1627.

himself relegated in the spring of 1628 to another spell of rural exile.[5]
For Quevedo, as for many others, it was the sword of Santiago which
had won for Castile its glorious victories against the Moors. Why
should St. James now be summarily stripped of his primacy, or subjected to the indignity of sharing his tutelary role with another? St.
Teresa was no doubt an authentically Castilian saint, but her sex
made her unsuited to the arduous task of defending Spain from its
foes. St. Teresa's supporters, on the other hand, argued that the course
of recent events pointed strongly to the need for a more effective
advocacy in high places. Were not the great floods of 1626, to take
only one example, a clear indication that all was not well? On the
contrary, Santiago's defenders replied, such calamities might reasonably be regarded as signs of the saint's displeasure at his threatened
displacement.

The controversy would eventually be resolved by a compromise
arrangement imposed by a papal brief in 1630, which left it to each
community to decide whether or not to elevate St. Teresa to co-
patronage with Santiago. But in the meantime the debate provoked
a bitterness and ferocity which suggest that a raw nerve in Castilian
society had somehow been touched. The ambiguities all too obvious
in the contorted character of Quevedo, who staunchly defended Santiago while simultaneously (if with many mental reservations) supporting Olivares, suggest that it would be unwise to attempt a simple
identification of the adherents of St. James with the Castilian tradition-
alists, and the adherents of St. Teresa with the partisans of reform.
But some element of this division of opinion may well have been
reflected in the controversy, if only because the challenge to St. James
was itself a 'novelty' in a society accustomed to thinking of novelties
as bad. *Converso* families, for their part, had a natural incentive to
support the claims of St. Teresa, as one of their own. At the same
time their best hope for the future lay with Olivares, the self-
appointed champion of their efforts to relax the stringent laws on
purity of blood.

Even if the confrontation between the two armed camps in defence
of the honour of the rival saints did not automatically extend to
the other great issues of the day, it hints at an unease in Castilian
society which cannot be entirely unrelated to the Count-Duke's
attempts to introduce change. Some of his proposed reforms constituted a direct challenge to old-established values and practices. His
invitation to the Portuguese *conversos* to serve as royal bankers was
a source of scandal to those who saw Spain's sole hope of salvation

[5] Francisco de Quevedo, 'Memorial por el patronato de Santiago', *Obras completas*, 1, pp.
765–87; J. H. Elliott, 'Quevedo and the Count-Duke of Olivares', *Quevedo in Perspective*,
ed. James Iffland (Newark, Delaware, 1982), p. 232.

in a rigid adherence to the purity of the faith. His failure to conjure back into the bottle the genie of *vellón* inflation so blithely conjured up at the beginning of the reign, cast serious doubts on his governmental capabilities, or his intentions, or both.

This disquiet was compounded by the apparently uncertain trajectory of his foreign policy. Impressive as were the triumphs of 1625, they had brought neither lasting victory nor peace. The war with England dragged on; the Dutch, as always, remained unsubdued. But the Count-Duke's critics were not privy to his plans. Surveying the options open to him for 1627, he had decided that the first and most important question demanding an answer was whether the trend of international events had now moved sufficiently in favour of Spain for peace talks to be opened with the Dutch, or the English, or both.[6] Answering his own question he concluded that Spain, as the greatest power in the world, needed peace more than anybody, and yet, for that same reason, could least afford to give the impression of seeking it. Like a lion in the forest it would always be friendless, and its survival depended on the fear and respect that it was capable of commanding among the lesser animals. On this analogy the Monarchy should never openly take the initiative by proposing peace, but while living in constant expectation of attack should be ready to grasp the chance of peace whenever it presented itself.

It was therefore 'hoping for peace but not proposing it' that he made his dispositions for 1627. His aim was to edge England and the United Provinces to the negotiating table, while simultaneously neutralizing France. This required a series of convolutions of exceptional complexity, which left the Count-Duke's friends and his enemies equally baffled. His diplomacy was never more complicated than in 1627, and its most startling feature was the apparent rejection of Madrid's traditional anti-French foreign policy, and its replacement by a working alliance with Richelieu.[7]

The opportunity for a possible rapprochement between France and Spain was provided by the rapid deterioration of France's relations with England soon after the marriage of Henrietta Maria to Charles I.[8] Richelieu would in any event have found it difficult, it not impossible, to maintain the precarious Anglo–French relationship once he had decided to give first priority to suppressing the Huguenots of La Rochelle. The prospect of conflict with England, together with his fears of finding France diplomatically isolated if Olivares

---

[6] AGS Est. leg. 2040, 'Parecer de SE el Conde-Duque...', 12 December 1626.

[7] For the history of this project, see Lutz, *Bagno*, pt. 2, chs. 2 and 3; Straub, *Pax et Imperium*, ch. 7; Ródenas Vilar, *La Política europea*, pp. 93–108; M. Devèze, *L'Espagne de Philippe IV* (Paris, 1970), 1, pp. 137–8.

[8] Lutz, *Bagno*, pp. 161 ff.

succeeded in cementing the close relationship between Madrid and Vienna with a formal League of Alliance, led the Cardinal to approach Olivares in July 1626, through his ambassador in Madrid, Du Fargis, about the possibilities of an alliance between France and Spain.[9]

Richelieu's was a purely tactical move, and Olivares responded in the same spirit. A Franco–Spanish alliance could only be directed against England, with which Spain was technically, although not very actively, at war; and nothing would suit the Count-Duke's purposes better than to see the French also embroiled in hostilities with the English. Above all, a united Franco–Spanish front against England would help to isolate the United Provinces, and compel them to drop some of their more objectionable terms for a peace settlement. Unfortunately, a formal alliance between Philip IV and Louis XIII was bound to arouse domestic opposition in Spain. For Richelieu, a switch of policy to alliance with Spain was easily managed since it coincided with the wishes of the powerful *dévot* faction at court which was scandalized by his support for foreign heretics, and believed that the only proper basis for the conduct of French foreign policy was a close understanding with Madrid that would reflect the 'natural' alliance of the two great Catholic powers. In Madrid, on the other hand, there was no *dévot* party. On the contrary, there was a deep-seated traditional distrust of France, and Olivares was faced with the difficult if ironic task of persuading the Catholic King and his Council of State to adopt a 'Catholic' foreign policy of alliance with the French.

Spain's ambassador in Paris, the Marquis of Mirabel, remained deeply suspicious of Richelieu's true intentions as the Cardinal discussed with him plans for a joint Franco–Spanish invasion of the British Isles, to be launched in the summer of 1627.[10] From Brussels, too, the Infanta warned the Count-Duke against France's machinations, recalling the maxim of her father, Philip II, that France and Spain were fundamentally irreconcilable powers.[11] But Olivares, who was handling the matter with a junta of ministers drawn from the Council of State,[12] was not to be deterred. On 20 March 1627 he and Du Fargis negotiated an offensive alliance against England, and one month later the treaty was ratified.

The Count-Duke was well aware that one of Richelieu's principal motives in agreeing to the treaty was to prevent a peace settlement between Spain and England, just as his own was to involve France and England in war. But this was a game that two could play. Over

[9] Straub, *Pax et Imperium*, pp. 245–6.
[10] Lutz, *Bagno*, pp. 232–3.
[11] AGS Est. leg. 2041, Isabella to Olivares, 12 March 1627.
[12] Straub, *Pax et Imperium*, p. 263 n. 9.

the winter of 1626–7, with the encouragement of Charles Emmanuel of Savoy, the Duke of Buckingham—now facing the prospect of war with France—had begun to think about mending his fences with Spain. He used for the purpose Balthazar Gerbier, who had been acting as his agent for the purchase of the splendid art collection of Peter Paul Rubens. Early exchanges between dealer and artist were sufficiently promising for Gerbier to come to Brussels in February 1627 with a letter from Buckingham to Rubens outlining the possibilities for an armistice between Spain, England, and England's allies, the United Provinces and Denmark. The Infanta Isabella, anxious about the weakness of the army of Flanders and the impact of the war on the Spanish Netherlands, was determined if she could to secure a general settlement in northern Europe, but without the permission of Madrid her hands were tied. Since, unknown to her, Madrid had already committed itself to a Franco–Spanish invasion of England, this was something of an embarrassment to Olivares, but he neatly resolved the problem by backdating to February 1626 the authorization for her to negotiate with Buckingham. This made it possible for discreet discussions to get under way in Brussels in the early summer of 1627 between Gerbier, the Abbot Alessandro Scaglia (the Duke of Savoy's ambassador to France), and Rubens, who was acting on behalf of the Infanta, in spite of Madrid's objections to the selection of a mere painter to discuss high matters of state, as being prejudicial to the reputation of the Spanish crown.[13]

Since Richelieu was simultaneously negotiating with the United Provinces for the renewal of the Franco–Dutch subsidy treaty,[14] the Count-Duke can have felt no great compunction about this double game. But sooner or later he might find himself compelled to deliver on his promises to France. The rebellion of La Rochelle and the despatch of an English fleet to its relief in July 1627 brought him face to face with his commitments to the French. With some involuntary assistance from the Duke of Buckingham, he had succeeded in his aim: England and France were at war. But did not Spain have an obligation to help France repel the English attack, in the name of the new-found unity of the Catholic powers? It was an awkward decision, not least because it was clearly to Madrid's advantage that Richelieu should be tied down by the Huguenots of La Rochelle for as long as possible.

Not surprisingly, there were misgivings in the Council of State

---

[13] G. Cruzada Villaamil, *Rubens, diplomático español* (Madrid, 1874), pp. 117–9. For the background to these negotiations see Lockyer, *Buckingham*, pp. 356–7 and 369; L. P. Gachard, *Histoire politique et diplomatique de Pierre-Paul Rubens* (Brussels, 1877), pp. 48–61; *The Letters of Peter Paul Rubens*, trans. and ed. Ruth Saunders Magurn (Cambridge, Mass., 1955), pp. 161–5.

[14] Lutz, *Bagno*, pp. 237–8; Alcalá-Zamora, *España, Flandes*, pp. 226–7.

over the prospect of offering military and naval assistance to Spain's traditional enemy. Don Pedro de Toledo, who had not been privy to the discussions on the French alliance, was deeply perturbed,[15] but the council approved the despatch of a fleet of twenty-six ships to assist the French at La Rochelle, although on the condition (which it may well have thought would not be fulfilled) that the French, for their part, should provide a similar number of ships. Richelieu, however, was determined to sabotage the Count-Duke's attempts to reach a settlement with England, and called Madrid's bluff by ordering the preparation of a powerful French fleet to match the Spanish squadron. As it became clear that Spain would after all have to keep its promise, a further debate in the Council of State on 14 August revealed a widespread unease.[16] Military assistance for the French represented, after all, a spectacular reversal of policy which it was not easy for the older generation of councillors in particular to understand. But Olivares clearly had his eye on the internal situation in France. The willingness of Philip IV to come to the help of his brother-in-law in his time of need might help to convince both Louis and the powerful *dévot* faction in the French court that a 'Catholic' foreign policy, based on the mutual friendship of France and Spain, was a practical possibility. If Paris were indeed persuaded of this, Richelieu would become the prisoner of *dévot* policies, and so be forced to abandon France's Protestant allies. If he failed to oblige he would be driven from power.

It was therefore essential to the Count-Duke's objectives that Spain should neither default, nor be seen to default, on the promises made to Paris. Here he could rely on the king's sense of obligation towards his royal commitments. Philip issued a sharp rebuke to the Council of State for prevaricating when the royal word was at stake,[17] and that same afternoon the council complied with the demands of an irate monarch by recommending the immediate despatch to La Rochelle of the fleet under the command of Don Fadrique de Toledo. But there was more than one way of frustrating the king's wishes. Don Fadrique de Toledo, the successful commander of the Bahía expedition, was the younger son of the violently anti-French Don Pedro de Toledo, whose death on 17 July came none too soon for the Count-Duke, with whom he was persistently at loggerheads.[18] As proud and intractable as his father, whose aversion to Olivares and his policies he shared, Don Fadrique made all due speed as slowly as possible, and had still not put to sea when the king recovered

[15] Ródenas Vilar, *La política europea*, p. 101; Straub, *Pax et Imperium*, pp. 272–3.
[16] Straub, p. 283.
[17] Straub, pp. 272–5; Ródenas Vilar, pp. 100–105.
[18] ASVen, Spagna, filza 62, despatch of Alvise Mocenigo, 24 July 1627.

from his illness in the second week of September.[19] It was not until late November that a fleet of forty-seven galleons under Don Fadrique's command finally set sail from Corunna for the gulf of Morbihan to join forces with the French, and by the time of its arrival its services had ceased to be necessary. The Duke of Buckingham had withdrawn his defeated and demoralized expeditionary force from the Ile de Ré earlier in the month, and only a token French fleet was there to greet the Spaniards.[20]

Still apparently unaware that Don Fadrique's fleet had arrived much too late to have the kind of impact on French policy and public opinion which he had so sedulously sought to create,[21] Olivares was determined to press ahead with plans for joint Spanish–French operations against the English. This would help to keep the war between France and England alive, while encouraging the British to reach an early accommodation with Spain. The 1625 plans for the invasion of the British Isles were therefore brought out of cold storage,[22] and on 20 November 1627 the Count-Duke settled down with his colleagues to consider how best to make use of Spain's growing naval capacity in the coming year.[23]

Although the Infanta failed to disguise her dislike of the whole idea, which would inevitably divert money and men from the war in Flanders, the Count-Duke outlined with every sign of conviction his plans for an assault on the England of Charles I. The possibility of French assistance obviously made it seem a more feasible project than it had appeared in the recent past. He was impressed, too, with the uniquely favourable conjuncture in which Catholic Europe now found itself. 'Never in history', he told his colleagues, 'has there been such a favourable season for the Catholic cause, with all its enemies defeated, and incapable of coming to each other's assistance.' The English, at war with France, were in no position to come to the help of the Dutch. The same was true of the French as long as they had the siege of La Rochelle and the war with England on their hands. This meant that the Dutch, in turn, would be in no position to rescue the Danes, any more than would the Swedes, who were being hard pressed by the Poles . . . This, then, was an opportunity not to be missed, and he proposed a specific timetable: a diversionary attack on Ireland in March; the capture of one of the Scottish islands in June; and then, in July, an assault on England itself.

---

[19] Straub, *Pax et Imperium*, p. 277.
[20] Devèze, *L'Espagne de Philippe IV*, 1, pp. 137–8; Lockyer, *Buckingham*, pp. 378–402 for the Ile de Ré expedition.
[21] Straub, *Pax et Imperium*, p. 283.
[22] Above, p. 249.
[23] AGS Est. leg. 2041, Junta, 20 November 1627.

The veteran Don Fernando Girón, whose long experience of the war in the Netherlands had made him a realist (or a defeatist) on matters of war and peace in northern Europe, argued that the scale and cost of the enterprise made it unthinkable before 1629. Given the failure to get Don Fadrique de Toledo's fleet to sea on time, he was almost certainly right. But here was the Count-Duke thinking out loud the unthinkable, with every impression of seriousness. Thinking out loud might, of course, serve as an effective substitute for action—a consideration that may have prompted his little lecture to the Genoese ambassador in his map-room in December on England's vulnerability if Spain should choose to invade.[24] It was as good a way as any of getting his message to London. The proposals were discussed that same month with France's special envoy Guillaume de Bautru, who had been sent to Madrid with news of the English defeat on the Ile de Ré. Richelieu in turn discussed them with Ambrosio Spínola and the Marquis of Leganés during their visit to the royal camp at La Rochelle in late January 1628 on their way from Flanders to Spain.[25]

It was obviously of advantage to both parties to keep the project alive, partly because neither wished to bear the onus of abandoning it, and partly because each was afraid that the other would go its own way and make a separate peace with England. The continued presence of Don Fadrique de Toledo's fleet in the gulf of Morbihan served as a hint to the French that Madrid still meant business, and Richelieu, however much he had come to distrust Olivares' intentions, may well have felt that the Spanish fleet might still come in useful if the English again attempted to come to the aid of La Rochelle.[26]

Olivares, for his part, badly needed to prove to Paris the strength of his commitment to the alliance and offset the unfortunate impression of Spanish duplicity caused by the late arrival of the fleet. It was therefore desirable for him to maintain the momentum by pressing ahead with plans for this new 'enterprise of England'. But it seems probable that he also had other considerations in mind. During those difficult autumn months of 1627 the world had gone sour on him. The course of events during the king's illness had revealed with a startling brutality the extreme unpopularity of his government. Everywhere he turned there was acrimony—over high taxation and high prices, over his conduct of foreign affairs, and even over the identity of Spain's patron saint. All this suggested the urgent need

---

[24] Above, p. 282.
[25] Lutz, *Bagno*, pp. 305, 311.
[26] *Ibid.*, p. 306.

for some spectacular success which would show that the government was indeed in good hands.

Spectacular success was more easily achieved abroad than at home, and at least to the Count-Duke it seemed tantalizingly close. When he wrote to the Infanta Isabella on 12 October complaining that all the world was against him,[27] he also asserted that, in spite of the fall of the important fortress town of Grol in Overijssel on 20 August,[28] the chances for a good peace with the Dutch had never been better. The actual course of hostilities in the Netherlands that summer would hardly seem to have borne him out. The army of Flanders, weakened by the Count-Duke's persistent attempts to pare down its size and its costs,[29] had had an unimpressive campaigning season. But in other respects the picture was more promising. The economy of the United Provinces was feeling the effects of blockade and counter-blockade;[30] and, if visits by Rubens to Holland in July of 1627 for further discussions with Gerbier had no very tangible results, they at least suggested that the Dutch had some interest in keeping the lines of diplomatic communication open.[31]

It was, however, the general direction in which events were moving that gave Olivares grounds for hope. Right across western and central Europe the tide was turning in favour of the House of Austria. By the autumn of 1627 the Danes had been routed by the Imperial army under the command of that enigmatic *condottiere*, Albrecht von Wallenstein, whose meteoric rise to fame and fortune had now brought him the title of Duke of Friedland. With each new Imperial victory, the Count-Duke's excitement increased. The Imperial forces and those of the Catholic League, he wrote to Aytona in November, had achieved an almost miraculous success, and it seemed as if God had chosen Ferdinand II as the *caudillo*, 'if not to uproot heresy from all Europe, at least to mortify it and give freedom to the Catholic religion in those areas where it is forbidden.'[32]

Olivares rightly saw a settlement in the Empire as the key to European peace. He had consistently supported the Emperor in his troubles, in the belief that a close understanding between Madrid and Vienna must be the cornerstone of Spain's foreign policy. Now that the cause of the House of Austria was triumphing, it was essential that vindictiveness should not enter the final settlement, or it would be no more than a prelude to new hostilities. This meant that some satisfaction must be given to England and to the family of the exiled

[27] Above, p. 317.
[28] Israel, *The Dutch Republic*, pp. 170–1.
[29] *Ibid.*, pp. 162–3.
[30] *Ibid.*, pp. 219–21.
[31] *Ibid.*, p. 225; Magurn, *Letters of Rubens*, pp. 163–5.
[32] ADM, leg. 79, Olivares to Aytona, 11 November 1627.

Elector Palatine in the matter of the Palatinate[33]—a delicate and highly controversial problem because of the Emperor's bestowal of the electoral title on Maximilian of Bavaria. It meant, too, that the security of the Lutheran princes, and with it the religious pluralism established by the Peace of Augsburg, must be guaranteed. This was to be the basis of a new and more harmonious relationship between the Emperor and the princes of Germany, who in due course would come to see that the King of Spain was their most reliable protector and friend. The union of Spain, the Emperor and the princes of the Empire, sanctified by a formal league of alliance, would check the ambitions of France, enable Madrid to secure a settlement with the Dutch on terms acceptable to both parties, and thus ensure the lasting peace of Christendom.[34]

It was a hazy vision, which left many points of substance unresolved; and it had the misfortune of running directly counter to the alternative vision for the peace of Christendom which Richelieu was simultaneously nurturing in Paris. The Cardinal, too, accepted the fact of religious pluralism, but saw in the overweening ambitions of the House of Austria a standing threat to the liberty of European princes, whose only hope of permanent security lay in the willingness and the capacity of the King of France to act as their natural protector.[35] At this moment, however, Richelieu had his hands fully occupied with the Huguenots of La Rochelle, and there was as yet no guarantee that he would succeed in overcoming his domestic difficulties, or in imposing his vision on the *dévots*, with their instinctive inclination for a close relationship with Catholic Spain. The field was therefore left clear to Olivares in the autumn of 1627 to make his bid for a European *pax austriaca*.

There was even a possible instrument to hand in the form of Wallenstein's victorious army. Over the last year or two the Count-Duke had been carefully laying the diplomatic groundwork for that grand Baltic design which was intended to settle the fate of the Dutch.[36] The Baltic, as he knew, was the key to Dutch survival. If the republic were cut off from the grain ports of Pomerania and Poland, and from the sources of the naval supplies, of the timber, tar and hemp

[33] '... that the King of England should receive a suitable and just satisfaction in the affairs and claims of his daughter and grandchildren, for having (at His Majesty's request) refrained from taking up arms on behalf of his son-in-law', Olivares to Khevenhüller on the guiding principles of Spanish policy in Germany, 20 October 1626 (State Archives, Prague. Mnichovo Hradiště, RA Valdstejnové, A II-288). Partially printed in *Documenta Bohemica Bellum Tricennale Illustrantia*, 4 (Prague, 1974, Doc. 349).

[34] See Straub, *Pax et Imperium*, pp. 232–4. Straub's assessment of Olivares' long-term programme for the peace of Christendom seems to me persuasive.

[35] Elliott, *Richelieu and Olivares*, pp. 100 and 123.

[36] Above, pp. 218–19 and 272.

that were indispensable for the construction and maintenance of its fleets, its days would be numbered. Expressing gratitude to Franz Christoph Khevenhüller, the Imperial ambassador, for his master's readiness to help Madrid secure one of the Baltic ports as a Spanish naval base, he remarked that as long as the Dutch had untrammelled access to their lucrative Baltic trade, they would never 'come to see reason and reconcile themselves to the peace we all desire.'[37] The Baron d'Auchy was in Warsaw negotiating with the Poles, and Gabriel de Roy was shuttling among the towns of the Hanseatic League,[38] but no one could be sure about the success of their diplomatic missions. The Hanseatic towns were deeply suspicious of Spain and had no wish to lose their lucrative neutrality. A more direct approach to the acquisition of a Baltic base was therefore an attractive possibility. In May 1627 Olivares had written to the Marquis of Aytona in Vienna, asking for confidential information on the 'condition' of the Duke of Friedland. Aytona's answer was encouraging. Wallenstein was the most loyal man he had ever known—a friend to the Spaniards, an enemy to the French. Surrounded by silent and terrified servants in a house as quiet as a convent, he was for ever machinating new schemes. But he was not, reported Aytona, a man to take grave military risks, because he believed that, if his army were once destroyed, the Emperor lacked the resources to put it together again.[39]

There were possibilities for both parties in this situation.[40] Wallenstein, appointed 'General of the Oceanic and Baltic seas' in April, needed a fleet to consolidate his position in the north. He was greedy, too, for Spanish silver and for the benefits of Spanish patronage. In return, he could render two signal services to Spain. The occupation of a Baltic port would give Spain a home for its projected trading company. Wallenstein might also be persuaded to turn his unemployed forces against the United Provinces by recovering the Imperial territory of East Friesland, which was still under Dutch occupation. In August 1627 he indicated that he might respond favourably to an approach from Madrid.[41] The Count-Duke saw that this was an opportunity not to be missed, and instructed Aytona to do everything

---

[37] Letter of 20 October 1626, cited note 33. This part of the letter is not reproduced in the transcript in *Documenta Bohemica*, 4, Doc. 349.

[38] See Ródenas Vilar, *La política europea*, pp. 113–19; Straub, *Pax et Imperium*, p. 295.

[39] ADM, leg. 90, *Registro de las cartas que el Marqués de Aytona escribió al Sr. Conde Duque*, Aytona to Olivares, 12 August 1627.

[40] See, in addition to the second part (1881) of Mareš, 'Die maritime Politik der Habsburger', Michael Roberts, *Gustavus Adolphus. A History of Sweden, 1611–1632*, 2 vols. (London, 1953–8), 2, pp. 346–50, for the revival of the Baltic scheme in 1627 and its outcome. Also Golo Mann, *Wallenstein* (Eng. trans., New York, 1976), pp. 364–8.

[41] Ródenas Vilar, *La política europea*, p. 120.

in his power to persuade Wallenstein to deploy his armies along the
eastern border of the United Provinces.[42] Almost simultaneously
Wallenstein made his own first approach to the Count-Duke about
the possibility of concerted action with the Spanish Crown. He
alluded to the prospects for a Baltic trading company, and to the
potential help that could be rendered by a fleet of twenty-four Spanish
ships in waging war on the Danes.[43]

If Spínola's army of Flanders could only keep up the pressure
on the Dutch until the Baltic and East Friesland schemes matured,
Olivares might well get peace with the United Provinces on better
terms than those of the humiliating truce of 1609. Exploratory talks
had in fact been taking place at Roosendael between representatives
of the Infanta and the United Provinces.[44] According to the instructions sent to the Infanta in 1625, the concessions expected of the
Dutch were to include not only the reopening of the Scheldt and
withdrawal from the Indies, but also some token acknowledgement
of Spanish sovereignty, and permission for Dutch Catholics to worship in public.[45] As yet there was no sign of a break, but an attack
on East Friesland and a threat to their Baltic interests might do much
to concentrate minds in the Dutch Republic.

Prospects, however, seemed less encouraging when viewed from
Brussels rather than Madrid. The Infanta and Spínola were understandably worried about the strains being imposed by continuous
warfare on the fragile social and economic fabric of the Spanish Netherlands, and wanted to reach a settlement with the Dutch as quickly
as they could. The arrival of Leganés in September 1627 with his
plans for introducing the Union of Arms[46] hardly suggested that
Madrid shared their sense of urgency. There was something unattrac-
tively permanent about the idea of defensive warfare, and in any
event even defensive warfare cost money. They concluded that the
only hope of bringing home to the king and his ministers the extreme
seriousness of the situation in the Netherlands was for Spínola to
visit Madrid. There was some hesitation at court about releasing such
an indispensable commander from his military duties,[47] but Olivares
had never met Spínola and welcomed the chance of personal discus-

---

[42] ADM, leg. 79, Olivares to Aytona, 11 November 1627.

[43] *Documenta Bohemica*, 4, Doc. 539.

[44] Joseph Cuvelier, 'Les négociations diplomatiques de Roosendael (1627–1630)', *Mélanges d'histoire offerts à Henri Pirenne*, 2 vols. (Brussels, 1926), 1, pp. 73–80.

[45] Israel, *The Dutch Republic*, p. 224; and see Lonchay and Cuvelier, *Correspondance*, 2, Doc. 759 (King to Infanta Isabella, 7 November 1625).

[46] Above, p. 275.

[47] Rodríguez Villa, *Ambrosio Spínola*, p. 473.

sions.[48] He was therefore granted three months' leave, and eventually left Brussels in company with Leganés on 3 January 1628.[49]

In December 1627, while Spínola was preparing for departure from a Netherlands which he would never see again, some Imperial contingents under the command of Tilly moved into East Friesland, and occupied a number of strongpoints near the Dutch border before taking up their winter quarters in the province.[50] This was a good beginning, and if everything went as the Count-Duke had planned, the coming year of 1628 would see the triumph of the Monarchy. France had been neutralized and England defeated. The Emperor and Wallenstein, fresh from their glorious run of victories in Germany, were poised to lend their support to Spain in its war against the Dutch, and help to drive them onto the defensive both on their own soil and in the Baltic. With a great combined effort by Spain and the Empire, the United Provinces might soon be suing for a peace on terms which Madrid would find acceptable.

But the kind of effort which the Count-Duke envisaged required a large expenditure of money, both for subsidies to the Emperor and for Spain's own military operations. Could the money be found? There were at least one or two hopeful signs. In June 1627 the crown's Genoese bankers had been forced to come to terms over the renegotiation of the royal debts. While the king's bankruptcy had seriously impaired their own solvency and so reduced their future usefulness,[51] the Count-Duke's manoeuvres had satisfactorily set the stage for the entry of the new consortium of Portuguese financiers, prepared to lend to the crown at less extortionate rates of interest.[52] The crown's bargaining position was further improved by the arrival in November of a well-stocked treasure-fleet,[53] and there seemed a good prospect, too, that remittances from the Union of Arms would soon begin to flow into the treasury in substantial quantities.[54]

On the other hand, confidence and credit were being mercilessly undermined by the rapid depreciation of Castile's *vellón* coinage. The Council of Castile's attempt to hold prices and restore Castile's economic health without resorting to currency reform was visibly failing, as Olivares had always predicted that it would. During the winter of 1627–8 conditions rapidly deteriorated. 'Everything is in an even

---

[48] National Maritime Museum, Greenwich, Ms. PHB/1a, Olivares to Leganés, 5 November 1627.
[49] Magurn, *Letters of Rubens*, p. 221.
[50] Israel, *The Dutch Republic*, p. 172.
[51] Boyajian, *Portuguese Bankers*, p. 40.
[52] ASG, Lettere Ministri, Spagna, 2434, despatch of 3 December 1627; AGS CJH, leg. 643, fos. 4 and 9, consultas of 26 December 1627 and 6 January 1628 for *asientos* for 1628.
[53] ASG, Lettere Ministri, Spagna, 2434, despatch of 27 November 1627.
[54] BL Add. Ms. 14,006, fo. 33, Olivares to Infanta, 29 October 1627.

worse state than usual', Lope de Vega wrote to his patron the Duke of Sessa in early January, 'because if there were formerly a few glimmers of hope, they have now been obscured by clouds of every sort. There is neither food, nor clothing, nor money.'[55] As fears grew that a currency reform was inevitable, tradesmen worried that they would be left with large stocks of unusable coins on their hands, and refused to sell their goods.[56]

The unhappy Cardinal Trejo, who as president of the Council of Castile was nominally responsible for Castile's economic well-being, was sent another stinging note by the Count-Duke on 19 January 1628 rebuking him for his council's failure to enforce the pragmatic that fixed a legal maximum on the silver premium. As the purchase of silver with *vellón* became more expensive by the day—the premium would reach 50% by April[57]—the costs of remitting funds to Spain's armies in Flanders or Milan threatened to become prohibitive.[58]

The Council of Castile was hopelessly divided on the question of currency reform, and Trejo himself was close to despair. Of the eighteen votes on the council, he needed twelve for a legally binding decision, and the only proposition capable of mustering twelve votes was an anodyne one which did no more than recognize the deleterious consequences of the existing currency arrangements. The problem, as always, revolved around the compensation to be given to holders of *vellón* if its tariff was reduced by 50% or 75%. Ten councillors were prepared to vote for such a reduction, but only if it was 'painless', and no one had yet succeeded in performing this kind of economic miracle. Trejo wrote despairingly to Olivares that he trembled at the prospect of revaluation, which threatened to be like the Day of Judgment.[59] Rumour had it that he was on the brink of resignation.[60]

It was against this background of rising silver costs and renewed domestic clamour over spiralling inflation that Olivares took the decisions that were to launch him into a foreign policy venture of momentous consequence. On 26 December 1627 the last of the male line of the Gonzagas, Duke Vincenzo II, died in Mantua. At a time when the Count-Duke's foreign policy had been directed almost exclusively to taking advantage of the uniquely favourable conjunc-

[55] Lope de Vega, *Cartas completas* (Buenos Aires, 1948), 2, letter 494, 8 January 1628.
[56] ASG, Lettere Ministri, Spagna, 2434, despatch of 1 February 1628.
[57] ASG, Lettere Ministri, Spagna, 2434, despatch of 12 April 1628.
[58] AHN Consejos, leg. 51,359, expte. 8, Olivares to Trejo, 19 January 1628.
[59] AHN Consejos, leg. 51,359, expte. 11, Trejo to Olivares, 31 January 1628, and *votos* of the councillors. The original responses of one of these, Dr. Pedro Marmolejo, are to be found in BL 1322.1.12 Ms. 4.
[60] ASL, Anziani al tempo della libertà, 647 (Lettere di Spagna), no. 55, Iacopo Arnolfini, 19 February 1628.

ture of events in northern and central Europe, new opportunities—
and with them new dangers—suddenly presented themselves in
northern Italy.

The Mantuan Affair

The problems likely to arise from the extinction of the male line
of the Gonzagas had for some time given cause for concern in the
courts of Europe. The succession itself raised some difficult juridical
questions, but their speedy resolution would not have been impossible
if major strategic and political considerations had not also been
involved. The Mantuan inheritance consisted of the duchy of Mantua
and the marquisate of Montferrat, both of which were fiefs of the
Empire. Duke Vincenzo left a niece, Princess Maria, the daughter
of his eldest brother, Duke Francis II, and granddaughter of the
maverick Charles Emmanuel of Savoy. Female succession, however,
while allowed in Montferrat was not allowed in Mantua. The strongest male candidate was the head of the French branch of the Gonzagas,
Charles, Duke of Nevers, but claims could also be put forward
with some show of plausibility by Ferrante, Duke of Guastalla, and
with less plausibility by Charles Emmanuel of Savoy and the Duke
of Lorraine.[61]

It was the strategic position of Mantua and Montferrat that gave
the question of the disputed inheritance its European importance.
The duchy itself lay to the southeast of the duchy of Milan, also
a fief of the Empire, held in this instance by the kings of Spain as
hereditary dukes. Milanese territory separated Mantua from the marquisate of Montferrat to the west, with its citadel of Casale dominating the valley of the Upper Po. Charles Emmanuel of Savoy, whose
territories bordered Montferrat, had for long cast covetous eyes on
the marquisate, and indeed temporarily succeeded in occupying it
in 1613 when the death of Francis II first raised the question of
the Mantuan succession. Charles Emmanuel's designs were on this
occasion blocked by Spain, which was naturally concerned for the
safety of Milan and would dearly have liked to get its own hands
on the fortress of Casale.[62] Since then there had been intense if sporadic
discussions about the possibility of readjusting Milan's western
frontiers through an exchange of territory which would transfer

[61] For the Mantuan Succession, see especially Manuel Fernández Álvarez, *Don Gonzalo Fernández de Córdoba y la guerra de sucesión de Mantua y del Monferrato, 1627–1629* (Madrid, 1955);
Romolo Quazza, *La guerra per la successione de Mantova e del Monferrato, 1628–1631*, 2 vols.
(Mantua, 1926); Straub, *Pax et Imperium*, ch. 8.
[62] For the Mantuan war of 1613–15, see Bombín Pérez, *La cuestión de Monferrato*.

Montferrat to Spain and the Milanese county of Cremona to the Duke of Mantua.[63] But nothing had been definitively agreed when Vincenzo II died on 26 December 1627.

The duke's death, although long anticipated, took Madrid by surprise. The Duke of Nevers, on the other hand, had already moved to make sure of his inheritance, by sending his son, Charles Duke of Rethel, to Mantua. Here, he was hastily married to Princess Maria, with the blessing of her uncle, Duke Vincenzo, who died three days later. Everything happened so quickly that there was no time to seek formal permission from the Emperor in his capacity as suzerain of Mantua, or to inform the court of Madrid. Immediately after the duke's death, the young Duke of Rethel took possession of Mantua and Montferrat in his father's name.

Madrid therefore found itself presented with a *fait accompli*. It had sent no clear instructions to Don Gonzalo de Córdoba, the governor of Milan, as to what action he should take in the event of the duke's death,[64] in spite of Don Gonzalo's previous warnings that Spain's position in northern Italy could be jeopardized if it failed to prevent the succession of the French-born Duke of Nevers. Although Madrid seems to have recognized the strength of Nevers' claims, it was naturally anxious to take advantage of the uncertainties attending his succession to improve its own position, and ward off, if possible, the serious danger of an understanding between the new duke on the one hand, and Louis XIII and the ever fickle Charles Emmanuel of Savoy on the other, which would leave Milan dangerously exposed and outflanked. But there is nothing to indicate that the Count-Duke and his colleagues had formulated a policy designed to meet the eventuality of the duke's death, and a Spanish envoy in Rome was still attempting at the time of his death to negotiate a dispensation for his marriage to his niece.[65]

The unfortunate Don Gonzalo de Córdoba, left largely to his own devices, took a number of precautionary measures as soon as he realized that the duke's death was imminent. The most pressing need was to forestall the Duke of Nevers' assumption of the Mantuan inheritance before the Emperor had been given the opportunity to pronounce on the case. Unfortunately the army of Milan was short of men and money, so that unilateral military action by Spain was likely to be difficult, if not impossible.[66] Charles Emmanuel of Savoy, however, was equally anxious to prevent Nevers' succession, and

[63] Ródenas Vilar, *La política europea*, pp. 152–3; AHN Est. lib. 869, fos. 48–50 (consulta of triumvirate, 1623); AGS Est. leg. 2853, *parecer* of Olivares, 5 March 1626.
[64] Fernández Álvarez, *Don Gonzalo de Córdoba*, pp. 41–2.
[65] *Ibid.*, p. 53.
[66] Gonzalo de Córdoba to king, 20 December 1627, in Fernández Álvarez, *Don Gonzalo de Córdoba*, Appendix 2, p. 139.

on the eve of the duke's death agreement was reached in Milan for Savoyard and Spanish troops to occupy Mantua and Montferrat in the name of the Emperor, and pending his decision.[67] The Imperial Commissioner, the Duke of Guastalla—himself a candidate for the inheritance—would hold Mantua with Spanish troops on the Emperor's behalf.[68]

Besides reaching an understanding with the Duke of Savoy, Don Gonzalo wrote to Spain's ambassador at the Imperial court, the Marquis of Aytona, asking him to secure the Emperor's formal authorization for Spanish military intervention and sequestration of the territories. A bolder man might have given marching orders to his troops as soon as news of the duke's death was received, but Don Gonzalo lacked the decisiveness of his illustrious forbear and namesake, and in any event is likely to have felt inhibited by the sorry condition of the army of Milan. Technically, too, he had every justification for delay. The King of Spain, in his capacity as Duke of Milan and consequently as a liege of the Emperor, was legally bound to act only as the Emperor directed.[69] But by waiting in order to comply with the requirements of the law, Don Gonzalo gave the Duke of Nevers precious weeks in which to consolidate his position. The new duke arrived in Mantua with a small contingent of soldiers early in January, and at once despatched an envoy to plead his case with the Emperor.

Still without orders from Madrid, Don Gonzalo continued to wait. The result of this long delay was that, when he finally moved, he did so as if unsure of himself and his cause, and forfeited in the process the decisive advantage of surprise. The Count-Duke's later behaviour suggests that he hoped, and indeed expected, that Don Gonzalo would move decisively on his own initiative, leaving Madrid without the onus of making a decision to intervene, but confident of the Emperor's retrospective authorization for an action so obviously beneficial to his authority and interests. If in any way the intervention misfired, it would be easy enough to make Don Gonzalo the scapegoat, and disclaim responsibility for something which had been done on local initiative without the knowledge or orders of the king.

If this was Olivares' purpose, things did not turn out as he had planned. According to a later statement by the Count-Duke,[70] ten ministers of the Council of State met as soon as the news of Duke Vincenzo's illness reached Madrid, and agreed that Nevers, although

---

[67] *Ibid.*, Appendix 4, for the agreement of 25 December 1625.
[68] *Ibid.*, p. 42.
[69] Straub, *Pax et Imperium*, p. 332.
[70] AGS Est. leg. 2331, fo. 48. Undated letter (December 1629?).

French, should be offered Spanish support for the succession and for his son's marriage to the Princess Maria. Despatches had been drawn up to this effect when that same night, 11 January 1628, news came from Italy of the Duke of Mantua's death, and of the moves master-minded by the French ambassador in Mantua for the hasty marriage of Charles of Rethel to the Princess Maria.

This account may well be true. The legal case for Nevers was strong, and the logical policy was for Spain to offer him its support, using its offer to extract some such concession as the exchange of Cremona for Casale, in the knowledge that the presence of Spanish troops would make it impossible for Nevers to refuse. But the news of Rethel's hasty wedding, celebrated without the prior approval of the Emperor, changed the complexion of events and suggested a different strategy. On 12 January the Count-Duke prepared a lengthy memorandum for the king.[71] While conceding that Nevers was the legitimate successor to Duke Vincenzo, Olivares argued that he had behaved with the greatest impropriety in rushing through his son's marriage without first seeking leave and approval from the Emperor and the King of Spain, or from the princess' grandfather, the Duke of Savoy. His precipitate behaviour had jeopardized the peace of Italy and the security of Milan. How, then, should His Majesty properly respond?

There was no doubt, according to Olivares, of the enormous advantage to be gained from annexing Montferrat to Milan. But since Nevers possessed legitimate rights, Philip would not be justified in declaring war; and in any event Spain lacked the resources for what could well be a two-years' war in Italy. Yet Nevers deserved some 'mortification' for his outrageous behaviour, and to teach him due respect for the King of Spain. What was needed was a 'middle way'— *medio camino*—that would rescue Spain's tarnished reputation while opening the door to a settlement which would not exclude the possibilities of territorial gain. The choice of a 'middle way' was characteristic of Olivares, and so, too, was the middle way that he chose on this occasion. A junta of theologians and jurists was to pronounce on how far the king could go in conscience. No reprimand should be sent to Don Gonzalo de Córdoba, although he had acted without orders (the Count-Duke was obviously assuming that by now he would indeed have acted). Nor was he to abandon a single battlement or bastion that he might have managed to capture. 'In conclusion, I would say that nothing is more important to Your Majesty than Montferrat, except for having justice on your side; that to mortify the Dukes of Nevers and Rethel is more than justified; and that if

---

[71] BL Eg. Ms. 2053, fos. 232–238v., *Voto del Conde Duque*, 12 January 1628.

this mortification should induce Nevers to settle by accepting some exchange of territory with Your Majesty, it would be both just and saintly to agree.'

The junta of theologians duly delivered its verdict. It decided that until such time as the Emperor declared Nevers the rightful successor to Mantua, the army of Milan should occupy part of Montferrat in the name of Ferdinand II, and lend its support to the Dukes of Savoy and Guastalla. All this, however, should be done without any thought of territorial gain for Spain, and with the sole object of upholding the Emperor's authority.[72] For Olivares this was a highly satisfactory judgment. The papal nuncio, who was busily attempting to avert Spanish military intervention, noted his smooth responses during an interview on Mantua and suspected the worst.[73]

To the nuncio there was a sharp contrast between the Count-Duke's controlled calm at their interview and the fuss he was reported to be making in the Council of State about the costs of possible military action in Italy. As so often at moments of decision, Olivares gives the impression of wanting to make the best of every world. He and his colleagues were deeply, and justifiably, concerned, about the possibility of the duchy of Mantua going to a client of France. The ideal solution would have been to find an Italian candidate with stronger claims than Nevers, but since this was impossible, the second best solution was to clip Nevers' wings so that he would constitute no threat to Spain's hold on Milan. Nevers' own behaviour opened the way to this, by providing a pretext for the temporary occupation of his territories by Spain and Savoy acting in the interests of the Emperor. But northern Italy was one of Europe's most sensitive regions, and the Court-Duke naturally hesitated to stir up passions which it would afterwards be difficult to calm. Legitimation of any Spanish military intervention by the Emperor was therefore indispensable.

Was it necessary, however, to take the threat from Nevers so seriously? There should, after all, have been ways of neutralizing any potential danger without the necessity for recourse to arms. The Empress Eleonora, Ferdinand II's second wife, was herself a Gonzaga, and the aunt of Princess Maria. The closeness of the family relationship suggests that the Austrian connection could have proved at least as strong as the French connection when questions of loyalty arose. Nor was the duke likely to want to see his duchy turned into the arena for a Bourbon-Habsburg struggle. Either, therefore, Olivares had persuaded himself of the dangers to Spain from Nevers'

[72] AGS Est. leg. 2331, fo. 48, Olivares letter.
[73] ASV, Spagna 66, fo. 295v., nuncio, 26 January 1628.

succession on the basis of arguments which seemed stronger at the
time than they seem in retrospect, or he had concluded that it lay
within his power to carry off a spectacular *coup* at very little risk.
All that was needed was to put up a smokescreen about the scandalous
mode of proceeding of the Duke of Nevers, giving Don Gonzalo
de Córdoba time to do what had to be done before the last puffs
of smoke blew away. Then, with a little luck, he would achieve
something which had eluded all his predecessors in the government
of Spain—the establishment of an impregnable Spanish position in
northern Italy.

The Count-Duke's foreign policy had not previously been characterized by a willingness to take gambles. On the contrary, his critics
accused him of excessive cautiousness, and of missing opportunities
for making bold pre-emptive strikes. Criticisms of this kind may
well have made him eager to prove that he was capable of bold action
when he judged the time right. A brilliant success like the acquisition
of Casale would silence at a stroke the critics of his foreign policy,
and reinforce his position at court at a moment when his domestic
programme seemed to be blocked at every turn. The prestige acquired
from a spectacular triumph in Italy might well give new momentum
to his projects for reform.

If these considerations were prominent in the Count-Duke's calculations, the exceptionally favourable international situation may also
have led him to underestimate the risks. The French ambassador had
warned him that Louis XIII would be obliged to support Nevers
in the event of a challenge to his succession,[74] but as long as the
French army was occupied outside the walls of La Rochelle this could
be dismissed as no more than an idle threat. More worrying was
the unreliability of the Duke of Savoy, but Spain's willingness to
make him an accomplice in the sequestration of the ducal territories
would, it was hoped, bind him with ties of gratitude to Madrid.
Everything therefore seemed set fair for the venture; and the papal
nuncio, writing on 19 February 1628, noted in the Count-Duke an
arrogance born of the Spanish and Imperial victories of the past
two years.[75]

At first glance, Olivares' confidence was justified, but the pope
and the other princes of Italy were bound to be disturbed by any
serious alteration to the balance of local power. Any action, therefore,
would have to be both swift and limited, if Madrid were not to
conjure up all the old spectres of Spanish domination. Two elements
were required for the success of Olivares' plan: Imperial authorization

---

[74] ASV, Spagna 66, fo. 291v., nuncio, 15 January 1628.
[75] ASV, Spagna 66, fo. 314, nuncio, 19 February 1628.

for Spanish military intervention which would justify it in the eyes of the world, and prompt and effective action by the army of Milan. Since (although Madrid remained unaware of this) Don Gonzalo hesitated to act unilaterally, the second of these conditions was dependent on the first.

It never seems to have occurred to Olivares and his colleagues that Ferdinand, after receiving so many benefits from Spain, would prove reluctant to authorize military intervention when his own interests were so clearly at stake. Yet this is exactly what occurred. In late January Don Gonzalo, now poised for intervention, was amazed to learn from Prague that the Emperor was not immediately prepared to countenance military action in the Mantuan affair.[76] Like everyone else Don Gonzalo had underestimated the influence exercised over Ferdinand II by his confessor and his wife. The hispanophile Johann Ulrich von Eggenberg, director of the Emperor's privy council, advocated a favourable response to Don Gonzalo's request, but was countered by Father Lamormaini, the Emperor's Jesuit confessor, whose high hopes of the French *dévots* made him anxious to avoid a rupture between Paris and Vienna.[77] For her part the Empress, naturally sympathetic to the claims of her niece, was attempting behind the scenes to steer her husband towards recognition of the Duke of Nevers' rights.[78] Wallenstein, too, was concerned that the Emperor should keep out of trouble in Italy while there was still unfinished business to attend to in the north.[79]

Just at the time, therefore, when Madrid, having informed Don Gonzalo that he would be receiving 50,000 *escudos* a month for the deployment of his army,[80] took it for granted that a substantial portion of the Duke of Mantua's territory would already be under Spanish control, the governor of Milan found the rug pulled from beneath his feet. The first intimations of the Emperor's surprising behaviour reached Madrid in February. There would still have been a chance to pull back, but questions of reputation were involved, and especially the commitment to Savoy. On 15 February the king wrote to Don Gonzalo saying that he assumed he would already be on campaign. If not, he was still to go ahead, subject to two provisos: that he should move his forces only into Montferrat, and that the Duke of Savoy should be induced to make the first move before the army of Milan followed suit.[81] This would justify Spanish intervention as

---

[76] Straub, *Pax et Imperium*, p. 333.
[77] Bireley, *Religion and Politics*, p. 97, for Lamormaini and the *dévots*.
[78] Fernández Álvarez, *Don Gonzalo de Córdoba*, p. 58.
[79] Straub, *Pax et Imperium*, p. 338.
[80] Fernández Álvarez, *Don Gonzalo de Córdoba*, p. 59.
[81] *Ibid.*

an attempt to forestall a Savoyard occupation of the entire territory before the Emperor made a formal declaration.

Madrid's orders reached Don Gonzalo on 2 March, and he embarked on the invasion of Montferrat on the 29th, a few days after the Duke of Savoy's army had entered the marquisate.[82] Three months had now passed since Duke Vincenzo's death. Even now, with limited financial resources and a depleted army, Don Gonzalo was reluctant to lay siege to Casale until reinforcements reached him from Genoa and Naples. This further delay, which gave Nevers time to entrench himself, was to prove fatal to the Spanish cause.

Olivares was later to claim that the Mantuan War of 1628–31, from which so many disasters were to flow, was approved by twelve of his colleagues and that 'he alone, by the grace of God, did not vote.'[83] On the other hand, shortly after the end of the war, the Count-Duke is said to have been walking with the English ambassador, Arthur Hopton, beneath the palace walls along the banks of the Manzanares. Pointing to a clump of trees close to a ruined stretch of wall, he amazed him by claiming with characteristic bravado that this was the very spot where the decision to intervene in Mantua had originally been taken.[84] The story has the ring of truth. Even if the Count-Duke, in his usual evasive fashion, contrived to leave the final decision to his colleagues, there is no escaping his own deep involvement in the chain of action and inaction which was to lead to a full-scale war in Italy. The succession crisis in Mantua had long been foreseen, and yet, in spite of this, the governor of Milan had received no clear instructions as to how he should conduct himself when the crisis came. This may have been the result of deliberate intent rather than inertia. But, if so, this would hardly excuse the failure to maintain the army of Milan at an adequate strength for intervention in Montferrat at the appropriate time. Nor would it excuse the failure to make sure in advance of the Emperor's approval. Madrid seems to have taken this for granted, just as it also seems to have taken for granted that Casale and the other strong points could be taken with relative ease. While Don Gonzalo's earlier despatches had helped to foster this impression, everything suggests that the Count-Duke allowed himself to be led on, in the hope and expectation of a bloodless *coup*, by a man who wanted Spain to inter-

---

[82] Ródenas Vilar, *La política europea*, p. 156.

[83] Cited Elliott, *Catalans*, p. 518.

[84] The Modenese envoy at the Spanish court in the early 1640's, Ippolito Guidi, claims to have had the story from Hopton himself, and recounts it in his *Relazione della corte di Spagna* (BAV Lat. Ms. 10,422, fo. 255). It was subsequently incorporated by Vittorio Siri into his *Mercurio*. See Francisco Silvela, *Cartas de la Venerable Sor María de Agreda y del Señor Rey Don Felipe IV*, 2 vols. (Madrid, 1885–6), 1, p. 38.

vene but who lacked the character and firmness of purpose required of a commander with much to win but even more to lose.

Don Gonzalo's army was only some seven thousand men strong, and it was not until mid-May 1628 that he made his first serious moves to lay siege to Casale.[85] Although by this time the Emperor had imposed a sequestration order on the Duke of Mantua's territories and replaced the Duke of Guastalla by Count John of Nassau as Imperial Commissioner, he still held back from authorizing Spain and Savoy to intervene in his name.[86] Sooner or later, no doubt, he would bow to Spanish pressure, but the delay was highly embarrassing to Madrid and revealed to the world the lack of unity between the two branches of the House of Austria. At the Imperial court the Marquis of Aytona worked hard to win the Emperor's support, but the rivalries and intrigues taxed his diplomatic skills to the limit. He reported that Ferdinand was under siege from his confessor Lamormaini, who regarded himself as a friend of Nevers, and also from the Empress. 'The Empress', he wrote three months later, 'is a terrible enemy.'[87]

The strains in the relationship between Vienna and Madrid would have been easier to bear if the siege of Casale had gone according to plan and the citadel had fallen quickly into Spanish hands. But precious time was lost in thwarting a relief attempt by an army hastily raised from Nevers' French estates, and Don Gonzalo's own forces proved inadequate for the rapid reduction of such a formidable fortress. Madrid sent him half a million ducats between January and July, but a substantial portion of this money was lost in conversion at unfavourable rates of exchange, or vanished into the pockets of a multitude of middlemen. As a result, Don Gonzalo and his men were perennially short of funds.[88]

As the siege faltered, the sense of urgency increased. The Venetians, who at first had been cowed by the Spanish and Savoyard intervention, began to recover their confidence. There were growing fears that they might send military help to Nevers, and there was talk among pro-Spanish circles at the Imperial court of launching an attack on Friuli to forestall such a move.[89] But Madrid's greatest source of worry was the possible reaction of the French. There was little danger of Richelieu giving effective help to Nevers as long as the army of Louis XIII was camped outside the walls of La Rochelle. But how much longer would the siege continue?

---

[85] Fernández Álvarez, *Don Gonzalo de Córdoba*, p. 66.
[86] Straub, *Pax et Imperium*, p. 339.
[87] ADM, leg. 90, Aytona to Olivares, 3 June and 6 September 1628.
[88] Fernández Álvarez, *Don Gonzalo de Córdoba*, p. 72.
[89] Straub, *Pax et Imperium*, p. 338.

One man capable of making a uniquely well-informed assessment was Ambrosio Spínola, the victorious commander at the siege of Breda. On his journey from Brussels to Madrid in January 1628 he and his future son-in-law, the Marquis of Leganés, were entertained at the royal camp outside La Rochelle and had the opportunity to inspect the siege operations at close quarters. The two men also held long secret discussions with Louis XIII and Richelieu, which left them in no doubt that France, in spite of its troubles with the Huguenots and the English, had no intention of abandoning Nevers' cause.[90] On 24 February, with their impressions of La Rochelle still fresh in their minds, they reached the outskirts of Madrid, where Olivares and all the grandees had gathered to meet them. While the rest of the company took the ordinary route into the capital, Spínola was accorded the unique honour of being invited into the Count-Duke's coach and riding with him across country direct to the palace, where the king was waiting to receive him.[91] It was a fitting tribute to a great commander, but whether the king and his minister would listen to what he had to tell them was another matter. Even if they did, there was little time to spare. Nine days had already passed since a courier had left Madrid with orders to Don Gonzalo to embark on the invasion of Montferrat.

Olivares and Spínola

Nearly eighteen months later, when Spínola himself was on the eve of departing for Italy to succeed Don Gonzalo de Córdoba as commander of the army of Milan, he confided to the papal nuncio that, as soon as he arrived in Madrid, he had seized the opportunity afforded by his first audiences with the king and the Count-Duke to beg them to countermand their orders for the invasion. He urged the same course on the Council of State and, by his own account, succeeded in persuading almost all the councillors. At Spínola's insistence—or so he told the nuncio—the Council of State decided to revoke Don Gonzalo's orders. A letter was drafted but its despatch was then postponed from one day to the next, on the pretext that a message was expected from Milan at any moment. When the message was finally delivered it held out such high hopes of a speedy occupation of Montferrat and Casale that the council had second thoughts, and decided to let Don Gonzalo's instructions stand.[92]

---

[90] Rodríguez Villa, *Ambrosio Spínola*, pp. 477–8.
[91] Magurn, *Letters of Rubens*, p. 247 (Rubens to Pierre Dupuy, 23 March 1628).
[92] ASV, Spagna 69, fo. 135v., nuncio, 14 July 1629.

Spínola's concern to prevent the outbreak of hostilities was motivated in part by his assessment of the mood of Louis XIII and Richelieu, and still more by his concern about the impact of a war in Italy on the conflict in the Netherlands. The Count-Duke shared Spínola's anxieties about Richelieu's intentions, but believed that Casale would fall before the Cardinal had time to move. As an additional precaution, he sent Lorenzo Ramírez de Prado on a special mission to Paris in February 1628 in order to keep alive the plans for the invasion of England, and above all to deepen the rift between the English and the French.[93] As long as Louis XIII and Charles I were busy fighting each other the French would be in no condition to send effective help to Nevers.

On the Netherlands, however, Spínola and the Count-Duke were far apart. Differences of personality were aggravated by the differences of perspective which came from viewing the world from the contrasting vantage-points of Brussels and Madrid. To Olivares, as he bent over his maps or eagerly perused the despatches flowing in from Spanish ambassadors and agents across the continent, there had never been a moment like the present for establishing the fortunes of the House of Austria on unshakable foundations. But in the eyes of Spínola, who had been immersed in the problems of the Netherlands for nearly thirty years, there was little room for optimism. He knew from first-hand experience the endless struggle involved in keeping the army of Flanders up to strength, and the sheer war-weariness of a civil population which found itself reluctantly caught up in an apparently interminable conflict. He also knew all too well that the figures so confidently reeled off by Madrid for the latest remittances of money to Antwerp bore very little relation either to receipts or to costs. Swallowed up in the payment of the premium on silver, and filtered through the hands of a host of parasites, they appeared woefully inadequate to army commanders charged with maintaining discipline among men whose pay was for ever in arrears. If Spínola, part soldier, part banker, struck Olivares as an incurable pessimist, his was a pessimism born of long experience both of the counting-house and the battlefield.

Looking back during the spring of 1630, when Spínola was no longer around to cast his spell over the Council of State, the Count-Duke wrote to the Marquis of Aytona that 'the ruin of this crown began with the arrival here of the Marquis Spínola.'[94] Four years later, the king echoed this sentiment when he observed of Spínola's arrival and its aftermath that this was the moment when 'my

---

[93] Straub, *Pax et Imperium*, p. 343.
[94] ADM, leg. 79, Olivares to Aytona, 31 March 1630.

Monarchy began visibly to decline.'[95] What prompted this bitter judgment on a great commander?

It is not clear which the king and the Count-Duke considered the more disastrous for the Monarchy—Spínola's absence from Flanders or his presence in Spain. There is no doubt that his departure from the Netherlands left a void which would remain unfilled until the Cardinal-Infante's arrival in Brussels seven years later. The Infanta was growing old, and, with Spínola gone, the balance of power at her court tilted towards Spain's ambassador in Brussels, Cardinal de la Cueva, whose Spanish attitudes and ways made him anathema to the local population. As a commander, too, Spínola was irreplaceable. No one could rival him in his unique combination of prestige, personal authority, and military and financial expertise. His disappearance from the scene was bound to encourage the Stadholder Frederick Henry at a difficult moment in the military fortunes of the United Provinces; and its effects were compounded by the division of the army command in Flanders between the Spanish veteran, Don Carlos Coloma, and a member of the local nobility, Count Henri de Bergh, with whom his personal relations were uniformly bad.[96]

If Spínola's departure produced demoralization in the Netherlands, his arrival in Spain soon led to demoralization in Madrid. He was received with acclaim at court, where his daughter's marriage to Leganés was celebrated with great pomp on 28 February, four days after his arrival.[97] He had long daily audiences with the king,[98] who appeared to hold him in the highest favour—an obvious cause of concern to the congenitally suspicious Olivares. Spínola had always been a good courtier, and as the Count-Duke looked around his colleagues he may well have had good reason for unease, especially in view of the recent death of his own close friend and Spínola's enemy, the Marquis of La Hinojosa.[99] As the weeks passed, Olivares began to find himself increasingly isolated. Spínola was all too persuasive, and his persuasiveness was having an unsettling effect on the Council of State.

Spínola brought with him from Brussels a simple message: that the army of Flanders was undermanned and underpaid. If he was right, Madrid had to make a choice. It could either—as Spínola himself wished—use the Roosendael negotiations to reach a settlement with the Dutch; alternatively it would have to send massive reinforce-

[95] AGS Est. leg. 2048, king on consulta of Council of State, 16 March 1634.
[96] BL Add. Ms. 28,708, fos. 266–71v., *Papel que escribió Don Carlos Coloma*.
[97] Hoz, p. 166; Magurn, *Letters of Rubens*, p. 244 (Rubens to Dupuy, 16 March 1628).
[98] *Ibid.*, p. 254 (Rubens to Dupuy, 30 March 1628).
[99] ADM, leg. 79, Olivares to Aytona, 1 March 1628 for the Count-Duke's sense of loss; Magurn, p. 244, for the enmity between Hinojosa and Spínola.

ments to Brussels to enable the army of Flanders to wage a more vigorous war.[100] There followed a brisk exchange of memoranda and counter-memoranda, in which the Count-Duke cast doubts on the accuracy of Spínola's calculations, and—while regretting his own lack of military training—was not above giving the veteran commander a few lessons in the art of war.[101]

It was always difficult for Olivares, working himself to the bone to provide men and money, to understand that statistics which seemed solid enough in Madrid looked a good deal less solid by the time they had been transformed into actual men on the battlefield. The Romans, he argued, had ruled the world with a hundred thousand men, and here was Spínola asking for almost ninety thousand for the Netherlands alone![102] In his view, Spínola was being promised financial support of unparalleled generosity. Any man given 3,700,000 *escudos* a year to maintain an army of 57,000 infantry and 4,000 cavalry should have money enough and to spare.[103] Privately he was convinced that hard-bought Spanish resources were being disgracefully squandered in Flanders. The army of Flanders, in his belief, could manage well enough with a streamlined mobile force of some 20,000 infantry and 4,000 cavalry, and perhaps a further 34,000 troops for garrison duty. Spínola, on the other hand, considered that the minimum figures should be 35,000 for the field force and 35,000 for the garrisons.[104] In fact by the spring of 1628 the army of Flanders, excluding the contingents quartered on the Middle Rhine, was apparently down to little more than 50,000 men—some thirty per cent fewer than in the early 1620's. This fall coincided with an increase in the size of the forces available to the Dutch, who now for the first time, as the result of Frederick Henry's efforts, had more men under arms than Spain.[105] Spínola's anxieties, therefore, were by no means unjustified.

But the differences between Olivares and Spínola extended beyond their disagreement over the size, potential or actual, of the army of Flanders. Both men entertained a high view of their own worth, and both had strong personalities. If Olivares, in Spínola's eyes, trespassed into areas beyond his expertise, Spínola was guilty in Olivares' eyes of exactly the same failing. Here was a military expert with a limited knowledge of the European political scene, filling the councillors of state with 'apprehensions' about Spain's prospects in northern Europe, at a time when he himself believed that a settlement

[100] Rodríguez Villa, *Ambrosio Spínola*, p. 480.
[101] *Ibid.*, pp. 484–500.
[102] *Ibid.*, p. 487.
[103] *Ibid.*, pp. 498–9.
[104] Israel, *The Dutch Republic*, p. 163.
[105] *Ibid.*, pp. 165 and 170.

on much better terms than those of 1609 was within his grasp. The agents of Philip IV and the Infanta—Jacques Bruneau, Count Octavio Sforza, Gabriel de Roy—were criss-crossing central and eastern Europe, attempting to persuade the Emperor, Wallenstein and the Duke of Bavaria to commit themselves. Wallenstein, as always, blew hot and cold, but the tenor of Aytona's letters from the Imperial court was distinctly encouraging. If the king, he wrote to Olivares in February, could manage to subsidize the Imperial and Catholic armies to the tune of a mere 800,000 or a million ducats a year in return for their being used against the Dutch, 'there is no doubt that—with the forces of the Empire and our sovereign the king united—we shall achieve in a very few years what we have failed to achieve in seventy years of war...'[106]

It is not therefore surprising that Olivares should have taken a generally uncompromising line in the special junta set up early in April 1628 to consider the whole question of whether, and on what terms, to treat with the Dutch. Hopes had been raised in Madrid by a report from Jean de Kesseler, the Infanta's representative at the Roosendael discussions, to the effect that the Dutch would no longer insist as a precondition for peace talks on Spanish acceptance of the article in the 1609 truce which declared the United Provinces to be 'free provinces'. The implication of this concession was that the States General of the United Provinces might be prepared to acknowledge at least a nominal relationship to Philip IV.[107] Spínola was quick to capitalize on this indication of a new flexibility on the Dutch side, but Olivares was wary about a 'concession' which could well be no more than a tactical manoeuvre at a time when the Dutch found themselves under pressure and dangerously isolated. Requested by the junta to draft a list of conditions for a settlement, he responded on 10 April with a list of twenty-three proposed articles which showed little sign of a corresponding flexibility on the part of Spain.[108] He insisted on a peace settlement rather than another temporary truce, and was adamant that the Dutch should recognize the King of Spain as their sovereign and protector. Spínola argued that this clause was enough by itself to wreck the chances of a settlement. Most of the councillors saw it as a maximum demand rather than a *sine qua non*, but Olivares was prepared to regard it as negotiable only if the Dutch conceded freedom of worship to the Catholics.

---

[106] ADM, leg. 90, Aytona to Olivares, 12 February 1628 (printed as letter 12 in Jesús Gutiérrez, 'Don Francisco de Moncada').

[107] Israel, p. 225; Cuvelier, 'Les négociations', p. 75.

[108] Lonchay, *Correspondance*, 2, Doc. 1197. Information about the Junta comes from AHN Est. lib. 697. This is a later seventeenth-century inventory summarizing the course of negotiations with England and the United Provinces from 1604–79. Under the heading of *treguas* there is a summary of the discussions which took place in Madrid in 1628.

In his reply to this *consulta*, the king laid down the indispensable conditions to be communicated to the Infanta in Brussels, and by her to Kesseler.[109] Following the hard line taken by Olivares, he declared that there was to be no question of a truce or armistice but only of a comprehensive peace settlement, and ordered the negotiations to be accompanied by an all-out military effort designed to wring as many concessions as possible from the Dutch. There was to be no weakening where questions of worship for Catholics were at issue, and on the matter of sovereignty he wanted the title of sovereign protector in perpetuity, although it would be understood that the Dutch would enjoy *de facto* absolute liberty and sovereign rights. They must also open the Scheldt to shipping, and accept their exclusion from America; and they were expected to keep Spain supplied with ships, munitions and naval stores at reasonable prices.

These conditions were forwarded to the Infanta on 1 May. Few secrets were kept for long from the papal nuncio, and he wrote to Rome the same day reporting that there was not the faintest chance of the Dutch accepting such terms.[110] Olivares, with the support of the Duke of Feria and the Marquis of Montesclaros, was banking on a sudden softening of Dutch intransigence when the United Provinces found themselves threatened by the onslaught of the combined forces of Spain and the Empire. In his view, the alleged concession reported by Kesseler was no more than a device by the Dutch to save themselves from the fate that awaited them.[111] If so, it was essential to Olivares' policy that there should be no signs of weakening in Madrid's resolve at this most critical of times. It was for this reason that Spínola's attempts to swing the Council of State behind a peace policy caused him such concern, for they would encourage the Dutch to play on the divisions among the king's advisers in order to avoid making real concessions. In a letter to Aytona on 6 May he warned against the Emperor and his councillors giving credence to any rumours they might hear about a forthcoming truce or peace treaty with the Dutch. 'His Majesty's resolution for this year is that there should be a massive military effort.'[112]

There was an obvious element of bluff in Olivares' tactics. By making extravagant demands, he clearly hoped to stampede the Dutch into assuming that he was virtually assured of military assistance from the Emperor. Spínola, however, was sceptical. In his view, there was no time to be lost. The army of Flanders lacked the capacity to undertake a new offensive, or even to resist an offensive

[109] Lonchay, *Correspondance*, 2, p. 382. Summary in AHN Est. lib. 697, *treguas*.
[110] ASV, Spagna, 66, fo. 341v.; Cuvelier, 'Les négociations', p. 77, note.
[111] AGS Est. leg. 2042, paper by Olivares, 23 April 1628.
[112] ADM, leg. 79, Olivares to Aytona, 6 May 1628.

launched by the Dutch.[113] While the Dutch might now be apprehensive about the dangers of attack by an Imperialist army, 'if they then see, as seems probable, that it is unlikely to do them serious harm, they will revert to their earlier stance.'[114]

The events of the spring and summer of 1628 were to prove Spínola right. The Infanta wrote to tell him at the end of May that Bruneau's negotiations in Prague made it clear that Spain would receive no help from the Emperor's forces during the current year.[115] Neither the Emperor himself, nor Wallenstein, nor the Catholic League could see any immediate benefits from embroiling themselves in war with the Dutch; and Aytona's attempts to get them to change their minds were not helped by the Spanish intervention in Mantua. Wallenstein, who supported the claims of Nevers, considered this intervention unjustified. 'The Germans', Aytona wrote, 'are very subtle theologians when it comes to our behaviour, but when it comes to their own, anything goes.'[116]

The Mantuan affair, therefore, was already beginning to have serious consequences for Olivares' northern policy, although Aytona believed that if Don Gonzalo de Córdoba could take Casale quickly, all would be well. But one might as well have urged a tortoise to hurry. As more and more of Spain's resources were diverted to Italy it became clear that a summer offensive by the army of Flanders was out of the question.[117] This meant that one vital component of the scheme to force peace upon the Dutch—the 'massive military effort' in the Netherlands—disappeared in the summer of 1628 along with a second, the threat of an imminent Imperial invasion. Simultaneously, the prospect of bringing into play the third component—the domination of the Baltic—dwindled almost to vanishing point. In February, Wallenstein's lieutenant, Hans Georg von Arnim, had embarked on the siege of Stralsund, which promised to be an ideal naval base for a Spanish Baltic fleet. On 23 June, Wallenstein himself arrived outside the city to preside over what were expected to be the final stages of the siege. But the arrival in July of Danish, and then of Swedish, reinforcements compelled the Imperialists to abandon the siege at the end of the month.[118] If Olivares was not yet prepared to abandon his Baltic design, he would certainly have to recast it on more modest lines.

Although Wallenstein's 'extravagance' posed constant problems for the Count-Duke, he knew that without Wallenstein the Emperor

[113] AGR, SEG, liasse 126, Spínola to Infanta, 1 May 1628.
[114] AGR, SEG, liasse 126, Spínola to Infanta, 30 April 1628.
[115] AGR, SEG, liasse 126, Infanta to Spínola, 31 May 1628.
[116] ADM, leg. 90, Aytona to Olivares, 3 June 1628.
[117] Alcalá-Zamora, España, Flandes, p. 286.
[118] Roberts, Gustavus Adolphus, 2, pp. 359–65.

was nothing. A junta of ministers meeting in his rooms on 27 June agreed that it would be far too dangerous to have the Duke of Friedland dismissed. 'Although', remarked Olivares, 'many things would be better if they were other than they are, to change them would be worse.'[119] But the divisions within the Empire placed Madrid in an awkward dilemma. If Spain used Wallenstein's troops against the United Provinces—and this was still the Count-Duke's hope—it would arouse the distrust of the Catholic League. But if he turned to Tilly and the Duke of Bavaria for help, it would antagonize Wallenstein and the Emperor. Reconciliation of the opposing factions around the Emperor was therefore the essential pre-condition for any union of Imperial and Spanish forces against the Dutch.

It would take Aytona time to achieve such a reconciliation, and Spínola for one had no time to spare. Olivares was now attempting to send him back to Flanders, where the effects of his absence were becoming daily more acute. But Spínola was determined not to leave Madrid until he had persuaded the king and his ministers to undertake serious negotiations with the Dutch, and he fought a long and successful battle against being ordered back to Brussels.[120] His activities in Madrid as an advocate of peace were aided by the willingness of the Dutch to go on talking at Roosendael. Pressures for peace within the United Provinces, and perhaps a latent fear that the Imperial army might yet attack, suggested to the States General that it would be wise to continue the negotiations, and perhaps even to offer some concessions, although it is not clear whether these were merely tactical or reflected a growing war-weariness. On 15 July the negotiators at Roosendael declared that they were ready to accept a twelve or twenty-year truce, during which peace terms could be worked out, and also to countenance a Spanish text which omitted any reference to their status as 'free provinces'.[121]

Any Dutch concessions were likely to find the majority of the Council of State in a receptive frame of mind. Spínola had been lobbying hard, and the success of his efforts can be gauged by the views expressed at a council meeting on 1 August.[122] There was now a strong majority in favour of a settlement with the Dutch. Some councillors, like Juan de Villela and Don Fernando de Girón—both of them with personal experience of the Netherlands—had for long been advocates of peace. Others were coming to accept its inevitability. Leganés, caught between his father-in-law, Spínola, and his

---

[119] AGS Est. leg. 2042, Junta del aposento del Conde Duque, 27 June 1628.
[120] Rodríguez Villa, *Ambrosio Spínola*, p. 534.
[121] Lonchay, *Correspondance*, 2, Doc. 1255; Cuvelier, 'Les négociations', p. 77.
[122] AGS Est. leg. 2042, consulta, 1 August 1628. This is a file of individual *votos*. That of Olivares is dated 30 August, but this appears to be a slip for 30 July.

patron, Olivares, came down on the side of the former. More strikingly, Montesclaros, not generally noted for pacifist inclinations,
ended an impressive survey by accepting that the war in the Netherlands was unwinnable, and that this was an opportune moment to
negotiate. Like others among his colleagues he was concerned at the
possibility of a retreat by Madrid on the question of freedom of
worship for Dutch Catholics, but this question seems to have exercised the lay members of the council more than their clerical colleagues. Fray Antonio de Sotomayor, the king's confessor, observed
that His Majesty's greatest gift to his Monarchy would be peace,
while Fray Iñigo de Brizuela, once the confessor of the Archduke
Albert and now Bishop of Segovia and President of the Council
of Flanders, expressed the view that a truce without an improvement
in the religious provisions for the Catholics was preferable to the
alternative, the total loss of Flanders.

Only two councillors stood firm against the prevailing trend—the
Duke of Feria, who expressed his views with characteristic bluntness,
and the Count-Duke, who expressed his with characteristic ambiguity. Both men were afraid of being trapped into a truce as disastrous
as that of 1609, and both remained hopeful that the Emperor would
still be prepared to join forces with Spain and to place the United
Provinces under an Imperial ban. The Count-Duke, speaking in rid-
dles, gives the impression of a man fighting a bitter rearguard action
to prevent his king and his colleagues from selling out to the Dutch.
Religion and reputation were both at stake, and neither could be
guaranteed by the kind of peace terms at present under discussion.
But confessing himself shaken by Spínola's new battery of arguments
about the impossibility of continuing the war in the Netherlands,
and anxious, as he said, that his own 'speculative reasons' should
not stand in the way of a possibly beneficial settlement, he declared
himself ready to fall in with any terms approved by the five veterans
of the Netherlands war in the Council of State: Spínola himself, Don
Agustín Mexía, Don Fernando Girón, the Marquis of Gelves and
the Marquis of Leganés.

Given the voting record of these five men, the Count-Duke was
clearly in retreat. He may have clutched at this device of a special
junta of the Flanders experts to cover himself in the event of a discreditable truce being agreed. He may also have been using it as a delaying
tactic, in the hope of gaining a few more precious weeks. If Casale
fell, as at any moment it might, the Mantuan question would be
as good as settled, resources would be freed for the Netherlands,
and the Emperor might be induced to look more kindly on Madrid's
plans for combined operations against the Dutch. The Count-Duke's
plans for a Baltic squadron, too, had not yet been abandoned,

although this was now beginning to be thought of more as a guarantee to the Poles and a deterrent to the Swedes than as a decisive weapon against the United Provinces.[123]

Olivares may well have reckoned during this first week of August that, if he could only buy time, the crown would soon be on the road to financial recovery. Throughout the spring and early summer the Council of Castile and the Cortes had been grappling with the problem of the inflation of *vellón* prices, which rose sharply with each new rumour of an imminent currency reform. It was fortunate for the government that, after two years of unseasonable rain and flooding, which were responsible for poor harvests and high grain prices, the spring of 1628 brought with it the prospect of bumper crops.[124] But it had become perfectly clear that sooner or later the crown and the urban patriciate of Castile would have to reach a compromise on the vexed question of the *vellón* coinage. The cities represented in the Cortes had made it plain that they had no intention of voting new taxes as long as the special banks—the *diputaciones*—for the 'consumption' of *vellón* remained in being. The fact that they were controlled by the Genoese and held a monopoly on loans made them anathema to the municipal oligarchies.

The continuing hostility of the cities to the currency banks suggested the outlines of a package deal which would give the crown the taxes it wanted, while securing in return the acquiescence of the cities in a deflationary policy, with or without compensation for the holders of *vellón*. Repeating its favourite tactic of attempting to outflank the Cortes, the crown wrote on 11 June to twenty-five cities asking for their views on a reduction in the nominal value of *vellón*, with or without compensation. Most of the cities, finding themselves in a situation in which 'nobody sells, nobody buys, and we all behave like Jews',[125] now declared themselves willing to accept a change in the value of the *vellón* coinage, although they were divided as to whether or not the holders of *vellón* should be indemnified. One exception was Lisón y Biedma's city of Granada, which opposed revaluation on the grounds that it was prices in *vellón* and not real prices that had risen, and that the *vellón* price rise was attributable to rumours of a revaluation which (if it occurred) would be the ruin of Castile's businessmen.[126]

[123] AGS Est. leg. 2328, La Junta del Mar Báltico, 16 September 1628; Alcalá-Zamora, *España, Flandes*, pp. 272–3.
[124] ASG, Lettere Ministri, Spagna, 2434, despatch of 19 April 1628. For climatic conditions and grain prices between 1626 and 1630, see Urgorri Casado, 'Ideas sobre el gobierno económico', pp. 196–202.
[125] Lope de Vega, *Cartas completas*, 2, letter 508 (to Duke of Sessa, early July 1628).
[126] AHN Consejos, leg. 51,359, expte. 18, replies of cities. See Domínguez Ortiz, *Política y hacienda*, p. 276 n. 19, and J. Vilar, 'Formes et tendances de l'opposition', p. 282 n. 4.

With the majority of the cities accepting the need for currency reform, at least in principle, a bargain could be struck. On 8 July the Cortes made their vote of 18 million ducats conditional on the crown revoking the charter of the currency banks.[127] On 15 July the crown accepted the condition. Three weeks later, on 7 August, a royal pragmatic abolished the banks, lifted the price-fixing decree of the previous autumn, and reduced the nominal value of copper *vellón* by half. This was insufficient, Olivares told Aytona, to produce a total cure, but anything more drastic would have been *rigorosísimo*, and it seemed advisable to adopt a more gentle approach.[128] In practice, even a 50% currency change proved *rigorosísimo* for some, since the crown left it to the individual cities to decide how the holders of *vellón* should be indemnified, and naturally the compensation was not forthcoming.[129] Those people who depended on *vellón* incomes or who happened to possess large holdings of *vellón* were therefore hit hard. But it is doubtful whether the large fish were caught. The Count-Duke, for instance, had warned his friend, the Duke of Alcalá, of the impending decree, and the advance notice gave him time to dispose of unwanted coins.[130]

Lope de Vega reported that the reform was in general well received, in spite of heavy personal losses. His own father-in-law had been caught with 300,000 *reales* in *cuartos* (4 maravedí pieces of *vellón*); but by the next day he was taking comfort from the thought that it would 'cure everything'.[131] He was not alone in this belief. Reactions tended to be over-optimistic, partly perhaps because of the crown's promise never again to alter the value of *vellón*.[132] But the spectacular deflation did bring relief to the royal treasury at a critical time. While the crown lost 1,100,000 ducats through the drastic reduction in value of tax receipts in *vellón* which happened at the moment of the decree to be in the hands of tax collectors and treasury officials,[133] it gained an immediate benefit from the sharp drop in its premium payments to the bankers: from 50% to 10% in a matter of days.[134] This alleviation of a heavy financial burden gave new hope to Olivares that it would, after all, be possible to pay the royal armies, and to hold out in Flanders while reducing Casale. Taken in conjunction with the suspension of payments in 1627, the deflationary policy of 1628,

---

[127] Ruiz Martín, 'La banca', p. 107.

[128] ADM. leg. 79, Olivares to Aytona, 20 August 1628.

[129] Antonio de León Pinelo, *Anales de Madrid*, ed. Pedro Fernández Martín (Madrid, 1971), p. 278.

[130] González Moreno, *Don Fernando Enríquez Ribera*, pp. 149–50.

[131] Lope de Vega, *Cartas completas*, 2, letter 511, mid-August 1628.

[132] Hamilton, *American Treasure*, p. 83.

[133] Domínguez Ortiz, *Política y hacienda*, p. 41.

[134] See Hamilton, *American Treasure*, Table 7.

however badly managed, offered a real possibility that the crown's finances might at last be stabilized.

It is probable that these considerations strengthened the Count-Duke's resolve to avoid a precipitate settlement with the Dutch which Spain would one day live to regret. All his instincts urged him to play for time. He had reason, for instance, to believe that peace with England was on the way. During the second week of September Rubens arrived in Madrid to report on the progress of his negotiations with the English court. Rubens was followed on 20 September by Endymion Porter, the personal emissary of Buckingham.[135] On the 28th Rubens was summoned to a meeting of the Junta de Estado at which it was decided that the negotiations with England should proceed.[136] Hardly had this decision been reached when news reached Madrid of the Duke of Buckingham's assassination. Even Olivares, who detested him, was disturbed. 'It would have come less badly for us at another time', he wrote, fearing that it would prejudice the chances of a settlement.[137] But his fears were misplaced. London, like Madrid, had an interest in peace which transcended personality.

The ending of hostilities with England would relieve Spain of one of its major preoccupations, while also helping to delay the Anglo-French rapprochement which Olivares always feared. The prospect of improved relations with Charles I was an additional argument against rushing into an agreement with the Dutch. But it is hard to know how far the Count-Duke's bitter opposition to serious negotiations with the United Provinces was dictated by questions of timing, and how far by questions of principle. That timing weighed heavily with him is clear from his insistence that there had never been a better moment for striking hard at the Dutch. His reading of the contemporary situation had clearly persuaded him that the Catholic and Habsburg forces stood on the brink of a decisive victory. At the same time he was sceptical, and not without reason, of Dutch good faith. To enter into serious peace negotiations without a prior guarantee of major concessions would merely encourage the army of Flanders to slacken its effort, and would suggest to the Dutch that Spain had lost its resolve to fight to the end. In any event, was there any real reason to believe that the United Provinces would not exploit another truce as they had exploited that of 1609? When he advised the Council of State on 1 August that a new truce would merely leave the Dutch free to come to the help of the Danes, he highlighted Madrid's dilemma—that the Dutch, whether at peace or war with Spain, would continue to behave like the Dutch. Any

[135] Gachard, *Histoire de Rubens*, pp. 95, 103; Magurn, *Letters of Rubens*, pp. 283–4.
[136] Gachard, pp. 102ff.
[137] ADM, leg. 79, Olivares to Aytona, 5 October 1628.

agreement which failed to remove the root causes of friction was therefore not worth the paper on which it was drafted.

Spínola and his colleagues, on the other hand, were by now so persuaded of the fatal consequences to Flanders and Spain itself of continuing the war in the Netherlands, that they were prepared to settle for a peace that fell short of the ideal, so long as it was peace. The risks which this entailed were obvious, but their policy allowed, as that of Olivares did not, for internal changes and a gradual evolution in the United Provinces that might work to Spain's advantage. The ending of the war might well, as Spínola argued, revive in a sharper form the feuds that had torn the United Provinces during the Twelve Years' Truce—religious feuds between Gomarists and Arminians, and political feuds between the House of Orange and the Estates.[138]

Spínola's arguments prevailed. The junta of the five Flanders veterans, meeting with the Count-Duke and Juan de Villela on 28 September, recommended that the Infanta be given full negotiating powers.[139] But the concession proved to be more nominal than real. To the Infanta's despair, serious negotiations were to be deferred until the Emperor broke with the Dutch.[140] She had good reason for her distress. During the summer of 1628 the dangers of the international situation had forced the Dutch to adopt a degree of flexibility; but during the autumn those dangers began to disappear.

The siege of Stralsund had already been lifted. Of the two other great sieges still under way—those of La Rochelle and Casale—the first was going better than the second. On 28 October, while Don Gonzalo de Córdoba was still camped outside the walls of Casale, La Rochelle surrendered to Louis XIII. Its surrender gave Richelieu more room for manoeuvre than at any time since his advent to power four years earlier. Almost simultaneously he was to be a principal beneficiary of a dramatic windfall. On 8 September a Dutch squadron under the command of Piet Heyn captured the New Spain treasurefleet as it lay in the Cuban harbour of Matanzas—a spectacular *coup* which would play havoc with Spanish finances. Between them, Matanzas and La Rochelle were to snatch the initiative from Olivares' hands and leave his grand design in shreds.

---

[138] AGS Est. leg. 2042, voto del marqués de los Balbases, 1 August 1628.
[139] Lonchay, *Correspondance*, 2, Doc. 1278, consulta, 28 September 1628.
[140] *Ibid.*, Doc. 1306, Infanta to king, 21 November 1628.

X

THE OPTIONS CLOSED (1629–1631)

The French intervention

During 1627 and 1628, the two most critical years in his twenty-two years of power, the Count-Duke had committed himself to certain courses of action from which there could be no turning back. On the domestic front he had moved, although late and clumsily, to bring inflation under control, but had been forced in the process to sacrifice his plans for a national banking scheme and for fiscal reform, which had been central to his grand design for the regeneration of Castile. He had also broken the monopoly of the Genoese over the crown's finances by turning for help to a group of Portuguese businessmen of dubious ancestry and orthodoxy, with whom his regime would henceforth be closely associated in practice, and still more closely in the popular imagination. In his foreign policy he had made two decisive choices which seem to have been inspired by a mixture of despair at his continuing failure to achieve domestic reform, and confidence (or possibly over-confidence) generated by the string of successes achieved by Spanish and Imperial arms: to engage the reputation of Spain in an uncertain adventure in Italy, which he believed would turn out well, and not to engage it in serious negotiations with the United Provinces, which he believed could only lead to disaster.

Statesmen are often, but not invariably, prisoners of circumstance. In his foreign policy decisions of 1628 Olivares made two clear choices, however much he tried to obfuscate them for the future record; and neither of these choices, as far as can be told, was forced upon him by the sheer logic of events. His sources of information may have been faulty, exaggerating at once the ease of the Italian adventure and the drawbacks to a negotiated settlement with the Dutch, but the final decision was his. It seems, too, to have been his almost alone, although sanctified by the stamp of approval from a king who, at the age of twenty-three, had yet to move beyond his massive shadow. Under the spell of Spínola's personality and arguments, the majority of his colleagues on the Council of State favoured a prompt settlement with the Dutch on terms which

Olivares declared himself unable to accept. The Council seems to have been rather more inclined to start a war in Italy than continue it in the Netherlands, but although it approved military intervention in Montferrat, its subsequent willingness to respond to the pleas of Spínola and countermand the orders for invasion[1] suggests that it felt no overwhelming enthusiasm for the enterprise.

Spínola's worries about Spain's military intervention in Mantua proved in the event to be fully justified, although with a more resolute commander of the army of Milan the story might have turned out very differently. Had Casale been swiftly captured, much might have been forgiven the Count-Duke, although the willingness of a hand-picked junta of toadying clerics to cast its blessing on the intervention fails to conceal the dubious morality of the resort to arms. Yet even success would have exacted its penalties by disturbing the precarious peace of Italy, which the Count-Duke always declared himself so anxious to preserve. Many years later, an older and sadder Philip IV, looking back over his tragic reign, would write to his confidante Sor María, that he had heard it said that the Italian wars resulting from Spain's intervention in Mantua could have been avoided; 'and although I have always followed the opinion of my ministers in matters of such importance, if I have erred in anything and given Our Lord cause for displeasure, it was in this.'[2]

In Mantua, Olivares made the unforgivable mistake of compounding immorality with failure. In the Netherlands, his position was more honourable, and the arguments more finely drawn. The United Provinces were deeply divided during these years over the issue of peace with Spain, the militant hispanophobia of Zeeland contrasting with the growing war-weariness of the eastern provinces of Overijssel and Gelderland.[3] But there could be no assurance that the peace party would carry the day. It was Olivares' judgment that any hint of concessions at this juncture would suggest a weakening of Spanish resolve which would strengthen the hand of the war party rather than that of its adversaries. It would also undermine Spain's entire position in northern Europe, which had never looked more promising, thanks to the Emperor's victories in Germany. However much he spoke of religion and reputation, his Netherlands policy had always been shaped by an acute perception of the economic basis of Dutch power and of its potentially disastrous consequences for Spain. Control of the carrying trade between the Baltic and the Mediterranean was the foundation of Dutch prosperity. In the circumstances of

---

[1] Above, p. 346.
[2] Silvela, *Cartas de Sor María de Agreda*, 1, letter 30 (20 July 1645).
[3] Israel, *The Dutch Republic*, pp. 227–36.

1625–8 it was not unreasonable to believe that Spain and its friends might snatch the control of that trade from the Dutch, thus depriving them of the Spanish silver which was essential to their continuing prosperity, and forcing them to accept a settlement less harmful to Spanish interests than that of 1609.

This commitment of Olivares to his great Baltic design, which assumed different aspects as circumstances changed but which never wavered from its principal object of undermining the commercial power of the Dutch, vividly illustrates the differences of approach that divided him from Spínola. For Spínola, the design—however splendid in principle—was a waste of money when resources were tight. For the Count-Duke, on the other hand, the design had a necessary and critical place in a global strategy in which it was taken for granted that no problem could be treated in isolation, but was intimately related to what was happening elsewhere. Spanish support for Sigismund of Poland, for instance, would help to keep the ambitions of Gustavus Adolphus in check, and in this way ward off the dangers of Swedish intervention in Germany. For this reason he continued through 1628 and the early part of 1629 to support the efforts of the baron d'Auchy and Gabriel de Roy to rescue something from the wreckage of Wallenstein's bid to secure a naval base at Stralsund. Auchy negotiated in Warsaw for a Polish squadron, while de Roy succeeded in hiring six ships from Lübeck. These vessels, which formed the potential nucleus for a Polish-Habsburg Baltic fleet based on the port of Wismar, actually captured some Dutch merchant ships early in 1629; but then, as Sigismund lost interest and moved towards a peace settlement with Sweden, the whole project slowly died of inertia, and Olivares was forced to accept defeat.[4]

It was a disappointing finale to a bold design on which the Count-Duke had set his heart. The shortage of money, Hanseatic suspicions of Spanish intentions, the different priorities of Spain, Poland, Wallenstein and the Empire, and the heavy-handedness of Spain's envoys in these sensitive northern regions—all these played their part in the failure of his Baltic project. Logistics no doubt were against it, but, as the Count-Duke argued at a meeting of the Council of State, while his colleagues might consider the Baltic 'remote', they should remember what trouble the Dutch were giving Spain in the Indies, 'which are far more distant from them than the Baltic is from us.'[5] As a statesman who spent long hours with his maps and his globes, he had come to think of the whole world as one single theatre in

[4] Alcalá-Zamora, *España, Flandes*, pp. 273–5; Jonathan Israel, 'The Politics of International Trade Rivalry'.
[5] AGS Est. leg. 2329, consulta, 19 February 1629.

which the drama of politics and war was played out. Spínola, on the other hand, with a vision focused intensely on the loyal provinces of the southern Netherlands and their sufferings, entertained a less grandiose vision of the world. There were many things in it, as he explained at the same meeting, which it would be excellent to do, but which were impossible because of lack of resources. His counting-house mentality, and his down-to-earth approach to the political and military realities of the local scene, made him sceptical of vast under-takings, and a partisan of a rapid settlement with the Dutch Republic which would involve no more than a few cosmetic improvements to the 1609 truce. Olivares, with a global vision that was always liable to sweep majestically over little local difficulties, chose to gamble for a bigger prize. But he allowed himself to be tripped by his Mantuan preoccupations, and his timing went badly awry. He was the victim, too, of an unprecedented stroke of bad luck. Who could have foretold that the silver fleet, after crossing the Atlantic in safety year after year, would in this year of all years succumb to a Dutch attack, and its contents fall into enemy hands?

Already during the late autumn of 1628 the mysterious non-appear-ance of the treasure fleet under the command of Don Juan de Bena-vides was giving cause for concern. Two days after the deflationary decree of 7 August the Council of Finance had reported that it was 600,000 ducats down on the *asientos* to date, and that there was likely to be a shortfall for the year of two million ducats, leaving nothing for Flanders in November and December.[6] News of the imminent arrival of the galleons would have eased the credit situation, but no news came. The Infanta wrote to Madrid in late November report-ing that disaster threatened because the army of Flanders was without its pay.[7] Similar complaints were coming by every post from Milan. Although Madrid had sent him over half a million ducats during the first half of the year,[8] Gonzalo de Córdoba felt that Olivares had got him deeply involved in an expensive enterprise, and then starved him of the money essential for its realization.[9]

Olivares, who had been working night and day to supply the armies with cash, took the urgent reproaches of Gonzalo de Córdoba in

---

[6] AGS CJH, leg. 643, fo. 177, consulta, 9 August 1628; Domínguez Ortiz, *Política y hacienda*, pp. 40–41.

[7] Lonchay, *Correspondance*, 2, Doc. 1304, Infanta to king, 21 November 1628.

[8] Fernández Álvarez, *Don Gonzalo de Córdoba*, p. 72.

[9] 'Correspondencia de D. Gonzalo Fernández de Córdoba . . .', *Codoin* 54, p. 369 (Don Gonzalo to his brother, Don Fernando, 16 December 1628). This volume contains numerous letters from Don Gonzalo to his brother written during his 1629 campaign.

good part; 'the galleons', he wrote on 19 December, 'have not arrived, and everything is very tight.'[10] It was only on 22 December that the news of the disaster of 8 September in the Bay of Matanzas became generally known in Madrid.[11] But rumours had been circulating, and the Count-Duke may well have had advance warning that something was amiss. The papal nuncio reported on 11 December that the previous evening, when Olivares was closeted with the French envoy Bautru discussing the affairs of Mantua, he had been handed the despatches from Paris, and had shown signs of great agitation on opening them. When asked by Bautru if they contained bad news of the fleet, he brushed the inquiry aside. From his reaction the nuncio deduced either that the silver-fleet had indeed been lost, or alternatively that the French army, released from La Rochelle, was on the move to Italy.[12]

From every point of view, financial, political and psychological, Piet Heyn's capture of the treasure fleet was a major disaster for Spain.[13] As a result of the cowardice of the captains and crews of the twenty-two ships when confronted by superior forces, almost the entire fleet, along with its contents, fell into the hands of the Dutch. The loss to the crown was put at one million ducats in silver, together with a further three million in ships and artillery, while the *consulado* of Seville set the figure for private losses as high as six million.[14] These losses came at a moment when Andalusia, which reacted more quickly than Castile, was suffering all the consequences of the brutal deflation of the preceding summer. Between 1628 and 1629 the Andalusian price index fell from 110.61 to 99.88.[15] To the disruption of commercial life caused by the sudden disappearance of easy money, was now added a temporary but paralyzing disruption of the transatlantic trade. The morale of Seville's merchant community, never very buoyant, was at a low ebb in 1629.

Five years after Matanzas, Don Juan de Benavides—imprisoned, and subjected to lengthy investigations—paid for the shame of that day with his life. The king and Olivares felt the disgrace deeply—the king later wrote that every time he thought of it, the blood raced

---

[10] AGS Est. leg. 2712, Olivares to Gonzalo de Córdoba, 19 December 1628. One of a series of draft letters in Carnero's hand, most of them in *legajo* 2713 and covering 1629, written by Olivares to Gonzalo de Córdoba, Monterrey and Spínola. These letters seem to have passed unnoticed when he had his papers removed to his private archive. No set of comparable drafts for other years appears to have survived in the Estado section at Simancas.

[11] Hoz, p. 171 (22 December 1628).

[12] ASV, Spagna 69, fo. 55v.

[13] For this episode and some of its consequences, see Chaunu, *Séville et l'Atlantique*, 8, 2 (2), pp. 1645–6, and Antonio Domínguez Ortiz, 'El suplicio de Don Juan de Benavides', *Archivo Hispalense*, p. 76 (1956).

[14] Domínguez Ortiz, *Política y hacienda*, p. 295 n. 13.

[15] Hamilton, *American Treasure*, pp. 215, 218.

through his veins[16]—but Rubens, who was in Madrid when the news of the disaster arrived, reported a very different reaction outside government circles: 'You would be surprised to see that almost all the people here are very glad about it, feeling that this public calamity can be set down as a disgrace to their rulers. So great is the power of hate that they overlook or fail to feel their own ills, for the mere pleasure of vengeance.'[17]

The Count-Duke, shaken by the disaster, and profoundly conscious of his own unpopularity, began to appear less frequently in public, and gave orders to tighten the control over posts and communications.[18] In an attempt to counter the flood of libels and satires which no censorship laws could check, he also recalled Quevedo from his exile and set him to work as a pamphleteer and publicist for the regime.[19] But not even the polemical skills of Quevedo could disguise the extent of the damage to Spain's resources and its reputation. It was the thought of this that most upset Olivares, and gave him—he told Gonzalo de Córdoba—the worst days he had experienced since entering the royal service.[20] But in spite of the loss of the silver, he managed to arrange in those first weeks of January 1629 *asientos* for 5,800,000 ducats,[21] although the terms on which they were negotiated were so unfavourable to the crown that the Genoese ambassador considered the sum involved to be merely notional.[22]

The Count-Duke responded to the loss of the Mexican silver by ordering the despatch of a powerful squadron to convoy the Tierra Firme fleet laden with the silver of Peru. He also seized the opportunity to attempt to inject new life into his flagging schemes for the creation of overseas trading companies—'a project so important that this unhappy event could even be termed happy if it resulted in its realization.'[23] These trading companies would—or so it was hoped—defeat the Dutch at their own game. No progress was made in establishing the proposed Levant Company in Barcelona, but the India Company, founded in Lisbon by royal decree in August 1628, duly embarked on its operations, although inadequate funding by the crown, and the lack of substantial private investment, got it off to an uncertain start and condemned it to a largely disappointing career.[24]

The inability of the Spanish crown to provide the new company

---

[16] Domínguez Ortiz, *Política y hacienda*, p. 288.

[17] Magurn, *Letters of Rubens*, p. 295.

[18] Novoa, *Codoin* 69, pp. 73 and 76.

[19] *Ibid.*

[20] AGS Est. leg. 2713, Olivares to Gonzalo de Córdoba, 19 January 1629.

[21] *Ibid.*

[22] ASG, Lettere ministri, Spagna, 2435, despatch of 6 January 1629.

[23] AGS Est. leg. 2713, Olivares to Gonzalo de Córdoba, 7 January 1629.

[24] For the history of the India Company see A. R. Disney, *Twilight of the Pepper Empire* (Cambridge, Mass., 1978).

in Lisbon with the funds which it had originally been promised was itself a reflection of the acute silver shortage created by the loss of the treasure fleet. The silver required to finance such domestic enterprises and to pay for the military operations planned for 1629 was simply not to be had. Worse still, it was in the hands of the enemy. The unexpected windfall immediately diminished Dutch interest in reaching an accommodation with a colossus whose feet were so plainly made of clay.[25] It also enabled Frederick Henry to plan a spring offensive; and the Infanta, correctly suspecting that Bois-le-Duc was the most likely target, warned Madrid that the army would be too short of funds to come to its relief.[26]

The repercussions of the disaster at Matanzas were felt, however, most immediately and most dangerously in Spain's relationship with France. Ever since the surrender of La Rochelle at the end of October there had been a possibility, if not a certainty, of French intervention in Italy on behalf of the Duke of Nevers. Bautru's mission to Madrid to discuss a Mantuan settlement with Olivares was no doubt partly intended to lull the Count-Duke into a false sense of security.[27] At a meeting of a special junta held in his rooms on 7 January, however, Olivares showed himself well aware of Richelieu's intentions. The French army, he told his colleagues, had begun to assemble on the very day when the news of the capture of the treasure fleet was confirmed.[28] From this it could be deduced that Louis XIII and Richelieu were in the process of reaching a settlement with the Huguenots—if indeed they had not already done so—and were planning to send their army across the Alps. All the traditions of French foreign policy pointed in this direction, and Spain's current monetary troubles and the loss of the treasure fleet made this an ideal moment.

The Count-Duke's response was to propose that the French should be given a solemn warning. In fact, he had already told the papal nuncio two days earlier that, if French troops entered Italy, Spanish troops would enter France, and he predicted—with uncanny accuracy—that it would be the beginning of a war that would last for thirty years.[29] He also said that ships and troops should be placed on stand-by orders, and that all licit measures should be considered for building up a party of opposition inside France. Since this was bound to involve dealings with heretics, certain tricky theological problems arose, but it was not long before they were satisfactorily

[25] Cuvelier, 'Les négociations', p. 79.
[26] Lonchay, *Correspondance*, 2, Doc. 1348, Infanta to king, 13 February 1629. In this book I have used the French name, Bois-le-Duc, rather than the Dutch, 's-Hertogenbosch, for a town known to the Spaniards as 'Bolduque'.
[27] Fernández Alvarez, *Don Gonzalo de Córdoba*, pp. 85–6.
[28] AGS Est. K.1437, fo. 9, consulta, 7 January 1629.
[29] ASV, Spagna, 69, fo. 61, nuncio, 5 January 1629.

resolved. The king summoned a junta of six theologians, including his own confessor and that of the Count-Duke, Hernando de Salazar, to advise whether he could in good conscience encourage and pay for a diversion inside France by the Huguenot Duke of Rohan if Louis XIII persisted in his Italian schemes and in giving help to the Dutch. The theologians, obliging as always, unanimously agreed that in the circumstances His Majesty had a positive obligation to make use of French heretics for diversionary purposes.[30] Three weeks later Olivares despatched 200,000 ducats to Gonzalo de Córdoba, with which to 'assist the Duke of Rohan's party, as the theologians have decided can and must be done on this occasion.'[31]

At the meeting of the junta on 7 January the Count-Duke had described Italy as 'the most important and sensitive part' of the Spanish Monarchy, and it was in accordance with this conventional judgment on the supreme importance of Italy to Spain that priorities were now determined. In the event of France declaring war, he recommended that the king should reach an agreement with the Dutch, irrespective of the difficulties.[32] In his view, however, it was essential not to leave the world with the impression that, with the loss of the treasure fleet, Spain had lost everything. This was no time to give the appearance of weakness; but during these difficult days of January 1629 he had to yield, at least momentarily, to the desire of the overwhelming majority in the Council of State for an immediate settlement with the Dutch. It was essentially a tactical retreat that he was now making, and one which, as he was well aware, could even be turned to Madrid's advantage, since the knowledge that Spain and the United Provinces were on the verge of agreement might well deter Richelieu from intervening in Italy.[33] The king's reluctance to compromise his honour through an unfavourable settlement with the Dutch still remained an obstacle, but Philip was induced to signify to the Infanta his willingness to approve an armistice of from two to six years, on the understanding that it would also extend to the Indies. But Amsterdam, as the Infanta felt bound to reply, was now in less of a hurry than Madrid for a settlement, and with good cause.[34]

For all Madrid's fears of French intervention in Italy, it had always been taken for granted that nothing would happen over the winter

[30] RAH 9-71-8-6, *Parecer de una junta de teólogos*, 25 January 1629. See Elliott, *Richelieu and Olivares*, pp. 126–7.
[31] AGS Est. leg. 2713, Olivares to Gonzalo de Córdoba, 18 February 1629.
[32] AGS Est. K.1437, fo. 35, consulta, 18 January 1629.
[33] Straub, *Pax et Imperium*, pp. 362–3.
[34] Lonchay, *Correspondance*, 2, Doc. 1349, king to Infanta, 14 February 1629; Doc. 1353, Infanta to king, 3 March 1629; Israel, *The Dutch Republic*, p. 227.

season,[35] and that Gonzalo de Córdoba still had a few months in which to redeem Spain's reputation by capturing Casale. But at the end of February Louis XIII led his army across the Alps through heavy snow. On 3 March the vanguard of the French army was within a mile or two of the frontier of Savoy. Charles Emmanuel of Savoy was not noted for his adherence either to his principles or his allies, and three days later, in a battle which may well have been stage-managed, his forces were defeated at Susa.[36] On the 7th he opened peace negotiations with the French. Ironically, Olivares wrote to Gonzalo de Córdoba on the very same day that if Louis XIII should have attacked Savoy, and if an armistice was reached in the Netherlands—and one was expected hourly—then France would be in trouble, with its north-eastern frontier wide open to a Spanish attack from Flanders.[37]

There was consternation at the court when the news of the defeat at Susa arrived. Olivares was perhaps more shaken than at any time since his rise to power. He saw little hope of escaping the 'total ruin' that threatened, unless the Emperor could be persuaded to order his troops at once into Italy.[38] A meeting of the Council of State, which lasted far into the night, was held in Olivares' rooms, with the king listening from behind a tapestry.[39] Nor was it only the fate of Italy that was at stake. The news that Frederick Henry was planning a spring offensive against Brabant with the silver captured by Piet Heyn had persuaded the crown that Flanders, too, was 'on the point of being lost'.[40] Olivares urged that Spínola should at once return to Brussels, before the expected offensive was launched.[41] At the same time, the Infanta was given a free hand to negotiate an armistice, or—still better—a truce, the only exception being that she should not deviate from her instructions on the question of sovereignty.[42]

The clouds momentarily lifted when news reached the court on 10 April that Tomás de la Raspuru's fleet, with its cargo of Peruvian silver, had arrived off Cadiz a month earlier than expected. Olivares thought there was ten to twelve million on board—enough to save the situation[43]—and allowed himself to be seen in public, going by coach down the Calle Mayor to give thanks at the church of Santa

[35] AGS Est. leg. 2328, king on consulta of 6 December 1628.
[36] Fernández Álvarez, *Don Gonzalo de Córdoba*, p. 89.
[37] AGS Est. leg. 2713, Olivares to Gonzalo de Córdoba, 7 March 1629.
[38] ADM, leg. 79, Olivares to Aytona, 26 March 1629.
[39] ASV, Spagna 69, fo. 109, nuncio, 28 March 1629; ASG, Lettere ministri, Spagna, 2435, despatch, 26 March 1629.
[40] Lonchay, *Correspondance*, 2, Doc. 1357, royal decree, 21 March 1629.
[41] AHN Est. leg. 727, *Papel del conde mi señor*, 2 April 1629.
[42] Lonchay, *Correspondance*, 2, Doc. 1369, king to Infanta, 5 April 1629.
[43] ADM, leg. 79, Olivares to Aytona, 13 April 1629.

María de Atocha.[44] In fact the fleet brought four million ducats, of which one million was for the king, and the remainder for private individuals.[45] Desperately pressed for funds, the crown ordered the sequestration of $1\frac{1}{2}$ million (later reduced to 1 million) as a forced loan,[46] and then, on 10 May, confiscated a year's interest on the *juros* held by foreigners. Of the 800,000 ducats involved, 700,000 belonged to the Genoese, although exemptions would reduce the figure substantially.[47]

These draconian measures were forced on the crown by what promised to be a total debacle in Italy. Rubens, just before leaving Madrid on 29 April for Brussels and London with instructions from Olivares for further peace negotiations with England and for talks with the Huguenot Duke of Soubise about the possibilities of provoking disturbances inside France,[48] wrote to a friend of the 'infamous' treaty which the Duke of Savoy had signed with the French, and which Gonzalo de Córdoba had ratified.[49] By the terms of the treaty of Susa, France offered Savoy some of the Duke of Nevers' territory in Montferrat, in return for granting French troops right of passage to Montferrat, and for helping to drive out Gonzalo de Córdoba's besieging army unless he saw fit to ratify the treaty. Short of money, as always, and fearing for the safety of Milan and Genoa, Gonzalo de Córdoba duly put his signature to the agreement, and ordered the lifting of the siege of Casale.[50]

The Council of State met daily, mornings and afternoons, for a whole week after the news of the treaty of Susa reached Madrid in late April. The king, burning with indignation at the behaviour of the French, went down with a fever, attributed to the bad news from Italy. Olivares declared himself struck to the heart at having lived to see his 'nation, which is still declining', overtaken by such ignominy. The blows of these last months had reduced him to such prostration that he could no longer support the burden. 'I have quite lost my navigating aids—my quadrant and compass.'[51] The immediate problem was obviously for the crown to extricate itself as best it could, without further loss of prestige.

Something might yet be saved from the wreckage if, as Olivares

[44] ASG, Lettere ministri, Spagna, 2435, despatch, 11 April 1629.

[45] AGS Est. leg. 2647, petition of prior and consuls of Seville, 16 May 1629.

[46] AGS Est. leg. 2647, consulta, 20 May 1629; Domínguez Ortiz, *Política y hacienda*, pp. 288–9.

[47] ASG, Lettere ministri, Spagna, 2435, despatch, 10 May 1629.

[48] AHN Consejos, leg. 12,010, expte. 8, draft of 'Lo que el Conde Duque de San Lúcar advierte al Sr. P. P. Rubens', 24 April 1629. I am grateful to Dr. Richard Kagan for bringing this document to my attention.

[49] Magurn, *Letters of Rubens*, letter 184.

[50] Fernández Álvarez, *Don Gonzalo de Córdoba*, pp. 90–94; Straub, *Pax et Imperium*, p. 364.

[51] AGS Est. leg. 2713, Olivares to Gonzalo de Córdoba, 4 May 1629.

hoped, the Emperor could be persuaded to intervene. In the wake of the currency reform and the capture of the silver fleet, a League of offensive and defensive Alliance with the Emperor and the German Catholic princes seemed to him the only viable alternative to peace with England and the Dutch.[52] As an earnest of Madrid's determination to work in close partnership with Vienna, the proxy marriage of the Infanta Doña María to the Emperor's son, the King of Hungary, was hastily celebrated on 25 April, in spite of Philip's indisposition.[53] It was no doubt hoped that the news of the marriage, coupled with the promise that the bride would soon be leaving for Vienna, would encourage the Emperor to do what was hoped of him—to send his troops into the Valtelline and Milan, and order a diversionary attack on France's eastern frontier.[54]

Olivares would spend much of his career waiting on the Emperor. The presumed identity of interests between Madrid and Vienna, and the overriding necessity of preserving unity between the two branches of the House of Austria, were central to all his thinking about Spain's international position. It was his constant refrain that 'not for anything must these two houses let themselves be divided.'[55] All too often his hopes would be defrauded: Vienna's priorities were not those of Madrid, and even on those occasions when the Emperor had the will, he rarely had the wherewithal. Either he lacked the money, or he was unable to persuade Wallenstein to move, or he could not carry Bavaria and the Catholic League with him, as in 1628 when Madrid solicited his help against the Dutch, and—as Girón warned in the Council of State—the German princes were unwilling to concur in a policy that threatened their own homes with fire and sword.[56] But by the spring of 1629 there was a real possibility that Olivares' hopes would, for once at least, not be misplaced. In March the Emperor, exultant over his victories, felt confident enough to impose his own settlement on Germany in the form of the Edict of Restitution.[57] He was on the verge, too, of peace with Denmark, which would be signed at Lübeck on 7 June.[58] Although Gustavus Adolphus had already taken his decision in principle to launch an invasion of Germany,[59] the north German situation looked sufficiently tranquil in the spring and summer of 1629 for the Emperor

[52] Olivares to Conde de Castro, March 1629, in Günter, *Die Habsburger-Liga*, Appendix 7.
[53] Hoz, p. 174.
[54] *Parecer del Conde-Duque*, 27 April 1629 (misdated 7 April), in Fernández Álvarez, *Don Gonzalo de Córdoba*, Appendix 11, p. 203.
[55] AGS Est. leg. 2331, Olivares in Council of State, 10 November 1630.
[56] AGS Est. leg. 2328, fos. 157–8, consulta, 10 November 1628.
[57] For the Edict of Restitution and reactions to it, see Bireley, *Religion and Politics*, especially pp. 78–9.
[58] Roberts, *Gustavus Adolphus*, 2, p. 387.
[59] *Ibid.*, p. 373.

to feel free to turn his attention to Italy. Even if there was strong support for Nevers inside the Imperial family itself, Ferdinand could hardly fail to be concerned by the way in which events there had developed. A French presence in northern Italy was no more to the liking of Vienna than it was to that of Madrid.

The obvious policy for Olivares and his colleagues was therefore to play for time while Spain's envoys in Vienna, the Marquis of Aytona and the Count of Castro, pressed home their appeals for help. Nothing could be done to prevent the siege of Casale from being raised, but a declaration of Spain's position, coupled with preparations for war, might help to tide over the weeks of waiting until the Emperor should decide to move. The Council of State's decision, which seems to have been inspired by Spínola, was for the king to refuse to ratify the treaty of Susa, but to accompany the refusal with a statement that Spain, acting alone, would not fight Nevers, nor go to war with France.[60] Meanwhile, further preparations were made for war. In addition to the sequestration of silver from the treasure fleet and the retention of half the interest on foreign-held *juros*, six members of the Council of Castile were deputed to tour the country requesting another voluntary *donativo* from corporations and private individuals, similar to that of 1624.[61] There followed, too, a string of new appointments. The Duke of Feria was made viceroy and captain-general of Catalonia, with responsibility for Spain's north-eastern frontier with France. Don Fernando Girón was appointed viceroy of another sensitive area, Navarre, but suspecting that this was an attempt by the Count-Duke to get him away from the Council of State, he declined the appointment and was given leave to retire.[62] The Marquis of Santa Cruz was given command of the Mediterranean galley fleet; and Spínola was chosen to replace Gonzalo de Córdoba as governor of Milan.[63]

Don Gonzalo's replacement was long overdue. 'His comedy is over', wrote Olivares, more in sorrow than in anger.[64] In letter after letter to his brother the governor of Milan had complained bitterly about the way in which he had been left in the lurch by Madrid, and his communications to the Count-Duke seem to have been couched in deliberately uncompromising language, in order to provoke him into ordering his dismissal.[65] Disheartened and demora-

---

[60] Consulta of 28 April 1629 in Fernández Álvarez, *Don Gonzalo de Córdoba*, Appendix 10; and see also Ródenas Vilar, *La política europea*, p. 187.
[61] ASG, Lettere ministri, Spagna, 2434, despatch, 21 April 1629; Domínguez Ortiz, *Política y hacienda*, pp. 299–300.
[62] ASG, Lettere ministri, Spagna, 2435, despatch, 2 June 1629.
[63] ASV, Spagna 69, fo. 116v., nuncio, 4 March 1629.
[64] ADM, leg. 79, Olivares to Aytona, 4 May 1629.
[65] 'Correspondencia', *Codoin* 54, p. 369 (letter of 16 December 1628).

lized, he was beginning to think of exchanging the life of a soldier for that of a friar—a vocation in which the Count-Duke had a mind to join him as more and more bad news arrived from Italy.[66] A distinguished military career was coming to a close in dishonour—a dishonour for which he held the Count-Duke personally responsible, by failing to keep him supplied with cash. In fact he received from Spain around $1\frac{1}{2}$ million ducats between February 1628 and January 1629, but delays in the despatch of the money and high interest payments deriving from his own lack of credit had eaten into the remittances to such an extent that sums which had seemed ample to Olivares in Madrid appeared totally inadequate for a commander in the field.[67] As an experienced soldier, Spínola for one knew what Olivares could never quite grasp: that 'when the moment comes, it will be found that much more money is needed than was originally anticipated, as always happens. Your Majesty has seen this now in relation to Italy, and will see it again as new occasions arise.'[68]

The ordeal of Don Gonzalo would last for some months yet. Spínola knew that these were critical days in Madrid, and was determined if possible to postpone his departure until a truce had been signed with the Dutch.[69] It was not until 29 July that he left Madrid, accompanied by Velázquez, who was paying his first visit to Italy. By 19 September he had only got as far as Genoa.[70] In the meantime, the regime had been considering its verdict on Don Gonzalo's share of responsibility for the Italian fiasco. In view of his accusations against the Count-Duke, it was first necessary for the Council of State to clear Olivares of any blame for the disaster. This was duly done, although with one dissentient, and the king ordered Villela to inform the favourite personally of his entire satisfaction with his conduct throughout the whole affair.[71] On the other hand, Philip expressed himself dissatisfied with the conduct of the governor of Milan, who now had to face fifteen charges assembled by a tribunal of councillors of state. But Don Gonzalo came from one of the great houses of Spain, glorious in the annals of its military history, and two years later the affair was quietly buried, with the verdict that if in some instances Don Gonzalo had lacked wisdom, he had never been wanting in zeal.[72]

---

[66] AGS Est. leg. 2713, Olivares to Monterrey, 1 May 1629.
[67] See Fernández Álvarez, *Don Gonzalo de Córdoba*, pp. 90–1, for the question of responsibility for the shortage of money.
[68] AGS Est. K.1437, Spínola in Council of State, 7 January 1629.
[69] AGR SEG, liasse 126, Spínola to Infanta, 20 June 1629.
[70] ASG, Lettere ministri, Spagna, 2435, despatch, 5 August 1629; Rodríguez Villa, *Ambrosio Spínola*, p. 548.
[71] Fernández Álvarez, *Don Gonzalo de Córdoba*, p. 111, and p. 116 n. 18.
[72] *Ibid.*, pp. 111–13.

The Count-Duke at bay

Although Olivares had once again received the approbation of his monarch, his position was less secure in the spring and summer of 1629 than this might suggest. Don Gonzalo de Córdoba's accusations against him for mismanagement of affairs in Italy were no secret in Madrid—indeed Don Gonzalo's brother seems to have made plans to publish his correspondence with the Count-Duke as a kind of manifesto[73]—and as one disaster followed another, the mounting chorus of complaint was bound sooner or later to have an impact on the young and still impressionable king. Nor could Olivares feel happy about the way his own authority had been eroded by the activities of Spínola, who seemed to be establishing himself increasingly as the supreme arbiter in matters of war and peace. The news from the Netherlands confirmed all his worst predictions about the likely consequences of Spínola's intervention to secure a rapid settlement. On 3 May the Infanta reported that the Dutch army had turned out in force, and was laying siege to Bois-le-Duc.[74] On 1 June her special emissary, Juan de Benavides, arrived in Madrid with an urgent request for help, and an additional letter dated 18 May reporting that the Dutch negotiators at Roosendael were now refusing any concessions on the question of sovereignty and were prepared only to accept a straight renewal of the truce of 1609.[75]

For Olivares, who had never been more busily occupied in self-justification than during these past few months, the latest despatch from Flanders confirmed everything he had ever said about the dangers of negotiating with the Dutch. The Infanta and Spínola had all along been misled by Kesseler, their representative at the peace talks, and the Dutch had simply been using the talks as a device to prevent Spain from waging a vigorous war. He had always known that this would happen, and had been so unhappy at the way in which Madrid's policy towards the Netherlands had been conducted under the influence of Spínola, that he had refrained from attending council meetings when Flanders was under discussion. Over the last four years, Spain had thrown away fourteen million ducats in the Low Countries, only to lose the loyal provinces of the southern Netherlands, along with its own reputation. Spínola should never have been present at council meetings on Netherlands policy. As for himself, he had never sought to influence anybody . . . His record was clear and open. Like so many distinguished councillors before him,

---

[73] ASG, Lettere ministri, Spagna, 2435, despatch, 25 March 1629.
[74] Lonchay, *Correspondance*, 2, Doc. 1384.
[75] Lonchay, *Correspondance*, 2, Docs. 1394 and 1404.

like his uncle Don Baltasar de Zúñiga, and the Marquis of Montesclaros, who had died unexpectedly and still comparatively young the preceding autumn,[76] he had consistently voted against the discreditable truce terms of 1609.[77]

The stridency of the Count-Duke's reaction to the news from Brussels suggests that he was acutely conscious that his long personal battle against a repetition of the 1609 truce was as good as lost. It was no use his insisting that 'this crown was never more at war, or spent more money', than during the truce years of 1609–21.[78] Shaken by the disaster in Italy, and the imminent threat of disaster in the Netherlands, the council was ready to follow Spínola's lead. 'All except one', wrote Spínola pointedly to the Infanta on 6 June, 'have recommended that we should agree to the truce, and His Majesty has told me personally that he knows it to be necessary.' But the Infanta must act at once.[79]

The king's readiness to consider as an unhappy necessity a truce which virtually repeated that of 1609 was itself an indication of how isolated the Count-Duke had become. Philip had for some months been taking a close personal interest in his ministers' discussions, and was now writing long replies to their *consultas* in his own hand.[80] Partly this reflected his own growing absorption in affairs of state. But it may also be seen as a response to the increasingly insistent demand that he should free himself from subservience to a favourite who was leading Spain to disaster.

However closely Olivares tried to seal off the king from undesirable contacts, total isolation was out of the question, even in the etiquette-bound court of Madrid. It is true that the queen, who was thought to have little liking for the Count-Duke, passed her days under the watchful gaze of the Countess of Olivares, while every move of the Infantes was reported by the Count-Duke's agents in their entourage. But for all this there were still ways of reaching the king. Cardinal Trejo, as president of the Council of Castile, enjoyed direct access. So, too, did Spínola. Even if the court clerics, beginning with the king's confessor, Fray Antonio de Sotomayor, tended to be Olivares' creatures, none was immune to external influences, and in particular to lobbying by the papal nuncios, the representatives of a pontiff whose 'extravagant judgments' were, in the eyes of Olivares, the

[76] Hoz, p. 170; ASG, Lettere ministri, Spagna, 2435, despatch, 14 October 1628.
[77] AHN Est. leg. 727, *Voto del Conde mi señor*, 2 June 1629; AGS Est. leg. 2043, fo. 62/1, *Parecer del Conde Duque*, 2 June 1629.
[78] AGS Est. leg. 2043, fo. 61/1, *parecer* of Olivares, 3 June 1629.
[79] AGR SEG, liasse 126, Spínola to Infanta, 6 June 1629.
[80] See especially his replies on the 1629 documents relating to the Dutch truce, in AGS Est. leg. 2043.

source of many of Spain's present misfortunes.[81] Nor was it possible for the Count-Duke, for all his army of informers, to check the flow of subversive pamphlets or ensure that occasional seditious pieces did not fall into the hands of his royal master.

It was in June 1629, when the fate of Flanders and Italy hung in the balance, that one such piece was brought to Philip's notice. At least two hundred copies were alleged to have found their way into circulation[82] of a manifesto against the Count-Duke attributed diversely to the *caballeros de España* and to the head of the Fernández de Córdoba family, the Duke of Sessa, who was said to have given it to the king.[83] *Traidor fuera a su rey*, it began: 'he would be a traitor to his king' who failed to warn him of impending ruin. The king loved the Count of Olivares, his good intentions, his desire to be of service. But against the Count's virtues must be set his 'insatiable ambition to govern', which impelled him to tyrannize over Philip and prevent access by anyone able to tell him the true state of affairs. Olivares was destroying king and country, not by deliberate intent, but through his 'presumption and *errada política*.'

His 'mistaken policies' included attempting to set the world to rights by means of 'imaginary and fantastical machinations', and the appointment of his own men to high office in order to keep himself in power. He was destroying Spain with his futile pragmatics, his ill-timed currency reform, his failure to prevent the loss of the silver fleet after receiving (or so the author alleged) advance notice of the enemy's intentions, and finally the war in Italy, capriciously begun, inadequately planned, and fought 'without troops, without money, without reason.' The result was that the people were oppressed, the princes of Italy disaffected, the pope hostile, and the French victorious.

This indictment of the Count-Duke, at once true and false, justified and grossly unfair, was followed by a powerful personal appeal to the king to restore genuine conciliar government in place of government by one man. Let him imitate his prudent grandfather—now it was the opposition and not the ministry which appealed to the memory of Philip II—and his glorious great-grandfather! 'Your Majesty is not a king, he is a person to whose conservation the Count looks in order to make use of the office of king, and a mere ceremonial ruler.' Grandees and good vassals stood ready to advise Philip. Let him turn to them!

[81] AGS Est. leg. 2713, Olivares to Monterrey, 1 May 1629.

[82] Conde de la Roca, 'Responde a un memorial divulgado contra el Conde Duque', in Ms. volume, *Fragmentos históricos de la Monarchia de España*, fo. 104v. (see Marañón, *Olivares*, bibliography, no. 301).

[83] BL Add. Ms. 6902, fos. 193–4v., dated June 1629; AAE Corresp. Espagne, no. 15, fos. 400–401v. (with Sessa's name). The text is also reproduced by Novoa in *Codoin* 69, pp. 74–6.

Was it by coincidence, or as a direct consequence of this aristocratic manifesto, that Philip displayed in June 1629 the first real signs of wanting to be something more than a 'mere ceremonial ruler'? Over the preceding twelve months there had already been some ominous stirrings, which began with the king's expressed wish to accompany his sister, the Queen of Hungary, to her port of embarkation. In July 1628 the Count-Duke had made clear to the king his disapproval of the whole idea. Travel was dangerous, his presence was essential in Madrid, and if he went to Barcelona and the Catalan Cortes again proved disobliging his prestige would suffer.[84] In spite of this, a royal visit to Barcelona was arranged for January, only to be called off because of lack of money.[85] But a trip to Barcelona was only the beginning of Philip's new-found ambitions. If his brother-in-law, Louis XIII, went victoriously to war, why should not he do the same? During the winter of 1628–9 he was talking about going to Italy at the head of an army,[86] and as he heard the praises of Louis as a warrior-king sung loudly in Madrid,[87] so his determination grew.

In an attempt to hold in check his master's awkward yearnings for glory on the battlefield, Olivares insisted that a military expedition to Italy under royal leadership, which would inevitably be a costly operation, was out of the question until a truce had been agreed in the Netherlands.[88] Now, in June of 1629, a truce was beginning to look possible, although only if Bois-le-Duc were not captured by the Dutch, since its fall was bound to weaken Spain's bargaining position. Agents from Brussels and Madrid had been working feverishly, although without proper co-ordination, to secure the help of a relief force from Germany. Maximilian of Bavaria was unwilling to oblige,[89] but Count Sforza managed to work out an agreement with Wallenstein, under which he would invade the United Provinces from East Friesland in return for a promise of Spanish help the following year in carving himself a principality out of Venetian territory.[90] Unfortunately, however, all this was negotiated without reference to the Emperor, with whom it found no favour.

Ferdinand, who was besought at one moment by Madrid to come to Spain's help in Italy, and the next in Flanders, had concluded that his own interests were best served by intervention in Mantua. By the end of May 15,000 infantrymen and a thousand cavalry had

---

[84] BL Add. Ms. 14,004, fos. 428–30v., draft consulta of Olivares, 6 July 1628.

[85] ASG, Lettere ministri, Spagna, 2434, despatch, 9 December 1628.

[86] AGS Est. leg. 2713, Olivares to Gonzalo de Córdoba, 7 January 1629; ASG, Lettere ministri, Spagna, 2435, despatch, 27 January 1629.

[87] Elliott, *Richelieu and Olivares*, p. 101.

[88] AGS Est. leg. 2713, Olivares to Spínola, 17 August 1629.

[89] Ródenas Vilar, *La política europea*, pp. 204–5.

[90] *Ibid.*, pp. 20–23; Straub, *Pax et Imperium*, p. 385.

negotiated the Grisons passes and were on their way to Milan. Early in June, with the Danish war over, Vienna decided to send a further 20,000 men to Italy.[91] The Emperor was at last doing what Olivares had urged and expected him to do twelve months earlier, by moving to assert the rights of Imperial jurisdiction in the Italian fiefs of the Empire.[92] If he could frighten the French into withdrawing their forces from Italy, he would be in a position to settle the Mantuan affair on his own terms before deploying his armies against Venice, which had sent soldiers to the help of Nevers and was the arch-instigator of anti-Habsburg policies in the eyes of Vienna and Madrid.

In mid-June Vienna appealed to Madrid to collaborate in this 'Venetian enterprise', 'without our having raised the question from this end', according to Olivares,[93] although this hardly seems likely, since the king had written to Aytona early in May saying that the Emperor should make peace with the Danes and war with the Venetians.[94] This appeal from the Emperor for joint action in northern Italy seemed irresistible to Philip, and it brought to a head the differences between him and his favourite which had begun with the disagreement over his expressed desire to escort his sister to Barcelona.

On 17 June Olivares presented the king with a series of questions on major matters of policy, asking Philip to write his answers in the margin.[95] The result is one of the few surviving documents to lift the veil covering the working relations of king and minister, but it is not clear whether the question-and-answer format constituted a normal method of communication between them, or whether the form of the document reflected some sudden new tension in their relationship. There is no doubt that they were seeing less of each other than in the first years of the reign, in part at least because of Olivares' relinquishment of his office of groom of the stole in favour of his son-in-law, Medina de las Torres, in 1626.[96] But in a letter written to the Count of Castro in August of 1629 Olivares complained of the king's incredible obstinacy, and spoke of himself as having been for the past three years 'so withdrawn from his person and from all questions having to do with his pleasure, that I know nothing at all about them. At the most I attend on him a quarter of an hour a day.'[97] Are we really to believe this? Castro was in Vienna as Spain's special envoy to the Emperor, and Olivares had nothing to lose by insisting on his own lack of influence with the

[91] Ródenas Vilar, pp. 189–90.
[92] Bireley, *Religion and Politics*, p. 94.
[93] AGS Est. leg. 2713, Olivares to Monterrey, 27 January 1629.
[94] Ródenas Vilar, p. 187 n. 465.
[95] *MC*, 2, Doc. I.
[96] Above, p. 278.
[97] *MC*, 2, Doc. VIII.

king at a time when relations between Vienna and Madrid were badly strained over Philip's apparent reluctance to let the Queen of Hungary set out on her journey to Austria. But it is perfectly plausible that a king in his early twenties, who was used to being told that he should take into his own hands the reins of government, should have been attempting, however hesitantly, to put some distance between himself and a favourite whose assistance he at once needed and resented.

What, asked Olivares in his memorandum, was Philip's intention as regards Mantua and Montferrat? 'It is my intention', Philip replied in the margin, 'that not a single Frenchman should remain in Italy, and that the affairs of Mantua and Montferrat should be placed in the hands of the Emperor, where they belong. Military means should be used to achieve this if there is no alternative.' Did the king intend to participate in the campaign in Italy proposed by the Emperor? 'I intend this for the coming year, by which time affairs in Flanders should be settled . . .' Did he intend to keep the peace with France, with or without a satisfactory settlement in Italy? 'My intention is to get my revenge on France for its recent behaviour, but I do not know when or how, as I intend first to go on the Venetian campaign . . . But I am determined to do something against the French, who deserve what is coming to them.'

The Count-Duke then turned to the Netherlands. If Bois-le-Duc were relieved, and the enemy should be unwilling to agree to a truce on the terms proposed by Madrid, even in exchange for the restoration of Breda, did the king intend to approve a renewal of the 1609 truce as the Infanta wanted, so as to free all his forces for the war in Italy, and then return later to the war in Flanders, since it was impossible to wage wars on both fronts simultaneously?

> The war in Flanders [the king replied] is one that brings us heavy losses and few gains, and therefore I wish, whatever happens, to reach a settlement with the Dutch . . . I must point out that the Venetian campaign is planned for next year when, God willing, I shall have a successor [the queen was pregnant], and Flanders will be at peace, and there will be two fine armies in Italy, my own and the Emperor's, and I shall be there in person. Fame, after all, cannot be gained without taking personal part in some great enterprise. This one will enhance my reputation, and I gather it should not be too difficult. As I tell you, I want to go in person, and once I have got to Italy with these armies and they have achieved their objective, I shall—with God's help—do what I want with the world. Give thought to it, and do everything possible to bring it about, because I fail to see how I can gain honour

without leaving Spain ... And if you try to tell me that there will be trouble in Spain if its king goes abroad, let me remind you that at the time when trouble was at its worst [Philip was here recalling the revolt of the Comuneros] there was no ruler of royal blood in the country, and no heir to the throne. Now, with God's favour, there will be an heir, and the queen will be there to manage the government. This is no laughing matter. You must take it seriously.

Olivares gave the king one final option, that of peace in both Flanders and Italy, whatever the price. To this Philip replied with a firm refusal: 'to secure a general peace, it is necessary first of all to fight a good and honourable war, in order to secure the best and most suitable outcome.'

The Count-Duke was obviously having to deal with a spoilt young man who had just begun to ask himself why his word should not be law in big things as well as small. Jealous of his French brother-in-law, and carried away by visions of military glory, he saw himself as another Charles V with the world at his feet. Disillusionment would come later. In the meantime, he had spoken, and it was up to his minister to obey. On 3 June the Infanta had sent from Brussels the final offer from the Dutch—a thirty-four or forty-year truce on the same terms as that of 1609, with the question of the Scheldt to be considered by a special commission.[98] The Council of State, meeting on 19 June, swallowed the terms, and the king agreed.[99] The humiliation could be borne if the truce were signed before Bois-le-Duc's resistance gave out, and if it gave him the opportunity to win his laurels in a triumphant campaign against Venice.

Whether the Dutch were willing and able to follow up on this offer remains an open question. It was obviously in Frederick Henry's interest to delay a settlement until he had captured Bois-le-Duc; but even had he been anxious for an immediate settlement, it would have been no easy matter to secure the approval of the individual provinces, some of which were bitterly opposed to any agreement with Spain.[100] But in Madrid at least a firm decision had been taken: the war in the Netherlands was to be wound up, even at the price of dishonour. However unhappy the Count-Duke may have been, he could only bow to his master's will and make the necessary dispositions required by Philip's determination to win his spurs in Italy. On 22 June, which must have been a day of feverish activity for his overworked secretary, Antonio Carnero, he dictated four memor-

---

[98] Lonchay, *Correspondance*, 2, Doc. 1405.
[99] *Ibid.*, Docs. 1415 and 1418; Alcalá-Zamora, *España, Flandes*, p. 307.
[100] Israel, *The Dutch Republic*, pp. 227–8.

anda on the subject.[101] The first and longest of these consisted of a summary of the instructions and despatches which would need to be prepared before the great machine could be set in motion. As he brooded on the details and on the enormous expense, Olivares did not conceal his intense dislike of the whole enterprise. 'This', he ended his memorandum, 'is the over-all plan for this movement, drafted by someone who is totally opposed to it, on the grounds that with eight years of peace and quiet we could do all this and much more without anxiety or difficulty.'[102]

What, then, was entailed? Spínola, who was to take $1\frac{1}{2}$ million ducats with him to Milan, was to base all his actions on the premise that the king had decided in favour of a truce in Flanders on the best available terms, even if this meant no more than a return to the truce of 1609, subject to Bois-le-Duc remaining in Spanish hands. Spain's two envoys at the Imperial court, the Marquis of Aytona and the Count of Castro, were to be told how the Emperor's decision to wage war against the Venetians had persuaded the king to settle with the Dutch on the 1609 terms. In return, the Emperor would be expected to enlist the help of the Imperial electors in the war with Venice, and to organize a large-scale diversion across the frontier into France. The Dukes of Savoy and Lorraine were to be induced to participate with offers of territorial compensation; and Abbot Scaglia, who had arrived in Madrid in January 1629 as the special envoy of the Duke of Savoy, was to go to London to tempt the English with the bait of the Spanish-occupied Rhine Palatinate. Heavy subsidies would be necessary—700,000 ducats a year each for the Dukes of Savoy and Lorraine, and 300,000 for the Huguenot Duke of Rohan. An army of 30,000 in Milan would cost 2 million ducats over the course of a year, and an army of similar size on the Catalan frontier with France another $2\frac{1}{2}$ million.[103]

Even as he drafted his plans, however, the Count-Duke had not despaired of changing the king's mind. One of his memoranda of 22 June attempted to spell out for the king some of the implications of his decision to leave home in pursuit of foreign glory. As far as costs were concerned, Philip would need at least $1\frac{1}{2}$ million ducats for household expenses if the court were transferred to Italy, over and above the 2 million needed for his army, and he would have to think in terms of a grand total of 15 million ducats over a two-year period. He needed to reflect, too, on the hazards of war, and the risk of losing everything. If the queen remained behind as regent, she would need wise heads to advise her, and where were these to

[101] MC, 2, Docs. II, III, V, VI.
[102] Ibid., p. 31.
[103] AHN Est. lib. 869, fos. 177–8v. List of expenses drawn up by Olivares.

be found? And how was a regency government to extract more cash from an exhausted country, without the risk of another revolt of the Comuneros? Nor could Naples, Milan and Sicily be expected to help—they, too, were exhausted. It was well enough for kings to leave Spain in time of peace to visit their other dominions, but this was a different matter.[104]

There was, however, a possible alternative—one that was still difficult, but at least manageable. This was for the king to go to Barcelona, conclude the Catalan Cortes, and build up an army on the Catalan frontier, which would be the obvious target for a French attack. Then the Spanish army under the royal command would strike against France, opening the way to an honourable and reasonable peace settlement between the two monarchs. When the French were thus suitably 'mortified', Philip could then pay a month's visit to Italy to review the army of Milan.

Olivares seems to have felt that in this scheme for a diversion against France from Catalonia he had hit on a plausible substitute for the wild projects of the king, and he accompanied it with a more detailed plan of action.[105] If the king really wanted to take his revenge against Louis XIII he must make careful preparations. This was not a matter for 'anger and precipitation, but for mature wisdom and constancy, and for extreme caution in not spending a single *real* unnecessarily.' Assuming that the plans for war against Venice went ahead, with the Emperor providing the bulk of the troops, the Count-Duke proposed the following timetable. The fortresses along the Catalan frontier should be strengthened during the course of the next few months. The Queen of Hungary should leave Madrid at the beginning of September on her journey to Vienna, while the king remained at court until his wife gave birth to the long-awaited heir. Then, in late October or early November, he should set off for Barcelona, securing promises of military assistance along the way in Aragon and Valencia. In Catalonia he would get the Cortes to vote the subsidy, and would raise the standards throughout the Crown of Aragon. Assisted by the Mediterranean galley fleet, he could then think about advancing into France if the moment seemed opportune. In order to make the idea more attractive, the Count-Duke thoughtfully enclosed a similar scheme, perhaps from his own archive, which the Prior Don Hernando de Toledo had drawn up for Philip II in 1572.[106] As the king would see, even this project was fraught with difficulties, but at least it was not 'utterly impossible and impracticable' like the one which His Majesty proposed.

---

[104] *MC*, 2, Doc. III.
[105] *MC*, 2, Doc. V.
[106] AHN Est. lib. 869, fos. 197–9v.

Overwhelmed by this bombardment from the Count-Duke's heavy artillery, Philip's defences collapsed. He replied that he was not for the time being contemplating a journey to Italy. His present intention was to launch in person an invasion of France from Catalonia in the coming year, in order to undo what the French had done in Italy. For this he had in mind an army of some 30,000 infantrymen and 5,000 cavalry. He also expected the Emperor and the Dukes of Savoy and Lorraine to attack France simultaneously. Only one of the Count-Duke's proposals did he reject out of hand. Nothing would stop him from accompanying his sister to her port of embarkation.[107]

The king's bid to assert his independence was over almost before it had begun. The strain may have been too much for him. On 29 June the first signs of a tertian fever appeared,[108] and for two weeks he was ill, although not too ill to listen in bed while Olivares lectured the papal nuncio and the Venetian ambassador on the overwhelming power of the combined forces of Spain and the Empire.[109]

The Count-Duke followed up his advantage with a further memorandum to the king on 21 July, which took the form of a disquisition on the problems of governing Castile even when the king was present.[110] Where in these times were good ministers to be found—men with the authority conferred by birth or experience, who possessed the intelligence and the capacity to serve the king well? As he examined the important offices of state and the men who might be called upon to fill them, he found the pool of talent sadly diminished. Since he used numbers rather than names, and the king alone had the key to the cypher, his assessments of his colleagues unfortunately remain obscure; but he was probably referring to Cardinal Trejo when he wrote that it was no longer possible to dissimulate with number 1 and that, if the king were to leave Madrid, it would be essential to remove him from office.

There was nothing obscure, however, about his views on the likely consequences of a royal journey which removed the king from his capital. Castile at present was in such a state that, so far from leaving it, the king should be prepared to travel all the way from China to set things right. The Count-Duke's summary of the condition of Castile in 1629 was so remote from the rosy survey which he had prepared for the king to deliver to his councillors in 1627[111] that

[107] *MC*, 2, pp. 41–2.
[108] AGS Est. leg. 2713, Olivares to Monterrey, 3 July 1629.
[109] ASG Lettere ministri, Spagna, 2435, despatch, 14 July 1629.
[110] AHN Est. lib. 869, fos. 91–102, *Papel del Conde Duque escrito en cifra tocante al gobierno.* The document is summarized in *MC*, 2, pp. 12–13.
[111] Above, p. 315.

he might have been describing a different kingdom. There were, he said, three outstanding problems, any one of which was capable of utterly destroying Castile. The administration of justice was in a terrible state—no action was ever taken against men of influence and position, and public sins went virtually unpunished. The condition of the currency was rather better than it had been, but everything would go to wrack and ruin if *vellón* were not phased out in favour of silver. As for business and trade, they were largely in ruins. All these problems were ones which could only be effectively tackled if the king were personally present. They were too serious to be left in the hands of ministers—all of them men of boundless ambition. It was the ambition, the greed and self-interest of ministers which were destroying the country. What better proof of this than the calculated and successful attempt to frustrate the fiscal reforms which would have brought some relief to the poor?

Even if, as Olivares conceded, there were some good ministers and officials in the Castile of the 1620's, he was no doubt correct in assuming that their number was limited. In a society where connections and influence were overwhelmingly important, disinterested service was not an ideal that was easily instilled. Olivares himself came closer to practising it than most, in part because the death of his daughter had deprived him of the prime incentive for family aggrandisement. But while this made it easier for him to identify himself with what he presumed to be the royal interest, it left him vulnerable to the more subtle temptation to assume that his own enemies were also the enemies of the king.

He was no doubt sincere in his conviction that for the king to go campaigning like Louis XIII could lead only to disappointment and perhaps to disaster. Any such enterprise was bound to be expensive, and it entailed obvious risks both to the king's reputation and to his health. But did he really believe that Castile would revolt almost as soon as the king's back was turned? Did he believe, too, that there were simply no ministers of sufficient stature to run the government while he and the king were away from Madrid? He was certainly persuaded of his own indispensability for the effective working of the governmental machine. He was also afraid, and not without reason, that his enemies would take advantage of his absence to strengthen their forces and present the king on his return with a demand for his dismissal that would prove impossible to resist.

Olivares' complaints about the scarcity of experienced ministers for a regency government were not entirely groundless. Over the past few years death had been thinning the ranks of the last generation to have served under Philip II. Of the prominent figures in the Council of State in the opening years of the reign, few now remained.

Gondomar and Don Diego de Ibarra had died in 1626,[112] and Don Pedro de Toledo, Marquis of Villafranca, that peppery veteran of so many campaigns, in 1627. The following year had seen the death in February of the Count-Duke's confidant, the Marquis of La Hinojosa, and in October of one of his more ambitious and clever rivals, the Marquis of Montesclaros, at the age of fifty-seven. While the Count-Duke had never really trusted Montesclaros, his long years of service in the American viceroyalties made him the kind of experienced councillor who spoke with authority on matters of state, and he possessed a global view of Spain's reputation and interests which made him a useful colleague when it was necessary to stiffen the resolution of the more pusillanimous councillors. Don Agustín Mexía, one of the council's Flanders veterans, and an advocate of a new truce with the Dutch, died on 11 March 1629.[113] His fellow-veteran, the Marquis of Gelves, survived until 1636, but he was already eighty, although a sufficiently young eighty to take a new wife.[114]

But it was not only death that depleted the Council of State. The Count-Duke might expatiate on the urgency of the need for great councillors and ministers, but he did not exactly encourage the presence of men of stature in his own proximity. Early in June 1629 the Genoese ambassador noted how the Council of State had been reduced to impotence.[115] Don Fernando Girón, always so defeatist when Flanders was discussed, had been honourably retired, and the outspoken Duke of Feria, who had seen eye to eye with the Count-Duke on Flanders before succumbing to Spínola's blandishments, had left for Catalonia at the end of May to take up his new post of viceroy. Spínola himself, the source of so much trouble to Olivares, was constantly being urged to pack his bags for Italy, and failed, in spite of all his wiles, to defer his departure beyond the month of July. Three of the remaining lay councillors, Leganés, the Marquis of Floresdávila and Don Juan Villela, were all, according to the Genoese envoy, mere spokesmen for Olivares. Of the two clerics, Sotomayor, the king's confessor, was the Count-Duke's tool, while the Inquisitor-General, Cardinal Zapata, who was now in his late seventies, rarely attended meetings. This left only two councillors prepared to speak their minds when the occasion demanded—the octogenarian Gelves, and the Count of Lemos. The latter, increasingly disillusioned with the world, turned his back on the court in September and became a Benedictine monk.[116]

---

[112] Sálazar y Castro, *Advertencias históricas*, pp. 227–37, for the date of death of these and other councillors of state appointed by Philip IV.

[113] *Ibid.*, p. 226.

[114] ASV, Spagna 69, fo. 128v., nuncio, 13 June 1629.

[115] ASG Lettere ministri, Spagna, 2435, despatch of 2 June 1629.

[116] ASG Lettere ministri, Spagna, 2435, despatch of 18 September 1629.

By the summer of 1629, therefore, Olivares had succeeded in acquiring a degree of personal control over the Council of State which made it a considerably less impressive and independent-minded body than it had been in the days of Feria, Montesclaros and Girón. It was generally assumed that the Count-Duke was anxious to remove potential rivals from Madrid at the earliest opportunity, but Spínola, Feria and Girón were all soldiers, and he could argue with some justification that they were more valuable serving the king in military commands than in the council chamber. But the effect of his policy was to leave himself as a giant surrounded by pygmies. If he then complained that there was no one capable of running the country if he accompanied the king to Italy, his own suspicious nature was at least partly to blame.

As a device for deterring Philip from leaving his capital, his argument proved less effective than he had hoped. Philip may have agreed under pressure to substitute the Pyrenees frontier for Italy as the setting for the next major campaign, but he was not prepared to abandon his military ambitions to please the Count-Duke. Nor, to Olivares' anguish, could he be shaken in his determination to accompany the Queen of Hungary at least to the coast. Noting the high deathrate among the Jesuits who travelled from Madrid to their house in Cartagena during the hot summer months, the Count-Duke lamented the folly of his royal master.[117] But he had never, he wrote to the Count of Castro, known anyone so set on having his own way as the king. The only concession Philip would make when warned of the risk to his life was to agree to postpone the journey from September to December.[118]

The king's obstinacy over his sister's journey promptly became a major political embarrassment to Olivares. It was not simply that he found himself seriously crossed by his sovereign for the first time since he had come to power. It also placed him in an extremely awkward position as he attempted to navigate the shoals of Madrid's always treacherous relationship with Vienna. The continuing postponement on one pretext or another of the Queen of Hungary's journey to join her new husband was beginning to exasperate the Imperial court. The Emperor was even reported to be threatening war if the Queen of Hungary was not despatched forthwith. It was, as Olivares commented, the most extraordinary affair that had ever been heard of;[119] and it could not have come at a more inopportune time. Quite apart from the problem of the Queen of Hungary, relations with Vienna had never been more delicate or more critical than in the

---

[117] ADM, leg. 79, Olivares to Aytona, 9 August 1629.
[118] MC, 2, p. 48 (Olivares to Castro, 13 August 1629).
[119] ADM, leg. 79, Olivares to Aytona, 12 August 1629.

summer of 1629. The first news of the descent of Imperial troops into Italy had been received with rapture in Madrid.[120] But there was growing preoccupation at court over the fate of Bois-le-Duc, and it was not long, as Olivares had feared, before the Emperor's action had a decisive impact on the war in the Netherlands. On 6 August the king was congratulating himself and the Infanta on the fact that his emissary, Court Sforza, had reached an agreement with Wallenstein for the despatch of part of his army to Friesland.[121] A week later the Infanta was writing to Philip to say that the Emperor had revoked Wallenstein's orders.[122]

The Count-Duke believed that Ferdinand's precipitate decision was likely to damage irreparably the chances both of relieving Bois-le-Duc and of reaching a settlement with the Dutch.[123] His continuing inability to coordinate the policies of Vienna and Madrid, and to bring into existence a 'universal league' between Spain, the Emperor and the German electors,[124] was a source of continuous disappointment and frustration. If only their forces would once close ranks, no power in Europe would be able to resist them. Now, in August 1629, the possibilities of success were once again being wrecked by confusion, malice, and sheer misunderstanding.

Amidst the confusion, the king was showing signs of unprecedented activity. He had created a special 'junta for the secret matter' to handle the arrangements for his Italian campaign, and the extent of his displeasure with the Count-Duke is suggested by the fact that he was not appointed to it. But finally, on the evening of 16 August, Olivares was invited to attend a special session.[125] At the end of the five hours of deliberations, to which the king and the Infantes listened from behind a private window into the council chamber, it was agreed that Olivares and the Count of Oñate should both draft papers. The following morning, however, as Olivares settled down to write, he was brought three pages written by the king in his own hand, which summarized the preceding day's discussions and concluded with the king's decision and his orders for action.

No doubt it gave Philip special satisfaction to have proved to the Count-Duke his ability to produce by himself a state document so well drafted that it could be passed at once to the secretariat without need for emendation. Olivares, for his part, expressed in letters to Spínola and Monterrey his astonishment and his admiration for the

[120] ASV, Spagna 69, fo. 129v., nuncio, 30 June 1629.
[121] Lonchay, *Correspondance*, 2, Doc. 1450, king to Infanta, 6 August 1629.
[122] *Ibid.*, Doc. 1453, Infanta to king, 14 August 1629.
[123] AGS Est. leg. 2713, Olivares to Spínola, 17 August 1629.
[124] Ródenas Vilar, *La política europea*, p. 205.
[125] AGS Est. leg. 2713, Olivares to Spínola, 17 August 1629, and further details in his letter of the same date to Monterrey.

king's remarkable intellectual feat. Not one of his predecessors since Ferdinand the Catholic would have been capable of drafting such a document without help, or so at least the Count-Duke thought. Indeed, it was doubtful if any king in the history of Castile could have produced anything comparable, at least without days of cogitation and hard work. In recounting the episode to Monterrey, the Count-Duke confided that over the past eight months the king had been sending him memoranda that were his own unaided work, and that only the other day he had been transacting business with the secretary of the French embassy without the Count-Duke knowing anything about it, and without having the benefit of a *consulta* to guide him. All of this suggested to Olivares that his services were no longer needed, and that he would at last be free to retire and nurse his shattered health in solitude . . .

So Olivares had realized his ambition of turning Philip IV into a royal bureaucrat on the model of Philip II. It was an alarming moment. It failed, however, to lead to any momentous change. Philip's newly-acquired taste for paperwork was to prove enduring, but Spain's massive bureaucracy could handle the working and the non-working monarch alike. For the next few months Philip would continue to show signs of the impulsiveness which had so disturbed the Count-Duke in the summer, but there was to be no open break between king and minister, and their disagreements were no more than passing storm-clouds. The Count-Duke's enemies, like those of Richelieu at the same moment, continued to live in hope and expectation that the king would open his eyes; and in January 1630, a few months before France's Day of the Dupes, Spain would have its own minor version of that fateful day.[126] But Philip knew his need of Olivares, just as Louis XIII knew his need of Richelieu. Here at least was a minister of proven integrity and ability, devoted to his service. Who could be called upon to replace him if he were dismissed? The Duke of Sessa and his friends wanted the king to govern by himself, with a consortium of councillors to advise. But Philip, for all his desire to cut a figure in the world, was intelligent enough to realize that it was one thing to draft a document without assistance, and quite another to take upon his own shoulders the crushing burden of government.

Flanders and Italy

Even if the king felt stirrings of independence, the summer of 1629 was hardly the best moment to dispense with the services of his

[126] Below, p. 395, and see Elliott, *Richelieu and Olivares*, ch. 4.

principal minister. The Monarchy was at war simultaneously on several fronts, and even if things had not been going well there was an obvious need for a strong central direction of the war effort. The Count-Duke had shown an undoubted capacity for keeping in motion Spain's cumbersome war machine, and he was perennially fertile in ideas and policies. In the spring of 1629 he might, as he confessed, have lost his aids to navigation, but by August he had made some progress in recharting the course.

In Italy, he hoped that Spínola, with the benefit of additional funds and his own immense prestige, would quickly be able to negotiate an honourable settlement leading to the withdrawal of the French. But Olivares was aware that the chances of a speedy settlement had, if anything, been complicated by the influx of so many Imperial troops. He had asked the Emperor for modest military assistance—some 12,000 men—largely as a symbol of solidarity in the question of the Mantuan succession. Instead, it looked as though some 70,000 men were in process of descending on the Italian peninsula, where the Emperor hoped to billet them at the expense of his Spanish nephew and the local population.[127]

In the Netherlands, as the Count-Duke told Spínola, he now supported measures to secure the truce he had 'for so long abominated', since the king had made his decision and there was no more to be said. But now that the Emperor had chosen to commit Wallenstein's army to the Italian front instead of the Dutch, he was sceptical of success.[128] The best remaining hope was that the Emperor, having made the terrible mistake of cancelling the orders for Wallenstein's forces to move into Friesland, might be induced to threaten the United Provinces with a declaration of war if they refused to agree to a truce.[129] If he did this, and a truce was achieved, then the proposed Venetian campaign of king and Emperor might become a practical possibility in the spring of 1630.

The Count-Duke's hopes at this moment were more fragile than his fears, and the events of the autumn of 1629 were to justify his pessimism. Since Nevers showed no inclination to accept a settlement, the Imperial army set about invading and ravaging his Duchy of Mantua, while Spínola reluctantly committed his troops—and his prestige—to a second siege of Casale. But it was in the Netherlands, as the Count-Duke had always feared, that the strain imposed by war on two fronts became suddenly unbearable. Spínola's commanding presence had never been more necessary than during that long summer of 1629 when the noose was being tightened around Bois-le-Duc.

---

[127] BL Add. Ms. 14,004, fo. 445 (Instructions for Queen of Hungary, December 1629).
[128] AGS Est. leg. 2713, Olivares to Spínola, 27 August 1629.
[129] ADM, leg. 79, Olivares to Aytona, 2 September 1629.

Count Henry van den Bergh proved a disastrous substitute as commander of the army of Flanders, and in organizing a spectacular but
useless diversion across the Ijssel into Dutch territory, allowed the
vital garrison town of Wesel, at the junction of the Rhine and the
Lippe, to fall to a surprise enemy attack.[130] The inexcusable loss of
Wesel on 19 August, and the imminent loss of Bois-le-Duc which
finally capitulated to Frederick Henry on 14 September, shattered
the fragile morale of the Spanish Netherlands. The smell of defeat
was in the air, and with it the smell of treachery. Already before
the fall of Bois-le-Duc it had been scented by the sensitive nose of
Cardinal de la Cueva, who, as the former Marquis of Bedmar of
the Venetian Conspiracy, was no novice when it came to plots. In
early September he wrote from Brussels to warn Madrid that there
was a danger of rebellion, and that the Infanta's government had
virtually collapsed.[131]

The despatches from Brussels reached Madrid on 22 September,
and so disturbed the king that he prepared on his own initiative a
lengthy statement for the Council of Castile, which he first sent in
draft to the Count-Duke with a covering note to the effect that the
cause of the recent disasters was 'your and my sins'.[132] The royal
statement, as the Count-Duke observed, was notable for its 'piety
and resignation'.[133] Large monarchies, Philip observed, were bound
to suffer setbacks and reverses, in the nature of things. But when
they multiplied, as was happening now, it was a clear sign of divine
punishment for public sins. 'I consider that God is angry with me
and my kingdoms for our sins.' The only way to placate His wrath
was for the Council of Castile to remind itself of its obligations and
make sure that justice was better administered and sinners punished.

Philip had obviously taken to heart the Count-Duke's observations
about the state of justice and morality in Castile.[134] He and his minister
took for granted the equation between national immorality and national
disaster, and both men felt a special degree of responsibility by virtue
of their exalted positions. Philip at least had good cause for self-
reproach. Private sins when committed by the vicegerent of the
Lord had a way of leading to public disasters; and as the disasters
accumulated over the years, so too did the self-recrimination and
guilt. Both king and minister came to feel with special intensity the

---

[130] Alcalá-Zamora, *España, Flandes*, p. 288; Israel, *The Dutch Republic*, pp. 176–9.
[131] Lonchay, *Correspondance*, 2, Doc. 1471, La Cueva to king, 9 September 1629.
[132] AHN Est lib. 857, fos. 180–3v. *Papel que escribió SM al consejo real . . . 1629.* Although
this bears no date, Olivares, in his letter of 25 September to Monterrey, writes of having
received it that morning.
[133] AGS Est. leg. 2713, Olivares to Monterrey, 25 September 1629.
[134] Above, p. 382.

burden of guilt that weighed upon them—a burden that no amount
of confession, penance and absolution could ever lift.

If private and public regeneration could alone turn back the anger
of the Lord, this did not preclude the resort to more mundane measures to confront the impending catastrophe, although Olivares
expressed deep discouragement over the fact that every remedial measure seemed to produce the exact reverse of what was intended, so
great, it seemed, was the wrath of God.[135] Of the imminence of
catastrophe he had no doubt. Catholicism in northern Europe he
now regarded as 'utterly lost'. It would not take much for France
to abandon the faith; and if the southern Netherlands fell into the
hands of the Dutch, they would soon be the masters of 'India and
the Empire'. He foresaw a new persecution of the church and 'the
total ruin of our religion'—all because the French had lent their support to the heretics, aided and abetted by a pope who put temporal
interests ahead of those of the faith.[136]

Nothing, perhaps, could prevent a mutiny in the army of Flanders
and a 'general revolution' in the southern Netherlands, but he examined in turn for the benefit of the king the various possible lines
of action.[137] One possibility, which Philip himself may well have
raised, was a royal visit to Flanders. But this required much preparation and the time was not ripe. A more feasible alternative would
be to send one of the Infantes—but would His Majesty be prepared
to see one of his brothers become a soldier before himself? Another
possibility was to press for a settlement with the United Provinces
'at any price'; but this would have to be done without repeating
the mistake made during the past eighteen months of assuming that
success was just round the corner, and so letting the army be lulled
into a false sense of security with disastrous results. Alternatively,
Spain should try to reach a settlement in Italy, again at any price,
thus allowing for transfer of Spínola to Flanders with a large contingent of his Italian army. This decision had already been made
in principle, but the chances of its taking effect were jeopardized
by the descent of the Imperial forces into the north Italian plain.
Failing Spínola, Flanders needed a soldier who was also a member
of the Council of State; but, as Olivares wrote, 'we have so few
from whom to choose', and he even speculated whether Gonzalo
de Córdoba, for all his hatred of the war in Flanders, could be induced
to accept the job. As for the civil administration, it had already been
decided that the Marquis of Aytona should be moved from the

[135] AHN Est. leg. 727, *Voto del Conde mi señor sobre cosas de Flandes* (undated), beginning
'Este correo de Flandes . . .'
[136] Olivares to Monterrey, 25 September 1629.
[137] *Voto del Conde mi señor . . .*

D. A. Van Dyck Eques Pinxit.
Vorsterman sculpsit.

EXCELL.^{MVS} D. FRANCISCVS DE MONCADA, MARCHIO AYTONÆ, COMES OSSONÆ, VICE-
COMES CABRERÆ ET BAAS, MAGNVS SENESCALCVS REGNI ARRAGONIÆ, PHILIPPO IV.
HISPANIAR. INDIARVMQ. REGI A CONSILIIS STATVS, EIVSDEMQ. LEGATVS EXTRAORDIN. ET
SVPREMVS MILITIÆ TERRA MARIQ. IN BELGIO PRÆFECTVS.

21. Don Francisco de Moncada, Marquis of Aytona, shown here in an engraving
after Van Dyck. Aytona moved from Vienna to Brussels in 1629 to become
ambassador at the court of the Infanta Isabella, and was the dominant figure
in the administration of the Spanish Netherlands until his death in 1635. The
Count-Duke, who had great respect for his abilities, maintained a long and important correspondence with him.

embassy in Vienna and proceed at once to Brussels, while Cardinal de la Cueva should be transferred to Rome (Pl. 21). Aytona's presence in the Spanish Netherlands had come to seem essential. The Count-Duke was now convinced that maladministration was at the root of the trouble in Flanders. Corruption, confusion and self-interest had undermined the government, sapped the determination of the army, and led to a squandering of the resources which Spain had lavished on Flanders at such cost to itself.[138]

While offering Philip a series of choices, the Count-Duke recognized that the fundamental choice lay between Flanders and Italy. It was out of the question, he wrote to Spínola, for the king to bear the brunt of supporting the Imperial army in Italy, and simultaneously to fight the Dutch, the French and the Venetians, all on different fronts.[139] His own inclinations were for peace in Italy and war in the Netherlands, but as long as it remained royal policy to seek a truce with the Dutch, he was prepared to abide by it.[140] But he knew perfectly well that events themselves were dictating the choice. The chances of a truce with the Dutch had dwindled to nothing and there was no alternative to continuing the war in the north. But the war, too, looked hopeless. Only intervention by the Emperor and the Catholic League could now save Flanders from being overrun by the Dutch.[141]

To secure that intervention he would pay almost any price, including the evacuation by Spanish troops of the Rhine Palatinate, and its transfer to Bavaria and the Catholic League in exchange for any territory taken by League forces when they moved into Dutch West Friesland.[142] Such was the danger from the United Provinces that it was essential, even if it involved enlisting the help of England and France, to dismantle that 'cuerpo infernal' which so obstinately aims at the Monarchy's ruin.' Was this the rhetoric of crisis, or did it reflect a clear perception that there would be no place for Spain in a world which danced to the tune of the Dutch?

The prospect of a total collapse of the loyal provinces of the southern Netherlands provoked a mood of crisis in Madrid which lasted all through October 1629. The king himself was deeply concerned, and anxious to play his part in stemming the tide of disaster. God, it

---

[138] AHN Est. leg. 727, *Voto del Conde mi señor* . . . (undated), beginning 'Aunque se entró . . .'

[139] AGS Est. leg. 2713, Olivares to Spínola, 1 October 1629.

[140] AGS Est. leg. 2713, Olivares to Spínola, 29 September 1629.

[141] ADM, leg. 79, Olivares to Aytona, 27 September 1629.

[142] AHN Est. leg. 2043, *Parecer del Conde Duque*, 18 October 1629. For the Palatinate proposal, already broached to Maximilian of Bavaria in the summer, see Ródenas Vilar, *La política europea*, pp. 199–200, Straub, *Pax et Imperium*, p. 387, and Albrecht, *Die auswärtige Politik*, p. 239.

seemed, approved his intention, for on 17 October the queen at last bore him a son and heir. The birth of prince Baltasar Carlos, celebrated with a Te Deum in the royal chapel and with fireworks and bonfires in the streets of Madrid, seemed—at least to the king—to remove one of the principal objections to his leaving Castile. With the succession assured, why should he not go to Flanders in person?

Philip's decision created a flurry of activity at court and considerable alarm in the Council of State.[143] On Saturday 27 October he summoned the presidents of the ten councils into his presence to inform them of his plan. First of all he would accompany his sister to the coast in the first week of December. In the meantime, all the councillors, individually and collectively in their respective councils, were to suggest ways of raising money to finance a possible royal visit to Flanders.[144] It was assumed that he would undertake this journey soon after his return from Barcelona where he hoped to conclude the Catalan Cortes. This part of the scheme, however, had to be abandoned almost at once. The news of the king's intended visit to Barcelona upset the exchange rates between silver and *vellón*, and it was decided to postpone the trip rather than run the risk of putting undue pressure on the Catalan Cortes to reach a speedy conclusion.[145] Instead, the king would accompany his sister to Cartagena, where, unlike Barcelona, court expenses could be paid in *vellón* rather than in silver.[146]

For Olivares the king's determination to go to Cartagena was bad enough, but his decision to visit Flanders was a disaster. It would be 'the ruin of everything, both here and there.' It all sprang, Olivares confided to Spínola, from the suggestion that one of the Infantes should join their aunt in Brussels, to be apprenticed in the art of government.[147] The thought that one or other of his brothers might actually have a chance to go on campaign before him filled the king with jealousy, and he seemed to think that no king of Castile had won glory without leaving the country. 'Although we try to remind him of the Catholic Kings, the Fernandos and Alfonsos, he replies that they had no Flanders.' Oh for peace this winter, so that the king could calm down and withdraw to the Escorial or one of his country estates and try to save money! Once this was achieved, Olivares could present him with proposals that would make him the most glorious king in the history of Spain.

[143] AGS Est. leg. 2043, consulta, 27 October 1629.

[144] AHN Est. leg. 727, *Orden de SM sobre su ida a Flandes*; ASG, Lettere ministri, Spagna, 2435, despatch, 29 October 1629.

[145] AGS Est. leg. 2713, Olivares to Spínola, 30 October 1629.

[146] ASG, Lettere ministri, Spagna, 2435, despatch, 14 November 1629.

[147] Olivares to Spínola, 30 October 1629. Similar sentiments are expressed in his letter to Monterrey of the same date, in AGS Est. leg. 2713.

Philip, however, remained adamant, and the preparations went ahead. Whatever happened, there was no possibility, as Olivares recognized, of the king being able to leave for Flanders before September or October 1630[148]—there was too much to be arranged, and the journey was out of the question until the treasure fleets arrived. But the Queen of Hungary's departure was close at hand, and he reluctantly wrestled with the problem of selecting the ministers who were to accompany the king, and those who were to stay behind in Madrid.[149] It was a difficult task, not least because the Council of State was now such a depleted body, and in the end he settled for the Count of Oñate and the Marquis of Gelves to accompany the king, although travelling expenses would have to be found for both of them, and he did not know where to turn. He also suggested the inclusion in the royal party his relative, Don García de Haro, the brother of the Marquis of Carpio, and the uncle of Don Luis de Haro.[150] The Count-Duke already had his eye on him for promotion to the Council of State, on the grounds that good men were in such short supply that it was necessary to select and train promising ones, even if it meant drawing them from the ranks of university-trained lawyers—the *togados*—rather than from the high nobility.

To remain in Madrid he proposed Cardinal Zapata and Don Juan de Villela, but Villela had been incapacitated by illness for most of the year, and he died on 3 January—his death accelerated by the burden of work as superintendent of the secretariat, a post in which he had never been happy.[151] The lack of experienced ministers who could be trusted to hold the fort in Madrid during the king's absence was clearly a source of deep concern to Olivares. In particular he worried about the President of the Council of Castile, Cardinal Trejo, who seemed singularly unwilling or unable to persuade his colleagues on the council to attend to the reform of administration and to carry out orders.[152] He had probably been contemplating for some time the possibility of ridding himself of Trejo by sending him to his diocese of Málaga, and the king's impending departure hastened the day of decision. Trejo apparently attempted to fight back, and gave the king in private a graphic account of the condition of his realms;[153] but on 24 November he found himself no longer president,[154] and

[148] Olivares to Monterrey, 30 October 1629.
[149] BL Add. Ms. 14,004, fos. 454–5v., *El Conde mi señor sobre las personas que han de ir a la jornada*, 18 November 1629.
[150] Above, p. 140.
[151] ASG, Lettere ministri, Spagna, 2434, despatch, 4 January 1630.
[152] AGS Est. leg. 2713, Olivares to Monterrey, 17 August 1629.
[153] Novoa, *Codoin* 69, p. 95.
[154] ASG, Lettere ministri, Spagna, 2435, despatch, 26 November 1629. The cessation of office is dated 24 November in Francisco Xavier de Garma y Durán, *Teatro universal de España* (Barcelona, 1751), 4, p. 262.

he died a few weeks later on the road to Málaga. His successor was an Aragonese, Miguel Santos de San Pedro, bishop of Solsona, and a former interim viceroy of Catalonia—a 'good man' admitted Novoa grudgingly, 'and a good Christian, but not for the pomp, and vanity—or rather, majesty—of that office.'[155]

While making his dispositions, the Count-Duke still hoped against hope that he could change the king's mind, and eagerly seized on each new argument that came to hand. Sir Francis Cottington was reported to be on his way from London as a special ambassador from Charles I to negotiate the long-awaited Anglo-Spanish peace treaty, and was expected to arrive in Madrid at a moment when Philip would already be on the road. Olivares argued that it would be extremely awkward if both the king and his principal minister—the only senior minister to know Cottington personally—were away from the capital just at this time. Delicacy forbade an invitation to Cottington to join the royal party, when its purpose was to accompany the former bride of the Prince of Wales on her wedding journey.[156]

But Philip refused to say his farewells to his sister in Madrid, and eventually it was settled that he should accompany her on at least the opening stage of her journey, while the Count-Duke remained in the capital. Escorted by her three brothers the Queen of Hungary left Madrid on 26 December.[157] She took as her confessor Father Diego de Quiroga, the head of the Capuchin province of Castile, who knew his way around the courts of Madrid and Vienna. By planting him at the very centre of the Imperial court, Olivares clearly hoped that he would be able to neutralize the pernicious influence of the Emperor's Jesuit confessor Lamormaini, whose enthusiastic advocacy of the extreme Catholic policies associated with the Edict of Restitution, and of friendship between the Empire and France, had so exasperated Madrid; and he also saw in Quiroga a potentially useful intermediary for negotiations with Wallenstein and Maximilian of Bavaria, a ruler notorious for his predilection for the Capuchins.[158]

The Count-Duke gave Quiroga as he began his journey what he euphemistically called a 'short paper' of instructions, in which he insisted on the interdependence of Spain and the Empire, since the

[155] Novoa, *Codoin* 69, p. 96.

[156] BL Add. Ms. 14,004, fos. 439–40v., Olivares to king, 18 November 1629.

[157] See the accounts of her departure by Juan Beltrán and Pedro de Robles in *Relaciones de actos públicos celebrados en Madrid (1541–1650)*, ed. José Simón Díaz (Madrid, 1982), pp. 393–5. See also Enriqueta Harris and John Elliott, 'Velázquez and the Queen of Hungary', *Burlington Magazine*, 118 (1976), pp. 24–6. The king's instructions for his sister are to be found in BL Add. Ms. 14,007, fos. 442–51.

[158] Bireley, *Religion and Politics*, pp. 160–1; Albrecht, *Die auswärtige Politik*, pp. 21–3. See also the entry under Quiroga in vol. 3 of the *Diccionario de historia eclesiástica de España*.

'decline' of one would infallibly lead to the ruin of the other. But there were constant misunderstandings between them, which he believed could only be averted by the conclusion of an offensive and defensive alliance. Negotiation by threats—of which there had been far too many in the complex bargaining that had accompanied the marriage and travel arrangements for the Queen of Hungary—was no way for friends to proceed. But above all Olivares was exasperated by the behaviour of the Catholic League, which in his opinion had become a serious threat to the Emperor's authority, thanks to the machinations of Maximilian of Bavaria. It was the Catholic League which, by insisting on neutrality in the face of heresy and rebellion, had made possible the Dutch capture of Wesel and Bois-le-Duc. Allies were needed who would be allies in practice as well as in name. 'The plain fact is', he told Quiroga, 'that we cannot bear any longer the burden of so many enemies without effective and substantial help from our friends.'[159]

The Count-Duke—once again ill and in low spirits and yearning for retirement, if his confidential letter to Quiroga is to be trusted— saw in the Queen of Hungary an instrument for strengthening the traditional relationship between the two branches of the House of Austria which time and misunderstanding had frayed. That was why he had worked so hard to bring about the marriage, although he felt badly used by all parties for his pains. But the Queen of Hungary seemed fated to bring him nothing but trouble, from the moment of her belated departure from court until the moment when, after endless delays along the route, she joined her husband in Vienna.

After stopping at Alcalá de Henares, where it was originally thought that the king and his two brothers would take leave of their sister, the royal party continued to Guadalajara. It was expected that the king and the Infantes would now say their farewells, but the Queen of Hungary was visibly distressed, and, instead of turning round at this point, the king gave orders for the whole party to go on to the border of Aragon. Here again he was expected to take his leave, but instead, to everybody's surprise, he ordered the party to proceed to Zaragoza. It was, wrote Matías de Novoa gloatingly, the first occasion on which Philip had ever deceived his favourite,[160] and the news caused intense excitement both inside and outside Spain.

The royal party arrived in Zaragoza on 7 January. The viceroy of Aragon was Don Fernando de Borja, who was thought to have had too much influence with Philip in the days when he was still heir to the throne, and had been despatched to Zaragoza after the

---

[159] BL Add. Ms. 24,909, fos. 136–41v., Olivares to Quiroga, 31 December 1629. A large part of this volume consists of Olivares' correspondence with Quiroga, much of it in cypher.
[160] Novoa, *Codoin* 69, p. 89.

'revolution of the keys' in 1618. Was it possible that the king was
at last about to cut the threads that tied him to Olivares? The tension
mounted as rumours circulated that the Count-Duke had been all
set to join the king, and had then cancelled his journey. There was
also speculation about the role of the Duke of Alba, whom the king
summoned to Zaragoza, saying that he was not as well served as
he ought to be.[161] On the face of it, there was nothing very unusual
about the call to Alba. In 1628, as his tour of duty as viceroy of
Naples came to an end, he had been appointed lord high steward—
mayordomo mayor—in succession to the Duke of Infantado.[162] It was
an appointment that had been promised him, and one which was
appropriate to the head of one of Castile's most distinguished houses,
but Olivares seems to have been uneasy about the presence of such
an independent grandee in this sensitive palace post, and set up a
junta of reformation for the office, which effectively tied the duke's
hands.[163] Although Alba put a brave face on the slight to his honour,
everyone knew that relations were not easy; and, to make matters
worse, his son and heir, the Constable of Navarre, had recently
clashed publicly with Olivares over his refusal to consider his claims
to one of the lucrative Italian appointments in the gift of the crown,
the embassy in Rome or the viceroyalty of Sicily.[164]

Was the call to Alba, then, part of the king's plan to rid himself
of the Count-Duke? After considering the various portents, the
Genoese ambassador, Giovanni Battista Saluzzo, decided that any
real novelty was improbable. In particular, he noted that the king
was accompanied by the Count-Duke's closest confidants among
the gentlemen of his household. Of those in attendance on the king
and his brothers—the Constable of Castile, the Duke of Medina de
las Torres, the Marquises of Camarasa and Carpio, and the Counts
of Sástago and La Puebla[165]—the first four were close relatives, or
formed part of the Guzmán family connection, while the Count of
La Puebla stood particularly high in the Count-Duke's favour.[166] With
the king so tightly hemmed in, it was hard to envisage a major political
upheaval.

Saluzzo's assessment proved correct. All the hopes and expectations

[161] ASG, Lettere ministri, Spagna, 2434, despatch of G. B. Saluzzo, 10 January 1630.
[162] Hoz, p. 169 (18 August 1628).
[163] Novoa, *Codoin* 69, pp. 90–2.
[164] Saluzzo's despatch, 10 January 1630.
[165] Biblioteca universitària de Barcelona, Ms. 1009, fos. 330–2, Pedro de Robles, *Jornada de la Infanta Doña María para embarcar*. I owe this document to the kindness of Xavier Gil Pujol.
[166] Don Lorenzo de Cárdenas, sixth Count of La Puebla del Maestre, after serving as *asistente* of Seville was given the presidency of the Council of the Indies in 1628 under the title of 'governor'. He died in 1637. He is not to be confused with Olivares' kinsman the Marquis of La Puebla (the brother of Leganés), who was appointed 'governor' of the Council of Finance in 1629.

generated by the king's journey to Zaragoza were to be as brutally
shattered as those of Richelieu's rivals during the illness of Louis
XIII a few months later. Too many mysteries had been created
where they did not exist. One of the reasons why Philip lingered
on the journey was that he found it hard to tear himself away from
a sister whom he knew he would never see again; and he summoned
the Duke of Alba because he wanted him to accompany her to Italy
and make sure that she travelled in appropriate state. Making the
most of precious moments, he and his brothers spent a week in Zaragoza. Then, hoping to save their sister the grief of a formal parting,
they left surreptitiously on the morning of 14 January without saying
their goodbyes, and turned back in the direction of Castile. They
were home in Madrid on the 19th—not a moment too soon for an
anxious Count-Duke.

He had described the king's absence as a serious embarrassment
when various grave matters of state were pending.[167] But the greatest
embarrassment was his own. By travelling as far as Zaragoza against
his known wishes Philip seems to have wished to snub him publicly,
in order to show both him and the world who was the real master.
No doubt it gave Philip, frustrated by his failure to get his way
in the matter of foreign campaigning, some personal satisfaction to
indulge in this symbolic act of defiance. Once it was done, the king
seems to have felt that he had proved his point to himself, the Count-
Duke and the world, and there were to be no more public displays
of royal independence until he relieved his minister of his duties thirteen years later. While lacking in the high drama that would characterize the Day of the Dupes ten months later in France, the royal journey
to Zaragoza in January 1630 shared many of the same features: the
high hopes of the minister's enemies that his downfall was imminent;
the vacillation of a monarch who at once longed to be free of servitude
to an authoritarian minister, and yet feared that very freedom; and
a dénouement in which the king, in retaining the services of his minister, in effect proclaimed his continuing confidence in him, to the
discomfiture of his enemies.

The little drama played out in Zaragoza—so significant for contemporaries, so inconsequential in retrospect—overshadowed the event
which had brought it about: the departure from Spain of the king's
sister to join her new husband, the King of Hungary. The marriage
itself was intended as a fresh pledge of the community of interest
between the Spanish and Austrian Habsburgs, but the Queen of
Hungary's departure did little to improve Madrid's difficult relations
with Vienna. It had cost the Count-Duke 'drops of blood', and the

---

[167] BL Add. Ms. 24,909, Olivares to Quiroga, 4 January 1630.

Castilian tax-payer 1½ million ducats to provide for her dowry and travelling expenses as far as Barcelona,[168] but there seemed to be no gratitude in Vienna. Olivares found himself having to answer complaints about the time wasted in Zaragoza by the king's prolonged leave-taking, and about the lack of money for the Queen of Hungary in Barcelona, or of galleys to transport her. It was in vain that he attempted to explain to the Imperial ambassador that, while there might have been two weeks' delay in getting ready cash to her, he had also been occupied in arranging 6 million *escudos* for this year alone for the war in Italy; 4 million for the war in Flanders; 2 million for a fleet for the defence of Brazil; ½ a million for Germany, and another ½ million in Genoa—and all this when the treasure fleets were still to arrive.[169] Each fresh delay by the Queen—first in Barcelona, and then a mysterious four months in Naples from August to December—brought further recriminations. This business of the Queen of Hungary's marriage and journey was killing him, the Count-Duke told Quiroga. Besieged by illness during the spring of 1630, and subjected to constant bleedings and purges—was it gout again?—he was deeply depressed and had lost all hope of life.[170]

For good or ill the fortunes of Spain and the Empire were, as the Count-Duke never let himself forget, inextricably intermeshed. The presence of a large Imperial army in northern Italy meant that there would be no repetition in 1630 of the humiliation suffered by the Spanish army of Milan when the French first came to the rescue of Nevers in the spring of 1629.[171] The intrigues of his brother Gaston d'Orléans prevented Louis XIII from leading a second rescue operation in person;[172] but in March 1630 a French army under the direction of Richelieu again crossed into Italy, advanced through Savoy, and on the 29th captured the fortress of Pinerolo.[173] But this time Charles Emmanuel, flanked by the armies of Spain and the Empire, was in less of a hurry to reach an accommodation with the French. Spínola had begun to press the siege against Casale, and prospects looked much brighter than they had the year before.

Yet once again Spain was to be cheated of success in Italy. Imperial forces under Collalto stormed and sacked the city of Mantua on 18 July, but Spínola, like Gonzalo de Córdoba before him, found Casale obstinately impervious to attack. Olivares hoped that, with the fall

[168] BL Add. Ms. 1404, fo. 453, Olivares to Alcalá (undated. October 1630).

[169] BL Add. Ms. 24,909, fos. 171–2v., Olivares to Khevenhüller, 27 April 1630.

[170] BL Add. Ms. 24,909, fo. 181, Olivares to Quiroga, 29 May 1630. The preceding letters contain several references to his illness.

[171] See Ródenas Vilar, *La política europea*, pp. 221ff.

[172] Georges Pagès, 'Autour du "grand orage". Richelieu et Marillac: deux politiques', *Revue Historique*, 179 (1937), pp. 79–80.

[173] Jacques Humbert, *Les Français en Savoie sous Louis XIII* (Paris, 1960), p. 77.

of Mantua, the surrender of Casale could not be long delayed.[174]
Again, however, he underestimated the difficulties of a besieging
army, and failed to allow for the impact of external events on the
Italian theatre of war. The German electors were assembled at
Regensburg for a meeting of the Imperial Diet. They were bent on
the removal of Wallenstein, whose army had dangerously increased
the power of the Emperor, and whose ambitions they mistrusted
and feared. In this they were abetted by Louis XIII's envoys, Nicolas
Brûlart and Father Joseph, whose aim was to isolate and weaken
the Emperor, and to prise away from him Maximilian of Bavaria
and the other members of the Catholic League.[175] On 13 August,
Ferdinand succumbed to the pressure from the electors, dismissed
his general, and agreed to drastic reductions in the size of the Imperial
army, which now had some 55,000 men serving in Italy.[176] The dismissal could hardly have been worse timed, for on 26 June the
Swedish army under the command of Gustavus Adolphus had landed
at Peenemünde, and the long-anticipated intervention of Sweden on
behalf of the Protestant cause in Germany was about to begin.

First reactions to the Swedish invasion were muted, largely perhaps
because any element of surprise had long since disappeared.[177] Gustavus spent some weeks establishing his base in Pomerania, and his
plans were still very uncertain; but Olivares, writing to the Marquis
of Aytona on 19 September, and still unaware of Wallenstein's dismissal, observed that 'the misfortune of the incursion of the Swedes
into Germany' was capable of causing a 'great change in the course
of affairs in every part.'[178] He was alarmed lest the new danger from
the north should push the Emperor into some precipitate decision
about Italy, without first consulting Madrid. The situation would
be less ominous if only Casale could be captured, but the siege operations were slow, and Spínola had fallen seriously ill.

A deep discouragement seems to have settled on Spínola following
his arrival in Italy. His relations with Duke Charles Emmanuel of
Savoy were difficult, and the duke's agent in Madrid, the Abbot
Scaglia, was busily intriguing against him. Scaglia, with his silken
manners and his subtle mind, seems to have made a deep impression
on the Count-Duke, who found him a man after his own heart,
and obviously decided in the course of their discussions to lure him,
if he could, into the service of the King of Spain, employing him

---

[174] ADM, leg. 79, Olivares to Aytona, 14 August 1630.
[175] Mann, *Wallenstein*, pp. 524–5; Gustave Fagniez, *Le Père Joseph et Richelieu*, 2 vols. (Paris,
1891–4), 2, p. 450; Georges Pagès, *La guerre de Trente Ans* (Paris, 1949), pp. 122–4.
[176] Roberts, *Gustavus Adolphus*, 2, pp. 437–9.
[177] Roberts, *Gustavus Adolphus*, 2, p. 426.
[178] ADM, leg. 79, Olivares to Aytona, 19 September 1630.

initially as an intermediary in the peace negotiations with England.[179] The abbot's criticisms of Spínola fell on ready ears. The Count-Duke had seen enough of him in Madrid to distrust his judgment, and to fear his charm. Although he had been sent to Italy with full powers to negotiate a peace settlement, these powers were withdrawn in the summer of 1630, and Madrid began to negotiate over his head.

In a conversation in his encampment outside Casale with the papal negotiator, Giulio Mazzarini (the future Cardinal Mazarin), Spínola could not conceal the extent of his bitterness at the treatment he had received from Madrid.[180] Ever since his arrival in Italy he had been struggling to induce the Count-Duke to send more supplies to his army. Now, as his men stood poised for success, Madrid, in limiting his plenipotentiary powers, had stripped him of his honour. The Count-Duke was of the opinion that Spínola was over-reacting, but professed to recognize that his great services, and continuing indispensability, made it necessary to handle him with kid gloves.[181] But he failed to take into account Spínola's general state of health and mind, and his profound sense of reputation, as finely tuned as his own. Weary, ill, and humiliated, the great commander seems in the end to have pined away. He died on 25 September.[182] It was, as the Count-Duke observed in a letter to Aytona, an inopportune death.[183] As an obituary, the comment left something to be desired, but it reflected the Count-Duke's own bitterness over what he regarded as the disastrous consequences for the Monarchy of Spínola's attempts to 'run the wars in Flanders and Italy simultaneously.'[184] The Duke of Feria, currently viceroy of Catalonia, was chosen to succeed Spínola as governor of Milan.[185] Feria was a man of some ability, but good generals were in short supply, and, where generalship was concerned, Spínola was irreplaceable.

The fate of Italy, in any event, was to be decided by what was happening elsewhere. Olivares' fears about the impact of the Swedish invasion of Germany on the Emperor and his advisers were realized all too soon. At Regensburg, on 13 October 1630, the Emperor agreed to a peace settlement in Italy with Father Joseph and Brûlart. By the terms of the agreement French troops would withdraw from Italy in return for the Imperial investiture of the Duke of Nevers,

---

[179] For Scaglia and his activities in the service of Spain, see Echevarría Bacigalupe, *La diplomacia secreta*, ch. 6. The papal nuncio reported on 31 May 1631 the formal transfer of Scaglia to Philip IV's service, with the permission of the Duke of Savoy (ASV, Spagna, 72, fo. 81).
[180] Georges Dethan, *Mazarin et ses amis* (Paris, 1968), pp. 228–9; Rodríguez Villa, *Ambrosio Spínola*, pp. 589–90.
[181] Rodríguez Villa, p. 590.
[182] Rodríguez Villa, p. 593.
[183] ADM, leg. 79, Olivares to Aytona, 22 October 1630.
[184] ADM, leg. 79, Olivares to Aytona, 31 March 1630.
[185] Hoz, p. 185.

and compensation would be given to the Duke of Guastalla and to Victor Amadeus who had succeeded to the duchy of Savoy on the death of his father, Charles Emmanuel, on 26 July. In agreeing to the treaty of Regensburg, even on a provisional basis, the French diplomats had exceeded their instructions; and the news of their action, which involved a renunciation of French support for allies and potential allies, reduced Richelieu to paroxysms of rage.[186] But the indignation was just as great in Madrid. It was, said Olivares, 'the most discreditable peace we have ever had.' Spain had spent ten million ducats on the war in Italy, and for all this it received nothing in return—not even the right to send troops through Montferrat. This was the third occasion on which the Emperor's ministers had deprived Spain of the chance of capturing Casale. Were it not for the fundamental importance of preserving unity between the two branches of the House of Austria, the Emperor's behaviour would be justification enough for war. But, as things were, it would be impolitic even to protest too loud.[187]

The Spain of Olivares could live neither with, nor without, the Empire; and nothing illustrated this better than the impotence of the Count-Duke's reaction to the news from Regensburg. He wanted a world in which his voice carried as much weight in Vienna as it did in Madrid. But this was impossible. Of the Emperor's advisers, he recognized that Spain had a good friend in Ulrich von Eggenberg—'the only minister there who is entirely devoted to His Majesty.'[188] Wallenstein he knew to be an eccentric and unreliable character, but this did not prevent him from believing that his dismissal was 'a terrible mistake', likely to 'sweep along in its wake all the aims and interests of the House of Austria.'[189] Otherwise, those who possessed any influence with Ferdinand were secretly or openly hostile to Spain, and as likely as not were suborned by the French and by the Elector of Bavaria.

It was difficult for the Count-Duke, just as it had been for Philip II, to appreciate that the Habsburgs of Vienna had their own traditions and their own priorities which did not coincide on all points with those of Madrid. It was even more difficult to accept that Madrid, after pouring so much money into the Emperor's coffers, should not be allowed a determining voice in his policies. Once again he had chosen to go his own way, and once again the Spanish crown—worried, as always, about Protestantism and the Dutch and the military routes that linked Milan to Brussels—had no alternative but

[186] See Jörg Wollenberg, *Richelieu* (Bielefeld, 1977), pp. 55–9.
[187] AGS Est. leg. 2331, fo. 126, consulta, 10 November 1630.
[188] BL Add. Ms. 24,409, fo. 269v., Olivares to Quiroga, 11 September 1632.
[189] AGS Est. leg. 2331, fo. 30, Olivares in Council of State, 10 November 1630.

to comply. For a moment, as Richelieu disavowed the settlement reached by his agents at Regensburg, it seemed as if Olivares would be able to bring the Emperor into line.[190] But Tilly, as commander of the Imperial army which would have to fight the Swedes, needed the troops that had been sent to Italy. Therefore it remained in Ferdinand's interest to settle, and the Mantuan question was finally disposed of by the two treaties of Cherasco of April and June 1631, which recognized the rights of a duly submissive Duke of Mantua, with some territorial compensation for Savoy.[191] Olivares accepted the settlement with resignation. It was not as great an improvement on the original agreements as it should have been, but nor was it so small as to justify a return to war.[192]

The peace of Cherasco of 1631 was no more than a coda to the long finale of the Mantuan affair, which had wound its way through 1630 towards its sad conclusion. But for all the Count-Duke's indignation, it was not really a conclusion with any surprises. As early as February 1630, before Richelieu's army had entered Savoy, Olivares confided to the Marquis of Aytona that all his information indicated how little was to be hoped of Italy. Either there would be a full-scale war, which would be bad, or an unauthorized peace, which would be worse; 'and it is certain that we shall not recover in Flanders the prestige we shall lose in Italy ... The probability is that we shall have military reverses, or conclude bad peace treaties, in both.'[193]

The Count-Duke was right about the peace in Italy, which was bad enough in itself for Spain after all the money and effort it had invested in the siege of Casale, and was made still worse in September 1631 when the French resorted to deception to keep the fortress of Pinerolo in their own hands, and contrived by this means to secure themselves a permanent stronghold on Italian soil. In Flanders, on the other hand, it proved impossible to conclude any peace at all, even a bad one. While Frederick Henry, triumphant from his summer campaign of 1629, seems to have felt that this was the moment to strike a bargain with Spain, he failed to break the deadlock between the peace and war parties in the United Provinces.[194] Although he continued to maintain his contacts with the Infanta in Brussels, the last chance of a settlement evaporated in March 1630 when the Dutch scored a further notable success, this time overseas, by capturing Olinda and Recife, in the captaincy of Pernambuco in north-eastern

[190] Ródenas Vilar, *La política europea*, p. 248.
[191] Quazza, *Preponderanza Spagnuola*, p. 474; Leman, *Urbain VIII*, pp. 2–3.
[192] AGS Est. leg. 3336, fo. 230, *Copia del voto del Señor Conde Duque*, 15 July 1631.
[193] ADM, leg. 79, Olivares to Aytona, 8 February 1630.
[194] Israel, *The Dutch Republic*, pp. 232–7.

Brazil. Even if, as Olivares was informed, the Portuguese had time to burn the sugar plantations before the arrival of the Dutch,[195] it was a devastating blow. An immediate response was required, and orders were given for the preparation of a new Spanish-Portuguese expeditionary force, like that which had so triumphantly recaptured Bahía in 1625. As long as Pernambuco remained in enemy hands it would be virtually impossible for Madrid—always sensitive to Portuguese reactions where the overseas possessions of the Portuguese crown were concerned—to conclude any treaty with the Dutch which did not include provisions for its return. The Dutch, for their part, were unlikely to show any great eagerness for peace with an enemy in such obvious disarray; and the Infanta had to report in July that the string of Dutch victories, together with the new Franco-Dutch subsidy treaty concluded a few weeks earlier, had led to the failure of the talks at Roosendael.[196]

This was hardly the moment for Madrid to launch a new peace initiative in the north, especially with the war in Italy drawing to a close. If and when the time should come to start new negotiations, Olivares hoped to be able to add at least one strong card to what now looked to be a very weak hand. On 15 November 1630 the long-awaited treaty of peace between England and Spain was at last signed.[197] It contained no reference to England's claims for the restoration of the Palatinate—'a point of great importance and reputation' for Spain, as Olivares observed.[198] But he had not yet finished with Cottington. As far as Spain was concerned, the ending of hostilities with England brought a major European power back into play. With the problem of the Palatinate still unresolved, some interesting bargaining possibilities lay ahead, and on 12 January 1631 the Count-Duke and Cottington signed a secret treaty, which had to be ratified by their respective monarchs before coming into force. By the terms of this treaty England and Spain would join in an offensive and defensive alliance against the United Provinces, with Spain promising England 100,000 *escudos* a month for the duration of the war, and the cession of the isle of Zeeland on its successful conclusion.[199]

It is not clear that Olivares had any belief in the immediate efficacy

[195] BL Add. Ms. 24,909, fo. 174, Olivares to Quiroga, 4 May 1630. For the fall of Olinda and Recife see C. R. Boxer, *The Dutch in Brazil, 1624–1654* (Oxford, 1957). Also for Pernambuco during these years, Evaldo Cabral de Mello, *Olinda restaurada. Guerra e Açúcar no Nordeste, 1630–1654* (São Paulo, 1975).
[196] Lonchay, *Correspondance*, 2, Doc. 1657, Infanta to king, 27 July 1630.
[197] Ródenas Vilar, *La política europea*, p. 249; Gardiner, *History of England*, 7, pp. 175–6; Martin J. Havran, *Caroline Courtier: the Life of Lord Cottington* (London, 1973), pp. 99–101.
[198] ADM, leg. 79, Olivares to Aytona, 19 September 1630.
[199] Gardiner, *History of England*, 7, p. 177; Havran, *Caroline Courtier*, p. 102. There is a copy of the treaty in ADM, leg. 86.

22. In this letter to the Infanta Isabella, written on 16 June 1631, in his own hand, the Count-Duke, in one of his moods of despair, defends himself against her reproaches for Madrid's rejection of terms being offered by a Capuchin, Father Philip, for a truce with the Dutch. He would rather die than serve a single day more; he has no strength to continue, and requests the Infanta's help in securing permission from the king to retire. 'I have served with much love and little interest, and have lost my life and my health tied to the oar (*asido al remo*), and I know that I get nothing right, and never will . . .'

of this highly secret document other than as a means of keeping Charles I in a state of expectant dependence on Madrid. One day English intervention against the Dutch on the side of Spain might transform the struggle in the north, but time would be needed to prepare the way. Charles I might dislike the Dutch, as Don Carlos Coloma would explain for the benefit of Spain's new resident envoy to London, but he was afraid to strike at them.[200] For the time being, the most urgent problem was to shore up the Infanta's wobbling administration in Brussels and hold the line in the loyal southern provinces of the Netherlands against the expected Dutch assault (Pl. 22).

The Marquis of Mirabel had been hastily despatched from the Paris embassy to lend his support to the Infanta, and in November 1629 the Marquis of Aytona replaced the detested Cardinal de la Cueva as Spain's ambassador in Brussels.[201] As a further reinforcement, Olivares' cousin and protégé, the Marquis of Leganés, who had been serving in Madrid as president of the Council of Flanders since 1628, was sent back to Brussels in February 1630.[202] Although his formal appointment was as general of the cavalry, and deputy to the still unappointed commander of the army of Flanders, his instructions from Olivares make it clear that he also had political functions as an adviser to Aytona, and as a liaison officer between Olivares and the Infanta.[203]

Spaniards, however, remained obstinately alien figures in the southern Netherlands, and Olivares badly needed a native-born minister on whom he could rely. One of the greatest weaknesses of the Brussels administration, as he saw it, was that it was packed with Spínola's friends, and while many of them had a distinguished record of service, they were hopelessly compromised by their association with the jobbery and corruption which had brought the crown's finances in Flanders to their present sorry pass.[204] It was the same problem of reforming an unreformed, and possibly unreformable, administration as Olivares faced in Castile. For some time he had had his eye on Pierre Roose, a Louvain-educated lawyer who had visited Madrid in 1628.[205] At the beginning of 1630 Roose was added

---

[200] ADI, Palafox Mss. leg. 94, fos. 136–8, *Instrucción de Don Carlos Coloma a un residente que iba a venir en Inglaterra*, 26 May 1631.

[201] Lonchay, *Correspondance*, 2, Doc. 1513, Infanta to king, 14 November 1629.

[202] ADM, leg. 79, Olivares to Aytona, 15 March 1630. For Council of Flanders presidency, Lonchay, *Correspondance*, 2, Doc. 1285.

[203] MC, 2, Doc. X (*Instrucción al Marqués de Leganés*).

[204] ADM, leg. 79, Olivares to Aytona, 14 April 1631.

[205] AHN Est. leg. 727, *Voto del Conde mi señor sobre materias de Flandes* (1629); René Delplanche, *Un légiste anversois au service d'Espagne. Pierre Roose, chef-président du Conseil-Privé des Pays-Bas, 1583–1673* (Brussels, 1945).

to the Council of State in Brussels,[206] and was called back to Madrid at the end of the year. The Count-Duke found in him a man very much to his liking—determined, loyal, and a firm believer in discipline and authority. Roose would be his chosen instrument for restoring good government in the loyal provinces, and when he returned to Brussels in 1632 to assume the presidency of the *conseil privé*, it was with the assurance that the Count-Duke would back him through thick and thin.[207]

The collapse of authority in Flanders was narrowly averted, but there were to be many difficult and dangerous days between the time of the military debacle of 1629 and the moment when the Cardinal-Infante reached the Netherlands in November 1634 to assume charge of the government in Brussels. The return of peace to Italy in 1631, however, did make it possible to order a massive redeployment of men and money from Milan to Flanders. In the summer of that year eight *tercios*—a total of 10,000 men—and twenty-two cavalry companies moved up from Lombardy to the Netherlands under the new commander of the army of Flanders, the Marquis of Santa Cruz, and Olivares' spirits visibly rose.[208]

But could anything make up for the mistakes and miscalculations of that terrible period from 1628 to 1631 when Spain found itself simultaneously engaged on two fronts, Flanders and Italy, and emerged with no more than a badly tarnished military reputation? The Count-Duke himself was painfully conscious of the humiliation and loss of prestige. 'In Flanders we have achieved nothing in the last six years, and goodness knows why', he wrote to Aytona in 1630, 'the last two of them because it was taken for granted that the truce was as good as agreed ... And neither in Flanders nor in Italy have we done anything except lose reputation.'[209] But where did the fault lie? Over and over again he laid the blame not on his own willingness to become involved in the Mantuan adventure, but on the sins of omission and commission of Ambrosio Spínola, whose absence from Flanders was generally agreed—or so he told Leganés— to have been the cause of the Monarchy's ruin. During all that time, and with twelve million ducats spent, not a single success had been achieved in Flanders, and Spain had lost its martial glory.[210]

The price of failure, as the Count-Duke appreciated, was heavy, and it was still far from being paid in full. By 1631 the international implications were becoming clear, and they contained little of comfort

[206] AGR CPE, Reg. 1502, fo. 2, Olivares to Roose, 10 February 1630.
[207] AGR CPE, Reg. 1502, fo. 5, Olivares to Roose, 24 October 1632.
[208] Israel, *The Dutch Republic*, p. 181; Alcalá-Zamora, *España, Flandes*, p. 292.
[209] ADM, leg. 79, Olivares to Aytona, 8 February 1630.
[210] *MC*, 2, p. 58.

for Madrid. Spain's abortive Mantuan adventure had brought four years of war and misery to northern Italy, disturbing the fragile political structure of the peninsula, and driving an alarmed Urban VIII into the anti-Spanish camp. It had wrecked the Count-Duke's carefully devised northern strategy for an honourable peace with the Dutch, by diverting men and supplies from the north to Italy at a critical moment, and forfeiting the chance of a cooperative military effort between Spain and the Empire designed to bring the Dutch to their senses. At the same time, it had subjected to acute strains the assumed 'natural alliance' between the Habsburgs of Vienna and Madrid, which was the foundation-stone of the Count-Duke's foreign policy.

The Mantuan venture, too, by broadening the area of confrontation between France and Spain, had sharpened the internal conflicts on both sides of the Pyrenees. Richelieu and Olivares, as the two royal favourites, had both become identified with aggressive foreign policies—policies of 'reputation' which, if pursued, could only lead to a full-scale Franco-Spanish conflict. In both France and Spain the policy of military intervention in Italy brought to a head the opposition to government by an authoritarian principal minister.[211] The 'mistaken policies' of which Olivares was accused in the nobles' manifesto of 1629 offered an excellent pretext for bringing pressure to bear on Philip IV to dispense with the services of his favourite, and subsequent events showed that the king was not entirely unmoved by the appeal to assert his independence. In France, Marillac and the other domestic opponents of the Cardinal resorted to comparable arguments to secure his dismissal, and came very close to success. Richelieu's domestic opposition was more formidable and better organized than that of Olivares, and its leader, Marillac, was able to articulate an alternative policy, based on peace and reform, which seems to have found no echo south of the Pyrenees. The battle in France, therefore, was longer and harder fought. But when Richelieu emerged victorious over his opponents at the end of 1630 he had to his credit, unlike the Count-Duke, a foreign policy and a military record which—for all the setbacks and disappointments—were beginning to bear the stamp of success. While Olivares lamented the failure of the army of Milan to take Casale after a long and laborious effort, Richelieu could point to the captured fortress of Pinerolo as visible proof that his costly policy of intervention in Italy had not been in vain.

Richelieu's victory over his enemies at once sanctioned and reinforced the anti-Habsburg foreign policy with which he had become

---

[211] See Elliott, *Richelieu and Olivares*, ch. 3.

identified. The effect of the Mantuan War was therefore in the long run to strengthen those forces in France which it was most in the Count-Duke's interest to discourage; and an increasingly confident Richelieu began to steer his country with growing assertiveness on a course that could only lead to confrontation with Spain. In April of 1631 Olivares was writing of 'the movements of France in every direction, its deceitfulness in the Italian peace settlement, its open and secret machinations in Germany, and the violent mode of proceeding of the cardinal.'[212] War with France was not a prospect to be faced with equanimity by a minister who had taken office as a dedicated reformer, and found with every passing year that the achievement of reform was slipping further and further from his grasp.

[212] ADM, leg. 79, Olivares to Aytona, 17 April 1631.

XI

A REGIME UNDER PRESSURE

The great depression (1629–31)

During the agitated summer of 1629, when Spanish forces found themselves embattled simultaneously in Italy and Flanders, the Count-Duke had sighed for 'eight years of peace and quiet' in which to put Spain to rights.[1] He would not get his wish. The war in Italy continued for a further two years; peace with the Dutch still eluded him; the activist foreign policy of Richelieu promised new and even more dangerous confrontations with France; and the Swedish intervention in Germany in the summer of 1630 transformed the situation in northern and central Europe overnight, challenging the supremacy established by the victorious Catholic forces, and threatening the Austrian Habsburgs with imminent debacle.

There could, then, be no peace for Spain. At the most, unnecessary foreign policy commitments might be avoided, and an impatient Philip IV be restrained from rash military ventures which would squander hard-won resources. It was with this at least partly in mind that the Count-Duke encouraged Philip to begin extending the modest royal apartments attached to the monastery of San Jerónimo on the eastern outskirts of Madrid and build for himself an attractive semi-rural residence surrounded by gardens where he could distract himself from the cares of office, forget for a time his military ambitions, and preside over court festivities befitting the brilliance of a 'Planet King'. Building work began in 1630 with funds from the king's secret expense account, and then, just as it seemed to be approaching completion, was suddenly expanded in 1632–3 to transform what had until then been little more than a suburban villa into an embryonic pleasure palace on a grandiose scale. This new palace, officially christened the Buen Retiro, and unofficially known as the *gallinero*—the chicken coop—after the iron aviary for exotic birds constructed in its gardens, would be ceremonially opened in December 1633 (Pl. 23).[2]

---

[1] Above, p. 379.
[2] See Brown and Elliott, *A Palace*, especially ch. 3, for the construction of the Buen Retiro.

In yearning for peace, even if it were no more than peace on a single front,[3] Olivares was acutely aware of the misery into which Castile had been plunged by perpetual war. He wrote feelingly in the autumn of 1629 of the desperate straits to which the king's Castilian subjects had been reduced, and of the need to cut down on unnecessary expenses and relieve the poor. 'The propertied among us know better how to ward off the impending thunderbolt than do the wretched poor whom we always condemn, because the *procuradores* of the Cortes and the town councillors—the people with the votes—cast their burden on the miserable plebs to escape paying themselves.'[4]

The strains created by financing the war of the Mantuan Succession were enhanced by the painful process of readjustment to the new deflationary era which had opened with the great *vellón* revaluation of August 1628. In June 1629 the Genoese ambassador in Madrid reported a general and acute shortage of credit: everybody wanted payment in cash.[5] With the value of the *vellón* coinage reduced by half, wrote a government minister in November 1629, 'the kingdom is in such necessity and so short of money that nobody pays, not even the wealthy. No letters of credit are accepted, and in many areas people are reduced to barter because of the lack of coins.'[6] Piet Heyn's capture of the 1628 silver fleet, and the crown's confiscation of a million ducats belonging to private individuals in the galleons which reached Sanlúcar from Havana in April 1629, had aggravated the situation by adding to the scarcity of silver for commercial transactions, and giving the demoralized Indies merchants of Seville fresh cause for nervousness. The years 1629 to 1631 saw a deep trough in the already depressed transatlantic trade.[7] What inducement was there, after all, to invest in the trade? Whether the silver was seized by the Dutch or sequestered by royal officials was of little moment. Robbery remained robbery, whatever it was called.

To the depression of confidence and depression of trade there was also added a major agricultural depression in the years between 1629 and 1632, reflected in exceptionally high mortality rates and extensive internal migration as the distressed inhabitants of central Castile moved southwards towards Andalusia.[8] The agrarian crisis seems to

---

[3] AGS Est. leg. 2713, Olivares to Spínola, 30 October 1629.

[4] AGS Est. leg. 2043, *Parecer del Conde-Duque en las cosas de Italia y Flandes*, 18 October 1629.

[5] ASG, Lettere Ministri, Spagna, 2435, despatch of 9 June 1629.

[6] AHN Est. lib. 856, fo. 181 (Don Antonio de Camporredondo).

[7] Chaunu, *Séville et l'Atlantique*, 8, 2 (2), p. 1654.

[8] García Sanz, *Desarrollo y crisis*, pp. 82–3; G. Anes and J. P. Le Flem, 'Las crisis del siglo XVII: producción agrícola, precios e ingresos en tierras de Segovia', *Moneda y Crédito*, 93 (1965), p. 17; Pérez Moreda, *Las crisis de mortalidad*, pp. 111, 299–300.

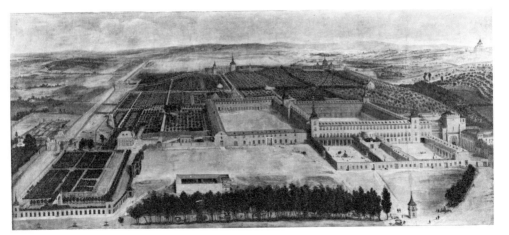

23. This painting of the king's pleasure palace of the Buen Retiro, attributed to Jusepe Leonardo, shows it as it was in 1636–7, after the completion of the major part of the complex and the landscaping of the grounds. The Count-Duke's 'hermitage' of San Juan is the free-standing house on the left of the main complex.

have been brought on by widespread drought in Castile: poor crops from parched soil led to famine prices. Although Andalusia, unlike Castile, had a good harvest in 1630, transport problems made it difficult to turn this to account. The government, deeply concerned about the scarcity of bread in the capital, calculated at the beginning of July that Andalusian corn could not reach Madrid in significant quantities before the end of August. The only solution was to relax the ban imposed at the request of the Cortes in 1626[9] and import foreign corn—in the first instance, if possible, from Sicily, Sardinia, and Oran, and, failing these, northern Europe and the Hanseatic cities. The corn imports would have to be paid for in silver and transported if necessary, as Olivares admitted, in ships of Dutch manufacture.[10]

Not all the agrarian problems of those years, however, could be blamed on the weather. The *Junta de Población* believed that the root cause was the determination of Castile's peasants and farmers to plant vines rather than corn, in the belief that the sale of wine could bring them higher profits.[11] There was nothing new about this analysis, and indeed the *tasa del trigo*—the legal maximum on grain prices—had been abolished in 1619 in an attempt to reverse the process by offering

[9] Israel, *The Dutch Republic*, p. 299.
[10] AHN Consejos, leg. 51,438, no. 3, consulta of Council of Castile, 2 July 1630.
[11] AHN Consejos, leg. 51,438, no. 3, consulta of Council of Castile, 22 August 1630.

the peasantry a free market in grain as an inducement to increase production. But in 1628 the coincidence of a grain shortage in Madrid with an unusually abundant harvest had led ministers to reconsider the effects of the free market system. They concluded that the law of 1619 had neither increased the amount of land under cultivation nor brought down the price of grain. Instead, the peasants had seized the opportunity to force up prices to artificial levels.[12] The 1619 law was therefore revoked on 11 September 1628, and producers were again to be held to the maximum prices fixed in 1605.[13] The corn-growers naturally responded to this fresh attempt at price-fixing by holding back their grain. This must explain at least in part the 'incredible' increasing in misery noted by Olivares in 1631, and the large and growing numbers of deaths attributable to starvation.[14] Under pressure from the Cortes, the crown repealed the 1628 legislation in 1632, and restored the free market in grain,[15] while reintroducing the prohibition on the import of foreign cereals. The four years of price-fixing had ended in failure.

By some miracle, the hunger-stricken Castile of 1629-31 escaped the plague that ravaged northern Italy, and spread through southern France into Catalonia during those same years.[16] But in other respects this was a disastrous moment in the economic and social fortunes of seventeenth-century Castile. It was in the later 1620's that Miguel Caxa de Leruela, a high official of the *Mesta*, was preparing his treatise on the state of the Castilian livestock industry, which he published in 1631 with a dedication to one of the ministers most consulted by Olivares on economic and financial matters, Francisco Antonio de Alarcón.[17] It was a desolate picture that he painted of the difficulties of the sheep-farmers and of the general decline of stock-raising, which he regarded as the principal cause of the depopulation of Castile. In Caxa de Leruela, as in most of the contemporary analysts of the condition of Castile, there was a strong element of special pleading on behalf of sectional interests, but he effectively brought ministerial attention to bear on a major social problem. Peasants who lost grazing rights through the alienation of common lands or their conversion to other uses, lost with their livestock their sole independent source of support. The government responded in 1633 with a new law which characteristically strengthened the regulatory powers of the great

---

[12] AHN Consejos, leg. 51,438, no. 3, consulta of Council of Castile, 23 August 1628.
[13] Gil Ayuso, *Noticia bibliográfica*, Doc. 940; Hamilton, *American Treasure*, p. 255.
[14] AGS GA leg. 1035, consulta of Council of State, 27 February 1631. *Voto* of Olivares.
[15] Hamilton, *American Treasure*, p. 256.
[16] Pérez Moreda, *Las crisis*, pp. 298–9. For Catalonia, see Elliott, *Catalans*, p. 273.
[17] *Restauración de la antigua abundancia de España* (Naples, 1631). See the 1975 edition by J. P. Le Flem for Caxa's analysis and proposals.

livestock corporation of the *Mesta*, but which also sought to restore to pasture all the common lands put to other uses since 1590.[18]

The efficacy of the 1633 legislation, like so many of the other economic reforms of the Olivares regime, remains open to question. It was too easy for the *poderosos* to circumvent the laws.[19] The intention, as so often, was enlightened, but the results all too liable to prove a disappointment. For all the efforts of the *Junta de Población*, that elixir the 'restoration of Spain', sought by *arbitristas* and government alike, continued to elude it. There are some indications in the opening years of the reign of incipient industrial recovery as Castilian manufactures, and especially textile manufactures, benefited from the regime's protectionist policies and from the closure of northern markets as a consequence of war.[20] Similarly, after a severe slump at the beginning of the decade, wool exports, that staple of Castile's export trade, showed a marked recovery from 1626.[21] But the consequent high price of wool threatened to wreck Olivares' plans for the revival of the textile industry by means of the introduction of foreign artisans and the establishment of new workshops, and in 1627 he secured permission from the crown to organize the import under licence of wool from Mexico and Peru to supplement Castilian stocks and so keep prices at a manageable level.[22]

Yet, so far as the limited evidence allows for judgment, proposal after proposal came to nothing. Engineers were brought from Flanders to advise on improvements to river navigation, and in some instances plans seem to have been well advanced, but in 1637 Olivares was complaining that opposition had forced their abandonment, because—as he explained—'anything that Spaniards who are uncouth or of only moderate intelligence do not grasp, they immediately mistrust.'[23] A similar fate seems to have befallen the schemes for creating a more industrious population. In 1627 the *Junta de Población*, following the recommendation of Don Andrés Gutiérrez de Haro, a citizen of Palencia, ordered the establishment in every city, town and village of Castile of a committee or *diputación* which would be responsible

---

[18] *Novísima recopilación*, lib. 7, tit. 25, ley 9. This decree, condemned as 'reactionary' by Klein, *The Mesta*, p. 125, is seen by Le Flem as making possible the development of non-migrant flocks in the period after the 1627 crisis (introduction to his edition of Caxa de Leruela, p.L). A similarly favourable view is taken by Henry Kamen, *Spain in the Later Seventeenth Century, 1665–1700* (London, 1980), pp. 99–100.

[19] See Klein, *The Mesta*, pp. 340–1.

[20] See Israel, *The Dutch Republic*, p. 154, but the evidence is thin.

[21] See Carla Rahn Phillips, 'The Spanish Wool Trade, 1500–1780', *Journal of Economic History*, 42 (1982), pp. 775–95, and Jonathan I. Israel, 'Spanish Wool Exports and the European Economy, 1610–40', *Economic History Review*, 33 (1980), pp. 193–211.

[22] AGI Indif. leg. 755, royal order of 26 April 1627 and consulta of Council of the Indies, 21 May 1627.

[23] *MC*, 2, p. 175 (consulta of 1637).

for gathering up abandoned and orphaned children, and training them in some useful occupation.[24] There is no indication that anything came of this order, any more than it came of the mass of proposals for poor relief, the employment of vagabonds and the encouragement of industry and trade found in the house of Olivares' adviser in such matters, Alamos de Barrientos, after his death in 1634.[25] One of the few schemes actually to come to fruition was a pilot project for the introduction of immigrant workers, and the results were not particularly encouraging. A colony of six hundred Walloon artisans was established in Arévalo, in Old Castile, in the hope that their habits of work would 'serve as an example, as against the idleness of the native population.' The experiment met with some initial success, and by 1629 the colony had seventy-four textile workshops in operation, but by now it was beset by financial troubles, and the Cortes were unable to produce the funds needed to ensure its survival.[26]

Over-ambitious schemes, shortage of funds, the opposition of vested interests, a resistance to innovation—all these inhibited the *Junta de Población*'s attempts to promote economic recovery in the Castile of the 1620's. Above all, its projects required time to establish themselves, and time was in short supply. The years 1627–31 seem in retrospect to have been the economic turning-point of the Olivares era. Even if a modest recovery was indeed under way in some areas of the economy, with or without the help of government measures for reform, it was quickly blighted by the impact of war taxation in the later 1620's, combined with high grain prices and a brutal deflation which drastically reduced the ability of the mass of the population to purchase cheap home-produced goods. It would be correspondingly harder to return to the path of recovery in the years ahead.

It was against this grim background of dislocation and distress that the Count-Duke sought to raise more money for war and national defence. Wherever possible he had recourse to the bankers, although, as he noted in a letter to Spínola in the autumn of 1629, so few were available that his task was very difficult.[27] He exploited to the full, however, such advantages as he had. The *vellón* revaluation achieved its purpose of bringing down the premium rates on silver from the dramatic levels of the mid-1620's, although the rate could not be held, as Olivares had hoped, to 10%. But, with the exception of a sudden and momentary rise in January 1629 to 30% in Madrid and 36% in Seville on the news of the capture of the treasure fleet,[28]

[24] AHN Osuna, leg. 3759, doc. 25, king to Duke of Béjar, enclosing copy of printed proposal by Gutiérrez de Haro. I owe this document to the kindness of Xavier Gil Pujol.
[25] ASF, Mediceo, filza 4960, despatch by Monanni, 28 April 1635.
[26] *Actas*, 48, pp. 208–18 for the project and its difficulties.
[27] AGS Est. leg. 2713, Olivares to Spínola, 30 October 1629.
[28] ASG, Lettere Ministri, Spagna, 2435, despatch, 20 January 1629.

it drifted only slowly upwards, first to 15% and subsequently, in the *asientos* of 1630, to 20%, a figure around which it hovered for the next four years.[29] By resorting to the Portuguese financial community the Count-Duke could also exercise some leverage over the Genoese, just as he had planned. In spite of their comparative lack of experience in transactions of this kind, the crown's Portuguese bankers were to perform with remarkable success throughout the 1630's. Between 1631 and 1640 they delivered some thirty million ducats to Spanish agents, and it was their presence alongside the crown's Genoese and German financiers which enabled Spain to sustain its war effort throughout the decade on such a massive scale.[30]

The bankers, however, had to be kept in funds; and in spite of the doubling of the *millones* by the Castilian Cortes of 1626 from two to four million ducats a year,[31] the inadequacy of the normal sources of revenue for the exceptionally heavy war expenditure of the later 1620's was glaringly apparent. But the event which forced on the ministers a general reappraisal of the crown's finances was the king's sudden decision in October 1629 to join his army in Flanders.[32] Philip's order to his various councils on 2 November 1629 to consider ways of raising revenue and cutting costs with an eye to his forthcoming voyage to Flanders provided opportunities for individual ministers not only to come forward with their own fiscal proposals, but also to make any general comments they wished on the condition of Castile.[33]

The exercise elicited one or two remarkably frank expressions of opinion, notably from the *licenciado* Berenguel Daoiz, a member of the Council of Castile, who wrote that the best remedy lay not in extracting more money but in good management, and made it clear that in his view the Mantuan war had been a grave mistake.[34] José González, Olivares' confidant, estimated that, of the ten million ducats a year paid in taxation by Castile, the king scarcely received three, while the ordinary annual expenditure on Flanders, the fleets, and the royal households came to five. 'It is difficult to think that the deficit can be made up by new taxes, because Castile is already paying what it can, and to attempt to increase the revenues from the other realms could raise serious problems.' The only solution

---

[29] Domínguez Ortiz, *Política y hacienda*, p. 258.

[30] See Boyajian, *Portuguese Bankers*, p. 71, and ch. 4, *passim*.

[31] Domínguez Ortiz, *Política y hacienda*, p. 235.

[32] Above, p. 392.

[33] These proposals and comments are to be found in AHN Est. lib. 856. This volume is an eighteenth-century copy of documentation relating to the Junta Grande of 1629–30. The existence of this junta has passed largely unnoticed, apart from a brief mention by Domínguez Ortiz, *Política y hacienda*, p. 185. Matías de Novoa speaks witheringly of this 'junta prodigiosa' (*Codoin* 69, pp. 93–4).

[34] AHN Est. lib. 856, fos. 157–60.

was peace on the most honourable terms obtainable, postponing new military ventures to more propitious times.[35]

The Count-Duke felt it incumbent upon him to respond with the other ministers to the royal decree, and submitted an unsigned paper containing an assortment of proposals.[36] He argued that Castile was in no state to pay more taxes, especially while its currency remained in such bad shape. His suggestions ranged from a new attempt to make economies in the royal households, 'where theft occurs on a massive scale . . . and everything is in disorder', to the sale of the staffs of office of *alguaciles mayores*, and (more unconventionally) the surrender by rural labourers in all the kingdoms of the Monarchy of ten holidays a year, which would be set aside for work for the crown. But he admitted that this would be a difficult reform to institute, requiring a high degree of 'harmony' and a great deal of administrative supervision. Two ideas particularly commended themselves to him: the Dutch device of stamped paper for public and official documents, and the imposition throughout the peninsula of a salt monopoly. He took the opportunity, too, to revert to his old preoccupation with the appropriation by the different regions and kingdoms of Spain of fixed and regular revenues for the peninsula's defence.

The mixed bag of proposals put forward by Olivares and his ministerial colleagues in what came to be known as the *Junta Grande*, was passed to a junta of eleven theologians, presided over by the royal confessor, Sotomayor, and including among their number the Count-Duke's confessor, Hernando de Salazar, whose ingenuity when it came to raising money was acknowledged by his friends, and even more by his enemies. It was the task of this junta to screen the proposals, and summarize for the king those which it regarded as morally justified. The document prepared by the theologians was ready for the Count-Duke's perusal on 3 January 1630, and was enthusiastically commended by him to the king.[37]

It was, wrote the Count-Duke, the best thing he had ever seen in his life, and the most important in the history of the Spanish Monarchy, or for that matter of any other. If the proposals were carried into effect—and because of their universal character they would first require the close attention of the councils of the non-Castilian realms—His Majesty would not only have the money for his expedition to Flanders, but would be wealthy enough to lay down the law for the world from his turret. He would have all the fleets

[35] AHN Est. lib. 856, fos. 197–204.

[36] AHN Est. lib. 856, fos. 91–4. His paper bears no name, but its authorship is clear both from the contents and from the deliberations of the junta.

[37] BL Add. Ms. 14,007, fos. 229–30v., Olivares (in his own hand) to king, 3 January 1630. The proposals approved by the theologians are to be found in AHN Est. lib. 856, fos. 3–10.

and the armies, the wars and the peace treaties that he wanted, although with the proviso that some of the additional funds would have to be used to straighten out the Castilian currency and establish the trading companies. But if all went well, there would be money and to spare ... It would not, however, be all plain sailing. His Majesty would have to work intensively, and place the whole weight of his authority behind the junta's document, knowing that it was going to offend many powerful people and that its most important recommendation, for the *desempeño* (redemption) of mortgaged royal revenues, would be regarded as utterly abhorrent. He concluded with the hope that God would so direct the business that it would redound to His own greater service and to the well-being and pleasure of the king. He himself did not expect to live much longer, but at least it would be a consolation to see the task well begun.

Philip, not surprisingly, expressed his eagerness to see this remarkable document, which offered him the hope of extracting 'a good sum of money both for the preservation and tranquillity of these realms and for making us feared in all parts of the world, and in some of them in person.' It was a nice way of telling his minister that he had no intention of renouncing his dreams of military glory. But whether the thirty-two recommendations submitted by the theologians would perform the miracle expected of them was another matter. The first of them, which was justified in a separate document,[38] was for the *desempeño* of the royal revenues, that will-of-the-wisp which had for so long been unsuccessfully pursued by the ministers of the crown. This time it was to be achieved by the retention of one fifth of the interest on *juros* and *censos* throughout the Monarchy, with the intention of building up funds for the redemption of the principal. Once the redemption was achieved, it would be possible to abandon the *millones*. The withholding of interest would naturally cause hardship, especially for religious and charitable foundations dependent on the interest from their *juros* and *censos*, but the theologians argued that in 1621 Castile had tolerated a 2% reduction of interest[39] without rising up in revolt, and this time the reduction would come to no more than 1%. They also pointed out, with some justification, that these instruments of credit were now so generally discredited that bonds bought at twenty were being sold at twelve, and that a vigorously pursued programme for paying off royal debts would help restore their value.

Other proposals of the junta included the withholding of 5% for

[38] AHN Est. lib. 856, fos. 13–26v., *Papel que habla más en particular sobre el modo de praticar el desempeño en el quinto de los juros* ...
[39] Above, p. 77.

five years on the income from all *mercedes*, and also on the income from the *encomiendas* of the military orders, subject to papal approval. Villages should be urged to put part of their common lands under the plough and contracts be sold for the right to work Spain's disused gold and silver mines. Economies were to be demanded in judicial and defence expenditure throughout the Monarchy, and there were to be reforms in the palace, with a reduction of posts. The money-making devices approved by the theologians included the schemes for stamped paper and for the sale of the staffs of office of *alguaciles mayores* in villages of more than five hundred inhabitants, along with the sale of other local offices and the creation of new ones. The theologians also accepted the idea of monopolies on salt and tobacco, and approved in principle the Count-Duke's scheme for regional responsibility for regular appropriations for self-defence, preferably financed from the new fiscal expedients proposed by the junta.

It was obvious from the beginning that several of these proposals would strike hard at the *poderosos*—the powerful ones—whom Olivares saw as holding Spain up to ransom. They were not likely to sit back impassively, for example, when faced with a compulsory reduction of their income from *mercedes* and *encomiendas*. Was the regime strong enough to resist the inevitable pressure from the numerous private and sectional interests that the fiscal proposals were bound to offend? It was already operating in a climate of intense hostility, and its recent policy failures had made it more than usually vulnerable.

It was the awareness of this that had induced Olivares to recall Quevedo from his rural exile.[40] The regime's case against the slanderers and the satirists could not be allowed to go by default. Quevedo now joined the ranks of those in the Count-Duke's entourage, like the Count of La Roca and the court poet and royal secretary, Antonio Hurtado de Mendoza,[41] who were happy to place their pens at their master's service. They seem to have been kept especially busy over the winter of 1629–30, when he was the recipient of 'disrespectful papers under the disguise of letters'.[42] One book in particular—an anonymous work—was the object of careful scrutiny. Mendoza described its subject as 'the most serious and complex imaginable', and its style 'the most contemptible and vulgar that can be found.'[43] The work in question was quite possibly a clandestine publication by

[40] Above, p. 364.

[41] Above, p. 175.

[42] ASG, Lettere Ministri, Spagna, 2435, despatch, 6 October 1629.

[43] *Discursos de Don Antonio de Mendoza*, ed. Marqués de Alcedo (Madrid, 1911), p. 73. Gareth Davies, *A Poet at Court*, pp. 52–3, tentatively dates this *discurso* to the mid-1630's, but it seems to me to complement Quevedo's *Chitón*, and I believe that Quevedo and Mendoza are preoccupied in their different ways with the same work.

that old and doughty adversary of Olivares, Mateo Lisón y Biedma, the former *procurador* of the Cortes for Granada.[44]

Mendoza responded philosophically to the charges of this and other detractors, pointing out that all great men were the targets of vicious attack. But he took care to defend the Count-Duke's record, setting it against the background of a depleted royal inheritance, and quoting the recent somewhat double-edged words of an unnamed 'great minister': 'It is true that we are approaching our end, but in other hands we would have perished faster.'[45] This was not perhaps the most effective rallying-cry for the faithful, and early in 1630 the reading public of Madrid was electrified by the appearance of a stinging piece of polemic described by Lope de Vega as 'the most satirical and poisonous since the world was created.'[46] This was Quevedo's anonymous *El Chitón de las Tarabillas*.[47]

Quevedo was scathing in his comments on the *licenciado* 'Know-all', the anonymous author who in his ignorance had set out to malign the king and his favourite. Apparently briefed by Hernando de Salazar,[48] he defended the monetary stabilization measures of 1628 as a liberation of Spain from the 'Moorish' tribute of the *vellón* coinage and 'the empire of one hundred per cent'.[49] Of course there had been setbacks, but—as Mendoza also argued—nobody considered the setbacks suffered by Charles V or Philip II to be a reflection on their glory. Misfortunes and reverses were part of life itself, and there were great triumphs to set against them: the victories of Breda and Brazil; the king's journey to the Crown of Aragon to inaugurate the Union of Arms; the foundation of the India Company; the 'miracle' of the suspension of payments to the bankers. What cause existed for complaint when Spain had a favourite so dedicated to the service of the king, and so immune to the vice to which favourites were commonly prone—the creation of new favourites and the enrichment of relatives?

Lisón, if he was indeed the *licenciado* 'Know-all', was quick to strike back. The *Chitón* was denounced to the Inquisition as being scandalous and seditious, and placed on the Index. The all-powerful Count-Duke was not, it seems, powerful enough to save a published defence of his own regime from the attentions of the Holy Office.

---

[44] The case for this is argued by Jean Vilar in his 'Formes et tendances de l'opposition'.

[45] Mendoza, *Discursos*, p. 93 ('Es así que nos vamos acabando, pero en otras manos hubiéramos perecido más presto.').

[46] Agustín González de Amezúa, *Epistolario de Lope de Vega Carpio*, 4 (Madrid, 1943), letter 523 (to Duke of Sessa, January–February 1630).

[47] Quevedo, *Obras completas. Prosa*, pp. 805–13. For the *Chitón* polemic, see Vilar's 'Formes et tendances', which I have followed here.

[48] See Astrana Marín, *Epistolario de Quevedo*, letter CII and note.

[49] *Obras completas*, p. 808.

Then came a written reply, the *Tapaboca*, which repaid Quevedo in his own coin.[50] After the obligatory trading of insults, the *Tapaboca* went on to develop themes espoused in the past by Lisón. Of what benefit, it asked, had the revaluation of the currency been to the royal treasury? In an imaginary interview with the Count-Duke, perhaps taking sweet revenge for that terrible real interview between the two men on 1 June 1627,[51] the author expounded his own economic remedies: fiscal restraint, economic protectionism, the reduction of expenses in the royal households, sumptuary restrictions, and an effort to set the able-bodied poor to work. The time had come to sweep away surplus offices, and abolish unjustified fiscal privileges. Ironically, these proposals were almost identical with those being simultaneously put forward by Olivares and the Junta Grande.

The *Tapaboca* culminated in a ferocious piece of satirical writing, in which Quevedo's claim that Olivares had passed over his own relatives in the distribution of favours and offices was refuted name by name: Medina de las Torres; Monterrey, Alcañices and Carpio; Don García de Haro, Carpio's younger brother; the Marquis of Camarasa (the Count-Duke's cousin) and his son, the Count of Ricla; and a whole bevy of Guzmanes—Alfonso, Pedro, Martín, Juan Claros—of varying degrees of kinship. The long litany of Olivares' kinsmen holding places of profit and honour under the crown made it devastatingly clear that this was as much a personal and family regime as any that had preceded it. But how could it be otherwise? Like any seventeenth-century minister, the Count-Duke had to turn to relatives and dependents to protect his position in the palace and to staff his administration. Since those terrible weeks of the king's illness in 1627 Olivares had tightened his grip on the royal household, but as long as the two Infantes remained at court, the only way to keep them from becoming a centre of faction was to surround them with courtiers loyal to himself. It was not until 1632 that the problem was resolved, with the unexpected death of Don Carlos at the end of July, and the despatch of the Cardinal-Infante to the viceroyalty of Catalonia and the governorship of Flanders.

In the administration, too, the Count-Duke had largely succeeded by the end of the decade in establishing an inner group of ministers on whose loyalty he could rely. The Council of State was now largely neutralized,[52] although it would take him another three or four years to ensure that its decisions were no longer leaked to prying foreign

---

[50] Only one copy of this is known. It was printed by Luis Astrana Marín as an appendix to his *Vida turbulenta de Quevedo* (2nd ed., Madrid, 1945).

[51] Above, p. 305 and see Vilar's 'Formes et tendances', pp. 263–6, for Lisón's verbatim account of the interview.

[52] Above, p. 383.

envoys.[53] The special juntas, packed with his own men, were being used to short-circuit the councils,[54] and as the presidents of the councils retired or died, they were replaced by 'governors' with more limited powers. The Count-Duke had also managed to assemble a team of loyal secretaries, whose power increased as that of the councils declined. These included his own personal secretaries under the charge of Antonio Carnero,[55] and those who belonged to the official secretariat. In February 1630, shortly after the death of Don Juan de Villela,[56] this was reorganized. The attempt to combine the secretariats of Italy and the North in the hands of a single individual, Villela, had not proved a success. The secretaryship of state was therefore again divided, but this time into three secretaryships instead of two. Italy went to Don Pedro de Arce, formerly secretary of the Council of War, and described by the Genoese ambassador as a man of 'rough disposition'. The North was given to Andrés de Rozas, who had been dealing with the business of Genoa and Milan in Olivares' own secretariat. But the real innovation was the creation of a third secretary, the *secretario de estado de España*. The man chosen for this critical appointment at the very heart of the royal administration was Don Jerónimo de Villanueva, Protonotario of the Crown of Aragon.[57]

The speed of Villanueva's rise was spectacular, but the appointment was logical if the affairs of Spain as a whole were to be concentrated in the hands of a single official. As Protonotario, Villanueva was already manipulating the levers of power in the Crown of Aragon, where he was quietly establishing a private network of friends and confidants.[58] In 1627, following the death of Juan de Insausti, he had been rewarded for his assiduous services during the king's visit to his Aragonese territories in the preceding year with the post of *secretario del despacho*. As such, he was the secretary directly attendant on the person of the king, and the essential link between the king and his favourite. In a poem of 1629, which contains a lively vignette of two crowded hours in the Count-Duke's working day, Quevedo

[53] ASF, Mediceo, filza 4959, despatch of Francesco Medici, 26 June 1632; ASVen, Spagna, filza 70, despatch, 11 March 1634.

[54] Above, p. 296.

[55] In an (undated) poem by Antonio Hurtado de Mendoza, entitled 'En un convite que hizo a los secretarios del Conde Duque de Olivares', the names of nine secretaries appear: Mendoza himself; the Protonotario; Baltasar Alamos de Barrientos; Antonio Carnero; Francisco Gómez de Lasprilla; Pedro Coloma; Pedro de Olivares; Pedro de Villanueva; Juan del Castillo (*Obras poéticas de Don Antonio Hurtado de Mendoza*, ed. Rafael Benítez Claros, Madrid, 1947–8, 1, pp. 241–4). One or two of these, notably Mendoza and the Protonotario, would more properly seem to have been secretaries of the king than of the Count-Duke.

[56] Above, p. 254.

[57] ASG, Lettere Ministri, Spagna, 2434, despatch of 9 February 1630, including the description of Arce; AGS Est. leg. 2714, draft despatch of 11 February 1630; Escudero, *Los secretarios de estado*, 1, pp. 244–5.

[58] AHN Osuna, leg. 554, expte. 9, Cardinal Borja to Duke of Gandía, 6 February 1642.

portrays Villanueva entering Olivares' study and dumping on him sixty packets of letters.[59] On assuming his new office in 1630 he continued in his busy post as *secretario del despacho*, and retained it until his fall in 1643.[60]

Concentrating in his own hands the control of all domestic official business and the private communications between the king and his principal minister, Don Jerónimo became in 1630 the most powerful man in Spain after Olivares. Yet in spite of his importance, and indeed notoriety, he remains a shadowy character. A bachelor, he was already wealthy enough by 1623 to become founder and patron of the fashionable Benedictine convent of San Plácido in Madrid. He was said to have been engaged for a time, before she took the habit, to its prioress, Doña Teresa Valle de la Cerda, sister of Don Pedro Valle de la Cerda, his brother-in-law.[61] His foundation was to become a source of anxiety rather than consolation to Villanueva when a scandal broke in 1628 and the Inquisition began ferreting into the affairs of a community of hysterical nuns who were believed to have fallen victim to the malign influences of witchcraft and Illuminism. By 1630, when Doña Teresa was relegated to a convent in Toledo, the Protonotario himself was too powerful to be touched. But his reputation, at least in the outside world, was now fatally compromised. His well-known addiction to astrology did not help his cause;[62] but in spite of any uneasiness the Count-Duke may have felt on this score,[63] he gave him unstinting support, and even seems to have pressed on Rome his claims to a cardinal's hat, on the grounds of his wealth, his learning and the goodness of his life.[64]

Villanueva's smooth efficiency, and his loyalty to his patron, clearly made him an indispensable member of the governmental machine, but his dubious reputation was an additional liability to an administration already subject to bitter attack. The association in the public mind between the Olivares regime and the strange happenings in San Plácido was made all the closer by the knowledge that the Count-Duke himself was a frequent visitor to the convent. In his desperate yearning for an heir, he often consulted the prioress, and asked her

[59] Quevedo, *Obra poética*, ed. Blecua, 3, no. 72 ('Fiesta de toros literal y alegórica'), lines 145–8.

[60] Escudero, *Los secretarios de estado*, 1, p. 257.

[61] For Villanueva and San Plácido, see Agulló y Cobo, 'El monasterio de San Plácido', and Gregorio Marañón, *Don Juan* (6th ed., Madrid, 1953), pp. 13–66 ('Los misterios de San Plácido').

[62] Above, p. 261.

[63] Antonio Carnero, in his deposition to the Inquisition on 19 May 1645 (AHN Inquis. leg. 3688², fo. 388v.), reports that on one occasion, when told that Villanueva was with an astrologer, Olivares asked: 'Is it possible that a man of sound judgment should waste his time on such vain things?'

[64] ASF, Mediceo, filza 4961, letter of Bernardo Monanni, 15 November 1636.

nuns for their prayers—a practice that gave rise to all manner of scabrous stories about immorality in high places.[65]

In seventeenth-century Madrid, as in every European court, personal and public failings were interchangeable subjects for scurrilous talk. Pasquinades and doggerel verses passed from hand to hand, or were recited with gusto, even if in lowered voice. The Count-Duke, with his personal idiosyncrasies and his authoritarian ways, presented an ideal target, and his 'creatures' could hardly expect to be immune to attack. Increasingly embattled as the years went by, they developed their own special camaraderie as martyrs in a virtuous cause. Motivated, as they saw it, by the highest sense of duty, and unswervingly loyal to their patron and his royal master, they stood shoulder to shoulder against an uncomprehending world.

But did this tight little coterie of the Count-Duke's men—Villanueva and José González, Antonio de Contreras and that *éminence grise*, Hernando de Salazar—really possess the political stamina and skill to push through the radical fiscal proposals of the Junta Grande? The junta, of forty or more ministers, was reported to be deliberating at the beginning of March 1630,[66] but seems thereafter to have disappeared from sight. According to the Mantuan envoy it refrained from issuing pragmatics in order to avoid antagonizing an already over-taxed populace.[67] Three years later, José González, referring to the central plank of the junta's fiscal programme, the reduction of interest rates on *juros* and *censos* from 5% to 4% and a systematic effort to free the royal revenues of debt, wrote that the king, although approving the proposal, had decided in his royal piety and grandeur to suspend its implementation in order to bring relief to his realms.[68] This was a euphemism for the abandonment of a reform which had come to be seen as politically impossible.

But if a serious onslaught on the problem of royal indebtedness proved to be out of the question, the Count-Duke did not abandon his hopes of increasing national wealth, and of finding new and more effective means of augmenting the royal revenues. The vicissitudes of the newly founded Portuguese India Company[69] had not shaken his faith in his plans for reviving Iberian trade by means of trading companies, and in 1630 he made a fresh attempt to infuse them with life. Discussions were held with naval experts and merchants,[70] and some of his principal advisers in matters of trade and finance—Francisco

---

[65] Above, p. 278 and see Marañón, *Olivares*, pp. 202–5.

[66] ASM, Archivio Gonzaga, Serie E.XIV.3, Busta 618, despatch, 2 March 1630.

[67] ASM, Archivio Gonzaga, Serie E.XIV.3, Busta 618, despatch, 18 May 1630.

[68] AHN Est. lib. 871, fo. 23, 17 April 1633.

[69] Above, p. 364.

[70] ASM, Archivio Gonzaga, Serie E.XIV.3, Busta 618, despatch, 18 May 1630.

de Tejada, José González, Alonso Guillén de la Carrera, Mendo da Mota, and Hernando de Salazar—met on 1 June to consider Spain's commercial decline.[71] They reiterated the need for a Levant Company based on Barcelona, and again insisted on the importance of giving trade a good name by conferring honours on merchants. A royal decree drafted by Olivares extolled the virtues of trading companies as the best means of securing a commercial revival,[72] but the proposed Levant company found more favour among the ministers in Madrid than the merchants of Barcelona, who—like their counterparts in Seville—were badly affected by the depression of trade.[73] Within a few months the papers and *consultas* were once again gathering dust on the shelves. Here, as in so much else, timing and confidence were paramount. The timing was wrong, the confidence non-existent.

It is not surprising if at times Olivares was deeply discouraged. His health seems to have been particularly bad in the early spring of 1630,[74] and in May he was again confined to bed, troubled—according to the Mantuan ambassador—partly by his bodily afflictions, but much more by an affliction of the spirit, 'seeing that everything turns out contrary to his intentions, and knowing that his mode of government is disapproved of by most people, not to say by everyone.'[75] He confided in a personal note to Father Quiroga during this same difficult period that he found himself in such low spirits that he had lost the will to live.[76] But in these moments of deep depression his sense of duty kept him going. The king's service must be done; his armies must be paid.

From the money-raising devices discussed by the Junta Grande he therefore struggled to fashion over the course of the next two years a coherent strategy designed at once to increase the royal revenues, rationalize their collection, and lighten wherever possible the burden on the tax-payers of Castile. He had tried without success in 1622–3 to introduce radical changes in the tax system, by proposing the abolition of the *millones* and the assignment to every Castilian town and village of responsibility for the upkeep of an agreed quota of soldiers.[77] In 1631–2 he tried again.

[71] BL Eg. Ms. 339, fos. 422–37, consulta, 1 June 1630, mistakenly attributed to the Council of Portugal.
[72] BL Eg. Ms. 2053, fos. 258–9, *decreto de SM redactado por el Conde Duque.*
[73] Elliott, *Catalans*, pp. 274–5.
[74] BL Add. Ms. 24,909, fos. 159, 160 and 163 (letters of 13 and 23 February and 9 March, to Fray Diego de Quiroga).
[75] ASM, Archivio Gonzaga, Serie E.XIV.3, Busta 618, despatch, 18 May 1630.
[76] BL Add. Ms. 24,909, fo. 181, 29 May 1630.
[77] Above, p. 122.

Church, state and Cortes (1631–1632)

On 3 January 1631 the crown announced the abolition of the old and new *millones* and the creation of a crown monopoly on salt.[78] Salt, as an essential commodity in universal use, seemed to offer an ideal basis for a reformed fiscal system in which a single tax replaced a multiplicity of imposts. Olivares' submission to the Junta Grande shows that he was well aware that the establishment of a French-style *gabelle* on salt was likely to require long and difficult negotiations, and that neither the outcome, nor the yield of the tax, could be safely predicted. But the sum involved was potentially large. The introduction of a salt tax would also spread the fiscal burden more evenly. The great wine and corn-producing regions of New Castile and Andalusia, which were heavy contributors to the *millones*, stood to gain significantly from the change. In northern Spain, on the other hand, salt was in great demand for feeding livestock and preserving fish; and some of the northern regions which had hitherto escaped lightly—notably Vizcaya, which had successfully used its historic rights of tax-exemption to resist the *millones*—were now liable to find themselves making substantial contributions to the royal treasury.[79]

One consequence of the abolition of the *millones* was the disappearance of monies at least notionally appropriated for the payment of garrison troops in Spain. The introduction of the salt tax therefore gave a fresh impetus to Olivares' long-cherished plans for reorganizing national defence on a sound fiscal basis. Worried by the aggressive behaviour of the French, he was anxious that Castile should levy 18,000 men, and the Crown of Aragon and Portugal a further 3,000 each. The traditional system of levying by recruiting captains was both oppressive and inefficient, and this made it all the more necessary to review the current method of raising and financing men to guard the coasts and frontiers.[80] The Council of Castile, under the presidency of Miguel Santos de San Pedro, was sympathetic to the Count-Duke's well-known wish to appropriate fixed annual sums for the fortresses and garrisons, and on 30 March 1631 recommended a new system designed to ensure regular military appropriations. The king would furnish 5,000 men; Castile's thirty-two archbishops and bishops, 254; the 241 grandees and titled nobles, 1,599; the 163 *comendadores* of the military orders, 850; the councils and chancelleries, 817. There

---

[78] Gil Ayuso, *Noticia bibliográfica*, Doc. 963.
[79] Domínguez Ortiz, *Política y hacienda*, p. 235.
[80] AGS GA leg. 1035, draft *consulta* of Council of State, 27 February 1631. For further details on the defence proposals of the early 1630's see *MC*, 2, pp. 104–10.

would be proportional allocations to other corporate bodies, like cathedral chapters and the universities, and the towns and larger villages would be called upon to maintain 8,375 men, every hundred householders being responsible for one soldier.[81]

The Count-Duke responded enthusiastically to the Council's proposal. For six years, he said, he had been clamouring for Spain's defences to be properly funded and manned by seasoned troops.[82] Under the new system, men would enlist voluntarily, assured of good pay, and it would be possible to keep the garrisons up to strength. The plan was approved by the crown, and the first attempts to win acceptance for it were made in the summer of 1631, with mixed success. Although the bishops concurred, there was trouble with some of the religious orders, notably the Theatines and the Carmelites.[83] While the reaction of the cities was apparently not unfavourable, the decision was deferred until the Cortes met again. In the end, it was not until 1634 that Olivares got his vote for a six-year appropriation for the support of 12,000 men. The Cortes made it a condition that the men were not to be used for service beyond the borders of Castile.[84]

Even in the Castile of Philip IV, long used to the relatively authoritarian exercise of power, the principle of consent still retained importance, however much the requirement was flouted in practice. The crown's decision to introduce the salt tax was unilateral, taken without consulting the Cortes, which had last been in session in 1629. In spite of this, the first auguries for the salt tax seemed good. The British agent in Madrid, Arthur Hopton, reported that the replacement of the *millones* by the salt tax was 'not much complained of by the subjects', and was likely to augment the royal revenues substantially, 'being payable by all sorts of people, and it was a pretty way of imposing upon the clergy and religious people without leave from the pope.'[85] His assessment proved to be over-sanguine.

The first signs of active resistance to the salt monopoly came from the clergy, who claimed that the crown, by making them pay the same price for salt as laymen (now to be forty *reales* a *fanega* instead of the customary eight), was imposing a new and unauthorized tax on the ecclesiastical estate. The introduction of the salt tax coincided with other intrusions by the state into areas of alleged clerical immunity, like the demand that the church should raise and support troops for the frontier posts, and the royal decree of May 1631 establishing

[81] AGS GA leg. 1035, consulta of Council of State, 30 March 1631.
[82] AGS GA leg. 1035, *voto* of Olivares, 2 April 1631.
[83] ASF, Mediceo, filza 4959, letter of Bernardo Monanni, 20 December 1631.
[84] ASVen, Spagna, filza 70, despatch, 10 April 1634.
[85] BL Eg. Ms. 1820, fo. 10, Hopton to Dorchester, 18 February 1631.

a new impost, the *media anata*.[86] One of the money-raising devices proposed by the Junta Grande, the *media anata* was a fee payable by every newly appointed office-holder, including holders of ecclesiastical benefices, on the first year's proceeds of his office. These various impositions raised once again in acute form the old question of clerical immunity and papal authority which had so often in the past produced confrontations between the Spanish crown and the papal see.

The Count-Duke, as a convinced regalist in the style exemplified by his father during his Roman embassy, was determined that the king should be absolute master in his own house. He had made as much clear in his Great Memorial of 1624.[87] Already in the 1620's he had had a number of brushes with Rome, in particular over the placing on the Roman Index in 1626 of works by Jerónimo de Ceballos, of whom he had a high opinion, and the Jesuit Juan Bautista Poza, whose extravagant defence of the Immaculate Conception had led him into propositions of dubious orthodoxy.[88] While charges and counter-charges were still being bandied between Rome and Madrid over the opinions and activities of Father Poza, a fresh dispute erupted over another Jesuit much closer to the Count-Duke than Poza—his own confessor, Hernando de Salazar. Since 1629 he had been trying to get Salazar appointed to a bishopric, but the papal dispensation required for the appointment of a Jesuit failed to arrive. As delay followed delay the king attempted to force the issue by naming Salazar bishop of Málaga in July 1630.[89] To Olivares' chagrin, however, a papal dispensation was refused, and in an interview to which he summoned the nuncio, Cesare Monti, in January 1631, he angrily warned the nuncio that a break between Spain and the papacy seemed imminent.[90]

Although the Count-Duke was exasperated by Urban VIII's reluctance to promote Salazar, his anger over the pope's behaviour was prompted by much more than personal pique, however much Monti might affect to believe the opposite.[91] The Salazar affair was in his eyes symptomatic of the profoundly anti-Spanish instincts of the reigning pontiff, which he believed were leading Christendom to disaster. He was convinced that the church in Spain, shielded by

---

[86] ASV, Spagna 72, fo. 79v., nuncio, 27 May 1631, enclosing royal decree on the *media anata*, dated 23 May; Domínguez Ortiz, *Política y hacienda*, p. 228.

[87] Above, pp. 182–4.

[88] Leturia, *Relaciones entre la Santa Sede e Hispanoamérica*, 1, p. 376; Barrera y Leirado, *Poesías de Don Francisco de Rioja*, pp. 55–61, for the Poza affair.

[89] AGS Est. leg. 2713, Olivares to Cardinal Borja, 20 December 1629; AGS Est. leg. 2714, draft letter from king to Count of Monterrey, 9 July 1630.

[90] ASV, Spagna 72, fo. 29v., nuncio, 14 January 1631.

[91] ASV, Spagna 72, fo. 126v., nuncio, 28 July 1631.

the pope, was not making a contribution to the war effort propor-
tionate to its wealth. He was also convinced, and with justification,
that papal diplomacy during the war of the Mantuan Succession had
been actively working in the interests of France.

In March 1631 he learnt through intercepted letters that secret
negotiations were under way between France and Bavaria, with the
papal nuncio in Paris, Cardinal Bagno, acting as an intermediary.
These negotiations, which would lead in May to the Franco-Bavarian
Treaty of Fontainebleau, had all the appearance of a great international
conspiracy against the House of Austria, with Cardinal Richelieu
pulling the strings.[92] Aided and abetted by papal diplomats,
Richelieu—as Olivares saw it—was attempting to reverse the military
verdict in Italy, detach Bavaria and the Catholic League from the
Emperor, split Vienna from Madrid, and in due course transfer the
Imperial title from the Austrian Habsburgs to the Bavarian Wittels-
bachs. Although the Count-Duke believed that Urban VIII was
motivated solely by his determination to harm Spanish interests, he
considered that for the time being it was necessary to 'dissimulate
and avoid irritating him.' But he recommended that a dossier should
be drawn up for future use, detailing all the points of juridical conflict
between the crown and the papacy throughout the Monarchy.[93]

The stage was therefore to be systematically prepared for a direct
challenge to Rome. The Count-Duke was willing to bide his time,
correctly suspecting that if the Swedes continued their run of victories, Urban would have no choice but to abandon his support for
a France that consorted with heretics, and return to the Habsburg
fold where he properly belonged. But he was not reluctant to begin
forcing the pace. He badly needed financial help from the Spanish
church, and Salazar and his friends had no difficulty in providing
him with the necessary theoretical weapons. In the summer of 1631
the nuncio noted that a 'detestable' doctrine had gained currency
at court. Originated by 'bad theologians', it held that, in questions
affecting the clergy, natural law permitted the crown to look to the
needs of the republic without first securing papal approval, since
the pope had shown himself motivated by partisan interests.[94]

In late July 1631 the councils were instructed to provide details
of any actions by the papacy and its agents that were prejudicial
to the rights of the crown.[95] The nuncio was convinced that Salazar,
who dominated the juntas and was the leader of all those disaffected

[92] Aldea Vaquero, 'Iglesia y estado en la época barroca', pp. 605–7, 616–17.
[93] AGS Est. leg. 2332, consulta, 31 March 1631.
[94] ASV, Spagna 72, fo. 122, nuncio, 26 July 1631.
[95] ASV, Spagna 72, fo. 126, nuncio, 28 July 1631, and see Aldea, *Iglesia y estado*, pp. 38ff.
for this and subsequent events.

to Rome and the clergy, was master-minding the whole affair.[96] When the cathedral chapter of Seville lodged its protest against the salt tax, a deputation consisting of the dean and three canons was ordered to present itself at court to explain. But hardly had the deputation begun its journey when the three canons were arrested in Carmona on 12 August, and summarily expelled from Castile. Olivares, in replying to Monti's protest, remarked acidly that the king was still king of the clergy, and that there were even precedents for the expulsion of nuncios.[97]

The arrest of the canons was followed by the appointment of a special 'Junta on the abuses of Rome and the nunciature', under the chairmanship of the king's confessor, Sotomayor. Its secretary was Don Diego de Saavedra Fajardo, who had recently returned from a post in the Spanish embassy in Rome, and who was soon to be launched by Olivares on a distinguished diplomatic career.[98] The President of the Council of Castile, Miguel Santos de San Pedro, was suspected of being too friendly with the nuncio, and was carefully kept off the junta, whose moving spirits were Salazar and José González.[99] The first session was held on 7 September, and some days later a deputation called on Monti to inform him on behalf of the king that he was to carry out his duties without meddling in the 'political and economic' affairs of the realm.[100] He went to see Olivares to expostulate, and found him in bed, 'as is his custom after lunch. His complexion was not good, and from time to time he would sigh. He spoke to me with humility, in a way that suggested numerous preoccupations and machinations going on in his head.'[101]

Olivares had good reason to sigh. The nuncio had excellent contacts, and knew everything that was going on in Madrid. Ironically, it was friends of the Count-Duke's son-in-law, the Duke of Medina de las Torres, who kept him informed of everything that was said in the junta.[102] Armed with all the information he needed, he was able to bring his influence to bear in high places when the moment was favourable. The Count-Duke, in planning his campaign against the papacy, had overlooked one vital element—the conscience of the king. The nuncio's trump card was his close relationship with the

[96] ASV, Spagna 72, fo. 126v., nuncio, 28 July 1631.
[97] ASV, Spagna 72, fo. 144, nuncio, 20 August 1631.
[98] For biographical details and bibliography, see the introduction to Saavedra Fajardo's *Empresas políticas. Idea de un príncipe político-cristiano*, ed. Quintín Aldea Vaquero, 2 vols. (Madrid, 1976).
[99] ASV, Spagna 72, fos. 158 and 166, nuncio, 26 August and 12 September 1631; Aldea, *Iglesia y estado*, pp. 39–40.
[100] ASV, Spagna 72, fo. 176, nuncio, 18 September 1631.
[101] ASV, Spagna 72, fo. 178v., nuncio, 20 September 1631.
[102] ASV, Spagna 72, fo. 172, nuncio, 16 September 1631.

king's formidable aunt, sister to the late Emperors Rudolph II and
Matthias, and for many years a nun in the convent of the Descalzas
in Madrid. The Infanta of the Descalzas, after a discreet approach
from the nuncio, duly talked to her nephew, who feared his aunt
more than his principal minister, and his God most of all. On 22
October Monti had the satisfaction of reporting to Rome that Olivares
had moderated the violence of his language, and that the storm
appeared to be over.[103]

In this the nuncio was not quite correct. The Count-Duke might
modify his tactics, but Cesare Monti's backstairs intrigues could not
conjure away the substantial points at issue between Spain and the
papacy. As Olivares had anticipated, the rapid advance of Gustavus
Adolphus through Germany was every day imposing tighter constraints on Urban's room for diplomatic manoeuvre. On 17 September the Swedes routed Tilly's army of the Catholic League at
Breitenfeld, and Swedish victory began to accomplish what Spanish
diplomacy had failed to achieve.

Only a few days earlier, the Count-Duke, exasperated by what
he regarded as the pernicious influence of the Jesuit Father Lamormaini over the Emperor, and convinced that the pope, the Jesuits,
Maximilian of Bavaria and Richelieu would stop at nothing to ruin
the House of Austria, had voiced his despair at the way in which
Spain was expected to save the Emperor while his alleged friends
would let him do nothing to save himself. If, remarked the Count-
Duke in an extraordinary aside, the conquest of America had reduced
the Monarchy 'to such a miserable state that a good case can be
made for saying that it would have been more powerful without
that New World', whatever would continuous assistance to the
Emperor do to it? And yet, he must be helped to the bitter end.
It was better, said the Count-Duke with characteristic bravura, to
'die attempting to put things right than to allow oneself to sink to
the bottom without doing anything.'[104]

Such desperate measures, however, were no longer quite so necessary, now that the Swedes were doing the Count-Duke's work for
him. A panic-stricken Maximilian of Bavaria begged the Emperor
to save him; as Spanish influence recovered at the Imperial court
while that of Lamormaini waned, the Emperor in turn did what
the Spaniards had long urged, and recalled Wallenstein to head an
Imperial army; and Urban VIII, under heavy pressure from the

[103] ASV, Spagna 72, fos. 189–90v., and 205–7.
[104] AGS Est. leg. 2332, consulta, 7 September 1631. Olivares' speech takes up the first 26
folios (i.e. 51 pages) of this consulta. See also for this speech, Aldea, *Iglesia y estado*, pp.
23ff.

powerful Spanish faction among the cardinals, found himself driven into a corner.[105]

Since the Count of Monterrey's departure in 1631 to become viceroy of Naples, Cardinal Gaspar de Borja, one of Olivares' Velasco cousins,[106] had been acting Spanish ambassador in Rome (Pl. 24). Arrogant and impulsive, he was the kind of man most likely to infuriate the equally self-opinionated Urban VIII. His instructions from Madrid were to put pressure on the pope to work for a coalition of Catholic princes against the Swedes. He was also to persuade Urban to send subsidies to the hard-pressed Emperor, and authorize a no less hard-pressed Philip IV to impose a three-year tax on the Spanish clergy.[107] One after another, between 29 January and 4 February 1632, the Spanish cardinals—Borja, Moscoso, Albornoz and Spínola—called on Urban to press Madrid's claims. But Urban was unwilling to authorize more than a one-year subsidy of 600,000 ducats, to be used exclusively to assist the Emperor. This was far from the massive outpouring of church wealth which Olivares had repeatedly demanded, including, if need be, the sale of communion plate.[108] At the secret consistory held on 8 March Borja read out a formal protest, to the fury of Urban who ordered him to be silent. There was nearly a general mêlée of the cardinals as Antonio Barberini, Cardinal of San Onofrio, laid hands on Borja in his efforts to stop him.[109]

Borja's famous protest, which scandalized Catholic Europe, did nothing to advance the cause of Madrid. The king showed his confidence in Borja by naming him ordinary ambassador, and his removal now became the principal object of Monti's activities at the Spanish court. The Count-Duke, however, seems to have decided that a more conciliatory approach would serve his purposes better. A commission of jurists and theologians was named to examine the outstanding issues between Spain and the papacy, and in July Olivares informed Monti that the king had decided to send Fray Diego Pimentel, bishop of Osma, and Don Juan Chumacero, of the Council of Castile, on a mission to Rome to attempt to resolve the points in dispute.[110] They did not in fact leave for Rome until more than a year later, in October 1633,[111] and the mission, after prolonged negotiations, proved a disappointment.

[105] See Pietro Redondi, *Galileo eretico* (Turin, 1983), p. 290, for the end of what he calls the 'via dell'appertura filofranca' in Rome.
[106] AGS Est. leg. 2998, Borja to Olivares, 14 March 1634, in which he addresses him as 'cousin'.
[107] Leman, *Urbain VIII*, pp. 119–28.
[108] AGS Est. leg. 2332, consulta, 20 December 1631 (Olivares' *voto*).
[109] Leman, *Urbain VIII*, pp. 134–5; Ludwig von Pastor, *The History of the Popes*, 18 (London, 1938), pp. 287–9.
[110] ASV, Spagna 345, fos. 14v. and 21, nuncio, 24 July and 7 August 1632.
[111] Leman, *Urbain VIII*, p. 339.

Some of the heat, however, had been taken out of the dispute, and even Borja adopted a conciliatory manner which seemed strangely out of character.[112] Spain and the papacy each had need of the other, and were compelled to get along together as best they could. But the problem of clerical taxation remained obstinately unresolved. Ecclesiastics continued to insist that they were not liable for higher salt prices without a grace from the pope, and the Salamanca clergy threatened to excommunicate any royal official who forced them to pay.[113]

By this time, however, the new salt tax had become a major domestic issue extending well beyond the sphere of church-state relations. In printed leaflets distributed to local magistrates the administration had sought to prepare public opinion for the substitution of the salt tax for the hated *millones*, while a breakdown of family budgets attempted to show the savings that would accrue to every Castilian household. On the assumption that the population of Castile exceeded 5,333,000—a figure based on the sale of bulls of the *cruzada* in 1629—it was argued that the rise in the price of salt should produce a yield of four million ducats a year for the crown, whereas the *millones*, and supplementary taxes, cost the Castilian tax-payers over thirteen million ducats a year, of which only $2\frac{1}{2}$ million ever reached the royal treasury.[114]

Something seems to have been at fault in these calculations, however, for within a few months of the introduction of the new salt prices at the start of 1631 there were indications that the yield would be substantially less than anticipated. The crown, having abolished the *millones* with a stroke of the pen, was finding itself unexpectedly short of revenue.[115] Ministers may well have overestimated the country's salt requirements. Certainly they underestimated the strength of feeling against the new monopoly, and the reluctance of local officials in some regions to enforce the new regulations. The Basque provinces in particular, already perturbed by the crown's attempts to collect a voluntary *donativo*, lodged an immediate protest against what they claimed to be a gross infringement of their liberties. Madrid ruled on 6 May 1631 that the establishment of a salt monopoly contravened no Basque *fueros*, and plans went ahead to set up the repositories—known as *alfolíes*—from which the salt was to be distributed. Although no serious attempt seems to have been made during

---

[112] *Ibid.*, p. 207.

[113] ASF, Mediceo, filza 4959, despatch of Francesco Medici, 14 August 1632.

[114] BL 593 h. 17 (96), 'Las utilidades que se siguen de aver Su Magd ... quitado los millones al Reyno con solo el crecimiento de la sal', in *Tratados históricos*, a printed tract of 4 pp. included among the 'Relaciones del año 1630'. See also Teófilo Guiard y Larrauri, *Historia de la noble villa de Bilbao* (Bilbao, 1906, repr. 1971), 2, pp. 51–5.

[115] ASV, Spagna 72, fo. 137v., nuncio, 15 August 1631.

24. After his tempestuous period of service as Spain's ambassador to the Holy See, Cardinal Borja, shown here in a drawing by Velázquez, returned to Madrid in 1636 and served as a faithful henchman of the Count-Duke in the Council of State, and as President of the Council of Aragon.

the summer of 1631 to enforce the new regulations, there were ominous rumblings from Vizcaya, and on 24 September a rowdy meeting of the Junta General was held at Guernica, with a large crowd accusing the oligarchy of selling out to Madrid for its own selfish reasons.[116]

The sudden fall produced in the crown's revenues by the abolition of the *millones* coincided with urgent calls on Madrid for higher military expenditures, provoked by the dramatic deterioration of the international situation in the winter of 1631–2. As Gustavus Adolphus continued his irresistible advance, the Emperor's ministers in their moment of extremity were again beginning to talk about the formation of a League of Alliance between the Emperor, the King of Spain, and any German princes willing to participate—that same scheme which had undergone so many vicissitudes since it was first mooted at the Treaty of Aranjuez in 1625.[117] Olivares was in no doubt as to where his master's duty lay. At all costs the Emperor and the Catholic cause must be saved. This would require regular and substantial subsidies to the Emperor and the King of Hungary, cash payments to the loyal electors of the Empire, and the build-up of a large Spanish army in the Palatinate. A strong Spanish presence in the Rhine Palatinate would guarantee the safety of the Rhineland passages. It would also provide teeth for the projected Habsburg league, help secure the election of the King of Hungary as King of the Romans, and enable Spanish forces to come to the assistance of the ecclesiastical electors and the Duke of Lorraine.[118] The total sum needed would be 1,700,000 ducats.[119]

But Richelieu, not for the first time, moved faster than Olivares. The decision-making process in France was less cumbersome, the lines of communication shorter. In December 1631 Louis XIII arrived on the German frontier, alleging the need to defend the ecclesiastical electors of the Empire from the Swedes. On the 17th a French besieging force occupied Moyenvic, a strategic town in the diocese of Metz, garrisoned by Imperial forces since early 1630. Charles, Duke of Lorraine, who was fatally compromised by his dealings with the Emperor and by his support for Gaston d'Orléans after his flight from France, now found himself in an impossible situation. On 27 December 1631 he was compelled to put his signature to the Treaty of Vic, the terms of which had been dictated by Richelieu. In it he promised to cease his activities on behalf of Gaston and the Queen Mother, Marie de Médicis, and to assist French troops

---

[116] 'Relación de lo sucedido', Guiard, *Historia de Bilbao*, 2, p. 90.
[117] AGS Est. leg. 2332, consulta, 20 December 1631; Günter, *Die Habsburger-Liga*, pp. 97–8.
[118] Roberts, *Gustavus Adolphus*, 2, p. 575.
[119] AGS Est. leg. 2332, consulta, 20 December 1631 (Olivares' *voto*).

with transport and supplies if they should move to the help of the German Catholics.[120]

Madrid was shaken by the news that the French were besieging the fortresses in the diocese of Metz, and that Gustavus Adolphus had crossed the Rhine, and blocked the route between Germany and Flanders. The *comedias* planned in the palace for the celebration of the season were immediately suspended,[121] and the ministers went into hurried consultation. They were persuaded that the progress of Gustavus Adolphus was in large part to be attributed to French diplomatic and financial assistance,[122] and were now faced with the sombre decision of whether to commit themselves to an open break with the King of France, who was described by Olivares as 'hurling himself against the Emperor and the House of Austria, in total indifference to God, law, reason and justice.'[123]

The ministers decided that Don Gonzalo de Córdoba, who had just been appointed commander of the army of the Palatinate, should be sent on a mission to Paris with proposals for keeping the peace. Meanwhile, the Cortes of Castile would be summoned to take the oath of allegiance to the two-year-old Prince Baltasar Carlos, and the king and his brothers would soon be on their way to Catalonia, where the Cortes—so abruptly terminated in 1626—were to be reconvened. At the same time, troops would be assembled to take up positions on the frontier, probably at Perpignan.[124]

The last thing the Count-Duke wanted, bearing in mind 'the state of all His Majesty's realms, and particularly of this miserable Castile', was open war with France. He obviously hoped that Don Gonzalo's mission would make it unnecessary to 'go to those extremes to which the French are pushing things.'[125] But it was clear that Spain had to be ready for war. Those January days of 1632 were agonizing days for him—he told Aytona he had never been more pressed for time or overburdened with work in all his years in the royal service[126]—and he had to be absolutely sure of whole-hearted support within the administration before embarking on any course that might lead irrevocably to war.

During the last part of January and early February of 1632 the councils were in constant session, as the ministers engaged in full-scale debate about the *pros* and *cons* of war with France, and the means of fighting it. The king, listening in from his window, heard contrary

[120] Roberts, *Gustavus Adolphus*, 2, p. 581; Leman, *Urbain VIII*, pp. 85-7.
[121] ASF, Mediceo, filza 4959, despatch of Francesco Medici, 10 January 1632.
[122] ASF, Mediceo, filza 4959, despatch of Francesco Medici, 24 January 1632.
[123] ADM, leg. 79, Olivares to Aytona, 14 January 1632.
[124] *Ibid.*
[125] ADM, leg. 79, Olivares to Aytona, 8 February 1632.
[126] ADM, leg. 79, Olivares to Aytona, 13 January 1632.

opinions expressed, and on 30 January summoned a combined meeting of the members of the Councils of State and Castile to thrash out the central problems at issue—whether France's attack on the Emperor and Spain's allies constituted an act of war against Spain; whether there was a case for a pre-emptive strike; and whether it was better to 'live at risk', in view of the 'difficulty or impossibility of finding resources', or to 'die, expending the last drop of blood in order to ensure an effective defence.'[127]

It was the beginning of a momentous debate, in which a wide range of opinions seems to have been freely expressed. Eleven ministers were of the opinion that a diversionary campaign against France was the best means of defence, but others had their doubts. That venerable councillor Don Diego de Corral, the author of the great reforming *consulta* of 1619, felt that the doctrine of a pre-emptive strike, even if adduced by great commanders from Quintus Fabius Maximus to the Great Captain and the Duke of Alba, had to be considered in the light of specific situations. Castile's lack of men and money was notorious. Should it really be allowed to waste its substance away in this fashion? José González, too, urged the king to consider the condition of Castile, and its inability to embark on a pre-emptive war. The most outspoken comments, however, came from Don Juan Chumacero y Carrillo, who was later to be chosen for the special diplomatic mission to Rome. Born in 1580, and a member of one of those bureaucratic dynasties which had succeeded in securing a tentacular grip over the Castilian body politic—he was a nephew of Don Fernando Carrillo, the influential president of the Councils of Finance and the Indies under Philip III—he had begun as a professor of law at Salamanca, and had risen by the usual stages on the judicial ladder to reach the position of Councillor of Castile in 1626. A dry, austere figure, whose obvious sense of rectitude pervades his correspondence, he was always a man to speak his own mind.[128]

Chumacero argued that with five million ducats needed to create an army, and another four to maintain it, there was neither the time nor the money to launch a diversionary campaign across the Pyrenees. Nor was there any guarantee that such a campaign would meet with success. The siege of Casale, of which such great things were promised, had been represented as an easy and risk-free operation. But it had cost ten million ducats *not* to take Casale, not to mention

---

[127] AGS Est. leg. 2650, consulta of Junta de los Consejeros de Estado y Castilla, 30 January 1632, for the king's order and the subsequent discussion.
[128] Fayard, *Les membres du Conseil de Castille*, p. 152; Escagedo Salmón, 'Los Acebedos', *Boletín de la Biblioteca Menéndez y Pelayo*, 8, p. 341, for the Carrillo connection. Chumacero's correspondence from Rome is to be found in BNM Ms. 10,984 (*Correspondencias de Don Juan Chumacero y Carrillo*).

the heavy losses in men and reputation. The abortive campaign in Mantua had been the source of 'all our present woes'. It had prompted the first military movements of the French, deprived the treasure fleet of effective protection against Piet Heyn's attack, and reduced the strength of the army of Flanders, provoking the unnecessary loss of major strongholds.

Chumacero cautioned, too, against underestimating Louis XIII, who had already sent his armies twice into Italy, and occupied the strongpoints that he wanted. It was also important to remember how war had changed its character. The age of conquest—of scaling ladders and sudden assaults—was over. Nowadays, sieges lasted for years, and cost millions, while the besieging army waited for the besieged to die of hunger. To launch an army of raw recruits on the invasion of France was therefore to run grave risks with little chance of good returns. It would be better to opt for defensive warfare wherever the enemy attacked, and avoid starting new wars where none existed. An improvement of Spain's own defences, and the despatch of troops as well as money to the Emperor, would be far less wasteful of resources than an invasion of France from Spanish soil.

The king, in replying to this *consulta*, came out against those of his ministers who opposed a diversionary campaign against the French, arguing, among other things, that the defensive measures proposed by members of the Council of Castile would cost more than the pre-emptive attack advocated by the Council of State. How he reached this conclusion is not clear. There were strong pressures for a pre-emptive strike, particularly from those members of the Council with military experience, like Don Gonzalo de Córdoba, and it was urged upon Olivares from Brussels by the Marquis of Aytona: 'Sir, I have always considered a break with France essential, because it is the source of all our troubles. This is a fundamental consideration, which I think admits of no dispute. The question really turns on two points—whether we have the resources for so many wars, and where we should make our incursion into France.'[129]

Even the king, anxious to lead a spectacular campaign against the French, had admitted that 'the whole thing turns on the degree of necessity which afflicts us', although only to conclude by asserting that it was not so great as to rule out an invasion of France. The Count-Duke for his part hedged so much that it is difficult to know what he believed. While he was always happy to make bellicose noises, his natural caution had been reinforced by the terrible failure of his one major attempt to seize the initiative—the war in Mantua—

---

[129] ADM, leg. 78, Aytona to Olivares, 10 April 1632.

and he, more than anyone, knew what it was to haggle with the *asentistas* and suffer the reproaches of army commanders for the inadequacy of their supplies. Of one thing above all he was painfully aware: that, whatever the final decision, it was always left to him to find the money. Everyone else could go home to supper and bed when the day's work was done, 'leaving the tempest to fall on me. God help me find some miserable corner. With so much work and so little help, I can't keep going .... I am incapable of making bread from stones.'[130]

Yet the making of bread from stones was rapidly becoming a full-time occupation of the Olivares regime. The task was now to be shared with the Cortes of Castile. A special Junta of the Council of State, with Olivares among its members, had recommended on 21 January 1632 the prompt convocation of the Cortes to suggest ways of raising money, and had also recommended that the *procuradores* should be ordered to come armed with full powers from their cities.[131] Two days later, the summons went out for convocation on 7 February, with a warning that *procuradores* who were bound by special instructions and oaths of obedience from their cities would not be admitted.[132] The king's speech, in which he announced that the Cortes had been convened to swear homage to the heir to the throne and give further financial assistance at a time when the House of Austria was assailed on all sides, was delivered on 21 February. On 7 March, in a solemn ceremony held in the monastery of San Jerónimo, the Infantes, the nobility and the Cortes of Castile on behalf of the realm swore fealty to Baltasar Carlos.[133]

The 1632 Cortes met in an atmosphere of financial crisis. 'This king is making the greatest preparations that ever were made in Spain for the assistance of the Emperor', Hopton wrote in early February. The collection of another 'voluntary' *donativo*—the third of the reign— was also in full swing this month, and, as Hopton reported, 'they have sent to the Duke of Béjar for 100,000 ducats, to the Duke of Medina Sidonia for much more, according to the proportion they send to others.'[134] Everyone in Castile was to be approached, including servants and children.[135] In addition to the new revenues to be provided by the *donativo*, the salt tax and the *media anata*, Olivares wanted nine million ducats from the Cortes, spread over three years.

---

[130] ADM, leg. 79, Olivares to Aytona, 16 and 31 March 1632.
[131] AHN Est. leg. 674, consulta, 21 January 1632.
[132] See Jago, 'Habsburg absolutism and the Cortes of Castile', pp. 321–2, and also Thompson, 'Crown and Cortes in Castile', p. 40, for the question of full powers.
[133] Danvila, *El poder civil*, 3, p. 85. For the ceremony of fealty, León Pinelo, *Anales de Madrid*, pp. 287–90, and Brown and Elliott, *A Palace*, pp. 55–6.
[134] BL Eg. Ms. 1820, fo. 145, Hopton to Sir Robert Anstruther, 9 February 1632.
[135] RAH 11–219, *Papeles varios*, fos. 334–5, Instructions for collection of *donativo*.

The attitude of the court was, on the whole, contemptuous of the Castilian Cortes. In a stinging note of rebuke to the Council of Castile for not having worked out in advance the financial measures to be put to the Cortes, Philip made it plain that he was not prepared to submit to the will of 'four or forty youths who come to these Cortes', when the honour of his person and his Monarchy was at stake.[136] But the 'youths' were not prepared to play their part with quite the whole-hearted enthusiasm required of them. The crown's demand that the *procuradores* should be sent with full powers had caused widespread indignation, and if some cities yielded to pressure from the court, several, including Seville, refused to comply.[137] In the course of their deliberations the Cortes made it clear that they could only give a provisional approval to a monetary grant, which itself would be conditional on a reduction in the price of salt.[138] But they found themselves under heavy pressure to give final and unconditional approval to the subsidy. Olivares professed himself scandalized that his native Seville should align itself with Segovia and Salamanca in refusing to serve the king. Having, as he remarked with blithe disregard for autobiographical truth, been born in the city, he would not even receive a deputation from it to explain such dishonourable procedure.[139]

A note from the king on 21 March expressing his displeasure at the delay in approving the subsidy[140] provoked mixed anger and anguish in the Cortes, but the king and the Count-Duke were in no mood for constitutional niceties. The news had just arrived that the New Spain treasure fleet, with two years' remittances of silver on board, had been lost at sea.[141] 'Everything depended on this financial nerve of the crown', the Count-Duke told an emergency meeting of the Council of State on 19 March.[142] With the king suddenly deprived of two million ducats in silver on which he had been counting for the year's expenditures, an immediate decision by the Cortes was required. The question of the king's right to insist on the *procuradores* having full powers was put to the Council of Castile, which ruled in his favour, and on 26 March the president of the Council ordered the Cortes to take a definitive vote that same day. In future,

---

[136] AHN Consejos, leg. 51,438, no. 3, royal order to Archbishop of Granada, president of Council of Castile, 9 February 1632.
[137] BL Eg. Ms. 1820, fo. 146, Hopton to Dorchester, 4 March 1632. Hopton's report indicates that not all the cities 'refrained from imposing special instructions and oaths on their delegates', as Jago suggests ('Habsburg absolutism', p. 321).
[138] *Actas*, 49, pp. 176ff.
[139] Biblioteca de la Universidad de Salamanca, Ms. 2066, no. 33, Olivares to the Vizconde de la Corcana, *asistente* of Seville, 16 March 1632.
[140] *Actas*, 49, pp. 231–2.
[141] Hoz, p. 194; ASF, Mediceo, filza 4959, despatch of Francesco Medici, 20 March 1632.
[142] AGS Est. leg. 2651, consulta, 19 March 1632.

all votes in the Cortes were to be definitive rather than merely consultative.[143] Faced with this ministerial onslaught, the resistance of the
Cortes on a point of major constitutional principle crumbled.
Although the crown's campaign on the powers of *procuradores* still
had to be carried to the cities, the surrender of the deputies in March
1632 marked an important, and possibly decisive, moment in the
institutional weakening of Castile's fragile parliamentary assembly.[144]

While the Cortes had now voted a subsidy of $2\frac{1}{2}$ million ducats
a year for the next three years, it still remained to be decided how
the money was to be raised. This would require protracted discussion,
and the king and the Count-Duke had business elsewhere. The
reported loss of the treasure fleet had finally persuaded the ministers
that they must go ahead with plans for the king to return to Barcelona
and reconvene the Catalan Cortes.[145] Having failed to vote a subsidy
in 1626, the Catalans (especially if handled with tact and given time
to deliberate) would surely not disappoint their prince a second time.
The king would have to attend the opening session in person, but
could then hand over to his second brother, the Cardinal-Infante,
who would remain in Barcelona to preside over the Catalan Cortes
and see them through to a successful conclusion. During Philip's
absence from Madrid, Castile would be governed by a junta presided
over by the queen, and the management of the Castilian Cortes would
be left to Don García de Haro, now Count of Castrillo, whom Olivares was systematically grooming for high office.[146]

The king, accompanied by both his brothers, set out from Madrid
on 12 April,[147] making first for Valencia, where there was momentary
alarm when the Count-Duke, finding that the wine tasted different
from the way he remembered it on his previous visit, announced
that he had been poisoned. Calm was restored when it was discovered
that the bottle had previously been used for vinegar and had not
been rinsed.[148] Without further mishap, the royal party reached Barcelona on 3 May, and with some difficulty the reluctant Catalans were
induced to accept the Cardinal-Infante as president of their Cortes.[149]

During his six weeks' absence from Madrid, Olivares kept in as
close touch with affairs of state and finance as the roads and posts
would allow. He fretted when a letter from the Count of Castrillo
took four days to reach him in Valencia,[150] although three to five

[143] *Actas*, 49, pp. 176ff.
[144] See Jago, 'Habsburg absolutism', pp. 322.
[145] Danvila, *El poder civil*, 6, Doc. 950, no. 1, consulta of Council of State, 23 March 1632.
[146] Above, p. 393. He succeeded to the title in 1629.
[147] Hoz, p. 198.
[148] ASF, Mediceo, filza 4959, despatch of Francesco Medici, 8 May 1632.
[149] Elliott, *Catalans*, pp. 272 and 275.
[150] AHN Est. lib. 864, fo. 243, Olivares to Castrillo, 19 April 1632.

days were normal for posts between Madrid and the Levantine coastal towns. Through his correspondence with Castrillo he followed closely the progress of the Castilian Cortes, where Castrillo soon found himself in trouble over the price of salt, and offered his own running commentary, liberally sprinkled with advice.[151]

On 19 April he was expressing agreement with Castrillo's view that salt prices must be fixed at a level which would produce a million ducats for the crown, and professed his inability to understand the workings of a proposed alternative tax on flour, although he suspected it would bear heavily on the poor.[152] The next day, after a disquisition on the beauties of the city of Valencia and its gardens, especially after a heavy night's rain, he expressed his confidence in Castrillo's handling of the salt tax problem, and congratulated him on his success in a recent transaction with the Fuggers: 'I cannot imagine how you scraped together so much money, unless you confer with the devil by night.'[153]

For all his confidence in Castrillo's skills, however, each new letter made it increasingly clear to the Count-Duke that there was strong opposition in the Cortes to the new salt prices. Already it was becoming obvious that the disappointingly low revenue being generated by the salt monopoly would leave the crown with no option but to restore the *millones*. The question now was whether salt prices could be held at a level which would yield as much as a million ducats. Castrillo himself had grave doubts, and hesitated to put the salt tax to a vote without specific orders.[154] Until now, he had been instructed to hold firm, but on receiving Castrillo's letter of 24 April the Count-Duke agreed that it had become necessary to show flexibility in the matter of prices if the entire project were not to be permanently becalmed.[155] On 2 May Castrillo was able to write that he had succeeded in negotiating prices for salt which would vary from region to region, but which should produce a clear 900,000 ducats a year for the crown.[156] This still had to be approved, but three days later, with twenty-one of thirty-four votes in favour, he reported success.[157] The news was received with heartfelt relief by Olivares in Barcelona. It was the end of a hard-fought battle, in which even

---

[151] Professor Domínguez Ortiz was the first to draw attention to this correspondence, preserved in AHN Est. lib. 864, and to publish part of it as Appendix V of his *Política y hacienda*. I am grateful to Dr. Renato Barahona for placing at my disposal a microfilm of the correspondence.

[152] AHN Est. lib. 864, fo. 243.

[153] AHN Est. lib. 864, fos. 183–8.

[154] AHN Est. lib. 864, fo. 197v., 24 April 1632.

[155] AHN Est. lib. 864, fo. 234v., Olivares to Castrillo, 29 April 1632.

[156] AHN Est. lib. 864, fos. 275v.–276.

[157] AHN Est. lib. 864, fos. 291–2, Castrillo to Olivares, 5 May 1632.

the crown's friends and dependents had wavered before the day was won.[158]

In May, 1632, therefore, it seemed that the vexed problem of the introduction of the salt monopoly had been satisfactorily resolved, even if with far less benefit to the crown that had originally been envisaged. But at least Spain, like every 'well-governed part of Europe',[159] now had its *gabelle*. The Castilian Cortes, although tiresome and obstinate, had been cowed. The same did not, however, prove true of the Catalan Cortes. In Castile, the crown was strong, in Catalonia it was weak; and Catalan constitutionalism had reserves of institutional strength which its Castilian counterpart lacked.

Provincial disobedience (1632)

The king and the Count-Duke returned from Barcelona on 31 May 1632, having left the Cardinal-Infante to bring the Catalan Cortes to a satisfactory conclusion with the assistance of one of the most experienced and well-travelled of all Philip's ministers, the Count of Oñate. As a former ambassador to the Imperial court, he was a practised negotiator. He also—or so he believed—knew how to handle Olivares, with whom it was necessary to 'insist on reason, answer back with it, speak softly, not be surprised when he gets angry, let the first outburst subside, and then return to the subject and get him to grasp it, making clear what is wanted.'[160] None of this valuable experience, however, had quite prepared him for dealing with the Catalans.

The early summer of 1632 was not the ideal moment to approach the Catalans for money. In Catalonia, as in Castile, a succession of poor harvests had reduced many to starvation, and trade with France and Italy had been disrupted by the Mediterranean plague of 1629–31.[161] The money on which Olivares had been counting to make good the sums lost with the treasure fleet was not likely in the circumstances to be easily accessible. In fact the news of the loss of the treasure fleet proved to be incorrect. The *Capitana* and the *Almiranta* had gone down off the coast of Campeche in October, but the remaining galleons had safely reached Havana, and they eventually cast anchor at Cadiz on 16 April, four days after the king's departure for Barcelona.[162] If they were indeed carrying $1\frac{1}{2}$ million

---

[158] AHN Est. lib. 864, fo. 313v., Olivares to Castrillo, 9 May 1632.

[159] King on consulta of Council of Castile, 22 March 1632 (AHN Consejos, leg. 7145, expte. 45).

[160] Archivo de los Condes de Oñate, leg. 104, expte. 1637, *Instrucción secreta* by Oñate.

[161] Elliott, *Catalans*, p. 273.

[162] Chaunu, *Séville et l'Atlantique*, 5, p. 221.

ducats in gold and silver for the king, as was reported,[163] the pressures to extract a subsidy from the Catalans at any price were at least reduced. This was all to the good, since Oñate was soon to discover that the Catalans were unwilling to oblige.

Although Olivares told Aytona that the king had returned 'contented and satisfied with the Catalans',[164] the contentment proved short-lived. Even before the royal party was back at court, trouble had broken out in Barcelona. A dispute over a question of etiquette, involving the alleged right of the Barcelona city councillors to remain covered in the presence of princes of the blood—in this instance the Cardinal-Infante—aroused powerful emotions in the city, and Barcelona made use of its influence in the Cortes to bring the entire proceedings to a halt.[165] The symbolic importance of ceremonial was great, and neither side was prepared to give ground. For Olivares, 'those people there are hard and terrible, because their form of government departs little, if at all, from that of a republic',[166] and any concessions would only make them more proud and independent. For Barcelona, the court's rejection of a historic right only confirmed the widespread conviction that the Count-Duke was determined to do away with Catalonia's liberties.

Throughout his ministry, two considerations guided the Count-Duke's policy towards the peripheral provinces of the Iberian peninsula. His long-term intention was to integrate them more closely with Castile and to mobilize their resources for the Union of Arms. At the same time, he regarded it as essential that the authority of his royal master should be at all times sustained, and wherever possible enhanced, in provinces where it was historically weak. In his scale of priorities, the maintenance of royal authority was even more important than the maintenance of royal solvency, although ultimately the one was dependent on the other. In matters of taxation, it might be necessary on occasion to retreat for tactical reasons, but even retreats had to be managed in such a way as to leave the authority of the crown intact.

But how was authority to be sustained in a province like Catalonia that was so nearly republican in its form of government, with only a viceroy and a handful of officials to symbolize the presence and power of the crown? This was an acute dilemma for Olivares, as it was for many another European statesman of the period, and its

---

[163] ASVen. Spagna, filza 69, despatch, 8 May 1632.

[164] ADM, leg. 79, Olivares to Aytona, 5 June 1632.

[165] See Elliott, *Catalans*, ch. 10 for the controversy between the crown and Barcelona. Great as was the importance of the symbolic issue, certain groups in Catalan society had their own reasons for frustrating the operations of an assembly which was displaying rather too much interest in the reform of local institutions.

[166] ADM. leg. 259, Olivares to Cardinal-Infante, 5 June 1632.

resolution depended on a balance of forces between the central government and outlying regions that was bound to fluctuate with the times and the seasons. One possibility was to resort to arms, as Richelieu had recently resorted to arms against the Huguenots of La Rochelle. But this involved risk and expense, and did not necessarily guarantee a lasting solution to a refractory problem.

Olivares found himself for the first time seriously confronted by this dilemma in his dealings with Catalonia in 1632. He could not run the risk of another rebuff like that suffered by the king in Barcelona in 1626, since it would compromise the crown's authority not only in Catalonia itself, but also in those other kingdoms and provinces—the Basque provinces, Aragon, Valencia and Portugal—where constitutional rights and liberties impeded the free exercise of royal power. On the other hand, he had to consider whether at this moment it was either desirable or feasible to deploy an army against a province which was showing a tiresome recalcitrance in matters of legitimate service to the crown, but had stopped well short of open revolt.

There were, however, intermediate stages before the full-scale deployment of military power. One possibility, mentioned by the Count-Duke in his Great Memorial of 1624,[167] was for the king, with an army on hand, to negotiate with recalcitrant vassals from a position of strength. If a large royal army had been assembled on the Catalan frontier for a pre-emptive strike against France, as the king had decided earlier in the year, this might indeed have been a possible solution in the summer of 1632. But in April, after the arrival of despatches from Vienna which made it clear that there was no chance of the Emperor joining Spain in war against the French, Madrid's enthusiasm for immediate action noticeably cooled, and the Council of State put the project on one side.[168] In July rumours were circulating at court that troops would be sent from Naples and Castile for use against the principality, and a contingent of Neapolitans did in fact reach Catalonia, where it was roughly handled by the peasantry.[169] But at this stage the Count-Duke seems to have made no serious contingency plans.

One of his difficulties was that he had so many other calls on his time and energies, and Madrid's resources were stretched to the limits. In Germany, the Swedes had been ravaging Bavaria, and only Wallenstein, always unpredictable and cautious to a fault, stood between Gustavus and total victory. Along France's eastern frontier, Louis XIII had sent his army into Lorraine again at the end of May

[167] Above, p. 198.
[168] Leman, *Urbain VIII*, p. 101.
[169] Elliott, *Catalans*, pp. 282–3.

and imposed a harsh new settlement on the Duke of Lorraine in the following month, while his troops cleared the Spaniards out of their garrisons in the electorate of Trèves.[170] But worst of all was the situation in the Netherlands, where Frederick Henry had launched a spring offensive designed to break the line of defences along the river Maas. Venlo and Roermond fell in quick succession, and Dutch forces appeared outside the walls of Maastricht on 10 June. That same month, Count Henry van den Bergh, whose inactivity had done much to facilitate the Dutch advance, fled to Liège, where he sought to persuade his compatriots in the Southern Netherlands to revolt against the domination of Spain.[171] His efforts, encouraged by Richelieu and the Dutch, met with no success, but militarily the damage was done. The whole Maas defensive system was crumbling during those summer months of 1632; and although Don Gonzalo de Córdoba returned at speed from the Palatinate, neither he nor Pappenheim was able to raise the siege of Maastricht, which fell on 22 August.

Faced with a renewed prospect of total collapse in the Netherlands, and bitterly regretting the abandonment of the project for an invasion of France from the Catalan frontier,[172] the Count-Duke was reluctant to push the conflict in Catalonia to an open confrontation. While some ministers might feel that the behaviour of Barcelona was sufficient to justify armed intervention, Olivares was well aware that he had neither the men nor the money for this. He believed that all the avenues of conciliation should first be explored in an effort to bring the Cortes to some sort of conclusion, even if this meant abandoning the hope of a substantial subsidy. But at the same time he recommended that arrangements be made for troops to stand by in Milan for despatch to the principality if it should be felt appropriate for the king to return there to conclude the Cortes in person.[173]

No doubt a conciliatory approach made sense if, as Olivares insisted, the Monarchy was in no fit state to allow of a prompt solution to the Catalan problem. But if this was to be the policy, it was not necessarily advantageous to make contingency plans for military intervention at some later date, unless there existed a firm determination to put them into effect. Such plans had no chance of remaining secret for long,[174] and the failure to implement them once they were

[170] P. Henrard, *Marie de Médicis dans les Pays-Bas, 1631–1638* (Antwerp, 1875), pp. 212–15; Leman, *Urbain VIII*, p. 217.

[171] A. Waddington, *La République des Provinces-Unies, la France et les Pays-Bas Espagnols de 1630 à 1650*, 2 vols. (Paris, 1895–7), 1, pp. 159–61; Israel, *The Dutch Republic*, pp. 185–6.

[172] ADM, leg. 79, Olivares to Aytona, 15 July 1632.

[173] Elliott, *Catalans*, p. 282.

[174] The British agent in Madrid reported on 23 September that the Catalans suspected that Madrid was planning armed intervention under cover of a campaign against France (BL Eg. Ms. 1820, fo. 209, Hopton to Coke).

known would only discredit still further the royal authority, and foster the very impression of weakness that Olivares was so anxious to avoid.

By threatening without performing—a technique that he was prone to employ in both domestic and foreign affairs—the Count-Duke damaged his own credibility. Ironically, his kid-glove handling of Catalonia contrasted with Richelieu's very different handling of a not dissimilar situation across the border in Languedoc at exactly this moment. In Languedoc, however, the prestige of the French crown was even more at stake than that of the Spanish crown in Catalonia, since Louis was faced with open revolt by the governor, Montmorency, who had risen in support of Gaston d'Orléans. Richelieu therefore had less room for prevarication than Olivares: the stakes were higher, the issue clear-cut. At the battle of Castelnaudary on 1 September, the French rebels were defeated by the royalist army, and Montmorency was taken prisoner.[175] Even now, Olivares could not believe that Richelieu would be so bold as to put Montmorency to death, since all the princes in France would rise up in revolt.[176] Two weeks after this confident judgment, Montmorency was executed in the courtyard of the Hôtel de Ville of Toulouse.

The Cardinal, unlike the Count-Duke, had behind him a string of recent foreign policy successes to strengthen his hand at home. The domestic opposition was demoralized, and Languedoc, although proud of its rights and privileges, lacked the strong institutional defences with which Catalonia could fend off assaults by the central government. These considerations all served as an encouragement to Richelieu to act quickly and decisively. But for Olivares, operating from a weaker position, the risks of action and inaction appeared finely balanced. If the king decided to return to the principality, supported by a greater or lesser display of strength, and his action subsequently misfired, the result would be to undermine his authority throughout the peninsula.[177] Yet if he did nothing, other regions of Spain might be tempted to follow the Catalan example and refuse to pay their taxes. It was not easy to decide which line of policy to adopt, especially when international tension was running so high. But it is possible that in playing for time the Count-Duke made the worst of every world.

Decisive action in Catalonia in 1632—the appearance of the king to close the Cortes, with soldiers discreetly, but not too discreetly, posted on the principality's borders—might have given Barcelona pause for thought, while simultaneously discouraging the imitation

[175] Georges Dethan, *Gaston d'Orléans. Conspirateur et Prince Charmant* Paris, 1959), pp. 116–7.
[176] AGR SEG, Reg. 596, Olivares to Abbot Scaglia, 13 October 1632.
[177] AHN Est. leg. 860, no. 22, paper by Olivares, 25 August 1632.

of Barcelona's behaviour elsewhere in Spain. In the event, no such action was taken. Instead, it was decided that the Cardinal-Infante should prorogue the Cortes and move to Gerona, on the pretext of inspecting the frontier defences.[178] The effective removal of the viceregal administration from the principality's capital was to mark the beginning of a long and inconclusive campaign by Olivares and Villanueva to reduce to obedience a city which they tended to think of as their own La Rochelle.[179]

Barcelona, however, was not the only great city to give them trouble in 1632. There had been difficulties with Seville over the salt tax, and now, in the autumn, it was to be the turn of northern Spain. It hardly seems a coincidence that trouble should have arisen in Bilbao at the moment when Barcelona's successful act of defiance had become a matter of public record. This at least was the conclusion of Arthur Hopton, as he surveyed the dispute in Catalonia. 'The voice of privilege', he wrote, 'spreads far, and it may have been an occasion of that which hath since happened in Biscay, from the town of Bilbao, upon occasion of establishing the new imposition of salt.'[180]

If he was faced with obstructionism in Catalonia, the Count-Duke found himself confronted with actual insurrection in Vizcaya, a region as insistent as Catalonia on the strict observance of its privileges. Madrid's attempt to raise money by increasing the price of salt looked to the Vizcayans like a planned assault on their laws and liberties. Their suspicions were confirmed when it became apparent that the Basque provinces were not included in the agreement reached between the Count of Castrillo and the Castilian Cortes in May 1632 to bring salt prices down.[181] As part of the bargain, the *millones*, which the Count-Duke had worked so hard to abolish, were restored again from 1 August 1632 at a rate of four million ducats a year for six years, some of it to be raised from the sale of salt at the compromise price that Castrillo had worked out with the Cortes.[182] While Vizcayan salt prices were also lowered in August, the crown was particularly anxious to ensure that the Vizcayans paid their salt tax in full, not least because they enjoyed exemption from the *millones*. It therefore kept in being the new monopolistic organization for salt collection and distribution, under the direction of the *Junta de la Sal* in Madrid.

---

[178] Elliott, *Catalans*, p. 285.

[179] For this campaign, see Elliott, *Catalans*, ch. 10.

[180] BL Eg. Ms. 1820, fo. 216, Hopton to Coke, 19 November 1632.

[181] Renato Barahona, *Histoire d'une révolte en Biscaye: Bilbao, 1631–4* (unpublished thesis), p. 48. I am deeply indebted to Dr Barahona for allowing me to make use of his thesis, which represents a valuable attempt to make sense of the Vizcayan troubles.

[182] Domínguez Ortiz, *Política y hacienda*, p. 235; Gil Ayuso, *Noticia bibliográfica*, Doc. 979.

Early in October a deputy *corregidor*, Don Juan Calderón de la Barca, arrived in Bilbao, and made it clear from the start that he intended to enforce the rights of the crown. The government of the Señorío of Vizcaya and the city council of Bilbao found themselves under intense popular pressure to resist Calderón and his infamous designs. The Bilbao riots of 20–22 October can be seen at one level as an uprising in defence of traditional Basque liberties. But at another they constituted a movement of popular protest against the domination of the region's life by an entrenched oligarchy—by town councillors, and rich merchants and the local nobility, who formed an intricate network of power and patronage. 'Since in Vizcaya we are all equal', the people were saying, 'property, too, should be equal. It is not right that they should be rich and we poor, and that they should eat chicken, and we sardines.'[183]

The news of the Basque disorders came as an additional embarrassment to the administration when things were already sufficiently bad. Enormous and by no means unsuccessful efforts had been made over the past few months to raise more money, and yet there was very little to show for all the pain and sacrifice. 'You get to the mountain-top', wrote Olivares to Aytona in early October, 'and then everything falls, everything goes wrong. We never see a comforting letter; not a despatch arrives that does not tell us that everything is lost because we had failed to provide the money.'[184] Now a new domestic crisis had broken.

The immediate responsibility for advising the king fell on the Council of Castile, which recommended for the time being a cautious and conciliatory approach. The Council suggested that the *corregidor* of Vizcaya, Don Lope de Morales, who had been attending the Cortes in Madrid as *procurador* for Soria, should return immediately to calm the province by assuring the populace that the king had no intention of contravening their *fueros*. But it also recommended giving secret consideration to the punitive measures to be adopted once Vizcaya had been pacified.[185]

If Olivares did not himself inspire the Council's recommendations, he undoubtedly approved them, as did the king, who wrote mournfully on the *consulta*: 'I have read this *consulta* and the accompanying documents with the sadness that comes of seeing something in Spain the like of which has not been seen in centuries.' In spite of the enormity of the offence, however, a measured response was to be the order of the day. As the secretary of the Tuscan embassy noted, it was not a time 'for introducing internal wars and giving the Catalans

[183] 'Relación de lo sucedido . . .', in Guiard, *Historia de Bilbao*, 2, pp. 102–3.
[184] ADM, leg. 79, Olivares to Aytona, 6 October 1632.
[185] AHN Consejos, leg. 12,479, consulta, 4 November 1632.

and others an opportunity to revolt . . . . This would have very serious consequences for the conduct of foreign affairs, which at present have priority over everything else.'[186]

The priority of foreign policy was in fact to be the key to much of the internal history of Spain during the second half of the Olivares regime. The looming prospect of war with France increasingly dominated the Count-Duke's actions and thoughts. In October he was contemplating the possibility of a French invasion of northern Spain,[187] and in the circumstances it was hardly politic to risk a conflict with the inhabitants of provinces so close to France. He therefore approached the Basque problem with extreme circumspection. But his initial measures were not a success. Morales failed to pacify the Basques. So too did the Duke of Ciudad Real, the most prominent member of the Vizcayan nobility, and the grandson of Philip II's minister, Juan de Idiáquez, who was despatched to the province in the hope that his local influence would allow him to sway the hearts and minds of his compatriots. It proved a vain hope. The duke came of a family which now belonged to the Hispano-Italian aristocracy, and the Basques did not see him as one of themselves. In a memorandum written for Olivares on the Vizcayan troubles, Antonio Hurtado de Mendoza observed that the province no longer had an influential nobility of ancient lineage.[188]

In spite of these setbacks, the Count-Duke continued to proceed with caution, well aware that the faults were not all on one side. The salt monopoly had spawned a host of new officials, whose corrupt and extortionate practices had done much to increase the general discontent. The situation was made worse by the fact that much of the tax-collecting apparatus in the Basque provinces, as elsewhere in Spain, had fallen into the hands of the crown's Portuguese bankers,[189] whose general unpopularity was reinforced by the knowledge of their dubious orthodoxy. The great *auto de fe* of a group of Judaizing Portuguese, held in the Plaza Mayor of Madrid on 4 July before the king, the queen, the Count-Duke and an enormous crowd,[190] had captured the popular imagination and placed the stamp of divine and ecclesiastical approval on the rising tide of anti-Portuguese sentiment in the country as a whole. On the outskirts of Bilbao a rich Portuguese, who had lived there for twenty-five years, had his house burnt to the ground; in the province of Guipúzcoa, bordering on Vizcaya, native Portuguese were forbidden on pain of life

---

[186] ASF, Mediceo, filza 4959, letter of Bernardo Monanni, 6 November 1632.
[187] ADM, leg. 79, Olivares to Aytona, 12 October 1632.
[188] *Discursos de Mendoza*, p. 139 ('Al Conde-Duque, cuando las alteraciones de Vizcaya').
[189] ASF, Mediceo, filza 4959, letter of Bernardo Monanni, 11 December 1632.
[190] See Yerushalmi, *From Spanish Court to Italian Ghetto*, pp. 105–22, for an account of this *auto* and the attendant circumstances.

and forfeiture of property to involve themselves in revenue-collect-ing.[191]

It remained the Count-Duke's firm policy to cast his mantle of protection over the king's Portuguese bankers, who had made themselves indispensable. But it would have been highly impolitic for him to risk a confrontation with the Inquisition over specific cases of Judaizing, especially at a time when the Council of Castile itself was hinting that with so many Portuguese Jews coming and going freely at court, it was scarcely surprising if God was punishing Castile for its sinfulness.[192] Nor was there any reason to be over-zealous in the protection of the horde of Portuguese agents and minions who extorted money for themselves under the guise of collecting taxes for the king. Where grievances were legitimate, justice must be done.

In February 1633, therefore, all the administrators of the salt monopoly were dismissed by royal decree, and were replaced by three royal appointees, including the ubiquitous and indispensable José González. At the same time, numerous minor officials were deprived of their jobs.[193] But a way still had to be found of bringing the Basques to heel. After consulting with the many Basques at court and in the royal administration, Olivares decided to try an economic boycott. The inspectors and officials of the Almirantazgo had always been refused entry into Vizcaya on the grounds that their activities would infringe the province's *fueros*. In March 1633 the crown ordered the rigorous enforcement of Almirantazgo regulations. The object of this order was to deter merchants from importing goods by way of Bilbao and other Basque ports, in the knowledge that any such goods would be confiscated as unregistered merchandise when they crossed the border into Castile.[194]

'The Biscayans have a hard choice', wrote Arthur Hopton.[195] For a region so dependent on trade, a boycott meant slow economic strangulation. By the end of 1633 it was all over. The movement of protest seems to have been largely confined to the city of Bilbao and its immediate region, and the lack of unity among the Basques contributed to the undermining of resistance to Madrid. By the summer of 1634 Hopton could report that the royal proclamation on trade 'hath brought them so low as they have been content with an accommodation upon any conditions.'[196] In fact Olivares, perhaps influenced by his Basque ministers and officials, refrained from

[191] ASF, Mediceo, filza 4959, letter of Bernardo Monanni, 11 December 1632.
[192] AHN Consejos, leg. 7145, expte. 45, consulta of Council of Castile, 22 March 1632.
[193] ASF, Mediceo, filza 4959, letter of Bernardo Monanni, 26 February 1633.
[194] ASF, Mediceo, filza 4959, letter of Bernardo Monanni, 16 April 1633.
[195] BL Eg. Ms. 1820, fo. 253, Hopton to Coke, 12 April 1633.
[196] BL Eg. Ms. 1820, fo. 354, Hopton to Coke, 18 June 1634.

administering the kind of penalties that his success would have made possible. By a royal decree of 12 May 1634 the king acceded to the pleas of his loyal Vizcayan vassals and, in recognition of their long record of service to the crown, consented to restore the system used for supplying and distributing salt before the notorious decree of 3 January 1631. He also granted a general pardon, excluding only twelve named ringleaders of the troubles, of whom six managed to escape.

The Count-Duke, then, sacrificed a fiscal device which had brought him little but headaches, but at the same time continued to reassert the royal authority in Vizcaya without resort to arms. The quiescence of the Basques during the remainder of his years in office suggests that he had handled an awkward situation with skill. The Catalans, however, were to prove considerably more intractable, and the fault may in part have lain with Madrid. The Basques, unlike the Catalans, were well represented in the royal administration, and Olivares had at hand Basque secretaries and ministers who could both interpret their compatriots' behaviour to him and plead on their behalf. The Catalans, significantly, had no such advocates in high places, and it was Villanueva, an Aragonese, who took upon himself the task of assessing Catalan behaviour and orchestrating the responses of the court.

But there was always more to be won, or lost, in Catalonia than in Vizcaya. The principality passed for a rich and populous province, capable of making a substantial contribution to the common war effort. To give up here, and leave the Catalans to their own devices, would be tantamount to abandoning that great project for the unification of Spain which Olivares regarded as essential for the Monarchy's survival. In Catalonia, then, whatever the temporary setbacks, there could be no long-term retreat. The proximity of a hostile France suggested the need for caution, but by one means or another Barcelona would have to be made as submissive as Bilbao, and the Catalans be shown that no provincial rights and liberties could be allowed to stand in the way of necessities of state.

The internal and international problems of 1632 took a heavy toll of the Count-Duke's spirits and his energies. His correspondence is that of a man weighed down by his intolerable burdens and despairing of ever finding a way of escape. But there were moments of cheerfulness as well as periods of gloom. In the middle of June 1632, for instance, Hopton 'never saw him merrier, nor with greater appearances of confidence', and 'laughing very heartily' about the King of Sweden.[197] It seems as if he was endowed with a remarkable resilience. Scarcely was some new disaster reported when he would be producing new schemes to recoup his losses; and, hard-pressed on every side with more demands for money, he would plunge into fresh negotiations with the bankers, and emerge triumphantly brandishing another *asiento*. It was an extraordinary display of determination and stamina, which over the years would provoke the sometimes bemused admiration of foreign envoys in Madrid.

Arthur Hopton, who was rather too inclined to take the Count-Duke's assessments of himself and his achievements at face value, frequently remarked on his 'zeal and industry in his master's service', although he also felt that Olivares was too preoccupied with the business of raising money from the bankers—a characteristic which his rival, Richelieu, did not share.[198] 'I think', wrote Hopton, 'he hath so much lent his understanding to the affairs of interest and merchants as his proceedings with princes have savoured thereof, which may have been a cause that he hath thriven so well in the one and so ill in the other.'[199] If Hopton meant by this that Olivares haggled too much when negotiating with foreign powers, the charge is equally difficult to prove and disprove. He was a hard bargainer, as his stubborn handling of the periodic negotiations with the Dutch makes clear; but, if such negotiations display the mentality of a merchant, they also betray an obsessive concern with that most unmercantile of objectives, 'reputation'.

If the Count-Duke spent a lot of time on money-matters, this was because the maintenance of Spain's far-flung armies and fleets was entirely dependent on the smooth and efficient working of the *asiento* system. Money, as he knew, spoke loud in international affairs. 'Everything', he wrote, 'yields and has always yielded to a superior power, and power is regulated by money.'[200] While he would leave the preliminary arrangements for *asientos* to the Council of Finance and to experts like López Pereira, he knew that there were moments when his intervention was needed to bring the whole weight of the royal authority to bear on some recalcitrant banker. One per cent less on the rate of interest charged by the *asentistas* could make all the difference. So, too, could the punctual return of the treasure fleet, well stocked with supplies of silver. His tragedy was that over and over again long-term economic considerations were forced to take second place to fiscal expediency. On the one hand, for example, he would be telling the Count of La Puebla, president of the Council

[197] BL Eg. Ms. 1820, Hopton to Cottington, 16 June 1632.
[198] Elliott, *Richelieu and Olivares*, p. 137.
[199] BL Eg. Ms. 1820, fo. 253, Hopton to Coke, 18 December 1632.
[200] AGR CPE, Reg. 1502, fo. 15, Olivares to Roose, 6 March 1633.

of the Indies, that everything depended on the health of the Indies trade, and on the other he would be ordering La Puebla to appropriate 200,000 ducats in silver from Seville's Indies merchants, reimbursing them with worthless slips of paper.[201]

But the intensive fiscalism of 1631–2, however prejudicial to the Count-Duke's cherished schemes for Castile's economic recovery, seems at least in the short run to have been remarkably productive. In 1634 Hopton was writing that the crown's revenues had doubled over the past four years.[202] The clerical subsidy, the *media anata*, the sale of offices, the new grant of *millones* from the Cortes of Castile with their component of money from the sale of salt, all helped to reinforce royal credit and expand royal income at a moment when the state of international affairs urgently demanded it. The situation in the Netherlands in particular was extremely grave. The fall of Maastricht in August 1632 was followed by the loss of Limburg— news which gave Olivares a sleepless night[203]—and all the Spanish strongpoints on the Rhine were now in danger.[204] The army of Flanders was in a state of disarray, the civil administration demoralized, the Infanta old and ailing. Under intense pressure from her own subjects to negotiate a peace settlement, she was pushed in September into convening a meeting of the States General in Brussels, without first securing the permission of Madrid.[205]

But even as Olivares agonized, the military situation in the Low Countries was being stabilized. Spanish reinforcements had arrived from the Palatinate, and the Marquis of Aytona and his military colleagues succeeded in checking further advances by the forces of Frederick Henry, which had been weakened by the prolonged siege of Maastricht.[206] More troops would be needed, however, to turn the tide, and it was decided that the Cardinal-Infante should leave Catalonia for the Netherlands, if possible by the end of the year, going by way of Milan, where he and the Duke of Feria would assemble a great army for the march to Flanders.[207]

The civil problem, however, remained acute, and the Count-Duke watched with alarm as the States General in Brussels seized the initiative. One of its first acts was to appoint three commissioners to

---

[201] Archivo del Duque de Alba, Caja 58, nos. 256 and 262, Olivares to La Puebla, 11 June and 31 August 1632.

[202] BL Eg. Ms. 1820, Hopton to Coke, 18 June 1634.

[203] ADM, leg. 79, Olivares to Aytona, 12 October 1632.

[204] Lonchay, *Correspondance*, 2, Doc. 1970, Isabella to king, 8 November 1632.

[205] Waddington, *La République des Provinces-Unies*, 1, p. 181. For a brief survey of the discontents of the southern Netherlands in these years, see Paul Janssens, 'L'échec des tentatives de soulèvement aux Pays-Bas sous Philippe IV (1621–1665)', *Revue d'Histoire Diplomatique*, 92 (1978), pp. 110–29.

[206] Israel, *The Dutch Republic*, p. 188.

[207] ADM, leg. 79, Olivares to Aytona, 6 October and ? October 1632.

go to Maastricht and sound out Frederick Henry on his terms for a truce.[208] With defeatism so widespread in the Southern Provinces anything could happen now that the States General had involved itself in the truce negotiations, and Madrid hastily revoked the Infanta's powers to conclude a settlement.[209] The Dutch demands were so exaggerated as to shake even the States General,[210] but the Count-Duke was bound to feel deep concern over this new manifestation of independent activity by local corporations and assemblies, of the kind that he was simultaneously confronting in Catalonia and Vizcaya.

Like the Vizcayans and the Catalans, the people of the southern Netherlands were suffering from what Olivares called 'the appetite for a delusive liberty'.[211] It was part of a universal problem that met him at every turn. There was no obedience left among the vassals of the king, he complained to the Cardinal-Infante, and unless it were restored, the ship was bound to sink.[212] The *procuradores* of the Castilian Cortes, the town councillors of Barcelona, nobles, courtiers and royal officials—all of them, to a man, were out for their own interests, and forgot their duty to the crown. 'We Spaniards are very good when we are subjected to rigorous obedience, but left to ourselves we are the worst people in the world.' The only solution was to revive that 'severity' which had prevailed under the greatest of all Spain's kings, Ferdinand the Catholic.

The Count-Duke's plea for 'severity', for discipline and obedience, smacks of the neo-Stoic teaching of Justus Lipsius, the intellectual father of the Olivares generation. The appeal of Lipsian doctrine to the seventeenth-century statesman lay precisely in its evident applicability to the government of societies in which disobedience, disorder and an unbridled pursuit of 'liberty' presented a continuous challenge to his carefully pondered plans. Human nature, left to its own devices, was naturally inclined to the bad, and it was therefore essential to subject it to rigorous control. It is not therefore surprising that the Count-Duke's growing concern in 1632 with the general problem of obedience—a problem brought to the fore by the resurgence, whether in Castile, the Spanish periphery and now the Netherlands, of a constitutionalist opposition insistent on its privileges and historic rights and liberties—should have turned his mind again to the education of the young.

It was only through education at an impressionable age that the

[208] Waddington, *La République des Provinces-Unies*, 1, p. 183.
[209] Lonchay, *Correspondance*, 2, Doc. 1962, decree of Philip IV, 4 November 1632.
[210] Israel, *The Dutch Republic*, p. 240.
[211] AGS Est. leg. 2151, draft *voto* of Olivares, 14 April 1633.
[212] *MC*, 2, Doc. XI, Olivares to Cardinal-Infante, 27 September 1632.

civic virtues of service and obedience could be properly instilled. The young, he complained in his letter to the Cardinal-Infante, were not being properly trained.[213] He had sought to remedy this by establishing the Colegio Imperial in Madrid, but by 1632 the new foundation was visibly failing.[214] What he now proposed was the setting up of academies on the lines of those to be found in France and the Venetian Republic. At court, in addition to the household for the royal pages which came under his supervision as master of the horse, there should be two such academies, and others should be founded in Seville, Granada, Valladolid, Lisbon, Pamplona, and in Aragon.[215] The purpose of these academies would be to provide a military and 'political' education, and—as Olivares' plans were later elaborated by a special *Junta de educación*[216]—they would combine practical training in the military arts with a theoretical training in mathematics, geography, mechanics, and 'the political and economic arts which train the mind for public and domestic government.'

Didactic by temperament, authoritarian in his responses, the Count-Duke was always struggling to reduce chaos to order and conform the world to his image. Disobedient nobles, obstructionist representative assemblies, unruly provinces must all be brought under the iron hand of discipline. But to find the disciplinarians was no easy task. That was why his spirits rose when he came across a man like Pierre Roose, the lawyer from Louvain, whom he singled out for promotion to the presidency of the *conseil privé* in Brussels.[217] Writing in December 1632 on his way from Spain to Brussels to take up his presidency, Roose showed that he fully appreciated what Olivares required of him when he sent him on his mission—the need for that 'extreme effort' which could alone shore up the crumbling edifice of Spanish administration in the Netherlands. His orders were to find a means of dissolving the States General, and reestablishing justice on a firm foundation. It was, Roose wrote, the lack of justice which was at the root of the trouble—of that justice which 'gave to the Romans discipline, economy, and—through them—universal empire.'[218] This was the kind of sentiment that the Count-Duke loved to hear. To do what had to be done, he needed a Roose in every province.

During the course of 1632 his government had been hard-pressed on every side as it struggled to mobilize the resources for a war

---

[213] *Ibid.*, p. 76.
[214] Above, p. 188.
[215] *MC*, 2, Doc. XIIC.
[216] Biblioteca de la Universidad de Salamanca, Ms. 2064, no. 4, consulta of *Junta de educación*, 12 January 1636. See also *MC*, 2, pp. 65–73, for these educational projects.
[217] Above, pp. 405–6.
[218] AGR CPE, Reg. 1502, fo. 8, Roose to Olivares, 15 December 1632.

which seemed to consist of nothing but reverses and disasters. But then, at the very end of the year, the clouds suddenly lifted to reveal the hidden uplands. On 25 December the first reports reached Madrid of the death on 16 November of Gustavus Adolphus on the battlefield of Lützen.[219] Two days later the news was confirmed, and was celebrated with fireworks, and a *Te Deum* in the royal chapel.[220] After all the misfortunes of 1632, Olivares wrote to Aytona, there was cheerful news at last.[221]

[219] ASF Mediceo, filza 4959, letters of Bernardo Monanni, 29 January and 5 February 1633.
[220] Hoz, p. 208.
[221] ADM, leg. 79, Olivares to Aytona, 4 January 1633.

XII

THE CONFRONTATION WITH FRANCE

Reopening the road

Anyone visiting the Count-Duke in his study in the palace had first
to pass through a small gallery, the walls of which were hung with
portraits of madmen and fools.[1] Presumably the Count-Duke had
arranged this somewhat bizarre decorative scheme as a reminder of
the vanity of the human intellect and the follies of hubris among
the mighty of this world. For all his awareness of the unpredictability
of events and the fallibility of men, there were moments when he
himself stood in need of the reminder. One of these moments came
with the news of the battle of Lützen. Carried away by an understandable elation, he told his colleagues at a meeting of the Council of
State on 9 January 1633 that 'this is the moment to finish everything
off and settle the affairs of the Empire, secure the election of [the
Emperor's son as] King of the Romans, achieve an honourable peace
with the Dutch, resolve the problems of Italy, restore Lorraine, and
sow in France the discord that it so handsomely deserves.'[2] The same
euphoria may have prompted the decision taken during these weeks
to expand dramatically the building works on the royal apartment
of San Jerónimo, and transform it at great expense into a palace
complex worthy of a triumphant King of Spain.[3]

As soon as the news of Gustavus Adolphus' death reached Madrid,
Olivares had begun to address his ingenious mind to the ways in
which the House of Austria could derive the maximum benefit from
this unforeseen event. As always, he had to bear in mind several
different but related theatres of conflict. There was Germany itself,
now miraculously saved when on the very brink of catastrophe. There
were the Netherlands, and, by overseas extension, Brazil, where the
Dutch were beginning to consolidate their hold. And there were
the marchlands between France and the Empire—Alsace, Lorraine,
the Rhine Valley region—where French encroachments had put at

---

[1] AAE, Correspondance politique, Espagne, tome 15, fo. 285v., M. de Bautru, *Relation
de la première conférence que j'ai eu avec M. le Comte-Duc*, 27 November 1628.
[2] AGS Est. leg. 2334, consulta, 9 January 1633.
[3] Brown and Elliott, *A Palace*, pp. 62–4.

risk the military corridors that allowed Spain to provision Flanders
from its bases in Italy.

It was Cardinal Richelieu whose machinations linked these three
theatres, seeking everywhere to foster resistance to the House of Austria, and quick to offer subsidies and encouragement when he saw
a chance of damaging Spain's interests. As soon as the Cardinal had
assessed the implications of Gustavus' death, he was at it again. He
told Louis that, while France should not shrink from open war with
Spain if this proved necessary, it was essential that the German Protestants and the United Provinces should not lay down their arms.[4]
Charnacé was therefore sent to the Hague to encourage the United
Provinces, which were deeply divided over the issue of war or peace,
to persist in their struggle; while the Marquis de Feuquières, who
was under instructions to strengthen the alliance with the German
Protestant princes, negotiated in February 1633 the League of Heil-
bronn, whereby the Swedes, under Oxenstierna's leadership, were
to take the lead in 'restoring the Imperial constitution', leaving France
discreetly in the shadows.[5]

Like Richelieu, the Count-Duke also seems by now to have decided
that, barring some unexpected turn of events, a Franco-Spanish war
was inevitable, but he, too, like Richelieu, hoped to defer it until
the time was right. His first task was to seize the opportunity afforded
by Lützen to restore peace to Germany. This in turn would release
the Imperial army under Wallenstein for further services to the House
of Austria, and specifically to Spain. For the two great objectives
of his German policy remained as fixed as ever: a great league or
confederation of Madrid, Vienna, and the German princes to hold
France in check; and the assistance of Imperial forces in reducing
the Dutch.

He explained his intentions in a cyphered letter of 23 January to
Father Quiroga.[6] The Emperor was to be offered large subsidies,
'paid for out of the blood of the king's vassals.' The supreme objective
at this most favourable of moments was to

> unite the Emperor, the Duke of Friedland, the Empire and our-
> selves in peace and war against the Dutch... If the two Houses
> do not pool their interests, both will be lost. We should repay
> God for the favours He has shown us on this occasion by securing
> for once and all the Catholic religion in Germany. The way to
> do this is to unite and incorporate the affairs of Holland and Flanders
> with those of the Empire... This is our chance to drive the blade

---

[4] Fagniez, *Le Père Joseph et Richelieu*, 2, pp. 108–9.
[5] Mann, *Wallenstein* p. 677; Victor L. Tapié, *La France de Louis XIII et de Richelieu* (Paris, 1967), p. 296.
[6] BL Add. Ms. 24,909, fos. 285–6, Olivares to Quiroga, 23 January 1633.

home (*apretar los puños*) . . . If things go wrong this year, everything is lost, and we shall be so debilitated by our heavy expenditure that we shall never recover.

To achieve all this, Olivares, like Richelieu, sent out his ambassadors. The Count of Oñate, growing old and touchy, reluctantly accepted a new assignment to return to Germany as ambassador extraordinary to the Emperor. The principal objects of his mission were to secure the King of Hungary's election as King of the Romans, thus ensuring the continuation of the Imperial title in the House of Austria; the reconciliation with the Emperor of the Lutheran Elector of Saxony; and the organization of a league or confederation of Spain, the Emperor and princes of the Empire, the exiled French Queen Mother, Gaston d'Orléans, and Charles, Duke of Lorraine.[7] Since Oñate's relations with Maximilian of Bavaria were notoriously bad, Don Diego de Saavedra Fajardo was sent to Munich, where it was hoped that a suitably chastened Maximilian would show himself more cooperative than in the past.[8] As for Wallenstein, the central figure in all the Count-Duke's calculations, a special envoy, Ottavio Villani, had already been chosen in the autumn of 1632,[9] and he reached Prague belatedly on 16 February after being laid up by a fall from his horse.[10]

These diplomatic moves were to be accompanied by a spectacular deployment of Spain's military might. The proposal that the Cardinal-Infante should join his aunt in Brussels had taken a long time to mature, not least because Swedish and French advances had blocked the military corridors from Lombardy to Flanders so that there was no safe land-route available. The decision taken in the autumn of 1632 that the Duke of Feria should assemble an army of 16,000 in Milan to accompany him on the journey[11] reflected these difficulties. During the winter of 1632–3, however, the already complex plans became more complex still. In November, Feria had received a letter from the Infanta asking if he could send help to the Franche-Comté, which she was in no position to defend from Flanders. In response to this plea, and to his own preoccupations about the need to clear a route for the Cardinal-Infante, he wrote to Madrid on 4 February 1633 proposing the formation of an army in Germany, along the lines of the Count-Duke's proposal of 1631 for an army of the

---

[7] AGS Est. leg. 2047, *Sobre los puntos sustanciales de la instrucción embiada al Conde de Oñate,* 1 February 1633.
[8] AGS Est. leg. 2334, consulta, 26 February 1633.
[9] AGS Est. leg. 2333, *Lo que parece al Conde-Duque se podría dar para instrucción al Regente Ottavio Vilani . . .* (October 1632).
[10] AGS Est. leg. 2334, Villani to Olivares, 1 March 1633.
[11] Above, p. 453.

Palatinate.[12] This army would defend the Franche-Comté, ensure the safety of the Tyrol, support the military efforts of the Emperor, and come to the help of Italy in case of need.

Hardly had Madrid had time to approve this proposal when Feria submitted new and still more ambitious plans. The army of Alsace, for which he had originally proposed 15,000 men, should be enlarged to 20,000 infantry and 4,000 cavalry. This, he believed, would be sufficient for him to be able to recover Alsace itself, ensure the safety of the Franche-Comté, and clear the Moselle and Rhine of enemy forces as far as Cologne.[13] The Council of State approved this revised scheme on 27 March, although with some anxiety about its implications for Spain's relations with its allies. It would be necessary, for instance, to force a passage through the Grisons, and for this the Emperor's permission would be needed. Olivares also emphasized the need to calm fears in Germany about the presence of a large Spanish army on German soil by appealing to the Emperor, the Duke of Bavaria and Wallenstein to give Feria all possible assistance.

The order for the formation of an army of Alsace of 24,000 men was sent out on 8 April, and the Cardinal-Infante, appointed general-issimo of all the armies, was ordered to leave at once for Flanders. He sailed from Barcelona on 11 April, and reached Genoa on 5 May.[14] The great machine was being laboriously set in motion—a machine designed to impress the world once again with the overwhelming power of Spain. The costs, inevitably, would be enormous, and Olivares believed that the Monarchy had never, even in its most flourishing days, made preparations on such a massive scale.[15] How to find the money remained, as always, a problem. In April a junta containing some of Olivares' closest confidants met to consider once again the question of desempeño, the redemption of crown debts. Some members of the junta questioned the feasibility of proceeding with the redemption of debts in time of war, but the king, recalling the decision of Hernán Cortés to scuttle his ships in Mexico, expressed his determination to go ahead, and appointed a three-man commission for the task. A financial reserve had to be built up, untouchable even in the most extreme emergency, since credit was the key to success.[16]

In a letter sent to the Marquis of Aytona in March explaining his military dispositions for the year, the Count-Duke expressed both

---

[12] Above. p. 434.

[13] AGS Est. leg. 3340, fo. 114, paper by Duke of Feria, 7 August 1633, summarizing history of army of Alsace.

[14] A. Van der Essen, Le Cardinal-Infant et la politique européenne de l'Espagne (Brussels, 1944), pp. 78–80.

[15] AGR CPE, Reg. 1502, fo. 14v., Olivares to Roose, 16 February 1633.

[16] AHN Est. lib. 871, fos. 17–36v., consulta of Junta, 17 April 1633.

his worries and his hopes.[17] It seemed impossible that human means alone could avert 'the final ruin', but prayers were being said in all the churches for the success of Spanish arms. With God's help, the Cardinal-Infante's army would succeed in 'opening the road, which would also open the way to the relief of the fortresses beyond the Meuse, and those along the Rhine.' But everyone was worried that the French would attack the Franche-Comté while the Dutch invested another garrison town. 'This is our supreme concern . . . Today everything is directed towards defending ourselves from France.' In February he had sent a new and intransigent ambassador to Paris, Cristóbal de Benavente y Benavides, with instructions to insist on territorial concessions by Louis XIII, and the abandonment of his Swedish allies.[18] But he confessed in a letter to Roose that, if only the French would leave Spain in peace and give up meddling in the affairs of the Netherlands, he would forgive them everything and agree to a firm treaty of peace and friendship. After twelve years of war he longed for a good peace. But if the French remained determined to take on Spain, as they seemed to be, they were running a great risk in challenging a power that was stronger than themselves.[19]

The French unfortunately showed no inclination to keep out of the affairs of others. Charnacé dangled before the Dutch the bait of a larger subsidy, and although they were in no great hurry to swallow it, the Count-Duke's insistence that the restoration of Pernambuco was essential for a settlement was a serious discouragement to the peace party in the northern provinces, and strengthened the French envoy's hand.[20] In the southern Netherlands Olivares was counting on Roose to prevent the delegates of the States General from agreeing to the intolerable conditions demanded by the Dutch. Yet even as he played for time while the Cardinal-Infante's army assembled for its march to Flanders, his fertile mind was toying with new ideas for relieving Spain of its burdensome northern commitment. If he could only find a way to establish an equilibrium between the United Provinces and the loyal provinces of the southern Netherlands, he was prepared to contemplate Spain's abandonment of the southern provinces, leaving it only with control of Antwerp, Namur, Cambrai and the Channel ports. Adopting any form of government they wished, the southern Netherlanders would be free to reach an accommodation with the Dutch, secure in the knowledge that Spain

---

[17] ADM leg. 79, Olivares to Aytona, ? March 1633.
[18] Leman, *Urbain VIII*, p. 278.
[19] AGR CPE, Reg. 1502, fos. 15–17, Olivares to Roose, 6 March 1633.
[20] Israel, *The Dutch Republic*, p. 245; Gabriel Hanotaux and the Duc de La Force, *Histoire du Cardinal de Richelieu*, 6 vols. (Paris, 1893–1947), 5 pp. 74–5; Henrard, *Marie de Médicis*, p. 355.

would guarantee their military security in the event of attack. 'In this way we should be incomparably better off than we are now, and the loss of reputation would be more than offset by the practical gains.'[21]

This is the first known occasion on which the Count-Duke openly considered the possibility of an eventual withdrawal from the Netherlands, even if only an incomplete withdrawal. But with the southern provinces so close to collapse, he was still a long way from attaining his essential precondition—a balance of power between north and south. Such a balance, however, might be achieved if the Cardinal-Infante arrived in Flanders at the head of a great new army, while the Imperial army under Wallenstein struck at the United Provinces from across their eastern border. Everything therefore turned on the ever-enigmatic Wallenstein, who stood at the centre of all the Count-Duke's calculations in these opening months of 1633.

Wallenstein, however, lived up to his reputation. A long letter from Ottavio Villani to Olivares, written in Prague on 1 March, reached Madrid on 30 April. Its contents, describing Villani's reception by Wallenstein, were deeply disturbing.[22] Although Wallenstein had made flattering remarks about the Count-Duke, he also left Villani in no doubt that there was no question of helping Spain fight the Dutch as long as the problems of the Empire remained unresolved. Villani suspected that money was at the bottom of it—he still had his territorial ambitions, he was very short of cash to pay his men, and he insisted that Spanish ministers had promised him a subsidy of 200,000 florins a month. Without this money his army would disintegrate and he would be driven to desperation.

Olivares was shaken. The situation in Germany proved to be so very different from what he had understood, not so much because of the strength of the enemy as of Wallenstein's shortage of funds for campaigning. But the Count-Duke reaffirmed his confidence in Wallenstein himself: 'That man is not mad, and has achieved great things in the world, many of them against all expectations. My only fear is lest his vast ambition causes us embarrassment and drags us into something from which there is no way of escape.' Olivares had in fact received private information from Dr. Agustín Navarro, Wallenstein's Spanish confidant, that the general had set his heart on acquiring the electorate of Brandenburg.[23] This was very worrying. 'If we oppose him on this, he will be driven to an act of desperation, and will lose everything in a day. But if we humour him we shan't

---

[21] AGS Est. leg. 2151, Draft by Olivares for consulta of Council of State, 14 April 1633.
[22] AGS Est. leg. 2334.
[23] See Emilio Beladiez, *España y el Sacro Imperio Romano Germánico. Wallenstein, 1583–1634* (Madrid, 1967), pp. 328–9.

be able to support him; and if he is lost we are all lost, since I can't see sufficient biscuit for such a long voyage.'[24]

With prospects of help from Wallenstein so uncertain, the Count-Duke looked for salvation to the embryonic army of Alsace. It was essential that the Cardinal-Infante and the Duke of Feria should get their army to Flanders before the States General of the southern provinces, seduced by the senior noble of Brabant, the Duke of Aerschot, and his pusillanimous or treacherous aristocratic friends, could sell out to the Dutch.[25] By the beginning of July the army of Alsace was almost ready, but then a new and unexpected difficulty arose. In a letter from Milan dated 5 July, which reached Madrid on the 17th, the Duke of Feria reported that the Emperor, bowing to pressure from Wallenstein, seemed unwilling to allow his army to enter Alsace.[26] His instructions had not taken into account the possibility of a refusal of transit facilities by the Emperor. With Alsace itself in danger of being totally lost to the enemy, and with the vital Rhine crossing at Breisach threatened by General Horn's Swedes, how was he to convey the Cardinal-Infante and his army to Flanders in the event of an official refusal arriving from Vienna?

All Wallenstein's suspicions of Spain had been revived by the prospect of another army on German soil, outside his own control. Sick and cantankerous, with his influence over his own officers and men visibly declining, he lashed out against the Spaniards and their aggressive, blundering ways.[27] But Wallenstein's increasingly eccentric behaviour was adding to the number of his enemies in Vienna, and its was always possible that Ferdinand, when pressed by Spain's envoys, the Count of Oñate and the Marquis of Castañeda, might agree to change his mind. At a meeting of the Council of State held on 19 August the Count-Duke argued in favour of forcing the issue. The Cardinal-Infante should be ordered to begin his northwards march, and the Emperor be told that if he was not prepared to send troops to ensure his safety on the journey, he would receive no more money from Madrid.[28]

Castañeda was able to report from Vienna in the second week of August that Ferdinand had indeed after all changed his mind.[29] Breisach and Constance were both in danger of falling to the Swedes, and Ferdinand had no choice in the circumstances but to allow the movement of Spanish forces from Italy into Alsace, however much Wallenstein might object. The Cardinal-Infante would remain for

[24] AGS Est. leg. 2334, consulta, 11 May 1633.
[25] AGS Est. leg. 2151, voto of Olivares, 30 May 1633.
[26] AGS Est. leg. 3339, fo. 163.
[27] Mann, Wallenstein, p. 713.
[28] AGS Est. leg. 3339, fo. 135, consulta, 19 August 1633.
[29] AGS Est. leg. 2334, consulta, 25 September 1633.

the time being in Milan, while the Duke of Feria would go to Breisach's relief with the help of German regiments under the command of Wallenstein's lieutenant, Aldringen, who had been seconded to Maximilian of Bavaria. The willingness of Maximilian to send Bavarians to Feria's aid suggests how far the ever-menacing presence of the Swedes had forced him to retreat from his pro-French stance.[30]

As Feria prepared himself for his march, the situation along the western frontier of the Empire was rapidly deteriorating. Louis XIII and Richelieu had grown exasperated with the behaviour of Charles, Duke of Lorraine, who had allowed Spain and the Emperor to raise troops on his lands, and was known to be conspiring with Gaston and the Spaniards.[31] On 31 August Louis appeared at the head of an army beneath the walls of Nancy. Charles, hoping in vain for help from Wallenstein, was unable to resist French demands, which included a thirty-year occupation of his capital. On 25 September Louis entered Nancy in state, and four months later the duke abdicated.

A strong French military presence in Lorraine was essential to Richelieu's anti-Habsburg strategy. At a meeting of the Spanish Council of State on 17 September, the Count-Duke angrily spelled out the implications of France's maltreatment of Duke Charles.[32] If, as already seemed probable, Louis seized Lorraine, he would have succeeded in cutting communications between Germany and the Netherlands except by way of Cologne. Already controlling Alsace and Breisgau, with the exception of the crossing-point at Breisach, he was poised to cut the final links between Italy and Germany. The geo-strategic considerations that were never far beneath the surface of the Count-Duke's mind were now uppermost in his thoughts.

> The King of France has entirely closed the Italy–Flanders route. France lies between Spain and Flanders, so that no help from Germany can reach either Flanders or Italy; none from Italy can reach Flanders; and none can reach Spain from Flanders or Flanders from Spain except by way of the Channel, bordered by French ports on one side and English ports on the other, and swarming with Dutch.

He saw the danger as even greater now than in the days of Gustavus Adolphus. In this terrible extremity there was no option but to 'die doing something' (*morir haciendo*), for to acquiesce in any settlement imposed on the Duke of Lorraine by the French was tantamount to acquiescence in the closure of the Milan to Brussels road.

---

[30] Leman, *Urbain VIII*, p. 305.
[31] Hanotaux, *Richelieu*, 5, p. 9; Carl J. Burckhardt, *Richelieu and his Age*, 3 vols. (London, 1940–71), 3, pp. 27–30.
[32] AGS Est. K.1416, fo. 56; Van der Essen, *Le Cardinal-Infant*, pp. 279–80.

To preserve the Spanish Road and recover Alsace, divine and human aid must alike be mobilized. In Spain itself a spiritual house-cleaning was needed, with the proclamation of public prayers for the Catholic cause, victory and peace, and a new campaign for the reformation of morals. War with France now seemed so close that the only remaining hope was to form a grand alliance for the restoration of peace in Christendom. This alliance should be headed by the pope, the King of Spain and the Emperor, and have at its disposal an army 40,000 strong under the supreme command of the Cardinal-Infante.[33] Wallenstein's participation was obviously problematic in view of his recent eccentric behaviour. The Marquis of Castañeda had relayed to Madrid the growing suspicions in Vienna about his loyalty to the Emperor, but Olivares, although now conceding that his capriciousness amounted to a form of madness, was still disposed to give him the benefit of the doubt. There was insufficient evidence to convict him of disloyalty, and even if there were, it would be prudent to dissimulate. The Count-Duke, indeed, professed himself more preoccupied with the vacillations of the Emperor than the vagaries of his general. But if the Duke of Feria succeeded in relieving Breisach and liberating Lorraine he would be in a strong position to persuade the Emperor to participate in an alliance against the Dutch.[34]

Feria had in fact crossed the Alps on 5 September with 8,000 infantry and 1,300 cavalry—some three weeks too late, according to Olivares' timetable, with the fate of Lorraine hanging in the balance.[35] The Count-Duke was prepared to promise him all the money he needed. The silver fleet had arrived on 13 July with seven million *pesos* registered, and a suspected three million in contraband.[36] In the third week of September *asientos* were concluded with the bankers for the whole of 1634, with the Genoese undertaking to provide some four million ducats and the Portuguese another 1,200,000.[37] With regular payments guaranteed there seemed a good chance that Madrid's high expectations of Feria's army would be realized, in spite of reports that it was badly equipped.[38]

Joined by Aldringen's Germans, Feria executed a skilful march that cleared the entire route from Constance to Breisach, which his forces relieved on 20 October.[39] The victories could hardly have come at a better moment. A new clandestine pamphlet had just found its

---

[33] Details of the alliance in Günter, *Die Habsburger-Liga*, Docs. 111 and 112.

[34] AGS Est. leg. 2334, consulta, 25 September 1633. See also Günter, Doc. 116.

[35] AGS Est. leg. 2334, consulta, 27 October 1633.

[36] ADM leg. 79, Olivares to Aytona, 19 July 1633.

[37] ASF, Mediceo, filza 4959, letter of Bernardo Monanni, 24 September 1633; AGS CJH leg. 711, *Consignaciones de las provisones generales del año de 1634*.

[38] Marrades, *El camino del Imperio*, p. 161.

[39] Mann, *Wallenstein*, p. 736.

way into the hands of the king and many of the court notables, attacking the Count-Duke and his government, and lamenting the decline of Spain's military prestige. The regime at once produced a six-page response, answering point by point.[40] It was just about this time that the great building works extending the king's quarters at the monastery of San Jerónimo into a suburban palace were nearing completion, and the great central hall of the new extension required decoration. Partly perhaps in order to counter criticisms of expenditure on frivolities in times of war, it was decided to provide the hall with a decorative scheme commemorating the power and extension of the Monarchy, the greatness of the dynasty and the glories of the reign. This hall, which came to be known as the Hall of Realms because the escutcheons of the various realms of the Monarchy were painted on its ceiling, was to be adorned with equestrian portraits of Philip III and Philip IV and their consorts, and of Baltasar Carlos, the heir to the throne. It was also to be decorated with scenes from the life of Hercules, the founding father of the dynasty; and along the two side walls, between the windows, were to hang twelve large paintings commemorating battles won by Spanish arms since the accession of Philip IV. A number of these paintings, especially commissioned from Spain's leading painters with Velázquez at their head, commemorated the victories of 1625, the *annus mirabilis*. But, as if in direct response to the charge that Spain's military reputation was on the wane, three of them were devoted to the Duke of Feria's triumphs at Constance, Rheinfelden and Breisach in these very months. The paintings were to prove more permanent than the victories they celebrated.[41]

In order to support Feria, Aldringen had been forced to move his men away from their defence posts along the Danube, and Bernard of Saxe-Weimar seized the opportunity to advance on Regensburg, which controlled the road to Vienna. Wallenstein responded too late to the appeals of the Emperor and Maximilian of Bavaria for help. On 14 November Regensburg fell.[42] During these months the Spanish ambassador in Vienna had been warning Madrid of Wallenstein's unreliability and of the hostility with which he was regarded at the Emperor's court. But there was a tendency in Madrid to discount Castañeda's warnings on the grounds that he had associated himself too closely with the King of Hungary, who hated Wallenstein, and in so doing had alienated Spain's staunchest friend among the

[40] ASF, Mediceo, filza 4959, letter of Bernardo Monanni, 15 October 1633. I have been unable to locate a copy either of the original attack or of the response.
[41] For a detailed description of the Hall of Realms and its decorative scheme, see Brown and Elliott, *A Palace*, ch. 6.
[42] Beladiez, *España y el Sacro Imperio*, pp. 345–6.

Emperor's advisers, Johann Ulrich von Eggenberg.[43] Father Quiroga, who still enjoyed Wallenstein's confidence, continued to assure Madrid that there were no grounds for believing that he was engaged in treasonable activities; and the Spanish ambassador extraordinary, Oñate, believed that Wallenstein's failure to relieve Regensburg was no more than a strategic error, although he also felt that he needed watching.[44]

As the Wallenstein drama approached its terrible climax, Madrid continued to operate on the assumption that this strange man could both be trusted and used. The news reaching court during the final weeks of 1633 seemed to make his help all the more necessary. It was only in mid-November, with despatches from Abbot Scaglia, now Spain's ambassador to Marie de Médicis in Brussels, that the full extent of the disaster that had overtaken the Duke of Lorraine became apparent. It broke his heart, Olivares said, that at a time of such critical danger the lack of news and the non-arrival of despatches from all over Europe made it almost impossible to assess the degree of damage. But the fall of Nancy, now belatedly confirmed, could only be regarded as a major disaster—a disaster that might have been averted, the Count-Duke hastened to add, if only the Council of State had accepted his advice in 1631 and approved the formation of an army of the Palatinate.[45]

More bad news arrived early in December with fresh despatches from Scaglia, this time reporting the discovery of a plot among the Flemish nobility to liberate the Netherlands from Spanish rule.[46] A special session of the Council of State was called on 8 December, probably the first to be held in the new palace of the Buen Retiro, where the king had taken up residence for the first time that week.[47] It was essential to shore up Spain's position in the Low Countries before it was too late. This required the dissolution of the States General, a Trojan horse in the eyes of the ministers in Madrid, and a determination to press ahead with the reformation of the army of Flanders. It also required a vigorous new attempt to realize the Count-Duke's dream of a deployment of Imperial forces against the Dutch. Oñate was therefore to approach Wallenstein, expressing Spain's willingness to consider his claims to the Rhine Palatinate, in spite of Bavarian and British interest in the Elector's lands. It was desirable, remarked Olivares a few weeks later, to 'do much' for Wallenstein, but without letting oneself be deceived by 'fantastic

[43] AGS Est. leg. 2334, consulta, 29 October 1633.
[44] Beladiez, *España y el Sacro Imperio*, p. 349.
[45] AGS Est. K.1416, fo. 71, consulta, 18 November 1633.
[46] Information about the conspiracy was revealed to Scaglia by Charles I's agent in Brussels, Balthazar Gerbier (Henrard, *Marie de Médicis*, p. 444).
[47] AGS Est. K.1416, fo. 72, consulta, 8 December 1633.

hopes and airy discourses, or being subjected to the heavenly constellations and mathematical computations.'[48]

Germany, as always, was the key to the Netherlands. All the reports flowing in to Madrid during these last weeks of 1633 suggested that France would declare war on Spain in the coming spring.[49] To save Flanders, the Count-Duke would have liked to strike against France from Spain, 'but we must disabuse ourselves that this is feasible in the present state of things', with all the expense of subsidies for Germany, the maintenance of Feria's army, the troubles in Flanders, and the organization of an expedition under Don Fadrique de Toledo for the recovery of Brazil. Everything therefore turned on the negotiations with the Emperor and Wallenstein.

These negotiations were to be governed by two important considerations. Simultaneous war against France and the United Provinces was out of the question without help from the Emperor and the Empire. But peace with the Dutch was equally out of the question unless they were willing to dissolve the West Indies Company, restore Pernambuco, and hand back Maastricht, perhaps in exchange for Breda and a cash payment of one million ducats. The second consideration was that, if Wallenstein insisted on pressing his claims to the Palatinate, they should be handled in such a way as to avoid antagonizing Charles I and Maximilian of Bavaria.

This was a tall order, even for a diplomat of Oñate's experience. Matters were made worse by the non-arrival of the silver galleons, which were delayed in Havana, and would not reach Cadiz until 15 February 1634.[50] Until they came, no funds were available for Germany. But the situation, already urgent, was made all the more so by the death of the Infanta in Brussels on 1 December 1633.[51] The secret instructions opened in Brussels as the Infanta lay dying made provision for the transfer of power to a five-man junta, but the king at once signed an order appointing the Marquis of Aytona interim governor general. The interim, however, was intended to be short. The Cardinal-Infante was to start as soon as possible on his hazardous journey to Flanders.[52]

Now that Lorraine was under French control, it was necessary to devise a safer, more easterly, route for the Cardinal-Infante—one which would take him through Bohemia and Saxony, and then westwards again to Cologne.[53] It was hoped that Wallenstein would provide an escort of 6,000 men for the occasion, and the indefatigable

[48] AGS Est. leg. 2335, consulta, 8 January 1634.
[49] AGS Est. leg. 2047, consulta, 27 December 1633.
[50] Chaunu, *Séville et l'Atlantique*, 5, p. 258.
[51] Hoz, p. 217 (the news reached Madrid on 18 January 1634).
[52] Alcalá-Zamora, *España, Flandes*, p. 340; Lonchay, *Correspondance*, 2, Doc. 2187.
[53] Mann, *Wallenstein*, p. 759.

Father Quiroga set off for Pilsen to put Madrid's request to the general-issimo. At a long interview on 4 January 1634 Wallenstein heard him out, but would have nothing to do with the scheme. As long as the Swedes remained undefeated, the suggested route was too dangerous, and the Cardinal-Infante's journey was best postponed.[54]

Ironically, on the very day of this interview at Pilsen, the Count-Duke was writing in a letter to the viceroy of Sicily, the Duke of Alcalá, that 'the affairs of this world seem to be turning rather more in favour of this Monarchy, for the Dukes of Friedland and Feria have been continuing their progress.'[55] But so far from continuing his progress, Wallenstein had made none, and was patently becoming an obstacle to Spanish designs. Feria, for his part, had come to a halt. As his troops were preparing to take up winter quarters, they were stricken by typhus, which scythed its way through their ranks. Feria himself contracted the disease, and—already gravely ill—was carried to Munich, where he died on 11 February 1634.[56] More a great proconsul than a great general, his death left a gaping void. In a letter from the court a contemporary described him, with par-donable exaggeration, as 'the first man in this Monarchy.'[57] There were all too few *cabezas*—too few real leaders—in the Spain of Olivares.

Even before the news of Feria's death reached Madrid, the Count-Duke was being notably cautious about a break with France. The French occupation of Pinerolo and Lorraine provided justification enough; but Castile was exhausted, and the country was in no condi-tion to embark on a new war.[58] The Count-Duke's natural inclination to temporize was reinforced by the news of Feria's death, which removed the last chance of an effective spring campaign by the ill-fated army of Alsace. Already the Swedes and the French were seizing the opportunity to reoccupy the ground lost in the autumn.[59] The unsettled condition of Flanders, too, held him back. Although the nobles' plot had been uncovered in time, the situation in Brussels remained very dangerous. Fortunately, the Infanta in the last weeks of her life had managed to get the most prominent member of the nobility, the Duke of Aerschot, out of the country on the pretext of sending him on an important mission to Madrid.[60]

---

[54] *Ibid.*, pp. 761–2; Beladiez, *España y el Sacro Imperio*, pp. 361–2.
[55] RAH 11-13-3, Olivares to Alcalá, 4 January 1634.
[56] Marrades, *El camino del Imperio*, p. 163. The news arrived in Madrid on 10 February (Hoz, p. 219).
[57] *MHE*, 13, p. 18 (*Cartas de algunos P.P. de la Compañía de Jesús*, 14 February 1634).
[58] AHN Est. leg. 864, fos. 124–144v., *El Conde-Duque sobre la materia de romper o no con Francia*, 26 January 1634 (original in AGS Est. K.1423).
[59] Van der Essen, *Le Cardinal-Infant*, pp. 375–6.
[60] Lonchay, *Correspondance*, 2, Doc. 2163, Infanta to Philip IV, 12 November 1633.

Aerschot had played a leading part in the peace initiatives undertaken by the States General of the Southern Provinces, and had therefore cast himself in the villain's role in the eyes of Olivares and his colleagues. When he arrived in Madrid they gave him a reception befitting his rank, but it seems to have been designed primarily to satisfy his vanity and lull his suspicions. At an interview on 2 February in the palace, the Count-Duke questioned him closely on peace prospects with the Dutch.[61] His responses were not reassuring. In the face of Olivares' scepticism about the genuineness of the Dutch desire for peace, he urged that negotiations should continue in spite of the Infanta's death, and seemed curiously naïf about the ambitions of the Dutch in Brazil. He also made it clear that, in the event of a truce or a peace, the Southern Provinces would have no great interest in serving as a base for a war against France.

Aerschot, with his honest and insouciant responses, was signing the warrant for his own political extinction. Olivares told the Council of State early in March that the duke was potentially very dangerous, and that the time had come to reach a decision on his future.[62] At a session of the Council of State on 16 March a full-scale debate was held on the prospects for a truce in the light of the evidence adduced by Aerschot.[63] The councillors followed the Count-Duke's lead in expressing their desire for an immediate truce, and their pessimism about the chances of attaining it on the terms outlined by Madrid. In replying to the *consulta*, the king reviewed with some bitterness the 'decline' of his Monarchy as a consequence of the peace initiatives begun six years previously with Spínola's arrival in Madrid. He minced no words about the activities of the States General in Brussels. Such bodies were 'pernicious in all times, in all ages, and in all monarchical governments without exception', and he deplored their conduct of negotiations with the Dutch. Reluctantly, however, he followed the advice of his council and approved a fresh attempt at a settlement. But not a word was to be breathed to Aerschot, and only six men were to know of the king's decision: the Counts of Castrillo and La Puebla, the Duke of Villahermosa, the Count-Duke himself, and those two indefatigable secretaries, the Protonotario and Antonio Carnero. The remainder of the Council of State—Cardinal Zapata, Alba, Alburquerque, Gelves, Leganés, Santa Cruz, Mirabel, and the royal confessor—were thus to be left in the dark.

While Aerschot's fate hung in the balance, sensational news arrived from Germany on 26 March.[64] Wallenstein had been found guilty

---

[61] AHN Consejos, leg. 12,444, account of meeting of 2 February 1634.
[62] AGS Est. leg. 2153, *voto* of Olivares for meeting of Council of State of 2 March 1634.
[63] AGS Est. leg. 2048, consulta, 16 March 1634. See also Henrard, *Marie de Médicis*, p. 450.
[64] Hoz, p. 222.

of treason to the Emperor, and had been assassinated at Eger on 25 February by officers under his own command. The Count-Duke, who had been insisting to the very end on the need to humour Wallenstein because of his indispensability to the Habsburg cause, seems to have been taken completely by surprise. Although Madrid had hesitantly authorized Oñate to secure the removal of Wallenstein, by death if necessary, in the event of an extreme emergency,[65] the slowness of communications between Vienna and Madrid had apparently left him in the dark about the recent turn of events. Oñate had become convinced that there was more than met the eye in Wallenstein's persistent opposition to Spanish plans to clear the Rhine route to Flanders and he joined forces with his old enemy, Maximilian of Bavaria, in working to destroy him.[66] Oñate's independent action won the Count-Duke's belated approval. Confronted by the evidence of treachery, he could only interpret the events at Eger as a providential liberation of the House of Austria from what would otherwise have been certain ruin. 'Friedland's ingratitude and infidelity have left us all amazed', he wrote to Abbot Scaglia. Thanks were due to God for His inestimable favours, and to the Count of Oñate for unmasking the villain.[67]

With Wallenstein's treachery uppermost in his mind, Olivares made his customary Holy Week retreat to the Retiro,[68] where a special 'hermitage', the Hermitage of San Juan, had been constructed for him in the palace grounds. A modest building, furnished with a library,[69] it was secluded enough to give him at least a temporary respite from the cares of office. His spiritual exercises, however, did not prevent him from attending an important meeting of the Council of State on 13 April to consider the international situation in the light of Oñate's despatches from Germany.[70] On Easter Sunday, 15 April, the Duke of Aerschot was placed under arrest on leaving the palace after an audience with the king. Six years later he died in captivity, the case against him still incomplete.[71]

---

[65] Albrecht, *Die auswärtige Politik*, pp. 368–9.
[66] Bireley, *Religion and Politics*, pp. 200–2; Beladiez, *España y el Sacro Imperio*, pp. 366–7. For a succinct recent account of the circumstances leading to Wallenstein's assassination, see Parker, *The Thirty Years' War*, pp. 137–9.
[67] AGR SEG, Reg. 596, fo. 61, 5 April 1634.
[68] ASF, Mediceo, filza 4960, letter from Bernardo Monanni, 15 April 1634; Novoa, *Codoin* 69, p. 352.
[69] See Brown and Elliott, *A Palace*, pp. 76–7.
[70] AGS Est. leg. 2335, consulta, 13 April 1634. See also Leman, *Urbain VIII*, pp. 381–2.
[71] Hoz, pp. 224–5; *MHE*, 13, pp. 38–9; Henrard, *Marie de Médicis*, p. 455; Novoa, *Codoin* 69, pp. 358–63 for details of the Aerschot case.

The Brink of War

At the special meeting of the Council of State held on 13 April 1634 to consider the implications of Wallenstein's death, the Count-Duke told his colleagues that the Monarchy was beset by unparalleled dangers. While Germany had been saved from disaster by the removal of Wallenstein, the fact remained that it was now left leaderless. Both in Germany and Italy the advances made by the King of France—'the sole mainstay of this whole conspiracy and of all the upheavals in Europe'—had rendered war inevitable. Justice, reason, the law of nations, the preservation of the Catholic faith and of the kingdoms and territories of the king and his house—all of these fully justified the resort to arms. But when resources were so limited, it remained an open question whether Spain should go to war forthwith, or wait for it to come. Pierre Roose in Brussels, and the Count of Monterrey in Naples, both advocated an immediate break with France, and the same was true of the majority of Spain's envoys in foreign parts. While delay would strengthen Spain's case in the court of European public opinion, it would also entail another year of heavy expenditure to no good purpose. On balance, the Count-Duke was inclined to believe that whatever Madrid decided would make very little difference. His assumption—fallacious, like so many of his assumptions about the reactions of Vienna—was that the Emperor, seeing Richelieu's hand in Wallenstein's treason, would already have decided in favour of war with France. On the whole, therefore, he preferred to wait on events, and in this his colleagues agreed with him.

Spain, then, would prepare for war with France, but not declare it. Its chances of success in such a war would be enormously strengthened by the liquidation of the war in the Netherlands, but the prospects for this seemed increasingly remote. The dissolution of the States General in Brussels shortly after the Infanta's death, and the subsequent arrest of Aerschot, had effectively ended the danger of a precipitate peace settlement on unacceptable terms. While the duke's arrest once again opened the way for an 'honourable' settlement, ministerial circles in Madrid seem to have been unanimous in their belief that no settlement could be regarded as honourable which undercut Seville's Atlantic monopoly by conceding to the Dutch commercial access to the Indies.[72] Madrid's clear reluctance to give any ground on this and other matters of substance progressively weakened the peace party in the United Provinces, which had already lost the support of the Stadholder, Frederick Henry.[73] On

[72] Israel, *The Dutch Republic*, pp. 302–3.
[73] *Ibid.*, p. 300.

15 April, the very day of Aerschot's arrest, Charnacé's efforts in the Hague bore fruit in a new subsidy treaty between the French and the Dutch. In return for an increase in their annual subsidy from one to 2.3 million *livres*, the United Provinces agreed to suspend all peace negotiations for the next eight months.[74] Frederick Henry, still uneasy about the pacifist tendencies of the Amsterdam regents, was anxious to go even further in committing France to his cause. The Dutch mission despatched to Paris at the end of May to ratify the treaty was instructed to seek a new offensive and defensive alliance with France. But Richelieu was wary. He was no more anxious than Olivares to commit himself irrevocably to open war.[75]

During this period of cold war preceding the official outbreak of hostilities in May 1635 the Cardinal and the Count-Duke were both manoeuvring for positions of advantage in the knowledge that, barring some miracle, a military confrontation was unavoidable. The two men profoundly distrusted each other—a fact which was hardly conducive to Urban VIII's efforts to bring about a reconciliation, although Olivares always insisted that, on his side at least, there was no personal animosity and that he took care to be guided solely by considerations of state.[76] In making the defeat of the House of Austria his first priority, Richelieu had established himself in Olivares' eyes as the principal obstacle to peace in Europe. Nothing would have suited him better than the Cardinal's overthrow by his domestic enemies, and the Day of the Dupes must have been as great a disappointment to him as it was to Marillac and his allies. Since that unhappy reversal of fortune in 1630 he had kept a continuous watch on events at the court of Louis XIII, drawing his information both from diplomatic despatches and from the reports of private agents and of confidants in the entourage of Louis' queen, Anne of Austria. But while well aware of the depth of hostility to the Cardinal among the malcontents, he was also alive to the dangers of associating himself too closely with the French opposition.

The flight to Brussels in July 1631 of France's Queen Mother, Marie de Médicis, came as a grave embarrassment. Everyone would assume, the Count-Duke pointed out, that she was acting in collusion with Spain, and the king could all too easily find himself committed to active support of her cause. It would be a terrible mistake to build any hopes either on her or on Gaston d'Orléans, who would prove as inveterate an enemy of Spain as Louis XIII if ever he succeeded to his brother's throne.[77] These were perceptive words, but the

---

[74] Henrard, *Marie de Médicis*, p. 460; Bonney, *The King's Debts*, p. 163.
[75] Pagès, *Guerre de Trente Ans*, pp. 177–8.
[76] Elliott, *Richelieu and Olivares*, p. 114.
[77] AGS Est. leg. 2045, consulta, 5 August 1631.

temptation to fish in France's troubled waters proved difficult to resist. The French, after all, were doing the same in the Spanish Netherlands, even while nominally still at peace with Spain. Although his conversations with Gaston's envoy in Madrid, Du Fargis, persuaded him that the prince's plans for a military incursion into France were 'very fragile', Olivares was ready by the summer of 1632 covertly to provide money and arms to assist Gaston's cause.[78] The subsequent collapse of Montmorency's revolt and the reconciliation of the royal brothers only confirmed the validity of his initial assessment. Yet hope, and with it temptation, revived almost immediately when Gaston once again fled to Flanders. This time the Count-Duke was unwilling to offer help until Gaston could guarantee the support of the Count of Soissons and other French malcontent nobles.[79]

Now, in the spring of 1634, as war approached, it became necessary to lay aside any remaining scruples and make sure of allies wherever they could be found. In January, Duke Charles of Lorraine, whose sister Margaret had married Gaston d'Orléans, abdicated in favour of his brother to save himself from the wrath of Louis XIII and Richelieu. In coming to the defence of the duke and his relatives, Spain could pose as a champion of the wronged house of Lorraine, and draw the fickle Gaston more tightly into its network of alliances. The process was assisted by the Duke of Savoy's younger brother, Prince Thomas, who turned up in Flanders in April and placed his services at the disposal of Philip IV. Prince Thomas, as brother-in-law of the Count of Soissons, had close connections with the French malcontents. Under his influence, Gaston broke with Marie de Médicis and signed a secret agreement with Spain on 12 May, in which he promised his support for the House of Austria in the event of war. In return he was to receive from Philip IV 15,000 men, who were to enter France at the end of September while Spanish forces invaded from across the Pyrenees.[80]

In attempting to construct an anti-French coalition to counter the anti-Spanish coalition that Richelieu was constructing, the Count-Duke was, as always, dependent on the reactions of Vienna. Once Oñate had finally got the Emperor's signature to the long-discussed League of Alliance with Spain, he would be committed to war with the Dutch and, when necessary, with the French.[81] But Ferdinand could never quite be brought to the point. The only explanation that

---

[78] AGS Est. K. 1415, fo. 95, consulta, 12 August 1623. Du Fargis, the former French ambassador in Madrid who had negotiated the treaty of Monzón in 1626, was an adherent of Gaston and had defected with him.
[79] Henrard, *Marie de Médicis*, p. 331.
[80] *Ibid.*, pp. 425–6.
[81] AGS Est. leg. 2335, consulta, 14 May 1634; and see Günter, *Die Habsburger-Liga*, pp. 178–9.

Madrid could find for his strange reluctance was that his advisers had been bribed by the French.[82] It was a dispiriting business attempting to bring home to the Emperor that the very salvation of the House of Austria required the closest confidence and coordination between the two branches of the family. At the very least, Ferdinand could surely offer help to the Duke of Lorraine and the malcontents.[83]

The English ambassador, observing the Count-Duke during these difficult days of May 1634 as he toiled to prepare Spain for war and bring the Emperor into line, noted how exhausted he appeared. 'The poor man is spent with the burden of business that lies on him, and deserves to be pitied if he would pity himself.'[84] He allowed himself little rest from his labours, although he would escape to his hermitage in the Retiro gardens whenever he could. In 1633 he had negotiated the purchase of the little town of Loeches to the east of Madrid, where he commissioned Alonso Carbonel, the architect of the Buen Retiro, to construct a modest 'palace' for his use, together with a convent of Dominican nuns.[85] He paid his first visit in February 1634 while the works were still in progress, and whenever he could he would make the two-hour journey to this country retreat.[86] But affairs of state were all absorbing. Yet, even as he struggled with the prevarications of the Emperor and pored over the plans for the projected expedition to Pernambuco and the Cardinal-Infante's march to Flanders, he still found time to attend to the building and furnishing of the Buen Retiro, writing to Florence to commission a large bronze equestrian statue of Philip IV,[87] and reporting to the king on the latest site developments after the return of the court from a stay at Aranjuez.[88]

Whether it was a question of acquiring tapestries for the Retiro, or preparing for the imminent war with France, he could never ignore for long the perennial shortage of cash. 'It is no wonder', observed Hopton, 'that many of their designs fail in the execution, for though this great vessel contains much water, yet it hath so many leaks as it is always dry. It is certain they have made *asientos* this year for thirteen millions, and are still treating of more, yet at the end of the year they will have neither money in their purses nor army

---

[82] Günter, p. 182.

[83] AGS Est. leg. 2335, consulta, 13 May 1634.

[84] BL Eg. Ms. 1820, fo. 351, Hopton to Cottington, 22 May 1634.

[85] Brown and Elliott, *A Palace*, p. 61. Carbonel was his special protégé, and his counter to the official court architect, Gómez de Mora, who was tarnished in his eyes by his association with the Duke of Lerma's building projects.

[86] ASF, Mediceo, filza 4960, despatch of Comendatore di Sorano, 11 February 1634. For the travelling time to Loeches, Marañón, *Olivares*, pp. 108–9.

[87] ASF, Mediceo, filza 4960, Olivares to Comendatore di Sorano, 2 May 1634.

[88] ASF, Mediceo, filza 4960, letter from Bernardo Monanni, 13 May 1634.

paid...'[89] In theory this was a problem for the Council of Finance. In practice it was more often than not a problem for the Count-Duke himself. On paper everything would seem to be satisfactorily arranged, but time after time the carefully constructed package of financial provisions would come apart in the ministers' hands.

The galleons that had belatedly reached Cadiz in February 1634 had unfortunately brought much less Peruvian silver than anticipated. The sum total registered in Seville at the beginning of March was only 2,248,532 ducats, almost equally divided between the crown and private owners, instead of the $8\frac{1}{2}$ million ducats said to have been put on board in Portobelo and Cartagena. The Council of Finance alleged large-scale fraud. The Council of the Indies, on the other hand, alleged special circumstances—the mercury shortage in Peru, which had restricted production in the mines, and the loss of confidence among merchants as a result of the high duties and confiscation by the crown. Unimpressed by these arguments, the administration sent Fernando Ramírez Fariñas to investigate on the spot.[90]

The disappointing figures had an immediate impact on the confidence and the lending capacity of the *asentistas*, who amazed the authorities by suspending payments. Scarcely had this been rectified when Olivares' confidential financial adviser, the *contador* Manuel López Pereira, reported that the Council of Finance was about to suspend even the ordinary payments for Flanders. The president of the council, the Marquis of La Puebla, categorically denied this when summoned into Olivares' presence, but suspension was only prevented by rapid action on the part of one of the *asentistas*, Julio César Scavola. But this was only the beginning of the Count-Duke's troubles with his cousin, the Marquis of La Puebla, whose council seemed in his eyes to be strangely negligent in fulfilling its prime duty of finding money for the crown. After further promptings from the Count-Duke late in April to make sure that all the payments for May and early June were covered, the Council of Finance reported on 10 May that everything was in order. It then transpired that this was simply not true, and the Count-Duke himself was forced to step in and issue the necessary letters of authorization.[91]

'I took the work into my own hands', wrote Olivares when recounting the sad story of the culpable negligence of the ministers of finance. It was always the same. Exasperated, impatient, intolerant of the mistakes or inefficiency of colleagues and subordinates, he was always having to take the work into his own hands. Although

[89] BL Eg. Ms. 1820, fo. 340, Hopton to Coke, 6 April 1634.
[90] AGS CJH leg. 714, no. 349, consulta of Council of Finance, 3 March 1634; AGI, Indif. leg. 758, consulta of Council of Indies, 7 March 1634.
[91] AHN Est. lib. 862, fos. 2–7, paper by Olivares, 23 May 1634.

endlessly lamenting the necessity for this, he may secretly have derived some satisfaction from the continuing evidence of his own indispensability. In fact he was right to think that only a first minister
with authority firmly concentrated in his own person could take the
actions that needed to be taken. In his determination to mobilize
the Monarchy's resources for war, he was placing enormous demands
on an administrative system which was so constructed as to require
constant pressure from above. He expected and demanded of others
the unstinting loyalty and dedicated hard work that he himself offered
the crown, forgetting that his subordinates—underpaid, harassed,
torn between their desire to earn the approval of their monarch and
their anxiety to avoid offending influential elements in the community
at large—tended to be less committed than himself to measures which
were devised without regard to the personal and social costs involved.
For him the requirements of the crown, as defined by himself and
a handful of trusted advisers, took precedence over everything else.
How then was it possible that bankers, or officials, or the Castilian
Cortes or the city of Barcelona, should resist or evade obligations
that were so patently legitimate?

Yet at every point he was liable to meet resistance, or, at the very
least, the most grudging acquiescence. Like Richelieu[92] he was deeply
exercised about the problem of disobedience to royal orders at every
level of society. The nobility, in particular, gave him nothing but
headaches. They were endlessly bickering over points of etiquette
and precedence, and taking offence at real or imagined slights at
the hands of each other, or of Olivares himself. Feuds among grandees
could be politically dangerous, like the one that broke out in Naples
in 1630 between the Duke of Alba, who was escorting the Queen
of Hungary on her journey to Vienna, and the man who had recently
succeeded him as viceroy of Naples, Olivares' fellow-magnate from
Seville, the Duke of Alcalá. The Councils of State, *cámara* and Italy
were hurriedly called into session to attempt to settle an affair which
the Count-Duke considered extremely serious, 'because, the day it
is made the subject of litigation, these two houses would become
irreconcilable, and these kingdoms would be threatened with serious
disturbance.'[93] Every quarrel, and every act of insubordination, therefore developed all too rapidly into an exercise in damage control.

There was even a partial estrangement from his own son-in-law,
the Duke of Medina de las Torres, who had come to the conclusion
that the only means of making his own way in the world was to
find a rich wife. The lady in question was a Neapolitan heiress to

[92] See Elliott, *Richelieu and Olivares*, pp. 132–3.
[93] BL Add. Ms. 24,909, fos. 187–v., Olivares to Padre Diego de Quiroga, 12 December
1630.

vast but neglected estates, Anna Carafa, Princess of Stigliano,[94] who made it a condition of the marriage that her future husband should reside in Naples and succeed to the viceroyalty. A marriage alliance of this kind between two great houses, one in Castile and one in Naples, had important national and international implications, but the duke appears to have embarked on the negotiations without taking his father-in-law into his confidence, counting on his mother-in-law's help to bring him round.[95] The Count-Duke was hostile to the marriage and offended by the insubordination of a young man whom he had raised from obscurity, and whom he wanted to keep at his side. In the circumstances, the marriage negotiations proved more than usually complicated, and depended for their resolution on the deliberations of a specially appointed junta and the good offices of the king. Always generous in such matters, he loaded the bridegroom with favours, including the reversionary succession to the viceroyalty of Naples, currently held by the Count of Monterrey.[96] When Medina de las Torres—his dispute with his father-in-law patched up—eventually departed for Italy early in 1636, he left vacant the court post of *sumiller de corps* which he had occupied since 1626. There were rumours that this would go to another of the Count-Duke's young protégés, Don Gaspar de Tebes, who had recently returned from a two-year mission to Germany, and was believed by some to be his illegitimate son.[97] Once again, however, Olivares did the unexpected. He arranged for the revival in his person of the old and more senior court office of grand chamberlain (*camarero mayor*), which had not been filled since the days of Charles V.[98] It was a neat device for keeping his finger on the pulse of the royal household once his son-in-law was gone.

The antipathy felt towards Olivares by so many of the representatives of the old houses of Castile made it all the harder for him to secure compliance with the orders of the king. In July 1634, for instance, he clashed violently with Don Fadrique de Toledo, who was only willing to accept the command of the projected naval expedition to expel the Dutch from Brazil on terms which the Count-Duke regarded as intolerable. After a shouting match in the Count-Duke's study, Don Fadrique was arrested, and the whole business was put

[94] See Alfred de Reumont, *Naples under Spanish Dominion. The Carafas of Maddaloni and Masaniello* (Eng. trans., London, 1853), pp. 221–5.
[95] ASF, Mediceo, filza 4960, despatch of Comendatore di Sorano, 15 April 1634.
[96] AGS Est. leg. 3332, fo. 151, paper by Olivares, 13 August 1634, and fo. 110 for certificate of *mercedes*, 20 December 1634; Stradling, 'A Spanish Statesman of Appeasement', pp. 5–6.
[97] ASF, Mediceo, filza 4961, despatch of Bernardo Monanni, 15 March 1636. For Tebes, see Marañón, *Olivares*, Appendix 9.
[98] ASF, Mediceo, filza 4961, despatch of Bernardo Monanni, 12 April 1636; Novoa, *Codoin* 77, p. 147.

in the hands of a newly constituted junta of the Council of Castile, the *Junta de Obediencia*, set up 'to punish those that slack in their obedience to the king's commands, which keeps them in awe.'[99] The entire house of Toledo, headed by the Duke of Alba, rallied to the support of the injured member of their clan, signalling their outrage by boycotting the court festivities at the Buen Retiro.[100] Relations had never been easy between Olivares and the Duke of Alba, and the favourite and the *mayordomo mayor* had long been watching each other warily.[101] The Count-Duke was no doubt happy to have an excuse to remove him from the palace, and at the end of October he was ordered to leave for his estates. When a grandee was punished in this way, it was customary for the king to bestow some favour on his sons; but Alba's son, the Constable of Navarre, refused the proffered honour and chose to accompany his father into exile. Alba's nephew, the Count of Oropesa, followed suit, as did other members of the Toledo family. Indeed, Alba's departure seems to have been followed by a mass exit of the grandees from the court, as a collective expression of their disgust with Olivares, and their unwillingness to provide the companies of cavalry and infantry requested of them by the king in anticipation of the coming war.[102]

The populace—and, it was rumoured, the queen—supported the Duke of Alba, but the Count-Duke remained unmoved, and there was no one left to challenge him on the Council of State. This was reduced to six active members apart from himself, all of them either his henchmen or too weak to be of any consequence: Cardinal Zapata, the Duke of Villahermosa, the royal confessor, and the Counts of Castrillo, Mirabel and La Puebla.[103] He was determined to secure obedience, and the unhappy Don Fadrique de Toledo was only spared by death from learning of the savage sentence passed upon him: the loss of all his offices and the income from his estates, and a fine of 10,000 ducats. The persecution was extended beyond the grave—he was denied a requiem mass in the church of the Colegio Imperial, and orders were given for the dismantling of his catafalque. If the king's enemies and Olivares' enemies were one and the same, they were pursued with a savagery which smacks of a personal vendetta.

Harshness might provoke fear, but it did not necessarily ensure obedience. The nobility showed at best a grudging acquiescence,

---

[99] BL Eg. Ms. 1820, fo. 393, Hopton to Windebank, 16 October 1634.

[100] See Brown and Elliott, *A Palace*, pp. 172–3, for the affair of Don Fadrique de Toledo.

[101] ASF, Mediceo, filza 4960, despatch of Comendatore di Sorano, 28 October 1634, and see above, p. 396.

[102] ASF, Mediceo, filza 4960, despatches of Monanni, 28 October and 4 November 1634.

[103] ASF, Mediceo, filza 4960, despatch of Comendatore di Sorano, 4 November 1634. The Marquis of Gelves was too old to attend, and the Duke of Alburquerque, feeling aggrieved, had left court.

prevaricating as best they could when faced with royal orders to produce men or money. In Madrid, where satire was a common response to the demands of those in authority, pasquinades appeared depicting Spain as a mule which Olivares held by the ears, or as a patient being told by his doctor that the only remedy left was the knife.[104] But the Count-Duke needed his money. The Cardinal-Infante began his great northwards march from Milan in July,[105] and this was one enterprise which could on no account be starved of funds. The king had made this clear in April when he asked the Cortes of Castile for four million ducats in silver to pay for the Cardinal-Infante's forthcoming campaign—a request said to have reduced it to a state of 'great affliction'.[106] The Count-Duke had no wish to bleed the Castilian tax-payer white, but in Castile, as in the France of Richelieu, the fiscal necessities of the state were paramount. Before committing themselves irrevocably, however, ministers were asked by the king to give a written opinion as to whether any territories should be abandoned as being too expensive to defend. The Council of State recommended defending everything to the last breath. In his own unsigned response Olivares argued that it would be a national indignity if Spain shrank from sacrifice at a time when the French were being taxed to the hilt, and when even their nobility were being subjected to a levy.[107]

An attempt was also made to estimate expenditures for the first year of the war:

	escudos
Flanders (for 1635)	3,700,000
Subsidies for princes and electors in Westphalia and Rhineland	500,000
Assistance for Germany (to be doubled if the proposed League came into being)	600,000
Assistance for Gaston d'Orléans (conditional on his launching a diversionary attack on France)	1,200,000
Invasion of France from Spain	500,000
Defence of Milan	600,000
Brazil expedition	1,000,000
Aid to Marie de Médicis, Gaston, and Prince Thomas	333,000
	8,433,000

Although this was an enormous sum, the Count-Duke remained convinced that it was not unrealistic if only the monies raised by

---

[104] *MHE*, 13, p. 87 (letter of 18 August 1634).
[105] Alcalá-Zamora, *España, Flandes*, p. 341.
[106] *MHE*, 13, p. 33 (letter of 4 April 1634).
[107] AGS Est. leg. 2152, royal order of 28 August 1634 and enclosed responses.

taxation were actually to reach the treasury instead of being diverted along the route. It was, he told a joint meeting of financial ministers and councillors of state on 22 September, the 'bosses (*mandones*), the *regidores*, the *poderosos* and the rich' who were the true enemies of the republic, and it was because of them that the crown received scarcely three millions a year in taxes out of the nine million being extracted from the population of Castile.[108]

In spite of the crown's reported success in doubling its revenues over the past four years,[109] there was a staggering loss of income through fraud, and the Council of State set up a junta of inquiry.[110] But at the same time it approved a whole series of new fiscal expedients, most of them consisting of the creation and sale of offices. The justification that would increasingly be offered for such unpalatable measures was that of 'necessity'—a conveniently flexible concept which was to prove as useful to the government of Philip IV in Spain as it was to that of Charles I in England and of Louis XIII in France. At the ministerial meeting held on 22 September, José González and Antonio de Contreras argued that it was for the king and his ministers, and not the people, to determine what constituted 'necessity'. Luis de Gudiel, on the other hand, spoke for the Castilian constitutional tradition when he said that, while it was true that vassals had an obligation to assist their prince, it was unjust to demand so much of them as to prejudice their chances of survival. 'If these kingdoms, which constitute the heart of the Monarchy, are lost, there is little point in hanging on to the rest.' Before there was a king, there must be a kingdom. Kings, he said, were instituted for the government and preservation of their peoples.

This was the kind of argument which that dogged patriot, Lisón y Biedma, had advanced at some personal cost in the 1620's, and Gudiel would have no more success with it than Lisón before him. However genuinely Olivares might sympathize with the wretched tax-payers of Castile, 'necessity' was paramount, and it was a necessity defined by himself. If a supreme effort were made now, extremes in the future could yet be avoided. One could always argue, as González and Contreras argued, that the crown's fiscal demands were more than offset by the peace enjoyed by Castile in time of general warfare, and that it was better to pay for war abroad than suffer it at home.

As if in confirmation of these ingenious arguments, the Cardinal-Infante's great victory over the Swedes at Nördlingen on 6 September

---

[108] AHN Est. lib. 862, fos. 24–70, consulta (summarized in Domínguez Ortiz, *Política y hacienda*, Appendix 9).
[109] Above, p. 453.
[110] AHN Est. lib. 862, fos. 18–22, consulta, 22 September 1634 (summarized in Domínguez Ortiz, *Política y hacienda*, Appendix 24).

brought new hope that all the sacrifice was not, after all, to be in vain. 'The greatest victory of our times', as the Count-Duke called it,[111] was an impressive reaffirmation of Spanish power at a time when many were beginning to wonder if it had not gone into eclipse. The Swedish army had been shattered. All southern Germany was occupied by the victors, and Sweden's allies among the North German princes were thrown into disarray. It was true that the most direct route from Italy to Flanders, by way of the Rhine and Lorraine, was even now not cleared—this would have meant immediate hostilities with the French, who were stationed in upper and lower Alsace, and at key points along the Rhine and Moselle.[112] But the Cardinal-Infante, with powerful reinforcements under his command, forced his way through to Flanders and entered Brussels in triumph on 4 November 1634 (Pl. 25).

For all his personal satisfaction at the Cardinal-Infante's success—a success which Don Fernando himself attributed to the Count-Duke's labours in providing him with sufficient men and money[113]—Olivares could not conceal a certain disappointment in the immediate aftermath of the victory. The Cardinal-Infante obeyed his instructions to the letter in continuing his march to Flanders; but had his orders been other than they were, and had time and supplies been sufficient, he and the King of Hungary might have dealt with Saxony, settled the German question for good and all at an Imperial diet, and then turned south to clear the Rhine. 'Then they would have been the masters of everything.' As it was, the situation was 'better, but still very dangerous', and the Emperor would still need substantial help for the coming year.[114]

The Count of Oñate seized the opportunity provided by Nördlingen to press the Emperor yet again to consent to a League of Alliance. Ferdinand, however, remained as cautious as ever. At least until the German lands were pacified he was reluctant to commit himself to war against the French, and the farthest he was prepared to go was to sign on 31 October, for later publication, a treaty of offensive and defensive alliance with Spain.[115] Under the terms of this treaty an army could be kept in Germany at Spain's expense, but the Emperor avoided any definite commitment to military intervention. His overwhelming concern was to make use of the defeat of the Swedes to ensure a favourable settlement of the religious and

---

[111] AGR CPE, Reg. 1502, fo. 75, Olivares to Roose, 29 September 1634.

[112] Pagès, *Guerre de Trente Ans*, pp. 182–3; Van der Essen, *Le Cardinal-Infant*, p. 454.

[113] BL Eg. Ms. 14,006, fo. 584v., Cardinal-Infante to king, 7 September 1634.

[114] AGS Est. leg. 2152, draft *voto* of Olivares for meeting of Council of State, 9 November 1634. Consulta in AGS Est. leg. 2048.

[115] Günter, *Die Habsburger-Liga*, p. 186; Leman, *Urbain VIII*, p. 430; Lonchay, *Correspondance*, 6, Doc. 939, Oñate to Cardinal-Infante, 8 November 1634.

25. Peter Paul Rubens, *Cardinal-Infante at Nördlingen*.

political affairs of the Empire, and there was no question of his engaging in military operations against the French or the Dutch until this had been achieved. His immediate object was to reach a settlement with the Elector of Saxony. A temporary truce was negotiated between the Emperor and the Elector at Pirna in November;[116] and a general settlement of Imperial affairs, acceptable to the other German Protestant princes, was formally agreed at the Peace of Prague on 30 May 1635.

The defection of Saxony from the anti-Habsburg cause was a measure of the change brought about by Nördlingen. The Swedes no longer had the power to sustain single-handed an anti-Habsburg coalition in Germany. Inexorably France was being pushed towards war, although it was still Richelieu's aim to hold back from conflict for as long as possible. The months that followed Nördlingen were to be months of intense diplomatic activity, with the papacy struggling to prevent a rupture between Paris and Madrid, and to organize a peace congress at which their claims and counter-claims could be settled by discussion and arbitration.[117] Both capitals, however, were busily engaged in making the final diplomatic and military preparations for the conflict—Olivares working to induce the Emperor to enter the fray, and Richelieu to rally the Swedes and the Dutch. On one issue in particular it was clear to the Cardinal that he must make at least a temporary concession. If war came, he could not afford to have Gaston d'Orléans in the Spanish Netherlands, serving as rallying-point for the French malcontents. Marie de Médicis could—and indeed must—be kept out of France; but somehow Gaston had to be brought home. On 1 October Louis XIII signed an agreement with Gaston's agents promising a full pardon to his errant brother. A week later Gaston slipped across the frontier and back into France.[118]

Olivares dismissed the news of Gaston's flight as of little importance. Marie de Médici's name was worth more than that of Gaston, and Philip IV was duly freed from all the commitments into which he had entered.[119] For Madrid the main priorities now were to make certain of the safety of the Netherlands; establish the League with the Emperor; exploit any domestic discontent inside France; strengthen Spain's naval effort in the Mediterranean, the Atlantic and the English Channel; and make all necessary financial arrangements. The Marquis of La Puebla was instructed to arrange an *asiento* of 7,256,000 ducats for the new financial year, which began on 1 November.

[116] Pagès, *Guerre de Trente Ans*, p. 193.
[117] Leman, *Urbain VIII*, pp. 434–8.
[118] Dethan, *Gaston d'Orléans*, pp. 131–2; Hanotaux, *Richelieu*, 5, pp. 48ff.
[119] AGS Est. leg. 2152, Olivares' *voto* for meeting of 9 November 1634.

This enormous sum, which was additional to the money that had to be provided for household expenses, was broken down into 5,656,000 for Flanders, 600,000 for Germany, and 500,000 each in Spain and Genoa. The marquis replied that it was impossible to arrange an *asiento* of this magnitude, and was curtly told by the king that the impossible must be made possible.[120]

Yet for all those massive war preparations in the autumn months of 1634, Hopton was still in two minds as to whether war would really come. For the time being at least, he saw little interest on the Spanish side in precipitating it, 'for the galleons having failed for this year, they are hard unto it to find moneys to defray their ordinary charges.'[121] The New Spain *flota* under the command of Don Lope de Hoces had in fact been caught by a storm in September, just after setting sail from Cuba, and it was only with difficulty that the scattered treasure-ships made their way back to Havana harbour. They would not put to sea again until the following spring, and only reached Cadiz, in company with the galleons from Tierra Firme, on 10 June 1635.[122]

The hazards of wind and wave seem not only to have given the Count-Duke pause for thought, but also to have influenced his metaphors. 'When matters are approaching their climacteric' he told the Council of State on 27 December, 'this is the season to draw in the sails of wrath' and survey matters dispassionately. 'I have therefore been continuously meditating these days on the best course of action, and I have been wondering whether Your Majesty might make a peace treaty with the King of France, leaving him in control of Pinerolo and Valdeperosa, and using for the fortification of the state of Milan the money that is being spent, or is about to be spent, on war.' He doubted, however, whether even this short-term solution, which would allow Spain a breathing-space of two or three years before it attempted to expel the French from Italy, would be sufficient to deflect Louis XIII and Richelieu from their intentions. If not, anything seemed better than the present state of affairs, in which the French made all the running.[123]

While this particular proposition does not seem to have been put to the French, papal diplomats were making intensive efforts to reconcile the two powers. Mazarin, who had been sent by Urban VIII to Paris as nuncio extraordinary, seized the opportunity afforded by the return of Leganés from Flanders in December after safely escorting

---

[120] AGS CJH leg. 714, Junta de Hacienda, 3 October 1634; Domínguez Ortiz, *Política y hacienda*, pp. 47–8.
[121] BL Eg. Ms. 1820, fo. 422, Hopton to Windebank, 31 December 1634.
[122] Chaunu, *Séville et l'Atlantique*, 5, pp. 262–3, 276.
[123] AGS Est. leg. 2048, consulta, 27 December 1634.

the Cardinal-Infante to Brussels, to arrange an interview between him and Richelieu as he passed through the French capital.[124] The closeness of Leganés to the Count-Duke made him an ideal channel for communication between the two ministers, but the interview produced no positive results. Hopton in Madrid was of the opinion that 'if they can by any means excuse it they will never break with France',[125] but as each side attempted to steal a march on the other, they moved inexorably closer to a break. On 22 December 1634 the French, who were continuing to take up positions beyond the Rhine, occupied Heidelberg.[126] In January, Imperial forces took Philippsburg, and then in March the Spaniards raided Trèves and carried off the Elector, who had placed himself under French protection.[127]

The seizure of the Elector of Trèves was to be used by Richelieu as the pretext he needed for a formal break with Spain. The decision to declare war was taken at an extraordinary meeting of the Council in Paris on 1 April 1635, but Richelieu preferred to postpone the declaration itself for a few more weeks. He had concluded a new alliance with the United Provinces on 8 February, but it was not until 28 April that a treaty of alliance was signed with the Swedes. Once his alliances were secured, the Cardinal was ready for the break. On 19 May a French herald arrived in Brussels to announce his master's intention to obtain satisfaction by force of arms for the King of Spain's unlawful detention of a sovereign prince.[128]

War aims and aspirations

While the French herald in Brussels was attempting, although without success, to deliver his proclamation to the Cardinal-Infante in person,[129] the courtiers in Madrid were enjoying their first sight of the Hall of Realms in all the glory of its new decoration. The battle paintings were now in place,[130] and the iconographic programme that stood revealed on its walls and ceiling seemed all the more appropriate now that Spain was entering on its decisive trial of strength with France. The vivid depictions of the triumphs of Spanish arms under the leadership of Philip IV—martially portrayed by Velázquez, baton in hand, on his splendid charger (Pl. 26)—were well calculated

---

[124] Leman, *Urbain VIII*, p. 452.

[125] BL Eg. Ms. 1820, fo. 428, Hopton to Windebank, 11 January 1635.

[126] Leman, *Urbain VIII*, p. 455.

[127] *Ibid.*, p. 473; Pagès, *Guerre de Trente Ans*, pp. 196–7.

[128] Pagès, pp. 196–7.

[129] The Cardinal-Infante refused to receive him, and he was reduced to hurling down a copy in Brussels, and posting up another on the frontier (José María Jover, *1635. Historia de una polémica y semblanza de una generación* [Madrid, 1959], p. 26 n. 43).

[130] Above, p. 466, and Brown and Elliott, *A Palace*, p. 142.

26. Velázquez's portrait of Philip IV on horseback was painted as a suitably martial image for the Hall of Realms in 1635, and shows the king in armour as captain-general, with red sash and baton.

to produce a surge of patriotic emotion at a moment when the tide of anti-French sentiment was running high. It remained to be seen whether those privileged enough to have access to the hall would also be prepared to accept some of the messages conveyed in the programme, especially those relating to the Count-Duke's wise guidance of the Monarchy, and to the virtues of a Union of Arms.[131]

If the programme of the Hall of Realms contained a didactic element, it also represented a statement in visual terms of how the Olivares' regime read the history of the reign of Philip IV. It had

[131] Brown and Elliott, ch. 6.

no doubt about the glories of the reign, nor about the values which the Spanish Monarchy was committed to uphold. Those values were now openly challenged by the King of France. Philip himself could hardly contain his indignation at his brother-in-law's behaviour. In responding to a *consulta* of the Council of State of 2 June 1635 recommending an embargo on French property in Spain, he wrote that 'the King of France, defying God, law and nature, has opened hostilities against me . . . At a time when I was attempting to rein in the heretics he has gone to war with me, without challenge or warning, in support of heresy.'[132]

The Count-Duke shared the same burning indignation against the French for what he regarded as behaviour unprecedented in the history of international relations.[133] His vision was of a Christendom—for the time being religiously divided, but not, he hoped, for ever—rejoicing in all the benefits of a *pax austriaca*. This *pax* would be guaranteed by the overwhelming power of the King of Spain, acting in close collaboration with the Emperor and a pope who placed the interests of the church above his own narrowly temporal concerns. Richelieu, although a cardinal of the church, had deliberately set out to wreck this noble vision. Since attaining power he had done nothing but challenge the legitimate rights of the House of Austria, aiding and abetting rebels and heretics whose overriding purpose was to destroy the power of Spain. Although the timing of the war was not of the Count-Duke's own choosing, the situation by the spring of 1635 had become intolerable. Milan, Flanders and Germany were all three in danger, and a major assault on any one of them would produce a chain of repercussions: 'Germany would be followed by Italy and Flanders, Flanders by the Indies, Milan by Naples and Sicily.' Spain herself was almost without allies, and those that remained were so terrorized by the French that they scarcely dared show their faces.[134] Now, by formally breaking with Spain, France had at last shown herself in her true colours, and the world would be able to judge for itself which of the two crowns was the real disturber of the peace of Christendom.

It might, however, require a little assistance. The Count-Duke was always conscious of the need to present Spain's case as effectively as possible in the court of European public opinion, especially when confronting a rival as skilled in the arts of propaganda as the Cardinal. He therefore took a close personal interest in the work of potential publicists and pamphleteers whose services might be harnessed to

[132] AGS Est. K.1644, fo. 15.
[133] AGS GA leg. 1120, *Papel del Conde-Duque*, for consideration at a Junta of 10 February 1635.
[134] *Ibid.*

the needs of the regime. In 1633 Saavedra Fajardo, who was well aware of this interest and had prepared a manuscript defence of Spanish policy in Italy, was careful to send the Count-Duke a copy interleaved with blank pages so that he could add his own comments.[135] A few months later Juan Adam de la Parra, *fiscal* of the Inquisition in Murcia, sought the permission of the Council of Castile to publish an anti-French tract, the *Conspiratio Haeretico-Christianissima*.[136] Olivares immediately took charge. He expressed his approval of Adam de la Parra's style, and recommended that he should be brought to Madrid where he could revise his tract and perhaps be commissioned to write a history.[137] Although the Count-Duke believed on first reading that Parra's treatise would 'mortify the enemies of the crown, and especially the French', he seems to have had second thoughts after its publication, and ordered the recall of all the copies in circulation to introduce further revisions.[138]

The formal outbreak of hostilities with France clearly demanded a special and concerted effort by a team of publicists.[139] There were French charges to be answered, and a European public to be reached. In a paper prepared for a meeting of the Council of State held on 2 June 1635 to discuss war preparations, the Count-Duke wrote of the need to produce a 'paper or general letter' addressed to the princes of Europe and the pope, and also *manifiestos* to be scattered through France.[140] He designated a junta to handle the manifestoes, and expressed his willingness to be a member of it, and have it meet in his study.[141] The secretary of the junta was to be the Sevillian man of letters and royal secretary, Francisco de Calatayud, whom Olivares usually employed in matters relating to culture and education. Its members included Alonso Guillén de la Carrera, a native of Seville and a Salamanca-trained lawyer whose expertise made him a useful polemicist in a dispute where so much turned on legal arguments,[142] and Juan de Palafox. The king and the Count-Duke had been much impressed by Palafox on their visit to Aragon in 1626, and as part of their attempt to break down the divisions between the different kingdoms had called him to Madrid, where they

[135] AGS Est. leg. 3339, fo. 44, Diego Saavedra Fajardo to Olivares, 19 April 1633.
[136] Juan Adam de la Parra, *Conspiración Herético-Cristianísima*, Spanish trans. Angeles Roda Aguirre (Madrid, 1943), p. xli.
[137] AGS Est. leg. 2335, consulta, 27 October 1634.
[138] ASV, Spagna 345, fo. 284, nuncio, 1 April 1635.
[139] For a detailed study of this effort, see Jover, *1635*.
[140] AGS Est. K.1644, fo. 11, *El Conde-Duque con ocasión del rompimiento de franceses en Flandes*.
[141] AGS Est. K.1644, fo. 16, *Adición que el Conde-Duque ha hecho para execución de lo propuesto en su voto*.
[142] Jover, *1635*, pp. 88–9; Bodleian Library, Ms. Add. C. 126, fos. 266–7v., Guillén de la Carrera to Olivares, 28 February 1641, recounting his career.

launched him on a career which would take him to the bishopric
of Puebla and the viceroyalty of Mexico.[143]

It was probably this team of publicists that was responsible for
the anonymous *Declaración de Don Felipe IV . . . al rompimiento de la
guerra*,[144] a manifesto designed to present in the 'theatre of the world'
the aggressive actions undertaken by the French. But Richelieu's men
moved faster than their Spanish counterparts, with the *Declaration
of Louis XIII*, dated 6 June 1635.[145] The battle-lines were now drawn
in what was to be a war of manifestoes, and fresh recruits—José
Pellicer, Saavedra Fajardo, Juan de Jáuregui—either volunteered or
were mobilized to beat back the French assault.

The battery of arguments deployed by Guillén de la Carrera and
his colleagues played over the whole range of the French positions,
and in particular the thesis that Spain aspired to universal monarchy.[146]
The Spanish polemicists represented the war as the Count-Duke
always represented it in his state papers—as an essentially defensive
war, a *guerra defensiva, santa y religiosa*, in Guillén's words.[147] As
viewed from the Madrid of Olivares the French had been persistent
violators of the *pax austriaca*, that beneficial ordering of Europe guaranteed by the indissoluble alliance of Vienna and Madrid. They had
broken the terms of the peace settlements of Vervins, Regensburg
and Cherasco, allied themselves with heretics and given succour and
support to the enemies of Spain—a strange way, indeed, to repay
the generosity of a king who had sent help to his brother-in-law
of France in 1628 against his own heretical rebels of La Rochelle!
The sole concern of Philip IV, the paladin of Christian rectitude,
was to come to the defence of those who were unjustly attacked,
and to fight, not for the expansion of his own dominions but for
the conservation of a European order that Louis XIII and his unscrupulous minister seemed determined to subvert.

It was, therefore, as the self-proclaimed defender of the European
status quo that the Spain of Olivares went to war with France. It
was ironical that the *Declaration* of Louis XIII argued from the same
basic principles. Richelieu and Olivares both saw themselves as reluctantly driven to take up arms against the measureless ambition of
an unprincipled rival; and both knew that this meant sacrificing
domestic reform, financial retrenchment, and all those hopes of peace
and renewed prosperity which they had held before their long-suffer-

---

[143] AHN Est. lib. 741, fo. 352, consulta, 20 October 1626. See also Francisco Sánchez-Castañer,
Don Juan de Palafox, virrey de Nueva España (Zaragoza, 1964).
[144] Partially reproduced in Jover, *1635*, pp. 505–11.
[145] Jover, pp. 71–2. Printed in the contemporary Spanish translation as Appendix 1 of Jover.
[146] See Jover for a detailed discussion of the polemic. Also Devèze, *L'Espagne de Philippe
IV*, 1, pp. 153–70.
[147] Jover, p. 253.

ing peoples as attainable objectives. Almost as soon as war broke out, both ministers were putting out tentative peace feelers, and the opening years of the war would see a series of unsuccessful attempts to bring about a reconciliation of the two crowns, either through papal mediation, or through direct negotiations between Paris and Madrid.[148] Neither party could afford to give the impression, either to its own subjects or to a war-weary Europe, that it had no interest in peace. Richelieu and Olivares alike, while proclaiming their confidence in ultimate victory, were anxious to see their careers crowned with peace, and were uneasily aware that, unless peace came quickly, their peoples might crack beneath the strain.

Of the necessity, and indeed the inevitability, of the war with France the Count-Duke seems to have had no doubt, just as he had no doubt about the innate loyalty and fighting qualities of the king's Castilian subjects. The nation, he told the council, had always been faithful to its king; and 'in spite of the extravagant upbringing of our youth, I vouch for it and the nation.'[149] The problem lay in how to tap that innate loyalty and use it to the best advantage. Castile could do much, but it could not do everything, and there were some who argued that it was now being called upon to do the impossible. In particular the Count-Duke's close friend and confidant, the Count of Humanes, was clearly uneasy. Less than three months before his death in the autumn of 1635 he wrote a remarkable document on the problems of the Monarchy, which in his view found itself in its present sorry state because of its persistent determination to cling to Flanders and Milan.[150] His remedy was to abandon the Spanish Netherlands, using the five or six million ducats a year saved in this way to improve the defences of Spain and the Indies. He also advocated that Milan, whose principal value to the crown was as a military base for the despatch of men to the Netherlands, should be ceded to the Cardinal-Infante as an independent duchy. The Monarchy, thus reduced to Spain, the Indies, Naples and Sicily, would then be easily defensible, and the king would in reality be more powerful than he found himself at present.

This radical proposal for withdrawal and retrenchment had no detectable influence on the thinking of Olivares. Nor do we know whether Humanes spoke only for himself—Hopton described him as a 'lover of *arbitrios*' who 'hath laid his ground according to the books he hath read, which may make him judge amiss'[151]—or whether his views reflected a wider current of opinion in Castile. But his

---

[148] The story of these negotiations is followed in Auguste Leman, *Richelieu et Olivarès* (Lille, 1938).

[149] AGS Est. K.1644, fo. 11, Olivares' paper *con ocasión del rompimiento de franceses*.

[150] ADI, Palafox Mss., leg. 91, fos. 429–32v., *Papel de Don Francisco de Eraso*, 8 July 1635.

[151] BL Eg. Ms. 1820, fo. 495, Hopton to Cottington, 13 June 1635.

memorandum to Olivares is valuable as an indication that the
unthinkable was in fact being thought in the Spain of the 1630's—that
a figure of some importance at court could argue the case for retreat
from empire, and explicitly defy the conventional assumption that
loss of territory necessarily implied loss of reputation. The nearest
Olivares himself ever seems to have come to this line of reasoning
was in April 1633 when he played with the idea of a partial Spanish
withdrawal from the Netherlands;[152] but in general he gives the
impression of being unable to reconsider the assumptions that had
traditionally governed the foreign policy of the Spanish Habsburgs:
that the Catholic cause and the stability of Europe depended on the
preservation of a close relationship between Vienna and Madrid; that
the Dutch, unless effectively restrained, constituted a mortal danger
to the Monarchy; that France was a natural enemy which must at
all times be held in check; and that the loss of any one of the king's
far-flung dominions could only be followed by a domino effect. The
Count-Duke, as heir to a great tradition which he had inherited by
way of his uncle, Don Baltasar de Zúñiga, gives no indication that
he was disposed to question it. If he differed from his predecessors,
it was not in the degree of commitment to that tradition, but in
the degree of vigour and ingenuity which he applied to the realization
of its aims.

He was, however, faced with a question of priorities. While the
Dutch problem inevitably coloured all his thinking, the France of
Richelieu was now openly challenging Spain for primacy in Europe.
The French invasion of Luxemburg at the beginning of the war, and
the union of the French army with that of the Dutch,[153] came as
an unpleasant reminder of the consequences of fighting both at once.
Peace with the United Provinces would enable him to concentrate
all his forces against France, and therefore became an even more
desirable prize than in earlier years. But he remained adamant that
it must be an honourable peace, which for him was one that preserved
the prestige of his sovereign, guaranteed Spain's vital interests (which
he defined as unhampered commerce with northern Europe and
uncontested possession of the Indies), and preserved the loyal provinces of the Southern Netherlands as a viable Catholic community
that retained some links with Spain. Such a settlement, he believed,
would only be possible if the army of Flanders went over again to
the offensive and achieved a substantial success.

He could therefore scarcely contain his excitement when the Cardinal-Infante's forces in a daring night attack on 26 July captured the
great Dutch fortress of Schenkenschans on the border of Cleves and

[152] Above, pp. 461–2.
[153] Henri Pirenne, *Histoire de Belgique* (3rd. ed., Brussels, 1927), 4, pp. 276–7.

Gelderland.[154] The Count-Duke was well-briefed on the strategic importance of the fortress by the viceroy of Navarre, the Chilean-born Marquis of Valparaíso, a Flanders veteran who had reconnoitred it more years ago than he cared to remember.[155] Standing at the confluence of the Waal and the Rhine, it was one of the keys to the United Provinces, and according to Valparaíso its possession was of more value to Spain than either Maastricht or Bois-le-Duc. As he pored over his maps, the Count-Duke could be forgiven for thinking that success in the Netherlands was at last within his grasp. Unfortunately the news of the victory was soon followed by that of the death of the Marquis of Aytona on 18 August.[156] Aytona, with whom Olivares had maintained a close correspondence over the years, had been an able proconsul in the Spanish Netherlands, and the Count-Duke described him as irreplaceable.[157] Although not a soldier, even in the military sphere his loss was keenly felt. A Sicilian engineer who arrived in Madrid with despatches from Flanders told Olivares that if Aytona had lived, the capture of Schenkenschans would have been followed within a week by that of Venlo. But in spite of this, the Count-Duke was quick, indeed too quick, to see the capture of the Dutch fortress as a turning-point. 'Your Majesty can be assured that neither your father nor your grandfather had the opportunity which you now have to settle the affairs of Holland with advantage and reputation, because God has been pleased to place the master-key in Your Majesty's hands.'[158]

If only the Cardinal-Infante could build on his success during the next campaigning season, the war in Flanders would be over, and the king could be assured of a 'long and secure truce, and even a most glorious peace.' This would allow Spain to concentrate all its forces on the war with France, which the Count-Duke knew must be quickly won if any real advantage were to be derived from the victory. In a special paper prepared for him before the French declaration of war, the Marquis of Valparaíso had argued that mere containment of the French was not enough.[159] It was essential to seize the offensive, and France could most easily be attacked from Flanders,

---

[154] Israel, *The Dutch Republic*, p. 253.
[155] Don Francisco de Andia Irarrázabal, created Marquis of Valparaíso in 1631, had crossed the Atlantic to serve in the army of Flanders in 1599. He became viceroy of Navarre in 1634. (AHN Est. lib. 738, fos. 311–12, consulta, 10 June 1623 on a *memorial* recounting his career.) See also 'Epistolario de la Familia Yrarrázaval en el siglo XVII', *Boletín de la Academia Chilena de la Historia*, 41 (1949), pp. 125–34.
[156] Archivo de la Casa de Miraflores, Madrid. Cardinal-Infante to Olivares, 20 August 1635.
[157] AGS Est. leg. 2050, consulta, 20 September 1635.
[158] AGS Est. leg. 2153, draft *voto* of Olivares, 16 November 1635.
[159] See Alfredo Sánchez Bella, 'El poderío español a mediados del siglo XVII, según el parecer de un chileno', *Boletín de la Academia Chilena de la Historia*, 57 (1957), pp. 47–59.

although diversionary attacks could also be launched from Catalonia and Guipúzcoa, while galleys based on Italy could provide cover for any uprising of Richelieu's enemies in Provence. All this, Valparaíso told him, would require an enormous military effort, which effectively precluded the immediate despatch of the expedition for the recapture of Brazil. But the effort was essential, for Spain's best hope lay in a prompt and massive assault on France.

Armed with Valparaíso's blueprint, the Count-Duke called the Council of State to action. This was no time, he told it, for 'consultas and delays.' Everything must now be directed to the execution of orders—ejecución. To this end he now produced thirty points, and then appended another paper containing the names of the ministers who were to take the necessary action.[160] It was important, the council was told, to refute a whole series of misconceptions: that the war would never come; that it was impossible to form an army inside Spain; that the nobility and people were already at their last gasp. Public prayers and the reformation of manners and morals were the first necessity, and must take precedence over everything else. Then followed the more mundane measures, beginning with the embargo of French property to counter the embargo already imposed by the French. The levies already ordered must be speeded up, the unemployed drafted into the army, the court nobility be ready to accompany the king on campaign. Twelve thousand infantrymen must be standing by in Catalonia by St. John's day, the Mediterranean fleet under the command of the Marquis of Villafranca be put on a state of alert, and the Cortes and the Council of Castile be ordered to devise new ways of raising funds.

In these early June days of 1635 the Count-Duke was clearly planning to rally the nation to arms behind a warrior king. Philip's long-standing ambition to lead his armies into battle had been sharpened by his younger brother's triumph at Nördlingen. The moment seemed ripe to let him have his head. On 14 June the Count-Duke dictated a long paper on the preparations that would be needed for a campaign by the king.[161] Catalonia was to become the *plaza de armas* of Spain, the assemblage point for an army of 40,000 men. Joined by the king as its commander, this army would be ready to invade France from Perpignan if the occasion demanded. The Count-Duke had in mind a massive three-pronged assault on France, from Flanders, the Empire, and across the Pyrenees, inspired perhaps by a proposal on these lines put forward by a secret French sympathizer of Spain,

---

[160] AGS Est. K.1644, fos. 11 and 16.
[161] AGS Est. leg. 2656, *El Conde-Duque sobre lo que se debe disponer para executar la jornada de VM*, 14 June 1635. See Elliott, *Catalans*, pp. 309–10.

and forwarded by Abbot Scaglia from Brussels with comments of his own.[162]

When his paper was finished, the Count-Duke scrawled a few words at the end. His head was aching, and both daylight and candle-light were more than he could stand. He was painfully aware how much was at stake. He was gambling everything on this throw—'religion, king, kingdom, nation, everything.' Either, he wrote, every-thing would be lost, or else the ship would be saved. Either Castile would have to bow down before the heretics 'which is what I consider the French to be', or else it would become 'head of the world, as it is already head of Your Majesty's monarchy.' Once again the whole burden seemed to rest upon his shoulders. He was beginning to dis-cover the trials and tribulations of a minister for war.

---

[162] See Echevarría Bacigalupe, *La diplomacia secreta*, pp. 209–11.

PART IV

THE LOSS OF REPUTATION (1635–1645)

XIII

MINISTER FOR WAR

Organizing for victory

The upsurge of anti-French sentiment in the wake of Louis XIII's declaration of war was strong enough to persuade Antonio Carnero that Philip IV's loyal subjects would willingly shed their own and their children's blood for the sake of so just a cause.[1] But how much did the Count-Duke's secretary, who spent most of the day closeted with his exacting master, really know about the sentiments of the population at large? How far indeed did anyone at court—in that tight little circle of overworked officials and palace sycophants—have any perception of the people of Castile and the extent of their sufferings? If, as Olivares had written, 'it is always necessary to pay attention to the voice of the people',[2] there was little chance of its being heard at court unless raised to a shout. The Cortes of Castile, by virtue of their restricted composition, spoke for the municipal oligarchies rather than the people. But the oligarchs could not entirely ignore the murmuring in the streets, and even at this moment of presumed popular emotion the Cortes proved unexpectedly reluctant to vote new subsidies. The outbreak of hostilities with France gave the crown a pretext to request nine million ducats payable over three years; but in spite of warnings from the Archbishop of Granada, president of the Council of Castile, that the deputies would be locked in until they voted the money, he was unable to get a majority, and it took several more days of pressure before the subsidy was approved on 9 July.[3]

The facts of war, as Olivares saw it, still had to be brought home to Castile. He himself prepared for it by taking lessons in the art of fortification. A distinguished mathematician, Father Antonio Camasa, a Neapolitan Jesuit who held the chair of military studies at the Colegio Imperial, was ordered to provide nightly instruction in a remote courtyard of the palace, where the king—unseen—could

---

[1] AGR CPE, Reg. 1504, fo. 92, Carnero to Roose, 3 June 1635.
[2] *MC*, 1, p. 62.
[3] AHN Consejos, leg. 50,038, fo. 24, Archbishop of Granada to Rafael Cornejo, 27 June 1635; *MHE*, 13, p. 201; Hoz, p. 238.

listen from a window.[4] It is probable that Philip proved a diligent if invisible pupil. He was determined to lead his armies into battle, and all the more so since his brother had won immortal fame on the field of Nördlingen. 'That the king will go himself in person to this war is the general opinion', wrote Arthur Hopton in June, 'and doubtless if he shall go he will appear a most gallant prince, for he hath as noble parts of body and mind as any king of this crown hath ever had, and being as he is exceeding industrious he cannot but with action improve himself to a very great perfection.'[5]

The king's thirst for military glory posed problems for his minister during the summer of 1635 comparable to those of 1629. Like the relationship between Louis XIII and Cardinal Richelieu, that between Philip and Olivares was also subject to periods of strain.[6] It would be surprising if in the course of daily intimacy, year in and year out, two men bound to each other by the complex and artificial ties of personal obligation and political necessity did not on occasion grate on each other's nerves. Philip was now thirty, Olivares forty-eight. The unequal years of master-pupil relationship were therefore a thing of the past. That relationship had been replaced by a genuine partnership, but a partnership between a king who had now reached maturity and wanted to make his own mark on the world, and a minister who—while not losing his skill and subtlety in handling his monarch—had to some extent been coarsened by the long exercise of power.

At such a sensitive point in the relationship there were bound to be tensions, and predictably it was the outbreak of the war with France that brought them to the surface. Philip's desire to emulate his brother—and his brother-in-law of France—by assuming personal command of his armies was understandable (Pl. 27). Military leadership was expected of kings; it corresponded with his own inclinations; and it was being urged upon him by the Count-Duke's enemies, who believed that it was the best, and perhaps the only way, to emancipate him from the Count-Duke's tutelage. The disappointing news from the various battle-fronts in the opening weeks of the war made him all the more impatient to lead his armies into action. Observers noted that he seemed out of humour with his minister, and ordered couriers to bring their despatches directly to him instead of the Count-Duke.[7]

---

[4] ASF, Mediceo, filza 4960, letter of Bernardo Monanni, 30 June 1635. Monanni calls him Gamasa. This is presumably the Father Camasa whom Leganés wished to take with him on the Nördlingen campaign, in order to let him gain experience of the less theoretical aspects of his subject (AGS Est. leg. 2335, consulta, 28 March 1634).

[5] BL Eg. Ms. 1820, fo. 490v., Hopton to Coke, 13 June 1635.

[6] See Elliott, *Richelieu and Olivares*, ch. 2.

[7] AS Modena, Spagna 45, despatch of Giovanni Battista Migliari, 8 July 1635.

27. Another representation of Philip IV in martial pose, by the Flemish artist Gaspar de Crayer, painter to the Cardinal-Infante.

With his king in such a testy mood, Olivares had to move with care, and he seems to have succeeded. In any event, there was apparently no repetition of the open confrontation of 1629–30. It was always assumed by his enemies that he would do everything possible to prevent the king from going on campaign, but it is by no means certain that their assumption was correct. His real concern was to prevent the king from going on an unsuccessful campaign, irreparably damaging his reputation in the world—something of far greater moment in the Count-Duke's eyes than his own personal future as the king's first minister. His statements and actions during these opening months of the war suggest that a campaign led in person by the king formed a genuine part of his plans.[8] But any such campaign must be meticulously prepared to produce the desired results, and one difficulty after another had first to be resolved.

On 21 June 1635 a proclamation ordered all *caballeros* and *hidalgos* to hold themselves ready to accompany the king on campaign, and the customary St. John's day festivities at the Buen Retiro were abruptly cancelled.[9] Throughout July there was much bustle over preparations for Philip's departure to Catalonia where he was to take command of the army for the invasion of France,[10] and on 26 August preparations were sufficiently advanced for the city of Barcelona to be officially informed of his impending return.[11] But then nothing happened. One reason seems to have been the sheer impracticability of mounting so elaborate a military machine at such short notice. The Tierra Firme treasure fleet and the remnants of the New Spain *flota* had reached Cadiz on 10 June,[12] but money remained impossibly tight.

Although the Cortes had voted nine million ducats, difficulties arose over the actual raising of the taxes.[13] After the excellent harvest of 1634, that of 1635 proved to be unusually poor.[14] This meant again importing grain at heavy expense from northern Europe—in Dutch ships, if need be, but on no account in French ones.[15] The total embargo on trade with France only aggravated the economic troubles of Castile and Vizcaya.[16] Olivares was in despair: 'there's no money, no bankers, no ministers, and they are leaving me to die . . .'[17] But,

[8] See Elliott, *Catalans*, pp. 309–14.
[9] *MHE*, 13, p. 200.
[10] AGR CPE, Reg. 1502, fo. 122v., Olivares to Roose, 17 July 1635.
[11] Elliott, *Catalans*, p. 310.
[12] Chaunu, *Séville et l'Atlantique*, 5, p. 276.
[13] *MHE*, 13, p. 218.
[14] ASF, Mediceo, filza 4960, letter of Bernardo Monanni, 11 August 1635. See also Anes and Le Flem, 'Las crisis del siglo XVII', for the high prices of 1635–6.
[15] AGS Est. leg. 2658, consulta, 1 April 1636.
[16] BL Eg. Ms. 1820, fo. 547, Hopton to Windebank, 15 September 1635.
[17] MSB, Cod. hisp. 22, fo. 1, Olivares to Cardinal-Infante, 13 October 1635.

where the Council of Finance had failed, he personally persuaded Carlos Strata, one of the most flamboyant of the Genoese bankers, to come to the crown's rescue and arrange an *asiento* for the enormous sum of 2,150,000 *escudos*.[18]

The shortage of money, however, was not the only reason for the postponement of the king's journey to Catalonia. The military enterprise had come to be inextricably entangled with the Catalan political problem.[19] The Catalan Cortes remained in a state of suspension, and if the king returned to the principality considerations of prestige required that he should bring them to a close. But any attempt to conclude the Cortes when he came accompanied by an army raised delicate issues which preoccupied an anxious Council of State during the month of November. The Duke of Alburquerque and the Count of Castrillo—a man who owed everything to Olivares but was beginning to reveal a mind of his own—spoke out against the royal expedition. The king indignantly responded that the thought of conquering Catalonia had never crossed his mind. At most the intention—or so he seemed to imply—was to hold an army in the wings while the Catalan Cortes voted their long overdue subsidy, and then to reaffirm his commitment to uphold the principality's laws and constitutions. On this understanding the ministers, other than Alburquerque, approved the expedition. The decision was reached in early December, and Olivares was planning for the royal party to leave on 15 January 1636 at the latest. But he made it clear that the trip would be impossible without the first round of three million ducats voted by the Cortes of Castile in June.[20] Yet in spite of the fact that ministers had been stumping the country for a 'voluntary' *donativo* to help towards this sum,[21] it had still not been raised, and more trouble with the Cortes followed in January 1636.[22] The decision to issue marching orders was taken on 21 January,[23] but the disagreements with the Castilian Cortes may explain why the expedition was once again postponed.

Although Olivares himself had no desire to return to Catalonia, and least of all when his health was so poor, he considered the king's journey politically and militarily essential. The Catalans could not be allowed to evade their obligations indefinitely.[24] But the king's

---

[18] AGS Est. leg. 2336, consulta, 27 November 1635; Domínguez Ortiz, *Política y hacienda*, p. 53.

[19] Elliott, *Catalans*, pp. 311–14.

[20] AHN Est. leg. 860, no. 39, Olivares on king's *jornada*, 12 December 1635.

[21] Domínguez Ortiz, *Política y hacienda*, pp. 302–3; ASF, Mediceo, filza 4961, letter from Bernardo Monanni, 22 September 1635.

[22] Antonio Rodríguez Villa, *La corte y monarquía de España* (Madrid, 1886), pp. 10 and 13.

[23] AGS Est. leg. 2658, consulta, 21 January 1636.

[24] MSB, Cod. hisp. 22, fo. 2v., Olivares to Cardinal-Infante, 10 December 1635.

presence with an army in Catalonia was also central to the Count-Duke's grand strategic design. In an extensive document of 13 January 1636 on military preparations in the coming months,[25] he continued to urge that everything should be kept ready for a rapid departure from Madrid. His aim had always been to strike hard and fast against France. That was why the war itself had in many ways come as a relief—at least it allowed of a rapid decision, unlike the fifteen years of nominal peace between the crowns, which had seen the Monarchy reduced to its present plight.[26]

During these winter months of 1635–6 the Dutch, temporarily chastened by the loss of Schenkenschans to the Cardinal-Infante, were again secretly talking to the Spaniards about the possibilities of peace.[27] If he could only detach the Dutch from the French and secure an honourable settlement in the Netherlands, the Count-Duke could turn the full weight of Spanish power against France. But once again—counting on further military successes by the Cardinal-Infante in the spring—he pitched his demands too high. In addition to the withdrawal of the Dutch from Brazil in return for financial and territorial compensation, the Spanish representatives at the peace talks wanted to see the treaty extended to Asia, where the Dutch East India Company was again on the offensive. In February 1636 the talks were broken off, with bad blood on both sides. Writing to the Cardinal-Infante on 14 March 1636 the Count-Duke gave vent to his many anxieties—the excessive cost of provisions for Germany, the lack of progress of the war in northern Italy—but made it clear that his greatest concern of all was for the safety of Schenkenschans. 'Without Schenk we have nothing, even if Paris falls.'[28] All too soon he was indeed 'without Schenk'. It fell to the besieging army of Frederick Henry on 30 April,[29] and the Count-Duke could scarcely believe his ears when he heard the news. The king had lost the 'brightest jewel' in the Netherlands. It was a 'terrible blow for the king our lord, and for all Spain.'[30]

What had gone wrong? No doubt Olivares, misled by his advisers and his maps, and perhaps also by his own tendency to build houses on sand, had overestimated the strategic and political significance of the Cardinal-Infante's original success. But the whole affair exposed what was to be a perennial problem for the Count-Duke—the extreme difficulty of planning and directing military operations from

[25] AGS Est. leg. 2658, *El Conde Duque sobre lo que conviene disponer y executar en los reynos de SM*, 13 January 1636.
[26] *Ibid.*, fo. 5.
[27] Israel, *The Dutch Republic*, pp. 304–8.
[28] MSB, Cod. hisp. 22, fo. 12v.
[29] Pirenne, *Histoire de Belgique*, 4, p. 278.
[30] MSB, Cod. hisp. 22, fo. 17v., Olivares to Cardinal-Infante, 25 May 1636.

Madrid. He would carefully draw up his plans for the coming year, laying down exact figures for the numbers of men and the sums of money required in each of the the theatres of war,[31] only to have his generals report that they lacked the men and resources to comply with their orders.

The Count-Duke's immediate reaction was to blame his generals, as he blamed Juan Cerbellón in 1635 for losing the Valtelline to a numerically inferior French army under the command of the Duke of Rohan.[32] If there is one recurring theme in his memoranda and correspondence during these years of total war, it is the lack of *cabezas*, or leaders: 'The lack of *cabezas* seems to me the most serious of our problems, because there are none, partly because of the number we have lost in the past two or three years, which is quite without precedent over many centuries, and partly because the war threatens the whole Monarchy, so that we need *cabezas* everywhere.'[33] '*Cabezas, señor, cabezas, señor*, this is what we lack', he wrote to the Cardinal-Infante on 25 May 1636, when blaming him (while pretending not to do so) for the loss of Schenkenschans. His complaint seems to have been justified. Once Spínola and the Duke of Feria disappeared from the scene, there was no outstanding general in the service of the King of Spain, although in the opening years of the war Richelieu too had good reason to distrust the capacity of his commanders.[34] In Flanders after the death of the Marquis of Aytona, the Cardinal-Infante appears dangerously isolated, both politically and militarily. No doubt the adhesion of Prince Thomas of Savoy to the Spanish cause[35] gave him a commander of some professional competence; but the prince's French connections through his eccentric wife, the Princess of Carignano, raised questions about his reliability which deterred the king from appointing him to the most responsible commands. In Italy, where the war had opened inauspiciously with the occupation of Breme by the forces of Victor Amadeus of Savoy,[36] the veteran Don Carlos Coloma (born in 1566) can hardly have been expected to measure up to his duties as *maestre de campo general* in Milan, the post to which he had been appointed in the previous year. Olivares himself described him as 'totally incapable, his understanding impaired, his memory gone, and quite unable to remain on horse-

---

[31] For example, AGS Est. leg. 2051, no. 26, *El Conde Duque sobre lo que se deve disponer para el año que viene de 1637* (1 October 1636), one of a series of annual surveys of this type. Others, for 1638 and 1639, in AGS Est. leg. 2053 and 2661.

[32] AGS Est. leg. 3342, fo. 147, paper by Olivares, 15 October 1635.

[33] AGS Est. leg. 2051, no. 19, *El Conde Duque sobre . . . despachos de Flandes*, 6 March 1636.

[34] Tapié, *La France de Louis XIII*, p. 312; Elliott, *Richelieu and Olivares*, pp. 130–1.

[35] Above, p. 474. For the prince's military service on behalf of Spain, Quazza, *Tomaso di Savoia-Carignano*.

[36] Quazza, *Preponderanza Spagnuola*, p. 484.

back.'[37] The man sent to replace him and restore Spain's fortunes in Lombardy was the Count-Duke's factotum, the Marquis of Leganés, who had yet to prove his capacity for supreme command.

Regretting his own lack of military experience, the Count-Duke had a tendency to make up for it by mentally fighting his generals' battles for them, and then expressing surprise and consternation when their despatches revealed that things were not as he imagined them. The Cardinal-Infante found it necessary to remind him on more than one occasion that 'there is a great difference in discoursing on affairs from afar.'[38] In theory the Count-Duke knew this. In practice he found its implications hard to accept. There was, too, another difficulty which hampered the accurate assessment of distant military operations—the time-factor. The ordinary delays and uncertainties in the system of communications that linked the outlying parts of the Monarchy to Madrid were greatly compounded by the outbreak of the war with France. Despatches from Flanders which had formerly been sent to Spain by way of France now had to take a longer and more roundabout route through Germany, unless some alternative could be found. Arrangements were in fact made with England for a Flanders-Corunna route by way of Plymouth,[39] but it was subject to the vagaries of wind, wave and enemy action. 'It is a long time since we have had any news from Flanders', Olivares wrote to the Marquis of Santa Cruz two months after the outbreak of the war with France, ' . . . and we live in perpetual desire of mail from those parts.'[40] The time-lag in the receipt of news from Flanders was little short of three months, he wrote to Roose in December 1635.[41] This contrasted with the twelve to sixteen days for official correspondence before the French route was interrupted.[42] The posts also became more than usually uncertain. On 14 July 1636 the Count-Duke wrote to thank the Cardinal-Infante for his letter of 26 May, but had to tell him that his previous letters had failed to arrive. With such a defective postal system, any close coordination of the different theatres of war was virtually impossible. Problems of communication made it considerably easier to run a war from Paris than Madrid.

Impatiently waiting for despatches that seemed interminably delayed, Olivares must have envied Richelieu the geographical advan-

---

[37] Olivares in Council of State, 15 October 1635 (AGS Est. leg. 3342, fo. 147). Coloma was relieved of his command and brought back to Madrid, where he served on a variety of juntas, including the *Junta de Ejecución*, for the remaining two years of his life (BL Add. Ms. 28,708, fos. 266–71v. *Papel que dexó escrito Don Carlos Coloma . . . de sus servicios*). He died in October 1637 at the age of seventy-one.

[38] Archivo de la Casa de Miraflores, Madrid. Cardinal-Infante to Olivares, 29 January 1637.

[39] Alcalá-Zamora, *España, Flandes*, pp. 357 and 363.

[40] Hispanic Society, New York, HC 397/207, 12 August 1635.

[41] AGR CPE, Reg. 1502, fo. 130, 4 December 1635.

[42] Alcalá-Zamora, *España, Flandes*, p. 96.

tages of Paris as a European news-gathering centre. But if most of the problems of remote control were quite insuperable, he had almost equally insuperable problems nearer home. How could a Castile that was already patently exhausted possibly be mobilized for the monumental war-effort that the Count-Duke now required of it? In the spring of 1635 Sir Arthur Hopton, reviewing the high cost and scarcity of 'arms and furniture', and the extreme misery of the Castilian conscripts, 'so unwilling to serve as they are carried like galley-slaves in chains', considered it 'almost impossible for them to make a lasting war.'[43]

Arms, ships, men—all were in short supply. In the earlier years of the Olivares regime, however, a serious attempt had been made to improve Spain's military and naval capacity. A Liège iron-founder, known in Spain as Juan Curcio, had been granted special privileges in 1622 for the manufacture of artillery and munitions, and the iron-works that he established at Liérganes in Santander became a major arsenal for the Spanish war effort in the 1630's and 1640's. The outbreak of war with France saw a massive increase both in demand and supply, and between 1635 and 1640 Liérganes furnished the crown with 939 large cannon, and substantial quantities of ammunition.[44]

As for ships, the Count-Duke had always been well aware that an increase in naval power was vital for the Monarchy's survival.[45] An elaborate new series of naval ordinances was promulgated in 1633, and strenuous efforts were made to strengthen and expand the Atlantic and Mediterranean fleets and the Dunkirk flotilla.[46] In his paper of 13 January 1636 on military and naval preparations, the Count-Duke detailed some of the orders already issued: Portugal to have ready an armada of 20,000 tons for the coming year; the Seville merchants to increase the escort fleet for the Indies galleons to 20,000 tons; the Atlantic fleet to be increased by 10,000 tons to a total of 30,000; a Cantabrian flotilla to be created, and the Dunkirk flotilla raised to forty vessels.[47] This kind of expansion could not conceivably be achieved in the short time available from Spanish resources alone. The peninsula was heavily dependent on northern Europe for naval supplies, and this dependence made an alliance with England all the more attractive to Madrid. English ships could carry Baltic wood and naval stores to Iberian ports, and—subject to agreement with London—might also assist in keeping open the shipping lanes in the

[43] BL, Eg. Ms. 1820, fo. 72, Hopton to Windebank, 31 May 1635.
[44] José Alcalá-Zamora y Queipo de Llano, *Historia de una empresa siderúrgica española: los altos hornos de Liérganes y La Cavada, 1622–1834* (Santander, 1974), pp. 82–91.
[45] Above, p. 142.
[46] See Alcalá-Zamora, *España, Flandes*, part 3, ch. 4.
[47] *El Conde Duque sobre lo que conviene disponer* . . . (AGS Est. leg. 2658).

Bay of Biscay and the Channel, and transporting men and supplies between Spain and Flanders with greater safety than Spanish ships in time of war. A naval alliance between Spain and England had been envisaged in the secret Cottington treaty of 1631, and the outbreak of war with France gave new urgency to Olivares' schemes for drawing England into Spain's orbit. It was agreed in the Council of State in 1636 that if only Spain's naval resources could be supplemented by those of England, 'we shall be masters of the sea.'[48] The Spanish embassy in London would make vigorous efforts in the years before the outbreak of the English civil war to bring this naval alliance into being.[49]

By 1638 the king could tell the Cortes of Castile that Spain's naval power had never been greater, and this assertion may well have been correct.[50] Certainly, large sums of money had been spent: a total of just over 11 million *escudos* between 1632 and 1638, of which some 2,600,000 were devoted to the ten Spanish and fourteen Genoese galleys, and the remaining 8,600,000 to the Atlantic fleet and special armadas.[51] It is always difficult to measure the true increase in the size of fleets and armies, however, since the figures so lavishly thrown around in Olivares' state papers tend to reflect hopes and expectations rather than realities. Time after time paper armies proved to be a very different matter from armies on the ground. The latter, unlike the former, were always being reduced by hunger, disease, desertion, and shortage of pay. Attempting to account for the fall of Schenkenschans the Cardinal-Infante explained to Olivares how it had only been possible to give the army of Flanders one month's pay over the past five months, how provisions were in such short supply that the cavalry had lost all its horses, and how only 4,000 infantrymen were left out of a force of 14,000.[52] Another problem was that such large numbers of men in the Netherlands were tied up in garrison duties that relatively few were available to go out on campaign. The muster taken in the Low Countries at the beginning of 1637 showed a total of 65,000 infantrymen on the books, of whom 55,000 were expected to be effective. But of these 55,000, no less than 44,000 were needed to guard the fortresses, so that only 11,000 were left for campaigning. It was hoped that levies and recruiting would produce another 12,000–13,000 men, but a further 13,000 to 14,000

[48] AGS Est. leg. 2521, consulta, 26 June 1636.
[49] See J. H. Elliott, 'The Year of the Three Ambassadors', in *History and Imagination. Essays in Honour of H. R. Trevor-Roper*, ed. Hugh Lloyd-Jones, Valerie Pearl and Blair Worden (London, 1981), ch. 13.
[50] See Alcalá-Zamora, *España, Flandes*, p. 358 n. 90.
[51] *Actas* 55, pp. 441–5.
[52] Archivo de la Casa de Miraflores, Madrid. Cardinal-Infante to Olivares, 2 May 1636.

would still be needed before the army of Flanders could take the offensive.[53]

In his paper of 1627 for the Council of Castile the king had boasted of having almost 300,000 men under arms,[54] but if this was meant to refer to effective soldiers, the figure seems wildly implausible. On the other hand, a suggested total for 1635 of 60,400 infantry (divided into forty-five regiments) and 27,500 cavalry[55] is unacceptably small, since the army of Flanders alone had at least 60,000 infantry on its books. The French had 132,000 infantry and 12–15,000 cavalry under arms in April 1635,[56] and Spain could hardly have had less. On the outbreak of the war, orders were issued that military establishments should be at the following strengths:

Germany	30,000 men
Milan	23,600
Naples	10,000
Catalonia (vanguard of royal army)	16,000
	79,600

When the army of Flanders is added to these totals, there would have been some 150,000 men under arms, excluding those on garrison duty or reserve in the Iberian peninsula, bringing the grand total to around 160,000–170,000.

Olivares, like Richelieu,[57] planned to mobilize the nobility for war. In 1634 the Council of State recommended the revival of a system whereby members of the titled nobility were appointed *coroneles*, with the obligation of maintaining regiments at their own expense. Predictably, one duke after another pleaded indebtedness, and several were banished to their estates for their unwillingness to oblige. The Count-Duke, however, formed his own regiment, 1,500 men strong, and there seems to have been no shortage of volunteers from among the principal families of Castile to serve beneath his standard.[58] But an attempt to mobilize the Castilian gentry under the pretext of the king's imminent departure for the battlefront yielded very little by way of practical results, in part, perhaps, because the king never actually left Madrid.[59] Equally abortive efforts in the succeeding years

[53] AGS Est. leg. 2051, no. 225, Report of Don Miguel de Salamanca, 8 February 1637. See also Parker, *Army of Flanders*, pp. 11–12.

[54] *MC*, 2, p. 244.

[55] See J. P. A. Bazy, *État militaire de la Monarchie Espagnole sous le règne de Philippe IV* (Poitiers, 1864).

[56] Bonney, *King's Debts*, p. 173 n. 3.

[57] Pagès, *La guerre de Trente Ans*, p. 207.

[58] *MC*, 2, p. 125, notes 36 and 37.

[59] See Antonio Domínguez Ortiz, 'La movilización de la nobleza castellana en 1640', *Anuario de historia del derecho español*, 25 (1955), pp. 799–824.

were to show that the *hidalgos* of Castile, like their counterparts in other West European societies, no longer found their *raison d'être* in war.

One of the principal obstacles to the effective mobilization of Castile's resources of manpower and money was the lack of up-to-date information to determine their extent. Ministers were very uncertain as to the number of towns and villages in Castile. In the early years of the reign the figure commonly given was 15,000,[60] but this dated from 1592, and a junta of 1637 advised Olivares that it should probably now be put at 10,000.[61] Since the junta was proposing that every centre of population should make the king a 'gift' of two hundred ducats, an arbitrary one-third reduction was clearly of some significance. Nobody doubted that Castile's population had declined since the days of Philip II, but the extent of the decline was the subject of wild guesswork. In 1634 two well-informed ministers, José González and Antonio de Contreras, put Castile's population at only three million.[62] On the other hand, a computation of 1630, based on the sale of bulls for the *cruzada*, put it at 'over 5,333,000 persons',[63] while the 1634 troop levies voted by the Cortes were distributed by provinces in accordance with a breakdown of population which gave Castile a grand total of 1,015,000 *vecinos*, or some four and a half million inhabitants on a basis of 4.5 to a household.[64]

With such a variety of estimates, any targets set by ministers either for taxes or for military levies were bound to be more or less arbitrary. The inevitable result was that an official bearing a commission to extract from some unfortunate village a predetermined number of conscripts or a fixed sum in cash was likely to find that he had been set an impossible task. As each new report of a shortfall in men or taxes reached the Count-Duke, he could find only one explanation—disobedience. 'I can do no more; I am all alone', he wrote in October 1635. 'Not one of Your Majesty's orders is obeyed.' No one, he continued, was prepared to risk an unpopularity comparable to his own, and most of the time he found himself having to bark at men whom he liked and respected, 'because I esteem Your Majesty's service a thousand times more highly than my own life. But I can do no more, and anyhow, this is not my job but the council's. And I solemnly protest before it that I can no longer

[60] Ceballos, *Arte real*, fo. 115; Julián del Castillo, *Historia de los reyes godos* (Madrid, 1624), p. 489.

[61] AGS CJH, leg. 773, Junta del aposento del Conde Duque, 27 July 1637.

[62] AHN Est. lib. 862, fo. 51, consulta, 22 September 1634.

[63] 'Las utilidades que se siguen de aver Su Magestad . . . quitado los millones al Reyno . . .' (See above, p. 432 n. 114). See also Domínguez Ortiz, *La sociedad española*, 1, p. 112.

[64] AGS GA leg. 1095, *Relación de la vecindad que ay en las provincias del Reyno* . . ., summarized in *MC*, 2, p. 110.

exceed my duty, or even perform it adequately, because my strength is gone, and overwork has left me utterly exhausted.'[65]

The Count-Duke's prostration was hardly surprising. The war had placed an enormous additional burden on his shoulders, forcing him—as it forced Richelieu[66]—to assume direct personal responsibility not only for grand strategy but also for the general oversight of the multitude of details inherent in the running of a military machine. The conciliar bureaucracy, with its standard procedures and its obsessive concern with the delimitation of boundaries, was ill adapted to meet the challenges of total war. There was an obvious need for more effective central planning, and for specialist bodies to handle with speed and efficiency the innumerable problems involved in mobilizing resources and ensuring that orders were obeyed. The councils were always better at discussion than action, and in military as in civil affairs the Count-Duke preferred to act through *ad hoc* bodies and juntas, consisting of small groups of ministers and the occasional expert. No less than fourteen special commissions were set up in 1634 to handle different aspects of the mobilization programme.[67] One was established to supervise the recruiting of cavalry companies; another to deal with arms and artillery; a third (consisting of Olivares, José González, three financial ministers and the crown's factor, Bartolomé Espínola) had overall responsibility for the general *asientos* with the bankers.

These various commissions seem to have been subordinated to a new defence junta, the *Junta de la ejecución de las prevenciones de la defensa*, which is described in 1635 as having twenty-four members, chosen for their governmental or military expertise.[68] As intended, the commissions took power away from the councils, which—as described by the Genoese ambassador—had ceased to transact really important business. But the ambassador added that such business was then 'settled in accordance with one man's wishes.'[69] This may well have been true, although the very multiplicity of juntas with their often overlapping spheres of interest was a recipe for confusion which could only be sorted out by a single powerful figure at the centre of the system. Once again, therefore, the Count-Duke was cast in the role of Atlas, bearing the burden of the world on his shoulders, just as he had been depicted on the title page of the Count of La Roca's *El Fernando* in 1632 (Pl. 7).

[65] AGS Est. leg. 2656, paper by Olivares, 2 October 1635.

[66] See Elliott, *Richelieu and Olivares*, pp. 130–32.

[67] AGS GA leg. 1099, *Instrucciones . . . tocantes a las comisiones . . .*, 14 December 1634.

[68] ASF, Mediceo, filza 4960, letter from Bernardo Monanni, 10 February 1635. For the composition of this Junta, see *MC*, 2, pp. 128–30.

[69] ASG, Lettere Ministri, Spagna, 2440, despatch by Giacomo De'Franchi, 26 May 1635.

Now that the composition of the Council of State was more to his liking, he attended its meetings with much greater frequency than during the 1620's, shaping its agenda and dominating its discussions with imperious ease.[70] But while it formulated, or rubber-stamped, a wide range of policy recommendations for submission to the king, who often responded at length in the margins of its *consultas*, it was not well adapted to rapid decision-making in times of war. For its part, the new defence junta was much too large and cumbersome. Eventually Olivares hit on the device of a small war cabinet, which came to be known as the Junta de Ejecución. The first known reference to this junta dates from January 1637, when a newsletter reports its existence and the speed with which it was despatching business. Its initial membership consisted of the Count-Duke, the Duke of Villahermosa, Don Carlos Coloma, and the Proto-notario.[71]

The purpose of this junta was to ensure that important policy decisions were taken rapidly and put into effect. In the Count-Duke's eyes, the failure to execute the king's orders threatened Spain with disaster. In a cogent paper written for the king in February 1636 he remorselessly detailed the shortcomings. Although the impending storm had been foreseen more than a year and a half in advance, and repeated orders had been given, there had been nothing but delay. The *donativo* approved on 3 June 1635—no action taken; the measures for raising three million ducats—no action after seven months; the vote on *donativos*—no action after five months. And so the litany continued.[72] 'We are sinking', he wrote, 'because orders are not being executed.'[73] Since he never spared himself, he expected everyone else to behave as he did, and was constantly having to rebuke, chastise and cajole when subordinates fell short of the exacting standards that he both set and demanded. By temperament he was more inclined to drive men than encourage them, although he seems to have made something of an exception for his protégé Pierre Roose, who suffered from bouts of depression similar to his own, and who was always

---

[70] Dr. Patrick Williams is at present engaged in drawing up attendance registers for the Council of State. First indications point to a striking increase in the number of verified attendances by Olivares in the 1630's, at least when Flanders was under discussion, although this may be unrepresentative because he was boycotting meetings in the Spínola period. Of 274 recorded meetings between 1623 and 1630, he attended 37; of 544 between 1631 and 1642, he attended 216 (a yearly average of 18 instead of 5). I am very grateful to Dr. Williams for providing me with these figures, which must be regarded as provisional.

[71] Rodríguez Villa, *La corte y monarquía*, p. 75.

[72] AGS Est. leg. 2337, fo. 54, paper by Olivares of 3 February 1636 incorporated into consulta of Council of State of 10 February.

[73] AGS Est. leg. 2658, *El Conde Duque sobre lo que falta de executar de lo resuelto*, 28 March 1636.

threatening to resign from his thankless duties in Brussels, where Olivares regarded his services as indispensable.[74]

In general it was a bleak vision of the world that the Count-Duke purveyed in his letters—a world of duty, sacrifice and suffering. He was working himself to the bone; he permitted himself few distractions, other than building or landscape-designing at the Retiro;[75] and the constant complaints of headaches suggest that the strain was beginning to tell. In 1637 people were saying that his judgment was gone, and darkly recalled that he had been the victim of periods of temporary mental instability in his childhood. Why else was he always making exaggerated bodily movements—his head, his arms, his legs—even while transacting serious affairs of state?[76] Yet it is hard to detect any change of tone or manner in his correspondence and in his *votos* for the Council of State and the juntas, at least before 1640–1. There is, as always, meandering rhetoric, but vigour and cogency remain very much to the fore. Nor do responsible outside observers give any impression that Olivares was entering a period of mental decline, although they do make it clear that his one-man style of government was taking its toll of his energies. Even then, Sir Walter Aston was able to write in the autumn of 1639 to Cottington, who had last been in Madrid in 1630, that Olivares 'seems younger than he did when your lordship was here, and I take him to be stronger, only that he grows excessive fat.'[77] This is hardly the impression conveyed by the Count-Duke's own letters, where he depicts himself as prostrated with exhaustion and with one foot in the grave (Pl. 28).

If these letters express agony, the task that confronted him was itself agonizing. He may have lacked accurate statistics, but his eyes and ears told him that he was engaged in a race with time. The burden was weighing with oppressive heaviness on the backs of those he most wished to spare, 'the miserable plebs'.[78] His aim, as always, was to shift it on to backs more capable of bearing it, but preferably through concealed or indirect taxation in order to avoid a confrontation with the tax-exempt sectors of Castilian society that was certain to be lost. A *donativo*, described by Novoa as 'immortal';[79] the withholding of interest payments on *juros*;[80] and the introduction at the beginning of 1637 of *papel sellado*, the notorious stamped paper,

---

[74] See his letter of 6 April 1640 to Roose (AGR CPE, Reg. 1502, fos. 259–61).
[75] AHN Est. lib. 981, Carnero to Miguel de Salamanca, 4 December 1638.
[76] ASF, Mediceo, filza 4963, enclosure with Monanni's letter of 14 November 1637 of a clandestine indictment, here given in Italian, of the Count-Duke and his government.
[77] PRO SP. 94.41, fo. 210, 5/15 October 1639.
[78] Above, p. 410.
[79] Novoa, *Codoin* 77, p. 232.
[80] Domínguez Ortiz, *Política y hacienda*, p. 319.

allegedly invented by Father Salazar[81]—such devices would, it was hoped, be both lucrative in themselves and less socially unfair than the normal subsidies voted by the Cortes of Castile.

Over and over again, however, the Count-Duke was driven in spite of himself to adopt fiscal measures that were bound to hurt most severely those he was most anxious to relieve. He had left the *vellón* coinage alone since the great deflation of 1628; but in the new circumstances created by the war with France, the king's promise of 1628 never again to interfere with the *vellón* tariff began to look increasingly untenable. On 11 March 1636, apparently at the instigation of the *factor general* Bartolomé Espínola and of Olivares' Portuguese financial adviser, Manuel López Pereira,[82] the crown ordered the holders of *calderilla*, the better quality *vellón* minted in the sixteenth century, to turn it in at the mints for restamping at three times its face value, the king being left with the profits of this transaction—some four million ducats.[83] The Count-Duke, writing three days later to the Cardinal-Infante, described interference with the value of money as 'the worst of methods', and the action he had just taken as 'the most harmful and unjust ever adopted', but defended it as the only way to ensure firm payments for the armies, at least until the end of September.[84] The immediate consequence, however, was to produce the worst monetary confusion of the reign, with the flight from *vellón* leading to a scarcity of goods and sharp price rises, which the government then attempted to curb by fixing a maximum of 25% for the premium on silver in terms of *vellón*.[85]

Accompanied as it was by harvest failure, the monetary confusion of 1636 had a drastic impact on wage-earners, and the next two or three years wiped out half the gain in real wages that they had made in the preceding seven.[86] But, as the war made the poor poorer, so also it created spectacular opportunities for others to grow rich. The crown's bankers, the military entrepreneurs, strategically placed ministers and royal officials, tax-collectors, the administrators of royal rents, and the *poderosos* of the towns and villages—all saw an opportunity in the crown's embarrassments to feather already well-feathered nests. Each time an office was sold, or crown revenues

---

[81] ASF, Mediceo, filza 4963, letter from Bernardo Monanni, 3 January 1627.

[82] ASF, Mediceo, filza 4963, letter from Bernardo Monanni, 29 March 1636. The 'Manuel Pereyra' of whom Monanni writes, and whom he describes as a wicked man, and an 'enemy both of Castilians and Christians', is presumably Manuel López Pereira, since there is no indication of a Manuel Pereyra among the crown's Portuguese *asentistas*.

[83] Hamilton, *American Treasure*, p. 84; Domínguez Ortiz, *Política y hacienda*, p. 258; BL Add. Ms. 36,450, fo. 30, Aston to Coke, 3 April 1636.

[84] MSB, Cod. hisp. 22, fo. 7v., 14 March 1636.

[85] ASF, Mediceo, filza 4962, letter from Bernardo Monanni, 29 March 1636; BL Add. Ms. 36,450, fo. 45, Aston to Coke, 29 May 1636.

[86] Hamilton, *American Treasure*, p. 281.

28. Diego de Velázquez, *Count-Duke of Olivares*, probably painted in 1638.

farmed out, new recruits were added to the already swollen ranks of intermediaries between crown and people. In a long memorandum of 1637, suffused with despair, the Count-Duke inveighed against 'the enemies of the *patria*, the local bosses, and iniquitous officials', whose pockets were overflowing with the taxes paid by the 'sad and miserable labourer.' 'It is very possible, sir, that seven million out of every ten are stolen, and all of them paid by the poor . . . Your vassals, sir, are perishing, and Castile approaches its end.'[87]

What was to be done? 'The principal source of our misfortunes', according to the Count-Duke's analysis, 'consists in our saying: "this is not the time; we'll do it when peace returns."' His reform programme, in other words, had been jettisoned for the sake of the war. But as he surveyed the dismal Castilian scene, Olivares was now passionately convinced that this had been a dreadful mistake— that war and reform were, after all, compatible, and indeed that victory abroad was impossible without reformation at home. Reformation meant a vigorous drive against every kind of fraud; it meant educating the new generation to place the public interest ahead of its own; and it meant a revival of those great projects of the 1620's— the schemes for repopulation, the plans for making waterways navigable, for abolishing customs barriers and setting the poor to work— which would generate an increase in national wealth and restore Castile's prosperity.

But it was a lost cause. The crown was so persistently short of ready cash to meet even its routine commitments that there was simply no possibility of finding additional sums to finance major undertakings, like transportation improvements, which would take time to yield a dividend. Nor did the crown have sufficient ministers and officials of the calibre needed for planning and executing the projects so dear to the Count-Duke's heart. It lacked, too, the strength and authority, especially in time of war, to confront the sectional interests that always stood ready to block efforts at reform. As a result, Olivares' passionate plea for a renewal of the reform campaign was no more than a monument to his good intentions, the last testament of a frustrated reformer.

The crown could not afford to be fastidious about its methods of raising men and money. This was the dominant fact of life as Olivares and his closest confidants—José González, Antonio de Contreras, Francisco Antonio de Alarcón—struggled to meet the urgent and despairing demands of the captains and commanders. The most remarkable feature of the later 1630's, however, was not so much the crown's shortage of funds, which was hardly a novelty in Habs-

---

[87] *MC*, 2, Doc. XIV. See especially pp. 171–2, and 158.

burg Spain, as the enormous sums that it remained able to mobilize. Between 1635 and the end of 1641 some thirty million *escudos* passed through the hands of the paymaster-general of the army of Flanders, and it is probable that 90% or more of this came to him from Spain.[88] That Spain, at the height of the war, should still have been able to send four million *escudos* a year to the Netherlands—remittances higher than at any period since the truce expired in 1621—is a remarkable testimonial both to the Count-Duke's determination, and to the continuing capacity of an apparently exhausted Spanish Monarchy to raise or mobilize funds.

This feat is all the more remarkable when the unhappy state of Seville's trade with the Indies is taken into account. During the 1630's the volume and value of the transatlantic trade continued to decline, although there seems to have been a brief spurt of vitality in 1636–7.[89] While 1636–7 was also to prove a period of relative military successes,[90] the relationship between transatlantic trade fluctuations and the fortunes of war seems at best a tenuous one. The crown's most immediate interest was in the silver remittances for the royal treasury, and the figures for these years were discouraging. The treasure fleets arrived irregularly—no fleets returned to Spain either in 1638 or 1640[91]—and the quantities actually received failed to live up to expectations. Two fleets from New Spain arrived together in August 1636 and between them only yielded 165 million maravedís (440,000 ducats) for the royal treasury, to the indignation of the king.[92] The total remittances for the crown over the five years 1636–40 came to just over $5\frac{1}{2}$ million ducats[93]—much the same figure as in the preceding five years, and only sufficient to meet Spain's disbursements in Flanders for a period of under two years.

Since the remittances of Peruvian silver to Seville rose to a high level in the 1630's—in part becuase of the energetic fiscal measures adopted by the viceroy, the Count of Chinchón[94]—the explanation of the disappointing figures is to be sought primarily in New Spain. Here, too, the level of taxation was rising, although in New Spain, as in Peru, the viceroys were careful to make haste slowly in complying with their orders to introduce the Union of Arms. But the increase

---

[88] Parker, *Army of Flanders*, p. 295; Domínguez Ortiz, 'Los caudales de Indias', p. 358.

[89] Chaunu, *Séville et l'Atlantique*, 8, 2 (2), part 5.

[90] *Ibid.*, 8, 2 (2), p. 1745.

[91] *Ibid.*, 5, pp. 336 and 374.

[92] AGS CJH leg. 750, consulta, 19 September 1636; Domínguez Ortiz, 'Los caudales', pp. 350–1.

[93] J. H. Elliott, *Imperial Spain, 1469–1716* (London, 1963; repr. Harmondsworth, 1970), Table 4 (Hamilton's figures, in *pesos*, converted into ducats).

[94] Carmen Báncora Cañero, 'Las remesas de metales preciosos desde el Callao a España en la primera mitad del siglo XVII', *Revista de Indias*, no. 75 (1959), pp. 35–88.

in taxes was offset by the declining yield of the Mexican silver mines, which took second place to the Peruvian mines in the allocation by Madrid of the limited supplies of European mercury available for the refining process.[95] The level of silver remittances to Spain, however, was not solely dictated by the level of production in the mines. Large quantities of Mexican and Peruvian silver were taking the trans-Pacific route by way of the Philippines to pay for oriental luxuries;[96] and further substantial amounts were being withheld by the American viceroys to meet the rising costs of imperial defence as the Dutch established themselves in north-eastern Brazil and the Antilles, where they were to be followed by the ships of other northern nations. The Count-Duke, when planning the expulsion of the Dutch from the Caribbean island of St. Martin in 1633, had declared that no quarter was to be given to 'the pirates and the [Dutch] rebels in the Indies', and ordered the waging of 'bloody war' against them.[97] But 'bloody war', even against privateers, could not be waged on the cheap, and it helped to divert to regional uses silver that might otherwise have gone back to Spain for expenditure on the battlefields of Europe.

The outbreak of war with France in 1635 added immeasurably to the already considerable expense of defending the Spanish Atlantic, and imposed new strains on Seville's trade and on Spain's limited stock of ships and skilled seamen.[98] It also imparted fresh urgency to a project long debated in Madrid for the creation of a special Caribbean defence squadron, the *armada de Barlovento*. The Count-Duke's protégé, Juan de Palafox, appointed to the Council of the Indies in 1633, was an enthusiastic advocate, and seems to have convinced his patron of the virtues of the project.[99] At a meeting of a junta held in his rooms on 8 March 1635 to discuss the recent Dutch capture of Curaçao, Olivares accepted the need for an *armada de Barlovento*, although arguing that it should be an escort squadron rather than being permanently stationed in the Caribbean, where he believed

[95] Bakewell, *Silver Mining*, p. 234.

[96] For the Philippines trade, see William L. Schurz, *The Manila Galleon* (1939, repr. New York, 1959), and Pierre Chaunu, *Les Philippines et le Pacifique des Ibériques: XVIᵉ, XVIIᵉ, XVIIIᵉ siècles* (Paris, 1960). For a discussion of the production and destination of New World silver in the seventeenth century, see John J. TePaske, and Herbert S. Klein, 'The seventeenth-century crisis in New Spain: myth or reality?', *Past and Present*, 90 (1981), pp. 116–35, and the ensuing debate, *Past and Present*, 97 (1982), pp. 144–61.

[97] AGI Indif. leg. 2568, paper by Olivares, 23 March 1633. For the Dutch occupation of St. Martin and the Spanish expedition for its recovery, commanded by the Marquis of Cadereita, see Vila Vilar, *Historia de Puerto Rico*, pp. 152 and 159–64, and Thomas G. Mathews, 'The Spanish Dominion of St. Martin, 1633–1648', *Caribbean Studies*, 9 (1969), pp. 3–23.

[98] Chaunu, *Séville et l'Atlantique*, 8, 2 (2), pp. 1743–4.

[99] Vila Vilar, *Historia de Puerto Rico*, pp. 164–8; Bibiano Torres Ramírez, *La Armada de Barlovento* (Seville, 1981), pp. 35–6.

that it would all too soon disintegrate.[100] It was to consist of eighteen galleons and four smaller vessels, with a complement of 1,300 men, and be financed from new taxes raised in the American viceroyalties, but the first ships were not ready for service until 1641.[101]

While the crown suffered directly from any diminution or diversion of the silver remittances due to it from the Indies, its fortunes, as the Count-Duke was well aware, were also bound up with the fortunes of the Indies trade as a whole. Since French textiles bulked large in transatlantic cargoes,[102] these were severely affected by the embargo on French trade. Seville was also highly sensitive to interference by the state. Between 1635 and 1637 two million ducats of silver belonging to private individuals were compulsorily exchanged for *vellón* at an artificially low premium of 25%.[103] On top of this, the crown approached the Seville *consulado* in 1636 for a loan of 800,000 ducats, and then attempted to levy another half million of privately owned silver in 1637. The Count of Castrillo, as president of the Council of the Indies, warned the king of the potentially disastrous impact of these arbitrary actions on the Indies trade, but Olivares, while 'deeply regretting that His Majesty's needs should compel him to do this', went ahead none the less.[104] As always, in any potential conflict of interest it was royal fiscalism that had the final word.

Trouble in Portugal (1637)

The intensive fiscalism of 1635–6 might be justified in terms of the need for short-term sacrifices in order to bring the war to an end in two or three years at the most; but how realistic was this goal? From the moment that France declared war, the Count-Duke was well aware of the urgent need for peace, but he was insistent that neither with the Dutch nor with the French could this be peace regardless of the cost. Criticizing the Cardinal-Infante in the spring of 1635 for writing a conciliatory letter to Frederick Henry, he explained that the king wanted 'a good truce at any price, but not just any truce.'[105] His aim was to ensure a 'good truce' or definitive settlement by bringing such massive pressure to bear on his opponents before

[100] AGI Indif. leg. 758, Junta particular de los consejos de estado y guerra, 8 March 1635.
[101] Torres Ramírez, *La Armada de Barlovento*, pp. 37–44.
[102] Chaunu, *Séville et l'Atlantique*, 5, p. 271.
[103] Domínguez Ortiz, *Política y hacienda*, p. 290.
[104] AGI Indif. leg. 761, consulta, 10 December 1637. See also Domínguez Ortiz, 'Los caudales de Indias', pp. 353–4.
[105] Consulta of Council of State, 31 March 1635, cited in Alcalá-Zamora, *España, Flandes*, p. 372.

they had time to coordinate their war effort, that one of them at least would be driven to settle and leave the other isolated.

In 1635–6 he still reckoned that he was powerful enough to achieve this, especially when it began to look as though Spain would not be fighting France single-handed. France had alienated Maximilian of Bavaria by its constant interference in the affairs of the Empire and its dispossession of Maximilian's cousin, Duke Charles of Lorraine.[106] At the Imperial court the Emperor's son, the King of Hungary, the Cardinal-Infante's companion in victory at Nördlingen, was less hesitant than his father about a confrontation with the French. With some uneasiness the Emperor formally declared war on France in March 1636. There was therefore a reasonable prospect of active Imperial cooperation with Spain against both the Dutch and the French, as long as the Swedes did not stage a recovery.[107]

If Olivares was gambling on a quick triumph over France, the resurgence of the Habsburg and Catholic forces in Germany in the wake of their victory at Nördlingen made 1635–6 as propitious a moment as any. He is also likely to have reckoned that, if Spain's situation was bad, that of France was no better. As viewed from Madrid, Richelieu was the enemy, and Richelieu's control was permanently at risk from the activities of his domestic enemies, although the Count-Duke would have nothing to do with possible attempts on the life of the Cardinal.[108] The French war machine, too, was inexperienced in comparison with that of Spain. France's commanders were still largely untried, and its soldiers unhardened by long campaigns. In the short run at least, Spain's forces were reckoned to be superior,[109] thanks in particular to the professional expertise of the Spanish and Italian regiments. It was by depending on the troops of these two 'nations', the Count-Duke told Philip, that he could best hope to preserve his Monarchy.[110] Suspicions of France's military vulnerability were increased by the events of the 1635 campaigning season. Richelieu had hoped to weaken Spain by a series of sudden strikes—in the Netherlands, Italy and the Valtelline—but he was disappointed by the meagre results.[111] Above all, Spain clearly possessed greater reserves of silver. In the opinion of the British ambassador in Madrid, the men who ruled Spain were genuinely anxious for peace, but if they failed to achieve it, they believed that 'their golden spring, which like Martial's *aqua perennis* runs from

[106] Parker, *Thirty Years' War*, p. 162.
[107] Bireley, *Religion and Politics*, p. 227.
[108] MSB, Cod. hisp. 22, fo. 26v., Olivares to Cardinal-Infante, 14 July 1636.
[109] Alburquerque in Council of State, 26 August 1635 (AGS Est. leg. 2336).
[110] AGS Est. leg. 2051, no. 26. *El Conde Duque sobre lo que se deve disponer para el año que viene de 1637* (October 1636).
[111] Parker, *Thirty Years' War*, pp. 148–51.

the Indies, will keep them fresh here when France will have spent itself dry.'[112]

The Count-Duke was therefore prepared to bide his time, although never entirely closing his lines of communication with Paris. Sometimes they ran by way of Rome, sometimes more directly.[113] The first attempts at direct negotiation between the two ministers came from Richelieu in 1636.[114] The Count of Salazar, on his way from Brussels to negotiate at Blois with Gaston d'Orléans, had been caught on French territory at the beginning of the war, and taken into custody. In the summer of 1636 Richelieu allowed Salazar to return to Madrid, bearing conciliatory messages to Olivares. The Cardinal insinuated that France might in certain circumstances be willing to abandon its Dutch allies; and while there could be no question of giving up Pinerolo or Lorraine, an accommodation might be reached over Alsace and the Valtelline.

The Count-Duke affected indignation at the form of Richelieu's minister-to-minister approach, which placed him—or so he said—in an impossible situation, especially having to negotiate with 'a man so wise and astute as the Cardinal.'[115] This little piece of self-depreciation was no doubt intended to elicit expressions of confidence from his colleagues. But it suited Olivares better at this moment to prevaricate by saying that everything should be left to the general peace conference that had been scheduled for Cologne. These were heady days in Madrid, when it seemed as if the forces of the Habsburgs might indeed be on the way to a quick and decisive victory. In order to relieve French pressure on the Franche-Comté, where Dôle was under siege, the Cardinal-Infante decided to launch a diversionary invasion of France.[116] What had originally been intended as no more than a preventive strike suddenly assumed major significance as French resistance crumbled. Bavarian light cavalry joined the Cardinal-Infante's army at La Capelle and on 15 August it captured the fortress of Corbie. The route to Paris lay open before it.

On 18 September Olivares was writing to congratulate the Cardinal-Infante 'a thousand times on these glorious events.' The king and his court were 'wild with delight' at the news that Condé had lifted the siege of Dôle.[117] With Spanish and Imperial forces on the advance, this was obviously not the moment to listen to peace

---

[112] BL Add. Ms. 36,449, fo. 64, Aston to Leicester, 30 June 1636.

[113] See Leman, *Richelieu et Olivarès*, for a detailed account of Franco-Spanish peace negotiations and initiatives.

[114] *Ibid.*, pp. 21–4.

[115] AGS Est. leg. 2051, no. 27, *voto del Conde Duque sobre el papel que ha dado el Conde de Salazar*, 1 October 1636.

[116] Archivo de la Casa de Miraflores, Madrid. Cardinal-Infante to Olivares, 6 July 1636.

[117] MSB, Cod. hisp. 22, fo. 27, Olivares to Cardinal-Infante, 18 September 1636.

overtures from Richelieu. But the Corbie campaign of 1636 proved to be no more than a short-lived pyrotechnical display. To the south, the Imperial army under Count Gallas crossed into Burgundy on 15 September, but its move came too late. The Cardinal-Infante, disappointed in his hopes of help from Gallas' Germans, lacked the forces to drive home his unexpected advantage, and prudently decided to withdraw when he saw the French rallying under the shock of the attack. The invasion of Burgundy achieved little but devastation, and Gallas had to be recalled to Germany when the Swedes defeated an Imperial and Saxon army at Wittstock in October. Corbie itself was lost to the French on 14 November. The Count-Duke, on hearing the news, wanted only to lie down and die.[118] He had claimed a few days earlier that his sole desire was for a real peace, which would allow the king's subjects to live in prosperity and justice—a peace in which his master would keep not a yard of territory that belonged to others.[119] Such a peace would not now be brought about by the sudden collapse of French arms.

In February 1637 the most lavish festivities ever seen in the Madrid of Philip IV were held in the Prado Alto de San Jerónimo—a large expanse of land adjoining the Buen Retiro, which had been specially levelled for the staging of tournaments and pageants. These festivities were held to celebrate the election in December 1636 of Ferdinand King of Hungary as King of the Romans,[120] and in effect as successor to his ailing father as Holy Roman Emperor. Among the principal inventions of the court stage designer, Cosimo Lotti, for the occasion were two enormous cars drawn by oxen. On the first rode Justice and Fury, symbolizing the triumph of war; on the second Religion and Spain, symbolizing the triumph of peace. The ponderous movement of the two cars was to be paralleled by the ponderous movement of Spain's efforts on behalf of war and peace in the long months ahead.

The Cardinal-Infante's invasion, and anti-fiscal revolts throughout south-west France,[121] had made 1636 an agonizing year for Richelieu. To make matters worse, Gaston d'Orléans and the dissident Count of Soissons were again conspiring to overthrow him. Olivares had nothing comparable to face in terms of aristocratic conspiracy or popular unrest, and it is not surprising that the Cardinal should have been the one to take the initiative in making peace overtures.[122] This

[118] MSB, Cod. hisp. 222, fo. 111, Olivares to Cardinal-Infante, 13 December 1636.
[119] AGS Est. leg. 2657, *voto* of Olivares, 1 December 1636.
[120] Brown and Elliott, *A Palace*, pp. 199–202.
[121] See Yves-Marie Bercé, *Histoire des croquants* (Geneva, 1974); also, Boris Porchnev, *Les soulèvements populaires en France de 1623 à 1648* (Paris, 1963), pp. 52–80, and Tapié, *La France de Louis XIII*, pp. 336–8.
[122] Leman, *Richelieu et Olivarès*, p. 38.

time the agent was the Baron de Pujols, a retainer of the house of Soissons, already well known to Olivares through a previous visit to Madrid on behalf of the Princess of Carignano and her husband, Prince Thomas of Savoy.[123] Pujols arrived in March 1637, and in private conversations with the Count-Duke expressed Richelieu's willingness to discuss conditions for peace, either at Cologne or on the Franco–Spanish border.[124]

The tortuous conversations and the exchange of cryptic messages between Paris and Madrid continued throughout 1637, in spite of Richelieu's discovery that the Queen of France was carrying on a secret correspondence with the Marquis of Mirabel, now serving as Spain's ambassador in Brussels.[125] But if the negotiations did not actually break down, they did little more than emphasize the extent and depth of the differences dividing Spain from France. Richelieu wanted a truce based on the status quo, Olivares a peace settlement based on the reciprocal restitution of conquests.[126] Failing a general settlement, each minister hoped to disrupt the alliances of the other— Richelieu to detach the Empire from Spain, Olivares to induce the French to abandon the Dutch. Distrust was deeply rooted, and neither party was prepared to make serious concessions when the war was going either unusually badly or unusually well.

The Count-Duke had high hopes for 1637. The Count of Monterrey was to send 8,000 men from Naples by sea to reinforce the army of Flanders for what was expected to be a critical campaigning season. Most of all, however, he was banking on the Mediterranean galleys and the army of Milan, which by his count numbered some 40,000 men. This army, commanded by the Marquis of Leganés, was in his view the key to victory, and he planned to unleash it in the spring for an attack on Marseilles or Narbonne. In combination with the army of Flanders it offered the 'infallible hope of a most glorious peace.'[127] But once again hope proved all too fallible. Leganés achieved some successes in Italy, where the death of Victor Amadeus brought civil war to Savoy; and Rohan's troops were driven from the Valtelline. Elsewhere, however, there was painfully little to show for Spain's massive investment in war. An attempt to invade France from the Principality of Catalonia ended in humiliating failure when Spain's army was defeated at Leucata on 27 September.[128] But it was in the

---

[123] A. Cánovas del Castillo, *Estudios del reinado de Felipe IV*, 2 vols. (Madrid, 1888), 1, pp. 390–3 (Nota de Cancillería, 1637).
[124] Leman, *Richelieu et Olivarès*, p. 40.
[125] Tapié, *La France de Louis XIII*, pp. 342–7.
[126] Leman, *Richelieu et Olivarès*, p. 52.
[127] AGS Est. leg. 2051, no. 26, *El Conde Duque sobre lo que se deve disponer para el año que viene de 1637.*
[128] Elliott, *Catalans*, pp. 324–6.

Netherlands that disappointment was keenest. The Dutch and French were beginning to learn how to cooperate. The French gained ground in Artois, while Frederick Henry's forces laid siege to Breda, the scene of Spínola's great triumph in 1625. On 10 October Breda fell. In a pathetic letter of self-exculpation to the Count-Duke, the Cardinal-Infante claimed that Breda's military value had been exaggerated, and reminded him of the season's successes, achieved with resources far smaller than he could possibly imagine.[129] But Breda was more than a fortress. It was a symbol of all that was most glorious in the reign of *Felipe el Grande*, and the king and the Count-Duke took its loss very hard. On 13 December, in a frame of mind very different from that of fifteen months before, Olivares commented in a letter to Roose that over the last few years none had been so disastrous for Spain as 1637.[130]

When he delivered himself of this summary judgment, the Count-Duke had in mind not only the double humiliation of Leucata and Breda, but also a deeply disturbing event close to home—insurrection in Portugal. His policy with the Portuguese, as with the Catalans, was to edge them little by little into the Union of Arms and give them some sense of participation in a Monarchy whose interests far transcended those of their own small corner of the world. The joint Castilian-Portuguese expedition for the recapture of Bahía in 1625 was a step in the right direction, and was proudly commemorated in Maino's splendid painting in the Hall of Realms. But the postponement of the projected Brazil relief expedition of 1634 had left it without a sequel. The Portuguese had still to become fully paid-up participants in the Union of Arms. Somehow they must be persuaded to bear their proper quota of expenses, but this was bound to be a delicate question in what Olivares described as 'kingdoms and provinces that have privileges, and are naturally inclined to insurrections.'[131]

A major problem in all such kingdoms and provinces was to find native ministers on whom he could rely. For the Netherlands, after a long search, he had found Pierre Roose, and for the Crown of Aragon Jerónimo de Villanueva. He needed a Villanueva for Portugal, and in 1631 he believed that he had discovered one. Diego Suárez was the son and grandson of royal officials serving in Lisbon. Finding himself at cross purposes with the Portuguese administration, he went to Madrid in 1631, apparently intending to resign his post. He had an interview with the Count-Duke and a few days later, perhaps

---

[129] Archivo de la Casa de Miraflores, Madrid. Cardinal-Infante to Olivares, 2 November 1637.
[130] AGR CPE, Reg. 1202, fo. 166.
[131] Letter to Roose, 13 December 1637.

to his own surprise as much as that of anyone else, was appointed secretary of state to the king for Portuguese affairs.[132] Having won the Count-Duke's support, he set out to build himself a formidable power base. He soon had the Council of Portugal in his pocket, and engineered the appointment of Miguel de Vasconcelos, who was both his brother-in-law and father-in-law, to the royal administration in Lisbon.[133] It was not long before Portuguese affairs were merrily revolving round the Suárez-Vasconcelos axis. Olivares both used and was used by Suárez, who in turn made use of Vasconcelos to implement the Count-Duke's policies in Portugal.

If Olivares now had satisfactory subordinates, he still had to devise a system of government that worked better than the triumvirate of governors introduced in 1621. The system had proved unpopular in Portugal, and unreliable from the standpoint of Madrid. In particular, the governors had shrunk from introducing the fixed annual contribution that Madrid wanted from the Portuguese as the price of participating in the benefits of the Union of Arms.[134] Olivares had long felt that the Portuguese would be more reconciled to their union with Castile if they were governed by a member of the royal family. Philip's brother, Don Carlos, was being groomed for the post at the time of his sudden death in 1632—a death which the malicious ascribed to poison administered at the behest of the Count-Duke, allegedly alarmed by the popularity which this feeble young man enjoyed among the dissident nobility.[135] Failing a suitable royal candidate, Olivares turned again to the Count of Basto, the sole survivor of the three governors of 1621. But although Basto commanded a certain respect in his native Portugal, and especially in his home city of Évora,[136] his viceroyalty of 1633–4 was a disappointment to Madrid. It was hoped that he would steer his compatriots into accepting new taxes designed to raise 500,000 *escudos* annually, to be used in the first instance for the recovery of Brazil. But efforts to raise money and men provoked sporadic outbursts of unrest,[137] and Basto himself wisely asked to be relieved of his duties.

At a time of unrest with obvious nationalist overtones, Olivares was bound to feel a certain unease about the attitude and intentions of the Duke of Braganza, a descendant of the country's ruling house who could well become a figure-head for Portuguese opposition to Castilian demands. The king offered him the governorship of Milan,

---

[132] BNM, Ms. 2363, fos. 128–217, *Memorial del secretario Diego Suárez*.

[133] Manuel de Melo, *Epanáforas*, pp. 16–17.

[134] The best general account of Portugal under Spanish rule is now Joaquim Veríssimo Serrão, *História de Portugal*, 4 (Lisbon, 1979), but the subject remains very inadequately studied.

[135] Marañón, *Olivares*, p. 250.

[136] Veríssimo Serrão, *História de Portugal*, 4, p. 115.

[137] ASF, Mediceo, filza 4960, letter from Bernardo Monanni, 21 October 1634.

but he turned it down. His ancestors, he said, had never left the soil of Portugal.[138] His answer earned him a fine from the newly created Junta for Obedience, and a summons to Madrid[139]—a summons which he excused himself from obeying. Braganza, as the Count-Duke was beginning to discover, was a slippery customer. His continuing presence on Portuguese soil only served to emphasize the importance of providing the country with a ruler of royal blood who would be in a position to upstage any attempt by Braganza to represent himself as an uncrowned king.

It was apparently the Duke of Villahermosa, a close friend of Olivares and president of the Council of Portugal, who came up with a solution. Having failed to secure the viceroyalty for his own brother, the Prince of Esquilache, he suggested calling from Italy the widowed Duchess of Mantua, Princess Margaret of Savoy.[140] As the great-granddaughter of the Empress Isabella, and the granddaughter of Philip II, she could claim Portuguese royal blood, but otherwise her credentials for this sensitive office were undistinguished.[141] The duchess arrived in Madrid from Italy on 4 November 1634, and was accorded a magnificent reception by the king, who greeted her at the Buen Retiro.[142] She left for Lisbon on 30 November, taking as her *mayordomo* and principal adviser the Marquis of La Puebla, who nominally retained his presidency of the Council of Finance.[143] Her instructions make it clear that she was to be kept on a tight rein by the marquis and by her newly appointed secretary, Gaspar Ruiz de Ezcaray, secretary of the Council of War. She was also expected to secure the prize that had consistently eluded her predecessors—a regular financial contribution for the recovery of Brazil.[144]

The princess' efforts, however, were not notably successful. In December 1636 the English ambassador reported that 'the king lately demanded a supply of 500,000 crowns from Portugal, and was absolutely denied it . . .'.[145] National opposition to the introduction of a tax which had not been submitted to the Portuguese Cortes for assent persuaded the ministers to adopt a different approach, allocating contributions on a regional basis, with each region making its own decision as to how to raise the money. It was the attempt of the corregidor of Évora to collect this money in the summer of 1637 that precipitated

[138] *MHE*, 13, p. 88 (23 August 1634).
[139] ASF, Mediceo, filza 4960, letter from Bernardo Monanni, 7 October 1634.
[140] Manuel de Melo, *Epanáforas*, pp. 12–14.
[141] There is a biography by Romolo Quazza, *Margherita di Savoia* (Turin, 1930), but it has little to say about her Portuguese period.
[142] *MHE*, 13, p. 107.
[143] *Ibid.*, p. 108.
[144] Instructions printed in Cánovas del Castillo, *Estudios*, 1, pp. 327–34.
[145] BL Add. Ms. 36,450, fo. 104, Aston to Coke, 13 December 1636.

a revolt which spread to most of the Alentejo, and to the Algarve and Ribatejo.[146] Olivares was indignant that this 'canaille', 'these rogues, . . . vassals who pay less in taxes than any people in Europe', should thwart the king's commands, and he urged the Count of Basto and his fellow-nobles to stand up to the mob, as he himself had fought off a student attack single-handed in his Salamanca days.[147]

The Évora riots were all the more disturbing because they occurred at a moment when, on the other side of the peninsula, the marked lack of enthusiasm of the Catalans for the Leucata campaign against the French had made Olivares uneasy about the loyalty of another group of recalcitrant vassals. If he used brutal language to demand that the Portuguese nobility crush the rebels and mete out exemplary punishment, it was partly because he was frightened of the bad example they could set for other reluctant tax-payers. But he proceeded more cautiously than the noise and bluster might suggest. He despatched in turn two personal envoys to Évora, the Jesuit Father Manso, and then a Dominican, Fray Juan de Vasconcellos, a native of the city, who suggested that the citizens should make a voluntary contribution in lieu of the tax. The rebels, however, would agree to nothing unless guaranteed a total amnesty.

Olivares' caution was motivated in part by his judgment that the rebellion was less a hunger riot than an uprising in defence of Portugal's laws and liberties—'*no es por el huevo sino por el fuero*', as he wrote to Vasconcellos, using a phrase later to be immortalized by Quevedo in his denunciation of the Catalan rebellion.[148] It was therefore very important to keep the Évora troubles localized. But he was also receiving conflicting advice from the Council of Portugal. The majority belonged to the Suárez-Vasconcelos faction, and wanted exemplary punishment for the rebels. But the Count of Linhares, who had recently joined the council after his six years of service as viceroy of Goa, blamed the riots on the tyrannical government of the two Portuguese secretaries, and argued that it was better to dismiss two unpopular ministers than run the risk of losing the kingdom.[149] While the Count-Duke seems to have respected Linhares,

---

[146] Manuel de Melo's account in the *Epanáforas* has been published separately with a valuable introduction by Joel Serrão, *Alterações de Évora, (1637)* (Lisbon, 1967). Further details in A. Viñas Navarro, 'El motín de Évora y su significación en la restauración portuguesa de 1640', *Boletín de la Biblioteca Menéndez y Pelayo*, 6 (1924), pp. 321–39, and 7 (1925), pp. 29–49.

[147] BL Add. Ms. 28,429, fos. 57–58v., and 60–61v., Olivares to Count of Basto, 16 and 26 November 1637; and see above, p. 18.

[148] Letter to Fray Juan de Vasconcellos, in Viñas Navarro, 'El motín', *Boletín de la Biblioteca Menéndez y Pelayo*, 7, p. 49. He uses the same phrase in a letter to the Count of Basto on 18 December 1637 (BL Add. Ms. 28,429, fo. 76). For Quevedo's use of it, see his *Obras completas. Prosa*, pp. 937–8.

[149] Manuel de Melo, *Epanáforas*, p. 60.

he was also well aware that, as a member of the pro-Braganza aristocratic faction, he shared the aristocracy's traditional resentment of
government by *letrados*. His instinct was always to support the
letrados. In Flanders he backed Roose against all his noble enemies. In
Portugal he threw his support to Suárez and Vasconcelos.

But all the time he was warily manoeuvring, hoping to contain
a potentially dangerous insurrection by a judicious combination of
pressure and conciliation. Orders were given for everything to be
made ready for a possible royal expedition to Portugal. The knights
of the military orders were to stand by to accompany the king;[150]
and the Duke of Medina Sidonia was instructed to raise a force of
6,000 men, while the army of Cantabria was sent south to Extrema-
dura to be ready to cross the frontier.[151] With the armies almost
ready to move, Olivares suddenly called into his presence the leading
Portuguese personalities at court. Francisco Manuel de Melo, who
was present, offers a vivid vignette of the scene.[152] The Count-Duke,
he tells us, 'was accustomed to hold audience in a long gallery ending
in a small and dark alcove, from where he replied like an oracle,
barely seen and heard.' The seating on this occasion was carefully
arranged for some fifty people, including the entire Council of Portugal and a selection of ministers from the Junta de Ejecución and the
Councils of State and Castile. Opposite the Count-Duke's chair
was a table at which sat Diego Suárez and Fernando Ruiz de Contreras,
secretary to the Council of War, with their backs to the assembled
company. Suárez rose to read aloud a document in Castilian, but
had some trouble with the language, and passed it to Contreras.
In it, the king asked for advice on how to calm the country and
punish the guilty. The Bishop of Portalegre followed with a nervous
speech urging the Portuguese nobility to approve firm action, and
take upon themselves the reduction of the rebels. Olivares made a
similar appeal, which was predictably greeted with an obsequious
response.

While the Portuguese nobility at court were easily persuaded to
concur in the use of force against the rebels, the Count-Duke was
taking no chances with that elusive figure-in-waiting, the Duke of
Braganza. From the start of the troubles he had been careful to keep
in touch with Braganza, but early in November he decided to send
a personal emissary in conditions of the utmost secrecy. His choice
fell on Don Miguel de Salamanca, a former inspector of the army
of Flanders who was about to return to Brussels as a political and

---

[150] AGS Est. leg. 2052, royal order, 16 November 1637; Rodríguez Villa, *La corte y monarquía*,
pp. 225–6.
[151] Manuel de Melo, *Epanáforas*, pp. 65–6.
[152] *Ibid.*, pp. 70ff.

military adviser to the Cardinal-Infante.[153] The Count-Duke's instructions for Don Miguel have a cloak-and-dagger air.[154] Accompanied only by a servant in the guise of a travelling companion he was to catch the first or second postal relay for Badajoz just outside Madrid. On reaching Badajoz the pair were to change to horses and make for Elvas and thence for Vila Viçosa, where they were to enter at nightfall and stable their horses at the inn. Going to the duke's house, Don Miguel was to ask for his secretary, explaining that he needed to request a favour of the duke. Once in Braganza's presence he could reveal that he came from the Count-Duke and brought with him expressions of esteem and gratitude.

Don Miguel was to ascertain Braganza's views on the Évora troubles and read him a detailed account, prepared by the Count-Duke, of events to date, insisting on the vital importance of having everything back to normal by the start of the new year, even if this should require the presence of the king. The Count-Duke's narrative of events began by explaining that little importance was attached to the first reports of unrest at Évora 'because popular tumults occur daily without giving cause for concern.' But the reactions of the Counts of Basto and Linhares had made the king anxious, and the narrative then recounted the subsequent developments at court—the deliberations of the councils, their decision that the expeditionary force for the recovery of Brazil should leave as soon as possible, and the consultations with Portuguese resident in Madrid. There followed a long and impressive list of the military preparations now under way, and the document ended with an expression of astonishment at the behaviour of the Portuguese, unwilling even to provide eight galleons for the recovery of a land that was theirs while Castilian tax-payers had so far contributed one and a half million ducats, and all to no effect.

The Count-Duke's message to Braganza was clearly designed to overawe him with its revelation of the king's military might, and ensure that he did not swerve from the path of loyalty. But while Olivares sought to rally Braganza and his fellow nobles in support of his military measures, he also aimed to secure their assistance in seeking a peaceful solution. At the suggestion of Diego Suárez, who was anxious to get him out of Madrid,[155] Linhares was despatched

---

[153] AGS Est. leg. 2052, consulta, 9 September 1637, and Salamanca to Olivares, 17 September 1637, attempting to excuse himself on the grounds of short-sightedness, which had given him 'a great aversion to writing and to handling papers.' Olivares found the excuse lame (note to Andrés de Rozas, 30 September 1637).

[154] AHN Est. lib. 961, fos. 53–5, *Lo que v.m. Sr. Don Miguel de Salamanca ha de hacer*, 6 November 1637, and fos. 56–9v. (*Relación*). I am indebted to Sr. Santiago de Luxán for bringing these important documents to my notice.

[155] Manuel de Melo, *Epanáforas*, p. 83.

first to Vila Viçosa to persuade Braganza to offer his services as a
mediator, and then to Évora to bargain with the rebels. But an angry
mob surrounded Linhares' house on New Year's night, and he hastily
removed himself to Lisbon. Conciliation had obviously failed; but
if repressive measures were to be adopted, it was important to act
before the new campaigning season began in Flanders and Italy.
Before leaving for Brussels Don Miguel de Salamanca was sent across
the border from Galicia to spy out the land. On 7 January 1638 the
king informed Princess Margaret in a letter that sterner measures
would be needed, since attempts at pacification had failed; and the
army of Cantabria, along with the troops that had assembled in Extre-
madura and Andalusia, crossed the frontier into Portugal.[156]

'If our lord the king cannot punish a sedition, riot or rebellion
extending over three whole Portuguese provinces', wrote Olivares
to the Count of Basto on 30 January, 'he is not King of Portugal,
and cannot be regarded as such.'[157] The determination to uphold the
king's authority was, as always, the paramount consideration in the
Count-Duke's mind. A failure of authority in one part of the
Monarchy was bound to have its repercussions in the rest, and this
was not a risk he was prepared to run. As the armies advanced,
opposition crumbled, and a new corregidor of Évora began to try
those of the delinquents who had failed to escape. The Marquis of
Valparaíso's men conducted themselves like an army of occupation
in the Algarve, and by early March the crown concluded that it had
made its point. A royal proclamation of pardon, excepting only the
ringleaders, was issued on 5 March. The 'troubles of Évora' were
at an end, and authority upheld.

The Count-Duke could congratulate himself on his handling of
the Évora affair; and later he proudly held it up, in a conversation
with the British ambassador, as a model for Charles I to follow
in his dealings with the Scots.[158] But he could not avoid a feeling
of unease about the underlying loyalty of the Portuguese, who had
not responded to the appeal of their monarch with that unreserved
enthusiasm normally expected of loyal vassals. The Portuguese nobility in general, and the Duke of Braganza in particular, had been
almost ostentatiously inactive. There were several other unresolved
mysteries about the business, including the relationship of the Jesuits
and the local clergy to the leaders of the rebellion. What part, too,
had the French played in stirring up trouble? The Portuguese *marrano*
community in France naturally remained in contact with its kinsmen
who had stayed behind in Portugal. One member of this community

[156] Viñas Navarro, 'El motin', *Boletin de la Biblioteca Menéndez y Pelayo*, 7, p. 34.
[157] BL Add. Ms. 28,429, fo. 95.
[158] PRO SP. 94.42. fo. 10, Hopton to Cottington, 15/25 July 1640.

was Richelieu's confidant, Alphonse Lopez, ostensibly an Aragonese Morisco, who was in touch with Olivares, and may or may not have been playing a double game.[159] Lopez could be expected to brief Richelieu on events in Portugal, and indeed early in 1638 the Cardinal sent a Franciscan on an unsuccessful mission to make contact with the Évora rebels.[160] Olivares may well have known of this mission. He had his own sources of information, and in any event would hardly have expected Richelieu to remain a passive bystander at a moment such as this.

The Évora insurrection therefore only served to confirm Olivares' feelings of insecurity about the Portuguese. He had originally placed high hopes in the government of Princess Margaret, which he believed would bring Portugal more closely under royal—and Castilian—control. But the princess' regime had proved a failure. The Portuguese and Castilian ministers squabbled ceaselessly, and Margaret herself had fallen out with her principal counsellor, the Marquis of La Puebla, and was alleged to be excessively susceptible to Portuguese influence.[161] The Portuguese, for their part, were profoundly antagonized by the monopoly of power and patronage exercised by that formidable pair, Suárez and Vasconcelos. The Count-Duke, aware of their resentment, had Suárez subjected to an investigation, which lasted for eight months, but ended by clearing his name.[162] The truth of the matter was that Suárez had made himself as indispensable to the Count-Duke in the government of Portugal as Villanueva in that of Aragon.

If the administration of Portugal was unsatisfactory, the relationship of the Portuguese to the Crown of Castile was, as Olivares saw it, even more to be deplored. For sixty years, he complained, Portugal had lived in a 'state of separation and division from the rest of the Monarchy and every part of it.' Portuguese soldiers were notoriously undisciplined, and the country showed a persistent reluctance to respond to royal appeals for help. It was hard enough even to extract a piece of amber for the queen![163] Something must be done, but he hesitated how to proceed. Eventually he decided to summon Portugal's most prominent clerics and nobles to court, nominally to seek their advice on the best way to improve the administration

---

[159] Elliott, *Richelieu and Olivares*, p. 116.
[160] See I. S. Révah, *Le Cardinal de Richelieu et la restauration du Portugal* (Lisbon, 1950), pp. 10–16.
[161] AGS Est. leg. 4047, no. 96, consulta, 25 January 1636, and no. 47, consulta, 17 December 1639.
[162] BNM Ms. 2363, fos 180–217. *Memorial del secretario Diego Suárez*. The *visita* papers relating to Suárez are to be found in the Archivo de los Condes de Bornos in Madrid.
[163] AGS Est. leg. 2660, paper by Olivares, (June) 1638.

and set about recovering Portugal's lost overseas territories.[164] The gathering which assembled in the summer of 1638 was less well attended than it might have been; and Braganza once again found a pretext for refusing the invitation to Madrid. Nor did anything much come of its deliberations, apart from a decision to abolish the Council of Portugal, and replace it with a Junta Grande of those who had been summoned to Madrid.[165] It is possible that the Count-Duke himself never expected much of it, and saw it as little more than a device for binding a number of eminent Portuguese personalities to the court with silken cords. Meanwhile, the affairs of Portugal remained in a state of dangerous suspension, dependent, like so much else, on the fortunes of war across the continent.

The war in the balance (1638–1639)

His cloak-and-dagger work in Portugal completed, Don Miguel de Salamanca set out in April 1638 on his journey to Brussels to take up his appointment with the Cardinal-Infante. But before leaving he was favoured with a personal letter from the Count-Duke.[166] While there are always limits to the Count-Duke's frankness, no surviving letter is more revealing of the man, and it offers a remarkable insight into his state of mind three years into the war with France.

He wanted to say to Don Miguel 'a few words about myself, as brief as possible, and as accurate and truthful as I can make them.' He began with his financial affairs. Lack of time to attend to his estates, together with his natural 'prodigality', had left him with 600,000 ducats of consolidated debts (at 5%, interest payments would have amounted to 30,000 ducats a year), and a further 300,000 in personal debts. Thanks to the generosity of the king he would in time be able to pay off 500,000 ducats out of the income from his *encomiendas* (the remainder being charged to the house of Olivares), and still have the San Lúcar estate and a few mementos to bequeath. But if his creditors pressed him there was nothing to be done.

'With this, and with no children or expectation of them, I find myself with no desire in this life but to go and die in the company of a few monks, in a spot that I have bought in the Tardón near Seville', assuming always that the king would give his permission. To make this desire credible to the Cardinal-Infante, Don Miguel was to describe to him the kind of life he was leading, 'finding myself

---

[164] AGS Est. leg. 2660, *Papel sobre cosas tocantes a Portugal.*
[165] AGS Est. leg. 2770, royal order, (March) 1639. For the Junta Grande, see Manuel de Melo, *Epanáforas*, p. 108, and Novoa, *Codoin* 77, p. 378.
[166] AHN Est. lib. 961, fos. 123–6v., Olivares to Miguel de Salamanca, 31 March 1638.

without the strength to continue, and assuring you that there is not a single night when I expect to be alive to see the dawn, nor a single morning when I expect to reach nightfall.'

Don Miguel knew, too, how little truck the Count-Duke had with the pomp and circumstance of his position, and how he took the burdens upon himself and left the pageantry to others:

> Where ministerial business is concerned, I hold audiences, see and vote on all the official despatches, and sweat over the *asientos* and the provision of funds. The work is as unbearable and the assistance I receive as limited as you have seen and everybody knows. Everything else is done by whoever is responsible, and ecclesiastical business is managed by His Majesty's confessor, without my knowing anything more about one or the other than is known by the secretaries and officials of the Protonotario's office, and a good deal less . . . This, Don Miguel, is a fact, and I resign myself to being called a liar if, since the days when kings began to reign on earth and had favourites and ministers, a single one of them has worked like me . . .

In performing his duties as master of the horse—for which he was paid a mere 500,000 *maravedís* a year—the Count-Duke also claimed to eschew all pomp, except when he had to accompany the king out riding or hunting. Since the beginning of the reign he had lacked both the spirit and the strength to break a lance, or shoot a stag in the royal forests, except out of duty. As grand chamberlain— an office 'into which I entered against my will'—he received no wages or perquisites, and performed only the 'mechanical' duties, again shunning the pageantry. The same held true of his duties as general of the Spanish cavalry, for which he likewise received no wages or emoluments. 'I have told you this to prove that I serve neither out of vanity nor interest, nor for any reason except the love, loyalty, esteem and gratitude that I owe to our master the king.'

Armed with this remarkable epistle, the burden of which he was expected to convey to the Cardinal-Infante, Don Miguel de Salamanca left for northern Europe, travelling overland by way of Paris. Here he had two interviews with Richelieu in May 1638.[167] These made it clear that France and Spain were as far apart as ever; and no doubt the recent events in Portugal gave added significance to Salamanca's insistence that peace with the Dutch was out of the question as long as they remained in Brazil. Richelieu replied that they would never agree to abandon Brazil, and that France for its part would never abandon the Dutch.[168] The Cardinal was now in a

---

[167] Leman, *Richelieu et Olivarès*, pp. 61–70.
[168] *Ibid.*, p. 68.

stronger bargaining position than he had been the year before. Dutch and French arms had scored important successes in 1637, and Louis XIII's authority at home had been reinforced by the crushing of the revolt of the Croquants in June, and the accommodation reached with the Count of Soissons in July.[169] Olivares for his part had taken the setbacks of 1637 very hard, and indulged—as he was always liable to do at moments of depression—in a round of self-flagellation. All the misfortunes of the year, he wrote to the Cardinal-Infante at the end of November, 'are my fault, and once I am thrown into the sea the storm will cease, and success and good fortune follow.'[170] It was that same image of Jonah which he had used in the crisis of the king's illness ten years earlier,[171] and it would continue to haunt him during his final years in power.

Although the Count-Duke's sense of personal responsibility for the misfortunes of his country was well-developed, the expressions of doom and despair which pervade his letters are not always to be taken at face value. His correspondence no doubt acted as a safety-valve, allowing him to work off the frustrations and feelings of help-lessness in the face of great events that periodically afflict any great minister of state in times of war and travail. He was undoubtedly tired, and often disillusioned, but the melodramatic outbursts were accompanied by an iron determination to maintain a rigid self-control whenever this was needed. Neither prosperity nor adversity must be permitted to cloud his judgment, and the former—at least for a man of his temperament—was the more dangerous of the two. He was aware of this, and took care to counteract its effects, remind-ing himself and others 'how unstable is everything in this life, and how necessary to think of ill fortune in time of good fortune; for it is my opinion that the strongest indication of a base spirit is to let oneself be elevated in time of prosperity, when one should take exactly the opposite line.'[172]

By the spring of 1638 he knew that the situation was grave, and that this would be a critical year for the restoration or ruin of the Monarchy's fortunes. Surveying the international scene in March, he judged that 'our own forces and those of our enemies are more or less balanced today.'[173] It was not only that the enemy had gained the advantage in Lorraine, Alsace and now Flanders, although this

[169] Porchnev, *Les soulèvements populaires*, p. 80; Hanotaux, *Histoire du Cardinal de Richelieu*, 5, pp. 211–13.

[170] MSB, Cod. hisp. 22, fo. 64, 29 November 1637.

[171] *MC*, 1, p. 227 (*Papel del Conde Duque . . . sobre los naturales de los señores infantes*, 10 October 1627).

[172] AGS Est. K.1419, fo. 81, Olivares to king, 14 May 1639.

[173] AGS Est. leg. 2053, *El Conde Duque sobre la materia del Palatinato* (for meeting of Council of State, 7 March 1638).

was serious enough. He was also deeply concerned that Spain had such 'few and tepid allies'. He was thinking especially of the Empire, where the accession of the King of Hungary as the Emperor Ferdinand III on the death of his father in February 1637 had not produced any notable accession of new energy in support of causes dear to Madrid. If something like a balance of military power now prevailed, the role of that unpredictable neutral, Charles I of England, could well prove decisive for the future of the continent.

Spain's military supply routes between Italy and the Netherlands were now either broken, or hopelessly vulnerable to French attack. The consequence was to redouble the importance of the sea-route to the Netherlands by way of the English Channel.[174] Ever since the Anglo-Spanish peace treaty of 1630 Spain had been using this route for the transport of men and bullion, which was landed at Dover to be ferried across to Flanders in English ships.[175] The critical importance of commanding the sea-lanes to northern Europe fully vindicated the Count-Duke's intensive efforts over the years to build up Spanish naval power, and these efforts were now beginning to yield dividends. In December 1637, for instance, at a moment when the Cardinal-Infante was desperate for reinforcements, a squadron under the command of Don Lope de Hoces managed to rush them in five days from Corunna to Dunkirk.[176] But the active support of England, or at least of the English fleet, was regarded by the Count-Duke as indispensable for the retention of those maritime life-lines whose loss or conservation would determine the fate of his policy for reaching an honourable settlement with the Dutch Republic.

In the hope of bringing the vacillating administration of Charles I more firmly into the Spanish camp, he decided in January 1638 to withdraw Spain's ambassador in London, the younger Count of Oñate, whom Charles I had never liked.[177] But it proved difficult to discover a suitable replacement, and Madrid eventually compromised by sending a temporary envoy, Don Alonso de Cárdenas, of non-ambassadorial rank.[178] It was hardly the ideal start for a major diplomatic offensive.

The difficulty in finding a suitable envoy for England was symptomatic of what had now come to preoccupy the Count-Duke almost

---

[174] See Parker, *The Army of Flanders*, p. 77.

[175] For this arrangement and its origins, see Harland Taylor, 'Trade, neutrality and the "English Road", 1630–1648', *The Economic History Review*, 25 (1972), pp. 236–60, and J. S. Kepler, *The Exchange of Christendom* (Leicester, 1976).

[176] Alcalá-Zamora, *España, Flandes*, p. 394.

[177] AGS Est. leg. 2651, consulta, 14 January 1638.

[178] AGS Est. leg. 2575, draft royal despatch of 7 March 1638. For Cárdenas' mission see Elliott, 'The Year of the Three Ambassadors'.

to the point of obsession: the lack of men of stature and experience to occupy the principal military, diplomatic and administrative posts in the Monarchy. When Leganés wrote home in 1637 asking to be relieved of his command in Milan because of ill-health, Olivares launched into a disquisition on what he called 'the sterility of qualified men'.[179] As he looked down the lists of cardinals and grandees, of titled nobles and ambassadors, he could not find six men among them whom he regarded as fit for high office. 'Where there are none, there are none (*donde no hay, no hay*), which is the worst thing that can befall any government.' There was a strong feeling in the inner circles of the administration, and perhaps outside it, that good men were indeed in short supply and that death had been taking an exceptionally heavy toll. Antonio Carnero commented on this in a letter of 1636 to Pierre Roose: 'Feria, Don Gonzalo [de Córdoba], Aytona, Lerma—four great Spaniards. And I promise you that few are left.'[180]

Unfortunately, as the Count-Duke liked to say, one could not create great men overnight. He was always quick to note men of promise, like the Portuguese Francisco de Melo, who was rising rapidly in his estimation, and was carefully groomed in 1637 and 1638 to fill the highest offices.[181] But men with *panache*, like Melo, were few and far between. 'The lack of qualified men makes almost all our preparations futile', he lamented at the beginning of 1638 as he outlined the military dispositions for the coming year.[182] The Council of State itself was so undermanned that on some days it was impossible to get a meeting together. There were only five councillors present at the session which made this complaint: Olivares himself, the Marquis of Santa Cruz, the Count of Castrillo, the Duke of Villahermosa, and the Marquis of Villafranca. Of these, Olivares was frequently too busy to attend, and Villafranca was liable to be away on military service. The king, in reply, confessed himself baffled as to where to find qualified councillors—men who had served as ambassadors and travelled outside Spain.[183] The Count-Duke for his part wondered whether it might not be worth taking a leaf out of the Venetians' book, and appointing an outer group of councillors to be consulted on some matters but not on others.[184]

[179] AGS Est. leg. 3345, fo. 133, paper by Olivares, 7 October 1637.
[180] AGR CPE, Reg. 1504, fo. 105v., ? January 1636. The third Duke of Lerma, who had just died, was the Cardinal-Duke's grandson, and a commander in the army of Flanders.
[181] AGS Est. leg. 2052, Olivares in Council of State, 25 July 1637; AGR CPE, Reg. 1504, fo. 125v., Carnero to Roose, 25 August 1637; AGS Est. leg. 3346, fo. 107, consulta, 15 March 1638. Francisco de Melo, who is now best remembered for his defeat at Rocroi, is not to be confused with his compatriot, Francisco Manuel de Melo, the author of the *Epanáforas* and of the *Guerra de Cataluña*.
[182] AGS Est. leg. 2053, consulta, 5 January 1638.
[183] AGS Est. leg. 3346, fo. 71, consulta, 3 March 1638.
[184] AGS Est. leg. 3346, fo. 72, *voto* of Olivares.

In Spain and out of it the story was the same. 'What really concerns me', the Count-Duke wrote to Roose on 15 February 1638, 'is to see how few *cabezas*—leaders—there are.' It was precisely to form a new generation of *cabezas* that he had put forward his abortive plans for the foundation of academies for young nobles. He took seriously his responsibility for the palace school for pages, and in 1639 he drafted new instructions for their education, which subjected them to an academic and military training of monastic intensity.[185] But numbers were small, and training took time. In the absence of qualified Spaniards of suitable rank to place in positions of military command, he found himself much too dependent on soldiers of fortune, and future prospects worried him deeply. He begged Roose to do everything in his power to make possible a 'good peace' in the Netherlands, because (and the words were written in code) 'our sufferings are such that we simply cannot go on.' Then he added in his own hand, nowadays a scratchy scrawl that resembled a seismograph: 'Put your shoulder to the wheel for the love of God. This is the year on which everything depends.'[186]

During 1638 the Cardinal-Infante succeeded in at least holding the line in the Netherlands, with the help of letters of exchange for three million *escudos* despatched to Flanders in December of 1637 on the arrival of the treasure fleet.[187] In June, Frederick Henry's attempt to capture Antwerp was thwarted by the defeat of his army at Kallo; and a month later, the French had to abandon the siege of St. Omer, after suffering heavy losses at the hands of Piccolomini and Prince Thomas of Savoy.[188] The simultaneous successes of Spanish arms in Italy, where Leganés captured in quick succession Breme and Vercelli,[189] seemed suddenly to be turning the war around. The Cardinal-Infante, writing in high spirits to Olivares from Brussels late in July, thought that the prospects for a 'good peace' were once again favourable,[190] and Olivares himself, in a letter to the Cardinal-Infante a few days later, was no less optimistic. If things continued the way they were now going, this would be the happiest year in the whole history of the Monarchy.[191]

He was writing, however, under the shadow of a French invasion. His own plan of campaign for that year had been to attack the French

---

[185] RAH, Salazar K-8, fos. 361-7, *Instrucción para la casa de los pajes*, 30 April 1639.
[186] AGR CPE, Reg. 1502, fos. 179-80.
[187] AGR CPE, Reg. 1504, fo. 133v., Carnero to Roose, 16 December 1637.
[188] Pirenne, *Histoire de Belgique*, 4, p. 278; Israel, *The Dutch Republic*, p. 259.
[189] Modesto Lafuente, *Historia General de España*, 11 (Barcelona, 1888), p. 276; Quazza, *Preponderanza Spagnuola*, p. 486.
[190] Archivo de la Casa de Miraflores, Madrid. Cardinal-Infante to Olivares, 20 July 1638.
[191] MSB, Cod. hisp. 22, fo. 77v., Olivares to Cardinal-Infante, 31 July 1638.

from Catalonia[192]—a plan which that wily old councillor, the Count of Oñate, considered highly imprudent in view of the Catalan aversion to anything that smacked of increased royal power in the principality.[193] But this was exactly what made the Count-Duke's plan so attractive to some of the other councillors, and especially to the Marquis of Villafranca, for whom a major cause of all the king's difficulties with the Catalans was that they had always got away with too much under the pretext of their privileges.[194] These conflicting views on the wisdom of a campaign from Catalonia were not, in the event, to be put to the test in 1638. Richelieu turned out to have his own plans for the 1638 campaigning season, and they were directed to the western end of the Pyrenees. In July, Condé's army crossed the border with Guipúzcoa at Irún, and laid siege, by land and sea, to Spain's frontier fortress of Fuenterrabía.

The French attack on Fuenterrabía took Madrid by surprise, although Novoa alleges that the Countess of Salvatierra passed to Olivares reports of French troop movements from the frontier region, only to find that he laughed off the warnings.[195] The Count-Duke, who was not usually one to acknowledge his mistakes, admitted on this occasion that he was wrong. He had been operating on the assumption that there was little love lost between Richelieu and Condé, and that Condé was an unlikely choice for an enterprise of this magnitude.[196] The invasion began just at the moment when a new session of the Cortes of Castile was starting in Madrid, preceded by an opening ceremony in the palace of the Buen Retiro.[197] The letter of convocation had insisted that the *procuradores* should come furnished with full powers from their cities, to avoid any question of reporting back for further instructions.[198] Several of the cities took strong exception to this condition and to the short notice given them, and only seven of them were represented when the session began.[199]

The Cortes were informed in the royal speech that the crown's expenditures from 1632 to the end of 1638 amounted to 72 million ducats, including 21 millions for *asientos* in Flanders, and 6 millions for Germany.[200] From the administration's standpoint the French invasion was conveniently timed. It was difficult for the *procuradores* to ignore appeals to their patriotism at a moment like this, whatever

[192] MSB, Cod. hisp. 22, fo. 72v., Olivares to Cardinal-Infante, 27 May 1638.
[193] AGS Est. leg. 2660, Junta del Aposento del Conde Duque, 12 March 1638; Elliott, *Catalans*, p. 332.
[194] AGS Est. leg. 2660, consulta, 9 April 1638.
[195] Novoa, *Codoin* 77, p. 441.
[196] MSB, Cod. hisp. 22, fo. 75, Olivares to Cardinal-Infante, 21 June 1638.
[197] Brown and Elliott, *A Palace*, p. 198.
[198] *Actas*, 55, pp. 347–9.
[199] Novoa, *Codoin* 77, pp. 418–19.
[200] *Actas*, 55, pp. 377–98.

their private feelings about the proposal of one of the Count-Duke's protégés, the spokesman for Burgos, Don Juan de Castro y Castilla, that his patron should be rewarded for his devoted services by being permitted to dine at the royal table once a year.[201] The Cortes promptly voted to raise six thousand paid men for a six months' period, and on 19 July they approved the renewal of the *millones* for a further six years, at the rate of four millions a year.[202] The Count-Duke had good reason to write to the Cardinal-Infante that the Cortes were 'doing marvellously.'[203]

The siege of Fuenterrabía, dragging on through July and August as the garrison put up a stout resistance, took a heavy toll of the Count-Duke's reserves of strength and energy. The king, turning the tables for once, refused to let him go to the front.[204] Thwarted in his ambition of serving on the battlefield, he threw himself into the task of organizing relief measures from the capital. The nobility were called to arms. The Admiral of Castile offered his services, and was followed to the front by other prominent nobles, all willing to serve with a pike.[205] Fifteen hundred Irish soldiers who had arrived in Corunna with the returning fleet of Don Lope de Hoces were sent to Fuenterrabía, and placed under the command of the Marquis of Mortara. The Vizcayans, the Catalans, the Navarrese were all ordered to send supplies and reinforcements, for here was the occasion to inaugurate a genuine Union of Arms.

In order to be able to follow the progress of the siege without distraction, the Count-Duke moved Fernando Ruiz de Contreras and his secretariat of war upstairs to the north gallery of the palace, a few yards from his own quarters.[206] Here that veteran councillor of war, Don Pedro Pacheco, Marquis of Castrofuerte, remained on constant duty, seeing that the Count-Duke's orders were put into effect. Olivares was a hard and impatient taskmaster, always on tenterhooks for the latest news of the siege, fulminating against the Vizcayans for their tardiness and inefficiency,[207] and fearful that the garrison, for all its courage, might at any moment be forced to surrender. But it hung on through August, though the price was high. Urgent orders were sent to Don Lope de Hoces in Corunna to break the blockade maintained by a French fleet under the command of the Archbishop of Bordeaux. In spite of having only twelve seaworthy galleons he obeyed his orders, and met with disaster in his

[201] *Ibid.*, pp. 404–9.
[202] *Actas*, 55, p. 418; Danvila, *El poder civil*, p. 88.
[203] MSB, Cod. hisp. 22, fo. 78, Olivares to Cardinal-Infante, 31 July 1638.
[204] The same (fo. 78v.).
[205] Cánovas del Castillo, *Estudios*, 1, pp. 122–3.
[206] Novoa, *Codoin* 77, p. 463.
[207] *Ibid.*, p. 458.

encounter with the French fleet at Guetaria on 22 August. Eleven of his twelve ships were lost, and with them three thousand men, including some of Spain's most experienced captains. Although the news of Guetaria was swiftly overshadowed by that of victory on the land, it was to prove of greater consequence in its impact on the war.[208]

By 9 September the Count-Duke was in despair. He was convinced that the days of Fuenterrabía's defenders were numbered, and begged the king in vain to let him go to Guipúzcoa for three weeks, or even two. While not a professional soldier, he told the Cardinal-Infante that he was sure that he could cope with the 'mechanical and economic aspects' of the war; and the happiest of all deaths would be death by a cannon-ball in the service of his king.[209] The self-sacrifice, however, proved not to be required. A few hours later word came that on 7 September Mortara's men had forced the besiegers' lines, and that Condé's panic-stricken soldiers had fled to the boats. Madrid went wild at the news. 'The night was turned into day', reported the British ambassador, 'by the many bonfires that were made.'[210]

The two months' agony of Fuenterrabía left the Count-Duke prostrate. Four months later he was still referring to the 'unbearable cares, fatigues and hardship of the Fuenterrabía affair', which had so burnt themselves into his blood that at his age—he wrote on his fifty-second birthday—he could see no possibility of recovery.[211] But officially at least the triumph of Fuenterrabía left him the hero of the hour, to the indignation of the Admiral of Castile and his friends.[212] The ministers fell over themselves to recommend honours for the favourite.[213] The Count-Duke himself commissioned Don Juan de Palafox to write a history of the campaign,[214] and it was probably to celebrate the victory that Velázquez executed his great painting of Olivares on horseback, his baton raised in imperious command (Pl. 1).[215] A grateful king commanded that on 7 September of every year in perpetuity the Count-Duke and the heirs to his title should dine at the royal table, and a toast be drunk from a cup of gold: '*A vos, duque, librador de la patria.*'[216] He was to be made hereditary governor of

[208] For Guetaria, see Alcalá-Zamora, *España, Flandes*, pp. 398–400.

[209] MSB, Cod. hisp. 22, fo. 82, Olivares to Cardinal-Infante, 9 September 1638.

[210] PRO SP. 94.40, fo. 208, Hopton to Coke, 31 August/10 September 1638.

[211] MSB, Cod. hisp. 22, fo. 88v., Olivares to Cardinal-Infante, 6 January 1639.

[212] Shaw, 'Olivares y el Almirante de Castilla', pp. 349–51.

[213] A malicious account in Novoa, *Codoin* 80, pp. 4ff.

[214] José Pellicer y Tovar, *Avisos históricos* (in Antonio Valladares, *Semanario erudito*, vols. 31 and 32, Madrid, 1790) 31, p. 14.

[215] Enriqueta Harris, *Velázquez* (Oxford, 1982), p. 100.

[216] PRO SP. 94.40, fo. 261, Hopton to Coke, 6/16 October 1638. Olivares lists his honours in a letter to the Cardinal-Infante of 9 February 1639 (MSB, Cod. hisp. 22, fo. 95).

the fortress of Fuenterrabía, and be granted 12,000 ducats a year
on *encomiendas* in the Indies as they fell vacant, and a thousand Andalusian vassals in the vicinity of Seville. Nor was political advantage
overlooked in this cascade of honours. The king informed the Cortes
in May 1639 that the Count-Duke and his heirs were to be accorded
a seat in the government of every city represented in the Cortes,
along with a seat in the Cortes itself. He was also appointed president
of the Commission of the *millones*, the committee which held the
key to the Cortes' tax-raising powers and political leverage.[217]

The regime and its friends lost no opportunity to broadcast the
triumph of Spanish arms to the world. On 24 September 1638 the
Duke of Modena, who had arrived in Madrid on a state visit, was
given a lavish reception and regally housed at the Buen Retiro.[218]
More celebrations followed for the baptism of the Infanta María
Teresa—the future instrument of Franco-Spanish reconciliation—
who was born on 20 September. All these festivities were designed
to impress public opinion both at home and abroad with an overwhelming demonstration of the wealth and magnificence of a victorious Spanish king. A court play was performed on the theme of
'the victories of 1638',[219] and Virgilio Malvezzi, discreetly described
by the English ambassador as 'being as well a courtier as an historian',
wrote an adulatory account of the government of Olivares, published
in the summer of 1639 under the title of *La Libra*.[220]

The publication in 1635 of his *Ritratto del privato politico cristiano*—a
flattering depiction of the Count-Duke—had won for Malvezzi an
invitation to leave his native Bologna and come to Madrid.[221] Here
he settled down happily to devote his literary skills to the service
of the minister whom he so greatly admired. His *Libra* purported
to be an impartial attempt to weigh in the scales the gains and losses
of Spanish power since the outbreak of the war with France, but
the author, never at a loss for clever rhetoric and ingenious argument,
left his readers in no doubt as to the side on which the scales came
down. Olivares, however, had learnt through bitter experience the
need to maintain a certain wariness in assessing the always unpredictable fortunes of war. In the midst of all the euphoria of that euphoric
autumn of 1638 he confessed to the Cardinal-Infante that the thought
of the coming year made him tremble.[222] He was right to be cautious.

---

[217] Cánovas del Castillo, *Estudios*, 1, pp. 125–7; Fernández Albaladejo, 'Monarquía, Cortes',
p. 30.
[218] Brown and Elliott, *A Palace*, pp. 195–6.
[219] Justi, *Diego Velázquez*, p. 196.
[220] PRO SP. 94.41, fo. 129, Hopton to Coke, 27 June/7 July 1639.
[221] For Malvezzi, see above, p. 17, and Elliott, 'The Year of the Three Ambassadors', pp.
171–2.
[222] MSB, Cod. hisp. 22, fo. 83v., Olivares to Cardinal-Infante, 22 October 1638.

The 1638 silver galleons failed to arrive, and the English ambassador, writing in mid-December, prophesied that there would be a 'great disorder' if they did not come, 'for the *asentistas* are at a stand'.[223] It turned out that the galleons, commanded by Don Carlos de Ibarra, had been involved in a successful engagement with the Dutch off Havana, but had then been held up awaiting the *flota* from New Spain, and that both fleets had been compelled to winter in Vera Cruz.[224] The news, as the Count-Duke remarked, was better than it might have been, but a disaster in comparison with what had been expected.[225] It left the crown short of 1,600,000 ducats in silver for its *asientos* with the bankers.

The news of the delayed return of the silver fleet came at the worst possible time. For the past few weeks all Europe had been watching the final stages of the great drama at Breisach, that supposedly impregnable fortress on the Rhine, which had been under siege by the forces of Bernard of Saxe-Weimar since June of 1638. On 17 December the garrison was starved into surrender. Breisach occupied a key position in Spanish grand strategy, guarding as it did two vital military corridors, one to the heart of the Empire, and the other to Flanders.[226] Despatches sent by Leganés from Milan on 17 and 18 December, and received in Madrid at the end of the first week of 1639, warned that the fall of Breisach was imminent. Olivares' reaction was that it would carry with it a large part of what was left and remove the last remaining chances of peace. With the Germans still sitting at home, it would also make the French the masters of the world. The only hope now was to raise a new army for despatch to Germany, and plan a multiple invasion of France before it was too late.[227]

Ten days later the Count-Duke wrote a paper to be read to the Council of State.[228] 'A great storm threatens us this year', it began. Surveying the international scene he emphasized how critical the role of England had become. In spite of Charles I's troubles with the Scots, a vigorous effort must be made to enlist English support. He also proposed a new mission by the much-travelled Gabriel de Roy, this time to Denmark to secure Danish mediation between the Emperor and the Swedes, and perhaps even a Danish declaration of war on France. As part of a grand peace offensive, new approaches were to be made to Venice and the papacy, and the foreign envoys

---

[223] PRO SP. 94.41, fo. 337, Hopton to Cottington, 8/18 December 1638.

[224] Chaunu, *Séville et l'Atlantique*, 5, p. 336 n. 5.

[225] AGS Est. leg. 2660, consulta, 3 January 1639.

[226] Pagès, *La guerre de Trente Ans*, p. 211; Parker, *Army of Flanders*, pp. 55–6.

[227] AGS Est. leg. 3349, fo. 17, *voto* of Olivares, 8 January 1639.

[228] BL Eg. Ms. 2053, fos. 1–5v., *Papel del Conde Duque* (copy of original in AGS Est. leg. 2340, no. 139. See Leman, *Richelieu et Olivarès*, p. 83).

in Madrid should be summoned to hear of the dangers that threatened to overwhelm Christendom if peace were not restored. When the Council of State met on 18 January to discuss this apocalyptic paper, the Count-Duke again insisted on the extreme dangers now facing Spain.[229] The fall of Breisach had dangerously unbalanced the scales, but there was one way in which the balance could be righted. This would be the invasion of France by an Imperial army, for the whole lesson of Fuenterrabía had been that no victory abroad—whether in Flanders, Italy or Brazil—could outweigh the effects of invading home territory. The one chance, then, was to press the French from all sides, while counting on the malcontents to come into the open against Richelieu's regime.

Once again, therefore, the Count-Duke was pinning his hopes on Imperial intervention. The Marquis of Villafranca expressed some scepticism about the new Emperor's enthusiasm for war, and believed, as did others of his colleagues, that the intervention of England was likely to prove more decisive than that of the Emperor. But could Charles I, now deeply embroiled with the Scots, ever be persuaded to intervene? It is some indication of the remoteness of Madrid from the British scene that such high hopes should have been built on such slender foundations. Nor was it clear what kind of inducement, other than the restitution of the Palatinate, might persuade Charles to throw in his lot with Spain—and, as Olivares never failed to point out, any Spanish move on the Palatinate would antagonize Bavaria. Despatches from Brussels, however, tended to encourage the ministers in their illusory hopes. The Cardinal-Infante's advisers did not share Madrid's fears about Bavarian reactions. They also believed that his troubles with the Scots were likely to predispose Charles I more favourably to foreign alliances, and that he would prefer a treaty with Spain to a treaty with France, which they suspected of giving covert help to the Scots. But they admitted that any British assistance was likely to be of only marginal use. On the other hand, a Madrid-London axis would frighten the enemy, and in this way strengthen the chances for peace. The Count-Duke allowed himself to be persuaded by these arguments, and orders were sent to the Cardinal-Infante to negotiate with Charles I.[230]

If England was to prove a disappointment for Madrid in its attempts to restore the military balance in Europe, the same was also true of the Empire. As the war began to slip out of control, it was inevitable that the Count-Duke should clutch increasingly at straws—England, the Empire, the French malcontents. If the fall

---

[229] *Ibid.*, fos. 5v.–10 (consulta, 18 January 1639).
[230] AGS Est. leg. 3860, Cardinal-Infante to king, 29 February 1639, and Olivares' *voto* of 29 March. See also Elliott, 'The Year of the Three Ambassadors'.

of Breisach were only to galvanize the indolent Ferdinand III into action, a disaster could yet be transformed into a blessing for Spain. But the despatches sent by the ambassador in Vienna, the Marquis of Castañeda, were hardly encouraging. Olivares was always liable to blame his ambassadors when they sent bad tidings, and Castañeda had never enjoyed his confidence.[231] But his harshest words were reserved for the Imperial councillors who, as he saw it, were always diverting their master from the line of duty. Count Trautmansdorff, Ferdinand's closest adviser, was particularly pernicious. 'His first maxim is that the Emperor should not be a partisan of ours, but merely Imperial, and neutral in everything else.' This was a point of view that the Count-Duke, with his almost mystical faith in Habsburg solidarity, found almost past comprehension. How could the Austrian Habsburgs fail to see that their only road to salvation lay through Madrid? 'The Emperor', he concluded, 'is lost. We must not let him be lost, in so far as it lies in our power to prevent this. He is under heavy pressure and in extreme need of men and money. He is badly served, with few or no friends, and is badly advised. We must first of all save his reputation, and this can only be achieved by sending him money.'[232] It was Madrid's traditional answer to every problem, and experience might have suggested that it was not infallible, especially when—as usually happened—the money that eventually arrived was too little and too late.

Olivares believed that it lay in Ferdinand III's power to save Germany, and all Christendom, by invading France. But while Ferdinand was always happy to pocket Spanish money, he had no wish to let his pocket dictate his policy. After the fall of Breisach he had more than enough difficulties of his own in Germany; and the closer he drew to Spain, the harder it would be for him to reach a settlement with France. Under Trautmansdorff's direction, Imperial policy was, as Olivares complained, becoming too exclusively Imperial. In Flanders, where the Cardinal-Infante was starved for men and money, there was growing resentment at the Emperor's behaviour.[233] At the start of the 1639 campaigning season, at a moment when the French were already in Artois, almost half the German troops serving in the Netherlands under Piccolomini's command were withdrawn.[234] Piccolomini still managed to defeat the French at Thionville on 7 June, but his success was offset three weeks later by the loss

[231] Cf. *El Conde Duque sobre el reparo de las cosas de Alemania*, 23 (?) October 1639 (AGS Est. leg. 2054).

[232] AGS Est. leg. 3860, *El Conde Duque sobre despachos de Alemania*, undated, for meeting of Council of State of 27 February 1639.

[233] Archivo de la Casa de Miraflores, Madrid. Cardinal-Infante to Olivares, 11 May 1639.

[234] *Ibid.*

of Hesdin.[235] Piccolomini's relations with the Cardinal-Infante and Prince Thomas of Savoy had never been easy, but in the five years during which he had commanded an Imperial contingent in Flanders, he had made an important contribution to the defence of the Spanish Netherlands. But at the beginning of October the Emperor recalled him, to the fury of Madrid.[236] At this moment it was not surprising that Olivares and his colleagues should have felt that the enormous sums of money they had poured into Vienna over the past two decades had been spent in vain.[237] Vienna and Madrid were moving inexorably towards that parting of the ways which was to occur nine years later at Westphalia.

With the Cardinal-Infante barely holding his own in the Netherlands, and Imperial authority again imperilled in Germany by Sweden's military revival, the Count-Duke's hopes that Habsburg fortunes could be restored in 1639 by a general assault on France seemed utopian even before the campaigning season got well under way. Spain's own contribution to the assault on France was to be an invasion from Catalonia. Olivares decided to mount his attack at the eastern rather than the western end of the Pyrenees partly because Guipúzcoa had borne the brunt of the war in 1638, while Catalonia was still relatively untouched, and partly because of his continuing determination to involve the Catalans more directly in the war with France as part of his grand design for bringing about a closer association of the Iberian peoples.[238] But the new viceroy of Catalonia, the native-born Count of Santa Coloma, felt bound to report that he found the principality hopelessly unprepared for war. The Catalans' previous experiences with the Olivares regime did not predispose them to provide money for the frontier fortresses or soldiers to defend them. In any event, an invading force from Catalonia would have to be stiffened by veteran regiments. During the winter, the Cardinal-Infante was ordered to send 2,000 Walloon soldiers to Spain[239] and Leganés to send 6,000 veterans from Milan. When he refused to denude Milan in this way, Olivares seized on his refusal to demand exemplary punishment. The security of Spain must take precedence, he insisted, over every other consideration.[240] But Leganés was astute enough to get his troops out early on campaign, and with the assistance of Prince Thomas of Savoy he won a string of spectacular victories. This 'inundation of victories', as the

[235] Pirenne, *Histoire de Belgique*, 4, p. 279.
[236] Pagès, *La Guerre de Trente Ans*, p. 213.
[237] Lonchay, *Correspondance*, 3, Doc. 1002, Philip IV to Cardinal-Infante, 9 October 1639.
[238] See Elliott, *Catalans*, pp. 360–1.
[239] Lonchay, *Correspondance*, 3, Doc. 838, Cardinal-Infante to Philip IV, reporting that the Walloons were ready for embarkation.
[240] AGS Est. leg. 3349, fo. 39, *voto* of Olivares, 21 January 1639.

Count-Duke called them,[241] was only checked by Leganés' acceptance of a suspension of arms between 14 August and 24 October, after his increasingly weary army had captured the city of Turin, but failed to take its fortress.[242]

Although the Count-Duke, finding it difficult to argue against success, temporarily condoned his cousin's disobedience,[243] he soon came to regret it. The absence of the Italian veterans made it impossible to execute his plan for an invasion of France from Catalonia, and it enhanced the principality's vulnerability to a French attack. After his rebuff at Fuenterrabía in 1638, Richelieu was naturally attracted to a plan of campaign designed to probe Spain's defences at the other end of the frontier. This entailed risks, since Languedoc's relations with Paris remained uneasy after the suppression of Montmorency's revolt. But the same was true of Catalonia's relations with Madrid, on which the Cardinal kept a wary eye. In 1634 his confidant, Father Joseph, had told the French envoy to Madrid that it was 'important to see if one can make use of the discontents of the Catalans and the Portuguese.'[244] Richelieu was willing to take the gamble. The army of Condé and Schomberg crossed the Roussillon frontier early in June 1639, outflanked the fortress of Opol, which surrendered without a fight, and laid siege to the more significant fortress of Salces. Although the Catalans were now flocking to the front, the royal army of 8,000 men that had been assembled in Catalonia was no match for a French army 16,000 strong. Salces surrendered on 19 July.[245]

The full implications of the fall of Salces would take time to reveal themselves. In 1638 Fuenterrabía held firm. In 1639 Salces surrendered after no more than brief resistance. This demoralizing loss of a major Spanish fortress placed an additional strain on the already brittle relations between the principality and the government in Madrid, which laid the blame for the disaster squarely on the Catalans.[246] Salces must at all costs be won back, and for six months, until the surrender of the French garrison on 6 January 1640, energy and acrimony were invested in the recovery of Salces in almost equal proportions. Faced with what he called an 'established war' (guerra asentada) inside the borders of Spain,[247] Olivares raged against the 'extrava-

[241] AGS Est. leg. 3349, fo. 230, voto of Olivares, 27 May 1639.
[242] AGS Est. leg. 3350, fo. 126, consulta, 2 September 1639.
[243] Olivares' voto of 27 May 1639.
[244] BNP, Fonds français, 10,759, fo. 199, Père Joseph to the Comte de Barrault, 16 October 1634.
[245] For the Salces campaign, see Charles Vasal-Reig, La guerre en Roussillon sous Louis XIII, 1635–1639 (Paris, 1934).
[246] Elliott, Catalans, pp. 365–6.
[247] MSB, Cod. hisp. 22, fo. 113v., Olivares to Cardinal-Infante, 18 September 1639.

gance' of the Catalans[248]—their dilatoriness in sending men and supplies to the front, their insistence that their beloved 'constitutions' should not be infringed, even amidst all the emergencies of war.

Some of the Count-Duke's ranting and raving was undoubtedly for effect. Upbraiding and harrying the Catalans in a despairing attempt to transform them into a nation of warriors, he hoped to extract the maximum sacrifice from a province that he regarded as persistently defaulting on its obligations to its king. If, as inevitably happened, the louder he shouted, the more the Catalans dragged their feet, this was almost a source of perverse satisfaction, since it confirmed what he had always said: that effective government was hopelessly hampered by laws and liberties which in his eyes were no more than antiquarian survivals. If their constitutions forbade the Catalans to transport corn at their own expense from the ports to the barracks, where it was needed by hungry soldiers fighting to save their own country from the enemy, then 'the devil take the constitutions and whoever observes them!'[249] Necessity knew no law but its own, and mere legal impediments could not be allowed to stand in the way of the prosecution of the war.

But the shrill, accusing voice of the Count-Duke was also the voice of a desperately tired and discouraged man. He could get almost no sleep; his head hurt; he was convinced that his days were numbered.[250] It seemed that there was no end to the battering he had to take, and nothing appeared to be going right. In the eyes of Sir Arthur Hopton, 'there wants nothing but fortune to make him the worthiest Favourite that any king hath had, but this hath not been propitious hitherto, nor I fear is likely to be.'[251] If things continued on their unpropitious course, this was largely because the Count-Duke was involved in the massive task of attempting to orchestrate what had become a global war against a background of growing economic dislocation and shrinking reserves of men, ships and money. It was true that 1639, unlike 1638, produced its treasure fleets—the delayed fleets under the command of Ibarra in mid-July, and the Tierra Firme galleons in late December[252]—but the silver was insufficient to cover assignations.[253] It also happened that 1638 and 1639 were two of 'the plentifullest years that have been seen', in the words of the British ambassador.[254] This relative abundance of

[248] MSB, Cod. hisp. 22, fo. 114v., Olivares to Cardinal-Infante, 23 October 1639.
[249] Olivares to Santa Coloma, 7 October 1639 (cited Elliott, *Catalans*, p. 375).
[250] Olivares to Cardinal-Infante, 23 October 1639.
[251] PRO SP. 94.41, fo. 211, Hopton to Cottington, 21/31 October 1639.
[252] Chaunu, *Séville et l'Atlantique*, 5, pp. 350 and 352.
[253] Domínguez Ortiz, *Política y hacienda*, p. 58.
[254] PRO SP. 94.41, fo. 211, Hopton to Cottington, 21/31 October 1639.

cereals in Castile brought prices down sharply in 1638–9,[255] blunting
the impact of the new taxes voted by the Cortes. It also reduced
the drain on reserves by saving on the import of foreign cereals.
But this was one of the very few pieces of good fortune that the
Count-Duke enjoyed at this most critical moment of the war, and
it provided no more than a temporary respite at best.

The unending succession of calls on Castile's shrunken resources,
and the vast extent of the area to be covered, made it impossible
to deal with each new emergency as it arose. The Count-Duke was
beginning to look like a fireman desperately running from one corner
of the building to another with his bucket of water as the flames
leapt from place to place. At one moment he was in despair over
Germany; the next he was having to organize the recovery of Salces,
only to be distracted by bad news from the Franche-Comté, or Italy,
or Brazil. There were, as he said, 'so many calamities everywhere',[256]
and 'bad news flies.'[257] Above all, what was becoming alarmingly
apparent in 1639 was the extreme length and fragility of Spain's lines
of communication in relation to those of the French. Distance had
always been the enemy, but never more so than after the fall of
Breisach in December 1638. The cutting of the land routes drove
Spain back to the sea to keep the life-lines open; and those life-lines
were now being put to unusually heavy use because the shortage
of seasoned veterans required the frequent transportation of men from
one theatre of war to another.

Although the increase in Spanish naval power in the 1630's had
been impressive, so also had the losses, as the Count-Duke acknowledged at the beginning of 1639, when reviewing the implications
of Ibarra's decision to winter with the treasure fleets in the Indies.[258]
Some of the losses could be made good by the peninsular shipyards,
and contracts were also made with foreign shipowners, like the Eng-
lishmen Benjamin Wright, for transporting men to Flanders in neutral
ships, following proposals to this effect made by the Count-Duke
at a meeting of the Council of State in the autumn of 1638.[259] A
neutral flag, however, proved less effective than Olivares had hoped.
Three of the five English ships which sailed from Cadiz for Mardick
in the summer of 1639 with 1,500 infantrymen on board were seized
by Tromp's squadron patrolling the Channel, while another was
forced to take refuge in the Isle of Wight.[260]

[255] Anes and Le Flem, 'Las crisis del siglo XVII', Appendix 6 (Mercurial de Segovia).
[256] MSB, Cod. hisp. 22, fo. 108, Olivares to Cardinal-Infante, 12 July 1639.
[257] MSB, Cod. hisp. 22, fo. 108, Olivares to Cardinal-Infante, 23 August 1639.
[258] AGS Est. leg. 2660, consulta, 3 January 1639.
[259] Alcalá-Zamora, España, Flandes, p. 396.
[260] Ibid., pp. 412–13.

The obvious hazards of the sea-route explain Madrid's anxiety to secure the active naval cooperation of Charles I in guarding the Channel passage. But the Count-Duke had been encouraged by the success of Spanish naval commanders in ferrying men to Flanders, and orders were given for the assembling of a massive armada, which would force its way through to Dunkirk, laden with troop reinforcements and bullion.[261] By July 1639 the Count-Duke could report to the Junta de Armadas that Don Antonio de Oquendo had twenty-four ships in Cadiz, and Don Lope de Hoces sixty-three in Corunna, with more expected from Naples, Cadiz and Cantabria.[262]

The details of the plan of campaign were finalized at a meeting of the Junta de Armadas in the Count-Duke's study on 7 August.[263] The task of the armada, which was to be commanded by Oquendo, was first of all to drive away or destroy the French flotilla which had been preying on shipping off the Cantabrian coast. It was then to transport the Spanish and Italian infantrymen, along with a consignment of Indies silver, to Dunkirk, where it would pick up the Walloon infantry needed for the Salces campaign.[264] But this was to be more than a mere transport operation. With so large a naval force assembled, Olivares proposed that it should challenge and destroy the Dutch fleet in the Channel. In effect this was to be a major bid for naval supremacy in North European waters.

It was an impressive fleet that eventually set sail from Corunna on 6 September. With around a hundred ships, totalling 36,000 tons, and carrying some two thousand cannon, it was not quite as large as the Invincible Armada of 1588, but its firepower was greater. It carried about the same number of men—20,000, of whom 6,000 were crew, 8,000 fighting men belonging to the warships, and 8,500 infantry for Flanders.[265] Enormous efforts had gone into its organization, and the Count-Duke was banking heavily on success. But once again an expected triumph turned to ashes in his hands.[266] For three days, from 16 to 18 September, Oquendo's ships were engaged in a running battle with those of Tromp. Badly damaged, they took refuge in the Downs, exactly where the Count-Duke had believed that a defeated Dutch fleet would be driven by the Spaniards. From

---

[261] *The Journal of Maarten Harpertszoon Tromp*, ed. C. R. Boxer (Cambridge, 1930), pp. 2–5; Alcalá-Zamora, *España, Flandes*, pp. 13–16; Israel, *The Dutch Republic*, pp. 268–9.
[262] Alcalá-Zamora, p. 420.
[263] *Ibid.*, p. 423.
[264] The assumption behind this transfer was that native troops fought better away from their home territory, where it was easy for them to desert. Walloon soldiers were despised in the Netherlands but highly prized in Mediterranean theatres of war, while Spaniards and Italians were the elite of the army of Flanders (see Parker, *The Army of Flanders*, pp. 30–1).
[265] Alcalá-Zamora, pp. 425–6.
[266] For a detailed account of the fate of the Armada, see chs. 3 and 4 of Boxer's introduction to Tromp's *Journal*. Also Alcalá-Zamora, *España, Flandes*, pp. 440–53.

here, fourteen ships, with 3,000 soldiers on board, succeeded in making the night crossing to Mardick. During the month in which the Spanish fleet sheltered in the Downs with the Dutch lying in wait, more soldiers crossed in fishing boats, and it is probable that the Cardinal-Infante received some 70–80% of his men. But the ships themselves deteriorated in their enforced confinement, and their crews fell sick.

In Madrid Olivares waited anxiously for news. 'It all depends on God', he wrote to the Cardinal-Infante on 2 November, 'and it is to be expected of Him that now that human hopes are so low, things will turn out better than when they were high.'[267] They did not. On 21 October, as Tromp's ships pressed in on the Spanish fleet, Oquendo decided to make a run for it. Brushing aside an unconvincing British effort to separate the fleets, a superior Dutch force bore down on the twenty-one Spanish galleons that made out into the open sea. Although Oquendo's flagship just succeeded in reaching Mardick, Lope de Hoces was killed on board the *Santa Teresa*, along with most of her crew. Nine Spanish galleons fell into the hands of the Dutch, although six of them sank before reaching harbour. Five of the six galleons of the Dunkirk squadron, and three Spanish galleons, managed to crawl into Mardick. Others, caught up in the storm which dispersed Tromp's fleet on the 22nd, were dashed against the coast of France.

The news of the catastrophe reached Madrid on 15 November.[268] 'I cannot deny to Your Highness', wrote Olivares to the Cardinal-Infante two weeks later, 'the extreme concern and distress with which the news of the great disaster of our armada has been received. There is indeed nothing we can do but bow our heads to the Lord's commands; and I really believe that our presumption in regard to this armada was such as to justify our punishment.'[269] The Count-Duke's response, however, was not as resigned as these words suggest. On 16 November he held an emergency meeting of ministers, at which he described the disaster as irreparable. But orders were at once given for ships, cannons and crews to be brought to Spain from Italy; the Cardinal-Infante was instructed to buy up ships wherever he could find them; and a fresh attempt was begun to persuade the English to guard the Channel route.[270]

At the same time, considerable efforts were made to doctor the news for home consumption.[271] This was nothing new. The Spain

[267] MSB, Cod. hisp. 22, fo. 115v., Olivares to Cardinal-Infante, 2 November 1639.
[268] Alcalá-Zamora, p. 457.
[269] MSB, Cod. hisp. 22, fo. 117v., Olivares to Cardinal-Infante, 29 November 1639.
[270] Alcalá-Zamora, pp. 457–8.
[271] *Ibid.*, pp. 460–2.

of Olivares had no regularly published gazette comparable to the *Gazette* founded in Paris by Théophraste Renaudot in 1631 and promptly taken under Richelieu's wing.[272] But it did have numerous irregularly published *relaciones*, produced by enterprising printers in the major cities of the peninsula. These *relaciones* gave readers an encouragingly reassuring interpretation of domestic and foreign news.[273] In response to the news of the battle of the Downs, the chief printer of the city of Seville, Juan Gómez de Blas, published a 'true relation of the great victory of Don Antonio de Oquendo over Dutch ships in the English Channel'. Meanwhile Malvezzi, following *La Libra* with *The Chiefe Events of the Monarchie of Spaine in the yeare 1639*, displayed his customary artifice in snatching victory from the jaws of defeat.[274]

The ministers at least were not deceived by their own propaganda, although they believed that the fleet could be built up again to sixty ships by the coming summer.[275] They were cheered by the news of the safe arrival of the silver galleons from the Indies in late December,[276] which accorded some minor compensation for the naval disaster and for the rising costs of the interminable siege of Salces. They still had hopes, too, of their second great fleet, sent out in the autumn of 1638 under the command of the Count of La Torre to recover Brazil. Again they were to be disappointed. After spending ten months to no great purpose in Bahía, Torre left for Pernambuco in November 1639 with eighty-six ships and 10,000 men. But the size of the fleet was more impressive than the capacity of its commander. An indecisive engagement with a Dutch fleet half its size off the island of Itamaracá on 12 January 1640 was sufficient to deter Torre from attacking Pernambuco. He returned to Bahía, and allowed his fleet to disperse.[277]

The Brazilian fiasco set the seal on the naval catastrophe that had overtaken the Spanish Monarchy in the course of eighteen months. Between Guetaria in August 1638 and Itamaracá in January 1640, the Spanish Ocean fleet had lost one hundred warships, twelve admirals, hundreds of officers, and some 20,000 seamen.[278] Surveying the scene at the beginning of 1640, the British ambassador decided that

[272] Howard M. Solomon, *Public Welfare, Science and Propaganda in Seventeenth Century France. The Innovations of Théophraste Renaudot* (Princeton, 1972), chs. 4 and 5.

[273] See Henry Ettinghausen, 'The News in Spain: *Relaciones de sucesos* in the Reigns of Philip III and IV', *European History Quarterly*, 14 (1984), pp. 1–20.

[274] Eng. trans. by Robert Gentilis (London, 1647) of *Sucesos principales de la Monarquía de España* (Madrid, 1640), p. 130.

[275] Alcalá-Zamora, p. 459.

[276] AGR CPE, Reg. 1504, fo. 176, Carnero to Roose, 24 December 1639.

[277] See Boxer, *Salvador de Sá*, pp. 117–120.

[278] Alcalá-Zamora, p. 459.

'they are likely to be ill provided at sea the next year, and so every year worse and worse, for this want of mariners is a terrible difficulty.'[279] It was true that all was not yet lost. The dockyards were again hard at work; it was still possible to run individual transport ships through to Flanders; and Spain still maintained a precarious control of its transatlantic routes. But Olivares' grand design to win from the Dutch an acceptable peace by means of a massive display of Spanish power in the north now lay in a thousand pieces, along with the fragments of Oquendo's ships, at the bottom of the Channel. Once again the Spanish Netherlands had become an exposed and vulnerable outpost, beating off Dutch and French attacks as best it could. With control of the northern waters now definitively lost to the Dutch, the Count-Duke found himself thrown back everywhere on the defensive as he entered 1640. Malvezzi's scales of war were tilting dangerously. Only a miracle, it seemed, could now restore the balance.

[279] PRO SP. 94.41, fo. 247, Hopton to Cottington, 25 December 1639/4 January 1640.

XIV

1640

Malaise in the Monarchy

On the night of 7 December 1639, three weeks after Madrid learnt of the disaster which had overtaken the fleet at the battle of the Downs, two *alcaldes de corte*, the officials responsible for maintaining law and order in the capital, entered the town house of the Duke of Medinaceli, where Don Francisco de Quevedo (Pl. 29) was living as a guest. While the poet was dressing, they ransacked the house for papers. Then they bundled him into a waiting coach, which drove out to the Toledo bridge. Here he was met by other officials, and transferred to a fresh coach. Still under cover of darkness, the heavily guarded cortege set out in a north-westerly direction, along the road that led to León. It eventually drew up at the convent of San Marcos in León, where Quevedo was to be incarcerated for nearly four years, to emerge in June 1643 a broken man. He spent the first two years of his confinement in total solitude in a dank cell, where he would have died of hunger and misery but for the support and encouragement of his ducal patron, who himself was banished from Madrid a few weeks after Quevedo's arrest. The papers seized in the duke's house were removed to the residence of José González, of the *cámara* and Council of Castile, the Count-Duke's confidant.[1]

The arrest and imprisonment of Spain's most brilliant and versatile writer, and especially of one who had so often placed his pen at the disposal of the Olivares regime, provided material for endless speculation. 'Some say that it was because he wrote satires against the monarchy, others because he spoke ill of the government; and others, with more certainty, or so I am told, that he suffered from the same disease as the nuncio, and that a certain Frenchman, a servant of Cardinal Richelieu, frequented his house.'[2] The reference was to the late papal nuncio Lorenzo Campeggi, who had died in Madrid that August. Relations between Spain and Rome, already strained

---

[1] Details of the affair are given in *MHE*, 15, pp. 374 and 411, and Pellicer, *Avisos*, 31, pp. 104–5. See also Quevedo, *Obras*, 1, pp. 19–20; Marañón, *Olivares*, ch. 11; Astrana Marín, *La vida turbulenta de Quevedo*, pp. 490ff; Elliott, 'Quevedo and the Count-Duke of Olivares'.

[2] Pellicer, *Avisos*, 31, pp. 104–5.

by the regalist attitudes of the Madrid government and its anger over what it believed to be the pro-French bias of Urban VIII's foreign policy, reached breaking-point when Campeggi's chaplain decamped with the cypher, which revealed that he was engaged in an incriminating correspondence with Louis XIII.[3] The government seized the opportunity afforded by his death to suspend the jurisdiction of the nunciature, and for over a year its tribunal was out of commission.[4] The Count-Duke was now brimming over with bitterness at what he regarded as the scandalous behaviour of Urban VIII. Presented this autumn with a papal brief by the new nuncio, Cesare Facchinetti, protesting against Madrid's most recent hostile act—the expulsion of the Apostolic Collector from Portugal—the Count-Duke threw down his hat and angrily exclaimed: 'So I am excommunicated!'[5]

Officially, silence reigned over the causes of Quevedo's arrest, and it was never broken. When the case was reviewed after the Count-Duke's fall, the king wrote laconically on the *consulta*: 'The imprisonment of Don Francisco was for grave cause.'[6] But what exactly was Quevedo's crime? At least a hint is provided by a letter of 19 October 1642 from Olivares to the king relating to the arrest of yet another man of letters and former protégé, Juan Adam de la Parra, on a charge of libelling ministers. The letter refers in passing to Quevedo's arrest three years earlier, and reveals that the action had been taken on the advice of the President of the Council of Castile and of José González after Quevedo's friend, the Duke of Infantado, had denounced him (very possibly under pressure) as 'disloyal, an enemy of the government and a murmurer against it, and finally as a confidant of France and in correspondence with Frenchmen.'[7]

To judge from this confidential note from the Count-Duke to Philip, court gossip was close to the mark. There were two principal charges against Quevedo: vilifying the government and making contact with the enemy. Of these, the first is more susceptible of proof than the second. Long tradition associates him with two verse satires, a glossed version of the Lord's Prayer and a *Memorial* to Philip IV, which the king is alleged to have found concealed under his tablenapkin in December 1639, and is said to have been the immediate cause of his arrest.[8] It so happens that Bernardo Monanni, the secretary

[3] *MHE*, 19, pp. 389–90, and Pellicer, *Avisos*, 31, pp. 54–5.

[4] Aldea, 'Iglesia y estado', *Historia de España*, 25, p. 628.

[5] Pastor, *History of the Popes*, 29, p. 199.

[6] Astrana Marín, ed., *Obras completas de Don Francisco Quevedo Villegas*, p. 1931.

[7] The text of this letter is given in *MC*, 2, Doc. XV, with an explanatory introduction, based on J. H. Elliott, 'Nueva luz sobre la prisión de Quevedo y Adam de la Parra', *BRAH*, 169 (1972), pp. 171–82, where the letter was first published and discussed.

[8] Egido, *Sátiras políticas*, nos. 23 and 24.

29. Follower of Diego de Velázquez, *Francisco de Quevedo*.

to the Tuscan embassy, took a close interest in the case, and his cyphered despatches make it clear beyond a doubt that Quevedo was indeed the author of the celebrated *Memorial*.[9]

These satirical poems shared a common theme: it was time for the king to wake up to what was happening around him. Castile and Andalusia were poverty-stricken, crushed by more taxes in a single reign than in the reigns of a hundred of Philip's predecessors taken together. As ministers and profiteers took their cut, the rich grew richer and the poor paid. In the words of the *Memorial*:

[9] See Shirley B. Whitaker, 'The Quevedo Case (1639): Documents from Florentine Archives', *Modern Language Notes*, 97 (1982), pp. 368–79.

We are all children consigned by God to your care;
To kill us like beasts of burden is unfair.

The attempts to wrest Mantua from its legitimate heir had begun an interminable war; and yet while money was needed for Flanders and Italy, millions were being squandered on the Buen Retiro. The original version of the *Memorial* may not have contained the famous lines comparing Philip the Great to a hole—the more taken from it, the greater it grows—but the Olivares regime is subjected in both poems to ferocious attack.

The attack, however, was not confined to verse. The papers seized from Quevedo may well have included the text of that devastating satirical piece, *La isla de los monopantos*, apparently composed before the birth of the future Louis XIV in 1638.[10] The governor of the island of the Monopantos was Pragas Chincollos, an anagrammatic allusion to the Count-Duke's Jewish ancestry.[11] When all the Jews of Europe sent their representatives to a sanhedrin in Salonika, Pragas Chincollos sent the six most learned men in his realm. Not all the identifications are certain, but they include the Protonotario (Arpio Trotono), José González (Pacos Mazo) and Hernando de Salazar (Alkemiastos), whose alleged responsibility for the invention of many of the more obnoxious fiscal devices introduced in recent years had made him one of the most unpopular figures in Spain. In this solemn conclave the participants discussed their plans for securing wealth and power. Characteristically it was José González who served as the spokesman for his master, and offered his help in coordinating the international Jewish conspiracy. It was González, too, who produced a volume, bound in sheepskin, of the works of Machiavelli.

Quevedo's attack on the Olivares camarilla—popularly known as the *sinagoga* because of the notorious *converso* origins of some of its members and the administration's close relationship with the crypto-Jewish Portuguese business community[12]—constitutes a part of his broad frontal assault on the times in *La hora de todos*. Reforming projects (*arbitrismo*), innovation of all sorts, and the exaltation of commercial values were corrupting the heroic virtues that had made Castile great. All of these were associated with the Count-Duke and his policies. The writer who had saluted Olivares in the early years of his government as the man who would 'restore' Spain,[13] and who

---

[10] For a discussion of the dating of this piece, included in Quevedo's *La hora de todos*, which was first published in 1650, see the introduction to the edition of the text, with French translation, by Jean Bourg, Pierre Dupont and Pierre Geneste: Francisco de Quevedo, *L'Heure de tous et la fortune raisonnable* (Paris, 1980), pp. 147–56.

[11] See above, p. 10.

[12] Bourg, Dupont and Geneste, *L'Heure de tous*, p. 497 (note 573), where possible identifications of the various characters are discussed.

[13] Quevedo, 'Epístola satírica y censoria contra las costumbres presentes de los castellanos', in *Obra poética*, ed. Blecua, 1, no. 146, line 203.

had lavished upon the minister and his policies encomiums of embarrassing adulation, had now turned violently against his patron. The Count-Duke and Quevedo had always enjoyed a somewhat wary relationship, based more on mutual need than mutual sympathy. Sooner or later there was bound to be a falling out, and the only surprise is that it should have been so long delayed.

While there are indications that Quevedo remained *persona grata* in the palace at least until the end of 1634,[14] he may already by that time have been cooling towards the regime. His alienation was probably enhanced by his growing intimacy with Don Antonio Juan Luis de la Cerda, seventh Duke of Medinaceli, whose estates neighboured Quevedo's property at La Torre de Juan Abad.[15] Medinaceli was a cultivated noble with a knowledge of Greek, Latin and Hebrew,[16] and during the 1630's a group of friends used to meet regularly in his house for literary and political discussions. They eagerly debated such subjects as whether kings should have favourites,[17] and presumably gave free rein to the hatred of the Count-Duke that pervaded aristocratic circles in Castile. Quevedo's famous sonnet on the death of Don Fadrique de Toledo in December 1634, hounded into the grave (and beyond it) by an implacable Olivares,[18] laments the death of an authentic Castilian hero in words that would have sounded as music to the ears of the nobility. In its ambiguous final words it also hints at the dangers of speaking out in the Spain of Olivares.

It is possible that Quevedo did not pay sufficient heed to his own warning. Olivares called him suddenly to Madrid in late February 1637, and then again in January 1639, this time accompanied by the Duke of Medinaceli.[19] Either the Count-Duke needed him for some new propaganda exercise, or he was growing anxious about the uses to which the poet was putting his pen in his rural retreat. The very fact that he had turned his back on the court and was now spending most of his time at La Torre de Juan Abad was obviously disturbing. Quevedo seems to have been experiencing a profound disillusionment with the regime which sprang either from some bitter personal experience, or from a loss of sympathy with its aims and policies. Given the character of the government in the 1630's this loss of sympathy is understandable. The Count-Duke appeared increasingly arbitrary

[14] See Elliott, 'Quevedo and the Count-Duke of Olivares', pp. 241–2.
[15] See *Le dialogue 'Hospital das Letras' de D. Francisco Manuel de Melo*, ed. Jean Colomès (Paris, 1970), p. 52.
[16] Astrana Marín, *La vida turbulenta de Quevedo*, p. 422.
[17] *Le dialogue*, p. 53.
[18] Above, p. 479. Text of the sonnet in *Obra poética*, ed. Blecua, 1, no. 264. For the circumstances surrounding its composition see James O. Crosby, *En torno a la poesía de Quevedo* (Madrid, 1967), pp. 31–7.
[19] Astrana Marín, *La vida turbulenta*, pp. 490 and 498.

and dictatorial. He was demanding more and more money from an oppressed people in the name (as the gloss on the Lord's Prayer put it) of *grave necesidad*.[20] He was surrounded by sycophantic ministers, who had grown rich as Castile grew poorer. His policies for the restoration of Spain had ended in abysmal failure; and, as Quevedo saw it, he had sold out to the enemies of Spain and the faith, especially to the Jews. He had turned to the heretical and rebellious Dutch for his reforming projects, and in attempting to put them into effect had corrupted the traditional values which had been the glory of Castile. The country's self-appointed saviour was fast leading it to destruction.

Quevedo's was a classic case of the politically disillusioned intellectual. The intensity of the hatred which he had come to feel for the Count-Duke and his men was that of a bitter and thwarted personality who saw his ideals betrayed. But was the bitterness so strong as to support the second charge against Quevedo—that he was in collusion with the French? This would have been an extraordinary volte-face for a man who had persistently lauded the virtues of patriotism, and who in 1635 had not only responded to the French manifesto in his open *Letter to Louis XIII* but had composed a vicious *Anatomy of the head of Cardinal Richelieu*.[21] Now, only four years later, he was— if Olivares is to be believed—'a confidant of France and in correspondence with Frenchmen.' The evidence for this dramatic transformation, if it ever existed, is unlikely to come to light, but the implausible is not by its nature beyond the bounds of possibility. That the twisted, corrosive, embittered Quevedo should have seen in the France of Louis XIII a possible instrument for the overthrow of a tyrannical minister who was leading his country to destruction is not wholly out of character. The occasional contact with a French agent would, in any event, surely do no harm. The behaviour of the French malcontents in these very years indicates that there was nothing very unusual about the domestic opponents of a hated minister responding to enemy overtures in the hope of finding a means to precipitate his downfall.

Quevedo's vendetta against the man who had once been his patron was unique in the vituperative brilliance of the polemical style in which it was pursued, but it was hardly unique in character. Year after year in the secrecy of his journal that disappointed courtier, Matías de Novoa, spewed forth his hatred of the all-powerful minister. The grandees, for their part, barely attempted to conceal their loathing of the man. In Madrid at large he was now so detested that he rarely showed himself. 'Of late', reported the English ambas-

---

[20] Egido, *Sátiras políticas*, no. 24, verse 10.
[21] *Obras completas*, 1, pp. 887–903, and 903–9.

sador in the summer of 1638, 'he hath wholly left the recreations he was wont to take in the field and in the Buen Retiro, and that upon some shows of unruliness in the people towards him.'[22] Alvise Contarini, Venice's ambassador in Madrid between 1638 and 1641, described Spain in his valedictory report as being ruled by force and fear.[23]

Exactly how much coercive power the Count-Duke had at his disposal is, however, unclear. Royal guards were available for the personal protection of the king and his minister; but the coercion must have rested primarily on the activities of the normal law-enforcing agencies of the crown, the *alcaldes de corte* and the judicial officers, and on an extensive spy network, presumably financed from the 'secret expense' account, held by the Protonotario. Yet the efficacy of these agencies is open to question. Contemporary accounts give the impression of a general decline of law and order in the Madrid of the late 1630's, provoked especially by soldiery confident in the protection afforded them by the *fuero militar*, the jurisdiction administered by the Council of War.[24] In two weeks of July 1639 soldiers in Madrid were responsible for seventy violent deaths.[25] The unwelcome presence of so many troops in the capital was in part the natural outcome of wartime conditions, as veterans, new recruits and deserters milled around the court. But it is also possible that the Count-Duke was stationing soldiers in and around the capital to reinforce his government's authority.

The administration, too, provided circuses, even if it could not always provide cheap bread, to keep the people docile. When an elaborate mock naval battle was staged on the lake of the Retiro during the festivities held in June 1639, the third performance was thrown open to the general public free of charge.[26] But the paradoxical result of this largesse may have been simply to increase the regime's unpopularity. There was continuous and mounting criticism of Olivares and his ministers for their squandering of precious resources on expensive royal pleasures.[27] An additional source of scandal and offence was the highly visible presence at court of Portuguese financiers of dubious orthodoxy. Both by the company it kept and the policies it pursued the regime had managed to isolate itself by the late 1630's from the society that surrounded it. The king, although he worked long hours at his papers, was universally regarded as

[22] PRO SP. 94.40, fo. 156, Hopton to Coke, 25 July/4 August 1638.

[23] Barozzi and Berchet, *Relazioni. Spagna*, 2, p. 86.

[24] See Pellicer, *Avisos*, 31, p. 21 (31 May 1639).

[25] *Ibid.*, p. 53. Further incidents of this type are scattered through the *Avisos*.

[26] *Ibid.*, p. 36. Stage performances held on the island of the Retiro lake were also open on occasions to the public (see Brown and Elliott, *A Palace*, p. 206).

[27] See Brown and Elliott, *A Palace*, especially pp. 228–34.

a puppet in the Count-Duke's hands, although Quevedo and many others still looked to him for salvation. The Count-Duke himself was feared and detested as a tyrant who had surrounded himself with time-servers, among them various members of the Guzmán-Haro-Zúñiga connection—notably the Count of Castrillo and the Count-Duke's sly and self-serving brother-in-law, the Count of Monterrey, back in the summer of 1638 with his booty from Naples.[28] The Council of State, which now took second place to the hand-picked Junta de Ejecución, was packed with sycophants, like the Duke of Villahermosa and Cardinal Borja, who had been welcomed like a returning hero on his entry into Madrid in 1636 after his celebrated confrontations with Urban VIII. The only member of that council to maintain any semblance of genuine independence was the aged and imperious Count of Oñate. Outside it, the Count-Duke had his close circle of intimate advisers, like the Protonotario, José González, Antonio de Contreras, and Hernando de Salazar, although the latter's heavy duties as a member of the Council of the Inquisition had led to his replacement as the Count-Duke's confessor in 1632 or 1633 by Father Francisco Aguado, a fellow-Jesuit who kept a lower profile.[29] Then, too, there were the secretaries, influential figures in the Madrid of the 1630's because of their close association with the all-powerful minister. These included the Count-Duke's personal secretaries, the indispensable Antonio Carnero and his promising new assistant, Jerónimo de Lezama, together with the principal secretaries of state—Andrés de Rozas for Flanders, Pedro de Arce for Italy, and Fernando Ruiz de Contreras, who occupied the increasingly important post of secretary to the Junta de Ejecución.

By 1640 these men constituted a rather self-consciously embattled group, very aware of the extent to which their own fortunes were tied to those of the favourite. In June 1640 Andrés de Rozas wrote to Don Miguel de Salamanca in Brussels, to tell him of a recent distribution of patronage by Olivares among his confidants and secretaries. He had allocated to them the seats in the municipal governments granted him by a grateful Castilian Cortes: 'Burgos for the Protonotario, Madrid for Antonio Carnero, Valladolid for Jerónimo de Lezama, Toro for Don Bartolomé de Lagarda, Murcia for me ... I am much consoled by his remembering me and counting me among his own, and in my heart no one will ever be more so than I, both now and for ever.'[30] If Rozas subsequently failed to live up to these protestations of undying loyalty, he clearly appreciated his identifica-

[28] *MHE*, 14, p. 434 (22 June 1638).
[29] Alonso de Andrade, *Vida del Venerable Padre Francisco de Aguado, provincial de la Compañía de Jesús* (Madrid, 1658), pp. 266–8.
[30] AHN Est. lib. 981, Rosas to Salamanca, 25 June 1640.

tion with a group of men who prided themselves on being the Count-Duke's 'creatures' or *hechuras*. Like the ebullient Don Francisco de Melo, who credited Olivares in 1642 with having 'taken me from the cradle, fed and sustained me',[31] they owed him everything. Now, as the skies grew dark, the moment had come to prove themselves worthy of his confidence.

The Count-Duke's clarion call to action required absolute dedication to the service of the king. No sacrifice could be too great when the survival of the Monarchy itself was at stake. This bleak appeal to sacrifice, especially when uttered by ministers who lived in considerable comfort and ostentation, was not calculated to add to the administration's popularity. But to Olivares, whose own austerity stood out in sharp contrast to the splendours of the court and the corruption of many of the most prominent figures in his government, unpopularity was a necessary fact of life, and indeed he almost gloried in it. When ministers were unpopular it showed that they were doing their duty. He was shocked when his own former son-in-law, Medina de las Torres, wrote from Naples, where he had succeeded Monterrey as viceroy after endless altercations and delays, to protest that Madrid was making impossible demands. It was his duty, according to Olivares, 'to search out ways in the midst of impossibility. This is the function of great ministers, and why they are needed'[32] (Pl. 30).

Ironically, Medina de las Torres, still little more than a playboy when he took over the viceroyalty from a reluctant Monterrey at the end of 1637, was at this moment acquiring in the harsh school of experience the first rudiments of a political sagacity that would one day make him a dominant figure in the government of Spain.[33] Olivares hoped to teach his ministers the art of the impossible. But there was nothing like a spell in one of the viceroyalties for learning the art of the possible. This was an art that Medina de las Torres was quickly mastering in his important new post. Naples was an indispensable source of revenue for the Spanish crown. The king had given orders in 1636 that nothing should be left undone to extract money from the kingdom, and the new viceroy, for all his protests, outdid even his predecessor in his money-raising efforts.[34] But he had to steer a careful course between the imperious orders of Madrid on the one hand, and the understandable resentment of the Neapolitan

---

[31] AGS Est. leg. 3860, Melo to Olivares, 5 January 1642.
[32] AGS Est. leg. 3262, fo. 167, Note from Olivares to king relating to letter of 26 June 1639 from Medina de las Torres.
[33] See Stradling, 'A Spanish Statesman of Appeasement'.
[34] See Rosario Villari, 'Baronaggio e finanza a Napoli alla vigilia della rivoluzione del 1647–8', *Studi Storici*, 3 (1962), pp. 259–305. See also the table of comparative contributions under Monterrey and Medina de las Torres in Giuseppe Coniglio, *Il viceregno di Napoli nel sec. XVII* (Rome, 1955), p. 272.

nobility and people on the other. In October 1639 the nobles chose one of their number, the Duke of Nochera, the newly-appointed viceroy of Aragon, to present their case to the government in Madrid.[35] Medina de las Torres was acutely sensitive to the pressures that were building up in his viceroyalty. 'In times when it is necessary to consider the imposition of extraordinary taxes', he wrote to the Count-Duke in the spring of 1640, 'it is also necessary to apply antidotes to moderate their effects', and he warned him of the growing malaise among the nobility, whose love for the king was cooling in proportion as their desire to do something for the relief of their *patria* intensified.[36]

The existence of a potential alternative focus of loyalty to the king, in the shape of a *patria* (however shadowy that *patria* might be), worried Medina de las Torres, as well it might. Naples, like the other kingdoms and provinces of the Monarchy, had its own customs, its own distinctive traditions, and its own political institutions, however much decayed. The Monarchy had held together for over a century because of the bonds of allegiance that tied it to the king, and because of the power, at once protective and threatening, of its dominant member, Castile. Except in the Netherlands under Philip II that power had generally not been asserted in such a way as to force the king's subjects to choose between their loyalty to him and their loyalty to their own national or local communities. Many of them, indeed, would have found it difficult to imagine an object of allegiance other than their king. The cumulative effect of Madrid's war-time fiscalism, however, was to impose intense strains on this loyalty to an absentee monarch whom few of them had seen, and to raise at least the possibility of a higher loyalty to an idealized community.

These strains were becoming increasingly apparent throughout the Monarchy—in Naples and Sicily, Vizcaya, Navarre, Portugal, the states of the Crown of Aragon, and even Mexico and Peru—as local populations sought to resist fiscal and military demands that appeared to them intolerably oppressive. The discontent was most obviously dangerous in those communities whose sense of communal identity was strengthened by the existence of laws, liberties and *fueros* restricting the possibilities of intervention by the central power. These local liberties, which complicated the task of raising the men and money needed by the crown, helped to define the responses of societies under pressure from the central government to those of their own community who were associated with its actions. In the Vizcayan disturbances of 1632 the angry crowds went hunting for 'traitors'.[37] The

[35] Villari, 'Baronaggio e finanza', p. 274.
[36] AGS Est. leg. 3263, fo. 59, Medina de las Torres to Olivares, 22 April 1640.
[37] Guiard, *Historia de Bilbao*, 2, p. 90.

30. The Count-Duke's son-in-law, the Duke of Medina de las Torres, a bust by Juan Melchor Pérez.

very concept of treachery presupposes a loyalty to Vizcaya itself, as a legal, political and historical entity. To Olivares, who could conceive of no loyalty in the Monarchy other than loyalty to the king, such attitudes were beyond the bounds of comprehension. On more than one occasion he spoke scornfully of those who gave way to the passions of nationality. When a bitter feud erupted in the royal army outside Salces between the native viceroy of Catalonia, the Count of Santa Coloma, and the Neapolitan *maestre de campo*, the Marquis of Torrecuso, he found it hard to contain his indignation. 'Cursed be nations, and cursed the men who are *nacionales*! . . . I love all the vassals of the king, and I love the Neapolitans enough to make Spaniards feel jealous, because they seem to me such a mighty pillar of the Monarchy. I am no *nacional*—that is for children.'[38]

In disdaining as unworthy of rational adults the assertion of sentiments of national or local pride, the Count-Duke may well have blinded himself to the impact that his own policies were having on the peoples of the Monarchy. When he discussed the government of Portugal in his Great Memorial of 1624, he had pronounced the heart of the Portuguese to be 'essentially loyal', and attributed any discontent they may have felt to the natural discontent of vassals ruled by an absentee king.[39] This judgment suggests a profound unawareness of the psychology of a proud people with a great imperial past, now reduced to dependence on a powerful neighbour. In the circumstances, it is hardly surprising that he misread the Évora disturbances of 1637. For him, they were the work of a handful of troublemakers, mere *canaille* who deserved to have their brains beaten out. While he was astute enough to realize that the Portuguese nobility represented a potential source of danger, and promptly sought to neutralize it, the effect upon him of Evora was simply to reinforce his conviction of the need to press ahead with his plans for a more effective integration of the Monarchy as a genuine partnership of kingdoms and provinces enjoying parity of opportunity and united in service to their king. Once parity was assured, there could be no legitimate cause for complaint.

For the same reason he seems to have ignored the warning signals that were flashing on the eastern side of the peninsula during the winter of 1639–40, as the royal army struggled to recapture Salces. At the best of times it would not have been easy to mobilize for war a society so little amenable to royal authority as that of Catalonia.

---

[38] BNM Ms. 1630, fos. 186–7v., Olivares to Torrecuso, 4 January 1640. A further example of his attitude is to be found in his letter to Father Quiroga of 31 December 1639, in which he writes: 'No me apassiono nazionalmente, teniendo esto por vanidad insustancial' (BL Add. Ms. 24,909, fo. 136v.).

[39] *MC*, 1, p. 92.

The powers of its viceroy, operating under instructions from the Council of Aragon in Madrid, were tightly circumscribed by the 'constitutions' which the king had sworn an oath to observe. All officials other than the viceroy himself had, by law, to be native Catalans, and their number—also restricted by law—was small. The principality had an *audiencia*, or supreme judicial tribunal, consisting of a president and seventeen judges; a governor with four senior subordinates; a handful of financial officers; and less than two hundred underpaid local officials of the crown, operating in a province with a population approaching 400,000.[40] Laws could only be changed with the approval of the Cortes, which since the beginning of the reign had met twice, in 1626 and 1632, and on both occasions abortively. Authority, such as it was, was shared uneasily between the viceregal administration, the municipal oligarchies—especially that of the powerful city of Barcelona with its strongly entrenched privileges—, the local baronage, which retained extensive rights of jurisdiction, and the *Diputació*, which, as the standing committee of the Cortes, served as the symbolic representative body of the Catalan community. During the first years of the Olivares regime the *Diputació*, consisting of three *diputats* and three *oidors*, had not revealed itself as a particularly effective institution on the occasions when Catalan liberties came under attack from agents of the crown. But in 1638 its presidency fell to Pau Claris, a canon of the cathedral chapter of the Pyrenean diocese of Urgell, whose fiery brand of patriotism had breathed new life into an ailing institution, and brought it into conflict with the government of the new and native-born viceroy, the Count of Santa Coloma.

The long succession of disputes between the Olivares regime and the Catalans had led to such ill-feeling on both sides that effective cooperation during the siege of Salces would have been a minor miracle. Many Catalans did indeed go to the front during those harrowing six months, and Catalan casualties were high—probably around 7,000, including two hundred nobles and gentry, or a quarter of the principality's nobility.[41] But much of the Catalan contribution to the war effort, which Madrid regarded as both tardy and inadequate, was secured with the greatest difficulty by royal officials and the judges of the *audiencia*, who were acting from October 1639 under orders to disregard any constitutions which impeded the mobilization of resources for the war. Inevitably the judges, pitched into the unfamiliar duties of recruiting sergeants and military purveyors, became marked men as they travelled round the principality, struggling to get men and supplies to the camp at Salces. By the time the siege

---

[40] For a detailed account of the administration see Elliott, *Catalans*, ch. 4.
[41] *Ibid.*, pp. 384–5.

drew to a successful but inglorious close on 6 January 1640 a swelling tide of mass popular indignation against these 'traitors' to the fatherland was already beginning to shake the whole precarious edifice of royal authority in Catalonia.

For six months Count-Duke had watched the unfolding of events in Catalonia with mounting exasperation. He was dependent for his information on the army commanders, who inevitably complained about the ineffective help they were receiving from the local population, and on the viceroy and judges of the *audiencia*, who naturally made the most of their difficulties in order to justify their own failures to meet the requirements of Madrid. His other preoccupations in any event left him with little time for the details of Catalan affairs. The Council of Aragon, under the presidency of Cardinal Borja, was in the pocket of the Protonotario, who was also a busy man. No doubt he had his private network of local informants in the principality, but they too had their own interests to promote. Neither the Count-Duke nor Villanueva had any love for the Catalans, especially after the experiences of the past few years, and nothing occurred in the course of the Salces campaign to shake their conviction that the laws and liberties of Catalonia represented an intolerable obstacle to efficient government and the effective prosecution of the war.

Neither man, therefore, was willing, or even perhaps able, to hear what the Catalans were trying to say. It was characteristic of their approach to Catalan sensibilities that at the moment of the victory of Salces, when the Catalans were preening themselves on their achievements, the king should have failed to send the principality or the city of Barcelona a letter of thanks. Instead, Santa Coloma was instructed to consider possible ways of raising 5,000 paid Catalan soldiers for the next campaign, and plans were prepared for a new session of the Catalan Cortes in April, which would be exclusively devoted to what Olivares euphemistically called 'the reform of government.'[42] He meant by this a revision of the Catalan constitutions in such a way as to compel the principality to contribute on a regular basis to the fiscal and military needs of the Monarchy. Now that the siege of Salces was over, he was clearly determined to forge ahead with the Union of Arms. In writing to Santa Coloma of the importance of getting the Catalans to raise two or three *tercios*, he described this as the 'remedy which has been adopted in Castile, Italy and Flanders', and as about to be adopted in Portugal, which would be asked this year to produce eight thousand men.[43] The time had come, he told an emergency meeting of the Council of State

[42] *Ibid.*, p. 388 (letter to Santa Coloma, 3 February 1640).
[43] Olivares to Santa Coloma, 14 January 1640, printed in appendix to Gaspar Sala, *Secrets Públichs* (Barcelona, 1641).

held a few days earlier to discuss the perilous state of Portuguese India, for Portugal to 'defend itself while simultaneously helping to defend Spain.' Spain's enemies, he reminded the council, had banded together to destroy the Monarchy, and the Monarchy itself must follow suit. Portugal's India trade should be thrown open to all the king's subjects, and trading companies established to help ensure that it did not fall into the hands of the Dutch.[44]

All the resources of the Monarchy had to be mobilized for a final supreme effort, designed to make 1640 the year of peace, and for any such effort, unity was paramount. Olivares was convinced that the only way to secure peace was to launch an assault on France itself. 'Unless war can be carried into its very entrails, all our efforts are useless.'[45] That peace was urgently necessary he now had no doubt. Any peace that was not 'very bad' would be acceptable, he wrote early in February 1640 in a memorandum for discussion by the Council of State, and it was clearly God's will, for He had 'absolutely and visibly deprived us of the means of making war by depriving us of all our military and civil leaders . . . In six years we have lost more *cabezas* than in the preceding sixty.' The Empire, for its part, was in even worse shape.[46]

The Council of State responded by drawing up proposals for a new peace mission to be headed by Joseph de Bergaigne, the Franciscan bishop of Bois-le-Duc. The Count-Duke meanwhile was busy with his plans for the invasion of France. In order to concentrate resources, Italy was to be reduced to a secondary theatre of war, and Leganés would have to limit his operations to sealing off Casale, since additional contingents from his army of Milan would be needed in the Iberian peninsula for the attack on France.[47]

An essential element for the projected invasion would be the royal army that had been campaigning in Catalonia during the winter. In addition to the cavalry, this contained some eight thousand infantrymen, including the Count-Duke's own regiment (a thousand strong), one Irish *tercio*, one Walloon *tercio*, and two *tercios* of Neapolitans.[48] These were seasoned veterans, some of the best men still in the royal service outside the army of Flanders, and Olivares was

[44] AGS Est. leg. 2664, consulta, 5 January 1640.

[45] AGS Est. leg. 3352, fo. 4, *El Conde-Duque sobre una carta del Marqués de Leganés que trata de lo que se puede obrar el año de 1640.*

[46] 'Informe presentado por el Conde-Duque al Rey', Cánovas del Castillo, *Estudios*, 1, pp. 414–15. Leman, *Richelieu et Olivarès*, p. 125 n.1, corrects Cánovas' dating of this document to March, and shows that it was prepared for a meeting of the Council of State held on 14 February.

[47] *El Conde-Duque sobre una carta del Marqués de Leganés.*

[48] Elliott, *Catalans*, pp. 392–3. The problems involved in billeting these troops, and the impact of the billeting on the principality, are examined in detail in Elliott, *Catalans*, chs. 14 and 15.

naturally concerned that they should be well rested before the new campaigning season opened. In view of the clashes between the Neapolitan and native Catalan contingents, and the general restiveness of the province, there was an obvious case for getting these men out of the principality. But Olivares saw no reason to relieve the Catalans of the additional burden of billeting the army that had defended them. Why should other provinces be called upon to make fresh sacrifices when the Catalans had so manifestly defaulted on their obligations? No doubt he also calculated that, if the king were to hold a session of the Cortes in April, the presence of an army quartered on the province for legitimate military reasons would provide the extra touch of authority required to enable him to bring the Cortes to a long overdue and satisfactory conclusion.

The Count of Santa Coloma, in his capacity as viceroy, was therefore ordered to get the army into winter quarters. 'I beg you on my knees, and from the bottom of my heart, to billet that army well', the Count-Duke wrote to him at the beginning of February.[49] This was asking a good deal. The forcible billeting of soldiers in private homes was one of the greatest causes of hardship and grievance in Early Modern Europe. There was no way, as Olivares himself once admitted in a letter to the Duke of Feria about the billeting of Spanish soldiers in Mantua, that a large body of men could be kept under such close discipline as not to provoke incidents among the local population.[50] To billet the army on Catalan peasants who had already seen their livestock and provisions requisitioned for the Salces campaign was therefore tempting providence. Moreover, these were peasants who knew their rights. Under the Catalan constitutions the formal obligations of a householder were limited to providing a soldier with a bed, a table, a light, and service, along with salt, vinegar and water. A veteran of the Italian or Flanders wars was unlikely to find this very nourishing fare. Madrid assumed that the local population would feed a billeted army at its own expense; but any such requirement could only be pronounced illegal under the Catalan constitutions by *Diputació* and *audiencia* alike. The army commanders for their part were interested only in getting their tired men housed and fed as quickly as possible, knowing that unless this happened they would resort to violence or desert.

As hungry soldiers clashed with angry householders, the Catalan authorities—the *diputats*, the Estates, the city council of Barcelona—sent deputations of protest to the viceroy against the contravention of the principality's laws. Santa Coloma, with much wringing of hands, kept Madrid informed of their behaviour, and commented

[49] *Ibid.*, p. 393.
[50] ASM, Archivio Gonzaga, Serie E.XIV.3, busta 616, Olivares to Feria, 5 January 1626.

with mounting alarm on the spreading movement of unrest. His letters, after initial discussion in the Council of Aragon, where Cardinal Borja and the Protonotario dominated the proceedings, were then passed to the Junta de Ejecución with the council's recommendations. Attendance at this junta varied. On occasions it rose to as many as thirteen, but it usually remained in single figures. Five members attended regularly during the first six months of 1640 when Catalan affairs were under discussion: Olivares himself; the Marquis of Castrofuerte, general of the Spanish artillery and a military expert; the Protonotario; Don Nicolás Cid of the Council of War, and Pedro de Arce, of the same council, whose brother was *maestre de campo* of the Count-Duke's regiment serving in Catalonia. These five were joined in the spring by José González, and by Ambrosio Spínola's son, the Marquis of Los Balbases, who had been commanding the royal army in Catalonia and returned to Madrid from Barcelona at the end of March. At times this small group was reinforced by senior ministers—Cardinal Borja, the Duke of Villahermosa, the Counts of Monterrey and Oñate, the Marquises of Mirabel and Santa Cruz. But in practice the day-to-day decisions on Catalonia were being taken by the Count-Duke and four or five colleagues, of whom the Protonotario was the one most conversant with Catalan affairs.

Olivares and his colleagues followed with growing indignation the reports of mounting agitation among the Catalans. In early February the court was busy with preparations for the king's projected visit to Catalonia to preside over the Cortes,[51] and now the clashes between peasantry and soldiers threatened to put the visit at risk. The court had taken up residence for Shrovetide at the Buen Retiro, where the splendid new theatre of the Coliseum had just been completed. Early in the morning of 20 February smoke was seen rising from the king's quarters, and the royal apartments were soon ablaze. The palace was hastily evacuated, furniture and pictures flung pell-mell from the windows, and all Madrid turned out to watch, and, when possible, to loot. The Count-Duke himself spent the whole day presiding over the fire-fighting operations, without even breaking off to eat. The following day the *comedias* went ahead as planned; the councils and the Cortes were immediately approached for money to pay for the reconstruction of the damaged quarters; and a large labour force was put to work to get the Retiro restored to its pristine state before the coming of Easter.[52]

The Count-Duke was soon to find that it was easier to quench the fires of the Retiro than those of Catalonia. His most immediate

[51] *MHE*, 15, p. 411 (11 February 1640).
[52] Brown and Elliott, *A Palace*, p. 101. Contemporary accounts in *MHE*, 15, pp. 412–14; Pellicer, *Avisos*, 31, pp. 142–4; Novoa, *Codoin* 81, pp. 191–2.

concern was for the well-being of the army which was beginning to disintegrate through lack of supplies and of adequate winter quarters. How could the Catalans be so blind as to allow the letter of their laws to stand between the principality and another French invasion? 'We always have to look and see if a constitution says this or that', he wrote to Santa Coloma on 29 February. 'We have to discover what the customary usage is, even when it is a question of the supreme law, of the actual preservation and defence of the province ... How is it possible that, of thirty-six ministers who have seen the despatches this morning, there is not one who is not clamouring, clamouring against Catalonia?'[53]

At a meeting on 27 February the Council of Aragon had already suggested draconian measures for restoring calm to the principality: one or more *diputats* should be arrested, an inquiry should be held into the recent seditious proceedings in the Barcelona city council, and troops should be quartered in Barcelona itself.[54] With alarming news arriving from Catalonia by every post, the king approved these measures, and Santa Coloma was ordered to put them into effect. At the same time the king sent a private missive, drafted by the Protonotario, to the Marquis of Los Balbases, telling him that his first priority was to make sure that the billeting was arranged, rather than use his troops to enforce compliance to the royal orders. But Balbases was also authorized, if he saw fit, to quarter his men in Barcelona, as a means of preventing the disintegration of the army, and of 'restraining' the populace.[55]

There was even some question of the Protonotario going in person to Catalonia to supervise the levying of 6,000 Catalans for service in Italy—a contribution towards the Union of Arms which the Junta de Ejecución regarded as essential, but which hardly seemed well timed.[56] But the Count-Duke could not dispense with the services of his right-hand man, and Villanueva was spared a journey which could well have cost him his life. The Catalans, who were kept well informed by agents and well-wishers of everything that was happening at court, were convinced that in the Count-Duke and the Protonotario they had two enemies who would stop at nothing to destroy their laws and liberties. Over the years they had received nothing but abuse and reproaches from the Count-Duke, and they knew enough about his projects for the closer union of the Monarchy to regard his behaviour as part of a carefully orchestrated plan to reduce them to the servitude that had overtaken Castile. It was now clear

[53] Elliott, *Catalans*, p. 401.
[54] *Ibid.*, p. 403.
[55] AGS Est. leg. 2721, draft despatch, 29 February 1640.
[56] Elliott, *Catalans*, pp. 403–4.

to Pau Claris and his friends that the king would never listen to their just complaints as long as Olivares remained at his side. The principality would have to look to itself—to its own traditional ideals and its own resources—to escape from the disaster that they saw hanging over it.

The events of March 1640 only served to confirm the accuracy of this diagnosis. Pau Claris, having got wind of the plans to arrest a *diputat*, absented himself from official business on the pretext of illness, and went into hiding. On 18 March his colleague in the *Diputació*, Francesc de Tamarit, was arrested by Santa Coloma in compliance with his orders from Madrid. The news of Tamarit's arrest came as a great relief to Olivares and his colleagues, although they were worried by Santa Coloma's failure to fulfil the second part of his instructions and get the arrested *diputat* out of Barcelona. But they were confident that the *Diputació* had been taught a lesson, and would now be more willing to cooperate in the billeting arrangements and in helping to recruit native troops for Italy.

The spring, after all, was approaching, and with it the new campaigning season. It was essential to the Count-Duke that Catalonia should be tranquil before it began. Frontier provinces were sensitive areas, and nothing must be allowed to divert energies and attention from the prosecution of the war. He needed, too, the help that the Catalans could give. Following the practice pursued by imperial Rome, he was juggling with troops from the different parts of the Monarchy, sending Italians to Catalonia and Flanders, Flemings to Spain, and—or so he hoped—Catalans and Portuguese to Italy, on the principle that it was wisest to employ soldiers well away from their province of origin. He was very conscious of the acute shortage of men and money for an effective attack on the French. The Cardinal-Infante had written in January that his forces were inadequate even to defend the Netherlands themselves, still less to embark on an early offensive, as the king had ordered.[57] At the present rate of desertion, the army in Catalonia would be equally unprepared for a spring campaign. If everything was to be got in order, there was no time to be lost.

A 'general rebellion'

Although Richelieu had for some time been keeping an eye on Catalonia, and French agents were operating in the principality,[58] there

[57] Archivo de la Casa de Miraflores, Madrid. Cardinal-Infante to Olivares, 17 January 1640.
[58] Elliott, *Catalans*, p. 469; José Sanabre, *La acción de Francia en Cataluña en la pugna por la hegemonía de Europe* (Barcelona, 1956), p. 88.

was as yet no indication of French involvement in Catalan affairs. But it would have been surprising if the Cardinal had not been probing for chinks in the Count-Duke's armour, whether by means of judicious contacts with opposition circles in Madrid, or by taking discreet soundings in the troubled border area of north-eastern Spain. The quickest way to bring the enemy to his knees was to foment and encourage domestic unrest. But this was as true of France as it was of Spain. The Count-Duke was hated, but so too was the Cardinal.[59] The government in France was no less oppressive than the government in Spain; domestic discontent was endemic, and found an outlet in a succession of tax-revolts, the most recent of them in Lower Normandy in the late summer and autumn of 1639;[60] and Richelieu's aristocratic enemies, unlike those of Olivares, had shown few inhibitions about resorting to conspiracy and armed insurrection to bring about his overthrow. The Count-Duke was well aware of the possibility of some great upheaval in France, and as Spain's military reverses multiplied, he came to bank increasingly on a change of regime in Paris.

The road to Paris led through London, which had become a haven for Richelieu's enemies since the Duke of Soubise had fled there on the fall of La Rochelle. He was joined in London early in 1638 by that arch-conspirator, Marie de Rohan, Duchess of Chevreuse, who descended on the court of Charles I after having made a dramatic flight from France and taken Madrid by storm.[61] In the autumn of 1638 she was followed by Marie de Médicis herself. Another exile to arrive at the English court that winter was the Duke of La Valette. The son of the elderly Duke of Épernon, whose native province of Guyenne had been uneasily quiescent since the peace of Alais between the crown and the Huguenots, La Valette fled the country after Richelieu made him the scapegoat for the failure of the siege of Fuenterrabía, and was condemned to death *in absentia* on a charge of lèse-majesté.[62] From London this émigré faction maintained close contacts with the dissidents in France, and especially with the Count of Soissons, who, after the latest round of troubles between Gaston d'Orléans and the king, had prudently retired to Sedan. As an independent territory under the sovereignty of the Duke of Bouillon this offered him a refuge against the Cardinal's revenge.[63]

---

[59] See Elliott, *Richelieu and Olivares*, especially ch. 5, for a comparison of the two regimes in the 1630's.

[60] See Madeleine Foisil, *La révolte des nu-pieds et les révoltes normandes de 1639* (Paris, 1970).

[61] See Victor Cousin, *Madame de Chevreuse* (7th ed., Paris, 1886), and Brown and Elliott, *A Palace*, p. 195. She entered Madrid on 6 December 1637 and left for England in February 1638 (*MHE*, 14, p. 332).

[62] Burckhardt, *Richelieu and his Age*, 3, p. 344.

[63] *Ibid.*, p. 338.

In the hornet's nest of émigrés who buzzed around the court of Charles and Henrietta Maria, it was the Duchess of Chevreuse who buzzed the loudest. In mid-December 1639 Spain's envoy in London, Cárdenas, had a three-hour conversation with her and La Valette. They had just come from a discussion with Soubise about possible ways of provoking trouble in France. Their plan was to seize La Rochelle, an operation for which they would require 12,000 men, the majority of them English. But they would also need the support of Spain, including financial support. This raised the usual delicate question of the legitimacy of the Catholic king offering help to Huguenots, but on previous occasions the theologians in Madrid had found no insuperable obstacle to bending religion to the needs of *raison d'état*.[64] Cárdenas reported these promising developments to Miguel de Salamanca in Brussels,[65] and on 30 December his letter was forwarded to Madrid with an enthusiastic endorsement from the Cardinal-Infante who believed that the project had a good chance of success and might well prove the instrument for restoring peace.[66]

The Duchess of Chevreuse followed up her talk with Cárdenas by sending a member of her household to Madrid to give the Count-Duke the benefit of her views on the London scene. La Valette she found somewhat irresolute, and Soubise distrustful of the chances of help from Madrid, and she suggested that Olivares should send a confidant to London to work out with him the terms of an agreement. She also reported on her attempts to persuade Charles I to stand up for himself and take revenge on the Dutch for their flagrant disrespect for his authority in attacking the Spanish fleet in British waters at the Downs. Spain, she urged, should send an ambassador to London to strengthen its ties with Charles I, perhaps by proposing a new Anglo-Spanish marriage.[67]

Olivares was effusive in his gratitude to the duchess, who was risking her life in the cause; 'and liberty is life, and without it all is nothing.'[68] He was in fact already well aware of the need for stronger diplomatic representation in London, even allowing for Cárdenas' success in establishing his position at the English court. He was confirmed in his views by the envoy's despatch of 21 December, which reached him on 6 February. This spoke of Charles I's growing difficulties with the Scots, whom he suspected of receiving assistance

[64] Above, p. 227.
[65] AHN Est. lib. 971, letter of 16 December 1639.
[66] AHN Est. lib. 971, Cardinal-Infante to king, 30 December 1639.
[67] AGS Est. K. 1420, fo. 19. Undated paper by Duchess of Chevreuse's agent, discussed in Council of State on 23 February 1640.
[68] AGS Est. K. 1420, fo. 18, Olivares to king (no date). 'Con la vida se alcanza todo, y con la libertad se vive, y todo es nada sin tenerla.'

from the French, and also of his decision to summon parliament.[69] While the Count-Duke thought this decision extremely unwise, he saw in it the prospect for a closer association between England and Spain. Charles, it seemed, was going to need Spanish help. All this suggested the need to reinforce Spain's presence in London, even though Cárdenas was about to be joined by the Marquis of Velada, who was coming over from Brussels to deal with problems over the disposal of Spanish men and ships after the disaster of the Downs. But who could be found for the post of ambassador extraordinary at this critical moment?

The Count-Duke racked his brain to think of a suitable envoy, and finally came up with a somewhat improbable choice—the court historian, Virgilio Malvezzi.[70] His study of the relevant documents for his history of the reign had left him with a good background knowledge of Anglo-Spanish relations; his post as a member of the Council of War had given him the necessary practical experience; and he was, in the Count-Duke's opinion, a most Christian *caballero*. The only problem was that he was physically so weak, he ate so little and suffered so acutely from sea-sickness, that it hardly seemed reasonable to risk the loss of a life so dedicated to the service of His Majesty.[71] Malvezzi, however, was willing to put his dedication to the test, and by 7 March the Protonotario had finished preparing draft instructions for his mission.[72]

These instructions left no doubt about the importance that Olivares attached to it. 'The impetuous progress of the King of France', with his 'pernicious designs against public peace and the Catholic religion', had made it essential to find ways of restraining him. The most effective method was to organize some diversion inside France itself, in order to keep his armies occupied at home. For this reason, Malvezzi was told, the scheme now proposed by La Valette and Soubise for the seizure of La Rochelle was of the highest importance, since the renewal of civil war in France provided an infallible means for securing peace. But there was no prospect of success without Huguenot assistance; and although all the leading theologians were agreed that in this case the end justified the means, the king would rather risk everything than go back on his firm resolve not to help heretics. Malvezzi was therefore instructed to sign the articles of agreement with La Valette, a Catholic, and not with the Huguenot Soubise. He was to be offered a subsidy of 60,000 ducats a month over a

---

[69] AGS Est. leg. 2565.
[70] For details of Malvezzi's London mission, see Elliott, 'The Year of the Three Ambassadors'.
[71] AGS Est. leg. 2521, consulta, 17 February 1640.
[72] AHN Est. leg. 3456, no. 11, draft instructions, partly in Villanueva's hand.

four month period, together with men and munitions if necessary, to help him put 10,000 infantry and 2,000 cavalry into the field.

Spain would give La Valette all the help it could, but the battle of the Downs had left it short of ships. It was here, in particular, that the English could be of use. But Olivares had his eyes on an even larger prize than the English fleet. Malvezzi was to emphasize to Charles I how acute was the danger in which he now found himself. The Dutch at the Downs had struck a savage blow at his reputation; the French had imprisoned the Elector Palatine; the parliaments assembled in his kingdoms threatened his authority. The only hope remaining to him in the midst of all his troubles was to join with Spain in its war against the Dutch. The alliance could be based on the secret treaty negotiated between the Count-Duke and Cottington in January 1631, with a promise to Charles of territorial satisfaction in Zeeland or the Palatinate, according to choice, and trading opportunities for British merchants in Spain. If Charles were to go still further and provide Spain with 20,000 men for service in Flanders, Spain in return would place 8,000 veterans at his disposal to fight against the Scots. With Spanish help he would recover the respect of his vassals; and his fleet, enlarged to fifty ships with the aid of Spanish subsidies, would be strong enough to prevent the passage of Dutch ships through the Channel, and perhaps also secure a port from which the malcontents could launch their diversion inside France.

It was heady vision, which was not inappropriately entrusted for its realization to a historian whose relationship to reality was always somewhat tenuous. On 20 March Malvezzi embarked nervously for northern Europe. Olivares, informing the Cardinal-Infante of his departure, observed that 'all the artillery of our negotiation is directed against England', at what he considered to be the most favourable moment there had ever been or could be.[73] But even if Malvezzi, who had once fought under Feria's command in the wars in Piedmont, had been equipped with a weapon more lethal than a pea-shooter, he could hardly have made much impression on the course of English policy in the extraordinary circumstances of the spring of 1640.

As might have been anticipated, negotiations with the French exiles in London went more smoothly than those with the British ministers. On 18 May Cárdenas was able to send to Madrid the articles of the agreement reached with La Valette.[74] La Valette himself had written to Olivares a few days earlier expressing his willingness to devote his life to the King of Spain's service, and begging him to act with all possible speed as there was not a moment to be lost.[75] But these

---

[73] MSB, Cod. hisp. 22, fo. 119v., Olivares to Cardinal-Infante, 24 March 1640.
[74] AGS Est. leg. 2521, Cárdenas to king, 18 May 1640.
[75] AGS Est. leg. 2521, La Valette to Olivares, 10 May 1640.

letters did not arrive until the end of June; and although Olivares
was delighted at the success of the envoys in London, it was already
clear that the shortage of ships and men ruled out any possibility
of launching the enterprise until winter at the earliest.[76]

La Valette was an easy fish to catch. The Earl of Strafford, for
all the acuteness of his own predicament, proved considerably more
slippery. There was some hard bargaining with the Spanish envoys
before he called at the Marquis of Velada's house on 21 May to say
that if Philip IV could lend Charles I 1,200,000 ducats there was
every prospect of an agreement which would infallibly lead in due
course to a break between England and the Dutch.[77] In his report
to Olivares Velada expressed scepticism about the possibility of a
declaration of war on the Dutch, but seems to have felt that Spain
would get a good bargain for its 1,200,000 ducats: 3,000 high quality
Irish soldiers, and convoys for the protection of the silver and men
shipped from Spain to Flanders. He also pointed out that both Strafford and the king were likely to be in great danger if the deal fell
through.[78]

Reports on the London negotiations reached the Count-Duke in
mid-June. He obviously thought that the English were offering too
little and asking too much. But he was prepared to keep the negotiations going, partly because he needed the ships and the Irishmen,
and partly because of his growing anxiety over the way that events
were moving in England. If there were to be a great rebellion culminating in the establishment of a republic, the southern Netherlands
would without a doubt be lost to Spain. Beyond that there was the
even more terrible prospect of a union of two heretical republics,
the English and the Dutch, so irresistibly powerful as to swamp
all Europe.[79] Negotiations, therefore, must continue. On the basis
of one of Malvezzi's despatches the Count-Duke decided that Strafford must be a man of parts, and took the trouble to write him
a personal letter.[80] To Strafford, Olivares' compliments must have
seemed a poor substitute for his cash.

By the time Olivares wrote his flattering letter of 25 June to Strafford, however, his worries about the prospects of an insurrection
in England were as nothing compared with those inspired by the
reality of what he was now calling a 'general rebellion'[81] inside Spain

[76] AGS Est. leg. 2521, undated paper by Olivares on the *capitulación asentada con el Duque
de La Valette.*
[77] AGS Est. leg. 2521, Marquis of Velada to king, 21 May 1640; and see Elliott, 'Three
Ambassadors', pp. 173–6, for the negotiations with Strafford.
[78] AGR SEG, Reg. 374, fos. 245–6v., Velada to Olivares, 26 May 1640.
[79] AGS Est. leg. 2521, *voto* of Olivares, 16 June 1640.
[80] AGS Est. leg. 2575, *El Conde Duque al Virrey de Irlanda,* 25 June 1640.
[81] MSB, Cod. hisp. 22, fo. 125v., Olivares to Cardinal-Infante, 24 June 1640.

itself. To his horror and astonishment the unrest in Catalonia had got dangerously out of hand. A sudden calm did indeed seem to fall on the principality following Tamarit's arrest on 18 March, and after immense efforts the *tercios* were billeted—the Italians and Walloons in north-eastern Catalonia, the Spaniards in the south and west. But desertions continued at such a heavy rate that it was decided in April to make the two halves of the army change places. The marching and counter-marching involved in this operation were hardly calculated to promote the tranquillity of the regions through which the soldiers passed. The men were hungry, the villages unwelcoming. On 30 April a royal official who had gone to the small town of Santa Coloma de Farners to arrange for the billeting of the Neapolitans was burnt to death in the local inn where he had taken refuge from an angry crowd.[82] In response to their appeals for help, the inhabitants were joined by armed bands of peasants and villagers from the surrounding region. All over the province of Gerona furious bands of peasants were now massing. The *tercios*, leaving a trail of destruction in their wake, regrouped as best they could. On 14 May, in a punitive action ordered by the viceroy, they returned to Santa Coloma de Farners, now silent and abandoned, and razed it to the ground. The countryside erupted in revolt; and as the *tercios* retreated towards the coast, a peasant army on the march was baying at their heels.

As bad news continued to pour in from Catalonia, the Count-Duke's overriding concern was for the survival of his veteran troops. He wrote to the Cardinal-Infante on 21 May to say that he still hoped that it would be possible to help the 'common cause' by undertaking some form of diversionary attack on France, but warned him that the troops had fared so badly at the hands of the Catalans that they had had no time for rest.[83] A few days later, however, he realized that more than the survival of the army was at stake. The Catalan insurgents, fortified by the bishop of Gerona's denunciation of the *tercios* for the desecration and destruction of churches along their route, now regarded themselves as engaged in a holy mission to clear the principality of its sacrilegious oppressors. Hearing that the city of Barcelona was in imminent danger from the *tercios*, the rebel forces from Vallès marched to the relief of the capital. On the morning of 22 May, after the city gates had been mysteriously opened to them, they forced their way in, and made for the prison. Before allowing themselves with surprising docility to be shepherded out of the city by the bishops of Barcelona and Vic, they freed Tamarit

[82] Elliott, *Catalans*, p. 420.
[83] MSB, Cod. hisp. 22, fo. 122, Olivares to Cardinal-Infante, 21 May 1640.

and two members of the city council who had been imprisoned with him.[84]

Santa Coloma's letter containing the news of Tamarit's release arrived in Madrid on 27 May. The immediate reaction of Cardinal Borja and the Protonotario was to see this as the long-awaited moment when the crown would be justified in using a demonstration of force against the Catalans. Once again, however, as so often in moments of crisis, the innate caution of the Count-Duke came to the fore. A combined meeting on the 27th of the members of the Council of State and the Junta de Ejecución unanimously approved his recommendation that the king should adopt a conciliatory approach. The advice of the Catalan authorities should be sought on how to pacify the peasantry, and grandees with Catalan estates who lived in Madrid should leave at once for the principality. These included the Duke of Sessa, whose relations with the Catalans had always been too close for the Count-Duke's liking, but who for this very reason could be expected to carry weight with them in any attempt at conciliation. The king should be willing, said Olivares, to accept the advice given him within the principality for the pacification of the peasants, since the Catalan question was far too complex to allow of a once-for-all solution.[85]

In rejecting a military solution—even though hoping and expecting that the provincial and local authorities in Catalonia would not handle their rebellious peasants with kid gloves—the Count-Duke was ruling out, at least for the time being, an option that he had been holding open ever since the breakdown of the Catalan Cortes in 1626. He may, as so often, have been playing for time; but the realization that Catalonia was on the brink of insurrection had clearly startled him. Only a few days earlier, the Junta de Ejecución had agreed that an insurrection in Catalonia, at this of all moments, would be extremely embarrassing, and that everything possible should be done to limit the disturbances.[86] The Count-Duke, however defective his understanding of the Catalan scene, was acutely aware that any mistake could now have disastrous repercussions on the war with France.

The wisdom of this decision of 27 May to have recourse to conciliation rather than force in Catalonia must have been confirmed by the arrival four days later of a letter from the Marquis of Leganés reporting that Spanish arms had suffered a 'great disaster' in Italy.[87] His army, which had been besieging Casale, had been forced to retreat with heavy losses following a combined attack by French and

[84] Elliott, *Catalans*, pp. 429–30.
[85] *Ibid.*, pp. 434–5.
[86] *Ibid.*, pp. 433–4.
[87] AGS Est. leg. 3352, fo. 131, Leganés to king, 3 May 1640 (received 31 May).

Savoyard troops under the command of Harcourt. It was one more blow to the Count-Duke's hopes of redressing the balance by maintaining pressure on France in every theatre of war. Instead, there was now a real danger that the French would begin massing troops on the Catalan frontier, seizing the opportunity provided by the peasant uprisings to launch a new invasion.

This prospect made it essential to reinforce the battered royal army in Catalonia. But the reinforcement of the *tercios* had ceased to be purely a matter of military routine. On 26 May the Catalan *diputats* wrote to their envoys in Madrid telling them that the only way to end the disturbances was to withdraw all the soldiers from the province and issue a general pardon.[88] But to the ministers in Madrid the evacuation of the principality was out of the question. How could it conceivably defend itself if the French attacked? In the circumstances it is not surprising that the first two weeks of June saw the regime in disarray, as it sought to reconcile the requirement of defence with that of pacification. Some ministers advocated an economic boycott of Catalonia like that which had reduced the Vizcayans to their senses in 1633. Others suggested concessions to the Catalans in order to buy the goodwill of the towns. Olivares himself, at a meeting of the Junta de Ejecución on 11 June, returned with great eloquence to one of the leading themes of his Great Memorial of 1624: no vassal of the crown should feel himself excluded from office or be treated as a foreigner simply because he was not a native of Castile. Equally, no Castilian should be excluded from the provincial councils.[89] The vision of a unified Monarchy never burned more brightly than at this moment, as disintegration threatened.

Suggestions of this kind, however, did nothing to resolve the immediate problem. Each new report from Barcelona indicated that the disorders, so far from abating, were continuing to spread. An insurrection that had begun in the countryside was now extending to the towns. In Vic, in Gerona, the city gates would be opened, groups of townsmen would make common cause with the rebels who entered from outside, and city officials and members of the urban patriciate who were in some way identified with the viceregal administration would be hounded down as 'traitors' to the Catalan fatherland. 'Long live the king! Death to traitors! Down with bad government!'[90]—these were the cries of the insurgents, the self-appointed defenders of the king's justice against the tyranny of his ministers.

Of all the ministers in the principality, Santa Coloma, as viceroy,

[88] Elliott, *Catalans*, p. 535.
[89] *Ibid.*, p. 441.
[90] *Ibid.*, p. 429.

was the one with most reason to fear for his life. As a native Catalan he was the arch-traitor, the man who had persistently played the Count-Duke's game. With no troops in Barcelona to guard him, he was dependent for his protection on the goodwill of the *diputats* and the municipal authorities, and there was no certainty of their willingness or ability to save him in an emergency. His letters to Madrid made it clear that he had lost both his authority and his nerve, and on 11 June the Junta de Ejecución decided to replace him by the man whom he had succeeded as viceroy two years previously, the Duke of Cardona. But events had already overtaken ministerial decisions. On 7 June, Corpus Christi day, armed rebels made their way into Barcelona along with the rural labourers, the *segadors*, who traditionally at this season came to the city to hire themselves out for harvesting. Once inside the city walls the insurgents turned their attention to the 'traitors', marching on the viceregal palace, which they just failed to set ablaze, and then venting their fury on the persons and houses of viceregal officials and judges of the *audiencia*. The wretched Santa Coloma himself, after failing to make his escape by sea, was caught and struck down by the rebels on the rocky shore.

The Count-Duke reacted with stunned disbelief to the news of the viceroy's murder. 'With the Casale affair, and now with Catalonia', he wrote to the Cardinal-Infante, he was surprised that he had not dropped dead. 'The troubles of Catalonia have reached an extreme, and I confess to Your Highness that, like family troubles, they are driving me out of my mind.'[91] It was as if he had been hit by an arquebus shot, he told the Catalan envoys at court. He was so out of his mind that he did not know whether he was sleeping or eating. To the representatives of the city of Barcelona, who brought with them a letter in self-defence, he cried three times 'Go away!' and refused to take the letter.[92] There may have been a deliberate element of theatre in his behaviour, but the news came as a shattering blow to a minister who knew that the fate of the Monarchy was now balanced on a knife-edge.

Others, however, reacted with less distress to the news from Catalonia. The Count-Duke's enemies at court could regard with a degree of equanimity a provincial revolt that seemed likely to hasten the demise of a detested regime. It was significant that four nobles, including two anti-Olivares grandees, the Dukes of Híjar and Sessa, greeted the ambassadors of the *Diputació* as they emerged from their audience with the Count-Duke and took them aside to give them some friendly advice on the best way for the Catalans to conduct

[91] MSB, Cod. hisp. 22, fos. 123–123v., Olivares to Cardinal-Infante, 14 June 1640.
[92] Elliott, *Catalans*, p. 452.

themselves in this dangerous juncture.[93] Among the Count-Duke's supporters, too, there may well have been a certain perverse satisfaction at the way in which events were developing. To those who resented the survival of provincial liberties, the viceroy's murder appeared to provide a convenient pretext for their abolition. The Marquis of Velada, for instance, writing privately from London, hoped that 'the mishap can be turned to account for our future security, with His Majesty ruling in that principality as he does in Castile.'[94]

But for the time being at least there was to be no deviation from the policy decisions taken in Madrid after reports had reached it of the viceroy's death. It was hoped that the personal authority of the new viceroy, Cardona, would be sufficient to restore order, with the assistance of the *Diputació* and the Catalan oligarchy. In any event the disarray of the *tercios* now sheltering in the ports left no alternative to this policy of playing for time and hoping that the problem would resolve itself. But this hope depended to a large extent on the correctness of the Count-Duke's diagnosis that this was a 'general rebellion without a leader and without any foreign intent, provoked solely by irritation with the soldiers, who, being leaderless, have given no little occasion for it.'[95]

This diagnosis, however, took no account of the intense hatred felt in the principality for the government in Madrid and for the Castilian connection. It ignored, too, the determination of at least a handful of prominent Catalans to press on towards open defiance of the crown if they failed to secure the redress for past wrongs and the guarantees for future security that they considered indispensable for Catalonia's survival. The *Diputació* under the leadership of Pau Claris had now built up a formidable dossier of infringements of the Catalan constitutions by ministers of the crown—a dossier which would justify the renunciation of the contractual relationship between Catalonia and Philip IV as its prince if the occasion should demand it. It is probable that Claris himself still shrank from so dangerous and drastic a step in June and July of 1640, but it seems likely that he had already tentatively moved to reinsure himself by sounding out the French about the possibilities of help if Barcelona should be driven to a formal break with Madrid.[96]

It was unfortunate for the Count-Duke that Cardona, at the time of his reappointment as viceroy, was already a dying man. In the few weeks that remained to him he did what he could to restore a semblance of order, but the task was beyond him. As long as the

[93] *Ibid.*, p. 453.
[94] AGR SEG, Reg. 378, fo. 66v., Velada to Don Miguel de Salamanca, 13 July 1640.
[95] MSB, Cod. hisp. 22, fo. 125v., Olivares to Cardinal-Infante, 24 June 1640.
[96] See Elliott, *Catalans*, pp. 469–72, and Sanabre, *La acción de Francia*, pp. 91–4.

members of the *audiencia* remained in hiding, it was impossible to reconstitute even a skeleton viceregal administration. During those summer months there was a power vacuum in the principality—the viceroyalty impotent, and the principality's natural ruling class held back either by fear or indecision. For the insurrection in the country-side, having begun as a movement of armed resistance against the depredations of an undisciplined soldiery, was now assuming the characteristics of a general movement of popular protest in town and country against the rich and well-connected who dominated the principality's public life. A 'Christian army' had sprung into exis-tence, whose commander threatened fire and slaughter to all 'trai-tors'.[97] Cardona failed to rally sufficient support to check the progress of this 'army', and in one of his last letters to Madrid before his death on 22 July complained bitterly of the uncooperative behaviour of the *diputats* and the city of Barcelona.[98]

As he watched the situation in Catalonia deteriorate day by day, Olivares had no doubt that a remedy must promptly be applied while there was still a chance to put matters right.[99] But to identify the correct remedy was no easy matter. 'Our ruler, wavering, and almost swamped by the weight of affairs', wrote Novoa, 'went around ask-ing how he could pacify Catalonia.'[100] The Duke of Sessa, no doubt acting as the mouthpiece of the Catalans, offered a suggestion. The king should go to the principality almost unaccompanied, in order to demonstrate his confidence in his Catalan subjects.[101] Sessa took as his example Charles V's reaction to the troubles in Flanders, but if he was thinking of 1540 he overlooked the inconvenient fact that the Emperor had entered the rebellious city of Ghent with an army behind him. This would have made the analogy more attractive to Olivares and his colleagues, for whom it was unthinkable that the king's personal safety should be jeopardized by sending him unpro-tected into a rebellious province.

In view of Cardona's failure it was difficult to see how the king's authority could now be restored in the principality without a show of force. Amidst great secrecy some military preparations were already under way when reports reached Madrid of a popular uprising on 21 July in Tortosa. Since Corpus day, Tortosa had replaced Barce-lona as the port from which troops and supplies were sent to Italy and to the remnants of the royal army in the Catalan border territory of Roussillon. The expulsion of the troops from Tortosa gave Olivares

[97] Elliott, *Catalans*, pp. 460–5.
[98] *Ibid.*, p. 467.
[99] MSB, Cod. hisp. 22, fo. 127, Olivares to Cardinal-Infante, 18 July 1640.
[100] Novoa, *Codoin* 80, p. 225.
[101] Pellicer, *Avisos*, 31, pp. 193–4 (31 July 1640).

a pretext for a decision which he had already in all probability taken in principle—to exchange conciliation for force. On 27 July he addressed the Junta de Ejecución on the need for a reappraisal of the government's Catalan policies in view of the extreme gravity of the new situation created by the loss to the crown of the port facilities offered by Tortosa.[102] At another meeting four days later the Count-Duke argued that the policy of conciliation had failed. The junta agreed with him that there was now no alternative to armed action, for unless the disorders were checked in Catalonia, a terrible example would have been set to the other kingdoms of the Monarchy. Without the complication of the war with France this would be an easy matter. As it was, a massive show of strength would be needed, and everything must be finished before the onset of winter. The plan devised by Olivares and his colleagues was for the king to convoke meetings of the Cortes of Aragon and Valencia, and announce a royal visit which was to include Catalonia once the province was pacified. The royal army would enter Catalonia with the declared aim of liberating the government, the clergy and the nobility from popular oppression. Once its work was completed the king would hold a new session of the Catalan Cortes, in which the necessary changes to the laws could be made.[103]

The Count-Duke's plans earned him the plaudits of his colleagues at a joint meeting of the Junta de Ejecución and councillors of state held the same day. All eleven of them accepted the necessity for force, and they fell over themselves to heap praise on the favourite, whose proposals, if José González is to be trusted, were inspired by the Holy Spirit.[104] The Count-Duke himself seems to have been less persuaded of the source of his inspiration than some of his colleagues. Even if he gave the impression that the despatch of an army to Tortosa would soon restore Catalonia to a proper respect for the royal authority, he was perfectly well aware of the additional strains that the operation would impose on Spain's over-extended forces. 'If only peace had been concluded', he had said in his letter of 18 July to the Cardinal-Infante, 'that is all I want.' But reports about the outcome of his latest peace initiatives were deeply discouraging. Richelieu had made it clear during the spring that the three-man peace mission to Paris headed by Joseph de Bergaigne would not be welcome.[105] Olivares responded by instructing Jacques de Brecht, secretary of the Council of Flanders, and one of the three designated members of the Bergaigne mission, to make the journey to France

[102] AGS GA, leg. 1329, consulta, 27 July 1640.
[103] AGS GA, leg. 1329, consulta, 31 July 1640.
[104] AGS GA, leg. 1339, consulta of Junta de Ejecución y Consejeros de Estado, 31 July 1640.
[105] Leman, *Richelieu et Olivarès*, pp. 133–5.

alone. He had few illusions. It was, he said in June, a question of negotiating '*in spe, contra spem.*'[106]

Brecht's first audience with the Cardinal, to whom he brought two letters from Olivares, was held on 13 June. In it he put forward Spain's conditions for peace: the restoration of Lorraine to its duke, and of Alsace and Breisach to the Emperor, the Dutch evacuation of Brazil in return for compensation, the dissolution of the Dutch East India Company, and the restoration of Maastricht and one of the Rhine crossings. The Cardinal rejected these demands as totally unacceptable and as designed merely to sow discord between France and her allies.[107] After a second and equally abortive audience on the following day, Brecht left for Spain, and gave the Count-Duke a personal account of his failed mission at an audience on 1 August.

Brecht's report produced gloom in the Council of State. The French, decided the councillors, had no interest in peace, and there was nothing for it now but to hope for a successful end to the campaigning season, and prepare for the coming year.[108] It was, therefore, under the depressing shadow of what now looked like becoming an interminable war, that the plans for a military operation against the Catalans were drawn up during the first week of August. The improbability of a general peace settlement made it essential to despatch the Catalan business as quickly as possible, but at the same time added enormously to the risks. There was confidence that the pacification of Catalonia could be accomplished with relative ease. But how permanently effective could it be, with a hostile power on the frontier, always ready to meddle? And how many troops would it tie down—troops that were badly needed for the main theatres of war?

Yet the risks of inaction seemed, if anything, greater still. At the beginning of August Don Francisco de Melo, viceroy of Sicily, reported in cypher on the 'evil humours and intentions' abroad in his island in the aftermath of the news from Barcelona.[109] Vizcaya, always a sensitive barometer, turned down the king's request for soldiers, and rumours were circulating in Madrid that it was on the verge of a new insurrection.[110] When a peasant accosted Philip IV as he was taking part in a procession accompanying the sacrament through the streets of Madrid in June, and told him that he was being deceived and that his Monarchy was nearing its end, the imper-

[106] AGS Est. K. 1419, fo. 165, Olivares to king, 14 June 1640. See also Leman, p. 151.
[107] Leman, pp. 142–3.
[108] *Ibid.*, pp. 152–3.
[109] AGS Est. leg. 3483, fo. 242, Melo to king, 1 August 1640.
[110] *MHE*, 15, p. 470 (25 August 1640).

turbable king had remarked: 'This man must be mad.'[111] But perhaps he was not so mad after all.

The Count-Duke knew that a spectacular reassertion of royal authority was required if he were to have any hope of halting the accelerating slide into the abyss. He therefore threw himself into the task of building up a massive army to march into Catalonia—an army that was to consist of 35,000 infantry and 2,000 cavalry[112]—an army so large for a mere punitive expedition that it surely could not fail. It was to start its operations on 1 October, and its commander was to be a noble who had just been selected for the post of *mayordomo mayor* of the Cardinal-Infante,[113] the Marquis of Los Vélez. The marquis, as the grandson of Requesens, Philip II's governor in the Netherlands, came from a family that was Catalan by origin. His experience, as a former viceroy of Valencia, Aragon and Navarre, was entirely political, but he would have experienced commanders to advise him, and the Count-Duke presumably reckoned that the pacification of Catalonia was more likely to need political than military gifts.[114]

The hand of God?

Outlining his plans to his colleagues on 11 August, Olivares gave them a solemn warning that if the punitive action in Catalonia, which they had unanimously approved, should in any way go wrong, it was 'very possible that all the kingdoms of Spain will either be (if I dare say this) absolutely lost or in such terrible danger, misery and tribulation that only a miracle would be capable of saving them, and our affairs abroad in such a terrible state that we should have to abandon all our allies in order to make peace, however infamous this might be.' He used this occasion to emphasize that there was no intention of abolishing Catalonia's constitutional system, but only of repealing those laws which prevented the principality from being treated on a basis of uniformity with the other territories of the Monarchy, and impeded the billeting of an army under satisfactory conditions. Even now, indeed, he was willing to pull back if only the Catalans would agree to a reasonable system of billeting.[115]

---

[111] *MHE*, 15, pp. 451–2 (19 June 1640).

[112] AGS GA, leg. 1329, *Relación de lo que SM tiene resuelto para castigo de lo sucedido en Tortosa y acudir al sosiego de las alteraciones de Cataluña.*

[113] AGR CPE, Reg. 1504, fo. 188v., Carnero to Roose, 18 May 1640.

[114] Francisco Manuel de Melo, *Historia de los movimientos, separación y guerra de Cataluña en tiempo de Felipe IV* (ed. Madrid, 1912), pp. 109–110.

[115] AGS GA, leg. 1329, paper by Olivares, 11 August 1640; Elliott, *Catalans*, pp. 497–8.

In principle the military operation seemed simple enough. The experts told the Count-Duke that it would take no more than fifteen days, and that, in the short time available, there was no chance of the French being in a position to mount an effective campaign in support of the Catalans. But the fact that Olivares twice took the opportunity in the course of his discussion to remind his colleagues of the unpredictability of all things human suggests a deep uncertainty about the action he was now proposing. His confidence was badly shaken, and with good reason, for it seemed that every fresh despatch brought further bad news.

Within a few days of the formal approval of the plans for the pacification of Catalonia, a letter of 7 August was received from the Cardinal-Infante to the effect that the army of Flanders had not succeeded in relieving the town of Arras, to which the French had laid siege. At the time of writing its fall appeared imminent, and the garrison surrendered two days later. This was devastating news, and all the more so for being quite unexpected. It was difficult to understand how the relief expedition could have failed. 'Some men are naturally unfortunate', the Count-Duke observed of Andrea Cantelmo, the commander of the relieving force,[116] but he might equally well have been speaking of himself. It was certainly one of the things said about him, even by his friends.[117] Cantelmo was the man who had lost Schenkenschans in 1636, and now he looked to be on the way to losing all Flanders.

What, then, was to be done? The Count-Duke's confessor, Father Aguado, was just at this moment in process of publishing a bulky volume of Exhortations, dedicated to the Countess of Olivares, Doña Inés. Exhortation XXX was concerned with times of war, and dwelt on the need to ensure divine help by means of constant prayer and supplication, 'persuading ourselves that prayer is a valiant arm for overcoming our enemies, and no less powerful than the sword and the lance.'[118] The Count-Duke had no need of the reminder. He was constantly making the point in his speeches and state papers, and never more vigorously than during this terrible season of military reverses. Yet sometimes God seemed to work in mysterious ways. The first priority, Olivares told his colleagues as they discussed the fall of Arras, was to 'give thanks continually to God for punishing us, if He wishes to punish us, because His divine will is done; and beseech Him to direct things in accordance with His service and offer us His protection and favour, for our cause is His.' The fall of Arras, coming on top of the earlier disasters of the year, was

---

[116] AGS Est. leg. 2055, consulta, 22 August 1640.
[117] See Elliott, *Richelieu and Olivares*, pp. 154–5.
[118] *Exhortaciones varias*, p. 431.

bringing him face to face with the fact of failure, and with the need to find an explanation for the apparently inexplicable. What did it mean to be 'naturally unfortunate' within the context of a Christian design? Theologically it was an awkward question, but the doctrine of divine punishment seemed to offer the glimmerings of an answer.

If Arras had indeed fallen, as Olivares hoped to God that it had not, then the cause of universal peace was hopelessly set back. Yet paradoxically—or so he believed—it might be thought to have enhanced the chances of achieving a separate peace settlement with the Dutch, if only because it would bring home to them that the French were becoming too powerful for their comfort. The moment, then, seemed opportune for seeking a 'reasonable truce' with the United Provinces. But there remained the overwhelming obstacle of the Dutch occupation of Brazil. It was characteristic of the Count-Duke that, even as he recommended the renewal of truce negotiations with the Dutch in the utmost secrecy, he should also recommend the equipping, in no less secrecy, of a new Brazilian armada of thirty-six ships. It was the old device of attempting to secure better peace terms by combining the negotiations with a fresh application of military or naval power. On paper it appeared reasonable enough, but the Cardinal-Infante, when informed of the plan, declared it to be 'in no way practicable.'[119]

Temperamentally, the Count-Duke seems to have found it hard to take clean, sharp decisions, without accompanying them with qualifying formulas and subsidiary proposals which either weakened or subverted the line of action he proposed to pursue. This had happened time and time again in his handling of relations with the Dutch. Hoping to get a better deal, he would throw away such chances as existed of securing any deal at all. Paradoxically, this unwillingness, or inability, to take a drastic risk may have involved him in greater risks than a bold decision, since all too often the price of procrastination proved high. It may well be that the Mantuan War—when he had indeed taken a risk, with most unfortunate consequences—had reinforced an instinctive caution which on that occasion failed him. As it was, he betrayed a persistent tendency to hold back, whether in his negotiations with the Dutch or his dealings with the Catalans, until, instead of choosing his policies, the policies chose him.

His fellow-councillors—Monterrey, Oñate, Santa Cruz, Mirabel, Villahermosa and Borja—all approved his proposition for new truce negotiations with the Dutch. So, too, did the king, who was now so thoroughly transformed into a royal bureaucrat that he would return the *consultas* with lengthy personal comments, like another

---

[119] AGS Est. leg. 3860, Cardinal-Infante to king, 11 December 1640.

Philip II. His comments, however, testified more to his conscientiousness than his perspicacity. He would reinforce the majority decision with dire warnings or imperious commands, but gave no sign of having an independent point of view. As always, it is impossible to know whether his orders on the *consultas* were made after consultation with Olivares, or without reference to him. The probability is that, after nearly twenty years of close collaboration with his principal minister, he had come to see the world from the same angle of vision. Long after Olivares had disappeared from the scene, Philip responded to situations as if the Count-Duke were still standing at his side.

Of all the councillors of state, the Count of Oñate was the only one to display a certain independence. The others were hacks or time-servers, who still fell over themselves to applaud the favourite to the skies, whatever doubts they may have secretly entertained. Oñate, with over fifty years in the service of the king, and with his long experience as ambassador in Germany, was prepared on occasions to speak his own mind. It was he, for instance, who disputed the wisdom of the Count-Duke's plan in 1638 to launch an invasion of France from Catalonia.[120] Contemporaries believed that he was opposed to the Count-Duke's proposal for military action against the Catalans; and Francisco Manuel de Melo, in his history of the revolt of Catalonia, puts into his mouth an eloquent plea for conciliation instead of recourse to arms.[121] The *consultas* of July and August, however, give no indication that Oñate objected to Olivares' policies; or, if he did, he failed to voice them in the council room, although it would not have been out of character if he had done so outside it. In spite of his advanced age, he still cherished political ambitions, and was manoeuvring with caution. The Count-Duke, who had made a careful study of his colleagues' characters, knew all this and took the necessary precautions. For many years Oñate had let it be known that he expected a grandeeship for his services. Long deferred, it came at last on 6 January 1640, when his name appeared on a list of ten new creations.[122] But even now there was a sting in the tail: the grandeeship was personal and not hereditary. It was a characteristic device for ensuring that he still remained dependent on the favour of the favourite.

In the grave circumstances created by the fall of Arras, the Count-Duke felt it expedient to invite Oñate to prepare a memorandum for the Council of State on the current situation and future prospects.

---

[120] Above, p. 538.
[121] Melo, *Guerra de Cataluña*, pp. 88–94.
[122] Pellicer, *Avisos*, 31, p. 120. For earlier efforts to secure the grandeeship, see AGS Est. leg. 2335, consultas of 24 September and 2 December 1634.

This paper, which was discussed on 24 August, was written with an elegance and lucidity that contrasted sharply with the prolix memorandum produced by the Count-Duke himself for the same occasion.[123] Oñate argued that Spain now lacked the resources to continue sending vast sums of money to Germany and Flanders, and that this made it essential to work for a general peace settlement. Failing this, one or two of the three wars in which the House of Austria was currently engaged must be terminated. The Emperor and Empire were at war with Sweden and France; Spain was at war with the Dutch Republic and France; and it was effectively, if not formally, at war with the Swedes, in the sense that a significant proportion of its resources was going to the Emperor to enable him to fight them. The Emperor's position, according to Oñate, had improved in recent years, and the whole Empire was weary of the war. He therefore proposed that Francisco de Melo (who held his post as viceroy of Sicily concurrently with the office of plenipotentiary to a general peace conference, if one should be assembled[124]) should immediately leave for Germany with Joseph de Bergaigne to attempt to negotiate a settlement between the Emperor and the Swedes. Once this had been achieved, Oñate thought that it would not be too difficult to persuade Ferdinand III to unleash all his forces against the French.

Oñate also proposed that the Cardinal-Infante should simultaneously begin negotiations for a truce with the Dutch. If this could be obtained in addition to a settlement between the Emperor and the Swedes, Richelieu would have to reduce his demands. If, on the other hand, an Imperial-Swedish settlement could not be reached, Oñate saw no alternative to a settlement with France. To reach this he would be prepared to sacrifice the Duke of Lorraine, who would be compensated for the loss of his duchy by being conceded the rights held by Philip IV in the Rhine Palatinate. The King of England was no longer in a position to contest this transfer.

Oñate's *tour d'horizon* covered ten pages. The Count-Duke's covered eighteen, without adding anything of great substance to what Oñate had said. But it did reveal the darker patches of his mind—those tortuous wrestlings and gropings which were becoming more pronounced as the cares of office overwhelmed him. The state of the world, he announced to his colleagues, was highly troubled and dangerous, for God had allowed four great misfortunes to occur, in places where in ordinary circumstances one might reasonably have expected success. Casale should have been captured; Turin, where

---

[123] AGS Est. leg. 2055, consulta, 24 August 1640, containing papers by both ministers.
[124] *MHE*, 15, p. 103 (17 November 1638).

Prince Thomas of Savoy was under siege, should have been relieved; Arras should have been saved; and the Catalans should never have resorted to a 'general rebellion' simply because the billeting arrangements for the army that had saved them from the French deviated here or there from the letter of their laws. How else could all this be explained but by the hand of God?

The king—the Count-Duke declared—was ready to lay down his life and lands to save the Faith at a time when heresy, with French help, was riding high throughout Europe, except in England, where God was making it confound itself. But in all this he glimpsed some cause for hope. 'Either the true Faith will fall, or the Divine Majesty, having punished us (as He most justly has), will turn again towards us in superabundance, and will rescue us from the travails and tribulations in which we find ourselves, for otherwise His Faith and His Law will collapse through lack of support, and heresy will dominate all Europe.' The Count-Duke therefore trusted that God would not fail to send help, and that, if necessary, He would perform miracles— and many of them—to repair such fearful losses. 'If His Divine Majesty', he continued, 'should work in our favour, then there will be little need for counsel. But if for His just reasons He should choose to delay His help, then we as ministers ... must work to restore things, and pay with our lives.'

How did the Count-Duke's colleagues react to this lengthy theological prelude to the business of the day? By now they must have been inured to the discursive reflections that prefaced and punctuated the official pronouncements of an overwrought minister to whom they were held in bondage by a combination of dependence and fear. The vigour, however, remained—the stamina and resilience which never ceased to amaze. As soon as he turned to practical details he was in his element. The first priority, he told his colleagues, was the 'reduction of Catalonia' to obedience to the king, and the viceroy of Naples must be ordered to send troops for the forthcoming campaign. This would require twenty-eight to thirty galleys, to transport the six thousand infantrymen that would be needed from Milan. In the second place, Melo was to leave at once for Germany as Oñate proposed, accompanied by Bergaigne, who would be given a bishopric in Italy or Spain. The Cardinal-Infante should begin talks with the Dutch, as 'the first priority in those parts today.' He agreed that it was essential to wind up two wars, or at least one. Then he was off again, moving troops and ships around the globe, totting up their numbers port by port. The appetite for facts and figures was, as always, voracious—the Count-Duke was never happier than when assembling paper armies and fleets. The care that he devoted to the execution of his designs was, as Cardinal Borja observed in congratulating him, 'always equal to the wisdom with which he thinks and plans.'

Yet for all the thinking and planning, nothing was ever ready on time. So it was with the army of Los Vélez, who was due to move against Catalonia on 1 October. But everything was in short supply— money, soldiers, artillery—and it was not until late in the month that Los Vélez was able to order his troops to move towards the Catalan border. The Catalans, as was only to be expected, made the most of the delay. Secret negotiations with the French had long since got under way, and on 7 September a written understanding was reached between the agent of Pau Claris and the Duke of Espenan, acting on behalf of Louis XIII.[125] During the following weeks Claris manoeuvred skilfully to prepare the principality for war. In response to the royal proclamation announcing the convocation of a Cortes, the *diputats* summoned their own meeting of the Catalan estates. These opened, although with a relatively poor attendance, on 10 September. A special defence committee was established, and the question of an approach to the French for military assistance was judiciously broached. On 24 September the *diputats* felt ready to present the French plenipotentaries with a formal request that Louis XIII should help the principality defend itself in the war that 'the ministers of Spain' were threatening to wage against it.[126]

The optimism in Paris[127] contrasted strikingly with the gloom that now pervaded Madrid, where the Count-Duke was approaching with mounting anguish the prospect of war in Catalonia. 'This year', he wrote in mid-September, before he was yet aware of the Catalan capitulation with France, 'can undoubtedly be considered the most unfortunate that this Monarchy has ever experienced ... because never have such great preparations been made in all theatres of war, and yet the results have been far worse than could ever have been imagined ... And all this together must be regarded as far less disastrous than the rebellion and obduracy of Catalonia, for one cannot talk of success in an action against one's own vassals, in which all gain must be loss. We have been reduced to a new war inside Spain which is already costing millions, at a time when we already find ourselves in terrible straits.'[128]

The Count-Duke's publicity machine was now hard at work, preparing justifications for the entry of Los Vélez's army.[129] The Catalans

[125] Sanabre, *La acción de Francia*, p. 94.
[126] Elliott, *Catalans*, p. 504.
[127] Sanabre, *La acción de Francia*, pp. 94–5.
[128] AHN Est. leg. 674, *El conde mi señor sobre el estado en que han quedado las armas este año* ..., cited Elliott, *Catalans*, p. 504.
[129] Elliott, *Catalans*, p. 506. A copy of Alonso Guillén de la Carrera's manifesto in *MHE*, 16, pp. 7–14.

must be made to see the error of their ways. Obdurate as they were, he still seems to have clung to the hope that the conflict could be avoided; and he obviously had difficulty in believing the news that belatedly reached him on 10 October of the agreement signed between the *Diputació* and the French. The whole affair, he told the Cardinal-Infante, must be God's doing, for the Catalans 'without human reason or occasion have thrown themselves into as established a rebellion as that of the Dutch.'[130] But what could he do? The Catalans said that they were prepared to reach an accommodation, but only on terms which appeared totally unacceptable to Madrid. They would consider returning to obedience if the king came to the principality without an army, or appointed the Admiral of Castile or the Duke of Sessa—both of them enemies of Olivares—as viceroy. On no account would they let Olivares himself, or the Protonotario, set foot on Catalan soil.[131]

Aware that the Catalans' distrust of himself was a major obstacle to a settlement, the Count-Duke induced his son-in-law, Medina de las Torres, to renounce in his own favour the post of treasurer-general of the Crown of Aragon which he had held since 1628. This gave him the opportunity to take the customary oath to observe the constitutions—a gesture which he hoped would persuade them of his good intentions. But the view of the Catalans was that, even if he took a hundred thousand more oaths, his record of hostility to the principality made it impossible to trust him.[132] They spelled out this record in their pamphlet, the *Proclamación Católica*, which was circulating in Madrid before the end of October.[133] Its author, Gaspar Sala, had skilfully linked the grievances of Catalonia to those of the other parts of the Monarchy—'Portugal restive, Castile weeping, Aragon and Valencia groaning, Catalonia clamouring to heaven.'[134] He also singled out for special mention the nobles who, by popular repute, had been dishonoured or driven to the grave by the treatment they had received at the Count-Duke's hands: Alcalá, Aytona, Feria, Don Gonzalo de Córdoba, the Duke of Osuna, Don Fadrique de Toledo, the Duke of Alba, the Admiral of Castile, the Duke of Cardona.[135] It was an impressive, if not entirely reliable, list, well designed to win the sympathy and perhaps the active support of an aristocracy who hated Olivares as intensely as the Catalans themselves.

[130] MSB, Cod. hisp. 22, fo. 130v., Olivares to Cardinal-Infante, 10 October 1640.
[131] ASVen, Spagna, filza 75, despatch, 17 October 1640.
[132] ASVen, Spagna, filza 75, despatch, 24 October 1640.
[133] Pellicer, *Avisos*, 31, pp. 229–30.
[134] *Proclamación católica a la Magestad piadosa de Felipe el Grande*, (ed. Lisbon, 1641), pp. 149–50 (ch. 33).
[135] *Ibid.*, pp. 152–3 (ch. 34).

The theme of Gaspar Sala's tract was that the Count-Duke and the Protonotario had ruined the Monarchy by their disastrous innovations and their ill-conceived policies. Olivares instructed his librarian, Francisco de Rioja, to reply to this attack. His pamphlet, the *Aristarco*, contained a point by point rebuttal of the Catalan charges.[136] The Count-Duke's policies were justified, as they had been so often justified in ministerial circles over the past few years, by the conveniently flexible doctrine of necessity. When ruin threatened, Rioja argued, the king was entitled to disregard privileges without formal dispensation. Billeting the troops in Catalonia was a clear case of necessity because natural law demanded self-defence, and this law took precedence over all others, including those agreed by mutual compact.[137]

'It is not licit', said the *Aristarco*, 'that for the convenience or comfort of a few, the whole Monarchy should be lost.' Catalonia's behaviour threatened that concept of reciprocity which was central to the Count-Duke's vision of the Monarchy. To the Catalans, this vision was utterly unrealistic. They condemned 'imaginary and Platonic policies', directed not towards vassals of the crown as they really were, but to imaginary vassals, capriciously dreamt up by the all-powerful minister.[138] But for Olivares this was not a matter of how the Monarchy should be, but of how it must be in order to survive. He was never more insistent on the need for parity of reward and sacrifice among the kingdoms of the Monarchy than in this terrible year, 1640, as it started to crumble. When Medina de las Torres, writing from Naples, reminded him of his plan in the 1626 Cortes of the Crown of Aragon to employ non-Castilians in the royal household, he spoke again of the need to 'mix by means of marriages, household offices and governmental and judicial posts, the vassals of those kingdoms, who do not see their king.' The Inquisitor General referred ominously to the unhappiness likely to be felt by the Castilians if 'what God created first for them were taken from them and given to foreigners'; but in spite of die-hard Castilian objections orders were despatched in September to Sicily, Flanders, Milan and Naples, for two carefully selected grooms and two 'very small' pages to be sent from each of them to the court in Madrid.[139]

If a handful of very small pages was all that the Olivares regime could manage after twenty years of lip-service to the ideal of appointment to office without discrimination, it is not surprising that the Count-Duke's professions of a fair deal for all the kingdoms of the Monarchy should have been greeted outside Castile with a certain

[136] BL Eg. Ms. 403, fos. 1–78v., *Aristarco o censura de la proclamación católica*.
[137] *Ibid.*, fo. 48v.
[138] *Proclamación católica*, p. 147 (ch. 32).
[139] AGS Est. leg. 3263, fo. 100, consulta, 30 August 1640 (and subsequent royal orders).

scepticism. The exclusivism of the Castilians, the dead weight of tradition, the rules of court protocol, all militated against his hopes of creating an international service nobility for the Spanish crown. While he had always been anxious to strengthen the bonds of loyalty between the different kingdoms, he had consistently failed to provide the offices, the honours, and the visible symbols of royal favour which alone could persuade the provincial nobilities of his concern for their well-being.

The defection of Catalonia painfully illustrated the consequences of the crown's failure to bind the principality's ruling class to it with the silken bonds of patronage. In the nearly twenty years since Philip IV's accession Madrid had managed to alienate in turn every section of Catalan society, including the nobility. As a result, the viceregal administration found itself without friends when rebellion came. By the autumn of 1640 there was a growing possibility that the story would repeat itself in Portugal, where the government of the Duchess of Mantua was universally unpopular. Here, too, the crown had signally failed to win the allegiance of the nobility, as Olivares was uncomfortably aware. The nobles had remained ominously passive during the Évora disturbances; and the Duke of Braganza always had an excuse ready when offered some post or other outside Portugal in the royal service.

Was it blindness or desperation with led Olivares to commit at this moment another fateful blunder by summoning the Portuguese nobility to take service with the king on the Catalan campaign? In mid-October there were rumours in Madrid that the *fidalgos* were not only ignoring the summons to arms, but were threatening any of their number who showed signs of obeying.[140] But if any concern was felt in ministerial circles about the reliability of the Portuguese, it found no echo in conciliar debates. On the contrary, the Junta de Ejecución on 27 October vigorously reaffirmed the principle that it was the obligation of the Portuguese to help the king suppress the Catalan revolt. One minister after another—Cid and Arce, the Protonotario, José González and the Marquises of Balbases and Castrofuerte—insisted that the cause was common, and that it was incumbent on all the provinces of the Monarchy to assist their king.[141] Olivares himself endorsed to the hilt his colleagues' arguments. It was precisely the opposite view—that Portugal was only responsible for Portugal and Aragon for Aragon—which had reduced the Monarchy to its present state, 'when these kingdoms should all be giving each other reciprocal assistance.' The Portuguese, he said, must help against the Catalans if they in turn wanted the help of others

---

[140] Pellicer, *Avisos*, 31, pp. 227–8 (16 October 1640).
[141] AGS GA, leg. 1331, consulta of Junta de Ejecución, 27 October 1640.

to recover Brazil from the Dutch. And might not this be the moment to introduce into Portugal the hearth tax which had recently been decided on for Castile? No tax, after all, was more productive and less burdensome.

The suppression of the Catalan rebellion, then, was to become a test case for the ability of the King of Spain to secure the effective cooperation of the different kingdoms of his Monarchy. Bearing in mind their sensitivity to any hint of danger to their laws and privileges, it was a reckless gamble to count on their willingness to support the king in imposing his authority on one of their number. The cause of Catalonia was the cause of each of them, even if none dared proclaim this out loud. The Duke of Nochera, the Neapolitan viceroy of Aragon, made one last attempt to dissuade Madrid from its course of action. Well aware of the rumblings of discontent in his viceroyalty, he tried to emphasize both the risks and the futility of the enterprise. Defeat would endanger both Aragon and Navarre, while victory would be the ruin of Catalonia. He still believed that an accommodation was possible, and warned the king of the risk he was running in using force against the Catalans when the French were on the doorstep.[142]

By early November, however, Olivares was in no mood to change his mind. By now he was desperate for a major success. He had just heard that Prince Thomas of Savoy had surrendered Turin to the French. The loss of Turin seems to have hit the king and his ministers even harder than the loss of Arras two months earlier.[143] A victory was more than ever needed, and the victory most nearly in the king's grasp was in Catalonia. Los Vélez's army was finally ready, and morale in the principality was reported to be low. When messages arrived from the widowed Duchess of Cardona that the Catalans were still willing to negotiate, the Junta de Ejecución dismissed the idea, on the grounds that if the army did not proceed on its march, it was likely to disperse and the opportunity be lost. The Catalans were demanding that the army should not cross their border; that the king should issue a general pardon, to exclude only the viceroy's murderers; that certain ministers in the viceregal administration should be removed from office; and that no troops should be quartered in the principality. Although Olivares again on this occasion professed his willingness to reach an agreement, the junta was sceptical about the genuineness of the Catalan offer, and anyhow considered it improper that vassals should dictate conditions to their lord.[144]

---

[142] Nochera to king, 6 November 1640, cited Elliott, *Catalans*, p. 511.
[143] ASVen, Spagna, filza 75, despatch, 31 October 1640.
[144] AGS GA, leg. 1331, consulta of Junta de Ejecución, 5 November 1640.

The need to reassert the royal authority had become an act of faith; and in the circumstances of 1640 it understandably seemed to offer ministers the only way of escape from their troubles. It was only the unrelenting pressure from above that had made it possible for the Monarchy to undertake the unprecedented military effort of the 1630's, and they feared that any sign of weakening might at once set off a chain reaction. Men were very conscious at this moment, whether in Madrid, or Paris, or London, of living in more than usually troubled times. Francisco de Melo, on his way northwards to Germany, commented on the age in a letter to Olivares: 'Like malign fevers, sir, the epilepsy of republics and disobedience to princes runs through the world.' In Sweden, England, Spain, Sicily, Naples, Milan, everywhere it was the same. The Count-Duke, observing carefully the remedies adopted by his neighbours, must select the best of them to effect the cure.[145] This indeed was what Olivares believed himself to be doing. He had seen the fatal surrender of the King of England to his subjects, and had no mind to follow suit. Catalonia must not become another Scotland; and as Los Vélez entered Tortosa without trouble on 23 November and took the oath as viceroy, there seemed every chance that this could be avoided.

Yet if to show weakness was to court disaster, it could also be argued that the determination to press unremittingly ahead with the fiscal and military policies agreed by the ministers risked imposing an intolerable strain on the fabric of a Monarchy now stretched to its limits. Even Castile and Andalusia, apparently so pliable, might not be able to resist indefinitely. The double consignments of American silver (those of 1638 and 1639) brought by the 1639 fleets were inadequate to meet the enormous expenditures of 1640; and in 1640 itself no treasure fleet arrived. The silver shortage was therefore acute, and the Seville merchants, their reserves seized by the crown for payments in Italy and Flanders, were reported on the verge of bankruptcy in August 1640.[146] The mechanism of Spain's transatlantic trade was visibly disintegrating under the pressure of war and royal fiscalism, and the ministers were frantically searching for alternative sources of revenue which would tide them over until the next fleet reached Seville. Early in November the crown announced a graduated hearth tax (a *donativo general por fuegos*) ranging from half a *real* to eight *reales*, to be collected monthly from every household in Castile.[147]

The new tax ran into trouble at once. By the first week of December

---

[145] AGS Est. leg. 3005, Melo to Olivares, 26 October 1640.

[146] Chaunu, *Séville et l'Atlantique*, 5, p. 368.

[147] Pellicer, *Avisos*, 31, p. 237 (6 November 1640); Domínguez Ortiz, *Política y hacienda*, p. 305.

reports were reaching Madrid of violent resistance to its collection, and in Tarifa, in the province of Cadiz, the population murdered the commissary who had been sent to collect it, and crossed *en masse* to North Africa, where they seized a Moorish fort and barricaded themselves against attack.[148] But there was worse to come. Suspicions were first aroused that all was not well in Lisbon when the regular mail failed to arrive, any more than the Portuguese sole traditionally sent for the royal table to celebrate the feast of the Immaculate Conception.[149] The news reached Madrid on 7 December—news of 'the greatest disaster that could befall this crown . . . The majority of the nobles have risen; the Princess Margaret has been put in a convent, and they have tumultuously turned to the Duke of Braganza, offering him possession of the kingdom . . . The motive was the express order sent by His Majesty to impose a hearth tax like the one they are now trying to raise in Castile.'[150]

The news of the Portuguese *coup d'état* of 1 December 1640—the murder of Vasconcelos, the proclamation of the Duke of Braganza as John IV of Portugal—seems to have been received with utter incredulity in Madrid. Jacques de Brecht, secretary to the Council of Flanders, who maintained a private correspondence with Pierre Roose, observed that it had caused 'great perturbation', and that it was totally incomprehensible unless Braganza had received assurances of foreign help.[151] The Venetian ambassador said that it had descended like a thunderbolt from the heavens, for how could a whole kingdom revolt without warning?[152] According to one account, the Count-Duke assumed a jaunty expression and went up to the king to tell him that he brought good news—he would now be absolute master of Portugal, since the Duke of Braganza had gone out of his mind, proclaimed himself king, and therefore automatically forfeited all his estates. Philip, it seems, was not taken in.[153]

The story has the ring of truth. Three months later, when more information was available about what had happened in Lisbon, the Count-Duke still seems to have found it impossible to believe. In an extraordinary letter to Malvezzi he described the Portuguese revolution as the work of five men: the Duke of Braganza, 'stupid and drunk, without a glimmer of intelligence'; the Marquis of Ferreira, so stupid that he would be incapable of finding Valladolid, and even

[148] PRO SP. 94.42, Hopton to Lord Treasurer, 28 November/8 December 1640.
[149] Novoa, *Codoin* 80, p. 392.
[150] ASVen, Spagna, filza 75, despatch, 8 December 1640.
[151] AGR CPE, Reg. 1506, fo. 195, Brecht to Roose, 16 December 1640.
[152] ASVen, Spagna, filza 75, despatch, 12 December 1640.
[153] Vittorio Siri, as reproduced in Guillaume de Valdory, *Anecdotes du ministère du comte duc d'Olivarés, tirées et traduites de l'Italien de Mercurio Siry, par Monsieur de Valdory* (Paris, 1722), pp. 364–5.

of learning how to do so; the Count of Vimioso, 'a chicken'; Don Antonio Vaz de Almada, whom the Count-Duke did not know, but who was reported to be totally ignorant; and the archbishop of Lisbon, a traitor and the son of a traitor, a virtuous cleric, a poor theologian, an ambitious man. Could these five really have challenged the might and majesty of the King of Spain?[154]

The Count-Duke's pathetic comments, at once jocular and bemused, suggest the extraordinary remoteness of the ministers in Madrid from the realities of the Monarchy they ruled. How was it possible that the Portuguese—discontented, perhaps, but famed for their loyalty—could have gone so far as to cast off their allegiance to their rightful king? The whole affair seemed so utterly incomprehensible that the immediate reaction in Madrid was to explain it in terms of a foreign plot. The principal instigator was believed to be Don Duarte, Braganza's brother, who had been serving in the army in Flanders and Germany; and the king sent secret instructions on 15 December to Don Juan Chumacero, Spain's ambassador extraordinary in Rome, to the effect that whoever killed Don Duarte, or took him alive, would receive a fitting reward.[155] On 17 December the Count-Duke summoned the eighty or so Portuguese nobles and prelates at court and vigorously denounced the abominable treachery of the Duke of Braganza and his wife, Doña Luisa de Guzmán, whose behaviour had so blemished the blood of the house of Guzmán that he had written to her brother, the Duke of Medina Sidonia, to order that her name should be expunged from the family records.[156]

The Count-Duke was clearly under terrible strain, not least because he was universally held responsible for the succession of disasters. The Venetian ambassador reported that he was the target of savage criticism, and that the Admiral of Castile was alleged to be thinking of calling together all the grandees to form a mass deputation to the king to request that he remove the Count-Duke from his side. A few days later the Admiral—always a thorn in the Count-Duke's flesh—was appointed viceroy of Sicily and ordered to leave for his new post at once.[157] Besides these stirrings in the ranks of the aristocracy, which hitherto had shown itself so politically ineffectual, there was also the most intense popular hostility to Olivares. Indeed, if the ambassador is to be believed, he was afraid to emerge from the palace for fear of assassination.[158] Not surprisingly, he showed signs of losing control of himself. At a meeting of the Junta de Ejecución

[154] MC, 2, Doc. XVI, p. 203.
[155] BNM, Ms. 10984, fo. 28, king to Chumacero, 15 December 1640.
[156] MHE, 16, pp. 100–101 (27 December 1640).
[157] MHE, 16, p. 95 (18 December 1640).
[158] ASVen, Spagna, filza 75, despatch, 12 December 1640.

summoned soon after the arrival of the news from Portugal, he spoke of the rebellion as an unprecedented act of treachery, carried out in extraordinary secrecy—the very reverse of what happened in Madrid, where everything, whether important or trivial, immediately became common property. Was it surprising, then, that ministers when they addressed the councils did not say what they thought, knowing that secrets would not be kept? He, for his part, always said what he thought. His hands were clean, his disinterest notorious. Why should he be blamed for everything that went wrong? It was not he who was responsible for the wars. Indeed, he loved peace so dearly that he would throw himself at the feet of anyone who could achieve it. But in his position he had to implement agreed policies, and if people took the trouble to read the relevant papers, they would see that he had never once voted in favour of war—neither the unfortunate Mantuan War, where there were twelve votes in favour and only his against, nor the war with France, where his record was plain to all.[159]

It was a rambling, hysterical, and dishonest defence, which his colleagues can hardly have found persuasive. But there was no indication that Philip was prepared to relinquish his minister, and the Count-Duke was still a formidable figure, even in defeat. The wounded stag had been brought to bay—or so at least his enemies must have thought in those December days of 1640. But this would not be the first time that they underestimated the stamina, the resilience, and the sheer indispensability of the man who had dominated their world for so long, and whom they now thought that they had it in their power to destroy.

---

[159] AGS GA, leg. 1331, consulta of Junta de Ejecución, 23 December 1640. Although the consulta is dated 23 December, the enclosed secret *voto* by Cardinal Borja, which refers to the Count-Duke's exhortation on secrecy as having been made 'this morning', bears the date of 13 December. The consulta itself speaks of eighteen days having passed since the revolt on 1 December. Since secret *votos* were requested from those who wished to produce them, and these bear various dates, I am inclined to think that the process of drafting the consulta went on for several days, and was not completed until 23 December.

XV

FOUNDERING

A question of survival

'In many centuries there cannot have been a more unlucky year than the present one . . . I propose peace, and more peace, and it is my understanding that powers to this effect have been sent to all parts . . . We must certainly beg God to give us a general peace, which, even if it is not good, or even average, would be better than the most advantageous war.' The Count-Duke wrote these words in mid-November 1640, shortly before the Lisbon *coup*. They were prompted by his concern over the crippling shortage of military leaders (*cabezas*), and by the 'the embarrassments of Catalonia, which have been the ruin of all our affairs.'[1]

The Portuguese revolt served only to underline the urgency of this passionate plea for peace. But it was easier to want peace than to obtain it. Since 1637 the Baron de Pujols had been intermittently acting as an intermediary in the negotiations between the courts of Madrid and Paris.[2] Fluent speakers of French were in short supply in Madrid—the Count-Duke's secretary, Antonio Carnero, who was half Flemish, was almost the only qualified Spaniard, and for obvious reasons could not be spared[3]—and Pujols had won Olivares' confidence sufficiently to be used as a go-between. After some hesitation, however, it was decided that a mission by Pujols to France would be premature, and instead he remained in Madrid to serve as a channel of communication between the Count-Duke and the Cardinal. In mid-November new peace proposals were transmitted to Paris through his agency. But, as Olivares' interest in an immediate peace settlement grew stronger, so Richelieu's declined, and the response sent by the French at the end of December proved deeply discouraging. Thereafter Pujols waited in vain for further communications from Paris.[4]

---

[1] AGS Est. leg. 2055, consulta, 17 December 1640. See also Leman, *Richelieu et Olivarès*, pp. 157–8.
[2] Above, p. 523.
[3] AGS Est. K. 1419, fo. 101, consulta, 22 August 1639.
[4] Leman, pp. 155–9.

With the prospect of a general peace settlement apparently remote, the ministers in Madrid were busily engaged in the last days of December 1640 and the first weeks of the new year in assessing the damage in the wake of the Portuguese revolt. A separate peace, or alternatively a truce, with the United Provinces headed their list of possible options. The Cardinal-Infante was already under orders to work for a settlement, and before the arrival of the news from Portugal the auguries looked good for a new initiative. The Stadholder Frederick Henry was increasingly at odds with the city of Amsterdam, which wanted to cut costs by reverting to a purely defensive war now that Spain had been weakened by the Catalan revolt.[5] In Madrid, the Council of State approved on 16 January 1641 a truce proposal under which both parties would retain any areas they had occupied in Europe and the Indies. By effectively partitioning Brazil with the Dutch, Spain would be formally accepting, for the first time ever, the presence of foreigners on American soil.[6]

Previous experience suggested that truce negotiations with the United Provinces were a slow and tortuous business, since the Stadholder and individual provinces tended to pull in different directions. The immediate effect of the Portuguese revolt was to strengthen Frederick Henry's hand and lend credibility to his arguments that with Spain so close to collapse this was no time to seek peace.[7] Sir Arthur Hopton, commenting from Madrid in the autumn of 1640 on the latest events in Catalonia, wrote with concern of their impact on 'the state of Christendom, which begins already to be unequally balanced.'[8] Failing a quick settlement with the Dutch, it was not easy to see how the balance could be redressed. The first task was somehow to extinguish the two rebellions before they had time to take hold. There was otherwise little prospect of mounting a major offensive against the French or the Dutch. The temptation in such circumstances was for Madrid to bank its hopes—too many of them—on a great domestic upheaval in France, and on the conspiracy that La Valette and Soubise were organizing from London.

Faced with the challenge of ending not one revolt but two, the regime had difficult decisions to take. At the present rate of progress, Barcelona would soon be in range of Los Vélez's army. In spite of this, a majority among the ministers, voting in secret between 13 and 16 December, favoured an immediate negotiated settlement with the Catalans.[9] Morale in the principality was collapsing as the

[5] Israel, *The Dutch Republic*, pp. 262–3.
[6] *Ibid.*, p. 314.
[7] *Ibid.*, p. 263.
[8] PRO SP. 94.41, fo. 51, Hopton to Vane, 22 September/2 October 1640.
[9] AGS GA leg. 1331, drafts of *votos*, and Elliott, *Catalans*, pp. 518–19.

royal army continued its northwards advance, and soundings taken by the widowed Duchess of Cardona suggested that some sort of accommodation between the king and the Catalans ought not to be impossible. This was the opinion, among others, of the Count of Castrillo whose consciousness of his own rectitude kept pace with his growing ministerial experience:

> Our misadventure in Portugal [he wrote] absolutely compels us to reach an immediate accommodation with the Catalans, without awaiting the outcome of the progress of our arms ... Nothing would be so disastrous as to remain at war with both Catalonia and Portugal, and we must therefore accept the best settlement we can get. This would save us from having to divide our army, which I fear would be unsatisfactory for both areas, Catalonia and Portugal, and would leave us with two wars on our hands, excluding any new ones. Then we should immediately transfer to Portugal all the troops now in Catalonia and try to smother that fire, too, before the conflagration spreads.

The Count-Duke took a different view. He accepted that recent events in Portugal made it imperative to settle with the Catalans, and believed that a settlement might be achieved by the king writing to the city of Barcelona, or by Don Luis de Haro writing to his mother-in-law, the Duchess of Cardona. But any such moves taken before the royal army reached the outskirts of Barcelona would be interpreted by the Catalans as a sign not of clemency but of weakness induced by the Portuguese revolt. In his view this made it more advisable to let another week or ten days pass before responding to Catalan peace overtures. The act of clemency would be all the more dramatic and effective if it were made at the very moment when the troops appeared before the city gates.

As so often in his political career, the Count-Duke was playing for time. He seems to have been confident that Catalan resistance would crumble in a matter of days, as indeed all the reports from the principality suggested. The Duke of Espenan, the French commander in Catalonia, was so discouraged by the unwillingness of the Catalans to defend their own territory that on 22 December he made a private agreement with Los Vélez to withdraw French forces from the principality, and two days later he surrendered Tarragona to the Spanish army.[10] Everything therefore seemed set fair for a settlement in Catalonia on terms that would not humiliate the crown. These terms, as drafted by the Count-Duke, and revised by Los Balbases, the Duke of Villahermosa, José González and the Protonotario,

---

[10] Sanabre, *La acción de Francia*, pp. 116–120.

stipulated that the Catalans should throw out the French and revoke all agreements with them; offer token assistance against the Portuguese; permit some six to eight thousand men to remain billeted in the Tortosa region for future use against the French, and provide assistance with the frontier defences. The king, for his part, would issue a general pardon, excepting only Santa Coloma's murderers, and would see that justice was done where soldiers and ministers of the Audiencia had offended. The Catalans would, of course, retain their rights and privileges.[11]

When news of the king's willingness to strike a deal with the Catalans reached the ears of the Marquis of Villafranca at Alfaques, where he was in command of the galleys, he wrote indignantly to Olivares, criticizing the decision and warning him of the dire consequences of letting the Catalans go unpunished. Since Spain's enemies could only get help to the Portuguese by sea, he thought it safe enough for the time being to leave Portugal to its own devices. The Catalan rebellion, on the other hand, was made exceptionally dangerous by the principality's proximity to France. Any attempt by the king to come to terms with the Catalans could well set off a series of revolts in his other dominions—in Naples and Sicily ('already suffering from a headache'), Lombardy ('tired of its army'), the Indies ('populated by rogues'), Valencia, Aragon and then the rest of Spain, starting at the Guadalajara gate in Madrid. This made it essential to crush Catalonia and mete out the kind of punishment that would serve as a warning to the other kingdoms of the Monarchy.[12]

In Madrid, however, ministers were drawing the opposite conclusion from a similar line of reasoning. The Marquis of Los Balbases was also of the opinion that the geographical situation of Catalonia made its pacification the first priority.[13] But he and his colleagues seem to have decided that this was no time to treat Catalonia as a conquered land. Where Portugal was concerned, they apparently had fewer scruples. When the Count-Duke asked his fellow ministers what should be done about Portugal after its recovery, his query elicited some sharp comments to the effect that the Portuguese had forfeited their privileges through their treachery, and would be at the king's mercy, like any other conquered people.[14]

Perhaps the most striking feature of this discussion was the optimistic assumption of the ministers that the revolts would soon be suppressed. Inevitably there was deep concern, but the climate of opinion in official circles in Madrid at the start of 1641 is reflected in a private

[11] AGS GA leg. 1331, consulta of Junta Grande, 23 December 1640.
[12] AGS GA leg. 1374, Villafranca to Olivares, 16 January 1641.
[13] AGS GA leg. 1331, consulta of Junta Grande, 29 December 1640.
[14] AGS GA leg. 1331, consulta of Junta Grande, 31 December 1640.

letter written by the Count-Duke's secretary Carnero to Pierre Roose on 27 January.[15] Troubles, he wrote, were piling up, with the revolt of Portugal, 'so much more serious in its import', following on the heels of that of Catalonia. But, he continued, the Catalan revolt should by this moment have been overcome, 'and with this we shall turn out attention to the west, since the business in the east can be regarded as over and done with. The whole affair, because of its very novelty, will cause much noise in the world, but there is no need for concern because the king without a doubt will punish that traitor [Braganza] and his followers.'

It was difficult for men living close to the king and accustomed to thinking in terms of the global power of Spain, to contemplate the possibility that he might not even be the master in his own house. Revolts, if they occurred, were seen as temporary aberrations—the work of a handful of conspirators operating for their own nefarious purposes, and carrying with them in the excitement of the moment the mischievous, the ignorant and the misinformed. In this reading it could only be a matter of time before the nobility in the rebellious provinces were recalled to a sense of their obligations, and the scales fell from the eyes of the people. But even as Carnero wrote, this comforting assumption was about to be shattered by developments in Catalonia. The craven surrender of Tarragona provoked savage mob violence in Barcelona. 'I do now begin to think', wrote Hopton, 'that this madness of the common people . . . will throw that principality into the hands of the French.'[16] He was right. With the populace in a state of high agitation and the royal army drawing closer and closer to Barcelona, Pau Claris made the one move capable of saving the rebel cause, and formally placed the principality under the protection of Louis XIII. Defences were thrown up around Barcelona with the help of the French, and on 26 January the Catalan-French defending force met the army of Los Vélez on the hill of Montjuic, outside the city walls. The marquis unaccountably allowed himself to be engaged in battle, and then, worried by the number of casualties and the shortage of supplies, gave the order to retreat. It would be another ten years before a Spanish army got as close again to Barcelona as the army of Los Vélez on the day of Montjuic.[17]

The astonishing news of Los Vélez's retreat shattered at least one of Madrid's illusions. The problem of Catalonia was not, after all, to be as rapidly resolved as the ministers had expected. This may have been a consequence of gross human error, but there was little point in recrimination. The Count-Duke recalled that Los Vélez was

[15] AGR CPE, Reg. 1504, fo. 205.
[16] PRO SP. 94.42, fo. 106, Hopton to Vane, 20/30 January 1641.
[17] Sanabre, *La acción de Francia*, pp. 129–38; Elliott, *Catalans*, pp. 521–2.

in the habit of saying that he would rather be a poor water-carrier than a soldier; but it was not necessary to be a professional soldier to realize that an army had to be kept supplied, and it passed his understanding how the marquis could have advanced on Barcelona without making sure of his provisions.[18] As for the immediate steps to be taken, the councillors of state and members of the Junta de Ejecución who together formed the so-called Junta Grande, the body which had apparently assumed overall responsibility for Catalan and Portuguese affairs, agreed that there should be no change in priorities, and that Catalonia should continue to take precedence over Portugal. It believed that the French were bound to take advantage of Spain's new vulnerability by concentrating their efforts on the Catalan front rather than Flanders in the coming campaign season. This called for a supreme effort to complete the unfinished Catalan business. The men from Los Vélez's army would have to be transported to the exposed frontier region of Roussillon, which still remained under Spanish control. But the 'first maxim today is negotiation.' The king, in signifying his approval, insisted that military preparations against the Portuguese must on no account be halted.[19]

The fact that the ministers still had high hopes of a Catalan settlement that would force the French to abandon the principality[20] suggests a continuing failure to appreciate the depth and intensity of Catalan feeling against the Count-Duke's government. Living in a world of rumour and speculation, and dependent on an erratic supply of information from sources that were frequently unreliable, they were taking their decisions in a mental universe in which reality and fantasy were not easily separated. Some of them were overworked and desperately tired. During those early weeks of 1641 the Count-Duke himself was staggering beneath the cares of business, and was described as 'not very well'.[21] 'My master', reported Carnero, 'although not defeated, is terribly hard pressed.'[22] Two weeks later, Hopton wrote in a cyphered despatch that 'the little prosperity of those two great businesses [Catalonia and Portugal] doth strangely afflict the Conde Duque de Olivares, inasmuch as his secretary Carnero hath said he believes it will either break his heart or drive him into a monastery.'[23]

The strains under which the Count-Duke was labouring were made painfully clear by two letters which he wrote on 10 March. The first

[18] AGS GA leg. 1374, consulta of Junta Grande, 15 February 1641.
[19] AGS GA leg. 1374, consulta of Junta Grande, 16 February 1641.
[20] AGS GA leg. 1374, consulta of Junta Grande, 16 February 1641.
[21] AGR CPE, Reg. 1506, fo. 206, Brecht to Roose, 24 January 1641.
[22] AGR CPE, Reg. 1504, fo. 206, Carnero to Roose, 25 January 1641.
[23] PRO SP. 94.42, fo. 113, Hopton to Secretary of State, 3/13 February 1641.

of these, written to Malvezzi in London, contained not only a withering account of the five men he held responsible for the secession of Portugal,[24] but also a description, heavy with forced irony, of the incomprehensible behaviour of the Marquis of Los Vélez outside the walls of Barcelona. 'Look, Sir, what happens for lack of a rational man.' But Catalonia, he predicted, would prove as useless to Louis XIII as it had been to Philip IV. Writing the same day to Don Miguel de Salamanca in Brussels,[25] he dismissed the Portuguese revolt as a matter of no consequence. Everyone with any knowledge of Portugal, he assured Don Miguel, thought that the only real risk lay in Braganza making his escape, 'and even that would be no great loss. On the contrary, it would represent a major gain, with the madness and blindness of that beast assuring us of absolute tranquillity in Portugal both now and for the future.'

The Count-Duke's actions, however, belied the blithe tone of his words. There are signs of panic and desperation in the counter-measures being adopted by Madrid against the Catalans and the Portuguese. On 27 February 1641 Pau Claris died suddenly in Barcelona. It may have been a natural death—his health had not been good—but there was a belief in French circles that he had been poisoned.[26] Reports of poisoning were common currency, but they gain some credibility from Madrid's determination to take Braganza's brother, Don Duarte, dead or alive.[27] When Don Francisco de Melo—himself under some suspicion as a native Portuguese—successfully appealed to the Emperor to have Don Duarte placed under arrest, Olivares was delighted but wanted him handed over to the Spaniards to ensure maximum security; and if the Emperor was unwilling to oblige, 'it would be best to make sure of him by killing him.'[28] If Olivares had his way, even the envoy sent by the new King of Portugal to England would not escape Spanish vengeance. The Count-Duke wondered whether his old English friend and protégé Endymion Porter might not be able to arrange for 'this traitor' to be murdered.[29] Times had changed since he had refused to countenance any attempt on the life of Cardinal Richelieu, or a plot to assassinate Gustavus Adolphus, on the grounds that this would be an act unbecoming to so great a king as Philip IV.[30]

[24] MC, 2, Doc. XVI, and see above, pp. 597–8.
[25] AHN Est. lib. 955.
[26] Sanabre, La acción de Francia, pp. 139–40.
[27] Above, p. 598, and Olivares to Cardinal-Infante, 23 March 1641 (MSB, Cod. hisp. 22, fo. 133).
[28] AGS Est. leg. 3860, consulta, 2 April 1641.
[29] AGS Est. leg. 2056, consulta, 31 May 1640.
[30] For Richelieu, above, p. 520; for Gustavus Adolphus, AGS Est. leg. 2333, fo. 78, consulta, 19 February 1632.

Not surprisingly, the Count-Duke and his colleagues saw conspiracy all around them. It was difficult for them at this moment to know who were their friends and who their enemies, especially with so many Portuguese holding high office in the Monarchy. The Marquis of Castel Rodrigo, who was ordered in the aftermath of the revolt to leave the Spanish embassy in Rome at short notice to attend the Diet of Regensburg, took this as a slur on his reputation, and, protesting his loyalty, demanded compensation (Pl. 31).[31] Considering his uneasy relationship with Olivares in earlier years there may have been some grounds for his suspicions. Like many of his compatriots he was paying a price not only for the revolt itself, but also for the very prominence of the Portuguese in the life of the Spanish Monarchy over the past two decades. In casting the mantle of its protection over the Portuguese banking and business community in Madrid, and creating new opportunities for Portuguese merchants—many of them suspected of crypto-Judaic practices—to participate in Spanish and Spanish-American commerce and finance, the Olivares regime had unwittingly fanned the flames of Castilian xenophobia. So far from familiarity promoting that 'union of hearts' between Castilians and non-Castilians that Olivares had always declared to be his dearest aim, it had merely served to accentuate the divisions between them.

The 1630's had been a decade of rising anti-Portuguese hysteria, tinged with anti-Semitism, both in the Iberian Peninsula and in the Spanish Indies. The remedy for Spain's economic woes, wrote José Pellicer in a virulently anti-Portuguese tract of 1640, had proved worse than the disease. It would be better to open Iberian and colonial trade to foreigners than leave it in the hands of the Portuguese, 'in their majority hidden Jews.'[32] As Spain's transatlantic trade contracted, so Spaniards both at home and in the New World were less and less willing to share it with Portuguese merchants who had taken advantage of the opportunities provided by the union of the crowns to insinuate themselves into its interstices. In this sense, 1640 represented a divorce between two parties who had grown weary of each other, and the Count-Duke's heavy-handed fiscalism may simply have accelerated the dissolution of a marriage that was already past salvation. Where Castilians resented the growing prominence of the Portuguese in an increasingly sour partnership, the Portuguese resented both the arrogance and hostility of an overbearing partner and the failure of the union to bring them greater advantages. The

---

[31] AGS Est. leg. 2059, consulta, 28 February 1643.
[32] *Comercio impedido*. A copy of this printed tract, dated 30 January 1640, is to be found, catalogued under Comercio, in BL 1445 f. 17 (13). It was reprinted in Juan Sempere y Guarinos, *Biblioteca española económico-política*, 3, (Madrid, 1804), cxxiii–clvii.

King of Spain, for all his vaunted power, had been unable to save Portuguese Asia from the Dutch. Nor, as the events of the 1630's showed, did he seem capable of saving Brazil, that other jewel in the Portuguese crown. In addition, it was being made abundantly clear to Portuguese merchants and settlers that they were not wanted in Mexico and Peru. On both sides, therefore, the separation of 1640 was being mentally rehearsed before it was enacted.[33]

Although individual Portuguese may have agonized over the conflict of loyalties that now confronted them, and many, especially in the upper classes, viewed Braganza's assumption of the crown with a distinct lack of enthusiasm, the new King of Portugal could set about building his regime on the basis of something approaching a national consensus inspired by disillusionment with the union of the crowns and hatred of Castile. In this task he enjoyed the support of the lower clergy and of the Jesuits, who proved to be among his most fervent advocates.[34] Olivares had high hopes that Brazil and Goa would remain loyal to Philip IV,[35] but the Jesuits in particular were active in securing the adherence to the rebel cause of Dom Jorge de Mascarenhas, the viceroy of Brazil, and Salvador de Sá, the governor of Rio de Janeiro. During February and March, to cries of 'Long live King Dom John the Fourth of Portugal!', Braganza was proclaimed in one town after another of Brazil; and in September Portuguese India followed suit.[36]

The adherence of Portugal's colonial empire to the Braganza regime was potentially critical for its future as an independent state. It held out the promise of continuing overseas wealth and trade, especially if the lost areas of Brazil could one day be recovered from the Dutch; and correspondingly it increased the interest of other European states in the new regime's survival. Already before news had reached Europe of reactions in Brazil and India to John IV's proclamation, the Dutch had begun to ship guns and munitions to Portugal, and Richelieu had offered a formal alliance to the new king's ambassadors.[37] The regime needed all the help it could get in these first months of independence. It was still exceptionally fragile, and it is hard to see how it could have survived in the event of an immediate Spanish invasion.

Yet no invasion came. In retrospect, the failure to strike hard against Portugal in January or February of 1641 looks like a fatal

---

[33] See Huguette and Pierre Chaunu, 'Autour de 1640: politiques et économiques atlantiques', *Annales*, 9 (1954), pp. 44–52.

[34] See Boxer, *Salvador de Sá*, pp. 142–4.

[35] Letter to Malvezzi of 10 March 1641 (*MC*, 2, p. 204).

[36] Veríssimo Serrão, *História de Portugal*, 5, pp. 102–4, 106–8.

[37] Israel, *The Dutch Republic*, p. 340; Révah, *Le Cardinal de Richelieu et la restauration du Portugal*, p. 45.

31. Don Manuel de Moura, Marquis of Castel Rodrigo. Initially an ally of Olivares, and then a major figure in the court intrigues of the 1620's to overthrow him, Castel Rodrigo was sent as ambassador to Rome in 1630 and served outside Spain for the remaining years of the Olivares ministry.

mistake by the Count-Duke and his colleagues. But the decision to give priority to Catalonia seemed a logical one, bearing in mind the danger of a French incursion from Catalonia into the very heart of Spain; and when on 16 February the Junta Grande confirmed this decision on learning of the disaster at Montjuic, and insisted on the importance of not dividing the army and forcing it to fight on two fronts simultaneously, it still expected preparations to go ahead with all speed for the creation of a new army to fight the Portuguese. But, as always, there were delays. With no treasure fleet arriving in 1640 money was tighter than ever. Jacques de Brecht writing (in invisible ink) to Pierre Roose in February, confessed that his spirits failed him as he saw what was happening. 'Here', he wrote, 'everything is a matter of demanding and extracting money with no exemptions permitted to anyone, and everywhere as necessities increase resources are diminishing. They have just doubled the *cuartos*, except those minted in Segovia. It pains me to see His Excellency, although he displays great courage and prudence in everything he does.'[38]

If shortage of money was one problem, shortage of men was another, although the Count-Duke told the Cardinal-Infante on 23 March that they were seeking to raise a battalion of two thousand cavalrymen in the court at Madrid for use in Catalonia or Portugal.[39] Attempts to mobilize the Castilian nobility had been proving singularly unsuccessful. In spite of the emergency created by the revolt of Catalonia, only 150 members of the military orders or their substitutes turned up for a troop review held by the king at the Buen Retiro at the end of September 1640.[40] Further problems arose over the command of the embryonic army of Portugal. The Count-Duke's brother-in-law, Monterrey, who had estates in Galicia, was appointed to the command with the title of lieutenant-general. His appointment was not to the liking of his fellow-grandees, who considered him their inferior. The new Duke of Alba, who had led a good number of men from his own estates to the borders of Portugal, returned home in high dudgeon, refusing to serve as Monterrey's subordinate; and the Dukes of Medina Sidonia, Medinaceli, Béjar and Arcos all followed suit.[41]

[38] AGR CPE, Reg. 1506, fos. 212v.–213, Brecht to Roose, 20 February 1641. Roose replied later that he had had difficulty in reading this letter, which was written in lemon juice, and which Brecht had asked him to burn. The doubling of the *cuartos* is a reference to the inflationary decree of 11 February, ordering the restamping of the 4-maravedí pieces first restamped in 1603. See Hamilton, *American Treasure*, pp. 85–6.
[39] MSB, Cod. hisp. 22, fo. 133.
[40] ASF Mediceo, filza 4965, letter from Bernardo Monanni, 6 October 1640; and see Domínguez Ortiz, 'La movilización de la nobleza castellana en 1640'.
[41] ASVen, Spagna, filza 75, despatches of 6 and 20 February 1641; PRO SP. 94.42, fo. 113, Hopton to Secretary of State, 3/13 February 1641.

In spite of the opposition of the grandees, however, Monterrey kept his command. Spanish troops, many of them raw recruits, started assembling in Badajoz, and the first border skirmishes took place around the beginning of April.[42] But it was a desultory start to the campaign. In part this can be explained by the priority given to the Catalan front, but it may also reflect the spreading demoralization in Castile, vividly described at just this moment by the British ambassador, Sir Arthur Hopton:[43]

> Concerning the state of this kingdom, I could never have imagined to have seen it as it now is, for their people begin to fail, and those that remain, by a continuance of bad success, and by their heavy burdens, are quite out of heart. They have not one man of quality fit to command an army. The king's revenues being paid in brass money will be lessened a third part being reduced to silver. They begin already to lay hands on the silver vessel of particular men, which, together with that in the churches, is all the stock of silver in the kingdom. Their trade must of necessity fail though the daily new burdens that are laid thereon, and the molestation of merchants ... Justice is quite extinguished here, and the people are become almost desperate, partly by the intolerable sisas they pay upon whatsoever they spend (bread only excepted) and partly by the great sums of money are daily extorted from them. Their provisions of shipping and mariners are not the tenth part of what they have been and what they ought to be, *and the greatest mischief of all is that the King of Spain knows little of all this, and the Count-Duke is so wilful as he will break rather than bend.* So as your honour may be confident this monarchy is in great danger to be ruined, and whether that will be good for us and the rest of Christendom is best known to your honour.

It was hard in these circumstances for the Count-Duke to maintain his own morale and that of the men around him. Little comfort remained to him other than his religion. At the beginning of the year he was reported to have been discovered kneeling in contemplation before a crucifix when the king sent for him. He failed to answer the royal summons, remaining 'as if exalted and in ecstasy'. Finally, when the king personally sought him out, he is said to have come round 'as if from the dead'.[44] There were one or two intimates to whom he could turn for solace, among them his old friend and the custodian of his library, Francisco de Rioja.[45] His inner circle was

---

[42] ASVen, Spagna, filza 75, despatch, 10 April 1641.
[43] PRO SP. 94.42, fo. 144, Hopton to Vane, 3/13 April 1641. (The italicized words are in cypher in the original.)
[44] ASF Mediceo, filza 4965, letter from Monanni, 2 January 1641.
[45] Above, p. 22.

strengthened, too, by the return this spring of the Marquis of Leganés from Italy.[46] Leganés rapidly became his closest collaborator, to the annoyance of the Protonotario who failed to hide his jealousy.[47] But no man was more conscious than the Count-Duke of the essentially solitary nature of his responsibilities. In a letter to Don Francisco de Melo he spoke of the agony of receiving bad news not just from one or two parts of the world—which might have been bearable—but from all of them at once. And yet, he concluded, 'it is not courage that fails me, but men, for everywhere we need great men and many of them, and we find ourselves with fewer than a few.'[48]

More often than in the past, too, he and his ministerial colleagues did not see eye to eye. On 19 June the Junta Grande again discussed the vexed question of whether the Catalan front should continue to take precedence over the Portuguese.[49] Although the Count-Duke had supported the policy of giving Catalonia priority, he had never in his own mind ruled out the possibility of sending an army into Portugal before the Catalans were defeated. Behind the scenes he had been working hard to raise troops for an invasion of Portugal, but he now discovered that some members of the Junta Grande— Balbases, Mirabel, Oñate, Villahermosa—were disinclined to use them.

The Count-Duke expressed indignation at what he regarded as a volte-face by his colleagues. If something was not done at once in Portugal, he told them, it would be impossible to recover it for many years to come. He added that although it was a wise maxim to avoid wars on two fronts simultaneously, there were times like the present when there was no option but to meet each new situation as it arose, and do the best one could. His remarks suggest that it was the shadow of Montjuic that divided him from his colleagues. The majority of them were clearly unwilling to run the risk of a repeat performance in Portugal, whereas the Count-Duke believed that the revolution had not yet taken deep root, and that the time to strike was now. Already the newly independent kingdom was beginning to achieve international recognition. A formal treaty between France and Portugal was signed on 1 June,[50] and on the 12th, temporarily sinking their differences over Brazil, the Dutch Republic and Portugal agreed to a ten-year truce.[51]

Any policy disagreement between the Count-Duke and his col-leagues, however, was dissipated by the euphoria generated by the

[46] *MHE*, 16, p. 129 (14 May 1641).
[47] ASF Mediceo, filza 4966, despatch from Ottavio Pucci, 11 September 1641.
[48] BL Add. Ms. 14,004, fos. 288–9, copy of letter from Olivares to Melo, 8 June 1641.
[49] AGS GA leg. 1376, consulta, 19 June 1641.
[50] Révah, *Le Cardinal de Richelieu et la restauration du Portugal*, p. 46.
[51] Roger Bigelow Merriman, *Six Contemporaneous Revolutions* (Oxford, 1938), p. 151.

news of a victory in Catalonia early in July. Following the death of Pau Claris, Richelieu was more than ever anxious to prove to the Catalans the continuing commitment of Louis XIII to their cause. He had originally planned a campaign for the conquest of Roussillon, where Spanish forces still held most of the eastern portion of the territory, including Perpignan and the principal frontier fortresses. But the forces intended for the Roussillon campaign were now ordered south into Catalonia to eject the remnants of Los Vélez's army, which had fallen back on Tarragona after its defeat at Montjuic.[52] During May and June the French tightened their land and sea blockade of Tarragona. On 4 July, however, the Marquis of Villafranca's galleys, reinforced by those of Genoa and Naples, defeated the French blockading fleet and ran in supplies to the besieged royal army.[53]

Although the siege would not be raised until August, Tarragona now seemed unlikely to fall to the French, and it was clear that Richelieu's plans for Catalonia had suffered a major reverse. It was a long time since Madrid had savoured the taste of success. The fourth of July was proclaimed a day of *fiesta* in perpetuity, and the ministers in the Junta Grande formally expressed to the king their recognition of the immense services rendered by the Count-Duke, whose untiring efforts in organizing the war effort had made the victory possible.[54] But would a single victory, however gratifying, be enough to compensate for the opportunities that had been lost in Catalonia and Portugal during those first six critical months of 1641?

Plots and counter-plots

While working day and night to build up the king's armies for the reconquest of his two rebellious provinces, the Count-Duke still clung to the hope that some sudden dramatic event might yet reverse the tide of the war. It had by now become clear even to Madrid that there was no chance of Charles I of England, beset by rebels of his own, entering the war on the side of Spain. Ministers were also resigned to the fact that at this stage France had no interest in further peace negotiations. Attempts by the papal nuncio and the Venetian ambassador in Paris to negotiate a general suspension of arms had proved fruitless, and the Count-Duke was particularly indignant that the French should take the cause of rebellious Catalans and Portuguese as their own. In these circumstances he looked to

---

[52] Sanabre, *La acción de Francia*, p. 153.
[53] *Ibid.*, pp. 158–9.
[54] AGS GA leg. 1376, consulta, 10 July 1641.

the French malcontent conspirators of Sedan—the Duke of Bouillon, the Count of Soissons and their friends[55]—as the 'sole means of salvation from shipwreck.'[56]

His spirits rose when he received from the Cardinal-Infante early in June the details of the agreement negotiated with the French conspirators. But he warned his colleagues that at all costs they must avoid the mistake of Philip II, whose attempts to reduce France to a dominion of Spain cost him the Netherlands, as well as France itself.[57] There was, however, to be no opportunity to avoid, or even to duplicate, Philip II's mistake. Richelieu had managed to penetrate the conspiracy, and Soissons and his friends were brought to battle by a royal army at La Marfée on 6 July. The king's forces, however, were so crushingly defeated that for one moment it looked as if the insurgents were indeed to be God's chosen instrument for the reversal of Spain's fortunes. An alarmed Richelieu now contemplated the possibility of a simultaneous offensive by Soissons and the Spaniards which might carry them all the way to Paris. But a chance shot was to save the day. As the victorious Soissons rode across the battlefield, his brains were blown out by a bullet, fired either by an assassin or by himself as he injudiciously raised his visor with the barrel of his pistol. Once their leader was dead, Soissons' supporters abandoned his cause.[58]

One more conspiracy had gone awry, destroying any immediate chance of Richelieu's overthrow. The Cardinal appeared to lead a charmed life, and the Count-Duke could hardly fail to contrast his own misfortunes and his rival's unbroken run of luck. Somehow the key to success consistently eluded him. The Council of Castile was repeatedly ordered to punish all public infringements of morality and to improve administration and justice, 'omitting nothing which can oblige and placate God', in the hope—as the king himself wrote—of inducing Him to 'come to our help in the miserable times that He has been pleased to give me.'[59] Yet neither prayer nor policy availed; and in this same month of July in which the Soissons conspiracy collapsed, another promising plot was also prematurely nipped in the bud.

In spite of the initial success of John IV of Portugal in rallying the country to his cause, the new regime in Lisbon was not without its enemies, especially among the nobility, the higher clergy, and merchants who had made large sums from their association with the

[55] Above, p. 572.
[56] AGS Est. leg. 3860, consulta of Council of State, 10 May 1641.
[57] AGS Est. leg. 2056, paper by Olivares, 14 June 1641.
[58] Burckhardt, *Richelieu and his Age*, 3, pp. 344–53.
[59] AHN Consejos, leg. 7137, consulta of Council of Castile, 8 July 1641, and king's response.

Spanish crown finances and tax administration. As the implications of a definitive termination of the union of the crowns gradually dawned upon them, they began to contemplate the possibility of a counter-revolution. During the spring and early summer of 1641 a plot was hatched to assassinate the new king and his wife and family. Its threads ran to and fro between Madrid and the Lisbon convent in which the deposed vicereine, the Duchess of Mantua, was confined,[60] and the list of conspirators included some of the most important names in the country, among them the archbishop of Braga, and the Marquis of Vila Real, along with his son, the Duke of Caminha.[61] But some time in July the plot was betrayed. Inquiries revealed that a number of secret meetings had been held at the home of a banker, Pedro de Baeça, the brother of one of the leading *asentistas* in Madrid, Jorge de Paz.[62] The involvement of Baeça, who had offered substantial sums to help finance the conspiracy, testifies to the deep rift in the Portuguese mercantile community at the time of the revolt. However unpopular the high financiers with their court connections may have been in Madrid, they were no less unpopular with members of their own community who had not enjoyed the lucrative benefits to be gained from collaboration with the Olivares regime. While the less privileged merchants threw in their lot with Braganza, the high financiers had too much at stake to cut their links with Philip IV. Caught in the coils of the international money market, Baeça paid for his involvement with his life. Together with Vila Real, Caminha and a handful of others he was executed on 29 August.

While the Count-Duke was doing his best to instigate or encourage conspiracy abroad, he was well aware of the need to protect his own flanks at home. The possibility of new regional revolts in the peninsula was a continuing nightmare. He was especially worried about the kingdom of Aragon, which could all too easily be infected by its Catalan neighbours, and he had no confidence in the Duke of Nochera, its Neapolitan viceroy, who had counselled him not to use force against Catalonia.[63] The head of the king's intelligence service, Marcelino de Fária, warned Olivares that the French, through their agents in Zaragoza, were attempting to foment rebellion in Aragon.[64] It was known that some years earlier Nochera had spent a few days in Paris on his journey back to Naples from Flanders,

---

[60] Veríssimo Serrão, *História de Portugal*, 5, pp. 28–9.
[61] Archivo del Duque de Alba, Madrid. Caja 96–15, no. 5711. *Memoria de las personas que el Duque de Braganza hizo prender en Lisboa . . . a los 28 de julio de este año.*
[62] For Baeça, see Boyajian, *Portuguese Bankers*, pp. 129–30.
[63] Above, p. 595.
[64] 'Copia de consulta de 3 de marzo de 1643', *Codoin* 81, p. 555. Another copy of this report by Fária on his services to the crown is to be found in the Archivo del Ministerio de Asuntos Exteriores, Ms. 39, fos. 1–6v.

and had adopted the French style of dress on returning home.[65] Taken in conjunction with the fact that during the spring of 1641 he had assumed the role of intermediary between the Catalans and the king,[66] these earlier francophile proclivities looked highly suspicious. Early in July he was taken into custody, and he died a year later in the fortress of Pinto.[67]

The Duke of Nochera is more likely to have been incautious than actively seditious, and even if Aragonese sympathy lay with the Catalans, memories of the army sent by Philip II to restore order in 1591 were strong enough to inhibit any immediate urge to follow the Catalan example. But Madrid was understandably taking no chances. In the climate of discontent and demoralization affecting Spain in 1641, treason was possible at any moment and in the most unlikely places—even, it now appeared, in the Count-Duke's own family. On 9 August Don Miguel de Salamanca sent him an urgent confidential letter containing a mysterious coded message from a Portuguese resident in the Hague, Manuel Botelo de Sossa. This warned that Duarte Díaz (Olivares) should at once send medical aid to Cadiz, and not make use of the leading doctor there, 'namely Medina'. Speed was essential because Pedro Váes (the king) could well die of the disease.[68] This letter brought unwelcome confirmation of news that Olivares had almost certainly already received from other sources—that a conspiracy was brewing in Andalusia, and that one of those involved in it was the head of the senior branch of the house of Guzmán, Don Gaspar de Guzmán y Sandoval, ninth Duke of Medina Sidonia.[69]

The ninth duke, Don Gaspar, had succeeded to the title on the death of his father, Don Juan Manuel, in 1636. There had been no love lost between Olivares, jealous of the pre-eminence of the senior branch of the family, and Don Juan Manuel, no less jealous as he watched the steady climb of its junior branch to fame and fortune, and observed the Count-Duke's endeavours to establish in Andalusia a ducal domain that threatened to overshadow his own.[70] But Olivares

---

[65] RAH Salazar, N-53, fos. 41–7, undated paper containing charges against Nochera by the *procurador fiscal* of the Council of Aragon.

[66] See his letter of 18 April to the Catalan *diputat*, José Quintana, in Sanabre *La acción de Francia*, Appendix 14.

[67] See Miguel Batllori and Ceferino Peralta, *Baltasar Gracián en su vida y en sus obras* (Zaragoza, 1969), p. 81. Nochera, or Nocera to give him his Italian title, was Gracián's patron.

[68] AHN Est. lib. 969, copy of letter from Manuel Botelo, with draft letter from Miguel de Salamanca to Olivares.

[69] The information that something was afoot had probably already reached him through a letter of 8 August sent to a royal official in Ayamonte, Don Antonio de Isasi, by Doña Clara Gonzaga de Valdés. See the account of the conspiracy by Antonio Domínguez Ortiz, 'La conspiración del Duque de Medina Sidonia y el Marqués de Ayamonte', in his *Crisis y decadencia*, pp. 113–53, and especially p. 129.

[70] Above, p. 165.

took care to observe the proprieties in his dealings with the eighth duke, whose enormous local influence made him a power to be reckoned with. Yet the duke himself noted that while any business transacted through Olivares was settled to his satisfaction, this did not hold true of other official business, which was handled in a way 'very different from what is owed to a person like myself.'[71] In spite of this, the eighth duke held his resentments in check. He knew that he was dependent on Olivares' advocacy at court, just as Olivares knew that he was dependent on Medina Sidonia's local influence for the smooth running of Andalusia and its coastal defences.

The ninth duke inherited his father's resentments but not his common sense. Like other members of the high nobility, he had seen his patrimony eroded by the endless succession of royal demands for military service and money, and by lawsuits intended to appropriate major sources of ducal income for the crown. He shared the hatred of his fellow-magnates for the Count-Duke's harsh and authoritarian style of government, and, like them, looked forward to the day when the tyrant would fall. His close regional ties with the Portuguese nobility, reinforced by his sister's marriage to the Duke of Braganza, made him naturally sympathetic to many of the aspirations of the Portuguese rebels; and even if he was required to expunge from the family records the name of Doña Luisa de Guzmán he can hardly have been displeased to see her become the Queen of Portugal.

Any incipient ideas of grandeur provoked by the accession of a member of the house of Guzmán to the ranks of European royalty are likely to have been fostered by another member of the same house, a border noble in impoverished circumstances, Don Francisco Antonio de Guzmán, sixth Marquis of Ayamonte.[72] Ayamonte probably took the lead in hatching a plot with his Portuguese friends on the other side of the frontier, and subsequently turned to his kinsman to provide the movement with an acceptable figurehead. The exact aims of the plot remain obscure, although rumour had it that the conspirators planned to proclaim Medina Sidonia 'King of Andalusia and the Indies'.[73] If so, it was a wild idea. Unlike Catalonia or Portugal, Andalusia lacked the sense of historical and corporate identity that was required for the launching of a movement of independence; and even if it had revolted, it had no means of carrying the Indies in its wake. The plotters seem to have been counting on outside help, not only from the Portuguese, who were expected to send their troops across the frontier, but also from the French and

---

[71] Archivo de los Duques de Medina Sidonia, Sanlúcar de Barrameda. Cartas de reyes 18, Medina Sidonia to Olivares, 11 October 1626.
[72] Domínguez Ortiz, 'La conspiración', pp. 125–6.
[73] ASF Mediceo, filza 4966, despatch of Ottavio Pucci, 4 September 1641.

the Dutch. Botelo's letter urging the king to make sure of Cadiz suggests that the plan was to coordinate an Andalusian uprising with a seaborne invasion. During these months a Dutch fleet was in fact cruising off the Portuguese coast, and Dutch and Franco-Portuguese squadrons were sighted off Cadiz in September.[74] According to the duke's subsequent confession the conspirators were to raise the nobility and people in revolt by promising to ease the burden of taxes; and they would press the king to remove the great inventor of taxes, the Count-Duke, from his side.[75]

On receiving the intelligence reports, the Count-Duke had Medina Sidonia summoned to Madrid. The duke later confessed to his panic on receiving the summons. The first thought of Ayamonte and himself was to disregard the summons, burn their papers, and warn the Dutch and Portuguese fleets to come immediately. But while the duke still hesitated, he received two more letters from Olivares in quick succession.[76] An observation in the first of these letters provides the key to Olivares' handling of this curious affair: 'It is impossible for Your Excellency's reputation to suffer without my own collapsing.'[77] Any public hint of disloyalty by the head of the house of Guzmán would tarnish the reputation of all its members, and most of all that of the Count-Duke himself. He would therefore do everything possible in the following weeks to conceal the enormity of his kinsman's crime from the world.

Reluctantly a frightened Duke of Medina Sidonia set out for Madrid, while the Count-Duke's nephew, Don Luis de Haro, was sent to Andalusia to make sure that he came.[78] The court by now was buzzing with rumour, but this seems to have been directed more to the family affairs of the house of Guzmán, than to any suspicion of wrong-doing by Medina Sidonia. It is not surprising that public attention should have been diverted in this way, for a bizarre story was being unfolded. It had suddenly become public knowledge—and the timing may not have been accidental—that the Count-Duke, without an heir of his body since his daughter's death in 1626, now claimed to be the father of a son.[79]

The young man in question, known as Don Julián de Guzmán, had seen a good deal of the world in his twenty-eight years. Many rumours, most of them without foundation, surrounded his origins.[80]

---

[74] Israel, *The Dutch Republic*, p. 325; Domínguez Ortiz, 'La conspiración', p. 127.
[75] BNM Ms. 6043, fos. 188–90, *Carte del papel que dió a Su Majestad el Duque de Medina Sidonia en 21 de setiembre de 1641*.
[76] Letters of 29 August and 1 September, reproduced in *MHE*, 16, pp. 161–4.
[77] *Ibid*, p. 162.
[78] Novoa, *Codoin* 80, p. 473.
[79] ASVen, Spagna, filza 76, despatch of 4 September 1641.
[80] For the affair of the bastard son, see Marañón, *Olivares*, ch. 20.

Nominally he was the son of Don Gonzalo de Guzmán Salazar and his wife, Doña Juana de Ocampo, but in fact he seems to have been the result of a liaison that occurred in 1612 between Olivares and a high-born lady at court. Olivares placed him in the care of a relative, Don Gonzalo de Guzmán, and then of a court official, Don Francisco Valcárcel, under whose surname Julián frequently appears in later accounts. As a young man he apparently went to Italy as a page to Don Diego de Guzmán, the archbishop of Seville, who was accompanying the Queen of Hungary on her journey to Vienna.[81] He then took passage to the Indies, where he lived the life of a vagrant and is reputed to have had a narrow escape from the gallows. Returning to Spain in 1636, he is said to have signed up as a soldier, and served in Italy and Flanders before turning up again at court in 1639. Here he fell in love with and precipitously married the daughter of a royal official, to the dismay of the Count-Duke, who by now had more grandiose plans for the future of this wastrel. Olivares' yearning for an heir was as intense as ever, and may indeed have intensified as political failure began to stare him in the face. The letter he wrote to Don Miguel de Salamanca in March 1638 shows that he had finally reconciled himself to the fact that Doña Inés would not bear him another child. Failing her death and a subsequent remarriage—and there had been no lack of speculation about possible candidates when she fell seriously ill and nearly died in 1636[82]—formal recognition of a bastard son appeared the only means of ensuring a direct succession to the duchy of San Lúcar.

The first step in the process was to dissolve Julián's unfortunate marriage. Happily there were certain irregularities in the marriage ceremony. The Count-Duke brought his formidable influence to bear on the ecclesiastical authorities, and by the summer of 1641 had made good progress towards his goal. Now, at the beginning of September, the butterfly was permitted to emerge from the chrysalis, resplendent under the new name of Don Enrique Felípez de Guzmán. The Venetian ambassador reported on 4 September that the Count-Duke had decided that Don Enrique should succeed to the duchy of San Lúcar, and that it was for this reason that the Duke of Medina Sidonia was being called to Madrid.[83] The smoke-screen, however, does not seem to have been very effective. Within a week the ambassador was reporting rumours of some secret understanding between Medina Sidonia and the new King of Portugal.[84]

Medina Sidonia arrived at court on 10 September, and had a long

---

[81] Novoa, *Codoin* 86, p. 6.
[82] Novoa, *Codoin* 77, p. 146.
[83] ASVen, Spagna, filza 76, despatch of Niccolò Sagredo.
[84] *Ibid*, despatch of 11 September 1641.

private interview with the Count-Duke in which he confessed under pressure to everything.[85] Before moving to the Count-Duke's country house at Loeches he was lodged in state at the Buen Retiro, as part of an elaborate effort to preserve appearances. By now the Venetian ambassador was speculating that Olivares was attempting to get revenge on the duke for crossing his plans for the future of Don Enrique. But he also reported in the same despatch the arrest in Andalusia of the Marquis of Ayamonte.[86] On the evening of 21 September, Medina Sidonia, accompanied by the Count-Duke, descended the secret staircase in the palace that led to the king's summer quarters, and throwing himself at the king's feet, confessed his crimes, placed the blame on the Marquis of Ayamonte, and begged for mercy. Taking him by the shoulders, Philip magnanimously forgave him.[87] But this was not the end of the melodrama. In order to silence the rumours, the duke issued on 29 September a manifesto challenging his brother-in-law, the Duke of Braganza, to a duel.[88] The Portuguese treated this document with the contempt it deserved, and responded with a challenge bearing the name of that illustrious knight, Don Quijote de la Mancha (Pl. 32).[89]

For the time being at least, the Medina Sidonia affair was closed, while the Marquis of Ayamonte, a less privileged malefactor, was locked up in a fortress, and, after seven years of agonized waiting, paid for his follies with his life. The whole affair left the Count-Duke shaken and profoundly scarred. The conjunction of public and private misfortune, of national disaster and family dishonour, seems to have been forcing upon him an agonizing re-appraisal of his life. In an interview at the end of August with the Venetian ambassador, who had come to congratulate him on the raising of the siege of Tarragona, he suddenly spoke with surprising frankness of himself:

> I must tell you in confidence that I have been the most ambitious man in the world. I confess that I never stopped machinating, I never slept at night, in the effort to advance my fortunes. I regarded the *privanza* as a state of incomparable felicity; I secured it; and I have held it for twenty years. And now—and God punish me if this is not the truth—my only desire is to conclude a peace, and then die. As regards the king, I owe him everything ... But for him I would almost not be a Christian, for whenever I pray

[85] Novoa, *Codoin* 80, pp. 474–5.

[86] ASVen, Spagna, filza 76, 18 September 1641.

[87] Note appended by the Protonotario to Medina Sidonia's letter of confession (BNM Ms. 6043, fo. 190).

[88] This strange document, of which numerous manuscript copies survive, is reproduced by Novoa, *Codoin* 80, pp. 476–8.

[89] *MHE*, 16, p. 189 n. 1.

32. A caricature taken from a satirical piece of 1641, of Portuguese origin, in which Don Quijote prepares to take revenge on behalf of Castile for Portugal's assertion of independence. The king is depicted as Don Quijote, and the Count-Duke as Sancho Panza.

to God it is for him . . . As for myself, I would be content to conclude a peace and then die . . . And here in my breast I have a sealed envelope whose contents describe the kind of life I have determined to live . . .'[90]

The sudden 'discovery' of his illegitimate son may well have been part of this attempt to give meaning to his life at the moment when defeat was staring him in the face. During these autumn months the Count-Duke appears to have been going through a deep mental and emotional upheaval. Writing in September of the mysteries surrounding the summoning of the Duke of Medina Sidonia to Madrid, the British ambassador remarked that 'in this business I find there is a great cabal, for I have observed in the Conde these two months an extraordinary sadness, and an utter neglect of all things but those of Andalusia.' Hopton suspected a plot by the grandees, and noted that the Count-Duke appeared to be taking precautionary measures, like placing Leganés in the king's chamber, and filling the juntas with his confidants. 'I hear it observed by some that converse with the Conde', he continued, 'that he is so overlaid with care . . . that his judgement begins to break, and that he is so intent upon his own conservation as all he doth in these great affairs is rather for show to content the king's eye, than to the effect of his service.'[91]

The king on campaign

When things were going badly in the monarchical societies of Early Modern Europe there was a tendency to assume that the truth was being concealed from the king, and that as soon as those who deceived him were removed from his presence he would assert his authority and rectify the wrongs. This had long been the assumption, and the hope, in the Spain of Philip IV. Although it was true that Philip had not moved beyond the environs of Madrid since his brief trip to Barcelona in 1632, his conscientious reading of state papers and foreign despatches can hardly have failed to convey a strong impression of the course of events in his Monarchy and in the wider world. While he was of course shielded by a screen of carefully selected nobles and officials from contact with those who might have brought him excessively unpleasant tidings, there were always ways of breaching the cordon, and in any event he was an intelligent enough man to make his own deductions. No doubt he had come with the passage of time to see the world through the Count-Duke's eyes. King and minister had laboured side by side long enough to rejoice together

[90] ASVen, Spagna, filza 76, despatch of Niccolò Sagredo, 28 August 1641.
[91] PRO SP. 94.42, fos. 211–13, Hopton to Vane, 14/24 September 1641.

at their increasingly rare successes, and grieve together as tribulations multiplied. But Philip had not been deceived by his minister's forced levity when he brought him the news of the Portuguese revolt, and, like the Count-Duke, he increasingly felt the oppressive burden of misfortune and defeat weighing down upon him.

The Tuscan ambassador, observing Philip's melancholy, noted that he seemed to be devoting all his time to preparing his will.[92] But this is to be explained as much by practical necessity as by the prevailing mood of gloom. From the beginning of the year the possibility of a royal visit to the Crown of Aragon had been under discussion.[93] Philip himself was anxious to go, and the Count-Duke's opponents were no less anxious that he should, in the belief that this would open his eyes to what was going on around him. The principal difficulty, as always, was money. Seville's Atlantic trade was in disarray.[94] The Tierra Firme fleet that finally reached port in July 1641 carried substantially the cargo which should have come in 1640, and yielded scarcely half a million ducats for the crown.[95] The New Spain fleet was still expected, but it departed late from the Indies, with many of its ships in poor condition, and was caught in a storm in the Bahamas channel late in September. As a result, most of it was lost.[96] Pending its expected arrival, the premium on silver in terms of *vellón* rose to 190%, and the government optimistically stepped in to reduce it to 50% by official decree.[97]

Until arrangements could be made with the bankers it was difficult to see how the king could travel to Aragon to raise the morale of his loyal subjects and join his forces on campaign. But it was agreed at a meeting on 28 August of the Junta de Ejecución that the king's departure should be fixed for not later than the end of September.[98] The king, therefore, expected to be going on campaign at any moment, and prepared his will in anticipation of this momentous event. As it happened, there was no need for undue haste. The non-arrival of the New Spain fleet made it impossible to arrange the *asientos*, and the Junta Grande on 25 September had to advise a post-

[92] ASF, Mediceo, filza 4966, despatch of Ottavio Pucci, 11 September 1641.
[93] AGS GA, leg. 1374, consulta of Junta Grande, 16 February 1641.
[94] Chaunu, *Séville et l'Atlantique*, 8, 2 (2), p. 1836.
[95] *Ibid*, p. 1840; Domínguez Ortiz, *Política y hacienda*, p. 291.
[96] Chaunu, 5, pp. 384–5.
[97] ASVen, Spagna, filza 76, despatch of 11 September 1641; Domínguez Ortiz, p. 262.
[98] AGS GA, leg. 1377, consulta of Junta de Ejecución attended by Olivares, the Protonotario, the Marquises of Los Balbases and Castrofuerte, and Don Nícolas Cid. On the king's orders this consulta was considered on 1 September by the Junta Grande, which was attended on this occasion by thirteen ministers: Cardinals Borja and Spínola, the Inquisitor General (Antonio de Sotomayor), the Count-Duke, the Count of Oñate, the Duke of Villahermosa, the Marquises of Los Balbases and Castrofuerte, José González, Alonso Guillén de la Carrera, Don Nicolás Cid, and Joseph de Nápoles. The procedure gives a good idea of the relationship, and the overlapping membership, of the two bodies.

ponement, although disagreeing with the Council of Castile's recommendation that the journey should be delayed until the spring.[99] The king ordered prayers for the speedy arrival of the fleet, and when Leganés kissed hands on receiving command of the army of Catalonia early in November, told him that he hoped to be following soon.[100]

As long as the fleet failed to arrive, the military apparatus of the Monarchy remained in a state of suspended animation. At the end of October the Count-Duke assured Pierre Roose that the Monarchy's problems, however difficult, were 'not incurable' if only they were handled with speed. It would be 'very easy' to deal with Portugal if prompt action were taken, and 'extremely difficult' if there were further delays. Continuing war in Spain was bound to weaken the Monarchy, but 'if God gives victory to our arms in Portugal and Catalonia' it would emerge stronger than before. The purpose behind these optimistic words was to persuade Roose that Flanders had an obligation at this moment of crisis to send help to Spain, in the form of veteran infantry and cavalrymen.[101] The Count-Duke was still clinging tenaciously to the central proposition of his political career that, if only resources could be mobilized through a Union of Arms, the Monarchy could weather the storm. Yet this was to assume that the resources existed, and all the information coming in to him from the different quarters of the globe was to the effect that they did not.[102]

This persistent conviction of the underlying power and potential of the Spanish Monarchy may well have made it difficult for the Count-Duke to settle for anything less than the ideal. The Tuscan ambassador certainly believed this to be so. He reported that the Spaniards themselves were drawing an unfavourable comparison between the 'political' approach of Richelieu, whose speed in moving to remedy disorders was bringing him obvious success, and the 'mature' approach of Olivares, 'based on always wanting to enjoy the benefit of time.' In the ambassador's view there were several occasions on which the Count-Duke could have settled the Catalan question with honour and advantage, and yet, in his desire to get everything, he had contrived only to be left with nothing. The same, he believed, was true of Portugal, where the disunity between nobility and people offered obvious possibilities. But Olivares' persistent underestimate of the enemy, and his well-known determination to make Portugal and Catalonia conform to the laws of Castile, were

[99] AGS GA, leg. 1377, consulta, 25 September 1641.
[100] ASF, Mediceo, filza 4966, despatch of 13 November 1641.
[101] AGR CPE, Reg. 1502, fos. 309–12, Olivares to Roose, 30 October 1641.
[102] See, for example, the consulta of the Council of Italy of 15 June 1641,'in AGS Est. leg. 3005.

likely to rule out any chance of a negotiated settlement. It was all very well to say that the two provinces remained useless as long as the king could not govern them with the same degree of authority as he exercised in Castile, but the conjuncture was not propitious for bringing this about.[103]

The Count-Duke's commitment to his great project for the unification of the Monarchy clearly remained unshaken by the events of 1640. But the same is likely to have been less true of the king. While Philip may initially have been captivated by the Count-Duke's plans to make him king of a united Spain, the very nature of his office ensured that he saw the peoples of his Monarchy in a rather different light. They stood to him in a special relationship, as children committed by God to his paternal care. When the Marquis of Villafranca earlier took the Count-Duke and his colleagues to task for attempting to strike a deal with rebellious vassals, the king wrote on the Junta Grande's *consulta* that there must be no alteration in the agreed policy of pardon for the Catalans, 'for any time the son chooses to come, I am ready to be the father.'[104] Emotionally, therefore, he was better prepared than the Count-Duke to welcome back the prodigal on the prodigal's terms.

In December Philip seems to have concluded that the moment was propitious for a new attempt to settle the Catalan question. He had just suffered a devastating personal blow in the death of his brother, the Cardinal-Infante, in Flanders—the culminating disaster of the year, as Olivares described it.[105] When the Count-Duke brought him the terrible news, Philip, who had schooled himself to maintain an absolute composure, broke down and sobbed.[106] For Olivares the death of 'so great a prince' was a grievous loss. After the initial period of distrust in the years when the Cardinal-Infante was growing up at court, the two men had come to develop at a distance a close personal relationship by means of a regular correspondence of surprising warmth.[107] The Count-Duke saw this new disaster as further evidence that his own sins were responsible for the woes of the Monarchy, and—as he told Roose—he had a strong apprehension that, with his own death, 'everything would quieten down, and our wishes be fulfilled.'

Don Fernando's death meant that, of the three royal brothers, only Philip remained. Like the Count-Duke he had come to see national

[103] ASF, Mediceo, filza 4966, despatch of Ottavio Pucci, 4 September 1641.
[104] AGS GA, leg. 1374, consulta of 26 January 1641.
[105] AGR CPE, Reg. 1502, fos. 323–5, Olivares to Roose, 8 December 1641.
[106] ASVen, Spagna, filza 76, despatch of 11 November 1641.
[107] Copies of the Count-Duke's letters in MSB, Cod. hisp. 22, and of the Cardinal-Infante's in the Archivo de la Casa de Miraflores, Madrid.

and personal misfortune as the direct consequence of his private sins, and the loss of his last surviving brother only served to intensify his sense of isolation, guilt and despair. He was well aware of the undercurrent of criticism at the way in which he devolved the duties of kingship on the Count-Duke, but at the same time remained deeply distrustful of his ability to bear the burden alone. Spurred now by private and public disaster he made a fresh attempt to rise to the occasion. Early in January it was noted that over the last few weeks he had been working alone on the *consultas* in the solitude of his study,[108] which suggests that his usual practice had been to go through them with the Count-Duke or the Protonotario at his side. As an early manifestation of this new attempt at personal involvement, he sent down for the consideration of the Junta Grande a paper he had drafted on the current state of affairs in Catalonia.[109]

The junta greeted the king's memorandum with a chorus of adulation, as being 'so admirable and superior as to make our principal task the offering of continuous thanks to God for having given these kingdoms a prince distinguished by so many virtues.' The royal document that elicited this paean of praise stated that the king's dearest wish was to settle the question of Catalonia. He believed that recent successes by royal troops in Roussillon and the plain of Tarragona made this a good moment, and there were encouraging reports from the Duchess of Cardona of persistent friction between the Catalans and their French protectors. This strengthened the case for a visit to Aragon before the spring, when the French would once again have their fleet off the Catalan coast. The junta responded that the silver galleons had yet to arrive, and it had so far proved impossible to make the necessary arrangements with the royal bankers. But José González and Cardinal Spínola both urged the king to leave at once, even if it meant requisitioning silver from the churches.

The king ordered González to take personal charge of the financial arrangements, but once again it proved necessary for the Count-Duke to intervene personally and twist the bankers' arms. At the beginning of February he could report that they were ready to supplement any shortfall in the February payments, and to cover the crown's expenses during the two succeeding months. His colleagues hailed this as nothing less than a miracle.[110] If so, it was a miracle wrought by the Portuguese businessmen who had remained in Castile. At a time when some of the major Genoese bankers of the reign, like Lelio Imvrea and Carlos Strata, had been removed from the scene by illness or death, while others were prudently cutting down on their transac-

---

[108] ASF Mediceo, filza 4966, letter from Bernardo Monanni, 8 January 1642.
[109] AGS GA, leg. 1378, consulta of Junta Grande, 27 December 1641.
[110] AGS GA, leg. 1422, consulta of Junta Grande, 4 February 1642.

tions with the government, the Portuguese came to Olivares' rescue yet again. Over 1641–2 they remitted twelve million ducats to the crown.[111] They presumably calculated—correctly as it proved—that the galleons would soon be arriving at Cadiz,[112] but they were also in no doubt that their own future was bound up with that of Olivares. Once he went, there might well be no one left to shield them from the hostility of the populace and the attentions of the Inquisition.

In spite of the king's apparent eagerness to be gone, and the agreement of the bankers to advance money to the crown, the passing weeks still found Philip in Madrid. On 21 March, however, Olivares wrote to Pierre Roose that the king had decided to leave for Aragon on 23 April in response to repeated reports that Louis XIII was on his way to join his army in Roussillon.[113] The continuing delays are to be ascribed, in part if not wholly, to the scale and complexity of the organization that had to be mounted whenever the king left his capital. Provisions had to be assembled for the large royal entourage, and in this instance, although the initial purpose of the journey was to raise the morale of his subjects in Aragon and Valencia, a whole army had to be collected, if the king were to make an appearance near the battle lines. The presence of Louis XIII outside Perpignan demanded nothing less. It was becoming clear with every day that passed that Perpignan was the prize French objective, and the growing urgency of the situation was underlined when a relieving force of a mere two thousand men under the command of Cardona's son, the Marquis of Povar, was roundly defeated on 31 March, shortly after setting out from Tarragona in a wild attempt to march through Catalonia to Roussillon.[114]

Arrangements had to be made, too, for the running of the government during the absence of the king and his principal minister from Madrid. There were also certain matters of more private concern. In a determination to tidy up his affairs before leaving on a journey from which he might not return, Philip—perhaps inspired by the example set by his minister—formally recognized as his son a boy, Juan José de Austria, born to the Madrid actress, La Calderona, in 1629, a few months before the birth of Baltasar Carlos.[115] There seems to have been growing impatience with these various delays. At the end of March a sermon was preached in the church of the Incarnation by Father Agustín de Castro, in which he gave his opinion 'with

---

[111] Boyajian, *Portuguese Bankers*, pp. 138–9.
[112] The fourteen galleons and two *pataches* of the Armada Real de las Indias reached port on 5 March 1642 (see Chaunu, *Séville et l'Atlantique*, 5, p. 398).
[113] AGR CPE, Reg. 1502, fo. 336.
[114] Sanabre, *La acción de Francia*, pp. 200–202, and 222.
[115] *MHE*, 16, pp. 300 and 306 (25 and 29 March 1642).

great clarity' on matters of government and the necessity of a royal visit to Aragon.

It was presumed that the preacher would not have gone so far without permission from the Count-Duke or the king.[116] But there was a widespread suspicion that the Count-Duke was doing his best to keep the king in Madrid. The truth of this allegation is difficult to determine. There is no doubt that his deteriorating health made him reluctant to subject himself to the rigours of travel. When the king named him lieutenant general for the forthcoming campaign, he wrote an extraordinary letter of response, arguing that frequent dizzy spells and heart pains made it impossible for him to fulfill his functions as grand chamberlain and master of the horse, or even assist at an audience with the king or accompany him to church, let alone undertake a journey of this kind. While he would rather 'die miserably in the sea' (that obsessively recurrent image) than fail in his obligations, he begged to be relieved of his ministerial duties, for the 'most wretched professor is retired after twenty years of service, and I have already served for twenty-one.'[117] Apart from considerations of health, he knew that his enemies at court would make the most of his absence from Madrid. But most of all he seems to have felt a deep foreboding about campaigning prospects. The opening rounds of the campaign were not auspicious and the news of the Marquis of Povar's defeat and the subsequent French capture of the border fortress of Cotlliure reduced the Count-Duke to tears. If, as the Venetian ambassador assumed, these reverses meant that Roussillon was now irreparably lost,[118] the king's presence was unlikely to salvage the Catalan campaign.

Whatever the Count-Duke's reservations, the king was determined to go. He left Madrid at last on 26 April. His plan was to visit Valencia and then go on to Huesca in Aragon, and the Count-Duke was to join him shortly. During her husband's absence the queen was appointed governor of the realm, assisted by Cardinal Borja and a small group of councillors, with the Count of Castrillo handling the financial arrangements.[119] Philip's decision was hailed as the first independent action he had taken in his life, although there was some scepticism as to whether the Count-Duke would permit the trip to be anything more than a brief promenade, well away from the danger zone.[120] The events of the next few weeks fully justified the sceptics. The first night of the royal journey was spent at Barajas and the

[116] MHE, 16, p. 306.
[117] MC, 2, Doc. XVIII (6 April 1642).
[118] ASVen, Spagna, filza 77, despatch of 16 April 1642.
[119] MHE, 16, pp. 345 and 364.
[120] ASVen, Spagna, filza 77, despatch of 23 April 1642.

second at Alcalá de Henares, which the king entered in suitably martial style on horseback, with pistols at his saddle-bow. This promised well, but any military ardour inspired by the unusual sight of a King of Spain setting out for war was quickly dissipated as Philip frittered away the succeeding weeks in the environs of Madrid. He was entertained for three days by the Countess of Olivares in the Count-Duke's house at Loeches and then moved to his own country seat of Aranjuez, where he devoted himself to his usual hunting and sporting activities.[121] It was not until 23 May that he actually set out for the Crown of Aragon with a vast entourage of officials and an enormous baggage train.[122]

The most plausible explanation of this leisurely response to a declared emergency is that the troops were not ready and the money was not there. With Indies silver in such short supply, the monetary disorder in Castile had become so acute as to threaten total paralysis. On inspection of the books, it transpired that only 300,000 ducats of silver had been registered in the name of private persons in the galleons that put in to Cadiz in March. The Junta de Ejecución, describing the figure as unprecedented in its meagreness, attributed the catastrophic decline in remittances to large-scale fraud, and recommended that, since most of the money was anyhow for foreigners, the king could safely appropriate the silver and compensate the owners in vellón.[123] This was hardly the way to revive the flagging Indies trade.

The consequences of the lack of silver, and of confidence, were painfully apparent. On 23 April the Venetian ambassador reported that, in the nine days since the king's journey had come to be regarded as a certainty, the premium on silver in terms of vellón had risen 50% and now stood at 300% or more. One consequence of the vertiginous fall in the value of vellón was that the prices of goods in the shops were purely arbitrary, and misery widespread. According to the Venetian ambassador's preceding despatch of 16 April, the clergy were denouncing the government from the pulpits, and Madrid and Seville were on the brink of revolt. The nobility, most of whose income was derived from payments on censos, juros and other instruments of credit, were desperately impoverished, and the king could not capitalize on his Castilian revenues, which tax-payers paid in vellón. The change of plan when Philip set out from Aranjuez on 23 May is itself an indication of the difficulties involved in financing his expedition. His first destination was no longer Valencia, where

[121] Novoa, Codoin 86, pp. 21–2.
[122] Ibid., p. 32.
[123] AGS GA, consulta, 4 April 1642.

he would have to pay his expenses in silver, but the Castilian town of Cuenca, still safely within the confines of the kingdom of *vellón*.[124]

Quite apart from any personal reluctance he may have felt about leaving for Aragon, the Count-Duke was kept fully occupied in Madrid by the pressing need to scrape up funds and assemble companies of soldiers to accompany the king. This year he did not take time for his customary Easter retreat in his Retiro hermitage, but he did withdraw there for two days to prepare his last will and testament, which he signed on 16 May.[125] Ironically, Cardinal Richelieu, who had fallen gravely ill at Narbonne, on his way to join Louis XIII and the French army besieging Perpignan, drafted his own last will and testament exactly one week later.[126] The Count-Duke's testament was characteristic of the man in its grandiose ambition to bend the future to his will, and perhaps too in the disparity between the elaborate character of its numerous provisions and the capacity of a heavily indebted estate to permit their realization. These provisions included the foundation of a Hieronymite convent, eight *montes de piedad* for the relief of the poor, a college at Salamanca, three pilgrim hostels in Santiago, Loreto and Jerusalem, one hospice and two hospitals for retired soldiers, and an endowment of 100,000 ducats for rebuilding and repopulating the town of Algeciras and maintaining a squadron of galleons to defend the Straits of Gibraltar and the Spanish coast. But the Count-Duke's principal intention, in the words of the will, was the establishment of his ducal estate of San Lúcar in such a way that his successors would 'have sufficient to serve the Kings of Castile and maintain the splendour of my line.' His wife was made the heiress to the title and estate, and after her death, in lieu of any legitimate heirs, they were to go to the bastard son, Don Enrique, and then to his descendants.

With his personal affairs arranged, the Count-Duke left for Aranjuez on 20 May to join the king. There were rumours of an imperious royal summons, and his departure may have been more hasty than he would have liked.[127] He set out, according to Novoa, with fear of assassination in his heart, and a gnawing anxiety about the company that his royal master was keeping.[128] In the preceding August, to his utter astonishment,[129] the Portuguese had allowed their former vicereine, the Duchess of Mantua, to escape. On arrival in Spain

---

[124] *MHE*, 16, p. 369.

[125] ASF, Mediceo, filza 4966, despatch of Ottavio Pucci, 21 May 1642. For the text of the will, see Matilla Tascón, *Testamentos de 43 personas del Madrid de los Austrias*, pp. 171–94.

[126] See Elliott, *Richelieu and Olivares*, pp. 149–50, for a comparison of the two wills.

[127] *MHE*, 16, pp. 363–4, and 384–5.

[128] Novoa, *Codoin* 86, pp. 23–5. See Marañón, *Olivares*, pp. 342–7, for the problem of distinguishing between truth and legend in the story of the king's journey to Aragon.

[129] ASVen, Spagna, filza 76, despatch of 28 August 1641.

she was lodged in the convent of Ocaña, not far from Aranjuez, and the king now used the opportunity to spend an evening in her company. She may well have seized the occasion, as Novoa alleged, to pour out her grievances, and tell the king things he did not know about the background to the Portuguese revolt. During these days the king also gave two long secret audiences to the Duke of Alba, who had been serving as captain-general of the army on the Portuguese frontier, following the recall in November 1641 of the Count of Monterrey, in semi-disgrace for his miserable conduct of the Portuguese campaign.[130] Since Alba was regarded as an open enemy of the Count-Duke, tongues began to wag,[131] but it is likely that Alba was at least as concerned with his own financial state as with the state of the nation. A few months earlier he had written to Olivares to complain of his poverty: troops had been billeted on his estates in Navarre, he had lost six thousand ducats annual income in silver paid by his Catalan properties, and the Council of the Indies owed him another six thousand ducats of income on the proceeds of fines and salaries.[132] His case was no different, except perhaps in scale, from that of the majority of his fellow magnates. For all of them, the years of the Count-Duke's government had been financially ruinous.[133]

Hardly had the royal party set out from Aranjuez for Cuenca when the papal dispensation arrived for the marriage of the Count-Duke's bastard son to Doña Juana de Velasco, the daughter of the Constable of Castile.[134] Don Enrique, who now bore the title of Marquis of Mairena, left at once for Madrid, and his wedding was celebrated a few days later in the palace.[135] After the sixteen years hiatus following the death of his daughter in 1626, the Count-Duke's family strategy was again on course. Once again he began to purchase estates in the region of Seville to consolidate the family properties,[136] and within a day to two of the marriage he was writing to the Constable looking forward to the birth of the first of many grandsons.[137] The marriage itself could be regarded as highly satisfactory, at least for

[130] ASF, Mediceo, filza 4966, despatch of Ottavio Pucci, 13 November 1641.
[131] ASVen, Spagna, filza 77, despatch of 25 May 1642. Marañón, *Olivares*, pp. 94–5, has doubts about the alleged enmity between Olivares and the sixth Duke of Alba, and publishes in Appendix 24 extracts from letters exchanged between them during this period which show the Count-Duke dealing in characteristically paternal style with an irritable younger man.
[132] AGS GA, leg. 1423, consulta of Junta de Ejecución, 12 March 1642.
[133] For other examples see Charles Jago, 'The "Crisis of the Aristocracy" in Seventeenth-Century Castile', *Past and Present*, 84 (1979), pp. 60–90.
[134] Archivo del Duque de Frías, Cat. 1, no. 2834, Olivares to Constable of Castile, 24 May 1642.
[135] Novoa, *Codoin* 86, p. 25.
[136] ASF, Mediceo, filza 4966, letter from Bernardo Monanni, 25 June 1642.
[137] Archivo del Duque de Frías, Cat. 1, no. 2834, letter of 5 June 1642.

the father of the bridegroom. Not only was his son marrying into one of the great houses of Castile, but the bride's mother, Doña Isabel de Guzmán, was the sister of the Duke of Medina de las Torres, his former son-in-law, so that two of the main branches of the Guzmán family were once again intertwined.[138] But not everyone in the family circle could take the same satisfaction in the marriage. The principal losers were the Haro family—the Count-Duke's sister, the Marchioness of Carpio, her brother-in-law, the Count of Castrillo, and, most of all, her son, Don Luis de Haro, who had expected the San Lúcar succession to devolve upon him by default. Don Luis was too smooth a courtier not to put a brave face on these untoward proceedings, although no one doubted the strength of the resentment beneath that bland exterior. But the marked signs of favour bestowed on him by the king at Aranjuez during the absence of his uncle, prompted speculation that, although one inheritance might be lost to him, a greater might soon come his way.[139]

The Count-Duke's relatives found themselves in an increasingly awkward situation. For years their fate had been bound up with his, and however exasperating they had found his capriciousness, the knowledge that they sank or swam together had imposed upon them an obvious circumspection. Beginning with the capture of the court and governmental apparatus from the Sandoval connection on the death of Philip III, the family solidarity of the Guzmán-Haro connection had brought it impressive rewards. While the Count-Duke had done what he could to hold the more rapacious of his relatives in check, ease of access to the fount of patronage had enabled them to accumulate lucrative offices and amass large personal fortunes at the expense of their rivals. Enjoying the Count-Duke's favour, if not always his confidence, Monterrey, Leganés, Medina de las Torres and Don Luis de Haro had become exceptionally wealthy men. None of them knew how much longer the Count-Duke would remain in power, but all of them, observing his increasingly erratic behaviour and his unbroken run of misfortune, could sense that an age was drawing to its close. Did the interests of the *parentela*—the clan—demand that they should stand beside him to the end? Or might they not be better advised, following the analogy so beloved of the Count-Duke himself, to fling this Jonah into the ocean in a bid to save their skins?

It was an awkward dilemma, not least because some sudden change in the direction of the winds might yet calm the storm-tossed seas. There were, for instance, persistent rumours that Richelieu was close

---

[138] Marañón, *Olivares*, p. 300.
[139] ASVen, Spagna, filza 77, despatch of 25 May 1642.

to death.[140] There was unexpectedly good news, too, from Flanders, where Don Francisco de Melo, who had assumed the post of governor on the Cardinal-Infante's death, won a striking victory over the French at Honnecourt on 26 May.[141] With the road to Paris open, Melo might well be in a position to replay the Cardinal-Infante's Corbie campaign of 1636. Even in Spain itself there was now a glimmer of hope. With an army of eight thousand infantry and another eight thousand cavalry assembled on the Valencian coast at Vinaroz under the command of Leganés,[142] and large numbers of men arriving from all over Spain at Molina in Aragon, to which the king removed from Cuenca at the end of June, prospects began to improve for the recovery of Catalonia. Each year, as the Tuscan ambassador pointed out, there was talk of one last great effort, but this year it seemed truer than ever, and he did not see how the Catalans could resist such an overwhelming force.[143] If Catalonia were recovered, the Count-Duke would survive.

Among his relatives, therefore, discretion remained the order of the day. But the Count-Duke had one kinsman who did not know the meaning of the word. The smoke-screen so carefully devised to conceal from the world the treasonable activities of the Duke of Medina Sidonia had been reasonably effective. While questions may have lingered in the public mind as to exactly what had happened in the summer of 1641, the duke seemed the very epitome of loyalty as he challenged the new King of Portugal to a personal duel, and then, when his challenge was contemptuously ignored, engaged himself and his vassals in the border war. These military activities, as the crown intended, took a heavy toll of the ducal income, and imposed massive burdens on the capital of his duchy, Sanlúcar de Barrameda. One of the conditions of his pardon was that he stayed away from Sanlúcar, but on 19 June he turned up in the town without warning, to receive an ecstatic welcome from his vassals.[144] This time there was no way in which the Count-Duke could save the family's honour. With the king away in Aragon, and with Andalusia 'half in revolt', as the Venetian ambassador had described it in the spring,[145] it was essential to forestall the duke before he built up a large popular following. Ordered to leave at once for Burgos, he was arrested at Vitoria, imprisoned in the castle of Coca, and subjected to a long

[140] *MHE*, 16, p. 391 (10 June 1642).
[141] Israel, *The Dutch Republic*, p. 316; AHN Osuna, leg. 554, Olivares to Duke of Gandía, 18 June 1642, announcing Melo's 'grande victoria', and sending him a dozen copies of Melo's letter for distribution, as a means of raising morale.
[142] *MHE*, 16, p. 391.
[143] ASF, Mediceo, filza 4967, despatch of Ottavio Pucci, 30 July 1642.
[144] *MHE*, 16, pp. 415–16; Domínguez Ortiz, 'La conspiración', pp. 133–8.
[145] ASVen, Spagna, filza 77, cyphered despatch of 30 April 1642.

judicial investigation, which would end in the compulsory incorporation of Sanlúcar into the royal demesne. Within a few weeks of
his arrest the secret was out, and the treachery of the preceding year
became public knowledge.[146] The Count-Duke never recovered from
the blow to the honour of the house of Guzmán. Writing to Antonio
Carnero after his fall from power, he worried that future historians
would record his own downfall as a direct consequence of the arrest
of Medina Sidonia and the Marquis of Ayamonte, and lead even
the most 'merciful' reader to cast doubt on his 'fame and honour'.[147]

These deep family worries clouded the Count-Duke's mind, and
perhaps his judgment, as he struggled with the problems of military
organization and campaign strategy at the king's temporary headquarters in Molina de Aragón. His anxieties were increased by a
curious incident on 17 July, when he was reviewing the troops outside
the city walls. As the company of the Marquis of Salinas fired a
salvo in his honour, a bullet hit the bar of his coach, and the flying
fragments struck and slightly wounded two of his companions, his
secretary Carnero and the dwarf known as El Primo, who was fanning
him in the heat of the day.[148] Although an unfortunate soldier was
put to the torture, it proved impossible to discover whether the shot
was fired by accident or design. The uncertainty only increased the
consternation in the Count-Duke's immediate circle, and while the
Count-Duke himself maintained his composure, there was talk of
an immediate return to Madrid. The news of the alleged attempt—if
such it was—travelled fast, provoking general regret that the tyrant
still lived and that the bullet had missed it mark.

In France, too, the tyrant still lived, in spite of all the efforts of
his enemies. On 28 February Olivares had received a letter, dated
3 February and reserved for his sight alone, written by Don Antonio
de Sarmiento, formerly *maestre de campo general* in the Franche-Comté
and now assisting Don Francisco de Melo in Brussels.[149] Sarmiento
wrote under oath of secrecy to report that Louis XIII's young
favourite, Cinq-Mars, was planning to 'destroy the Cardinal', and
that a conspiracy was being hatched with the Queen of France's knowledge.[150] The conspirators sent an emissary to Madrid by a covert
route. This was the hunchback Marquis de Fontrailles, a dependent

[146] ASF, Mediceo, filza 4967, letter of Bernardo Monanni, 6 August 1642.
[147] AHN Est. lib. 869, fo. 248, Olivares to Carnero, 16 February 1644.
[148] Novoa, *Codoin* 86, p. 47, and see Marañón, *Olivares*, pp. 338–40 for this incident. El
Primo is the subject of a famous portrait by Velázquez.
[149] AGS Est. leg. 2057, Sarmiento to Olivares, 3 February 1642, with consulta of Council
of State, 6 March 1642.
[150] For the Cinq-Mars conspiracy, see Philippe Erlanger, *Cinq-Mars ou la passion et la fatalité*
(Paris, 1962); also Burckhardt, *Richelieu and his Age*, 3, pp. 426–53, and Elliott, *Richelieu and
Olivares*, pp. 146–8.

of the ever unreliable Duke of Orléans, who was deputed to request military assistance from Spain, although apparently without revealing the complicity of Cinq-Mars in the plot. The Count-Duke seems to have concealed Sarmiento's letter from his colleagues on the Council of State, which was asked only to pronounce on whether to approve a formal agreement with Orléans. After what seemed to Fontrailles an eternity of waiting, the treaty was at last signed on 13 March, and he hurried back to France.

By ways which have never been firmly established, the text of the treaty fell into Richelieu's hands. Many influential figures, and possibly even Louis XIII himself, had an inkling that something was afoot. There was a profound war-weariness in France; Richelieu, who was a dying man, was detested; and a *coup* designed to overthrow his regime and replace it with one which would actively seek peace with Spain would have been widely welcomed. It is possible that Anne of Austria herself revealed the secret to the Cardinal, as a means of retaining control over her children and securing the regency in the event of her husband's death.[151] By 11 June, the Cardinal, who was at Arles, had in his hands the evidence he needed. The next day it was presented to the king at Narbonne, and Cinq-Mars and his fellow conspirators were arrested. Early in July the Duke of Orléans, confronted with irrefutable proof of his complicity in the plot, fled to Savoy. Once again, the Cardinal had foiled his enemies, and once again the Count-Duke saw his hopes of his rival's downfall dashed, and with them any prospect of an early end to the war.

In spite of the massive military and naval effort being made by Spain that summer, the news from the front was full of disappointments. A powerful French army, under the command of La Mothe-Houdancourt, had established its base at Lérida in the spring, and from there had crossed the frontier into Aragon. Late in June it captured Monzón, the scene of so many sessions of the Cortes. It then advanced on Fraga, but abandoned its attempts to take the town when the Spanish army under Leganés reported progress in the plain of Tarragona.[152] If the advance of Leganés provided temporary relief for Aragon, there was deep concern at the king's headquarters in Molina about the course of events in Roussillon. Although Louis XIII had left the camp early in June, disappointed at the slow progress of the siege of Perpignan, the noose was tightening round the beleaguered city as French ships, engaged in a running battle with a large Spanish squadron, blocked the coastal approaches and prevented the defenders from receiving supplies.

---

[151] Dethan, *Gaston d'Orléans*, pp. 271–4.
[152] Sanabre, *La acción de Francia*, pp. 210–11.

Frustration at the failure to achieve some spectacular success only added to the tensions in the royal entourage, where nerves were more than usually taut following the Count-Duke's narrow escape from death. Nearly two months had passed since the king had left Aranjuez, and so far there was nothing to show for the expense and discomfort of his trip to Aragon. What indeed was he supposed to be doing there, and did his journey serve any useful purpose at all? It had originally been intended that he should proceed from Cuenca to the city of Valencia, where his presence was expected to arouse the enthusiasm of his Valencian vassals, and induce them to contribute generously to the campaign against the Catalans. The change of plan that brought him to Molina de Aragón was not well received in Valencia, and contributions lagged. Olivares wrote in July to the viceroy of Valencia, the Duke of Gandía, that it broke his heart to see the Marquis of Torrecuso unable to launch a new campaign in the plain of Tarragona because of the lack of Valencian troops—and this at a time when the Monarchy was 'on the point of foundering'.[153]

The king's move to Molina de Aragón seems to have come about at the insistence of the newly appointed Imperial ambassador, the Marquis of Grana. A professional soldier whose experience had earned from Philip an invitation to accompany him on the journey as a military adviser,[154] Grana was highly critical of the way in which affairs were being managed. At one of the council meetings he apparently argued that instead of visiting Valencia, the king should establish his headquarters in Aragon, with his armies close at hand. It is not clear whether the ambassador was simply giving a soldier's blunt appraisal of the situation, or was speaking for others—for those who hoped that Philip would rise to the occasion as a warrior-king, and in the process free himself from the clutches of his favourite. His argument involved him in a bitter clash with the Count-Duke's confidant, José González, who spoke forcefully but unsuccessfully in favour of a royal visit to Valencia. The Venetian ambassador, in reporting this clash, noted that Grana was linked by ties of blood and friendship to Don Luis de Haro.[155] Is it possible that Don Luis was already manoeuvring with an eye to the succession?

On 27 July, coming a little closer to the scene of action, the king and court moved to Zaragoza, where they would remain for the rest of the season. The city overflowed with nobles, courtiers and

[153] AHN Osuna, leg. 554, no. 78, Olivares to Gandía, 19 July 1642.
[154] ASF, Mediceo, filza 4966, despatch of Ottavio Pucci, 6 November 1641, written just after Grana's arrival in Madrid as the Emperor's new ambassador, and Novoa, *Codoin* 86, p. 35.
[155] ASVen, Spagna, filza 77, despatch of Venetian ambassador, 21 July 1642, reporting Grana's return to Molina after two days of seclusion in Madrid. See also Marañón, *Olivares*, p. 346 for this episode.

captains, all of them with time hanging heavy on their hands.[156] Once again all the sound and fury of military preparations translated into nothing. The army of Aragon obstinately refused to take shape.[157] All the action was away to the northeast, in Roussillon, where the defenders of Perpignan were slowly being starved into submission. During that summer Richelieu directed his failing energies to the reduction of Perpignan, the traditional key to Spain.[158] Its surrender to the French army, on 10 September, was a devastating blow to Spanish morale. According to the Venetian ambassador, the Count-Duke entered the king's chamber, his face bathed in tears, and kneeling at the king's feet begged him, without explanation, to let him throw himself out of the window. He wanted, he said, only to die; no consolation was left to him in this world; he was the most unfortunate man ever to be born; and he besought His Majesty to allow him to kill himself, or at least, with his customary benignity, to give him leave to bury himself in some remote corner of the world where he would never again be seen. The startled monarch, still ignorant of what this scene was all about, finally extracted from his minister the news of Perpignan's fall. He tearfully consoled and embraced him, assuring him that this was all God's will, and that he had in no way failed in his obligations.[159]

In his distress at the loss of Perpignan, Philip gave orders for the immediate preparation of the army for an assault on Lérida, in spite of the lateness of the campaigning season. While the army commanded by the Marquises of Torrecusa and Mortara, and encamped in the plain of Tarragona, was to advance on Lérida from the south, the troops assembled in Zaragoza were to approach it from the west, by way of Fraga. To the king's annoyance, their commander, Leganés, seemed in no hurry to be gone, but by the end of the month he was on the move.[160] The subsequent brief campaign was a disaster. After skirmishes along the road, the two Spanish armies, totalling 20,000 men, met La Mothe's army of 12,000 French and 1,000 Catalans on the outskirts of Lérida on 7 October. There were heavy casualties on both sides—in dead, wounded and prisoners Leganés lost a quarter of his men—and at the end of the day the battlefield remained in the hands of the French.[161]

When the news of the defeat reached Zaragoza, the king seems to have subsided into a profound melancholy. His personal responsi-

---

[156] Novoa, *Codoin* 86, pp. 51–3.
[157] *Ibid.*, p. 55.
[158] Sanabre, *La acción de Francia*, p. 230.
[159] ASVen, Spagna, filza 77, despatch of Niccolò Sagrado, 17 September 1642.
[160] Novoa, *Codoin* 86, pp. 62–3.
[161] Sanabre, *La acción de Francia*, pp. 211–12.

bility for the campaign, coupled with the numerical inferiority of the victorious French army, made its outcome an even greater humiliation than the fall of Perpignan.[162] In the words of Matías de Novoa, 'the honour of the nation and the reputation of Spain were lost', and the army, with nothing accomplished, and with provisions running short, began to disintegrate.[163] During the following weeks there was much debate as to whether the king's continuing presence in Zaragoza served any useful purpose, while the subject of these discussions sat brooding in his apartments.[164]

Inevitably, there was an intense post-mortem analysis of the disastrous campaign, conducted both openly and in secret. Sheer technical incompetence undoubtedly played some part in the miserable showing of the Spanish forces. The cosmographer royal, the Flemish Jesuit Jean-Charles della Faille, was shocked at the lack of up-to-date maps of both Catalonia and Portugal. 'I am not surprised that our enemies, with fewer men, have the advantage over us, because I can see that *ingenio* and science are despised, and in matters of war these are of no less importance than military strength.'[165] Behind the technical incompetence lay personal incompetence, and Leganés was held responsible for the failure of the campaign. For some months he lived in a state of suspended disgrace, to be relieved of his command in the spring of 1643, after the Count-Duke's fall.[166] In the meantime, it was noted that the Count-Duke seemed to be turning his back on the man whom he held (in the words of his recent will) 'in place of a son',[167] while his real or putative son, Don Enrique, now a gentleman of the king's chamber, rarely left the king's side and was riding high at court.[168]

In distancing himself from Leganés, the Count-Duke was tacitly recognizing his own vulnerability following the abysmal failure of the Aragonese campaign. Half of him wanted it all to be over and done with for ever. He was demoralized, exhausted, and—as he approached his fifty-sixth year—his health was collapsing. In a letter written to the Tuscan ambassador on 19 November he complained of leg and back pains, headaches and dizziness. He was, he said, in such distress that he did not know whether he was coming or

[162] ASVen, Spagna, filza 77, despatch of 22 October 1642.
[163] Novoa, *Codoin* 86, p. 66.
[164] ASVen, Spagna, filza 77, despatch of 26 November 1642.
[165] Omer Van de Vyver S. I., 'Lettres de J-Ch.Della Faille S. I., cosmographe du roi à Madrid, à M-F. Van Langren, cosmographe du roi à Bruxelles, 1634–1645', *Archivum Historicum Societatis Iesu*, 46 (1977), p. 172 (19 October 1642).
[166] AS Modena, Spagna B.53, despatch of Ippolito Camilo Guidi, 1 April 1643; *MHE*, 17, p. 64 (2 April 1643).
[167] Matilla Tascón, *Testamentos*, p. 174.
[168] ASVen, Spagna, filza 77, despatch of 17 December 1642.

going.[169] Yet the other half of him refused to abandon the struggle. In part this was because he could not bring himself to face the shame and humiliation of leaving office with his work in ruins. But he had also come to think of himself as utterly indispensable to the royal service, and could not conceive how the monarch to whom he had devoted every waking hour of his ministerial career could ever manage without him. At all costs—and his own life was the least of these—the king's service must be done.

Sniffing treachery everywhere, but determined to hold on, the Count-Duke started preparing for the king's return to Madrid. Before the next campaigning season, new troops would have to be levied, and new funds raised; and, as the king told his disappointed Aragonese vassals, this could only be done in Castile.[170] On 1 December Philip and his entourage left Zaragoza. At Alcalá de Henares, on the last stage of a rough and uncomfortable journey, the students shouted insults as the Count-Duke's coach passed through the streets, and accused him of cowardice in running away from the war. He had the coach curtains drawn, and, cancelling his plans to dine in Alcalá, gave orders to press on to Madrid, where he arrived a little ahead of the king. At midday on 6 December Philip reached the Retiro, and was reunited with the queen. That night he returned to his palace of the Alcázar under cover of darkness. The Count-Duke chose to enter Madrid by an unfrequented gate, following the back streets to reach the Alcázar. It was a dispiriting return, and yet, when he appeared in public again, observers were amazed. He seemed serene, confident, and even cheerful, and addressed the grandees in tones of superiority unusual even for him.[171] Whatever the future held in store, the Count-Duke still had his pride.

---

[169] ASF, Mediceo, filza 4966, copy of letter from Olivares to Ottavio Pucci, 19 November 1642. 'Asseguro a VS. que me hallo con tal aprieto que no sé donde estoy de la cabeza'.
[170] Novoa, *Codoin* 86, p. 71.
[171] ASVen, Spagna, filza 77, despatch of 12 December 1642.

XVI

SHIPWRECK

Fall from power

It was very unfortunate, confessed the Count-Duke in an end-of-the-year letter to Pierre Roose, that, in spite of the large armies that had been assembled, His Majesty had not returned from Aragon 'with the glory that had been expected'.[1] This was a notable understatement. The campaign had been nothing short of ignominious, and if the Count-Duke was universally held responsible for the fiasco, Philip himself did not escape unscathed. His passivity in the face of grave national crisis stood in sharp contrast to the vigour with which the queen had carried out her duties as governor of the realm during her husband's absence from Madrid. During her months of regency, Elizabeth of Bourbon—known to Spaniards as Isabel de Borbón—emerged from the shadows to which court protocol normally confined queens of Spain, and revealed qualities of energy and determination which impressed her advisers, and turned her overnight into a popular heroine (Pl. 33).[2] Where her Spanish counterpart in France, Anne of Austria, was usually privy to the intrigues of Richelieu's enemies and was incessantly meddling in political affairs, there is no indication that Isabel had ever done the same. She was believed to resent the Count-Duke's influence over her husband, but the close supervision of the Countess of Olivares, her mistress of the robes, severely restricted her freedom of action, and any injudicious word was unlikely to be kept from him for long. The outward demeanour of this long-suffering woman, whose natural gaiety of spirit had been slowly worn down by the cavalier treatment she received from a notoriously unfaithful husband, was in any event impeccable, and Olivares himself always spoke of her with the utmost respect and veneration. When she died two years later, he wrote from his exile to Antonio Carnero to say that not a day or an hour would pass in which she would not be sorely missed.[3]

[1] AGR CPE, Reg. 1502, fo. 350, Olivares to Roose, 30 December 1642.

[2] ASG, Lettere Ministri, Spagna, 2445, despatch of Constantino Doria, 22 January 1643. The queen's comportment in the period before Olivares' fall is examined by Marañón in *Olivares*, pp. 348–52.

[3] AHN Est. lib. 869, fo. 282, letter of 12 October 1644.

33. Diego de Velázquez and workshop, *Queen Isabella*.

Court gossip and popular legend credited the queen with playing the leading part in the Count-Duke's overthrow. In contemporary accounts she is depicted as the central figure in a 'conspiracy of the women', in which the embittered Duchess of Mantua, the king's old nurse, Doña Ana de Guevara, and his future confidante, Sor María, the mother superior of the Aragonese convent of Agreda, also participated.[4] She had undoubtedly acquired a new authority, and perhaps also a new self-confidence, through her recent experience of government, and since the Count-Duke's fate rested in the hands of the king, it was inevitable that anyone actively working to get rid of the minister would seek to enlist her support. Among the councillors of state attending on her in Madrid during the king's absence, the one most interested in securing the Count-Duke's smooth and expeditious removal from office was his kinsman, the Count of Castrillo, whom he had left in charge of day-to-day financial arrangements.

Since 1632 Castrillo had presided over the Council of the Indies, and in the past few years he had shouldered heavy administrative duties for Olivares, who was impressed by his capacity for work. It was presumably as a reward for his labours, and as an expression of the Count-Duke's complete confidence in his dependability, that he was appointed in 1640 to the key palace post of *mayordomo mayor* which the death of the fifth Duke of Alba in the preceding year had left unoccupied.[5] The papal nuncio described him as 'capable, and totally dependent on the Count-Duke', but thought him imperious, although he walked circumspectly where his own concerns were not involved.[6] According to the Earl of Clarendon, who came to know him in Madrid a few years later, 'he was a man of great parts, and a very wise man, grave and eloquent in his discourse, and understood the state of Spain better than any man. He lived within himself, as if he had a mind to be rich.'[7] While he cherished private ambitions, it seems likely that at this stage he was acting in collusion with his nephew, Don Luis de Haro, to whom otherwise, in the words of Clarendon, he was 'of no kind of kin'. The king's affection since boyhood days for Don Luis, who was of much the same age as himself, made a working partnership of uncle and nephew—like that of Zúñiga and Olivares a generation earlier—a sensible arrangement if the Count-Duke's political legacy were to be kept in the family's hands. But Castrillo, assiduously cultivating the queen, was laying the foundations of a power-base of his own. In the end his efforts

---

[4] See Marañón, *Olivares*, ch. 24.
[5] *MHE*, 15, p. 434 (27 March 1640).
[6] ASV, Spagna 85, fo. 71, despatch of Mgr. Panziroli, 22 October 1642.
[7] *History of the Rebellion*, 5, p. 95.

were to be frustrated by the premature death of his royal patron. He was, wrote Clarendon, 'much trusted by the late Queen, after the disgrace of the conde duke, to which he was thought to [have contributed] very much, that if she had lived and held that power which she had newly got he was very like to be the first minister; which did him no good when he missed it.'

Circumstances, however, as much as conspiracy, were working to topple the Count-Duke from power. Not the least of these was the precarious state of his mental and physical health, although once back in Madrid he seemed his old self again. Characteristically he at once threw himself into the business of arranging the *asientos* with the bankers for the coming year, and generally displayed a frenetic energy which belied his complaints of exhaustion. Why, he wanted to know, were the orders issued in Zaragoza being disregarded— orders for production to continue at full pace in the powder factories of Aragon, Valencia and Navarre, in the Plasencia arms works and the Liérganes iron foundries? Why were steps not being taken to halt mass desertions from the frontier armies? Already nine days had passed since the king's return to Madrid, and yet 'nothing has been done, nothing is being done, and everything has come to a standstill— and this at a time when we need recruits, cavalry horses and every- thing else.' After 'twenty-two years of labouring at the oar, and always against the wind and fortune, thanks to my own sins, and those of many others' he could no longer keep going at his old pace.[8]

Observers at court had the impression that the Count-Duke stood higher in the royal favour than ever, and that the king seemed to be sliding back into the lazy and compliant ways of his earlier years.[9] This could well have been his way of responding to the mounting pressures for the dismissal of his minister. It was easier to take refuge in court amusements than face unwelcome decisions. The long years of dependence made it difficult for Philip to imagine life without the Count-Duke at his side, and he had no confidence in his own ability to manage affairs of state unaided. For the first two or three weeks after his return to Aragon he may have wanted to give his minister the benefit of the doubt, as if determined to express to the last possible moment his continuing confidence in the man who had for so many years guided the affairs of his state. Yet he was intelligent enough to read the portents, and pyschologically he may have been adjusting himself to the change that lay ahead.

Late in December there was a reorganization of the central organs of government, which bears all the marks of the Court-Duke's

[8] *MC*, 2, Doc. XIX (15 December 1642).
[9] ASVen, Spagna, filza 77, desparch of 17 December 1642.

capricious hand.[10] The principal policy-making body of the last few years, the Junta de Ejecución, was dissolved, presumably in response to demands for a restoration of authority to the councils, which the Count-Duke had done so much to weaken and undermine. The Marquis of Grana, the Imperial ambassador, was saying nothing new when he wrote that it had consisted of the Count-Duke's adherents, who always knew what he wanted before they cast their votes. But those who expected the Council of State to recover its powers were to be quickly disabused. A plenary session was held in the presence of the king, but it concluded its business in under an hour, and apparently decided nothing of moment.

In place of the Junta de Ejecución, three new committees, or *salas*, were created—the obnoxious word *junta* was apparently to be dropped. The first and most important of these was the *sala de gobierno*, which was to meet in the Count-Duke's rooms and under his presidency. It was expected to handle the whole range of government business, but its composition hardly suggested an improvement on what had gone before. The Duke of Villahermosa had always been one of the Count-Duke's most sycophantic followers. The Marquis of Castrofuerte, according to the Marquis of Grana, enjoyed a similar reputation, and anyhow was eighty years old, and totally deaf. The third member, Don Cristóbal de Benavente y Benavides, while better qualified, was working his passage back into favour. The second *sala* was to handle the militia levies, under the presidency of the Count of Monterrey, described by Grana as a 'capital enemy' of the Count-Duke, whose confidence he had never enjoyed. But while he was hoping for his brother-in-law's downfall, he was too scared to speak out. Its other members were the Protonotario, and the elderly secretary, Pedro de Arce. The third *sala*, for 'provisioning the armies of Spain, Italy and Flanders', was to be presided over by the Marquis of Castañeda, who had returned to court in 1640 from his embassy to Vienna. Its membership consisted of the Count of Miranda, another of the Count-Duke's creatures, and that indispensable Genoese business-man, Bartolomé Espínola. The king seems to have insisted that there should be no repetition of the incompetence that had dogged the Aragonese campaign, but observers might well be forgiven for assuming that the three *salas* together were no more than the old Junta de Ejecución in another guise.

---

[10] ASVen, Spagna, filza 77, despatch of 31 December 1642. A fuller account, giving personal details, is supplied by the Imperial ambassador, the Marquis of Grana, in a despatch of 16 January 1643 (Österreichisches Staatsarchiv, Vienna, Abteilung Haus-, Hof-und Staatsarchiv, Spanien Diplomatische Korrespondenz, Kart. 27, Mappe 491). I am much indebted to Magdalena Sánchez for providing me with copies of this and other despatches from the Marquis of Grana.

This restructuring of the administration hardly suggested that the Count-Duke's downfall was imminent. But as 1642 drew to a close there were one or two straws in the wind. Once again the ministers disagreed over the perennial question of whether to give priority to Catalonia or Portugal. The Count-Duke wanted to launch a campaign against Portugal early in the new year, but his fellow-ministers had their usual reservations about dividing Spain's forces, especially with hunger and misery thinning the ranks of the army of Aragon.[11] The Count of Oñate, who was prevented by gout from attending the Council of State, apparently produced a written statement in which he took sharp issue with the plans for a Portuguese campaign.[12] The king was reported by the papal nuncio to have decided in favour of prosecuting a vigorous war against the Catalans, in defiance of Olivares. It was this, said the nuncio, that first opened the Count-Duke's eyes to what was happening.[13]

It is difficult to sift fact from fiction in the court gossip relayed by foreign ambassadors in Madrid in the weeks surrounding the Count-Duke's departure from office. The most sensational letters were those written by Father Ippolito Camillo Guidi, the Modenese envoy, whose *Caduta del Conte d'Olivares* would become the standard contemporary account of his fall from power.[14] In despatches dated 7 January 1643, however, three ambassadors—the Modenese, Tuscan and Venetian—all give the impression that major events were in the making, although they disagreed on the details. The sudden departure of the Duchess of Mantua from her convent at Ocaña and her dramatic appearance at court on the night of 3 January were thought to presage no good for the Count-Duke, and there was much speculation about the efforts of the queen to make her husband reflect on the sad state of the Spanish Monarchy. According to the Venetian ambassador, the king resolved to talk to his minister, who threw himself at his feet, begged for leave to retire, and then had all the current *consultas* and state papers sent over to the king's rooms. At the sight of so much paper covering every table in his apartments, Philip took fright, and returned all the documents to the Count-Duke, ordering him to continue in office. He then left the palace to go hunting.[15]

---

[11] ASG, Spagna, filza 2444, despatch of 31 December 1642.

[12] ASF, Mediceo, filza 4966, despatch of 7 January 1643.

[13] ASV, Spagna 85, despatch of 28 January 1643.

[14] The *editio princeps* was published at Ivrea in 1644. See A. Morel-Fatio, 'Caduta del Conte d'Olivares', *Bulletin Italien*, 12 (1912), pp. 27–49, 136–56, 224–37, and Werner, 'Caída del Conde-Duque de Olivares', pp. 1–156, for the text of the Spanish version. The origins and reliability of the various accounts of Olivares' fall are discussed in Marañón, *Olivares*, Appendix 2.

[15] ASVen, Spagna, filza 77, despatch of 7 January 1643. The Marquis of Grana tells the same story in his despatch of 16 January.

Whatever the truth of this engaging story, there is no doubt that the Count-Duke's position was becoming untenable, and it seems likely that, even inside the palace itself, his authority was slipping. The Count of Castrillo, as *mayordomo mayor*, was well placed to influence by a word or a whisper the gentlemen in waiting and the king's closest servants, who were now moving through their ritual functions in the echoing silences of a half-empty palace. Since the return from Zaragoza, the grandees had taken to boycotting court activities, and on Christmas day only the young Count of Santa Coloma took his place in the grandees' pew of the royal chapel.[16] The court preachers, meanwhile, denounced the government openly.[17] If nobility and church were ranged against him, the Count-Duke could certainly expect no sympathy from the populace of Madrid. Royal and municipal taxes, all the more galling when they were raised to pay for the king's diversions in the Buen Retiro, were bitterly resented. To them were added a currency that was more than usually chaotic. On 15 September 1642, in an attempt to curb the violent inflation of *vellón* prices of 1641–2 brought about by its tampering with the coinage, the government had resorted to deflation on a massive scale. Pieces of twelve and eight *maravedís* were reduced to two, those of six and four to one, and those of one to a *blanca*, or half a *maravedí*.[18] Since copper was the normal day-to-day currency, the social and economic consequences were calamitous.

Over the winter months of 1642–3 a pall of despair seems to have descended on the cities of Castile. Life was made intolerable by the lack of coins for ordinary transactions, and poverty was acute.[19] What Antonio Carnero described as 'the extreme tightness and inconvenience caused by the reduction in the value of *vellón*'[20] also made it more than usually difficult to conclude the *asientos* with the bankers, since tax yields were much reduced. Royal requests for fifteen million ducats for 1643 had to be scaled down to six million and then to four million,[21] and negotiations once again continued well into the new year, although on 16 January Carnero thought that they were close to being concluded. The Count-Duke, he told Roose, still kept swimming, but the waters were nearly over his head. 'The storm', he went on, 'is great, but God is above all, and one single event can change everything for the better and give us the peace that is the only remedy.'

[16] Werner, 'Caída del Conde-Duque de Olivares', p. 121.
[17] ASVen, Spagna, filza 77, despatch of 21 January 1643.
[18] Hamilton, *American Treasure*, p. 86; Domínguez Ortiz, *Política y hacienda*, p. 262.
[19] ASVen, Spagna, filza 77, despatch of 19 November 1642; and see Domínguez Ortiz, pp. 262–3.
[20] AGR CPE, Reg. 1504, fo. 238v., Carnero to Roose, 16 January 1643.
[21] ASV, Spagna 85, nuncio's despatch of 24 December 1642.

That 'single event' might indeed already have occurred. Definitive news of the death of Cardinal Richelieu in Paris on 4 December 1642 seems to have reached Madrid only in January. On the 10th the Count-Duke received a letter from Don Francisco de Melo, written in Brussels on 11 December, confirming his death and assessing its implications for Spain.[22] In Melo's opinion it was bound to weaken France's military efforts, since the Cardinal's successor, Mazarin, for all his acuteness and political skills, lacked both his predecessor's authority, and his 'vehemence and violence in following a course once chosen.' In addition, Louis XIII was sinking, and did not have long to live. All this was bound to improve the prospects for peace. The Count-Duke fully concurred in this diagnosis. In what may well have been his last state paper, drafted on 10 January and discussed the same day in the Council of State, he urged his colleagues on the occasion of the news from France to reflect on the acute situation in which the Monarchy found itself. Now was the time to do everything possible to secure a peace treaty, even at the cost of some indignity.[23] The Council of State, observing that the peoples of both France and Spain were yearning for peace, found itself in full agreement with Olivares, perhaps for the last time.

The death of the Count-Duke's great rival might yet save the Monarchy, but it came too late to save the Count-Duke himself. To some extent it may even have weakened his position, by suggesting the possibility of a new beginning on both sides of the Pyrenees. The implications for Catalonia and Portugal increased his vulnerability. The ministers felt that the two rebellious provinces might be brought to their senses if advantage were taken of the news of Richelieu's death to drop hints of a forthcoming peace treaty between the French and Spanish crowns. But it was hard to believe that the Catalans would have any confidence in a settlement with Madrid to which the Count-Duke was a party. Indeed, it would not be surprising if there were informal contacts between high-placed Catalans and Olivares' enemies in Madrid about the possibilities of a deal, in which the removal of the Count-Duke from office was made the *quid pro quo* for the principality's return to obedience.[24]

The Count-Duke, therefore, had become a dangerously isolated figure, and all the more so as, in his last days in office, he insisted

[22] AGS Est. leg. 3860.

[23] AGS Est. leg. 3860, undated paper of Olivares and consulta of 10 January 1643; and see Elliott, *Richelieu and Olivares*, pp. 153–4.

[24] There are hints to this effect in an obscure letter of 2 February 1644, in which Antonio Carnero, the brother of the Count-Duke's secretary, whose name he confusingly shared, considers the possibility that the king might recall the Count-Duke, and speaks of 'the reduction of Catalonia, which they offered him as the price for retiring him.' (AHN Est. lib. 869, fo. 274.)

on handling everything himself. On 14 January 1643 the Genoese
ambassador had a confidential talk with a minister, who told him
that Olivares refused to take anyone into his confidence. Official
business traditionally moved at a snail's pace in Spain—the ambassador was still awaiting a reply to three memoranda submitted in September 1641—but the delays were becoming intolerable now that
the Count-Duke attempted to transact affairs single-handed, leaving
almost everyone dissatisfied.[25] Yet as long as the king was unwilling
to move, the world could only wait and watch. On Saturday 17
January, from the safety of his hunting-lodge of the Torre de la Parada,
Philip at last nerved himself to act. The exact circumstances in which
he brought himself to admit the necessity of dispensing with the
Count-Duke's services remain a matter of dispute. Father Guidi attributed a major part in the final decision to the Imperial ambassador,
who is alleged to have persuaded his master to write Philip a private
letter, warning him that his Monarchy would be ruined unless he
changed his government.[26] But Guidi's Venetian colleague was sceptical, noting that Grana was among the last ambassadors to learn of
the Count-Duke's fall.[27] There were also stories in circulation that
the king and his minister had fallen out over the establishment of
a separate household for Prince Baltasar Carlos, and that the difficulties raised by the Count-Duke precipitated the final break. The king
was even said to have asked, with a lack of grace quite out of keeping
with his character, if there were any reason why the prince should
not take over the Count-Duke's apartments, which had traditionally
been occupied by the heir to the throne.[28]

It is more likely to have been in pity than in anger that the king
reached his decision to let his minister go. From the Torre de la
Parada on the 17th he sent the Count-Duke a note saying that he
was prepared to accede to his repeated requests for permission to
retire.[29] Three days later, Philip wrote a letter to the Duke of Medina
de las Torres in Naples to let him know what had happened.[30]
Although the purpose of the letter was to assure the duke that he
could count on continuing royal favour in spite of his father-in-law's
departure from office, it also gives some insight into the king's motivation. Using some of the phrases which would appear in his formal

[25] ASG, Lettere Ministri, Spagna, 2445, cyphered despatch of 14 January 1643.
[26] AS Modena, Spagna B.53, cyphered despatch of 21 January 1643.
[27] ASVen, Spagna, filza 77, 21 January 1643.
[28] Werner, 'Caída', p. 127; and see also León Pinelo, *Anales de Madrid*, p. 323, for this reputed
disagreement between king and minister.
[29] The events of 17 January and the succeeding days are well chronicled in Marañón, *Olivares*,
pp. 358–62.
[30] AHN Est. lib. 869, copy of letter from king to Medina de las Torres, 20 January 1643.

communication of 24 January to the Consejo de la Cámara announcing the Count-Duke's retirement,[31] the king wrote that

> for many days the Count has been pressing me for leave to retire
> and take a rest from the many labours he has performed in my
> service and to my entire satisfaction, on the grounds that he is
> tired, and that his poor state of health prevents him from working
> as actively and vigorously as hitherto. I have held off granting
> him this permission because of the void that his departure will
> create, and the loneliness that his absence will cause me. But during
> the last few days he has urged me so insistently to concede it that
> I have agreed, and have left it to him to make use of this permission
> when he wishes, or when his health compels it. Because I imagine
> that an event of this kind will be talked about everywhere, with
> some saying one thing and some another, I decided to write to
> you in my own hand to tell you what has happened, and at the
> same time to let you know, since it was through the Count that
> you became my creature (hechura), that although he will be away
> from my presence while he is recuperating, I remain here to favour
> and honour you as always. And I will give you whatever support
> you may need, since the burden of government and the manage-
> ment of affairs will now depend directly on my person, for with
> the Count gone I dare not entrust to anybody what I entrusted
> to him.

In spite of the king's obvious anxiety to reassure Medina de las
Torres, there seems no reason not to take at face value the statements
of fact in this remarkable letter. The most significant of these were
that, over the last few days, the Count-Duke had made several
requests to be allowed to withdraw from the royal service because
his health was failing; that the king was acceding to them with the
greatest reluctance; and that he hoped the Count-Duke would return
to his service when he was fully recovered. Even if this last was
at best a pious hope, it would hardly have been necessary for the
king to go so far in his expressions of reluctance and regret if he
did not mean what he said. The enforced separation from the man
who had scarcely left his side over a period of more than twenty
years, and who had worked for him with unswerving devotion, even
if with results that were hardly commensurate with his efforts, can
hardly have failed to be a wrenching experience for the king. His
decision to write the Count-Duke a note rather than give him the
news to his face possibly reflected a feeling that the occasion could
prove too much for both of them. Yet Philip may also have distrusted

---

[31] Printed in Marañón, *Olivares*, Appendix 28.

his own response if the Count-Duke took it into his head to go
back on his request. For if the king meant what he said, it is by
no means certain that the same held true of his minister. He had
made a practice of offering his resignation, secure in the knowledge
that it would be refused. How would he react if this time he were
taken at his word?

On receiving the king's note, the Count-Duke immediately sent
a message to his wife at Loeches, and she hurried back to court.
By Sunday the 18th rumours of his impending departure were all
over Madrid, and the courtyards and environs of the palace were
thronged. But inside the Alcázar life continued as usual, and on the
Monday the Count-Duke even presided over a meeting of one of
the juntas, although reportedly in a very black mood. Amidst mounting uncertainty as to whether the rumours of the Count-Duke's dismissal were true, the king departed for the Escorial on the Wednesday
for a few days hunting. Meanwhile, accompanied by his governess,
the Countess of Olivares, Prince Baltasar Carlos left for the palace
of the Zarzuela, built by his late uncle, the Cardinal-Infante, on
the outskirts of Madrid. Here he received a note in which the Count-
Duke explained that he could not bring himself to pay a farewell
visit, and begged him to continue his favours to the countess. In
his reply, the thirteen-year-old prince promised to oblige. He fully
appreciated that it was the Count-Duke's affection for him and his
parents that prevented him from taking leave in person.[32]

On 22 January, amidst signs of growing impatience among the
populace and the grandees, the king returned to the palace. In a
movement orchestrated by the Duke of Híjar a number of grandees
went out in their coaches to greet him,[33] and Philip apparently showed
some irritation on learning that his minister was still in residence.
The Count-Duke, who protested that he had not been well enough
to leave, spent the night with Carnero and the Protonotario sorting
his papers and burning any that were felt to be incriminating.[34] The
following morning, Friday, 23 January 1643, saw the publication
of a list of honours for the Count-Duke's closest servants, including
Antonio Carnero, and Simón Rodríguez, the valet who had guarded
the entry to his apartments during his long years in power and was
reputed to have used his position to amass more than 100,000 ducats
in gifts and bribes.[35] At eleven o'clock that morning, in the presence
only of his librarian Rioja and the comptroller of the queen's household, an old family servant, he toyed with a meal, which he took

[32] Exchange of letters published in Marañón, *Olivares*, p. 255.
[33] Novoa, *Codoin* 86, p. 83.
[34] Werner, 'Caída', p. 132.
[35] Novoa, *Codoin* 86, pp. 84–5.

in absolute silence.[36] It seems to have been decided that the presence of angry crowds would make a public exit from the palace dangerous. Instead, he was carried in his chair down a secret staircase, accompanied by Don Luis de Haro—chivalrous to the last—, his friend the Count of Grajal (one of his Borja relatives), and the Jesuit Father Juan Martínez Ripalda, who was to succeed Aguado as his confessor. A carriage with closed curtains was awaiting him at the door, and it set off at once for Loeches. A little later a cortège of carriages left the palace by the principal gateway, among them the Count-Duke's. But as people craned their necks to get a last glimpse of the fallen tyrant, they found that they had been cheated. There was no one in the coach.

The defence of a ministry

In concluding a personal letter of 20 January to the governor of the Netherlands, Don Francisco de Melo, almost identical to the one he wrote on the same day to the Duke of Medina de las Torres, the king wrote the brave words *Yo tomo el remo*—'I am taking over the oar'.[37] It was the oar at which the Count-Duke had been labouring for twenty-two years,[38] and to which he had once told Gondomar he would still be clinging as the ship went down.[39] The day after the Count-Duke's covert departure for Loeches Philip informed the Consejo de la Cámara of the reasons for his minister's retirement and of his determination to be his own minister.[40] The news was greeted with vast enthusiasm. At last the king would be a king, and rule without a *privado*.

Everywhere, after the oppressive years of the Count-Duke's government, people were looking for changes, but these proved to be disconcertingly slow in coming. The king, it was true, was displaying unwonted signs of energy. He presided at meetings of the Council of State, attended juntas, and had the secretarial offices moved from the lower floor of the palace to the little tower that led to his own apartments, so that he could visit them at any hour of the day.[41] The grandees were now assiduous in their attendance at the palace, and there were promising indications that prominent figures who for one reason or another had fallen foul of the Count-Duke would

[36] *MHE*, 16, p. 504 (letter of 27 January 1643).
[37] *MHE*, 16, p. 502.
[38] Above, p. 643.
[39] Above, p. 231
[40] Marañón, *Olivares*, p. 464.
[41] ASG, Lettere Ministri, Spagna, 2445, despatches of 28 January and 18 February 1643.

soon be rehabilitated. The first to be restored to favour were two distinguished commanders. The hot-tempered Marquis of Villa-franca, who had been relieved of his post for insubordination in the preceding year and imprisoned for the past ten months in the fortress of Odón, was reappointed to the command of the Spanish galleys with wider powers.[42] Ironically, he would soon be giving as much trouble to the Count-Duke's successors as he ever gave the Count-Duke,[43] but his release and rehabilitation symbolized the return to favour of the house of Toledo, which had lived for the last twenty years in the shadow of the Count-Duke's hostility. Also released at the same time was Don Felipe de Silva, formerly general of the cavalry in Flanders. As a Portuguese, and a relative of the Duke of Braganza, he had fallen under suspicion of disloyalty, but it was widely assumed that he had been taken into custody for daring to contradict the Count-Duke's opinions.[44] In March he left for Zara-goza to take over command of the army of Aragon from Leganés, who was recalled in disgrace and relegated to virtual confinement at Ocaña while a judicial committee looked into his management of the Aragonese campaign and his handling of the army's funds.[45]

There were some hints, too, of a general stock-taking in the fields of policy and administration. On 3 February the Council of State, attended by Cardinal Borja, the Counts of Monterrey and Oñate, and the Marquis of Castañeda, met in the king's presence to deliberate on the current state of the Monarchy's affairs, and on possible ways in which it might begin to extricate itself from its troubles.[46] In reality, however, the councillors, although released from the oppressive presence of the Count-Duke, had nothing new to propose. It was reaffirmed that Richelieu's death improved the prospects for negotiations with France, but it might have been Olivares speaking when Oñate advised proceeding cautiously and 'giving time to time'. After listening to the discussion Philip wrote on the *consulta* that everything 'decent and possible' should be done to initiate negotiations with the French and the Dutch. Subsequent events, however, were to show that the 'decent and possible' would continue to be rigidly interpreted when it came to specific points at issue. The war with the Dutch Republic would continue for a further five years, and with France for a further sixteen.

[42] *MHE*, 17, pp. 11 and 34. The marquis was also known by his other title of Duke of Fernandina.

[43] BL Eg. Ms. 2081, fos. 166–8, *Junta particular sobre las conversaciones del Marqués de Villafranca tocantes al estado de la monarchía*, 1 September 1643.

[44] AS Modena, Spagna B.53, despatch of 4 March 1643.

[45] *MHE*, 17, pp. 61–2; ASG, Lettere Ministri, Spagna, 2445, despatch of 8 April 1643. It took Leganés a year to clear his name. Generals were in short supply, and he would again be given military commands, first in Portugal, and then in Catalonia.

[46] AGS Est. leg. 2059, consulta, 3 February 1643.

There was certainly no indication in these first weeks of the post-Olivares era that his enemies were possessed of some grand design for an alternative foreign policy. The war was to continue as before, until a satisfactory peace became possible. Inside the peninsula, following the wishes of the king, the reduction of Catalonia was to take priority over that of Portugal—a policy from which the Count-Duke seems to have been moving away at the time of his fall from power. But domestically it was in the system of government that the pressures for change were strongest. No aspect of the Count-Duke's regime had been more unpopular than his method of governing through special juntas and his downgrading of the councils. On 26 February the king ordered a general review of government by junta, and—no doubt with unconscious irony—appointed a junta to undertake the task. It reported back on 8 March, listing no less than thirty-one existing juntas, ranging from the junta for stamped paper to such cherished creations of the Count-Duke's regime as the junta for population. One or two of these juntas were allowed to remain in being, like the Junta de Armadas for the management of the fleets, which was retained at the king's request. But the majority were to be dissolved, and their business returned to the councils from which it had originally been taken.[47] Their dissolution marked the triumph of the conciliar bureaucracy over government by *ad hoc* committee.

For over twenty years the Count-Duke had struggled to subordinate the grandees and the conciliar bureaucracy to the authority of the crown. Now, within days of his fall, the aristocrats and the bureaucrats were again asserting themselves, and almost from the first there were doubts about the king's ability to exercise his authority to the full and govern without a *privado*. The Venetian ambassador reported that while he seemed like a 'new man', and those who observed him in action praised his sense of justice and his willingness to listen to the arguments presented to him, they also accused him of 'irresolution and of such a lack of self-confidence that he is always worrying about making mistakes.' This suggested that he would always be dependent on someone. In these first few days after the Count-Duke's departure he was turning to the queen, who herself turned to the Count of Castrillo.[48] But institutional as well as personal factors militated from the start against the attempt at direct government by the king. The administrative structure had become too massive, and the demands upon it too complex and urgent, for a monarch—even one with more energy and firmness of character than Philip IV—to manage it unaided. Guidi, commenting in April on

---

[47] AHN Consejos, leg. 12,432, consulta of Junta particular, 8 March 1643.
[48] ASVen, Spagna, filza 77, despatch of 4 February 1643.

the total lack of effective government since the Count-Duke's fall, recognized this unpleasant truth, which flew in the face of cherished contemporary assumptions about the duty of kings to be kings. 'Experience', he wrote, 'makes it clear that it is morally impossible for such a great king to be without a favourite, for everything has remained in suspense since the time of the Count's fall, and it takes for ever to despatch business which was easily and quickly transacted by a minister with authority putting all his weight behind it.'[49]

The Count-Duke, in other words, might have gone, but he left a large space to be filled. No one, however, wanted to see a repetition of the experience of the past twenty-two years. The kind of *privanza* now required, as Guidi said, was a modified and more 'suave' version of the one that had just come to an end. An Olivares had succeeded a Lerma, and now a Lerma was again needed to succeed an Olivares. There was certainly no lack of candidates, although it remained to be seen how 'suave' they would be once they attained high office, and indeed whether 'suave' authority could be effective authority in the deeply troubled Spain of the mid-seventeenth century.

The struggle for the Count-Duke's succession began as soon as he left the palace, although the rivals had to move warily for fear of giving the impression that they were trespassing on the king's new-found authority. Covertly battling between themselves, they were solicitous in their attendance on the king at lunch and dinner, using the transaction of business as their pretext.[50] At the beginning, it was noted that four ministers were called in more frequently for consultation by Philip than the others. Oñate was thought to enjoy the most authority, followed by Monterrey. Castrillo was the dominant figure in domestic affairs, while the Marquis of Castañeda, who was not regarded as a serious candidate for the *privanza*, seems to have been used by Philip as a convenient sounding-board.[51] All these men, however, had their disabilities. Oñate was old and infirm, and seems to have demanded too many *mercedes* too soon. The king did not love Monterrey as much as Monterrey loved himself. Castrillo was too inflexible, Castañeda too capricious. Others remained on the fringes of the contest—Cardinals Borja and Spínola, and the Count of Chinchón, who had returned in 1640 from his viceroyalty of Peru. And smoothly moving about the palace was to be seen that epitome of the suave courtier, the Count-Duke's nephew, Don Luis de Haro.[52]

[49] AS Modena, Spagna B.53, despatch of 27 April 1643.
[50] ASV, Spagna 85, fo. 229v., nuncio's despatch of 13 May 1643.
[51] ASV, Spagna 85, fo. 145, nuncio's despatch of 4 February 1643.
[52] Described by Guidi as 'l'idea del vero cavaliere', and therefore highly acceptable, in his despatch of 27 April 1643. (AS Modena, Spagna B.53.)

While these court personalities manoeuvred with varying degrees of discretion for the favour of the king, the Count-Duke's men still continued to operate the levers of the administration, although suffering one or two minor casualties. Don Diego de Castejón, who had been President of the Council of Castile since 1639 and was much despised for his toadying to the Count-Duke, was pushed out of office in March, and accepted without enthusiasm the bishopric of Tarazona. His place was to be taken by that grim guardian of public morals, Don Juan Chumacero, recently returned from his Roman embassy.[53] Potentially more significant was a change in the status of the most unpopular of all the Count-Duke's men, the Protonotario. On 27 April a royal decree, after expressing the king's complete satisfaction at the way in which Villanueva had performed his duties, announced his removal from the royal secretariat and his seat in the Council of Aragon, on the grounds that he lacked the confidence of the Catalans, whose return to allegiance the king wished to hasten. In compensation he was given a seat in the Council of the Indies.[54] While this was a demotion, it was certainly not the disgrace for which his enemies had been praying. But he enjoyed the support of the queen and Castrillo,[55] and nothing less than the intervention of the Inquisition would be required to shake his hold on office.

Not only did the Count-Duke's men—the Protonotario, José González, Diego Suárez, Antonio Carnero, Francisco Antonio de Alarcón—remain in positions of authority, but they were suspected of deliberately holding up urgent government business in a bid to present the fallen regime in a more favourable light.[56] Not surprisingly, disillusionment spread as people saw that change appeared to mean no change, and that even the Countess of Olivares and the Count-Duke's bastard son, the Marquis of Mairena, still kept their household appointments. Already by the late spring the king's new popularity was fading, and there were mutterings that 'the House of Austria has always been weak and has never known how to act with vigour and resolution.'[57] There was even an uneasy suspicion that the king was planning to recall Olivares to office. No doubt it was a good sign that the contents of the Count-Duke's great library were being packed into crates—a hundred of them—so that it could form part of the new apartments designated for Prince Baltasar Carlos,[58] but this was little consolation as long as their owner sat brooding in solitary silence only a few miles from Madrid.

[53] ASG, Spagna, filza 2444, despatch of 4 March 1643.
[54] See Elliott, *Catalans*, p. 529.
[55] AHN Est. lib. 869, fo. 217v., Carnero to Olivares, 24 February 1644.
[56] AS Modena, Spagna B.53, despatch from Guidi, 27 April 1643.
[57] ASV, Spagna 85, fo. 233, nuncio's despatch of 13 May 1643.
[58] AS Modena, Spagna B.53, despatch of 9 May 1643.

Since his move to Loeches the Count-Duke had refused to have any contact with his friends at court, leaving them, as Carnero complained, in 'solitude and sorrow'.[59] When he was not resting he was reported to be spending most of his time at his devotions.[60] He wanted now only to be left to die in peace, and peace did not come easily. He was a deeply embittered man; he was worried about his wife, son and daughter-in-law, and the humiliations to which they were exposed in the palace; and he was well aware that his enemies, not satisfied with his departure from the court, were baying for his blood.[61]

In February a printed pamphlet appeared, containing a series of accusations against the Count-Duke.[62] Its author, Andrés de Mena, seems to have been a former royal official who had served in 1633–4 as the Duke of Béjar's agent at the court.[63] The pamphlet was essentially a recapitulation of the criticisms levelled against the Count-Duke by his aristocratic enemies during his years in office. He was blamed for ending the truce with the Dutch in 1621, and for involving Spain in the war of the Mantuan Succession. He was held responsible for the rebellion of the Catalans, which in turn had encouraged the Duke of Braganza to declare Portugal independent. At home he had played havoc with the coinage, squandered money on the unnecessary building of the palace of the Buen Retiro, persecuted the grandees, and reserved the royal bounty for his own friends and clients. Inevitably, too, his system of government came under attack—his recourse to juntas, his appointment of foreigners to the councils, and his dependence on *letrados* and bureaucrats who had grown fat on the pickings of office, while the grandees were left to starve. Comparing the Count-Duke's record unfavourably with that of Cardinal Richelieu, the pamphlet urged the king to institute a judicial inquiry into his actions and those of his ministers. This was the time for Philip to rise to new heights of kingship. He must restore power to the councils

[59] AGR CPE, Reg. 1504, fo. 241, Carnero to Roose, 7 March 1643.

[60] ASVen, Spagna, filza 77, despatch of 4 February 1643.

[61] Evidence for his state of mind in the period between his fall from power and his death is provided by the correspondence he maintained with Antonio Carnero during these two years, of which many letters have survived. Forty-four of them, preserved in the archive of the Ministry of Foreign Affairs in Madrid, were published with an introduction by Miguel Santiago Rodríguez under the title of 'Cartas del Conde-Duque de Olivares escritas después de su caída', in *Revista de Archivos, Bibliotecas y Museos*, 66 (1973), pp. 323–404. Another forty-four, along with several letters from Carnero to the Count-Duke, are to be found in AHN Est. lib. 869, and remain unpublished.

[62] The first known version, dated 18 February 1643, appeared under the title of *Memorial dado al rey don Felipe IV por un ministro antiguo*. Later versions are entitled *Cargos contra el Conde Duque*, and it is by this title that the document is generally known. It is reproduced as Doc. XXa of *MC*, 2, as a companion piece to the Count-Duke's reply, the *Nicandro*, preceded by an introduction in which the two pamphlets are analysed and discussed.

[63] Jago, 'Crisis of the aristocracy', p. 68 n. 24.

and in future select for his service only those who enjoyed the approval of the people.

Mena's barrage of accusations demanded a vigorous response. This appeared in May under a clandestine imprint bearing the title of the *Nicandro*.[64] Nicander, a Greek physician of the second century BC, was the author of the *Alexipharmaca*, a treatise on poisons and their antidotes. The 1531 Cologne edition was to be found in the Count-Duke's library,[65] and it seems likely that his librarian, Rioja, prepared this forceful antidote to Mena's poison, perhaps with José González and Olivares' new confessor, Father Martínez Ripalda, helping to stir the pot. Yet if the prose in which the *Nicandro* is written is too limpid to belong to the Count-Duke, there is no escaping his hovering influence. This is the defence of his twenty-two years of government, presented with the air of a man who saw nothing in his record for which to apologize.

The counter-arguments to Mena that appear in the *Nicandro* are largely predictable. The author reminded his readers that the Twelve Years' Truce with the Dutch had few supporters in 1621, and that Don Baltasar de Zúñiga was in charge of policy when it was allowed to expire. Similarly the regime's military failures could be ascribed to the mistakes of the commanders—Don Gonzalo de Córdoba, or the Marquis of Los Vélez. The *Nicandro* is less interesting for these debating-points than for its introduction of historical and political perspectives which suggest some of the influences that shaped the Count-Duke's policies and determined the constraints under which he operated. It claimed, for instance, in defence of the Count-Duke's administrative style, that government by junta was not his invention, but had been systematically practiced since the Duke of Lerma's rise to power. It also claimed with some justice that Ferdinand and Isabella had made a practice of raising *letrados* to positions of eminence and that they had never enjoyed more power and authority than in the reign of Philip II.[66] But the *Nicandro* is at its most revealing when it turns to the defence of the Count-Duke's policies towards Catalonia and Portugal.

On his Catalan policy, as on everything else, Olivares was unrepentant. His Majesty, the *Nicandro* said, was well aware of the cost to his ancestors of Catalonia's *fueros*. Had not Isabella the Catholic spoken of the need to 'conquer' Catalonia? He also had before his eyes the bitter experience of his grandfather, Philip II, who time and time again had been deceived by his subjects in the Netherlands.

[64] *MC*, 2, Doc. XXb.
[65] BAV, Barb. Lat. Ms. 3098, fo. 27.
[66] *MC*, 2, pp. 257–8.

'When subjects rebel, the rebellion must be put down at once, without giving them time to arm themselves.' It was precisely to avoid a repetition of what had happened in the Netherlands that the Count-Duke had sent a powerful army into Catalonia under the command of the Marquis of Los Vélez. It was wrong, the *Nicandro* continued, to believe that in such dangerous times the Monarchy could survive when it was constituted of 'such disproportionate parts, without union or conformity between them.' The only hope was to 'reduce them to union and equality in laws, customs and form of government.' The same held true of Portugal, where Philip II had been disastrously lax in failing to break down the trade barriers with Castile and in omitting to appoint Portuguese to high office in the Crown of Castile and its dependent territories; and 'Ferdinand the Catholic should have done the same with Aragon and Catalonia.' If the Count-Duke had attempted to achieve 'such an essential point of empire', he had only acted as befitted a 'great minister'.[67]

This spirited defence of his cherished policy of union and uniformity was unlikely to win the Count-Duke new friends at a time when the policy had so resoundingly failed. In a graphic image Matías de Novoa summarized the common view of the Count-Duke's personal responsibility for the catastrophes of 1640. By attempting to gather the whole Monarchy into his hand and hold it tight with fist clenched, he had let a large part of it slip and fall from his grasp.[68] Not surprisingly, the very magnitude of the disaster had utterly discredited the Count-Duke's policy for unifying the kingdoms of the Monarchy, and the post-Olivares era would be one of elaborately paraded respect for the principle of diversity. It was significant that Juan de Palafox, whose career the Count-Duke had done so much to foster, should in his later years have come down decisively against this central tenet of his patron's programme. In a 'Private and Secret Opinion on the Monarchy, written for myself alone', he argued that one of the principal causes of the Monarchy's sickness was the doctrine that nations so diverse in character should be subjected to a single form of government, law and obedience. He admitted that the attempt to achieve this had been inspired by the best of intentions— namely to 'achieve unity in government and exclude the diversity which is liable to be the mother of discord'. But since God had created them different—Valencia grew oranges but not chestnuts, and Vizcaya chestnuts but not oranges—it was essential that the laws under

---

[67] *MC*, 2, pp. 251–2.
[68] Novoa, *Codoin* 80, p. 14. José María Jover Zamora draws attention to this passage in 'Sobre los conceptos de monarquía y nación en el pensamiento político español del XVII', *Cuadernos de Historia de España*, 13 (1950), pp. 101–50, See p. 132 n. 53.

which they lived should conform to the principles of nature, and their differences be respected.[69]

As the Count-Duke saw it, this traditional type of justification for maintaining the laws and liberties of the various kingdoms and provinces of the Monarchy took no account of contemporary realities, and above all of the reality of seventeenth-century warfare. 'All great monarchies', stated the *Nicandro*, 'are founded on men, money and an abundance of such things as are required for the preparation of great armies to defeat the enemy.' Foreign statesmen, who took careful note of such matters, had seen how the various provinces of the Monarchy failed to come to their king's assistance in time of need, and had not unreasonably concluded that it was a 'phantom' (*cuerpo fantástico*) protected more by reputation than substance. This was the intolerable situation that the Count-Duke had sought to rectify.[70] It was true that in this, as in other things, he had not always been successful; but at least—or so the *Nicandro* argued—his chosen methods had conformed to the requirements of 'God, religion and the House of Austria', whereas Richelieu, who had been 'fortunate in many things', had used 'detestable methods' to achieve them.[71] How, then, were the misfortunes of his later years to be explained? According to the *Nicandro*, even those who applauded Olivares' care and vigilance in the management of affairs had failed to give due account to the 'universal providence of things', which had led in these last years to great public calamities: 'all the north in commotion... England, Ireland and Scotland aflame with civil war... The Ottomans tearing each other to pieces... China invaded by the Tartars, Ethiopia by the Turks, and the Indian kings who live scattered through the region between the Ganges and the Indus all at each other's throats...'[72] In effect, the Count-Duke and his friends were adducing the theory of a general crisis to account for the disasters of his final years in office.

Not surprisingly, this impenitent and sometimes brazen apology for the Count-Duke's ministerial career evoked howls of protest. Guidi wrote that in his three years in Madrid he had never seen the court in such a commotion. It was the boldest and most

---

[69] See pp. 145–6 of Juan de Palafox y Mendoza, 'Juicio interior y secreto de la monarquía para mí solo', text as established by Jover in 'Sobre los conceptos de monarquía y nación', cited in the preceding note. It is not clear whether this treatise dates from the 1640's, when Palafox was in Mexico, serving first as bishop of Puebla, and then as interim viceroy (1642) and archbishop of Mexico, or whether it was composed after his return to Spain in 1649. He died as bishop of Osma in 1659.

[70] *MC*, 2, pp. 269–70.

[71] *Ibid.*, p. 268.

[72] *Ibid.*, p. 275.

imprudent pamphlet ever penned, and reeked of arrogance.[73] For the Count-Duke's enemies, frustrated by their inability to break the hold of the *olivaristas* on the court and the administration, the *Nicandro* came as a happy windfall. But it seems to have left the king unmoved—he is said to have considered it a very superficial defence of his fallen minister. Its circulation, however, had aroused such emotions that he felt obliged to authorize the seizure of as many copies as could be found, and to order an investigation to discover those responsible.[74] Inquiries led to the arrest of Don Juan de Ahumada, the tutor of Juan José de Austria, Philip's bastard son, for complicity in the authorship. Some weeks later he was dismissed from his post. The court *alcalde* Lezama—the brother of the Count-Duke's secretary Jerónimo de Lezama—was also taken into custody under suspicion of having authorized the printing. In due course, relatively light sentences were imposed on Mateo Fernández and one of the Count-Duke's servants, Domingo de Herrera, for respectively printing and distributing the pamphlet. The degree of influence still enjoyed by the Count-Duke's partisans in judicial and administrative circles is suggested by the fact that the author of the original charges, Andrés de Mena, was savagely punished with a fine and a sentence of six years exile in Oran, and his printer was more heavily penalized than the printer of the *Nicandro*.[75]

As was only to be expected, the arrest of a few minor personalities proved insufficient to calm the storm. The Count-Duke's enemies among the grandees were bent on revenge—notably the Dukes of Infantado and Medinaceli, the Count of Lemos, and that perennial intriguer, the Duke of Híjar, who saw himself in the role of royal *privado*.[76] The grandees as a class were indignant at the slanders to which the *Nicandro* had subjected them, and some of them had personal grounds for complaint, like the Duke of Osuna, who bitterly resented the imputations against his father.[77] In a mass deputation they went to see the king, although characteristically the Duke of Alba—no friend to the Count-Duke—preferred to stand aloof. By nature benign and easy-going, Philip had no desire to encourage a witch-hunt against his fallen minister, but circumstance and character made his situation not unlike that of Charles I with the Earl of Strafford two years earlier. The pressure was less overwhelming than in England, and Philip's retreat from his word of honour correspond-

[73] AS Modena, Spagna B.53, despatch of 3 June 1643.

[74] ASV, Spagna 345, fos. 237 and 242v., nuncio's despatches of 20 and 27 May 1643.

[75] *MHE*, 17, p. 157 (21 July 1643); Marañón, *Olivares*, pp. 379–80.

[76] For Don Rodrigo Sarmiento de Silva, Duke of Híjar, whose ambitions led him into a disastrous conspiracy in 1648, see Ramón Ezquerra Abadía, *La conspiración del Duque de Híjar [1648]* (Madrid, 1934).

[77] Novoa, *Codoin* 86, pp. 121–2.

ingly less precipitate than that of Charles I, but there can be no certainty that the Count-Duke, if he had lived, would have escaped the Earl of Strafford's fate.

The grandees were persuaded that the king would never break free from Olivares' malign influence as long as he was at Loeches and his wife in the Alcázar. To judge from some obscurely phrased letters sent by Olivares to Carnero, a royal message may have been privately conveyed to the effect that it would be more seemly if the countess were to go and live with him at Loeches.[78] The Count-Duke reacted bitterly. The king had made an unconditional promise that his retirement from office should not affect the position of his wife and family; and in any event, because of their age, he and the countess had long since ceased to live together as man and wife. The king cast doubt on the Count-Duke's repeated complaints that his enemies were conspiring against him, and even asked rather naively who these enemies were. The very question made the Count-Duke laugh. What about Monterrey's corruption and his dissolute life, so graphically documented in papers shown by Olivares to the king? What about the Count of Oñate, three times imprisoned? Or Castrillo, or Castañeda, whom he had summarily recalled to Madrid? 'His Majesty has forgotten so much that he asks who my enemies are, when in fact they are his.'

In his anguish over what might become of his wife and son, and over the blow to his honour if they should be expelled from the palace, he looked for help to his nephew, Don Luis de Haro, whom he regarded as honourable and upright.[79] His relationship with his nephew and potential heir had never been easy, but there was no one else in the king's confidence whom he could trust, and least of all the man now moving into the position of royal confessor, Fray Juan de Santo Tomás, whom he suspected of being the author of his present misfortunes.[80] The ties that still bound uncle and nephew made Don Luis a natural intermediary between the king and his former minister. Presumably hoping to sweeten the pill that he was about to administer, the king sent Don Luis to Loeches on Sunday 24 May, accompanied by one of the Count-Duke's most loyal

[78] AHN Est. lib. 869, fo. 266, Olivares to Carnero, 21 May 1643; Santiago Rodríguez, 'Cartas', nos. 1, 2 and 3, 20 and 21 May 1643.

[79] Postscript to letter of 21 April 1643, Santiago Rodríguez, no. 2.

[80] Santiago Rodríguez, 'Cartas', no. 7, Olivares to Carnero, 24 May 1643. Santo Tomás was in the process of replacing the octogenarian Fray Antonio de Sotomayor, generally regarded as a tool of the Count-Duke. In June Sotomayor would also be forced to relinquish the post of Inquisitor-General which he had held since 1632. He survived in retirement for another five years, dying in September 1648. See José Espinosa Rodríguez, Fray Antonio de Sotomayor y su correspondencia con Felipe IV (Vigo, 1944). This volume unfortunately contains no correspondence before 1643.

dependents, Don Francisco Antonio de Alarcón, newly promoted
to the presidency of the Council of Finance. An elaborately courteous
but none the less painful meeting took place in a deserted spot in
the country outside Loeches—the Count-Duke waiting alone in his
coach with the mules tethered some distance away, Don Luis coming
over to join him, and at one stage consulting his watch as the Count-
Duke poured forth his woes.[81] If he felt awkward in his uncle's company, this was hardly surprising in view of the nature of his mission.
He was deputed to explain that the circumstances attending the publication of the *Nicandro* left the king no choice but to order the Count-
Duke to leave Loeches for Seville or one of his Andalusian estates.[82]

The Count-Duke at first found it impossible to believe that the
king whom he had 'served and adored' for so long should bring
him so low. He had deprived him of his honour.[83] The next day
he despatched Father Martínez Ripalda to Haro with a letter protesting
that Andalusia would be ruinous to his health, and asking that he
should be allowed to live in a northern city—Toro or León—where
the air was better. It was ironical that in León at this very moment
one of his most illustrious victims, Francisco de Quevedo, was on
the point of recovering his freedom after his three years of harsh
imprisonment in the convent of San Marcos. On 7 June, after José
González—another survivor among the *olivaristas*—had conducted
a review of his case, Quevedo's release was recommended by the
new president of the Council of Castile, Don Juan Chumacero, and
approved by the king.[84] Over the last twenty years the lives of the
statesman and the satirist had crossed and recrossed time and time
again. Now, with both of them approaching death, one was leaving
his exile for home, the other his home for exile.

In the end, however, the Count-Duke's choice fell not on León
but Toro, where his recently widowed sister Doña Inés, Marchioness
of Alcañices, offered him the use of her palace. On 12 June he set
out from Loeches, accompanied by a guard of fifty men. His health
was crumbling—he described himself as being as yellow as a candle,[85]
and those who saw him reported that he was bent almost double
and his hair had turned white[86]—and since he was forbidden to enter
Madrid he was forced to make a detour. But his wife and Don Luis

[81] Santiago Rodríguez, 'Cartas', no. 9, Olivares to Carnero, 24 May 1643.
[82] See the account in *MHE*, 17, pp. 105–9, and Marañón, *Olivares*, pp. 371–2. Marañón
was unaware of the correspondence between the Count-Duke and Carnero, which mentions
Haro referring to his watch.
[83] Letter to Carnero of 24 May 1643.
[84] Archivo del Ministerio de Asuntos Exteriores, Madrid, Ms. 39 (Papeles de Don Juan Chumacero), fos. 15–15v.
[85] Santiago Rodríguez, 'Cartas', no. 20, Olivares to Carnero, 2 June 1643.
[86] AS Modena, Spagna B.53, despatch of 17 June 1643.

de Haro both came out to see him. His route nearly crossed with that of his other surviving sister, Doña Leonor, the Countess of Monterrey, but there was no love lost between them now, and each took avoiding action.[87] On the 20th he reached the little provincial city of Toro, which was overwhelmed at having such a distinguished figure in its midst and received him with every honour. Here, in his sister's house, with his little court around him, he was to spend the two remaining years of his life, attempting without success to banish the ghosts that crowded in upon him.

The death of a tyrant

Although the Count-Duke was now well away from Madrid, his enemies were not satisfied. They wanted, if they could, to bring him to trial; they had not yet succeeded in getting his wife out of the palace; and the Count-Duke's men continued to occupy some of the most powerful positions in the court and the royal administration. Haro had given him a verbal promise on behalf of the king that if he moved to Toro there would be no change in the situation of the countess, or of his son, the Marquis of Mairena, and his daughter-in-law, Doña Juana de Velasco.[88] But it was doubtful whether Haro had the power, or even perhaps the will, to ward off the pressure for further reprisals.

The king left again for the front in Aragon on 1 July, making some new administrative appointments just before his departure which did not augur well for the Count-Duke and his friends. Some major changes were announced in the royal secretariat. The secretary for northern affairs, Andrés de Rozas, relegated to the sidelines during the last years of the Count-Duke's government,[89] was appointed principal secretary of state in the place of Jerónimo de Villanueva; and Antonio Carnero, who displayed a remarkable capacity for survival in spite of his closeness to his master, ceased to be secretary for the king's secret correspondence, but retained the post of patronage secretary of the Consejo de Cámara of Castile given him on Olivares' last day in office—a not unattractive position for a man so heavily burdened with children.[90] At the same time there was a radical overhaul of the Commission of the *millones*—the powerful tax-raising

---

[87] Marañón, *Olivares*, p. 382.
[88] The promise is recorded in a *Memorial* presented to the king a few months after the Count-Duke's move to Toro by Father Martínez Ripalda, and summarized in Appendix 31 of Marañón, *Olivares*. See, for this promise, pp. 473–4.
[89] AHN Est. lib. 981, Rozas to Don Miguel de Salamanca, 23 December 1640.
[90] *MHE*, 17, p. 132 (23 June 1643) for these appointments, and Novoa, *Codoin* 86, pp. 129–31.

committee of the Cortes of Castile which the Count-Duke, in his role as president, had bent to his own will during his final years in office.[91] Its members included those trusted confidants of the Count-Duke, José González and Nicolás Cid. All of them were replaced, and an investigation launched into the activities of the commission's dominant figure, the king's *factor general* Bartolomé Espínola, who had run the crown's financial operations for Olivares during the previous fifteen years.[92]

These changes were bound to increase the Count-Duke's unease as he adjusted to his new life in Toro. He asked the faithful Carnero to offer the countess what comfort he could, but warned him not to visit her more than once a week.[93] Any indiscretion, as he knew, would at once be used by his enemies against him, and they were numerous. On his entry into each new town in Aragon Philip was greeted with cries of 'Long live the king, and death to the Conde Duque!'[94] Shielded in his little enclave at Toro from the immediate onslaught of popular hatred and aristocratic venom, the Count-Duke worried about his wife and his honour, and tried hard to forget. 'I must frankly confess to you', he wrote to Carnero on 22 July, 'that I am so far removed from the world that I think I must be dreaming'; or again, in October, 'God give me the grace to die well, knowing nothing of the world, nor the world of me.'[95] Yet he looked to Carnero for news of the world he was so anxious to forget, and commented where appropriate on items of special importance—the latest events in Flanders after the resounding defeat in May of the Spanish *tercios* at Rocroi under the command of his protégé Francisco de Melo; or in Germany, where in his opinion things were going very badly for the Emperor, 'without leaders, without government, and with everything in utter confusion'; or in England, where things were going no less badly for 'that king', because 'the parliamentarians have been recovering strength.'[96]

Meanwhile, the jockeying went on in Aragon for the royal favour. Guidi, the Modenese ambassador, was scathing in his comments. The affairs of Spain, he wrote, could not be in worse shape than they now were. 'His Majesty has no spirit, and was born to be ruled rather than to rule. This looks to me more like an aristocracy than a monarchy, because in effect Haro, Monterrey, Oñate and Castrillo do everything they wish, and do it badly... The new government

[91] Above, p. 541.
[92] AS Modena, Spagna B.53, despatch of 8 July 1643.
[93] AHN Est. lib. 869, fos. 271 and 117, Olivares to Carnero, 22 July and 12 August 1643.
[94] AS Modena, Spagna B.53, despatch of 5 August 1643.
[95] AHN Est. lib. 869, fo. 259, letter of 14 October 1643.
[96] AHN Est. lib. 869, fo. 115v., Olivares to Carnero, 12 August 1643.

34. The 'Fraga' portrait of Philip IV, painted by Velázquez in the summer of 1644, when the king was with his army in Aragon.

follows the same maxims as the Count-Duke, but without his rigour . . .'[97] The Count-Duke and his immediate family had become mere pawns in this struggle for power at court. On 3 November the long anticipated blow fell. The Countess of Olivares was ordered out of the palace; and in Zaragoza on the same day, the Marquis of Mairena was told that, in view of the Count-Duke's illness, the countess was leaving Madrid to care for him, and that he was to join them forthwith.[98]

The Count-Duke saw the dismissal of his wife and son from their palace duties as a humiliation which had destroyed the reputation of his family. He was left, in the words of the *Memorial* of protest presented for him by Martínez Ripalda, 'without honour and discredited in the eyes of the world.' Never before had a royal *privado* of his quality and standing been brought so low.[99] But it was possible to protest too much, as Don Luis de Haro warned Carnero that December, after the king and court had returned from Aragon. The Count-Duke's enemies, Haro told him, were attempting to bring down not only the Count-Duke, but all his 'creatures' and relations.[100] In another brief conversation with Carnero in February, just as the king was leaving again for Aragon, Haro insisted on the extent of the 'great conspiracy' against the Count-Duke and his men, and represented himself as having saved Carnero and Villanueva from dismissal from office and expulsion from the court.[101]

While Don Luis was no doubt attempting to cover himself for his failure to protect the countess, Carnero was probably correct in his assessment that he could be relied upon to do his best on the Count-Duke's behalf, since his own credit was also at stake. Haro's position was in fact not yet assured. At this very moment a conspiracy was being hatched against him by the Duke of Híjar and a band of fellow-nobles—the Dukes of Infantado, Osuna, and Montalto, and the Count of Lemos—with the apparent intention of putting the Count of Oñate in his place.[102] Haro got wind of what was afoot and foiled the conspirators, but it was only by slow degrees that he established himself over rivals like Monterrey and Oñate as the nearest political equivalent to his fallen uncle and the principal recipient of the royal favour.

The Count-Duke continued to follow Carnero's letters closely, but more and more his thoughts were turning from this life to the

---

[97] AS Modena, Spagna B.53, despatch of 9 September 1643.
[98] *MHE*, 17, pp. 356–8.
[99] Marañón, *Olivares*, p. 474.
[100] AHN Est. lib. 869, fos. 139–41, Carnero to Olivares, 16 December 1643.
[101] AHN Est. lib. 869, fos. 118–23, Carnero to Olivares, 10 February 1644.
[102] Ezquerra, *La conspiración*, pp. 127–8; Novoa, *Codoin* 86, pp. 162–5.

next. All he desired, he told him, was to see that day of absolute peace for which he had been yearning.[103] The years in that 'babylon' of the court had become for him no more than an 'enchantment and a dream'.[104] But if there were growing signs of incoherence in his letters, the practical man of action, the reformer and improver, was still very much alive. In the spring of 1644, with time hanging heavy on his hands, he was negotiating for the purchase of 'a very bad' tract of dry land which he planned to irrigate with a system of pumps,[105] just like the old days when he had created the splendid gardens of the Buen Retiro. Over the months he seems to have been coming to terms with his new existence in Toro, where he could live the life of a great man in a small town. The countryside was looking 'like a garden' in the fair spring weather, and now that gout, corpulence and old age kept him confined to a chair, he hoped to get good views of it from the piece of land that he planned to buy.[106]

Yet always the memories and the self-reproaches were liable to return. He was not the man, he wrote, to whom Carnero should turn for advice. After all, he had lost his way while navigating, and this was all the more reprehensible when he had boarded ship 'so free of ambition'.[107] He wanted only to forget, as if the past had never been; and he did not dare open his writing cabinet or his boxes for fear of seeing all those state papers again.[108] He ruminated on the inconstancy of things and the ingratitude of man, and on his fatal mistake in placing his trust in men rather than in God.[109] Yet in the end he remained baffled and bemused: 'My understanding is that I never understood anything, and now much less than ever.'[110]

But even if he wanted to forget, the world would not let him. In the spring of 1644 he had been forced to relinquish his position as Grand Chancellor of the Indies, and to resign his post as master of the horse, which went to Don Luis de Haro's father, the Marquis of Carpio. The indignity and humiliation were almost more than he could bear. He complained to Don Luis that he was despised and treated like a delinquent—exiled, dishonoured, and with his enemies sitting in judgment on his case. Even a galley slave was given a fairer deal.[111] Then on 31 August there came another shattering blow: Jerónimo de Villanueva was arrested on the orders of the

---

[103] AHN Est. lib. 869, fo. 248, Olivares to Carnero, 16 February 1644.
[104] *Ibid.*, fo. 130, letter of 7 March.
[105] *Ibid.*, fos. 267–8 and 142–3, letters of 21 April and 2 May.
[106] *Ibid.*, fo. 111v., letter of 9 May 1644. For his gout and other ailments, see Marañón, *Olivares*, pp. 393–7.
[107] AHN Est. lib. 869, fo. 233v., Olivares to Carnero, 24 May 1644.
[108] *Ibid.*, fos. 135 and 254, letters of 7 and 25 July 1644.
[109] *Ibid.*, fo. 287, letter of 8 August 1644, and see Elliott, *Richelieu and Olivares*, p. 172.
[110] *Ibid.*, fo. 284, letter of 30 August 1644.
[111] Archivo del Duque de Alba, caja 220–14, Olivares to Don Luis de Haro, 17 May 1644.

Inquisition, and taken to Toledo, where he was confined in a narrow cell.[112] The arrest had been prompted by the revival of the investigation into the scandalous happenings in Villanueva's convent of San Plácido more than ten years earlier,[113] but the prime motivation for reopening the case was political. Not only was Villanueva's continuing influence at court a source of exasperation to the Count-Duke's enemies, but there was every reason to assume that he had in his possession highly sensitive papers which might be effectively used against his fallen patron. The dismissal of Sotomayor from the post of Inquisitor-General in June 1643, and the appointment of Diego de Arce y Reynoso, bishop of Plasencia, in his stead, provided the perfect opportunity to secure a new and more vigorous investigation of the San Plácido affair, which was bound to implicate Villanueva, and—with luck—Olivares too.

The Count-Duke was shocked but not entirely surprised by the news of Villanueva's arrest. He suspected that his rather light-hearted approach to serious matters had done him no good. Nor had he helped himself by speaking disrespectfully of the Council of the Inquisition and the learning of its councillors. But he found it impossible to believe that there was any malice in the man. 'Ignorance and lack of discretion, perhaps, and these are things that we his friends cannot deny.'[114] But if the Count-Duke's first thought was for the man himself and the gravity of his situation, another aspect of the arrest came to fill him with foreboding. What instructions had the king given about the disposal of Villanueva's papers? No royal official, after all, knew as many of the secrets of the Olivares regime as the Protonotario. The thought that the papers might fall into the wrong hands was deeply disturbing.[115] The Count-Duke had every reason to be worried. Villanueva did indeed have highly sensitive material in his possession; and apparently nearly two years elapsed before an order was given for the offical papers found in his house to be transferred from the hands of the inquisitors to those of Don Fernando Ruiz de Contreras, the successor of Andrés de Rozas as principal secretary of state.

The eventual fate of these papers remains a mystery, but an inventory of them—which, ironically, seems to have been drawn up for the occasion by none other than that great survivor, Antonio Carnero—suggests something of the richness of the documentation kept by Villanueva in his house.[116] It included files on the dispute between

---

[112] For the Villanueva case, see Lea, *History of the Inquisition*, 2, pp. 133–58.
[113] Above, p. 422.
[114] AHN Est. lib. 869, fos. 235–6 and 234, Olivares to Carnero, 5 and 7 September 1644.
[115] *Ibid.*, fo. 148, letter of 14 September 1644.
[116] AHN Inquis. leg. 3687(3), *Inventario de los papeles que se hallaron en casa de Don Gerónimo Villanueva*.

Monterrey and Medina de las Torres, his successor as the viceroy of Naples, and also on the Duke of Medina Sidonia's conspiracy. Both these files were mysteriously tampered with between the time the inventory was taken and the moment when the papers were passed to Ruiz de Contreras.[117] There were papers, too, about the Count-Duke's illegitimate son (these also disappeared); documents relating to the War of the Mantuan Succession, to the death of the Infante Don Carlos (where foul play had been suspected), and to the troubles in Vizcaya and the affairs of Catalonia. There were two bundles of drafts relating to the king's will; the papers of the junta appointed to free the Count-Duke's estate from its burden of debt; and a *consulta* in which it was decided that the Count of Linhares, the former Portuguese viceroy of Goa, should attempt to procure the death of the Duke of Braganza. There were also 884 *consultas* addressed by the Count-Duke to the king, consisting of 2,668 pages in all—*consultas* that no doubt contained the hidden history of the Olivares regime.

The arrest of Villanueva marked the beginning of a bizarre and protracted case in which the victim showed that not for nothing had he occupied during the best part of two decades what he liked to call 'the second place in the Monarchy'.[118] He was still fighting to clear his name at the time of his death in 1653, but after three years of imprisonment his extraordinary skill in pulling strings enabled him to fight the Inquisition to a standstill, and transformed his case into a major issue in Spain's relations with the papacy. In the months immediately following his arrest, however, the dramatic resurrection of the San Plácido affair once again served—as the Count-Duke's enemies intended—to cast a lurid light on what contemporaries liked to consider one of the darkest and most diabolical mysteries of the Olivares regime. In one of his letters to Carnero shortly after the arrest, the Count-Duke wrote that he was unacquainted with any of the nuns of San Plácido, because 'on the few occasions that I went to see them I was so overawed by their sanctity and virtue that I did not dare look them in the face.'[119] But this was not how his connections with San Plácido were seen by the world at large, and in December, back in his home at La Torre de Juan Abad, Quevedo picked up the news that an inquisitor had left Toledo for Toro on an unknown mission.[120]

The investigations into the Count-Duke's orthodoxy, however,

---

[117] AHN Inquis. leg. 3690, Inquisitor-General to king, 16 September 1647.
[118] Cited by Agulló y Cobo, 'El monasterio de San Plácido', p. 64.
[119] AHN Est. lib. 869, fo. 240, letter of 11 September 1644.
[120] Quevedo, *Epistolario completo*, letter CCLX (24 December 1644), pp. 478–9. See also the letter dated 22 November 1644 in *MHE*, 17, p. 506, which reports that a secretary of the Inquisition, a *fiscal* and an inquisitor from Valladolid had held a long private interview with Olivares in the Cistercian convent of La Espina.

seem to have dragged, possibly because of delaying action by the new Inquisitor General, Arce y Reynoso, whose career had prospered in the years of his government.[121] During the last months of Olivares' life the pressures seem to have been mounting for some action by the Inquisition, but it was not until the spring of 1646, some nine months after his death, that he was posthumously denounced before the tribunal by a certain Juan Vidés for reading the Koran and the works of Luther.[122] Eventually the case petered out. The alleged heretic had already gone before a higher tribunal.

Already at the time of the Count-Duke's interview with the inquisitors, his physical and mental health were visibly failing, and it was obvious that he did not have long to live. In February 1645 Carnero paid another visit to Don Luis de Haro in the hope of securing authorization for him to end his days in Loeches. Don Luis, as always, was bland and courteous. He could not deny that he stood higher than anyone else in the royal favour, and he was well aware that he owed everything to the Count-Duke who was the 'author of such fortune as he had, since he had brought him and his father to the place in which they now found themselves.' But this was not something that he had the power to settle on his own, and nor was this the time to press so delicate a point.[123] So the Count-Duke seemed destined to die in exile in Toro, unless his enemies should succeed before then in bringing him to book.

The opening of the Inquisition proceedings makes it clear that there were some who would stop at nothing to extract their revenge, and there was always a possibility that the king would succumb to the pressures for summary justice against his fallen minister. According to popular report the Count-Duke's final illness was in fact brought on by the receipt of a letter from Zaragoza in which the king told him that the Aragonese were only prepared to take the oath of allegiance to Prince Baltasar Carlos if they were given his head in return. But the story sounds apocryphal, and is best taken as an indication of the intensity of the hatred that still surrounded the Count-Duke. No doubt it reflects, too, a natural wish to provide a fittingly spectacular finale to a spectacular career.[124]

The reality of the Count-Duke's last days appears to have been more mundane.[125] On 15 July he felt indisposed while out in the

---

[121] Marañón, *Olivares*, pp. 179 and 390.

[122] AHN Inquis. leg. 1867, no. 36. *Delación contra el Conde Duque de Olivares, difunto*.

[123] AHN Est. lib. 869, fos. 260–3v., Carnero to Olivares, 22 February 1645.

[124] BL Eg. Ms. 26,558, fos. 266–8, *Muerte del Conde de Olivares sucedido en Toro a 22 de julio de 1645*. For this and other stories about the contents of the alleged letter, see Marañón, *Olivares*, pp. 391–2.

[125] His last illness and death are described in ch. 29 of Marañón, who also offers a posthumous diagnosis.

countryside and was taken back to his house. That evening his conversation became wild, and it was obvious that something in his mind had finally snapped. In his incoherent ramblings during that last week of his life he referred over and over again to 'my wife, my wife'; and his last recorded words, 'when I was rector, when I was rector' suggest that he had drifted back into his Salamanca days. The local doctors from Toro, and the eminent Don Cipriano de Maroja, who was summoned post haste from Valladolid, were unable to check the fever and delirium, and he died at nine or ten in the morning of Saturday 22 July 1645, at the age of fifty-eight.

For some days the embalmed body lay in state on a gold brocade, dressed in doublet and hose of gold and mother-of-pearl, the cloak of the Order of Alcántara, a white hat adorned with four tawny-coloured feathers, and white boots with golden spurs. A general's baton lay at its side.[126] It was then taken to the church of San Ildefonso in Toro where masses were incessantly intoned, while permission was awaited from the king for it to be taken back for burial at Loeches, to which the Countess of Olivares had returned on 5 August. In due course a macabre procession set out for the slow journey home, with thunder and lightning appropriately playing overhead as it stopped on the outskirts of Madrid.[127] On the last stage of its journey it was accompanied by the coffin of the Count-Duke's daughter María, which was taken from its temporary resting-place in the Madrid church of Santo Tomás. In a somewhat disorganized ceremony in the convent church at Loeches the bodies of father and daughter were buried side by side.

With the Count-Duke safely buried, the relatives swooped down. Predictably, there was indescribable confusion over the inheritance. For some reason, his wife seems to have been unaware that he had made a will in the spring of 1642, and in his final illness, rightly suspecting that there would be protracted suits over the succession, she obtained powers to have a last will and testament drawn up in his name.[128] The illegitimacy of the Marquis of Mairena left him in a weak position, and Don Luis de Haro, the Count-Duke's sole nephew, was politically well placed to ensure his own succession as the Count of Olivares. Within a few days the king had raised him to a grandeeship under the title of Duke of Olivares,[129] and henceforth he was formally styled 'Conde Duque de Olivares',[130]

[126] Marañón, p. 404.
[127] *MHE*, 18, pp. 136–7 (letter of 23 August 1645).
[128] Archivo Histórico Provincial de Zamora. Sección protocolos (Toro), leg. 3881, fos. 205–6v. *Poder del Excmo. Sr. Conde Duque para hacer su testamento*, 19 July 1645. See Marañón, *Olivares*, Appendix 32 for the litigation over the inheritance.
[129] *MHE*, 18, p. 138.
[130] See, for example, *Defensas legales por la Señora D. Inés de Zúñiga y Velasco*.

although characteristically, and presumably by choice, he continued
to be known simply as Don Luis de Haro. But there was also the
dukedom of San Lúcar la Mayor, held by the Count-Duke's widow
for the two remaining years of her life. The Marquis of Mairena
predeceased her in 1646, leaving a sickly son who survived for only
two years. Don Luis de Haro was induced to renounce his claims
to this dukedom, for which the prime contestants were the Marquis
of Leganés and the Duke of Medina de las Torres, who returned
to Spain from Naples in 1644. After a long and complicated suit,
the dukedom was finally adjudged to Medina de las Torres.[131]

No inventory of the Count-Duke's possessions at the time of his
death has yet come to light, but it is not clear that he had much
to leave other than titles and heavily encumbered estates. While he
had received handsome grants from the crown during the years of
his ministry, he had also spent lavishly—often, as in maintaining
his own regiment of soldiers, in the royal service. Father Martínez
Ripalda calculated that it would have cost ten million ducats to carry
out all the bequests listed in his testament of 1642, and pithily, if
unkindly, summarized his views both of that strange document and
its author in the memorable words: 'the gentleman who made this
will governed the Monarchy for nineteen years in the same style
as he bequeathed his inheritance.'[132] Among the more substantial of
his remaining assets, however, were his library and his papers.

The Count-Duke had made the most meticulous provisions for
the preservation of his precious library, which was to be moved
to Seville to form part of the entailed estate of the ducal house of
San Lúcar. Many of the books were already in temporary deposit
in the Alcázar of Seville, while the bulk of the rest of the library
was stored at Loeches. The Countess of Olivares, whose priorities
were not the same as her husband's, began disposing of large parts
of the collection as soon as he was dead—largely, it seems, as gifts
to monasteries and convents in order to pay for masses for his soul.[133]
Most of the ancient codices, however, went to Don Luis de Haro.
He transferred them to his son, Don Gaspar de Haro, Marquis of
Heliche, who in turn presented two thirds of the collection to the
king.

The Count-Duke's personal archive—that great repository of the
history of his ministry—suffered a no less chequered fate. The Countess of Olivares died in September 1647, and in the same month

---

[131] Diego Ortiz de Zúñiga, *Anales eclesiásticos y seculares de la muy noble y muy leal ciudad de Sevilla*, 4 (Madrid, 1796), pp. 386–7.

[132] Quoted Marañón, *Olivares*, p. 479. The 'twenty-nine years' in the quotation as cited by Marañón would more plausibly read 'nineteen'.

[133] See Andrés, 'Historia de la biblioteca del Conde-Duque de Olivares', part 2, for the story of the library's dispersal.

the king ordered an inventory to be taken of all his papers and possessions. The books and papers were consigned by a royal decree of 1650 to Don Luis de Haro, and in due course were inherited by his son. On Don Gaspar de Haro's death in 1687 there was a great auction of his effects, including his library, which was put up for sale by lots in his garden at the Puerta de San Bernardino. There an observer saw 'ancient and modern volumes of manuscripts of great consideration, composed of *consultas* and original papers on the gravest and most arcane affairs of the Monarchy, which were bought by ambassadors, and by ministers, both foreign and Spanish'. He also reports that, some years after the sale, members of the community of one of the convents of the Descalzos in Madrid went for a day's recreation to this same garden, where a gardener unlocked a room for them to while away their siesta. The room was stacked high with papers, and the friars spent the afternoon tearing out the blank pages, which they carried off, along with several of the volumes, in triumph to their convent.[134]

It is doubtful, however, whether the papers subjected to this unworthy fate represented more than a small portion of the Count-Duke's enormous archive. The bulk of it seems to have passed by inheritance to the ducal house of Alba. Two great fires—apparently the result of arson—consumed it all, with the exception of a single volume, in 1795 and 1796.[135] It was a perhaps not inappropriate fate for the records of a minister whom contemporaries would do their utmost to forget, and whose dark and disastrous years of government would be obliterated as far as possible from Spain's collective memory.

---

[134] 'Informe que hizo a Su Majestad en 16 de junio de 1726 Don Santiago Agustín Riol', Valladares, *Semanario erudito*, 3, p. 197.

[135] Duque de Berwick y Alba, *El archivo de la Casa de Alba* (Madrid, 1953), p. 19.

EPILOGUE

'The day of the Magdalene', wrote Quevedo to a friend, 'must be a memorable one, for it saw the end, with the Count-Duke's life, of all those threats, those hatreds and those acts of revenge which promised to go on for eternity . . . These are mighty secrets of God. I who was dead on the day of St. Mark have lived to witness the end of a man who liked to say that he would witness mine, captive and in chains.'[1] How far it all seems from that lyrical effusion with which, twenty-four years earlier, he had greeted the dawn of a new age in his *Grand Annals of Fifteen Days*! But Quevedo, with only a few more weeks to live, may be permitted his brief moment of triumph. He had survived, if barely—survived those nightmare years of the Olivares ministry which had begun amidst such high hopes only to end in defeat and disillusionment.

Quevedo's reaction to the news of the Count-Duke's death seems to have been shared by the majority of his compatriots. The country heaved an almost audible sigh of relief as the news spread. But was it true or false? Even in death the Count-Duke, so crafty and deceitful, was not entirely to be trusted. 'At last', runs one of those ballads which made the rounds in Castile whenever great events were in the air, 'the Count-Duke is dead. Please heaven it be true. If true it is, congratulations, Spain! If not, loyalty and patience.'[2] If the Spaniards of the 1640's were united in anything, it was in their desire never again to repeat the experience of the Olivares years. 'The kings of Castile' wrote the chronicler Gil González Dávila at the time of his fall, 'have had nineteen favourites from the reign of Don Pedro to that of Don Felipe, and it would be hard to level against all of them together half as many charges as against this one alone.'[3]

A similar sense of relief—of a heavy burden lifted—had greeted the death of Richelieu in France. For the best part of twenty years

[1] Quevedo, *Epistolario completo*, letter CCLXXXVII, to Don Francisco de Oviedo, 1 August 1645.
[2] 'A la muerte del Conde-Duque. Romance', in Egido, *Sátiras políticas*, no. 38, p. 174.
[3] BNM Ms. 8389, fo. 38, Gil González Dávila to Dr. Juan Francisco Andrés, 21 February 1643.

the rival monarchies of France and Spain had been governed by two harsh and authoritarian ministers who had seemed prepared to stop at nothing in their determination to exalt their king's authority and wage his wars to the last drop of blood.[4] Up to a point their authoritarianism reflected their elevated sense of mission in the royal service, and the sternness of their temperaments. But it also derived from their conviction that national survival depended on the mobilization of all conceivable human and fiscal resources for the purposes of war. In attempting to achieve the degree of mobilization to which they aspired, they ran up against obstacles of every kind—corporate and regional privileges, practical and legal limitations on the royal sovereignty, the arrogance of blue-blooded commanders, the inertia of incompetent and corrupt officials, the greed of urban oligarchs, the sullen, and sometimes explosive, resistance of the peasantry. Year after year they struggled to impose themselves on societies that seemed deaf to their message, bullying, harrying and cajoling until they came to symbolize in their own persons what was widely seen to be the capricious and arbitrary power of the crown. By their insistent imperiousness they had made themselves intolerable, and those who had suffered under their tyranny—almost the entire population—were glad to see them gone.

Yet there were important differences in their legacies. While Richelieu left France with at least a glimpse of final victory, the Spain of Olivares was staring defeat in the face. To some extent, however, the following years would see a redressing of the balance. Castile, unlike France, experienced no Fronde. Philip IV's dismissal of his hated minister helped reduce the tension before breaking-point was reached; and Don Luis de Haro—supple, like Mazarin, although lacking his intelligence—did not have to grapple with the problems of a royal minority. Philip IV ruled for twenty-two years with the Count-Duke beside him; he would rule for another twenty-two after the Count-Duke was gone. This continuity provided a stabilizing element during the turbulent decade of the 1640's, and helped create the conditions in which Spain could take advantage of French weakness and recoup some of the losses of the Olivares years. Although Portugal proved to be beyond recovery, the return of Catalonia to obedience in 1652 made the final balance-sheet less distressing when France and Spain compared accounts in 1659 and agreed to call it quits.

No cataclysm, then, engulfed the Spanish Monarchy in the wake of Olivares' fall. Castile—loyal, long-suffering, bound by a tangled web of allegiances to a central royal authority—stood firm. The

---

[4] See Elliott, *Richelieu and Olivares*, for a more extended parallel between the two statesmen.

Monarchy, despite upheavals in Naples and Sicily in 1647–8, fragmented no further. And if the peace settlement with the Dutch in
1648 was a bitter and humiliating conclusion to eighty years of conflict, the peace with France in 1659 preserved at least the trappings
that passed for 'reputation'. But two central facts had emerged by
the time of Olivares' fall, and nothing that occurred between 1643
and the death of Philip IV in 1665 proved capable of changing them.
In Europe, the pre-eminence so long enjoyed by the Spanish crown
was passing to the French. Within the Monarchy itself, the crown
had failed in its efforts to reshape the administrative, constitutional
and economic order in a bid to sustain its credibility in a changing
world. These were defeats from which Habsburg Spain would not
recover. The loss of hegemony proved definitive; and until the advent
of a new dynasty in 1700 no ministry dared embark on reforms as
radical as those of Olivares.

The impact of Richelieu's government on France proved very different. The violence of the reaction to the Cardinal's regime in the
aftermath of his death might force his immediate successor into a
temporary retreat, but the power and prestige he had conferred on
the crown by virtue of its victories enabled it to hold to the path
that he had chosen for it. This alone was sufficient to ensure him
posthumous respect. The Count-Duke, on the other hand, by virtue
of his failure, had discredited many of the policies with which he
was associated. It would be some time before his successors in office
would shake themselves free of this incubus of failure; and when
subsequent generations borrowed, as they did, from his reforming
projects, they tended to pass over in silence the identity of their
author. To all intents and purposes he had become a non-person—
literally, indeed, in a copy of Velázquez's painting of *Prince Baltasar
Carlos in the Riding School*, from which his portly figure has been
obliterated (Pls. 35 and 36).[5] When his name did happen to be mentioned, the reference was unlikely to be flattering. Perhaps the most
dispassionate comment came some thirty years after his death from
the Sevillian chronicler Ortiz de Zúñiga: 'a great man who knew
how to make gigantic designs, but he lacked aptitude (*disposición*)
in the means of achieving them and felicity in the outcome.'[6]

The very magnitude of the failure enhances the difficulty of assessing the man. No doubt, at least in comparison with the political
skills of Richelieu, there was a lack of 'aptitude'. The Mantuan affair
was badly bungled, and more skilful handling of the Catalans might

---

[5] For the two versions of the painting see Enriqueta Harris, 'Velázquez's Portrait of Prince
Baltasar Carlos in the Riding School', *The Burlington Magazine*, 118 (1976), pp. 266–75.
[6] *Anales de Sevilla*, 4, p. 388. Ortiz de Zúñiga seems to have been compiling his annals
in the 1670's.

have made some difference. When the fate of the Monarchy was so finely balanced, questions of timing were paramount and even minor differences could have major consequences. Yet, irrespective of his own skills or the lack of them, the Count-Duke often gives the impression of a man struggling against impossible odds. This seems to have been the view of some of those around him, like the 'great minister' who observed that 'it is true that we are approaching our end, but in other hands we would have perished faster.'[7] He himself in his darker moments apparently felt the same. Had he not, after all, largely concurred in Gondomar's grim assessment that the ship was going down?[8]

Decline, then, was not simply the context into which later generations chose to set him. It was also the context in which he and his ministerial colleagues were consciously operating as they framed their policies. Indeed, the Count-Duke's ministerial career can be interpreted as a long and ultimately unsuccessful struggle to find the right responses to a perceived challenge of decline. When he came to power in 1621–2 a number of deeply unfavourable long-term trends were working against the capacity of Spain—or more accurately Castile—to sustain the part it had chosen to play in the theatre of the world. The costs of defending a far-flung empire were mounting as the enemies of the Monarchy, in the first instance the Dutch, encroached with growing confidence on its outer edges. The silver remittances of the Indies, that perennial stand-by of the Spanish crown, were no longer what they had been in the days of Philip II. Decades of deficit financing had given rise to massive crown indebtedness, which diverted capital from economically productive investment, and generated a whole series of fiscal distortions that were progressively crippling Castile's capacity for economic revival. In the cities and countryside of Castile, as in the royal administration, an oligarchy of interlocking families had accumulated a power and an influence that were eroding little by little the crown's authority and limiting its room for manoeuvre as a potential force for change. Beyond the confines of Castile, the rigid administrative and constitutional structure of the Monarchy had brought the crown to the point where any significant increase in the rate of contributions to the central treasury could be bought only by a surrender to powerful local elites or a major confrontation.

Inevitably the Count-Duke was to a large extent a prisoner of these trends, which he and others interpreted as manifestations of sickness and decline. One possible response was to bow to them, making limited adjustments wherever possible. Cautious responses

---

[7] Above, p. 419.
[8] Above, p. 231.

35 and 36. The Count-Duke becomes a non-person. In Velázquez's *Baltasar Carlos in the Riding School* (Pl. 35), probably executed in 1636, the prince is about to practice running at the ring. His valet hands the lance to Olivares, who himself, as the prince's instructor, will hand it to Baltasar Carlos. In the copy (Pl. 36), probably made between the time of Olivares' fall in 1643 and the prince's death in 1646, the figure of the Count-Duke has disappeared.

of this kind were traditional among rulers of the Spanish Monarchy, where in any event vast distances and a slow-moving bureaucracy made caution a natural way of life. An alternative response was to move boldly and decisively in the direction of change, taking risks where necessary. The Count-Duke by instinct was canny and cautious, but he was also by temperament one of nature's activists. The first approach, in his eyes, could only lead to creeping paralysis and a lingering death. His own assessment of the gravity of Castile's condition, his activist temperament, and his burning desire to restore his monarch to his rightful position in the world, all led him to place himself squarely in the ranks of the reformers.

He was shrewd enough, in effect, to see that survival demanded adaptation, and it was the urgency of this vision which he tried, without much success, to communicate to others. Domestically he committed himself to a policy of change and innovation, with a consistency of thought and action during his twenty years of power that makes his political career all of a piece from the beginning to the end. Over and over again the same themes recur: the need for strong kingship and national regeneration; the imposition of unity and uniformity on a fragmented Monarchy; the importance of educating a new generation to higher ideals of service; a widening of the ranks of the elite to include those unjustifiably excluded as a result of their provincial, non-Castilian, origins, or their 'tainted' blood; and a willingness, where necessary, to borrow the ideas and techniques of foreigners (even heretics) in order to generate the new sources of wealth and enterprise that he regarded as indispensable for the Monarchy's survival in an unfriendly world. Events might force upon him tactical retreats, or even the temporary abandonment of one or other of his cherished projects, but the defiant tones of the *Nicandro* proclaim his undying commitment to the programme that he had made his own.

His task was made the harder by the fact that Spanish society, like all European societies of the seventeenth century, was instinctively resistant to the very idea of 'innovation'. When innovations were also foreign-inspired they became doubly detestable. To turn 'Spaniards into merchants', for instance, was to turn them into imitation Dutchmen, and in the process to repudiate those distinctive qualities which were thought to be the glory of Castile. The violent diatribes in Quevedo's *La hora de todos* against new-fangled foreign notions are symptomatic of the reactions of a society that felt itself under threat, and responded to the challenge of innovation as many a future society would respond to that of modernization—by vigorous reaffirmation of its traditional values.

But, faithfully reflecting the tensions in Castilian society of the early seventeenth century, this radical reformer was also a profound traditionalist. Imbued with a deep sense of Castilian history, he was as much concerned to reinvigorate traditional values as to innovate and change. While aligning himself with the fragile but tenacious Castilian reformist tradition that looked abroad to Italy or the Netherlands for the most up-to-date guidance on such matters as making rivers navigable,[9] he was also at one with that tradition in looking back to a past when the virtues of honour and austerity, prowess in arms, and devotion to the faith had made Castile great. Behind the innovator stood the conservative and patriot, whose dearest ambition was to restore Castile to its ancient grandeur as the head and the heart of a world-wide Monarchy through the restoration of its moral values. The very conceptualization of Castile's current difficulties in terms of decline carried with it the idea of restoration—of recreating a past that had been lost through the pride, sloth and sinfulness of later generations. This circumscribed within strict limits the areas in which he was capable of contemplating change, since Castile had risen to greatness through victory in war. Reformist policies at home, then, meant no change in national goals, and were intended solely to make them more attainable. The maintenance of 'reputation' abroad was central to his programme, and in a state with as many foreign commitments as Spain, the maintenance of 'reputation' left little room for flexibility.

Consequently, the daring policy innovations in his programme for the government of Spain found no parallel in his conduct of foreign affairs, and he approached with deep caution all questions that affected his master's standing in the world. There was to be no deviation from the traditional lines of Habsburg foreign policy, no departure from Madrid's commitment to the Austrian branch of the dynasty, and no humiliating compromise with the Dutch of the kind that had been so damaging to the prestige of the Monarchy in the reign of Philip III. But if the policies were traditional, they were pursued with all the tenacious ingenuity that was the hallmark of the man. The child of his age in this, as in so much else, he revelled in the complexities of grandiose designs—Baltic schemes, and economic blockades, and the deployment of fleets and armies over vast areas of space. The Count-Duke was probably the first ruler of the Spanish Monarchy to think in genuinely global terms, and it is no accident that he should have felt at home with that bold adventurer, Sir Anthony Sherley, who would spin the globe with confidence and offer to reveal the secret strengths and weaknesses of every kingdom and sultanate between the Danish Sound and the coast of Malabar.

---

[9] For an early example see the *Memorial del Contador Luis Ortiz* (1558; ed. Madrid 1970), p. 75.

Policies of reform at home and reputation abroad were not necessarily mutually exclusive, and could indeed be used to support each other. The maintenance of 'reputation' was an essential weapon in the armoury of any statesman concerned to protect what were perceived as the vital interests of his king and state; and any sign of weakness, as the Count-Duke appreciated, would only be an inducement to Spain's enemies to display a greater boldness. If he could only sustain his king's reputation abroad, he would be well positioned to carry through his programme of reform in the Monarchy—a programme which itself would raise his master's reputation to still greater heights. In an age when obedience to royal commands was not easily assured, a monarch crowned with the laurels of victory acquired a potent new authority in deploying to the full his prerogative at home. War, under the right conditions, could both facilitate and accelerate reform, while reform could pay for war.

To some extent, indeed, this was happening in the Spain of Olivares, as the urgent requirements of warfare compelled the introduction of fiscal and administrative measures which promised to bring in their wake far-reaching social and political change. The fiscal expedients adopted by his regime were gradually eroding, in practice if not in theory, the traditional tax-exempt status of the privileged classes of Castile. The levelling process of royal fiscalism inside Castile itself was complemented by the levelling process of royal fiscalism as it affected the relationship between Castile and the other regions of the peninsula, which saw their traditional exemptions being similarly eroded by steady pressure from Madrid. But such reforms were highly selective, and were pursued at the cost of other elements of the Count-Duke's reform programme, less immediately relevant to the waging of war. They also depended for their ultimate success on the achievement of victory, and year after year the victory for which he was looking somehow managed to elude his grasp.

With victory and a few years of peace, what could he not achieve! One of the few lasting successes of his ministry—his projection of Philip IV as a patron of the arts of peace—suggests the kind of accomplishments that might have been within his reach in happier times. The knowledge of this tore at him, and gives his career its special poignancy. 'Fame', he told his colleagues after the capture of Breda, 'is achieved through the good government of what one possesses, and from this the reputation of princes is born.'[10] But 'the good government of what one possesses' was made difficult, if not impossible, by the demands of war. In retrospect it is easy to say that he should have cut his losses and made peace with the

---

[10] AGS Est. leg. 2309, consulta, 29 June 1625; and see above, p. 234.

Dutch on the best terms possible in the 1620's, or certainly before becoming involved in full-scale war with France. He himself had pointed out on the occasion of the Mantuan crisis that the Monarchy lacked the resources to wage war on two fronts for any length of time. But at the time the arguments *pro* and *con* appeared finely balanced, and it was his judgment—sometimes against that of the majority of his colleagues—that more would be lost by a settlement than by continuing the war. As the heir to a great tradition he could not bring himself to deviate from the positions of the past. The room he gave himself for manoeuvre was too narrowly defined.

Failing to settle on terms that he could regard as consonant with the honour of his king, he put himself increasingly at the mercy of events, until he, and much of what he had stood for, were swept away by rebellion and defeat. But the effects of his departure from the centre of the stage were not confined to the abandonment of reform for a generation or more. His determined assertion of the royal authority had put some brake on the process by which the oligarchical forces in Castilian society—the *poderosos*, as he liked to call them—were accumulating in their own hands more and more economic, social and political power. Once this brake was removed, the process resumed at a gathering pace, making the kinds of reform he had envisaged still more difficult to achieve. Between them, the bureaucrats and the aristocrats, united by a solidarity of interests, blocked the path to change, exploiting the processes of the conciliar bureaucracy to restrain the royal prerogative and prevent the alteration of a status quo that worked to their advantage.[11] As a result, the Bourbons would inherit in 1700 an old regime society with one or two incipient signs of renewal,[12] but one which, in comparison with its European rivals, looked antiquated and ill-equipped to meet the challenges of a changing world. By 1700 the relative decline which the Count-Duke had detected and struggled to reverse in the 1620's had spread to almost every area of Spanish life and thought.

To reverse the trajectory of a nation through revolution from above demands a high degree of discontinuity, with all the consequent strains on the fabric of society. In the circumstances of the seventeenth century the kind of social engineering required to produce such discontinuity was neither intellectually conceivable nor within the realms of administrative possibility. The ordering of society was God-given,

[11] See the perceptive review article by I. A. A. Thompson, 'The Rule of the Law in Early Modern Castile', *European History Quarterly*, 14 (1984), pp. 221–34.

[12] See Henry Kamen, *Spain in the Later Seventeenth Century*, which, however, does not make an entirely persuasive case for regeneration in the reign of Carlos II. The degree to which the men trained by Olivares succeeded in keeping alive the reforming tradition in the unfavourable climate of the later seventeenth century remains to be explored.

and its vision of the future was bounded by its veneration of the past. At best, the would-be reformer could do little more than seek to purge excesses, remove abuses, and introduce more or less piecemeal certain administrative, economic and institutional changes which might with the passage of time help to modify or alter the attitudes of society at large. The Count-Duke of Olivares correctly identified some of the central ills afflicting Castile and the Spanish Monarchy, and offered a number of antidotes which—if better administered or applied in happier circumstances—might have produced beneficial effects. As it was, many of them failed, others cancelled themselves out, and still others wrought greater damage than any that they were designed to repair, since the body politic and the body social proved unready to receive them. As he ruefully confessed in a letter to Carnero a year before he died: 'We were trying to achieve miracles and reduce the world to what it cannot be.'[13]

The price of action can be high, although not necessarily as high as the price of inaction; but even unsuccessful reforms have a habit of acquiring an existence of their own. In the 1620's and 1630's a Spain in urgent need of remedies had felt its first touch of reforming government. What had been attempted once could be attempted again, and since the problems remained the same, so too did many of the answers. The decrees of the *Nueva Planta* of 1707–16 by which the victorious new dynasty of the Bourbons abolished the constitutional rights and liberties of the Crown of Aragon, closely followed the Count-Duke's plans for the introduction of unity and uniformity among the different realms of the Iberian peninsula, even to the stipulation that the imposition of Castilian legal and administrative forms was to be accompanied by open access to offices and honours irrespective of the province of origin.[14]

While the degree of direct borrowing still remains to be established, there was scarcely one of the reforming projects of Olivares, from repopulation projects to plans for fiscal reform, which did not resurface in one shape or another in the great reforming movement of the eighteenth century. One of the principal reformers of that century, the Count of Campomanes, acknowledged the importance of seventeenth-century precedent when he described Philip IV's letter of 1622 to the cities of Castile as containing 'everything that has since been discussed on simplifying and reducing provincial revenues to one single and unique contribution.'[15] Although new-style reform might clothe itself in the international language of the Enlightenment, much

---

[13] AHN Est. lib. 869, fo. 287, Olivares to Carnero, 8 August 1644.
[14] *Novísima recopilación*, lib. III, tit. III, ley I.
[15] See the 'Notas de Campomanes' to the *Memoriales y discursos de Francisco Martínez de Mata*, ed. Gonzalo Anes (Madrid, 1971), Appendix 9, note 304 (p. 582).

of its content was indigenous. For the Spain of the old regime had developed its own tradition of reform; and behind it in the shadows, his reputation lost, loomed the unmistakable figure of the Count-Duke of Olivares.

BIBLIOGRAPHY

Manuscript sources

This book is based primarily on manuscript sources from numerous archives, both inside and outside Spain. The following is a select list of some of the more useful series consulted in the course of my researches. See J. H. Elliott and José F. de la Peña, *Memoriales y Cartas del Conde Duque de Olivares* (*MC*) for the sources of some of the Count-Duke's most important papers, and Appendix VI of J. H. Elliott, *The Revolt of the Catalans*, for those relating to his Catalan policy.

SPAIN

Archivo de la Casa del Duque de Alba, Madrid
Alba, caja 99–25; Carpio, caja 220–14; Monterrey, caja 96–17; Olivares, cajas 58, 96–14, 96–15, 100.

Archivo del Duque de Frías, Montemayor
Papeles personales de Don Luis Carrillo y Toledo, Marqués de Caracena (1 *carpeta*)

Archivo del Duque del Infantado, Madrid (ADI)
Montesclaros Mss., libs. 25, 26, 29, 31, 56, 59, 63, 125, 130.
Palafox Mss., legs. 91, 94, 95, 96.

Archivo del Duque de Medinaceli, Seville (ADM)
Archivo Histórico, legs. 78, 79, 90 (correspondence between Olivares and the Marquis of Aytona); 259 (correspondence between Olivares and Cardinal-Infante, 1632).

Archivo de los Duques de Medina Sidonia, Sanlúcar de Barrameda
Cartas de reyes, 15, 17, 18.

Archivo de la Casa de Miraflores, Madrid
Copias de cartas que el seteníssimo señor Cardenal Infante escribió de su mano a Don Gaspar de Guzmán, Conde Duque de Olivares, 1635–41.

Archivo de los Condes de Oñate, Madrid
leg. 104 (consultas)

Archivo General de Indias, Seville (AGI)
Indiferente (Indif.), legs. 755, 758, 761, 2658.

Archivo General de Simancas (AGS)
Consejo y Juntas de Hacienda (CJH), annual documentation, 1598–1643.
Estado (Est). España; Portugal; Flandes; Alemania; Francia; Inglaterra; Roma; Nápoles; Sicilia; Milán; Venecia; Génova; selected *legajos*, 1621–43.
Gracia y Justicia, legs. 621, 889.
Guerra Antigua (GA), selected *legajos*, 1621–43.
Patronato real, leg. 91 (replies of cities to royal letter of 20 October 1622).

Archivo Histórico Nacional, Madrid (AHN)
Consejos, legs. 7137, 7145, 7157, 12,444, 12,479 (Vizcaya, 1632), 51,359, 51,438.
Estado (Est), legs. 1427, 1428, 12,010; libs. 697, 726, 729, 737–742, 856, 864 (Olivares–Castrillo correspondence, 1632), 869 (Olivares–Carnero correspondence, 1643–5), 894, 904, 910, 955 (Olivares–Malvezzi correspondence), 959 and 969 (minutes of letters from Don Miguel de Salamanca, 1640 and 1641), 981 (correspondence of Andrés de Rozas, 1638–41).
Inquisición, legs. 494, 1867 no. 36 (Olivares and the Inquisition), 3687–3688 (Villanueva and the Inquisition).
Osuna, leg. 554 (Letters from Olivares to Duke of Gandía).

Archivo Histórico de Protocolos, Madrid (AHP)
1718 (notary, Juan de Santillana). Olivares legal and estate documents, 1622–6.

Archivo Municipal de Toledo (AMT)
Cartas y varios (1621–1630).

Biblioteca del Escorial
Ms. K.1.17, Index of Count-Duke's papers (1622–5) by Fray Lucas de Alaejos.

Biblioteca Nacional, Madrid (BNM)
Mss. 1630 (Olivares–Torrecuso correspondence), 2237 (Joseph Pellicer de Tovar, *Templo de la fama, alcázar de la fortuna, levantado a las acciones de Don Gaspar de Guzmán*), 2258 (Juan Alonso Martínez Sánchez de Calderón, *Epítome de las historias de la gran casa de Guzmán*, vol. 3), 2,352–2,366 (annual *sucesos*), 10,984 (Olivares–Chumacero correspondence).

Biblioteca del Palacio, Madrid (BPM)
Ms. 1817 (Olivares–Gondomar correspondence).

Real Academia de la Historia, Madrid (RAH)
G.43 D. J. Dormer, *Anales de la Corona de Aragón en el reinado de Felipe IV el Grande*.
9–71–8–6 (consulta of Junta of Theologians, 25 January 1629, on aid to Huguenots).
11–13–3 (Olivares correspondence with Duke of Alcalá).
Salazar, M-189 (Olivares' will).

AUSTRIA

Österreichisches Staatsarchiv, Vienna.
Abteilung Haus-, Hof-und Staatsarchiv, Spanien Diplomatische Korrespondenz, Kart. 27, Mappen 491, 498 (despatches of Marquis of Grana, 1642–3).

BELGIUM

Archives Générales du Royaume, Brussels (AGR)
Conseil Privé Espagnol (CPE), Regs. 1502 (Olivares–Roose correspondence), 1504 (Carnero–Roose correspondence), 1506–7 (Roose–Brecht correspondence).
Secrétairerie d'État et de Guerre (SEG), Regs. 126 (Spínola letters), 301–2 (Correspondence of Infanta Isabella and Cardinal-Infante with Olivares), 374–8 (Malvezzi, Velada, Cárdenas correspondence, 1639–41), 596–9 (Olivares–Scaglia correspondence).

FRANCE

Archives du Ministère des Affaires Étrangères, Paris (AAE)
Correspondance politique, Espagne, vols. 13–18.
Bibliothèque Nationale, Paris (BNP)
Fonds français, 10,759.

GERMANY

Bayerische Staatsbibliothek, Munich (MBS)
Cod. Hisp. 22 (Olivares' letters to Cardinal-Infante, 1635–41).

GREAT BRITAIN

British Library, London (BL)
Additional Mss. (Add), 6,902, 9,936, 13,997 (Union of Arms), 14,004,
    14,006, 14,007 (letters to Cardinal-Infante), 14,015, 14,017, 24,909 (letter-
    book of Padre Diego de Quiroga, 1629–46), 25,688–9 (papers on and
    by Olivares), 28,452, 36,449–50 (letter-books of Sir Walter Aston, British
    ambassador in Madrid, 1620–25, 1635–8).
Egerton Mss. (Eg), 315, 332, 335, 338, 339, 340, 347 (major Olivares papers),
    403, 1820 (notebook of Sir Arthur Hopton, British agent in Madrid,
    1631–6), 2052, 2053, 2079, 2081.

Public Record Office, London (PRO)
State Papers, Spain (SP) 94.40, 41, 42 (letters from Sir Arthur Hopton fol-
    lowing his return to Madrid in 1638).

ITALY

Archivio di Stato, Florence (ASF)
Mediceo, filza 4949, 4959, 4960, 4961, 4963, 4964, 4965, 4966, 4967 (diplo-
    matic despatches from Madrid for selected years between 1619 and 1643,
    and correspondence of Bernardo Monanni, secretary to Tuscan legation).
Archivio di Stato, Genoa (ASG)
Lettere Ministri, Spagna, 2429–2445 (despatches from Madrid, 1617–43).
Archivio di Stato, Lucca (ASL)
Anziani al tempo dalla libertà, 647 (Lettere di Spagna, 1615–34).
Archivio di Stato, Mantua (ASM)
Archivio Gonzaga, Serie E.XIV.3 (Carteggio di inviati dalla Spagna), busta
    615 (1621–2), 616 (1623–5), 617 (1626–8), 618 (1629–30).
Archivio di Stato, Modena
Cancelleria ducale. Estero. Cart. Ambasciatori Spagna, busta 45 (1634–6),
    46 (1636), 48 (1638–9), 53 (Guidi's correspondence, 1643).
Archivio Segreto Vaticano, Rome (ASV)
Nunziatura di Spagna, 65–69 (1623–9), 72 (1630–1), 345 (1632–4), 76
    (1634–5), 77 (1635), 78 (1636–7), 85 (1642–3).
Biblioteca Apostolica Vaticana, Rome (BAV)
Barberini Lat. Ms. 3098 (catalogue of Olivares library), 8321, 8599–8600
    (Olivares correspondence with Rome, 1622–42).

Archivio di Stato, Venice (ASVen)
Senato. Dispacci degli ambasciatori, filza 69 (1632–3), 70 (1633–5), 75 (1640–1), 76 (1641–2), 77 (1642–3).

PORTUGAL

Ajuda Palace, Lisbon
Correspondence of Olivares with Count of Castro.

USA

Bancroft Library, Berkeley
Ms. MM 1755, papers by Olivares.
Hispanic Society of America, New York
Ms. HC 380/80, Baltasar Alamos de Barrientos, *Advertencias políticas sobre lo particular y público de esta monarchia.*

Printed sources

Las Actas de las Cortes de Castilla, 60 vols. (Madrid, 1877–1974).

Adams, Simon. 'Spain or the Netherlands? The Dilemmas of Early Stuart Foreign Policy', *Before the English Civil War*, ed. Howard Tomlinson (New York, 1984).

Aguado, Francisco. *Exhortaciones varias, dotrinales* (Madrid, 1641).

Agulló y Cobo, Mercedes. 'El monasterio de San Plácido y su fundador, el madrileño Jerónimo de Villanueva, protonotario de Aragón', *Villa de Madrid*, 13 (1975), pp. 59–68.

Alamos de Barrientos. *L'Art de Gouverner*, ed. J. M. Guardia (Paris, 1867).

——. *Tácito español* (Madrid, 1614).

Albrecht, Dieter. *Die auswärtige Politik Maximilians von Bayern, 1618–1635* (Göttingen, 1962).

Alcalá-Zamora y Queipo de Llano, José. *Historia de una empresa siderúrgica española: los altos hornos de Liérganes y La Cavada, 1622–1834* (Santander, 1974).

——. *España, Flandes y el mar del norte, 1618–1639* (Barcelona, 1975).

Alcedo, Marqués de. *Olivares et l'Alliance Anglaise* (Bayonne, 1905).

—— ed. *Discursos de Don Antonio de Mendoza* (Madrid, 1911).

Aldea Vaquero, Quintín. *Iglesia y estado en la España del siglo XVII* (Comillas, 1961).

——. 'Iglesia y estado en la época barroca', *Historia de España Ramón Menéndez Pidal*, 25 (Madrid, 1982).

Allen, John J. *The Reconstruction of a Spanish Golden Age Playhouse. El Corral del Príncipe, 1583–1744* (Gainesville, 1983).

Almansa y Mendoza, Andrés. *Cartas de Andrés de Almansa y Mendoza* (Madrid, 1886).

Álvarez y Baena, Joseph Antonio. *Hijos de Madrid*, 4 vols. (Madrid, 1789–91; repr. Madrid, 1972–3).

Anderson, Ruth Matilda. *The Golilla: a Spanish Collar of the Seventeenth*

Century, Hispanic Society of America, New York, n.d. Reprinted from *Waffen-und Kostümkunde*, 11 (1969).

Andrade, Alonso de. *Vida del Venerable Padre Francisco de Aguado, provincial de la Compañía de Jesús* (Madrid, 1658).

Andrés, Gregorio de. 'Historia de la biblioteca del Conde-Duque de Olivares y descripción de sus códices', *Cuadernos Bibliográficos* 28 (1972).

Anes, G. and Le Flem, J. P. 'Las Crisis del siglo XVII: producción agrícola, precios e ingresos en tierras de Segovia', *Moneda y Crédito*, no. 93 (1965), pp. 3–55.

Assarino, Luca. *Le rivolutioni di Catalogna* (Bologna, 1648).

Astrana Marín, Luis. *La vida turbulenta de Quevedo* (Madrid, 1945).

Atienza Hernández, Ignacio. 'La "quiebra" de la nobleza castellana en el siglo XVII. Autoridad real y poder señorial: el secuestro de los bienes de la casa de Osuna', *Hispania*, 44 (1984), pp. 49–81.

Aubrun, Charles Vincent. *La Comédie Espagnole, 1600–1680* (Paris, 1966).

Bakewell, P. J. *Silver Mining and Society in Colonial Mexico* (Cambridge, 1971).

Báncora Cañero, Carmen. 'Las remesas de metales preciosos desde el Callao a España en la primera mitad del siglo XVII', *Revista de Indias*, no. 75 (1959), pp. 35–88.

Barahona, Renato. *Histoire d'une révolte en Biscaye: Bilbao, 1631–4* (unpublished thesis).

Barozzi, N. and Berchet, G. *Relazioni degli stati europei*. Serie 1, *Spagna*, 2 (Venice, 1860).

Barrera y Leirado, Cayetano Alberto de la. *Poesías de Don Francisco de Rioja* (Madrid, 1867).

Bataillon, Marcel. *Études sur Bartolomé de las Casas* (Paris, 1965).

Batllori, Miguel and Peralta, Ceferino. *Baltasar Gracián en su vida y en sus obras* (Zaragoza, 1969).

Bazy, J. P. A. *État militaire de la Monarchie Espagnole sous le règne de Philippe IV* (Poitiers, 1864).

Beladiez, Emilio. *España y el Sacro Imperio Romano Germánico. Wallenstein, 1583–1634* (Madrid, 1967).

Bennassar, Bartolomé. *La España del siglo de oro* (Barcelona, 1983) (Spanish translation of *Un siècle d'or espagnol*, Paris, 1982).

———. *Recherches sur les grandes epidémies dans le nord de l'Espagne à la fin du XVIe siècle* (Paris, 1969).

Bercé, Yves-Marie. *Histoire des croquants* (Geneva, 1974).

Bermúdez de Pedraza, Francisco. *El secretario del rey* (Madrid, 1620; facsimile reprint, Madrid, 1973).

Berwick y Alba, Duque de. *Discursos leídos ante la Real Academia de Bellas Artes de San Fernando en la recepción pública del Excmo. Sr. Duque de Berwick y de Alba* (Madrid, 1924).

———. *El archivo de la Casa de Alba* (Madrid, 1953).

Bireley, Robert. *Religion and Politics in the Age of the Counterreformation* (Chapel Hill, 1981).

Bolzern, Rudolf. *Spanien, Mailand und die katholische Eidgenossenschaft* (Luzern/Stuttgart, 1982).

Bombín Pérez, Antonio. *Los caminos del imperio español* (inaugural lecture, Vitoria, 1974).

——. *La cuestión de Monferrato, 1613–1618* (Vitoria, 1975).

Bonney, Richard. *The King's Debts. Finance and Politics in France, 1589–1661* (Oxford, 1981).

Botero, Giovanni. *The Reason of State*, trans. and ed. P. J. and D. P. Waley (London, 1956).

Bourcier, Elisabeth, ed. *The Diary of Sir Simonds D'Ewes, 1622–1624* (Paris, 1974).

Boxer, C. R. *Salvador de Sá and the Struggle for Brazil and Angola, 1602–1686* (London, 1952).

——. *The Dutch in Brazil, 1624–1654* (Oxford, 1957).

—— ed. *The Journal of Maarten Harpertszoon Tromp* (Cambridge, 1930).

Boyajian, James C. *Portuguese Bankers at the Madrid Court, 1626–1650* (New Brunswick, 1982).

Braudel, Fernand. 'En Espagne au temps de Richelieu et d'Olivarès', *Annales*, 2 (1947), pp. 354–8.

Brightwell, Peter. 'The Spanish Origins of the Thirty Years' War', *European Studies Review*, 9 (1979), pp. 409–31.

——. 'Spain and Bohemia: the Decision to Intervene', *European Studies Review*, 12 (1982).

——. 'Spain, Bohemia and Europe, 1619–1621', *European Studies Review*, 12 (1982), pp. 371–99.

——. 'The Spanish System and the Twelve Years Truce', *English Historical Review*, 89 (1974), pp. 270–92.

——. 'Spain and the Origins of the Thirty Years' War', unpublished Cambridge Ph.D. thesis (1967).

Bronner, Fred. 'La Unión de las Armas en el Perú. Aspectos político-legales', *Anuario de Estudios Americanos*, 24 (1967), pp. 1133–71.

Brouwers, L. *Carolus Scribani SJ., 1561–1629* (Antwerp, 1961).

——. *Brieven van Carolus Scribani (1561–1629)* (Antwerp, 1972).

Brown, Jonathan. *Images and Ideas in Seventeenth-Century Spanish Painting* (Princeton, 1978).

——. *Velázquez, Painter and Courtier* (New Haven and London, 1986).

——. 'A Portrait Drawing by Velázquez', *Master Drawings*, 14 (1976), pp. 46–51.

Brown, Jonathan and Elliott, J. H. *A Palace for a King* (New Haven and London, 1980).

Burckhardt, Carl, J. *Richelieu and His Age*, 3 vols. (London, 1940–71).

Cabral de Mello, Evaldo. *Olinda restaurada. Guerra e Açúcar no Nordeste, 1630–1654* (São Paulo, 1975).

Cabrera de Córdoba, Luis. *Relaciones de las cosas sucedidas en la corte de España desde 1599 hasta 1614* (Madrid, 1857).

Cabrillana, Nicolás. 'Un noble de la decadencia: el virrey marqués de Montesclaros, 1571–1628', *Revista de Indias*, 29 (1969), pp. 107–50.

Calvo Serraller, Francisco. *Teoría de la pintura del siglo de oro* (Madrid, 1981).

Campanella, Thomas. *A Discourse Touching the Spanish Monarchy* (Eng. trans., London, 1654).

——. *La Monarquía hispánica* (Spanish trans., Primitivo Mariño, Madrid, 1982).

Cánovas del Castillo, A. *Historia de la decadencia española* (Madrid, 1854).

——. *Bosquejo histórico de la Casa de Austria* (Madrid, 1869).

——. *Estudios del reinado de Felipe IV*, 2 vols. (Madrid, 1888).

Cansino, Jacob. *Extremos y grandezas de Constantinopla* (Madrid, 1638).

Caramuel y Lobkowitz, Juan de. *Declaración mystica de las armas de España invictamente belicosas* (Brussels, 1636).

Carnero, Antonio. *Historia de las guerras civiles que ha avido en los Estados de Flandes* (Brussels, 1625).

Caro Baroja, Julio. *Los judíos en la España moderna y contemporánea*, 2 vols. (Madrid, 1962).

——. 'La sociedad criptojudía en la corte de Felipe IV', in *Inquisición, brujería y criptojudaismo* (2nd. ed., Barcelona, 1972).

Carrera Pujal, Jaime. *Historia de la economía española*, 1 (Barcelona, 1943).

Cartas de algunos PP. de la Compañía de Jesús entre los años de 1634 y 1648 (*Memorial Histórico Español*, 13–19 [Madrid, 1861–5]).

Carter, Charles Howard. *The Secret Diplomacy of the Habsburgs, 1598–1625* (New York and London, 1964).

Casey, James. *The Kingdom of Valencia in the Seventeenth Century* (Cambridge, 1979).

——. 'Spain: a Failed Transition', *The European Crisis of the 1590s*, ed. P. Clark (London, 1985).

Castellanos, Basilio Sebastián. *El Bibliotecario* (Madrid, 1841).

Castillo, Julián del. *Historia de los reyes godos* (Madrid, 1624).

Castro, Adolfo de. *El Conde-Duque de Olivares y el Rey Felipe IV* (Cadiz, 1846).

Castro, Américo. *La realidad histórica de España* (3rd ed., Mexico, 1966).

Cavillac, Michel. *Gueux et marchands dans le 'Guzmán de Alfarache', 1599–1604* (Brussels, 1983).

Caxa de Leruela, Miguel. *Restauración de la abundancia de España* (1631), ed. Jean Paul Le Flem (Madrid, 1975).

Ceballos, Jerónimo de. *Arte real para el buen govierno de los reyes y príncipes, y de sus vasallos* (Toledo, 1623).

Céspedes y Meneses, Gonzalo. *Historia de Don Felipe IV, Rey de las Españas* (Barcelona, 1634).

Chaunu, Huguette and Pierre. 'Autour de 1640: politiques et économiques atlantiques', *Annales*, 9 (1954), pp. 44–52.

Chaunu, Pierre. *Séville et l'Atlantique, 1504–1650*, 8 vols. (Paris, 1955–9).

——. *Les Philippines et le Pacifique des Ibériques: XVIᵉ, XVIIᵉ, XVIIIᵉ siècles* (Paris, 1960).

Chudoba, Bohdan. *Spain and the Empire, 1519–1643* (Chicago, 1952).

Church, William F. *Richelieu and Reason of State* (Princeton, 1972).

Ciasca, Raffaele. *Istruzioni e Relazioni degli Ambasciatori Genovesi*, 2 (*Spagna*) 2 vols. (Rome, 1955).

Cirot, Georges. *Mariana, historien* (Paris, 1905).

Clarendon, Edward, Earl of. *The History of the Rebellion and Civil Wars in England*, ed. W. D. Macray, 5 (Oxford, 1888).

Clark, Peter, ed. *The European Crisis of the 1590s* (London, 1985).

Colmeiro, Manuel. *Historia de la economía política en España*, ed. Gonzalo Anes Álvarez, 2 vols. (Madrid, 1965).

Colmenares, Diego de. *Historia de la insigne ciudad de Segovia*, 3 vols. (Segovia, 1637; ed. Segovia, 1970–5).

Coniglio, Giuseppe. *Il viceregno di Napoli nel sec. XVII* (Rome, 1955).

Córdoba Ronquillo, Luis de. *Sermones funebres predicados dominica infra octava de todos santos de 1624 años en la provincia del andalucia del orden de la Santísima Trinidad de Redemptores . . . recopilados por el muy reverendo maestro fray Luis de Cordova Ronquillo* (Seville, 1624).

Corral y Maestro, León. *Don Diego de Corral y Arellano, y los Corrales de Valladolid* (Valladolid, 1905).

Cousin, Victor. *Madame de Chevreuse* (7th ed., Paris, 1886).

Crosby, James O. *En torno a la poesía de Quevedo* (Madrid, 1967).

Cruzada Villaamil, G. *Rubens, diplomático español* (Madrid, 1874).

Cuvelier, Joseph. 'Les négociations diplomatiques de Roosendael (1627–1630)', *Mélanges d'histoire offerts à Henri Pirenne*, 2 vols. (Brussels, 1926), 1, pp. 73–80.

Danvila y Collado, Manuel. *El poder civil en España*, 6 vols. (Madrid, 1885–6).

Davies, Gareth. *A Poet at Court: Antonio Hurtado de Mendoza* (Oxford, 1971).

——. 'The Influence of Justus Lipsius on Juan de Vera y Figueroa's *Embaxador* (1620)', *Bulletin of Hispanic Studies*, 42 (1965), pp. 160–73.

Defensas legales por la Señora D. Inés de Zúñiga y Velasco . . . contra el Señor Don Luis Méndez de Haro, Conde Duque de Olivares (Madrid, 1646).

Delplanche, René. *Un légiste anversois au service d'Espagne. Pierre Roose, chef-président du Conseil-Privé des Pays-Bas, 1583–1673* (Brussels, 1945).

Dethan, Georges. *Mazarin et ses amis* (Paris, 1968).

——. *Gaston d'Orléans. Conspirateur et Prince Charmant* (Paris, 1959).

Devèze, M. *L'Espagne de Philippe IV*, 2 vols. (Paris, 1970).

Diccionario de historia eclesiástica de España, 4 vols. (Madrid, 1972–5), ed. Aldea Vaquero, Quintín, *et al.*

Díez Borque, José María. *Sociología de la comedia española del siglo XVII* (Madrid, 1976).

Disney, A. R. *Twilight of the Pepper Empire* (Cambridge, Mass., 1978).

Documenta Bohemica Bellum Tricennale Illustrantia, 7 vols. (Prague, 1971–81).

Domínguez Ortiz, Antonio and Aguilar Piñal, Francisco. *Historia de Sevilla*, 4, *El Barroco y la Ilustración* (Seville, 1976).

Domínguez Ortiz, Antonio. *Política y hacienda de Felipe IV* (Madrid, 1960).

——. *La sociedad española en el siglo XVII*, 2 vols. (Madrid, 1963–70).

——. *Crisis y decadencia de la España de los Austrias* (Madrid, 1969).

——. *The Golden Age of Spain, 1516–1659* (London, 1971).

——. *Los judeoconversos en España y América* (Madrid, 1971).

——. 'El almirantazgo de los países septentrionales y la política économica de Felipe IV', *Hispania* 7 (1947), pp. 272–90.

——. 'La movilización de la nobleza castellana en 1640', *Anuario de Historia del Derecho Español*, 25 (1955), pp. 799–824.

——. 'Los caudales de Indias y la política exterior de Felipe IV', *Anuario de Estudios Americanos*, 13 (1956), pp. 311–83.

——. 'El suplicio de Don Juan de Benavides', *Archivo Hispalense* (1956), 159–71.

Echevarría Bacigalupe, Miguel Angel. *La diplomacia secreta en Flandes, 1598–1643* (Bilbao, 1984).

Egido, Teófanes. *Sátiras políticas de la España moderna* (Madrid, 1973).

Egler, Anna. *Die Spanier in der Linksrheinischen Pfalz, 1620–1632* (Mainz, 1971).

Eiras Roel, Antonio. 'Desvío y "mudanza" de Francia en 1616', *Hispania*, 25 (1965), pp. 521–60.

——. 'Política francesa de Felipe III: las tensiones con Enrique IV', *Hispania*, 31 (1971), pp. 245–336.

Elliott, J. H. *The Revolt of the Catalans* (Cambridge, 1963).

——. *Imperial Spain, 1469–1716* (London, 1963).

——. *El Conde-Duque de Olivares y la herencia de Felipe II* (Valladolid, 1977).

——. *Richelieu and Olivares* (Cambridge, 1984).

——. 'The Decline of Spain', *Past and Present*, 20 (1961), pp. 52–75.

——. 'Nueva luz sobre la prisión de Quevedo y Adam de la Parra', *Boletín de la Real Academia de la Historia*, 169 (1972), 171–82.

——. 'Self-perception and Decline in Early Seventeenth-Century Spain', *Past and Present*, 74 (1977), pp. 41–61.

——. 'Philip IV of Spain. Prisoner of Ceremony', *The Courts of Europe*, ed. A. G. Dickens (London, 1977).

——. 'The Year of the Three Ambassadors', in *History and Imagination. Essays in Honour of H. R. Trevor-Roper*, ed. Hugh Lloyd-Jones, Valerie Pearl and Blair Worden (London, 1981).

——. 'El programa de Olivares y los movimientos de 1640', *Historia de España Ramón Menéndez Pidal*, 25 (Madrid, 1982).

——. 'Quevedo and the Count-Duke of Olivares', *Quevedo in Perspective*, ed. James Iffland (Newark, Delaware, 1982).

——, and Brown, Jonathan. *A Palace for a King. See under* Brown.

——, and Peña, José F. de la. *Memoriales y cartas del Conde Duque de Olivares*, 2 vols. (Madrid, 1978–80).

'Epistolario de la Familia Yrarrázaval en el siglo XVII', *Boletín de la Academia Chilena de la Historia*, 41 (1949), pp. 125–34.

Escagedo Salmón, Mateo. 'Los Acebedos', *Boletín de la Biblioteca Menéndez y Pelayo*, 5–9 (1923–7).

Escudero, José Antonio. *Los secretarios de estado y del despacho*, 4 vols. (Madrid, 1969).

Espejo, Cristóbal. 'Enumeración y atribuciones de algunas juntas de la administración española desde el siglo XVI hasta el año 1800', *Revista de la Biblioteca, Archivo y Museo*, Año VIII, 32 (1931), pp. 325–62.

Espinosa Rodríguez, José. *Fray Antonio de Sotomayor y su correspondencia con Felipe IV* (Vigo, 1944).

Ettinghausen, Henry. 'The News in Spain; *Relaciones de sucesos* in the Reigns of Philip III and IV', *European History Quarterly*, 14 (1984), pp. 1–20.

Evans, R. J. W. *The Making of the Habsburg Monarchy, 1550–1700* (Oxford, 1979).

Ezquerra Abadía, Ramón. *La conspiración del Duque de Híjar [1648]* (Madrid, 1934).

Fagniez, Gustave. *Le Père Joseph et Richelieu*, 2 vols. (Paris, 1891–4).

Fayard, Janine. *Les membres du Conseil de Castille à l'époque moderne (1621–1746)* (Geneva, 1979).

——. 'José González (1583?–1668) "créature" du comte-duc d'Olivares et conseiller de Philippe IV', in *Hommage a Roland Mousnier*, ed. Yves Durand (Paris, 1981).

Fernández Albaladejo, Pablo. 'Monarquía, Cortes y "cuestión constitucional" en Castilla durante la edad moderna', *Revista de las Cortes Generales*. 1. *Estudios* (1984), pp. 11–34.

Fernández Álvarez, Manuel. *Don Gonzalo Fernández de Córdoba y la guerra de sucesión de Mantua y del Monferrato, 1627–1629* (Madrid, 1955).

Fernández Duro, C. *Armada española*, 4 (Madrid, 1898).

——. *El Gran Duque de Osuna y su marina* (Madrid, 1885).

Fernández Navarrete, Pedro. *Conservación de monarquías* (Madrid, 1626).

Fernández-Santamaría, J. A. *Reason of State and Statecraft in Spanish Political Thought, 1595–1640* (Lanham, 1983).

Flores, Xavier-A., ed. *Le "Peso político de todo el mundo" d'Anthony Sherley* (Paris, 1963).

Foisil, Madeleine. *La révolte des nu-pieds et les révoltes normandes de 1639* (Paris, 1970).

Ford, Richard. *A Handbook for Travellers in Spain* (London, 1845).

Fortea Pérez, José Ignacio. *Córdoba en el siglo XVI. Las bases demográficas y económicas de una expansión urbana* (Córdoba, 1981).

Fumaroli, Marc. *L'âge de l'éloquence* (Geneva, 1980).

Gállego, Julián. *Velázquez en Sevilla* (Seville, 1974).

Gachard, L. P. *Histoire politique et diplomatique de Pierre-Paul Rubens* (Brussels, 1877).

García, Carlos. *La oposición y conjunción de los dos grandes luminares de la tierra, o la antipatía de franceses y españoles*, ed. Michel Bareau (Edmonton, 1979).

García Sanz, Angel. *Desarrollo y crisis del Antiguo Régimen en Castilla la Vieja* (Madrid, 1977).

Gardiner, S. R. *History of England from the Accession of James I to the Outbreak of the Civil War, 1603–1642*, 10 vols. (London, 1899–1901; repr. New York, 1965).

Garma y Durán, Francisco Xavier. *Teatro universal de España*, 4 (Barcelona, 1751).

Gil Ayuso, Faustino. *Noticia bibliográfica de textos y disposiciones legales de los reinos de Castilla impresos en los siglos XVI y XVII* (Madrid, 1935).

Gil-Bermejo, Juana. 'Olivares y su colegial', *El Correo de Andalucía*, 29 December 1971.

Girard, Albert. 'La saisie des biens des français en Espagne en 1625', *Revue d'Histoire Économique et Sociale*, 19 (1931), pp. 279–315.

Gómez del Campillo, Miguel. 'El espía mayor y el conductor de embajadores', *Boletín de la Real Academia de la Historia*, 119 (1946).

Gómez Solís, Duarte. *Discursos sobre los comercios de las dos Indias* (Madrid, 1622; new ed. by Moses Bensabat Amzalak, Lisbon, 1943).

Gondomar, Count of. *Correspondencia Oficial de don Diego Sarmiento de Acuña, Conde de Gondomar* in *Documentos inéditos para la historia de España*, 4 vols. (Madrid, 1936–45).

González Dávila, Gil. *Teatro de las Grandezas de Madrid* (Madrid, 1623).

González de Amezúa, Agustín. *Epistolario de Lope de Vega Carpio*, 3 and 4 (Madrid, 1941–3).

González de la Calle, Urbano. *Relaciones del Conde Duque de Olivares con la Universidad de Salamanca* (Madrid, 1931).

González de Cellorigo, Martín. *Memorial de la política necessaria y útil restauración a la república de España* (Valladolid, 1600).

González Moreno, Joaquín. *Don Fernando Enríquez de Ribera, tercer duque de Alcalá de los Gazules, 1583–1637* (Seville, 1969).

González Palencia, Angel. *La Junta de Reformación* (Valladolid, 1932).

——. *Noticias de Madrid, 1621–1627* (Madrid, 1942).

——. 'Quevedo, Tirso y las comedias ante la Junta de Reformación', *Boletín de la Real Academia Española*, 25 (1946), pp. 43–84.

Gordon, Michael D. 'Morality, Reform and the Empire in Seventeenth-Century Spain', *Il Pensiero Politico*, 11 (1978), pp. 3–19.

Gottigny, Jean. 'Juste-Lipse et l'Espagne', unpublished doctoral thesis (Louvain, 1968).

Guiard y Larrauri, Teófilo. *Historia de la noble villa de Bilbao*, 2 (Bilbao, 1906; repr. 1971).

Guichot y Parodi, Joaquín. *Historia del excelentísimo ayuntamiento de . . . Sevilla*, 1 (Seville, 1896).

Guidi, Ippolito Camillo. *Caduta del Conte d'Olivares* (Ivrea, 1644).

Günter, Heinrich. *Die Habsburger-Liga, 1625–1635* (Berlin, 1908).

Gutiérrez, Jesús. 'Don Francisco de Moncada, el hombre y el embajador. Selección de textos inéditos', *Boletín de la Biblioteca de Menéndez Pelayo* (1980), pp. 3–72.

Hamilton, Earl J. *American Treasure and the Price Revolution in Spain, 1501–1650* (Cambridge, Mass., 1934).

——. 'The Decline of Spain', *Economic History Review*, 8 (1938), pp. 168–79.

——. 'Spanish Banking Schemes before 1700', *The Journal of Political Economy*, 47 (1949), pp. 134–56.

Hanotaux, Gabriel and La Force, Duc de. *Histoire du Cardinal de Richelieu*, 6 vols. (Paris, 1893–1947).

Harris, Enriqueta and Elliott, J. H. 'Velázquez and the Queen of Hungary', *Burlington Magazine*, 118 (1976), pp. 24–6.

Harris, Enriqueta. *Velázquez* (Oxford, 1982).

——. 'Velázquez's Portrait of Prince Baltasar Carlos in the Riding School', *The Burlington Magazine*, 118 (1976), pp. 266–75.

Havran, Martin J. *Caroline Courtier: the Life of Lord Cottington* (London, 1973).

Henrard, P. *Marie de Médicis dans les Pays-Bas, 1631–1638* (Antwerp, 1875).

Herrera, Antonio de. *Elogio a Don Baltasar de Zúñiga* (Madrid, 1622).

Herrera García, Antonio. *El Aljarafe sevillano durante el antiguo régimen. Un estudio de su evolución socioeconómica en los siglos XVI, XVII y XVIII* (Seville, 1980).

Herrera y Sotomayor, Jacinto de. *Jornada que Su Magestad hizo a la Andaluzia* (Madrid, 1624).

Herrero García, Miguel. *Ideas de los Españoles del siglo XVII* (2nd. ed., Madrid, 1966).

Howell, James. *Epistolae Ho-Elianae* (11th ed., London, 1754).

Humbert, Jacques. *Les Français en Savoie sous Louis XIII* (Paris, 1960).

Hume, Martin. *The Court of Philip IV* (2nd. ed., London, 1928).

Hurtado de Mendoza, Antonio. *Discursos de Don Antonio de Mendoza*, ed. Marqués de Alcedo (Madrid, 1911).

——. *Obras poéticas de Don Antonio Hurtado de Mendoza*, ed. Rafael Benítez Claros, 2 vols. (Madrid, 1947–8).

Huxley, Gervas. *Endymion Porter* (London, 1959).

Iffland, James, ed. *Quevedo in Perspective* (Newark, Delaware, 1982).

Israel, J. I. *Race, Class and Politics in Colonial Mexico, 1610–1670* (Oxford, 1975).

——. *The Dutch Republic and the Hispanic World, 1606–1661* (Oxford, 1982).

——. 'A Conflict of Empires: Spain and the Netherlands, 1618–1648', *Past and Present*, 76 (1977), pp. 34–74.

——. 'Spain and the Dutch Sephardim, 1609–1660', *Studia Rosenthaliana*, 12 (1978), pp. 1–61.

——. 'The States General and the Strategic Regulation of the Dutch River Trade, 1621–1636', *Bijdragen en Mededelingen Betreffende de Geschiedenis der Nederlanden*, 95 (1980), pp. 461–91.

——. 'Spanish Wool Exports and the European Economy, 1610–40', *Economic History Review*, 33 (1980), pp. 193–211.

——. 'The Politics of International Trade Rivalry during the Thirty Years' War: Gabriel de Roy and Olivares' Mercantilist Projects (1623–45)', forthcoming in *The International History Review*.

Jago, Charles. 'The Influence of Debt on the Relations between Crown and Aristocracy in Seventeeth-Century Castile', *Economic History Review*, 26 (1973), pp. 218–36.

——. 'The "Crisis of the Aristocracy" in Seventeenth-Century Castile', *Past and Present*, 84 (1979), pp. 60–90.

——. 'Habsburg Absolutism and the Cortes of Castile', *American Historical Review*, 86 (1981), pp. 307–86.

Jammes, Robert. *Études sur l'oeuvre poétique de Don Luis de Góngora y Argote* (Bordeaux, 1967).

Janssens, Paul. 'L'échec des tentatives de soulèvement aux Pays-Bas sous Philippe IV (1621–1665)', *Revue d'Histoire Diplomatique*, 92 (1978), pp. 110–29.

Jesús, Fray Francisco de. *Narrative of the Spanish Marriage Treaty*, ed. S. R. Gardiner (Camden Society, vol. 101, 1869).

Jordán de Urriés y Azara, José. *Biografía y estudio crítico de Jáuregui* (Madrid, 1899).

Jover Zamora, José María. *1635. Historia de una polémica y semblanza de una generación* (Madrid, 1959).

——. 'Sobre los conceptos de monarquía y nación en el pensamiento político español del XVII', *Cuadernos de Historia de España*, 13 (1950), pp. 101–50.

Justi, Carl. *Diego Velázquez and his Times* (London, 1889).

Kagan, Richard L. *Students and Society in Early Modern Spain* (Baltimore, 1974).

Kamen, Henry. *Spain in the Later Seventeenth Century, 1665–1700* (London, 1980).

——. *Spain, 1469–1714. A Society of Conflict* (London, 1983).

——. *Inquisition and Society in Spain in the Sixteenth and Seventeenth Centuries* (London, 1985).

Kendrick, T. D. *Saint James in Spain* (London, 1960).

Keniston, Hayward. *Francisco de los Cobos* (Pittsburgh, 1960).

Kennedy, Ruth Lee. *Studies in Tirso, I: The Dramatist and his Competitors, 1620–26* (Chapel Hill, 1974).

——. '"El condenado por desconfiado"; its ambient and date of composition', *Homenaje a Guillermo Gustavino* (Madrid, 1974).

——. '"La Estrella de Sevilla", reinterpreted', *Revista de Archivos, Bibliotecas y Museos*, 78 (1975), pp. 385–408.

Kepler, J. S. *The Exchange of Christendom* (Leicester, 1976).

Kessel, Jürgen. *Spanien und die geistlichen Kurstaaten am Rhein während der Regierungszeit der Infantin Isabella, 1621–1633* (Frankfurt, 1979).

Khevenhüller, Franz Christoph. *Annales Ferdinandei*, 4 vols. (Leipzig, 1724–6).

Klein, Julius. *The Mesta. A Study in Spanish Economic History, 1273–1836* (Cambridge, Mass., 1920).

Koenigsberger, H. G. *The Government of Sicily under Philip II of Spain* (London, 1951). Emended version, *The Practice of Empire* (Ithaca, 1969).

——. 'The Statecraft of Philip II', *European Studies Review*, 1 (1971), pp. 1–21.

Lafuente, Modesto, *Historia General de España*, 11 (Barcelona, 1888).

Lario Ramírez, Dámaso de. *Cortes del reinado de Felipe IV. 1. Cortes Valencianas de 1626* (Valencia, 1973).

——. 'Cortes valencianas de 1626: problemas en torno al pago del servicio ofrecido', *Estudis*, 4 (1975), pp. 115–27.

——. 'Un conato de revuelta social en Valencia bajo el reinado de Felipe IV', in *Homenaje al Dr. Juan Reglà Campistol* (Valencia, 1975).

Larraz López, José. *La época del mercantilismo en Castilla, 1500–1700* (Madrid, 1943).

Larruga, Eugenio. *Memorias políticas y económicas*, 11 (Madrid, 1791).

Layna Serrano, Francisco. *Historia de Guadalajara y sus Mendozas en los siglos XV y XVI*, 3 (Madrid, 1942).

Lea, Henry Charles. *A History of the Inquisition of Spain*, 4 vols. (New York, 1906–7).

Leman, Auguste. *Urbain VIII et la rivalité de la France et de la Maison d'Autriche de 1631 à 1635* (Lille, 1920).

——. *Richelieu et Olivarès* (Lille, 1938).

León Pinelo, Antonio. *El Gran Canciller de Indias*, ed. Guillermo Lohmann Villena (Seville, 1953).

——. *Anales de Madrid* (Madrid, 1971).

Leturia, S. J., Pedro de. *Relaciones entre la Santa Sede e Hispanoamérica*, 1 (Analecta Gregoriana 101, Rome, 1959).

Lisón y Biedma, Mateo de. *Discursos y apuntamientos* (no place or date of publication).

Lleó Cañal, Vicente. *Nueva Roma: mitología y humanismo en el renacimiento sevillano* (Seville, 1979).

Lockyer, Roger. *Buckingham. The Life and Political Career of George Villiers, First Duke of Buckingham, 1592–1628* (London, 1981).

Lonchay H. and Cuvelier J., *Correspondance de la cour d'Espagne sur les affaires des Pays-Bas au XVIIᵉ siècle*, 6 vols. (Brussels, 1923–37).

Loomie, Albert J. 'The *Conducteur des Ambassadeurs* of Seventeenth Century France and Spain', *Revue belge de philologie et d'histoire*, 43 (1975), pp. 333–56.

López de Toro, José. 'Respuesta del cardenal Trejo a una carta de Tomás Campanella', *Revista de Estudios Políticos* 122 (1962), pp. 161–78.

López Madera, Gregorio. *Excelencias de la monarquía y reyno de España* (Madrid, 1625).

Lublinskaya, A. D. *French Absolutism: the Crucial Phase, 1620–1629* (Cambridge, 1968).

Lutz, George. *Kardinal Giovanni Francesco Guidi di Bagno* (Tübingen, 1971).

Lynch, John. *Spain under the Habsburgs*, 2 vols. (1969; 2nd. ed. Oxford, 1981).

Madre de Dios, Efrén de la, and Steggink, O. *Tiempo y vida de Santa Teresa* (Madrid, 1968).

Madruga Real, Angela. *Arquitectura barroca salamantina. Las Agustinas de Monterrey* (Salamanca, 1983).

Magurn, Ruth Saunders, trans. and ed. *The Letters of Peter Paul Rubens* (Cambridge, Mass., 1955).

Maloney, James C. *A Critical Edition of Mira de Amescua's "La Fe de Hungría" and "El Monte de la Piedad"* (Tulane Studies in Romance Languages and Literature, no. 7, 1975).

Malvezzi, Virgilio. *Historia de los primeros años del reinado de Felipe IV*, ed. D. L. Shaw (London, 1968).

——. *Il Ritratto del Privato Politico Christiano* (Bologna, 1635; Eng. trans. *The Pourtract of the politicke Christian-favourite*, London, 1647).

——. *La libra de Grivilio Vezzalmi* (Pamplona, 1639).

——. *Sucesos principales de la Monarquía de España* (Madrid, 1640. Eng. trans. Robert Gentilis, *The Chiefe Events of The Monarchie of Spain*, London, 1647).

Mann, Golo. *Wallenstein* (Frankfurt, 1971; Eng. trans., New York, 1976).

Manrique, Angel. *Socorro del clero al estado* (Salamanca, 1624; repr. Madrid, 1814).

Manuel de Melo, Franciso. *Alterações de Évora (1637)*, ed. Joel Serrão (Lisbon, 1967).

———. *Epanáforas*, ed. E. Prestage (Coimbra, 1931).

———. *Historia de los movimientos, separación y guerra de Cataluña en tiempo de Felipe IV* (ed. Madrid, 1912).

———. *Le dialogue 'Hospital das Letras' de D. Francisco Manuel de Melo*, ed. Jean Colomès (Paris, 1970).

Marañón, Gregorio. *El Conde-Duque de Olivares* (3rd. ed., Madrid, 1952).

———. *Don Juan* (6th ed., Madrid, 1953).

———. 'La biblioteca del Conde-Duque de Olivares', *Boletín de la Real Academia de la Historia* 107 (1935), pp. 677–92.

Maravall, José Antonio. *La Philosophie Politique Espagnole au XVIIᵉ siècle* (Paris, 1955).

———. *Teatro y literatura en la sociedad barroca* (Madrid, 1972).

———. *Poder, honor y elites en el siglo XVII* (Madrid, 1979).

———. *La cultura del barroco* (2nd. ed., Madrid, 1980).

———. *Estudios de historia del pensamiento español*, 3 vols. (Madrid, 1984).

Mareš, F. 'Die maritime Politik der Habsburger in den Jahren 1625–1628', *Mitteilungen des Instituts für Oesterreichische Geschichtsforschung*, 1 (1880), pp. 541–78, and 2 (1881), pp. 49–82.

Mariana, Juan de. *Obras* (*Biblioteca de Autores Españoles*, 31 (Madrid, 1854).

———. *La dignidad real y la educación del rey*, ed. Luis Sánchez Agesta (Madrid, 1981).

Marichal, Juan. *La voluntad del estilo* (Madrid, 1971).

Márquez, Juan. *El governador christiano* (Salamanca, 1612).

Marrades, Pedro. *El camino del imperio* (Madrid, 1943).

Martínez de Mata, Francisco. *Memoriales y discursos de Francisco Martínez de Mata*, ed. Gonzalo Anes (Madrid, 1971).

Martínez Val, José María and Margarita Peñalosa E.-Infantes. *Un epistolario inédito del reinado de Felipe IV* (Ciudad Real, 1961).

Martyr Rizo, Juan Pablo. *Historia de la vida de Mecenas* (Madrid, 1626).

Mateos, Juan. *Origen y dignidad de la caza* (Madrid, 1634; new ed., Madrid, 1928).

Mathews, Thomas G. 'The Spanish Dominion of St. Martin, 1633–1648', *Caribbean Studies*, 9 (1969), pp. 3–23.

Matilla Tascón, Antonio, ed. *Testamentos de 43 personas del Madrid de los Austrias,* (Madrid, 1943).

Mattingly, Garrett. *Renaissance Diplomacy* (London, 1955).

McKendrick, Melveena. *Women and Society in the Spanish Drama of the Golden Age* (Cambridge, 1974).

Menéndez Pidal, Ramón. *Historia de España Ramón Menéndez Pidal*, 24 (Madrid, 1979), 25 (Madrid, 1982).

Menor Fuentes, José Carlos. *El linaje toledano de Santa Teresa de Jesús y de San Juan de la Cruz* (Toledo, 1970).

Merriman, Roger Bigelow. *Six Contemporaneous Revolutions* (Oxford, 1938).

Metford, J. C. J. 'Tirso de Molina and the Conde-Duque de Olivares', *Bulletin of Hispanic Studies*, 36 (1959), pp. 15–27.

Mira de Amescua, Antonio. *Comedia famosa de Ruy López de Avalos (Primera parte de don Albaro de Luna)*, ed. Nellie E. Sánchez-Arce (México, 1965).

Moll, Jaime. 'Diez años sin licencias para imprimir comedias y novelas en los reinos de Castilla: 1625–1634', *Boletín de la Real Academia Española*, 54 (1974), pp. 97–103.

Moncada, Sancho de. *Restauración política de España* (1619; ed. Jean Vilar, Madrid, 1974).

Morel-Fatio, A. 'Caduta del Conte d'Olivares', *Bulletin Italien*, 12 (1912), pp. 27–49, 136–56, 224–37.

Mout, M. E. H. N. '"Holendische Propositiones". Een Habsburgs plan tot vernietiging van handel, visserij en scheepvaart der Republiek (ca.1625)', *Tijdschrift voor Geschiedenis*, 95 (1982), pp. 345–62.

Muñoz de San Pedro, Miguel. 'Un extremeño en la corte de los Austrias', *Revista de Estudios Extremeños*, 2 (1946), pp. 390–3.

Muto, Giovanni. *Le finanze pubbliche napoletane tra riforme e restaurazione, 1520–1634* (Naples, 1980).

Nadal, Jordi. *La población española. Siglos XVI a XX* (2nd. ed., Barcelona, 1984).

Novísima recopilación de las leyes de España, 3 vols. (Madrid, 1805).

Novoa, Matías de. *Historia de Felipe III, rey de España (Colección de documentos inéditos para la historia de España*, 60, 61 [Madrid, 1875]).

——. *Historia de Felipe IV, rey de España (Colección de documentos inéditos para la historia de España*, 69, 77, 80, 86 [Madrid, 1876–86]).

Núñez de Salcedo, Pedro. 'Relación de los títulos que hay en España', *Boletín de la Real Academia de la Historia* (1918), pp. 468–92.

Oestreich, Gerhard. *Neostoicism and the Early Modern State* (Cambridge, 1982).

Ortiz, Luis. *Memorial del Contador Luis Ortiz a Felipe II* (1558; ed. Madrid, 1970).

Ortiz de Zúñiga, Diego. *Anales eclesiásticos y seculares de la muy noble y muy leal ciudad de Sevilla*, 4 (Madrid, 1796).

Ossorio, Angel. *Los hombres de toga en el proceso de D. Rodrigo Calderón* (Madrid, 1918).

Pagès, Georges. *La Guerre de Trente Ans* (Paris, 1949).

——. 'Autour du "grand orage". Richelieu et Marillac: deux politiques', *Revue Historique*, 179 (1937), pp. 63–97.

Parker, Geoffrey. *The Army of Flanders and the Spanish Road, 1567–1659* (Cambridge, 1972).

——. *The Dutch Revolt* (Ithaca, 1977).

——. *Spain and the Netherlands, 1559–1659* (London, 1979).

——. *The Thirty Years' War* (London, 1984).

Parra, Juan Adam de la. *Conspiración Herético-Cristianísima*, Spanish trans. Angeles Roda Aguirre (Madrid, 1943).

Pastor, Ludwig von. *The History of the Popes*, 18 (London, 1938).

Pellegrini, Amadeo. *Relazioni inedite di Ambasciatori Lucchesi alla corte di Madrid* (Lucca, 1903).

Pellicer de Tovar, José. *Comercio impedido* (Madrid, 1640).

——. *Avisos históricos* (in Antonio Valladares, *Semanario erudito*, 31 and 32 [Madrid, 1790]).

Pelorson, Jean-Marc. *Les Letrados, juristes castillans sous Philippe III* (Le Puy-en-Velay, 1980).

Peña, José F. de la. *Oligarquía y propiedad en Nueva España* (Mexico City, 1981).

Pérez Bustamante, C. *Felipe III. Semblanza de un monarca y perfiles de una privanza* (Madrid, 1950).

Pérez Escolano, Víctor. *Juan de Oviedo y de la Bandera* (Seville, 1977).

Pérez Martín, María Jesús. *Margarita de Austria, Reina de España* (Madrid, 1961).

Pérez Moreda, Vicente. *Las crisis de mortalidad en la España interior, siglos XVI–XIX* (Madrid, 1980).

Phillips, Carla Rahn. 'The Spanish Wool Trade, 1500–1780', *Journal of Economic History*, 42 (1982), pp. 775–95.

Pike, Ruth. *Aristocrats and Traders. Sevillian Society in the Sixteenth Century* (Ithaca, 1972).

Pirenne, Henri. *Histoire de Belgique*, 4 (3rd. ed., Brussels, 1927).

Pithon, Rémy. 'Les débuts difficiles du ministère de Richelieu et la crise de Valteline, 1621–1627', *Revue d'Histoire Diplomatique*, 74 (1960), pp. 289–322.

Poelhekke, J. J. *'t Uytgaen van den Treves. Spanje en de Nederlanden in 1621* (Groningen, 1960).

Polisensky, J. V. *The Thirty Years War* (London, 1971).

Porcar, Pedro Juan. *Coses evengudes en la ciutat y regne de València*, ed. V. Castañeda Alcover, 2 vols. (Madrid, 1934).

Porchnev, Boris. *Les soulèvements populaires en France de 1623 à 1648* (Paris, 1963).

Proclamación católica a la Magestad piadosa de Felipe el Grande, (ed. Lisbon, 1641).

Prontuario de los tratados de paz, 4 vols. (Madrid, 1749–52).

Pujades, Jeroni. *Dietari de Jeroni Pujades*, ed. Josep Maria Casas Homs, 4 vols. (Barcelona, 1975–6).

Quazza, Romolo. *La guerra per la successione de Mantova e del Monferrato, 1628–1631*, 2 vols. (Mantua, 1926).

——. *Margherita di Savoia* (Turin, 1930).

——. *Tomaso di Savoia-Carignano nelle campagne di Fiandra e di Francia, 1635–1638* (Turin, 1941).

——. *Storia Politica d'Italia. Preponderanza Spagnuola, 1559–1700* (2nd. ed., Milan, 1950).

Quevedo, Francisco de. *Epistolario completo de Don Francisco de Quevedo Villegas*, ed. Luis Astrana Marín (Madrid, 1946).

——. *Obras completas de Don Francisco de Quevedo Villegas. Obras en prosa*, ed. Luis Astrana Marín (2nd ed., Madrid, 1941).

——. *Obras completas*, ed. Felicidad Buendía, 2 vols. (6th ed., Madrid, 1966–7).

——. *Obra poética*, ed. José Manuel Blecua, 3 vols. (Madrid, 1969–71).

——. *La hora de todos*, French trans., Jean Bourg, Pierre Dupont, and Pierre Geneste, *L'Heure de tous et la fortune raisonnable* (Paris, 1980).

Rafal, Marqués de (Alfonso Pardo Manuel de Villena). *Un mecenas español del siglo XVII. El conde de Lemos* (Madrid, 1911).

Ramírez, Alejandro. *Epistolario de Justo Lipsio y los Españoles, 1577–1606* (Madrid, 1966).

Redondi, Pietro. *Galileo eretico* (Turin, 1983).

Rennert, Hugo Albert. *The Life of Lope de Vega, 1562–1635* (Glasgow, 1904).

Reumont, Alfred de. *Naples under Spanish Dominion. The Carafas of Maddaloni and Masaniello* (Eng. trans., London, 1853).

Révah, I. S. *Le Cardinal de Richelieu et la restauration du Portugal* (Lisbon, 1950).

—— 'Le plaidoyer en faveur des *Nouveaux Chrétiens* portugais du licencié Martín González de Cellorigo', *Revue des Études Juives*, 4ᵉ série, 2 (1963), pp. 279–398.

Ringrose, David R. *Madrid and the Spanish Economy, 1560–1850* (Berkeley and Los Angeles, 1983).

Roberts, Michael. *Gustavus Adolphus. A History of Sweden, 1611–1632*, 2 vols. (London, 1953–8).

Robles, Juan de. *Tardes del Alcázar, doctrina para el perfecto vasallo*, ed. Miguel Romero Martínez (Seville, 1948).

Roca, Count of La. *See* Vera y Figueroa.

Roco de Campofrío, Juan. 'Relación de la jornada que su alteza el Archiduque Alberto . . . hizo a Flandes en el año de 1595', published under the title of *España en Flandes* (Madrid, 1973).

Ródenas Vilar, Rafael. *La política europea de España durante la Guerra de Treinta Años, 1624–1630* (Madrid, 1967).

Rodríguez Villa, Antonio. *La corte y monarquía de España* (Madrid, 1886).

——. *Ambrosio Spínola, primer marqués de los Balbases* (Madrid, 1904).

——. *Etiquetas de la casa de Austria* (Madrid, 1913).

Rooses, Max. *Correspondance de Rubens*, 3 (Antwerp, 1900).

Rosaldo Jr., Renato I. 'Lope as a poet of history and ritual in *El testimonio vengado*', *Estudios de Hispanófila* (1978), pp. 9–32.

Rott, Edouard. 'Philippe III et le duc de Lerme', *Revue d'Histoire Diplomatique*, 1 (1887), pp. 201–16, and 363–84.

Rubens, Peter Paul. *See* Magurn; Rooses.

Rubio, Julián María. *Los ideales hispanos en la tregua de 1609 y en el momento actual* (Valladolid, 1937).

Ruigh, Robert E. *The Parliament of 1624* (Cambridge, Mass., 1971).

Ruiz Martín, Felipe. *Lettres marchandes échangées entre Florence et Medina del Campo* (Paris, 1965).

——. 'La banca en España hasta 1782', in F. Ruiz Martín *et al.*, *El banco de España: una historia económica* (Madrid, 1970).

——. 'Pastos y ganaderos en Castilla; La Mesta, 1450–1600', in M. Spallanzini (ed.), *La lana come materia prima* (Florence, 1974).

Russell, Conrad. 'Monarchies, Wars and Estates in England, France, and Spain, c.1580–c.1640', *Legislative Studies Quarterly*, 7 (1982).

Saavedra Fajardo, Diego. *Empresas políticas. Idea de un príncipe político-cristiano*, ed. Quintín Aldea Vaquero, 2 vols. (Madrid, 1976).

Sala, Gaspar. *Secrets Públichs* (Barcelona, 1641).

Salazar, Fray Juan de. *Política española* (1619; ed. Miguel Herrero García, Madrid, 1945).

Salazar y Castro, Luis de. *Advertencias históricas* (Madrid, 1688).

Salomon, Noël. *La campagne de Nouvelle Castille à la fin du seizième siècle d'après les 'Relaciones topográficas'* (Paris, 1964).

Sanabre, José. *La acción de Francia en Cataluña en la pugna por la hegemonía de Europa* (Barcelona, 1956).

Sánchez Bella, Alfredo. 'El poderío español a mediados del siglo XVII, según el parecer de un chileno', *Boletín de la Academia Chilena de la Historia*, 57 (1957), pp. 47–59.

Sánchez-Castañer, Francisco. *Don Juan de Palafox, virrey de Nueva España* (Zaragoza, 1964).

Sanmartí Boncompte, Francisco. *Tácito en España* (Barcelona, 1951).

Santa María, Juan de. *República y policía christiana* (ed. Lisbon, 1621).

Santiago Rodríguez, Miguel. 'Cartas del Conde-Duque de Olivares escritas después de su caída', in *Revista de Archivos, Bibliotecas y Museos*, 66 (1973), pp. 323–404.

Schäfer, Ernesto. *El Consejo Real y Supremo de las Indias*, 2 vols. (Seville, 1935–47).

Schurz, William L. *The Manila Galleon* (1939, repr. New York, 1959).

Scribani, Carolus. *Politico-Christianus* (Antwerp, 1624).

Seco Serrano, Carlos, ed., *Cartas de Sor María de Ágreda y de Felipe IV*, 2 vols. (*Biblioteca de Autores Españoles*, 108 and 109, Madrid, 1958).

Sempere y Guarinos, Juan. *Biblioteca española económico-política*, 3, (Madrid, 1804).

Shaw, D. L. 'Olivares y el Almirante de Castilla (1638)', *Hispania* 27 (1967), pp. 342–53.

Shergold, N. D. *A History of the Spanish Stage from Medieval Times until the End of the Seventeenth Century* (Oxford, 1967).

Sherley, Sir Anthony. *See* Flores.

Silvela, Francisco. *Cartas de la Venerable Sor María de Agreda y del Señor Rey Don Felipe IV*, 2 vols. (Madrid, 1885–6).

Simón-Díaz, José. *Historia del Colegio Imperial de Madrid*, 1 (Madrid, 1952).

—— ed. *Relaciones de actos públicos celebrados en Madrid (1541–1650)* (Madrid, 1982).

——. 'El arte en las mansiones nobiliarias madrileñas de 1626', *Goya* 154 (1980), pp. 200–5.

——. 'La estancia del Cardenal Legado Francesco Barberini en Madrid el año 1626', *Anales del Instituto de Estudios Madrileños*, 17 (1980), pp. 159–213.

——. 'Dos privados frente a frente: el Cardenal F. Barberini y el Conde-Duque de Olivares (Madrid, 1626)', *Revista de la Biblioteca, Archivo y Museo*, 7–8 (1980), pp. 7–53.

Siri, Vittorio. *Mercurio* (2nd. ed., Casale, 1648), 2.

Skinner, Quentin. *The Foundations of Modern Political Thought*, 2 vols. (Cambridge, 1978).

Solomon, Howard M. *Public Welfare, Science and Propaganda in Seventeenth Century France. The Innovations of Théophraste Renaudot* (Princeton, 1972).

Steensgaard, Niels. *The Asian Trade Revolution of the Seventeenth Century* (Chicago, 1974).

Stols, Eddy. *De Spaanske Brabanders of de Handelsbetrekkingen der Zuidelijke Nederlanden met de Iberische Wereld, 1598–1648,* 2 vols. (Brussels, 1971).

Stradling, R. A. *Europe and the Decline of Spain* (London, 1981).

——. 'A Spanish Statesman of Apppeasement: Medina de las Torres and Spanish Policy, 1639–1670', *Historical Journal,* 19 (1976), pp. 1–31.

——. 'The Spanish Dunkirkers, 1621–1648: a record of plunder and destruction', *Tijdschrift voor Geschiedenis,* 93 (1980), pp. 541–58.

Straub, Eberhard. *Pax et Imperium* (Paderborn, 1980).

Suárez Fernández, Luis. *Notas a la política anti-española del Cardenal Richelieu* (Valladolid, 1950).

Tapia, Juan de. *Ilustración del renombre de grande* (Madrid, 1638).

Tapié, Victor L. *La France de Louis XIII et de Richelieu* (Paris, 1967).

Taylor, Harland. 'Trade, Neutrality and the "English Road", 1630–1648', *The Economic History Review,* 25 (1972), pp. 236–60.

Téllez, Fr. Gabriel. *Historia General de la Orden de Nuestra Señora de las Mercedes,* ed. Fray Manuel Penedo Rey, 2 vols. (Madrid, 1973–4). *See also* Tirso de Molina.

TePaske, John J. and Klein, Herbert S. 'The Seventeenth-Century Crisis in New Spain: Myth or Reality?', *Past and Present,* 90 (1981), pp. 116–35.

Thompson, I. A. A. *War and Government in Habsburg Spain, 1560–1620* (London, 1976).

——. 'Crown and Cortes in Castile, 1590–1665', *Parliaments, Estates and Representation,* 2 (1982), pp. 29–45.

——. 'The Rule of the Law in Early Modern Castile', *European History Quarterly,* 14 (1984), pp. 221–34.

——. 'The Impact of War', *The European Crisis of the 1590's,* ed. P. Clark.

Tierno-Galván, Enrique. 'Acerca de dos cartas muy poco conocidas del Conde Duque de Olivares', *Anales de la Universidad de Murcia* (1951–2), pp. 71–6.

Tirso de Molina. *Obras dramáticas completas,* ed. Blanca de los Ríos, 3 vols. (3rd. ed. Madrid, 1969). *See also* Téllez, Fray Gabriel.

Tomás Valiente, Francisco. *Los validos en la monarquía española* (Madrid, 1963).

Tormo y Monzó, Elías. *Pintura, escultura y arquitectura en España* (Madrid, 1949).

Torras i Elías, Jaume. 'L'economia castellana el segle XVI', *Recerques,* 16 (1984), pp. 159–69.

Torres Ramírez, Bibiano. *La Armada de Barlovento* (Seville, 1981).

Trevor-Roper, H. R. 'Spain and Europe 1598–1621', *The New Cambridge Modern History,* 4 (Cambridge, 1970).

Ulloa, Modesto. *La hacienda real de Castilla en el reinado de Felipe II* (Madrid, 1977).

Urgorri Casado, Fernando. 'Ideas sobre el gobierno económico de España en el siglo XVII', *Revista de la Biblioteca, Archivo y Museo* (Ayuntamiento de Madrid), 19 (1950), pp. 123–230.

Valdory, Guillaume de. *Anecdotes du ministère du comte duc d'Olivarés, tirées et traduites de l'Italien de Mercurio Siry, par Monsieur de Valdory* (Paris, 1722).

Valgoma y Díaz-Varela, Dalmiro de la. *Norma y ceremonia de las reinas de la casa de Austria* (Madrid, 1958).

Valladares de Sotomayor, Antonio. *Semanario erudito*, 34 vols. (Madrid, 1787–91).

Valle de la Cerda, Luis. *Desempeño del patrimonio de su Majestad . . .* (Madrid, 1600).

Van der Essen, A. *Le Cardinal-Infant et la politique européenne de l'Espagne* (Brussels, 1944).

Van de Vyver S. I., Omer. 'Lettres de J-Ch. Della Faille S. I., cosmographe du roi à Madrid, à M-F. Van Langren, cosmographe du roi a Bruxelles, 1634–1645', *Archivum Historicum Societatis Iesu*, 46 (1977), pp. 73–183.

Vasal-Reig, Charles. *La guerre en Roussillon sous Louis XIII, 1635–1639* (Paris, 1934).

Vassberg, David E. *Land and Society in Golden Age Castile* (Cambridge, 1984).

Vázquez de Prada, V. *Historia económica y social de España*, 3 (*Los siglos XVI y XVII*) (Madrid, 1978).

Vega Carpio, Lope de. *Cartas completas*, 2 vols. (Buenos Aires, 1948).

——. *Epistolario de Lope de Vega Carpio*, ed. Agustín González de Amezúa, 3 and 4 (Madrid, 1941–3).

Velázquez y Sánchez, José. *Estudios históricos* (Seville, 1864).

Vera y Figueroa, Juan Antonio de, Count of La Roca. *El Fernando, o Sevilla restaurada* (Milan, 1632).

——. *Fragmentos históricos de la vida de D. Gaspar de Guzmán*, Valladares, *Semanario Erudito*, 2.

—— (under name of Vera y Zúñiga). *El enbaxador* (Seville, 1620; facsimile ed. Madrid, 1947).

Veríssimo Serrão, Joaquim. *História de Portugal*, 4 and 5 (Lisbon, 1979–80).

Vila Vilar, Enriqueta. *Historia de Puerto Rico, 1600–1650* (Seville, 1974).

——. 'Las ferias de Portobelo: apariencia y realidad del comercio con Indias', *Anuario de Estudios Americanos*, 39 (1982).

Vilar, Jean. *Literatura y economía* (Madrid, 1973).

——. 'Docteurs et marchands: l'"école" de Tolède', communication to Fifth International Congress of Economic History (Moscow, 1970).

——. 'Formes et tendances de l'opposition sous Olivares: Lisón y Viedma, *Defensor de la Patria*', *Mélanges de la Casa de Velázquez*, 7 (1971).

——. 'Una pauta del pensamiento monetarista castellano: la "proposición" Cardona, 1618–1628', reprinted from *Dinero y Crédito* (*siglos XVI al XIX*), ed. Alfonso de Otazu (Madrid, 1978).

Villari, Rosario. 'Baronaggio e finanza a Napoli alla vigilia della rivoluzione del 1647–8', *Studi Storici*, 3 (1962), pp. 259–305.

Viñas Mey, Carmelo. 'Cuadro económico-social de la España de 1627–8', *Anuario de Historia Económica y Social*, 1 (1968), pp. 720–5.

Viñas Navarro, A. 'El motín de Évora y su significación en la restauración portuguesa de 1640', *Boletín de la Biblioteca Menéndez y Pelayo*, 6 (1924), pp. 321–39, and 7 (1925), pp. 29–49.

Voiture, Vincent. *Les Oeuvres de M. de Voiture*, 2 vols. (Paris, 1691).

Volk, Mary C. 'New Light on a 'Seventeenth-Century Collector: the Marquis of Leganés', *Art Bulletin*, 52 (1980), pp. 256–68.

Vosters, Simon A. *La rendición de Bredá en la literatura y el arte de España* (London, 1973).

Waddington, A. *La République des Provinces-Unies, la France et les Pays-Bas Espagnols de 1630 à 1650*, 2 vols. (Paris, 1895–7).

Wedgwood, C. V. *The Thirty Years' War* (London, 1938).

Weiss, C. *España desde el reinado de Felipe II* (Madrid, 1846).

Weisser, Michael. 'The Decline of Castile Revisited: the Case of Toledo', *The Journal of European Economic History*, 2 (1973), pp. 614–40.

Werner, Ernst. 'Caída del Conde-Duque de Olivares', *Revue Hispanique*, 71 (1927), pp. 1–156.

Whitaker, Shirley B. 'The First Performance of Calderón's *El sitio de Bredá*', *Renaissance Quarterly*, 31 (1978), pp. 515–31.

——. 'The Quevedo Case (1639): Documents from Florentine Archives', *Modern Language Notes*, 97 (1982), pp. 368–79.

Williams, P. L. 'Philip III and the Restoration of Spanish Government, 1598–1630', *The English Historical Review*, 88 (1973), pp. 751–69.

——. 'The Court and Councils of Philip III of Spain' (University of London, doctoral dissertation, 1973).

Willson, D. H. *King James VI and I* (London, 1956).

Wollenberg, Jörg. *Richelieu* (Bielefeld, 1977).

Wright, L. P. 'The Military Orders in Sixteenth and Seventeenth Century Spanish Society', *Past and Present*, 43 (1969), pp. 34–70.

Yáñez, Juan. *Memorias para la historia de don Felipe III* (Madrid, 1723).

Yerushalmi, Yosef Hayim. *From Spanish Court to Italian Ghetto* (New York, 1971).

Zudaire Huarte, Eulogio. *El Conde-Duque y Cataluña* (Madrid, 1964).

——. 'Un error de inercia: el supuesto Conde-Duque de Olivares', *Hidalguía*, 11 (1963), pp. 599–610.

——. 'Ideario político de D. Gaspar de Guzmán, privado de Felipe IV', *Hispania*, 25 (1965), pp. 413–25.

INDEX